Lecture Notes in Computer Science　　10205

Commenced Publication in 1973
Founding and Former Series Editors:
Gerhard Goos, Juris Hartmanis, and Jan van Leeuwen

Advanced Research in Computing and Software Science
Subline of Lecture Notes in Computer Science

More information about this series at http://www.springer.com/series/7407

Axel Legay · Tiziana Margaria (Eds.)

Tools and Algorithms for the Construction and Analysis of Systems

23rd International Conference, TACAS 2017
Held as Part of the European Joint Conferences
on Theory and Practice of Software, ETAPS 2017
Uppsala, Sweden, April 22–29, 2017
Proceedings, Part I

 Springer

Editors
Axel Legay
Inria
Rennes Cedex
France

Tiziana Margaria
University of Limerick and Lero - The Irish
   Software Research Center
Limerick
Ireland

ISSN 0302-9743   ISSN 1611-3349 (electronic)
Lecture Notes in Computer Science
ISBN 978-3-662-54576-8   ISBN 978-3-662-54577-5 (eBook)
DOI 10.1007/978-3-662-54577-5

Library of Congress Control Number: 2017935566

LNCS Sublibrary: SL1 – Theoretical Computer Science and General Issues

Printed on acid-free paper

This Springer imprint is published by Springer Nature
The registered company is Springer-Verlag GmbH Germany
The registered company address is: Heidelberger Platz 3, 14197 Berlin, Germany

ETAPS Foreword

Welcome to the proceedings of ETAPS 2017, which was held in Uppsala! It was the first time ever that ETAPS took place in Scandinavia.

ETAPS 2017 was the 20th instance of the European Joint Conferences on Theory and Practice of Software. ETAPS is an annual federated conference established in 1998, and consists of five conferences: ESOP, FASE, FoSSaCS, TACAS, and POST. Each conference has its own Program Committee (PC) and its own Steering Committee. The conferences cover various aspects of software systems, ranging from theoretical computer science to foundations to programming language developments, analysis tools, formal approaches to software engineering, and security. Organizing these conferences in a coherent, highly synchronized conference program enables participation in an exciting event, offering the possibility to meet many researchers working in different directions in the field and to easily attend talks of different conferences. Before and after the main conference, numerous satellite workshops take place and attract many researchers from all over the globe.

ETAPS 2017 received 531 submissions in total, 159 of which were accepted, yielding an overall acceptance rate of 30%. I thank all authors for their interest in ETAPS, all reviewers for their peer reviewing efforts, the PC members for their contributions, and in particular the PC (co-)chairs for their hard work in running this entire intensive process. Last but not least, my congratulations to all authors of the accepted papers!

ETAPS 2017 was enriched by the unifying invited speakers Kim G. Larsen (Aalborg University, Denmark) and Michael Ernst (University of Washington, USA), as well as the conference-specific invited speakers (FoSSaCS) Joel Ouaknine (MPI-SWS, Germany, and University of Oxford, UK) and (TACAS) Dino Distefano (Facebook and Queen Mary University of London, UK). In addition, ETAPS 2017 featured a public lecture by Serge Abiteboul (Inria and ENS Cachan, France). Invited tutorials were offered by Véronique Cortier (CNRS research director at Loria, Nancy, France) on security and Ken McMillan (Microsoft Research Redmond, USA) on compositional testing. My sincere thanks to all these speakers for their inspiring and interesting talks!

ETAPS 2017 took place in Uppsala, Sweden, and was organized by the Department of Information Technology of Uppsala University. It was further supported by the following associations and societies: ETAPS e.V., EATCS (European Association for Theoretical Computer Science), EAPLS (European Association for Programming Languages and Systems), and EASST (European Association of Software Science and Technology). Facebook, Microsoft, Amazon, and the city of Uppsala financially supported ETAPS 2017. The local organization team consisted of Parosh Aziz Abdulla (general chair), Wang Yi, Björn Victor, Konstantinos Sagonas, Mohamed Faouzi Atig, Andreina Francisco, Kaj Lampka, Tjark Weber, Yunyun Zhu, and Philipp Rümmer.

The overall planning for ETAPS is the main responsibility of the Steering Committee, and in particular of its executive board. The ETAPS Steering Committee consists of an executive board, and representatives of the individual ETAPS conferences, as well as representatives of EATCS, EAPLS, and EASST. The executive board consists of Gilles Barthe (Madrid), Holger Hermanns (Saarbrücken), Joost-Pieter Katoen (chair, Aachen and Twente), Gerald Lüttgen (Bamberg), Vladimiro Sassone (Southampton), Tarmo Uustalu (Tallinn), and Lenore Zuck (Chicago). Other members of the Steering Committee are: Parosh Abdulla (Uppsala), Amal Ahmed (Boston), Christel Baier (Dresden), David Basin (Zurich), Lujo Bauer (Pittsburgh), Dirk Beyer (Munich), Giuseppe Castagna (Paris), Tom Crick (Cardiff), Javier Esparza (Munich), Jan Friso Groote (Eindhoven), Jurriaan Hage (Utrecht), Reiko Heckel (Leicester), Marieke Huisman (Twente), Panagotios Katsaros (Thessaloniki), Ralf Küsters (Trier), Ugo del Lago (Bologna), Kim G. Larsen (Aalborg), Axel Legay (Rennes), Matteo Maffei (Saarbrücken), Tiziana Margaria (Limerick), Andrzej Murawski (Warwick), Catuscia Palamidessi (Palaiseau), Julia Rubin (Vancouver), Alessandra Russo (London), Mark Ryan (Birmingham), Don Sannella (Edinburgh), Andy Schürr (Darmstadt), Gabriele Taentzer (Marburg), Igor Walukiewicz (Bordeaux), and Hongseok Yang (Oxford).

I would like to take this opportunity to thank all speakers, attendees, organizers of the satellite workshops, and Springer for their support. Finally, a big thanks to Parosh and his local organization team for all their enormous efforts enabling a fantastic ETAPS in Uppsala!

April 2017   Joost-Pieter Katoen

Preface

TACAS 2017 was the 23rd edition of the International Conference on Tools and Algorithms for the Construction and Analysis of Systems. The conference took place during April 2017, in the Uppsala Concert and Congress Hall as part of the 19th European Joint Conferences on Theory and Practice of Software (ETAPS 2017).

TACAS is a forum for researchers, developers, and users interested in rigorously based tools and algorithms for the construction and analysis of systems. The conference aims to bridge the gaps between different communities with this common interest and to support them in their quest to improve the utility, reliability, flexibility, and efficiency of tools and algorithms for building systems.

As in former years, TACAS 2017 solicited four types of submissions:

- Research papers, identifying and justifying a principled advance to the theoretical foundations for the construction and analysis of systems, where applicable supported by experimental validation
- Case-study papers, reporting on case studies and providing information about the system being studied, the goals of the study, the challenges the system poses to automated analysis, research methodologies and approaches used, the degree to which goals were attained, and how the results can be generalized to other problems and domains
- Regular tool papers, presenting a new tool, a new tool component, or novel extensions to an existing tool, with an emphasis on design and implementation concerns, including software architecture and core data structures, practical applicability, and experimental evaluation
- Short tool-demonstration papers, focusing on the usage aspects of tools

This year, 181 papers were submitted to TACAS, among which 167 were research, case study, or tool papers, and 14 were tool demonstration papers. After a rigorous review process followed by an online discussion, the Program Committee accepted 48 full papers and four tool demonstration papers. This volume also includes an invited paper by the ETAPS unifying speaker Kim. G. Larsen titled "Validation, Synthesis, and Optimization for Cyber-Physical Systems" and an invited paper by TACAS invited speaker Dino Distefano titled "The Facebook Infer Static Analyzer."

TACAS 2017 also hosted the 6th International Competition on Software Verification (SV-COMP), chaired and organized by Dirk Beyer. The competition again had a high participation: 32 verification tools from 12 countries were submitted for the systematic comparative evaluation, including two submissions from industry. This volume includes an overview of the competition results, and short papers describing 12 of the participating verification systems. These papers were reviewed by a separate Program Committee; each of the papers was assessed by four reviewers. One session in the TACAS program was reserved for the presentation of the results: the summary by the SV-COMP chair and the participating tools by the developer teams.

Many people worked hard and offered their valuable time generously to make TACAS 2017 successful. First, the chairs would like to thank the authors for submitting their papers to TACAS 2017. We are grateful to the reviewers who contributed to nearly 550 informed and detailed reports and discussions during the electronic Program Committee meeting. We also sincerely thank the Steering Committee for their advice. We also acknowledge the work of Parosh Aziz Abdulla and the local organizers for ETAPS 2017. Furthermore, we would like to express a special thanks to Joost-Pieter Katoen, who answered many of our questions during the preparation of TACAS 2017. Finally, we thank EasyChair for providing us with the infrastructure to manage the submissions, the reviewing process, the Program Committee discussion, and the preparation of the proceedings.

April 2017

Dirk Beyer
Axel Legay
Tiziana Margaria
Dave Parker

Organization

Program Committee

Gilles Barthe	IMDEA Software Institute, Spain
Dirk Beyer	LMU Munich, Germany
Armin Biere	Johannes Kepler University Linz, Austria
Radu Calinescu	University of York, UK
Franck Cassez	Macquarie University, Australia
Swarat Chaudhuri	Rice University, USA
Alessandro Cimatti	FBK-irst, Italy
Rance Cleaveland	University of Maryland, USA
Byron Cook	University College London, UK
Leonardo de Moura	Microsoft Research
Cezara Dragoi	IST Austria
Cindy Eisner	IBM Research, Haifa, Israel
Martin Fränzle	Carl von Ossietzky Universität Oldenburg, Germany
Sicun Gao	MIT CSAIL, USA
Susanne Graf	Universite Joseph Fourier, CNRS, VERIMAG, France
Orna Grumberg	Technion, Israel Institute of Technology, Israel
Kim Guldstrand Larsen	Aalborg University, Denmark
Klaus Havelund	Jet Propulsion Laboratory, California Institute of Technology, USA
Holger Hermanns	Saarland University, Germany
Falk Howar	TU Clausthal/IPSSE, Germany
Thomas Jensen	Inria, France
Jan Kretinsky	Masaryk University, Czech Republic
Salvatore La Torre	Università degli studi di Salerno, Italy
Axel Legay	IRISA/Inria, Rennes, France
P. Madhusudan	University of Illinois at Urbana-Champaign, USA
Pasquale Malacaria	Queen Mary University of London, UK
Tiziana Margaria	Lero, Ireland
Darko Marinov	University of Illinois at Urbana-Champaign, USA
Dejan Nickovic	Austrian Institute of Technology AIT, Austria
David Parker	University of Birmingham, UK
Charles Pecheur	Université catholique de Louvain, Belgium
Kristin Yvonne Rozier	University of Cincinnati, USA
Natasha Sharygina	Università della Svizzera italiana (USI Lugano, Switzerland), Switzerland
Bernhard Steffen	University of Dortmund, Germany
Stavros Tripakis	University of California, Berkeley, USA
Jaco van de Pol	University of Twente, The Netherlands
Thomas Wies	New York University, USA

Additional Reviewers

Adir, Allon
Aleksandrowicz, Gadi
Almagor, Shaull
Alt, Leonardo
Aniculaesei, Adina
Asadi, Sepideh
Ashok, Pranav
Bacci, Giorgio
Bacci, Giovanni
Bansal, Suguman
Barnat, Jiri
Barringer, Howard
Bartocci, Ezio
Bensalem, Saddek
Berthomieu, Bernard
Biewer, Sebastian
Bloemen, Vincent
Blom, Stefan
Bogomolov, Sergiy
Busard, Simon
Butkova, Yuliya
Ceska, Milan
Chadha, Rohit
Chothia, Tom
Clemente, Lorenzo
Courtieu, Pierre
Da Silva, Carlos Eduardo
Daca, Przemyslaw
Dang, Thao
Dangl, Matthias
Daniel, Jakub
Dantam, Neil
de Ruiter, Joeri
Della Monica, Dario
Delzanno, Giorgio
Demasi, Ramiro
Doyen, Laurent
Dräger, Klaus
Duedder, Boris
Dureja, Rohit
Echahed, Rachid
Ehlers, Rüdiger
Ellis, Kevin

Ellison, Martyn
Emmi, Michael
Faella, Marco
Fahrenberg, Uli
Falcone, Ylies
Fazekas, Katalin
Fedyukovich, Grigory
Ferrara, Anna Lisa
Finkbeiner, Bernd
Flores-Montoya, Antonio
Fogarty, Seth
Fontaine, Pascal
Fox, Gereon
Frehse, Goran
Freiberger, Felix
Frenkel, Hadar
Friedberger, Karlheinz
Frohme, Markus
Ganty, Pierre
Gao, Yang
Genet, Thomas
Gentilini, Raffaella
Gerasimou, Simos
Gerhold, Marcus
Gerwinn, Sebastian
Giacobbe, Mirco
Giantamidis, Georgios
Gillard, Xavier
Given-Wilson, Thomas
Gligoric, Milos
Graf-Brill, Alexander
Gregoire, Benjamin
Grigore, Radu
Gyori, Alex
Hadzi-Tanovic, Milica
Hahn, Ernst Moritz
Hartmanns, Arnd
Hashemi, Vahid
Hatefi, Hassan
Hyvärinen, Antti
Inverso, Omar
Islam, Md. Ariful
Ivrii, Alexander

Jabbour, Fadi
Jaeger, Manfred
Jaksic, Stefan
Jasper, Marc
Jensen, Peter Gjøl
Johnson, Kenneth
Kaminski, Benjamin Lucien
Kang, Eunsuk
Kauffman, Sean
Keefe, Ken
Keidar-Barner, Sharon
Khouzani, Arman Mhr
Kikuchi, Shinji
King, Tim
Konnov, Igor
Koskinen, Eric
Koukoutos, Manos
Krenn, Willibald
Kumar, Rahul
Kupferman, Orna
Lacerda, Bruno
Laporte, Vincent
Le Guernic, Colas
Leroux, Jérôme
Leue, Stefan
Limbrée, Christophe
Lipskoch, Kinga
Lorber, Florian
Mahmood, Muhammad Suleman
Marescotti, Matteo
Marin, Paolo
Martinelli Tabajara, Lucas
Maudoux, Guillaume
Mauritz, Malte
Meel, Kuldeep
Meggendorfer, Tobias
Meijer, Jeroen
Meller, Yael
Meyer, Philipp J.
Micheli, Andrea
Mikučionis, Marius
Miner, Andrew
Mogavero, Fabio
Muniz, Marco
Nevo, Ziv
Nies, Gilles

Norman, Gethin
O'Kelly, Matthew
Oliva, Paulo
Oortwijn, Wytse
Orni, Avigail
Palmskog, Karl
Paoletti, Nicola
Paterson, Colin
Peled, Doron
Peters, Henrik
Phan, Quoc-Sang
Pinisetty, Srinivas
Preiner, Mathias
Preoteasa, Viorel
Pulina, Luca
Quilbeuf, Jean
Rajhans, Akshay
Rasin, Dan
Ravanbakhsh, Hadi
Reger, Giles
Reynolds, Andrew
Rezine, Ahmed
Rival, Xavier
Rothenberg, Bat-Chen
Roveri, Marco
Rozier, Eric
Ruijters, Enno
Rüthing, Oliver
Sangnier, Arnaud
Sankur, Ocan
Schivo, Stefano
Schwarzentruber, Francois
Schwoon, Stefan
Sebastiani, Roberto
Sergey, Ilya
Shi, August
Shmarov, Fedor
Shudrak, Maksim
Sighireanu, Mihaela
Sinn, Moritz
Sosnovich, Adi
Sproston, Jeremy
Srba, Jiri
Strub, Pierre-Yves
Taankvist, Jakob Haahr
Tarrach, Thorsten

Tautschnig, Michael
Théry, Laurent
Tonetta, Stefano
Traonouez, Louis-Marie
Trostanetski, Anna
Tzevelekos, Nikos
Urbain, Xavier
Valero, Pedro
van der Berg, Freark
van Dijk, Tom
Vizel, Yakir

Wendler, Philipp
Westphal, Bernd
Widder, Josef
Xue, Bai
Xue, Bingtian
Yorav, Karen
Zhai, Ennan
Zhang, Lingming
Ziv, Avi
Zuliani, Paolo

Abstracts of Invited Talks

Validation, Synthesis and Optimization for Cyber-Physical Systems

Kim Guldstrand Larsen

Department of Computer Science, Aalborg University,
Selma Lagerlöfs Vej 300, 9220 Aalborg East, Denmark
kgl@cs.aau.dk

Abstract. The growing complexity of Cyber-Physical Systems increasingly challenges existing methods and techniques. What is needed is a new generation of scalable tools for model-based learning, analysis, synthesis and optimization based on a mathematical sound foundation, that enables trade-offs between functional safety and quantitative performance. In paper we illustrate how recent branches of the UPPAAL tool suit are making an effort in this direction.

This work is partly funded by the ERC Advanced Grant LASSO: Learning, Analysis, SynthesiS and Optimization of Cyber-Physical Systems as well as the Innovation Center DiCyPS: Data-Intensive Cyber Physical Systems.

The Facebook Infer Static Analyser

Dino Distefano

Facebook Inc., Menlo Park, USA

Abstract. Infer is an open-source static analyser developed at Facebook [1]. Originally based on Separation Logic [2, 3], Infer has lately evolved from a specific tool for heap-manipulating programs to a general framework which facilitates the implementation of new static analyses.

In this talk, I will report on the Infer team's experience of applying our tool to Facebook mobile code, each day helping thousands of engineers to build more reliable and secure software [4]. Moreover, I will discuss the team's current effort to turn Infer into a static analysis platform for research and development useful both to academic researchers and industrial practitioners.

References

1. http://fbinfer.com
2. Calcagno, C., Distefano, D., O'Hearn, P.W., Yang, H.: Compositional shape analysis by means of bi-abduction. In: POPL, pp. 289–300. ACM (2009)
3. Calcagno, C., Distefano, D.: Infer: an automatic program verifier for memory safety of C programs. In: Bobaru, M., Havelund. K., Holzmann, G.J., Joshi, R. (eds.) NFM 2011. LNCS, vol. 6617, pp. 459–465. Springer, Heidelberg (2011)
4. Calcagno, C., Distefano, D., Dubreil, J., Gabi, D., Hooimeijer, P., Luca, M., O'Hearn, P.W., Papakonstantinou, I., Purbrick, J., Rodriguez, D.: Moving Fast with Software Verification. In: Havelund, K., Holzmann, G., Joshi, R. (eds.) NFM 2015. LNCS, vol. 9058, pp. 3–11. Springer, Switzerland (2015)

Contents – Part I

Hybrid Systems

Contents – Part II

Invited Talk

Validation, Synthesis and Optimization for Cyber-Physical Systems

Kim Guldstrand Larsen[(✉)]

Department of Computer Science, Aalborg University,
Selma Lagerlöfs Vej 300, 9220 Aalborg East, Denmark
kgl@cs.aau.dk

Abstract. The growing complexity of Cyber-Physical Systems increasingly challenges existing methods and techniques. What is needed is a new generation of scalable tools for model-based learning, analysis, synthesis and optimization based on a mathematical sound foundation, that enables trade-offs between functional safety and quantitative performance. In paper we illustrate how recent branches of the UPPAAL tool suit are making an effort in this direction.

Cyber-Physical Systems

The term Cyber-Physical Systems (CPS) describes systems that combine computing elements with dedicated hardware and software having to monitor and control a particular physical environment. This combination of the physical with a virtual world provides the digital foundation for smart solutions throughout society and within all sectors. The constant demand for increased functionality and performance that needs to be produced with tight time schedules and cost budges without compromising dependability of the final products constitutes a significant software engineering challenge.

What is needed are mathematically well-founded, scalable methods, tools and techniques that support the development of CPS. For this we have over more than 20 years pursued a model-based approach for the design of dependable and optimal CPS, supported by tools that are based on efficient algorithms and datastructures for analysis of semantically well-founded models. This has been the guiding pricinple behind the UPPAAL suite (www.uppaal.org) [54] which by now have been applied to a wide range of industrial applications from the domains of Embedded Systems and Cyber-Physical Systems.

The first version of the UPPAAL tool was presented at the very first TACAS conference in 1995 in Aarhus, Denmark. During the first several years the tool was developed in tight collaboration between Uppsala University, Sweden and Aalborg University, Denmark. Over the years a number branches has been developed, some of which will be described in the following sections.

This work is partly funded by the ERC Advanced Grant LASSO: Learning, Analysis, SynthesiS and Optimization of Cyber-Physical Systems as well as the Innovation Center DiCyPS: Data-Intensive Cyber Physical Systems.

A. Legay and T. Margaria (Eds.): TACAS 2017, Part I, LNCS 10205, pp. 3–20, 2017.
DOI: 10.1007/978-3-662-54577-5_1

1   The UPPAAL Tool Suite

UPPAAL. The underlying formalism of UPPAAL is that of timed automata with the tool providing support for model checking of hard real-time properties. Since the introduction of the tool in 1995, significant effort have been put into development and implementation of improved datastructures and algorithms for the analysis of timed automata. This includes guided search algorithms using heuristics from AI [6,40,46,47], fully symbolic datastructures [9], minimal constraint normal forms [50], as well as a new symblistic DART datastructure [43,45] making usefull tradeoffs between the effectiveness of discrete and symbolic semantics. Also, this research has included the development of a series of exact abstractions (or extrapolation) that not only ensures finiteness of the symbolic semantics, but also provide significant performance improvements [3,4,42]. Besides these advance with respect to the verification engine, significant effort has over the years been put on the graphical interface of the tool (e.g. [7]), and on the modelling side the introduction of user-defined, structured datatypes and procedures has undoubtedly made the tool significantly more usable in modeling real control programs and communication protocols [6].

UPPAAL CORA. Motivated by the need for addressing (optimal) usage of resource, extension of priced timed automata was introduced in 2001 with [2,8] (independently) demonstrating decidability of cost-optimal reachability. Soon after efficient priced extension of the symbolic zone datastructures was implemented in the branch UPPAAL CORA, which combined with a symbolic A* algorithm providing a new generic tool for cost-optimal planning competetive to traditional OR methods such as Mixed-Integer Linear Programming [49]. Most recently new efficient extrapolation methods for priced timed automata has been introduced [17] and UPPAAL CORA has been used for the optimal planning of missions for battery-powered nano-satelittes [12].

UPPAAL TRON. In 2004 the branch UPPAAL TRON was introduced offering the possibility of performing on-line conformance testing of *real* real-time systems with respect to timed input-output automata [51,56]. UPPAAL TRON implements a sound and (theoretically) complete randomized testing algorithm, and uses a formally defined notion of correctness to assign verdicts: i.e. relativized timed input/output conformance providing a timed extension of Jan Tretmans ioco [58]. Using online testing, events are generated and simultaneously executed on the system under test. UPPAAL TRON has been succesfully applied to a number of industrial case studies including an advanced electronic thermostat regulator sold world-wide in high volume by the Danish company Danfoss [52].

UPPAAL TIGA. In 2005 - encouraged by suggestions from Tom Henzinger – the branch UPPAAL TIGA was released, allowing for control strategies to be synthesized from timed games, i.e. two-player games played on a timed automata [5,24]. The branch implements an efficient symbolic on-the-fly algorithm for synthesizing winning strategies for reachability, safety as well as Büchi objectives and taking possible partial observability into account [25]. The branch marks a disruptive direction with respect to development of control programs for embedded systems: rather than manually developing the control program with subsequent model checking (and correction), UPPAAL TIGA provides a fully automatic method for deriving a correct-by-construction control program. In particular, this method allows for easy personalization of control program simply by modification of the objective. The branch has so far been industrially applied to the automatic synthesis of control strategies for zone-base climate control in pigsties [44] and safe and optimal operation of hydralic pumps [26].

UPPAAL ECDAR. In 2010 the branch UPPAAL ECDAR was introduced supporting a scalable methodology for compositional development and stepwise refinenemet of real-time systems [36,38]. The underlying specification theory is that of timed I/O automata being essentially timed games (with inputs being controllable, and outputs being uncontrollable) equipped with suitable methods for refinement checking (in terms of an alternating simulation between two timed game specifications), consistency checking, logical as well as structural composition. The UPPAAL ECDAR branch uses heavily the UPPAAL TIGA engine to solve various games that arise in the computing the various composition operators and refinements. For a full account of UPPAAL ECDAR we refer the reader to the tutorial [35].

2   UPPAAL SMC

One of most recent branches of the UPPAAL tool suite – UPPAAL SMC introduced in 2011 – allows for performance evaluation the much richer formalisms of stochastic hybrid automata and games [33,34] and has by now been widely applied to analysis of a variety of case studies ranging from biological examples [32], schedulability for mixed-critical systems [13,37], evaluation of controllers for energy-aware buildings [28], social-technical attacks in security [39] as well as performance evaluation of a variety of wireless communication protocols [59]. Also the statistical model checking engine of UPPAAL SMC is supported by a distributed implementation [23], and allows for the statistical model checking of a large subset of MITL [21,22]. For a full account of UPPAAL SMC we refer the reader to the recent tutorial [31].

The modeling formalism of UPPAAL SMC is based on a stochastic interpretation and extension of the timed automata formalism used in the classical model checking version of UPPAAL. For individual components the stochastic interpretation replaces the nondeterministic choices between multiple enabled transitions by probabilistic choices (that may or may not be user-defined). Similarly, the non-deterministic choices of time-delays are refined by probability distributions, which at the component level are given either uniform distributions in cases with time-bounded delays or exponential distributions (with user-defined rates) in cases of unbounded delays.

To illustrate the features of UPPAAL SMC let us consider the example in Fig. 1, providing an "extended" timed automata based model of a car, that needs to make it from its initial position Start to the final position End. In the model the driver of the car twice needs to make a choice between using a high road (H1 and H2) or a low road (L1 and L2). The four roads differ in their travel-times between 0 and 100 min (respective 0 and 50 min) as reflected by the invariants on the clock x). Also the roads differ in fuel-consumption reflected by the difference in the rate of the continuous variable fc (representing the total amount of fuel consumed). The model is in fact a priced timed automaton (as supported by the branch UPPAAL CORA) with the total time that it will take to make it to End ranging between 0 and 200, and total fuel-consumption ranging between 0 and 900. However, interpreted as a *stochastic* priced timed automaton, the discrete choice betweeen the high and the low roads are made based on a (uniform) random choice. Similary, the travel times of the 4 roads are resolved using uniform distributions of the respect travel-time intervals.

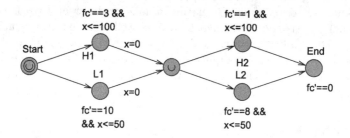

Fig. 1. The stochastic route model for a car

Now assume that we are interested in the expected fuel-consumption before reaching the goal End. Given the described stochastic semantics of the priced timed automaton in Fig. 1 this is easily seen to be the value of the following expression:

$$\left(0.5 \cdot \int_{t=0}^{100} 3t \cdot 0.01 dt + 0.5 \cdot \int_{t=0}^{50} 10t \cdot 0.02 dt\right) +$$
$$\left(0.5 \cdot \int_{t=0}^{100} 1t \cdot 0.01 dt + 0.5 \cdot \int_{t=0}^{50} 8t \cdot 0.02 dt\right) = 325$$

For this model the above expression giving the desired expectation was particularly easy as the clock x is reset. In general – and formally – the stochastic semantics of a stochastic (priced) timed automata is given by a probability measure assigning probabilities to (certain) sets of runs, being countable unions or complements of so-called cylinder-sets, i.e. sets of runs that follow the same prefix of edges in the automaton. In general, the probability of such a cylinder will be a nested integral (the nesting depth being the length of the path in the automaton). When considering *networks* of stochastic timed automata, the probability measure will moreover reflect a repeated race between components (for who is to perform the next discrete action) of the networks. Decidability (and undecidability) results for the stochastic interpretation of timed automata have so far – despite significant research – only given few conclusive results, e.g. that qualitative reachability (i.e. probability of reachability is 0 or 1) is decidable for one-clock stochastic timed automata [11, 14], or for acyclic models [55]. Instead, the statistical model checking engine of UPPAAL SMC resorts to simulation in order to settle a large range of quantitative questions, e.g. reachability probability or expectations. Being based on simulation, the results are however approximate (e.g. confidence intervals) but come with a statistically assured level of confidence. As an example, the UPPAAL SMC query

```
Pr[<=100](<> Car.End)
```

will after some 7382 random runs of the model (made according to the stochastic semantic described) return the 95% confidence interval [0.735636, 0.755635] as the probability that the location End is reached within 100 minutes. Addressing our original problem the query

```
E[<=200; 5000](max: fc)
```

will return the value 322.565 ± 4.70747 as an estimate of the expected fuel-comsumption based on 5000 random runs of the model. In Fig. 2 we see the additional plots offered by UPPAAL SMC for the cumulative probability of the time for reaching End and the frequency count of the fuel-consumption over 5000 random runs.

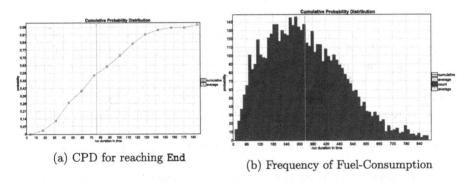

(a) CPD for reaching End   (b) Frequency of Fuel-Consumption

Fig. 2. Performance evaluation of stochastic car model.

3   UPPAAL Stratego

UPPAAL STRATEGO from 2014 [29, 30] is the most recent branch of the UPPAAL tool suite that allows to generate, optimize, compare and explore consequences and performance of strategies synthesized for stochastic priced timed games (SPTG) in a user-friendly manner. In particular, UPPAAL STRATEGO comes with an extended query language (see Table 1), where strategies are first class objects

Table 1. Various types of UPPAAL STRATEGO queries: "`strategy S =`" means strategy assignment and "`under S`" is strategy usage via strategy identifier `S`. Here the variables `NS`, `DS` and `SS` correspond to non-deterministic, deterministic and stochastic strategies respectively; `bound` is a bound expression on time or cost like `x<=100` and `n` is the number of simulations.

Strategy generators using [29]:	
Minimize objective:	`strategy DS = minE (expr) [bound]: <> prop`
Maximize objective:	`strategy DS = maxE (expr) [bound]: <> prop under NS`
Strategy generators using UPPAAL TIGA:	
Guarantee objective:	`strategy NS = control: A<> prop`
Guarantee objective:	`strategy NS = control: A[] prop`
Statistical model checking queries:	
Hypothesis testing:	`Pr[bound](<> prop)>=0.1 under SS`
Evaluation:	`Pr[bound](<> prop) under SS`
Comparison:	`Pr[bound](<> prop1) under SS1 >= Pr[<=20](<> prop2) under SS2`
Expected value:	`value E[bound;n](min: prop) under SS`
Simulations	`simulate n [bound] { expr1, expr2 } under SS`
Symbolic model checking queries:	
Safety:	`A[] prop under NS`
Liveness:	`A<> prop under NS`
Infimum of value:	`inf { condition } : expression`
Supremum of value:	`sup { condition } : expression`

that may be constructed, compared, optimized and used when performing (statistical) model checking of a game under the constraints of a given synthesized strategy. As such UPPAAL STRATEGO may be seen as a superset of UPPAAL TIGA and UPPAAL SMC.

To illustrate the features of UPPAAL STRATEGO, let us revise our running example of the car-route-problem as illustrated in in Fig. 3. Again there are four different roads with their individual required travel-times.

However, whereas the choice of road is up to the driver of the car to control (indicated by the solid transitions), the actual travel-time of the road is uncontrollable (indicated by the dashed transitions) reflecting the uncertainty of the amount of traffic on the particular day. In one scenario, the objective of the car it to choose the combination of roads that will ensure the shortest overall travel-time even in the most hostile traffic situation on the four roads. Under this interpretation, Fig. 3 represents a timed game. Clearly the strategy that would ensure the smallest worst-case travel-time is to take the two low roads, giving a guaranteed arrival time in 100 min. Taking the rates for the cost variable `fc` into account, makes Fig. 3 describe a priced time game, where the problem is to determine the best strategy in terms of minimizing the worst-case fuel-consumption. For our model this best strategy clearly consists in consistently choosing the

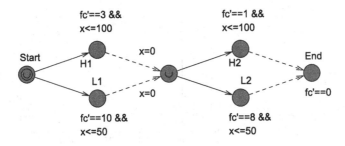

Fig. 3. The stochastic decision model for a car.

high roads. Unfortunaltely, cost-optimal winning strategies for priced games is undecidable in general when the underlying timed automata has three or more clocks [20]. Decidability results have been provided for one-clock priced timed games [19] and for so-called strongly cost-non-zeno priced timed games [15,16]; also approximate algorithms have been proposed [18].

However in UPPAAL STRATEGO, the model of Fig. 3 is interpreted as a *stochastic* priced timed game (SPTG), assuming that the travel-times of the four roads are chosen by uniform distributions, and the objective of the control strategy is to minimize the expected overall travel-time, or the expected overall fuel-consumption (e.g. the rate or fuel-consumption `fc'==3` on the first high road `H1` indicates that the cost variable `fc` grows with rate 3 in this location).

We are interested in synthesizing strategies for various objectives. Being primarily concerned with fuel-consumption we may want to determine the strategy that will minimize the expected fuel-consumption. For our simple decision model Fig. 3 this is clearly given by the following expression:

$$min\left\{ \int_{t=0}^{100} 3t \cdot 0.01 dt, \int_{t=0}^{50} 10t \cdot 0.02 dt \right\} +$$
$$min\left\{ \int_{t=0}^{100} 1t \cdot 0.01 dt, \int_{t=0}^{50} 8t \cdot 0.02 dt \right\} = 200$$

However, possing the UPPAAL STRATEGO query

```
strategy Opt = minE (fc) [<=200] : <> Car.End
```

will provide (by reinforcement learning[1]) the strategy `Opt`, that minimizes the expected total fuel-consumption, learning from runs which are maximally 200 time units long. The relativized query `E[<=200 ; 1000] (max: fc)` under `Opt`, generates 1000 runs of length 200 time units and then averages the maximum value of `fc` from each run. this is used to estimate the expected cost to be `200.39`. Figure 4a summarizes 10 random runs according `Opt` illustrating fuel-consumption. None of the runs had a fuel consumption of 400 indicating that we

---

[1] The reinforcement learning uses machine learning techniques to learn strategies from sets of randomly generated runs. See [29] for more details.

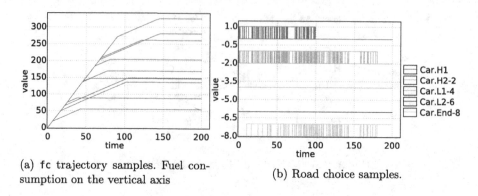

(a) fc trajectory samples. Fuel consumption on the vertical axis

(b) Road choice samples.

Fig. 4. Evaluation of strategy Opt via simulation.

always choose the energy-efficient roads. In Fig. 4b we see that this is actually the case as the simulations always choose to go to locations H1 and H2, which models the energy-efficient roads.

Now, assume that the task *must* be completed before 150 time-units. From Fig. 4 it can be seen that the strategy Opt unfortunately does not guarantee this, as there are a few runs which exceeds 150 before reaching End. However, the query

$$\text{strategy Safe = control: A<> Car.End and time<=150}$$

will generate the most permissive (non-deterministic) strategy Safe that guarantees this bound but unfortunately with a high expected total fuel-consumption of 342.19. However, the relativized learning query

$$\text{strategy OptSafe = minE (fc) [<=200] : <> Car.End under Safe}$$

will provide a sub-strategy OptSafe that minimizes the expected total fuel-consumption – here found to be 279.87 – subject to the constraints of Safe. Figure 5 summarizes 10 random runs according to SafeOpt, incidating that only road L1 is never choosen. Also, the failed model checking of E<> Car.H2 and time>=51 and Car.x==0 under Safe reveals that the high road H2 may only be choosen in case the first phase is completed before 50 time-units, confirming the observations from the simulations.

For learning the strategy OptSafe the reinforcement learning method required 5 iterations each with 1000 runs. We illustrate in Fig. 6 the outcome of the runs in the last 3 iterations focusing on the choice, time and resulting fuel-consumption at the choice-point between H2 and L2. As can be seen the method correctly learns to take the low road whenever the choice point is reached before a total time of 50 min (leaving enough time to guarantee that End will be reached within 150 min.

In general, as shown in the overview Fig. 7, UPPAAL STRATEGO will start from a SPTG $\mathcal{P}$. It can then abstract $\mathcal{P}$ into a timed game (TGA) $\mathcal{G}$ by simply ignoring

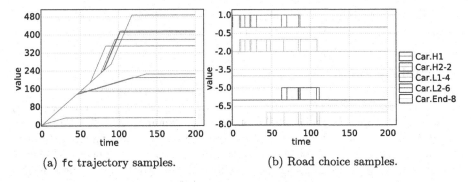

(a) fc trajectory samples.   (b) Road choice samples.

Fig. 5. Evaluation of strategy OptSafe via simulation.

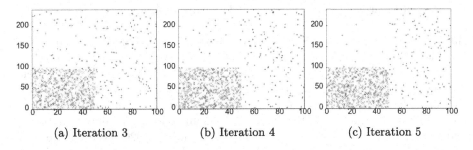

(a) Iteration 3   (b) Iteration 4   (c) Iteration 5

Fig. 6. Total fuel-consumption versus time at mid-location for runs 1000 runs choosing between H2 and L2 towards learning the strategy OptSafe.

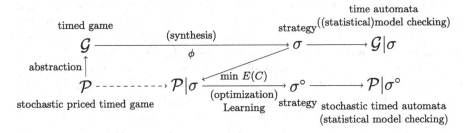

Fig. 7. Overview of UPPAAL STRATEGO

prices and stochasticity in the model. Using $\mathcal{G}$, UPPAAL TIGA [5] may now be used to (symbolically) synthesize a (most permissive) strategy σ meeting a required safety or (time-bounded) liveness constraint ϕ. The TGA $\mathcal{G}$ under σ (denoted $\mathcal{G}|\sigma$) may now be subject to additional (statistical) model checking using classical UPPAAL [54] and UPPAAL SMC [31,34]. Similarly, the original STGA $\mathcal{P}$ under σ may be subject to statistical model checking. Now using reinforcement learning [29], we may synthesize near-optimal strategies that minimizes (maximizes) the expectation of a given cost-expression *cost*. In case the learning is performed from $\mathcal{P}|\sigma$, we obtain a sub-strategy σ^o of σ that optimizes the expected value of *cost* subject to the hard constraints guaranteed by σ. Finally, given σ^o, one may perform additional statistical model checking of $\mathcal{P}|\sigma^o$.

4   Applications

The importance of CPS is clear within the domains of energy and transport with the emergence Smart Grid, Home Automation, Autonomous Driving, Advanced Driver Assistance and Intelligent Traffic Control where optimizing critical functionality is provided by intelligent and flexible software components. UPPAAL stratego has already been applied to a number of case studies including synthesis of a safe and optimal adaptive cruice control [53], synthesis of optimal floor heating system [48], and most recently synthesis of optimal control of traffic lights in intersections as described in the following sub-sections.

Adaptive Cruice Control. These days the Google Self-Driving car is about to become a reality: legislation has been passed in several U.S. states allowing driverless cars, in April 2014, Google announced that their vehicles had been logging nearly 1.1 million km, and it is forecast that Google's self-driving cars will hit the roads this summer. Also, in Europe driverless cars have been actively pursued, both by the automotive industry itself and within a number of national and European research projects (e.g. FP7 and Horizon2020). With more and more traffic, European roads are becoming increasingly congested, polluted and unsafe. One potential solution to this growing problem is seen to be the use of small, automated, low-polluting vehicles for driverless transport in (and between) cities. Within the last decade, a number of European projects have been launched for making transport systems capable of fully automated driving, energy efficient and environmentally friendly while performing. In addition, many individual driving assistant systems based on suitable sensors have been developed for cars.

In [53], we have considered a small part of lane-change manoeuvres, namely the existence of a safe-distance controller (assumed in the above work of Olderog et al.). In particular, we demonstrated how UPPAAL STRATEGO may be applied to automatically obtain a safe yet optimal adaptive strategy `safe` for the cruice control. Modelling the cruice control as a game with a car in front a *safe* strategy was synthezed ensuring that the distance to the front care would never get below 5 meters. In fact utilizing the distinct feature of UPPAAL STRATEGO – allowing additional properties to be verified of a synthesized strategy – we may verify the smallest distance possible to the front care which will not violate the `safe` as shown in Fig. 8.

Now asking for a sub-strategy `safeFast` of `safe` that will minimize the expected accumulated distance to the front care yields a substantial improvement as seen in Fig. 9.

Home Automation. Home automation includes the centralized control of a number of functionalities in a house such as lighting, HVAC (heating, ventilation and air conditioning), appliances, security locks of gates and doors as well as other

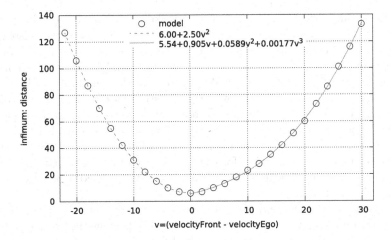

Fig. 8. Smallest distance possible under the `safe` strategy as a function of speed difference computed using `inf{velocityFront-velocityEgo==v}: distance under safe` for each v value. Connecting lines are from linear regression analysis.

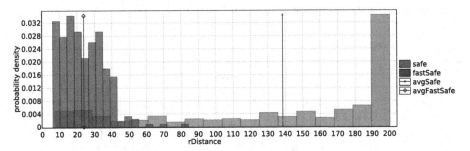

Fig. 9. The probability density distribution over `rDistance` at `time >= 100` thus after 100 time units under the strategies `safe` and `safeFast`. The (dark) red bars for `safe` and the (light) green bars for `safeFast`. (Color figure online)

systems. The overall goal is to achieve improved convenience, comfort, energy efficiency as well as security. The popularity of home automation has increased significantly in recent years through affordable smartphone and tablet connectivity. Also the emergence of "Internet of Things" has tied in closely with the popularization of home automation.

In [48] we collaborated with the Danish company Seluxit within the European project CASSTING[2]. The focus was on the floorheating system of a family house, where each room of the house has its own hot-water pipe circuit. These are controlled through a number of valves based on information about room temperatures communicated wirelessly (periodically due to energy considerations) from a number of temperature sensors. In the existing system, a simple

---

[2] http://www.cassting-project.eu/.

"Bang-Bang"-like strategy is applied, however, there are though several problems with this strategy, as experienced by the house owner: it completely disregards the interaction between rooms in terms of heat-exchange, the impact of the outside temperature and weather forecast as well as information about movements in the house. Taking this knowledge into account should potentially enable the synthesis of significantly improved control strategies. Unfortunately, direct application of UPPAAL STRATEGO does not scale: due to the enormous number of control modes it is virtually impossible to learn optimal control. Instead, we proposed a novel on-line synthesis methodology, where we periodically—and on-line—learn the optimal controller for the near future based on the current sensor readings. For additional scalability, we proposed and applied a novel compositional synthesis approach.

In particular, the strategy provided by UPPAAL STRATEGO takes weather information into account, as illustrated by Fig. 10 showing the spring stability scenario. From points of time between 0 and 500 min, the outside temperature increases and exceeds the target temperature. We observe that since the controller synthesized by UPPAAL STRATEGO is able to look at the weather forecast for the next 45 min, it shuts down the valves much earlier than the other controllers. This results in energy savings and increased comfort.

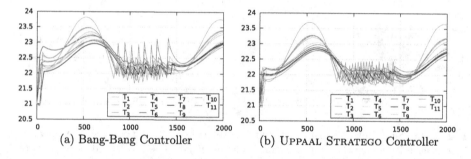

(a) Bang-Bang Controller   (b) UPPAAL STRATEGO Controller

Fig. 10. Room temperatures in the spring stability scenario

Intelligent Control of Trafic Light. The Danish Congestion Commission calls in its recent report for improved traffic signal control in order to reduce congestion, travel time and energy consumption. This project has been formulated to contribute to a more efficient utilisation of the existing infrastructure by improving traffic signal control. However, modern traffic lights use information from induction loops and to some extend radar information. Recent developments in radar technology has made it possible to obtain more detailed information relevant to the control mechanism of the traffic light. Unfortunately much of the current controllers do not profit from this additional information. Using this information could minimize waiting times and energy waste.

Within the Innovation Center DiCyPS[3] we have collaborated with researchers in traffic control to apply UPPAAL STRATEGO to the synthesis of an efficient

---

[3] Center for Data-Intensive Cyber-Physical Systems, www.dicyps.dk.

Fig. 11. Intersection between Nylandsvej and Værkstedvej at Køge municipality. Layout of loops and radar area.

traffic signal control strategy that takes advantage of the continuous traffic monitoring made available by radar detectors. The purpose of the strategy is to optimize the total traffic flow in the junction, i.e. to reduce the total delay, queue length and the number of stops. The synthesis of UPPAAL STRATEGO is done on-line offering every 5 s a new updated optimal strategy for the next operation of a signalized intersection in the municiplaity of Køge, Denmark, Fig. 11. In doing so the UPPAAL STRATEGO model takes into account the random generation of traffic in the various directions. The on-line strategy generated is fed to a richer simulation engine in SUMO, an open source tool which allows to model and simulate traffic systems. SUMO also provides a number of supporting tools which allow for visualization, network transformation, waiting time calculations, traffic light performance, etc.

In the resulting evaluation shown in Fig. 2 we have compared the performance of a so-called Static controller, the Loop Controller and the UPPAAL STRATEGO controller. In the most demanding MAX scenario – with highest intenty of traffic – it is clear that the UPPAAL STRATEGO controller is performining significantly better than any of the others. For MID scenario the findings are similar and for the LOW scenario all the controllers perform quite similar, but the Loop controller is in general the best (Table 2).

Table 2. Results of the experiments. We show the mean and the 95 percentile for respectively the waiting time of the cars and the queue length. This is done for each controller in all scenarios.

Scenario	Direction	Delay in Seconds (Waiting Time)						Queue Length in Meters					
		Mean			95p			Mean			95p		
		Static	Loop	STRATEGO	Static	Loop	STRATEGO	Static	Loop	STRATEGO	Static	Loop	STRATEGO
MAX	A1	19	7	10	69	49	52	23	10	13	67	45	60
	A2	25	8	9	87	50	47	31	11	12	105	45	54
	B1	69	89	25	221	300	77	24	31	8	142	188	45
	B2	108	169	28	263	389	88	44	68	11	188	286	53
	ALL	38	37	13	162	242	61	31	30	11	144	195	52
MID	A1	13	8	8	40	36	32	17	11	11	52	38	39
	A2	13	10	7	49	42	33	17	14	10	54	52	37
	B1	15	25	21	43	63	57	5	8	7	22	30	30
	B2	26	38	25	82	105	64	10	15	10	37	52	30
	ALL	15	14	11	48	61	44	12	12	10	45	45	37
LOW	A1	7	6	5	22	25	23	6	5	4	23	22	22
	A2	5	4	5	22	21	22	4	4	4	15	15	22
	B1	11	11	16	33	38	45	2	2	2	7	15	15
	B2	13	9	16	35	30	45	3	2	3	15	15	15
	ALL	7	6	8	29	26	30	4	3	4	15	15	15

References

1. Third International Conference on the Quantitative Evaluation of Systems (QEST 2006), Riverside, California, USA, 11–14 September 2006. IEEE Computer Society (2006)

2. Alur, R., La Torre, S., Pappas, G.J.: Optimal paths in weighted timed automata. In: Benedetto, M.D., Sangiovanni-Vincentelli, A. (eds.) HSCC 2001. LNCS, vol. 2034, pp. 49–62. Springer, Heidelberg (2001). doi:10.1007/3-540-45351-2_8. [10]

3. Behrmann, G., Bouyer, P., Fleury, E., Larsen, K.G.: Static guard analysis in timed automata verification. In: Garavel, H., Hatcliff, J. (eds.) TACAS 2003. LNCS, vol. 2619, pp. 254–270. Springer, Heidelberg (2003). doi:10.1007/3-540-36577-X_18

4. Behrmann, G., Bouyer, P., Larsen, K.G., Pelánek, R.: Lower and upper bounds in zone-based abstractions of timed automata. STTT $8(3)$, 204–215 (2006)

5. Behrmann, G., Cougnard, A., David, A., Fleury, E., Larsen, K.G., Lime, D.: UPPAAL-tiga: time for playing games! In: Damm, W., Hermanns, H. (eds.) CAV 2007. LNCS, vol. 4590, pp. 121–125. Springer, Heidelberg (2007). doi:10.1007/978-3-540-73368-3_14. [29]

6. Behrmann, G., David, A., Larsen, K.G., Håkansson, J., Pettersson, P., Yi, W., Hendriks, M.: UPPAAL 4.0. In: Third International Conference on the Quantitative Evaluation of Systems (QEST 2006), Riverside, California, USA, 11–14 September 2006, pp. 125–126 (2006). [1]

7. Behrmann, G., David, A., Larsen, K.G., Pettersson, P., Yi, W.: Developing UPPAAL over 15 years. Softw. Pract. Exp. $41(2)$, 133–142 (2011)

8. Behrmann, G., Fehnker, A., Hune, T., Larsen, K., Pettersson, P., Romijn, J., Vaandrager, F.: Minimum-cost reachability for priced time automata. In: Benedetto, M.D., Sangiovanni-Vincentelli, A. (eds.) HSCC 2001. LNCS, vol. 2034, pp. 147–161. Springer, Heidelberg (2001). doi:10.1007/3-540-45351-2_15. [10]

9. Behrmann, G., Larsen, K.G., Pearson, J., Weise, C., Yi, W.: Efficient timed reachability analysis using clock difference diagrams. In: Halbwachs, N., Peled, D. (eds.)

CAV 1999. LNCS, vol. 1633, pp. 341–353. Springer, Heidelberg (1999). doi:10.1007/3-540-48683-6_30

10. Benedetto, M.D., Sangiovanni-Vincentelli, A. (eds.): HSCC 2001. LNCS, vol. 2034. Springer, Heidelberg (2001)

11. Bertrand, N., Bouyer, P., Brihaye, T., Markey, N.: Quantitative model-checking of one-clock timed automata under probabilistic semantics. In: Fifth International Conference on the Quantitative Evaluaiton of Systems (QEST 2008), Saint-Malo, France, 14–17 September 2008, pp. 55–64. IEEE Computer Society (2008)

12. Bisgaard, M., Gerhardt, D., Hermanns, H., Krčál, J., Nies, G., Stenger, M.: Battery-aware scheduling in low orbit: the GoMX–3 case. In: Fitzgerald, J., Heitmeyer, C., Gnesi, S., Philippou, A. (eds.) FM 2016. LNCS, vol. 9995, pp. 559–576. Springer, Heidelberg (2016). doi:10.1007/978-3-319-48989-6_34

13. Boudjadar, A., David, A., Kim, J.H., Larsen, K.G., Mikucionis, M., Nyman, U., Skou, A.: Degree of schedulability of mixed-criticality real-time systems with probabilistic sporadic tasks. In: 2014 Theoretical Aspects of Software Engineering Conference, TASE 2014, Changsha, China, 1–3 September 2014, pp. 126–130. IEEE Computer Society (2014)

14. Bouyer, P., Brihaye, T., Jurdzinski, M., Menet, Q.: Almost-sure model-checking of reactive timed automata. In: Ninth International Conference on Quantitative Evaluation of Systems, QEST 2012, London, United Kingdom, 17–20 September 2012, pp. 138–147. IEEE Computer Society (2012)

15. Bouyer, P., Cassez, F., Fleury, E., Larsen, K.G.: Optimal strategies in priced timed game automata. In: Lodaya, K., Mahajan, M. (eds.) FSTTCS 2004. LNCS, vol. 3328, pp. 148–160. Springer, Heidelberg (2004). doi:10.1007/978-3-540-30538-5_13

16. Bouyer, P., Cassez, F., Fleury, E., Larsen, K.G.: Synthesis of optimal strategies using hytech. Electr. Notes Theor. Comput. Sci. **119**(1), 11–31 (2005)

17. Bouyer, P., Colange, M., Markey, N.: Symbolic optimal reachability in weighted timed automata. In: Chaudhuri, S., Farzan, A. (eds.) CAV 2016. LNCS, vol. 9779, pp. 513–530. Springer, Heidelberg (2016). doi:10.1007/978-3-319-41528-4_28

18. Bouyer, P., Jaziri, S., Markey, N.: On the value problem in weighted timed games. In: Aceto, L., de Frutos-Escrig, D. (eds.) 26th International Conference on Concurrency Theory, CONCUR 2015, Madrid, Spain, 1–4 September 2015. LIPIcs, vol. 42, pp. 311–324. Schloss Dagstuhl - Leibniz-Zentrum fuer Informatik (2015)

19. Bouyer, P., Larsen, K.G., Markey, N., Rasmussen, J.I.: Almost optimal strategies in one clock priced timed games. In: Arun-Kumar, S., Garg, N. (eds.) FSTTCS 2006. LNCS, vol. 4337, pp. 345–356. Springer, Heidelberg (2006). doi:10.1007/11944836_32

20. Brihaye, T., Bruyère, V., Raskin, J.-F.: On optimal timed strategies. In: Pettersson, P., Yi, W. (eds.) FORMATS 2005. LNCS, vol. 3829, pp. 49–64. Springer, Heidelberg (2005). doi:10.1007/11603009_5

21. Bulychev, P., David, A., Larsen, K.G., Legay, A., Li, G., Poulsen, D.B.: Rewrite-based statistical model checking of WMTL. In: Qadeer, S., Tasiran, S. (eds.) RV 2012. LNCS, vol. 7687, pp. 260–275. Springer, Heidelberg (2013). doi:10.1007/978-3-642-35632-2_25

22. Bulychev, P., David, A., Larsen, K.G., Legay, A., Li, G., Poulsen, D.B., Stainer, A.: Monitor-based statistical model checking for weighted metric temporal logic. In: Bjørner, N., Voronkov, A. (eds.) LPAR 2012. LNCS, vol. 7180, pp. 168–182. Springer, Heidelberg (2012). doi:10.1007/978-3-642-28717-6_15

23. Bulychev, P., David, A., Larsen, K.G., Legay, A., Mikučionis, M., Poulsen, D.B.: Checking and distributing statistical model checking. In: Goodloe, A.E., Person,

S. (eds.) NFM 2012. LNCS, vol. 7226, pp. 449–463. Springer, Heidelberg (2012). doi:10.1007/978-3-642-28891-3_39

24. Cassez, F., David, A., Fleury, E., Larsen, K.G., Lime, D.: Efficient on-the-fly algorithms for the analysis of timed games. In: Abadi, M., Alfaro, L. (eds.) CONCUR 2005. LNCS, vol. 3653, pp. 66–80. Springer, Heidelberg (2005). doi:10.1007/11539452_9

25. Cassez, F., David, A., Larsen, K.G., Lime, D., Raskin, J.-F.: Timed control with observation based and stuttering invariant strategies. In: Namjoshi, K.S., Yoneda, T., Higashino, T., Okamura, Y. (eds.) ATVA 2007. LNCS, vol. 4762, pp. 192–206. Springer, Heidelberg (2007). doi:10.1007/978-3-540-75596-8_15

26. Cassez, F., Jessen, J.J., Larsen, K.G., Raskin, J.-F., Reynier, P.-A.: Automatic synthesis of robust and optimal controllers – an industrial case study. In: Majumdar, R., Tabuada, P. (eds.) HSCC 2009. LNCS, vol. 5469, pp. 90–104. Springer, Heidelberg (2009). doi:10.1007/978-3-642-00602-9_7

27. Damm, W., Hermanns, H. (eds.): CAV 2007. LNCS, vol. 4590. Springer, Heidelberg (2007)

28. David, A., Du, D., Larsen, K.G., Mikucionis, M., Skou, A.: An evaluation framework for energy aware buildings using statistical model checking. Sci. China Inf. Sci. 55(12), 2694–2707 (2012)

29. David, A., Jensen, P.G., Larsen, K.G., Legay, A., Lime, D., Sørensen, M.G., Taankvist, J.H.: On time with minimal expected cost! In: Cassez, F., Raskin, J.-F. (eds.) ATVA 2014. LNCS, vol. 8837, pp. 129–145. Springer, Heidelberg (2014). doi:10.1007/978-3-319-11936-6_10

30. David, A., Jensen, P.G., Larsen, K.G., Mikučionis, M., Taankvist, J.H.: UPPAAL STRATEGO. In: Baier, C., Tinelli, C. (eds.) TACAS 2015. LNCS, vol. 9035, pp. 206–211. Springer, Heidelberg (2015). doi:10.1007/978-3-662-46681-0_16

31. David, A., Larsen, K.G., Legay, A., Mikucionis, M., Poulsen, D.B.: Uppaal SMC tutorial. STTT 17(4), 397–415 (2015)

32. David, A., Larsen, K.G., Legay, A., Mikucionis, M., Poulsen, D.B., Sedwards, S.: Statistical model checking for biological systems. STTT 17(3), 351–367 (2015)

33. David, A., Larsen, K.G., Legay, A., Mikučionis, M., Poulsen, D.B., Vliet, J., Wang, Z.: Statistical model checking for networks of priced timed automata. In: Fahrenberg, U., Tripakis, S. (eds.) FORMATS 2011. LNCS, vol. 6919, pp. 80–96. Springer, Heidelberg (2011). doi:10.1007/978-3-642-24310-3_7

34. David, A., Larsen, K.G., Legay, A., Mikučionis, M., Wang, Z.: Time for statistical model checking of real-time systems. In: Gopalakrishnan, G., Qadeer, S. (eds.) CAV 2011. LNCS, vol. 6806, pp. 349–355. Springer, Heidelberg (2011). doi:10.1007/978-3-642-22110-1_27. [41]

35. David, A., Larsen, K.G., Legay, A., Nyman, U., Traonouez, L.-M., Wasowski, A.: Real-time specifications. STTT 17(1), 17–45 (2015)

36. David, A., Larsen, K.G., Legay, A., Nyman, U., Wasowski, A.: Timed I/O automata: a complete specification theory for real-time systems. In: Johansson, K.H., Yi, W. (eds.) Proceedings of the 13th ACM International Conference on Hybrid Systems: Computation and Control, HSCC 2010, Stockholm, Sweden, 12–15 April 2010, pp. 91–100. ACM (2010)

37. David, A., Larsen, K.G., Legay, A., Mikučionis, M.: Schedulability of herschel-planck revisited using statistical model checking. In: Margaria, T., Steffen, B. (eds.) ISoLA 2012. LNCS, vol. 7610, pp. 293–307. Springer, Heidelberg (2012). doi:10.1007/978-3-642-34032-1_28

38. David, A., Larsen, K.G., Legay, A., Nyman, U., Wasowski, A.: ECDAR: an environment for compositional design and analysis of real time systems. In: Bouajjani, A., Chin, W.-N. (eds.) ATVA 2010. LNCS, vol. 6252, pp. 365–370. Springer, Heidelberg (2010). doi:10.1007/978-3-642-15643-4_29

39. David, N., David, A., Hansen, R.R., Larsen, K.G., Legay, A., Olesen, M.C., Probst, C.W.: Modelling social-technical attacks with timed automata. In: Bertino, E., You, I. (eds.) Proceedings of the 7th ACM CCS International Workshop on Managing Insider Security Threats, MIST 2015, Denver, Colorado, USA, 16 October 2015, pp. 21–28. ACM (2015)

40. Dierks, H., Kupferschmid, S., Larsen, K.G.: Automatic abstraction refinement for timed automata. In: Raskin, J.-F., Thiagarajan, P.S. (eds.) FORMATS 2007. LNCS, vol. 4763, pp. 114–129. Springer, Heidelberg (2007). doi:10.1007/978-3-540-75454-1_10. [57]

41. Gopalakrishnan, G., Qadeer, S. (eds.): CAV 2011. LNCS, vol. 6806. Springer, Heidelberg (2011)

42. Herbreteau, F., Srivathsan, B., Walukiewicz, I.: Better abstractions for timed automata. Inf. Comput. **251**, 67–90 (2016)

43. Jensen, P.G., Larsen, K.G., Srba, J., Sørensen, M.G., Taankvist, J.H.: Memory efficient data structures for explicit verification of timed systems. In: Badger, J.M., Rozier, K.Y. (eds.) NFM 2014. LNCS, vol. 8430, pp. 307–312. Springer, Heidelberg (2014). doi:10.1007/978-3-319-06200-6_26

44. Jessen, J.J., Rasmussen, J.I., Larsen, K.G., David, A.: Guided controller synthesis for climate controller using UPPAAL TIGA. In: Raskin, J.-F., Thiagarajan, P.S. (eds.) FORMATS 2007. LNCS, vol. 4763, pp. 227–240. Springer, Heidelberg (2007). doi:10.1007/978-3-540-75454-1_17. [57]

45. Jørgensen, K.Y., Larsen, K.G., Srba, J.: Time-darts: a data structure for verification of closed timed automata. In: Cassez, F., Huuck, R., Klein, G., Schlich, B. (eds.) Proceedings Seventh Conference on Systems Software Verification, SSV 2012, Sydney, Australia, 28–30 November 2012. EPTCS, vol. 102, pp. 141–155 (2012)

46. Kupferschmid, S., Hoffmann, J., Dierks, H., Behrmann, G.: Adapting an AI planning heuristic for directed model checking. In: Valmari, A. (ed.) SPIN 2006. LNCS, vol. 3925, pp. 35–52. Springer, Heidelberg (2006). doi:10.1007/11691617_3

47. Kupferschmid, S., Wehrle, M., Nebel, B., Podelski, A.: Faster than UPPAAL? In: Gupta, A., Malik, S. (eds.) CAV 2008. LNCS, vol. 5123, pp. 552–555. Springer, Heidelberg (2008). doi:10.1007/978-3-540-70545-1_53

48. Larsen, K.G., Mikučionis, M., Muñiz, M., Srba, J., Taankvist, J.H.: Online and compositional learning of controllers with application to floor heating. In: Chechik, M., Raskin, J.-F. (eds.) TACAS 2016. LNCS, vol. 9636, pp. 244–259. Springer, Heidelberg (2016). doi:10.1007/978-3-662-49674-9_14

49. Larsen, K.G., Behrmann, G., Brinksma, E., Fehnker, A., Hune, T., Pettersson, P., Romijn, J.: As cheap as possible: effcient cost-optimal reachability for priced timed automata. In: Berry, G., Comon, H., Finkel, A. (eds.) CAV 2001. LNCS, vol. 2102, pp. 493–505. Springer, Heidelberg (2001). doi:10.1007/3-540-44585-4_47

50. Larsen, K.G., Larsson, F., Pettersson, P., Yi, W.: Efficient verification of real-time systems: compact data structure and state-space reduction. In: Proceedings of the 18th IEEE Real-Time Systems Symposium (RTSS 1997), San Francisco, CA, USA, 3–5 December 1997, pp. 14–24. IEEE Computer Society (1997)

51. Larsen, K.G., Mikucionis, M., Nielsen, B.: Online testing of real-time systems using UPPAAL. In: Grabowski, J., Nielsen, B. (eds.) FATES 2004. LNCS, vol. 3395, pp. 79–94. Springer, Heidelberg (2005). doi:10.1007/978-3-540-31848-4_6

52. Larsen, K.G., Mikucionis, M., Nielsen, B., Skou, A.: Testing real-time embedded software using UPPAAL-TRON: an industrial case study. In: Wolf, W.H. (ed.) Proceedings of the 5th ACM International Conference On Embedded Software EMSOFT 2005, Jersey City, NJ, USA, 18–22 September 2005 , pp. 299–306. ACM (2005)

53. Larsen, K.G., Mikučionis, M., Taankvist, J.H.: Safe and optimal adaptive cruise control. In: Meyer, R., Platzer, A., Wehrheim, H. (eds.) Correct System Design. LNCS, vol. 9360, pp. 260–277. Springer, Heidelberg (2015). doi:10.1007/978-3-319-23506-6_17

54. Larsen, K.G., Pettersson, P., Yi, W.: UPPAAL in a nutshell. STTT $1(1–2)$, 134–152 (1997)

55. Maler, O., Larsen, K.G., Krogh, B.H.: On zone-based analysis of duration probabilistic automata. In: Chen, Y.-F., Rezine, A. (eds.) Proceedings 12th International Workshop on Verification of Infinite-State Systems, INFINITY 2010, Singapore, Singapore, 21 September 2010. EPTCS, vol. 39, pp. 33–46 (2010)

56. Mikucionis, M., Larsen, K.G., Nielsen, B.: T-UPPAAL: online model-based testing of real-time systems. In: 19th IEEE International Conference on Automated Software Engineering (ASE 2004), Linz, Austria, 20–25 September 2004, pp. 396–397. IEEE Computer Society (2004)

57. Raskin, J.-F., Thiagarajan, P.S. (eds.): FORMATS 2007. LNCS, vol. 4763. Springer, Heidelberg (2007)

58. Tretmans, J.: A formal approach to conformance testing. In: Rafiq, O. (ed.) Protocol Test Systems, VI, Proceedings of the IFIP TC6/WG6.1 Sixth International Workshop on Protocol Test systems, Pau, France, 28–30 September 1993. IFIP Transactions, vol. C-19, pp. 257–276. North-Holland (1993)

59. van Glabbeek, R.J., Höfner, P., Portmann, M., Tan, W.L.: Modelling and verifying the AODV routing protocol. Distrib. Comput. $29(4)$, 279–315 (2016)

Verification Techniques I

An Abstraction Technique for Parameterized Model Checking of Leader Election Protocols: Application to FTSP

Ocan Sankur[1]([✉]) and Jean-Pierre Talpin[2]

[1] CNRS, Irisa, Rennes, France
ocan.sankur@irisa.fr
[2] Inria, Rennes, France

Abstract. We consider distributed timed systems that implement leader election protocols which are at the heart of clock synchronization protocols. We develop abstraction techniques for parameterized model checking of such protocols under arbitrary network topologies, where nodes have independently evolving clocks. We apply our technique for model checking the root election part of the flooding time synchronisation protocol (FTSP), and obtain improved results compared to previous work. We model check the protocol for all topologies in which the distance to the node to be elected leader is bounded by a given parameter.

1 Introduction

One of the apparently simplest services in any loosely-coupled distributed system is the time service. Usually, a client in such a system, e.g. your laptop, simply posts an NTP (network time protocol) request to any registered server and uses the first reply. In many such systems, however, the accuracy and reliability of the time service are critical: clients of traffic and power grids, banking and transaction networks, automated factories and supply plants, acutely depend on a reliable and accurate measure of time.

To make things worse, most cyber-physical system in such distributed networks rely on a quasi-synchronous hypothesis that critically relies on drift and jitter bounds provided by time synchronisation protocols. In a remedy for this Achille's heel of the "Internet of things", fault-tolerant and self-calibrating protocols have been proposed, such as the open source *flooding time synchronisation protocol (FTSP)* of Tiny OS, Google's True Time API, as well as commercial solutions, such as IGS' Real-Time Service. It is critical to provide such services to the 21st Century's Internet as is it to provide proof of their correctness.

Our goal is to develop both modular and scalable verification techniques for time synchronisation protocols. Towards this aim, in this paper, we concentrate on leader election protocols which are at the basis of several time synchronisation protocols where the nodes in the network synchronise their clocks to that of the elected leader. Leader election protocols pose exciting benchmarks and case

© Springer-Verlag GmbH Germany 2017
A. Legay and T. Margaria (Eds.): TACAS 2017, Part I, LNCS 10205, pp. 23–40, 2017.
DOI: 10.1007/978-3-662-54577-5_2

studies to the verification of distributed systems design. These have been the subject of formal proofs or model-checking, *e.g.* Chang-Robert's algorithm [6,15], and that of Dolev-Klaweh-Rodeh [13,17].

The root election part of FTSP [20], available in open-source in the implementation of Tiny OS, has drawn attention from the formal verification community. Kusy and Abdelwahed [19] model-check FTSP root election using SPIN, showing that a 4-node FTSP network is guaranteed to converge to a single root node. McInnes [21] verifies root-convergence for 7-node models using the FDR2 model checker, and also considers time-convergence properties, *i.e.* whether all nodes agree on the time of the root node. Tan et al. [28] use timed automata to introduce a more realistic simulation model of wireless sensor networks (WSN) with transmission delays and node failures and check the FTSP against these. They identify an error in a scenario where two root nodes fail continuously.

Parameterized Verification. The major issue when model checking such distributed protocols is the state explosion problem due to the large number of nodes in the protocol. Several works have concentrated on given network topologies, for instance, a grid of fixed size, *e.g.* [21]. To model check properties for an arbitrary number of nodes, parameterized verification techniques have been considered. Although the general problem is undecidable [2], decidability has been shown in several cases, by proving cutoffs [14] either on fully connected topologies or particular ones such as rings. Compositional model checking techniques were used in [22] for model checking a cache coherence protocol.

Contributions. We present an abstraction technique for the parameterized verification of distributed protocols with unique identifiers and apply it for model checking the leader election part of the FTSP. Our model for FTSP is more precise compared to the previous works in several aspects. In fact, we consider asynchronous communication between nodes rather than instantaneous broadcasts, and we model the periodically executed tasks as run with local clocks that are subject to imperfections. We were able to model check that a unique leader is elected starting at an *arbitrary* configuration, assuming no fault occurs during this period. This corresponds to checking fault recovery, that is, proving the protocol correct following an arbitrary fault. Thus, if we prove that the leader is elected within N steps in this setting, then following any fault, a unique leader is elected again within N steps in the worst case.

Our parameterized verification algorithm allows us to check FTSP (a) for *arbitrary* topologies in which the maximal distance to the future leader is at most K, (b) where each node evolves under clock deviations whose magnitude can be adjusted, (c) where communication between nodes are either synchronous or asynchronous. As an example, we were able to model check the protocol for $K = 7$ in the synchronous case, and for $K = 5$ in the asynchronous case. Graphs with $K = 7$ include 2D grids with 169 nodes (or 3D grids with 2197 nodes), where the future leader is at the middle. For $K = 5$, these include 2D grids with 81 nodes (and 729 in 3D). Observe that grids of size 60 were considered for simulation in [20], which is out of the reach of previous model checking attempts.

We believe our parameterized verification technique can be adapted to other distributed protocols that work in a similar fashion, *e.g.* [29]. Our project is to extend our technique by integrating non-functional characteristics that have an impact on the accuracy and reliability of these protocols: electronic hazards (inaccuracy in physical clocks fabric), environmental hazards (temperature of clients environment), power hazards (capacity and stability of clients power source). Protocols accounting for such cyber-physical characteristics are being developed in the NSF Roseline and our goal is to prove their correctness.

More on Related Work. Our parameterized verification approach is inspired by [7] where an abstraction technique is given for parameterized model checking against *safety* properties in cache coherence protocols. Using the fact that such systems are *symmetric*, the main idea is to isolate a pair of nodes and abstract away other nodes as an abstract environment. In our work, the systems we consider are not symmetric since the nodes have unique identifiers which influence their behaviors and the network topology is arbitrary. We thus deal with these issues in order to lift the technique in our case. Another work introduces a refinement of existential abstraction for parameterized model checking: in [8], an abstraction is obtained by isolating a component, and abstracting away the other nodes by summarizing which control states are occupied by some component, which is similar to counter abstraction [25]. Parameterized verification techniques have been studied for fault-tolerant distributed systems with Byzantine or other types of failures [16]. Such protocols often consider *threshold guards*, which are used to make sure that a given number of messages have been received from different processes. The authors define abstractions on the set of participating nodes with predicates that use these thresholds. This approach is not applicable in our case due to our network topologies, and that the nodes do not use such thresholds. Parameterized verification results on processes with unique identifiers are more rare but decidability was obtained under some restrictions [11].

Overview of the Abstraction Technique. Let us give an overview of our parameterized verification technique. Let us call *future leader* the node that is expected to become the leader. We consider classes of graphs $\mathcal{G}_K$ in which the maximal distance from the future leader is K. We show how to verify the protocol for *all* network topologies in $\mathcal{G}_K$, for given K, essentially in two steps:

1. We apply abstractions on local variables including node identifiers, which reduce the state spaces and renders all nodes anonymous except for the future leader. In fact, the variables storing node ids are mapped to a Boolean domain; encoding whether the node id is that of the future leader or not.
2. We then pick a shortest path of length K from the future leader. We derive an abstract model where all nodes that appear on this path are kept as concrete, but all other nodes have been abstracted away.

For each K, we thus construct a model $\mathcal{A}(K)$ and prove that it is an over-approximation of the protocol on *all* topologies in $\mathcal{G}_K$. We make sure that $\mathcal{A}(K)$ does not depend on the choice of the shortest path; if the property holds on $\mathcal{A}(K)$, it holds on the whole network. The approach is illustrated in Fig. 1.

Clock Deviations. We are interested in protocols where each node executes a periodic action with identical period. However, this period is subject to small

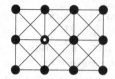   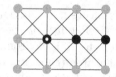

(a) A network with a grid topology. The future root, that is, the node with the smallest ID is shown with a white dot.

(b) We choose a path from the future root to some node

(c) We model all nodes on the path concretely, and summarize the behavior of all other nodes by one abstract node

Fig. 1. Shortest-path abstraction illustrated on a grid topology with $K = 3$.

deviations due to environment and hardware differences. Rather than using real-time verification techniques [1], we use a recent and simple way of modeling behaviors under such conditions. In [12], it is shown that an *approximately synchronous* semantics, where one bounds the progress of each process with respect to that of others, over-approximates the behaviors under bounded clock deviations, which makes it possible to use finite-state model checking techniques and tools.

Incremental Verification. We use an incremental proof technique for model checking $\mathcal{A}(K)$ for increasing values of K, as follows. To check $\mathcal{A}(K+1)$, we first model check $\mathcal{A}(K)$, proving that all nodes eventually agree on the leader. Our abstraction method implies that the first K components in $\mathcal{A}(K+1)$ eventually agree on the leader since their part of the graph belongs to $\mathcal{G}_K$. Thus, to check $\mathcal{A}(K+1)$, we initialize the first K nodes at states where they have agreed on the future leader. This significantly simplifies the verification process.

Overview. Section 2 presents definitions for the formalization of our approach. We describe FTSP in detail in Sect. 3, as well as the abstraction steps explained above, and the incremental verification result. A semi-algorithm for model checking and experimental results on FTSP are presented in Sect. 4.

2 Definitions

Communicating Processes. A *process* is an automaton $\mathcal{A} = (S, s_{\mathsf{init}}, \delta, \Sigma)$ where S are states, $s_{\mathsf{init}} \subseteq S$ are the initial states, and $\delta \subseteq S \times \Sigma \times S$ a transition relation, with alphabet Σ. A transition $(s, a, s') \in \delta$ is also written $\delta(s, a, s')$ or $s \xrightarrow{a} s'$, and we write $s \not\xrightarrow{a}$ to mean that there is no s' such that $\delta(s, a, s')$. We consider predicates that are evaluated on the states of a given process. Let $\mathcal{P}$ be a finite number of predicates where each $p \in \mathcal{P}$ is a subset $p \subseteq S$, representing states in which the predicate is satisfied. We write $s \models p$ if $s \in p$.

We define *simulation* between two processes as follows. Consider process $\mathcal{A} = (S, s_{\mathsf{init}}, \delta, \Sigma)$ with predicates $\mathcal{P}$ and $\mathcal{A}' = (S', s'_{\mathsf{init}}, \delta', \Sigma')$ with predicates $\mathcal{P}'$, an alphabet $\Sigma'' \subseteq \Sigma$, and any function $\alpha : \Sigma'' \to \Sigma'$. Assume that $\mathcal{P}$ and $\mathcal{P}'$ are in bijection denoted by $p \mapsto p'$ for each $p \in \mathcal{P}$. We say that $\mathcal{A}'$ (Σ'', α)-*simulates* $\mathcal{A}$, written $\mathcal{A} \sqsubseteq_{\Sigma'',\alpha} \mathcal{A}'$ if there exists $R \subseteq S \times S'$ such that $s_{\text{init}} \times s'_{\text{init}} \subseteq R$ and $\forall (s,s') \in R, \forall a \in \Sigma'', t \in S, \delta(s,a,t) \Rightarrow \exists t' \in S', \delta'(s', \alpha(a), t') \wedge (t,t') \in R$, and moreover for all $(s,s') \in R$ and $p \in \mathcal{P}$, $s \models p \Leftrightarrow s' \models p'$. When α is the identity and $\Sigma'' = \Sigma$, this is the usual simulation notion, and we write $\sqsubseteq_{\Sigma''}$. Given a process $\mathcal{A}$, let us define *the mapping of $\mathcal{A}$ by α* the process obtained by $\mathcal{A}$ by replacing the transitions δ by $\delta' = \{(s, \alpha(a), s') \mid (s,a,s') \in \delta\}$. It is clear that the mapping $\mathcal{A}'$ (Σ, α)-simulates $\mathcal{A}$.

For any positive integer N, we write $\mathcal{A} \sqsubseteq^N_{\Sigma'',\alpha} \mathcal{A}'$ if there exist $R_1, \ldots, R_N \subseteq S \times S'$ such that $s_{\text{init}} \times s'_{\text{init}} \subseteq R_1$ and for all $1 \leq i \leq N-1$, $\forall (s,s') \in R_i, \forall a \in \Sigma'', t \in S, \delta(s,a,t) \Rightarrow \exists t' \in S', \delta'(s', \alpha(a), t') \wedge (t,t') \in R_{i+1}$; and for all $(s,s') \in R_1 \cup \ldots \cup R_N$, $s \models p \Leftrightarrow s' \models p'$. The latter relation is called *simulation up to N*.

We define a particular alphabet Σ to model synchronization by rendez-vous. Let us fix $n > 0$, and define the set of *identifiers* $\mathsf{Id} = \{1, \ldots, n\}$. Consider also an arbitrary set Msg of message contents. We denote $[1,n] = \{1, \ldots, n\}$. We define the alphabet $\Sigma(\mathsf{Id}, \mathsf{Msg}) = \{i!(j,m) \mid i \in \mathsf{Id}, j \in \mathsf{Id}, m \in \mathsf{Msg}\} \cup \{j?(i,m) \mid i,j \in \mathsf{Id}, m \in \mathsf{Msg}\} \cup \{\tau\}$. We let $\Sigma = \Sigma(\mathsf{Id}, \mathsf{Msg})$. We will later use different sets Id and Msg to define alphabets. Intuitively, the label $i!(j,m)$ means that a process with id i sends message m to process with id j, while $j?(i,m)$ means that process j receives a message m from process i. The special symbol τ is an internal action. For a subset $I \subseteq \mathsf{Id}$, let $\Sigma_I(\mathsf{Id}, \mathsf{Msg}) = \{\tau\} \cup \{i!(j,m), i?(j,m) \in \Sigma(\mathsf{Id}, \mathsf{Msg}) \mid i \in I, j \in \mathsf{Id}, m \in \mathsf{Msg}\}$. These are the actions where the senders and receivers have ids in I. A τ-*path* of $\mathcal{A}$ is a sequence $s_1 s_2 \ldots$ of states such that for all $i \geq 1$, $\delta(s_i, \tau, s_{i+1})$. An *initialized* τ-path is such that $s_1 \in s_{\text{init}}$.

Graphs. To formalize network topologies, we consider undirected graphs. A graph is a pair $G = (V, E)$ with $V = \{1, \ldots, n\}$ and $E \subseteq V \times V$ which is symmetric. Let $\mathcal{G}(n)$ the set of graphs on vertex set $\{1, \ldots, n\}$. In our setting, a node will be identified with a process id. For a graph $G = (V, E)$, and node i, let $\mathcal{N}_G(i) = \{j \in V, (i,j) \in E\}$, the *neighborhood* of i. We define the following subclass of graphs. For any positive number $K \geq 0$, let $\mathcal{G}_K(n)$ denote the set of graphs of $\mathcal{G}(n)$ in which the longest distance between node 1 and any other node is at most K. Here, distance is the length of the shortest path between two nodes.

Asynchronous Product. We now define the product of two processes $\mathcal{A}$ and $\mathcal{A}'$ following CCS-like synchronization [23]. Intuitively, processes synchronize on send $i!(j,m)$ and receive $j?(i,m)$, and the joint transition becomes a τ-transition.

Definition 1. *Consider $\mathcal{A} = (S, s_{\text{init}}, \delta, \Sigma_J(\mathsf{Id}, \mathsf{Msg}))$ and $\mathcal{A}' = (S', s'_{\text{init}}, \delta', \Sigma_{J'}(\mathsf{Id}, \mathsf{Msg}))$ where $J, J' \subseteq \{1, \ldots, n\}$ with $J \cap J' = \emptyset$. Let $G = (V, E) \in \mathcal{G}(n)$. We define the product $\mathcal{A}'' = \mathcal{A} \parallel^G \mathcal{A}'$ as $(S'', s''_{\text{init}}, \delta'', \Sigma_{J \cup J'})$ where $S'' = S \times S'$, $s''_{\text{init}} = s_{\text{init}} \times s'_{\text{init}}$, and δ'' is defined as follows. There are four types of transitions.*

Internal transitions are defined by $(s_1, s'_1) \xrightarrow{\tau} (s_2, s'_2)$ whenever $\delta(s_1, \tau, s_2) \wedge s'_1 = s'_2$ or $\delta'(s'_1, \tau, s'_2) \wedge s_1 = s_2$.

Synchronizing transitions *are defined as* $(s_1, s_1') \xrightarrow{\tau} (s_2, s_2')$ *whenever* $\exists i \in J, j \in J', m \in \mathsf{Msg}$ *with* $i \in \mathcal{N}_G(j)$, *s.t. either* $s_1 \xrightarrow{i!(j,m)} s_2$ *and,* $s_1' \xrightarrow{j?(i,m)} s_2'$; *or,* $s_1' \xrightarrow{j!(i,m)} s_2'$, *and* $s_1 \xrightarrow{i?(j,m)} s_2$.

Sending transitions without matching receive *is defined as* $(s_1, s_1') \xrightarrow{i!(j,m)} (s_2, s_2')$ *whenever* $i \in J, j \notin J', m \in \mathsf{Msg}, i \in \mathcal{N}_G(j)$ *s.t. either* $s_1 \xrightarrow{i!(j,m)} s_2, s_1' = s_2'$; *or,* $i \in J', j \notin J, s_1' \xrightarrow{i!(j,m)} s_2', s_1 = s_2$.

Receive transitions without matching send *are defined, for all* $i, j \in \mathsf{Id}$ *and* $m \in \mathsf{Msg}$, $(s_1, s_1') \xrightarrow{i?(j,m)} (s_2, s_2')$ *whenever* $i \in \mathcal{N}_G(j)$ *and either* $i \in J$, $j \notin J', s_1 \xrightarrow{i?(j,m)} s_2, s_1' = s_2'$, *or* $i \in J', j \notin J, s_1' \xrightarrow{i?(j,m)} s_2', s_1 = s_2$.

The composition operation $\|^G$ is commutative and associative by definition. We will thus write the product of several processes as $\mathcal{A}_1 \|^G \ldots \|^G \mathcal{A}_n$, or $\|_{i=1\ldots n}^G \mathcal{A}_i$.

Predicates and LTL Satisfaction. We will use LTL for our specifications [24] which use the predicates $\mathcal{P}$ we consider for our model. We assume the reader is familiar with this logic, and refer to [10,24] otherwise. We just need the *eventually* (F), and *globally* (G) modalities. Given an LTL formula ϕ, we write $\mathcal{A} \models \phi$ if all initialized τ-paths satisfy ϕ.

Abstractions and Simulation. A *label abstraction function* is defined by $\alpha : \mathsf{Id} \to \mathsf{Id}^\sharp$, and $\alpha : \mathsf{Msg} \to \mathsf{Msg}^{\sharp 1}$. This function is uniquely extended to $\Sigma(\mathsf{Id}, \mathsf{Msg})$ by $\alpha(\tau) = \tau$, $\alpha(i!(j,m)) = \alpha(i)!(\alpha(j), \alpha(m))$, and $\alpha(i?(j,m)) = \alpha(i)?(\alpha(j), \alpha(m))$. We will see examples of label abstractions later in this paper.

Lemma 1. *Let* $\mathcal{A}_i = (S_i, s_{\mathsf{init}}^i, \delta_i, \Sigma_{J_i}(\mathsf{Id}, \mathsf{Msg}))$ *for* $i \in [1, n]$, *with pairwise disjoint* $J_i \subseteq \mathsf{Id}$, *and* $G \in \mathcal{G}(m)$ *with* $\cup_i J_i \subseteq \{1, \ldots, m\}$. *Consider a label abstraction function* α, *s.t.* $\alpha(J_i) \cap \alpha(J_j) = \emptyset$ *for all* $i \neq j \in [1, n]$; *and mappings* $\mathcal{A}_i'$ *of* $\mathcal{A}_i$ *by* α *so that* $\mathcal{A}_i \sqsubseteq_{\Sigma_{J_i}(\mathsf{Id}, \mathsf{Msg}), \alpha} \mathcal{A}_i'$. *Then,* $\|_{i=1\ldots n}^G \mathcal{A}_i \sqsubseteq_{\{\tau\}} \|_{i=1\ldots n}^G \mathcal{A}_i'$.

Notice that when $A \sqsubseteq_{\{\tau\}} B$, all LTL formulas that hold in B also hold in A (see *e.g.* [3]) since simulation implies trace inclusion. Thus, to prove that A satisfies a given property, it suffices to verify B.

An abstraction can also be obtained by relaxing the graph G.

Lemma 2. *Consider* $\mathcal{A}_i = (S_i, s_{\mathsf{init}}^i, \delta_i, \Sigma_{J_i}(\mathsf{Id}, \mathsf{Msg}))$ *for* $i \in [1, n]$, *where* $J_i \subseteq \mathsf{Id}$ *are pairwise disjoint, and* $G, G' \in \mathcal{G}(m)$ *where* $\cup_i J_i \subseteq \{1, \ldots, m\}$. *We write* $G = (V, E)$ *and* $G' = (V, E')$. *If* $E \subseteq E'$, *then* $\|_{i=1\ldots n}^G \mathcal{A}_i \sqsubseteq_{\{\tau\}} \|_{i=1\ldots n}^{G'} \mathcal{A}_i$.

Approximate Synchrony. We recall the results of [12] where a finite-state scheduler is defined for concurrent processes which run a periodic action with an approximately equal period. This is the case in FTSP since all nodes run processes that wake up and execute an action with an identical nominal period T. Since each node is executed on a distinct hardware with a local clock, the

---

[1] Both are denoted α. Formally, α can be defined on the disjoint union of these sets.

observed period is only approximately equal to T. Thus, some nodes can execute faster than other nodes. In our model, we would like to include different interleavings that can be observed due to clock rate changes. Let us assume that the actual period lies in the interval $[\sigma^l, \sigma^u]$ (which contains T). However, not all interleavings between processes can be observed. In particular, if $|\sigma^u - \sigma^l|$ is small, the periods of different processes will be close, so they will be *approximately synchronous*: within one period of a process, another process cannot execute several periods. This restricts considerably the interleavings to be considered for model checking. Following [12], we define a scheduler that generates at least all interleavings that can be observed during the first N periods, when the clock rates are within a given interval.

We give two schedulers to model such approximately periodic behaviors. We will later instantiate these again for the particular case of FTSP. Let us consider $\mathcal{A}_1, \ldots, \mathcal{A}_n$, and an additional process $\mathcal{S}$ which will be used to schedule processes $\mathcal{A}_i$. Let us add a label $\texttt{tick}_i?$ to each $\mathcal{A}_i$, and $\{\texttt{tick}_i!\}_{1 \leq i \leq n}$ to $\mathcal{S}$; this models the periodic task of the node i.[2] Let us assume that all states of $\mathcal{A}_i$ accept a transition with $\texttt{tick}_i?$.

Real-Time Scheduler. We define a *concrete* scheduler $\mathcal{S}_t$ which describes the executions generated by local clocks. We define $\mathcal{S}_t$ with an infinite state space, $S_{\mathcal{S}} = [0, \sigma_u]^n$, where the i-th component is the elapsed time since the latest execution of $\texttt{tick}_i?$ in process $\mathcal{A}_i$. We allow two kinds of transitions that alternate. There are *time elapse* transitions $(t_1, \ldots, t_n) \xrightarrow{\tau} (t'_1, \ldots, t'_n)$ if for some $d \geq 0$, $\forall 1 \leq i \leq n,\, t'_i = t_i + d$, and $\forall 1 \leq i \leq n, t'_i \leq \sigma_u$. Second, we have the transition $(t_1, \ldots, t_n) \xrightarrow{\texttt{tick}_i!} (t'_1, \ldots, t'_n)$ where $t'_j = t_j$ for all $j \neq i$ and $t'_i = 0$ if $t_i \in [\sigma_l, \sigma_u]$. Thus, $\mathcal{S}_t$ describes the executions where each process is executed with a period that varies within $[\sigma_l, \sigma_u]$.

Abstract Scheduler. Although the scheduler $\mathcal{S}_t$ above describes the behaviors we are interested in, its state space is continuous, and one would need a priori timed or hybrid automata to model it precisely. In this work, we prefer using finite-state model checking techniques for better efficiency, thus we now describe a simple abstraction of $\mathcal{S}_t$ using finite automata.

For each process i, and time t, let us denote by $N_i(t)$ the number of transitions $\texttt{tick}_i?$ that was executed in $\mathcal{A}_1 \parallel \ldots \parallel \mathcal{A}_n \parallel \mathcal{S}_t$ up to time t. We define the *abstract scheduler* $\mathcal{S}_a(\Delta)$ on a finite state-space, given integer Δ, which ensures that, at any time point t, for all pairs of processes i, j, we have $|N_i(t) - N_j(t)| \leq \Delta$. Intuitively, $\mathcal{S}_a(\Delta)$ describes the behaviors in which a fast process can execute at most Δ periods within one period of a slow process. Notice that $\mathcal{S}_a(\Delta)$ can be defined simply by counting the number of times each process has executed $\texttt{tick}_i?$ One can actually use bounded counters in $[0, \Delta]$; in fact, it is sufficient to keep the relative values of $N_i(t)$ with respect to the smallest one, so $\mathcal{S}_a(\Delta)$ can be defined as a finite automaton.

---

[2] These labels can actually be defined within $\Sigma(\mathsf{Id}, \mathsf{Msg})$ by adding a special message content $\texttt{tick}$ to Msg, and setting $\texttt{tick}_i! = (n{+}1)!(i, \texttt{tick})$ where $n{+}1$ is the identifier of $\mathcal{S}$. We will write them simply as $\texttt{tick}_i?$ and $\texttt{tick}_i!$ to simplify the presentation.

The intuition behind $S_a(\Delta)$ is that, given the bounds $[\sigma_l, \sigma_u]$ on the observable periods, all interleavings up to some length N under S_t are also present in $S_a(\Delta)$. That is, $S_a(\Delta)$ over-approximates S_t for finite executions. We will show how one can choose N. Let us denote Ticks = $\{\text{tick}_i!\}_{1 \leq i \leq n}$. We have the following correspondance between S_t and S_a:

Lemma 3 ([12]). *Consider $\Delta > 0$, and interval $[\sigma_l, \sigma_u]$. Let N_f be the minimal integer satisfying the following constraints: $N_f \geq N_s, N_f - N_s > \Delta, \sigma_l N_f + \sigma_u \leq \sigma_u N_s$, and $N_f, N_s \geq 1$. Then, we have $S_t \sqsubseteq_{Ticks}^{N_f-1} S_a(\Delta)$.*

In the above lemma, N_f represents the number of steps performed by the fastest processes, and N_s is that of the slowest processes. Minimizing N_f means that we look for the earliest step where $N_f - N_s > \Delta$ holds, so that the simulation holds up to $N_f - 1$ steps. Hence, we can use $S_a(\Delta)$ for model checking rather than S_t for N steps, where N is determined by Δ and σ_l, σ_u.

3 Parameterized Model Checking of FTSP

In the FTSP, each node has a unique identifier, and the nodes dynamically elect the node with the least id as the *root*. The root regularly sends messages to its neighbors, which forward it to their own neighbors and so on. These messages contain time information which is used by the nodes to adjust their clocks. If the root node fails, that is, stops transmitting messages, then other nodes eventually time out and declare themselves as roots, and the protocol makes sure that a unique root is eventually elected if no more faults occur during a period of time.

More precisely, each node has an identifier ID, and executes the periodic action send, depicted in Fig. 2 in which it increments a "heart beat" counter b. This counter is reset to 0 if the node receives a certain message via the receive function: this can happen either when the node first hears about a node with a smaller ID ri than the currently known one, stored in r, or when the currently known root sends a *new* message with a larger sequence number si than that of the latest message s. The sequence numbers are used to distinguish new messages from the old ones that originate from a root node; a lexicographic order is used so that smaller root IDs with higher sequence numbers are preferred. A node declares itself root if the counter b exceeds the threshold FTO; and it only broadcasts messages if it is root, or if it has received at least LIM messages from some root. We refer the reader to [20] for the details on FTSP.

Both functions send and receive are executed atomically. Thus, the effects of each function on local variables are self-explanatory. The operation $o!!(r, s)$ means broadcast: it is a system call to broadcast the message (r, s) to all the neighbors of the node. This operation is non-blocking: when the function send returns, the node sends the message to each neighbor in an arbitrary order. We assume the broadcast data is stored in a variable m which takes values from the set $\{\bot\} \cup 2^{ld} \times \text{Msg}$. Here $\bot$ means that there is no ongoing broadcast, and a pair (I, m) means that processes with ids in I are still to receive the message m. That is, the operation $o!!(r, s)$ actually just assigns the value (r, s) to local variable m.

The node can receive messages and execute **receive** before its own broadcast is over. We just make the following assumption on broadcasts, which is justified by the fact that the typical period of the **send** events is about 30 s [20].

Assumption: Any broadcast started by a node is completed before the node executes the next **send** event.

3.1 Concrete Model

We fix a graph $G \in \mathcal{G}(n)$ with n nodes, and set $\mathsf{Id} = \{1, \ldots, n\}$, and $\mathsf{Msg} = \mathsf{Id} \times \mathbb{N}$. In Msg, the first component of a message is the ID of the root node which has generated the message (and not the ID of the node that forwards the message), while the second component is the sequence number. Each process $\mathcal{A}_i$ is a node in the protocol in which the variable ID is i, and executes functions **receive** and **send** of Fig. 2. We define $\mathcal{A}_i = (S_i, s_{\mathsf{init}}^i, \delta_i, \Sigma_{\{i\}}(\mathsf{Id}, \mathsf{Msg}))$, with $S_i = V_i \times (2^n \cup \{\bot\})$ where V_i are the set of valuations for all local variables. For any variable a, and state $s \in S_i$, we write $s(\mathsf{a})$ for the value of a in s (we also write $v(\mathsf{a})$ for $v \in V_i$). The second component of a state $s \in S_i$ denotes whether the process is currently broadcasting: if it is $\bot$, there is no broadcast occurring and $s(\mathsf{m}) = \bot$; if it is $I \subseteq 2^{\mathsf{Id}}$, then message $s(\mathsf{m})$ is to be received by processes in I. We denote by $s[\mathsf{a} \leftarrow a]$ the state obtained from s by assigning a to a.

Since each function is executed atomically, in $\mathcal{A}_i$, a single transition corresponds to an uninterrupted execution of **send** or **receive**, or to a communication. For any $m \in \mathsf{Msg}$, let us define the relation $\mathbf{receive}_i(m) \subseteq V_i \times V_i$ (resp. send) as $(v, v') \in \mathbf{receive}_i(m)$ (resp. $(v, v') \in \mathbf{send}_i$) if, and only if there is an execution of this function from state v to state v', when the node ID is i. These relations are functions since $\mathbf{receive}_i$ and $\mathbf{send}_i$ are deterministic; however, subsequent abstractions will transform these into nondeterministic programs, thus we will obtain relations instead of functions. Thus, δ_i is defined as follows:

```
1  #define MAX   6  /* MAX_ENTRIES      */    1   byte b;  /* heartBeats */
2  #define LIM   3  /* ENTRY_SEND_LIMIT*/    2   byte e;  /* numEntries */
3  #define MIN   2  /* IGNORE_ROOT_MSG */    3   byte r;  /* outgoingMsg.rootID */
4  #define FTO   8  /* ROOT_TIMEOUT     */    4   byte s;  /* outgoingMsg.seqNum */
5  extern int ID   /* TOS_NODE_ID      */    5   chan o;  /* Output channel */
6  #define NIL 255                            6
7                                             7   void send () {
8  void receive (byte ri, byte si) {          8     if(b >= FTO){
9    if(ri < r && !(b < MIN && r==ID))        9       if(r == NIL){ s = 0; }
10     || (ri == r && si - s > 0){           10       else { b = 0; s++; }
11     r = ri;                               11       r = ID
12     s = si;                               12     }
13     if(r < ID){b = 0;}                    13     b++;
14     if(e < MAX){e++;}                     14     if(r == ID){ o !! (r, s); s++; }
15   }                                       15     else if(e >= LIM){ o !! (r, s) }
16  }                                        16   }
```

Fig. 2. Pseudocode of the main send and receive functions in FTSP

$$(v, \perp) \xrightarrow{\texttt{tick}_i?} (v', \mathcal{N}_G(i)) \Leftrightarrow (v, v') \in \texttt{send}_i \wedge v'(\texttt{m}) \neq \perp,$$

$$(v, \perp) \xrightarrow{\texttt{tick}_i?} (v', \perp) \Leftrightarrow (v, v') \in \texttt{send}_i \wedge v'(\texttt{m}) = \perp,$$

$$(v, \emptyset) \xrightarrow{\texttt{tock}_i?} (v[\texttt{m} \leftarrow \perp], \perp),$$

$$(v, I) \xrightarrow{j?(i,m)} (v', I) \Leftrightarrow (v, v') \in \texttt{receive}_i(m) \wedge j \in \mathcal{N}_G(i),$$

$$(v, I) \xrightarrow{i!(j,m)} (v, I \setminus \{j\}) \Leftrightarrow m = v(\texttt{m}) \neq \perp \wedge j \in I,$$

where the last two lines are defined for all $I \in \{\perp\} \cup 2^{\texttt{Id}}$.

Notice that we separate the execution of the body of the two functions and the broadcast operations. A broadcast operation is completed between the $\texttt{tick}_i?$ and $\texttt{tock}_i?$ events. Hence, the broadcast can be interrupted with a receive event, but another send event cannot be executed before the broadcast is complete, which conforms to our assumption above. The role of $\texttt{tick}_i$ and $\texttt{tock}_i$ signals will be clear in the next paragraph where the schedulers are defined. The initial states are the set of all valuations since we assume that the network starts in an arbitrary configuration. Now, $\|_{i=1...n}^G \mathcal{A}_i$ defines the protocol on the given topology G. It remains to define the schedulers.

Schedulers and Two Communication Semantics. We define schedulers which determine when each process can execute its **send** event, and how the communication is modeled. We sketch our schedulers with two communication models.

Synchronous Communication. In the first model, we assume that communication between the sender and *all* receivers occur simultaneously. So, one step consists in a node executing **send** followed by all its neighbors immediately receiving the message by executing **receive**. This is the *synchronous communication model* as considered in previous works [19,21,28].

To implement synchronous communication, we introduce the signal $\texttt{tock}_i!$, and force the whole communication initiated by node i to happen uninterrupted between $\texttt{tick}_i!$ and $\texttt{tock}_i!$ signals. We define $\mathcal{S}_{t,\text{syn}}$ by modifying the real-time scheduler $\mathcal{S}_t$ defined above by requiring that each $\texttt{tick}_i!$ is immediately followed by a corresponding $\texttt{tock}_i!$, and by disallowing any other $\texttt{tick}_j!$ inbetween. We also define $\mathcal{S}_{a,\text{syn}}^{\text{ftsp}}(\Delta)$ from $\mathcal{S}_a(\Delta)$ using the alternating $\texttt{tick}_i$ and $\texttt{tock}_i$ signals.

Asynchronous Communication. The second type of schedulers we define implement asynchronous communication, and is more faithful to the real behavior e.g. in the TinyOS implementation. In this setting, both events **send** and **receive** are still atomic, but the broadcast is concurrent: while the sender is broadcasting the message to its neighbors, other nodes can execute their own **send** action or receive other messages. We call this the *asynchronous communication model.*

We define $\mathcal{S}_{t,\text{asyn}}$ by adding to $\mathcal{S}_t$ self-loops labeled by $\texttt{tock}_i!$ to all states for all $i \in \texttt{Id}$. (Note that $\texttt{tock}_i!$ signals are useless here, but we keep them so that both schedulers have a uniform interface). We define the scheduler $\mathcal{S}_{a,\text{asyn}}^{\text{ftsp}}(\Delta)$ similarly, by adding self-loop $\texttt{tock}_i!$ to all states of $\mathcal{S}_a(\Delta)$.

The next developments are independent from the communication model.

Complete Model and Property to be Verified. Given a graph $G \in \mathcal{G}(n)$ let $\mathcal{A}_1, \ldots, \mathcal{A}_n$ denote the processes thus defined, and write $\mathcal{A}(G) = \|_{i=1 \ldots n}^{G} \mathcal{A}_i$. We let $\mathcal{M}_{\bowtie}^{\mathrm{conc}}(G) = \mathcal{A}(G) \parallel \mathcal{S}_{t,\bowtie}$, for $\bowtie \in \{\mathsf{syn}, \mathsf{asyn}\}$, which is the *concrete* protocol under the real-time scheduler $\mathcal{S}_t$ defined above. This model defines the behaviors we would like to verify. For each $i \in \mathsf{Id}$, let us add a counter c_i to the model that counts the number of times $\mathsf{tick}_i!$ is executed, and define $c = \max_i c_i$, which will be used in the specifications.

The property we want to check is that all nodes eventually agree on a common root. Let FRID denote the constant 1, which stands for the *future root id*. In fact, according to the protocol, $\mathcal{A}_1$ is expected to become the root since it has the least id. We will call $\mathcal{A}_1$ the *future root*. Define P_i as the set of states in which the local variable r of process i has value FRID. We consider the property $\mathcal{P}(N) = \mathsf{F}(c \leq N \wedge \wedge_{i=1}^{n} P_i)$ for some N. Thus, along all executions, before any process has executed more than N tick_i's, all processes agree on FRID to be the root. Thus, our goal is to show that $\mathcal{M}_{\bowtie}^{\mathrm{conc}}(G) \models \mathcal{P}(N)$ for some $N > 0$. By Lemma 3, given Δ, it suffices to find $N > 0$ for each $\bowtie \in \{\mathsf{syn}, \mathsf{asyn}\}$, such that $\mathcal{A}(G) \parallel \mathcal{S}_{a,\bowtie}^{\mathrm{ftsp}}(\Delta) \models \mathcal{P}(N)$.

3.2   Abstractions on Individual Nodes

We now present the abstraction steps we use before model checking. We will abstract our variables and statements involving these using *data abstraction*: we map the domain of the variables to a smaller set, and redefine the transitions using *existential abstraction* so that the abstract program is an over-approximation in the sense that the original process is simulated by the existential abstraction. This is a standard abstraction technique; we refer the reader to [9] for details.

More precisely, the applied abstraction steps are the following.

1. Add a redundant variable imroot that stores the value of the predicate r == ID, that is, whether the node is currently root.
2. Relax the behaviors of both functions in the case $\mathsf{r} \neq \mathsf{FRID} \wedge \mathsf{ri} \neq \mathsf{FRID} \wedge \mathsf{ID} \neq \mathsf{FRID}$ by abstracting the variables s and e away (*i.e.* we assume their values change arbitrarily at any time).
3. Map the variables r and ri in the abstract domain $\{\mathsf{FRID}, \mathsf{NRID}\}$ in each node. Also map b to the bounded integer domain $\{0, \mathsf{FTO}\}$, e to $\{0, \ldots, \mathsf{LIM}\}$.

The resulting pseudocode is shown in Fig. 3. Here, the value $\bot$ represents *any value*, which make any comparison operation nondeterministic. The constant NRID we introduce stands for *non-root id*, and is an abstract value that represents all ids different than FRID.

Note that the second step always yields an over-approximation, independently from the if-then-else condition chosen to separate the concrete and abstract cases in Fig. 3. In fact, the concrete case is identical to the original code, while the abstract case is an over-approximation by data abstraction. In Fig. 3, the abstractions of the predicates on variables r and ri are

```
 1  #define LIM  3  /* ENTRY_SEND_LIMIT */
 2  #define MIN  2  /* IGNORE_ROOT_MSG  */
 3  #define FTO  8  /* ROOT_TIMEOUT     */
 4  #define NIL  255
 5  extern int ID; /* TOS_NODE_ID      */
 6  #define FRID 0  /* FUTURE ROOT ID   */
 7  #define NRID 1  /* Abstract ID for
 8                     all other nodes > FRID */
 9
10  void receive (byte ri, byte si) {
11    /* Concrete case */
12    if (r ==  FRID || ri ==
        FRID || ID == FRID){
13      if ("ri < r" && !( b < MIN && imroot
14         || "ri == r" && si - s > 0 )){
15        r = ri;
16        s = si;
17        imroot = (ID ==  FRID);
18        if ("r < ID" ) b = 0;
19        if (e < LIM) e++;
20      }
21    } else {
22    /* Abstract case */
23      if ("ri < r" && !(b < MIN && imroot
24         || ("ri == r" && *)){
25        r = ri;
26        s = ⊥;
27        imroot = "r == ID";
28        if ("r < ID" ) b = 0;
29        e = ⊥;
30  }}}
```

```
 1  byte b; /* heartBeats */
 2  byte e; /* numEntries */
 3  byte r; /* outgoingMsg.rootID */
 4  byte s; /* outgoingMsg.seqNum */
 5  chan i, o; /* IO channels */
 6  byte imroot; /* Predicate: r == ID */
 7
 8  void send () {
 9    /* Concrete case */
10    if(r ==  FRID || ID ==  FRID){
11      if(b >= FTO){
12        if ("r == NIL") s = 0;
13        if ("r! = ID") { b = 0; s++; }
14        r = ID;
15        imroot = 1;
16      }
17      b++;
18      if(imroot){ o !! (r, s); s++; }
19      else if(e >= LIM){ o !! (r, s); }
20    } else {
21    /* Abstract case */
22      if(b >= FTO){
23        if("r! = ID") { b = 0; s = ⊥; }
24        r = ID;
25        imroot = 1;
26      }
27      if (b < FTO) b++;
28      if(imroot){ o !! (r, *); s = ⊥; }
29      else if(*){ o !! (r, *); }
30  }}
```

Fig. 3. After the second and third steps of the abstraction. The behavior of `receive` is relaxed when `r != FRID` or the received message (`ri,si`) is such that `ri != FRID`. Similarly, the behavior of `send` is relaxed when `r != FRID` and `ID != FRID`. For both functions, we redefine the behaviors of the protocol by disregarding the variables `e` and `s`. The updates and tests on these variables become completely non-deterministic. In particular, nodes in such states can send more often messages with arbitrary sequence numbers. Then, the variables `r,ri` are mapped to the domain {FRID, NRID}. The variable `b` is mapped to $\{0, 1, \ldots, \text{MAX}\}$, and `e` to $\{0, 1, \ldots, \text{LIM}\}$.

represented in quotes. They represent non-deterministic transitions as follows. The comparison relation becomes non-deterministic: we have FRID < NRID and FRID = FRID, but, for instance, a comparison between NRID and NRID can yield both true and false. As an example, "`r == ri`" stands for `r = FRID && ri = FRID || r = NRID && ri = NRID && *`, `*` being a nondeterministic Boolean value.

Let $S_i' = V_i' \times (2^n \cup \{\bot\})$ where V_i' is the set of valuations of node variables (with given id i), with the abstract domains we have described. Let us define the relations $\textsf{receive}_i' \subseteq V_i' \times V_i'$ and $\textsf{send}_i' \subseteq V_i' \times V_i'$, similarly as before, e.g. $(s, s') \in \textsf{receive}_i'$ if, and only if there is an execution of $\textsf{receive}_i'$ from s yielding s'. Let $\mathcal{A}_i'$ denote the process defined just like $\mathcal{A}_i$ in Subsect. 3.1 but using the new relations $\textsf{receive}_i'$ and $\textsf{send}_i'$. We state the relation between $\mathcal{A}_i$ and $\mathcal{A}_i'$ using a label abstraction function α. We let α be the identity over $\textsf{Id}$, and set $\textsf{Msg}^\# = \{\text{FRID}, \text{NRID}\} \times (\mathbb{N} \cup \{\bot\})$ with $\alpha((k, s)) = (\text{FRID}, s)$ if $k = \text{FRID}$, and $\alpha((k, s)) = (\text{NRID}, \bot)$ otherwise.

Lemma 4. *For all i, $\mathcal{A}_i \sqsubseteq_{\Sigma_i(\textsf{Id}, \textsf{Msg}), \alpha} \mathcal{A}_i'$.*

By Lemma 1, it follows that $\|_{i=1 \ldots n}^G \mathcal{A}_i \sqsubseteq_{\{\tau\}} \|_{i=1 \ldots n}^G \mathcal{A}_i'$.

3.3   Abstraction on Network Topology: Shortest-Path Abstraction

Recall that our model has a network topology $G \in \mathcal{G}_K(n)$. Consider an arbitrary shortest path $\mathcal{A}_{i_1} \mathcal{A}_{i_2} \ldots \mathcal{A}_{i_m}$ with $m \leq K$, where $i_1 = 1$. Let $C = \{i_2, \ldots, i_m\}$, that is, all nodes on this path but the future root. Define $O = \mathsf{Id} \setminus C$. Let us relax the graph $G = (V, E)$ into $G' = (V, E')$ by $E' = E \cup O \times O \cup O \times C \cup C \times O$. Thus, we render the graph complete within O, and add all edges between O and C. Let us write $\mathcal{A}'_C = \|_{i \in C}^{G'} \mathcal{A}'_i$, and $\mathcal{A}'_O = \|_{i \in O}^{G'} \mathcal{A}'_i$. By Lemma 2, these are over-approximations of the products defined for G.

We define $\mathcal{A}''_O$ as a single-state process with alphabet $\Sigma_O(\mathsf{Id}, \mathsf{Msg}^\sharp)$ which can send any message to any other node. We clearly have $\mathcal{A}'_O \sqsubseteq_{\Sigma_O(\mathsf{Id},\mathsf{Msg}^\sharp)} \mathcal{A}''_O$.

We now get rid of the identifiers outside $C \cup \{1\}$ by defining a label abstraction function $\alpha' : \mathsf{Id} \to \mathsf{Id}^\sharp$ with $\mathsf{Id}^\sharp = C \cup \{\mathcal{O}, 1\}$ where $\mathcal{O}$ is a fresh symbol. We let $\alpha'(i) = i$ for all $i \in C \cup \{1\}$, and $\alpha'(i) = \mathcal{O}$ for all $i \in O \setminus \{1\}$. So, all nodes outside $C \cup \{1\}$ are merged into one identifier $\mathcal{O}$. Let $\mathcal{B}_O$ be the mapping of $\mathcal{A}''_O$ by α', and $\mathcal{B}_C$ that of $\mathcal{A}'_C$, so that we have $\mathcal{A}'_O \sqsubseteq_{\Sigma_O(\mathsf{Id},\mathsf{Msg}^\sharp)} \mathcal{A}''_O \sqsubseteq_{\Sigma_O(\mathsf{Id},\mathsf{Msg}^\sharp),\alpha'} \mathcal{B}_O$ and $\mathcal{A}'_C \sqsubseteq_{\Sigma_C(\mathsf{Id},\mathsf{Msg}^\sharp),\alpha'} \mathcal{B}_C$.

We need to adapt the scheduler so that it does not keep track of the offset of the processes represented by $\mathcal{O}$. Let $\mathcal{S}'^{\mathsf{ftsp}}_{a,\mathsf{syn}}(\Delta)$ and $\mathcal{S}'^{\mathsf{ftsp}}_{a,\mathsf{asyn}}(\Delta)$ defined similarly as before which track the offsets of all nodes in $C \cup \{1\}$, but have a self-loop with label $\mathtt{tick}_\mathcal{O}!$ at all states. We thus have $\mathcal{S}^{\mathsf{ftsp}}_{a,\bowtie}(\Delta) \sqsubseteq_{\mathtt{Ticks},\alpha'} \mathcal{S}'^{\mathsf{ftsp}}_{a,\bowtie}(\Delta)$ for both $\bowtie \in \{\mathsf{syn}, \mathsf{asyn}\}$.

By Lemmas 1–2, $\mathcal{A}'_O \|^G \mathcal{A}'_C \|^G \mathcal{S}^{\mathsf{ftsp}}_{a,\bowtie}(\Delta) \sqsubseteq_{\{\tau\},\alpha'} \mathcal{B}_O \|^{G'} \mathcal{B}_C \|^{G'} \mathcal{S}'^{\mathsf{ftsp}}_{a,\bowtie}(\Delta)$.

We need another abstraction to obtain a finite model: The variable $\mathbf{s}$ is a priori unbounded in each process; however, the only applied operations are incrementation (by $\mathtt{FRID}$ only), assignment, and comparison. Therefore, we can shift the values so that the minimal one is always 0; thus limiting the maximal value that is observed. We modify our process to map these variables to a finite domain $\{0, 1, \ldots, \mathtt{SeqMax}, \bot\}$ and *normalize* their values after each transition: we make sure that at any step, the values taken by $\mathbf{s}$ at all nodes define a set $X \cup \{\bot\}$ for some $0 \in X \subseteq \{0, 1, \ldots, \mathtt{SeqMax}\}$.

We summarize all the steps of the abstractions as follows. Given graph $G \in \mathcal{G}_K(n)$, a path π of length K from node 1, let $\mathcal{M}^{\mathsf{abs}}_{\bowtie}(G, \pi, \Delta) = \mathcal{B}_O \|^{G'} \mathcal{B}_C \|^{G'} \mathcal{S}'^{\mathsf{ftsp}}_{a,\bowtie}(\Delta)$ where $\bowtie \in \{\mathsf{syn}, \mathsf{asyn}\}$.

Lemma 5. *For all $n, K > 0$, and all $G \in \mathcal{G}_K(n)$, let π be any shortest path from node 1. Let C be the nodes of π except 1, and $O = [1, n] \setminus C$. We have, for all $\bowtie \in \{\mathsf{syn}, \mathsf{async}\}$, $\mathcal{M}^{\mathsf{conc}}_{\bowtie}(G) \sqsubseteq_{\{\tau\}} \mathcal{M}^{\mathsf{abs}}_{\bowtie}(G, \pi, \Delta)$.*

Notice that in $\mathcal{M}^{\mathsf{abs}}_{\bowtie}(G, \pi, \Delta)$, all node ids are in the set $\{\mathtt{FRID}, \mathtt{NRID}\}$. Thus, given two different paths π, π', $\mathcal{M}^{\mathsf{abs}}_{\bowtie}(G, \pi, \Delta)$ and $\mathcal{M}^{\mathsf{abs}}_{\bowtie}(G, \pi', \Delta)$ are identical up to the renaming of their channel numbers since both models still contain labels of the form $i!(j, m)$ and $i?(j, m)$. However, these numbers i, j only define the topology and do not affect the behaviors. Let us state this formally as follows:

Lemma 6. *For all $K, n > 0$, graph $G \in \mathcal{G}_K(n)$, and paths π, π' of same length from node 1, we have $\mathcal{M}^{\mathsf{abs}}_{\bowtie}(G, \pi, \Delta) \sqsubseteq_{\{\tau\}} \mathcal{M}^{\mathsf{abs}}_{\bowtie}(G, \pi', \Delta)$.*

From the above lemma, it follows that for verification purposes (against LTL), the model $\mathcal{M}^{abs}_{\bowtie}(G, \pi, \Delta)$ is actually independent of the chosen path π, but only depends on the length of π. For each $K > 0$, let us pick one such model with $|\pi| = K$ and name it $\mathcal{M}^{abs}_{\bowtie}(K, \Delta)$. Then, we have $\mathcal{M}^{abs}_{\bowtie}(G, \pi, \Delta) \sqsubseteq_{\{\tau\}}$ $\mathcal{M}^{abs}_{\bowtie}(K, \Delta)$ for all $G \in \mathcal{G}_K(n)$ and $\Delta > 0$. It follows that model checking a property in $\mathcal{M}^{abs}_{\bowtie}(K, \Delta)$ proves it on all graphs $G \in \mathcal{G}_K(n)$ and all paths π.

In the rest, w.l.o.g. let us assume that $C = \{2, \ldots, K\}$. Our goal is to check $\mathcal{M}^{abs}_{\bowtie}(K, \Delta) \models \mathcal{P}^K(N)$ for some N, where $\mathcal{P}^K(N) = \mathsf{F}(\mathsf{c} \leq N \wedge \bigwedge_{i=1}^{K} P_i)$.

3.4   Incremental Verification Technique and Refinement

We explain an incremental approach to model-check our system for successive values of K. Intuitively, we assume that we have proved the root election property for K, and we want to prove it for $K + 1$. For K, if we prove the property is *persistent*, that is, holds forever after some point in time, then, we can prove the property for $K + 1$ as follows: initialize the first K nodes in $\mathcal{M}^{abs}_{\bowtie}(K + 1, \Delta)$ to a state in which they agree on the future root, and the $K + 1$-th node in an arbitrary state; then verify the property for the last process only:

Lemma 7. *Consider processes $\mathcal{R}_1, \ldots, \mathcal{R}_n$, and $\mathcal{S}_1, \ldots, \mathcal{S}_n$. For some graph G, let $\mathcal{R}(K) = \|_{i=0\ldots K}^{G} \mathcal{R}_i$. Assume that $\mathcal{R}(K + 1) \|^{G} \mathcal{S}_{K+1} \sqsubseteq_\tau \mathcal{R}(K) \|^{G} \mathcal{S}_K$ for all K. Consider predicate Q_i for each $\mathcal{R}_i$, and define $Q(K) = \wedge_{i=1}^{K} Q_i$. Consider $\mathcal{R}'(K+1)$ obtained from $\mathcal{R}(K+1)$ by restricting the states to $Q(K)$ (That is, we remove all states outside and all transitions that leave outside this set:), where the initial state set is $Q(K)$. We have that $\mathcal{R}(K) \| \mathcal{S}_K \models \mathsf{FG}Q(K) \wedge \mathcal{R}'(K+1) \| \mathcal{S}_{K+1} \models \mathsf{FG}Q_{K+1}$ implies $\mathcal{R}(K + 1) \| \mathcal{S}_{K+1} \models \mathsf{FG}Q(K + 1)$.*

Here is how we apply the above lemma in our case. Let $\mathcal{R}_i = \mathcal{A}'_{i+1}$ for $i = 1 \ldots K$. We write $S_K = \mathcal{S}'^{\mathsf{ftsp}}_{a,\mathsf{asyn}}(\Delta)$ defined for $C = \{1, \ldots, K\}$ in Sect. 3.3, and let $\mathcal{S}_K = \mathcal{A}''_{O_K} \| S_K$ with $O_K = \mathsf{Id} \setminus \{2, \ldots, K\}$. We have $\mathcal{A}''_{O_{K+1}} \sqsubseteq_{\Sigma(O_{K+1}, \mathsf{Msg}^\sharp)}$ $\mathcal{A}''_{O_K}$ and $S_{K+1} \sqsubseteq_{\mathsf{Ticks}} S_K$ by definition, so these processes do satisfy the relation $\mathcal{R}(K + 1) \| \mathcal{S}_{K+1} \sqsubseteq_\tau \mathcal{R}(K) \| \mathcal{S}_K$. As properties to satisfy, we consider $Q_i = P_i \wedge \mathsf{b}_i \leq \mathsf{FTO} - 1 \wedge \mathsf{e} \geq \mathsf{LIM}$, and also define $Q(K, N) = (\mathsf{c} \leq N \wedge \wedge_{i=1}^{K} Q_i)$. Notice that $Q(K, N)$ implies $\mathcal{P}^K(N)$.

Assume we have proved the following statements: $\mathcal{M}'^{abs}_{\bowtie}(1, \Delta) \models \mathsf{FG}Q(1, n_1)$, $\mathcal{M}'^{abs}_{\bowtie}(2, \Delta) \models \mathsf{FG}Q(2, n_2)$, ..., $\mathcal{M}'^{abs}_{\bowtie}(K - 1, \Delta) \models \mathsf{FG}Q(K - 1, n_{k-1})$, and $\mathcal{M}'^{abs}_{\bowtie}(K, \Delta) \models \mathsf{FG}Q(K, n_k)$. Then, by the previous lemma, $\mathcal{M}^{abs}_{\bowtie}(K, \Delta) \models \mathsf{FG}Q(K, N)$ for $N = n_1 + \ldots + n_k$, which means $\mathcal{P}^K(N)$. Note that the last property to be proven can also be chosen as $\mathsf{F}P_K$ which might be satisfied earlier than $\mathsf{FG}Q(K, n_k)$.

Non-interference Lemma. The first verification attempts reveal a spurious counter-example: the non-deterministic process $\mathcal{B}_O$ can send a node in C a message (r, s) with $r = \mathsf{FRID}$ and s large enough so that the node will ignore all messages for a long period of time, causing a timeout; this causes the violation of $\mathsf{FG}P_i$. However, intuitively, a node should not be able to send a message with $r =$ FRID with a newer sequence number than what has been generated by the root itself. Following [7], we use *guard strengthening*: We require that all messages that come from the process $\mathcal{B}_O$ must satisfy that either $r \neq$ FRID or s is at most equal to the variable s of the root. Let this condition be ϕ. We thus constrain the transitions of our model to satisfy ϕ, which eliminates this spurious counter-example. Property ϕ is also called a *non-interference lemma* [7]. However, we also need to actually prove ϕ. As it turns out, one can prove ϕ on the very same abstraction obtained by strenghtening. The works [7,18] explain why the apparently circular reasoning is correct. We do not detail this technique further since this is now a well-known result; see also [5,27].

4   Algorithm and Experimental Results

Semi-Algorithm for FG *Properties with Optimal Bound Computation.* Model checking algorithms consist in traversing the state space while storing the set of visited states so as to guarantee termination. However, this set can sometimes become prohibitively large. We introduce a simple semi-algorithm for properties of type FG p where we do not store all states: at iteration i, we just store the states reachable in i steps exactly, and only if all these satisfy p, do we start a fixpoint computation from these states. The resulting semi-algorithm is more efficient and allows us to find the smallest i in one shot.

We implemented the semi-algorithm in NuSMV 2.5.4[3]. We model-checked the property $\mathcal{P}(N)$, and computed the bounds N using our semi-algorithm. The models are initialized in an arbitrary state, so our results show that the network recovers from any arbitrary fault within the given time bound. We summarize our results in Fig. 4. We distinguish the best values for N in both communication models for different values of K. Missing rows mean timeout of 24 h.

We observe that the time for the root election N differs in the two communication semantics. This value is higher in the asynchronous case since it contains all behaviors that are possible in the synchronous case. Observe that the largest network topology that had been model checked for FTSP contained 7 nodes [21] with synchronous communication. In our case, we prove the property for $K = 7$, which means that it holds on two dimensional grids with 169 nodes (13×13) when the root is at the middle (and three-dimensional grids with 2197 nodes), and 49 nodes if it is on a corner (and 343 nodes in three dimensions). In the asynchronous case, we prove the property for $K = 5$, *e.g.* 2D grids of size 81 nodes where the root is at the middle.

	synchronous		asynchronous	
K	N	time	N	time
1	8	0s	8	0s
2	14	1s	14	1s
3	23	1s	25	28s
4	35	3s	39	130s
5	54	16s	63	65mins
6	67	76s		
7	107	13mins		

Fig. 4. Verification results for the property $\mathcal{P}(N)$, obtained with the semi-algorithm. For each K and communication model, the best derived N is given.

---

[3] The source code and models are available at https://github.com/osankur/nusmv/tree/ftsp.

This implies the following bounds on clock rates: by Lemma 3, for $N = 107$, property $\mathcal{P}(N)$ is guaranteed on $\mathcal{M}^{conc}_{\bowtie}(G)$ for all $G \in \mathcal{G}_K$ and $[\sigma_l, \sigma_u] = [29.7, 30.3]$ which is the case when the clock rates are within 1 ± 10^{-2}.

5   Conclusion

We presented an environment abstraction technique inspired from [7] for processes with unique identifiers, arbitrary network topologies, and drifting clocks. We introduced an incremental model checking technique, and gave an efficient semi-algorithm that can compute bounds for the eventually properties in one shot. We applied our technique to model check the root election part of FTSP and obtained significant improvements over previous results.

An important future work will be to automatize the presented abstraction method. Several steps of our abstractions, such as data abstractions, can easily be automatized with minimal user intervention. We would like to go further following [5], and consider automatic abstractions of the network topology.

Our aim is to address the case of more elaborate time synchronisation protocols based on interval methods, such as Sugihara and Gupta's [26] that are able to implement TSP in WSN without making assumptions on bounded drift, but simply on precise thermal and cristal oscillator specifications of the WSN hardware. We would like to obtain formal bounds on time precision guaranteed by a protocol under various assumptions on environment.

We believe our shortest-path abstraction technique can be used to verify different distributed protocols in which an information is forwarded in layers through the network such as [4,29]. An interesting future work would be to consider protocols that construct a spanning tree of the network in which case shortest paths would be replaced by a richer subgraph of the network topology.

References

1. Alur, R., Dill, D.L.: A theory of timed automata. Theoret. Comput. Sci. **126**(2), 183–235 (1994)
2. Apt, K.R., Kozen, D.C.: Limits for automatic verification of finite-state concurrent systems. Inf. Process. Lett. **22**(6), 307–309 (1986)
3. Baier, C., Katoen, J.-P.: Principles of Model Checking. MIT press, Cambridge (2008)
4. Bakhshi, R., Bonnet, F., Fokkink, W., Haverkort, B.: Formal analysis techniques for gossiping protocols. ACM SIGOPS Oper. Syst. Rev. **41**(5), 28–36 (2007)
5. Bingham, J.: Automatic non-interference lemmas for parameterized model checking. In: Proceedings of the 2008 International Conference on Formal Methods in Computer-Aided Design, FMCAD 2008, Piscataway, NJ, USA, pp. 11:1–11:8. IEEE Press (2008)
6. Chang, E., Roberts, R.: An improved algorithm for decentralized extrema-finding in circular configurations of processes. Commun. ACM **22**(5), 281–283 (1979)

7. Chou, C.-T., Mannava, P.K., Park, S.: A simple method for parameterized verification of cache coherence protocols. In: Hu, A.J., Martin, A.K. (eds.) FMCAD 2004. LNCS, vol. 3312, pp. 382–398. Springer, Heidelberg (2004). doi:10.1007/978-3-540-30494-4_27

8. Clarke, E., Talupur, M., Veith, H.: Proving ptolemy right: the environment abstraction framework for model checking concurrent systems. In: Ramakrishnan, C.R., Rehof, J. (eds.) TACAS 2008. LNCS, vol. 4963, pp. 33–47. Springer, Heidelberg (2008). doi:10.1007/978-3-540-78800-3_4

9. Clarke, E.M., Grumberg, O., Long, D.E.: Model checking and abstraction. ACM Trans. Program. Lang. Syst. (TOPLAS) 16(5), 1512–1542 (1994)

10. Clarke Jr., E.M., Grumberg, O., Peled, D.A.: Model Checking. MIT Press, Cambridge (1999)

11. Delzanno, G., Sangnier, A., Traverso, R.: Parameterized verification of broadcast networks of register automata. In: Abdulla, P.A., Potapov, I. (eds.) RP 2013. LNCS, vol. 8169, pp. 109–121. Springer, Heidelberg (2013). doi:10.1007/978-3-642-41036-9_11

12. Desai, A., Seshia, S.A., Qadeer, S., Broman, D., Eidson, J.C.: Approximate synchrony: an abstraction for distributed almost-synchronous systems. In: Kroening, D., Păsăreanu, C.S. (eds.) CAV 2015. LNCS, vol. 9207, pp. 429–448. Springer, Cham (2015). doi:10.1007/978-3-319-21668-3_25

13. Dolev, D., Klawe, M., Rodeh, M.: An o (n log n) unidirectional distributed algorithm for extrema finding in a circle. J. Algorithms 3(3), 245–260 (1982)

14. Emerson, E.A., Namjoshi, K.S.: Reasoning about rings. In: Proceedings of the 22nd ACM SIGPLAN-SIGACT Symposium on Principles of Programming Languages, POPL 1995, pp. 85–94. ACM, New York (1995)

15. Garavel, H., Mounier, L.: Specification and verification of various distributed leader election algorithms for unidirectional ring networks. Sci. Comput. Program. 29(1), 171–197 (1997)

16. John, A., Konnov, I., Schmid, U., Veith, H., Widder, J.: Parameterized model checking of fault-tolerant distributed algorithms by abstraction. In: FMCAD, pp. 201–209 (2013)

17. Fredlund, L., Groote, J.F., Korver, V.: Formal verification of a leader election protocol in process algebra. Theoret. Comput. Sci. 177(2), 459–486 (1997)

18. Krstic, S.: Parameterized system verification with guard strengthening and parameter abstraction. In: Automated Verification of Infinite State Systems (2005)

19. Kusy, B., Abdelwahed, S.: FTSP protocol verification using SPIN, May 2006

20. Maróti, M., Kusy, B., Simon, G., Lédeczi, A.: The flooding time synchronization protocol. In: Proceedings of the 2nd International Conference on Embedded Networked Sensor Systems, SenSys 2004, pp. 39–49. ACM, New York (2004)

21. McInnes, A.I.: Model-checking the flooding time synchronization protocol. In: IEEE International Conference on Control and Automation, ICCA 2009, pp. 422–429, December 2009

22. McMillan, K.L.: Parameterized verification of the FLASH cache coherence protocol by compositional model checking. In: Margaria, T., Melham, T. (eds.) CHARME 2001. LNCS, vol. 2144, pp. 179–195. Springer, Heidelberg (2001). doi:10.1007/3-540-44798-9_17

23. Milner, R.: A Calculus of Communicating Systems. Springer, New York (1982)

24. Pnueli, A.: The temporal logic of programs. In: 18th Annual Symposium on Foundations of Computer Science, pp. 46–57, October 1977

25. Pnueli, A., Xu, J., Zuck, L.: Liveness with (0,1, ∞)- counter abstraction. In: Brinksma, E., Larsen, K.G. (eds.) CAV 2002. LNCS, vol. 2404, pp. 107–122. Springer, Heidelberg (2002). doi:10.1007/3-540-45657-0_9
26. Sugihara, R., Gupta, R.K.: Clock synchronization with deterministic accuracy guarantee. In: Marrón, P.J., Whitehouse, K. (eds.) EWSN 2011. LNCS, vol. 6567, pp. 130–146. Springer, Heidelberg (2011). doi:10.1007/978-3-642-19186-2_9
27. Talupur, M., Tuttle, M.R.: Going with the flow: parameterized verification using message flows. In: Formal Methods in Computer-Aided Design, FMCAD 2008, pp. 1–8, November 2008
28. Tan, L., Bu, L., Zhao, J., Wang, L.: Analyzing the robustness of FTSP with timed automata. In: Proceedings of the Second Asia-Pacific Symposium on Internetware, Internetware 2010, pp. 21:1–21:4. ACM, New York (2010)
29. Vasudevan, S., Kurose, J., Towsley, D.: Design and analysis of a leader election algorithm for mobile ad hoc networks. In: Proceedings of the 12th IEEE International Conference on Network Protocols, ICNP 2004, pp. 350–360. IEEE (2004)

Combining String Abstract Domains for JavaScript Analysis: An Evaluation

Roberto Amadini[1]([⊠]), Alexander Jordan[2], Graeme Gange[1],
François Gauthier[2], Peter Schachte[1], Harald Søndergaard[1],
Peter J. Stuckey[1], and Chenyi Zhang[2,3]

[1] Department of Computing and Information Systems,
The University of Melbourne, Melbourne, VIC 3010, Australia
roberto.amadini@unimelb.edu.au
[2] Oracle Labs Australia, Brisbane, QLD 4000, Australia
[3] College of Information Science and Technology, Jinan University,
Guangzhou, China

Abstract. Strings play a central role in JavaScript and similar scripting languages. Owing to dynamic features such as the eval function and dynamic property access, precise string analysis is a prerequisite for automated reasoning about practically any kind of runtime property. Although the literature presents a considerable number of abstract domains for capturing and representing specific aspects of strings, we are not aware of tools that allow flexible combination of string abstract domains. Indeed, support for string analysis is often confined to a single, dedicated string domain. In this paper we describe a framework that allows us to combine multiple string abstract domains for the analysis of JavaScript programs. It is implemented as an extension of SAFE, an open-source static analysis tool. We investigate different combinations of abstract domains that capture various aspects of strings. Our evaluation suggests that a combination of a few, simple abstract domains suffice to outperform the precision of state-of-the-art static analysis tools for JavaScript.

1 Introduction

JavaScript is a highly dynamic and flexible language. Flexibility has a price: features such as dynamic property access and code execution, prototype-based inheritance, profligate coercion, and reflection combine to make the static analysis of JavaScript very challenging.[1]

Precise reasoning about *strings* is especially critical in JavaScript analysis. A coarse treatment of string values, and in particular of property names, may result in an inefficient and less than useful analysis. For example, consider the

---

[1] In JavaScript, an object is a map that associates *property names* to values. The *prototype* of an object is instead the object from which it inherits (possibly recursively) methods and properties. Each object has a property named __proto__ (standardized in ECMAScript6, even if deprecated) which points to its prototype.

© Springer-Verlag GmbH Germany 2017
A. Legay and T. Margaria (Eds.): TACAS 2017, Part I, LNCS 10205, pp. 41–57, 2017.
DOI: 10.1007/978-3-662-54577-5_3

dynamic access obj[x] for property name x of object obj. Since the value of x can be unknown (or difficult to know) at compile time, a rough static analysis may approximate x with the set of *all* possible string values. This can lead to a dramatic loss of precision (and, consequently, of efficiency) since obj[x] would point to *any* property of obj and any property of its prototype.

In this paper we consider static analysis of string values by means of abstract interpretation [8], a well-known theory of reasoning with approximations. Informally, each JavaScript string is approximated by an abstract counterpart, an "abstract" string. The abstract values used for abstracting a "concrete" string constitute a string abstract domain, or just *string domain*.

State-of-the-art JavaScript static analysers such as TAJS [11], JSAI [13], and SAFE [15] use similar, yet slightly different, abstract domains for representing string values. However, each commits to *one* single string domain defined *ad hoc* for JavaScript analysis. The precision of such JavaScript-specific domains is often limited, e.g., for most of the web applications relying on the well-known jQuery library [12], owing to the inherently dynamic nature of such libraries. On the other hand, the literature contains proposals for a large variety of general-purpose string domains [6,7,14,16,17].

Here we describe a usable and open-source tool which implements and integrates several string domains. The tool is built on top of SAFE and we refer to it as $SAFE_{str}$. It allows a user to use *combinations* of different string domains for the analysis of JavaScript programs. Analysis with $SAFE_{str}$ is not limited to a single specific string domain but allows arbitrary combination of string domains. This is useful, since a large number of string abstract domains have been proposed. It facilitates experiments with different combinations and investigation into the (complementary) advantages of different domains.

We have validated the performance of $SAFE_{str}$ on different JavaScript programs, most of which rely on the jQuery library. Our experiments suggest that the use of a single domain often leads to a severe loss of precision, whereas a suitable combination of relatively simple string domains can match, and sometimes outperform the precision of state-of-the-art JavaScript analysers.

The contributions of this paper are:

- a detailed discussion of state-of-the-art string domains, useful also in contexts beyond JavaScript, that we have integrated into $SAFE_{str}$;
- a description of $SAFE_{str}$, a major extension and re-engineering of SAFE which enables the tuning of different string abstract domains;
- an empirical evaluation of $SAFE_{str}$ on different JavaScript benchmarks that shows the impact and the benefits of combining string domains.

Paper Structure. Section 2 recapitulates string analysis concepts and gives examples. Section 3 discusses a range of string domains we have implemented and evaluated. Section 4 describes $SAFE_{str}$. Section 5 reports on the experimental results. Section 6 discusses related work and Sect. 7 concludes.

2   Preliminaries

JavaScript is a high-level, dynamic, and untyped language. It has been standardised in the ECMAScript language specification [10]. The flexibility of JavaScript is a double-edged sword that might surprise the user with unexpected behaviours.

Consider the snippet of code in Fig. 1. The value of variable res will be the string __proto__. This is due to the coercion of numbers to strings for property access, including not only digits but also special literals. For instance, the numerical expressions 1/0 and Math.pow(2, 1024) both evaluate to the Infinity string literal, while 0/0 turns into the string NaN.

In this case, the value of res can be statically determined since all the accesses to the properties of obj are known at compile time. Unfortunately, as we shall see, this is not always the case.

```
var obj = {0: "pr", 1: "to"};
obj[0/0] = "_";
obj[Math.pow(2, 1024)] = function(i) {
   return obj[obj[i]/i] + obj["0"] +"o"+ obj[i] + obj[obj[-i]]
};
obj.undefined = obj[0 * 1/0] + obj[1/0 - 1/0]
var res = "_" + obj[1/0](1);
```

Fig. 1. Unusual but legal property access in JavaScript

```
function lookup(o, x) {
   while (x.length < N)
      x = "0" + x;
   return o[x]
}
var v = lookup(obj, "123");
```

```
function update(o, x, v) {
   while (x.length < N)
      x = "0" + x;
   o[x] = v
}
update(obj, "123", "foo");
```

Fig. 2. A lookup function (left) and an update function (right)

Example 1. Consider Fig. 2(left). The call to lookup returns the value of property $0^n 123$ of object obj (that we assumed defined somewhere in the code) where $n = \max\{0, N-3\}$ and N is a value unknown at compile time (it may be a random-generated number or an input value provided by the user). This function might encode the lookup to a dictionary where the keys are numbers of at least N digits. A precise string analysis should be able to infer that $x = 0^n 123$. Unfortunately, static analysis often results in over-approximations and thus imprecision, so it is possible that a sound analysis says that x can be any string and therefore the function lookup(obj, x) points to any of the properties of obj, including all the properties of the prototype hierarchy of obj.   □

Example 2. Dynamic writes can be even nastier, since JavaScript enables to override properties dynamically. Consider the code in Fig. 2 (right) which acts analogously to `lookup`. The `update` function might encode the update of a value in a dictionary where the input key is padded to length N with $n = \max\{0, N-3\}$ leading zeros. In this case `obj[0`^{n}`123]` is set to value `"foo"`. If the analysis can not say anything about `x`, we have a situation where any property of object `obj` (including special property `__proto__`) can be *overwritten* by `"foo"`. In our example, this raises a false alarm that a coarse analysis cannot avoid.   □

For the static analysis of string-manipulation we take advantage of the *abstract interpretation* framework [8].

Let Σ be the set of characters allowed in JavaScript. We define the *concrete domain* as the lattice $\langle \mathcal{P}(\Sigma^*), \subseteq, \emptyset, \Sigma^*, \cap, \cup \rangle$ where Σ^* is the set of all the strings of Σ, $\mathcal{P}(\Sigma^*)$ is its powerset, and $\subseteq, \emptyset, \cap,$ and $\cup$ have the usual set-theoretic meanings. We define a *string (abstract) domain* as a lattice $\langle \mathcal{S}, \sqsubseteq, \bot, \top, \sqcap, \sqcup \rangle$ where each abstract string $\hat{s} \in \mathcal{S}$ denotes a set of concrete strings $\gamma(\hat{s}) \in \mathcal{P}(\Sigma^*)$ via a *concretisation function* γ such that $\hat{s} \sqsubseteq \hat{s}' \Rightarrow \gamma(\hat{s}) \subseteq \gamma(\hat{s}')$. Hence $\sqsubseteq$ captures the relation *"is at least as precise as"* on $\mathcal{S}$.

Often we require that γ has a (lower) adjoint $\alpha : \mathcal{P}(\Sigma^*) \rightarrow \mathcal{S}$, the so-called *abstraction function.*[2] In this case, every k-ary "concrete operation" $f : \mathcal{P}(\Sigma^*)^k \rightarrow \mathcal{P}(\Sigma^*)$ has a unique optimal counterpart on $\mathcal{S}$, namely the "abstract operation" $\hat{f}$ such that $\hat{f}(\hat{s_1}, \ldots, \hat{s_k}) = (\alpha \circ f)(\gamma(\hat{s_1}), \ldots, \gamma(\hat{s_k}))$.

Now suppose we have $n \geq 1$ string abstract domains $\langle \mathcal{S}_i, \sqsubseteq_i, \bot_i, \top_i, \sqcap_i, \sqcup_i \rangle$, each abstracting the concrete domain $\mathcal{P}(\Sigma^*)$. We can define their *direct product* as a structure $\langle \mathcal{S}, \sqsubseteq, \bot, \top, \sqcap, \sqcup \rangle$ such that:

- $\mathcal{S} = \mathcal{S}_1 \times \cdots \times \mathcal{S}_n$
- $(\hat{s}_1, \ldots, \hat{s}_n) \sqsubseteq (\hat{s}'_1, \ldots, \hat{s}'_n) \iff \hat{s}_1 \sqsubseteq_1 \hat{s}'_1 \wedge \ldots \wedge \hat{s}_n \sqsubseteq_n \hat{s}'_n$
- $\bot = (\bot_1, \ldots, \bot_n)$ and $\top = (\top_1, \ldots, \top_n)$
- $(\hat{s}_1, \ldots, \hat{s}_n) \sqcap (\hat{s}'_1, \ldots, \hat{s}'_n) = (\hat{s}_1 \sqcap_1 \hat{s}'_1, \ldots, \hat{s}_n \sqcap_n \hat{s}'_n)$
- $(\hat{s}_1, \ldots, \hat{s}_n) \sqcup (\hat{s}'_1, \ldots, \hat{s}'_n) = (\hat{s}_1 \sqcup_1 \hat{s}'_1, \ldots, \hat{s}_n \sqcup_n \hat{s}'_n)$
- $\gamma(\hat{s}_1, \ldots, \hat{s}_n) = \bigcap_{i=1}^{n} \gamma_i(\hat{s}_i)$ and $\alpha(S) = (\alpha_1(S), \ldots, \alpha_n(S))$

The direct product simply captures an analysis which acts componentwise on the Cartesian product $\mathcal{S}_1 \times \cdots \times \mathcal{S}_n$. A drawback of the direct product is that γ may not be injective, even if all of $\gamma_1, \ldots, \gamma_n$ are. This may give rise to a not optimal, but still sound, precision of the analysis.

3   String Domains

This section summarises the string domains we have integrated in SAFE$_{str}$. We show how they behave in analysis of the programs from Fig. 2, assuming that `lookup(obj, "123")` is called after `update(obj, "123", "foo")` on an initially empty object `obj`, in a context where N has an unknown value.

---

[2] In this case α and γ form a *Galois connection*, i.e., $\alpha(S) \sqsubseteq \hat{s} \iff S \subseteq \gamma(\hat{s})$.

3.1   The String Set and Constant String Domains

The *String Set* (SS_k) enables precise representation of at most $k \geq 1$ concrete strings. Formally, $SS_k = \{\top_{SS_k}\} \cup \{S \in \mathcal{P}(\Sigma^*) \mid |S| \leq k\}$ and the lattice operations $\sqsubseteq_{SS_k}, \sqcap_{SS_k}, \sqcup_{SS_k}$ correspond to $\subseteq, \cap, \cup$ respectively ($\bot_{SS_k} = \emptyset$).

The concretisation function is: $\gamma_{CS}(S) = S$, if $S \neq \top_{SS_k}$; Σ^* otherwise. The abstraction function is: $\alpha_{CS}(S) = S$, if $|S| \leq k$; $\top_{SS_k}$ otherwise. The abstract concatenation is $S \odot_{SS_k} S' = \{s \cdot s' \mid s \in S, s' \in S'\}$. If the set resulting from an abstract operation exceeds k strings, $\top_{SS_k}$ is returned.

One instance of SS_k is the *Constant String* (CS) domain, which is able to represents a single concrete string exactly (i.e., $CS = SS_1$). Despite the limited expressive power, this domain is commonly used, as pointed out in [16].

The SS_k domain is clearly more expressive than CS, and for some analysis a well picked value of k can be enough for achieving high precision. Unfortunately, when analysing loops with an unknown number of iterations, it is often no more expressive. This is the case of the **update** function of Fig. 2, where the abstract value of variable x becomes $\top$ and thus string "foo" might potentially be assigned to any property of obj. As a consequence, lookup(obj, "123") returns not only "foo" but also *all* the properties of the prototype of obj.

3.2   The Character Inclusion Domain

The *Character Inclusion* (CI) domain tracks the characters occurring in a string. Each abstract string has the form $[L, U] = \{X \in \mathcal{P}(\Sigma) \mid L \subseteq X \subseteq U\}$. The lower bound L contains the characters that *must* occur in the concrete string(s), while the upper bound U represents the characters that *may* appear.

Formally, $CI = \{\bot_{CI}\} \cup \{[L, U] \mid L, U \in \mathcal{P}(\Sigma), L \subseteq U\}$ and $[L, U] \sqsubseteq_{CI} [L', U'] \iff L' \subseteq L \wedge U \subseteq U'$. The meet operation is $[L, U] \sqcap_{CI} [L', U'] = [L \cup L', U \cap U']$ while the join is $[L, U] \sqcup_{CI} [L', U'] = [L \cap L', U \cup U']$.

Let $chars : \Sigma^* \rightarrow \mathcal{P}(\Sigma)$ return the set of characters occurring in a string. The abstraction function is $\alpha_{CI}(S) = [\bigcap C_S, \bigcup C_S]$, where $C_S = \{chars(w) \mid w \in S\}$, while $\gamma_{CI}([L, U]) = \{w \in \Sigma^* \mid L \subseteq chars(w) \subseteq U\}$. Abstract concatenation is $[L, U] \odot_{CI} [L', U'] = [L \cup L', U \cup U']$.

This domain completely ignores the structure of the concrete strings it approximates. But, CI is in general computationally cheap and sometimes provides very useful information. For example, for the **update** function in Fig. 2 we have that $\alpha_{CI}(\text{x}) = [\{1, 2, 3\}, \{0, 1, 2, 3\}]$. This information is enough to avoid the assignment of $\alpha_{CI}(\text{"foo"})$ to all the properties of obj and to restrict the (string) return value of the lookup function to $\alpha_{CI}(\text{"foo"}) = [\{f, o\}, \{f, o\}]$.[3]

3.3   The Prefix-Suffix Domain

An element of the *Prefix-Suffix* (PS) domain is a pair $\langle p, s \rangle \in \Sigma^* \times \Sigma^*$, corresponding to all the concrete strings that start as p and end as s. The domain is

---

[3] This is actually the only possible *string* value. However, SAFE also tracks possible non-string results (such as the special value **undefined**).

$\mathcal{PS} = \{\bot_{\mathcal{PS}}\} \cup (\Sigma^* \times \Sigma^*)$. Let $lcp(S)$ (respectively $lcs(S)$) be the longest common prefix (suffix) of a set of strings S. Then $\langle p, s \rangle \sqsubseteq_{\mathcal{PS}} \langle p', s' \rangle \iff lcp(\{p, p'\}) = p' \wedge lcs(\{s, s'\}) = s'$, the join is $\langle p, s \rangle \sqcup_{\mathcal{PS}} \langle p', s' \rangle = \langle lcp\{p, p'\}, lcs\{s, s'\} \rangle$, and the meet $\sqcap_{\mathcal{PS}}$ is naturally induced by $\sqsubseteq_{\mathcal{PS}}$.

Abstraction is defined by $\alpha_{\mathcal{PS}}(S) = \langle lcp(S), lcs(S) \rangle$ while concretisation is $\gamma(\langle p, s \rangle) = \{p \cdot w \mid w \in \Sigma^*\} \cap \{w \cdot s \mid w \in \Sigma^*\}$. The abstract concatenation is $\langle p, s \rangle \odot_{\mathcal{PS}} \langle p', s' \rangle = \langle p, s' \rangle$.

The $\mathcal{PS}$ domain can not keep track of concrete strings. Nonetheless, as for $\mathcal{CI}$, this domain is able to increase the precision of $\mathcal{SS}_k$. Indeed, for the update function we have that $\alpha_{\mathcal{PS}}(\mathbf{x}) = \langle \epsilon, 123 \rangle$ which allows to restrict the string return value of the lookup function to $\alpha_{\mathcal{PS}}(\text{"foo"}) = \langle \text{"foo"}, \text{"foo"} \rangle$.

3.4 The String Hash Domain

The *String Hash* ($\mathcal{SH}$) domain was proposed by Madsen and Andreasen [16]. For some fixed integer range $U = [0, b]$ and hash function $h : \Sigma^* \to U$, a concrete string s is mapped into a "bucket" of U according to the sum of the character codes of s, i.e., $\alpha(S) = \bigcup_{s \in S} h(\Sigma_{c \in chars(s)} I(c))$ where $I : \Sigma \to \mathbb{N}$ maps a character of alphabet Σ to the corresponding code (e.g., ASCII or Unicode). The concretisation function is $\gamma_{\mathcal{SH}}(X) = \{s \in \Sigma^* \mid h(\Sigma_{c \in chars(s)} I(c)) \in X\}$.

The abstract concatenation requires the hash function to be distributive. A linear-time implementation is possible (see [16] for details). This is one of the main strengths of $\mathcal{SH}$, together with its ability to infer string disequality: if $\alpha_{\mathcal{SH}}(s) \sqcap_{\mathcal{SH}} \alpha_{\mathcal{SH}}(s') = \emptyset$ then we can safely conclude that $s \neq s'$.

Unfortunately, $\mathcal{SH}$ can display slow convergence when analysing loops (in the worst case we may generate all elements of U before reaching a fixed point) and its precision appears limited. As with $\mathcal{CS}$ and $\mathcal{SS}_k$, this domain loses all information when analysing the programs in Fig. 2.

3.5 JavaScript-Specific Domains

The string domains we have seen so far are "general-purpose", rather than tailored for specific applications. We now discuss three simple domains, $\mathcal{UO}$, $\mathcal{NO}$, and $\mathcal{NS}$, that constitute the bases for the string domains of the TAJS, SAFE, and JSAI static analysers. Although easily extensible to other languages, these domains are in fact JavaScript-specific.

The *Unsigned-or-Other* ($\mathcal{UO}$) domain used by TAJS (see Fig. 3) discriminates between strings representing an *unsigned integer* and all the other JavaScript strings. TAJS uses this domain to better analyse array indexing. Note that if we concatenate two unsigned integers we do not necessarily get a valid unsigned integer since we might exceed the maximum unsigned integer $2^{32} - 1$. Also, if we concatenate an unsigned i with a string x we can still have i if $x = \epsilon$. However, concatenating two non-unsigned always results in a non-unsigned.

The *Number-or-Other* ($\mathcal{NO}$) domain used by SAFE (see Fig. 4) is very similar to $\mathcal{UO}$: the only difference is that it discriminates between *numeric strings* and

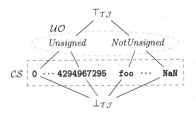

Fig. 3. TAJS string domain

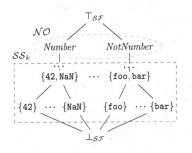

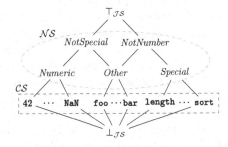

Fig. 4. SAFE string domain   **Fig. 5.** JSAI string domain

other strings. Literals like -3, 0.1, or NaN are considered numeric strings. In this case the concatenation is even more imprecise: we can get a numeric string by concatenating two non-numeric strings (e.g., "N" and "aN").

The *Number-Special-or-other* ($\mathcal{NS}$) domain used by JSAI (see Fig. 5) generalises $\mathcal{NO}$ by also distinguishing *special* JavaScript strings.[4] Concatenating a special string with another special string or a numeric string always results in an "*Other*" string, i.e., a string neither special nor numeric. Concatenating a special string with *Other* always results in a non-numeric string.

Although these domains are useful to capture specific aspects of JavaScript they have little meaning when used stand-alone. In the next section we show how TAJS, SAFE, and JSAI combine them with the $\mathcal{CS}$ and $\mathcal{SS}_k$ lattices.

3.6   The TAJS, SAFE and JSAI Domains

The string domains adopted by TAJS, SAFE, and JSAI are built respectively on top of the $\mathcal{UO}$, $\mathcal{NO}$, and $\mathcal{NS}$ domains from Sect. 3.5 in combination with the $\mathcal{CS}$ and $\mathcal{SS}_k$ domains from Sect. 3.1. The $\mathcal{TJ}$ domain used by TAJS is shown in Fig. 3. First, the analysis is conducted with the constant domain $\mathcal{CS}$. Then, when there is more than one constant string to track, $\mathcal{TJ}$ falls back to the $\mathcal{UO}$ domain trying to discriminate if all such strings are definitely unsigned or definitely not

---

[4] Namely, length, concat, join, pop, push, shift, sort, splice, reverse, valueOf, toString, indexOf, lastIndexOf, constructor, isPrototypeOf, toLocaleString, hasOwnProperty, and propertyIsEnumerable.

unsigned integers. If such a distinction is not possible (e.g., $-1 \sqcup_{\mathcal{TJ}} 1$) then $\top_{\mathcal{TJ}}$ is returned.

The $\mathcal{SF}$ domain used by SAFE (Fig. 4) uses a similar logic. The difference is that the analysis is conducted with the string set domain $\mathcal{SS}_k$ (for a certain value of $k \geq 1$) and then, when we have more than k constant strings to track, it falls back to the $\mathcal{NO}$ domain trying to discriminate if such strings are numeric or not. This is not a generalisation of $\mathcal{TJ}$: indeed, let us suppose $k = 2$ and $S = \{\texttt{foo}, \texttt{bar}, \texttt{-1}\}$. We have $\alpha_{\mathcal{SF}}(S) = \top_{\mathcal{SF}}$ and thus $\gamma_{\mathcal{SF}}(\alpha_{\mathcal{SF}}(S)) = \Sigma^*$. Instead, $\alpha_{\mathcal{TJ}}(S) = NotUnsigned$ so $\gamma_{\mathcal{TJ}}(\alpha_{\mathcal{TJ}}(S)) = \Sigma^* \setminus \{0, \dots, 4294967295\}$.

Being built on top of $\mathcal{SS}_k$, $\mathcal{SF}$ is also parametric. When the set size is not specified, we will assume $k = 1$ (which is the default value in SAFE).

The $\mathcal{JS}$ domain used by JSAI (Fig. 5) acts analogously to $\mathcal{SF}$. However, like $\mathcal{TJ}$, a single constant string is tracked instead of a set of k strings. When we have more than one constant string to track, the $\mathcal{JS}$ domain falls back to the $\mathcal{NS}$ domain (which actually generalises $\mathcal{NO}$, so we can say that $\mathcal{JS}$ generalises $\mathcal{SF}$ if and only if $k = 1$ for the $\mathcal{SS}_k$ domain of $\mathcal{SF}$).

Even if not strictly comparable, $\mathcal{TJ}$, $\mathcal{SF}$ and $\mathcal{JS}$ are very similar. Their JavaScript-driven nature is however not helpful for analysing the programs in Fig. 2. Indeed, when we call $\texttt{update(obj,"123", "foo")}$ we have that the abstract value of property x at the end of the loop is $\top$ for both $\mathcal{TJ}$ and $\mathcal{SF}$ (as seen in Sect. 3.5, they lose all the information when concatenating two numbers) while $\alpha_{\mathcal{JS}}(\texttt{x}) = NotSpecial$. However, this information is not enough to prevent the return of all the properties of $\texttt{obj}$ and its prototypes (except for those corresponding to the special strings) when $\texttt{lookup(obj, "123")}$ is called.

3.7   Direct Products and the Hybrid Domain

So far we have seen several string domains, some general, some JavaScript specific. We observed that each has its strengths and weaknesses. A natural extension is to *combine* different string domains into a single, compound string domain that generalises them in order to improve the precision of the analysis.

In Sect. 2 we introduced the direct product $\mathcal{S} = \mathcal{S}_1 \times \dots \times \mathcal{S}_n$ for systematically composing n string domains. We can thus apply this definition for combining the string domains we have seen so far. Clearly, while the precision of $\mathcal{S}$ is never lower than for a component domain $\mathcal{S}_i$, it may be the case that the direct product does not bring any benefit. For instance, $\mathcal{SH} \times \mathcal{TJ} \times \mathcal{SF} \times \mathcal{JS}$ is not beneficial for analysing the Examples 1 and 2. Conversely, $\mathcal{CI} \times \mathcal{PS}$ significantly increases the precision: if we consider $\alpha(\texttt{x})$ as the abstraction of property x of Examples 1 and 2 we have $\alpha(\texttt{x}) = (\alpha_{\mathcal{CI}}(\texttt{x}), \alpha_{\mathcal{PS}}(\texttt{x})) = ([\{\texttt{1},\texttt{2},\texttt{3}\}, \{\texttt{0},\texttt{1},\texttt{2},\texttt{3}\}], \langle \epsilon, \texttt{123} \rangle)$, so by definition the corresponding concretisation is $\gamma(\alpha(\texttt{x})) = \gamma_{\mathcal{CI}}(\alpha_{\mathcal{CI}}(\texttt{x})) \cap \gamma_{\mathcal{PS}}(\alpha_{\mathcal{PS}}(\texttt{x})) = \{x \cdot \texttt{123} \mid x \in \{\texttt{0},\texttt{1},\texttt{2},\texttt{3}\}^*\}$.

The *Hybrid* ($\mathcal{HY}$) string domain [16] is defined as the product of character inclusion, string set, and string hash: $\mathcal{HY} = \mathcal{CI} \times \mathcal{SS}_k \times \mathcal{SH}$. This domain appears to perform well, so we consider it in our evaluation of Sect. 5.

As mentioned in Sect. 2, the systematic combination via direct product does not always reach the optimal precision. For example, at first it may appear that $\mathcal{SF} = \mathcal{SS}_k \times \mathcal{NO}$ but this is not the case, as the following example shows.

Example 3. Consider the following JavaScript statement, where E is unknown:

$$x = \text{"0"}; \quad \text{if (E)} \quad x = x + \text{"1"};$$

If we approximate x with $\mathcal{SS}_1 \times \mathcal{NO}$ we have $(\{1\}\sqcup_{\mathcal{SS}_1}\{01\}, Number\sqcup_{\mathcal{NO}}\top_{\mathcal{NO}}) = (\top_{\mathcal{SS}_1}, \top_{\mathcal{NO}})$ after the statement. Conversely, even if the default $\mathcal{SF}$ domain can not represent the set $\{0,01\}$, it can infer from it that x is a *Number*.   □

To avoid these precision leaks when combining different domains, the *reduced product* [4,9] has been introduced as a refinement of the direct product.

Figure 6 concludes the section with a diagram summarising the string domains we have encountered so far. There is an upward edge between domain $\mathcal{S}$ and domain $\mathcal{S}'$ if and only if $\mathcal{S}$ is never less precise than $\mathcal{S}'$.

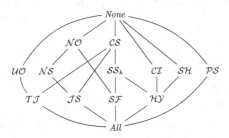

Fig. 6. String abstract domains

4   Implementation

We now describe SAFE$_{str}$, the extension of the SAFE tool in which we have implemented all the string domains discussed in Sect. 3.

SAFE [15] is a static analyser for ECMAScript developed for the JavaScript community. We chose it as a starting point for our analyser because it is open-source, under active development, exhaustively implements the DOM semantics, and utilises loop-sensitive analysis.

The execution flow of SAFE is structured into three main parts. First, the input JavaScript program is parsed and translated into a simplified Abstract Syntax Tree (AST). Then, the AST is translated into an Intermediate Representation (IR). Finally, the IR is used to build the Control Flow Graph (CFG). The CFG is the best representation for tracing control flows of a program, and in fact is used by SAFE to perform a type-based analysis of JavaScript programs. SAFE is implemented in Scala (with some modules written in Java).

The static analysis performed by SAFE relies on the string abstract domain described in Sect. 3.6 to model primitive JavaScript strings as well as for the lookup and update of properties in abstract JavaScript objects. The user can tune the size k of the underlying SS_k domain, but can not choose among other string domains. We therefore re-engineered and extended this tool to enable the user to combine all the domains described in Sect. 3. The resulting tool, SAFE$_{str}$, is a major extension of SAFE with improved usability, flexibility, and—as we shall see in Sect. 5—precision of the static analysis.

Table 1 lists the Scala classes that we have implemented in SAFE$_{str}$. The AbsString represents the *base* class, from which every other string domain inherits. AbsString has methods for the lattice operations (e.g., $\sqcup$, $\sqcap$, $\sqsubseteq$), for the abstraction/concretisation functions α and γ, for abstracting string operations (e.g., concatenation, trimming, slicing) and for general utility (e.g., toString or equals). Each class that implements a string domain must be a subclass of AbsString, and possibly overrides its methods.

Table 1. Scala classes implementing string domains into SAFE$_{str}$

Class	Description	Class	Description
AbsString	Base class	AbsStringHash	$\mathcal{SH}$
AbsStringConst	$\mathcal{CS}$	AbsStringSet	$\mathcal{SS}_k$
AbsStringPrefSuff	$\mathcal{PS}$	AbsStringCharIncl	$\mathcal{CI}$
AbsStringUnsOth	$\mathcal{UO}$	AbsStringTAJS	$\mathcal{TJ}$
AbsStringNumOth	$\mathcal{NO}$	AbsStringSAFE	$\mathcal{SF}$
AbsStringNumSplOth	$\mathcal{NS}$	AbsStringJSAI	$\mathcal{JS}$
AbsStringProd	Direct product of AbsString domains		

The new design of SAFE$_{str}$ is suitable for combining different string domains. An important novelty is the AbsStringProd class—which is itself a subclass of AbsString—that allows the user to systematically combine an arbitrary collection of AbsString classes. AbsStringProd can be *specialised* for refining the direct product of different string domains (see Example 3). For example, the $\mathcal{TJ}$, $\mathcal{SF}$, and $\mathcal{JS}$ domains are now specialised subclasses of AbsStringProd since they actually combine other basic domains (as shown in Figs. 3, 4, and 5). Furthermore, the $\mathcal{HY}$ domain does not need to be implemented at all: it is enough to define it as an AbsStringProd object consisting of AbsStringCharIncl, AbsStringSet, and AbsStringHash domains.

We implemented the string domains in SAFE$_{str}$ trying to be as un-intrusive as possible and to preserve the original structure of SAFE. In this we faced a number of design choices. For instance, SAFE analysis is not sound unless the target string domain is able to keep track of a single, concrete string. With SAFE$_{str}$ it is trivial to ensure this by just adding (via direct product) a new constituent domain like $\mathcal{CS}$ or $\mathcal{SS}_k$. Another crucial point for SAFE analysis is the ability to distinguish whether an abstract string is definitely numeric or not numeric. Again, with $SAFE_{str}$ it is easy to enrich a given domain by composing it with $\mathcal{NO}$ or $\mathcal{NS}$ for discriminating numeric strings.

The $SAFE_{str}$ tool can be imported into a Scala application or used as a standalone analyser from the command line. Notably, the user can choose and configure the string domains for an analysis run via command line options. $SAFE_{str}$ is open-source and can be downloaded from https://git.io/vPH9w.

5 Evaluation

In this section we evaluate the string domains that we implemented in $SAFE_{str}$. The default configuration for $SAFE_{str}$ tries to be as precise as possible. In particular, like SAFE, it uses a loop-sensitive analysis with a context-depth of 10 (see [18] for more details). While $SAFE_{str}$ diverged from the version of SAFE in [17], we tried to resemble the evaluation environment as closely as possible. We evaluated $SAFE_{str}$ on two benchmark sets from the literature:[5]

- JQUERY, a set of 61 JavaScript programs from a jQuery tutorial[6]. All the programs of this benchmark, adopted also in [17], use jQuery version 1.7.0 without any modification.
- JSAI, a set of 11 JavaScript sources made available with the JSAI tool [13]. Because of their JSAI-specific modelling, we made some minor modifications to conform with $SAFE_{str}$. Seven programs of JSAI are Firefox browser add-ons, while the remaining four come from the linq.js project.[7]

We stress that the goal of the evaluation is not to assess the performance of different analysis tools. Rather, our focus is on evaluating (the composition of) different string domains *within* the $SAFE_{str}$ environment. Note that we are comparing the implementation of TAJS and JSAI domains in $SAFE_{str}$, not the TAJS and JSAI tools themselves. A direct comparison with such tools is impracticable since a fair measurement of their performance requires knowledge, and modification, of their internals.

Measuring the precision within a complex static analysis framework like SAFE is inherently difficult. Simple metrics, such as runtime of the analysis or reachable program states provide glib information at best. To measure the overall performance we adopted three metrics—used in [17] and, with modifications, in [18]—that count 'how much imprecision' occurs during the static analysis. In more detail, the metrics are:

Multiple dereference (MD) : The number of program points where dereferencing an abstract object leads to more than one object value.

Multiple call (MC) : The number of program points where dereferencing an abstract function object leads to more than one function.

Non-concrete property access (PR) : The number of program points where an object property is accessed with a non-concrete abstract string, i.e., with an abstract string representing an infinite set of concrete strings.

Static analysis of non-trivial programs often involves the handling of failures and timeouts. In particular, owing to the dynamic nature of JavaScript, a lack of static boundaries like types or modules can cause the imprecision to spread explosively, causing the analysis to become infeasible or its results to be unusable.

We devised a mechanism to possibly terminate the analysis early, thus avoiding getting stuck in a non-meaningful analysis. We use empirically determined bounds to trigger an "imprecision stop", e.g., when the number of possible call targets for a function encountered during analysis becomes greater than 20.[8]

Unfortunately, since MD, MC, and PR do not have a reasonable upper bound, choosing a "penalty value" for these metrics when the analysis fails is not trivial. To overcome this problem, inspired by the MiniZinc Challenge [20], we defined a scoring system where we compare pairs of domains on each benchmark program.

Let $\mathbb{P}$ be a benchmark set of programs and $\mathbb{D}$ a collection of string domains. For each program $P \in \mathbb{P}$ and each domain $\mathcal{S} \in \mathbb{D}$ we define the *imprecision index* of $\mathcal{S}$ on P as: $IMP_{\mathcal{S}}(P) = \mathsf{MD}_{\mathcal{S}}(P) + \mathsf{MC}_{\mathcal{S}}(P) + \mathsf{PR}_{\mathcal{S}}(P)$, if the analysis of P using domain $\mathcal{S}$ terminates normally; $IMP_{\mathcal{S}}(P) = \infty$ if the imprecision stop is triggered. Given two distinct domains $\mathcal{S}$ and $\mathcal{S}'$ we define a scoring function:

$$Score_{\mathcal{S}}(P, \mathcal{S}') = \begin{cases} 0 & \text{if } IMP_{\mathcal{S}}(P) = \infty \vee IMP_{\mathcal{S}}(P) > IMP_{\mathcal{S}'}(P) \\ 0.5 & \text{if } IMP_{\mathcal{S}}(P) = IMP_{\mathcal{S}'}(P) \neq \infty \\ 1 & \text{if } IMP_{\mathcal{S}}(P) < IMP'_{\mathcal{S}}(P) \end{cases}$$

Finally, the overall score of the domain $\mathcal{S}$ on benchmark $\mathbb{P}$ is the sum of each $Score_{\mathcal{S}}(P, \mathcal{S}')$ value, for each $P \in \mathbb{P}$ and for each $\mathcal{S} \in \mathbb{D}$ such that $\mathcal{S} \neq \mathcal{S}'$.

We analysed all the domains depicted in Fig. 6. As mentioned in Sect. 4, because of the internal design of SAFE (which we did not want to modify), the static analysis in SAFE$_{str}$ needs a string abstract domain able to track (at least) a single constant string. For each $\mathcal{S} \in \{\mathcal{PS}, \mathcal{CI}, \mathcal{SH}, \mathcal{NO}, \mathcal{NS}, \mathcal{JS}\}$ we therefore evaluated the domain extension $\overline{\mathcal{S}} = \mathcal{S} \times \mathcal{CS}$ instead of $\mathcal{S}$. Note that this did not require any additional effort, since SAFE$_{str}$ allows the user to specify the preferred domain combination on the command line.

Similarly, instead of the original TAJS domain $\mathcal{TJ}$ we actually considered $\mathcal{TJ}^* = \mathcal{TJ} \times \mathcal{NO}$. This is because the underlying $\mathcal{UO}$ domain allows to discriminate only strings representing unsigned integers, but can not deal with numeric strings in general (e.g., floats or negative numbers). Since SAFE's design relies heavily on the distinction between numeric and other strings, the $\mathcal{TJ}$ domain is inevitably penalised when used by SAFE$_{str}$. This is arguably due to the SAFE structure, and not necessarily a weakness of TAJS. Thus, we took advantage of SAFE$_{str}$ for automatically combining $\mathcal{TJ}$ with $\mathcal{NO}$.

In addition, we evaluated the *All* baseline, i.e., the direct product of all the implemented domains, and a *new hybrid domain*, namely $\mathcal{HY}^* = \mathcal{CI} \times \mathcal{NO} \times \mathcal{SS}_k$.

---

[8] We noticed that imprecision stops only occurred in the analysis of JQUERY.

That is, we replace the more complex $\mathcal{SH}$ domain of $\mathcal{HY}$ by the simpler $\mathcal{NO}$. For $\mathcal{HY}^*$, as well as for SS_k, we used the default set size of the $\mathcal{HY}$ domain, $k = 3$. For $\mathcal{SF}$ we instead used the default set size of SAFE, $k = 1$. As we shall see, the difference turned out to be irrelevant.

Table 2a shows the overall performance of the string domains. ALL is the union of JQUERY and JSAI, thus consisting of $61 + 11 = 72$ programs.[9]

Table 2. Performance of string domains

Domain	Score			Fails [%]		
	JQUERY	JSAI	ALL	JQUERY	JSAI	ALL
All, $\mathcal{HY}^*$	418.5	99.0	517.5	49.2	18.2	44.4
$\mathcal{HY}$	337	58.5	395.5	52.5	18.2	47.2
$\overline{\mathcal{CI}}$	330	58.5	388.5	52.5	18.2	47.2
$\mathcal{TJ}^*, \mathcal{SF}, \mathcal{JS},$						
$\mathcal{NO}, \mathcal{NS}$	154	99.0	253.0	68.9	18.2	61.1
$\mathcal{CS}, SS_k, \overline{\mathcal{PS}},$						
$\overline{\mathcal{SH}}, \overline{\mathcal{UO}}$	0	7.5	7.5	100	72.7	95.8

(a) Scores and fail percentages

Domain	JQUERY	JSAI	ALL
$\mathcal{HY}^*$	321.6	137.2	293.1
All	323	142.1	295.4
$\mathcal{HY}$	339.1	182.8	315.2
$\overline{\mathcal{CI}}$	339.7	179.6	315.6
$\mathcal{TJ}^*$	435	136.2	389.4
$\mathcal{NS}$	435.8	140.0	390.6
$\mathcal{JS}$	436.4	136.9	390.6
$\mathcal{NO}$	436.3	138.3	390.7
$\mathcal{SF}$	436.9	137.4	391.1

(b) Average runtimes (s)

The "Score" column summarises the overall score of each domain. We note that $\mathcal{HY}^*$ has the same performance as *All*. Hence, at least for our benchmarks, it sufficient to combine three simple domains, namely $\mathcal{CI}$, $\mathcal{NO}$, and SS_k, to reach the same precision as the combination of all the domains. However, if we consider such domains independently the precision is far lower and often results in imprecision stops (especially for JQUERY, see the bottommost row of Table 2a). This shows the potential of combining different string domains.

The $\mathcal{HY}^*$ domain outperforms $\mathcal{HY}$. Why is replacing the String Hash domain by the Numeric-or-Other domain advantageous? In our context, $\mathcal{SH}$ appears to be unfruitful, but the $\mathcal{NO}$ domain is essential for detecting (non-)numeric strings. While that other $\mathcal{HY}^*$ component, $\mathcal{CI}$, can be helpful in this regard (as noticed in Sect. 3.2), it is often not enough. For example, let x be a variable representing a string in $S = \{-1,0,1\}$. Its abstraction is $\alpha_{\mathcal{CI}}(S) = [\emptyset, \{-,0,1\}]$, but this does not suffice to state that x is a number (e.g., the string - belongs to $\alpha_{\mathcal{CI}}(S)$ but it is not a number). However, $\alpha_{\mathcal{NO}}(S) = Number$.

The benefits of $\mathcal{NO}$ are noticeable especially for the JSAI benchmark, while for JQUERY, $\mathcal{CI}$ remains important. $\mathcal{CI}$ never causes a loss of precision in abstract concatenation, and this is very important, especially when concatenating an unknown string (as often happens when generating the jQuery.expando property). Overall, $\mathcal{HY}^*$ scores better than $\mathcal{HY}$ and $\mathcal{CI}$ for 40 programs (31 of JQUERY and 9 of JSAI) and is never worse than any other domain.

---

[9] We have run all the experiments with a timeout of $T = 600$ seconds on Ubuntu 15.10 machines with 16 GB of RAM and 2.60 GHz CPU.

The $\mathcal{HY}$ domain is better than $\mathcal{CI}$ for only seven programs of JQUERY. This is the only benefit that $\mathcal{SS}_3$ has brought to the analysis, compared to the constant domain $\mathcal{CS}$. We tried to investigate this aspect further, by performing a sensitivity analysis on the k parameter of $\mathcal{SS}_k$ for all the domains we implemented, varying $k \in \{8, 16, 32, 64, 128\}$. No improvement was observed for larger k.

If we look at the domains used by TAJS, SAFE, and JSAI, we observe a substantial equivalence. They are all very effective on the JSAI benchmark, but they have rather poor performance for the problems of JQUERY. We believe that this happens because these domains fail when concatenation involves an unknown string. Note that, in spite of Example 3 highlighting their difference, $\mathcal{SF}$ and $\overline{\mathcal{NO}} = \mathcal{NO} \times \mathcal{CS}$ have identical performance. Similarly, $\mathcal{JS}$ and $\overline{\mathcal{NS}}$ perform equally well.

Looking at the bottom of the table, apart from the aforementioned $\mathcal{SH}$, $\mathcal{SS}_k$ and $\mathcal{UO}$, we see that $\mathcal{PS}$ too has a rather poor performance. This was somewhat unexpected, considering the benefits seen in Examples 1 and 2. One explanation is that $\mathcal{PS}$ is less precise than $\mathcal{CI}$ when joining different abstract strings, and it loses all the information about the 'inner' structure of the string. A curious drawback of $\mathcal{PS}$ is that abstracting the empty string means losing all information, since $\alpha_{\mathcal{PS}}(\epsilon) = \langle \epsilon, \epsilon \rangle = \top_{\mathcal{PS}}$.

The "Fails" column of Table 2 shows, in percentage, the number of times the analysis failed due to imprecision stops or timeouts. Again in this case we see the advantage of combining the string domains. For example, while the analysis using the TAJS, SAFE, or JSAI domains often fail, the $\mathcal{HY}^*$ domain we introduced significantly improve on them (in particular for JQUERY benchmark). Nevertheless, even for $\mathcal{HY}^*$ we still notice a remarkable number of cases (about 44%) where the analysis fails. This calls for further investigation.

Although in this work we are more concerned in the precision of the analysis, it is clear that also efficiency plays an important role. Table 2b reports the average analysis time, where we assign a penalty of $T = 600$ seconds when the analysis fails. We see that in this case $\mathcal{HY}^*$ slightly *outperforms* the combination of all the domains. This is due to its lighter composition (only three domains). On average, the analysis with $\mathcal{HY}^*$ takes about 100 seconds less than analysing programs with the TAJS, SAFE, or JSAI domains.

Let us finally compare our evaluation with that of [16]. In that work, 12 string domains (including $\mathcal{HY}$, referred as $\mathcal{H}$ in the paper) are proposed and compared. We note that, while the dynamic analysis evaluation of [16] is exhaustive, the static analysis evaluation is limited: it is performed on only 10 JavaScript programs (for which sources are not available) and $\mathcal{HY}$ is only compared against the constant domain $\mathcal{CS}$ (which is inherently less precise than $\mathcal{HY}$). The more comprehensive evaluation we provide in this paper in part confirms the good intuition of [16] of including the $\mathcal{CI}$ domain within a collection of other domains.

6   Related Work

Our work has taken the SAFE framework [15] as inspiration and starting point. There are other well-engineered mature analysis frameworks such as TAJS [11],

WALA [19], and JSAI [13]. We chose SAFE because of its conformance with the latest ECMAScript standard, formal specification, loop-sensitivity [18], accessibility, and active development (SAFE 2.0 was released in October 2016).

The number of (string) abstract domains that have been proposed is surprisingly large. In [1,2] the configurable program analysis (CPA) and the dynamic precision adjustment (CPA+) frameworks are introduced to make the analysis configurable and possibly improve its precision.

Many of the domains we have evaluated were discussed by Madsen and Andreasen [16] who cover 12 string domains, half of which were new. Costantini et al. [5,7] discuss two domains whose product amounts to $\mathcal{PS}$, the $\mathcal{CI}$ domain, and two additional (rather more complex) string domains. In the context of Java analysis, Choi *et al.* [3] have used restricted regular expressions as an abstract domain. Sets of strings are approximated by sets of "regular string expressions". Such expressions are liberally defined and allow for nesting of Kleene stars. However, regular expressions of the form r^* cannot be juxtaposed. So while a^*ab^* is a valid regular string expression, aa^*b^* is not, and the latter, should it arise, will effectively be "flattened" into the coarser $a(a + b)^*$. Excessive nesting of stars is curbed through widening, which similarly flattens expressions at a certain star-depth.

Park et al. [17] use a stricter variant of this idea, with a more clearly defined string abstract domain. Here sets of strings are approximated by sets of "atomic" regular expressions. A regular expression is atomic (over alphabet $\Sigma = \{a_1, \ldots, a_n\}$) iff it can be generated by the grammar

$$S \rightarrow `\epsilon' \mid `\Sigma^{*'} \mid A\,S \mid `\Sigma^{*'}A\,S \qquad A \rightarrow a_1 \mid \ldots \mid a_n$$

Quotes indicate that ϵ and Σ^* are not meta-symbols, but terminals. This abstract domain is more restrictive than that of Choi *et al.* [3]. What is gained by this is faster analysis, and in particular tractability of the inclusion relation.

The number and richness of different string abstract domains provides a rich seam for experimental work and comparative evaluation. In spite of that, the number of systematic studies is very limited. An exception is the work by Madsen and Andreasen [16] which, in the static analysis evaluation, compares the precision of $\mathcal{HY}$-based analysis against $\mathcal{CS}$.

7 Conclusion

We have presented SAFE$_{str}$, an extension of the SAFE JavaScript static analysis tool. SAFE$_{str}$ provides support for a number of string analysis domains, as well as for analysis using arbitrary combinations of these domains. Precise string analysis is of paramount importance in a programming language like JavaScript, because almost any other kind of analysis relies heavily on the quality of string analysis to aid it; without precise string analysis, control and data flow information is weak; for example, field access becomes ambiguous. The required precision is ultimately achieved through the combination of a variety of string domains, each capturing some relevant aspect of strings and, accordingly, the literature is replete with proposals for string abstract domains.

We have used SAFE$_{str}$ to conduct the first systematic comparison of a broad range of such string abstract domains for the static analysis of JavaScript programs. We have measured precision and analysis time over two established benchmark sets. The results suggest that there is little value in maintaining string sets (elements of $\mathcal{SS}_k$) of cardinality $k > 3$; and that the relatively simple combination $\mathcal{CI} \times \mathcal{NO} \times \mathcal{CS}$ achieves higher precision than the various combinations proposed elsewhere—in fact, for our sets of benchmarks, it achieves as high precision as the combination of *all* of the string domains we have studied.

Future work will focus on the evaluation, and the combination, of new domains over new benchmarks. In particular, we wish to compare the use of direct products with reduced products [9] of string abstract domains.

Acknowledgements. This work is supported by the Australian Research Council (ARC) through Linkage Project Grant LP140100437.

References

1. Beyer, D., Henzinger, T.A., Théoduloz, G.: Configurable software verification: concretizing the convergence of model checking and program analysis. In: Damm, W., Hermanns, H. (eds.) CAV 2007. LNCS, vol. 4590, pp. 504–518. Springer, Heidelberg (2007). doi:10.1007/978-3-540-73368-3_51
2. Beyer, D., Henzinger, T.A., Théoduloz, G.: Program analysis with dynamic precision adjustment. In: 23rd IEEE/ACM International Conference on Automated Software Engineering (ASE 2008), pp. 29–38 (2008)
3. Choi, T.-H., Lee, O., Kim, H., Doh, K.-G.: A practical string analyzer by the widening approach. In: Kobayashi, N. (ed.) APLAS 2006. LNCS, vol. 4279, pp. 374–388. Springer, Heidelberg (2006). doi:10.1007/11924661_23
4. Cortesi, A., Costantini, G., Ferrara, P.: A survey on product operators in abstract interpretation. In: Semantics, Abstract Interpretation, and Reasoning About Programs: Essays Dedicated to David A. Schmidt on the Occasion of his Sixtieth Birthday, pp. 325–336 (2013)
5. Costantini, G.: Lexical and numerical domains for abstract interpretation. Ph.D. thesis, Università Ca' Foscara Di Venezia (2014)
6. Costantini, G., Ferrara, P., Cortesi, A.: Static analysis of string values. In: Qin, S., Qiu, Z. (eds.) ICFEM 2011. LNCS, vol. 6991, pp. 505–521. Springer, Heidelberg (2011). doi:10.1007/978-3-642-24559-6_34
7. Costantini, G., Ferrara, P., Cortesi, A.: A suite of abstract domains for static analysis of string values. Softw. Pract. Exp. **45**(2), 245–287 (2015)
8. Cousot, P., Cousot, R.: Abstract interpretation: a unified lattice model for static analysis of programs by construction or approximation of fixpoints. In: Proceedings of the Fourth ACM Symposium on Principles of Programming Languages, pp. 238–252. ACM Publication (1977)
9. Cousot, P., Cousot, R.: Systematic design of program analysis frameworks. In: Proceedings of the Sixth Annual ACM Symposium on Principles of Programming Languages, pp. 269–282. ACM Publication (1979)

10. ECMAScript 2016 language specification. http://www.ecma-international.org/publications/files/ECMA-ST/Ecma-262.pdf
11. Jensen, S.H., Møller, A., Thiemann, P.: Type analysis for JavaScript. In: Palsberg, J., Su, Z. (eds.) SAS 2009. LNCS, vol. 5673, pp. 238–255. Springer, Heidelberg (2009). doi:10.1007/978-3-642-03237-0_17
12. jQuery JavaScript library. https://jquery.com/
13. Kashyap, V., Dewey, K., Kuefner, E.A., Wagner, J., Gibbons, K., Sarracino, J., Wiedermann, B., Hardekopf, B.: JSAI: A static analysis platform for JavaScript. In: Proceedings of the 22nd ACM SIGSOFT International Symposium on Foundations of Software Engineering, pp. 121–132. ACM Publication (2014)
14. Kim, S.-W., Chin, W., Park, J., Kim, J., Ryu, S.: Inferring grammatical summaries of string values. In: Garrigue, J. (ed.) APLAS 2014. LNCS, vol. 8858, pp. 372–391. Springer, Cham (2014). doi:10.1007/978-3-319-12736-1_20
15. Lee, H., Won, S., Jin, J., Cho, J., Ryu, S.: SAFE: formal specification and implementation of a scalable analysis framework for ECMAScript. In: Proceedings of the 19th International Workshop on Foundations of Object-Oriented Languages (FOOL 2012) (2012)
16. Madsen, M., Andreasen, E.: String analysis for dynamic field access. In: Cohen, A. (ed.) CC 2014. LNCS, vol. 8409, pp. 197–217. Springer, Heidelberg (2014). doi:10.1007/978-3-642-54807-9_12
17. Park, C., Im, H., Ryu, S.: Precise and scalable static analysis of jQuery using a regular expression domain. In: Proceedings of the 12th Symposium on Dynamic Languages, DLS 2016, Amsterdam, The Netherlands, 1 November 2016, pp. 25–36 (2016)
18. Park, C., Ryu, S.: Scalable and precise static analysis of JavaScript applications via loop-sensitivity. In: Boyland, J.T. (ed.) Proceedings of the 29th European Conference on Object-Oriented Programming (ECOOP 2015), Leibniz International Proceedings in Informatics, pp. 735–756. Dagstuhl Publishing (2015)
19. Sridharan, M., Dolby, J., Chandra, S., Schäfer, M., Tip, F.: Correlation tracking for points-to analysis of JavaScript. In: Noble, J. (ed.) ECOOP 2012. LNCS, vol. 7313, pp. 435–458. Springer, Heidelberg (2012). doi:10.1007/978-3-642-31057-7_20
20. Stuckey, P.J., Feydy, T., Schutt, A., Tack, G., Fischer, J.: The MiniZinc challenge 2008–2013. AI Mag. **35**(2), 55–60 (2014)

Invariant Checking of NRA Transition Systems via Incremental Reduction to LRA with EUF

Alessandro Cimatti[1], Alberto Griggio[1], Ahmed Irfan[1,2(✉)],
Marco Roveri[1], and Roberto Sebastiani[2]

[1] Fondazione Bruno Kessler, Trento, Italy
{cimatti,griggio,irfan,roveri}@fbk.eu
[2] University of Trento, Trento, Italy
{ahmed.irfan,roberto.sebastiani}@unitn.it

Abstract. Model checking invariant properties of designs, represented as transition systems, with non-linear real arithmetic (NRA), is an important though very hard problem. On the one hand NRA is a hard-to-solve theory; on the other hand most of the powerful model checking techniques lack support for NRA. In this paper, we present a counterexample-guided abstraction refinement (CEGAR) approach that leverages linearization techniques from differential calculus to enable the use of mature and efficient model checking algorithms for transition systems on linear real arithmetic (LRA) with uninterpreted functions (EUF). The results of an empirical evaluation confirm the validity and potential of this approach.

1 Introduction

Invariant checking for infinite-state transition systems is a fundamental research area. Based on the recent improvements of SMT technologies, effective approaches have been developed for the case of transition systems with dynamics over Linear Real Arithmetic [4,9,18,21]. However, many real-world industrial designs (e.g. aerospace, automotive) require modeling as transition systems over non-linear arithmetic (NRA). Although both problems are undecidable, proving properties of the NRA transition systems turns out to be much harder than the linear case, and has in fact received much less attention. Approaches based on BMC and k-induction [15,29] are possible, so that non-linearity is handled at the SMT-level, by means of an SMT(NRA) solver (e.g. Z3 [13], nlSAT [20], Yices [14], SMT-RAT [1]). Their power is however limited. Consider the following simple transition system: initially, $x \geq 2 \wedge y \geq 2 \wedge z = x * y$; the transition relation is defined by $x' = x + 1 \wedge y' = y + 1 \wedge z' = x' * y'$. The property "*it is always the case that* $z \geq x + y$" is not k-inductive, not even for a very large value of k. Thus, the typical proving techniques that are based on k-induction using an SMT(NRA) solver will not be able to prove it. In principle, it is also possible to

---

This work was performed as part of the H2020-FETOPEN-2016-2017-CSA project SC² (712689).

A. Legay and T. Margaria (Eds.): TACAS 2017, Part I, LNCS 10205, pp. 58–75, 2017.
DOI: 10.1007/978-3-662-54577-5_4

lift other approaches (e.g. interpolation, IC3 [9,26]) to handle non-linearities at
the level of the solver. However, this requires the SMT(NRA) solver to carry out
interpolation or quantifier elimination, and to proceed incrementally. These extra
functions are usually not available, or they have a very high computational cost.

In this paper, we propose a completely different approach to tackle invariant
checking for NRA transition systems. Basically, we work with an abstract version
of the transition system, expressed over LRA with EUF, for which we have
effective verification tools [9]. In the abstract space, nonlinear multiplication
is modeled as an uninterpreted function. When spurious counter-examples are
found, the abstraction is tightened by the incremental introduction of linear
constraints, including tangent planes resulting from differential calculus, and
monotonicity constraints.

We implemented the approach on top of the NUXMV model checker [7], leveraging the IC3 engine with Implicit Abstraction [9] for invariant checking of transition systems over LRA with EUF. We compared it, on a wide set of benchmarks, against multiple approaches working at NRA level, including BMC and
k-induction using SMT(NRA), the recent interpolation-based ISAT3 engine [24],
and the static abstraction approach proposed in [8]. The results demonstrate substantial superiority of our approach, that is able to solve the highest number of
benchmarks.

The effectiveness of our approach is possibly explained with the following
insights. On the one hand, in contrast to LRA, NRA is a hard-to-solve theory: in practice, most available complete solvers rely on CAD techniques [12],
which require double exponential time in worst case. Thus, we try to avoid NRA
reasoning, trading it for LRA and EUF reasoning. On the other hand, proving
properties of practical NRA transition systems may not require the full power
of non-linear solving. In fact, some systems are "mostly-linear" (i.e. non-linear
constraints are associated to a very small part of the system), an example being
the Transport Class Model (TCM) for aircraft simulation from the Simulink
model library [19]. Furthermore, even NRA transition systems with significant
non-linear dynamics may admit a piecewise-linear invariant of the transition
system that is strong enough to prove the property.

Structure. In Sect. 2 we discuss the related work, and in Sect. 3 introduce some
background. In Sect. 4 we discuss the approach in the setting of SMT(NRA).
In Sect. 5 we present the verification algorithm for NRA transition systems.
In Sect. 6 we describe the results of the experimental evaluation. In Sect. 7 we
conclude and outline the directions for future research.

2   Related Work

There are not many tools that deal with NRA transition systems. The most relevant is the recently proposed ISAT3 [28], that uses an interpolation-based [23,24]
approach to prove invariants. In addition to NRA, it also supports trascendental
functions and some form of differential equations. ISAT3 is built on an SMT
solver based on numeric techniques (interval arithmetic), and is able to provide
results that are accurate up to the specified precision. In fact, in addition to

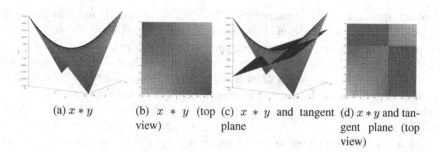

(a) $x * y$ (b) $x * y$ (top (c) $x * y$ and tangent (d) $x * y$ and tan-
           view)   plane   gent plane (top
                                                 view)

Fig. 1. Multiplication function and tangent plane.

"safe" and "unsafe" answers, ISAT3 may return "maybe unsafe" when it finds an envelope of given precision that may (but is not guaranteed to) contain a counterexample. Another relevant tool is DREACH [22], a bounded model checker implemented on top of the DREAL [16] SMT solver, that adopts numerical techniques similar to ISAT3. DREACH has an expressiveness similar to ISAT3, but being a bounded model checker it is unable to prove properties.

The work in [8] follows a reduction-based approach to check invariants of NRA transition systems. It over-approximates the non-linear terms with a coarse abstraction, encoding into LRA some weak properties of multiplication like identity and sign. Another reduction-based approach is presented in [25] in the context of program analysis. The idea is to find a (tighter) convex approximation of polynomials in form of polyhedra, thus obtaining a conservative linear transition system. The key differences of our approach with respect to [8,25] are that we iteratively refine the abstraction, and we adopt a reduction to LRA+EUF. Furthermore, to the best of our knowledge, there is no available implementation of the approach [25] in a program analysis tool – it has been only shown to work on SMT problems.

The idea of approximating a univariate function (in particular the natural logarithm ln) with tangent lines is used in [30]. Here we abstract a bivariate function (multiplication), and use tangent planes for the refinement. We also exploit other properties (e.g. monotonicity) to derive additional axioms. The idea of using tangent planes (spaces) has been explored in [27], limited to the case of SMT solving. Another key differences is that the tangent planes area used to under-approximate predicates, while we use them to refine the over-approximation of the multiplication function.

3   Background

Properties of the Multiplication Function. Geometrically, the surface generated by the multiplication function $f(x, y) \stackrel{\text{def}}{=} x * y$ is shown in Fig. 1a and b. This kind of surface is known in geometry as hyperbolic paraboloid. A hyperbolic paraboloid is a doubly-ruled surface, i.e. for every point on the surface, there are two distinct lines projected from the surface such that they pass through the point. In case of the multiplication surface, the projected lines basically lie on the surface.

Tangent Plane. The tangent plane to a surface at a point of interest (a, b) is a plane that "just touches" the surface at the point. The tangent planes can be used to linearly approximate the surface at the point of interest. An important property of the tangent plane to a hyperbolic paraboliod is that the two projected lines from the surface are also in the tangent plane, and they define how the plane cuts the surface (see Fig. 1c and d). The tangent plane $Tmul_{a,b}(x, y)$ to the multiplication function $f(x, y)$ at point (a, b) is calculated as follows:

$$Tmul_{a,b}(x, y) \stackrel{\text{def}}{=} f(a, b) + \frac{d}{dx}f(x, y)|_{(a,b)} * (x - a) + \frac{d}{dy}f(x, y)|_{(a,b)} * (y - b)$$

where $\frac{d}{dx}f(x, y)|_{(a,b)}$ and $\frac{d}{dy}f(x, y)|_{(a,b)}$ are the first-order partial derivatives of $f(x, y)$ w.r.t. x and y respectively, evaluated at (a, b). $Tmul_{a,b}(x, y)$ simplifies to:

$$Tmul_{a,b}(x, y) \stackrel{\text{def}}{=} b * x + a * y - a * b \tag{1}$$

Logic and Satisfiability. We assume the standard first-order quantifier-free logical setting and standard notions of theory, model, satisfiability, and logical consequence. If φ is a formula, we denote with $\text{vars}(\varphi)$ the set of its variables, and with $\text{atoms}(\varphi)$ the set of its atoms. We write $\varphi(X)$ to denote that $\text{vars}(\varphi) \subseteq X$. If x and y are two variables, we denote with $\varphi\{x \mapsto y\}$ the formula obtained by replacing all the occurrences of x in φ with y. We extend this notation to ordered sequences of variables in the natural way. If μ is a model and x is a variable, we write $\mu[x]$ to denote the value of x in μ, and we extend this notation to terms in the usual way. If X is a set of variables, we denote with X' the set obtained by replacing each element $x \in X$ with x', and with $X^{\langle i \rangle}$ the set obtained by replacing x with $x^{\langle i \rangle}$. If Γ is a set of formulas, we write $\bigwedge \Gamma$ to denote the formula obtained by taking the conjunction of all its elements. If $\bigwedge \Gamma$ is unsatisfiable (modulo some theory T), an unsatisfiable core is a set $C \subseteq \Gamma$ such that $\bigwedge C$ is still unsatisfiable.

Symbolic Transition Systems. A symbolic transition system $\mathcal{S} \stackrel{\text{def}}{=} \langle X, I, T \rangle$ is a tuple where X is a finite set of (state) variables, $I(X)$ is a formula denoting the initial states of the system, and $T(X, X')$ is a formula expressing its transition relation. A state s_i of $\mathcal{S}$ is an assignment to the variables X. A path (execution trace) $\pi = s_0, s_1, s_2, \ldots, s_{k-1}$ of length k (possibly infinite) for $\mathcal{S}$ is a sequence of states such that $s_0 \models I$ and $s_i \wedge s_{i+1}\{X \mapsto X'\} \models T$ for all $0 \leq i < k - 2$. We call an unrolling of $\mathcal{S}$ of length k the formula $I\{X \mapsto X^{\langle 0 \rangle}\} \wedge \bigwedge_{i=0}^{k-1} T\{X \mapsto X^{\langle i \rangle}\}\{X' \mapsto X^{\langle i+1 \rangle}\}$.

Let $P(X)$ be a formula whose assignments represent a property (good states) over the state variables X. The invariant verification problem, denoted with $\mathcal{S} \models P$, is the problem of checking if for all the finite paths $s_0, s_1, \ldots, s_k$ of $\mathcal{S}$, for all i, $0 \leq i \leq k$, $s_i \models P$. Its dual formulation in terms of reachability of $\neg P$ is the problem of finding a path $s_0, s_1, \ldots, s_k$ of $\mathcal{S}$ such that $s_k \models \neg P$. P represents the "good" states, while $\neg P$ represents the "bad" states.

```
bool SMT-NRA-check-abstract (φ):
1.   φ̂ = initial-abstraction(φ)
2.   res, data = SMT-NRA-check-abstract-ext(φ̂)
3.   return res

⟨bool, axiom set or model⟩ SMT-NRA-check-abstract-ext (φ̂):
4.   Γ = ∅
5.   while true:
6.        if budget-exhausted(): abort
7.        res, μ̂ = SMT-LRA+EUF-check(φ̂ ∧ ⋀ Γ)
8.        if not res: return false, Γ
9.        ok, μ = get-NRA-model(φ̂, μ̂)
10.       if ok: return true, μ
11.       else: Γ = Γ ∪ refine(μ̂)
```

Fig. 2. Solving SMT(NRA) via abstraction to SMT(LRA+EUF).

4   Solving SMT(NRA) via SMT(LRA+EUF)

Top-Level Algorithm. The main idea of this paper is that of solving an SMT formula containing non-linear polynomial constraints (i.e., expressed in the NRA theory) by overapproximating it with a formula over the combined theory of linear arithmetic and uninterpreted functions (LRA+EUF). Our main SMT solving procedure follows a classic abstraction refinement loop, in which at each iteration the current overapproximation of the input SMT formula is refined by adding new constraints that rule out one (or possibly more) spurious solutions, until one of the following occurs: (i) the SMT formula becomes unsatisfiable in the LRA+EUF theory; or (ii) the LRA+EUF model for the current overapproximation can be lifted to an NRA model for the original SMT formula; or (iii) the resource budget (e.g. time, memory, number of iterations) is exhausted.

The pseudocode for the top-level algorithm is shown in Fig. 2. We provide more details about its main components in the rest of this section.

Initial Abstraction. The function initial-abstraction takes as input an SMT(NRA) formula φ and returns an overapproximation $\widehat{\varphi}$ of it in the LRA+EUF theory.

First, each multiplication expression $x * y$ between two variables[1] occurring in φ is replaced by $fmul(x, y)$, where $fmul()$ is a binary uninterpreted function returning a real. We remark that this happens only for non-linear multiplications: expressions like $c * x$ or $x * c$ in which c is a constant are not rewritten.

Then, some simple axioms about multiplication are added to $\widehat{\varphi}$ via static learning. For each $fmul(x, y) \in \widehat{\varphi}$, we add the following axioms:

---

[1] To simplify the presentation, we assume (here and in the rest of the paper) that all multiplications in φ are either between two variables or between one constant and one variable.

Commutativity: $fmul(x, y) = fmul(y, x)$

Sign: $fmul(x, y) = fmul(-x, -y) \wedge fmul(x, y) = -fmul(-x, y) \wedge$
$fmul(x, y) = -fmul(x, -y)$

Zero: $((x = 0 \vee y = 0) \leftrightarrow fmul(x, y) = 0) \wedge$
$(((x > 0 \wedge y > 0) \vee (x < 0 \wedge y < 0)) \rightarrow fmul(x, y) > 0) \wedge$
$(((x < 0 \wedge y > 0) \vee (x < 0 \wedge y > 0)) \rightarrow fmul(x, y) < 0)$

Abstraction Refinement. If the SMT check on the LRA+EUF abstraction returns false (line 7 of Fig. 2), we can conclude that the input formula is unsatisfiable. In this case, Γ contains all the lemmas (discussed later in this section) that were added in the earlier refinements (line 11 of Fig. 2).

Otherwise, we have to check whether the model $\widehat{\mu}$ found for $\widehat{\varphi}$ is also a model for the original NRA formula φ. Let $Fmuls$ be the set of all $fmul(x, y)$ terms occurring in $\widehat{\varphi}$. In its simplest version, the function get-NRA-model checks whether, for all $fmul(x, y)$ in $Fmuls$, $\widehat{\mu}[fmul(x, y)] = \widehat{\mu}[x] * \widehat{\mu}[y]$. If this is the case, then $\widehat{\mu}$ is also a model for the original formula, and get-NRA-model returns true. (We present more sophisticated versions of get-NRA-model below.) Otherwise, let $CFmuls$ be the set of all $fmul(x, y)$ terms whose value in $\widehat{\mu}$ is different from $\widehat{\mu}[x] * \widehat{\mu}[y]$. The function refine generates a set of axioms Γ' such that there exists at least one element $fmul(x, y)$ of $CFmuls$ such that the formula $\widehat{\varphi} \wedge \bigwedge \Gamma'$ has no model $\widehat{\mu}'$ that agrees with $\widehat{\mu}$ on the values of x, y and $fmul(x, y)$ (i.e. such that $\widehat{\mu}'[fmul(x, y)] = \widehat{\mu}[fmul(x, y)]$, $\widehat{\mu}'[x] = \widehat{\mu}[x]$ and $\widehat{\mu}'[y] = \widehat{\mu}[y]$). Intuitively, the axioms Γ' block the bad model values for $fmul(x, y)$, making the abstraction more precise by restricting the set of spurious solutions.

In our current implementation, two kinds of lemmas are generated during refinement: *tangent lemmas* and *monotonicity lemmas*.

Tangent Lemmas. We use the model values $\widehat{\mu}[fmul(x, y)]$, $\widehat{\mu}[x]$ and $\widehat{\mu}[y]$ and (1) to generate tangent plane lemmas for $fmul(x, y)$:

$$fmul(a, y) = a * y \quad \wedge \quad fmul(x, b) = b * x \quad \wedge$$
$$(((x > a \wedge y < b) \vee (x < a \wedge y > b)) \rightarrow fmul(x, y) < Tmul_{a,b}(x, y)) \wedge \quad (2)$$
$$(((x < a \wedge y < b) \vee (x > a \wedge y > b)) \rightarrow fmul(x, y) > Tmul_{a,b}(x, y))$$

where we can choose a and b as:

$$a \stackrel{\text{def}}{=} \widehat{\mu}[x] \text{ and } b \stackrel{\text{def}}{=} \widehat{\mu}[y] \tag{3}$$

$$a \stackrel{\text{def}}{=} \frac{1}{\widehat{\mu}[fmul(x, y)]} \text{ and } b \stackrel{\text{def}}{=} \widehat{\mu}[y] \tag{4}$$

$$a \stackrel{\text{def}}{=} \widehat{\mu}[x] \text{ and } b \stackrel{\text{def}}{=} \frac{1}{\widehat{\mu}[fmul(x, y)]}. \tag{5}$$

Basically the equalities in the tangent lemma are providing multiplication lines that enforce the correct value of $fmul(x, y)$ when $x = a$ or $y = b$. Moreover, the inequalities of the tangent lemma are providing bounds for $fmul(x, y)$ when x and y are not on the multiplication lines.

⟨**bool**, model⟩ get-NRA-model ($\widehat{\varphi}$, $\widehat{\mu}$):

1. $\widehat{\psi}$ = get-assignment($\widehat{\mu}$) *# truth assignment induced by $\widehat{\mu}$ on the atoms of $\widehat{\varphi}$*
2. ψ = concretize($\widehat{\psi}$) *# replace each $fmul(x,y)$ in $\widehat{\psi}$ with $x * y$*
3. **return** SMT-NRA-check (ψ) *# check with a complete NRA solver*

Fig. 3. A complete procedure using an NRA solver.

Monotonicity Lemmas. Let $fmul(x,y)$ and $fmul(w,z)$ be two terms in $\widehat{\varphi}$, such that $|\widehat{\mu}[x]| \leq |\widehat{\mu}[w]|$, $|\widehat{\mu}[y]| \leq |\widehat{\mu}[z]|$, and $|\widehat{\mu}[fmul(x,y)]| > |\widehat{\mu}[fmul(w,z)]|$. Then, we add the monotonicity lemma

$$(abs(x) \leq abs(w) \wedge abs(y) \leq abs(z)) \rightarrow abs(fmul(x,y)) \leq abs(fmul(w,z)), \quad (6)$$

where $abs(t)$ stands for $\mathsf{ite}(t < 0, -t, t)$.

Finding Models. It is easy to see that our algorithm is expected to perform much better for unsatisfiable instances than for satisfiable ones. The algorithm can return true (meaning that the formula is satisfiable) only if the LRA+EUF solver "guesses" a model that is consistent with all the nonlinear multiplications. In an infinite and dense domain like the reals, the chances that this will happen are close to zero in general.

Moreover, our approach is inherently limited, because it can only find models over the rationals. If the input formula is satisfiable, but all its models contain some irrational values, then our algorithm will always abort (or never terminate, if there is no resource budget set). In practice, it is very likely that the same will happen even for formulas admitting a rational solution.

One possibility for addressing this limitation would be to couple our procedure with a complete solver for NRA, to be used for detecting satisfiable cases, in order to implement a more effective version of get-NRA-model. One such possibility is shown in Fig. 3, where we extract the truth assignment $\widehat{\psi}$ induced by the LRA+EUF model $\widehat{\mu}$ on the atoms of $\widehat{\varphi}$:

$$\widehat{\psi} \stackrel{\text{def}}{=} \bigwedge_{[\widehat{a_i} \in \text{atoms}(\widehat{\varphi}) \ s.t. \ \widehat{\mu} \models \widehat{a_i}]} \widehat{a_i} \ \wedge \bigwedge_{[\widehat{a_i} \in \text{atoms}(\widehat{\varphi}) \ s.t. \ \widehat{\mu} \not\models \widehat{a_i}]} \neg \widehat{a_i}, \quad (7)$$

We concretize it by replacing each $fmul(x,y)$ in $\widehat{\psi}$ with $x * y$, and invoke the complete NRA theory solver on the resulting conjunction of NRA-literals ψ, to check whether it contains at least one solution. Although in general the problem is expected to be simpler than the original input formula because the Boolean structure of φ is disregarded, invoking a complete NRA theory solver at each loop iteration of SMT-NRA-check-abstract-ext could be very expensive. Moreover, this would still require a complete NRA theory solver, which might not always be available.

As an alternative, we propose the procedure outlined in Fig. 4, where we extract the truth assignment $\widehat{\psi}$ induced by the LRA+EUF model $\widehat{\mu}$ on the atoms of $\widehat{\varphi}$, and we conjoin to it the *multiplication lines*:

⟨**bool**, model⟩ get-NRA-model ($\widehat{\varphi}$, $\widehat{\mu}$):
1. $\widehat{\psi}$ = get-assignment($\widehat{\mu}$)   *# truth assignment induced by $\widehat{\mu}$ on the atoms of $\widehat{\varphi}$*
2. $\widehat{\psi}^*$ = $\widehat{\psi}$ ∧ linearization-axioms($\widehat{\psi}$)   *# add multiplication-line axioms to $\widehat{\psi}$*
3. **return** SMT-LRA+EUF-check ($\widehat{\psi}^*$)

Fig. 4. An incomplete procedure using an SMT(LRA+EUF) solver.

$$\widehat{\psi}^* = \widehat{\psi} \wedge \bigwedge_{fmul(x,y) \in Fmuls} \left(\begin{array}{l} (x = \widehat{\mu}[x] \wedge fmul(x,y) = \widehat{\mu}[x] * y) \vee \\ (y = \widehat{\mu}[y] \wedge fmul(x,y) = \widehat{\mu}[y] * x) \end{array} \right), \quad (8)$$

Fmuls being the usual set of all $fmul(x,y)$ terms occurring in $\widehat{\varphi}$.

The main idea is to build an LRA+EUF underapproximation $\widehat{\psi}^*$ of the NRA formula ψ of Fig. 3, in which all multiplications are forced to be linear. Compared to the previous solution, this has the advantage of requiring a complete SMT(LRA+EUF) solver rather than a (much more expensive) complete NRA solver. Moreover, given the simplicity of the Boolean structure of the underapproximated formula, the check should in general be very cheap. The drawback is that this is (clearly) still an incomplete procedure. However, in our experiments (for which we refer to Sect. 6) we have found it to be surprisingly effective for many problems.

Unlike with the basic implementation of get-NRA-model which considers only one single candidate model at a time, the implementations in Figs. 3 and 4 consider an infinite amount of them, drastically increasing the chances of finding a model.

Correctness and Progress. We notice that the procedure in Fig. 2 is *correct*. In fact, it returns false only if φ is NRA-unsatisfiable because by construction $\widehat{\varphi}$ is an over-approximation of φ, and all axioms in Γ are valid in any theory interpreting $fmul(x,y)$ as $x*y$. Also, it returns true only if φ is NRA-satisfiable:

- if get-NRA-model is based only on evaluation, then by construction μ is an LRA+EUF-model for $\widehat{\varphi}$ s.t. each $fmul(x,y)$ equals $x*y$ in μ, so that μ is also a model for φ;
- if get-NRA-model is as in Fig. 3, then μ is an NRA-model of a conjunction of literals ψ which tautologically entails φ, so that μ is a model for φ;
- if get-NRA-model is as in Fig. 4, then μ is an LRA+EUF-model of a conjunction of literals $\widehat{\psi}^*$ which tautologically entails $\widehat{\varphi}$ and it is s.t. each $fmul(x,y)$ equals $x*y$ in μ, so that μ is a also model for φ.

We also notice that the progress of the procedure in Fig. 2 is guaranteed by the refinement step, which rules out significant parts of the search space at every loop by means of the added lemmas.

Important Heuristics for Refinement. The description of refine provided above leaves some flexibility in deciding what axioms to add (and how many of

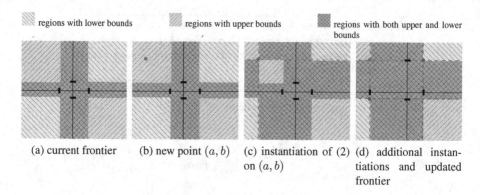

(a) current frontier　　(b) new point (a, b)　　(c) instantiation of (2) on (a, b)　　(d) additional instantiations and updated frontier

Fig. 5. Illustration of the tangent lemma frontier strategy.

them) at each iteration. It is possible to conceive strategies with an increasing degree of eagerness, from very lazy (e.g. adding only a single axiom per iteration) to more aggressive ones. In our current implementation, we eagerly add all the axioms (2)–(6) that are violated by the current abstract solution $\widehat{\mu}$, leaving the investigation of alternative strategies as future work. However, we found the following two strategies to be crucial for performance.

Tangent Lemma Frontiers. The tangent lemmas of (2) for a given point (a, b) are based on the fact that the multiplication function $x * y$ is a hyperbolic paraboloid surface, and a tangent plane to such surface cuts the surface into four regions such that in two of the regions the tangent plane is above the surface, whereas in the other two regions the tangent plane is below the surface (see Fig. 1). Each instantiation of (2) for a given point, therefore, can only provide either a lower or an upper bound for a given region. In some cases, this might lead to an infinite refinement loop in which at each iteration the "wrong" bound is refined. In order to address the problem, we use the following strategy. For each $fmul(x, y)$ in the input formula, we maintain a *frontier* $\langle l_x, u_x, l_y, u_y \rangle$ with the invariant that whenever x is in the interval $[l_x, u_x]$ or y is in the interval $[l_y, u_y]$, then $fmul(x, y)$ has both an upper and a lower bound. Initially, the frontiers are set to $\langle 0, 0, 0, 0 \rangle$. Whenever a lemma (2) for $fmul(x, y)$ is instantiated on a point (a, b), we generate further instantiations of (2) and update the frontier as follows:

case $a < l_x$ **and** $b < l_y$: instantiate (2) on (a, u_y) and on (u_x, b), and set the frontier to $\langle a, u_x, b, u_y \rangle$;

case $a < l_x$ **and** $b > u_y$: instantiate (2) on (a, l_y) and on (u_x, b), and set the frontier to $\langle a, u_x, l_y, b \rangle$;

case $a > u_x$ **and** $b > u_y$: instantiate (2) on (a, l_y) and on (l_x, b), and set the frontier to $\langle l_x, a, l_y, b \rangle$;

case $a > u_x$ **and** $b < l_y$: instantiate (2) on (a, u_y) and on (l_x, b), and set the frontier to $\langle l_x, a, b, u_y \rangle$.

Figure 5 shows a graphical illustration of the strategy.

Tangent Lemma Rounding. The instantiation of a tangent lemma at the point (a, b) has the side-effect of adding the rational constants a, b and $a * b$ to the formula that is solved by the LRA+EUF solver. If such values have large numerators and/or denominators, they might be a source of a significant slow-down for the LRA solver (which works on exact, arbitrary-precision rational arithmetic). We address this issue by observing that, in order to block a bad model $\hat{\mu}$ such that $\hat{\mu}[fmul(x, y)] \neq \hat{\mu}[x] * \hat{\mu}[y]$, it is sufficient to add one of the two equalities of (2); therefore, instead of instantiating a tangent lemma at (a, b), we can instantiate it at either $(a + \delta, b)$ or at $(a, b + \delta)$, for any value of δ. In practice, if a (resp. b) is a rational constant with a very large numerator or denominator, instead of instantiating a tangent lemma at (a, b), we instantiate two tangent lemmas at $(\lfloor a \rfloor, b)$ and $(\lceil a \rceil, b)$.

5   From Satisfiability to Verification

We now move from satisfiability checking to verification.

Overview. In principle, the solver described in the previous section could be integrated as a "black box" in any off-the-shelf SMT-based verification algorithm, such as BMC, k-induction, or one of the many extensions of IC3 to the SMT case (e.g. [4,9,18,21]). In practice, however, such black-box integration would hardly be effective, especially in the case of state-of-the-art algorithms like IC3. IC3 requires a very incremental interaction with the underlying SMT engine, which is asked to solve a large number of relatively-cheap queries. The procedure of Sect. 4, however, can be very expensive, especially for satisfiable queries, which are very common in an IC3-like algorithm.[2] Moreover, some of the IC3 extensions mentioned above require the ability of performing (approximated) quantifier eliminations, a functionality not provided by the algorithm of Fig. 2.

We propose therefore a white-box integration, in which we lift the abstraction refinement approach of Sect. 4 at the transition system level. We generate an abstract LRA+EUF version of the input NRA transition system, which is then checked with the IC3-based procedure of [9]. In case a counterexample is produced, we use the SMT-NRA-check-abstract-ext algorithm of Fig. 2 to check whether it is spurious. If so, the axioms generated by SMT-NRA-check-abstract-ext are then used to refine the abstraction of the transition system. The pseudo-code of this algorithm is reported in Fig. 6. Similarly to the satisfiability checking case, the initial-abstraction function replaces every non-linear multiplication $x*y$ in the input transition system and property with a $fmul(x, y)$ term, and adds some simple axioms about the behaviour of multiplication to the initial-state and transition-relation formulas of the transition system (see Sect. 4). In the rest of this section, we describe the abstraction refinement algorithm in more detail.

---

[2] In fact, as already discussed in Sect. 4, the procedure is biased towards unsatisfiable instances, and might easily diverge on satisfiable ones.

```
bool IC3-NRA-prove (S : transition system ⟨X, I, T⟩, φ : invariant property):
1.    Ŝ, φ̂ = initial-abstraction(S, φ)
2.    while true:
3.        if budget-exhausted(): abort
4.        ok, π̂ = IC3-LRA+EUF-prove(Ŝ, φ̂)
5.        if ok: return true  # property proved
6.        ψ = get-cex-formula(Ŝ, φ̂, π̂)
7.        is_cex, Γ = SMT-NRA-check-abstract-ext(ψ)
8.        if is_cex: return false  # counterexample found
9.        else: Ŝ = refine-transition-system(Ŝ, Γ)
```

Fig. 6. Verification of NRA transition systems via abstraction to LRA+EUF.

Counterexample Checking and Refinement. When IC3-LRA+EUF-prove returns a counterexample trace $\hat{\pi}$ for the abstract system $\hat{S}$, we use SMT-NRA-check-abstract-ext to check for its spuriousness. The function get-cex-formula builds a formula ψ to feed to SMT-NRA-check-abstract-ext, whose unsatisfiability implies that $\hat{\pi}$ is spurious. The formula ψ is built by unrolling the transition relation of $\hat{S}$, and optionally adding constraints that restrict the allowed transitions to be compatible with the states in $\hat{\pi}$. Various heuristics are possible, trading generality for complexity: ψ could be fully constrained by the states in $\hat{\pi}$ (thus checking only one abstract counterexample path per iteration); it could be only partially constrained (e.g. by considering only the Boolean variables and/or the state variables occurring only in linear constraints); or it could be left unconstrained, considering only the length of the abstract counterexample. In our current implementation (see Sect. 6), we use the last option, i.e. we only consider the length of $\hat{\pi}$ to build a BMC formula that checks for any counterexample of the given length, leaving the investigation of alternative strategies to future work.

If SMT-NRA-check-abstract-ext returns true, the property is violated. In this case, we can use the model found by SMT-NRA-check-abstract-ext to build a counterexample trace for the input system and property.

If SMT-NRA-check-abstract-ext returns false, we use the axioms Γ produced during search to refine the transition system $\hat{S}$, using the procedure shown in Fig. 7. Essentially, refine-transition-system translates back the axioms from their unrolled version (i.e. on variables $X^{\langle 0 \rangle}, X^{\langle 1 \rangle}, \ldots$) to their "single step" version (on variables X and X'), adding each of them either to the initial-states formula or to the transition relation formula. In case an axiom γ spans more than a single transition step (lines 9–10 of Fig. 7), we arbitrarily choose to map the variables with the lowest index as current state variables X, and all the others as next-state variables X'. Notice that this might cause some refinement failure, as discussed in the next paragraph.

Reducing the Number of Axioms to Add. In general, not all the axioms generated during a call to SMT-NRA-check-abstract-ext are needed to successfully block a counterexample, especially if eager strategies like those described in Sect. 4 are

---

transition system refine-transition-system ($\widehat{S}$: transition system, Γ : set of axioms):
1. **let** $\langle X, \widehat{I}, \widehat{T} \rangle = \widehat{S}$
2. $\Gamma_I, \Gamma_T = \emptyset, \emptyset$
3. **for each** γ in Γ:
4.   **if** vars$(\gamma) \subseteq X^{\langle 0 \rangle}$:
5. $\Gamma_I = \Gamma_I \cup \{\gamma\{X^{\langle 0 \rangle} \mapsto X\}\}$
6.   **else if** there exists $i > 0$ s.t. vars$(\gamma) \subseteq X^{\langle i \rangle}$:
7. $\Gamma_T = \Gamma_T \cup \{\gamma\{X^{\langle i \rangle} \mapsto X\}, \gamma\{X^{\langle i \rangle} \mapsto X'\}\}$
8.   **else**
9.   **let** i be the smallest index s.t. vars$(\gamma) \cap X^{\langle i \rangle} \neq \emptyset$
10. $\Gamma_T = \Gamma_T \cup \{\gamma\{X^{\langle i \rangle} \mapsto X\}\{X^{\langle i+1 \rangle} \cup \ldots \cup X^{\langle i+k \rangle} \mapsto X'\}\}$
11. **return** $\langle X, \widehat{I} \wedge \bigwedge \Gamma_I, \widehat{T} \wedge \bigwedge \Gamma_T \rangle$

Fig. 7. Refinement of the LRA+EUF transition system.

---

transition system reduce-axioms $(\langle X, \widehat{I}, \widehat{T} \rangle, \widehat{\varphi}, \widehat{\pi}, \langle \Gamma_I, \Gamma_T \rangle)$:
1. $\psi = $ get-cex-formula$(\langle X, \widehat{I} \wedge \bigwedge \Gamma_I, \widehat{T} \wedge \bigwedge \Gamma_T \rangle, \widehat{\pi})$
2. **if not** SMT-LRA+EUF-check(ψ)
3.   **let** C be an unsatisfiable core of ψ
4. $\Gamma_I = \{\gamma \in \Gamma_I \mid \gamma\{X \mapsto X^{\langle 0 \rangle}\} \in C\}$
5. $\Gamma_T = \{\gamma \in \Gamma_T \mid \exists j > 0 \text{ s.t. } \gamma\{X \mapsto X^{\langle j \rangle}\}\{X' \mapsto X^{\langle j+1 \rangle}\} \in C\}$
6.   **return** $\langle X, \widehat{I} \wedge \bigwedge \Gamma_I, \widehat{T} \wedge \bigwedge \Gamma_T \rangle$
7. **else**
8.   **abort** *# refinement failure*

Fig. 8. Reducing the axioms needed for refinement.

---

used. In the long run, having a large number of redundant axioms can be quite harmful for performance. In order to mitigate this problem, we apply a filtering strategy (based on unsatisfiable cores) to the set of axioms, before adding them to the transition system. Instead of adding Γ_I and Γ_T directly to $\widehat{S}$, we invoke the function shown in Fig. 8. Note that due to the flattening of multi-step axioms described above (lines 9–10 of Fig. 7), the refinement might fail. In this case, our current implementation simply aborts the execution.[3]

6 Experimental Analysis

Implementation and Comparisons. We have implemented a prototype of the IC3-NRA-prove procedure using the IC3 engine of NUXMV [7] for IC3-LRA+EUF-prove. The code is written in Python, using the PYSMT library [17]. Our implementation, benchmarks, and experimental data are available at https://es-static.fbk.eu/people/griggio/papers/tacas17-ic3-nra.tar.gz. We have used the following tools for our evaluation.

NUXMV-*LRA-static:* we apply the upfront abstraction of NRA to LRA proposed in [8], running the IC3 engine of NUXMV on the resulting transition system.

---

[3] We remark however that so far we have never observed this behaviour during our experiments.

NRA-BMC-{z3, DREAL} and NRA-K-induction-{z3, DREAL}: we have implemented the BMC [3] and k-induction [29] algorithms in Python (using PYSMT), using either z3 (NRA) or DREAL (NRA) as back-end SMT solver.

iSAT3[1e-1] and iSAT3[1e-9]: we have used the latest version of the iSAT3 solver [24], which combines an SMT solver integrating CDCL and interval constraint propagation techniques with an interpolation-based abstraction/refinement algorithm for verification. iSAT3 supports both transition systems and software programs encoded as control flow graphs. Similarly to DREAL, iSAT3 may return a "maybe unsafe" answer and provide a candidate solution identifying the upper and lower bounds on the variables. In the experiments, iSAT3[1e-1] is the configuration suggested by the iSAT3 authors[4] and iSAT3[1e-9] is the same except that the *minimum splitting width* (msw) parameter is set to 10^{-9}. We have used a smaller value for the msw to get more precise answers, i.e. "safe" or "unsafe", as suggested in the iSAT3 user manual.

Benchmarks. We have collected a total of 114 NRA benchmarks from various sources.

Handcrafted. This set contains 14 hand-written instances, 13 safe and 1 unsafe.

HyComp. The second set contains 7 benchmarks (3 safe, 4 unsafe) which are taken from [11] and converted to NRA transition systems using HYCOMP [10].

HYST. This is the biggest set, consisting of 65 benchmarks. These are generated from the Hybrid examples that come with the HYST [2] distribution, by approximating the continuous time by sampling at a fixed time interval. This process is done automatically using an extended version of HYST. Since the generated benchmarks are approximations, we do not know their safety status. The benchmarks contain mostly non-linear behaviour.

iSAT3 and iSAT3-CFG. The 11 benchmarks in this set (7 safe, 4 unsafe) are taken from [24] and the iSAT3 examples available online.

nuXmv. In this set, we have 2 safe benchmarks which we collected from the nuXmv users' mailing list. These benchmarks have complex boolean structure.

SAS13. These 13 benchmarks are generated from the C programs used in [5], but interpreted over NRA instead of the theory of IEEE floating-point numbers. This makes some of the instances unsafe.

TCM. We have generated 2 safe benchmarks from the Simulink models (taken from the case study [6]) by first generating the C code using the Embedded Coder[5] and then encoding the program into a symbolic transition system.

Results. We ran our experiments on a cluster of machines with 2.67 GHz Xeon X5650 CPUs and 96 GB of RAM, running Scientific Linux 6.7. We used 6 GB memory limit and 3600 s CPU timeout.

---

[4] `-I --use-craig-interpolation --use-cegar --cegar-abstraction-inductive --interpolant-rules-mcmillan --interpolant-a-biased --interpolation-offset --interpolant-offset 2.`
[5] https://www.mathworks.com/products/embedded-coder/.

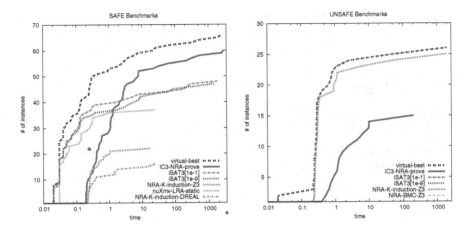

Fig. 9. Plots of SAFE and UNSAFE results.

Table 1. Summary of experimental results.

	Total	Handcrafted	HyComp	HYST	ISAT3	ISAT3-CFG	nuXmv	SAS13	TCM
	(114)	(14)	(7)	(65)	(1)	(10)	(2)	(13)	(2)
IC3-NRA-prove	60/15	9/1	3/0	33/7	0/0	6/2	2/0	5/5	2/0
iSAT3[1e-1]	48/2(47)	2/0(8)	0/0(3)	34/2(23)	0/0	6/0(4)	0/0	4/0(9)	2/0
iSAT3[1e-9]	47/2(19)	2/0(3)	0/0(2)	32/2(3)	0/0	6/0(3)	0/0	5/0(8)	2/0
NRA-K-induction-Z3	22/25	2/1	0/2	12/15	0/0	6/2	0/0	0/5	2/0
NUXMV-LRA-static	37/0	4/0	1/0	19/0	0/0	4/0	2/0	5/0	2/0
NRA-BMC-Z3	0/26	0/1	0/2	0/15	0/0	0/3	0/0	0/5	0/0
NRA-K-induction-DREAL	16/0(32)	2/0(4)	0/0(2)	9/0(19)	0/0	5/0(2)	0/0	0/0(5)	0/0
NRA-BMC-DREAL	0/0(39)	0/0(8)	0/0(2)	0/0(19)	0/0	0/0(3)	0/0	0/0(7)	0/0
virtual-best	66/26	9/1	3/2	38/15	0/0	7/3	2/0	5/5	2/0

Each column shows a benchmark family, and each entry gives the number of safe/unsafe instances found. For tools working over interval arithmetic, the number of "maybe unsafe" is reported in parentheses.

The results are summarized in Tables 1 and 2 and in Fig. 9. The plots show the time to solve an instance on the x-axis and the total number of solved instances on the y-axis. Table 1 reports a summary of the solved instances by family, whereas Table 2 shows a comparitive analysis by reporting for each tool the number of uniquely solved instances and the difference of solved instances w.r.t IC3-NRA-prove. We can make the following observations from the experimental results:

Table 2. Comparitive summary of total solved benchmarks.

	# Solved	# Uniquely Solved	Difference wrt. IC3-NRA-prove	Gained	Lost
IC3-NRA-prove	60/15	9/0	-	-	-
NUXMV-LRA-static	37/0	0/0	-38	1/0	24/15
iSAT3[1e-1]	48/2(47)	4/0	-25	4/0	16/13
iSAT3[1e-9]	47/2(19)		-26	3/0	16/13
NRA-K-induction-Z3	22/25	0/11	-28	2/11	40/1
NRA-BMC-Z3	0/26		-49	0/11	60/0
NRA-K-induction-DREAL	16/2(32)	0/0	-59	2/0	46/15
NRA-BMC-DREAL	0/0(39)		-75	0/0	60/15
virtual-best	66/26	-	17	6/11	0

- IC3-NRA-prove is the best performer overall, and it significantly outperforms all the other approaches on safe instances (where it can solve 9 problems that are out of reach for all the other tools). Interestingly, despite its simplicity, our model finding approach (as outlined in Sect. 4) is surprisingly effective, allowing IC3-NRA-prove to find 15 counterexample traces.
- The simple abstraction proposed in [8] is quite effective for many families, allowing NUXMV-LRA-static to verify more properties than the approaches based on K-induction with an NRA solver. However, IC3-NRA-prove results in a clear and very significant improvement, solving more than twice as many instances than NUXMV-LRA-static (and losing only 1).
- None of the other tools (with the exception of NUXMV-LRA-static) is able to solve any safe benchmark in the HyComp and nuXmv families. These benchmarks have a non-trivial Boolean structure and a significant linear component. Both IC3-NRA-prove and NUXMV-LRA-static are able to fully exploit the effectiveness of the underlying IC3 engine of NUXMV, outperforming the competitors. However, IC3-NRA-prove is very competitive also on the HYST family, whose instances are mostly non-linear and have very little Boolean structure.
- Increasing the default precision of iSAT3 significantly reduces the number of "maybe unsafe" answers, but it doesn't seem to help in solving more benchmarks. In fact, we remark that even with the increased precision iSAT3[1e-9] classifies 2 safe instances as "maybe unsafe" (whereas in the default configuration, 6 safe instances are classified as "maybe unsafe").

7   Conclusions and Future Work

We presented a novel abstraction-refinement approach to the verification of transition systems with nonlinear dynamics expressed in the NRA theory. We abstract non-linear multiplication as an uninterpreted function, leveraging efficient invariant checkers for transition systems over LRA and EUF to solve the problem in the abstract space. In case of spurious counterexample, the abstraction of multiplication is incrementally refined by introducing suitable axioms, based on the idea of tangent planes. An extensive experimental evaluation demonstrates that the proposed approach is significantly more effective than approaches directly based on SMT(NRA) solving.

This work opens up several important directions. First, we are going to improve the implementation, by integrating all the steps within the NUXMV [7] model checker, and to perform a thorough analysis of the various heuristic choices. Second, we will investigate the potential of the approach for SMT, both for other theories (e.g. NIA) and for extended functionalities (e.g. interpolation). We will also extend the scope of the approach to deal with transcendental functions, look-up tables, and partially axiomatized functions (e.g. gain functions known to be monotonic and of restricted co-domain).

Finally, we are going to investigate the generalization of the approach from transition systems to continuous-time hybrid systems with nonlinear characteristic functions.

Acknowledgement. We greatly thank the ISAT3 team for providing the latest ISAT3 executable and iSAT3-CFG benchmarks. We also thank James Davenport for the fruitful discussions on CAD techniques and finding solutions in NRA.

References

1. Ábrahám, E., Corzilius, F., Loup, U., Sturm, T.: A lazy SMT-solver for a nonlinear subset of real algebra. In: Dagstuhl Seminar Proceedings. Schloss Dagstuhl-Leibniz-Zentrum f A1/4r Informatik (2010)
2. Bak, S., Bogomolov, S., Johnson, T.T.: HYST: a source transformation and translation tool for hybrid automaton models. In: Proceedings of the 18th International Conference on Hybrid Systems: Computation and Control, pp. 128–133. ACM (2015)
3. Biere, A., Cimatti, A., Clarke, E., Zhu, Y.: Symbolic model checking without BDDs. In: Cleaveland, W.R. (ed.) TACAS 1999. LNCS, vol. 1579, pp. 193–207. Springer, Heidelberg (1999). doi:10.1007/3-540-49059-0_14
4. Birgmeier, J., Bradley, A.R., Weissenbacher, G.: Counterexample to induction-guided abstraction-refinement (CTIGAR). In: Biere, A., Bloem, R. (eds.) CAV 2014. LNCS, vol. 8559, pp. 831–848. Springer, Cham (2014). doi:10.1007/978-3-319-08867-9_55
5. Brain, M., D'Silva, V., Griggio, A., Haller, L., Kroening, D.: Interpolation-based verification of floating-point programs with abstract CDCL. In: Logozzo, F., Fähndrich, M. (eds.) SAS 2013. LNCS, vol. 7935, pp. 412–432. Springer, Heidelberg (2013). doi:10.1007/978-3-642-38856-9_22
6. Brat, G., Bushnell, D., Davies, M., Giannakopoulou, D., Howar, F., Kahsai, T.: Verifying the safety of a flight-critical system. In: Bjørner, N., de Boer, F. (eds.) FM 2015. LNCS, vol. 9109, pp. 308–324. Springer, Heidelberg (2015). doi:10.1007/978-3-319-19249-9_20
7. Cavada, R., et al.: The NUXMV symbolic model checker. In: Biere, A., Bloem, R. (eds.) CAV 2014. LNCS, vol. 8559, pp. 334–342. Springer, Cham (2014). doi:10.1007/978-3-319-08867-9_22

8. Champion, A., Gurfinkel, A., Kahsai, T., Tinelli, C.: CoCoSpec: a mode-aware contract language for reactive systems. In: De Nicola, R., Kühn, E. (eds.) SEFM 2016. LNCS, vol. 9763, pp. 347–366. Springer, Cham (2016). doi:10.1007/978-3-319-41591-8_24

9. Cimatti, A., Griggio, A., Mover, S., Tonetta, S.: IC3 modulo theories via implicit predicate abstraction. In: Ábrahám, E., Havelund, K. (eds.) TACAS 2014. LNCS, vol. 8413, pp. 46–61. Springer, Heidelberg (2014). doi:10.1007/978-3-642-54862-8_4

10. Cimatti, A., Griggio, A., Mover, S., Tonetta, S.: HyComp: an SMT-based model checker for hybrid systems. In: Baier, C., Tinelli, C. (eds.) TACAS 2015. LNCS, vol. 9035, pp. 52–67. Springer, Heidelberg (2015). doi:10.1007/978-3-662-46681-0_4

11. Cimatti, A., Mover, S., Tonetta, S.: A quantifier-free SMT encoding of non-linear hybrid automata. In: Formal Methods in Computer-Aided Design (FMCAD), pp. 187–195. IEEE (2012)

12. Collins, G.E.: Quantifier elimination for real closed fields by cylindrical algebraic decomposition-preliminary report. SIGSAM Bull. 8(3), 80–90 (1974). http://doi.acm.org/10.1145/1086837.1086852

13. Moura, L., Bjørner, N.: Z3: an efficient SMT solver. In: Ramakrishnan, C.R., Rehof, J. (eds.) TACAS 2008. LNCS, vol. 4963, pp. 337–340. Springer, Heidelberg (2008). doi:10.1007/978-3-540-78800-3_24

14. Dutertre, B.: Yices 2.2. In: Biere, A., Bloem, R. (eds.) CAV 2014. LNCS, vol. 8559, pp. 737–744. Springer, Heidelberg (2014). doi:10.1007/978-3-319-08867-9_49

15. Eén, N., Sörensson, N.: Temporal induction by incremental SAT solving. Electron. Notes Theor. Comput. Sci. 89(4), 543–560 (2003)

16. Gao, S., Kong, S., Clarke, E.M.: dReal: an SMT solver for nonlinear theories over the reals. In: Bonacina, M.P. (ed.) CADE 2013. LNCS (LNAI), vol. 7898, pp. 208–214. Springer, Heidelberg (2013). doi:10.1007/978-3-642-38574-2_14

17. Gario, M., Micheli, A.: PySMT: a solver-agnostic library for fast prototyping of SMT-based algorithms. In: Proceedings of the 13th International Workshop on Satisfiability Modulo Theories (SMT), pp. 373–384 (2015)

18. Hoder, K., Bjørner, N.: Generalized property directed reachability. In: Cimatti, A., Sebastiani, R. (eds.) SAT 2012. LNCS, vol. 7317, pp. 157–171. Springer, Heidelberg (2012). doi:10.1007/978-3-642-31612-8_13

19. Hueschen, R.M.: Development of the Transport Class Model (TCM) aircraft simulation from a sub-scale Generic Transport Model (GTM) simulation. Technical report, NASA Langley Research Center (2011)

20. Jovanović, D., Moura, L.: Solving non-linear arithmetic. In: Gramlich, B., Miller, D., Sattler, U. (eds.) IJCAR 2012. LNCS (LNAI), vol. 7364, pp. 339–354. Springer, Heidelberg (2012). doi:10.1007/978-3-642-31365-3_27

21. Komuravelli, A., Gurfinkel, A., Chaki, S.: SMT-based model checking for recursive programs. Form. Methods Syst. Des. 48(3), 175–205 (2016)

22. Kong, S., Gao, S., Chen, W., Clarke, E.: dReach: δ-reachability analysis for hybrid systems. In: Baier, C., Tinelli, C. (eds.) TACAS 2015. LNCS, vol. 9035, pp. 200–205. Springer, Heidelberg (2015). doi:10.1007/978-3-662-46681-0_15

23. Kupferschmid, S., Becker, B.: Craig interpolation in the presence of non-linear constraints. In: Fahrenberg, U., Tripakis, S. (eds.) FORMATS 2011. LNCS, vol. 6919, pp. 240–255. Springer, Heidelberg (2011). doi:10.1007/978-3-642-24310-3_17

24. Mahdi, A., Scheibler, K., Neubauer, F., Fränzle, M., Becker, B.: Advancing software model checking beyond linear arithmetic theories. In: Bloem, R., Arbel, E. (eds.) HVC 2016. LNCS, vol. 10028, pp. 186–201. Springer, Heidelberg (2016). doi:10.1007/978-3-319-49052-6_12

25. Maréchal, A., Fouilhé, A., King, T., Monniaux, D., Périn, M.: Polyhedral approximation of multivariate polynomials using Handelman's theorem. In: Jobstmann, B., Leino, K.R.M. (eds.) VMCAI 2016. LNCS, vol. 9583, pp. 166–184. Springer, Heidelberg (2016). doi:10.1007/978-3-662-49122-5_8

26. McMillan, K.L.: Interpolation and SAT-based model checking. In: Hunt, W.A., Somenzi, F. (eds.) CAV 2003. LNCS, vol. 2725, pp. 1–13. Springer, Heidelberg (2003). doi:10.1007/978-3-540-45069-6_1

27. Nuzzo, P., Puggelli, A., Seshia, S.A., Sangiovanni-Vincentelli, A.: CalCS: SMT solving for non-linear convex constraints. In: Proceedings of the 2010 Conference on Formal Methods in Computer-Aided Design, pp. 71–80. FMCAD Inc. (2010)

28. Scheibler, K., Kupferschmid, S., Becker, B.: Recent improvements in the SMT solver iSAT. MBMV 13, 231–241 (2013)

29. Sheeran, M., Singh, S., Stålmarck, G.: Checking safety properties using induction and a SAT-solver. In: Hunt, W.A., Johnson, S.D. (eds.) FMCAD 2000. LNCS, vol. 1954, pp. 127–144. Springer, Heidelberg (2000). doi:10.1007/3-540-40922-X_8

30. Tiwari, A.: Time-aware abstractions in HybridSal. In: Kroening, D., Păsăreanu, C.S. (eds.) CAV 2015. LNCS, vol. 9206, pp. 504–510. Springer, Heidelberg (2015). doi:10.1007/978-3-319-21690-4_34

Bounded Quantifier Instantiation for Checking Inductive Invariants

Yotam M.Y. Feldman[1]([✉]), Oded Padon[1], Neil Immerman[2], Mooly Sagiv[1], and Sharon Shoham[1]

[1] Tel Aviv University, Tel Aviv, Israel
yotam.feldman@gmail.com
[2] UMass, Amherst, USA

Abstract. We consider the problem of checking whether a proposed invariant φ expressed in first-order logic with quantifier alternation is *inductive*, i.e. preserved by a piece of code. While the problem is undecidable, modern SMT solvers can sometimes solve it automatically. However they employ powerful quantifier instantiation methods that may diverge, especially when φ is not preserved. A notable difficulty arises due to counterexamples of infinite size.

This paper studies *Bounded-Horizon instantiation*, a natural method for guaranteeing the termination of SMT solvers. The method bounds the depth of terms used in the quantifier instantiation process. We show that this method is surprisingly powerful for checking quantified invariants in uninterpreted domains. Furthermore, by producing partial models it can help the user diagnose the case when φ is not inductive, especially when the underlying reason is the existence of infinite counterexamples.

Our main technical result is that Bounded-Horizon is at least as powerful as *instrumentation*, which is a manual method to guarantee convergence of the solver by modifying the program so that it admits a purely universal invariant. We show that with a bound of 1 we can simulate a natural class of instrumentations, without the need to modify the code and in a fully automatic way. We also report on a prototype implementation on top of Z3, which we used to verify several examples by Bounded-Horizon of bound 1.

1 Introduction

This paper addresses a fundamental problem in automatic program verification: how to prove that a piece of code preserves a given invariant. In Floyd-Hoare style verification this means that we want to automatically prove the validity of the Hoare triple $\{P\}C\{P\}$ where P is an assertion and C is a command. Alternatively, this can be shown by proving the unsatisfiability of the formula $P(V) \wedge \delta(V, V') \wedge \neg P(V')$ (the *verification condition*) where $P(V)$ denotes the assertion P before the command, $P(V')$ denotes the assertion P after the command, and $\delta(V, V')$ is a formula expressing the meaning of the command C as a transition relation between pre- and post-states. When C is a loop body, such

© Springer-Verlag GmbH Germany 2017
A. Legay and T. Margaria (Eds.): TACAS 2017, Part I, LNCS 10205, pp. 76–95, 2017.
DOI: 10.1007/978-3-662-54577-5_5

a P is an inductive invariant and can be used to prove safety properties of the loop (if it also holds initially and implies the desired property).

For programs with infinite state space, proving the validity of $\{P\}C\{P\}$ is generally undecidable even when C does not include loops. Indeed, existing SMT solvers can diverge even for simple assertions and simple commands. Recent attempts to apply program verification to prove the correctness of critical system's design and code [16] identify this as the main hurdle for using program verification.

The difficulty is rooted in powerful constructs used in SMT-based verification of interesting programs. Prominent among these constructs are arithmetic and other program operations modeled using background theories, and logical quantifiers. In this paper we target the verification of applications in which the problem can be modeled without interpreted theories. This is in line with recent works that show that although reasoning about arithmetic is crucial for low-level code, in many cases the verification of high-level programs and designs can be performed by reasoning about quantification in uninterpreted theories. Specifically, the decidable Effectively Propositional logic (EPR) has been successfully applied to domains such as linked-list manipulation [21], Software-Defined Networks [6] and some distributed protocols [29]. Without interpreted theories it remains to address the complications induced by the use of quantifier alternation.

In the presence of quantifier alternation, the solver's ability to check assertions is hindered by the following issues: (1) an infinite search space of proofs that needs to be explored for correct assertions, a problem which is sometimes manifested in matching loops [12], and (2) a difficulty of finding counterexamples for invalid assertions, notably when counterexamples may be of infinite size. Current SMT techniques often fail to produce models of satisfiable quantified formulas [15,34], which is somewhat unfortunate since one of the main values of program verification is early detection of flaws in designs and programs. The existence of infinite counterexamples is a major complication as they are difficult to find. In uninterpreted domains, infinite counterexamples usually do not indicate a real violation of the verification conditions and are counterintuitive to programmers, yet render assertions invalid in the context of general first-order logic (on which SMT proof techniques are based). Hence infinite counter-models pose a real problem in the verification process.

Previous work on EPR [6,21,29] used universally quantified invariants with programs expressed by $\exists^*\forall^*$ formulas[1], in which case checking inductive invariants is decidable, hence problems (1) and (2) do not occur. In particular, EPR enjoys the finite-model property and so counterexamples are of finite size. EPR programs are in fact Turing-complete [29], but universal invariants are not always sufficient to express the required program properties.

For example, [16] describes a client server scenario where the invariant is "For every reply message sent by the server, there exists a corresponding request

---

[1] Automated tools that extract EPR transition relation from code exist for C code manipulating linked lists [21–23] and for the modeling language RML [29] which is Turing-complete.

message sent by a client". (See Example 1 for further details.) This invariant is $\forall^*\exists^*$ and thus leads to verification conditions with quantifier alternation. This kind of quantifier alternation may lead to divergence of the solver as problems (1) and (2) re-emerge.

The current work aims to expand the applicability of the EPR-based verification approach to invariants of more complex quantification. We focus on the class $\forall^*\exists^*$ invariants, which arise in interesting programs. As we show, checking inductiveness of invariants in this class is undecidable. We thus study problems (1),(2) above for this setting using the notion of *bounded quantifier instantiations*, which we term *Bounded-Horizon*.

Main Results. This paper explores the utility of limited quantifier instantiations for checking $\forall^*\exists^*$ invariants, and for dealing with the problems that arise from quantifier alternation: divergence of the proof search and infinite counter-models.

We consider instantiations that are *bounded in depth* of terms. Bounded instantiations trivially prevent divergence while maintaining soundness. Although for a given bound the technique is not complete, i.e. unable to prove every correct invariant, we provide completeness guarantees by comparing bounded instantiations to the method of *instrumentation*, a powerful technique implicitly employed in previous works [21,23,29]. Instrumentation tackles a $\forall^*\exists^*$ invariant by transforming the program in a way that allows the invariant to be expressed in a universal form, and, accordingly, makes the verification conditions fall in EPR. We show that for invariants that can be proven using a typical form of instrumentation, bounded instantiations of a small bound are also complete. Namely, they are sufficiently powerful to prove the original program without modifications and in a fully automatic way. This is encouraging since instrumentation is labor-intensive and error-prone while bounded instantiations are completely automatic.

This result suggests that in many cases correct $\forall^*\exists^*$ invariants of EPR programs can be proven using a simple proof technique. Typically in such cases tools such as Z3 will also manage to automatically prove the verification conditions. However, bounded instantiations guarantee termination a-priori even when the invariant is not correct. When it terminates, the procedure returns a logical structure which is not necessarily a true counterexample but "approximates" it, as it satisfies all the bounded instantiations. Interestingly, this suggests a way to overcome the problem of infinite models. This problem arises when the user provides an invariant that is correct for finite models but is incorrect in general first-order logic. In such cases, state-of-the-art SMT solvers typically produce "unknown" or timeout since they fail to find infinite models. Thus the user is left with very little aid from the solver when attempting to make progress and successfully verify the program. In contrast, bounded quantifier instantiation can be used to find finite models with increasing sizes, potentially indicating the existence of an infinite model, and provide hints as to the source of the error. This information allows the user to modify the program or the invariant to exclude the problematic models. We demonstrate this approach on a real example in which such a scenario occurred in one of our verification attempts. We show that the provided models assist in identifying and fixing the error, allowing the user to successfully verify the program.

We also implemented a prototype tool that performs bounded instantiations of bound 1, and used it to verify several distributed protocols and heap manipulating programs. The implementation efficiently reduces the problem of checking inductiveness with bound 1 to a Z3 satisfiability check on which the solver always terminates, thereby taking advantage of Z3's instantiation techniques while guaranteeing termination.

2 Preliminaries

In this section we provide background and explain our notation. Σ will always denote a relational first-order vocabulary, which may contain constant symbols, c_i, and relation symbols, r_j, but no function symbols. For a formula φ we denote by $const[\varphi]$ the set of constants that appear in φ. We write that $\varphi \in \exists^*(\Sigma)$ to mean that φ is an *existential* formula defined over vocabulary Σ. Similarly, the class of *universal* formulas is denoted by $\forall^*(\Sigma)$. We say that φ is *quantifier-free*, denoted $\varphi \in QF(\Sigma)$ if it contains no quantifiers, and that it is *alternation free*, denoted $\varphi \in AF(\Sigma)$, if it can be written as a Boolean combination of formulas in $\exists^*(\Sigma)$. $FOL(\Sigma)$ stands for arbitrary first-order formulas over Σ. A *sentence* is a closed formula.

EPR. The effectively-propositional (EPR) fragment of first-order logic, also known as the Bernays-Schönfinkel-Ramsey class, consists of $\exists^*\forall^*(\Sigma)$ sentences. Such sentences enjoy the *small model property*. Thus satisfiability of EPR sentences is decidable [31].

EPR Transition Relation. We specify a transition relation via an EPR sentence, δ, over a vocabulary $\Sigma \uplus \Sigma'$ where Σ is a relational vocabulary used to describe the source state of a transition and $\Sigma' = \{a' \mid a \in \Sigma\}$ is used to describe the target state.

Inductive Invariants. A first-order sentence I over Σ is an *inductive invariant* for δ if $I \wedge \delta \to I'$ is valid, or, equivalently, if $I \wedge \delta \wedge \neg I'$ is unsatisfiable[2], where I' results from substituting every constant and relation symbol in I by its primed version.

Skolemization. Let $\varphi(z_1, \ldots, z_n) \in FOL(\Sigma)$. The *Skolemization* of φ, denoted φ_S, is a universal formula over $\Sigma \uplus \Sigma_S$, where Σ_S consists of fresh constant symbols and function symbols, obtained as follows. We first convert φ to negation normal form (NNF) using the standard rules. For every existential quantifier $\exists y$ that appears under the scope of the universal quantifiers $\forall x_1, \ldots, \forall x_m$, we introduce a fresh function symbol $f_y \in \Sigma_S$ of arity $n + m$. We replace each bound occurrence of y by $f_y(z_1, \ldots, z_n, x_1, \ldots, x_m)$, and remove the existential

---

[2] In this paper, satisfiability and validity refer to general models, not restricted to finite models.

quantifier. If $n + m = 0$ (i.e., φ has no free variables and $\exists y$ does not appear in the scope of a universal quantifier) a fresh constant symbol is used to replace y. It is well known that $\varphi_S \rightarrow \varphi$ is valid and φ_S and φ are equi-satisfiable.

3   Bounded-Horizon

In this section, we define a systematic method of quantifier instantiation called *Bounded-Horizon* as a way of checking the inductiveness of first-order logic formulas, and explore some of its basic properties. We start with the undecidability of the problem.

Undecidability of Inductiveness. For a universal formula $I \in \forall^*(\Sigma)$, checking inductiveness amounts to checking unsatisfiability of an EPR formula, and is therefore decidable. The same holds for $I \in AF(\Sigma)$. However, this is no longer true when quantifier alternation is introduced. For example, checking inductiveness of $I \in \forall^*\exists^*(\Sigma)$ amounts to checking unsatisfiability of a formula in a fragment for which satisfiability is undecidable. In fact we prove that:

Theorem 1. *The problem of determining on input $I \in \forall^*\exists^*(\Sigma)$ and $\delta \in \exists^*\forall^*$ (Σ, Σ'), whether I is an inductive invariant for δ, is undecidable.*

Proof Sketch. The proof is by reduction from the halting problem, which can be encoded using a $\forall^*\exists^*$ formula via tiling (see e.g. [20]). For the setting of checking invariants, we start with a Turing machine M, and construct $\delta \in \exists^*\forall^*(\Sigma, \Sigma')$, and $I \in \forall^*\exists^*(\Sigma)$ s.t. I is an inductive invariant for δ iff M halts on the empty tape. In case M does not halt, the counter-model that shows that I is not inductive is an infinite structure which encodes an infinite run of M. □

Bounded-Horizon Instantiations. Let $\delta \in \exists^*\forall^*(\Sigma, \Sigma')$ be an EPR transition relation and $I \in \mathrm{FOL}(\Sigma)$ a candidate invariant. We would like to check the satisfiability of $I \wedge \delta \wedge \neg I'$, and equivalently of $Ind = I_S \wedge \delta_S \wedge (\neg I')_S$. Recall that φ_S denotes the Skolemization of φ, and note that I_S and $(\neg I')_S$ possibly add Skolem functions to the vocabulary. Roughly speaking, for a given $k \in \mathbb{N}$, Bounded-Horizon instantiates the universal quantifiers in Ind, while restricting the instantiations to produce ground-terms of function nesting at most k.

Below we provide the formal definitions and discuss soundness and (in)completeness. We start with the notion of instantiations, and recall Herbrand's theorem which establishes completeness of proof by (unrestricted) instantiations. Suppose that some vocabulary $\tilde{\Sigma}$ including constants and function symbols is understood (e.g., $\tilde{\Sigma} = \Sigma \uplus \Sigma_S$, where Σ_S includes Skolem constants and function symbols).

Definition 1 (Instantiation). *Let $\varphi(\overline{x}) \in \forall^*(\tilde{\Sigma})$ be a universal formula with n free variables and m universal quantifiers. An instantiation of φ by a tuple $\overline{t}$ of $n + m$ ground terms, denoted by $\varphi[\overline{t}]$, is obtained by substituting $\overline{t}$ for the free variables and the universally quantified variables, and then removing the universal quantifiers.*

Note that an instantiation is a quantifier-free sentence.

Theorem 2 (Herbrand's Theorem). *Let $\varphi \in \forall^*(\tilde{\Sigma})$. Then φ is satisfiable iff the (potentially infinite) set $\left\{\varphi[\bar{t}] \mid \bar{t} \text{ is a tuple of ground terms over } \tilde{\Sigma}\right\}$ is satisfiable.*

We now turn to restrict the depth of terms used in instantiations.

Definition 2 (Bounded-Depth Terms). *For every $k \in \mathbb{N}$, we define BHT_k to be the set of ground terms over $\tilde{\Sigma}$ with function symbols nested to depth at most k. BHT_k is defined by induction over k. Let C be the set of constants in $\tilde{\Sigma}$, F the set of functions, and for every $f \in F$ let Arity_f be the arity of f. Then $\mathrm{BHT}_0 = C$ and for $k > 0$:*

$$\mathrm{BHT}_k = \mathrm{BHT}_{k-1} \cup \{f(t_1, \ldots t_m) \mid f \in F, \ m = \mathrm{Arity}_f, \ t_1, \ldots, t_m \in \mathrm{BHT}_{k-1}\}.$$

We will also write $\bar{t} \in \mathrm{BHT}_k$ for a tuple of terms $\bar{t}$, to mean that every entry of $\bar{t}$ is in BHT_k (the number of elements in $\bar{t}$ should be clear from the context). Note that the set of ground terms is $\mathrm{BHT}_\infty = \bigcup_{k \in \mathbb{N}} \mathrm{BHT}_k$.

Definition 3 (Depth of Instantiation). *Let $\varphi \in \forall^*(\tilde{\Sigma})$ and $\bar{t} \in \mathrm{BHT}_\infty$. The depth of instantiation, denoted $depth(\varphi[\bar{t}])$, is the smallest k such that all ground terms that appear in $\varphi[\bar{t}]$ are included in BHT_k.*

Bounded-Horizon Algorithm. Given a candidate invariant $I \in \mathrm{FOL}(\Sigma)$, a transition relation δ over $\Sigma \uplus \Sigma'$, and $k \in \mathbb{N}$, the Bounded-Horizon algorithm constructs the formula $Ind = I_S \wedge \delta_S \wedge (\neg I')_S$, and checks if the set

$$\left\{ Ind[\bar{t}] \mid \bar{t} \in \mathrm{BHT}_k, \ depth(Ind[\bar{t}]) \leq k \right\} \tag{1}$$

is unsatisfiable. If it is, then I is provably inductive w.r.t. δ with Bounded-Horizon of bound k. Otherwise we report that I is not known to be inductive.

Note that the satisfiability check performed by Bounded-Horizon is decidable since the set of instantiations is finite, and each of them is a ground formula.

Bounded-Horizon for $\forall^*\exists^*$ Invariants. We illustrate the definition of Bounded-Horizon in the case that $I \in \forall^*\exists^*(\Sigma)$. Assume that $I = \forall \bar{x}. \exists \bar{y}. \ \alpha(\bar{x}, \bar{y})$ where $\alpha \in \mathrm{QF}$. Then $I_S = \forall \bar{x}. \ \alpha(\bar{x}, \bar{f}(\bar{x}))$ where $\bar{f}$ are new Skolem function symbols. δ_S introduces Skolem constants but no function symbols, and in this case so does $(\neg I')_S$. Bounded-Horizon check of bound k can be approximately understood as checking the satisfiability of

$$\Big(\bigwedge_{\bar{t} \in \mathrm{BHT}_{k-1}} I_S[\bar{t}] \Big) \wedge \Big(\bigwedge_{\bar{t} \in \mathrm{BHT}_k} \delta_S[\bar{t}] \Big) \wedge \Big(\bigwedge_{\bar{t} \in \mathrm{BHT}_k} (\neg I')_S[\bar{t}] \Big). \tag{2}$$

(In fact, it is possible that I_S contains sub-formulas for which instantiations of depth k do not increase the total depth of instantiations beyond k, and are thus also included.)

Lemma 1 (Soundness). *For every $k \in \mathbb{N}$, Bounded-Horizon with bound k is sound, i.e., if it reports that $I \in \mathrm{FOL}(\Sigma)$ is inductive w.r.t. δ, then I is indeed inductive.*

Proof. Assume that I is not inductive w.r.t. δ, so there is a structure $\mathcal{A}$ such that $\mathcal{A} \models I_S \wedge \delta_S \wedge (\neg I')_S$. In particular $\mathcal{A} \models Ind[\bar{t}]$ for every $\bar{t} \in \mathrm{BHT}_\infty$ and in particular for every $\bar{t} \in \mathrm{BHT}_k$ such that $\mathrm{depth}(Ind[\bar{t}]) \leq k$. Hence, Bounded-Horizon of bound k will not report that I is inductive. $\qquad\square$

```
req := ∅;  resp := ∅;  match := ∅;
action new_request(u) {
    q := new request;
    req := req ∪ {(u, q)}
    /@   r := r ∪ {(u, y) | match(q, y)}
}
action respond(u, q) {
    assume req(u, q);
    p := new response;
    match := match ∪ {(q, p)};
    /@   r := r ∪ {(x, p) | req(x, q)}
    resp := resp ∪ {(u, p)}
}
```

```
action check(u, p) {
    if resp(u, p) ∧ ∀q. req(u, q) → ¬match(q, p)
    /@ ↪ if resp(u, p) ∧ ¬r(u, p)
        then abort
}
```

$$\text{Invariant } I = \forall u, p.\, resp(u, p) \rightarrow$$
$$\exists q.\, req(u, q) \wedge match(q, p)$$
/@ $r(x, y) \equiv \exists z.\, req(x, z) \wedge match(z, y)$
/@   Invariant $\widehat{I} = \forall u, p.\, resp(u, p) \rightarrow r(u, p)$

Fig. 1. Example demonstrating a $\forall^* \exists^*$ invariant that is provable with bound 1. The reader should first ignore the instrumentation code denoted by /@ (see Example 2). This example is inspired by [16]. The complete program is provided in [2] (files `client_server_ae.ivy`, `client_server_instr.ivy`).

Example 1. Figure 1 presents a simple model of the client server scenario described in [16]. The program induces an EPR transition relation, and its invariant is provable by Bounded-Horizon of bound 1.

We first explain this example ignoring the annotations denoted by "/@". The system state is modeled using three binary relations. The *req* relation stores pairs of users and requests, representing requests sent by users. The *resp* relation similarly stores pairs of users and replies, representing replies sent back from the server. The *match* relation maintains the correspondence between a request and its reply.

The action **new_request** models an event where a user u sends a new request to the server. The action **respond** models an event where the server responds to a pending request by sending a reply to the user. The request and response are related by the *match* relation. The action **check** is used to verify the safety property that every response sent by the server has a matching request, by aborting the system if this does not hold.

A natural inductive invariant for this system is

$$I = \forall u, p.\, resp(u, p) \rightarrow \exists q.\, req(u, q) \wedge match(q, p).$$

The invariant proves that the **then** branch in action **check** will never happen and thus the system will never abort. This invariant is preserved under execution of all actions, and is provable by Bounded Horizon of bound 1.

Lemma 2 (Completeness for some k). *If $I \in \mathrm{FOL}(\Sigma)$ is inductive w.r.t. δ then there exists $k \in \mathbb{N}$ s.t. I is provably inductive w.r.t. δ with Bounded-Horizon of bound k.*

Proof. From Theorem 2 and compactness there is a finite set S of instantiations that is unsatisfiable. Take k to be the maximal depth of instantiations in S. □

For example, if $I \in \forall^*$ then Bounded-Horizon of bound 0 is complete. However, as expected due to the undecidability of checking inductiveness, for arbitrary invariants Bounded-Horizon is *not* necessarily complete for a given k: An example for which a bound of 1 is insufficient appears in the extended version [1].

Small Bounded-Horizon for $\forall^*\exists^*$ Invariants. Despite the incompleteness, we conjecture that a small depth of instantiations typically suffices to prove inductiveness. The intuition is that an EPR transition relation has a very limited "horizon" of the domain: it interacts only with a small fraction of the domain, namely elements pointed to by program variables (that correspond to logical constants in the vocabulary).

When performing the Bounded-Horizon check with bound 1 on a $\forall^*\exists^*$ invariant $I = \forall \overline{x}.\ \exists \overline{y}.\ \alpha(\overline{x}, \overline{y})$, we essentially assume that the existential part of the invariant $\psi(\overline{x}) = \exists \overline{y}.\ \alpha(\overline{x}, \overline{y})$ holds on all program variables—but not necessarily on all elements of the domain — and try to prove that it holds on all elements of the domain after the transition. We expect that for most elements of the domain, the correctness of ψ is maintained simply because they were not modified at all by the transition. For elements that are modified by the transition, we expect the correctness after modifications to result from the fact that ψ holds for the elements of the domain that the transition directly interacts with. If this is indeed the reason that ψ is maintained, a bound of 1 sufficiently uses ψ in the pre-state to prove the invariant in the post-state, i.e. it is inductive.

This is the case in Example 1. Additional examples are listed in Sect. 6.

4   Power of Bounded-Horizon for Proving Inductiveness

We now turn to investigate the ability of Bounded-Horizon to verify inductiveness. In this section we provide sufficient conditions for its success by relating it to the notion of instrumentation (which we explain below). We show that Bounded-Horizon with a low bound of 1 or 2 is as powerful as a natural class of sound program instrumentations, those that do not add existential quantifiers. Section 6 demonstrates the method's power on several interesting programs we verified using Bounded-Horizon of bound 1.

4.1   Instrumentation

We present our view of the instrumentation procedure used in previous works [21,23,29] to eliminate the need for quantifier-alternation, thus reducing the verification task to a decidable fragment. The procedure begins with a program that induces a transition relation $\delta \in \exists^*\forall^*(\Sigma \cup \Sigma')$. The purpose of instrumentation is to modify δ into another transition relation $\widehat{\delta}$ that admits an inductive invariant with simpler quantification (e.g., universal, in which case it is decidable to check). We note that instrumentation is generally a manual procedure. For simplicity, we describe the instrumentation process informally, but provide the semantic soundness requirement in Definition 4. The instrumentation procedure consists of the following three steps:

1. Identify a formula $\psi(\overline{x}) \in \mathrm{FOL}(\Sigma)$ (usually ψ will be existential) that captures information that is needed in the inductive invariant. Extend the vocabulary with an instrumentation relation $r(\overline{x})$ that intentionally should capture the derived relation defined by $\psi(\overline{x})$. Let $\widehat{\Sigma} = \Sigma \cup \{r\}$ denote the extended vocabulary[3].
2. Add update code that updates r when the original ("core") relations are modified, and maintains the meaning of r as encoding ψ. The update code must not block executions of real code, and can possibly be a sound approximation. Sometimes it can be generated automatically via finite differencing [32].
3. Modify the program to use r. Often this is performed by rewriting some program conditions, keeping in mind that r encodes ψ. This means replacing some quantified expressions by uses of r.

Example 2. In the example of Fig. 1, to achieve a universal invariant we add an instrumentation relation r defined by $r(x,y) \equiv \exists z.\ req(x,z) \wedge match(z,y)$ (step 1). The simple form of ψ allows us to obtain precise update code, which appears as annotations marked with /@ in lines that mutate *req* and *match* (step 2). We also replace the **if** condition in the action **check** by an equivalent condition that uses r (step 3). The line marked with /@ $\hookrightarrow$ in the **check** action replaces the line above it. The resulting program has the invariant $\widehat{I} = \forall u, p.\ resp(u,p) \rightarrow r(u,p)$, which is universal.

Let $\widehat{\delta} \in \exists^*\forall^*(\widehat{\Sigma} \cup \widehat{\Sigma}')$ denote the transition relation induced by the modified program (modifications occur in steps 2, 3). The soundness of the instrumentation procedure is formalized in the following connection between ψ, δ, and $\widehat{\delta}$:

Definition 4 (Sound Instrumentation). $\widehat{\delta} \in \exists^*\forall^*(\widehat{\Sigma} \cup \widehat{\Sigma}')$ *is a sound instrumentation for* $\delta \in \exists^*\forall^*(\Sigma \cup \Sigma')$ *and* $\psi \in \mathrm{FOL}(\Sigma)$ *if* $(\forall \overline{x}.\ r(\overline{x}) \leftrightarrow \psi(\overline{x})\ \wedge$ $\delta \wedge \forall \overline{x}.\ r'(\overline{x}) \leftrightarrow \psi'(\overline{x})) \rightarrow \widehat{\delta}$ *is valid, or equivalently,* $\delta \rightarrow \widehat{\delta}[\psi/r, \psi'/r']$ *is valid.*

---

[3] It is also possible to instrument the program with constants. This can be emulated by adding a unary relation $c(x)$ representing the constant, and adding the assumption that c contains exactly one element to the invariant. This is also aligned with the conditions of Theorem 5.

Definition 4 ensures that the instrumented program includes at least all the behaviors of the original program, when r is interpreted according to ψ. Thus, if the instrumented program is safe, then it is sound to infer that the original program is safe.

The instrumentation procedure does not require the user to know an inductive invariant for the original program. However, if a sound instrumentation which leads to an invariant exists, then an inductive invariant for the original δ can be produced by substituting back the "meaning" of r as ψ (thus, safety of the original program is implied):

Lemma 3. *Let $\widehat{\delta}$ be a sound instrumentation for δ and ψ, and $\widehat{I} \in \mathrm{FOL}(\widehat{\Sigma})$ be an inductive invariant for $\widehat{\delta}$. Then $I = \widehat{I}[\psi/r]$ is inductive w.r.t. δ.*

Proof. $\widehat{I} \wedge \widehat{\delta} \to \widehat{I}'$ is valid, thus, so is $(\widehat{I} \wedge \widehat{\delta} \to \widehat{I}')[\psi/r, \psi'/r']$. $\widehat{\delta}$ is a sound instrumentation for δ, so (using Definition 4) $I \wedge \delta \to I'$ is valid.   □

Note that typically the quantification structure of I is more complex than that of $\widehat{I}$.

Instrumentation Without Additional Existential Quantifiers. In order to relate instrumentation to Bounded-Horizon instantiations, we consider the typical case where the instrumentation process of δ does not add new existential quantifiers to $\widehat{\delta}$. This happens when the update code does not introduce additional existential quantifiers. Formally:

Definition 5 (Existential Naming). *Let $\widehat{\delta} = \exists z_1, \ldots z_m. \varphi(z_1, \ldots, z_m)$ where $\varphi \in \forall^*(\widehat{\Sigma}, \widehat{\Sigma}')$. An existential naming η for $(\widehat{\delta}, \delta)$ is a mapping $\eta : \{z_1, \ldots, z_m\} \to const[\delta_S] \cup const[\widehat{\delta}_S]$. We define $\eta(\widehat{\delta})$ to be $\varphi[\eta(z_1)/z_1, \ldots, \eta(z_m)/z_m]$.*

An existential naming provides a Skolemization procedure which uses existing constants rather than fresh ones. If such η exists, it maps the (Skolemized) existential quantifiers in $\widehat{\delta}$ to their counterparts in δ. For example, the instrumentation in Fig. 1 results in $\widehat{\delta}$ that has an existential naming w.r.t. the original δ. Note that it is possible that $\widehat{\delta}$ has in fact *fewer* existential quantifiers than δ, for example due to the rewriting of conditions (as happens in the example of Fig. 1—see the `if` statement in action `check`).

Definition 6 (Instrumentation Without Additional Existenials). *$\widehat{\delta}$ is a sound instrumentation without additional existentials for δ if there exists an existential naming η such that $\delta_S \to \eta(\widehat{\delta})[\psi/r, \psi'/r']$ is valid.*

4.2   From Instrumentation to Bounded-Horizon

The results described in this section show that if there is an instrumentation without additional existentials, then Bounded-Horizon with a low bound is able to prove the original invariant, without specific knowledge of the instrumentation and without manual assistance from the programmer. This is the case in the example of Fig. 1, which admits an instrumentation that transforms the invariant to a universal invariant (see Example 2) in a form that matches Theorem 3, and indeed the original invariant is provable by Bounded-Horizon of bound 1.

Interestingly, in case Bounded-Horizon with a small bound does not prove inductiveness (see the example in the extended version [1]), the results imply that either the invariant is not inductive or *no instrumentation* that does not add existential quantifiers can be used to show that it is inductive (even with the programmer's manual assistance).

In the remainder of this section we will assume that $\widehat{\delta}$ is a sound instrumentation without additional existentials for δ, and η is the corresponding naming of existentials. Further, we assume that $\widehat{I}$ is an inductive invariant for $\widehat{\delta}$ and denote $I = \widehat{I}[\psi/r]$.

The following theorems state our results for $I \in \forall^* \exists^*$.

Theorem 3. *Let $\widehat{I} \in \forall^*$. Assume $\psi \in \exists^*$ and r appears only positively in $\widehat{I}$, or $\psi \in \forall^*$ and r appears only negatively in $\widehat{I}$. Then $I = \widehat{I}[\psi/r]$ is inductive for δ with Bounded-Horizon of bound 1. (Note that $I \in \forall^* \exists^*$.)*

Proof Sketch. Let $I = \forall \overline{x}.\ \alpha(\overline{x})$ where $\alpha \in \exists^*$. Assume for the sake of contradiction that I is not inductive for δ with Bounded-Horizon of bound 1. By the assumptions on ψ and $\widehat{I}$, this means that there is a structure $\mathcal{A}$ such that

$$\mathcal{A} \models \left(\bigwedge_{\overline{c}} \alpha(\overline{c}) \right) \wedge \delta_S \wedge (\neg I')_S.$$

From the assumption (Definition 6) and properties of Skolemization, it follows that

$$\mathcal{A} \models \left(\bigwedge_{\overline{c}} \alpha(\overline{c}) \right) \wedge \left(\eta(\widehat{\delta}) \right)[\psi/r, \psi'/r'] \wedge \left((\neg \widehat{I'})_S \right)[\psi/r, \psi'/r'].$$

From the assumptions on the way ψ appears in $\widehat{I}$, when we write $\widehat{I} = \forall \overline{x}.\ \widehat{\alpha}(\overline{x})$ where $\widehat{\alpha} \in \mathrm{QF}$ we have $\alpha = \widehat{\alpha}[\psi/r]$. Thus, from properties of substitution (interpreting r, r' according to ψ, ψ' in $\mathcal{A}$) it follows that there is a structure $\widehat{\mathcal{A}}$ such that

$$\widehat{\mathcal{A}} \models \left(\bigwedge_{\overline{c}} \widehat{\alpha}(\overline{c}) \right) \wedge \eta(\widehat{\delta}) \wedge (\neg \widehat{I'})_S.$$

By reducing $\widehat{\mathcal{A}}$'s domain to the constants we have that $\left(\forall \overline{x}.\ \widehat{\alpha}(\overline{x}) \right) \wedge \eta(\widehat{\delta}) \wedge (\neg \widehat{I'})_S$ is satisfiable. (This is a use of complete instantiation for universal formulas.)

This in turn implies (by properties of Skolemization) that $\widehat{I} \wedge \widehat{\delta} \wedge \neg \widehat{I'}$ is satisfiable, which is a contradiction to the assumption that $\widehat{I}$ is inductive for $\widehat{\delta}$. □

Theorem 4. *Let $\widehat{I} \in \forall^*$. If $\psi \in \mathrm{AF}$ then $I = \widehat{I}[\psi/r]$ is inductive for δ with Bounded-Horizon of bound 2. (Note that $I \in \forall^* \exists^*$.)*

The following theorem generalizes the above result to *1-alternation invariants*. A formula is 1-alternation if it can be written as a Boolean combination of $\forall^* \exists^*$ formulas.

Theorem 5. *Let $\widehat{I} \in \mathrm{AF}$. If $\psi \in \mathrm{AF}$ then $I = \widehat{I}[\psi/r]$ is inductive for δ with Bounded-Horizon of bound 2. (Note that $I \in$ 1-alternation.)*

The full proofs appear in the extended version [1]. The results of this section also apply when multiple instrumentation relations $\psi_1, \ldots, \psi_t \in \mathrm{FOL}(\Sigma)$ are simultaneously substituted instead of the relation symbols $r_1, \ldots, r_t$ in $\widehat{\delta}$ and $\widehat{I}$.

Instrumentations for Higher Bounds. While instrumentation that does not add existentials is at most as powerful as Bounded-Horizon with a low bound, sound instrumentations that do add existentials to the program (thereby not satisfying Definition 6) can be used to simulate quantifier instantiation of an arbitrary depth. A simple way is to add r as an instrumentation that tracks the existential part of a $\forall^*\exists^*$ invariant. Instantiations are performed by introducing existentially quantified variables to the program and using **assume** statements to make these variables function as witnesses for a tuple of variables that instantiate the universal quantifiers. Doing this recursively generates instantiations of an arbitrary depth. See the extended version [1] for further details.

5   Partial Models for Understanding Non-Inductiveness

When conducting SMT-based deductive verification (e.g., using Dafny [26]), the user constructs both the formal representation of the system and its invariants. In many cases, the invariant I is initially not inductive w.r.t. the given program, due to a bug in the program or in the invariant. Therefore, deductive verification is typically an iterative process in which the user attempts to prove inductiveness, and, when this fails, adapts the program, the invariant, or both.

In such scenarios, it is extremely desirable to present the user with a *counterexample to induction* in the form of a state that satisfies I but makes a transition to a state that violates it. Such a state can be obtained from a model of the formula $Ind = I \wedge \delta \wedge \neg I'$ which is used to check inductiveness. It explains the error, and guides the user towards fixing the program and/or the invariant [13,26]. However, in many cases where the check involves quantifier alternation, current SMT solvers are unable to produce counterexamples. Instead, SMT solvers usually diverge or report "unknown" [15,33]. In such cases, Bounded-Horizon instantiations can be used to present a concrete logical structure which is comprehensible to the user, and is obtained as a model of the (finite) instantiations of the formula Ind. While this structure is not a true counterexample (as it is only a model of a subset of the instantiations of the formula), it can still guide the user in the right direction towards fixing the program and/or the invariant.

We illustrate this using a simple leader-election protocol in a ring [10], whose model is presented in Fig. 2(a). The protocol assumes that nodes are organized in a directional ring topology with unique IDs, and elects the node with the highest ID as the leader. Each node sends its own ID to its successor, and forwards messages when they contain an ID higher than its own ID. A node that receives its own ID is elected as leader. We wish to prove a termination property which states that once all nodes have sent their ID, and there are no pending messages in the network, then there is an elected leader. To verify this we use a

```
pending := ∅;
... # ring topology

action send_packet(n) {
  assume ring_next(n, m)
  pending := pending ∪ {(n, m)}
  sent := sent ∪ {n}
}

action receive_packet(n, m) {
  assume pending(m, n)
  pending := pending \ {(m, n)}
  if m = n then
    leader := leader ∪ {n}
  else
    if n < m then
      assume ring_next(n, n₀)
      pending := pending ∪ {(m, n₀)}
    else # do not forward
}
```

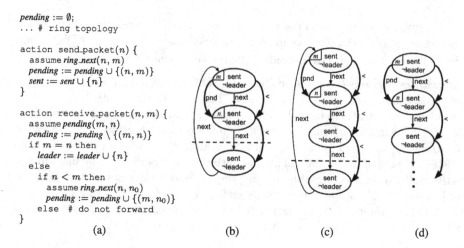

| (a) | (b) | (c) | (d) |

Fig. 2. Leader-election in a ring protocol as an illustration of the use of partial models for incorrect programs and invariants. (a) sketches the protocol (the complete program appears in [2], file `ring_leader_termination.ivy`). (b), (c) show partial models of bound 1 and 2, respectively, and (d) illustrates an infinite structure that explains the root cause of the non-inductiveness.

relational model of the protocol similar to [29], and specify the property via the following formula:

$$(\exists n. \; leader(n)) \vee (\exists n_1, n_2. \; \neg sent(n_1) \vee pending(n_1, n_2)) \qquad (3)$$

A natural attempt of proving this using an inductive invariant is by conjoining Eq. (3) (which is not inductive by itself) with the following property (this was the authors' actual next step in proving this termination property):

$$\forall n_1. \; sent(n_1) \wedge \neg leader(n_1) \rightarrow ((\exists n_2. \; pending(n_1, n_2)) \vee (\exists n_2. \; n_1 < n_2)) \qquad (4)$$

meaning that if a node has sent its own ID but has not (yet) become leader, then there is either a message pending in the network with the node's ID, or a node with a higher ID.

Alas, the conjunction of Eqs. (3) and (4) is still not an inductive invariant for the protocol (as we explain below). Since Eq. (4) contains $\forall^* \exists^*$ quantification, the associated inductiveness check is outside of the decidable EPR fragment. Indeed, Z3 diverges when it is used to check *Ind*. This is not surprising since the formula has no satisfying finite structures, but has an infinite model (a scenario that is not unusual for $\forall^* \exists^*$ formulas).

On the other hand, applying Bounded-Horizon (with any bound) to *Ind* results in a formula that has finite models. These concrete models are *partial models* of *Ind*. Figure 2(b) and (c) show partial models (restricted to the pre-states) obtained with bounds of 1 and 2, respectively, on this example.

These models are not true counterexamples to induction: the sub-formula of Eq. (4) residing under the universal quantifier does not hold for all the elements of the domain. It does, however, hold for all elements with which the quantifier was instantiated, which are the elements above the dashed line. These elements have all sent their own ID, which was blocked by their successor that has a higher ID, so none of them is the leader. In a finite model, this has to end somewhere, because one of the nodes must have the highest ID. Hence, no finite counter-model exists. However, extrapolating from Fig. 2(b) and (c), we can obtain the infinite model depicted in Fig. 2(d). This model represents an infinite ("open") ring in which each node has a lower ID than its successor. This model is a true model of the formula *Ind* generated by the invariant in Eqs. (3) and (4), but the fact that it is infinite prevented Z3 from producing it.

Since we use tools that check general (un)satisfiability, which is not limited to finite structures, the only way to prove that an invariant is inductive is to exclude infinite counterexamples to induction as well. Using Bounded-Horizon instantiations, we are able to obtain meaningful partial models that provide hints to the user about what is missing. In this case, the solution is to add an axiom to the system model which states that there is a node with maximal ID: $\exists n_1. \forall n_2. n_2 \leq n_1$. With this additional assumption, the formula *Ind* is unsatis-fiable so the invariant is inductive, and this is proven both by Z3's instantiation heuristics and by Bounded-Horizon with a bound of 1. This illustrates the use-fulness of Bounded-Horizon when the invariant is not inductive.

6   Implementation and Initial Evaluation

We implemented a prototype of Bounded-Horizon of bound 1 on top of Z3 [11] and used it within Ivy [29] and the framework of [21]. We applied the procedure to the incorrect example of Sect. 5, and successfully verified several correct pro-grams and invariants using bound 1. These examples are (the examples' code can be found in [2]):

- The client-server example of Fig. 1.
- List reverse [21], where the invariant states that the n edges ("next" pointers) are reversed. The invariant is $\forall^* \exists^*$ due to the encoding of n via n^* as explained in [21].
- Learning switch [6], where the invariant states every routing node has a successor.
- Hole-punching firewall [6], where the invariant states that every allowed exter-nal node was contacted by some internal node. We explored two modeling alternativies: using a ghost history relation, or existensially quantifying over time.
- Leader election in a ring [10,29] with the invariant discussed in Sect. 5.

An initial evaluation of the method's performance appears in Table 1.

Our implementation works by adding "guards" that restrict the range of uni-versal quantifiers to the set of constants where necessary. Technically, recall that we are considering the satisfiability of $Ind = I_S \wedge \delta_S \wedge (\neg I')_S$. Let $\forall x.\ \theta$ be a

Table 1. Experimental results.

Program	#∀	#Func	#Consts	#∀$^↓$	B1 Total	B1 Solve	Baseline Z3
Client-server	14	1	15	2	58 ms	3 ms	3 ms
List reverse	47	3	15	4	319 ms	211 ms	50 ms
Learning switch	70	1	7	37	245 ms	65 ms	33 ms
Hole-punching firewall with ghost	15	1	18	3	75 ms	4 ms	4 ms
Hole-punching firewall ∃ time	32	2	21	3	102 ms	4 ms	4 ms
Leader-election in a ring (correct)	41	1	21	1	113 ms	36 ms	27 ms
Leader-election in a ring (incorrect)	40	1	20	1	1112 ms	1008 ms	—

B1 Total is the time in milliseconds for the bound 1 implementation. It is compared to **Baseline Z3** which is the solving time in milliseconds of *Ind* as is (with quantifier alternation) by Z3. **B1 Solve** measures the solving time of the formula restricted to bound 1, which demonstrates that most of the overhead occurs when constructing the formula. #∀ is the number of universal quantifiers in *Ind*, **#Func** the number of different Skolem function symbols, and **#Consts** the number of constants. #∀$^↓$ is the number of universally quantified variables that were restricted in the bound 1 check. Measurements were performed on a 3.5GHz Intel i5-4690 CPU with 8GB RAM running Linux 3.13 x86_64.

subformula of *Ind*. If θ contains function symbol applications[4], we transform the subformula to $\forall x. \left(\bigvee_c x = c \right) \rightarrow \theta$ where c ranges over $const[Ind]$. The resulting formula is then dispatched to the solver. This is a simple way to encode the termination criterion of bound 1 while leaving room for the solver to perform the necessary instantiations cleverly. The translation enlarges the formula by $O(\#Consts \cdot \#\forall)$ although the number of bounded instantiations grows exponentially with $\#\forall$. The exponential explosion is due to combinations of constants in the instantiation, a problem we defer to the solver.

Z3 terminates on the class of formulas because during the Model-Based Quantifier Instantiation process every instantiation of a universally quantified formula has the same truth value in the model as an instantiation using one of the existing ground terms (constants and then BHT_1 terms). Z3's instantiation engine will produce instantiations using existing terms rather than create superfluous new terms [8].

The results are encouraging because they suggest that the termination strategy of Bounded-Horizon, at least for bound 1, can be combined with existing instantiation techniques to assure termination with only a slight performance penalty. Most encouraging is the satisfiable example of Sect. 5. On this instance, Z3 was able to return "sat" within seconds, although to do so, in theory, the solver must exhaust the entire set of bounded instantiations. This suggests that the Bounded-Horizon termination criterion might indeed be useful for "sat" instances on which the solver may diverge.

A different approach to the implementation is to integrate the termination criterion of the bound with the solver's heuristics more closely (see [7]).

---

[4] This in fact implements the approximation as of Eq. (2). The exact bound 1 per Eq. (1) can be implemented by a more careful consideration of which universally quantified variables should be restricted, but this was not necessary for our examples.

7   Related Work

Quantifier Instantiation. The importance of formulas with quantifier-alternations for program verification has led to many developments in the SMT and theorem-proving communities that aim to allow automated reasoning with quantifier-alternations. The Simplify system [12] promoted the practical usage of quantifier triggers, which let the user affect the quantifier instantiation in a clever way. Similar methods are integrated into modern SMT solvers such as Z3 [11]. Recently, a method for annotating the source code with triggers has been developed for Dafny [27]. The notion of instantiation depth is related to the notions of matching-depth [12] and instantiation-level [14] which are used for prioritization within the trigger-based instantiation procedure.

In addition to user-provided triggers, many automated heuristics for quantifier instantiation have been developed, such as Model-Based Quantifier Instantiation [15]. Even when quantifier instantiation is refutation-complete, it is still important and challenging to handle the SAT cases, which are especially important for program verification. Accordingly, many works (e.g., [33]) consider the problem of model finding.

Local Theory Extensions and Psi-Local Theories [7,19,36] identify settings in which limited quantifier instantiations are complete. They show that completeness is achieved exactly when every partial model can be extended to a (total) model. In such settings Bounded-Horizon instantiations are complete for invariant checking. However, Bounded-Horizon can also be useful when completeness cannot be guaranteed.

Classes of SMT formulas that are decidable by complete instantiations have been studied by [15]. In the uninterpreted fragment, a refined version of Herbrand's Theorem generates a finite set of instantiations when the dependencies are stratified. Bounded-Horizon is a way to bound unstratified dependencies.

Natural Proofs. Natural proofs [30] provide a sound and incomplete proof technique for deductive verification. The key idea is to instantiate recursive definitions over the terms appearing in the program. Bounded-Horizon is motivated by a similar intuition, but focuses on instantiating quantifiers in a way that is appropriate for the EPR setting.

Decidable Logics. Different decidable logics can be used to check inductive invariants. For example, Monadic second-order logic [17] obtains decidability by limiting the underlying domain to consist of trees only, and in particular does not allow arbitrary relations, which are useful to describe properties of programs. There are also many decidable fragments of first-order logic [9]. Our work aims to transcend the class of invariants checkable by a reduction to the decidable logic EPR. We note that the example of Sect. 5 does not fall under the Loosely-Guarded Fragment of first-order logic [18] due to a use of a transitivity axiom, and does not enjoy the finite-model property.

Abstractions for Verification of Infinite-State Systems. Our work is closely related to abstractions of infinite state systems. These abstractions aim at automatically inferring inductive invariants in a sound way. We are interested in checking if a given invariant is inductive either for automatic and semi-automatic verification.

The View-Abstraction approach [3–5] defines a useful abstraction for the verification of parameterized systems. This abstraction is closely related to universally quantified invariants. An extension of this approach [5] adds contexts to the abstraction, which are used to capture $\forall^*\exists^*$ invariants in a restricted setting where nodes have finite-state and are only related by specific topologies. Our work is in line with the need to use $\forall^*\exists^*$ invariants for verification, but applies in a more general setting (with unrestricted high-arity relations) at the cost of losing completeness of invariant checking.

Our work is related to the TVLA system [28, 35] which allows the programmers to define instrumentation relations. TVLA also employs finite differencing to infer sound update code for updating instrumentation relations [32], but generates non-EPR formulas and does not guarantee completeness. The focus operation in TVLA implements materialization which resembles quantifier-instantiation. TVLA shows that very few built-in instrumentation relations can be used to verify many different programs.

Instrumentation and Update Formulas. The idea of using instrumentation relations and generating update formulas is not limited to TVLA and was also used for more predictable SMT verification [24, 25].

8   Conclusion

We have provided an initial study of the power of bounded instantiations for tackling quantifier alternation. This paper shows that quantifier instantiation with small bounds can simulate instrumentation. This is a step in order to eliminate the need for instrumenting the program, which can be error-prone. The other direction, i.e. simulating quantifier instantiation with instrumentation, is also possible but is less appealing from a practical point of view, and is presented in the extended version [1].

We are encouraged by our initial experience that shows that various protocols can be proven with small instantiation bounds, and that partial models are useful for understanding the failures of the solver to prove inductiveness. Some of these failures correspond to non-inductive claims, especially those due to infinite counterexamples. In the future we hope to leverage this in effective deductive verification tools, and explore meaningful ways to display infinite counterexamples to the user.

Acknowledgments. We would like to thank Nikolaj Bjørner, Shachar Itzhaky, and Bryan Parno for helpful discussions, and Gilit Zohar-Oren for help and feedback. The research leading to these results has received funding from the European Research Council under the European Union's Seventh Framework Programme (FP7/2007-2013)/ERC grant agreement no [321174]. This research was partially supported by BSF grant no. 2012259, and by Len Blavatnik and the Blavatnik Family foundation.

References

1. Extended version. http://www.cs.tau.ac.il/research/yotam.feldman/papers/tacas17/tacas17-extended.pdf
2. Full code materials. http://www.cs.tau.ac.il/research/yotam.feldman/papers/tacas17/examples-code.zip
3. Abdulla, P., Haziza, F., Holík, L.: Parameterized verification through view abstraction. Int. J. Softw. Tools Technol. Transf. 1–22 (2015). http://dx.doi.org/10.1007/s10009-015-0406-x
4. Abdulla, P.A., Haziza, F., Holík, L.: All for the price of few. In: Giacobazzi, R., Berdine, J., Mastroeni, I. (eds.) VMCAI 2013. LNCS, vol. 7737, pp. 476–495. Springer, Heidelberg (2013). doi:10.1007/978-3-642-35873-9_28
5. Abdulla, P.A., Haziza, F., Holík, L.: Block me if you can!. In: Müller-Olm, M., Seidl, H. (eds.) SAS 2014. LNCS, vol. 8723, pp. 1–17. Springer, Heidelberg (2014). doi:10.1007/978-3-319-10936-7_1
6. Ball, T., Bjørner, N., Gember, A., Itzhaky, S., Karbyshev, A., Sagiv, M., Schapira, M., Valadarsky, A.: VeriCon: towards verifying controller programs in software-defined networks. In: ACM SIGPLAN Conference on Programming Language Design and Implementation, PLDI 2014, Edinburgh, United Kingdom, 09–11 June 2014, pp. 31 (2014)
7. Bansal, K., Reynolds, A., King, T., Barrett, C., Wies, T.: Deciding local theory extensions via E-matching. In: Kroening, D., Păsăreanu, C.S. (eds.) CAV 2015. LNCS, vol. 9207, pp. 87–105. Springer, Cham (2015). doi:10.1007/978-3-319-21668-3_6
8. Bjørner, N.: Personal communication (2017)
9. Börger, E., Grädel, E., Gurevich, Y.: The Classical Decision Problem. Perspectives in Mathematical Logic. Springer, Berlin (1997)
10. Chang, E., Roberts, R.: An improved algorithm for decentralized extrema-finding in circular configurations of processes. Commun. ACM 22(5), 281–283 (1979)
11. de Moura, L., Bjørner, N.: Z3: an efficient SMT solver. In: Ramakrishnan, C.R., Rehof, J. (eds.) TACAS 2008. LNCS, vol. 4963, pp. 337–340. Springer, Heidelberg (2008). doi:10.1007/978-3-540-78800-3_24
12. Detlefs, D., Nelson, G., Saxe, J.B.: Simplify: a theorem prover for program checking. J. ACM 52(3), 365–473 (2005)
13. Flanagan, C., Leino, K.R.M., Lillibridge, M., Nelson, G., Saxe, J.B., Stata, R.: Extended static checking for Java. In: Proceedings of the 2002 ACM SIGPLAN Conference on Programming Language Design and Implementation (PLDI), Berlin, Germany, 17–19 June 2002, pp. 234–245 (2002)
14. Ge, Y., Barrett, C.W., Tinelli, C.: Solving quantified verification conditions using satisfiability modulo theories. Ann. Math. Artif. Intell. 55(1–2), 101–122 (2009)
15. Ge, Y., de Moura, L.: Complete instantiation for quantified formulas in satisfiability modulo theories. In: Bouajjani, A., Maler, O. (eds.) CAV 2009. LNCS, vol. 5643, pp. 306–320. Springer, Heidelberg (2009). doi:10.1007/978-3-642-02658-4_25
16. Hawblitzel, C., Howell, J., Kapritsos, M., Lorch, J.R., Parno, B., Roberts, M.L., Setty, S.T.V., Zill, B.: IronFleet: proving practical distributed systems correct. In: Proceedings of the 25th Symposium on Operating Systems Principles, SOSP, pp. 1–17 (2015)
17. Henriksen, J.G., Jensen, J., Jørgensen, M., Klarlund, N., Paige, R., Rauhe, T., Sandholm, A.: Mona: monadic second-order logic in practice. In: Brinksma, E., Cleaveland, W.R., Larsen, K.G., Margaria, T., Steffen, B. (eds.) TACAS 1995. LNCS, vol. 1019, pp. 89–110. Springer, Heidelberg (1995). doi:10.1007/3-540-60630-0_5

18. Hodkinson, I.: Loosely guarded fragment of first-order logic has the finite model property. Stud. Logica. **70**(2), 205–240 (2002)
19. Ihlemann, C., Jacobs, S., Sofronie-Stokkermans, V.: On local reasoning in verification. In: 14th International Conference Tools and Algorithms for the Construction and Analysis of Systems, TACAS 2008, Held as Part of the Joint European Conferences on Theory and Practice of Software, ETAPS 2008, Budapest, Hungary, March 29-April 6 2008. Proceedings, pp. 265–281 (2008)
20. Immerman, N., Rabinovich, A., Reps, T., Sagiv, M., Yorsh, G.: The boundary between decidability and undecidability for transitive-closure logics. In: Marcinkowski, J., Tarlecki, A. (eds.) CSL 2004. LNCS, vol. 3210, pp. 160–174. Springer, Heidelberg (2004). doi:10.1007/978-3-540-30124-0_15
21. Itzhaky, S., Banerjee, A., Immerman, N., Nanevski, A., Sagiv, M.: Effectively-propositional reasoning about reachability in linked data structures. In: Sharygina, N., Veith, H. (eds.) CAV 2013. LNCS, vol. 8044, pp. 756–772. Springer, Heidelberg (2013). doi:10.1007/978-3-642-39799-8_53
22. Itzhaky, S., Bjørner, N., Reps, T., Sagiv, M., Thakur, A.: Property-directed shape analysis. In: Biere, A., Bloem, R. (eds.) CAV 2014. LNCS, vol. 8559, pp. 35–51. Springer, Cham (2014). doi:10.1007/978-3-319-08867-9_3
23. Karbyshev, A., Bjørner, N., Itzhaky, S., Rinetzky, N., Shoham, S.: Property-directed inference of universal invariants or proving their absence. In: Kroening, D., Păsăreanu, C.S. (eds.) CAV 2015. LNCS, vol. 9206, pp. 583–602. Springer, Cham (2015). doi:10.1007/978-3-319-21690-4_40
24. Lahiri, S.K., Qadeer, S.: Verifying properties of well-founded linked lists. In: Proceedings of the 33rd ACM SIGPLAN-SIGACT Symposium on Principles of Programming Languages, POPL 2006, Charleston, South Carolina, USA, 11–13 January 2006, pp. 115–126 (2006)
25. Lahiri, S.K., Qadeer, S.: Back to the future: revisiting precise program verification using SMT solvers. In Proceedings of the 35th ACM SIGPLAN-SIGACT Symposium on Principles of Programming Languages, POPL 2008, San Francisco, California, USA, 7–12 January 2008, pp. 171–182 (2008)
26. Leino, K.R.M.: Dafny: an automatic program verifier for functional correctness. In: Clarke, E.M., Voronkov, A. (eds.) LPAR 2010. LNCS (LNAI), vol. 6355, pp. 348–370. Springer, Heidelberg (2010). doi:10.1007/978-3-642-17511-4_20
27. Leino, K.R.M., Pit-Claudel, C.: Trigger selection strategies to stabilize program verifiers. In: Chaudhuri, S., Farzan, A. (eds.) CAV 2016. LNCS, vol. 9779, pp. 361–381. Springer, Cham (2016). doi:10.1007/978-3-319-41528-4_20
28. Lev-Ami, T., Sagiv, M.: TVLA: a system for implementing static analyses. In: Palsberg, J. (ed.) SAS 2000. LNCS, vol. 1824, pp. 280–301. Springer, Heidelberg (2000). doi:10.1007/978-3-540-45099-3_15
29. Padon, O., McMillan, K.L., Panda, A., Sagiv, M., Shoham, S.: Ivy: safety verification by interactive generalization. In: Proceedings of the 37th ACM SIGPLAN Conference on Programming Language Design and Implementation, PLDI 2016, Santa Barbara, CA, USA, 13–17 June 2016, pp. 614–630 (2016)
30. Qiu, X., Garg, P., Stefanescu, A., Madhusudan, P.: Natural proofs for structure, data, and separation. In: ACM SIGPLAN Conference on Programming Language Design and Implementation, PLDI 2013, Seattle, WA, USA, 16–19 June 2013, pp. 231–242 (2013)
31. Ramsey, F.P.: On a problem of formal logic. Proc. Lond. Math. Soc. **s2-30**(1), 264–286 (1930)
32. Reps, T.W., Sagiv, M., Loginov, A.: Finite differencing of logical formulas for static analysis. ACM Trans. Program. Lang. Syst. **32**(6), 24:1–24:55 (2010)

33. Reynolds, A., Tinelli, C., Goel, A., Krstić, S.: Finite model finding in SMT. In: Sharygina, N., Veith, H. (eds.) CAV 2013. LNCS, vol. 8044, pp. 640–655. Springer, Heidelberg (2013). doi:10.1007/978-3-642-39799-8_42

34. Reynolds, A., Tinelli, C., Goel, A., Krstić, S., Deters, M., Barrett, C.: Quantifier instantiation techniques for finite model finding in SMT. In: Bonacina, M.P. (ed.) CADE 2013. LNCS (LNAI), vol. 7898, pp. 377–391. Springer, Heidelberg (2013). doi:10.1007/978-3-642-38574-2_26

35. Sagiv, S., Reps, T.W., Wilhelm, R.: Parametric shape analysis via 3-valued logic. ACM Trans. Program. Lang. Syst. 24(3), 217–298 (2002)

36. Sofronie-Stokkermans, V.: Hierarchic reasoning in local theory extensions. In: Nieuwenhuis, R. (ed.) CADE 2005. LNCS (LNAI), vol. 3632, pp. 219–234. Springer, Heidelberg (2005). doi:10.1007/11532231_16

Verification Techniques II

Proving Termination Through Conditional Termination

Cristina Borralleras[1], Marc Brockschmidt[2], Daniel Larraz[3], Albert Oliveras[3],
Enric Rodríguez-Carbonell[3(✉)], and Albert Rubio[3]

[1] Universitat de Vic - Universitat Central de Catalunya, Vic, Spain
[2] Microsoft Research, Cambridge, UK
[3] Universitat Politècnica de Catalunya, Barcelona, Spain
erodri@cs.upc.edu

Abstract. We present a constraint-based method for proving conditional termination of integer programs. Building on this, we construct a framework to prove (unconditional) program termination using a powerful mechanism to combine conditional termination proofs. Our key insight is that a conditional termination proof shows termination for a subset of program execution states which do not need to be considered in the remaining analysis. This facilitates more effective termination as well as non-termination analyses, and allows handling loops with different execution phases naturally. Moreover, our method can deal with sequences of loops compositionally. In an empirical evaluation, we show that our implementation VeryMax outperforms state-of-the-art tools on a range of standard benchmarks.

1 Introduction

Proving program termination requires not only synthesizing termination arguments, but also reasoning about reachability of program states, as most nontrivial programs contain subprocedures or loops that only terminate for the executions that actually reach them. Thus, a termination prover has to segment the program state space according to its termination behavior, ignoring nonterminating but unreachable states. Recent advances in termination proving try to tackle this problem by abducing conditions for non-termination, and focusing the termination proof search on the remaining state space [25,32]. However, these techniques rely on relatively weak non-termination proving techniques. Furthermore, different termination arguments may be required depending on how a loop or subprocedure is reached, and thus, even though no non-termination argument can be found, the state space needs to be segmented.

This work was partially supported by the project TIN2015-69175-C4-3-R (MINECO/FEDER) and by the European Research Council (ERC) under the European Union's Horizon 2020 research and innovation programme (grant agreement ERC-2014-CoG 648276 AUTAR).

© Springer-Verlag GmbH Germany 2017
A. Legay and T. Margaria (Eds.): TACAS 2017, Part I, LNCS 10205, pp. 99–117, 2017.
DOI: 10.1007/978-3-662-54577-5_6

In this work, we propose to use preconditions for *termination* to drive the unconditional termination proof. The key insight is that a condition ϕ implying termination allows a termination prover to focus on those program states in which $\neg\phi$ holds. To obtain preconditions for termination, we introduce a new constraint-based method that analyzes program components (i.e., loops or subprocedures) independently and synthesizes termination arguments together with a conditional supporting invariant [12]. To prove full program termination, we use a novel program transformation we call *unfolding* which syntactically splits terminating from potentially non-terminating states using the generated termination conditions. This allows us to combine several conditional termination arguments, each obtained for a small component of the program independently, into a proof for the input program. In summary, we present the following contributions:

- A new method based on Max-SMT for finding preconditions for termination (cf. Sect. 3 and Algorithm 1).
- A framework to prove termination or non-termination by repeatedly simplifying the program analysis task by combining conditional termination arguments using the *unfolding* transformation (cf. Sect. 4 and Algorithm 2).
- An implementation of the technique in our tool VeryMax for C++ input programs and an extensive experimental evaluation showing that it is not only more powerful than existing tools, but also more efficient (cf. Sect. 5).

2   Preliminaries

SAT, Max-SAT, and Max-SMT. Let $\mathcal{P}$ be a fixed set of *propositional variables*. For $p \in \mathcal{P}$, p and $\neg p$ are *literals*. A *clause* is a disjunction of literals $l_1 \vee \cdots \vee l_n$. A (CNF) *propositional formula* is a conjunction of clauses $C_1 \wedge \cdots \wedge C_m$. The problem of *propositional satisfiability (SAT)* is to determine whether a propositional formula F has a *model*, i.e., an assignment M that satisfies F, denoted by $M \models F$. An extension of SAT is *Satisfiability Modulo Theories (SMT)* [6], where one checks the satisfiability of a formula with literals from a given background theory. Another extension is *(weighted partial) Max-SAT* [6], where some clauses in the input formula are *soft clauses* with an assigned weight, and the others are *hard clauses*. Here, we look for a model of the hard clauses that maximizes the sum of the weights of the satisfied soft clauses. Finally, *Max-SMT* combines Max-SAT and SMT. In a *Max-SMT* problem a formula is of the form $H_1 \wedge \ldots \wedge H_n \wedge [S_1, \omega_1] \wedge \ldots \wedge [S_m, \omega_m]$, where the hard clauses H_i and the soft clauses S_j (with weight ω_j) are disjunctions of literals over a background theory, and the aim is to find a model of the hard clauses that maximizes the sum of the weights of the satisfied soft clauses.

Programs and States. We fix a set of integer program *variables* $\mathcal{V} = \{v_1, \ldots, v_n\}$ and denote by $F(\mathcal{V})$ the conjunctions of linear inequalities over the variables $\mathcal{V}$.

Let $\mathcal{L}$ be the set of program *locations*, which contains a *canonical initial location* ℓ_{init}. Program *transitions* are tuples (ℓ_s, ρ, ℓ_t), where ℓ_s and $\ell_t \in \mathcal{L}$ are the source and target locations respectively, and $\rho \in F(\mathcal{V} \cup \mathcal{V}')$ describes the transition relation. Here $\mathcal{V}' = \{v'_1, \ldots, v'_n\}$ represent the values of the program variables after the transition.[1]

A *program* $\mathcal{P}$ is a set of transitions.[2] The set of locations in these transitions is denoted by $\mathcal{L}(\mathcal{P})$. We identify a program with its *control-flow graph* (CFG), a directed graph in which nodes are the locations and edges are the transitions.[3] A *program component* $\mathcal{C}$ of a program $\mathcal{P}$ is the set of transitions of a *strongly connected component* (SCC) of the CFG of $\mathcal{P}$. Its *entry transitions* $\mathcal{E}_{\mathcal{C}}$ are those transitions $\tau = (\ell_s, \rho, \ell_t)$ such that $\tau \notin \mathcal{C}$ but $\ell_t \in \mathcal{L}(\mathcal{C})$ (and in this case ℓ_t is called an *entry location*), while its *exit transitions* $\mathcal{X}_{\mathcal{C}}$ are such that $\tau \notin \mathcal{C}$ but $\ell_s \in \mathcal{L}(\mathcal{C})$ (and then ℓ_s is an *exit location*).

A *state* $s = (\ell, v)$ consists of a location $\ell \in \mathcal{L}$ and a valuation $v : \mathcal{V} \to \mathbb{Z}$. *Initial* states are of the form (ℓ_{init}, v). We denote a *computation step* with transition $\tau = (\ell_s, \rho, \ell_t)$ by $(\ell_s, v) \to_{\tau} (\ell_t, w)$, where $(v, w) \models \rho$. We use $\to_{\mathcal{P}}$ if we do not care about the executed transition of $\mathcal{P}$, and $\to_{\mathcal{P}}^{*}$ to denote the transitive-reflexive closure of $\to_{\mathcal{P}}$. Sequences of computation steps are called *computations*.

Safety and Termination. An *assertion* (ℓ, φ) is a pair of a location ℓ and a formula $\varphi \in F(\mathcal{V})$. A program $\mathcal{P}$ is *safe* for the assertion (ℓ, φ) if for every computation starting at an initial state s_0 of the form $s_0 \to_{\mathcal{P}}^{*} (\ell, v)$, we have that $v \models \varphi$ holds. Safety can be proved using *conditional invariants* [12], which like ordinary invariants are inductive, but not necessarily initiated in all computations.

Definition 1 (Conditional Inductive Invariant). *Let $\mathcal{P}$ be a program. We say a map $\mathcal{Q} : \mathcal{L}(\mathcal{P}) \to F(\mathcal{V})$ is a* conditional (inductive) invariant *for $\mathcal{P}$ if for all $(\ell_s, v) \to_{\mathcal{P}} (\ell_t, w)$, we have $v \models \mathcal{Q}(\ell_s)$ implies $w \models \mathcal{Q}(\ell_t)$.*

A program $\mathcal{P}$ is *terminating* if any computation starting at an initial state is finite. An important tool for proving termination are *ranking functions*:

Definition 2 (Ranking Function). *Let $\mathcal{C}$ be a component of a program $\mathcal{P}$, and $\tau = (\ell_s, \rho, \ell_t) \in \mathcal{C}$. A function $\mathcal{R} : \mathbb{Z}^n \to \mathbb{Z}$ is a ranking function for τ if:*

$$- \rho \models \mathcal{R} \geq 0 \qquad\qquad \textit{[Boundedness]}$$
$$- \rho \models \mathcal{R} > \mathcal{R}' \qquad\qquad \textit{[Decrease]}$$

and for every $(\hat{\ell}_s, \hat{\rho}, \hat{\ell}_t) \in \mathcal{C}$,

$$- \hat{\rho} \models \mathcal{R} \geq \mathcal{R}' \qquad\qquad \textit{[Non-increase]}$$

---

[1] For $\varphi \in F(\mathcal{V})$, we denote by $\varphi' \in F(\mathcal{V}')$ the version of φ using primed variables.
[2] Hence in our programming model procedure calls are not allowed. Note however that programs with non-recursive calls can also be handled by inlining the calls.
[3] Since we label transitions only with conjunctions of linear inequalities, disjunctive conditions are represented using several transitions with the same source and target location. Thus, $\mathcal{P}$ is actually a multigraph.

The key property of ranking functions is that if a transition admits one, then it cannot be executed infinitely.

A core concept in our approach is *conditional termination*, i.e., the notion that once a condition holds, a program is definitely terminating. As we make heavy use of the program's control flow graph structure, we introduce this concept as location-dependent.

Definition 3 (Conditional Termination). *We say that a program $\mathcal{P}$ is (ℓ, φ)-conditionally terminating if every computation that contains a state (ℓ, v) with $v \models \varphi$ uses transitions from $\mathcal{P}$ only a finite number of times. In that case the assertion (ℓ, φ) is called a* precondition *for termination.*

3   Synthesizing Conditional Termination Arguments

Our approach for synthesizing conditional termination arguments works on one program component at a time. As proving that a program terminates is equivalent to showing that there is no program component where a computation can stay indefinitely, this turns out to be a convenient way to decompose termination proofs.

For a fixed program component $\mathcal{C}$, a conditional lexicographic termination argument is constructed iteratively by transition elimination as follows. In each iteration, we synthesize a linear ranking function together with supporting conditional invariants, requiring that they show that at least one transition of $\mathcal{C}$ is *finitely executable*, i.e., can only occur a finite number of times in any execution. The intuition here is that once we have proven that a transition τ can only be used finitely often, we only need to consider (possibly infinite) suffixes of program executions in which τ cannot appear anymore. If after some iterations no transition of $\mathcal{C}$ can be executed infinitely anymore, then the conjunction of all conditional invariants obtained at an entry location of $\mathcal{C}$ yields a precondition for termination. Indeed, once the conditional invariants hold at that entry location, then by inductiveness they hold from then on at all locations of $\mathcal{C}$, and hence the termination argument applies.

Example 1. Consider the program in Fig. 1 and its CFG, with initial location $\ell_{\text{init}} = \ell_0$. We want to find a precondition for termination of the component $\mathcal{C} = \{\tau_1, \tau_2\}$, corresponding to the **while** loop.

In a first iteration, we generate the ranking function y for τ_2, together with the supporting conditional invariant $z < 0$. Note that $z < 0$ is indeed a conditional invariant: it is preserved by τ_2 as z decreases its value, and is also trivially preserved by τ_1 since this transition is in fact disabled if $z < 0$. Under the condition $z < 0$, y is bounded and decreases in τ_2, and τ_1 is disabled and so finitely executable. Hence, $(\ell_1, z < 0)$ is a precondition for termination.   ∎

As observed in [9, 30], synthesizing lexicographic termination arguments together with supporting invariants requires to keep several copies of the program under analysis. Thus, in the analysis of a component $\mathcal{C}$, we keep a set $\mathcal{M}$ of

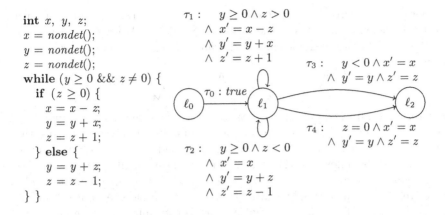

Fig. 1. Program and its CFG.

possibly infinitely executable transitions (i.e., those for which we have not proved conditional termination yet), called the *termination component*. Nonetheless, to compute sound invariants (i.e., soundly reason about reachable states), we need to take all transitions into account. However, these transitions can be strengthened with the supporting invariants that we synthesized in earlier proof steps. Hence, we keep another copy $\mathcal{I}$, called the *conditional invariant component*, which is like the original component $\mathcal{C}$, except for the addition of the conditional invariants found in previous iterations. Initially both the termination and the conditional invariant components are identical copies of the component $\mathcal{C}$.

The proposed method for generating preconditions for termination is an extension of the constraint-based approach for proving (unconditional) termination presented in [30]. The individual constraints used in our method are displayed in Fig. 2, corresponding to the standard constraints employed in constraint-based techniques [8]. For all locations ℓ in $\mathcal{C}$, we introduce templates I_ℓ corresponding to fixed-length conjunctions of linear inequalities on the program variables; i.e., I_ℓ is of the form $\bigwedge_{1 \leq i \leq k}(a_i + \sum_{v \in \mathcal{V}} a_{i,v} v \leq 0)$ for some k and where the a_* are integer template variables that do not appear in $\mathcal{V}$.

For $\tau = (\ell_s, \rho, \ell_t)$:

Initiation:	$\mathbb{I}_\tau$	$\stackrel{def}{=}$	ρ	$\Rightarrow I'_{\ell_t}$
Consecution:	$\mathbb{C}_\tau$	$\stackrel{def}{=}$	$I_{\ell_s} \wedge \rho$	$\Rightarrow I'_{\ell_t}$
Boundedness:	$\mathbb{B}_\tau$	$\stackrel{def}{=}$	$I_{\ell_s} \wedge \rho$	$\Rightarrow R \geq 0$
Decrease:	$\mathbb{D}_\tau$	$\stackrel{def}{=}$	$I_{\ell_s} \wedge \rho$	$\Rightarrow R > R'$
Non-increase:	$\mathbb{N}_\tau$	$\stackrel{def}{=}$	$I_{\ell_s} \wedge \rho$	$\Rightarrow R \geq R'$

Fig. 2. Constraints used for generating preconditions for termination.

Furthermore, we also define a template R for a linear ranking function[4] with integer coefficients, i.e., R is of the form $a + \sum_{v \in \mathcal{V}} a_v v$. For a given component $\mathcal{C}$ with entries $\mathcal{E}_\mathcal{C}$, we combine these constraints in the (non-linear) formula $\mathbb{F}$ as follows:

$$\mathbb{F} \stackrel{def}{=} \bigwedge_{\tau \in \mathcal{E}_\mathcal{C}} \mathbb{I}_\tau \wedge \bigwedge_{\tau \in \mathcal{I}} \mathbb{C}_\tau \wedge \bigwedge_{\tau \in \mathcal{M}} \mathbb{N}_\tau \wedge \bigvee_{\tau \in \mathcal{M}} (\mathbb{B}_\tau \wedge \mathbb{D}_\tau).$$

However, not all of these constraints are treated as hard constraints. Most notably, we turn $\bigwedge_{\tau \in \mathcal{E}_\mathcal{C}} \mathbb{I}_\tau$ into soft constraints. Intuitively this means that, if possible, we want to synthesize a true (unconditional) supporting invariant, but will also allow invariants that do not always hold. However, we keep $\bigwedge_{\tau \in \mathcal{I}} \mathbb{C}_\tau$ as a hard constraint, ensuring that our conditional invariants are indeed inductive, i.e., keep on holding after they have been satisfied once. Similarly, $\bigwedge_{\tau \in \mathcal{M}} \mathbb{N}_\tau \wedge \bigvee_{\tau \in \mathcal{M}} (\mathbb{B}_\tau \wedge \mathbb{D}_\tau)$ are kept as hard constraints, enforcing that a true ranking function is found, though it may only hold in those cases where the supporting invariant is initiated. The conditions for the supporting invariants will eventually become our preconditions for termination.

Algorithm 1 shows our procedure CondTerm for generating preconditions for termination. It takes as inputs the component $\mathcal{C}$ under consideration and its entry transitions $\mathcal{E}_\mathcal{C}$, and returns a conditional invariant $\mathcal{Q}$ that ensures that no infinite computation can remain within $\mathcal{C}$.

Algorithm 1. Procedure CondTerm for computing preconditions for termination

---

Input: component $\mathcal{C}$, entry transitions $\mathcal{E}_\mathcal{C}$
Output: None | $\mathcal{Q}$, where $\mathcal{Q}$ maps locations in $\mathcal{L}(\mathcal{C})$ to conjunctions of inequalities
1: $(\mathcal{I}, \mathcal{M}) \leftarrow (\mathcal{C}, \mathcal{C})$
2: $\mathcal{Q} \leftarrow \{\, \ell \mapsto true \mid \ell \in \mathcal{L}(\mathcal{C}) \,\}$
3: **while** $\mathcal{M} \neq \varnothing$ **do**
4:     construct formula $\mathbb{F}$ from $\mathcal{I}, \mathcal{M}, \mathcal{E}_\mathcal{C}$
5:     $\sigma \leftarrow$ Max-SMT-solver$(\mathbb{F})$
6:     **if** σ is a solution **then**
7:         $\mathcal{I} \leftarrow \{\, (\ell_s, \ \rho \wedge \sigma(I_{\ell_s}), \ \ell_t) \mid (\ell_s, \rho, \ell_t) \in \mathcal{I} \,\}$
8:         $\mathcal{M} \leftarrow \{\, (\ell_s, \ \rho \wedge \sigma(I_{\ell_s}), \ \ell_t) \mid (\ell_s, \rho, \ell_t) \in \mathcal{M} \,\}$
9:         $\mathcal{M} \leftarrow \mathcal{M} - \{\, \tau \in \mathcal{M} \mid \sigma(R) \text{ is a ranking function for } \tau \,\}$
10:       $\mathcal{Q} \leftarrow \{\, \ell \mapsto \mathcal{Q}(\ell) \wedge \sigma(I_\ell) \mid \ell \in \mathcal{L}(\mathcal{C}) \,\}$
11:     **else return** None
12: **return** $\mathcal{Q}$

In Algorithm 1, we continue to extend the termination argument as long as there are still potentially infinitely executable transitions (line 3). For this, we build a Max-SMT problem $\mathbb{F}$ to generate a ranking function and its supporting

---

[4] While using a different ranking function for each program location is possible, we have found that the added power does not justify the increased complexity of the ensuing SMT problem.

conditional invariants. If no solution can be found, then the procedure gives up (line 11). Otherwise, a solution σ to $\mathbb{F}$ yields a linear function $\sigma(R)$ (the instantiation of the template ranking function R determined by σ) together with conditional invariants $\sigma(I_{\ell_s})$. Since the $\sigma(I_{\ell_s})$ are conditional invariants, they can be used to strengthen transitions $\tau = (\ell_s, \rho, \ell_t)$ by conjoining $\sigma(I_{\ell_s})$ to ρ, both in the conditional invariant component and in the termination component (lines 7–8). Most importantly, we identify the subset of the transitions τ from $\mathcal{M}$ for which $\sigma(R)$ is a ranking function, and hence can be removed from $\mathcal{M}$ (line 9). Finally, conditional invariants from previous iterations are accumulated so that, in the end, a global conjunction can be returned (lines 10 and 12).

In essence, this process corresponds to the step-wise construction of a lexicographic termination argument. For a location ℓ at which the component $\mathcal{C}$ is entered, the conjunction of all obtained $\sigma(I_\ell)$ is then a precondition for termination. The following theorem states the correctness of procedure CondTerm:

Theorem 1 (CondTerm soundness). *Let $\mathcal{P}$ be a program, $\mathcal{C}$ a component, and $\mathcal{E}_\mathcal{C}$ its entry transitions. If the procedure call $\mathsf{CondTerm}(\mathcal{C}, \mathcal{E}_\mathcal{C})$ returns $\mathcal{Q} \neq \mathsf{None}$, then $\mathcal{C}$ is $(\ell, \mathcal{Q}(\ell))$-conditionally terminating for any $\ell \in \mathcal{L}(\mathcal{C})$.*

Of course, Algorithm 1 is an idealized, high-level description of our procedure. In an implementation of the procedure CondTerm, a number of small changes help to improve the overall number of solved instances.

Constraint Strengthening. Additional constraints can be added to formula $\mathbb{F}$ to favor conditional invariants that are more likely to be useful. In particular, a constraint requiring that the conditional invariants are compatible with the entry transitions and with the previously generated conditional invariants has proven useful, i.e.

$$\bigvee_{(\ell_s, \rho, \ell_t) \in \mathcal{E}_\mathcal{C}} \exists \mathcal{V}, \mathcal{V}' \left(I'_{\ell_t} \wedge \rho \wedge \mathcal{Q}(\ell_t)' \right).$$

Constraint Softening. Similarly, we can increase the allowed range of models by turning more of the clauses into soft clauses. For example, this can be used to allow *quasi-ranking functions* [30] in addition to ranking functions. Quasi-ranking functions are functions that satisfy the non-increase condition, but may fail to decrease or be bounded, or both. By using them to partition transitions and perform case analysis, programs can also be shown to be terminating.

Pseudo-Invariants of Termination Component. In some circumstances, inductive properties of the termination component $\mathcal{M}$ (i.e., satisfying **Consecution** only for transitions in $\mathcal{M}$) can be sound and useful; namely, when the complement of the property disables a transition.

Formally, let $\mathcal{Q}$ be a map from $\mathcal{L}(\mathcal{P})$ to $F(\mathcal{V})$ such that $\mathcal{Q}(\tilde{\ell}_s) \wedge \tilde{\rho} \Rightarrow \mathcal{Q}(\tilde{\ell}_t)'$ for all $(\tilde{\ell}_s, \tilde{\rho}, \tilde{\ell}_t) \in \mathcal{M}$, and $\neg \mathcal{Q}(\ell_s) \wedge \rho \models \mathit{false}$ for some $\tau = (\ell_s, \rho, \ell_t) \in \mathcal{M}$. Moreover, assume that $\mathcal{Q}$ supports a ranking function $\mathcal{R}$ for τ. Then τ can only be used finitely often. To see this, assume that there is an infinite computation in which τ occurs infinitely often. Then there is a state at location ℓ_s in the computation from which only transitions in $\mathcal{M}$ are taken. Since $\mathcal{Q}$ is inductive over transitions in $\mathcal{M}$, if $\mathcal{Q}(\ell_s)$ holds at that state then it holds from then on, and therefore $\mathcal{R}$ proves that τ cannot be executed an infinite number of times. Otherwise, if $\mathcal{Q}(\ell_s)$ does not hold, then τ cannot be executed at all. This weaker requirement on $\mathcal{Q}$ allows removing transitions from $\mathcal{M}$ and is easier to satisfy. Still, it is insufficient to do a case analysis as a full conditional invariant allows.

4   Proving Termination Using Conditional Termination

Our key contribution is to leverage conditional termination arguments to perform a natural case analysis of program executions. In this way, as our analysis progresses, more and more program runs are excluded from the program analysis, allowing the method to focus on those parts of the program for which termination has not been guaranteed yet. The core component of this is a syntactic program transformation we call *unfolding* that implements the semantic intuition of distinguishing program states for which termination has not been proven yet.

4.1   Program Unfoldings

We begin this subsection with an example that illustrates how conditional invariants can be used to unfold the component under consideration.

Example 2. Consider the program from Fig. 1 again. In Example 1 it was shown that all computations for which $z < 0$ holds at location ℓ_1 are finite. In fact, a byproduct of the proof was that $z < 0$ is a conditional invariant at location ℓ_1. We show how to exploit this to prove *unconditional* termination next.

Following the intuition of a case analysis, we unfold the program component by introducing a copy of it in which we assume that the conditional invariant holds. In our example, we duplicate the location ℓ_1, introducing a copy denoted by $\widehat{\ell_1}$. We also duplicate all transitions in, from and to the component, using the newly introduced location. However, all copied transitions should also reflect our case analysis, and are thus strengthened by the conditional invariant $z < 0$. In our case analysis, the original component now corresponds to the case that the conditional invariant does *not* hold, and thus, all of the original transitions are strengthened to assume the negation of the conditional invariant. Finally, to allow for computations where the invariant eventually becomes true, we add copies of the transitions from the original component to the copied location, again strengthened by the invariant. The resulting program is shown in Fig. 3(a).

The original program and its unfolding behave equivalently, in particular regarding termination. However, we already know from Example 1 that under the assumption $z > 0$, the new component has no infinite executions. Hence, we can *narrow* the set of potentially infinite computations and focus on the program shown in Fig. 3(b), obtained by removing all known-terminating locations

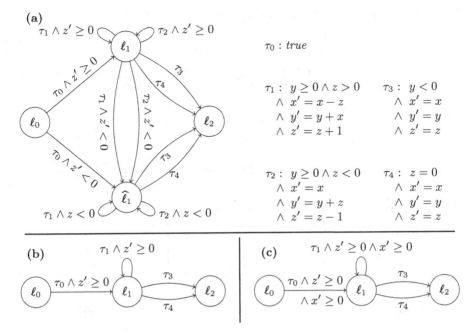

Fig. 3. Unfolding of the program from Fig. 1 for conditional invariant $z < 0$ at ℓ_1 (a), ensuing narrowing/simplification (b) and narrowing after unfolding for $x < 0$ at ℓ_1 (c).

(i.e., $\widehat{\ell_1}$) from the unfolding and simplifying. If this narrowed program terminates, we can conclude that the original program terminates too.

Synthesizing another conditional termination argument for the program from Fig. 3(b) now yields the ranking function y, supported by the conditional invariant $x < 0$ at ℓ_1. Then we can unfold with $x < 0$ again and narrow, obtaining the program in Fig. 3(c). Finally this program can be proven terminating with ranking function x without the need of any conditional invariant and, hence, without precondition. This concludes the proof of termination of the original program.

Note that the unfolding/narrowing mechanism provides not only a termination proof but also a characterization of the program execution phases. In particular, our example can be viewed to have three phases, corresponding to the unfoldings we have applied. One phase corresponds to the case where $z < 0$ (where the **else**-block is repeatedly used), one to the case $z > 0 \land x < 0$, and finally, one corresponds to the case $z > 0 \land x \geq 0$. ∎

To formalize this execution phase-structured proof technique, we first define the *unfolding* program transformation:

Definition 4. *Let* $\mathcal{P}$ *be a program,* $\mathcal{C}$ *a component of* $\mathcal{P}$*,* $\mathcal{E}_\mathcal{C}$ *its entry transitions,* $\mathcal{X}_\mathcal{C}$ *its exit transitions, and* $\mathcal{Q} : \mathcal{L}(\mathcal{C}) \to F(\mathcal{V})$ *a conditional invariant for* $\mathcal{C}$*. The unfolding of* $\mathcal{P}$ *is*

$$\widehat{P} = \quad \{ \, (\ell_s, \; \rho \wedge \neg \, \mathcal{Q}(\ell_t)', \; \ell_t),$$
$$(\ell_s, \; \rho \wedge \quad \mathcal{Q}(\ell_t)', \; \widehat{\ell_t}),$$
$$(\widehat{\ell_s}, \; \rho \wedge \quad \mathcal{Q}(\ell_s), \; \widehat{\ell_t}) \mid (\ell_s, \rho, \ell_t) \in \mathcal{C} \, \}$$
$$\cup \{ \, (\ell_s, \; \rho \wedge \neg \mathcal{Q}(\ell_t)', \; \ell_t),$$
$$(\ell_s, \; \rho \wedge \quad \mathcal{Q}(\ell_t)', \; \widehat{\ell_t}) \mid (\ell_s, \rho, \ell_t) \in \mathcal{E}_{\mathcal{C}} \, \}$$
$$\cup \{ \, (\ell_s, \; \rho, \ell_t),$$
$$(\widehat{\ell_s}, \; \rho, \ell_t) \mid (\ell_s, \rho, \ell_t) \in \mathcal{X}_{\mathcal{C}} \, \}$$
$$\cup \{ \tau \mid \tau \in \mathcal{P} \backslash (\mathcal{C} \cup \mathcal{E}_{\mathcal{C}} \cup \mathcal{X}_{\mathcal{C}}) \}$$

where for each $\ell \in \mathcal{L}(\mathcal{C})$ there is a fresh location $\widehat{\ell}$ such that $\widehat{\ell} \notin \mathcal{L}(\mathcal{P})$.

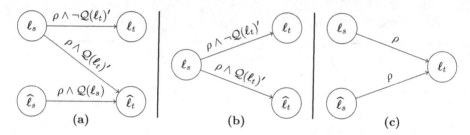

Fig. 4. Transitions in unfolding $\widehat{\mathcal{P}}$ for conditional invariant $\mathcal{Q}$ corresponding to a transition $\tau = (\ell_s, \rho, \ell_t) \in \mathcal{P}$, depending on whether (a) $\tau \in \mathcal{C}$, (b) $\tau \in \mathcal{E}_{\mathcal{C}}$, (c) $\tau \in \mathcal{X}_{\mathcal{C}}$.

Figure 4 represents graphically how a transition of the original program is transformed, depending on whether it is a transition of the component, an entry transition, or an exit transition. The following result states that a program and its unfolding are semantically equivalent, i.e., that the encoded case analysis is complete.

Theorem 2. *Given states (ℓ_0, v_0) and (ℓ_k, v_k) such that $\ell_0, \ell_k \in \mathcal{L}(\mathcal{P})$, there is a computation in $\mathcal{P}$ of length k of the form $(\ell_0, v_0) \to_{\mathcal{P}}^* (\ell_k, v_k)$ if and only if there is a computation in $\widehat{\mathcal{P}}$ of length k of the form $(\ell_0, v_0) \to_{\widehat{\mathcal{P}}}^* (\ell_k, v_k)$ or of the form $(\ell_0, v_0) \to_{\widehat{\mathcal{P}}}^* (\widehat{\ell_k}, v_k)$.*

Now we are ready to formally define the narrowing of a program:

Definition 5. *Let $\mathcal{P}$ be a program, $\mathcal{C}$ a component of $\mathcal{P}$, $\mathcal{E}_{\mathcal{C}}$ its entry transitions, and $\mathcal{Q} : \mathcal{L}(\mathcal{C}) \to F(\mathcal{V})$ a conditional invariant for $\mathcal{C}$. The* narrowing *of $\mathcal{P}$ is:*

$$narrow(\mathcal{P}) = \{ \, (\ell_s, \; \rho \wedge \neg \, \mathcal{Q}(\ell_t)', \; \ell_t) \mid (\ell_s, \rho, \ell_t) \in \mathcal{C} \cup \mathcal{E}_{\mathcal{C}} \, \} \cup$$
$$\{ \tau \mid \tau \in \mathcal{P} - (\mathcal{C} \cup \mathcal{E}_{\mathcal{C}}) \}$$

The narrowing of a program can be viewed as the result of eliminating the copies $\widehat{\ell}$ of the locations $\ell \in \mathcal{L}(\mathcal{C})$ in the unfolding $\widehat{\mathcal{P}}$ and their corresponding transitions. Alternatively, one may take the original program $\mathcal{P}$ and consider that for any transition $\tau = (\ell_s, \rho, \ell_t) \in \mathcal{C} \cup \mathcal{E}_{\mathcal{C}}$, the relation is replaced by $\rho \wedge \neg \, \mathcal{Q}(\ell_t)'$.

The intuition is that, if a call to CondTerm$(\mathcal{C}, \mathcal{E}_C)$ has been successful (i.e., $\mathcal{Q} \stackrel{def}{=}$ CondTerm$(\mathcal{C}, \mathcal{E}_C) \neq$ None), by the inductiveness of $\mathcal{Q}$ a computation that satisfies $\mathcal{Q}(\ell)$ for a certain $\ell \in \mathcal{C}$ cannot remain within $\mathcal{C}$ indefinitely. Hence we only need to consider computations such that whenever a location $\ell \in \mathcal{C}$ is reached, we have that $\mathcal{Q}(\ell)$ does not hold.

Corollary 1. *Let $\mathcal{P}$ be a program, $\mathcal{C}$ a component of $\mathcal{P}$, $\mathcal{E}_C$ its entry transitions, and $\mathcal{Q} : \mathcal{L}(\mathcal{C}) \rightarrow F(\mathcal{V})$ a conditional invariant for $\mathcal{C}$ obtained from a call to* CondTerm$(\mathcal{C}, \mathcal{E}_C)$. *There is an infinite computation in $\mathcal{P}$ that eventually only uses transitions from $\mathcal{C}$ if and only if there is such a computation in narrow$(\mathcal{P})$ using transitions from narrow$(\mathcal{C})$.*

Proof. The right to left implication holds by Theorem 2 as narrow$(\mathcal{P}) \subseteq \widehat{\mathcal{P}}$. For the left to right implication, by Theorem 2 an infinite computation of $\mathcal{P}$ staying in $\mathcal{C}$ yields an infinite computation of $\widehat{\mathcal{P}}$ staying in $\widehat{\mathcal{C}}$. By induction, for any location $\ell \in \mathcal{L}(\mathcal{C})$ we have that $\mathcal{Q}(\ell)$ is an (unconditional) invariant at location $\widehat{\ell}$ of $\widehat{\mathcal{P}}$: now the initiation condition also holds by definition because all transitions arriving at $\widehat{\ell}$ require $\mathcal{Q}(\ell)$ to hold. By Theorem 1, no infinite computation in $\widehat{\mathcal{P}}$ staying in $\widehat{\mathcal{C}}$ can reach a location of the form $\widehat{\ell}$, where $\ell \in \mathcal{L}(\mathcal{C})$. So such an infinite computation is a computation of narrow$(\mathcal{P})$ that eventually only uses transitions from narrow$(\mathcal{C})$. $\square$

Our termination proofs are sequences of relatively simple program transformations and termination proving techniques. This formal simplicity allows one to easily implement, extend and certify the technique. As discussed in Example 2, the unfolding/narrowing mechanism provides not only a termination proof, but also a characterization of the execution phases. In contrast to other works [37], these phases are obtained semantically from the generated conditional invariants, and do not require syntactic heuristics.

4.2   Proving Program Termination

So far we have discussed the handling of a single component at a time. By combining our method with an off-the-shelf safety checker, full program termination can be proven too. The next example illustrates this while comparing with previous Max-SMT-based techniques for proving termination [30].

Example 3. The method from [30] considers components following a topological ordering. Each component is dealt with locally: only its transitions and entries are taken into account, independently of the rest of the program. The analysis of a component concludes when the

```
int x = nondet();
int y = nondet();
int z = nondet();
assume(x > z && z ≥ 0);
while (z > 0) {
    x = x − 1;
    z = z − 1; }
ℓ : while (y < 0)
    y = y + x;
```

Fig. 5. Program that cannot be proven terminating with the approach in [30].

Algorithm 2. Procedure Term for proving or disproving program termination

---

Input: program $\mathcal{P}$
Output: Yes (resp., No) if $\mathcal{P}$ terminates (resp., does not terminate), or $\bot$ if unknown
1: $\mathcal{S} \leftarrow$ stack of components of $\mathcal{P}$
2: **while** $\mathcal{S} \neq \emptyset \wedge \neg timed\_out()$ **do**
3:     $\mathcal{C} \leftarrow \text{Pop}(\mathcal{S})$
4:     $\mathcal{E} \leftarrow \mathcal{E}_{\mathcal{C}}$
5:     $\mathcal{Q} \leftarrow \text{CondTerm}(\mathcal{C}, \mathcal{E})$
6:     **while** $\mathcal{Q} \neq$ None **do**
7:         **if** $\forall \ell \in \mathcal{L}(\mathcal{C}) \cap \mathcal{L}(\mathcal{E})$: $\mathcal{P}$ is safe for assertion$(\ell, \mathcal{Q}(\ell))$ **then**   {Call safety check}
8:             **break**
9:         $\mathcal{C} \leftarrow \{ (\ell_s, \ \rho \wedge \neg \mathcal{Q}(\ell_t)', \ \ell_t) \ | \ (\ell_s, \rho, \ell_t) \in \mathcal{C} \}$ {Narrow component}
10:         $\mathcal{E} \leftarrow \{ (\ell_s, \ \rho \wedge \neg \mathcal{Q}(\ell_t)', \ \ell_t) \ | \ (\ell_s, \rho, \ell_t) \in \mathcal{E} \}$ {Narrow entries}
11:         $\mathcal{Q} \leftarrow \text{CondTerm}(\mathcal{C}, \mathcal{E})$
12:     **if** $\mathcal{Q} =$ None **then return** (ProvedNonTermination$(\mathcal{C}, \mathcal{E}, \mathcal{P})$? No : $\bot$)
13: **return** ($\mathcal{S} = \emptyset$? Yes : $\bot$)

---

component is proven (unconditionally) terminating. Hence, for the program in Fig. 5, the first loop is proven terminating using the ranking function z. However, if no additional information is inferred, then the proof of termination of the second loop cannot succeed: the necessary invariant that $x \geq 1$ between the two loops, at program location ℓ, is missing.

On the other hand, the approach proposed here is able to handle this program successfully. Indeed, the first loop can be proven terminating with z as a ranking function as observed above. Regarding the second loop, the conditional invariant $x \geq 1$ together with the ranking function $-y$ are generated. To prove $x \geq 1$ holds at ℓ a safety checker may be used, which then makes a global analysis to verify the truth of the assertion. Finally full termination can be established. Note that components may be considered in any order, not necessarily a topological one.   ∎

Example 3 illustrates that combining our conditional termination proving technique with a safety checker is necessary to efficiently handle long and complex programs.

It is also important to note that, as the proof of Corollary 1 indicates, the narrowed program is termination-equivalent to the original program. In particular, this means that a non-termination proof for the narrowed program is a non-termination proof for the original program, as only terminating computations have been discarded by the transformation. Further, our program transformation does not only add information to the entry transitions (as in [32]) but also to all transitions occurring in the component under analysis. This significantly improves the precision of our otherwise unchanged non-termination analysis (cf. Sect. 5).

Altogether, our procedure for proving or disproving program termination is described in Algorithm 2. It takes as input a program $\mathcal{P}$ and returns Yes if the program can be proved to terminate, No if it can be proved not to terminate, or $\bot$ otherwise. Components are handled in sequence one at a time provided the time limit has not been exceeded (line 2). For each component, preconditions for termination are computed (lines 5 and 11), which are then checked to hold by calling an external safety checker (line 7). If this test is passed, the component is guaranteed to terminate and the next one can be considered. Otherwise narrowing is applied (lines 9–10) and the process is repeated. If at some point the generation of preconditions for termination fails, then non-termination is attempted by calling an out-of-the-box non-termination prover (line 12). Note that the outer loop can easily be parallelized (i.e., all components can be considered at the same time), and that similarly, the generation of more preconditions can be attempted in parallel to the safety checks for already generated termination conditions. The correctness of Algorithm 2 follows directly from Corollary 1.

5 Related Work and Experimental Results

We build on a rich tradition of methods to prove termination [1, 10, 16, 18, 21, 22, 25, 26, 28, 32, 36, 39, 42–44] and non-termination [4, 13, 14, 24, 29, 46] of imperative programs. Most notably, our constraint-based approach to conditional termination is an extension of existing work on ranking function synthesis using constraint solvers [2, 3, 5, 8, 23, 30, 33, 35], and is most closely related to our earlier work on using Max-SMT solving to infer quasi-ranking functions [30]. There, an independent invariant generation procedure was used before unconditional termination arguments were synthesized for program components. Thus, invariants were not generated "on demand" and the method fails on examples such as Example 3.

The key contribution of our method is to use conditional termination arguments to segment the state space for the remainder of the analysis. A related idea was used in TRex [25] and HipTNT+ [32], which alternate termination and non-termination proving techniques in their proof search. However, both approaches only use preconditions for *non-termination* to segment the state space, and thus are reliant on non-termination techniques. As finding non-termination arguments is an $\exists\forall\exists$ problem (there exists a state set such that for all its states there exists a computation leading back to it), these methods tend to be significantly weaker in practice than those based on termination, which is an $\exists\forall$ problem (there exists a ranking function such that all computations decrease it).

A related idea is counterexample-guided termination proving [10, 16, 26, 28, 36], in which a speculated termination argument is refined until it covers all program executions. Thus, these methods *grow* a set of terminating program states, whereas our method *shrinks* the set of potentially non-terminating states. In practice, "ignoring" the terminating states in a safety prover is often a non-trivial semantic operation, in contrast to the effects of our syntactic *narrowing* operation.

Proving conditional termination has seen less interest than full termination analysis. A first technique combined constraint-based methods for finding potential ranking functions with quantifier elimination [15] to infer preconditions. More recently, policy iteration-based methods [34], backwards reasoning in the abstract interpretation framework [45] and an adaptation of conflict-driven learning from satisfiability solving [17] have been adapted to find conditions for termination. Our algorithm CondTerm differs in its relative simplicity (by delegating the majority of the work to a constraint solver), and our procedure Term could combine it with or replace it by other approaches. Finally, in a related line of work, decision procedures for conditional termination on restricted programming languages (e.g., only using linear or affine operations) have been developed [7].

Evaluation. To evaluate our method, we have implemented Algorithm 2 in the tool VeryMax, using it as a safety prover [12] and a non-termination prover [29]. The effectiveness of VeryMax depends crucially on the underlying non-linear Max-SMT solver, described in [31]. All experiments were carried out on the StarExec cluster [40], whose nodes are equipped with Intel Xeon 2.4GHz processors.[5] We have compared VeryMax with a range of competing termination provers on three benchmark sets. The first two example sets are the benchmark suites INTEGER TRANSITION SYSTEMS and C INTEGER used in termCOMP 2016 [41], on which we compare with a superset of the tools [22,26,27,32,44] that competed in these categories in the 2016 edition[6]. Following the rules of the competition, we use a wall clock timeout of 300s for the C INTEGER benchmark set, and a wall clock timeout of 30s for the INTEGER TRANSITION SYSTEMS benchmark set. The results of these experiments are displayed in Table 1, where the "Term" (resp. "NTerm") column indicates the number of examples proven terminating (resp. non-terminating), "Fail" any kind of prover failure, and "TO"

Table 1. Experimental results on benchmarks from termCOMP 2016.

Tool	C INTEGER					INTEGER TRANSITION SYSTEMS				
	Term	NTerm	Fail	TO	Total (s)	Term	NTerm	Fail	TO	Total (s)
AProVE	210	73	39	13	7547.68	623	386	11	202	9651.05
Ctrl	–	–	–	–	–	348	0	421	453	17229.10
HipTNT+	210	95	25	5	2615.80	–	–	–	–	–
SeaHorn	171	73	19	72	22499.33	–	–	–	–	–
Ultimate	208	98	23	6	4745.79	–	–	–	–	–
VeryMax	**213**	**100**	**22**	**0**	**2354.94**	**620**	**412**	**103**	**87**	**8481.39**

---

[5] A binary of VeryMax as well as the detailed results of the experiments can be found at http://www.cs.upc.edu/~albert/VeryMax.html.

[6] Due to incompatibilities of input formats, some tools could not be run on some of the benchmark sets. This is indicated in the tables with a dash −.

the number of times the timeout was reached. Finally, "Total (s)" indicates the total time spent on all examples, in seconds.

We additionally evaluated our tool on the examples from the TERMINATION category of the Software Verification Competition 2016, comparing to the participants in 2016 [22, 26, 44] with a CPU timeout of 900 s. As VeryMax has no support for recursion and pointers at the moment, we removed 273 examples

Table 2. Results on SV-COMP benchmarks.

Tool	Term	NTerm	Fail	TO	Total (s)
AProVE	222	76	41	19	10235.44
SeaHorn	189	75	22	72	34760.69
Ultimate	224	103	25	6	7882.13
VeryMax	**231**	**101**	**26**	**0**	**2444.29**

using these features and tested the tools on the remaining 358 examples. The results of this experiment are shown in Table 2. Altogether, the overall experimental results show that our method is not only the most powerful combined termination and non-termination prover, but also more efficient than all competing tools.

Moreover, to analyze the effect of our narrowing technique on non-termination proofs, we experimented with the INTEGER TRANSITION SYSTEMS benchmark set. Namely, in Table 3 we compare the performance

Table 3. Impact of narrowing on non-termination proofs.

	NTerm	Exclusive
Narrowing	412	82
Original	334	4

of VeryMax when trying to prove non-termination of narrowed components (Narrowing row) against using the original component (Original row). For each case, column "NTerm" indicates the examples proven non-terminating, and column "Exclusive" identifies those that could only be proven with that approach. The results show that removing (conditionally) terminating computations from the analysis significantly improves the effectiveness of the analysis. Still, the more complex narrowed components make the non-termination procedure in VeryMax time out in 4 cases that are otherwise proved non-terminating when using the original program components.

Finally, we studied the gain obtained with constraint strengthening, constraint softening and pseudo-invariants of the termination component (see Sect. 3). While constraint softening and pseudo-invariants help in proving termination in few cases at the cost of a time overhead, constraint strengthening significantly improves both the number of problems proved terminating and the time required to do so.

6   Conclusions and Future Work

We have proposed a new method for modular termination proofs of integer programs. A program is decomposed into program components, and conditional termination arguments are sought for each component separately. Termination arguments are synthesized iteratively using a template-based approach with a Max-SMT solver as a constraint solving engine. At each iteration, conditional invariants and ranking functions are generated which prove termination for a subset of program execution states. The key step of our technique is to exclude these states from the remaining termination analysis. This is achieved by narrowing, i.e., strengthening the transitions of the component and its entry transitions with the negation of the conditional invariant. This operation of narrowing can be viewed as unfolding the program in two phases, namely when the conditional termination argument holds and when it does not, and focusing on the latter, for which termination is not guaranteed yet.

In the future, we want to remove some of the limitations of our method. For example, we do not support the heap at this time, and combining our conditional termination proving procedure with a heap analysis would greatly extend the applicability of our approach. Moreover, as in many other techniques, numbers are treated as mathematical integers, not machine integers. However, a transformation that handles machine integers correctly by inserting explicit normalization steps at possible overflows [19] could be added. We are also interested in formally verifying our technique and to produce certificates for termination that can be checked by theorem provers [11]. Finally, we plan to extend our technique to proving bounds on program complexity. Finding such bounds is closely related to termination proving, and also requires to distinguish different phases of the execution precisely [20,38]. Our termination proving method does this naturally, and an adaption to complexity could thus yield more precise bounds.

References

1. Albert, E., Arenas, P., Codish, M., Genaim, S., Puebla, G., Zanardini, D.: Termination analysis of Java Bytecode. In: Barthe, G., Boer, F.S. (eds.) FMOODS 2008. LNCS, vol. 5051, pp. 2–18. Springer, Heidelberg (2008). doi:10.1007/978-3-540-68863-1_2

2. Alias, C., Darte, A., Feautrier, P., Gonnord, L.: Multi-dimensional rankings, program termination, and complexity bounds of flowchart programs. In: Cousot, R., Martel, M. (eds.) SAS 2010. LNCS, vol. 6337, pp. 117–133. Springer, Heidelberg (2010). doi:10.1007/978-3-642-15769-1_8

3. Bagnara, R., Mesnard, F., Pescetti, A., Zaffanella, E.: A new look at the automatic synthesis of linear ranking functions. IC **215**, 47–67 (2012)

4. Bakhirkin, A., Piterman, N.: Finding recurrent sets with backward analysis and trace partitioning. In: Chechik, M., Raskin, J.-F. (eds.) TACAS 2016. LNCS, vol. 9636, pp. 17–35. Springer, Heidelberg (2016). doi:10.1007/978-3-662-49674-9_2

5. Ben-Amram, A.M., Genaim, S.: On the linear ranking problem for integer linear-constraint loops. In: POPL (2013)

6. Biere, A., Heule, M.J.H., van Maaren, H., Walsh, T. (eds.): Handbook of Satisfiability. IOS Press, Amsterdam (2009)

7. Bozga, M., Iosif, R., Konecný, F.: Deciding conditional termination. LCMS **10**(3), 1–61 (2014)

8. Bradley, A.R., Manna, Z., Sipma, H.B.: Linear ranking with reachability. In: Etessami, K., Rajamani, S.K. (eds.) CAV 2005. LNCS, vol. 3576, pp. 491–504. Springer, Heidelberg (2005). doi:10.1007/11513988_48

9. Brockschmidt, M., Cook, B., Fuhs, C.: Better termination proving through cooperation. In: Sharygina, N., Veith, H. (eds.) CAV 2013. LNCS, vol. 8044, pp. 413–429. Springer, Heidelberg (2013). doi:10.1007/978-3-642-39799-8_28

10. Brockschmidt, M., Cook, B., Ishtiaq, S., Khlaaf, H., Piterman, N.: T2: temporal property verification. In: Chechik, M., Raskin, J.-F. (eds.) TACAS 2016. LNCS, vol. 9636, pp. 387–393. Springer, Heidelberg (2016). doi:10.1007/978-3-662-49674-9_22
11. Brockschmidt, M., Joosten, S.J., Thiemann, R., Yamada, A.: Certifying safety and termination proofs for integer transition systems. In: WST (2016)
12. Brockschmidt, M., Larraz, D., Oliveras, A., Rodríguez-Carbonell, E., Rubio, A.: Compositional safety verification with Max-SMT. In: FMCAD (2015)
13. Brockschmidt, M., Ströder, T., Otto, C., Giesl, J.: Automated detection of nontermination and NullPointerExceptions, for JBC. In: Beckert, B., Damiani, F., Gurov, D. (eds.) FoVeOOS 2011. LNCS, vol. 7421, pp. 123–141. Springer, Heidelberg (2011). doi:10.1007/978-3-642-31762-0_9
14. Chen, H.-Y., Cook, B., Fuhs, C., Nimkar, K., O'Hearn, P.: Proving nontermination via safety. In: Ábrahám, E., Havelund, K. (eds.) TACAS 2014. LNCS, vol. 8413, pp. 156–171. Springer, Heidelberg (2014). doi:10.1007/978-3-642-54862-8_11
15. Cook, B., Gulwani, S., Lev-Ami, T., Rybalchenko, A., Sagiv, M.: Proving conditional termination. In: Gupta, A., Malik, S. (eds.) CAV 2008. LNCS, vol. 5123, pp. 328–340. Springer, Heidelberg (2008). doi:10.1007/978-3-540-70545-1_32
16. Cook, B., Podelski, A., Rybalchenko, A.: Termination proofs for systems code. In: PLDI (2006)
17. D'Silva, V., Urban, C.: Conflict-driven conditional termination. In: Kroening, D., Păsăreanu, C.S. (eds.) CAV 2015. LNCS, vol. 9207, pp. 271–286. Springer, Cham (2015). doi:10.1007/978-3-319-21668-3_16
18. Falke, S., Kapur, D., Sinz, C.: Termination analysis of C programs using compiler intermediate languages. In: RTA (2011)
19. Falke, S., Kapur, D., Sinz, C.: Termination analysis of imperative programs using bitvector arithmetic. In: Joshi, R., Müller, P., Podelski, A. (eds.) VSTTE 2012. LNCS, vol. 7152, pp. 261–277. Springer, Heidelberg (2012). doi:10.1007/978-3-642-27705-4_21
20. Flores-Montoya, A., Hähnle, R.: Resource analysis of complex programs with cost equations. In: Garrigue, J. (ed.) APLAS 2014. LNCS, vol. 8858, pp. 275–295. Springer, Cham (2014). doi:10.1007/978-3-319-12736-1_15
21. Ganty, P., Genaim, S.: Proving termination starting from the end. In: Sharygina, N., Veith, H. (eds.) CAV 2013. LNCS, vol. 8044, pp. 397–412. Springer, Heidelberg (2013). doi:10.1007/978-3-642-39799-8_27
22. Giesl, J., Brockschmidt, M., Emmes, F., Frohn, F., Fuhs, C., Otto, C., Plücker, M., Schneider-Kamp, P., Ströder, T., Swiderski, S., Thiemann, R.: Analyzing program termination and complexity automatically with AProVE. JAR (2016, to appear)
23. Gonnord, L., Monniaux, D., Radanne, G.: Synthesis of ranking functions using extremal counterexamples. In: PLDI (2015)
24. Gupta, A., Henzinger, T.A., Majumdar, R., Rybalchenko, A., Xu, R.-G.: Proving non-termination. In: POPL (2008)
25. Harris, W.R., Lal, A., Nori, A.V., Rajamani, S.K.: Alternation for termination. In: Cousot, R., Martel, M. (eds.) SAS 2010. LNCS, vol. 6337, pp. 304–319. Springer, Heidelberg (2010). doi:10.1007/978-3-642-15769-1_19
26. Heizmann, M., Hoenicke, J., Podelski, A.: Termination analysis by learning terminating programs. In: Biere, A., Bloem, R. (eds.) CAV 2014. LNCS, vol. 8559, pp. 797–813. Springer, Cham (2014). doi:10.1007/978-3-319-08867-9_53
27. Kop, C., Nishida, N.: Constrained term rewriting tool. In: Davis, M., Fehnker, A., McIver, A., Voronkov, A. (eds.) LPAR 2015. LNCS, vol. 9450, pp. 549–557. Springer, Heidelberg (2015). doi:10.1007/978-3-662-48899-7_38

28. Kroening, D., Sharygina, N., Tsitovich, A., Wintersteiger, C.M.: Termination analysis with compositional transition invariants. In: Touili, T., Cook, B., Jackson, P. (eds.) CAV 2010. LNCS, vol. 6174, pp. 89–103. Springer, Heidelberg (2010). doi:10.1007/978-3-642-14295-6_9

29. Larraz, D., Nimkar, K., Oliveras, A., Rodríguez-Carbonell, E., Rubio, A.: Proving non-termination using Max-SMT. In: Biere, A., Bloem, R. (eds.) CAV 2014. LNCS, vol. 8559, pp. 779–796. Springer, Cham (2014). doi:10.1007/978-3-319-08867-9_52

30. Larraz, D., Oliveras, A., Rodríguez-Carbonell, E., Rubio, A.: Proving termination of imperative programs using Max-SMT. In: FMCAD (2013)

31. Larraz, D., Oliveras, A., Rodríguez-Carbonell, E., Rubio, A.: Minimal-model-guided approaches to solving polynomial constraints and extensions. In: Sinz, C., Egly, U. (eds.) SAT 2014. LNCS, vol. 8561, pp. 333–350. Springer, Cham (2014). doi:10.1007/978-3-319-09284-3_25

32. Le, T.C., Qin, S., Chin, W.: Termination and non-termination specification inference. In: PLDI (2015)

33. Leike, J., Heizmann, M.: Ranking templates for linear loops. In: Ábrahám, E., Havelund, K. (eds.) TACAS 2014. LNCS, vol. 8413, pp. 172–186. Springer, Heidelberg (2014). doi:10.1007/978-3-642-54862-8_12

34. Massé, D.: Policy iteration-based conditional termination and ranking functions. In: McMillan, K.L., Rival, X. (eds.) VMCAI 2014. LNCS, vol. 8318, pp. 453–471. Springer, Heidelberg (2014). doi:10.1007/978-3-642-54013-4_25

35. Podelski, A., Rybalchenko, A.: A complete method for the synthesis of linear ranking functions. In: Steffen, B., Levi, G. (eds.) VMCAI 2004. LNCS, vol. 2937, pp. 239–251. Springer, Heidelberg (2004). doi:10.1007/978-3-540-24622-0_20

36. Podelski, A., Rybalchenko, A.: ARMC: the logical choice for software model checking with abstraction refinement. In: Hanus, M. (ed.) PADL 2007. LNCS, vol. 4354, pp. 245–259. Springer, Heidelberg (2007). doi:10.1007/978-3-540-69611-7_16

37. Sharma, R., Dillig, I., Dillig, T., Aiken, A.: Simplifying loop invariant generation using splitter predicates. In: Gopalakrishnan, G., Qadeer, S. (eds.) CAV 2011. LNCS, vol. 6806, pp. 703–719. Springer, Heidelberg (2011). doi:10.1007/978-3-642-22110-1_57

38. Sinn, M., Zuleger, F., Veith, H.: A simple and scalable static analysis for bound analysis and amortized complexity analysis. In: Biere, A., Bloem, R. (eds.) CAV 2014. LNCS, vol. 8559, pp. 745–761. Springer, Cham (2014). doi:10.1007/978-3-319-08867-9_50

39. Spoto, F., Mesnard, F., Payet, É.: A termination analyser for Java Bytecode based on path-length. TOPLAS 32(3), 8:1–8:70 (2010)

40. Stump, A., Sutcliffe, G., Tinelli, C.: StarExec: a cross-community infrastructure for logic solving. In: Demri, S., Kapur, D., Weidenbach, C. (eds.) IJCAR 2014. LNCS (LNAI), vol. 8562, pp. 367–373. Springer, Cham (2014). doi:10.1007/978-3-319-08587-6_28

41. Termination   Competition.   http://termination-portal.org/wiki/Termination_Competition

42. Tsitovich, A., Sharygina, N., Wintersteiger, C.M., Kroening, D.: Loop summarization and termination analysis. In: Abdulla, P.A., Leino, K.R.M. (eds.) TACAS 2011. LNCS, vol. 6605, pp. 81–95. Springer, Heidelberg (2011). doi:10.1007/978-3-642-19835-9_9

43. Urban, C.: The abstract domain of segmented ranking functions. In: Logozzo, F., Fähndrich, M. (eds.) SAS 2013. LNCS, vol. 7935, pp. 43–62. Springer, Heidelberg (2013). doi:10.1007/978-3-642-38856-9_5

44. Urban, C., Gurfinkel, A., Kahsai, T.: Synthesizing ranking functions from bits and pieces. In: Chechik, M., Raskin, J.-F. (eds.) TACAS 2016. LNCS, vol. 9636, pp. 54–70. Springer, Heidelberg (2016). doi:10.1007/978-3-662-49674-9_4

45. Urban, C., Miné, A.: A decision tree abstract domain for proving conditional termination. In: Müller-Olm, M., Seidl, H. (eds.) SAS 2014. LNCS, vol. 8723, pp. 302–318. Springer, Cham (2014). doi:10.1007/978-3-319-10936-7_19

46. Velroyen, H., Rümmer, P.: Non-termination checking for imperative programs. In: Beckert, B., Hähnle, R. (eds.) TAP 2008. LNCS, vol. 4966, pp. 154–170. Springer, Heidelberg (2008). doi:10.1007/978-3-540-79124-9_11

Efficient Certified Resolution Proof Checking

Luís Cruz-Filipe[1]([⊠]), Joao Marques-Silva[2], and Peter Schneider-Kamp[1]

[1] Department of Mathematics and Computer Science,
University of Southern Denmark, Odense, Denmark
{lcf,petersk}@imada.sdu.dk
[2] LaSIGE, Faculty of Science, University of Lisbon, Lisbon, Portugal
jpms@ciencias.ulisboa.pt

Abstract. We present a novel propositional proof tracing format that eliminates complex processing, thus enabling efficient (formal) proof checking. The benefits of this format are demonstrated by implementing a proof checker in C, which outperforms a state-of-the-art checker by two orders of magnitude. We then formalize the theory underlying propositional proof checking in Coq, and extract a correct-by-construction proof checker for our format from the formalization. An empirical evaluation using 280 unsatisfiable instances from the 2015 and 2016 SAT competitions shows that this certified checker usually performs comparably to a state-of-the-art non-certified proof checker. Using this format, we formally verify the recent 200 TB proof of the Boolean Pythagorean Triples conjecture.

1 Introduction

The practical success of Boolean Satisfiability (SAT) solvers cannot be overstated. Generally accepted as a mostly academic curiosity until the early 1990s, SAT solvers are now used ubiquitously, in a variety of industrial settings, and with an ever increasing range of practical applications [6]. Several of these applications are safety-critical, and so in these cases it is essential that produced results have some guarantee of correctness [37].

One approach investigated over the years has been to develop formally derived SAT solvers [7,32,34,35,39]. These works all follow the same underlying idea: formally specify SAT solving techniques within a constructive theorem prover and apply program extraction (an implementation of the Curry–Howard correspondence) to obtain a certified SAT solver. Unfortunately, certified SAT solvers produced by this method cannot match the performance of carefully hand-optimized solvers, as these optimizations typically rely on low-level code whose correctness is extremely difficult to prove formally, and the performance gap is still quite significant.

An alternative approach that has become quite popular is to *check* the results produced by SAT solvers, thus adding some level of assurance regarding the computed results. This line of work can be traced at least to the seminal work of Blum and Kannan [8], with recent work also focusing on certifying algorithms

© Springer-Verlag GmbH Germany 2017
A. Legay and T. Margaria (Eds.): TACAS 2017, Part I, LNCS 10205, pp. 118–135, 2017.
DOI: 10.1007/978-3-662-54577-5_7

and their verification [1, 36]. Most SAT checkers expect the SAT solver to produce a witness of its result, and then validate the witness against the input formula. For satisfiable instances, this is a trivial process that amounts to checking the computed satisfying assignment against the input formula. For unsatisfiable instances, since SAT is known to be in NP and believed not to be in coNP, it is unlikely that there exist succinct witnesses, in the worst case. As a result, the solution in practice has been to output a *trace* of the execution of the SAT solver, which essentially captures a resolution proof of the formula's unsatisfiability. Although this approach finds widespread use [5, 18, 20–24, 26–28, 38, 40, 44–47], and has been used to check large-scale resolution proofs [9, 25, 29–31], its main drawback is that there still is effectively no guarantee that the computed result is correct, since the proof checker has again not been proven correct.

Combining these two approaches, several authors [2, 16, 17, 23, 43, 44] have experimented with the idea of developing *certified* proof checkers, i.e. programs that check traces of unsatisfiability proofs and that have themselves been formally proven correct. However, all these approaches are limited in their scalability, essentially for one of two reasons: (1) information about deletion of learned clauses is not available nor used [2, 16, 17, 43]; and (2) the formats used to provide proof traces by SAT solvers still require the checker to perform complex checking steps [22, 23, 44, 46], which are very difficult to optimize.

In this paper we examine the fundamental reasons for why these attempts do not scale in practice, and propose a resolution proof trace format that extends the one developed in recent work [21–23, 45] by incorporating enough information to allow the reconstruction of the original resolution proof with minimum computational effort. This novel proof trace format impacts resolution proof checking in a number of fundamental aspects. First, we show how we can implement an (uncertified, optimized) proof checker in C whose run times are negligible when compared to those of state-of-the-art checkers, in particular drat-trim [19, 45][1]. Second, we capitalize on the simplicity of the new proof format to formalize the proof verification algorithm inside the theorem prover Coq. Third, we extract a certified checker from this formalization and show that it performs comparably with drat-trim on a number of significant test cases. As a consequence, this certified checker is able to verify, in reasonable time, the currently largest available resolution proof, namely the 200 TB proof of the unsatisfiability of a SAT encoding of the Boolean Pythagorean Triples conjecture [25].

The paper is organized as follows. Section 2 briefly summarizes basic SAT and proof checking definitions, and presents a brief overview of the Coq theorem prover and its extraction mechanism. Section 3 provides an overview of the best known resolution proof formats proposed in the recent past. Section 4 introduces the novel resolution proof trace format and outlines the pseudo-code of a verification algorithm, which is then implemented in C. Section 4 also compares its performance to that of drat-trim [45]. Section 5 then describes a formalization of the SAT problem in Coq, which includes a specification of the pseudo-code in the previous section and a proof of its soundness. By applying the program

---

[1] The sole purpose of comparing two checkers with different aims and based on different formats is to motivate the development of the efficient certified checker.

extraction capabilities of Coq, we obtain a certified checker in OCaml, which we evaluate on the same test set as our uncertified C checker. Section 6 details the performance of the certified checker on the verification of the proof of the Pythagorean Boolean Triples conjecture. The paper concludes in Section 7.

2   Preliminaries

Standard Boolean Satisfiability (SAT) definitions are assumed throughout [6]. Propositional variables are taken from a set X. In this work, we assume $X = \mathbb{N}^+$. A literal is either a variable or its negation. A clause is a disjunction of literals, also viewed as a set of literals. A conjunctive normal form (CNF) formula is a conjunction of clauses, also viewed as a set of clauses. Formulas are represented in calligraphic font, e.g. $\mathcal{F}$, with var($\mathcal{F}$) denoting the subset of X representing the variables occurring in $\mathcal{F}$. Clauses are represented with capital letters, e.g. C. Assignments are represented by a mapping $\mu : X \to \{0, 1\}$, and the semantics is defined inductively on the structure of propositional formulas, as usual. The paper focuses on CDCL SAT solvers [6]. The symbol $\vDash$ is used for entailment, whereas $\vdash_u$ is used for representing the result of running the well-known unit propagation algorithm.

This paper develops a formalized checker for proofs of unsatisfiability of propositional formulas using the theorem prover Coq [4]. Coq is a type-theoretical constructive interactive theorem prover based on the Calculus of Constructions (CoC) [10] using a propositions-as-types interpretation. Proofs of theorems are terms in the CoC, which are constructed interactively and type checked when the proof is completed; this final step ensures that the correctness of the results obtained in Coq only depends on the correctness of the type checker – a short piece of code that is much easier to verify by hand than the whole system.

A particular feature of Coq that we make use of in this paper is program extraction [33], which is an implementation of the Curry–Howard correspondence for CoC and several functional programming languages (in our case, OCaml). Programs thus obtained are correct-by-construction, as they are guaranteed to satisfy all the properties enforced by the Coq term they originate form. The CoC includes a special type `Prop` of propositions, which are understood to have no computational content; in particular, it is not allowed to define computational objects by case analysis on a term whose type lives in `Prop`. This allows these terms to be removed by program extraction, making the extracted code much smaller and more efficient; however, all properties of the program that they express are still valid, as stated by the soundness of the extraction mechanism.

3   Propositional Proof Trace Formats

The generation of resolution proof traces for checking the results of SAT solvers has been actively studied since the early 2000s [18,47]. Over the course of the years, different resolution proof tracing formats and extensions have been proposed [5,18,20–24,26,27,38,40,42,44–47]. These all boil down to listing information about the clauses learned by CDCL SAT solvers, with recent efforts allowing an extended set of operations [22,44]. Resolution proof traces can list the literals of each learned clause [21,23,40,42,45,46], the labels of the clauses used for learning each clause, or both [5,40,42]. Moreover, the checking of proof traces can traverse the trace from the start to the end, i.e. *forward checking*, or from end to the start, i.e. *backward checking*. In addition, the checking of proof traces most often exploits one of two key mechanisms. One validation mechanism uses trivial resolution steps (TVR) [3]. This is a restriction over the already restricted input resolution [42]. For proof checking purposes it suffices to require that every two consecutively listed clauses *must* contain a literal and its complement (and obviously not be tautologous). Another validation mechanism exploits the so-called reverse unit propagation (RUP) property [18]. Let $\mathcal{F}$ be a CNF formula, and C be a clause learned from $\mathcal{F}$. Thus, we must have $\mathcal{F} \vDash C$. The RUP property observes that, since $\mathcal{F} \wedge \neg C \vDash \bot$, then it is also true that $\mathcal{F} \wedge \neg C \vdash \bot$. The significance of the RUP property is that proof checking can be reduced to validating a sequence of unit propagations that yield the empty clause. More recent work proposed RAT property[2] checking [22,46]. The resulting format, DRAT, enables extended resolution proofs and, as a result, a wide range of preprocessing techniques [22,24,45].

A few additional properties of formats have important impact on the type of resulting proof checking. Some formats do not allow for clause deletion. This is the case with the RUP [40,42] and the *trace* [5] formats. For formats that generate clause dependencies, some will allow clauses *not* to be ordered, and so the checker is required to infer the correct order of steps.

Example 1. Figure 1 samples the proof tracing formats RUP, trace, and DRUP. (Compared to DRUP, the DRAT format is of interest when extended resolution is used. Every DRUP proof is by definition also a DRAT proof.) With the exception of the more verbose RES format, earlier formats did not allow for clause deletion. The DRUP format (and the more recent DRAT format) allow for clause deletion. A number of different traces would represent DRAT traces, including the DRUP trace shown.

Table 1 summarizes some of the best known formats, and their drawbacks. RES [40,42] is extremely verbose, separately encoding each resolution step, and is not in current use. RUP [40,42] and trace [5] do not consider clause deletion, and so are inadequate for modern SAT solvers. DRUP addresses most of the drawbacks of earlier formats, and has been superseded by DRAT, which provides an extended range of operations besides clause learning.

A number of guidelines for implementing resolution proof trace checking have emerged over the years. First, backward checking is usually preferred, since only the clauses in some unsatisfiable core need to be checked. Second, RUP is preferred over checking TVR steps [21–23,45,46], because the format becomes more flexible. Third, the SAT solver is often expected to minimize the time spent generating the proof trace. This means that, for formats that output clause dependencies, these are in general unordered. Moreover, modern checkers also carry out the validation of the RAT property [22,45,46]. These observations also

---

[2] We do not detail the RAT property here, as it is immaterial for our development.

```
problem CNF      RUP format      tracecheck         DRUP format

p cnf 3 5        1  0            1  1  2 0 0           1  0
  1  2 0         2  0            2 -1  2 0 0         d 1  2 0
 -1  2 0         3  0            3  1 -2 0 0         d 1 -2 0
  1 -2 0         0              4 -1  3 0 0           2  0
 -1  3 0                        5 -2 -3 0 0         d -1 2 0
 -2 -3 0                        6  1  0 1 3 0          3  0
                                7  2  0 2 6 0       d -1 3 0
                                8  3  0 4 6 0       d 1  0
                                9  0  5 7 8 0          0
```

Fig. 1. Examples of trace formats (example adapted from [23]; with original clauses in green, deletion information in blue, learnt clauses in red, and unit propagation information in yellow) (Color figure online)

Table 1. Comparison of some of the best known proof tracing formats

Format	Clause dependencies	Clause literals	Clause deletion	Clause reordering	RAT checking	Drawbacks
RES [40,42]	Yes	Yes	Yes	No	No	Size, RAT
RUP [40,42]	No	Yes	No	No	No	Deletion, RAT
trace [5]	Yes	Yes	No	Yes	No	Deletion, reordering, RAT
DRUP [21,23]	No	Yes	Yes	Yes	No	RAT, reordering
DRAT [45,46]	No	Yes	Yes	No	Yes	Complex checking

indicate that recent work on checking of resolution proof traces has moved in the direction of more complex checking procedures.

Besides efficient checking of resolution proof traces, another important line of work has been to develop certified checkers. Different researchers exploited existing proof formats to develop certified proof checkers [2,16,17,43]. The main drawback of this earlier work is that it was based on proof formats that did not enable clause deletion. For large proofs, this can result in unwieldy memory requirements. Recent work addressed this issue by considering proof formats that enable clause deletion [22,44,46]. Nevertheless, this recent work builds on complex proof checking (see Table 1) and so does not scale well in practice.

Given past evidence, one can argue that, in order to develop efficient certified resolution proof checkers, proof checking *must* be as simple as possible. This has immediate consequences on the proof format used, and also on the algorithm used for checking that format. The next section details our proposed approach. The proposed format requires enough information to enable a checking algorithm that minimizes the processing effort. The actual checking algorithms exploits the best features of TVR and RUP, to enable what can be described as *restricted reverse unit propagation*.

4   Introducing the GRIT Format

As described in the section above, an important aspect in the design of propositional proof trace formats has been the desire to make it easy for SAT solvers to produce a proof in that format. As a consequence, all the major proof trace formats have left some complex processing to the proof checker:

- The DRUP and DRAT formats specify the clauses learnt, but they do not specify the clauses that are used in reverse unit propagation to verify redundancy of these clauses. Thus, proof checkers need to implement a full unit-propagation algorithm. Our results suggest that even state-of-the-art implementations of such algorithms underperform our approach.
- The *trace* format specifies which clauses are used in reverse unit propagation, but it deliberately leaves the order of these undetermined. Thus, proof checkers still need to implement a unit-propagation algorithm, though limited to the clauses specified.

Experience from recent work verifying large-scale proof [14, 15], co-authored by two of the authors of this work, suggests that fully eliminating complex processing is a key ingredient in developing efficient proof checkers that scale to very large proofs. Furthermore, in the concrete case of unit-propagation, efficient algorithms rely on pointer structures that are not easily ported to the typical functional programming setting used in most theorem provers.

Based on these observations, as well as on the importance of deleting clauses that are no longer needed [21, 22], we propose a novel proof trace format that includes deletion and fully eliminates complex processing, effectively reducing unit-propagation to simple pre-determined set operations.

4.1   The Format

The *Generalized ResolutIon Trace (GRIT)* format builds on the *trace* format with its unique clause identifiers, but with two fundamental changes:

- We fix the order of the clauses dependencies given as a witness for each learnt clause to be: an order in which unit propagation produces the empty clause. This is a *restriction* of the freedom allowed by the *trace* format.
- In addition to the two types of lines specifying original and learnt clauses, we *extend* the format with a third type of line for deletions. These lines start with a 0 followed by a list of clause identifiers to delete and end with a 0, and are thus easily distinguishable from the other two types of lines that start with a positive integer.

These changes are minimal w.r.t. achieving the integration of deletion and the elimination of complex processing, and in particular the new lines keep some of the properties that make the *trace* format easy to parse (two zeroes per line; the integers between those zeroes are clause identifiers). In this way, the changes follow the spirit of the extension of the RUP format to DRUP and later DRAT, just with *trace* as the point of departure.

problem CNF	tracecheck	DRUP format	GRIT format
p cnf 3 5	1 1 2 0 0	1 0	1 1 2 0 0
1 2 0	2 -1 2 0 0	d 1 2 0	2 -1 2 0 0
-1 2 0	3 1 -2 0 0	d 1 -2 0	3 1 -2 0 0
1 -2 0	4 -1 3 0 0	2 0	4 -1 3 0 0
-1 3 0	5 -2 -3 0 0	d -1 2 0	5 -2 -3 0 0
-2 -3 0	6 1 0 1 3 0	3 0	6 1 0 1 3 0
	7 2 0 2 6 0	d -1 3 0	0 1 3 0
	8 3 0 4 6 0	d 1 0	7 2 0 6 2 0
	9 0 5 7 8 0	0	0 2 0
			8 3 0 6 4 0
			0 4 6 0
			9 0 7 8 5 0

Fig. 2. Synthesis of the GRIT format (with original clauses in green, deletion information in blue, learnt clauses in red, and unit propagation information in yellow). (Color figure online)

$\langle proof \rangle$	= $\{\langle line \rangle\}$	$\langle clause \rangle$	= $\{\langle lit \rangle\},"0"$
$\langle line \rangle$	= $(\langle original \rangle \mid \langle learnt \rangle \mid \langle delete \rangle),"\backslash n"$	$\langle idlist \rangle$	= $\langle id \rangle, \{\langle id \rangle\}$
$\langle original \rangle$	= $\langle id \rangle, \langle clause \rangle,"0","0"$	$\langle id \rangle$	= $\langle pos \rangle$
$\langle learnt \rangle$	= $\langle id \rangle, \langle clause \rangle,"0",\langle idlist \rangle,"0"$	$\langle lit \rangle$	= $\langle pos \rangle \mid \langle neg \rangle$
$\langle delete \rangle$	= $"0",\langle idlist \rangle,"0"$	$\langle pos \rangle$	= $"1" \mid "2" \mid \ldots$
		$\langle neg \rangle$	= $"-",\langle pos \rangle$

Fig. 3. EBNF grammar for the GRIT format. (Color figure online)

Figure 2 shows how the GRIT version of our running example from Fig. 1 incorporates the deletion information from the DRUP format into a *trace*-style proof, where the clause dependencies have been reordered to avoid the complexity of checking the RUP property by full unit propagation, instead facilitating the application of restricted reverse unit propagation.

The full syntax of the GRIT format is given by the grammar in Fig. 3, where for the sake of sanity whitespace (tabs and spaces) is ignored. Here, additions with respect to the original *trace* format are given in green. In addition to the extension with delete information, there is a semantic restriction on the list of clause identifiers marked in red, namely that the clause dependencies represented are in the order as specified above. Existing parsers for the *trace* format should be easy to extend to this syntax.

4.2   The Checker

To obtain an empirical evaluation of the potential of the GRIT format, we implemented a proof checking algorithm based on restricted reverse unit propagation in C. The source code is available from [13]. While the C code is quite optimized, the general algorithm follows the pseudo code given in Fig. 4 as 25 lines of fully-functional Python (also available from [13]).

The set of instances we considered consists of the 280 instances from the 2015 and 2016 main and parallel tracks of the SAT competition that could be shown

```python
def parse(line):
  ints = [int(s) for s in line.split()]
  i0 = ints.index(0)
  return ints[0], set(ints[1:i0]), ints[i0+1:-1]
def verify(file):
  cs = {}
  for id, c, ids in (parse(line) for line in file):
    if not id:     # delete clauses
      for id in ids: del cs[id]
    elif not ids:  # add original clause
      cs[id] = c
    else:          # check & add learnt clause
      d = c.copy()
      for i in ids:
        e = cs[i]-d
        if e:
          d.add(-e.pop()) # propagate
          assert not e   # is unit?
        else:  # empty clause reached
          cs[id] = c
          if not c:  return "VERIFIED"
          break
  return "NOT VERIFIED"
import sys
print(verify(open(sys.argv[1])))
```

Fig. 4. Fully functional checker for the GRIT format written in Python.

to be UNSAT within 5000 s using the 2016 competition version of lingeling. For each of these instances, the original CNF and proof trace are trimmed and optimized using drat-trim in backward checking mode. This is a side-effect of using drat-trim to generate proof traces in the GRIT format, and was applied in the same way to generate DRAT files from the original RUP files in order to ensure a level playing field. In this way, the RUP steps required are the same for both GRIT and DRAT checkers.

The C-checker successfully verifies all 280 GRIT files in just over 14 min (843.64 s), while drat-trim requires more than a day to solve the corresponding DRAT files (109214.08 s) using backward mode. Executing drat-trim in forward mode incurred a runtime overhead of 15% on the total set of trimmed and optimized instances. As expected, the overhead was even bigger when working on the original CNFs and proof traces. The quantitative results are summarized in the plots of Fig. 5, with details available from [13].

This two-orders-of-magnitude speedup demonstrates the potential of using a file format for propositional resolution proof checking by restricted reverse unit propagation. Note that we currently do *not* output the GRIT format directly, but require a modified version of drat-trim as a pre-processor[3] in order to determine

---

[3] The modified version essentially uses drat-trim's tracecheck output, interleaving it with deletion information. The modified source code is available from [13].

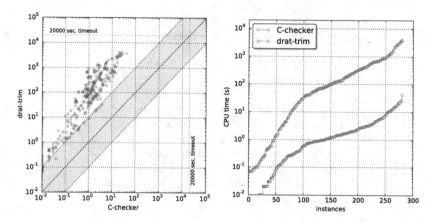

Fig. 5. Scatter and cactus plot comparing the runtime of the C-checker on GRIT files and drat-trim on the corresponding DRAT files.

both the order of clauses used in unit propagation, the set of original and learnt clauses relevant, and the deletion of clauses that are no longer needed. We stress the importance of this additional information in obtaining the performance gains we measure. Additional experiments (whose results we do not detail for space constraints) show that deletion of clauses alone is responsible for a speedup of more than one order of magnitude for the larger instances, when using the certified checker we develop in the next section. In this way, deletion is essential for making certified checking feasible on the largest available instances.

While it is in principle thinkable to modify a SAT solver to output the GRIT format directly, building on [41], in this work our focus is on enabling sufficiently efficient certified proof checking. To this end, it seems fully acceptable to run an uncertified proof checker as a pre-processor to generate the oracle data enabling the application of restricted reverse unit propagation in a certified checker.

5   Coq Formalization

We now show how to obtain a certified checker of unsatisfiability proofs. Rather than verify the code of the C checker developed earlier, we formalize the underlying algorithm in Coq and extract a new certified checker. This approach has the benefits of being simpler and less dependent on the soundness of the underlying software stack.

We follow the strategy outlined in [14,15]: first, we formalize the necessary theoretical concepts (propositional satisfiability, entailment and soundness of unit propagation); then, we naively specify the verification algorithm; finally, we optimize this algorithm using standard computer science techniques to obtain feasible runtimes. In the interest of succintness, we only present the formalization obtained at the end of this process. The source files can be obtained from [13].

5.1   Formalizing Propositional Satisfiability

We identify propositional variables with Coq's binary natural numbers (type positive), and define a literal to be a signed variable. The type of literals is thus isomorphic to that of integers (excluding zero).

```
Inductive Literal : Type :=
  | pos : positive → Literal
  | neg : positive → Literal.
```

A clause is a set of literals, and a CNF is a set of clauses. For efficiency, there are two different definitions of each type, with mappings between them. A Clause is a list Literal, and is the type preferably used in proofs due to its simplicity; it is also the type used for inputting data from the oracle. A CNF is a BinaryTree Clause, where the dependent type BinaryTree implements search trees over any type with a comparison operator. This is the type of the CNF given as input to the algorithm, which is built once, never changed, and repeatedly tested for membership. The working set uses two different representations of these types. A SetClause is a BinaryTree Literal, where in particular set differences can be computed much more efficiently than using Clause. Finally, an ICNF is a Map {cl:SetClause | SC_wf cl}, where Map is the Coq standard library's implementation of Patricia trees. The elements of an ICNF must be well-formed search trees (ensured by the condition in the definition of subset type); proofs of well-formedness do not contain computational meaning and are removed by extraction.[4] In particular, every SetClause built from a Clause is well-formed.

A valuation is a function from positive numbers to Booleans. Satisfaction is defined for literals, clauses and CNFs either directly (as below) or by translating to the appropriate type (for SetClause and ICNF).

```
Definition Valuation := positive → bool.
```

```
Fixpoint L_satisfies (v:Valuation) (l:Literal) : Prop :=
  match l with
  | pos x ⇒ if (v x) then True else False
  | neg x ⇒ if (v x) then False else True
  end.
```

```
Fixpoint C_satisfies (v:Valuation) (c:Clause) : Prop :=
  match c with
  | nil ⇒ False
  | l :: c' ⇒ (L_satisfies v l) ∨ (C_satisfies v c')
  end.
```

```
Fixpoint satisfies (v:Valuation) (c:CNF) : Prop :=
  match c with
  | nought ⇒ True
  | node cl c' c'' ⇒ (C_satisfies v cl) ∧ (satisfies v c') ∧ (satisfies v c'')
  end.
```

---

[4] Soundness of extraction implies that these trees are well-formed.

Definition unsat (c:CNF) : Prop := ∀ v:Valuation, ~(satisfies v c).

Definition entails (c:CNF) (c':Clause) : Prop :=
  ∀ v:Valuation, satisfies v c → C_satisfies v c'.

We then prove the intuitive semantics of satisfaction: a clause is satisfied if one of its literals is satisfied, and a CNF is satisfied if all its clauses are satisfied. Other properties that we need include: the empty clause is unsatisfiable; every non-empty clause is satisfiable; a subset of a satisfiable CNF is satisfiable; and a CNF that entails the empty clause is unsatisfiable.

Lemma C_satisfies_exist : ∀ (v:Valuation) (cl:Clause),
  C_satisfies v cl → ∃ l, In l cl ∧ L_satisfies v l.

Lemma satisfies_remove : ∀ (c:CNF) (cl:Clause) (v:Valuation),
  satisfies v c → satisfies v (CNF_remove cl c).

Lemma unsat_subset : ∀ (c c':CNF),
  (∀ cl, CNF_in cl c → CNF_in cl c') → unsat c → unsat c'.

Lemma CNF_empty : ∀ c, entails c nil → unsat c.

5.2 Soundness of Unit Propagation

The key ingredient to verifying unsatisfiability proofs in GRIT format is being able to verify the original unit propagation steps. Soundness of unit propagation relies on the following results, formalizing the two relevant outcomes of resolving two clauses: a unit clause and the empty clause.

Lemma propagate_singleton : ∀ (cs:CNF) (c c':SetClause), ∀ l,
  entails cs (SetClause_to_Clause (SC_add (negate l) c')) →
  SC_diff c c' = (node l nought nought) → entails (CNF_add c cs) c'.

Lemma propagate_empty : ∀ (cs:CNF) (c c':SetClause),
  SC_diff c c' = nought → entails (BT_add Clause_compare c cs) c'.

We then define a function propagate that receives an ICNF, a SetClause and a list of indices (of type ad, used in the implementation of Map) and returns true if reverse unit propagation from the given clause using the clauses referred to by the given indices reaches the empty clause.[5] Concretely, we take the clause in the ICNF corresponding to the first index and check whether the set difference between it and the given clause is (i) the empty clause, in which case we return true, (ii) a singleton, in which case we add the negation of the derived literal to the clause, remove the index from the list and recur, or (iii) a longer list of literals, and we return false. We omit the formal definition of propagate, and reproduce only the lemma stating its soundness.

---

[5] The function propagate actually implements a restricted version of reverse unit propagation analogous to the one in our C-checker, which in particular avoids complex processing to determine the next clause to use in unit propagation.

Lemma propagate_sound : ∀ (cs:ICNF) (c:SetClause) (is:list ad),
  propagate cs c is = true → entails cs c.

To check that a given formula is unsatisfiable, we start with an empty working set, and iteratively change it by applying actions given by the oracle. These actions form a type `Action` with three constructors: delete a clause; add a clause from the original CNF; or extend it with a clause that is derivable by unit propagation (together with the indices of the clauses that should be used in this derivation).

Inductive Action : Type :=
  | D : list ad → Action
  | O : ad → Clause → Action
  | R : ad → Clause → list ad → Action.

Definition Answer := bool.

We then define a function `refute` that processes a list of `Actions` (the oracle), starting from a given CNF. This function starts with an empty ICNF, and processes each `Action` as expected: it deletes the clause with the given index from the ICNF (doing nothing if the index does not occur); it adds a clause from the argument CNF (checking that it occurs there, and failing otherwise); or add a clause to the ICNF after using `propagate` to ensure that it is entailed by the ICNF (and failing otherwise).

The list of `Actions` is actually defined to be a lazy list. Lazy lists are defined exactly as lists with constructors `lnil` and `lcons`, but with the second argument of `lcons` inside an invocation of an identity function. Likewise, additional functions for deferring or forcing evaluation inside `refute` are defined as the identity. These additions are necessary to be able to extract a memory-efficient checker to OCaml. On extraction, these functions are mapped to the adequate OCaml constructs implementing laziness; although in principle this approach could break soundness of extraction, these constructs do indeed behave as identities. Without them, the extracted checker attempts to load the entire oracle data at the start of execution, and thus risks running out of memory for larger proofs.[6]

The following result states soundness of `refute`: if `refute c O` returns `true`, then c is unsatisfiable. Since O is universally quantified, the result holds even if the oracle gives incorrect data. (Namely, because `refute` will output `false`.)

Theorem refute_correct : ∀ c O, refute c O = true → unsat (make_CNF c).

5.3   Experimental Evaluation

In order to evaluate the efficiency of our formalized checker, we extracted it to OCaml. The extraction definition is available in the file `Extraction.v` from [13]. As is customary, we extract the Coq type `positive`, used for variable and clause

---

[6] Targeting a lazy language like Haskell would not require this workaround. However, in our context, using OCaml reduced computation times to around one-fourth.

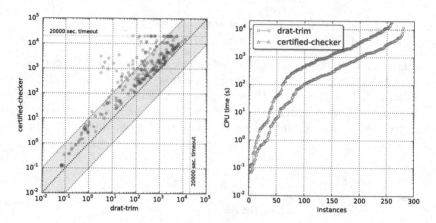

Fig. 6. Scatter and cactus plot comparing the runtime of our certified checker (including pre-processing) and drat-trim on the original proof traces from lingeling.

identifiers, to OCaml's native integers, and the comparator function on this type to a straightforward implementation of comparison of two integers. This reduces not only the memory footprint of the verified checker, but also its runtime (as lookups in ICNFs require comparison of keys). It is routine to check that these functions are correct. Furthermore, as described above, we extract the type of lazy lists to OCaml's lazy lists.

We ran the certified extracted checker on the same 280 unsatisfiable instances as in the previous section, with a timeout of 20,000 s, resulting in 260 successful verifications and 20 timeouts. On the 260 examples, the certified checker runs in good 4 days and 18 h (412469.50 s) compared to good 2 days and 17 h (234922.46 s) required by the uncertified checker drat-trim. The pre-processing using our modified version of drat-trim adds another 2 days and 19 h (241453.84 s) for a total runtime of 7 days and good 13 (653923.34 s). Thus, the extra degree of confidence provided by the certified checker comes at the price of approx. 2.8 times slower verification for these instances (180% overhead).

The quantitative results on all 280 instances are summarized in the plots of Fig. 6, where we added the pre-processing time to the time of the certified checker, with details available from [13].

The reason for the 20 timeouts can be found in the set implementation of our formalization. If we extract Coq sets to native OCaml sets, there are no time-outs. We extracted such a version of the certified checker in order to check this hypothesis, as well as to assess the performance impact. And indeed, this version of our checker successfully verifies all 280 GRIT files in less time (186599.20 s) than it takes to pre-process them using our modified drat-trim version (281516.13), and consequently the overhead of running a certified checker instead of an uncertified checker is down to 75%. The quantitative results for this variant are summarized in the plots of Fig. 7, with details available from [13].

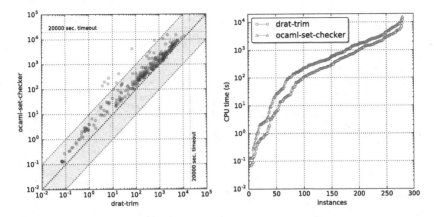

Fig. 7. Scatter and cactus plot comparing the runtime of a certified checker using OCaml sets (including pre-processing) and drat-trim on the original proof traces from lingeling.

6 Veryifing the Boolean Pythagorean Triples Proof

As a large-scale litmus test of our formally verified checker, we reconstituted the recent SAT-based proof of the Boolean Pythagorean Triples conjecture [25] (508 CPU days) using the incremental SAT solver *iGlucose*, transformed it into the GRIT format (871 CPU days) using our modified version of drat-trim, and formally verified that all 1,000,000 cases ("cubes") cover the entire search space (12 min), and that they are all indeed unsatisfiable (2608 days) using our certified checker (the original version, where all data structures except integers are extracted). This amounts to formally verifying the Boolean Pythagorean Triples conjecture (provided that its encoding as a propositional formula is correct).

The cactus plot in Fig. 8 visualizes the distribution of runtime on the 1,000,000 cubes. The size of the reconstituted proof traces in RUP format was measured to be 175 TB. After transformation to the more detailed GRIT format, the proof traces filled a total 389 TB. During runtime, the maximum resident memory usage of the incremental SAT solver was 237 MB, while drat-trim in backward mode used up to 1.59 GB. Our certified checker reached a maximum of 67 MB of resident memory usage thanks to laziness. Details on this experiment are available from [12].

7 Conclusions and Research Directions

This paper revisits past work on proof checking, aiming at developing high-performance certified proof checkers. It proposes a new format, which enables a very simple proof checking algorithm. This simple algorithm is formalized in the Coq theorem prover, from which an OCaml executable is then extracted.

The experimental results amply demonstrate the validity of the proposed approach. The C implementation of the checker is on average two orders of magnitude faster than what can be considered a reference C-implemented proof

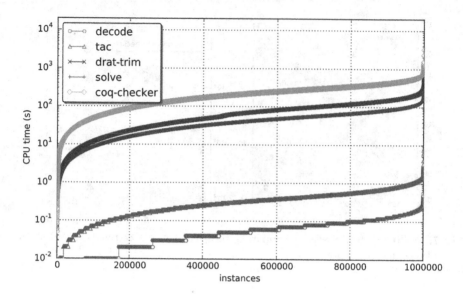

Fig. 8. Cactus plot comparing the runtimes for reconstituting the proof (decode and solve), transforming it into GRIT (drat-trim and tac), and formally verifying the GRIT files using our certified checker.

checker, drat-trim [19, 45]. This represents an essential requirement for developing an efficient certified proof checker. More importantly, the certified OCaml version of the checker performs comparably with drat-trim on problem instances from the SAT competitions. Perhaps more significantly, the certified checker has been used to formally verify the 200 TB proof of the Boolean Pythagorean Triples conjecture [25], in time comparable to the non-certified drat-trim checker.

Future work will address existing limitations of the approach. Currently, a modified version of drat-trim is used to generate the GRIT format. This can impact the overall running time, especially if the C-implemented checker for the GRIT format is to be used. This also includes modifying top performing SAT solvers to output the GRIT format, potentially based on A. Van Gelder's approach [41, 42].

A natural continuation of this work is the extension of GRIT to a format as general as DRAT, in particular by including support for the RAT property. This task is quite challenging, as verifying the RAT property requires global checks on the whole CNF – unlike the properties describable by GRIT, which are locally verified. Preliminary results regarding the extension of GRIT to the RAT property can be found in [11].

Acknowledgements. The authors thank M. Heule for comments on an early draft of this paper. This work was partially supported by the Danish Council for Independent Research, Natural Sciences, grant DFF-1323-00247. Computational resources on the Abacus 2.0 supercomputer were provided by the DeIC National HPC Centre at the University of Southern Denmark.

References

1. Alkassar, E., Böhme, S., Mehlhorn, K., Rizkallah, C.: A framework for the verification of certifying computations. J. Autom. Reason. **52**(3), 241–273 (2014)
2. Armand, M., Faure, G., Grégoire, B., Keller, C., Théry, L., Werner, B.: A modular integration of SAT/SMT solvers to Coq through proof witnesses. In: Jouannaud, J.-P., Shao, Z. (eds.) CPP 2011. LNCS, vol. 7086, pp. 135–150. Springer, Heidelberg (2011). doi:10.1007/978-3-642-25379-9_12
3. Beame, P., Kautz, H.A., Sabharwal, A.: Towards understanding and harnessing the potential of clause learning. J. Artif. Intell. Res. (JAIR) **22**, 319–351 (2004)
4. Bertot, Y., Castéran, P.: Interactive Theorem Proving and Program Development. Texts in Theoretical Computer Science. Springer, Heidelberg (2004)
5. Biere, A.: PicoSAT essentials. JSAT **4**(2–4), 75–97 (2008)
6. Biere, A., Heule, M., van Maaren, H., Walsh, T. (eds.): Handbook of Satisfiability. Frontiers in Artificial Intelligence and Applications, vol. 185. IOS Press, Amsterdam (2009)
7. Blanchette, J.C., Fleury, M., Weidenbach, C.: A verified SAT solver framework with learn, forget, restart, and incrementality. In: Olivetti, N., Tiwari, A. (eds.) IJCAR 2016. LNCS (LNAI), vol. 9706, pp. 25–44. Springer, Cham (2016). doi:10.1007/978-3-319-40229-1_4
8. Blum, M., Kannan, S.: Designing programs that check their work. In: STOC, pp. 86–97 (1989)
9. Bras, R.L., Gomes, C.P., Selman, B.: On the Erdős discrepancy problem. In: CP, pp. 440–448 (2014)
10. Coquand, T., Huet, G.P.: The calculus of constructions. Inf. Comput. **76**(2/3), 95–120 (1988)
11. Cruz-Filipe, L., Heule, M., Hunt, W., Kaufmann, M., Schneider-Kamp, P.: Efficient certified RAT verification. CoRR, abs/1610.06984 (2016)
12. Cruz-Filipe, L., Schneider-Kamp, P.: Checking the Boolean Pythagorean Triples conjecture. http://imada.sdu.dk/~petersk/bpt/
13. Cruz-Filipe, L., Schneider-Kamp, P.: Grit format, formalization, and checkers. http://imada.sdu.dk/~petersk/grit/. Source codes also available from: https://github.com/peter-sk/grit
14. Cruz-Filipe, L., Schneider-Kamp, P.: Formalizing size-optimal sorting networks: extracting a certified proof checker. In: Urban, C., Zhang, X. (eds.) ITP 2015. LNCS, vol. 9236, pp. 154–169. Springer, Cham (2015). doi:10.1007/978-3-319-22102-1_10
15. Cruz-Filipe, L., Schneider-Kamp, P.: Optimizing a certified proof checker for a large-scale computer-generated proof. In: Kerber, M., Carette, J., Kaliszyk, C., Rabe, F., Sorge, V. (eds.) CICM 2015. LNCS (LNAI), vol. 9150, pp. 55–70. Springer, Cham (2015). doi:10.1007/978-3-319-20615-8_4
16. Darbari, A., Fischer, B., Marques-Silva, J.: Formalizing a SAT proof checker in Coq. In: First Coq Workshop (2009)
17. Darbari, A., Fischer, B., Marques-Silva, J.: Industrial-strength certified SAT solving through verified SAT proof checking. In: Cavalcanti, A., Deharbe, D., Gaudel, M.-C., Woodcock, J. (eds.) ICTAC 2010. LNCS, vol. 6255, pp. 260–274. Springer, Heidelberg (2010). doi:10.1007/978-3-642-14808-8_18
18. Goldberg, E.I., Novikov, Y.: Verification of proofs of unsatisfiability for CNF formulas. In: DATE, pp. 10886–10891 (2003)

19. Heule, M.: The DRAT format and DRAT-trim checker. CoRR, abs/1610.06229 (2016). https://github.com/marijnheule/drat-trim
20. Heule, M., Biere, A.: Proofs for satisfiability problems. In: All About Proofs, Proofs for All (APPA), July 2014. http://www.easychair.org/smart-program/VSL2014/APPA-index.html
21. Heule, M., Hunt Jr., W.A., Wetzler, N.: Trimming while checking clausal proofs. In: FMCAD, pp. 181–188 (2013)
22. Heule, M.J.H., Hunt, W.A., Wetzler, N.: Verifying refutations with extended resolution. In: Bonacina, M.P. (ed.) CADE 2013. LNCS (LNAI), vol. 7898, pp. 345–359. Springer, Heidelberg (2013). doi:10.1007/978-3-642-38574-2_24
23. Heule, M., Hunt Jr., W.A., Wetzler, N.: Bridging the gap between easy generation and efficient verification of unsatisfiability proofs. Softw. Test. Verif. Reliab. **24**(8), 593–607 (2014)
24. Heule, M.J.H., Hunt, W.A., Wetzler, N.: Expressing symmetry breaking in DRAT proofs. In: Felty, A.P., Middeldorp, A. (eds.) CADE 2015. LNCS (LNAI), vol. 9195, pp. 591–606. Springer, Cham (2015). doi:10.1007/978-3-319-21401-6_40
25. Heule, M.J.H., Kullmann, O., Marek, V.W.: Solving and verifying the boolean pythagorean triples problem via cube-and-conquer. In: Creignou, N., Le Berre, D. (eds.) SAT 2016. LNCS, vol. 9710, pp. 228–245. Springer, Cham (2016). doi:10.1007/978-3-319-40970-2_15
26. Heule, M., Seidl, M., Biere, A.: Efficient extraction of skolem functions from QRAT proofs. In: FMCAD, pp. 107–114 (2014)
27. Jussila, T., Biere, A., Sinz, C., Kröning, D., Wintersteiger, C.M.: A first step towards a unified proof checker for QBF. In: Marques-Silva, J., Sakallah, K.A. (eds.) SAT 2007. LNCS, vol. 4501, pp. 201–214. Springer, Heidelberg (2007). doi:10.1007/978-3-540-72788-0_21
28. Jussila, T., Sinz, C., Biere, A.: Extended resolution proofs for symbolic SAT solving with quantification. In: Biere, A., Gomes, C.P. (eds.) SAT 2006. LNCS, vol. 4121, pp. 54–60. Springer, Heidelberg (2006). doi:10.1007/11814948_8
29. Konev, B., Lisitsa, A.: Computer-aided proof of Erdős discrepancy properties. CoRR, abs/1405.3097 (2014)
30. Konev, B., Lisitsa, A.: A SAT attack on the Erdős discrepancy conjecture. In: Sinz, C., Egly, U. (eds.) SAT 2014. LNCS, vol. 8561, pp. 219–226. Springer, Cham (2014). doi:10.1007/978-3-319-09284-3_17
31. Konev, B., Lisitsa, A.: Computer-aided proof of Erdős discrepancy properties. Artif. Intell. **224**, 103–118 (2015)
32. Lescuyer, S., Conchon, S.: Improving Coq propositional reasoning using a lazy CNF conversion scheme. In: Ghilardi, S., Sebastiani, R. (eds.) FroCoS 2009. LNCS (LNAI), vol. 5749, pp. 287–303. Springer, Heidelberg (2009). doi:10.1007/978-3-642-04222-5_18
33. Letouzey, P.: Extraction in Coq: an overview. In: Beckmann, A., Dimitracopoulos, C., Löwe, B. (eds.) CiE 2008. LNCS, vol. 5028, pp. 359–369. Springer, Heidelberg (2008). doi:10.1007/978-3-540-69407-6_39
34. Maric, F.: Formal verification of a modern SAT solver by shallow embedding into Isabelle/HOL. Theor. Comput. Sci. **411**(50), 4333–4356 (2010)
35. Maric, F., Janicic, P.: Formalization of abstract state transition systems for SAT. LMCS **7**(3:19), 1–37 (2011)
36. McConnell, R.M., Mehlhorn, K., Näher, S., Schweitzer, P.: Certifying algorithms. Comput. Sci. Rev. **5**(2), 119–161 (2011)

37. Shankar, N.: Trust and automation in verification tools. In: Cha, S.S., Choi, J.-Y., Kim, M., Lee, I., Viswanathan, M. (eds.) ATVA 2008. LNCS, vol. 5311, pp. 4–17. Springer, Heidelberg (2008). doi:10.1007/978-3-540-88387-6_3

38. Sinz, C., Biere, A.: Extended resolution proofs for conjoining BDDs. In: Grigoriev, D., Harrison, J., Hirsch, E.A. (eds.) CSR 2006. LNCS, vol. 3967, pp. 600–611. Springer, Heidelberg (2006). doi:10.1007/11753728_60

39. Smith, D.R., Westfold, S.J.: Synthesis of satisfiability solvers. Technical report, Kestrel Institute (2008)

40. Van Gelder, A.: Verifying RUP proofs of propositional unsatisfiability. In: ISAIM (2008)

41. Gelder, A.: Improved conflict-clause minimization leads to improved propositional proof traces. In: Kullmann, O. (ed.) SAT 2009. LNCS, vol. 5584, pp. 141–146. Springer, Heidelberg (2009). doi:10.1007/978-3-642-02777-2_15

42. Van Gelder, A.: Producing and verifying extremely large propositional refutations - have your cake and eat it too. Ann. Math. Artif. Intell. **65**(4), 329–372 (2012)

43. Weber, T., Amjad, H.: Efficiently checking propositional refutations in HOL theorem provers. J. Appl. Logic **7**(1), 26–40 (2009)

44. Wetzler, N., Heule, M.J.H., Hunt, W.A.: Mechanical verification of SAT refutations with extended resolution. In: Blazy, S., Paulin-Mohring, C., Pichardie, D. (eds.) ITP 2013. LNCS, vol. 7998, pp. 229–244. Springer, Heidelberg (2013). doi:10.1007/978-3-642-39634-2_18

45. Wetzler, N., Heule, M.J.H., Hunt, W.A.: DRAT-trim: efficient checking and trimming using expressive clausal proofs. In: Sinz, C., Egly, U. (eds.) SAT 2014. LNCS, vol. 8561, pp. 422–429. Springer, Cham (2014). doi:10.1007/978-3-319-09284-3_31

46. Wetzler, N.D.: Efficient, mechanically-verified validation of satisfiability solvers. Ph.D. thesis, The University of Texas at Austin (2015)

47. Zhang, L., Malik, S.: Validating SAT solvers using an independent resolution-based checker: practical implementations and other applications. In: DATE, pp. 10880–10885 (2003)

Precise Widening Operators for Proving Termination by Abstract Interpretation

Nathanaël Courant[1] and Caterina Urban[2]([⊠])

[1] École Normale Supérieure, Paris, France
nathanael.courant@ens.fr
[2] ETH Zurich, Zurich, Switzerland
caterina.urban@inf.ethz.ch

Abstract. FUNCTION is a static analyzer designed for proving conditional termination of C programs by means of abstract interpretation. Its underlying abstract domain is based on piecewise-defined functions, which provide an upper bound on the number of program execution steps until termination as a function of the program variables.

In this paper, we fully parameterize various aspects of the abstract domain, gaining a flexible balance between the precision and the cost of the analysis. We propose heuristics to improve the fixpoint extrapolation strategy (i.e., the widening operator) of the abstract domain. In particular we identify new widening operators, which combine these heuristics to dramatically increase the precision of the analysis while offering good cost compromises. We also introduce a more precise, albeit costly, variable assignment operator and the support for choosing between integer and rational values for the piecewise-defined functions.

We combined these improvements to obtain an implementation of the abstract domain which subsumes the previous implementation. We provide experimental evidence in comparison with state-of-the-art tools showing a considerable improvement in precision at a minor cost in performance.

1 Introduction

Programming errors which cause non-termination can compromise software systems by making them irresponsive. Notorious examples are the Microsoft Zune Z2K bug[1] and the Microsoft Azure Storage service interruption[2]. Termination bugs can also be exploited in denial-of-service attacks[3]. Therefore, proving program termination is important for ensuring software reliability.

The traditional method for proving termination is based on the synthesis of a *ranking function*, a well-founded metric which strictly decreases during the program execution. FUNCTION [36] is a static analyzer which automatically infers

---

[1] http://techcrunch.com/2008/12/31/zune-bug-explained-in-detail/.

[2] http://azure.microsoft.com/blog/2014/11/19/update-on-azure-storage-service-interruption/.

[3] http://cve.mitre.org/cgi-bin/cvename.cgi?name=CVE-2009-1890.

© Springer-Verlag GmbH Germany 2017
A. Legay and T. Margaria (Eds.): TACAS 2017, Part I, LNCS 10205, pp. 136–152, 2017.
DOI: 10.1007/978-3-662-54577-5_8

ranking functions and sufficient precondition for program termination by means of abstract interpretation [13]. The tool is based on the abstract interpretation framework for termination introduced by Cousot and Cousot [14].

The underlying abstract domain of FUNCTION is based on *piecewise-defined ranking functions* [40], which provide an upper bound on the number of program execution steps until termination as a function of the program variables. The piecewise-defined functions are represented by *decision trees*, where the decision nodes are labeled by linear constraints over the program variables, and the leaf nodes are labeled by functions of the program variables.

In this paper, we fully parameterize various aspects of the abstract domain, gaining a flexible balance between the precision and the cost of the analysis. We propose options to tune the representation of the domain and value of the ranking functions manipulated by the abstract domain. In particular, we introduce the support for using rational coefficients for the functions labeling the leaf nodes of the decision trees, all the while strengthening their decrease condition to still ensure termination. We also introduce a variable assignment operator which is very effective for programs with unbounded non-determinism. Finally, we propose heuristics to improve the widening operator of the abstract domain. Specifically, we suggest an heuristic inspired by [1] to infer new linear constraints to add to a decision tree and two heuristics to infer a value for the leaf nodes on which the ranking function is not yet defined. We identify new widening operators, which combine these heuristics to dramatically increase the precision of the analysis while offering good cost compromises.

We combined these improvements to obtain an implementation of the abstract domain which subsumes the previous implementation. We provide experimental evidence in comparison with state-of-the-art tools [21,22,34] showing a considerable improvement in precision at a minor cost in performance.

Outline. Sect. 2 offers a glimpse into the theory behind proving termination by abstract interpretation. In Sect. 3, we recall the ranking functions abstract domain and we discuss options to tune the representation of the piecewise-defined functions manipulated by the abstract domain. We suggest new precise widening operators in Sect. 4. Section 5 presents the result of our experimental evaluation. We discuss related work in Sect. 6 and Sect. 7 concludes.

2   Termination and Ranking Functions

The traditional method for proving program termination dates back to Turing [35] and Floyd [17]. It consists in inferring a *ranking function*, namely a function from the program states to elements of a well-ordered set whose value decreases during program execution. The best known well-ordered sets are the natural numbers $\langle \mathbb{N}, \leq \rangle$ and the ordinals $\langle \mathbb{O}, \leq \rangle$, and the most obvious ranking function maps each program state to the number of program execution steps until termination, or some well-chosen upper bound on this number.

In [14], Cousot and Cousot formalize the notion of a most precise ranking function w for a program. Intuitively, it is a partial function defined starting from the program final states, where it has value zero, and retracing the program backwards while mapping each program state definitely leading to a final state (i.e., a program state such that all program execution traces to which it belongs are terminating) to an ordinal representing an upper bound on the number of program execution steps remaining to termination. The domain dom(w) of w is the set of states from which the program execution must terminate: all traces branching from a state $s \in$ dom(w) terminate in at most $w(s)$ execution steps, while at least one trace branching from a state $s \notin$ dom(w) does not terminate.

Example 1. Let us consider the following execution traces of a given program:

The most precise ranking function for the program is iteratively defined as:

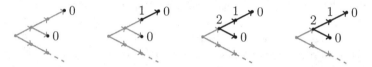

where unlabelled states are outside the domain of the function.

The most precise ranking function w is sound and complete to prove program termination [14]. However, it is usually not computable. In the following sections we recall and present various improvements on decidable approximations of w [40]. These *over-approximate* the value of w and *under-approximate* its domain of definition dom(w). In this way, we infer sufficient preconditions for program termination: if the approximation is defined on a program state, then all execution traces branching from that state are terminating.

3   The Ranking Functions Abstract Domain

We use abstract interpretation [13] to approximate the most precise ranking function mentioned in the previous section. In [40], to this end, we introduce an abstract domain based on *piecewise-defined ranking functions*. We recall here (and in the next section) the features of the abstract domain that are relevant for our purposes and introduce various improvements and parameterizations to tune the precision of the abstract domain. We refer to [37] for an exhaustive presentation of the original ranking functions abstract domain.

The elements of the abstract domain are piecewise-defined partial functions. Their internal representation is inspired by the space partitioning trees [18] developed in the context of 3D computer graphics and the use of decision trees in program analysis and verification [3,24]: the piecewise-defined partial functions are represented by *decision trees*, where the decision nodes are labeled by linear

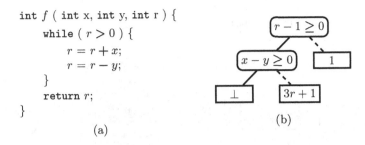

```
int f ( int x, int y, int r ) {
    while ( r > 0 ) {
        r = r + x;
        r = r − y;
    }
    return r;
}
```

(a)

(b)

Fig. 1. Decision tree representation (b) of the piecewise-defined ranking function for a simple C function (a). The linear constraints are satisfied by their left subtree, while their right subtree satisfies their negation. The leaves of the tree represent partial functions the domain of which is determined by the constraints satisfied along the path to the leaf node. The leaf with value ⊥ explicitly represents the undefined partition of the partial function.

constraints over the program variables, and the leaf nodes are labeled by functions of the program variables. The decision nodes recursively partition the space of possible values of the program variables and the functions at the leaves provide the corresponding upper bounds on the number of program execution steps until termination. An example of decision tree representation of a piecewise-defined ranking function is shown in Fig. 1.

The partitioning is dynamic: during the analysis, partitions (resp. decision nodes and constraints) are split (resp. added) by tests, modified by variable assignments and joined (resp. removed) when merging control flows. In order to minimize the cost of the analysis, a widening limits the height of the decision trees and the number of maintained partitions.

The abstract domain is parameterized in various aspects. Figure 2 offers an overview of the various parameterizations currently available. We discuss here options to tune the representation of the domain and value of the ranking functions manipulated by the abstract domain. The discussion on options to tune the precision of the widening operator is postponed to the next section.

3.1   Domain Representation

The domain of a ranking function represented by a decision tree is partitioned into pieces which are determined by the *linear constraints* encountered along the paths to the leaves of the tree. The abstract domain supports linear constraints of different expressivity. In the following, we also propose an alternative strategy to modify the linear constraints as a result of a variable assignment. We plan to support non-linear constraints as part of our future work.

Linear Constraints. We rely on existing numerical abstract domains for labeling the decision nodes with the corresponding linear constraints and for manipulating them. In order of expressivity, we support interval [12] constraints (i.e., of

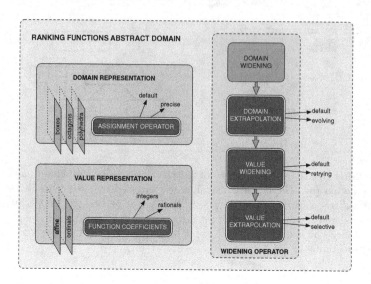

Fig. 2. Overview of the various parameterizations for the components of the ranking function abstract domain. Highlighted with a double border are the components for which new parameterizations are introduced in this paper.

the form $\pm x \leq c$), octagonal [30] constraints (i.e., of the form $\pm x_i \pm x_j \leq c$), and polyhedral [15] constraints (i.e., of the form $c_1 \cdot x_1 + \cdots + c_k \cdot x_k \leq c_{k+1}$). As for efficiency, contrary to expectations, octagonal constraints are the costliest labeling in practice. The reason for this lies in how constraints are manipulated as a results of a variable assignment which amplifies known performance drawbacks for octagons [19,26]. We expand on this shortly.

Assignment Operator. A variable assignment might impact some of the linear constraints within the decision nodes as well as some functions within the leaf nodes. The abstract domain now supports two strategies to modify the decision trees as a result of a variable assignment:

- The default strategy [40] consists in carrying out a variable assignment independently on each linear constraint labeling a decision node and each function labeling a leaf of the decision tree. This strategy is cheap since it requires a single tree traversal. It is sometimes imprecise as shown in Fig. 3.
- The new precise strategy consists in carrying out a variable assignment on each partition of a ranking function and then merging the resulting partitions. This strategy is costlier since it requires traversing the initial decision tree to identify the initial partitions, building a decision tree for each resulting partition, and traversing these decision trees to merge them. Note that building a decision tree requires sorting a number of linear constraints possibly higher than the height of the initial decision tree [37]. However, this strategy is much more precise as shown in Fig. 3.

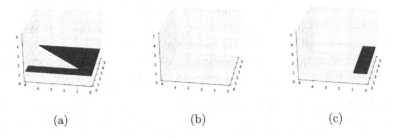

(a)   (b)   (c)

Fig. 3. Impact of the non-deterministic variable assignment x = ? (which resets the value of x to a randomly chosen value) on a ranking function (a) using the default assignment strategy (b) and the precise assignment strategy (c). Note that the default assignment strategy loses all information.

Both strategies do not work well with octagonal constraints. It is known that the original algorithms for manipulating octagons do not preserve their sparsity [19,26]. An immediate consequence of this is that a variable assignment on a single octagonal constraints often yields multiple linear constraints. This effect is particularly amplified by the default assignment strategy described above. The precise assignment strategy suffers less from this but the decision trees still tend to grow considerably in size. We plan to support sparsity-preserving algorithms for octagonal constraints as part of our future work.

3.2 Value Representation

The functions used for labeling the leaves of the decision trees are *affine functions* of the program variables (i.e., of the form $m_1 \cdot x_1 + \cdots + m_k \cdot x_k + q$), plus the special elements $\bot$ and $\top$ which explicitly represent undefined functions (cf. Fig. 1b). The element $\top$ shares the same meaning of $\bot$ but is only introduced by the widening operator. We expand on this in the next section. More specifically, we support *lexicographic* affine *functions* $(f_k, \ldots, f_1, f_0)$ in the isomorphic form of ordinals $\omega^k \cdot f_k + \cdots + \omega \cdot f_1 + f_0$ [29,39]. The *maximum degree* k of the polynomial is a parameter of the analysis. We leave non-linear functions for future work.

The coefficients of the affine functions are by default integers [40] and we now also support rational coefficients. Note that, when using rational coefficients, the functions have to decrease by at least one at each program execution step to ensure termination. Indeed, a decreasing sequence of rational number is not necessarily finite. However, the integer parts of rational-valued functions which decrease by at least one at each program step yield a finite decreasing sequence.

4   The Widening Operator on Ranking Functions

The widening operator ∇ tries to predict a value for the ranking function over the states on which it is not yet defined. Thus, it has more freedom than traditional widening operators, in the sense that it is temporarily allowed to *under-approximate* the value of the most precise ranking function w (cf. Sect. 2) or *over-approximate* its domain of definition dom(w), or both — in contrast with the observation made at the end of Sect. 2. The only requirement is that these discrepancies are resolved before the analysis stabilizes.

In more detail, give two decision trees t_1 and t_2, the widening operator will go through the following steps to compute $t_1 \triangledown t_2$ [40]:

Domain Widening. This step resolves an eventual over-approximation of the domain dom(w) of w following the inclusion of a program state from which a non-terminating program execution is reachable. This discrepancy manifests itself when a leaf in t_1 is labeled by a function and its corresponding leaf in t_2 is labeled by $\bot$. The widening operator marks the offending leaf in t_2 with $\top$ to prevent successive iterates of the analysis from mistakenly including again the same program state into the domain of the ranking function.

Domain Extrapolation. This step extrapolates the domain of the ranking functions over the states on which it is not yet defined. The default strategy consists in dropping the decision nodes that belong to t_2 but not to t_1 and merging the corresponding subtrees[4]. In this way we might lose information but we ensure convergence by limiting the size of the decision trees.

Value Widening. This step resolves an eventual under-approximation of the value of w and an eventual over-approximation of the domain dom(w) of w following the inclusion of a non-terminating program state. These discrepancies manifest themselves when the value of a function labeling a leaf in t_1 is smaller than the value of the function labeling the corresponding leaf in t_2. In this case, the default strategy consists again in marking the offending leaf in t_2 with $\top$ to exclude it from the rest of the analysis.

Value Extrapolation. This step extrapolates the value of the ranking function over the states that have been added to the domain of the ranking function in the last analysis iterate. These states are represented by the leaves in t_2 that are labeled by a function and their corresponding leaves in t_1 are labeled by $\bot$. The default heuristic consists in increasing the gradient of the functions with respect to the functions labeling their adjacent leaves in the decision tree. The rationale being that programs often loop over consecutive values of a variable, we use the information available in adjacent partitions of the domain of the ranking function to infer the shape of the ranking function for the current partitions. An example is shown in Fig. 4.

In the rest of the section, we suggest new heuristics to improve the default strategies used in the last three steps performed by the widening operator. These yield new widening operators which combine these heuristics to dramatically increase the precision of the analysis while offering good cost compromises.

Note that, to improve precision, it is customary to avoid the use of the widening operator for a certain number of analysis iterates. In the following, we refer to this number as *delay threshold*.

---

[4] We requires the decision nodes belonging to t_1 to be a subset of those belonging to t_2. This can always be ensured by computing $t_1 \triangledown (t_1 \sqcup t_2)$ instead of $t_1 \triangledown t_2$.

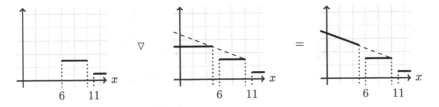

Fig. 4. Example of *value extrapolation*. The default heuristics increases the slope of the function defined for $x < 6$ with respect to the value of the function defined in its adjacent partition (i.e., for $6 \le x < 11$).

4.1 Domain Extrapolation

The default strategy for the *domain extrapolation* never infers new linear constraints and this hinders proving termination for some programs. In the following, we propose an alternative strategy which limits the number of decision nodes to be dropped during the analysis and labels them with new linear constraints. It is important to carefully choose the new added constraints to avoid slowing down the analysis unnecessarily and to make sure that the analysis still converges.

We suggest here a strategy inspired by the *evolving rays* heuristic presented in [1] to improve the widening operator of the polyhedra abstract domain [15]. The evolving strategy examines each linear constraint c_2 in t_2 (i.e., the decision tree corresponding to the last iterate of the analysis) as if it was generated by *rotation* of a linear constraint c_1 in t_1 (i.e., the decision tree corresponding to the previous iterate of the analysis). This rotation is formalized as follows [1]:

$$\text{evolve}(u, v) = w$$
$$\text{where } w_i = \begin{cases} 0 & \text{if } \exists j \in \{1, \ldots, n\}.(u_i v_j - u_j v_i)u_i u_j < 0 \\ u_i & \text{otherwise} \end{cases}$$

where u and w are the vectors of coefficients of the linear constraints c_2 in t_2 and c_1 in t_1, respectively. In particular, evolve sets to zero the components of u that match the direction of rotation. Intuitively, the evolving strategy continues the rotation of c_2 until one or more of the non-null coefficients of c_2 become zero. The new constraint reaches one of the boundaries of the orthant where c_2 lies without trespassing it. This strategy is particularly useful in situations similar to the one depicted in Fig. 5a: the ranking function is defined over increasingly smaller pieces delimited by different rotations of a linear constraint. In such case, the evolving strategy infers the linear constraints highlighted in red in Fig. 5b, thus extrapolating the domain of the ranking function up to the boundary of the orthant where the function is defined.

More specifically, the evolving strategy explores each pair of linear constraints on the same path in the decision tree t_2 and modifies them as described above to obtain new constraints. The strategy then discards the less frequently obtained constraints. The relevant frequency is a parameter of the analysis which in the

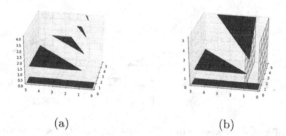

(a)   (b)

Fig. 5. The ranking function (b) obtained after widening using the evolving strategy on a given ranking function (a). Highlighted in red are the linear constraints inferred by the strategy, which limit the domain extrapolation to the increasingly smaller pieces on which the given ranking function is defined. (Color figure online)

following we call the *evolving threshold*. In our experience, it is usually a good choice to set the evolving threshold to be equal to the delay threshold of the widening. The remaining constraints are used to substitute the linear constraints that appear in t_2 but not in t_1, possibly merging the corresponding subtrees.

Note that, by definition, the number of new linear constraints that can be added by the evolving strategy is finite. The strategy then defaults to the default strategy and this guarantees the termination of the analysis.

4.2   Value Widening

The default strategy for the *value widening* marks with $\top$ the leaves in t_2 (i.e., the decision tree corresponding to the last iterate of the analysis) labeled with a larger value than their corresponding leaves in t_1 (i.e., the decision tree corresponding to the previous iterate of the analysis). This resolves eventual discrepancies in the approximation of the most precise ranking function w at the cost of losing precision in the analysis. As an example, consider the situation shown in Fig. 6: Fig. 6a depicts the most precise ranking function for a program and Fig. 6b depicts its approximation at the iterate immediately after widening. Note that one partition of the ranking function shown in Fig. 6b under-approximates the

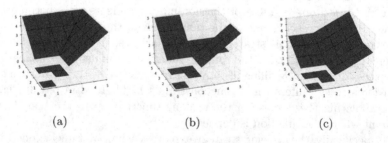

(a)   (b)   (c)

Fig. 6. The ranking function (c) obtained after widening using the retrying strategy on a given ranking function (b). Note that the given ranking function (b) under-approximates the value of the ranking function shown in (a).

value of the ranking function shown in Fig. 6a. The default strategy would then label the offending partition with $\top$, in essence giving up on trying to predict a value for the ranking function on that partition.

A simple and yet powerful improvement is to maintain the values of the offending leaves in t_2 and continue the analysis. In this way, the analysis can do various attempts at predicting a stable value for the ranking function. Note that using this retrying strategy without caution would cause the analysis to not converge for a number of programs. Instead, we limit the number of attempts to a certain *retrying threshold*, and then revert to the default strategy.

The retrying strategy for ordinals of the form $\omega^k \cdot f_k + \cdots + \omega \cdot f_1 + f_0$ (cf. Sect. 3.2) behaves analogously to the other abstract domain operators for manipulating ordinals [39]. It works in ascending powers of ω carrying to the next higher degree when the *retrying threshold* has been reached (up to the maximum degree for the polynomial, in which case we default to $\top$).

4.3   Value Extrapolation

The default heuristic for the *value extrapolation* consists in increasing the gradient of the ranking function with respect to its value in *adjacent* partition of its domain. Note that, many other heuristics are possible. In fact, this step only affects the precision of the analysis, and not its convergence or its soundness.

In this paper, we propose a selective extrapolation heuristic, which increases the gradient of the ranking function with respect to *selected* partitions of its domain. More specifically, the heuristic selects the partitions from which the current partition is reachable in one loop iteration. This strategy is particularly effective in combination with the evolving strategy described in Sect. 4.1. Indeed, the evolving strategy often splits partitions by adding new linear constraints and, in some cases, this affects the precision of the analysis since it alters the adjacency relationships between the pieces on which the ranking function is defined.

We plan to investigate other strategies as part of our future work.

5   Implementation and Experimental Evaluation

The ranking functions abstract domain and the new parameterizations introduced in this paper are implemented in FUNCTION [36] and are available online[5]. The implementation is in OCAML and consists of around 3K lines of code. The current front-end of FUNCTION accepts programs written in a (subset of) C, without struct and union types. It provides only a limited support for arrays, pointers, and recursion. The only basic data type are mathematical integers, deviating from the standard semantics of C. The abstract domain builds on the numerical abstract domains provided by the APRON library [25].

The analysis proceeds by structural induction on the program syntax, iterating loops until a fixpoint is reached. In case of nested loops, a fixpoint on the inner loop is computed for each iteration of the outer loop, following [4,31]. It is also possible to refine the analysis by only considering the reachable states.

---

[5] https://github.com/caterinaurban/function.

Experimental Evaluation. The ranking functions abstract domain was evaluated on 242 terminating C programs collected from the *5th International Competition on Software Verification (SV-COMP 2016)*. Due to the limitations in the current front-end of FUNCTION we were not able to analyze 47% of the test cases. The experiments were performed on a system with a 3.20 GHz 64-bit Dual-Core CPU (Intel i5-3470) and 6 GB of RAM, running Ubuntu 16.04.1 LTS.

We compared multiple configurations of parameters for the abstract domain. We report here the result obtained with the most relevant configurations. Unless otherwise specified, the common configuration of parameters uses the default strategy for handling variable assignments (cf. Sect. 3.1), a *maximum degree* of two for ordinals using integer coefficients for affine functions (cf. Sect. 3.2), and a *delay threshold* of three for the widening (cf. Sect. 4). Figure 7 presents the results obtained using polyhedral constraints. Figure 8 shows the successful configura-

N	Value		Widening				Assignment		Success	Time	TO
	$\mathbb{N}$	$\mathbb{Q}$	delay	retrying	evolving	selective	default	precise			
1	✓							✓		128	0.35s	5
									140	0.44s	3
2		✓						✓		124	0.35s	5
									138	0.78s	3
3	✓			✓				✓		138	0.40s	6
									152	0.48s	3
4	✓				✓			✓		125	1.28s	11
									127	1.01s	10
5	✓					✓		✓		118	0.28s	5
									106	0.21s	3
6	✓			✓	✓			✓		136	1.74s	17
									139	1.18s	14
7	✓			✓		✓		✓		129	0.35s	5
									124	0.26s	4
8	✓				✓	✓		✓		116	0.92s	11
									102	0.31s	10
9	✓			✓	✓	✓		✓		134	1.40s	16
									123	0.63s	19
10	✓			✓	✓	✓		✓		128	1.41s	18
									120	0.48s	16
11	✓			✓					✓	133	3.41s	50
									132	6.59s	56
12	✓	6		✓					✓	122	8.70s	92
									120	6.22s	98

Fig. 7. Evaluation of FUNCTION using polyhedral constraints. For each configuration N, the bottom row corresponds to the results obtained by restricting the analysis to the reachable states, and the top row to the results obtained without reachability information. Highlighted in blue is the best configuration in terms of number of successes. Time is the mean time per successful test case. (Color figure online)

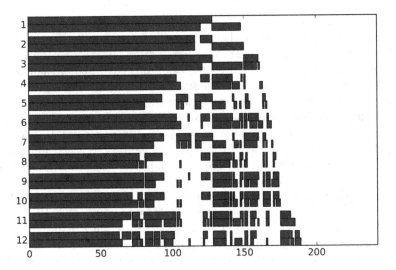

Fig. 8. Test case coverage for the evaluation of FUNCTION using polyhedral constraints. The horizontal axis enumerates the test cases. For each configuration of FUNCTION given on the vertical axis (without and with reachability information, as in Fig. 7), a colored area corresponds to successful test cases. (Color figure online)

tions for each test case. Using interval constraints yields fewer successful test cases (around 50% less successes) but it generally ensures better runtimes. The exception is a slight slowdown of the analysis when using rational coefficients, which is not observed when using polyhedral constraints. We did not evaluate the use of octagonal constraints due to the performance drawbacks discussed in Sect. 3.1. We used a time limit of 300 s for each test case.

We can observe that using the retrying strategy always improves the overall analysis result: configurations 3, 6, 7, and 9are more successful than the corresponding configurations 1, 4, 5, and 8, which instead use the default strategy. In particular, configuration 3 is the best configuration in terms of number of successes (cf. Fig. 7). However, in general, improving the precision of the widening operator does not necessarily improve the overall analysis result. More specifically, configurations 4 to 9 seem to perform generally worse than configuration 1 and 3 both in terms of number of successes and running times. However, although these configurations are not effective for a number of programs for which configuration 1 and 3 are successful, they are not subsumed by them since they allow proving termination of many other programs (cf. Fig. 8).

Another interesting observation is that using rational coefficients in configuration 2 worsens the result of the analysis compared to configuration 1 which uses integer coefficients (cf. Fig. 8). Instead, using rational coefficients in configuration 10 allows proving termination for a number of programs for which configuration 9 (which uses integer coefficients) is unsuccessful.

The configurations using the evolving strategy (i.e., 4, 6, 8, 9, and 10) tend to be slower than the configurations which use the default strategy. As a consequence, they suffer from a higher number of timeouts (cf. Fig. 7). Even worse is the slowdown caused by the precise strategy to handle variable assignments (cf. configurations 11 and 12) and a higher *delay threshold* for the widening (cf. configuration 12). We observed that a *delay threshold* higher than six only marginally improves precision while significantly worsening running times.

Finally, we observed that there are some configurations for which decreasing the precision of the linear constraints (from polyhedral to interval constraints) allows proving termination of some more programs. In particular, this concerns configuration 2 as well as some of the other configurations when limiting the analysis to the reachable states. However, this happens very rarely: overall, only three programs can be proven terminating only using interval constraints.

We also compared FUNCTION against the tools participating to *SV-COMP 2016*: APROVE [34], SEAHORN [21,38] and UAUTOMIZER [22]. We did not compare with other tools such as T2 [6] and 2LS [9] since FUNCTION does not yet support the input format of T2 and bit-precise integer semantics (like 2LS does). As we observed that most of the parameter configurations of the abstract domain do not subsume each other, for the comparison, we set up FUNCTION to use multiple parameter combinations successively, each with a time limit of 25 s. More specifically, we first use configuration 3, which offers the best compromise between number of successes and running times. We then move onto configurations that use the evolving strategy and the selective strategy, which are successful for other programs at the cost of an increased running time. Finally, we try the even more costly configurations that use the precise strategy for handling variable assignments and a higher *delay threshold* for the widening.

We ran FUNCTION on the same machine as above, while for the other tools we used the results of *SV-COMP 2016* since our machine was not powerful enough to run them. The time limit per test case was again 300 s. Figure 9 shows the result of the comparison and Fig. 10 shows the successful tools for each test case. We can observe that, despite being less successful than APROVE or UAUTOMIZER, FUNCTION is able to prove termination of an important number of programs (i.e., 80% of the test cases, cf. Fig. 9). Moreover, FUNCTION is generally faster than all other tools, despite the fact that these were run on

	■	▲	✕	○	Success	Time	TO
FUNCTION	–	–	–	–	195	5.25s	7
APROVE [34]	7	36	188	11	224	15.66s	15
SEAHORN [21,38]	31	22	164	25	186	8.57s	52
UAUTOMIZER [22]	10	36	185	11	221	14.04s	6

Fig. 9. Comparison of FUNCTION against tools participating in SV-COMP 2016. ■ denotes the number of programs for which only FUNCTION was successful, ▲ the number of programs for which only the other tool was successful, ✕ the number for which both tools were successful and ○ the number for which neither tool was. Time corresponds to the mean time per success of the tool.

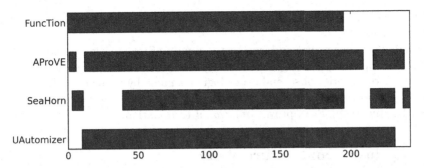

Fig. 10. Test case coverage for the comparison of FUNCTION against tools participating in SV-COMP 2016. The horizontal axis enumerates the test cases. Each colored area corresponds to successful test cases. (Color figure online)

more powerful machines. Finally, we can observe in Fig. 10, that for each tool there is a small subset of the test cases for which it is the only successful tool. The four tools together are able to prove termination for all the test cases.

6 Related Work

In the recent past, termination analysis has benefited from many research advances and powerful termination provers have emerged over the years.

APROVE [34] is probably the most mature tool in the field. Its underlying theory is the size-change termination approach [27], originated in the context of term rewriting systems, which consists in collecting a set of size-change graphs (representing function calls) and combining them into multipaths (representing program executions) in such a way that at least one variable is guaranteed to decrease. Compared to size-change termination, FUNCTION avoids the exploration of the combinatorial space of multipaths by manipulating ordinals.

TERMINATOR [10] is based on the transition invariants method introduced in [33]. More specifically, the tool iteratively constructs transition invariants by searching within a program for single paths representing potential counterexamples to termination, computing a ranking function for each one of them individually (as in [32]), and combining the obtained ranking functions into a single termination argument. Its successor, T2 [6], has abandoned the transition invariants approach in favor of lexicographic ranking functions [11] and has broadened its scope to a wide range of temporal properties [7].

UAUTOMIZER [22] is a software model checker based on an automata-theoretic approach to software verification [23]. Similarly to TERMINATOR, it reduces proving termination to proving that no program state is repeatedly visited (and it is not covered by the current termination argument), and composes termination arguments by repeatedly invoking a ranking function synthesis tool [28]. In contrast, the approach recently implemented in the software model checker SEAHORN [21] systematically samples terminating program executions and extrapolates from these a ranking function [38] using an approach which resembles the *value extrapolation* of the widening operator implemented in FUNCTION.

Finally, another recent addition to the family of termination provers is 2LS [9], which implements a *bit-precise* inter-procedural termination analysis. The analysis solves a series of second-order logic formulae by reducing them to first-order using polyhedral templates. In contrast with the tools mentioned above, both 2LS and FUNCTION prove *conditional* termination.

7   Conclusion and Future Work

In this paper, we fully parameterized various aspects of the ranking function abstract domain implemented in the static analyzer FUNCTION. We identified new widening operators, which increase the precision of the analysis while offering good cost compromises. We also introduced options to tune the representation of the ranking functions manipulated by the abstract domain. In combining these improvements, we obtained an implementation which subsumes the previous implementation and is competitive with state-of-the-art termination provers.

In the future, we would like to extend the abstract domain to also support non-linear constraints, such as congruences [20], and non-linear functions, such as polynomials [5] or exponentials [16]. In addition, we plan to support sparsity-preserving algorithms for manipulating octagonal constraints [19,26]. We would also like to investigate new strategies to predict a value for the ranking function during widening. Finally, we plan to work on proving termination of more complex programs, such as heap-manipulating programs. We would like to investigate the adaptability of existing methods [2] and existing abstract domains for heap analysis [8], and possibly design new techniques.

References

1. Bagnara, R., Hill, P.M., Ricci, E., Zaffanella, E.: Precise widening operators for convex polyhedra. Sci. Comput. Program. **58**(1–2), 28–56 (2005)
2. Berdine, J., Cook, B., Distefano, D., O'Hearn, P.W.: Automatic termination proofs for programs with shape-shifting heaps. In: Ball, T., Jones, R.B. (eds.) CAV 2006. LNCS, vol. 4144, pp. 386–400. Springer, Heidelberg (2006). doi:10.1007/11817963_35
3. Bertrane, J., Cousot, P., Cousot, R., Feret, J., Mauborgne, L., Miné, A., Rival, X.: Static analysis and verification of aerospace software by abstract interpretation. In: AIAA (2010)
4. Bourdoncle, F.: Efficient chaotic iteration strategies with widenings. In: Bjørner, D., Broy, M., Pottosin, I.V. (eds.) Formal Methods in Programming and Their Applications. LNCS, vol. 735, pp. 128–141. Springer, Heidelberg (1993). doi:10.1007/BFb0039704
5. Bradley, A.R., Manna, Z., Sipma, H.B.: The polyranking principle. In: Caires, L., Italiano, G.F., Monteiro, L., Palamidessi, C., Yung, M. (eds.) ICALP 2005. LNCS, vol. 3580, pp. 1349–1361. Springer, Heidelberg (2005). doi:10.1007/11523468_109

6. Brockschmidt, M., Cook, B., Fuhs, C.: Better termination proving through cooperation. In: Sharygina, N., Veith, H. (eds.) CAV 2013. LNCS, vol. 8044, pp. 413–429. Springer, Heidelberg (2013). doi:10.1007/978-3-642-39799-8_28

7. Brockschmidt, M., Cook, B., Ishtiaq, S., Khlaaf, H., Piterman, N.: T2: temporal property verification. In: Chechik, M., Raskin, J.-F. (eds.) TACAS 2016. LNCS, vol. 9636, pp. 387–393. Springer, Heidelberg (2016). doi:10.1007/978-3-662-49674-9_22

8. Chang, B.E., Rival, X.: Modular construction of shape-numeric analyzers. In: Festschrift for Dave Schmidt, pp. 161–185 (2013)

9. Chen, H.Y., David, C., Kroening, D., Schrammel, P., Wachter, B.: Synthesising interprocedural bit-precise termination proofs. In: ASE, pp. 53–64 (2015)

10. Cook, B., Podelski, A., Rybalchenko, A.: TERMINATOR: beyond safety. In: Ball, T., Jones, R.B. (eds.) CAV 2006. LNCS, vol. 4144, pp. 415–418. Springer, Heidelberg (2006). doi:10.1007/11817963_37

11. Cook, B., See, A., Zuleger, F.: Ramsey vs. lexicographic termination proving. In: Piterman, N., Smolka, S.A. (eds.) TACAS 2013. LNCS, vol. 7795, pp. 47–61. Springer, Heidelberg (2013). doi:10.1007/978-3-642-36742-7_4

12. Cousot, P., Cousot, R.: Static determination of dynamic properties of programs. In: Symposium on Programming, pp. 106–130 (1976)

13. Cousot, P., Cousot, R.: Abstract interpretation: a unied lattice model for static analysis of programs by construction or approximation of fixpoints. In: POPL, pp. 238–252 (1977)

14. Cousot, P., Cousot, R.: An abstract interpretation framework for termination. In: POPL, pp. 245–258 (2012)

15. Cousot, P., Halbwachs, N.: Automatic discovery of linear restraints among variables of a program. In: POPL, pp. 84–96 (1978)

16. Feret, J.: The arithmetic-geometric progression abstract domain. In: Cousot, R. (ed.) VMCAI 2005. LNCS, vol. 3385, pp. 42–58. Springer, Heidelberg (2005). doi:10.1007/978-3-540-30579-8_3

17. Floyd, R.W.: Assigning meanings to programs. In: Proceedings of Symposium on Applied Mathematics, vol. 19, pp. 19–32 (1967)

18. Fuchs, H., Kedem, Z.M., Naylor, B.F.: On visible surface generation by a priori tree structures. SIGGRAPH Comput. Graph. **14**(3), 124–133 (1980)

19. Gange, G., Navas, J.A., Schachte, P., Søndergaard, H., Stuckey, P.J.: Exploiting sparsity in difference-bound matrices. In: Rival, X. (ed.) SAS 2016. LNCS, vol. 9837, pp. 189–211. Springer, Heidelberg (2016). doi:10.1007/978-3-662-53413-7_10

20. Granger, P.: Static analysis of arithmetic congruences. Int. J. Comput. Math. **30**, 165–199 (1989)

21. Gurfinkel, A., Kahsai, T., Navas, J.A.: SeaHorn: a framework for verifying C programs (competition contribution). In: Baier, C., Tinelli, C. (eds.) TACAS 2015. LNCS, vol. 9035, pp. 447–450. Springer, Heidelberg (2015). doi:10.1007/978-3-662-46681-0_41

22. Heizmann, M., Dietsch, D., Greitschus, M., Leike, J., Musa, B., Schätzle, C., Podelski, A.: Ultimate automizer with two-track proofs. In: Chechik, M., Raskin, J.-F. (eds.) TACAS 2016. LNCS, vol. 9636, pp. 950–953. Springer, Heidelberg (2016). doi:10.1007/978-3-662-49674-9_68

23. Heizmann, M., Hoenicke, J., Podelski, A.: Software model checking for people who love automata. In: Sharygina, N., Veith, H. (eds.) CAV 2013. LNCS, vol. 8044, pp. 36–52. Springer, Heidelberg (2013). doi:10.1007/978-3-642-39799-8_2

24. Jeannet, B.: Representing and approximating transfer functions in abstract interpretation of hetereogeneous datatypes. In: Hermenegildo, M.V., Puebla, G. (eds.) SAS 2002. LNCS, vol. 2477, pp. 52–68. Springer, Heidelberg (2002). doi:10.1007/3-540-45789-5_7

25. Jeannet, B., Miné, A.: APRON: a library of numerical abstract domains for static analysis. In: Bouajjani, A., Maler, O. (eds.) CAV 2009. LNCS, vol. 5643, pp. 661–667. Springer, Heidelberg (2009). doi:10.1007/978-3-642-02658-4_52

26. Jourdan, J.-H.: Sparsity preserving algorithms for octagons. In: NSAD (2016)

27. Lee, C.S., Jones, N.D., Ben-Amram, A.M.: The size-change principle for program termination. In: POPL, pp. 81–92 (2001)

28. Leike, J., Heizmann, M.: Ranking templates for linear loops. In: Ábrahám, E., Havelund, K. (eds.) TACAS 2014. LNCS, vol. 8413, pp. 172–186. Springer, Heidelberg (2014). doi:10.1007/978-3-642-54862-8_12

29. Manna, Z., Pnueli, A.: The Temporal Verification of Reactive Systems: Progress (1996)

30. Miné, A.: The octagon abstract domain. High.-Order Symb. Comput. 19(1), 31–100 (2006)

31. Muthukumar, K., Hermenegildo, M.V.: Compile-time derivation of variable dependency using abstract interpretation. J. Log. Program. 13(2/3), 315–347 (1992)

32. Podelski, A., Rybalchenko, A.: A complete method for the synthesis of linear ranking functions. In: Steffen, B., Levi, G. (eds.) VMCAI 2004. LNCS, vol. 2937, pp. 239–251. Springer, Heidelberg (2004). doi:10.1007/978-3-540-24622-0_20

33. Podelski, A., Rybalchenko, A.: Transition invariants. In: LICS, pp. 32–41 (2004)

34. Ströder, T., Aschermann, C., Frohn, F., Hensel, J., Giesl, J.: AProVE: termination and memory safety of C programs. In: Baier, C., Tinelli, C. (eds.) TACAS 2015. LNCS, vol. 9035, pp. 417–419. Springer, Heidelberg (2015). doi:10.1007/978-3-662-46681-0_32

35. Turing, A.: Checking a large routine. In: Report of a Conference on High Speed Automatic Calculating Machines, pp. 67–69 (1949)

36. Urban, C.: FuncTion: an abstract domain functor for termination. In: Baier, C., Tinelli, C. (eds.) TACAS 2015. LNCS, vol. 9035, pp. 464–466. Springer, Heidelberg (2015). doi:10.1007/978-3-662-46681-0_46

37. Urban, C.: Static analysis by abstract interpretation of functional temporal properties of programs. Ph.D. thesis, École Normale Supérieure, July 2015

38. Urban, C., Gurfinkel, A., Kahsai, T.: Synthesizing ranking functions from bits and pieces. In: Chechik, M., Raskin, J.-F. (eds.) TACAS 2016. LNCS, vol. 9636, pp. 54–70. Springer, Heidelberg (2016). doi:10.1007/978-3-662-49674-9_4

39. Urban, C., Miné, A.: An abstract domain to infer ordinal-valued ranking functions. In: Shao, Z. (ed.) ESOP 2014. LNCS, vol. 8410, pp. 412–431. Springer, Heidelberg (2014). doi:10.1007/978-3-642-54833-8_22

40. Urban, C., Miné, A.: A decision tree abstract domain for proving conditional termination. In: Müller-Olm, M., Seidl, H. (eds.) SAS 2014. LNCS, vol. 8723, pp. 302–318. Springer, Cham (2014). doi:10.1007/978-3-319-10936-7_19

Automatic Verification of Finite Precision Implementations of Linear Controllers

Junkil Park[1]([✉]), Miroslav Pajic[2], Oleg Sokolsky[1], and Insup Lee[1]

[1] Department of Computer and Information Science,
University of Pennsylvania, Philadelphia, USA
{park11,sokolsky,lee}@cis.upenn.edu
[2] Department of Electrical and Computer Engineering,
Duke University, Durham, USA
miroslav.pajic@duke.edu

Abstract. We consider the problem of verifying finite precision implementation of linear time-invariant controllers against mathematical specifications. A specification may have multiple correct implementations which are different from each other in controller state representation, but equivalent from a perspective of input-output behavior (e.g., due to optimization in a code generator). The implementations may use finite precision computations (e.g. floating-point arithmetic) which cause quantization (i.e., roundoff) errors. To address these challenges, we first extract a controller's mathematical model from the implementation via symbolic execution and floating-point error analysis, and then check approximate input-output equivalence between the extracted model and the specification by similarity checking. We show how to automatically verify the correctness of floating-point controller implementation in C language using the combination of techniques such as symbolic execution and convex optimization problem solving. We demonstrate the scalability of our approach through evaluation with randomly generated controller specifications of realistic size.

1 Introduction

Most modern safety- and life-critical embedded applications rely on software-based control for their operation. When reasoning about safety of these systems, it is extremely important to ensure that control software is correctly implemented. In this paper, we study the problem of whether a given piece of software is a faithful representation of an abstract specification of the control function.

We assume a commonly used development approach, where control systems are developed in a model-driven fashion. The model captures both the dynamics of the "plant", the entity to be controlled, and the controller itself, as mathematical expressions using well established tools, such as Simulink and Stateflow. Control theory offers a rich set of techniques to determine these expressions, determine their parameters, and perform analysis of the model to conclude whether the plant model adequately describes the system to be controlled and

© Springer-Verlag GmbH Germany 2017
A. Legay and T. Margaria (Eds.): TACAS 2017, Part I, LNCS 10205, pp. 153–169, 2017.
DOI: 10.1007/978-3-662-54577-5_9

whether the controller achieves the desired goals of the control system. In this work, we assume that such control design activities have been performed, achieving the acceptable degree of assurance for the control design. In other words, we assume that the mathematical model of the controller is correct with respect to any higher-level requirements and can be used as the specification for a software implementation of the controller.

Typically, control software is obtained by code generation from the mathematical model. Code generation tools such as Embedded Coder are widely used. Ideally, we would like to have these code generation tools to be verified, that is, to offer guarantees that generated code correctly computes the control function. In this case, no verification of the control code would be needed. However, commercially available code generators are complex black-box tools and are generally not amenable to formal verification. Subtle bugs have been found in commercially available code generators in the past [25]. In the absence of verified code generators, we would like to be able to verify instances of generated code with respect to their mathematical specification.

In our past work [26, 28], we explored several approaches to the verification of implementations of linear time invariant (LTI) controllers. In LTI controllers, the relationships between the values of inputs and state variables, and between state variables and outputs, are captured as linear functions, and coefficients of these functions are constant (i.e., time-invariant). The main limitation in all of these approaches is the assumption that the calculations are performed using real numbers. Of course, real numbers are a mathematical abstraction. In practice, software performs calculations using a limited-precision representation of numbers, such as the floating-point representation. The use of floating-point numbers introduces errors into the computation, which have to be accounted for in the verification process.

In this paper, we build on the work of [28], which follows an *equivalence checking* approach. We apply symbolic execution to the generated code, which calculates symbolic expressions for the values of state and output variables in the code at the completion of the invocation of the controller. We use these symbolic values to reconstruct a mathematical representation of the control function. We introduce error terms into this representation that characterize the effects of numerical errors. The verification step then tries to establish the approximate equivalence between the specification of the control function and the reconstructed representation. In [28], we considered two promising alternatives for assessing the equivalence: one based on SMT solving and the other one based on convex optimization. Somewhat surprisingly, when the error terms that account for floating-point calculations are added, the SMT-solving approach becomes impractical, while the optimization-based approach suffers minimal degradation in performance.

The paper is organized as follows: Sect. 2 provides background of LTI systems. Section 3 describes how to extract a model from the controller code. Section 4 presents the approximate equivalence checking. Section 5 evaluates the scalability of our approach. Sections 6 and 7 provide an overview of related work and conclude the paper.

2   Preliminaries

This section presents preliminaries on LTI controllers and their software implementations. We also introduce two real-world examples that motivate the problem considered in this paper, as well as the problem statement.

2.1   Linear Feedback Controller

The goal of feedback controllers is to ensure that the closed-loop systems have certain desired behaviors. In general, these controllers derive suitable control inputs to the plants (i.e., systems to control) based on previously obtained measurements of the plant outputs. In this paper, we consider a general class of feedback controllers that can be specified as linear time-invariant (LTI) controllers in the standard *state-space representation* form:

$$\mathbf{z}_{k+1} = \mathbf{A}\mathbf{z}_k + \mathbf{B}\mathbf{u}_k$$
$$\mathbf{y}_k = \mathbf{C}\mathbf{z}_k + \mathbf{D}\mathbf{u}_k. \tag{1}$$

where $\mathbf{u}_k \in \mathbb{R}^p$, $\mathbf{y}_k \in \mathbb{R}^m$ and $\mathbf{z}_k \in \mathbb{R}^n$ are the input vector, the output vector and the state vector at time k respectively. The matrices $\mathbf{A} \in \mathbb{R}^{n \times n}$, $\mathbf{B} \in \mathbb{R}^{n \times p}$, $\mathbf{C} \in \mathbb{R}^{m \times n}$ and $\mathbf{D} \in \mathbb{R}^{m \times p}$ together with the initial controller state $\mathbf{z}_0$ completely specify an LTI controller. Thus, we use $\mathbf{\Sigma}(\mathbf{A}, \mathbf{B}, \mathbf{C}, \mathbf{D}, \mathbf{z}_0)$ to denote an LTI controller, or just use $\mathbf{\Sigma}(\mathbf{A}, \mathbf{B}, \mathbf{C}, \mathbf{D})$ when the initial controller state $\mathbf{z}_0$ is zero.

During the control-design phase, controller $\mathbf{\Sigma}(\mathbf{A}, \mathbf{B}, \mathbf{C}, \mathbf{D}, \mathbf{z}_0)$ is derived to guarantee the desired closed-loop performance, while taking into account available computation and communication resources (e.g., finite-precision arithmetic logic units). This model (i.e., controller specification) is then usually 'mapped' into a software implementation of a *step function* that: (1) maintains the state of the controller, and updates it every time new sensor measurements are available (i.e., when it's invoked); and (2) computes control outputs (i.e., inputs applied to the plant) from the current controller's state and incoming sensor measurements. In most embedded control systems, the step function is periodically invoked, or whenever new sensor measurements arrive. In this work, as in our previous work [28], we assume that data is exchanged with the step function through global variables.[1] In other words, the input, output and state variables are declared in the global scope, and the step function reads both input and state variables, and updates both output and state variables as the effect of its execution. It is worth noting however that this assumption does not critically limit our approach because it can be easily extended to support a different code interface for the step function.

2.2   Motivating Examples

To motivate our work, we introduce two examples from [26,28]. These examples illustrate limitations of the standard verification techniques that directly utilize

---

[1] This convention is used by Embedded Coder, a code generation toolbox for Matlab/Simulink.

the mathematical model from (1), in cases when controller software is generated by a code generator whose optimizations potentially violate the model while still ensuring the desired control functionality.

A Scalar Linear Integrator. Consider a simple controller that computes control input u_k as a scaled sum of all previous sensor data $y_i \in \mathbb{R}, i = 0, ..., k-1$ – i.e.,

$$u_k = \sum_{i=0}^{k-1} \alpha y_i, k > 1, \quad \text{and}, \quad u_0 = 0. \tag{2}$$

Now, if we use the Simulink Integrator block with Forward Euler integration to implement this controller, the resulting controller model will be $\Sigma(1, \alpha, 1, 0)$, – i.e., $z_{k+1} = z_k + \alpha y_k, u_k = z_k$. On the other hand, a realization $\hat{\Sigma}(1, 1, \alpha, 0)$ – i.e., $z_{k+1} = z_k + y_k, u_k = \alpha z_k$, of the controller would introduce a reduced computational error when finite precision arithmetics is used [10]. Thus, controller specification (2) may result in two different software implementations due to the use of different code generation tools. Still, it is important to highlight that these two implementations would have identical input-output behavior – the only difference is whether they maintain a scaled or unscaled sum of the previous sensor measurements.

Multiple-Input-Multiple-Output Controllers. Now, consider a more general Multiple-Input-Multiple-Output (MIMO) controller with two inputs and two outputs which maintains five states

$$\mathbf{z}_{k+1} = \underbrace{\begin{bmatrix} -0.500311 & 0.16751 & 0.028029 & -0.395599 & -0.652079 \\ 0.850942 & 0.181639 & -0.29276 & 0.481277 & 0.638183 \\ -0.458583 & -0.002389 & -0.154281 & -0.578708 & -0.769495 \\ 1.01855 & 0.638926 & -0.668256 & -0.258506 & 0.119959 \\ 0.100383 & -0.432501 & 0.122727 & 0.82634 & 0.892296 \end{bmatrix}}_{\mathbf{A}} \mathbf{z}_k +$$

$$+ \underbrace{\begin{bmatrix} 1.1149 & 0.164423 \\ -1.56592 & 0.634384 \\ 1.04856 & -0.196914 \\ 1.96066 & 3.11571 \\ -3.02046 & -1.96087 \end{bmatrix}}_{\mathbf{B}} \mathbf{u}_k \tag{3}$$

$$\mathbf{y}_k = \underbrace{\begin{bmatrix} 0.283441 & 0.032612 & -0.75658 & 0.085468 & 0.161088 \\ -0.528786 & 0.050734 & -0.681773 & -0.432334 & -1.17988 \end{bmatrix}}_{\mathbf{C}} \mathbf{z}_k \tag{4}$$

The controller has to perform $25 + 10 = 35$ multiplications as part of the state $\mathbf{z}$ update in every invocation of the step function. On the other hand, the following controller requires only $5 + 10 = 15$ multiplications for state update.

$$\hat{\mathbf{z}}_{k+1} = \underbrace{\begin{bmatrix} 0.87224 & 0 & 0 & 0 & 0 \\ 0 & 0.366378 & 0 & 0 & 0 \\ 0 & 0 & -0.540795 & 0 & 0 \\ 0 & 0 & 0 & -0.332664 & 0 \\ 0 & 0 & 0 & 0 & -0.204322 \end{bmatrix}}_{\hat{\mathbf{A}}} \hat{\mathbf{z}}_k +$$

$$+ \underbrace{\begin{bmatrix} 0.822174 & -0.438008 \\ -0.278536 & -0.824313 \\ 0.874484 & 0.858857 \\ -0.117628 & -0.506362 \\ -0.955459 & -0.622498 \end{bmatrix}}_{\hat{\mathbf{B}}} \mathbf{u}_k, \tag{5}$$

$$\mathbf{y}_k = \underbrace{\begin{bmatrix} -0.793176 & 0.154365 & -0.377883 & -0.360608 & -0.142123 \\ 0.503767 & -0.573538 & 0.170245 & -0.583312 & -0.56603 \end{bmatrix}}_{\hat{\mathbf{C}}} \hat{\mathbf{z}}_k \tag{6}$$

The above controllers Σ and $\hat{\Sigma}$ are *similar*,[2] which means that the same input sequences $\mathbf{y}_k$ delivered to both controllers, would result in identical outputs of the controllers. Note that the controller's states will likely differ. Consequently, the 'diagonalized' controller $\hat{\Sigma}$ results in the same control performance and thus provides the same control functionality as Σ, while violating the state evolution model of the initial controller Σ. The motivation for the use of the diagonalized controller comes from a significantly reduced computational cost that allow for the utilization of resource constrained embedded platforms. In general, any controller (1), would require $n^2 + np = n(n + p)$ multiplications to update its state. This can be significantly reduced when matrix $\mathbf{A}$ in (1) is diagonal – in this case only $n + np = n(p + 1)$ multiplications are needed.

2.3   Problem Statements

As illustrated with the motivating examples, the initial controller model and its implementation (i.e., step function) may be different from each other in representation (i.e., controller parameters, state representation) due to the optimization of code generators, while being functionally equivalent from the input-output perspective. Thus, we would like to develop the verification technique that is not sensitive to the state representation of the controller. Moreover, the controller software for embedded systems uses a finite precision arithmetic which introduces rounding errors in the computation. Thus, it is necessary to analyze the effect of rounding errors in the verification process. This work focuses on the controller implementations using floating-point arithmetic, but can be easily extended to the setup for fixed-point arithmetic. Consequently, our problem statements are as follows: given an LTI model, a step function using floating-point arithmetic and an approximate equivalence precision, verify if the step

---

[2] Similarity transform is formally defined in Sect. 4.

function is approximately equivalent to the initial LTI model from the input-output perspective.

3 Extracting Model from Floating-Point Controller Implementation

Our approach to the verification of a controller implementation against its mathematical model takes two steps: we first extract a model from the finite precision implementation (i.e., step function using floating-point arithmetic), and then compare it with the original model. This approach is an extension of [28] to consider the quantization error in the finite-precision implementation. To obtain a model from the step function, we employ the symbolic execution technique [7, 21], which allows us to identify the computation of the step function (i.e., the big-step transition relation on global states between before and after the execution of the step function). From the transition relation, we extract a mathematical model for the controller implementation. Since the implementation has floating-point quantization (i.e., roundoff) errors, the representation of the extracted model includes roundoff error terms, thus being different from the representation of the initial LTI model (1). We will describe the representation of extracted models in the next subsection.

3.1 Quantized Controller Model

A finite precision computation (e.g., floating-point arithmetic) involves rounding errors, which makes the computation result slightly deviated from the exact value that might be computed with the infinite precision computation. The floating-point rounding error can be modeled with the notions of both *absolute error* and *relative error*. The absolute error is defined as the difference between an exact number and its rounded number. The relative error defines such difference relative to the exact number. To model quantized controller implementations, we extend the representation of LTI model (1) with the new terms of absolute errors and relative errors, and obtain the following representation of quantized controller model:

$$
\begin{aligned}
\hat{\mathbf{z}}_{k+1} &= (\hat{\mathbf{A}} + \mathbf{E_A})\hat{\mathbf{z}}_k + (\hat{\mathbf{B}} + \mathbf{E_B})\mathbf{u}_k + \mathbf{e_z} \\
\mathbf{y}_k &= (\hat{\mathbf{C}} + \mathbf{E_C})\hat{\mathbf{z}}_k + (\hat{\mathbf{D}} + \mathbf{E_D})\mathbf{u}_k + \mathbf{e_y}.
\end{aligned}
\tag{7}
$$

where $\hat{\mathbf{A}}$, $\hat{\mathbf{B}}$, $\hat{\mathbf{C}}$ and $\hat{\mathbf{D}}$ are controller parameters. $\mathbf{E_A}$, $\mathbf{E_B}$, $\mathbf{E_C}$ and $\mathbf{E_D}$ are the relative errors regarding the state and input variables which are bounded by the relative error bound b_{rel} such that $\|\mathbf{E_A}\|, \|\mathbf{E_B}\|, \|\mathbf{E_C}\|, \|\mathbf{E_D}\| \leq b_{rel}$ where $\|\cdot\|$ is the L_∞ norm operator. In addition, $\mathbf{e_z}$ and $\mathbf{e_y}$ are the absolute errors which are bounded by the absolute error bound b_{abs} such that $\|\mathbf{e_x}\|, \|\mathbf{e_y}\| \leq b_{abs}$. In the rest of this section, we explain how to extract a quantized controller model $(\hat{\mathbf{A}}, \hat{\mathbf{B}}, \hat{\mathbf{C}}, \hat{\mathbf{D}}, b_{rel}, b_{abs})$ from the floating-point controller implementation via symbolic execution and floating-point error analysis techniques.

3.2   Symbolic Execution of Floating-Point Controller Implementation

In our approach, the symbolic execution technique [7,21] is employed to analyze the step function C code. We symbolically execute the step function with symbolic values such as symbolic inputs and symbolic controller states, and examine the change of the program's global state where the output and new controller state are updated with symbolic expressions in terms of the symbolic values. The goal of the symbolic execution in our approach is to find symbolic formulas that concisely represent the computation of the step function C code that originally has loops and pointer arithmetic operations. The idea behind this symbolic execution process is that the linear controller implementations that we consider in this work have simple control flows for the sake of deterministic real-time behaviors (e.g., fixed upper bound of loops), thus being amenable to our symbolic execution process. Consequently, the symbolic execution of linear controller implementations yield finite and deterministic symbolic execution paths [28].

However, unlike [28], our work herein newly considers the effect of floating-point rounding errors in the step function. Thus it is necessary to pay special attention (e.g., normalization [6]) to the floating-point computation in symbolic execution. When symbolic expressions are constructed with floating-point operators in the course of symbolic execution, the evaluation order of floating-point operations should be preserved according to the floating-point program semantics, because floating-point arithmetic does not hold basic algebraic properties such as associativity and distributivity in general.

Once the symbolic execution is completed, symbolic formulas are produced. The symbolic formulas represent the computation of the step function in a concise way (i.e., in the arithmetic expression form without loops, function calls and side effects). The produced symbolic formula has the following form, which we call *transition equation*:

$$v^{(new)} = f(v_1, v_2, \ldots, v_t) \tag{8}$$

where $v^{(new)}$ is a global variable which is updated with the symbolic expression, v_i are the initial symbolic values of the corresponding variables before the symbolic execution of the step function. $f(v_1, v_2, \ldots, v_t)$ is the symbolic expression that consists of floating-point operations where t is the number of variables used in f. This expression should preserve the correct order of evaluation according to the floating-point semantics of the step function C code.

For example, consider the step function in [27], which is generated by Embedded Coder (the code generator of MATLAB/Simulink) for the LTI controller models (5) and (6). We illustrate one of the transition equations obtained from the symbolic execution of the step function as follows:

$$\begin{aligned} \mathbf{y[1]}^{(new)} = {} & (((((0.503767 \otimes \mathbf{x}[0]) \oplus (-0.573538 \otimes \mathbf{x}[1])) \oplus (0.170245 \otimes \mathbf{x}[2])) \\ & \oplus (-0.583312 \otimes \mathbf{x}[3])) \oplus (-0.56603 \otimes \mathbf{x}[4])). \end{aligned} \tag{9}$$

where $\mathbf{x}$ is the shortened name for LTIS_DW.Internal_DSTATE, and $\mathbf{y}$ is the shortened name for LTIS_Y.y for presentation purposes only, and $\oplus$, $\ominus$ and $\otimes$ are floating-point operators corresponding to $+$, $-$ and $\times$ respectively. In the next subsection, we explain how to extract the quantized model (17) from the symbolic expressions.

3.3 Quantization Error Analysis and Model Extraction

This subsection explains how to extract the quantized controller model (17) from a set of symbolic expressions (8) obtained from the step function. The symbolic expression consists of floating-point operations of symbolic values and numeric constants. We first describe how to analyze the floating-point quantization (i.e., roundoff) error in the symbolic expression evaluation. Since we only consider linear controller implementations rejecting nonlinear cases in the symbolic execution phase, the symbolic expression f obtained from the step function has the following syntax, thus guaranteeing the linearity:

$$f := v \mid f \oplus f \mid f \ominus f \mid f \circledast f_c \mid f_c \circledast f$$
$$f_c := c \mid f_c \circledast f_c$$

where v is a variable (i.e., the initial symbolic value of the variable), c is a constant, and $\circledast \in \{\oplus, \ominus, \otimes\}$. f_c is a sub-expression which contains no variable, thus being evaluated to a constant, while f contains at least one variable. The multiplication operation $\otimes$ appears only when at least one operand is a constant-expression f_c, thus preventing the expression from being nonlinear (i.e., the product of two symbolic values).

In order to simplify a certain program analysis problem, a common assumption is often made in the literature [14,28] that the floating-point operations (e.g., $\oplus$, $\ominus$ and $\otimes$) behave the same way as the real operations (e.g., $+$, $-$ and $\times$) with no rounding. Under this assumption, the Eq. (8) can be represented in the following canonical form [28]:

$$v^{(new)} = \sum_{i=1}^{t} c_i v_i \tag{10}$$

where t is the number of product terms, v, v_i are variables, and c_i is the coefficient. In reality, however, floating-point numbers have limited precision, and the floating-point operations involve rounding errors. In this work, we consider the effect of such floating-point rounding errors in the verification.

The IEEE 754 standard [1] views a finite precision floating-point operation as the corresponding real operation followed by a rounding operation:

$$x_1 \circledast x_2 = rnd(x_1 * x_2) \tag{11}$$

where $\circledast \in \{\oplus, \ominus, \otimes\}$ and $*$ is the corresponding real arithmetic operation to $\circledast$. A rounding operator rnd is a function that takes a real number as input and returns as output a floating-point number that is closest to the input real number, thus causes a quantization error (i.e., rounding error) in the floating-point operation. There are multiple common rounding operators (e.g. round to the nearest, ties to even) defined in the IEEE 754 standard [1]. A rounding operator can be modeled as follows [15]:

$$rnd(x) = x(1 + e) + d \tag{12}$$

for some e and d where e is a relative error, d is an absolute error, and $|e| \leq \epsilon$ and $|d| \leq \delta$. ϵ and δ can be determined according to the rounding mode and the precision (i.e., the number of bits) of the system. For example, $\epsilon = 2^{-53}$ and $\delta = 2^{-1075}$ for the double precision (i.e., 64 bits) rounding to the nearest [33]. Combining the two Eqs. (11) and (12), we have the following model for the floating-point operations:

$$x_1 \circledast x_2 = (x_1 * x_2)(1 + e) + d \tag{13}$$

After rewriting the symbolic expression of the transition equation (8) applying the Eq. (13), suppose that we have the following equation form:

$$v^{(new)} = \sum c_i v_i + err_{rel} + err_{abs} \tag{14}$$

where $\sum c_i v_i$ is the exact expression as (10), and err_{abs} is the absolute error term bounded by b_{abs} such that $|err_{abs}| \leq b_{abs}$. err_{rel} is the relative error term which is related to the variables $\{v_i\}$ (i.e., symbolic values). We rewrite err_{rel} as $\sum err_i v_i$ where err_i is the relative error term specific to the variable v_i, and b_i is the upper bound for err_i such that $|err_i| \leq b_i$. We relax the equation by over-approximating each err_i as follows:

$$v^{(new)} = \sum c_i v_i + \sum err_i v_i + err_{abs}$$
$$= \sum c_i v_i + err \sum v_i + err_{abs} \tag{15}$$

where err is bounded by b_{rel} such that $|err| \leq b_{rel}$ where b_{rel} is defined as $b_{rel} = \max\{b_i\}$.

We now rearrange and group the product terms by variable names such as the state variables and the input variables. We assume that the names of input and output variables are given as the interface of the step function. The state variables can be identified as the variables appearing in the transition equations which are not input variables nor output variables. In addition to the rearrangement, by transforming the sum of products into a form of scalar product of vectors, we have:

$$v^{(new)} = [c_1, c_2, ..., c_n]\mathbf{x} + [err, err, ..., err]\mathbf{x}$$
$$+ [c'_1, c'_2, ..., c'_p]\mathbf{u} + [err, err, ..., err]\mathbf{u} + err_{abs} \tag{16}$$

where $\mathbf{x}$ is the vector of state variables, and $\mathbf{u}$ is the vector of input variables.

Finally, we rewrite the transition equations as two matrix equations as follows:

$$\mathbf{x}^{(new)} = (\hat{\mathbf{A}} + \mathbf{E_A})\mathbf{x} + (\hat{\mathbf{B}} + \mathbf{E_B})\mathbf{u} + \mathbf{e_x}$$
$$\mathbf{y}^{(new)} = (\hat{\mathbf{C}} + \mathbf{E_C})\mathbf{x} + (\hat{\mathbf{D}} + \mathbf{E_D})\mathbf{u} + \mathbf{e_y}. \tag{17}$$

where $\hat{\mathbf{A}} \in \mathbb{R}^{n \times n}$, $\hat{\mathbf{B}} \in \mathbb{R}^{n \times p}$, $\hat{\mathbf{C}} \in \mathbb{R}^{m \times n}$ and $\hat{\mathbf{D}} \in \mathbb{R}^{m \times p}$. The matrices for the relative errors are bounded by b_{rel}^* such that $\|\mathbf{E_A}\|, \|\mathbf{E_B}\|, \|\mathbf{E_C}\|, \|\mathbf{E_D}\| \leq b_{rel}^*$. The absolute error vectors $\mathbf{e_x}$ and $\mathbf{e_y}$ are bounded by b_{abs}^* such that $\|\mathbf{e_x}\|, \|\mathbf{e_y}\| \leq b_{abs}^*$. Note that b_{rel}^* and b_{abs}^* can be easily determined using b_{rel} and b_{abs} obtained from the floating-point error analysis for each transition equation.

For example, consider the transition equation (9), from which via the floating-point error analysis, we have:

$$
\begin{aligned}
\mathbf{y}[1]^{(new)} &= (((((0.503767 \otimes \mathbf{x}[0]) \oplus (-0.573538 \otimes \mathbf{x}[1])) \oplus (0.170245 \otimes \mathbf{x}[2])) \\
&\quad \oplus (-0.583312 \otimes \mathbf{x}[3])) \oplus (-0.56603 \otimes \mathbf{x}[4])) \\
&= 0.503767 \cdot \mathbf{x}[0] + -0.573538 \cdot \mathbf{x}[1] + 0.170245 \cdot \mathbf{x}[2] \\
&\quad + -0.583312 \cdot \mathbf{x}[3] + -0.56603 \cdot \mathbf{x}[4] + err_{rel} + err_{abs} \qquad (18) \\
&= 0.503767 \cdot \mathbf{x}[0] + -0.573538 \cdot \mathbf{x}[1] + 0.170245 \cdot \mathbf{x}[2] \\
&\quad + -0.583312 \cdot \mathbf{x}[3] + -0.56603 \cdot \mathbf{x}[4] \\
&\quad + err(\mathbf{x}[0] + \mathbf{x}[1] + \mathbf{x}[2] + \mathbf{x}[3] + \mathbf{x}[4]) + err_{abs}
\end{aligned}
$$

where $|err| \leq \frac{988331}{250000}\epsilon \div (1 - 4\epsilon) = b_{rel}$, and $|err_{abs}| \leq 4 \cdot (1 + \epsilon)^4 \cdot \delta = b_{abs}$. For the double precision (i.e., 64 bits) rounding to nearest (i.e., $\epsilon = 2^{-53}$ and $\delta = 2^{-1075}$), $b_{rel} \approx 4.389071 \times 10^{-16}$ and $b_{abs} \approx 1.235164 \times 10^{-323}$.

4   Approximate Input-Output Equivalence Checking

In order to verify a finite precision implementation of the linear controller, the previous section described how to extract the quantized controller model from the implementation. In this section, we introduce how to compare the extracted model (17) and the initial model (1) with a notion of approximate input-output (IO) equivalence.

4.1   Approximate Input-Output Equivalence

This subsection defines an approximate IO equivalence relation, inspired by the similarity transformation of LTI systems [30]. In order for two LTI systems to be IO equivalent to each other, there must exist an invertible linear mapping $\mathbf{T}$ from one system's state $\mathbf{z}$ to another system's state $\hat{\mathbf{z}}$ such that $\mathbf{z} = \mathbf{T}\hat{\mathbf{z}}$ and $\hat{\mathbf{z}} = \mathbf{T}^{-1}\mathbf{z}$. The matrix $\mathbf{T}$ is referred to as the *similarity transformation matrix* [30]. Assuming that a proper $\mathbf{T}$ is given, we substitute $\mathbf{z}_k$ by $\mathbf{T}\hat{\mathbf{z}}$ in the initial LTI model (1), thus having:

$$\mathbf{T}\hat{\mathbf{z}}_{k+1} = \mathbf{AT}\hat{\mathbf{z}}_k + \mathbf{Bu}_k, \quad \mathbf{y}_k = \mathbf{CT}\hat{\mathbf{z}}_k + \mathbf{Du}_k.$$

or

$$\hat{\mathbf{z}}_{k+1} = (\mathbf{T}^{-1}\mathbf{AT})\hat{\mathbf{z}}_k + (\mathbf{T}^{-1}\mathbf{B})\mathbf{u}_k, \quad \mathbf{y}_k = (\mathbf{CT})\hat{\mathbf{z}}_k + \mathbf{Du}_k. \qquad (19)$$

By the similarity transformation, two LTI systems (1) and (19) are *similar*, meaning that they are IO equivalent. We now compare the transformed initial

LTI model (19) and the quantized controller model (17) that is extracted from the step function. Equating the corresponding coefficient matrices of the two models (19) and (17), we have:

$$\mathbf{T}^{-1}\mathbf{AT} = \hat{\mathbf{A}} + \mathbf{E_A}, \quad \mathbf{T}^{-1}\mathbf{B} = \hat{\mathbf{B}} + \mathbf{E_B}, \quad \mathbf{CT} = \hat{\mathbf{C}} + \mathbf{E_C}, \quad \mathbf{D} = \hat{\mathbf{D}} + \mathbf{E_D}$$

or

$$\mathbf{AT} = \mathbf{T}\hat{\mathbf{A}} + \mathbf{TE_A}, \quad \mathbf{B} = \mathbf{T}\hat{\mathbf{B}} + \mathbf{TE_B}, \quad \mathbf{CT} = \hat{\mathbf{C}} + \mathbf{E_C}, \quad \mathbf{D} = \hat{\mathbf{D}} + \mathbf{E_D} \quad (20)$$

However, the equality of the exact equivalence condition (20) will never hold because of the floating-point error terms (e.g., $\mathbf{E_A}$) and the numerical errors in the implementation's controller parameters (e.g., $\hat{\mathbf{A}}$) due to the optimization of the code generator. To overcome this problem, we define and use an approximate equivalence relation $\approx_\rho$ on matrices such that $\mathbf{M} \approx_\rho \hat{\mathbf{M}}$ if and only if $\left\| \mathbf{M} - \hat{\mathbf{M}} \right\| \leq \rho$ where ρ is a given precision (i.e., threshold for approximate equivalence). Note that the approximate equivalence relation $\approx_\rho$ is not transitive, thus not an equivalence relation unless $\rho = 0$. With $\approx_\rho$ for a precision ρ, the Eq. (20) are relaxed as follows:

$$\mathbf{AT} \approx_\rho \mathbf{T}\hat{\mathbf{A}} + \mathbf{TE_A}, \quad \mathbf{B} \approx_\rho \mathbf{T}\hat{\mathbf{B}} + \mathbf{TE_B}, \quad \mathbf{CT} \approx_\rho \hat{\mathbf{C}} + \mathbf{E_C}, \quad \mathbf{D} \approx_\rho \hat{\mathbf{D}} + \mathbf{E_D} \quad (21)$$

Finally, we say that the initial LTI model (1) and the quantized model (17) extracted from the implementation are approximately IO equivalent with precision ρ if there exists a similarity transformation matrix $\mathbf{T}$ which satisfies (21), and the absolute errors of the floating-point computations are negligible (i.e., $\mathbf{e_z} \approx_\rho \mathbf{0}$ and $\mathbf{e_y} \approx_\rho \mathbf{0}$). Note that the problem of checking the approximate IO equivalence is the problem of finding a proper similarity transformation matrix. In the rest of this section, we explain how to find the similarity transformation matrix using a satisfiability problem formulation and a convex optimization problem formulation.

4.2 Satisfiability Problem Formulation

This section discusses the satisfiability problem formulation for the approximate IO equivalence checking. To find the similarity transformation matrix using existing SMT solvers, the problem can be formulated roughly as follows:

$$\exists \mathbf{T} : \forall \mathbf{E_A}, \mathbf{E_B}, \mathbf{E_C}, \mathbf{E_D} : \|\mathbf{E_A}\|, \|\mathbf{E_B}\|, \|\mathbf{E_C}\|, \|\mathbf{E_D}\| \leq b_{rel} \implies (21) \text{ holds}$$

In this formulation, the variable $\mathbf{T}$ and the relative error variables (e.g., $\mathbf{E_A}$) are quantified alternately, thus requiring exists/forall (EF) problem solving. Moreover, the formula involves the non-linear real arithmetic (NRA) due to the terms $\mathbf{TE_A}$ and $\mathbf{TE_B}$ in (21). For these reasons, the scalability of this SMT formulation-based approach is questionable because the current SMT solvers rarely supports EF-NRA problem solving with scalability. In the next subsection, we describe a more efficient approach based on convex optimization as an alternative method.

4.3   Convex Optimization Formulation

This subsection describes the convex optimization-based approach to the approximate IO equivalence checking. Since the relative error variables $\mathbf{E_A}$ make the condition (21) inappropriate to be formulated as a convex optimization problem, our approach is to derive a sufficient condition for (21). By over-approximating the error terms and removing the error variables, we derive such a sufficient condition for (21) which is formulated as a convex optimization problem as follows:

$$
\begin{aligned}
&\text{variables} && e \in \mathbb{R}, \mathbf{T} \in \mathbb{R}^{n \times n} \\
&\text{minimize} && e \\
&\text{subject to} && \left\| \hat{\mathbf{A}}\mathbf{T} - \mathbf{T}\mathbf{A} \right\|_\infty + n^2 \left\| \mathbf{T} \right\|_\infty b_{rel} \le e \\
& && \left\| \hat{\mathbf{B}} - \mathbf{T}\mathbf{B} \right\|_\infty + n^2 \left\| \mathbf{T} \right\|_\infty b_{rel} \le e \\
& && \left\| \hat{\mathbf{C}}\mathbf{T} - \mathbf{C} \right\|_\infty + n \cdot b_{rel} \le e, \quad \left\| \hat{\mathbf{D}} - \mathbf{D} \right\|_\infty + n \cdot b_{rel} \le e
\end{aligned}
\tag{22}
$$

The idea behind this formulation is to use convex optimization to find the minimum precision e and then check whether $e \le \rho$ where ρ is the given precision.

Remark 1. Our verification method is sound (i.e., no false positive) but not complete. Due to the relaxations both in the floating-point error approximation and the approximate IO equivalence checking, there might be a case with a model and a correct implementation where our method remains indecisive in the equivalence decision. This can be potentially improved by tightening the relaxations in future work. In addition, a larger ρ can make the approximate equivalence decision positive, which is not with a smaller ρ. The IO equivalence with a large ρ may not guarantee the controller's well-behavedness. Relating the approximate equivalence precision ρ and the performance of the controller (e.g., robustness) is an avenue of future work.

5   Evaluation

This section presents our toolchain for the verification of finite precision controller implementations, and evaluates its scalability. We also evaluate computational overhead (i.e., running time) over our own earlier work [28] which assumes that the computations of controller implementations have no rounding errors.

5.1   Toolchain

This subsection presents the verification toolchain (shown in Fig. 1) that we implemented based on our method described in this paper. The toolchain is an extension of [28] to consider the floating-point error of step function in verification. The toolchain takes as input a step function C code and an LTI model specification. We use the off-the-shelf symbolic execution tool PathCrawler [37] to symbolically execute the step function and produce the transition equations

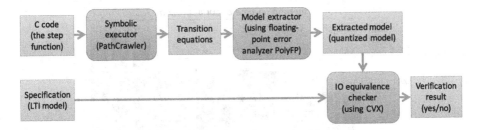

Fig. 1. The verification toolchain

for the step function. From the transition equations, the model extractor based on Sect. 3.3 extracts the quantized controller model using the floating-point error analysis tool PolyFP [2]. Finally, the extracted quantized model is compared with the given specification (i.e., LTI model) based on the approximate IO relation defined in Sect. 4. The approximate IO equivalence checker uses the convex optimization solver CVX [17] to solve the formulas in Sect. 4.3.

5.2 Scalability Analysis

This subsection evaluates the scalability of our approach/toolchain presented in this paper. To evaluate, we use the Matlab function `drss` to randomly generate discrete stable linear controller specifications (i.e., the elements of $\Sigma(\mathbf{A}, \mathbf{B}, \mathbf{C}, \mathbf{D})$) varying the controller dimension n from 2 to 14. To obtain an IO equivalent implementation, we perform an arbitrary similarity transformation on Σ, and yield the transformed model $\hat{\Sigma}$. We use an LTI system block of Simulink to allow the Embedded Coder (i.e., code generator of Matlab/Simulink) to generate a floating-point implementation (i.e., step function in C) for $\hat{\Sigma}$. Note that the generated step function has multiple loops and pointer arithmetic operations as illustrated in the step function in [27]. We employ our toolchain to verify that the generated step function correctly implements the original controller model. We pick the precision ρ to be 10^{-6} to tolerate both numerical errors in the similarity transformation and the floating-point controller implementation.

We now evaluate the scalability of our approach running our toolchain with the random controller specifications and their implementations generated. We measure the running time of the front-end and the back-end of our approach separately. The front-end refers to the process of symbolic execution of the step function (using PathCrawler) and model extraction using the floating-point analysis (using PolyFP). The back-end refers to the approximate IO equivalence checking using convex optimization problem solving (using CVX). The scalability analysis result is shown in Fig. 2, which demonstrates that our approach is scalable for the realistic size of controller dimension.

We now evaluate the overhead of our approach compared to the previous work [28] where the verification problem is simpler than our verification problem herein because the previous work [28] assumes that the computation of step function C code is exact without having any roundoff error. Our approach herein provides a higher assurance for the finite precision controller implementations considering the rounding errors in computation. Figure 3 shows the computational

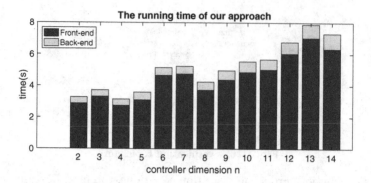

Fig. 2. The running time of both the front-end and the back-end of our approach

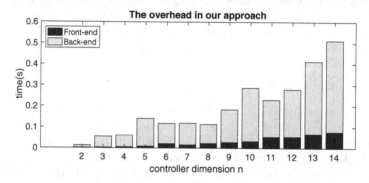

Fig. 3. The overhead in both the front-end and the back-end of our approach

overhead (i.e., the increase of running time) in our approach as a result of considering the floating-point roundoff error in controller implementation verification. We observe that the overhead of the floating-point error analysis in the front-end is marginal. The running time of the back-end increases because the convex optimization problem formulation for approximate IO equivalence requires more computations to solve. Finally, the total running time only increases marginally from 0.4% to 7.5% over the previous work [28] at a cost of providing higher assurance for the correctness of the finite precision computations of controller implementations.

6   Related Work

High-assurance control software for cyber physical systems has received much attention recently (e.g., [3, 10, 12, 22–24, 32]). Focusing on robust controller implementation, [22, 32] provide simulation-based robustness analysis tools, while [3, 10, 12, 24] studies issues related to fixed-point controller design. [4] presents a theorem proving method to verify the control related properties of Simulink models.

Moreover, there also has been work focusing on the code-level verification of controller implementation. [23, 31] propose methods to check a Simulink diagram and the generated code based on the structure of the diagram and the code, instead of input-output equivalence checking. [14,18,35,36] apply the concept of proof-carrying code to control software verification. Their approach is to annotate the code based on Lyapunov function, and prove the properties using the PVS linear algebra library [18]. However, they only consider stability and convergence properties rather than the equivalence between controller specifications and the implementations. Moreover, their verification approach may not be applicable to the code generated by existing off-the-shelf code generators because it requires the internal control of the code generators. Our own earlier work [26,28] presents methods to verify controller implementations against mathematical models, yet ignores the rounding errors in the finite precision computations of controller software implementations. There has been static analysis techniques (e.g., [5,13,16]) developed for the analysis of finite precision numerical programs, but they focus on verifying properties such as numerical stability, the absence of buffer overflow and the absence of arithmetic exception rather than verifying the equivalence between code and a dynamical system model as the specification of the controller. Finally, there has been software verification work using the model extraction technique [8,19,20,29,34], and the floating-point roundoff error estimation has been studied in [9,11,33].

7   Conclusion

We have presented an approach for the verification of finite precision implementations of linear controllers against mathematical specifications. We have proposed the use of a combination of techniques such as symbolic execution and floating point error analysis in order to extract the quantized controller model from finite precision linear controller implementations. We have defined an approximate input-output equivalence relation between the specification model (i.e., linear time-invariant model) and the extracted model (i.e., quantized controller model), and presented a method to check the approximate equivalence relation using the convex optimization formulation. We have evaluated our approach using randomly generated controller specifications and implementations by MATLAB/Simulink/Embedded Coder. The evaluation result shows that our approach is scalable for the realistic controller size, and the computational overhead to analyze the effect of floating-point error is negligible compared to our own earlier work. Future work includes the verification of a broader class of controller implementations.

Acknowledgments. This work was supported in part by NSF CNS-1505799, NSF CNS-1505701, and the Intel-NSF Partnership for Cyber-Physical Systems Security and Privacy. This material is based on research sponsored by DARPA under agreement number FA8750-12-2-0247. The U.S. Government is authorized to reproduce and distribute reprints for Governmental purposes notwithstanding any copyright notation thereon. The views and conclusions contained herein are those of the authors and should not be interpreted as necessarily representing the official policies or endorsements, either expressed or implied, of DARPA or the U.S. Government. This research was supported in part by Global Research Laboratory Program through the National Research Foundation of Korea (NRF) funded by the Ministry of Science, ICT and Future Planning (2013K1A1A2A02078326) with DGIST.

References

1. IEEE standard for floating-point arithmetic. IEEE Std 754-2008, pp. 1–70 (2008)
2. PolyFP. https://github.com/monadius/poly_fp. Accessed 2016
3. Anta, A., Majumdar, R., Saha, I., Tabuada, P.: Automatic verification of control system implementations. In: Proceedings of 10th ACM International Conference on Embedded Software, EMSOFT 2010, pp. 9–18 (2010)
4. Araiza-Illan, D., Eder, K., Richards, A.: Formal verification of control systems' properties with theorem proving. In: UKACC International Conference on Control (CONTROL), pp. 244–249 (2014)
5. Blanchet, B., Cousot, P., Cousot, R., Feret, J., Mauborgne, L., Miné, A., Monniaux, D., Rival, X.: A static analyzer for large safety-critical software. ACM SIGPLAN Not. **38**, 196–207 (2003). ACM
6. Botella, B., Gotlieb, A., Michel, C.: Symbolic execution of floating-point computations. Softw. Test. Verif. Reliab. **16**(2), 97–121 (2006)
7. Clarke, L.: A system to generate test data and symbolically execute programs. IEEE Trans. Softw. Eng. **3**, 215–222 (1976)
8. Corbett, J.C., Dwyer, M.B., Hatcliff, J., Laubach, S., Păsăreanu, C.S., Bby, R., Zheng, H.: Bandera: extracting finite-state models from Java source code. In: Proceedings of the 2000 International Conference on Software Engineering, pp. 439–448. IEEE (2000)
9. Darulova, E., Kuncak, V.: Sound compilation of reals. ACM SIGPLAN Not. **49**, 235–248 (2014). ACM
10. Darulova, E., Kuncak, V., Majumdar, R., Saha, I.: Synthesis of fixed-point programs. In: Proceedings of 11th ACM International Conference on Embedded Software, EMSOFT 2013, pp. 22:1–22:10 (2013)
11. Daumas, M., Melquiond, G.: Certification of bounds on expressions involving rounded operators. ACM Trans. Math. Softw. (TOMS) **37**(1), 2 (2010)
12. Eldib, H., Wang, C.: An SMT based method for optimizing arithmetic computations in embedded software code. IEEE Trans. Comput. Aided Des. Integr. Circuits Syst. **33**(11), 1611–1622 (2014)
13. Feret, J.: Static analysis of digital filters. In: Schmidt, D. (ed.) ESOP 2004. LNCS, vol. 2986, pp. 33–48. Springer, Heidelberg (2004). doi:10.1007/978-3-540-24725-8_4
14. Feron, E.: From control systems to control software. IEEE Control Syst. **30**(6), 50–71 (2010)
15. Goualard, F.: How do you compute the midpoint of an interval? ACM Trans. Math. Softw. (TOMS) **40**(2), 11 (2014)
16. Goubault, E., Putot, S.: Static analysis of finite precision computations. In: Jhala, R., Schmidt, D. (eds.) VMCAI 2011. LNCS, vol. 6538, pp. 232–247. Springer, Heidelberg (2011). doi:10.1007/978-3-642-18275-4_17
17. Grant, M., Boyd, S.: CVX: Matlab software for disciplined convex programming, version 2.1. http://cvxr.com/cvx
18. Herencia-Zapana, H., Jobredeaux, R., Owre, S., Garoche, P.L., Feron, E., Perez, G., Ascariz, P.: PVS linear algebra libraries for verification of control software algorithms in C/ACSL. In: NASA Formal Methods, pp. 147–161 (2012)
19. Holzmann, G.J., Smith, M.H.: Software model checking: extracting verification models from source code. Softw. Test. Verif. Reliab. **11**(2), 65–79 (2001)
20. Holzmann, G.J., Smith, M.H.: An automated verification method for distributed systems software based on model extraction. IEEE Trans. Softw. Eng. **28**(4), 364–377 (2002)

21. King, J.C.: Symbolic execution and program testing. Commun. ACM **19**(7), 385–394 (1976)

22. Majumdar, R., Saha, I., Shashidhar, K., Wang, Z.: CLSE: closed-loop symbolic execution. In: NASA Formal Methods, pp. 356–370 (2012)

23. Majumdar, R., Saha, I., Ueda, K., Yazarel, H.: Compositional equivalence checking for models and code of control systems. In: 52nd Annual IEEE Conference on Decision and Control (CDC), pp. 1564–1571 (2013)

24. Majumdar, R., Saha, I., Zamani, M.: Synthesis of minimal-error control software. In: Proceedings of 10th ACM International Conference on Embedded Software, EMSOFT 2012, pp. 123–132 (2012)

25. Mathworks: Bug Reports for Incorrect Code Generation. http://www.mathworks.com/support/bugreports/?product=ALL&release=R2015b&keyword=Incorrect+Code+Generation

26. Pajic, M., Park, J., Lee, I., Pappas, G.J., Sokolsky, O.: Automatic verification of linear controller software. In: 12th International Conference on Embedded Software (EMSOFT), pp. 217–226. IEEE Press (2015)

27. Park, J.: Step function example. http://dx.doi.org/10.5281/zenodo.44338

28. Park, J., Pajic, M., Lee, I., Sokolsky, O.: Scalable verification of linear controller software. In: Chechik, M., Raskin, J.-F. (eds.) TACAS 2016. LNCS, vol. 9636, pp. 662–679. Springer, Heidelberg (2016). doi:10.1007/978-3-662-49674-9_43

29. Pichler, J.: Specification extraction by symbolic execution. In: 2013 20th Working Conference on Reverse Engineering (WCRE), pp. 462–466. IEEE (2013)

30. Rugh, W.J.: Linear System Theory. Prentice Hall, Upper Saddle River (1996)

31. Ryabtsev, M., Strichman, O.: Translation validation: from Simulink to C. In: Bouajjani, A., Maler, O. (eds.) CAV 2009. LNCS, vol. 5643, pp. 696–701. Springer, Heidelberg (2009). doi:10.1007/978-3-642-02658-4_57

32. Sangiovanni-Vincentelli, A., Di Natale, M.: Embedded system design for automotive applications. IEEE Comput. **10**, 42–51 (2007)

33. Solovyev, A., Jacobsen, C., Rakamarić, Z., Gopalakrishnan, G.: Rigorous estimation of floating-point round-off errors with symbolic Taylor expansions. In: Bjørner, N., de Boer, F. (eds.) FM 2015. LNCS, vol. 9109, pp. 532–550. Springer, Heidelberg (2015). doi:10.1007/978-3-319-19249-9_33

34. Wang, S., Dwarakanathan, S., Sokolsky, O., Lee, I.: High-level model extraction via symbolic execution. Technical reports (CIS) paper 967, University of Pennsylvania, (2012). http://repository.upenn.edu/cis_reports/967

35. Wang, T., Jobredeaux, R., Herencia, H., Garoche, P.L., Dieumegard, A., Feron, E., Pantel, M.: From design to implementation: an automated, credible autocoding chain for control systems (2013). arXiv preprint: arXiv:1307.2641

36. Wang, T.E., Ashari, A.E., Jobredeaux, R.J., Feron, E.M.: Credible autocoding of fault detection observers. In: American Control Conference (ACC), pp. 672–677 (2014)

37. Williams, N., Marre, B., Mouy, P., Roger, M.: PathCrawler: automatic generation of path tests by combining static and dynamic analysis. In: Cin, M., Kaâniche, M., Pataricza, A. (eds.) EDCC 2005. LNCS, vol. 3463, pp. 281–292. Springer, Heidelberg (2005). doi:10.1007/11408901_21

Learning

Learning Symbolic Automata

Samuel Drews[(⊠)] and Loris D'Antoni

University of Wisconsin–Madison, Madison, USA
sedrews@wisc.edu

Abstract. Symbolic automata allow transitions to carry predicates over rich alphabet theories, such as linear arithmetic, and therefore extend classic automata to operate over infinite alphabets, such as the set of rational numbers. In this paper, we study the foundational problem of learning symbolic automata. We first present Λ^*, a symbolic automata extension of Angluin's L^* algorithm for learning regular languages. Then, we define notions of learnability that are parametric in the alphabet theories of the symbolic automata and show how these notions nicely compose. Specifically, we show that if two alphabet theories are *learnable*, then the theory accepting the Cartesian product or disjoint union of their alphabets is also learnable. Using these properties, we show how existing algorithms for learning automata over large alphabets nicely fall in our framework. Finally, we implement our algorithm in an open-source library and evaluate it on existing automata learning benchmarks.

1 Introduction

Finite automata are a ubiquitous formalism that is simple enough to model many real-life systems and phenomena, and they enjoy a large variety of theoretical properties: automata are closed under Boolean operations, have decidable emptiness and equivalence checking procedures, and *can be learned* [3]. This last problem on automata learning is the focus of this paper; learning has been studied extensively for several variations of finite automata [4,9] and has found many applications in program verification [2] and program synthesis [15].

Unfortunately, finite automata have an inherent limitation: they can only operate over finite (and typically small) alphabets. Symbolic finite automata (s-FA) allow transitions to carry predicates over rich alphabet theories, such as linear arithmetic, and therefore extend classic automata to operate over infinite alphabets, such as the set of rational numbers. Existing automata algorithms rely on the alphabet being finite, and generalizing them to the symbolic setting is not a trivial task. However, algorithms have been proposed for s-FA equivalence, for minimization, and for performing Boolean operations. In this paper, we study the foundational problem of learning symbolic automata.

We start by extending Angluin's L^* algorithm [3] for learning regular languages to symbolic automata. L^* iteratively updates a table of evidence, conjectures an automaton, and then if that conjecture is not correct, repeats with new evidence. However, at every step it must make a *query* to an oracle for each character in an alphabet; thus it does not scale in practice on alphabets that are

© Springer-Verlag GmbH Germany 2017
A. Legay and T. Margaria (Eds.): TACAS 2017, Part I, LNCS 10205, pp. 173–189, 2017.
DOI: 10.1007/978-3-662-54577-5_10

large and cannot be run on those that are infinite. Our algorithm, Λ^*, operates in a largely similar manner, except that the queries are asked only for a small set of representatives, and then there is an additional stage after updating the table of evidence during which the evidence is *generalized* into symbolic predicates; these predicates form the transitions for the symbolic automaton.

We then define notions of learnability that are parametric in the alphabet theory of the symbolic automata and show that these notions compose. For example, if two alphabet theories are *learnable*, then the theory accepting the Cartesian product of their alphabets is also learnable. We use these properties to show how existing algorithms for learning automata over large alphabets nicely fall in our framework: e.g., Maler and Mens present an ad hoc method for learning automata over the alphabet $\mathbb{Z} \times \mathbb{Z}$ [13], which we show is learnable because it is the Cartesian product of the alphabet $\mathbb{Z}$—which itself is learnable.

Finally, we implement our algorithm in an open-source symbolic automata library and evaluate it on existing automata learning benchmarks from [13]. The implementation is modular and only requires the programmer to provide learnable Boolean algebras as input to the learner; the disjoint union and product algebras are implemented as meta-algebras that can be instantiated arbitrarily. Our implementation, despite its generality, can learn the benchmarks appearing in [13] using a similar number of equivalence and membership queries.

In summary, our contributions are:

- An algorithm for learning Symbolic Finite Automata (Sect. 3).
- A notion of learnability parametric in the alphabet theory that composes over the Cartesian product and disjoint union of Boolean algebras (Sect. 4).
- A modular implementation of our algorithm in an existing open-source library and an evaluation on existing benchmarks (Sect. 5).

2   Preliminaries

In symbolic automata, transitions carry predicates over a decidable Boolean algebra. An *effective Boolean algebra* $\mathcal{A}$ is a tuple $(\mathfrak{D}, \Psi, [\![\_]\!], \bot, \top, \vee, \wedge, \neg)$ where $\mathfrak{D}$ is a set of *domain elements*; Ψ is a set of *predicates* closed under the Boolean connectives, with $\bot, \top \in \Psi$; $[\![\_]\!] : \Psi \to 2^{\mathfrak{D}}$ is a *denotation function* such that (i) $[\![\bot]\!] = \emptyset$, (ii) $[\![\top]\!] = \mathfrak{D}$, and (iii) for all $\varphi, \psi \in \Psi$, $[\![\varphi \vee \psi]\!] = [\![\varphi]\!] \cup [\![\psi]\!]$, $[\![\varphi \wedge \psi]\!] = [\![\varphi]\!] \cap [\![\psi]\!]$, and $[\![\neg\varphi]\!] = \mathfrak{D} \setminus [\![\varphi]\!]$.

Example 1 (Equality Algebra). The *equality algebra* for an arbitrary set $\mathfrak{D}$ has predicates formed from Boolean combinations of formulas of the form $\lambda c.\, c = a$ where $a \in \mathfrak{D}$. Formally, Ψ is generated from the Boolean closure of $\Psi_0 = \{\varphi_a \mid a \in \mathfrak{D}\} \cup \{\bot, \top\}$ where for all $a \in \mathfrak{D}$, $[\![\varphi_a]\!] = \{a\}$. Example predicates in this algebra include the predicates $\lambda c.\, c = 5 \vee c = 10$ and $\lambda c.\, \neg(c = 0)$.

Example 2 (Interval Algebra). The finite union of left-closed right-open intervals over non-negative integers (i.e. $\mathbb{N}$) also forms a Boolean algebra: take the Boolean closure of $\Psi_0 = \{\varphi_{ij} \mid i, j \in \mathbb{N} \wedge i < j\} \cup \{\bot, \top\}$ where $[\![\varphi_{ij}]\!] = [i, j)$. Example predicates in this algebra include those (written as their denotation) of the form $[0, 5) \cup [10, 15)$ or $[50, \infty)$.

Definition 1 (Symbolic Finite Automata). *A symbolic finite automaton (s-FA) M is a tuple $(\mathcal{A}, Q, q_{init}, F, \Delta)$ where $\mathcal{A}$ is an effective Boolean algebra, called the* alphabet; *Q is a finite set of states; $q_{init} \in Q$ is the* initial state; *$F \subseteq Q$ is the set of* final states; *and $\Delta \subseteq Q \times \Psi_{\mathcal{A}} \times Q$ is the transition relation consisting of a finite set of* moves *or* transitions.

Characters are elements of $\mathfrak{D}_{\mathcal{A}}$, and *words* are finite sequences of characters, or elements of $\mathfrak{D}_{\mathcal{A}}^*$. The empty word of length 0 is denoted by ϵ. A move $\rho = (q_1, \varphi, q_2) \in \Delta$, also denoted $q_1 \xrightarrow{\varphi} q_2$, is a transition from the *source* state q_1 to the *target* state q_2, where φ is the *guard* or *predicate* of the move. A move is *feasible* if its guard is satisfiable. For a character $a \in \mathfrak{D}_{\mathcal{A}}$, an *$a$-move* of M, denoted $q_1 \xrightarrow{a} q_2$ is a move $q_1 \xrightarrow{\varphi} q_2$ such that $a \in [\![\varphi]\!]$.

An s-FA M is *deterministic* if, for all transitions $(q, \varphi_1, q_1), (q, \varphi_2, q_2) \in \Delta$, $q_1 \neq q_2 \rightarrow [\![\varphi_1 \wedge \varphi_2]\!] = \emptyset$; i.e., for each state q and character a there is at most one a-move out of q. An s-FA M is *complete* if, for all $q \in Q$, $\bigvee_{(q,\varphi_i,q_i) \in \Delta} \varphi_i = \top$; i.e., for each state q and character a there exists an a-move out of q. Throughout the paper we assume all s-FAs are deterministic and complete, since determinization and completion are always possible [8]. An example s-FA is $\mathbf{M_{11}}$ in Fig. 2. This s-FA has 4 states and it operates over the interval algebra from Example 2.

Given an s-FA $M = (\mathcal{A}, Q, q_{init}, F, \Delta)$ and a state $q \in Q$, we say a word $w = a_1 a_2 \ldots a_k$ is *accepted at state* q if, for $1 \leq i \leq k$, there exist moves $q_{i-1} \xrightarrow{a_i} q_i$ such that $q_0 = q$ and $q_k \in F$. We refer to the set of words accepted at q as the *language accepted at* q, denoted as $\mathcal{L}_q(M)$; the *language accepted by M* is $\mathcal{L}(M) = \mathcal{L}_{q_{init}}(M)$. The s-FA $\mathbf{M_{11}}$ in Fig. 2 accepts, among others, words consisting only of numbers accepted by the predicate $[0, 51) \cup [101, \infty)$ and rejects, among others, the word $51, 25$.

3 Learning Algorithm

Here we present our algorithm, Λ^*, for learning symbolic automata. The premise is that the automaton to be learned, called the *target*, is hidden in a black box, so knowledge of it comes from some *oracle* that admits two kinds of queries: *membership queries* that ask whether a word is in the language of the target, and *equivalence queries* that ask whether a conjectured automaton is equivalent to the target—if not, a counterexample is provided. Λ^*, which builds upon L^* [3], maintains an *observation table* that comprises its knowledge about the target. The observation table is used to build the intermediary guesses of the target automaton and, eventually, the final automaton. It is assumed that the learner knows both the alphabet and the Boolean algebra in question.

3.1 Observation Table

The observation table consists of rows of prefixes and columns of suffixes. Each entry determines whether the target automaton accepts the word formed by concatenating the prefix and suffix. Intuitively, prefixes provide knowledge about words that lead to states, and suffixes help differentiate those states.

Definition 2 (Observation Table). *An observation table T for an s-FA M is a tuple (Σ, S, R, E, f) where Σ is a potentially infinite set called the* alphabet; $S, R, E \subset \Sigma^*$ *are finite subsets of words: S is called the set of* prefixes, *R is called the* boundary, *and E is called the set of* suffixes; *$f : (S \cup R) \cdot E \to \{0, 1\}$ is a* classification function[1] *such that for a word $w \cdot e \in (S \cup R) \cdot E$, $f(w \cdot e) = 1$ if $w \cdot e \in \mathcal{L}(M)$, and $f(w \cdot e) = 0$ if $w \cdot e \notin \mathcal{L}(M)$.[2] Additionally, (i) S and R are disjoint, (ii) $S \cup R$ is prefix-closed and $\epsilon \in S$, (iii) for all $s \in S$, there exists a character $a \in \Sigma$ such that $s \cdot a \in R$, and (iv) $\epsilon \in E$.*

Table $\mathbf{T_1}$ in Fig. 2 is an example observation table: The rows begin with elements of $S \cup R$, where the elements in S are shown above the horizontal divider and the elements in R below, and the columns begin with elements of E.

The observation table induces the construction of an automaton. For intuition, each $s \in S$ corresponds to a state q such that s is a string of moves from q_{init} to q. The boundary R gives information about the transitions between states. The states are differentiated by the strings in E and the classification function f, as if there exist $s_1, s_2 \in S$ and $e \in E$ such that $f(s_1 \cdot e) \neq f(s_2 \cdot e)$, then s_1 and s_2 *behave* differently and must lead to different states. We use the notation $row(w)$ for $w \in S \cup R$ to denote the vector indexed by $e \in E$ of $f(w \cdot e)$.

Λ^* manipulates the observation table and eventually conjectures an s-FA. For this to happen, the table must first satisfy certain properties—we call such a table *cohesive*—that are established through membership queries to the oracle. The cohesive observation table is used to construct an intermediary automaton that is ultimately used to produce a conjectured s-FA. An observation table is *closed* if for each $r \in R$ there exists $s \in S$ such that $row(s) = row(r)$; in other words, each element in the boundary corresponds to a state. An observation table is *reduced* if for all $s_1, s_2 \in S$, $row(s_1) \neq row(s_2)$, meaning each state is uniquely characterized by f and E. An observation table is *consistent* if for all $w_1, w_2 \in S \cup R$, if $a \in \Sigma^*$ and $w_1 \cdot a, w_2 \cdot a \in S \cup R$ and $row(w_1) = row(w_2)$, then $row(w_1 \cdot a) = row(w_2 \cdot a)$. A table being consistent means that if the words w_1 and w_2 are equivalent according to f and E, then $w_1 \cdot a$ and $w_2 \cdot a$ ought to be equivalent as well, and thus there is no evidence to the contrary.[3] An observation table is *evidence-closed* if for all $e \in E$ and $s \in S$, $s \cdot e \in S \cup R$. An observation table is *cohesive* if it is closed, reduced, consistent, and evidence-closed.

Consider, for example, the observation tables in Fig. 2. $\mathbf{T_2}$ is not closed, since $row(51) = -$ and there is no $s \in S$ with $row(s) = -$. Table $\mathbf{T_5}$ is not consistent because $row(51) = - = row(51, 0)$, but $row(51 \cdot 0) = - \neq + = row(51, 0 \cdot 0)$. Table $\mathbf{T_{11}}$ is closed, reduced, consistent, and evidence-closed.

If an observation table is cohesive, then it admits the construction of an *evidence automaton* that classifies words $w \in \Sigma^*$ equivalently to the observation table's classification function f.

---

[1] We also use $\{-, +\}$ to denote the range of f.

[2] We use $\cdot$ to denote both the concatenation of strings and its lifting to sets of strings, as is standard.

[3] We use $a \in \Sigma^*$ for the definition of *consistent*, but since the table is prefix-closed by definition, it is equivalent to consider only single-characters $a \in \Sigma$.

Definition 3 (Evidence Automaton). *An evidence automaton is a tuple* $(\Sigma, Q, q_{init}, F, \Delta)$ *where* Σ *is a set;* Q *is a finite set of states;* $q_{init} \in Q$ *is the initial state;* $F \subseteq Q$ *is the set of* final *states;* $\Delta \subseteq Q \times \Sigma \times Q$ *is the* transition relation.

A move $\rho = (q_1, a, q_2)$, also denoted $q_1 \xrightarrow{a} q_2$, is a transition from q_1 to q_2 using the character a. A word $w = a_1 a_2 \ldots a_k$ is *accepted at state* q if for $1 \leq i \leq k$ there exist moves $q_{i-1} \xrightarrow{a_i} q_i$ such that $q_0 = q$ and $q_k \in F$. Conversely, if that $q_k \notin F$, then w is *not* accepted at q. If there is no path through the automaton for w, then the acceptance is undefined. An evidence automaton differs from an s-FA in that transitions carry characters in Σ instead of predicates in a Boolean algebra over the domain Σ. Additionally, the evidence automaton can be deliberately sparse: it is not *complete*, and we avoid the notion that a state q does not accept a character a if there is no q' such that $(q, a, q') \in \Delta$—as stated above, such a case simply indicates the behavior of a at q is undefined.

Given a cohesive observation table $T = (\Sigma, S, R, E, f)$, we build an evidence automaton $A = (\Sigma, Q, q_{init}, F, \Delta)$ as follows: for each $s \in S$, we introduce a state $q_s \in Q$. q_{init} is assigned to q_ϵ. The final state set F contains all q_s such that $s \in S$ and $f(s) = 1$. Since the observation table is closed and reduced, there exists a function $g : S \cup R \to S$ such that $g(w) = s$ if and only if $row(w) = row(s)$. This function allows us to define the transition relation of A: if $w \cdot a \in S \cup R$ for $w \in \Sigma^*$ and $a \in \Sigma$, then $(q_{g(w)}, a, q_{g(w \cdot a)}) \in \Delta$. In Fig. 2, the automaton $\mathbf{M_1^e}$ (resp $\mathbf{M_{11}^e}$) is the evidence automaton corresponding to cohesive table $\mathbf{T_1}$ (resp. $\mathbf{T_{11}}$).

Lemma 1 (Evidence compatibility). *Given a cohesive observation table* $T = (\Sigma, S, R, E, f)$, *if* $M_{evid} = (\Sigma, Q, q_{init}, F, \Delta)$ *is the evidence automaton construction of* T, *then for all* $w \cdot e \in (S \cup R) \cdot E$, *if* $f(w \cdot e) = 1$ *then* M_{evid} *accepts* $w \cdot e$, *and if* $f(w \cdot e) = 0$ *then* M_{evid} *does not accept* $w \cdot e$.

3.2 Separating Predicates

Given an evidence automaton with an alphabet Σ, we require two pieces to build an s-FA: (*i*) a Boolean algebra $\mathcal{A}$ with $\mathfrak{D}_A = \Sigma$, and (*ii*) a partitioning function P for $\mathcal{A}$, which we define below. This latter component, the partitioning function, is the key insight to Λ^*'s generalization of L^*.

Definition 4 (Partitioning function). *A partitioning function for a Boolean algebra* $\mathcal{A} = (\mathfrak{D}, \Psi, [\![\_]\!], \bot, \top, \vee, \wedge, \neg)$ *is a function* $P : (2^{\mathfrak{D}})^* \to \Psi^*$ *that takes as input a list* $L_{\mathfrak{D}} = \ell_1 \ldots \ell_k$ *of disjoint sets of elements in* $\mathfrak{D}$, *and returns a parallel list* $L_\Psi = \varphi_1 \ldots \varphi_k$ *of predicates in* Ψ *such that*

- $\bigvee_{\varphi_i \in L_\Psi} \varphi_i = \top$
- $\varphi_i \wedge \varphi_j = \bot$ *for all* $\varphi_i, \varphi_j \in L_\Psi$ *with* $i \neq j$
- *for each* $\ell_i \in L_{\mathfrak{D}}$ *corresponding to* $\varphi_i \in L_\Psi$, *all* $a \in \ell_i$ *are such that* $a \in [\![\varphi_i]\!]$.

Example 3 (Equality Algebra Separating Predicates). We can construct a partitioning function for the equality algebra: given a list $L_\mathfrak{D} = \ell_1 \ldots \ell_k$ we construct a list $L_\Psi = \varphi_1 \ldots \varphi_k$ where each φ_i has $[\![\varphi_i]\!] = \ell_i$. We choose a j with maximal $|\ell_j|$ and update $\varphi_j \leftarrow \varphi_j \vee \bigwedge_{1 \leq i \leq k} \neg\varphi_i$. In the concrete case of $\mathfrak{D} = \mathbb{Z}$ and $L_\mathfrak{D} = [\{2\}, \{3\}, \emptyset, \{0, 5\}]$, the partitioning function would produce (after simplification) $L_\Psi = [\lambda a.\, a = 2, \lambda a.\, a = 3, \bot, \lambda a.\, a \neq 2 \wedge a \neq 3]$.

At a high level, as long as the s-FA is consistent with the evidence automaton, it will be consistent with the observation table. The words in the remainder of Σ^*—for which the evidence automaton has unspecified classification—can be assigned to paths in a largely arbitrary manner. The partitioning function handles generalizing the concrete evidence by creating *separating predicates*, in effect specifying the behavior for the remaining words. Ideally, this generalization allows an automaton to be learned with a relatively small observation table, even if the alphabet is large—or even infinite.

Given an evidence automaton $A = (\Sigma, Q, q_{\text{init}}, F, \Delta)$, a Boolean algebra $\mathcal{A}$ with domain Σ, and an appropriate partitioning function P, we build an s-FA $M = (\mathcal{A}, Q, q_{\text{init}}, F, \Delta_M)$ using that Boolean algebra and that exact configuration of states. All that remains is the construction of the transition relation Δ_M.

For each $q \in Q$, we perform the following. We gather all evidence transitions out of q into a set $\Delta_q = \{(q, a, q') \in \Delta\}$ and construct a list L_Σ indexed over the states $q_i \in Q$, where each set in L_Σ is $\ell_i = \{a \mid (q, a, q_i) \in \Delta_q\}$. We apply the partitioning function to get a list of separating predicates $L_{\Psi_\mathcal{A}} = P(L_\Sigma)$ which is also indexed over $q_i \in Q$, and add (q, φ_i, q_i) to Δ_M for each $\varphi_i \in L_{\Psi_\mathcal{A}}$.

Lemma 2 (s-FA evidence compatibility). *Given a cohesive observation table $T = (\Sigma, S, R, E, F)$, if $M_{evid} = (\Sigma, Q, q_{init}, F, \Delta)$ is the evidence automaton construction of T, and $M = (\mathcal{A}, Q, q_{init}, F, \Delta)$ is produced from M_{evid} using a partitioning function, then for all $w \cdot e \in (S \cup R) \cdot E$, if $f(w \cdot e) = 1$ then $w \cdot e \in \mathcal{L}(M)$, and if $f(w \cdot e) = 0$ then $w \cdot e \notin \mathcal{L}(M)$.*

An example observation table, its corresponding evidence automaton, and a resultant s-FA are shown in the last row of Fig. 2.

3.3 Algorithm Description

We now present a description of Λ^* and an example execution. The algorithm begins by initializing an observation table with $S = \{\epsilon\}$, $R = \{a\}$ for an arbitrary $a \in \Sigma$, and $E = \{\epsilon\}$. f is initially undefined. The knowledge of the table is grown using the operations *fill*, *close*, *evidence-close*, and *make-consistent*.

The operation *fill* asks a membership query for all $w \cdot e \in (S \cup R) \cdot E$ for which f is undefined and then adds those results to f; in this way, it ensures f is defined over the entire domain of the observation table.

The operation *close* checks for the existence of an $r \in R$ such that for all $s \in S$, $row(r) \neq row(s)$. Such an r is moved from R to S, and $r \cdot a$ is added to R for some arbitrary $a \in \Sigma$.

The operation *evidence-close* ensures for all $e \in E$ and $s \in S$ that $s \cdot e \in S \cup R$ by adding to R all $s \cdot e$ that are not. It also adds to R any necessary prefixes so that $S \cup R$ is prefix-closed.

The operation *make-consistent* operates as follows: if there exist $w_1, w_2 \in S \cup R$ and $w_1 \cdot a, w_2 \cdot a \in S \cup R$ for some $a \in \Sigma$ such that $row(w_1) = row(w_2)$ but $row(w_1 \cdot a) \neq row(w_2 \cdot a)$, then w_1 and w_2 actually lead to different states; using the $e \in E$ such that $f(w_1 \cdot a \cdot e) \neq f(w_2 \cdot a \cdot e)$, it is clear $a \cdot e$ thus differentiates those states. Accordingly, $a \cdot e$ is added to E. Additionally, we then add $(\{u_2 \cdot b \mid u_1 \cdot b \in S \cup R\} \cup \{u_1 \cdot b \mid u_2 \cdot b \in S \cup R\}) \setminus S$ to R for all pairs $u_1, u_2 \in S \cup R$ such that before adding e to E, $row(u_1) = row(u_2)$, but $f(u_1 \cdot e) \neq f(u_2 \cdot e)$ (this includes the pair w_1, w_2). This operation *distributes* the old evidence leading out of the amalgamated state between the newly differentiated states, simplifying the constructions in Sect. 4.

Upon receiving a counterexample $c \in \Sigma^*$ from an equivalence query sent to the oracle, all prefixes of c are added to R (except those already present in S). There are two cases for a counterexample: one of the predicates in the s-FA needs refinement, which is facilitated by adding those new words to the table, or a new state must exist in the automaton, which is handled by *make-consistent*.

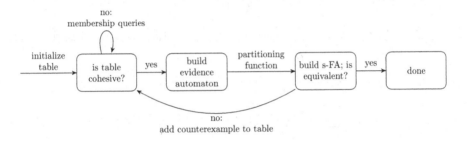

Fig. 1. Overview of the learning algorithm Λ^*.

Figure 1 shows an overview of the learning algorithm: after the table is initialized, the operations *make-consistent*, *evidence-close*, and *close* are applied until the table is cohesive.[4] (*Fill* is applied throughout whenever a change is made to the table.) An s-FA M is then conjectured from the table, and an equivalence query is performed: if M is equivalent to the target automaton, then the algorithm terminates. Otherwise, a counterexample is produced and processed, and the procedure repeats.

Λ^* can be thought of as a lazily-evaluated version of L* with the additional generalization step, and therefore it maintains the property of L* that the learned automaton has a minimal number of states.

Theorem 1 (Λ^* minimality). *When Λ^* terminates it returns a minimal s-FA.*

---

[4] It is an invariant of the initialization of the table and of the operations applied to it that the observation table is always reduced.

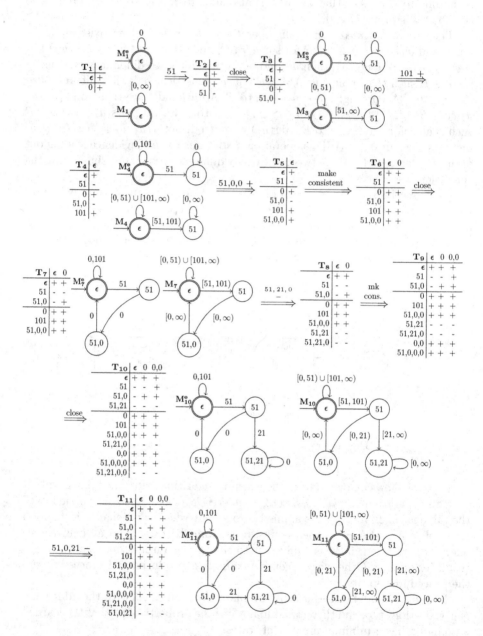

Fig. 2. An example run of the Λ^* algorithm.

3.4 Worked Example

Suppose we invoke Λ^* to learn the automaton over non-negative integers that accepts all words *except* those that contain a number between 51 and 100 that is not immediately followed by two numbers between 0 and 20.

The Boolean algebra we use is the union of left-closed right-open intervals. We fix a partitioning function P that assumes that if $a \in \ell$, $b \in \ell'$, and there are no c in the input sets such that $a < c < b$, then the whole interval $[a, b)$ behaves equivalently to a. For example, $P(\{0\}, \{10\}) = [0, 10), [10, \infty)$ and $P(\{0, 20\}, \{10\}) = [0, 10) \cup [20, \infty), [10, \infty)$.

The trace of the algorithm is illustrated in Fig. 2. Λ^* begins by initializing an observation table so that $S = \{\epsilon\}$, $R = \{0\}$ (the 0 is an arbitrary character from Σ and is used purely so that the table contains $\epsilon \cdot a$ for some a), and $E = \{\epsilon\}$. The appropriate membership queries are made to the oracle, resulting in the table T_1. T_1 is cohesive, so it is used to construct the evidence automaton M_1^e, and by calling the partitioning function P on the outgoing transitions of each state in M_1^e—in this case just $P(\{0\}) = [0, \infty)$—the s-FA M_1 is conjectured. The oracle is given M_1 as an equivalence query, and it returns the single-character word 51 as a counterexample. 51 is added to R in the observation table, as would all of its prefixes if it were a word of length greater than one, and a membership query is asked for $51 \cdot \epsilon$, resulting in table T_2.

T_2 is not closed, since $row(51) = -$ and there is no $s \in S$ with $row(s) = -$. Accordingly, 51 represents a path to a new state, so it is moved from S to R, and a continuation $51, 0$ is added to R. This produces table T_3, which is now cohesive and thus admits the construction of the evidence automaton M_3^e and ultimately the s-FA M_3 through the use of the partitioning function: for example, for the outgoing transitions of the initial state, $P(\{0\}, \{51\}) = [0, 51), [51, \infty)$. An equivalence query sent to the oracle returns the counterexample of 101.

Adding 101 to R results in the cohesive table T_4 and the s-FA M_4, and the oracle provides the counterexample $51, 0, 0$. $51, 0, 0$ is added to R (all of its prefixes are already present in $S \cup R$), resulting in the table T_5 which is not consistent: observe that $row(51) = - = row(51, 0)$, but $row(51 \cdot 0) = - \neq + = row(51, 0 \cdot 0)$. This means that 51 and $51, 0$ actually lead to different states, which will be addressed in two stages. First, following the rule *make-consistent*, since $f(51 \cdot 0 \cdot \epsilon) \neq f(51, 0 \cdot 0 \cdot \epsilon)$, we add $0 \cdot \epsilon$ to E to distinguish the states led to by 51 and $51, 0$, which produces table T_6. Applying *close* to T_6 results in T_7, which is then cohesive (we added an element to E, which would normally require applying *evidence-close*, but it happens to be that T_7 is already evidence-closed) and produces an s-FA M_7. The counterexample $51, 21, 0$ requires adding it as well as the prefix $51, 21$ to R, producing table T_8.

T_8 is also inconsistent, since $row(51) = -, - = row(51, 21)$ but $row(51 \cdot 0) = -, + \neq -, - = row(51, 21 \cdot 0)$. Since $f(51 \cdot 0 \cdot 0) \neq f(51, 21 \cdot 0 \cdot 0)$, we add $0 \cdot 0$ to E to distinguish 51 from $51, 21$, and evidence-close the table to get T_9. Closing and evidence-closing this table results in T_{10}, the conjecture M_{10}, the counterexample $51, 0, 21$, the table T_{11}, and finally the automaton M_{11} which passes the equivalence query.

4   Learnability and Its Properties

Whether an s-FA can be learned and, if so, the complexity of learning that s-FA, depends on a more fundamental property concerning the *learnability* of the underlying Boolean algebra. In Λ^*, this notion of learnability determines the complexity of the algorithm. We first provide a definition for an algebra's learnability with respect to the inputs given to a partitioning function and then connect these inputs to the queries given to the oracle during the learning algorithm.

4.1   Learnability of a Boolean Algebra

Fix a partitioning function P over a Boolean algebra $\mathcal{A}$. Let C denote a concept class for which each concept $c \in C$ is a finite partition of $\mathfrak{D}_{\mathcal{A}}$ using predicates in $\Psi_{\mathcal{A}}$, and let G denote the set of *generators* which, informally, provide a sequence of counterexamples—elements in $\mathfrak{D}_{\mathcal{A}}$—to update the sets given to P. We analyze how many times a generator g must make an update before P learns a desired partition. A generator $g \in G$ can be thought of as a function that takes as input a tuple $(L, c_{\text{guess}}, c_{\text{target}})$—where L is the list of subsets of $\mathfrak{D}_{\mathcal{A}}$ given as input to P, $c_{\text{guess}} \in C$ is a partition of $\mathfrak{D}_{\mathcal{A}}$ consistent with L, and $c_{\text{target}} \in C$ is the target partition—and outputs a new list L' of $\mathfrak{D}_{\mathcal{A}}$-subsets. We say g provides sets to P to refer to the iterative process in which $L_0 = [\emptyset]$ and $L_{i+1} = g(L_i, P(L_i), c_{\text{target}})$. Intuitively, a generator iteratively updates a list of sets to be given to a partitioning function so that the output of that function approaches the target partition.

Additionally, the generators are subject to the following restrictions that ensure a sense of monotonicity: (*i*) the output L' is *greater than* the input L in the sense that $\forall a \in \mathfrak{D}_{\mathcal{A}}[(\exists \ell \in L. a \in \ell) \to (\exists \ell' \in L'. a \in \ell')]$ (a character present in the input will always be present in future iterations); (*ii*) if $a_1 \in \ell_i \in L$ and $a_2 \in \ell_j \in L$ and $i \neq j$, then it cannot be that there is some $\ell' \in L'$ and both $a_1 \in \ell'$ and $a_2 \in \ell'$ (if the generator says two elements belong to different sets in a partition, that must be true for all future iterations); and (*iii*) either the number of sets in L' is larger than the number of sets in L, or at least one $a \in \mathfrak{D}_{\mathcal{A}}$ that was not present in any $\ell \in L$ is present in some $\ell' \in L'$ Also, the inputs to the generator are subject to a notion of consistency: if $a_1 \in \ell_i \in L$ and $a_2 \in \ell_j \in L$ such that $i \neq j$, then there is no $\varphi \in c_{\text{target}}$ such that $\{a_1, a_2\} \subseteq [\![\varphi]\!]$.

This definition of a generator exactly captures the high-level process of updating the observation table in our algorithm via queries to the oracle and *projecting* those changes onto the individual lists of sets that are given to the partitioning function for the creation of the conjectured s-FA. For example, in Fig. 2, the evidence for the outgoing transitions of the ϵ-state is provided by a generator such that $L_1 = [\{0\}]$, $L_2 = [\{0\}, \{51\}]$, and $L_3 = [\{0, 101\}, \{51\}]$. Below we will formalize a notion of learnability with respect to these generators, and it will thus bear a close correspondence to the complexity of learning an s-FA.

Definition 5 (s_g-learnability). *Given a Boolean algebra $\mathcal{A}$, a partitioning function P, and a generator $g \in G$, we say the pair $(\mathcal{A}, P)$ is s_g-learnable if there exists an implicit function $s_g : C \to \mathbb{N}$ such that P needs as input a list of sets, provided by g, with total size at most $s_g(c)$ to discover a target partition $c \in C$. Furthermore, we say $\mathcal{A}$ itself is s_g-learnable if there exists a partitioning function P such that $(\mathcal{A}, P)$ is s_g-learnable.*

We also classify $\mathcal{A}$ as belonging to a *learning class* that depends on these s_g functions—but first we need an auxiliary notion of the *size* of a partition.

Definition 6 (DNF-Size of a partition). *Let C be the set of partitions of $\mathcal{A}$. Each $c \in C$ is a list $\varphi_1, \ldots, \varphi_n$: we can expand each φ_i to a minimal disjunctive-normal-form formula $\bigvee_j \psi_{i,j}$ such that $c' = \psi_{1,1}, \ldots, \psi_{1,m_1}, \ldots, \psi_{n,1}, \ldots, \psi_{n,m_n}$ is a partition of $\mathcal{A}$ that is at least as fine as c. We say the DNF-size of c is the length of the list of such a minimal c'.*

Example 4. The partition $\{x < 5 \vee x > 10, 5 \leq x \wedge x \leq 10\}$ has DNF-size 3.

Definition 7 (Learning Class). *For a fixed Boolean algebra $\mathcal{A}$ if there exists a $g \in G$ such that $\mathcal{A}$ is s_g-learnable, then*

- *if s_g is a constant function, i.e. $\exists k \forall c.\, s_g(c) = k$, we say $\mathcal{A} \in \mathcal{C}^{\exists}_{const}$*
- *if s_g is a function only of the DNF-size of c, we say $\mathcal{A} \in \mathcal{C}^{\exists}_{size}$*
- *if s_g is otherwise unconstrained, we say $\mathcal{A} \in \mathcal{C}^{\exists}_{finite}$*

Additionally, for some fixed partitioning function P, if for all $g \in G$, $(\mathcal{A}, P)$ is s_g-learnable, then

- *if each s_g is a constant function, we say $\mathcal{A} \in \mathcal{C}^{\forall}_{const}$*
- *if each s_g is a function only of the DNF-size of c, we say $\mathcal{A} \in \mathcal{C}^{\forall}_{size}$*
- *if each s_g is otherwise unconstrained, we say $\mathcal{A} \in \mathcal{C}^{\forall}_{finite}$*

$$\begin{array}{ccccc} \mathcal{C}^{\forall}_{const} & \subseteq & \mathcal{C}^{\forall}_{size} & \subseteq & \mathcal{C}^{\forall}_{finite} \\ \cap & & \cap & & \cap \\ \mathcal{C}^{\exists}_{const} & \subseteq & \mathcal{C}^{\exists}_{size} & \subseteq & \mathcal{C}^{\exists}_{finite} \end{array}$$

Fig. 3. Learning classes.

Observe that learning classes are partially-ordered by the subset relation shown in Fig. 3. This categorization is convenient for reasoning about different instantiations of domains and oracles. For example: (*i*) When $\mathcal{A} \in \mathcal{C}^{\forall}_{const}$, learning a partition over $\mathfrak{D}_\mathcal{A}$ is equivalent to the machine-learning notion of a mistake-bound [12]. (*ii*) The equality algebra for any finite alphabet is in $\mathcal{C}^{\forall}_{const}$. (*iii*) The interval algebra over the integers or rationals is in $\mathcal{C}^{\exists}_{size}$; if the oracle provides lexicographically minimal counterexamples, the number of times the partitions must be updated through the generator is determined by the number of connected regions in the partition, as illustrated in [13] and as applicable for Fig. 2. The integer case is also in $C^\forall_{finite}$, since after arbitrary counterexamples are found beyond the least and greatest finite bounds in the partition, m and M respectively, at most $M - m$ more counterexamples are required. (iv) Using enumeration, linear rational arithmetic is in $C^\forall_{finite}$.

Since for each state in an s-FA, the set of outgoing transitions forms a partition of the alphabet, i.e. a concept in C, the number of counterexamples needed to learn the entire automaton is related to the sum of $s_g(c)$ for each state's outgoing transitions. Hence, the complexity of learning depends on (i) the choice of the partitioning function and, potentially, (ii) the quality of counterexamples provided by the oracle.

Theorem 2 (SFA Learnability). *If M is an s-FA over a learnable Boolean algebra $\mathcal{A}$ with n states, then the number of equivalence queries needed to learn M is bounded above by $n^2 \sum_{q_i \in Q} s_{g_i}(c_i)$, where s_{g_i} is the projection of the oracle onto learning the partition c_i for the outgoing transitions of state q_i.*

The notion of an algebra's learning class can have powerful ramifications in conjuction with the result of Theorem 2. For example, if an s-FA uses a Boolean algebra contained in $C^\forall_{finite}$, then the use of the appropriate partitioning function guarantees termination of the learning algorithm, independent of the quality of counterexamples produced from equivalence queries. Investigating which of the subset relations in Fig. 3 are strict subsets, as well as what (if any) algebras fall outside of $C^\exists_{finite}$ are interesting future problems.

4.2 Composing Learnable Algebras

The definition of learnability described prior has the remarkable property that it is preserved by some constructions that combine Boolean algebras, such as the *disjoint union* and the *cartesian product*. In these cases, a partitioning function for the resultant algebra can be constructed by using partitioning functions for the original algebras as black boxes; This allows us to phrase the learnability of the constructed algebra in terms of the learnability of the individual algebras.

Definition 8 (Disjoint Union Algebra). *Let $\mathcal{A}_1, \mathcal{A}_2$ be boolean algebras. Their disjoint union algebra $\mathcal{A}_\uplus = (\mathfrak{D}, \Psi, [\![\text{-}]\!], \bot, \top, \vee, \wedge, \neg)$, which we denote $\mathcal{A}_\uplus = \mathcal{A}_1 \uplus \mathcal{A}_2$, is constructed as follows:*[5]

$$\mathfrak{D} = \mathfrak{D}_{\mathcal{A}_1} \uplus \mathfrak{D}_{\mathcal{A}_2} \quad \Psi = \Psi_{\mathcal{A}_1} \times \Psi_{\mathcal{A}_2} \quad [\![(\varphi_{\mathcal{A}_1}, \varphi_{\mathcal{A}_2})]\!] = [\![\varphi_{\mathcal{A}_1}]\!]_{\mathcal{A}_1} \uplus [\![\varphi_{\mathcal{A}_2}]\!]_{\mathcal{A}_2}$$
$$\bot = (\bot_{\mathcal{A}_1}, \bot_{\mathcal{A}_2}) \quad \top = (\top_{\mathcal{A}_1}, \top_{\mathcal{A}_2}) \quad \neg(\varphi_{\mathcal{A}_1}, \varphi_{\mathcal{A}_2}) = (\neg_{\mathcal{A}_1} \varphi_{\mathcal{A}_1}, \neg_{\mathcal{A}_2} \varphi_{\mathcal{A}_2})$$
$$(\varphi_{\mathcal{A}_1}, \varphi_{\mathcal{A}_2}) \vee (\varphi'_{\mathcal{A}_1}, \varphi'_{\mathcal{A}_2}) = ((\varphi_{\mathcal{A}_1} \vee_{\mathcal{A}_1} \varphi'_{\mathcal{A}_1}), (\varphi_{\mathcal{A}_2} \vee_{\mathcal{A}_2} \varphi'_{\mathcal{A}_2}))$$
$$(\varphi_{\mathcal{A}_1}, \varphi_{\mathcal{A}_2}) \wedge (\varphi'_{\mathcal{A}_1}, \varphi'_{\mathcal{A}_2}) = ((\varphi_{\mathcal{A}_1} \wedge_{\mathcal{A}_1} \varphi'_{\mathcal{A}_1}), (\varphi_{\mathcal{A}_2} \wedge_{\mathcal{A}_2} \varphi'_{\mathcal{A}_2}))$$

---

[5] In our definition, we use $\mathfrak{D}_{\mathcal{A}_1} \uplus \mathfrak{D}_{\mathcal{A}_2}$ to denote the disjoint union of sets; rigorously, when the sets are not already disjoint, this is constructed by taking $(\mathfrak{D}_{\mathcal{A}_1} \times \{1\}) \cup (\mathfrak{D}_{\mathcal{A}_2} \times \{2\})$ and lifting all the remaining constructs appropriately.

If $\mathcal{A}_1$ has partitioning function P_1 and $\mathcal{A}_2$ has partitioning function P_2, then we can construct a partitioning function $P_\uplus$ for $\mathcal{A}_\uplus = \mathcal{A}_1 \uplus \mathcal{A}_2$: $P_\uplus$ takes as input a list $L_\uplus$ of sets where each set $\ell_{\uplus_i} \subset \mathfrak{D}_{\mathcal{A}_1} \uplus \mathfrak{D}_{\mathcal{A}_2}$. We decompose $L_\uplus$ into $L_{\mathfrak{D}_1}$ and $L_{\mathfrak{D}_2}$, two lists of sets of $\ell_{1_i} \subset \mathfrak{D}_{\mathcal{A}_1}$ and $\ell_{2_i} \subset \mathfrak{D}_{\mathcal{A}_2}$, respectively: for each $a \in \ell_{\uplus_i}$, if $a \in \mathfrak{D}_{\mathcal{A}_1}$, then we add a to ℓ_{1_i}, and otherwise if $a \in \mathfrak{D}_{\mathcal{A}_2}$, then we add a to ℓ_{2_i}. We obtain $L_{\Psi_1} = P_1(L_{\mathfrak{D}_1})$ and $L_{\Psi_2} = P_2(L_{\mathfrak{D}_2})$. We construct $L_{\Psi_\uplus}$ by taking $\varphi_{\uplus_i} = (\varphi_{1_i}, \varphi_{2_i})$ for all i, return $L_{\Psi_\uplus}$, and terminate.

The disjoint union is useful since, for example, we can represent arbitrary intervals over the integers as the disjoint union of (i) intervals over non-negative integers and (ii) intervals over negative integers. In other words, a partitioning function suited for a single notion of ∞ can be extended to capture two.

Theorem 3 (Disjoint Union Algebra Learnability). *Given Boolean algebras $\mathcal{A}_1, \mathcal{A}_2$ with partitioning functions P_1, P_2, $(\mathcal{A}_1, P_1)$ is s_{g_1}-learnable and $(\mathcal{A}_2, P_2)$ is s_{g_2}-learnable if and only if there exists $g_\uplus$ such that their disjoint union algebra $(\mathcal{A}_\uplus, P_\uplus)$ is $s_{g_\uplus}$-learnable, where $s_{g_\uplus}(c) = s_{g_1}(c_1) + s_{g_2}(c_2)$ and c_1 and c_2 are the restrictions of c to $\mathfrak{D}_{\mathcal{A}_1}$ and $\mathfrak{D}_{\mathcal{A}_2}$, respectively.*

Corollary 1. *If $\mathcal{A}_1$ and $\mathcal{A}_2$ are in learning class $\mathcal{C}$, then their disjoint union $\mathcal{A}_\uplus$ is also in learning class $\mathcal{C}$.*

We present a similar construction for the *product* of two Boolean algebras.

Definition 9 (Product Algebra). *Let $\mathcal{A}_1, \mathcal{A}_2$ be boolean algebras. Their product algebra $\mathcal{A}_\times = (\mathfrak{D}, \Psi, [\![\_]\!], \bot, \top, \vee, \wedge, \neg)$, which we denote $\mathcal{A}_\times = \mathcal{A}_1 \times \mathcal{A}_2$, is constructed as follows:*

$$\mathfrak{D} = \mathfrak{D}_{\mathcal{A}_1} \times \mathfrak{D}_{\mathcal{A}_2} \quad \Psi = 2^{\Psi_{\mathcal{A}_1} \times \Psi_{\mathcal{A}_2}} \quad [\![\{(\varphi_{\mathcal{A}_1 i}, \varphi_{\mathcal{A}_2 i})\}_i]\!] = \bigcup_i [\![\varphi_{\mathcal{A}_1 i}]\!]_{\mathcal{A}_1} \times [\![\varphi_{\mathcal{A}_2 i}]\!]_{\mathcal{A}_2}$$

$$\bot = \{(\bot_{\mathcal{A}_1}, \bot_{\mathcal{A}_2})\} \quad \top = \{(\top_{\mathcal{A}_1}, \bot_{\mathcal{A}_2})\}$$

$$\neg\{(\varphi_{\mathcal{A}_1 i}, \varphi_{\mathcal{A}_2 i})\}_i = \bigwedge_i \{(\neg_{\mathcal{A}_1} \varphi_{\mathcal{A}_1 i}, \top_{\mathcal{A}_2}), (\top_{\mathcal{A}_1}, \neg_{\mathcal{A}_2} \varphi_{\mathcal{A}_2 i})\}$$

$$\{(\varphi_{\mathcal{A}_1 i}, \varphi_{\mathcal{A}_2 i})\}_i \vee \{(\varphi'_{\mathcal{A}_1 j}, \varphi'_{\mathcal{A}_2 j})\}_j = \{(\varphi_{\mathcal{A}_1 i}, \varphi_{\mathcal{A}_2 i})\}_i \cup \{(\varphi'_{\mathcal{A}_1 j}, \varphi'_{\mathcal{A}_2 j})\}_j$$

$$\{(\varphi_{\mathcal{A}_1 i}, \varphi_{\mathcal{A}_2 i})\}_i \wedge \{(\varphi'_{\mathcal{A}_1 j}, \varphi'_{\mathcal{A}_2 j})\}_j = \{(\varphi_{\mathcal{A}_1 i} \wedge_{\mathcal{A}_1} \varphi'_{\mathcal{A}_1 j}, \varphi_{\mathcal{A}_2 i} \wedge_{\mathcal{A}_2} \varphi'_{\mathcal{A}_2 j}) \mid \forall i, j\}$$

If $\mathcal{A}_1$ has partitioning function P_1 and $\mathcal{A}_2$ has partitioning function P_2, then we can construct a partitioning function $P_\times$ for $\mathcal{A}_\times = \mathcal{A}_1 \times \mathcal{A}_2$: $P_\times$ takes as input a list $L_\times$ of sets where each set $\ell_{\times_i} \subset \mathfrak{D}_{\mathcal{A}_1} \times \mathfrak{D}_{\mathcal{A}_2}$. We first take the set $D_1 = \{d_1 \mid (d_1, d_2) \in \ell_{\times_i}$ for some $\ell_{\times_i} \in L_\times\}$, turn it into a list $D'_1 = \{d_{1,1}\}, \ldots, \{d_{1,n}\}$, and compute a partition $L_1 = P_1(D'_1)$. Then for each $d_i \in D_1$, we construct a list D_{2,d_i} where the j-th element is the set $\{d_2 \mid (d_i, d_2) \in \ell_{\times_i}\}$ and compute a partition $L_{2,d_i} = P_2(D_{2,d_i})$. Finally, we initialize the list of predicates to be returned $L_{\Psi_\times} = \varphi_{\times_1}, \ldots, \varphi_{\times_k}$ so that initially each $\varphi_{\times_i} = \bot$. Then for all i and each $(d_1, d_2) \in \ell_{\times_i}$, let φ_{d_1} be the predicate in L_1 corresponding to $\{d_1\}$ in D'_1 and let φ_{d_2} be the predicate in L_{2,d_1} corresponding to the set of D_{2,d_1} that contains d_2; update $\varphi_{\times_i} \leftarrow \varphi_{\times_i} \vee (\varphi_{d_1}, \varphi_{d_2})$. Return $L_{\Psi_\times}$ and terminate.

Example 5. Suppose we want to find a partition over $(x, y) \in \mathbb{Z} \times \mathbb{Z}$ where each component uses the interval algebra, and suppose the input sets are $L_\times = [\{(0,0), (1,0), (1,2)\}, \{(0,2)\}]$. Then $D'_1 = [\{0\}, \{1\}]$ and perhaps

$L_1 = P_1(D_1') = [x \leq 0, x > 0]$. Then we have $D_{2,0} = [\{0\}, \{2\}]$ and $D_{2,1} = [\{0, 2\}, \emptyset]$. Perhaps $L_{2,0} = P_2(D_{2,0}) = [y \leq 1, y > 1]$ and $L_{2,1} = P_2(D_{2,1}) = [\top, \bot]$. Then (without simplification) $L_{\Psi_x} = [(x \leq 0, y \leq 1) \vee (x > 0, \top) \vee (x > 0, \top), (x \leq 0, y > 1)]$.

Theorem 4 (Product Algebra Learnability). *Given Boolean algebras A_1, A_2 with partitioning functions P_1, P_2 and their product algebra $A_\times$ with the composite partitioning function $P_\times$, let $c \in C_\times$ be the target partition over the product algebra, let $c_1 \in C_1$ be the minterms of the A_1-components of c, and let $c_2 \in C_2$ be the minterms of the A_2-components of c. (i) If (A_1, P_1) is s_{g_1}-learnable and (A_2, P_2) is s_{g_2}-learnable, then there exists $g_\times$ such that $(A_\times, P_\times)$ is $s_{g_\times}$-learnable where $s_{g_\times}(c) = s_{g_1}(c_1)s_{g_2}(c_2)$. (ii) If $(A_\times, P_\times)$ is $s_{g_\times}$-learnable, then there exist g_1, g_2 such that (A_1, P_1) is s_{g_1}-learnable and (A_2, P_2) is s_{g_2}-learnable where $s_{g_\times}(c) = s_{g_1}(c_1) = s_{g_2}(c_2)$.*

Corollary 2. *If A_1 and A_2 are in learning class C, then their product $A_\times$ is also in learning class C.*

Since learnability is closed under disjoint union and product, symbolic automata over non-recursive data types can be learned using partitioning functions for the component types, as opposed to necessitating specialized partitioning functions.

5   Implementation

We implemented Λ^* in the open-source Java library Symbolic Automata. Our modular implementation only requires the programmer to provide learnable Boolean algebras as input to the learner; we have already implemented the equality and interval algebras as well as the disjoint union and product algebras—which are implemented as meta-algebras and can be instantiated arbitrarily.

We evaluated our algorithm on the examples presented by Maler and Mens [13], who proposed two extensions of L^* for learning s-FAs where 1) predicates are union of intervals in $\mathbb{N}$, or 2) predicates are union of intervals over $\mathbb{N} \times \mathbb{N}$. Their algorithms assume that the oracle always provides lexicographically minimal counterexamples, so that every counterexample identifies a boundary in a partition. They evaluate their techniques on two automata: one over the alphabet $\mathbb{N}$ (Ex. 4.1 [13]) and one over the alphabet $\mathbb{N} \times \mathbb{N}$ (Ex. 5.1 [13]).

We implemented a partitioning function equivalent to their characterization of the interval algebra over $\mathbb{N}$. While, to learn automata over $\mathbb{N} \times \mathbb{N}$, [13] introduces an ad-hoc separate technique that requires the oracle to always give locally minimal counterexamples, in our setting, the algebra for pairs can be trivially implemented as the Cartesian product of the interval algebra over $\mathbb{N}$ with itself.

We learn the first automaton using 8 equivalence and 23 membership queries, while their algorithm only requires 7 and 17, respectively. The former difference is due to their algorithm adding a different suffix to E than ours, which happens to discover two new states instead of one and ultimately saves them an equivalence query. The latter is due to a more refined handling of counterexamples (more in our related work). Similarly, we learn the second automaton using 28 equivalence and 43 membership queries, while their algorithm only requires 18 and 20, respectively. In this case, the discrepancy is amplified because the algorithm in [13] uses a specialized implicit partitioning function that avoids the quadratic blowup caused by the Cartesian product construction in Theorem 4. We implemented an analogous specialized partitioning function directly on the product algebra and were able to learn the same example using 19 equivalence and 30 membership queries.

6 Related Work

Λ^* builds on L^* [3], for which many extensions have been proposed, the most advanced one being TTT [1, 11]. While these extensions could be applied to Λ^* to potentially improve the size of the observation table, the number of membership queries is dictated by the amount of evidence needed for the partitioning function to generalize. Our algorithm opens new questions: Can we efficiently store intermediate predicates computed by the partitioning functions? Can separating predicates be computed incrementally?

Our paper is the first one to provide: (i) an algorithm for learning symbolic automata over arbitrary alphabet theories, with a notion of learnability that is parametric in both the alphabet theory and the oracle (through its projection onto generators), and (ii) compositionality properties that permit combining learnable algebras. We detail our comparison against the most relevant works.

Isberner et al. augment L^* with abstractions to learn automata over potentially infinite alphabets [10]. The algorithm creates abstract symbols to generalize sets of characters, and the final automaton operates over these abstract symbols. Abstractions can cause non-determinism that is resolved using refinement operators. This approach differs from ours in two aspects. First, while the final output of Λ^* is a symbolic automaton over the target Boolean algebra, the output in [10] is an automaton operating over a separate abstract alphabet that is discovered during the learning process and might not necessarily form a Boolean algebra. Second, our algorithm enjoys well-defined learnability and compositionality properties over the input Boolean algebras, while the one in [10] does not provide any such properties. Maler and Mens [13] instantiate the algorithm proposed in [10] and learn automata over the interval algebra for integers and pair of integers. As we discussed throughout the paper, their results are special cases of our formulation. In fact, their specialized algorithm for learning automata over pairs of integers is a special case of our Cartesian product of two algebras. Using our technique, we can also drop the assumption that the oracle provides lexicographically minimal counterexamples, which simply causes a change to the s_g functions and learnability.

Argyros et al. [5] present an algorithm for learning symbolic automata where the learnability is parametric with respect to a *guardgen* method, which is an equivalent formulation of our partitioning function. Their definition of learnability only captures our learning class $\mathcal{C}_{const}^\forall$ and can therefore only describe Boolean algebras operating over finite alphabets or with finitely many predicates. Our work introduces generators, proposes a deeper analysis of the learnability of a Boolean algebra, and shows how learnable algebras can be composed.

The Sigma* algorithm [6] is a practical algorithm for learning symbolic transducers, but it does not have learnability guarantees. Other algorithms can learn nominal [14] and register automata [7]. In these models, the alphabet is infinite but not structured (i.e., it does not form a Boolean algebra) and characters at different positions can be compared using binary relations (typically equality or simple arithmetic relations). These models are orthogonal to symbolic automata.

Acknowledgements. We would like to thank Alexandra Silva, Joshua Moerman, and Nimit Singhania for their feedback on an early version of this paper.

References

1. LearnLib, a framework for automata learning. http://learnlib.de/
2. Alur, R., Černý, P., Madhusudan, P., Nam, W.: Synthesis of interface specifications for Java classes. SIGPLAN Not. **40**(1), 98–109 (2005)
3. Angluin, D.: Learning regular sets from queries and counterexamples. Inf. Comput. **75**(2), 87–106 (1987)
4. Angluin, D., Eisenstat, S., Fisman, D.: Learning regular languages via alternating automata. In: Proceedings of the 24th International Conference on Artificial Intelligence, IJCAI 2015, pp. 3308–3314. AAAI Press (2015)
5. Argyros, G., Stais, I., Kiayias, A., Keromytis, A.D.: Back in black: towards formal, black box analysis of sanitizers and filters. In: IEEE Symposium on Security and Privacy, SP 2016, San Jose, CA, USA, 22–26 May 2016, pp. 91–109 (2016)
6. Botincan, M., Babic, D.: Sigma*: symbolic learning of input-output specifications. In: The 40th Annual ACM SIGPLAN-SIGACT Symposium on Principles of Programming Languages, POPL 2013, Rome, Italy, 23–25 January 2013, pp. 443–456 (2013)
7. Cassel, S., Howar, F., Jonsson, B., Steffen, B.: Active learning for extended finite state machines. Formal Aspects Comput. **28**(2), 233–263 (2016)
8. D'Antoni, L., Veanes, M.: Minimization of symbolic automata. SIGPLAN Not. **49**(1), 541–553 (2014)
9. García, P., de Parga, M.V., Álvarez, G.I., Ruiz, J.: Learning regular languages using nondeterministic finite automata. In: Ibarra, O.H., Ravikumar, B. (eds.) CIAA 2008. LNCS, vol. 5148, pp. 92–101. Springer, Heidelberg (2008). doi:10.1007/978-3-540-70844-5_10
10. Isberner, M., Howar, F., Steffen, B.: Inferring automata with state-local alphabet abstractions. In: Brat, G., Rungta, N., Venet, A. (eds.) NFM 2013. LNCS, vol. 7871, pp. 124–138. Springer, Heidelberg (2013). doi:10.1007/978-3-642-38088-4_9
11. Isberner, M., Howar, F., Steffen, B.: The TTT algorithm: a redundancy-free approach to active automata learning. In: Bonakdarpour, B., Smolka, S.A. (eds.) RV 2014. LNCS, vol. 8734, pp. 307–322. Springer, Heidelberg (2014). doi:10.1007/978-3-319-11164-3_26
12. Littlestone, N.: Learning quickly when irrelevant attributes abound: a new linear-threshold algorithm. Mach. Learn. **2**(4), 285–318 (1988)

13. Mens, I., Maler, O.: Learning regular languages over large ordered alphabets. Logical Methods Comput. Sci. **11**(3) (2015)
14. Moerman, J., Sammartino, M., Silva, A., Klin, B., Szynwelski, M.: Learning nominal automata. In: Proceedings of the 44th ACM SIGPLAN-SIGACT Symposium on Principles of Programming Languages (POPL) (2017)
15. Yuan, Y., Alur, R., Loo, B.T.: NetEgg: programming network policies by examples. In: Proceedings of the 13th ACM Workshop on Hot Topics in Networks, HotNets-XIII, pp. 20:1–20:7. ACM, New York (2014)

ML for ML: Learning Cost Semantics by Experiment

Ankush Das[(✉)] and Jan Hoffmann

Carnegie Mellon University, Pittsburgh, USA
ankushd@cs.cmu.edu

Abstract. It is an open problem in static resource bound analysis to connect high-level resource bounds with the actual execution time and memory usage of compiled machine code. This paper proposes to use machine learning to derive a cost model for a high-level source language that approximates the execution cost of compiled programs on a specific hardware platform. The proposed technique starts by fixing a cost semantics for the source language in which certain constants are unknown. To learn the constants for a specific hardware, a machine learning algorithm measures the resource cost of a set of training programs and compares the cost with the prediction of the cost semantics. The quality of the learned cost model is evaluated by comparing the model with the measured cost on a set of independent control programs. The technique has been implemented for a subset of OCaml using Inria's OCaml compiler on an Intel x86-64 and ARM 64-bit v8-A platform. The considered resources in the implementation are heap allocations and execution time. The training programs are deliberately simple, handwritten micro benchmarks and the control programs are retrieved from the standard library, an OCaml online tutorial, and local OCaml projects. Different machine learning techniques are applied, including (weighted) linear regression and (weighted) robust regression. To model the execution time of programs with garbage collection (GC), the system combines models for memory allocations and executions without GC, which are derived first. Experiments indicate that the derived cost semantics for the number of heap allocations on both hardware platforms is accurate. The error of the cost semantics on the control programs for the x86-64 architecture for execution time with and without GC is about 19.80% and 13.04%, respectively. The derived cost semantics are combined with RAML, a state-of-the-art system for automatically deriving resource bounds for OCaml programs. Using these semantics, RAML is for the first time able to make predictions about the actual worst-case execution time.

1 Introduction

Motivated by longstanding problems such as performance bugs [32], side-channel attacks [10,31], and to provide development-time feedback to programmers, the programming language community is developing tools that help programmers understand the resource usage of code at compile time. There has been great progress on automatically determining loop bounds in sequential

A. Legay and T. Margaria (Eds.): TACAS 2017, Part I, LNCS 10205, pp. 190–207, 2017.
DOI: 10.1007/978-3-662-54577-5_11

C-like programs [13,15,22,35], deriving, solving recurrence relations [4,6,9,19], and automating amortized analysis [23–25]. There exist several tools that can automatically derive loop and recursion bounds, including SPEED [21,22], KoAT [13], PUBS [5], Rank [7], ABC [11], LOOPUS [35,38], C4B [14], and RAML [23,24].

Most of these resource analysis tools use high-level cost models, like number of loop iterations and function calls, and it is often unclear how the derived bounds relate to the machine code executing on a specific hardware. To make the connection, one has to take into account compilation, hardware specific cache and memory effects, instruction pipelines, and garbage collection cycles. While there exist tools and techniques for analyzing low-level assembly code to produce worst-case execution time bounds for concrete hardware [37], they are limited in their expressive power, as analyzing assembly code is a complicated problem.

In this article, we propose a novel technique to derive cost models that can link high-level resource bounds to the execution of low-level code. We present a simple operational cost semantics for a subset of OCaml [20] that have been learned using standard machine learning techniques like linear regression. The resources we are considering are heap allocations, execution time without garbage collection (GC), and execution time with GC. The subset of OCaml we are considering is purely functional and includes lists, tuples and pattern matching. However, the technique is also applicable to programs with side effects.

To learn a cost semantics, we first define an operational big-step semantics that assign a parametric cost expression to a well-formed expression. This cost expression is parametric in (yet unknown) constants that correspond to high-level constructs in OCaml. The assumption is that the number of executions of each of these constructs constitutes the majority of the execution time of the expression. We keep track of the number of executions of each of these constructs in the cost semantics, which has been implemented in an OCaml interpreter. Our semantics then models the execution time of the program as a linear sum of the number of executions of each construct. The (unknown) coefficients of this linear function intuitively represent the execution time of each construct.

We then determine the average values of the coefficients on a specific hardware by experiment. We carefully select a set of relatively simple training programs and measure the median execution time of these programs on the hardware of interest. To this end, each program is executed with the OCaml native code compiler 500 times on an Intel x86-64 and a ARM 64-bit v8-A platform. We then apply machine learning techniques, such as linear regression [30], on the linear functions obtained by running the cost semantics to determine the constant costs of the constructs by fitting the prediction of the cost semantics to the measured costs. We measure the execution time using the Unix library in OCaml, which is hardware independent. We measure the number of allocation by relying on the OCaml GC library, which is again hardware independent. As a result, our approach is completely hardware independent and can be easily extended to different architectures, as we demonstrate in this work.

Of course, the execution time of, say, an addition cannot be described by a constant. In fact, it can vary by a large margin depending on whether the arguments are stored on the stack or in a register. Similarly, a cons operation can be costly if one of the arguments is not in the cache has to be fetched from memory. So the constants that we learn in our experiment will represent roughly the *average cost* of the operations on the training programs.

Once we have learned these cost coefficients for a specific hardware and resource metric, we validate our cost with control (or test) programs, retrieved from the standard library, an OCaml online tutorial, and local OCaml projects. Each control program is first compiled and executed on the hardware and the median execution cost is measured in the same way we did for training programs. The program is then run on the interpreter to obtain the parametric linear cost function. By plugging in the learned coefficients, we get a prediction for the execution time or memory usage. We compare the predictions of the cost semantics with the median cost, and report the percentage error on test programs. We use the median instead of the mean because it is more resilient against outliers which are often caused by context switches in the OS.

The result of the experiments with the control programs are surprisingly encouraging. We precisely learn the amount of memory that is allocated by each construct. For execution time of programs that do not trigger GC, the error of our model is up to 43%, for all but one program.

In memory intensive programs, the impact of garbage collection cycles on the execution time is significant. So, we adapt our cost semantics to account for the time taken by the GC. We make two simplifying assumptions to model the GC time. One of them is that the time taken by each GC cycle is a constant and the other is that each GC cycle starts with a full heap, and ends with an empty heap. These assumptions, as we will see in the experiments and the OCaml documentation, are quite close to the collections of the *minor heap*. To model this behavior, we combine the cost semantics for memory allocations and the cost semantics for programs without GC. Since the GC cycle occurs periodically when the minor heap is full, we can predict the number of minor GC cycles in the lifetime of a program using the allocation semantics. To determine the time needed for a minor garbage collection, we just measure the median GC time taken by a GC cycle for the training programs.

The main application of our cost semantics is the integration into Resource Aware ML (RAML), a state-of-the-art tool for automatic resource analysis. Using the semantics for execution time on x86, RAML can automatically derive worst-case bounds for many functions that are close to the measured execution time of the compiled code. Our results are precise enough, to statically determine the faster versions of different implementations of list append, Sieve of Eratosthenes, and factorial.

2   Method and Experimental Setup

In this section, we describe our experimental setup and training method. The main hypothesis, going into this experiment, is that the resource consumption of a program, whether time or memory, is a linear combination of the number of executions of each construct in the program. Moreover, the time (or memory) consumed by each construct is averaged out to be a constant. Hence, the execution time of a program is

$$T = \sum_{c \in \mathcal{C}} n_c T_c \qquad (1)$$

where $\mathcal{C}$ represents the set of constructs and n_c is the count of each construct during program execution, and T_c is the execution time of the respective construct. Clearly, these assumptions do not, in general, hold for most of the relevant platforms. Hence, we will analyze the error incurred by these simplifying assumptions on the execution time (or memory allocation) of a program.

Consider the following OCaml program, which computes the factorial.

let rec fact n = **if** (n = 0) **then** 1 **else** n * fact (n−1);;
(fact 10);;

In the above program, if we count the number of high level constructs, we get 10 function calls, 11 equality checks, 10 subtractions and multiplications and 1 "let rec" that defines the function. In our model the execution time of a program is the sum of the execution time of each construct multiplied by the number of times that construct is executed. For the above program, the total execution time is $11 * T_{FunApp} + 11 * T_{IntEq} + 10 * T_{IntSub} + 10 * T_{IntMult} + 1 * T_{letrec}$.

We are interested in the resources costs T_i that best approximate the actual cost. With this representative example, we describe our experimental setup.

Language Description. We have chosen a subset of OCaml as our modeling language. In this subset, we include the following program constructs: recursive functions, conditionals, boolean, integer and float comparisons and arithmetic, pattern matching and tuples. With this fairly general subset, we can write a variety of programs including list manipulation, matrix operations and other numeric programs, as we will demonstrate in our results. We chose OCaml as the source language for several reasons. For one, OCaml is a widely used language for functional programming which is quite efficient in practice. Moreover, we wanted to demonstrate that it is possible to define a practical cost semantics for a high-level functional language with a sophisticated compiler and automatic memory management. We assume that defining such a semantics would be easier for imperative programs, which are closer to assembly code.

A major obstacle when analyzing high-level languages is compiler optimization. The resource usage of the generated target assembly code depends greatly on the choices that are made by the compiler and cannot directly be derived from the original OCaml program. Hence, the cost semantics need to account for compiler optimizations. In our experience, we found two compiler optimizations with a significant impact on the execution time.

- *Tail Call Optimization* [36] - If the final action of a function body is a function call, it is optimized to a jump instruction. This is relevant for the cost semantics because a jump is faster than a call, hence we need two different costs for usual function calls and tail calls. Moreover, separating these costs in the semantics will later help us validate the claim that tail call optimization indeed reduces the execution time.
- *Function Inlining* [16] - OCaml compiler inlines functions as an optimization. Instead of accounting for inlining in our interpreter, we forced the compiler to

not inline any function when generating the native code. We will demonstrate the effect of this optimization when describing training programs. Conceptually, inlining is not a problem for our approach since it is possible to track at compile time which function applications have been inlined.

Training Algorithm. We formally describe the algorithm we use to learn the values of the constructs. Consider again our cost expression $T = \sum_{c \in \mathcal{C}} n_c T_c$. Essentially, we execute the native code obtained from the compiler to obtain the value T, and we execute the program on the interpreter to obtain the values n_c. Let there be P training programs and suppose we generate M instances of training data from each training program using the above method. We denote the count of each construct and execution time of the i-th instance of training data generated by j-th training program by $(n_c^{(i,j)})_{c \in \mathcal{C}}$ and $T_{(i,j)}$ respectively. Since we need to learn a linear model on T_c's, linear regression is the natural choice of machine learning algorithm. A simple linear regression [33] would produce the following objective function.

$$S = \sum_{j=1}^{P} \sum_{i=1}^{M} \left(T_{(i,j)} - \sum_{c \in \mathcal{C}} n_c^{(i,j)} T_c \right)^2.$$

where T_c are the unknowns that need to be learned. However, this approach is useful only when the error is additive, i.e. the error is independent of n_c. Unfortunately, in our case, each instruction has an inherent noise, which depends on the instruction, the operating system and synchronization overhead, measurement error and possibly other factors. So, as the number of instructions executed increases, the error in execution time also increases. Such an error is called *multiplicative*, and a solution by simple linear regression is skewed towards the constructs which have a higher cost, leading to inaccurate results. To overcome this problem, we need to normalize our objective function. We normalize the objective function by the sum of the execution time for each training program over all inputs. Hence, the new objective function is

$$S = \sum_{j=1}^{P} \sum_{i=1}^{M} \left(\frac{T_{(i,j)}}{S_j} - \sum_{c \in \mathcal{C}} \frac{n_c^{(i,j)}}{S_j} T_c \right)^2.$$

where $S_j = \sum_{i=1}^{M} T_{(i,j)}$, i.e. the total execution time of the j-th training program. We learn the cost of each construct using the weighted linear regression technique. In addition to the above method, we also employ two other regression techniques. One is robust regression [34], where the objective function is the L_1-norm, instead of the L_2-norm (written as S_{RR} below).

$$S_{RR} = \sum_{j=1}^{P} \sum_{i=1}^{M} \left| \frac{T_{(i,j)}}{S_j} - \sum_{c \in \mathcal{C}} \frac{n_c^{(i,j)}}{S_j} T_c \right|.$$

And the other is the non-negative least squares method [28], where the sum of squares is minimized under the constraint that all constants need to be non-negative. We evaluate each algorithm, and compare the results obtained for each regression technique in Sect. 7.

Training Programs. The main goal of training is to learn appropriate values T_c for each program construct c in the language described above. Since we have $|\mathcal{C}|$ variables that we need to learn, all we need is at least $|\mathcal{C}|$ training programs to get a feasible cost semantics. However, there is a pitfall here that we want to avoid. Most of the typical machine learning algorithms suffer from the problem of overfitting, i.e. when the model learned is biased towards the training data, and performs poorly on the testing data. Specifically, in our case, the function call construct exists in all the training programs, hence, the learning algorithm overfits the data w.r.t. the cost for function call. Moreover, the regression algorithm is unaware of the fact that these costs need to all be positive. To overcome these issues, we need to linearly separate out the cost of each construct. To this end, we create one training program for each construct. Such a program has a significant count of one construct while being moderate in other constructs. For example, the training program for function call is

let id n = n;;
let rec fapp x = if (x = 0) then 0 else fapp (id (id (id (id (x−1))))));

If we don't account for function inlining, the function id gets inlined, and the above is treated as 1 application instead of 5. This massively impacts our training, and we obtain an incorrect cost for function application. Similarly, the training program for integer addition is

let rec fintadd x = if (x = 0) then 0 else x + x + x + x + fintadd (x−1);;

Once we decided the training programs, we ran each training program with 20 inputs, ranging from 1000 to 20000. In this experiment, we have a total of 36 programs, and with 20 inputs for each program, we have a total of 720 training points for our linear regression algorithm. With this small training set, the regression techniques learn the cost model in less than 1 s. This training set might appear overly simplistic but our results show that this simple setup produces already surprisingly satisfying results.

Hardware Platforms. All of the above experiments have been performed on two separate platforms. One is an Intel NUC5i5RYH which has a 1.6 GHz 5th generation Intel Core i5-5250U processor based on the x86-64 instruction set. Another is a Raspberry Pi 3 which has a 1.2 GHz 64-bit quad-core ARM Cortex-A53 processor based on the ARM v8-A instruction set. We will report the results for both these platforms.

3 Operational Cost Semantics

In the following, we define the big-step operational cost semantics. A value environment V maps variables to values. An evaluation judgment $V \vdash e \Downarrow v \mid t$ denotes that in the environment V, the expression e evaluates to the value v

$$\frac{V \vdash e_1 \Downarrow v_1 \mid t_1 \qquad V \vdash e_2 \Downarrow v_2 \mid t_2 \qquad v_1, v_2 \in \mathbb{B}}{V \vdash e_1 \mathrel{\&\&} e_2 \Downarrow v_1 \mathrel{\&\&} v_2 \mid t_1 + t_2 + T_{BoolAnd}} \text{ (BoolAnd)}$$

$$\frac{V \vdash e_1 \Downarrow v_1 \mid t_1 \qquad V \vdash e_2 \Downarrow v_2 \mid t_2 \qquad v_1, v_2 \in \mathbb{Z}}{V \vdash e_1 + e_2 \Downarrow v_1 + v_2 \mid t_1 + t_2 + T_{IntAdd}} \text{ (IntAdd)}$$

$$\frac{V \vdash e_1 \Downarrow v_1 \mid t_1 \quad \ldots \quad V \vdash e_n \Downarrow v_n \mid t_n}{V \vdash (e_1, \ldots, e_n) \Downarrow (v_1, \ldots, v_n) \mid t_1 + \ldots + t_n + T_{tupleHead} + n T_{tupleElem}} \text{ (Tuple)}$$

$$\frac{V \vdash tup \Downarrow (v_1, \ldots v_n) \mid t_1 \quad V[x_1 \mapsto v_1] \ldots [x_n \mapsto v_n] \vdash e \Downarrow v \mid t_2}{V \vdash \text{let } (x_1, \ldots, x_n) = tup \text{ in } e \Downarrow v \mid t_1 + t_2 + n \, T_{tupleMatch}} \text{ (TupleMatch)}$$

$$\frac{v = (V, \lambda x.e) \quad |FV(e) \setminus \{x\}| = n}{V \vdash \lambda x.e \Downarrow v \mid T_{funDef} + n \, T_{closure}} \text{ (Closure)}$$

$$\frac{\begin{array}{c} V \vdash e_1 \Downarrow (V', \lambda x.e') \mid t_1 \quad V \vdash e_2 \Downarrow v_2 \mid t_2 \\ V'[x \mapsto v_2] \vdash e' \Downarrow v \mid t_3 \quad \text{tag}(e_1) = \text{tail} \end{array}}{V; TM \vdash \text{app}(e_1, e_2) \Downarrow v \mid t_1 + t_2 + t_3 + T_{TailApp}} \text{ (TailApp)}$$

$$\frac{\begin{array}{c} V \vdash e_1 \Downarrow (V', \lambda x.e') \mid t_1 \quad V \vdash e_2 \Downarrow v_2 \mid t_2 \\ V'[x \mapsto v_2] \vdash e' \Downarrow v \mid t_3 \quad \text{tag}(e_1) = \text{normal} \end{array}}{V; TM \vdash \text{app}(e_1, e_2) \Downarrow v \mid t_1 + t_2 + t_3 + T_{FunApp}} \text{ (FunApp)}$$

Fig. 1. Selected rules of the big-step operational cost semantics.

with resource cost t. To differentiate between normal function calls and tail calls, we perform a semantics-preserving program transformation, which adds a tag to all function calls. A tag `tail` is added to tail calls and a tag `normal` is added to all other function calls. Our decision to give a positive cost to the constructs below, while a zero cost to other constructs comes from analyzing the compiled assembly code. Only the constructs below generated assembly instructions with a significant relative execution time. Intuitively, the cost of other constructs can be thought of as absorbed in these constructs. For example, the cost for addition absorbs the cost for loading the two addends.

Figure 1 contains illustrative example rules of the big-step cost semantics. The rules for operations on booleans and integers are very similar to BoolAnd and IntAdd. For tuples, we introduce two constants $T_{tupleHead}$ and $T_{tupleElem}$. $T_{tupleHead}$ is counted every time we create a tuple, and $T_{tupleElem}$ is counted for the length of the tuple. Similarly, for tuple matching, we count a $T_{tupleMatch}$ for every element in the tuple being matched. When creating a tuple, there is an additional instruction, which assigns a tag to the tuple that represents the tuple constructor. Since there is no such instruction during a tuple match, we have an extra $T_{tupleHead}$ for creating tuples, but not when matching on it.

Since we support higher order functions, the rule Closure for function definitions accounts for the cost of creating closures. We again introduce two constants to deal with function definitions, T_{funDef} for creating a function, and $T_{closure}$ for creating a closure and capturing the free variables. Here, $FV(e)$ denotes the set of free variables of e. Since x is already bounded as the function argument, we remove it from the set of free variables of e. Rules TAILAPP and FUNAPP distinguish the cost of tail calls from the cost of regular function calls.

Lastly, we added a constant T_{base} to account for initializations made by each program, irrespective of the program code. Hence, we say that the execution cost of program p is $t + T_{base}$ if $\cdot \vdash p \Downarrow v \mid t$. With these evaluation rules for the cost semantics, we are ready to train our model by learning the values of the constructs described in this section.

4   Learning Memory Allocations

Before analyzing execution times, we will demonstrate the effectiveness of our approach by learning a cost semantics for memory allocations. We realized that our experiments did not lead to accurate results for floating point and tuple operations because they are generally stored on the heap, but often, optimized to be stored on the stack or the registers:

- The OCaml compiler performs constant propagation to determine which floats and tuples can be treated as globals, and need not be allocated on the heap, every time they are defined.
- If tuples only appear as arguments of a function, they are passed via registers and not allocated on the heap.

To accurately learn a cost semantics for floats and tuples we would need feedback from the OCaml compiler about the optimizations that have been performed. That is why, for the memory semantics only, we leave floats and tuples to future work and focus on booleans, integers, and lists. We use the cost semantics that is described in the previous section. According to this semantics, M, the number of bytes allocated by a program is a linear combination $M = \sum_{c \in C} n_c M_c$.

We use the same training programs for learning memory allocations as for execution times. An interesting point is that the count n_c for each construct remains the same whether executing the training programs for time or memory. Hence, while performing the linear regression, we only need to execute the program on the interpreter once to obtain the counts n_c. We then use the Gc module in OCaml to obtain the number M of bytes allocated by the program. Since the memory allocation of a program is constant over different runs, we only need to measure the memory consumption once. For the Intel x86-64 platform, the memory costs of each construct obtained by the linear regression are as follows where $M_x = 0.00$ for all constants M_x that are not listed.

$$M_{base} = 96.03 \quad M_{FunDef} = 24.00 \quad M_{closure} = 7.99 \quad M_{cons} = 24.00$$

An analysis of the OCaml compiler indicates that rounding the learned constants to the nearest integer corresponds exactly to the number of bytes that are allocated by the corresponding construct. For example, our model implies that integers and booleans are not stored on the heap. And the OCaml manual [20] indeed confirms that all integers and booleans are immediate, i.e., stored in registers and on the stack. The value 96 for the constant M_{base} is also confirmed as each program, even without memory allocations, has an initial heap consumption of 96 bytes. The cost $M_{FunDef} = 24$ and $M_{closure} = 8$ for function closures is also confirmed by the OCaml manual. If there are free variables trapped in the closure of a function, there is an additional memory allocation of 24 bytes on the heap to indicate that the program has a non-empty closure. Every cons constructor consumes 24 bytes on the heap; 8 bytes each for the head and tail, and 8 bytes for the tag to indicate the cons constructor. The empty list ([]) is represented as an immediate integer 0. Hence, the memory consumption of a list of size n is $24n$ bytes. Similarly, for the ARM v8-A platform, the memory costs of the non-zero constants obtained by the same linear regression are as follows. The results are also as expected and the data size seems to be 4 words.

$$M_{base} = 64.05 \quad M_{FunDef} = 12.00 \quad M_{closure} = 3.99 \quad M_{cons} = 12.00$$

We prefer learning the memory semantics instead of using them directly from the OCaml manual, because our technique is hardware-independent and can be extended in the event of creation of new architectures. It is notable that we can learn OCaml's heap model by performing a simple regression without the constraint that the learned coefficients need to be integral or non-negative.

5   Learning Execution Times

As mentioned earlier, we used several regression techniques to train our cost semantics: linear regression, robust regression, and non-negative least squares. The accuracy of all three approaches is similar. Also, we train on the median execution times since they are less prone to noise than the mean. Below we give the cost of each high-level construct (in nanoseconds) trained using the normalized linear regression technique for the Intel x86-64 architecture. Intuitively, these constants define the median execution time of the respective construct on this specific platform.

$T_{base} = 832.691$	$T_{FunApp} = 1.505$	$T_{TailApp} = 0.156$
$T_{FunDef} = 0.000$	$T_{closure} = 2.921$	$T_{BoolNot} = 0.424$
$T_{BoolAnd} = 0.184$	$T_{BoolOr} = 0.183$	$T_{IntUMinus} = 0.419$
$T_{IntAdd} = 0.297$	$T_{IntSub} = 0.278$	$T_{IntMult} = 1.299$
$T_{IntMod} = 19.231$	$T_{IntDiv} = 19.011$	$T_{FloatUMinus} = 1.232$
$T_{FloatAdd} = 2.102$	$T_{FloatSub} = 2.116$	$T_{FloatMult} = 1.737$
$T_{FloatDiv} = 8.575$	$T_{IntCondEq} = 0.382$	$T_{IntCondLT} = 0.381$
$T_{IntCondLE} = 0.381$	$T_{IntCondGT} = 0.375$	$T_{IntCondGE} = 0.381$
$T_{FloatCondEq} = 0.582$	$T_{FloatCondLT} = 0.619$	$T_{FloatCondLE} = 0.625$
$T_{FloatCondGT} = 0.585$	$T_{FloatCondGE} = 0.629$	$T_{letdata} = 2.828$
$T_{letlambda} = 1.312$	$T_{letrec} = 1.312$	$T_{patternMatch} = 0.223$
$T_{tupleHead} = 5.892$	$T_{tupleElem} = 1.717$	$T_{tupleMatch} = 0.237$

We make several qualitative observations about the learned cost semantics.

- $T_{FunApp} > T_{TailApp}$ indicates that a tail call is cheaper than a normal function call, confirming that tail call optimization reduces the execution time.
- $T_{BoolOr} \approx T_{BoolAnd}$, which is again expected as the && and || operators just place jump instructions at appropriate locations in the assembly.
- $T_{IntMod} \approx T_{IntDiv} \gg T_{IntMult} > T_{IntAdd} \approx T_{IntSub}$. This is again expected, since whenever we perform integer division or modulo, a check is performed to see if the denominator is 0 and raise an appropriate exception. Hence, division and modulo are much more expensive than multiplication. The latter is more expensive than addition and subtraction.
- $T_{IntCondEq} \approx T_{IntCondLE} \approx T_{IntCondLT} \approx T_{IntCondGT} \approx T_{IntCondGE}$ is confirmed by studying the generated assembly code. A comparison is compiled to comparing the two integers and storing the result in a register, followed by a conditional jump. The analogous observation holds for floating point comparisons.

6 Garbage Collection

The OCaml garbage collector (GC) has 2 major components, the variable size major heap and the fixed size minor heap. Allocations occur first on the minor heap. If the minor heap is full, the GC is invoked. Roughly, the GC frees unreachable cells, and promotes all live variables on the minor heap to the major heap, essentially emptying the minor heap. OCaml employs a generational hypothesis, which states that young memory cells tend to die young, and old cells tend to stay around for longer than young ones.

We roughly model this behavior of the GC. Our hypothesis is that every call to the GC roughly starts with the full minor heap and empties the minor heap. We currently do not model the major heap. Hence, the time taken for each call to the GC in our model is roughly the same. We need two parameters to model the time taken by the GC, one is n_{gc}, which is the number of calls to the GC, and the other is T_{gc}, which is the time taken by 1 call to the GC. Our hypothesis states that $n_{gc} = \left\lfloor \frac{M}{H_0} \right\rfloor$, where H_0 is the size of the minor heap, and M is the total number of memory allocations. Since we can already model the number of heap allocations, all we need is the size of the minor heap.

Consequently, the two parameters T_{gc} and H_0 can be learnt from our training programs. OCaml offers a Gc module, which provides the number of calls to the GC. We use this module to find out the first call to the GC, the number of memory allocations and the time taken by the GC call, thereby learning H_0, which is equal to the number of memory allocations (due to our hypothesis), and T_{gc}. With these parameters learned, the total execution time of the program is

$$T = \sum_{c \in \mathcal{C}} n_c T_c + \left\lfloor \frac{\sum_{c \in \mathcal{C}} n_c M_c}{H_0} \right\rfloor \cdot T_{gc}$$

7 Experiments with Control Programs

For our testing experiment, we used programs from the standard *List* library [2] and an OCaml tutorial [1].

Testing Method. For each test program, we first fix inputs of different sizes. For input i, we execute the compiled test program 500 times, measure the execution time, and compute the median T_i^{actual}. We then execute the test program on our interpreter to obtain the count of each construct n_c for $c \in C$, and calculate $T_i^{expected} = \sum_{c \in C} n_c T_c$. The average percentage error for each test program is

$$\text{Error}(\%) = \frac{1}{n} \left(\sum_{i=1}^{n} \frac{|T_i^{actual} - T_i^{expected}|}{T_i^{actual}} \right) \times 100$$

Experiments. Figure 2 shows the results on a compilation of control programs. The horizontal(x) axis represents the input size, while the vertical(y) axis represents the execution times. `factorialTR` is a tail recursive implementation of factorial. `append` concatenates two lists. `map` is a higher-order function, which maps a list of integers to booleans. Positive integers are mapped to `true` and the rest to `false`. `bubblesort` sorts a list using the bubblesort algorithm.

The measurement noise is significant, particularly in cases where high overhead is caused by context switches in the OS. Nevertheless, our prediction is surprisingly accurate given the simplicity of our model, particularly for functions without allocations, like `factorialTR`. For `append` our prediction is very accurate till the point of the first GC cycle ($x \approx 2.9$). The execution time after the first GC cycle is very unpredictable with frequent unexpected jumps (e.g. $x \approx 7$) and drops (e.g. $x \approx 14$). For `bubblesort` the GC jumps become invisible since the runtime of the GC is dominated by the actual computation. We can always very accurately predict the input size at which the GC cycles are triggered. This validates the accuracy of our model for learning memory allocations.

Table 1 summarizes the results obtained by evaluating our approach on 43 control programs. We implemented 3 different training algorithms for training in programs without GC, linear regression (LR), robust regression (RR) and nonnegative least squares (NNLS). Each column represents the average percentage error for both architectures. We also tested all memory-intensive programs with larger inputs to evaluate our cost model for the GC. The last column presents the percentage error for programs with GC cycles, trained using linear regression. Note that the error increase of programs with GC cycles is not significant, and it indeed decreases for ARM architecture, indicating that our model for GC cycles is also accurate. However, in about 5% of the programs, the error is quite high (error above 50%). This is usually caused by an unmodeled compiler optimization, causing a significant reduction in execution time.

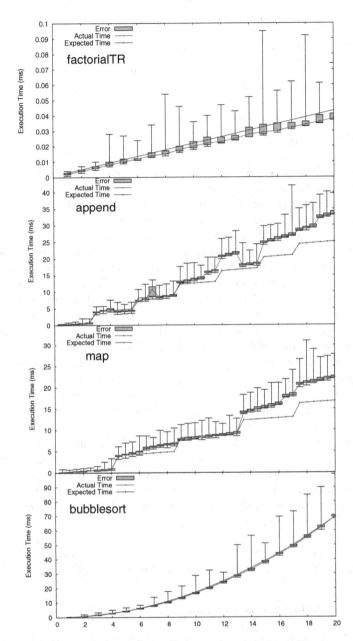

Fig. 2. Graph showing actual and expected time for factorialTR (input sizes $\times 10^3$) (top), append (input $\times 10^4$) (2nd), map (input $\times 10^4$) (3rd), and bubblesort (input $\times 10^2$) (bottom). The red and blue lines denote the actual and expected times, respectively. The vertical bars show the inherent noise in execution time. The lower and upper end of the vertical line denote the minimum and maximum execution time, while the lower and upper end of the box denotes the 1st and 3rd quartile of the execution time. (Color figure online)

Table 1. Results on x86-64 and ARM architectures

Architecture	Err (LR)	Err (RR)	Err (NNLS)	Err (GC)
x86-64	13.29	13.04	13.32	19.80
ARM v8-A	21.81	22.94	21.36	20.12

8 Applications

Integration with Resource Aware ML. We have integrated our learned cost semantics into Resource Aware ML [24], a static resource analysis tool for OCaml. RAML is based on an automatic amortized resource analysis (AARA) [23–25] that is parametric in a user defined cost metric. Such a metric can be defined by providing a constant cost (in floating point) for each syntactic form. This parametricity in a resource metric, and the ability to provide a cost to each syntactic form makes RAML very suitable for our integration purposes. Given an OCaml function, a resource metric, and a maximal degree of the search space of bounds, RAML statically derives a *multivariate resource polynomial* that is an upper bound on the resource usage as defined by the metric. The resource polynomial is parametric in the input sizes of the functions and contains concrete constant factors. The analysis is fully automatic and reduces bound inference to off-the-shelf LP solving. The subset of OCaml that is currently supported by RAML contains all language constructs that we consider in this paper. We used the experiments performed for this work to further refine the cost semantics and automatic analysis. For example, we added an analysis phase prior to the analysis that marks tail calls.

With the new cost metrics, we can use RAML for the first time to make predictions about the worst-case behavior of compiled code. For example, if we use the new execution-time metric (without GC) for x86 then we derive the following bounds in Table 2. The variables in the bounds are the input sizes. The table also contains runtime of the analysis and the number of generated constraint (cumulative for both bounds).

We can also use RAML to predict the execution time of programs with GC. To this end, we just derive two bounds using the execution metric and the metric for the number of allocations, respectively. We then combine the two bounds

Table 2. Symbolic bounds from RAML on x86-64

Program	Time bound (ns)	Heap bound (B)	Time (s)	#Cons
append	$0.45 + 11.28M$	$24M$	0.02	50
map	$0.60 + 13.16M$	$24M$	0.02	59
insertion sort	$0.45 + 6.06M + 5.83M^2$	$12M + 12M^2$	0.04	298
echelon	$0.60 + 17.29LM^2 + 23.11M + 37.38M^2$	$24LM^2 + 24M + 72M^2$	0.59	16297

using our model for GC which basically, accounts for a constant cost after a constant number of allocations. For example for **append** we obtain the following bound (heap size = 2097448 bytes, GC cycle = 3125429.15 ns on x86).

$$0.45 + 11.28M + \left\lfloor \frac{3125429.15 \times 24M}{2097448} \right\rfloor$$

Since the derived bounds for execution time and allocations are tight, this bound precisely corresponds to the prediction of our model as plotted in Fig. 2.

Qualitative Analysis. In addition to quantitative validation, we can also infer qualitative results from our learned cost semantics. For instance, we can compare two semantically-equivalent programs, and determine which one is more efficient on a specific hardware. Our model, predicts for example correctly the fastest version of different implementations of *factorial, append,* and *sieve of Eratosthenes.* Consider for example our Intel x86 machine and the following versions of **append**.

```
let rec append1 l1 l2 =
  match l1 with
  | [] -> l2
  | hd::tl -> hd::(append1 tl l2);;
```

```
let rec append2 l1 l2 = match l1 with
  | [] -> l2
  | x::[] -> x::l2
  | x::y::[] -> x::y::l2
  | x::y::tl -> x::y::(append2 tl l2);;
```

The trade-off in the above implementations is that the first has twice the number of function calls but half the number of pattern matches, as the second one. Since $T_{FunApp} = 1.505 > 4 \times 0.223 = 2 \times T_{patternMatch}$, hence, using our cost semantics concludes that the second version is more efficient. To reach this conclusion we can now analyze the two programs in RAML and automatically derive the execution-time bounds $0.45 + 11.28M$ and $0.45 + 10.53M$ for append1 and append2, respectively. The fact that append2 is faster carries over to the execution-time bounds with GC since the memory allocation bound for both functions is $24M$ bytes.

9   Related Work

The problem of modeling and execution time of programs has been extensively studied for several decades. Static bound analysis on the source level [4,6,9,13, 15,19,22,25,35] does not take into account compilation and concrete hardware.

Closer related are analyses that target real-time systems by modeling and analyzing worst case execution times (WCET) of programs. Wilhelm et al. [37] provides an overview of these techniques, which can be classified into static [18], measurement-based methods, and simulation [8]. Lim et al. [29] associate a worst case timing abstraction containing detailed information of every execution path to get tighter WCET bounds. Colin and Puaut [17] study the effect of branch prediction on WCET. The goals of our work are different since we are not aiming at a sound bound of the worst-case but rather an approximation of the average case. Advantages of our approach include hardware independence, modeling of GC, and little manual effort after the cost semantics is defined.

Lambert and Power [27] introduced a hardware independent method of estimating time cost of Java bytecode instructions. Unlike our work, they do not take into account GC and compilation. Huang et al. [26] build accurate prediction models of program performance using program execution on sample inputs using sparse polynomial regression. The difference to our work is that they build a model for one specific program, are not interested in low-level features, and mainly want to predict the (high-level) execution time for a given input.

Acar et al. [3] learn cost models for execution time to determine whether tasks need to run sequentially or in parallel. They observe executions to learn the cost of one specific program. In contrast, we build a cost semantics to make predictions for all programs. There exist many works that build on high-level cost semantics [23], for instance to model cache and I/O effects [12]. However, these semantics do not incorporate concrete constants for specific hardware.

10   Conclusion and Future Work

We have presented an operational cost semantics learned using standard machine learning techniques, like linear regression, robust regression, etc. These semantics were able to model the execution time of programs with surprising accuracy; even in the presence of compilation and garbage collection. Since all the three models can be learned without relying on hardware specifics, our method is completely hardware independent and easily extensible to other hardware platforms. We have also presented an integration of the cost semantics with RAML, hence, allowing static analyzers to predict the execution time and heap allocations of assembly code for the first time.

One of the significant future directions is a more precise model for the garbage collector. Our model is limited to the minor heap, we need a model for the major heap and heap compactions as well. The size of the major heap is variable, hence, modeling the major heap is an important and complicated problem. We also need to incorporate other language features, especially user-defined data types in our semantics. Another challenge with real-world languages is compiler optimizations. We modeled one optimization (and suppressed another) in these semantics, but we should extend our semantics to incorporate more. Since these optimizations are performed at compile time, using static analysis techniques, it should be possible to model all of them. Finally, we think that it is possible to extend this technique to other programming languages, and we only need an appropriate interpreter to achieve that. We would like to validate this claim. We believe this connection between high-level program constructs and low-level program resources like time and memory is a first step towards connecting theoretical features of a language and its practical applications.

Acknowledgments. This article is based on research that has been supported, in part, by AFRL under DARPA STAC award FA8750-15-C-0082, by NSF under grant 1319671 (VeriQ), and by a Google Research Award. Any opinions, findings, and conclusions contained in this document are those of the authors and do not necessarily reflect the views of the sponsoring organizations.

References

1. 99 problems (solved) in OCaml. https://ocaml.org/learn/tutorials/99problems. html. Accessed 16 Aug 2016
2. Module list. http://caml.inria.fr/pub/docs/manual-ocaml/libref/List.html. Accessed 16 Aug 2016
3. Acar, U.A., Charguéraud, A., Rainey, M.: Oracle scheduling: controlling granularity in implicitly parallel languages. In: Proceedings of the 2011 ACM International Conference on Object Oriented Programming Systems Languages and Applications, OOPSLA 2011, pp. 499–518. ACM, New York (2011)
4. Albert, E., Arenas, P., Genaim, S., Gómez-Zamalloa, M., Puebla, G.: Automatic inference of resource consumption bounds. In: Bjørner, N., Voronkov, A. (eds.) LPAR 2012. LNCS, vol. 7180, pp. 1–11. Springer, Heidelberg (2012). doi:10.1007/978-3-642-28717-6_1
5. Albert, E., Arenas, P., Genaim, S., Puebla, G., Zanardini, D.: Cost analysis of Java bytecode. In: Nicola, R. (ed.) ESOP 2007. LNCS, vol. 4421, pp. 157–172. Springer, Heidelberg (2007). doi:10.1007/978-3-540-71316-6_12
6. Albert, E., Fernández, J.C., Román-Díez, G.: Non-cumulative resource analysis. In: Baier, C., Tinelli, C. (eds.) TACAS 2015. LNCS, vol. 9035, pp. 85–100. Springer, Heidelberg (2015). doi:10.1007/978-3-662-46681-0_6
7. Alias, C., Darte, A., Feautrier, P., Gonnord, L.: Multi-dimensional rankings, program termination, and complexity bounds of flowchart programs. In: Cousot, R., Martel, M. (eds.) SAS 2010. LNCS, vol. 6337, pp. 117–133. Springer, Heidelberg (2010). doi:10.1007/978-3-642-15769-1_8
8. Austin, T., Larson, E., Ernst, D.: Simplescalar: an infrastructure for computer system modeling. Computer 35(2), 59–67 (2002)
9. Avanzini, M., Lago, U.D., Moser, G.: Analysing the complexity of functional programs: higher-order meets first-order. In: 29th International Conference on Functional Programming (ICFP 2015) (2012)
10. Backes, M., Doychev, G., Köpf, B.: Preventing side-channel leaks in web traffic: a formal approach. In: Proceedings of 20th Network and Distributed Systems Security Symposium (NDSS) (2013)
11. Blanc, R., Henzinger, T.A., Hottelier, T., Kovács, L.: ABC: algebraic bound computation for loops. In: Clarke, E.M., Voronkov, A. (eds.) LPAR 2010. LNCS (LNAI), vol. 6355, pp. 103–118. Springer, Heidelberg (2010). doi:10.1007/978-3-642-17511-4_7
12. Blelloch, G.E., Harper, R.: Cache and I/O efficent functional algorithms. In: Proceedings of the 40th Annual ACM SIGPLAN-SIGACT Symposium on Principles of Programming Languages, POPL 2013, pp. 39–50. ACM, New York (2013)
13. Brockschmidt, M., Emmes, F., Falke, S., Fuhs, C., Giesl, J.: Alternating runtime and size complexity analysis of integer programs. In: Ábrahám, E., Havelund, K. (eds.) TACAS 2014. LNCS, vol. 8413, pp. 140–155. Springer, Heidelberg (2014). doi:10.1007/978-3-642-54862-8_10
14. Carbonneaux, Q., Hoffmann, J., Shao, Z.: Compositional certified resource bounds. In: 36th Conference on Programming Language Design and Implementation (PLDI 2015) (2015)
15. Černý, P., Henzinger, T.A., Kovács, L., Radhakrishna, A., Zwirchmayr, J.: Segment abstraction for worst-case execution time analysis. In: Vitek, J. (ed.) ESOP 2015. LNCS, vol. 9032, pp. 105–131. Springer, Heidelberg (2015). doi:10.1007/978-3-662-46669-8_5

16. Chen, W.Y., Chang, P.P., Conte, T.M., Hwu, W.W.: The effect of code expanding optimizations on instruction cache design. IEEE Trans. Comput. **42**(9), 1045–1057 (1993)
17. Colin, A., Puaut, I.: Worst case execution time analysis for a processor with branch prediction. Real-Time Syst. **18**(2), 249–274 (2000)
18. Cousot, P., Cousot, R.: Abstract interpretation: a unified lattice model for static analysis of programs by construction or approximation of fixpoints. In: Proceedings of the 4th ACM SIGACT-SIGPLAN Symposium on Principles of Programming Languages, POPL 1977, pp. 238–252. ACM, New York (1977)
19. Danner, N., Licata, D.R., Ramyaa, R.: Denotational cost semantics for functional languages with inductive types. In: 29th International Conference on Functional Programming (ICFP 2015) (2012)
20. Doligez, D., Frisch, A., Garrigue, J., Rémy, D., Vouillon, J.: The OCaml system release 4.03. http://caml.inria.fr/pub/docs/manual-ocaml/
21. Gulwani, S., Mehra, K.K., Chilimbi, T.M.: SPEED: precise and efficient static estimation of program computational complexity. In: 36th ACM Symposium on Principles of Programming Languages (POPL 2009), pp. 127–139 (2009)
22. Gulwani, S., Zuleger, F.: The reachability-bound problem. In: Conference on Programming Language Design and Implementation (PLDI 2010), pp. 292–304 (2010)
23. Hoffmann, J., Aehlig, K., Hofmann, M.: Multivariate amortized resource analysis. In: 38th Symposium on Principles of Programming Languages (POPL 2011) (2011)
24. Hoffmann, J., Das, A., Weng, S.: Towards automatic resource bound analysis for OCaml. In: Proceedings of the 44th ACM SIGPLAN Symposium on Principles of Programming Languages, POPL 2017, Paris, France, 18–20 January 2017, pp. 359–373 (2017)
25. Hofmann, M., Jost, S.: Static prediction of heap space usage for first-order functional programs. In: 30th ACM Symposium on Principles of Programming Languages (POPL 2003), pp. 185–197 (2003)
26. Huang, L., Jia, J., Yu, B., Chun, B.G., Maniatis, P., Naik, M.: Predicting execution time of computer programs using sparse polynomial regression. In: Lafferty, J.D., Williams, C.K.I., Shawe-Taylor, J., Zemel, R.S., Culotta, A. (eds.) Advances in Neural Information Processing Systems 23, pp. 883–891. Curran Associates, Inc., Red Hook (2010)
27. Lambert, J.M., Power, J.F.: Platform independent timing of Java virtual machine bytecode instructions. Electron. Notes Theor. Comput. Sci. **220**, 97–113 (2008)
28. Lawson, C., Hanson, R.: Solving Least Squares Problems. Classics in Applied Mathematics. Society for Industrial and Applied Mathematics, Philadelphia (1995)
29. Lim, S.S., Bae, Y.H., Jang, G.T., Rhee, B.D., Min, S.L., Park, C.Y., Shin, H., Park, K., Moon, S.M., Kim, C.S.: An accurate worst case timing analysis for RISC processors. IEEE Trans. Softw. Eng. **21**(7), 593–604 (1995)
30. Neter, J., Kutner, M.H., Nachtsheim, C.J., Wasserman, W.: Applied Linear Statistical Models, vol. 4. Irwin, Chicago (1996)
31. Ngo, V.C., Dehesa-Azuara, M., Fredrikson, M., Hoffmann, J.: Quantifying and Preventing Side Channels with Substructural Type Systems (2016). Working paper
32. Olivo, O., Dillig, I., Lin, C.: Static detection of asymptotic performance bugs in collection traversals. In: Conference on Programming Language Design and Implementation (PLDI 2015), pp. 369–378 (2015)
33. Rencher, A.C., Christensen, W.F.: Multivariate regression, pp. 339–383. Wiley (2012). http://dx.doi.org/10.1002/9781118391686.ch10
34. Rousseeuw, P.J., Leroy, A.M.: Robust Regression and Outlier Detection. Wiley, New York (1987)

35. Sinn, M., Zuleger, F., Veith, H.: A simple and scalable static analysis for bound analysis and amortized complexity analysis. In: Biere, A., Bloem, R. (eds.) CAV 2014. LNCS, vol. 8559, pp. 745–761. Springer, Heidelberg (2014). doi:10.1007/ 978-3-319-08867-9_50

36. Steele Jr., G.L.: Debunking the 'expensive procedure call' myth or, procedure call implementations considered harmful or, LAMBDA: the ultimate GOTO. In: Proceedings of the 1977 Annual Conference, ACM 1977, pp. 153–162. ACM, New York (1977)

37. Wilhelm, R., et al.: The worst-case execution-time problem – overview of methods and survey of tools. ACM Trans. Embed. Comput. Syst. **7**(3), 36:1–36:53 (2008)

38. Zuleger, F., Gulwani, S., Sinn, M., Veith, H.: Bound analysis of imperative programs with the size-change abstraction. In: Yahav, E. (ed.) SAS 2011. LNCS, vol. 6887, pp. 280–297. Springer, Heidelberg (2011). doi:10.1007/978-3-642-23702-7_22

A Novel Learning Algorithm for Büchi Automata Based on Family of DFAs and Classification Trees

Yong Li[1,2], Yu-Fang Chen[3], Lijun Zhang[1,2(✉)], and Depeng Liu[1,2]

[1] State Key Laboratory of Computer Science,
Institute of Software, CAS, Beijing, China
zhanglj@ios.ac.cn
[2] University of Chinese Academy of Sciences, Beijing, China
[3] Institute of Information Science, Academia Sinica, Taipei, Taiwan

Abstract. In this paper, we propose a novel algorithm to learn a Büchi automaton from a teacher who knows an ω-regular language. The algorithm is based on learning a formalism named *family of DFAs* (FDFAs) recently proposed by Angluin and Fisman [10]. The main catch is that we use a *classification tree* structure instead of the standard *observation table* structure. The worst case storage space required by our algorithm is quadratically better than the table-based algorithm proposed in [10]. We implement the first publicly available library ROLL (Regular Omega Language Learning), which consists of all ω-regular learning algorithms available in the literature and the new algorithms proposed in this paper. Experimental results show that our tree-based algorithms have the best performance among others regarding the number of solved learning tasks.

1 Introduction

Since the last decade, learning-based automata inference techniques [7,11,30,36] have received significant attention from the community of formal system analysis. In general, the primary applications of automata learning in the community can be categorized into two: *improving efficiency and scalability of verification* [6,15,17,19,21,23,25,33] and *synthesizing abstract system model for further analysis* [1,5,16,18,22,24,26,35,37,40].

The former usually is based on the so called *assume-guarantee* compositional verification approach, which divides a verification task into several subtasks via a composition rule. Learning algorithms are applied to construct environmental assumptions of components in the rule automatically. For the latter, automata learning has been used to automatically generate interface model of computer programs [5,22,26,37,41], a model of system error traces for diagnosis purpose [16], behavior model of programs for statistical program analysis [18], and model-based testing and verification [24,35,40].

Besides the classical finite automata learning algorithms, people also apply and develop learning algorithm for richer models for the above two applications. For example, learning algorithms for register automata [27,28] have been developed and applied to synthesis system and program interface models. Learning

© Springer-Verlag GmbH Germany 2017
A. Legay and T. Margaria (Eds.): TACAS 2017, Part I, LNCS 10205, pp. 208–226, 2017.
DOI: 10.1007/978-3-662-54577-5_12

algorithm for timed automata has been developed for automated compositional verification for timed systems [33]. However, all the results mentioned above are for checking *safety properties* or synthesizing *finite behavior models* of systems/programs. Büchi automaton is the standard model for describing liveness properties of distributed systems [4]. The model has been applied in automata theoretical model checking [39] to describe the property to be verified. It is also often used in the synthesis of reactive systems. Moreover, Büchi automata have been used as a means to prove program termination [31]. However, unlike the case for finite automata learning, learning algorithms for Büchi automata are very rarely used in our community. We believe this is a potentially fertile area for further investigation.

The first learning algorithm for the full-class of ω-regular languages represented as Büchi automata was described in [20], based on the L^* algorithm [7] and the result of [14]. Recently, Angluin and Fisman propose a new learning algorithm for ω-regular languages [10] using a formalism called a *family of DFAs* (FDFAs), based on the results of [34]. The main problem of applying their algorithm in verification and synthesis is that their algorithm requires a teacher for FDFAs. In this paper, we show that their algorithm can be adapted to support Büchi automata teachers.

We propose a novel ω-regular learning algorithm based on FDFAs and a *classification tree* structure (inspired by the tree-based L^* algorithm in [30]). The worst case storage space required by our algorithm is quadratically better than the table-based algorithm proposed in [10]. Experimental results show that our tree-based algorithms have the best performance among others regarding the number of solved learning tasks.

For regular language learning, there are robust and publicly available libraries, e.g., libalf [12] and LearnLib [29]. A similar library is still lacking for Büchi automata learning. We implement the first publicly available Büchi automata learning library, named ROLL (Regular Omega Language Learning, http://iscasmc.ios.ac.cn/roll), which includes all Büchi automata learning algorithms of the full class of ω-regular languages available in the literature and the ones proposed in this paper. We compare the performance of those algorithms using a benchmark consisting of 295 Büchi automata corresponding to all 295 LTL specifications available in BüchiStore [38].

To summarize, our contribution includes the following. (1) Adapting the algorithm of [10] to support Büchi automata teachers. (2) A novel learning algorithm for ω-regular language based on FDFAs and classification trees. (3) The publicly available library ROLL that includes all Büchi automata learning algorithms can be found in the literature. (4) A comprehensive empirical evaluation of Büchi automata learning algorithms.

2 Preliminaries

Let A and B be two sets. We use $A \oplus B$ to denote their *symmetric difference*, i.e., the set $(A \setminus B) \cup (B \setminus A)$. Let Σ be a finite set called *alphabet*. We use ϵ

to represent an empty word. The set of all finite words is denoted by Σ^*, and the set of all infinite words, called ω-words, is denoted by Σ^ω. Moreover, we also denote by Σ^+ the set $\Sigma^* \setminus \{\epsilon\}$. We use $|u|$ to denote the length of the finite word u. We use $[i \cdots j]$ to denote the set $\{i, i+1, \cdots, j\}$. We denote by $w[i]$ the i-th letter of a word w. We use $w[i..k]$ to denote the subword of w starting at the i-th letter and ending at the k-th letter, inclusive, when $i \leq k$ and the empty word ϵ when $i > k$. A *language* is a subset of Σ^* and an ω-*language* is a subset of Σ^ω. Words of the form uv^ω are called *ultimately periodic* words. We use a pair of finite words (u, v) to denote the ultimately periodic word $w = uv^\omega$. We also call (u, v) a *decomposition* of w. For an ω-language L, let $\mathrm{UP}(L) = \{uv^\omega \mid u \in \Sigma^*, v \in \Sigma^+, uv^\omega \in L\}$, i.e., all ultimately periodic words in L.

A *finite automaton* (FA) is a tuple $A = (\Sigma, Q, q_0, F, \delta)$ consisting of a finite alphabet Σ, a finite set Q of states, an initial state q_0, a set $F \subseteq Q$ of accepting states, and a transition relation $\delta \subseteq Q \times \Sigma \times Q$. For convenience, we also use $\delta(q, a)$ to denote the set $\{q' \mid (q, a, q') \in \delta\}$. A *run* of an FA on a finite word $v = a_1 a_2 a_3 \cdots a_n$ is a sequence of states $q_0, q_1, \cdots, q_n$ such that $(q_i, a_{i+1}, q_{i+1}) \in \delta$. The run v is *accepting* if $q_n \in F$. A word u is accepting if it has an accepting run. The language of A, denoted by $L(A)$, is the set $\{u \in \Sigma^* \mid u \text{ is accepted by } A\}$. Given two FAs A and B, one can construct a product FA $A \times B$ recognizing $L(A) \cap L(B)$ using a standard product construction.

A *deterministic finite automaton* (DFA) is an FA such that $\delta(q, a)$ is a singleton for any $q \in Q$ and $a \in \Sigma$. For DFA, we write $\delta(q, a) = q'$ instead of $\delta(q, a) = \{q'\}$. The transition can be lifted to words by defining $\delta(q, \epsilon) = q$ and $\delta(q, av) = \delta(\delta(q, a), v)$ for $q \in Q, a \in \Sigma$ and $v \in \Sigma^*$. We also use $A(v)$ as a shorthand for $\delta(q_0, v)$.

A *Büchi automaton* (BA) has the same structure as an FA, except that it accepts only infinite words. A run of an infinite word in a BA is an infinite sequence of states defined similarly to the case of a finite word in an FA. An infinite word w is accepted by a BA iff it has a run visiting at least one accepting state infinitely often. The language defined by a BA A, denoted by $L(A)$, is the set $\{w \in \Sigma^\omega \mid w \text{ is accepted by } A\}$. An ω-language $L \subseteq \Sigma^\omega$ is ω-regular iff there exists a BA A such that $L = L(A)$.

Theorem 1 (Ultimately Periodic Words of ω-Regular Languages [13]). *Let L, L' be two ω-regular languages. Then $L = L'$ if and only if $\mathrm{UP}(L) = \mathrm{UP}(L')$.*

Definition 1 (Family of DFAs (FDFA) [10]). *A family of DFAs $\mathcal{F} = (M, \{A^q\})$ over an alphabet Σ consists of a leading automaton $M = (\Sigma, Q, q_0, \delta)$ and progress DFAs $A^q = (\Sigma, Q_q, s_q, \delta_q, F_q)$ for each $q \in Q$.*

Notice that the leading automaton M is a DFA without accepting states. Each FDFA $\mathcal{F}$ characterizes a set of ultimately periodic words $\mathrm{UP}(\mathcal{F})$. Formally, an ultimately periodic word w is in $\mathrm{UP}(\mathcal{F})$ iff it has a decomposition (u, v) accepted by $\mathcal{F}$. A decomposition (u, v) is accepted by $\mathcal{F}$ iff $M(uv) = M(u)$ and $v \in L(A^{M(u)})$. An example of an FDFA $\mathcal{F}$ is depicted in Fig. 1. The leading automaton M has only one state ϵ. The progress automaton of ϵ is A^ϵ. The word $(ba)^\omega$ is in $UP(\mathcal{F})$ because it has a decomposition (ba, ba) such that $M(ba \cdot ba) = M(ba)$ and $ba \in L(A^{M(ba)}) = L(A^\epsilon)$. It is easy to see that the decomposition (bab, ab) is not accepted by $\mathcal{F}$ since $ab \notin L(A^{M(bab)}) = L(A^\epsilon)$.

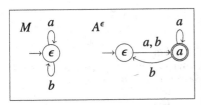

Fig. 1. An example of an FDFA

For any ω-regular language L, there exists an FDFA $\mathcal{F}$ such that $UP(L) = UP(\mathcal{F})$ [10]. We show in Sect. 6 that it is not the case for the reverse direction. More precisely, in [10], three kinds of FDFAs are suggested as the canonical representations of ω-regular languages, namely *periodic* FDFA, *syntactic* FDFA and *recurrent* FDFA. Their formal definitions are given in terms of *right congruence*.

An equivalence relation $\backsim$ on Σ^* is a right congruence if $x \backsim y$ implies $xv \backsim yv$ for every $x, y, v \in \Sigma^*$. The index of $\backsim$, denoted by $|\backsim|$, is the number of equivalence classes of $\backsim$. We use $\Sigma^*/_\backsim$ to denote the equivalence classes of the right congruence $\backsim$. A *finite right congruence* is a right congruence with a finite index. For a word $v \in \Sigma^*$, we use the notation $[v]_\backsim$ to represent the class of $\backsim$ in which v resides and ignore the subscript $\backsim$ when the context is clear. The right congruence $\backsim_L$ of a given ω-regular language L is defined such that $x \backsim_L y$ iff $\forall w \in \Sigma^\omega.xw \in L \Longleftrightarrow yw \in L$. The index of $\backsim_L$ is finite because it is not larger than the number of states in a deterministic Muller automaton recognizing L [34].

Definition 2 (Canonical FDFA [10]). *Given an ω-regular language L, a periodic (respectively, syntactic and recurrent) FDFA $\mathcal{F} = (M, \{A^q\})$ of L is defined as follows. The leading automaton M is the tuple $(\Sigma, \Sigma^*/_{\backsim_L}, [\epsilon]_{\backsim_L}, \delta)$, where $\delta([u]_{\backsim_L}, a) = [ua]_{\backsim_L}$ for all $u \in \Sigma^*$ and $a \in \Sigma$.*
We define the right congruences $\approx_P^u, \approx_S^u$, and $\approx_R^u$ for progress automata A^u of periodic, syntactic, and recurrent FDFA respectively as follows:

$$x \approx_P^u y \text{ iff } \forall v \in \Sigma^*, u(xv)^\omega \in L \Longleftrightarrow u(yv)^\omega \in L,$$
$$x \approx_S^u y \text{ iff } ux \backsim_L uy \text{ and } \forall v \in \Sigma^*, uxv \backsim_L u \Longrightarrow (u(xv)^\omega \in L \Longleftrightarrow u(yv)^\omega \in L), \text{ and}$$
$$x \approx_R^u y \text{ iff } \forall v \in \Sigma^*, uxv \backsim_L u \wedge u(xv)^\omega \in L \Longleftrightarrow uyv \backsim_L u \wedge u(xv)^\omega \in L.$$

The progress automaton A^u is the tuple $(\Sigma, \Sigma^*/_{\approx_K^u}, [\epsilon]_{\approx_K^u}, \delta_K, F_K)$, where $\delta_K([u]_{\approx_K^u}, a) = [ua]_{\approx_K^u}$ for all $u \in \Sigma^*$ and $a \in \Sigma$. The accepting states F_K is the set of equivalence classes $[v]_{\approx_K^u}$ for which $uv \backsim_L u$ and $uv^\omega \in L$ when $K \in \{S, R\}$ and the set of equivalence classes $[v]_{\approx_K^u}$ for which $uv^\omega \in L$ when $K \in \{P\}$.

In this paper, by an abuse of notation, we use a finite word u to denote the state in a DFA in which the equivalence class $[u]$ resides.

Lemma 1 [10]. *Let $\mathcal{F}$ be a periodic (syntactic, recurrent) FDFA of an ω-regular language L. Then $UP(\mathcal{F}) = UP(L)$.*

Lemma 2 [9]. *Let $\mathcal{F}$ be a periodic (syntactic, recurrent) FDFA of an ω-regular language L. One can construct a BA recognizing L from $\mathcal{F}$.*

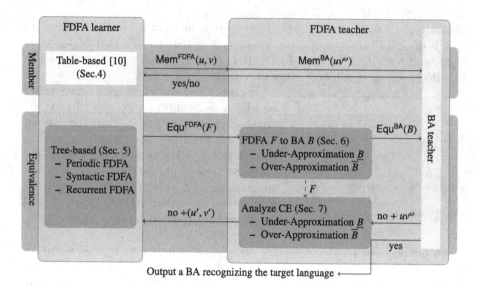

Fig. 2. Overview of the learning framework based on FDFA learning. The components in ▭ boxes are results from existing works. The components in ⬭ boxes are our new contributions. (Color figure online)

3 Büchi Automata Learning Framework Based on FDFA

We begin with an introduction of the framework of learning BA recognizing an unknown ω-regular language L.

Overview of the Framework: First, we assume that we already have a BA teacher who knows the unknown ω-regular language L and answers *membership* and *equivalence* queries about L. More precisely, a membership query $\mathsf{Mem}^{\mathsf{BA}}(uv^\omega)$ asks if $uv^\omega \in L$. For an equivalence query $\mathsf{Equ}^{\mathsf{BA}}(B)$, the BA teacher answers "yes" when $L(B) = L$, otherwise it returns "no" as well as a counterexample $uv^\omega \in L \oplus L(B)$.

The framework depicted in Fig. 2 consists of two components, namely the FDFA *learner* and the FDFA *teacher*. Note that one can place any FDFA learning algorithm to the FDFA learner component. For instance, one can use the FDFA learner from [10] which employs a table to store query results, or the FDFA learner using a classification tree proposed in this paper. The FDFA teacher can be any teacher who can answer membership and equivalence queries about an unknown FDFA.

FDFA Learners: The FDFA learners component will be introduced in Sects. 4 and 5. We first briefly review the table-based FDFA learning algorithms [10] in Sect. 4. Our tree-based learning algorithm for canonical FDFAs will be introduced in Sect. 5. The algorithm is inspired by the tree-based L^* learning algorithm [30]. Nevertheless, applying the tree structure to learn FDFAs is not a trivial task. For example, instead of a binary tree used in [30], we need to use a K-ary tree to learn syntactic FDFAs. The use of K-ary tree complicates the procedure of refining the classification tree and automaton construction. More details will be provided in Sect. 5.

FDFA Teacher: The task of the FDFA teacher is to answer queries $\mathsf{Mem}^{\mathsf{FDFA}}(u, v)$ and $\mathsf{Equ}^{\mathsf{FDFA}}(F)$ posed by the FDFA learner. Answering $\mathsf{Mem}^{\mathsf{FDFA}}(u, v)$ is easy. The FDFA teacher just needs to redirect the result of $\mathsf{Mem}^{\mathsf{BA}}(uv^{\omega})$ to the FDFA learner. Answering equivalence query $\mathsf{Equ}^{\mathsf{FDFA}}(F)$ is more tricky.

From an FDFA F to a BA B: The FDFA teacher needs to transform an FDFA F to a BA B to pose an equivalence query $\mathsf{Equ}^{\mathsf{BA}}(B)$. In Sect. 6, we show that, in general, it is impossible to build a BA B from an FDFA F such that $\mathrm{UP}(L(B)) = \mathrm{UP}(F)$. Therefore in Sect. 6, we propose two methods to approximate $\mathrm{UP}(F)$, namely the *under-approximation* method and the *over-approximation* method. As the name indicates, the under-approximation (respectively, over-approximation) method constructs a BA B from F such that $\mathrm{UP}(L(B)) \subseteq \mathrm{UP}(F)$ (respectively, $\mathrm{UP}(F) \subseteq \mathrm{UP}(L(B))$). The under-approximation method is modified from the algorithm in [14]. Note that if the FDFAs are the canonical representations, the BAs built by the under-approximation method recognize the same ultimately periodic words as the FDFAs, which makes it a complete method for BA learning (Lemmas 1 and 2). As for the over-approximation method, we cannot guarantee to get a BA B such that $\mathrm{UP}(L(B)) = \mathrm{UP}(F)$ even if the F is a canonical representation, which thus makes it an incomplete method. However, in the worst case, the over-approximation method produces a BA whose number of states is only quadratic in the size of the FDFA. In contrast, the number of states in the BA constructed by the under-approximation method is cubic in the size of the FDFA.

Counterexample Analysis: If the FDFA teacher receives "no" and a counterexample uv^{ω} from the BA teacher, the FDFA teacher has to return "no" as well as a valid decomposition (u', v') that can be used by the FDFA learner to refine F. In Sect. 7, we show how the FDFA teacher chooses a pair (u', v') from uv^{ω} that allows FDFA learner to refine current FDFA F. As the dashed line with a label F in Fig. 2 indicates, we use the current conjectured FDFA F to analyze the counterexample. The under-approximation method and the over-approximation method of FDFA to BA translation require different counterexample analysis procedures. More details will be provided in Sect. 7.

Once the BA teacher answers "yes" for the equivalence query $\mathsf{Equ}^{\mathsf{BA}}(B)$, the FDFA teacher will terminate the learning procedure and outputs a BA recognizing L.

Due to the lack of space, all missing proofs and details for our Büchi learning algorithm are provided in [32].

4   Table-Based Learning Algorithm for FDFAs

In this section, we briefly introduce the table-based learner for FDFAs [10]. It employs a structure called *observation table* [7] to organize the results obtained from queries and propose candidate FDFAs. The table-based FDFA learner simultaneously runs several instances of DFA learners. The DFA learners are very similar to the L^* algorithm [7], except that they use different conditions to decide if two strings belong to the same state (based on Definition 2). More precisely, the FDFA learner uses one DFA learner L_M^* for the leading automaton M, and for each state u in M, one DFA learner $L_{A^u}^*$ for each progress automaton A^u. The table-based learning procedure works as follows. The learner L_M^* first closes the observation table by posing membership queries and then constructs a candidate for leading automaton M. For every state u in M, the table-based algorithm runs an instance of DFA learner $L_{A^u}^*$ to find the progress automaton A^u. When all DFA learners propose candidate DFAs, the FDFA learner assembles them to an FDFA $\mathcal{F} = (M, \{A^u\})$ and then poses an equivalence query for it. The FDFA teacher will either return *"yes"* which means the learning algorithm succeeds or return *"no"* accompanying with a counterexample. Once receiving the counterexample, the table-based algorithm will decide which DFA learner should refine its candidate DFA. We refer interested readers to [10] for more details of the table-based algorithm.

5   Tree-Based Learning Algorithm for FDFAs

In this section, we provide our tree-based learning algorithm for FDFAs. To that end, we first define the classification tree structure for FDFA learning in Sect. 5.1 and present the tree-based algorithm in Sect. 5.2.

5.1   Classification Tree Structure in Learning

Here we present our classification tree structure for FDFA learning. Compared to the classification tree defined in [30], ours is not restricted to be a binary tree. Formally, a classification tree is a tuple $\mathcal{T} = (N, r, L_n, L_e)$ where $N = I \cup T$ is a set of nodes consisting of the set I of *internal nodes* and the set T of *terminal nodes*, the node $r \in N$ is the root of the tree, $L_n : N \rightarrow \Sigma^* \cup (\Sigma^* \times \Sigma^*)$ labels an internal node with an *experiment* and a terminal node with a *state*, and $L_e : N \times D \rightarrow N$ maps a parent node and a label to its corresponding child node, where the set of labels D will be specified below.

During the learning procedure, we maintain a *leading tree* $\mathcal{T}$ for the leading automaton M, and for every state u in M, we keep a *progress tree* $\mathcal{T}_u$ for the progress automaton A^u. For every classification tree, we define a tree experiment function **TE** : $\Sigma^* \times (\Sigma^* \cup (\Sigma^* \times \Sigma^*)) \rightarrow D$. Intuitively, **TE**$(x, e)$ computes the entry value at row (state) x and column (experiment) e of an observation table in table-based learning algorithms. The labels of nodes in the classification tree $\mathcal{T}$ satisfy the follow invariants: Let $t \in T$ be a terminal node labeled with a state $x = L_n(t)$. Let $t' \in I$ be an ancestor node of t labeled with an experiment $e = L_n(t')$. Then the child of t' following the label $\mathbf{TE}(x, e)$, i.e., $L_e(t', \mathbf{TE}(x, e))$, is either the node t or an ancestor node of t.

Leading Tree $\mathcal{T}$: The leading tree $\mathcal{T}$ for M is a binary tree with labels $D = \{F, T\}$. The tree experiment function $\mathbf{TE}(u, (x, y)) = T$ iff $uxy^\omega \in L$ (recall the definition of $\backsim_L$ in Sect. 2) where $u, x, y \in \Sigma^*$. Intuitively, each internal node n in $\mathcal{T}$ is labeled by an experiment xy^ω represented as (x, y). For any word $u \in \Sigma^*$, $uxy^\omega \in L$ (or $uxy^\omega \notin L$) implies that the equivalence class of u lies in the T-subtree (or F-subtree) of n.

Progress Tree $\mathcal{T}_u$: The progress trees $\mathcal{T}_u$ and the corresponding function $\mathbf{TE}(x, e)$ are defined based on the right congruences $\approx_P^u$, $\approx_S^u$, and $\approx_R^u$ of canonical FDFAs in Definition 2.

<u>Periodic FDFA:</u> The progress tree for periodic FDFA is also a binary tree labeled with $D = \{F, T\}$. The experiment function $\mathbf{TE}(x, e) = T$ iff $u(xe)^\omega \in L$ where $x, e \in \Sigma^*$.

<u>Syntactic FDFA:</u> The progress tree for syntactic FDFA is a K-ary tree with labels $D = Q \times \{A, B, C\}$ where Q is the set of states in the leading automaton M. For all $x, e \in \Sigma^*$, the experiment function $\mathbf{TE}(x, e) = (M(ux), t)$, where $t = A$ iff $u = M(uxe) \wedge u(xe)^\omega \in L$, $t = B$ iff $u = M(uxe) \wedge u(xe)^\omega \notin L$, and $t = C$ iff $u \neq M(uxe)$.

For example, assuming that M is constructed from the right congruence $\backsim_L$, for any two states x and y such that $\mathbf{TE}(x, e) = \mathbf{TE}(y, e) = (z, A)$, it must be the case that $ux \backsim_L uy$ because $M(ux) = z = M(uy)$. Moreover, the experiment e cannot distinguish x and y because $uxe \backsim_L u \backsim_L uye$ and both $u(xe)^\omega, u(ye)^\omega \in L$.

<u>Recurrent FDFA:</u> The progress tree for recurrent FDFA is a binary tree labeled with $D = \{F, T\}$. The function $\mathbf{TE}(x, e) = T$ iff $u(xe)^\omega \in L \wedge u = M(uxe)$ where $x, e \in \Sigma^*$.

5.2   Tree-Based Learning Algorithm

The tree-based learning algorithm first initializes the leading tree $\mathcal{T}$ and the progress tree $\mathcal{T}_\epsilon$ as a tree with only one terminal node r labeled by ϵ.

From a classification tree $\mathcal{T} = (N, r, L_n, L_e)$, the learner constructs a candidate of a leading automaton $M = (\Sigma, Q, \epsilon, \delta)$ or a progress automaton $A^u = (\Sigma, Q, \epsilon, \delta, F)$ as follow. The set of states is $Q = \{L_n(t) \mid t \in T\}$. Given $s \in Q$ and $a \in \Sigma$, the transition function $\delta(s, a)$ is constructed by the following procedure. Initially the current node $n := r$. If n is a terminal node, it returns $\delta(s, a) = L_n(n)$. Otherwise, it picks a unique child n' of n with $L_e(n, \mathbf{TE}(sa, L_n(n))) = n'$, updates the current node to n', and repeats the procedure[1]. By Definition 2, the set of accepting states F of a progress automaton can be identified from the structure of M with the help of membership

---

[1] For syntactic FDFA, it can happen that $\delta(s, a)$ goes to a "new" terminal node. A new state for the FDFA is identified in such a case.

queries. For periodic FDFA, $F = \{v \mid uv^\omega \in L, v \in Q\}$ and for syntactic and recurrent FDFA, $F = \{v \mid uv \backsim_M u, uv^\omega \in L, v \in Q\}$.

Whenever the learner has constructed an FDFA $\mathcal{F} = (M, \{A^u\})$, it will pose an equivalence query for $\mathcal{F}$. If the teacher returns "no" and a counterexample (u, v), the learner has to refine the classification tree and propose another candidate of FDFA.

Definition 3 (Counterexample for FDFA Learner). *Given the conjectured FDFA $\mathcal{F}$ and the target language L, we say that the counterexample*

- *(u, v) is positive if $uv \backsim_M u$, $uv^\omega \in UP(L)$, and (u, v) is not accepted by $\mathcal{F}$,*
- *(u, v) is negative if $uv \backsim_M u$, $uv^\omega \notin UP(L)$, and (u, v) is accepted by $\mathcal{F}$.*

We remark that in our case all counterexamples (u, v) from the FDFA teacher satisfy the constraint $uv \backsim_M u$, which corresponds to the *normalized factorization* form in [10].

Counterexample Guided Refinement of $\mathcal{F}$: Below we show how to refine the classification trees based on a negative counterexample (u, v). The case of a positive counterexample is symmetric. By definition, we have $uv \sim_M u$, $uv^\omega \notin UP(L)$ and (u, v) is accepted by $\mathcal{F}$. Let $\tilde{u} = M(u)$, if $\tilde{u}v^\omega \in UP(L)$, the refinement of the leading tree is performed, otherwise $\tilde{u}v^\omega \notin UP(L)$, the refinement of the progress tree is performed.

Refinement for the Leading Tree: In the leading automaton M of the conjectured FDFA, if a state p has a transition to a state q via a letter a, i.e., $q = M(pa)$, then pa has been assigned to the terminal node labeled by q during the construction of M. If one also finds an experiment e such that $\mathbf{TE}(q, e) \neq \mathbf{TE}(pa, e)$, then we know that q and pa should not belong to the same state in a leading automaton. W.l.o.g., we assume $\mathbf{TE}(q, e) = \mathrm{F}$. In such a case, the leading tree can be refined by replacing the terminal node labeled with q by a tree such that (i) its root is labeled by e, (ii) its left child is a terminal node labeled by q, and (iii) its right child is a terminal node labeled by pa.

Below we discuss how to extract the required states p, q and experiment e. Let $|u| = n$ and $s_0 s_1 \cdots s_n$ be the run of M over u. Note that $s_0 = M(\epsilon) = \epsilon$ and $s_n = M(u) = \tilde{u}$. From the facts that (u, v) is a negative counterexample and $\tilde{u}v^\omega \in UP(L)$ (the condition to refine the leading tree), we have $\mathbf{TE}(s_0, (u[1 \cdots n], v)) = \mathrm{F} \neq \mathrm{T} = \mathbf{TE}(s_n, (\epsilon, v)) = \mathbf{TE}(s_n, (u[n + 1 \cdots n], v))$ because $uv^\omega \notin UP(L)$ and $\tilde{u}v^\omega \in UP(L)$. Recall that we have $w[j \cdots k] = \epsilon$ when $j > k$. Therefore, there must exist a smallest $j \in [1 \cdots n]$ such that $\mathbf{TE}(s_{j-1}, (u[j \cdots n], v)) \neq \mathbf{TE}(s_j, (u[j + 1 \cdots n], v))$. It follows that we can use the experiment $e = (u[j + 1 \cdots n], v)$ to distinguish $q = s_j$ and $pa = s_{j-1}u[j]$.

Example 1. Consider a conjectured FDFA $\mathcal{F}$ in Fig. 1 produced during the process of learning $L = a^\omega + b^\omega$. The corresponding leading tree $\mathcal{T}$ and the progress tree $\mathcal{T}_\epsilon$ are depicted on the left of Fig. 3. The dashed line is for the F label and the solid one is for the T label. Suppose the FDFA teacher returns a negative counterexample (ab, b). The leading tree has to be refined since

$M(ab)b^\omega = b^\omega \in L$. We find an experiment (b, b) to differentiate ϵ and a using the procedure above and update the leading tree $\mathcal{T}$ to $\mathcal{T}'$. The leading automaton M constructed from $\mathcal{T}'$ is depicted on the right of Fig. 3.

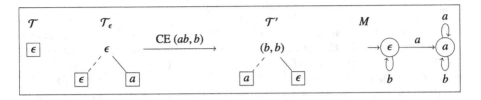

Fig. 3. Refinement of the leading tree and the corresponding leading automaton

Refinement for the Progress Tree: Here we explain the case of periodic FDFAs. The other cases are similar and we leave the details in [32]. Recall that $\tilde{u}v^\omega \notin \mathrm{UP}(L)$ and thus the algorithm refines the progress tree $\mathcal{T}_{\tilde{u}}$. Let $|v| = n$ and $h = s_0 s_1 \cdots s_n$ be the corresponding run of $A^{\tilde{u}}$ over v. Note that $s_0 = A^{\tilde{u}}(\epsilon) = \epsilon$ and $s_n = A^{\tilde{u}}(v) = \tilde{v}$. We have $\tilde{u}(\tilde{v})^\omega \in \mathrm{UP}(L)$ because $\tilde{v}$ is an accepting state. From the facts that $\tilde{u}v^\omega \notin \mathrm{UP}(L)$ and $\tilde{u}(\tilde{v})^\omega \in \mathrm{UP}(L)$, we have $\mathbf{TE}(s_0, v[1\cdots n]) = \mathrm{F} \neq \mathrm{T} = \mathbf{TE}(s_n, \epsilon) = \mathbf{TE}(s_n, v[n+1\cdots n])$. Therefore, there must exist a smallest $j \in [1\cdots n]$ such that $\mathbf{TE}(s_{j-1}, v[j\cdots n]) \neq \mathbf{TE}(s_j, v[j+1\cdots n])$. It follows that we can use the experiment $e = v[j+1\cdots n]$ to distinguish $q = s_j$, $pa = s_{j-1}v[j]$ and refine the progress tree $\mathcal{T}_{\tilde{u}}$.

Optimization: Example 1 also illustrates the fact that the counterexample (ab, b) may not be eliminated right away after the refinement. In this case, it is still a valid counterexample (assuming that the progress tree $\mathcal{T}_\epsilon$ remains unchanged). Thus as an optimization in our tool, one can repeatedly use the counterexample until it is eliminated.

6   From FDFA to Büchi Automata

Since the FDFA teacher exploits the BA teacher for answering equivalence queries, it needs first to convert the given FDFA into a BA. Unfortunately, with the following example, we show that in general, it is impossible to construct a *precise* BA B for an FDFA $\mathcal{F}$ such that $\mathrm{UP}(L(B)) = \mathrm{UP}(\mathcal{F})$.

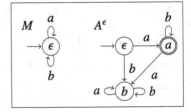

Fig. 4. An FDFA $\mathcal{F}$ such that $\mathrm{UP}(\mathcal{F})$ does not characterize an ω-regular language

Example 2. Consider a non-canonical FDFA $\mathcal{F}$ in Fig. 4, we have $\mathrm{UP}(\mathcal{F}) = \bigcup_{n=0}^{\infty} \{a, b\}^* \cdot (ab^n)^\omega$. We assume that $\mathrm{UP}(\mathcal{F})$ characterizes an ω-regular language L. It is known that the periodic FDFA recognizes exactly the ω-regular language and the index of each right congruence is finite [10]. However, we can show that the right congruence $\approx_P^\epsilon$ of a periodic FDFA of L is of infinite index. Observe that $ab^k \not\approx_P^\epsilon ab^j$ for any $k, j \geq 1$ and $k \neq j$, because $\epsilon \cdot (ab^k \cdot ab^k)^\omega \in \mathrm{UP}(\mathcal{F})$ and $\epsilon \cdot (ab^j \cdot ab^k)^\omega \notin \mathrm{UP}(\mathcal{F})$. It follows that $\approx_P^\epsilon$ is of infinite index. We conclude that $\mathrm{UP}(\mathcal{F})$ cannot characterize an ω-regular language.

We circumvent the above problem by proposing two BAs $\underline{B}, \overline{B}$, which under- and over-approximate the ultimately periodic words of an FDFA. Given an FDFA $\mathcal{F} = (M, \{A^u\})$ with $M = (\Sigma, Q, q_0, \delta)$ and $A^u = (\Sigma, Q_u, s_u, \delta_u, F_u)$ for all $u \in Q$, we define $M_v^s = (\Sigma, Q, s, \delta, \{v\})$ and $(A^u)_v^s = (\Sigma, Q_u, s, \delta_u, \{v\})$, i.e., the DFA obtained from M and A^u by setting their initial and accepting states as s and $\{v\}$, respectively. Define $N_{(u,v)} = \{v^\omega \mid uv \curvearrowright_M u \wedge v \in L((A^u)_v^{s_u})\}$. Then $\mathrm{UP}(\mathcal{F}) = \bigcup_{u \in Q, v \in F_u} L(M_u^{q_0}) \cdot N_{(u,v)}$.

We construct $\overline{B}$ and $\underline{B}$ by approximating the set $N_{(u,v)}$. For $\overline{B}$, we first define an FA $\overline{P}_{(u,v)} = (\Sigma, Q_{u,v}, s_{u,v}, \{f_{u,v}\}, \delta_{u,v}) = M_u^u \times (A^u)_v^{s_u}$ and let $\overline{N}_{(u,v)} = L(\overline{P}_{(u,v)})^\omega$. Then one can construct a BA $(\Sigma, Q_{u,v} \cup \{f\}, s_{u,v}, \{f\}, \delta_{u,v} \cup \delta_f)$ recognizing $\overline{N}_{(u,v)}$ where f is a "fresh" state and $\delta_f = \{(f, \epsilon, s_{u,v}), (f_{u,v}, \epsilon, f)\}$. For $\underline{B}$, we define an FA $\underline{P}_{(u,v)} = M_u^u \times (A^u)_v^{s_u} \times (A^u)_v^v$ and let $\underline{N}_{(u,v)} = L(\underline{P}_{(u,v)})^\omega$. One can construct a BA recognizing $\underline{N}_{(u,v)}$ using a similar construction to the case of $\overline{N}_{(u,v)}$. In Definition 4 we show how to construct BAs $\overline{B}$ and $\underline{B}$ s.t. $\mathrm{UP}(L(\overline{B})) = \bigcup_{u \in Q, v \in F_u} L(M_u^{q_0}) \cdot \overline{N}_{(u,v)}$ and $\mathrm{UP}(L(\underline{B})) = \bigcup_{u \in Q, v \in F_u} L(M_u^{q_0}) \cdot \underline{N}_{(u,v)}$.

Definition 4. *Let $\mathcal{F} = (M, \{A^u\})$ be an FDFA where $M = (\Sigma, Q, q_0, \delta)$ and $A^u = (\Sigma, Q_u, s_u, F_u, \delta_u)$ for every $u \in Q$. Let $(\Sigma, Q_{u,v}, s_{u,v}, \{f_{u,v}\}, \delta_{u,v})$ be a BA recognizing $\underline{N}_{(u,v)}$ (respectively $\overline{N}_{(u,v)}$). Then the BA $\underline{B}$ (respectively $\overline{B}$) is defined as the tuple*

$$\left(\Sigma, Q \cup \bigcup_{u \in Q, v \in F_u} Q_{u,v}, q_0, \bigcup_{u \in Q, v \in F_u} \{f_{u,v}\}, \delta \cup \bigcup_{u \in Q, v \in F_u} \delta_{u,v} \cup \bigcup_{u \in Q, v \in F_u} \{(u, \epsilon, s_{u,v})\} \right).$$

Lemma 3 (Sizes and Languages of $\underline{B}$ and $\overline{B}$). *Let $\mathcal{F}$ be an FDFA and $\underline{B}$, $\overline{B}$ be the BAs constructed from $\mathcal{F}$ by Definition 4. Let n and k be the numbers of states in the leading automaton and the largest progress automaton of $\mathcal{F}$. The number of states of $\underline{B}$ and $\overline{B}$ are in $\mathcal{O}(n^2 k^3)$ and $\mathcal{O}(n^2 k^2)$, respectively. Moreover, $\mathrm{UP}(L(\underline{B})) \subseteq \mathrm{UP}(\mathcal{F}) \subseteq \mathrm{UP}(L(\overline{B}))$ and we have $\mathrm{UP}(L(\underline{B})) = \mathrm{UP}(\mathcal{F})$ when $\mathcal{F}$ is a canonical FDFA.*

The properties below will be used later in analyzing counterexamples.

Lemma 4. *Given an FDFA $\mathcal{F} = (M, \{A^u\})$, and $\underline{B}$ the BA constructed from $\mathcal{F}$ by Definition 4. If (u, v^k) is accepted by $\mathcal{F}$ for every $k \geq 1$, then $uv^\omega \in \mathrm{UP}(L(\underline{B}))$.*

Lemma 5. *Given an ω-word $w \in \mathrm{UP}(L(\overline{B}))$, there exists a decomposition (u, v) of w and $n \geq 1$ such that $v = v_1 \cdot v_2 \cdots v_n$ and for all $i \in [1 \cdots n]$, $v_i \in L(A^{M(u)})$ and $uv_i \curvearrowright_M u$.*

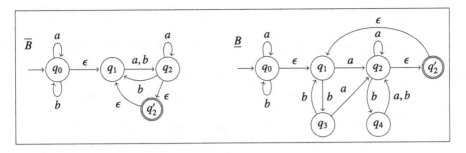

Fig. 5. NBA $\overline{B}$ and $\underline{B}$ for $\mathcal{F}$ in Fig. 1

Figure 5 depicts the BAs $\overline{B}$ and $\underline{B}$ constructed from the FDFA $\mathcal{F}$ in Fig. 1. In the example, we can see that the $b^\omega \in \mathrm{UP}(\mathcal{F})$ while $b^\omega \notin \mathrm{UP}(L(\underline{B}))$.

7   Counterexample Analysis for FDFA Teacher

During the learning procedure, if we failed the equivalence query for the BA B, the BA teacher will return a counterexample uv^ω to the FDFA teacher.

Definition 5 (Counterexample for the FDFA Teacher). *Given the conjectured BA $B \in \{\underline{B}, \overline{B}\}$, the target language L, we say that*

- *uv^ω is a* positive *counterexample if $uv^\omega \in UP(L)$ and $uv^\omega \notin UP(L(B))$,*
- *uv^ω is a* negative *counterexample if $uv^\omega \notin UP(L)$ and $uv^\omega \in UP(L(B))$.*

Obviously, the above is different to the counterexample for the FDFA learner in Definition 3. Below we illustrate the necessity of the counterexample analysis by an example.

Example 3. Again, consider the conjectured FDFA $\mathcal{F}$ depicted in Fig. 1 for $L = a^\omega + b^\omega$. Suppose the BA teacher returns a negative counterexample $(ba)^\omega$. In order to remove $(ba)^\omega \in \mathrm{UP}(\mathcal{F})$, one has to find a decomposition of $(ba)^\omega$ that $\mathcal{F}$ accepts, which is the goal of the counterexample analysis. Not all decompositions of $(ba)^\omega$ are accepted by $\mathcal{F}$. For instance, (ba, ba) is accepted while (bab, ab) is not.

A positive (respectively negative) counterexample uv^ω for the FDFA teacher is *spurious* if $uv^\omega \in \mathrm{UP}(\mathcal{F})$ (respectively $uv^\omega \notin \mathrm{UP}(\mathcal{F})$). Suppose we use the under-approximation method to construct the BA $\underline{B}$ from $\mathcal{F}$ depicted in Fig. 5. The BA teacher returns a spurious positive counterexample b^ω, which is in $\mathrm{UP}(\mathcal{F})$ but not in $\mathrm{UP}(L(\underline{B}))$. We show later that in such a case, one can always find a decomposition, in this example (b, bb), as the counterexample for the FDFA learner.

Given FDFA $\mathcal{F} = (M, \{A^u\})$, in order to analyze the counterexample uv^ω, we define:

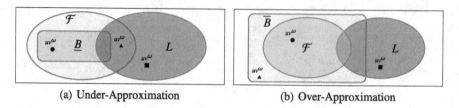

(a) Under-Approximation   (b) Over-Approximation

Fig. 6. The Case for Counterexample Analysis

- an FA $\mathcal{D}_{u\$v}$ with $L(\mathcal{D}_{u\$v}) = \{u'\$v' \mid u' \in \Sigma^*, v' \in \Sigma^+, uv^\omega = u'v'^\omega\}$,
- an FA $\mathcal{D}_1$ with $L(\mathcal{D}_1) = \{u\$v \mid u \in \Sigma^*, v \in \Sigma^*, uv \curvearrowright_M u, v \in L(A^{M(u)})\}$, and
- an FA $\mathcal{D}_2$ with $L(\mathcal{D}_2) = \{u\$v \mid u \in \Sigma^*, v \in \Sigma^*, uv \curvearrowright_M u, v \notin L(A^{M(u)})\}$.

Here \$ is a letter not in Σ. Intuitively, $\mathcal{D}_{u\$v}$ accepts every possible decomposition (u', v') of uv^ω, $\mathcal{D}_1$ recognizes every decomposition (u', v') which is accepted by $\mathcal{F}$ and $\mathcal{D}_2$ accepts every decomposition (u', v') which is not accepted by $\mathcal{F}$ yet $u'v' \curvearrowright_M u'$.

Given a BA $\underline{B}$ constructed by the under-approximation method to construct a BA $\underline{B}$ from $\mathcal{F}$, we have that $\mathrm{UP}(L(\underline{B})) \subseteq \mathrm{UP}(\mathcal{F})$. Figure 6(a) depicts all possible cases of $uv^\omega \in \mathrm{UP}(L(\underline{B})) \oplus \mathrm{UP}(L)$.

U1: $uv^\omega \in \mathrm{UP}(L) \wedge uv^\omega \notin \mathrm{UP}(\mathcal{F})$ (square). The word uv^ω is a positive counterexample, one has to find a decomposition (u', v') such that $u'v' \curvearrowright_M u'$ and $u'v'^\omega = uv^\omega$. This can be easily done by taking a word $u'\$v' \in L(\mathcal{D}_{u\$v}) \cap L(\mathcal{D}_2)$.

U2: $uv^\omega \notin \mathrm{UP}(L) \wedge uv^\omega \in \mathrm{UP}(\mathcal{F})$ (circle). The word uv^ω is a negative counterexample, one needs to find a decomposition (u', v') of uv^ω that is accepted by $\mathcal{F}$. This can be done by taking a word $u'\$v' \in L(\mathcal{D}_{u\$v}) \cap L(\mathcal{D}_1)$.

U3: $uv^\omega \in \mathrm{UP}(L) \wedge uv^\omega \in \mathrm{UP}(\mathcal{F})$ (triangle). The word uv^ω is a spurious positive counterexample. Suppose the decomposition (u, v) of uv^ω is accepted by $\mathcal{F}$, according to Lemma 4, there must exist some $k \geq 1$ such that (u, v^k) is not accepted by $\mathcal{F}$. Thus, we can also use the same method in U1 to get a counterexample (u', v').

We can also use the over-approximation construction to get a BA $\overline{B}$ from $\mathcal{F}$ such that $\mathrm{UP}(\mathcal{F}) \subseteq \mathrm{UP}(L(\overline{B}))$, and all possible cases for a counterexample $uv^\omega \in \mathrm{UP}(L(\overline{B})) \oplus \mathrm{UP}(L)$ is depicted in Fig. 6(b).

O1: $uv^\omega \in \mathrm{UP}(L) \wedge uv^\omega \notin \mathrm{UP}(\mathcal{F})$ (square). The word uv^ω is a positive counterexample that can be dealt with the same method for case U1.

O2: $uv^\omega \notin \mathrm{UP}(L) \wedge uv^\omega \in \mathrm{UP}(\mathcal{F})$ (circle). The word uv^ω is a negative counterexample that can be dealt with the same method for case U2.

O3: $uv^\omega \notin \mathrm{UP}(L) \wedge uv^\omega \notin \mathrm{UP}(\mathcal{F})$ (triangle). In this case, uv^ω is a spurious negative counterexample. In such a case it is possible that we cannot find a valid decomposition of uv^ω to refine $\mathcal{F}$. By Lemma 5, we can find a decomposition (u', v') of uv^ω such that $v' = v_1 v_2 \cdots v_n$, $u'v_i \curvearrowright_M u'$, and $v_i \in L(A^{M(u')})$ for some $n \geq 1$. It follows that (u', v_i) is accepted by $\mathcal{F}$. If we find some

$i \in [1 \cdots n]$ such that $u'v_i^\omega \notin \mathrm{UP}(L)$, then we return (u', v_i), otherwise, the algorithm aborts with an error.

Finally, we note that determining whether $uv^\omega \in \mathrm{UP}(L)$ can be done by posing a membership query $\mathsf{Mem}^{\mathsf{BA}}(uv^\omega)$, and checking whether $uv^\omega \in \mathrm{UP}(\mathcal{F})$ boils down to checking the emptiness of $L(\mathcal{D}_{u\$v}) \cap L(\mathcal{D}_1)$. The construction for $\mathcal{D}_{u\$v}$, $\mathcal{D}_1$, and $\mathcal{D}_2$, and the correctness proof of counterexample analysis are given in [32].

8   Complexity

We discuss the complexity of tree-based FDFA learning algorithms in Sect. 5. Let $\mathcal{F} = (M, \{A^u\})$ be the corresponding periodic FDFA of the ω-regular language L, and let n be the number of states in the leading automaton M and k be the number of states in the largest progress automaton A^u. We remark that $\mathcal{F}$ is uniquely defined for L and the table-based algorithm needs the same amount of equivalence queries as the tree-based one in the worst case. Given a counterexample (u, v) returned from the FDFA teacher, we define its *length* as $|u| + |v|$.

Theorem 2 (Query Complexity). *Let (u, v) be the longest counterexample returned from the FDFA teacher. The number of equivalence queries needed for the tree-based FDFA learning algorithm to learn the periodic FDFA of L is in $\mathcal{O}(n + nk)$, while the number of membership queries is in $\mathcal{O}((n + nk) \cdot (|u| + |v| + (n + k) \cdot |\Sigma|))$.*

For the syntactic and recurrent FDFAs, the number of equivalence queries needed for the tree-based FDFA learning algorithm is in $\mathcal{O}(n + n^3k)$, while the number of membership queries is in $\mathcal{O}((n + n^3k) \cdot (|u| + |v| + (n + nk) \cdot |\Sigma|))$.

The learning of syntactic and recurrent FDFAs requires more queries since once their leading automata have been modified, they need to redo the learning of all progress automata from scratch.

Theorem 3 (Space Complexity). *For all tree-based algorithms, the space required to learn the leading automaton is in $\mathcal{O}(n)$. For learning periodic FDFA, the space required for each progress automaton is in $\mathcal{O}(k)$, while for syntactic and recurrent FDFAs, the space required is in $\mathcal{O}(nk)$. For all table-based algorithms, the space required to learn the leading automaton is in $\mathcal{O}((n + n \cdot |\Sigma|) \cdot n)$. For learning periodic FDFA, the space required for each progress automaton is in $\mathcal{O}((k + k \cdot |\Sigma|) \cdot k)$, while for syntactic and recurrent FDFAs, the space required is in $\mathcal{O}((nk + nk \cdot |\Sigma|) \cdot nk)$.*

Theorem 4 (Correctness and Termination). *The BA learning algorithm based on the under-approximation method always terminates and returns a BA recognizing the unknown ω-regular language L in polynomial time. If the BA learning algorithm based on the over-approximation method terminates without reporting an error, it returns a BA recognizing L.*

Given a canonical FDFA $\mathcal{F}$, the under-approximation method produces a BA $\underline{B}$ such that $\mathrm{UP}(\mathcal{F}) = \mathrm{UP}(L(\underline{B}))$, thus in the worst case, FDFA learner learns a canonical FDFA and terminates. In practice, the algorithm very often finds a BA recognizing L before converging to a canonical FDFA.

9   Experimental Results

The ROLL library (http://iscasmc.ios.ac.cn/roll) is implemented in JAVA. The DFA operations in ROLL are delegated to the *dk.brics.automaton* package, and we use the RABIT tool [2,3] to check the equivalence of two BAs. We evaluate the performance of ROLL using the smallest BAs corresponding to all the 295 LTL specifications available in BüchiStore [38], where the numbers of states in the BAs range over 1 to 17 and transitions range over 0 to 123. The machine we used for the experiments is a 2.5 GHz Intel Core i7-6500 with 4 GB RAM. We set the timeout period to 30 min.

The overall experimental results are given in Table 1. In this section, we use $L^\$$ to denote the ω-regular learning algorithm in [20], and L^{Periodic}, $L^{\mathrm{Syntactic}}$, and $L^{\mathrm{Recurrent}}$ to represent the periodic, syntactic, and recurrent FDFA learning algorithm introduced in Sects. 4 and 5. From the table, we can find the following facts: (1) The BAs learned from $L^\$$ have more states but fewer transitions than their FDFA based counterpart. (2) L^{Periodic} uses fewer membership queries comparing to $L^{\mathrm{Syntactic}}$ and $L^{\mathrm{Recurrent}}$. The reason is that $L^{\mathrm{Syntactic}}$ and $L^{\mathrm{Recurrent}}$ need to restart the learning of all progress automata from scratch when the leading automaton has been modified. (3) Tree-based algorithms always solve more learning tasks than their table-based counterpart. In particular, the tree-based $L^{\mathrm{Syntactic}}$ with the under-approximation method solves all 295 learning tasks.

Table 1. Overall experimental results. We show the results of 285 cases where all algorithms can finish the BA learning within the timeout period and list the number of cases cannot be solved (#Unsolved). The mark n^*/m denotes that there are n cases terminate with an error (in the over-approximation method) and it ran out of time for $m - n$ cases. The rows #St., #Tr., #MQ, and #EQ, are the numbers of states, transitions, membership queries, and equivalence queries. Time$_{eq}$ is the time spent in answering equivalence queries and Time$_{total}$ is the total execution time.

Models	$L^\$$		L^{Periodic}				$L^{\mathrm{Syntactic}}$				$L^{\mathrm{Recurrent}}$			
Struct. & Approxi.	Table	Tree	Table		Tree		Table		Tree		Table		Tree	
			Under	Over	Under	Over	Under	Over	Under	Over	Under	Over	Under	Over
#Unsolved	4	2	3	0/2	2	0/1	1	4*/5	0	3*/3	1	0/1	1	0/1
#St	3078	3078	2481	2468	2526	2417	2591	2591	**2274**	**2274**	2382	2382	2400	2400
#Tr	10.6k	**10.3k**	13.0k	13.0k	13.4k	12.8k	13.6k	13.6k	12.2k	12.2k	12.7k	12.7k	12.8k	12.8k
#MQ	105k	114k	86k	85k	69k	**67k**	236k	238k	139k	139k	124k	124k	126k	126k
#EQ	**1281**	2024	1382	1351	1950	1918	1399	1394	2805	2786	1430	1421	3037	3037
Time$_{eq}$ (s)	146	817	580	92	186	159	111	115	**89**	91	149	149	462	465
Time$_{total}$ (s)	183	861	610	114	213	186	140	144	**118**	120	175	176	499	501
EQ (%)	79.8	94.9	95.1	80.7	87.3	85.5	79.3	79.9	**75.4**	75.8	85.1	84.6	92.6	92.8

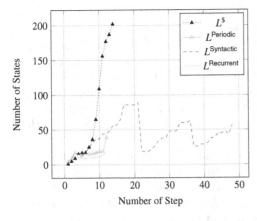

Fig. 7. Growth of state counts in BA.

In the experiment, we observe that table-based $L^\$$ has 4 cases cannot be finished within the timeout period, which is the largest number amount all learning algorithms[2]. We found that for these 4 cases, the average time required for $L^\$$ to get an equivalence query result is much longer than the FDFA algorithms. Under scrutiny, we found that the growth rate of the size (number of states) of the conjectured BAs generated by table-based $L^\$$ is much faster than that of table-based FDFA learning algorithms.

In Fig. 7, we illustrate the growth rate of the size (number of states) of the BAs generated by each table-based learning algorithm using one learning task that cannot be solved by $L^\$$ within the timeout period. The figures of the other three learning tasks show the same trend and hence are omitted. Another interesting observation is that the sizes of BAs generated by $L^{\text{Syntactic}}$ can decrease in some iteration because the leading automaton is refined and thus the algorithms have to redo the learning of all progress automata from scratch.

It is a bit surprise to us that, in our experiment, the size of BAs $\overline{B}$ produced by the over-approximation method is not much smaller than the BAs $\underline{B}$ produced by the under-approximation method. Recall that the progress automata of $\overline{B}$ comes from the product of three DFAs $M_u^u \times (A^u)_v^{s_u} \times (A^u)_v^v$ while those for $\underline{B}$ comes from the product of only two DFAs $M_u^u \times (A^u)_v^{s_u}$ (Sect. 6). We found the reason is that very often the language of the product of three DFAs is equivalent to the language of the product of two DFAs, thus we get the same DFA after applying DFA minimizations. Nevertheless, the over-approximation method is still helpful for L^{Periodic} and $L^{\text{Recurrent}}$. For L^{Periodic}, the over-approximation method solved more learning tasks than the under-approximation method. For $L^{\text{Recurrent}}$, the over-approximation method solved one tough learning task that is not solved by the under-approximation method.

As we mentioned at the end of Sect. 5.2, a possible optimization is to reuse the counterexample and to avoid equivalence query as much as possible. The optimization helps the learning algorithms to solve nine more cases that were not solved before.

10   Discussion and Future Works

Regarding our experiments, the BAs from LTL specifications are in general simple; the average sizes of the learned BAs are around 10 states. From our

---

[2] Most of the unsolved tasks using the over-approximation method are caused by the situation that the FDFA teacher cannot find a valid counterexample for refinement.

experience of applying DFA learning algorithms, the performance of tree-based algorithm is significantly better than the table-based one when the number of states of the learned DFA is large, say more than 1000. We believe this will also apply to the case of BA learning. Nevertheless, in our current experiments, most of the time is spent in answering equivalence queries. One possible direction to improve the scale of the experiment is to use a PAC (probably approximately correct) BA teacher [8] instead of an exact one, so the equivalence queries can be answered faster because the BA equivalence testing will be replaced with a bunch of BA membership testings.

There are several avenues for future works. We believe the algorithm and library of learning BAs should be an interesting tool for the community because it enables the possibility of many applications. For the next step, we will investigate the possibility of applying BA learning to the problem of reactive system synthesis, which is known to be a very difficult problem and learning-based approach has not been tried yet.

Acknowledgement. This work has been supported by the National Basic Research (973) Program of China under Grant No. 2014CB340701, the CAS Fellowship for Visiting Scientists from Taiwan under Grant No. 2015TW2GA0001, the National Natural Science Foundation of China (Grants 61532019, 61472473), the CAS/SAFEA International Partnership Program for Creative Research Teams, the Sino-German CDZ project CAP (GZ 1023), and the MOST project No. 103-2221-E-001-019-MY3.

References

1. Aarts, F., Jonsson, B., Uijen, J., Vaandrager, F.: Generating models of infinite-state communication protocols using regular inference with abstraction. Formal Methods Syst. Des. **46**(1), 1–41 (2015)
2. Abdulla, P.A., Chen, Y.-F., Clemente, L., Holík, L., Hong, C.-D., Mayr, R., Vojnar, T.: Simulation subsumption in Ramsey-based Büchi automata universality and inclusion testing. In: Touili, T., Cook, B., Jackson, P. (eds.) CAV 2010. LNCS, vol. 6174, pp. 132–147. Springer, Heidelberg (2010). doi:10.1007/978-3-642-14295-6_14
3. Abdulla, P.A., Chen, Y.-F., Clemente, L., Holík, L., Hong, C.-D., Mayr, R., Vojnar, T.: Advanced Ramsey-based Büchi automata inclusion testing. In: Katoen, J.-P., König, B. (eds.) CONCUR 2011. LNCS, vol. 6901, pp. 187–202. Springer, Heidelberg (2011). doi:10.1007/978-3-642-23217-6_13
4. Alpern, B., Schneider, F.B.: Recognizing safety and liveness. Distrib. Comput. **2**(3), 117–126 (1987)
5. Alur, R., Černý, P., Madhusudan, P., Nam, W.: Synthesis of interface specifications for Java classes. In: POPL, pp. 98–109 (2005)
6. Alur, R., Madhusudan, P., Nam, W.: Symbolic compositional verification by learning assumptions. In: Etessami, K., Rajamani, S.K. (eds.) CAV 2005. LNCS, vol. 3576, pp. 548–562. Springer, Heidelberg (2005). doi:10.1007/11513988_52
7. Angluin, D.: Learning regular sets from queries and counterexamples. Inf. Comput. **75**(2), 87–106 (1987)
8. Angluin, D.: Queries and concept learning. Mach. Learn. **2**(4), 319–342 (1988)
9. Angluin, D., Boker, U., Fisman, D.: Families of DFAs as acceptors of omega-regular languages. In: MFCS, pp. 11:1–11:14 (2016)

10. Angluin, D., Fisman, D.: Learning regular omega languages. In: Auer, P., Clark, A., Zeugmann, T., Zilles, S. (eds.) ALT 2014. LNCS (LNAI), vol. 8776, pp. 125–139. Springer, Cham (2014). doi:10.1007/978-3-319-11662-4_10

11. Bollig, B., Habermehl, P., Kern, C., Leucker, M.: Angluin-style learning of NFA. In: IJCAI, pp. 1004–1009 (2009)

12. Bollig, B., Katoen, J.-P., Kern, C., Leucker, M., Neider, D., Piegdon, D.R.: libalf: the automata learning framework. In: Touili, T., Cook, B., Jackson, P. (eds.) CAV 2010. LNCS, vol. 6174, pp. 360–364. Springer, Heidelberg (2010). doi:10.1007/978-3-642-14295-6_32

13. Büchi, J.R.: On a decision method in restricted second order arithmetic. In: 1960 International Congress on Logic, Methodology and Philosophy of Science, vol. 44, pp. 1–11 (2016)

14. Calbrix, H., Nivat, M., Podelski, A.: Ultimately periodic words of rational ω-languages. In: Brookes, S., Main, M., Melton, A., Mislove, M., Schmidt, D. (eds.) MFPS 1993. LNCS, vol. 802, pp. 554–566. Springer, Heidelberg (1994). doi:10.1007/3-540-58027-1_27

15. Chaki, S., Clarke, E., Sinha, N., Thati, P.: Automated assume-guarantee reasoning for simulation conformance. In: Etessami, K., Rajamani, S.K. (eds.) CAV 2005. LNCS, vol. 3576, pp. 534–547. Springer, Heidelberg (2005). doi:10.1007/11513988_51

16. Chapman, M., Chockler, H., Kesseli, P., Kroening, D., Strichman, O., Tautschnig, M.: Learning the language of error. In: Finkbeiner, B., Pu, G., Zhang, L. (eds.) ATVA 2015. LNCS, vol. 9364, pp. 114–130. Springer, Cham (2015). doi:10.1007/978-3-319-24953-7_9

17. Chen, Y.-F., Farzan, A., Clarke, E.M., Tsay, Y.-K., Wang, B.-Y.: Learning minimal separating DFA's for compositional verification. In: Kowalewski, S., Philippou, A. (eds.) TACAS 2009. LNCS, vol. 5505, pp. 31–45. Springer, Heidelberg (2009). doi:10.1007/978-3-642-00768-2_3

18. Chen, Y.-F., Hsieh, C., Lengál, O., Lii, T.-J., Tsai, M.-H., Wang, B.-Y., Wang, F.: PAC learning-based verification and model synthesis. In: ICSE, pp. 714–724 (2016)

19. Cobleigh, J.M., Giannakopoulou, D., Păsăreanu, C.S.: Learning assumptions for compositional verification. In: Garavel, H., Hatcliff, J. (eds.) TACAS 2003. LNCS, vol. 2619, pp. 331–346. Springer, Heidelberg (2003). doi:10.1007/3-540-36577-X_24

20. Farzan, A., Chen, Y.-F., Clarke, E.M., Tsay, Y.-K., Wang, B.-Y.: Extending automated compositional verification to the full class of omega-regular languages. In: Ramakrishnan, C.R., Rehof, J. (eds.) TACAS 2008. LNCS, vol. 4963, pp. 2–17. Springer, Heidelberg (2008). doi:10.1007/978-3-540-78800-3_2

21. Feng, L., Kwiatkowska, M., Parker, D.: Automated learning of probabilistic assumptions for compositional reasoning. In: Giannakopoulou, D., Orejas, F. (eds.) FASE 2011. LNCS, vol. 6603, pp. 2–17. Springer, Heidelberg (2011). doi:10.1007/978-3-642-19811-3_2

22. Giannakopoulou, D., Rakamarić, Z., Raman, V.: Symbolic learning of component interfaces. In: Miné, A., Schmidt, D. (eds.) SAS 2012. LNCS, vol. 7460, pp. 248–264. Springer, Heidelberg (2012). doi:10.1007/978-3-642-33125-1_18

23. Grumberg, O., Meller, Y.: Learning-based compositional model checking of behavioral UML systems. Dependable Softw. Syst. Eng. 45, 117 (2016)

24. Hagerer, A., Hungar, H., Niese, O., Steffen, B.: Model generation by moderated regular extrapolation. In: Kutsche, R.-D., Weber, H. (eds.) FASE 2002. LNCS, vol. 2306, pp. 80–95. Springer, Heidelberg (2002). doi:10.1007/3-540-45923-5_6

25. He, F., Gao, X., Wang, B., Zhang, L.: Leveraging weighted automata in compositional reasoning about concurrent probabilistic systems. In: POPL, pp. 503–514 (2015)

26. Howar, F., Giannakopoulou, D., Rakamarić, Z.: Hybrid learning: interface generation through static, dynamic, and symbolic analysis. In: ISSTA, pp. 268–279 (2013)

27. Howar, F., Steffen, B., Jonsson, B., Cassel, S.: Inferring canonical register automata. In: Kuncak, V., Rybalchenko, A. (eds.) VMCAI 2012. LNCS, vol. 7148, pp. 251–266. Springer, Heidelberg (2012). doi:10.1007/978-3-642-27940-9_17

28. Isberner, M., Howar, F., Steffen, B.: Learning register automata: from languages to program structures. Mach. Learn. **96**(1–2), 65–98 (2014)

29. Isberner, M., Howar, F., Steffen, B.: The open-source LearnLib. In: Kroening, D., Păsăreanu, C.S. (eds.) CAV 2015. LNCS, vol. 9206, pp. 487–495. Springer, Cham (2015). doi:10.1007/978-3-319-21690-4_32

30. Kearns, M.J., Vazirani, U.V.: An Introduction to Computational Learning Theory. MIT Press, Cambridge (1994)

31. Lee, C.S., Jones, N.D., Ben-Amram, A.M.: The size-change principle for program termination. In: POPL, pp. 81–92 (2001)

32. Li, Y., Chen, Y., Zhang, L., Liu, D.: A novel learning algorithm for Büchi automata based on family of DFAs and classification trees. CoRR, abs/1610.07380 (2016)

33. Lin, S.-W., André, E., Liu, Y., Sun, J., Dong, J.S.: Learning assumptions for compositional verification of timed systems. IEEE Trans. Softw. Eng. **40**(2), 137–153 (2014)

34. Maler, O., Staiger, L.: On syntactic congruences for ω-languages. In: Enjalbert, P., Finkel, A., Wagner, K.W. (eds.) STACS 1993. LNCS, vol. 665, pp. 586–594. Springer, Heidelberg (1993). doi:10.1007/3-540-56503-5_58

35. Peled, D., Vardi, M.Y., Yannakakis, M.: Black box checking. J. Automata Lang. Comb. **7**(2), 225–246 (2002)

36. Rivest, R.L., Schapire, R.E.: Inference of finite automata using homing sequences. In: STOC, pp. 411–420 (1989)

37. Sun, J., Xiao, H., Liu, Y., Lin, S.-W., Qin, S.: TLV: abstraction through testing, learning, and validation. In: FSE, pp. 698–709 (2015)

38. Tsay, Y.-K., Tsai, M.-H., Chang, J.-S., Chang, Y.-W.: Büchi store: an open repository of Büchi automata. In: Abdulla, P.A., Leino, K.R.M. (eds.) TACAS 2011. LNCS, vol. 6605, pp. 262–266. Springer, Heidelberg (2011). doi:10.1007/978-3-642-19835-9_23

39. Vardi, M.Y., Wolper, P.: An automata-theoretic approach to automatic program verification. In: LICS, pp. 322–331 (1986)

40. Wang, F., Wu, J.-H., Huang, C.-H., Chang, K.-H.: Evolving a test oracle in black-box testing. In: Giannakopoulou, D., Orejas, F. (eds.) FASE 2011. LNCS, vol. 6603, pp. 310–325. Springer, Heidelberg (2011). doi:10.1007/978-3-642-19811-3_22

41. Xiao, H., Sun, J., Liu, Y., Lin, S.-W., Sun, C.: Tzuyu: learning stateful typestates. In: ASE, pp. 432–442 (2013)

Synthesis I

Hierarchical Network Formation Games

Orna Kupferman[1(✉)] and Tami Tamir[2]

[1] School of Engineering and Computer Science, Hebrew University,
Jerusalem, Israel
orna@cs.huji.ac.il
[2] School of Computer Science, The Interdisciplinary Center,
Herzliya, Israel
tami@idc.ac.il

Abstract. Classical *network-formation games* (NFGs) are played on directed graphs, and are used in network design and analysis. Edges in the network are associated with costs and players have reachability objectives, which they try to fulfill at a minimal cost. When several players use the same edge, they share its cost. The theoretical and practical aspects of NFGs have been extensively studied and are well understood. All studies of NFGs, however, consider an *explicit* representation of the network. In practice, networks are often built in a *hierarchical* manner. Technically, some of the vertices in the network are *boxes*, associated with nested sub-networks, where a sub-network may be "called" by several boxes in the network. This makes hierarchical networks exponentially more succinct than traditional "flat" networks.

We introduce *hierarchical network formation games* (HNFGs) and study theoretical and practical aspects of the hierarchical setting. Different applications call for different cost-sharing mechanisms, which define how edge-formation costs are shared by their users. Indeed, in some applications, cost sharing should refer to the flat expansion of the network and in some it should take into account the hierarchical structure of the network. We study properties of HNFGs like stability and equilibrium inefficiency in the different mechanisms. We also study computational aspects of HNFGs, where the principal question is whether their exponential succinctness with respect to NFGs leads to an exponential increase in the complexity of reasoning about them. This question is analogous to research done in the formal-verification community about the ability to model-check hierarchical systems in their succinct presentation. We show that the picture is diverse and depends on the mechanism applied.

1 Introduction

Network design is a fundamental well-studied problem. A game-theoretic approach to network design has become especially relevant with the emergence of

The research leading to this paper has received funding from the European Research Council (FP7/2007-2013)/ERC grant agreement No. 278410, and from The Israel Science Foundation (grant No. 1229/10). Due to lack of space, some proofs are omitted and can be found in the full version in the authors' URLs.

A. Legay and T. Margaria (Eds.): TACAS 2017, Part I, LNCS 10205, pp. 229–246, 2017.
DOI: 10.1007/978-3-662-54577-5_13

the Internet, where different users share resources like software or communication channels [1,7,18,21]. In *network-formation games* (NFGs, for short) [7], the network is modeled by a weighted directed graph. The weight of an edge indicates the cost of activating the transition it models, which is independent of the number of times the edge is used. Players have reachability objectives, each given by a source and a target vertex. A strategy for a player is a path from the source to the target. Under the common fair cost-sharing mechanism, the cost of an edge is shared evenly by the players that use it.

Since the players attempt to minimize their own costs, rather than to optimize some global objective, they *selfishly* select a path instead of being assigned one by a central authority. The focus in game theory is on the *stable* outcomes of a given setting. The most prominent stability concept is that of a Nash equilibrium (NE): a profile (vector of strategies, one for each player) such that no player can decrease his cost by unilaterally deviating from his current strategy; that is, assuming that the strategies of the other players do not change.[1] A *best-response* (BR) for a player is a move that results in a profile with a reduced cost for the player. Thus, an NE can be viewed as a profile in which no player has a BR move. A *social optimum* (SO) is a profile that minimizes the total cost of the edges used by all players; thus the one obtained when the players obey some centralized authority.

Research on NFGs involves conceptual questions about them, like the existence of an NE or an analysis of *equilibrium inefficiency*. It is well known that decentralized decision-making may lead to solutions that are sub-optimal from the point of view of society as a whole. The inefficiency incurred due to selfish behavior is reflected in the *price of stability* (PoS) [7], namely the ratio between the costs of the best NE and the SO, and the *price of anarchy* (PoA) [26,33], namely the ratio between the costs of the worst NE and the SO. Research also concerns computational problems, like finding an SO, BR moves, and an NE. In NFGs, the picture is well understood. Every NFG has an NE; In a k-player game, the PoS and PoA are $O(\log k)$ and k, respectively; the problem of finding an SO is NP-complete, a single best-response move can be found in polynomial time; and the problem of finding an NE is PLS-complete [24,31,37].

To the best of our knowledge, all studies of NFGs consider an *explicit* representation of the network: it is given by means of its underlying weighted graph, and reasoning about it involves algorithms applied to explicitly-represented graphs. In practice, however, networks are often structured and given in some succinct presentation. This calls for a fresh examination of NFGs. First, the source for the succinctness may require new and more suitable cost-sharing mechanisms. In addition, the computational aspects of NFGs should be examined in terms of their succinct presentation.

In this paper we introduce and study *hierarchical network formation games* (HNFGs). Essentially, HNFGs are NFGs in which some of the vertices in the

---

[1] Throughout this paper, we consider *pure* strategies, as is the case for the vast literature on cost-sharing games. Unlike mixed strategies, pure strategies may not be random, or drawn from a distribution.

network may "call" (that is, be substituted by) nested sub-networks. Since a sub-network may be called by several vertices in the network, an HNFG may be exponentially more succinct than the NFG obtained by its "flattening".

Before we describe HNFGs and the challenges they bring with them in more detail, let us survey briefly the analogous research in *model checking*, where the study of succinct presentations and symbolic algorithms is a major research area. In model checking, we verify that a system meets its specification by translating the system to a finite state machine (FSM), translating the specification to a temporal-logic formula, and checking that the FSM satisfies the formula [17]. The translation of a high-level description of a system to an FSM involves a blow-up, and the size of the FSM is typically the computational bottleneck in model-checking algorithms. There are several sources of the blow-up that the translation of systems to FSMs involves. One is the ability of components in the system to work in parallel and communicate with each other, possibly using variables [19,20,34]. Another source has to do with the ability of a high-level description of a system to reuse the same component in different contexts (say, by calling a procedure). Researchers have studied *hierarchical FSMs*, in which some of the states of the FSM are boxes, which correspond to nested FSMs. The naive approach to model checking such systems is to "flatten" them. This, however, may involve an exponential blow up in the state space. In [5], it is shown that for LTL model checking, one can avoid this blow-up altogether, whereas for CTL, one can trade it for an exponential blow-up in the (often much smaller) size of the formula and the maximal number of exits of sub-structures. Likewise, it is shown in [6] that hierarchical parity games can be solved in PSPACE, also leading to a PSPACE model checking algorithm for the μ-calculus. In other words, while hierarchical FSMs are exponentially more succinct than flat FSMs [4], in many cases the complexity of the model-checking problem is not exponentially higher in the hierarchical setting. Thus, there is clear motivation not to flatten the FSM before model checking it. The hierarchical setting is appealing in the context of network design, as many networks are structured in a hierarchical manner.[2] In addition, understanding which types of problems can be solved in the hierarchical setting is of general interest to the formal-verification community.

The fact that box-vertices may be "called" by several vertices in the network motivates new cost-sharing mechanisms – ones that take the hierarchy into account when defining how edge-formation costs are shared by their users. We suggest three different cost-sharing mechanisms. In the *flat* mechanism, the hierarchical structure is flattened and the costs refer to the resulting network. The flat mechanism corresponds to the traditional setting of NFGs, and is suitable

---

[2] We note that different types of hierarchies, mainly ones that refer to a partition of the network to levels, have already been studied. In particular, in [35,36], it is shown how these levels induce a hierarchical game (also termed "hierarchical NFG", but with the adjective "hierarchical" describing the game rather than the network), leading to a clever decomposition of the game. Our notion of hierarchy is different and refers to nesting of sub-networks. In particular, in earlier work there is no notion of a flat extension, which is the key issue in our games.

in applications in which the traversal of edges corresponds to the utilization of consumable resources. For example, when the network models a hardware design that is built from a library of components, or when the network models a communication system in which local routing is performed by local networks that are composed into a global one. In the *hierarchical* approach, the cost of forming an edge in a sub-network is charged only once, regardless of the number of times it is used in different calls. The hierarchical approach is suitable in applications in which the traversal of edges corresponds to the utilization of non-consumable resources. Thus, repeated calls to a resource do not require its re-formation. For example, when the network models a software design that is built from a library of procedures and functions. The emergence of the OOP programming paradigm makes the hierarchical approach common [27,30]. In this approach, we study both a *uniform hierarchical* (UH) cost-sharing mechanism, where all players that use an edge share its cost evenly, and a *proportional hierarchical* (PH) cost-sharing mechanism, where the cost of an edge is shared among its users in proportion to their demand: each player may use each sub-network a different number of times. In the PH mechanism, this number influences the cost of using the sub-network. Note that the PH mechanism is related to a resource-allocation game in which players' strategies are *multisets* of resources [9,10].

After introducing HNFGs and the possible cost-sharing mechanisms, we study stability and equilibrium inefficiency in the different mechanisms. In particular, we show that while in HNFGs with the flat or UH mechanism, an NE always exists, this is not the case for the PH mechanism. Likewise, while the PoS and PoA in HNFGs with the flat or UH mechanisms agree with these known for NFGs, HNFGs with the PH mechanism are less stable, and we prove that their PoS may be the number of players. Then, we study the computational aspects of HNFG. The main questions that we answer refer to the ability to reason about an HNFG without first flattening it, which may involve an exponential blow-up. This question is analogous to research done in the formal-verification community about the ability to model-check hierarchical FSMs in their succinct presentation. We observe that the challenge of efficient reasoning about HNFGs starts already with a symbolic presentation of strategies. For the UH and PH mechanisms, we prove that it is sound to restrict attention to *homogeneous* strategies. Intuitively, in such strategies, repeated sub-objectives defined with respect to nested sub-networks are fulfilled in the same way. We show that homogeneous strategies can be represented and operated efficiently. This implies that the problems of finding an SO or a BR move in HNFGs is in NP, and we show matching lower bounds, already for very restricted classes of HNFGs. For the flat mechanism, we focus on HNFGs in which each sub-network has a constant number of exit vertices. We show that for such HNFGs, the problems of finding an SO or an NE are not more complex than these in the non-hierarchical setting.

Many variants of cost-sharing games have been studied. A generalization of the network-formation game of [7] in which players are weighted and a player's share in an edge cost is proportional to its weight is considered in [16], where it is shown that the weighted game does not necessarily have a pure NE. In *congestion games*, sharing of a resource increases its cost. Studied variants of congestion games include settings in which players' payments depend on the resource they choose to use, the set of players using this resource, or both [22,28,29,32]. In some of these variants a pure NE is guaranteed to exist while in others it is not. The three different ideas behind cost sharing, namely flat, UH, and PH, can be combined with other games.

We view this work as another chain in an exciting transfer of concepts and ideas between the areas of game theory and formal verification: logics for specifying multi-agent systems [3,14], studies of equilibria in games related to synthesis and repair problems [2,12,13,23], an extension of NFGs to objectives that are richer than reachability [9], studies of non-zero-sum games in formal methods [11,15], augmentation of the problem of synthesis from component libraries with costs [8], and more.

2 Preliminaries

2.1 Hierarchical Graphs

A *weighted graph* is $G = \langle V, E, c \rangle$, where V is a set of *vertices*, $E \subseteq V \times V$ is a set of *directed edges*, and $c : E \to \mathbb{R}_{\geq 0}$ is a *cost function* that maps each edge to a non-negative cost. When $c(e) = 0$, we say that e is *free*. A path in G is a sequence $\rho = e_1, e_2, \ldots, e_m$ of adjacent edges in G. For two vertices $s, t \in V$, we say that ρ is an (s, t)-path if it connects s to t.

A *hierarchical graph* consists of a vector of subgraphs that together compose a graph. A subgraph may be used several times in the composition. Technically, this is done via special vertices, called *boxes*, that are substituted in the composition by other subgraphs. In order to ensure a finite nesting depth of substitutions, the subgraphs are indexed, and a box of a graph can only *call* (that is, be substituted by) subgraphs with a strictly bigger index. Formally, a hierarchical graph is a tuple $\mathcal{G} = \langle G_1, \ldots, G_n \rangle$, where each subgraph is $G_j = \langle V_j, B_j, in_j, Exit_j, \tau_j, E_j \rangle$, where V_j and B_j are sets of vertices and boxes, respectively. We assume that $B_n = \emptyset$ and that $V_1, \ldots, V_n, B_1, \ldots, B_{n-1}$ are pairwise disjoint. Then, $in_j \in V_j$ is an entry vertex for G_j, and $Exit_j \subseteq V_j$ is a set of exit vertices for G_j. The function $\tau_j : B_j \to \{j+1, \ldots, n\}$ maps each box of G_j to an index greater than j. If $\tau_j(b) = \ell$, we say that the box b is substituted by G_ℓ in G_j. Finally, E_j is an edge relation. Each edge in E_j is a pair $\langle u, v \rangle$ with source u and target v. The source u is either a vertex of G_j, or a pair (b, x), where $b \in B_j$ and $x \in Exit_{\tau_j(b)}$. That is, u may be a box b coupled with an exit vertex of the subgraph by which b is about to be substituted. The target v is a vertex or a box of G_j. Formally, $E_j \subseteq (V_j \cup (\bigcup_{b \in B_j} (\{b\} \times Exit_{\tau_j(b)}))) \times (V_j \cup B_j)$. The *depth* of $\mathcal{G}$ is the number n of subgraphs. A *weighted hierarchical graph* is a hierarchical graph with cost functions $c_j : E_j \to \mathbb{R}_{\geq 0}$ that map the edges in each subgraph to costs.

A subgraph without boxes is *flat*. Every hierarchical graph can be transformed to an equivalent flat graph, referred to as its *flat expansion*, by recursively substituting each box by a copy of the corresponding subgraph. Formally, given a hierarchical graph $\mathcal{G}$, we inductively define for each subgraph G_j its flat expansion $G_j^f = \langle V_j^f, in_j, Exit_j, E_j^f \rangle$, where $V_j^f = V_j \cup (\bigcup_{b \in B_j} (\{b\} \times V_{\tau_j(b)}^f))$. Note that different boxes in G_j can be substituted by the same subgraph. This is why we preserve b as an identifier when we substitute it by the flat expansion of $\tau_j(b)$. The edge relation E_j^f includes the following edges, which we partition into four classes.

- **[Top]:** $\langle u, v \rangle$ such that $u, v \in V_j$ and $\langle u, v \rangle \in E_j$,
- **[Call]:** $\langle u, (b, v) \rangle$ such that $u \in V_j$, $v = in_{\tau_j(b)}$, and $\langle u, b \rangle \in E_j$,
- **[Return]:** $\langle (b, u), v \rangle$ such that $u \in Exit_{\tau_j(b)}$, $v \in V_j$, and $\langle (b, u), v \rangle \in E_j$, and
- **[Internal]:** $\langle (b, u), (b, v) \rangle$ such that $u, v \in V_{\tau_j(b)}^f$ and $\langle u, v \rangle \in E_{\tau_j(b)}^f$.

Note that each edge in E_j^f originates from an edge $\langle u, v \rangle \in E_{j'}$ for some $j' \geq j$. Indeed, in top, call, and return edges, we have that $j' = j$, and in internal edges, we have that j' is the subgraph from which the edge $\langle u, v \rangle$ originates (recursively) in $E_{\tau_j(b)}^f$. Formally, let $E = \bigcup_{1 \leq j \leq n} E_j$ and $E^f = \bigcup_{1 \leq j \leq n} E_j^f$. Then, the function $orig : E^f \to E$ is defined recursively as follows. For a top edge $e = \langle u, v \rangle$ or a return edge $e = \langle (b, u), v \rangle$, we have $orig(e) = e$. For a call edge $e = \langle u, (b, v) \rangle$, we have $orig(e) = \langle u, b \rangle$. Then, for an internal edge $e = \langle (b, u), (b, v) \rangle$, we have $orig(e) = orig(\langle u, v \rangle)$. The graph G_1^f is the flat expansion of $\mathcal{G}$, and we denote it by $\mathcal{G}^f$. For an edge e in $\mathcal{G}^f$, we refer to $orig(e)$ as the *origin* of e in $\mathcal{G}^f$. Consider a path $\rho = e_1, e_2, \ldots, e_m$ in $\mathcal{G}^f$. For a set $\pi \subseteq E$ of edges in $\mathcal{G}$, we say that ρ is *covered by* π if for all $1 \leq i \leq m$, we have $orig(e_i) \in \pi$.

A *multiset* over a set E of elements is a generalization of a subset of E in which each element may appear more than once. For a multiset π over E and an element $e \in E$, we use $\pi(e)$ to denote the number of times e appears in π. For two multisets π_1 and π_2, the union of π_1 and π_2 is the multiset $\pi_1 \cup \pi_2$ in which for all $e \in E$, we have $(\pi_1 \cup \pi_2)(e) = \pi_1(e) + \pi_2(e)$. Then, the difference between p_1 and p_2 is the multiset $\pi_1 \setminus \pi_2$ in which for all $e \in E$, we have $(\pi_1 \setminus \pi_2)(e) = \max\{0, \pi_1(e) - \pi_2(e)\}$. A multiset π is given as a set of its members, with each member e followed by a binary (or decimal) encoding of $\pi(e)$. Accordingly, we define the length of π by $\sum_{e \in \pi} \log \pi(e)$. Consider a path $\rho = e_1, e_2, \ldots, e_m$ in $\mathcal{G}^f$ and a multiset π over E; that is, π is a multiset of edges in $\mathcal{G}$. We say that ρ is *covered by* π if for every edge $e \in E$, the number of edges in ρ whose origin is e is at most the number of times that e appears in π. Formally, for every $e \in E$, we have that $|\{1 \leq i \leq m : orig(e_i) = e\}| \leq \pi(e)$.

Example 1. Figure 1 presents a weighted hierarchical graph $\mathcal{G} = \langle G_1, G_2 \rangle$ with $\tau_1(b_1) = \tau_1(b_2) = G_2$. The flat expansion $\mathcal{G}^f$ of $\mathcal{G}$ appears on the right.

The path $\rho = \langle s, (b_1, u_1) \rangle, \langle (b_1, u_1), (b_1, u_2) \rangle, \langle (b_1, u_2), (b_1, u_4) \rangle, \langle (b_1, u_4), (b_2, u_1) \rangle, \langle (b_2, u_1), (b_2, u_2) \rangle, \langle (b_2, u_2), (b_2, u_4) \rangle, \langle (b_2, u_4), t_2 \rangle$ in $\mathcal{G}^f$ is covered by the set $\pi = \{\langle s, b_1 \rangle, \langle (b_1, u_4), b_2 \rangle, \langle (b_2, u_4), t_2 \rangle, \langle u_1, u_2 \rangle, \langle u_2, u_4 \rangle\}$. Note that each of the edges $\langle s, b_1 \rangle$, $\langle (b_1, u_4), b_2 \rangle$, and $\langle (b_2, u_4), t_2 \rangle$ in π serve as the origin of a single edge in ρ, whereas each of the edges $\langle u_1, u_2 \rangle$ and $\langle u_2, u_4 \rangle$ serve as the origin of two edges in ρ. Accordingly, ρ is covered by the multiset $\pi = \{\langle s, b_1 \rangle^1, \langle (b_1, u_4), b_2 \rangle^1, \langle (b_2, u_4), t_2 \rangle^1, \langle u_1, u_2 \rangle^2, \langle u_2, u_4 \rangle^2\}$.

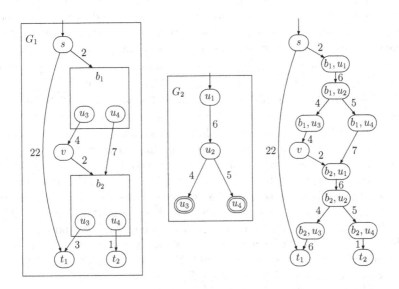

Fig. 1. An example of a hierarchical graph and its flat expansion.

We define the size of a hierarchical graph $\mathcal{G}$ by $|\mathcal{G}| = \sum_{j=1}^{n}(|V_j| + |B_j|)$. The size of its flat expansion, denoted $|\mathcal{G}^f|$, is the number of vertices in $|\mathcal{G}^f|$. Note that $|\mathcal{G}^f| = \sum_{j=1}^{n}(|V_j| + \sum_{b \in B_j} |G^f_{\tau_j(b)}|)$. It is not hard to see that the hierarchical setting is exponentially more succinct. Formally, we have the following.

Observation 1. *Flattening a hierarchical graph may involve an exponential blow up. That is, $\mathcal{G}^f$ may be exponentially larger than $\mathcal{G}$. In fact, the exponential blow-up applies already to the diameter of the graph, and applies even when all the subgraphs in $\mathcal{G}$ have a single exit vertex.*

2.2   Network Formation Games

For an integer $k \in \mathbb{N}$, let $[k] = \{1, \ldots, k\}$. A *network-formation game* (NFG, for short) [7] is $\mathcal{N} = \langle k, G, \langle s_i, t_i \rangle_{i \in [k]} \rangle$, where k is the number of players, $G = \langle V, E, c \rangle$ is a weighted graph, and for each $i \in [k]$, the pair $\langle s_i, t_i \rangle \in V \times V$ describes the objective of Player i, namely forming a path from his source vertex s_i to his target vertex t_i.

A *strategy* of a player $i \in [k]$ is a path from s_i to t_i. A *profile* in $\mathcal{N}$ is a tuple $P = \langle \pi_1, \ldots, \pi_k \rangle$ of strategies for the players. That is, for $1 \leq i \leq k$, we have that π_i is a path from s_i to t_i. Consider a profile $P = \langle \pi_1, \ldots, \pi_k \rangle$. Recall that c maps each edge to a cost, intuitively standing for the cost of its formation. The players aim at fulfilling their objective with minimal cost. Since all costs are positive, we can restrict attention to strategies in which the paths chosen by the players are simple. Then, we can also ignore the order between edges in the paths and assume that for all $i \in [k]$, we have that $\pi_i \subseteq E$ is a set of edges that compose a path from s_i to t_i. For an edge $e \in E$, we denote the number of players that use e in P by $load_P(e)$. Formally, $load_P(e) = |\{i : e \in \pi_i\}|$. Players that share an edge also share its formation cost. Thus, the cost of Player i in the profile P is $cost_i(P) = \sum_{e \in \pi_i} \frac{c(e)}{load_P(e)}$. Finally, the cost of a profile P is the sum of the costs of all the players in P. Thus, $cost(P) = \sum_{i \in [k]} cost_i(P)$. Note that $cost(P)$ is equal to the sum of costs of edges that participate in some strategy in P.

For a profile P and a strategy π of player $i \in [k]$, let $[P_{-i}, \pi]$ denote the profile obtained from P by replacing the strategy for Player i by π. For two strategies π_i and π'_i of Player i, we say that π_i is *dominated by* π'_i, if for every profile P in which Player i uses π_i, we have that $cost_i([P_{-i}, \pi'_i]) \leq cost_i(P)$. A *best response* (BR) for Player i is a strategy π_i that minimizes $cost_i([P_{-i}, \pi_i])$. A profile P is said to be a *(pure) Nash equilibrium* (NE) if none of the players in $[k]$ can benefit from an unilateral deviation from his strategy in P to another strategy. In other words, for every player i and every strategy π that Player i can deviate to from his current strategy in P, it holds that $cost_i([P_{-i}, \pi]) \geq cost_i(P)$. The set of NEs of the game $\mathcal{N}$ is denoted by $\Gamma(\mathcal{N})$.

A *social optimum* (SO) of a game $\mathcal{N}$ is a profile that attains the lowest cost. We denote by $OPT(\mathcal{N})$ the cost of an SO profile; i.e., $OPT(\mathcal{N}) = \min_P cost(P)$. A social optimum may be achieved by a centralized authority and need not be a NE. The following parameters measure the inefficiency caused as a result of the selfish interests of the players. First, the *price of stability* (PoS) [7] of an NFG $\mathcal{N}$ is the ratio between the minimal cost of an NE and the cost of a social optimum of $\mathcal{N}$. That is, $PoS(\mathcal{N}) = \min_{P \in \Gamma(\mathcal{N})} cost(P)/OPT(\mathcal{N})$. Then, the *price of anarchy* (PoA) [33] of $\mathcal{N}$ is the ratio between the maximal cost of an NE and the cost of the social optimum of $\mathcal{N}$. That is, $PoA(\mathcal{N}) = \max_{P \in \Gamma(\mathcal{N})} cost(P)/OPT(\mathcal{N})$.

2.3 Hierarchical Network Formation Games

A *hierarchical network-formation game* (HNFG, for short) $\mathcal{N} = \langle k, \mathcal{G}, \langle s_i, t_i \rangle_{i \in [k]} \rangle$, is similar to an NFG, except that the underlying graph is hierarchical. The objective of Player i is to form a path from s_i to t_i in the flat expansion of $\mathcal{G}$. We assume that the objectives of all players are in $\{in_1\} \times Exit_1$, for the entry vertex in_1 and the set $Exit_1$ of exit vertices in the "outer" subgraph G_1. While this strictly restricts the class of games, it is very easy to extend our results to a setting in which the objectives involve arbitrary vertices in $\mathcal{G}$. Essentially, our algorithms proceed from the innermost sub-graph G_n to G_1. The assumption above saves a special treatment for G_1.

We introduce and study three cost-sharing mechanisms for HNFGs. Consider an HNFG $\mathcal{N} = \langle k, \mathcal{G}, \langle s_i, t_i \rangle_{i \in [k]} \rangle$. Let $\mathcal{G} = \langle G_1, \ldots, G_n \rangle$, with

$G_j = \langle V_j, B_j, in_j, Exit_j, \tau_j, E_j, c_j \rangle$. Also, let $\mathcal{N}^f = \langle k, \mathcal{G}^f, \langle s_i, t_i \rangle_{i \in [k]} \rangle$ be the NFG obtained from $\mathcal{N}$ by replacing $\mathcal{G}$ by its flat expansion.

The Flat Cost-Sharing Mechanism. In the flat cost-sharing mechanism (Flat-mechanism, for short), the strategies and the costs of the players are defined with respect to $\mathcal{N}^f$. Thus, the only affect of the hierarchical structure in the flat approach is its succinctness. The flat mechanism fits settings in which the traversal of edges corresponds to the formation of physical channels or the utilization of consumable resources. For example, when the network models a hardware design that should be built from a library of components.

Consider, for example, the graph $\mathcal{G} = \langle G_1, G_2 \rangle$ in Fig. 1. Let $\mathcal{N} = \langle 2, \mathcal{G}, \{\langle s, t_1 \rangle, \langle s, t_2 \rangle\} \rangle$. Then, the game is played on the flat graph $\mathcal{G}^f$ on the right. Consider the profile $P = \langle \pi_1, \pi_2 \rangle$ in which Player 1 takes the path that traverses both boxes and in both calls to G_2 takes the u_3 exit, and Player 2 takes the path that traverses both boxes and in both calls to G_2 takes the u_4 exit. Then, the players share the edges $\langle s, (b_1, u_1) \rangle$, $\langle (b_1, u_1), (b_1, u_2) \rangle$, and $\langle (b_2, u_1), (b_2, u_2) \rangle$. Accordingly, $cost_1(P) = \frac{2}{2} + \frac{6}{2} + 4 + 4 + 2 + \frac{6}{2} + 4 + 3 = 24$ and $cost_2(P) = \frac{2}{2} + \frac{6}{2} + 5 + 7 + \frac{6}{2} + 5 + 1 = 25$. This is not a stable profile, as Player 1 can reduce his cost to 22 by deviating to the edge $\langle s, t_1 \rangle$. Also, Player 2 can join Player 1 in the first box and reduce his cost to $\frac{2}{2} + \frac{6}{2} + \frac{4}{2} + \frac{4}{2} + \frac{2}{2} + \frac{6}{2} + 5 + 1 = 18$. Note that this deviation also reduces the cost of Player 1, to 19.

The Uniform Hierarchical Cost-Sharing Mechanism. Recall that $E = \bigcup_{1 \le j \le n} E_j$. In the uniform hierarchical (UH) cost-sharing mechanism, a strategy for Player i is a set $\pi_i \subseteq E$ of edges in the hierarchical graph $\mathcal{G}$ such that π_i covers a path from s_i to t_i in $\mathcal{G}^f$. Players' costs in a profile $P = \langle \pi_1, \ldots, \pi_k \rangle$ are defined as follows: For a subgraph G_j and an edge $e \in E_j$, we define the load on e, denoted $load_P(e)$, as the number of strategies in P that include e. Thus, $load_P(e) = |\{i \in [k] : e \in \pi_i\}|$. The cost of an edge is shared evenly by the players that use it. Thus, the cost of Player i in P is $cost_i(P) = \sum_{e \in \pi_i} \frac{c(e)}{load_P(e)}$.

The UH mechanism corresponds to settings in which the traversal of edges corresponds to the utilization of non-consumable resources. Thus, repeated calls to the resource do not require its re-formation. For example, when the network models a software design that should be build from a library of components. In the uniform sharing rule, we care for the binary information of whether or not a player has used the resource, and we do not distinguish between light and heavy users of the resource.

Consider again the HNFG $\mathcal{N}$, now with the UH mechanism. Let $P = \langle \pi_1, \pi_2 \rangle$ be the profile in which Player 1 takes the path that traverses both boxes and in both calls to G_2 takes the u_3 exit, and Player 2 takes the path that traverses both boxes and in both calls to G_2 takes the u_4 exit. Thus, $\pi_1 = \{\langle s, b_1 \rangle, \langle (b_1, u_3), v \rangle, \langle v, b_2 \rangle, \langle (b_2, u_3), t_1 \rangle, \langle u_1, u_2 \rangle, \langle u_2, u_3 \rangle\}$ and $\pi_2 = \{\langle s, b_1 \rangle, \langle (b_1, u_4), b_2 \rangle, \langle (b_2, u_4), t_2 \rangle, \langle u_1, u_2 \rangle, \langle u_2, u_4 \rangle\}$. The load on $\langle s, b_1 \rangle$ and $\langle u_1, u_2 \rangle$ is 2, and the load on all other edges used in P is 1. Accordingly, $cost_1(P) = \frac{2}{2} + 4 + 2 + 3 + \frac{6}{2} + 4 = 17$ and $cost_2(P) = \frac{2}{2} + 7 + 1 + \frac{6}{2} + 5 = 17$.

Now, Player 1 has no incentive to deviate to $\langle s, t_1 \rangle$. However, P is not a NE as Player 2 can join Player 1 in the first box and reduce his cost. Indeed, let $\pi_2' = \{\langle s, b_1 \rangle, \langle (b_1, u_3), v \rangle, \langle v, b_2 \rangle, \langle (b_2, u_4), t_2 \rangle, \langle u_1, u_2 \rangle, \langle u_2, u_3 \rangle, \langle u_2, u_4 \rangle\}$. Then, in the profile $P' = \langle \pi_1, \pi_2' \rangle$, we have that $cost_2(P') = \frac{2}{2} + \frac{4}{2} + \frac{2}{2} + 1 + \frac{6}{2} + \frac{4}{2} + 5 = 15$. Note that Player 1 also benefits from this move, as $cost_1(P') = 12$. This example demonstrates that, even-though players have incentive to use an edge multiple times, the optimal strategy of a player in a subgraph G_i need not induce a single path from in_i to some vertex in $Exit_i$. Rather, it is sometimes beneficial for the players to pay for accessing several exit vertices.

The Proportional Hierarchical Cost-Sharing Mechanism. Like the UH mechanism, the proportional hierarchical (PH) cost-sharing mechanism corresponds to settings in which the traversal of edges corresponds to the utilization of a non-consumable resources. Here, however, we care for the number of times such resources are used by the players, as their costs are proportional to the use. In the PH mechanism, a strategy for Player i is a *multiset* π_i of edges in the hierarchical graph $\mathcal{G}$ such that π_i covers a path from s_i to t_i in $\mathcal{G}^f$. Players' costs in a profile $P = \langle \pi_1, \ldots, \pi_k \rangle$ are defined as follows: For a subgraph G_j and an edge $e \in E_j$, we define the weighted load on e, denoted $wload_P(e)$, as the number of times e appears in all the strategies in P. Recall that for a multiset π, we denote by $\pi(e)$ the number of times an element e appears in π. Then, $wload_P(e) = \sum_{i \in [k]} \pi_i(e)$, and the cost of Player i in P is $cost_i(P) = \sum_{e \in \pi_i} \frac{\pi_i(e) \cdot c(e)}{wload_P(e)}$.

Back to our example $\mathcal{N}$, the profile P with the PH mechanism consists of the strategies $\pi_1 = \{\langle s, b_1 \rangle^1, \langle u_1, u_2 \rangle^2, \langle u_2, u_3 \rangle^2, \langle (b_1, u_3), v \rangle^1, \langle v, b_2 \rangle^1, \langle (b_2, u_3), t_1 \rangle^1\}$ and $\pi_2 = \{\langle s, b_1 \rangle^1, \langle u_1, u_2 \rangle^2, \langle u_2, u_4 \rangle^2, \langle (b_1, u_4), b_2 \rangle^1, \langle (b_2, u_4), t_2 \rangle^1\}$. Now, $wload_P(\langle s, b_1 \rangle) = wload_P(\langle u_2, u_3 \rangle) = wload_P(\langle u_2, u_4 \rangle) = 2$, $wload_P(\langle u_1, u_2 \rangle) = 4$, and the weighted load on all other edges used in P is 1. Accordingly, every traversal of $\langle u_1, u_2 \rangle$ costs $\frac{6}{4}$, and similarly for the other edges. Hence, $cost_1(P) = \frac{2}{2} + 2 \cdot \frac{6}{4} + 4 + 4 + 2 + 3 = 17$ and $cost_2(P) = \frac{2}{2} + 2 \cdot \frac{6}{4} + 5 + 7 + 1 = 17$. While Player 1 has no incentive to deviate to $\langle s, t \rangle$, Player 2 can reduce his cost by deviating to a path that joins Player 1 in b_1. Indeed, let $\pi_2' = \{\langle s, b_1 \rangle^1, \langle u_1, u_2 \rangle^2, \langle u_2, u_3 \rangle^1, \langle (b_1, u_3), v \rangle^1, \langle v, b_2 \rangle^1, \langle u_2, u_4 \rangle^1, \langle (b_2, u_4), t_2 \rangle^1\}$. Then, in the profile $P' = \langle \pi_1, \pi_2' \rangle$, we have $wload_P(\langle v_1, b_1 \rangle) = 2$, $wload_P(\langle u_1, u_2 \rangle) = 4$, $wload_P(\langle u_2, u_3 \rangle) = 3$, $wload_P(\langle (b_1, u_3), v \rangle) = 2$, $wload_P(\langle v, b_2 \rangle) = 2$, and the weighted load on all other edges used in P is 1. Accordingly, $cost_2(P') = \frac{2}{2} + 2 \cdot \frac{6}{4} + \frac{4}{3} + \frac{4}{2} + \frac{2}{2} + 5 + 1 = 14\frac{1}{3}$. Note that Player 1 also benefits from this move, as $cost_1(P') = \frac{2}{2} + 2 \cdot \frac{6}{4} + 2 \cdot \frac{4}{3} + \frac{4}{2} + \frac{2}{2} + 3 = 12\frac{2}{3}$.

3   Stability Existence and Inefficiency

In this section we study the stability of HNFGs. We show that the cost-sharing mechanism is crucial in this analysis. Specifically, HNFGs with the Flat or the UH mechanism have an NE and their PoA and PoS are identical to the bounds known for NFGs. On the other hand, we show that even simple instances of

HNFGs with the PH mechanism need not have an NE, and there are games for which the only stable profile is k times more expensive than the SO.

We start with the stability existence question. The proof of the following theorem is based on converting every HNFG with the flat or the UH mechanism to an equivalent resource-allocation game, which is known to have an NE. As we show, the relation with resource-allocation games also induces potential functions for HNFGs in the flat and UH mechanisms.

Theorem 2. *Every HNFG with the flat or UH mechanism has an NE.*

For the PH mechanism, we present a negative result.

Theorem 3. *An HNFG with the PH mechanism need not have an NE.*

Proof. Consider the hierarchical graph $\mathcal{G} = \langle G_1, G_a, G_b, G_c \rangle$ depicted in Fig. 2. Let $\mathcal{N} = \langle 2, \mathcal{G}, \{\langle s, t_i \rangle\}_{i \in \{1,2\}} \rangle$. For every $\sigma \in \{a, b, c\}$, we have that $\tau_1(b_\sigma) = G_\sigma$. In the figure, edges that are not labeled are free. Thus, Player 1 needs to select in G_1 one of the two paths $\rho_1^1 = (s, b_a, b_c, t_1)$ and $\rho_1^2 = (s, b_b, t_1)$, and Player 2 needs to select one of two paths $\rho_2^1 = (s, b_a, b_a, b_a, t_2)$ and $\rho_2^2 = (s, b_c, b_a, b_a, t_2)$.

We show that $\mathcal{N}$ with the PH mechanism does not have an NE. Recall that a strategy for Player i is a multiset π_i over edges in $\mathcal{G}$ such that π_i covers a path from s to t_i in $\mathcal{G}^f$. Since all the edges in E_1 are free, we describe the players' strategies as multisets that include only the edges in the subgraphs G_a, G_b, and G_c. Denote by e_a, e_b, and e_c the (only) edge in G_a, G_b and G_c respectively. Thus, for Player 1, we have strategies $\pi_1^1 = \{e_a, e_c\}$ and $\pi_1^2 = \{e_b\}$, and for Player 2 we have $\pi_2^1 = \{e_a, e_a, e_a\}$ and $\pi_2^2 = \{e_c, e_a, e_a\}$.

Table 1 describes the players' costs in the four possible profiles. Note that $c(e_a) = 36, c(e_b) = 12$ and $c(e_c) = 2$. Consider for example the top left profile $P = \langle \pi_1^1, \pi_2^1 \rangle$. In this profile, the edge e_a is traversed four times, e_b is not traversed at all, and e_c is traversed once. Thus, $wload_P(e_a) = 4$. This implies that every traversal of e_a costs $c(e_a)/wload_P(e_a) = 36/4 = 9$. Since $wload_P(e_c) = 1$ and $e_c \in \pi_1^1$, Player 1 should also cover the cost of e_c. Hence, $cost_1(P) = 9 + 2 = 11$ and $cost_2(P) = 3 \cdot 9 = 27$. The players' costs in all other profiles are calculated in a similar way. The costs in the table imply that players benefit from changing strategies in counter clockwise direction, thus no NE exists. □

A natural question arising from the above theorem is whether we can distinguish between instances that have or do not have a stable profile. In the full version of this paper we show that we can do it in Σ_P^2, yet this is an NP-hard task.

We turn to analyze the equilibrium inefficiency. Once again, the fact that each HNFG with the flat or the UH mechanism has an equivalent resource-allocation cost-sharing game enables us to adopt the upper bounds known for resource-allocation games to our setting. Matching lower bounds then follow from the known bounds on NFGs and the fact that every NFG can be viewed as an HNFG with no nesting of subgraphs.

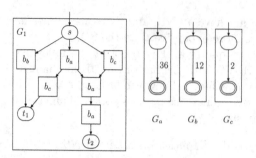

Table 1. Players' costs in $\mathcal{N}$ with the PH mechanism. Each entry describes the cost of Player 1 followed by the cost of Player 2.

	$\{e_a, e_c\}$	$\{e_b\}$
$\{e_a, e_a, e_a\}$	11, 27	12, 36
$\{e_c, e_a, e_a\}$	13, 25	12, 38

Fig. 2. An HNFG $\mathcal{N}$ that has no NE with the PH mechanism.

Theorem 4. *The PoS and PoA of k-player HNFGs with the flat or the UH mechanism are $O(\log k)$ and k, respectively.*

For the PH mechanism, we show that stability may came with a high cost, strictly higher than the one known for NFGs.

Theorem 5. *The PoS and PoA of k-player HNFGs with the PH mechanism are k.*

Proof. Similar to the analysis of many other cost-sharing games, PoA $\leq k$ as otherwise, some player in some NE profile P is paying more than the SO, and can benefit from deviating to his strategy in the SO, whose cost is not larger than the cost of the whole SO profile. This contradicts the stability of P. Combining the fact that PoA $\geq$ PoS, it is sufficient to show that PoS $\geq k$ in order to establish the tight bounds.

For every $k > 1$, we describe a k-player HNFG $\mathcal{N}_k$ such that the cost of the only NE in $\mathcal{N}_k$ is kM, for some large constant M, whereas the SO is $M + \epsilon''$, for a small constant ϵ''. Assume first that k is even. Partition the set $[k]$ of players into pairs $\langle 2\ell - 1, 2\ell \rangle$ for $1 \leq \ell \leq \frac{k}{2}$. Let $\mathcal{N}^\ell$ be a 2-player HNFG with no NE, with the costs of its edges multiplied by a small constant ϵ. In particular, we refer to the HNFG described in the proof of Theorem 3.

The HNFG $\mathcal{N}_k$ is played on the hierarchical graph $\mathcal{G} = \langle G_0, \{G_1^\ell, G_a^\ell, G_b^\ell, G_c^\ell\}_{1 \leq \ell \leq k/2} \rangle$, where G_0 is depicted in Fig. 3, and the other components consists of $k/2$ copies of the graphs G_1, G_a, G_b, and G_c, described in Fig. 2, with all costs multiplied by ϵ. The graph G_0 includes an edge $\langle s, t \rangle$ of cost kM, an edge $\langle s, v \rangle$ of cost M, and $k/2$ free edges $\langle v, s_\ell \rangle$ leading the copies G_1^ℓ for $1 \leq \ell \leq \frac{k}{2}$.

For simplicity, we assume that each player can choose between one of two targets. It is easy to see that this assumption can be removed by adding a new target connected from the two targets by free edges. Consider the ℓ-th pair of players. The target vertices of the first player in the pair are t and t_1^ℓ. The target vertices of the second player are t and t_2^ℓ. Thus, every player has three strategies: the path consisting of the edge $\langle s, t \rangle$ and the paths starting with s, v, s_ℓ and continuing with one of the two strategies in G_1^ℓ, as detailed in the proof of Theorem 3.

The SO of $\mathcal{N}_k$ consists of edges from the right side of the network: the edges $\langle s, v \rangle$, $\{\langle v, s_\ell \rangle_{1 \leq \ell \leq k/2}\}$, and edges forming an SO for each of the disjoint $\frac{k}{2}$ games (the latter consists of the edges e_a^ℓ, e_c^ℓ, and additional free edges from G_1^ℓ). The cost of the SO is then $M + \frac{\epsilon' k}{2}$, for $\epsilon' = 38\epsilon$.

We show that the only NE in $\mathcal{N}_k$ is the profile in which all the players share the edge $\langle s, t \rangle$. This profile is indeed an NE, as the cost of every player is exactly M, and by deviating to the right side of the network, a player must pay the cost of $\langle s, v \rangle$ plus the cost of his chosen path in some G_1^ℓ, which together exceeds M. Moreover, this is the only NE since in every other profile, players would benefit from leaving the edge $\langle s, t \rangle$ and reaching $\mathcal{N}^\ell$ – our familiar no-NE game described in the proof of Theorem 3. The cost of this NE profile is kM, implying that the PoS is $\frac{Mk}{M+19k\epsilon}$, which tends to k.

Finally, if the number k of players is odd, we define for the unpaired player two strategies: one is the path $\langle s, t \rangle$, and the other is a path s, v, u for a new vertex u. By setting to ϵ the cost of $\langle u, v \rangle$, it still holds that $\langle s, t \rangle$ is the only NE profile. The PoS for an odd k is therefore $\frac{Mk}{M+(19k+1)\epsilon}$, which tends to k.   □

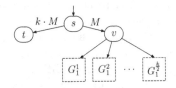

Fig. 3. An HNFG $\mathcal{N}_k$ for which PoS $= k$. Every G_1^ℓ is a copy of G_1 depicted in Fig. 2.

4   Computational Complexity

In this section we study the complexity of reasoning about HNFGs in the different cost-sharing mechanisms. The principal question is whether the exponential succinctness of HNFGs leads to an exponential increase in the complexity of reasoning about them.

4.1   The UH and PH Mechanisms

Recall that a strategy for Player i in the UH or PH mechanism is a set or a multiset π_i over E. A strategy is *feasible* if there is a path ρ from s_i to t_i in $\mathcal{G}^f$ such that ρ is covered by π_i. In traditional NFGs, it is easy to check in polynomial time whether a given set of edges is a feasible strategy. Indeed, there, the underlying graph is given explicitly. This is not the case in HNFGs: given π_i, a naive check that π_i indeed covers a path from s_i to t_i in $\mathcal{G}^f$ involves a construction of $\mathcal{G}^f$, which may be exponential in $\mathcal{G}$. An efficient checking that a given strategy π_i is feasible requires a clever encoding of π_i, involving a restriction to a subset of all possible strategies. We first define this subset and prove that it is dominating, that is, every Player has a best-response move to a homogeneous strategy.

Recall that π_i is feasible if there is a path ρ from s_i to t_i in $\mathcal{G}^f$ such that ρ is covered by π_i. The path ρ may traverse subgraphs G_j of $\mathcal{G}$ several times (in fact, per Observation 1, even exponentially many times). In each traversal, the path ρ may exit G_j through different exit vertices. For example, in the HNFGs described in Sect. 2.3, we showed that the players benefit from taking a strategy that exits G_2 from both u_3 and u_4. Thus, restricting attention to strategies in which all the traversals of G_j use the same exit vertex is not sound (and in fact may affect not only the cost of Player i but also cause t_i not to be reachable from s_i). Consider now two traversals of the subgraph G_j in which Player i chooses to exit G_j through the same exit vertex $u \in Exit_j$. Here too, Player i may choose to fulfill this repeated "nested sub-objective" in different ways. We say that a strategy for Player i is *homogeneous* if for every $j \in [n]$ and every $u \in Exit_j$, whenever Player i traverses the subgraph G_j through exit u it uses the same $\langle in_j, u \rangle$-path. We claim that restricting attention to homogeneous strategies is sound, and also leads to an efficient feasibility check. Intuitively, in the UH mechanism, the proof of the dominance is easy, as by repeating the same path a player can only reduce the set of edges in his strategy, which results in reduced payment. Thus, in the UH mechanism, the used $\langle in_j, u \rangle$-path can be chosen arbitrarily. In the PH mechanism, the proof is more involved, as moving to the chosen $\langle in_j, u \rangle$-path may increase the payment for other uses of this path. Accordingly, not all choices of a $\langle in_j, u \rangle$-path are beneficial. We show, however, that at least one choice is beneficial. In addition, checking the feasibility of homogeneous strategies requires only one check for each subgraph G_j and exit vertex $u \in Exit_j$, which can be done in polynomial time. Hence we have the following:

Lemma 1. *Consider an HNFG $\mathcal{N}$ with the UH or PH mechanism, and a player $i \in [k]$.*

1. *Every non-homogeneous strategy for Player i is dominated by a homogeneous one.*
2. *Checking that a homogeneous strategy of Player i is feasible can be done in polynomial time.*

We proceed to study the complexity of finding a BR and an SO in HNFGs with the UH or PH mechanism. For NFGs, a BR move can be found in polynomial time, and the problem of finding an SO is NP-complete [31]. For the lower bound, we show two reductions, both with a single-player HNFG. One, for the case the depth of the HNFG is a constant, is from the *directed Steiner tree* problem; and one, for the case the number of exit vertices is a constant, is from the *hitting-set* problem.

Theorem 6. *The problem of finding a BR move for a HFNG with the UH or PH mechanism is NP-complete. NP-hardness holds already for single-player HNFGs of a constant depth or with a constant number of exit vertices.*

Thus, the exponential succinctness of HNFGs makes the BR problem for the UH and PH mechanisms exponentially more complex than the one for NFGs.

Since the BR problem in single-player HNFGs coincides with the SO problem, Theorem 6 immediately implies the lower bound in the following theorem. The upper bound follows from the fact that a witness to the SO consists of listing the set of edges purchased in every subgraph. It is easy to see that there exists an SO in which every player is assigned a homogeneous strategy, therefore, the SO's feasibility is tractable.

Theorem 7. *The problem of finding an SO for an HNFG with the UH or PH mechanism is NP-complete. NP-hardness holds already for single-player HNFGs of a constant depth or with a constant number of exit vertices.*

4.2   The Flat Mechanism with a Constant Number of Exit Vertices

Consider an HNFG played over a hierarchical graph $\mathcal{G}$. Recall that in the flat mechanism, costs are calculated with respect to $\mathcal{G}^f$, which is exponentially larger than $\mathcal{G}$. While the exponential blow-up applies already for hierarchical graphs in which the number of exit vertices in each subgraph is a constant (in fact, per Observation 1, is 1), experience in formal verification of hierarchical systems shows that reasoning about hierarchical-FSMs in which each subgraph has a constant number of exit vertices does make verification easier [5,6]. In this section we consider HNFGs that are played over hierarchical graphs in which each subgraph has a constant number of exit vertices. We denote this class by CE-HNFGs. We note that CE-HNFGs are common in practice: in software, procedures typically have a constant number of returns, and in hardware, nested boxes are plugged in via a constant number of connections.

Before we describe our results for CE-HNFGs, let us point out that there are additional aspects in which the flat mechanism is computationally easier than the UH and PH mechanisms. For example, while the problem of finding an SO in HNFGs in the UH or PH mechanism is NP-complete already for single-player CE-HNFGs (as we proved in Theorem 7), for the flat mechanism, the single-player instance is easy even without restricting to CE-HNFGs. Indeed, let $\mathcal{N} = \langle 1, \mathcal{G}, \langle s, t \rangle \rangle$, with $\mathcal{G} = \langle G_1, \ldots, G_n \rangle$. Starting with G_n, we recursively replace each box that calls a subgraph G_j by a tree of depth 1 with root in_j and edges to all exit vertices $t \in Exit_j$. The cost of such an edge is the cost of the shortest path from in_j to t, which we need to calculate only once (and after boxes in G_j have been recursively replaced by trees of depth 1). Thus, we have,

Theorem 8. *The problem of finding an SO in a single-player HNFG with the flat mechanism can be solved in polynomial time.*

For $k > 1$ players, finding an SO is still tractable, but the algorithm is more involved:

Theorem 9. *The problem of finding an SO in CE-HNFGs with the flat mechanism can be solved in polynomial time.*

Proof. Let $\mathcal{N}$ be a CE-HNFG with $\mathcal{G} = \langle G_1, \ldots, G_n \rangle$, where $G_j = \langle V_j, B_j, in_j, Exit_j, \tau_j, E_j, c_j \rangle$. A profile of $\mathcal{N}$ utilizes a subset of the edges in $\mathcal{G}$. In fact, for every box in $\mathcal{G}$ that calls a subgraph G_j, the utilized edges form a Steiner tree connecting in_j with a set $T \subseteq Exit_j$ of exit vertices. Our algorithm is based on the fact that these Steiner trees can be enumerated, and that the minimum Steiner tree problem can be solved efficiently when the number of terminals is a constant [25].

For $j \in [n]$ and a set $T \subseteq Exit_j$, we define the HNFG $\mathcal{N}_{j,T} = \langle |T|, \mathcal{G}_j, \langle in_j, t \rangle_{t \in T} \rangle$, where $\mathcal{G}_j = \langle G_j, G_{j+1}, \ldots, G_n \rangle$. That is, $\mathcal{N}_{j,T}$ is a $|T|$-player game, where each player tries to reach from in_j to a different exit vertex $t \in T$. Note that an SO in $\mathcal{N}_{j,T}$ is a profile that minimizes the cost required for forming paths from in_j to all vertices in T in the flat expansion of $\mathcal{G}_j$. Now, let G'_j be a weighted tree of depth 1 with root in_j and leaves in 2^{Exit_j}, where the cost of an edge $\langle in_j, T \rangle$, for $T \subseteq Exit_j$, is the SO in $\mathcal{N}_{j,T}$. Thus, G'_j describes, for every subset $T \subseteq Exit_j$, the cost of covering paths from in_j to all vertices in T in the flat expansion of $\mathcal{G}_j$. Note that since $|Exit_j|$ is constant, so is the size of G'_j.

We argue that for all $j \in [n]$ and $T \subseteq Exit_j$, there is an algorithm that finds an SO in $\mathcal{N}_{j,T}$ and constructs G'_j in polynomial time. In particular, taking $j = 1$ and $T = \cup_{i \in [k]} \{t_i\}$, we can find the SO of $\mathcal{N}$ in polynomial time. The algorithm is omitted from this extended abstract. $\square$

We turn to the problem of calculating an NE. A well-known approach for calculating an NE in NFGs is *best-response dynamics* (BRD): starting with an arbitrary profile, we let players perform BR moves until an NE is reached. The complexity class PLS contains local search problems with polynomial time searchable neighborhoods [24]. Essentially, a problem is in PLS if there is a set of feasible solutions for it such that it is possible to find, in polynomial time, an initial feasible solution and then iteratively improve it, with each improvement being performed in polynomial time, until a local optimum is reached. While every iteration of BRD takes polynomial time, the number of iterations needs not be polynomial. The problem of finding an NE in NFGs is known to be PLS-complete. We show how to implement BRD in CE-HNFGs in a way that keeps the polynomial time-complexity for each improvement step. The idea is to use a succinct representation of a profile in a CE-HNFG, and to restrict attention to a limited class of profiles that are guaranteed to include an NE.

Theorem 10. *The problem of finding an NE in CE-HNFGs with the flat mechanism is PLS-complete.*

References

1. Albers, S., Elits, S., Even-Dar, E., Mansour, Y., Roditty, L.: On Nash equilibria for a network creation game. In: Proceedings of 7th SODA, pp. 89–98 (2006)
2. Almagor, S., Avni, G., Kupferman, O.: Repairing multi-player games. In: Proceedings of 26th CONCUR, pp. 325–339 (2015)
3. Alur, R., Henzinger, T.A., Kupferman, O.: Alternating-time temporal logic. J. ACM **49**(5), 672–713 (2002)

4. Alur, R., Kannan, S., Yannakakis, M.: Communicating hierarchical state machines. In: Wiedermann, J., Emde Boas, P., Nielsen, M. (eds.) ICALP 1999. LNCS, vol. 1644, pp. 169–178. Springer, Heidelberg (1999). doi:10.1007/3-540-48523-6_14
5. Alur, R., Yannakakis, M.: Model checking of hierarchical state machines. ACM TOPLAS 23(3), 273–303 (2001)
6. Aminof, B., Kupferman, O., Murano, A.: Improved model checking of hierarchical systems. J. Inf. Comput. 210, 68–86 (2012)
7. Anshelevich, E., Dasgupta, A., Kleinberg, J., Tardos, E., Wexler, T., Roughgarden, T.: The price of stability for network design with fair cost allocation. SIAM J. Comput. 38(4), 1602–1623 (2008)
8. Avni, G., Kupferman, O.: Synthesis from component libraries with costs. In: Baldan, P., Gorla, D. (eds.) CONCUR 2014. LNCS, vol. 8704, pp. 156–172. Springer, Heidelberg (2014). doi:10.1007/978-3-662-44584-6_12
9. Avni, G., Kupferman, O., Tamir, T.: Network-formation games with regular objectives. Inf. Comput. 251, 165–178 (2016)
10. Avni, G., Kupferman, O., Tamir, T.: Congestion games with multisets of resources and applications in synthesis. In: Proceedings of 35th FST and TCS. LIPIcs, pp. 365–379 (2015)
11. Brihaye, T., Bruyère, V., De Pril, J., Gimbert, H.: On subgame perfection in quantitative reachability games. LMCS 9(1), 1–32 (2012)
12. Chatterjee, K.: Nash equilibrium for upward-closed objectives. In: Ésik, Z. (ed.) CSL 2006. LNCS, vol. 4207, pp. 271–286. Springer, Heidelberg (2006). doi:10.1007/11874683_18
13. Chatterjee, K., Henzinger, T.A., Jurdzinski, M.: Games with secure equilibria. Theoret. Comput. Sci. 365(1–2), 67–82 (2006)
14. Chatterjee, K., Henzinger, T.A., Piterman, N.: Strategy logic. In: Caires, L., Vasconcelos, V.T. (eds.) CONCUR 2007. LNCS, vol. 4703, pp. 59–73. Springer, Heidelberg (2007). doi:10.1007/978-3-540-74407-8_5
15. Chatterjee, K., Majumdar, R., Jurdziński, M.: On Nash equilibria in stochastic games. In: Marcinkowski, J., Tarlecki, A. (eds.) CSL 2004. LNCS, vol. 3210, pp. 26–40. Springer, Heidelberg (2004). doi:10.1007/978-3-540-30124-0_6
16. Chen, H., Roughgarden, T.: Network design with weighted players. Theor. Comput. Syst. 45(2), 302–324 (2009)
17. Clarke, E.M., Grumberg, O., Peled, D.: Model Checking. MIT Press, Cambridge (1999)
18. Correa, J.R., Schulz, A.S., Stier-Moses, N.E.: Selfish routing in capacitated networks. Math. Oper. Res. 29, 961–976 (2004)
19. de Roever, W.-P., Langmaack, H., Pnueli, A. (eds.): COMPOS 1997. LNCS, vol. 1536. Springer, Heidelberg (1998). doi:10.1007/3-540-49213-5
20. Drusinsky, D., Harel, D.: On the power of bounded concurrency I: finite automata. J. ACM 41(3), 517–539 (1994)
21. Fabrikant, A., Luthra, A., Maneva, E., Papadimitriou, C., Shenker, S.: On a network creation game. In: ACM PODC, pp. 347–351 (2003)
22. Feldman, M., Tamir, T.: Conflicting congestion effects in resource allocation games. J. Oper. Res. 60(3), 529–540 (2012)
23. Fisman, D., Kupferman, O., Lustig, Y.: Rational synthesis. In: Esparza, J., Majumdar, R. (eds.) TACAS 2010. LNCS, vol. 6015, pp. 190–204. Springer, Heidelberg (2010). doi:10.1007/978-3-642-12002-2_16
24. Johnson, D.S., Papadimitriou, C.H., Yannakakis, M.: How easy is local search? J. Comput. Syst. Sci. 37, 79–100 (1988)

25. Kimelfeld, B., Sagiv, Y.: New algorithms for computing Steiner trees for a fixed number of terminals (2006). http://www.cs.huji.ac.il/bennyk/papers/steiner06.pdf
26. Koutsoupias, E., Papadimitriou, C.: Worst-case equilibria. Comput. Sci. Rev. **3**(2), 65–69 (2009)
27. Lustig, Y., Vardi, M.Y.: Synthesis from component libraries. STTT **15**(5–6), 603–618 (2013)
28. Mavronicolas, M., Milchtaich, I., Monien, B., Tiemann, K.: Congestion games with player-specific constants. In: Kučera, L., Kučera, A. (eds.) MFCS 2007. LNCS, vol. 4708, pp. 633–644. Springer, Heidelberg (2007). doi:10.1007/978-3-540-74456-6_56
29. Milchtaich, I.: Weighted congestion games with separable preferences. Games Econ. Behav. **67**, 750–757 (2009)
30. Mitchell, J.C.: Concepts in Programming Languages. Cambridge University Press, Cambridge (2003)
31. Meyers, C.A., Schulz, A.S.: The complexity of welfare maximization in congestion games. Networks **59**(2), 252–260 (2012)
32. Monderer, D., Shapley, L.: Potential games. Games Econ. Behav. **14**, 124–143 (1996)
33. Papadimitriou, C.H.: Algorithms, games, and the internet. In: Proceedings of STOC, pp. 749–753 (2001)
34. Pnueli, A.: In transition from global to modular temporal reasoning about programs. In: Apt, K.R. (ed.) Logics and Models of Concurrent Systems. NATO Advanced Science Institutes, vol. 13, pp. 123–144. Springer, Heidelberg (1985). doi:10.1007/978-3-642-82453-1_5
35. Rose, L., Belmega, E.V., Saad, W., Debbah, M.: Pricing in heterogeneous wireless networks: hierarchical games and dynamics. IEEE Trans. Wireless Commun. **13**(9), 4985–5001 (2014)
36. Saad, W., Zhu, Q., Basar, T., Han, Z., Hjørungnes, A.: Hierarchical network formation games in the uplink of multi-hop wireless networks. In: Proceedings of GLOBECOM, pp. 1–6. IEEE (2009)
37. Tardos, E., Wexler, T.: Network formation games and the potential function method. In: Algorithmic Game Theory. Cambridge University Press (2007)

Synthesis of Recursive ADT Transformations from Reusable Templates

Jeevana Priya Inala[1](✉), Nadia Polikarpova[1], Xiaokang Qiu[2],
Benjamin S. Lerner[3], and Armando Solar-Lezama[1]

[1] MIT, Cambridge, USA
{jinala,polikarn,asolar}@csail.mit.edu
[2] Purdue University, West Lafayette, USA
xkqiu@purdue.edu
[3] Northeastern University, Boston, USA
blerner@ccs.neu.edu

Abstract. Recent work has proposed a promising approach to improving scalability of program synthesis by allowing the user to supply a syntactic template that constrains the space of potential programs. Unfortunately, creating templates often requires nontrivial effort from the user, which impedes the usability of the synthesizer. We present a solution to this problem in the context of recursive transformations on algebraic data-types. Our approach relies on *polymorphic synthesis constructs*: a small but powerful extension to the language of syntactic templates, which makes it possible to define a program space in a concise and highly reusable manner, while at the same time retains the scalability benefits of conventional templates. This approach enables end-users to reuse predefined templates from a library for a wide variety of problems with little effort. The paper also describes a novel optimization that further improves the performance and the scalability of the system. We evaluated the approach on a set of benchmarks that most notably includes desugaring functions for lambda calculus, which force the synthesizer to discover Church encodings for pairs and boolean operations.

1 Introduction

Recent years have seen remarkable advances in tools and techniques for automated synthesis of recursive programs [1,4,8,13,16]. These tools take as input some form of *correctness specification* that describes the intended program behavior, and a set of building blocks (or *components*). The synthesizer then performs a search in the space of all programs that can be built from the given components until it finds one that satisfies the specification. The biggest obstacle to practical program synthesis is that this search space grows extremely fast with the size of the program and the number of available components. As a result, these tools have been able to tackle only relatively simple tasks, such as textbook data structure manipulations.

Syntax-guided synthesis (SyGuS) [2] has emerged as a promising way to address this problem. SyGuS tools, such as SKETCH [18] and Rosette [20,21]

© Springer-Verlag GmbH Germany 2017
A. Legay and T. Margaria (Eds.): TACAS 2017, Part I, LNCS 10205, pp. 247–263, 2017.
DOI: 10.1007/978-3-662-54577-5_14

leverage a user-provided syntactic *template* to restrict the space of programs the synthesizer has to consider, which improves scalability and allows SyGus tools to tackle much harder problems. However, the requirement to provide a template for every synthesis task significantly impacts usability.

This paper shows that, at least in the context of recursive transformations on algebraic data-types (ADTs), it is possible to get the best of both worlds. Our first contribution is a new approach to making syntactic templates highly reusable by relying on *polymorphic synthesis constructs* (*PSCs*). With *PSCs*, a user does not have to write a custom template for every synthesis problem, but can instead rely on a generic template from a library. Even when the user does write a custom template, the new constructs make this task simpler and less error-prone. We show in Sect. 4 that all our 23 diverse benchmarks are synthesized using just 4 different generic templates from the library. Moreover, thanks to a carefully designed type-directed expansion mechanism, our generic templates provide the same performance benefits during synthesis as conventional, program-specific templates. Our second contribution is a new optimization called *inductive decomposition*, which achieves asymptotic improvements in synthesis times for large and non-trivial ADT transformations. This optimization, together with the user guidance in the form of reusable templates, allows our system to attack problems that are out of scope for existing synthesizers.

We implemented these ideas in a tool called SYNTREC, which is built on top of the open source SKETCH synthesis platform [19]. Our tool supports expressive correctness specifications that can use arbitrary functions to constrain the behavior of ADT transformations. Like other expressive synthesizers, such as SKETCH [18] and Rosette [20,21], our system relies on exhaustive bounded checking to establish whether a program candidate matches the specification. While this does not provide correctness guarantees beyond a bounded set of inputs, it works well in practice and allows us to tackle complex problems, for which full correctness is undecidable and is beyond the state of the art in automatic verification. For example, our benchmarks include desugaring functions from an abstract syntax tree (AST) into a simpler AST, where correctness is defined in terms of interpreters for the two ASTs. As a result, our synthesizer is able to discover Church encodings for pairs and booleans, given nothing but an interpreter for the lambda calculus. In another benchmark, we show that the system is powerful enough to synthesize a type constraint generator for a simple programming language given the semantics of type constraints. Additionally, several of our benchmarks come from transformation passes implemented in our own compiler and synthesizer.

2   Overview

In this section, we use the problem of desugaring a simple language to illustrate the main features of SYNTREC. Specifically, the goal is to synthesize a function dstAST desugar(srcAST src) {...}, which translates an expression in source AST into a semantically equivalent expression in destination AST. Data type definitions for the two ASTs are shown in Fig. 1: the type srcAST has five *variants* (two

```
adt srcAST{                              adt dstAST{
  NumS{ int v; }                           NumD{ int v; }
  TrueS{ }                                  BoolD{ bit v; }
  FalseS{ }                                 BinaryD{ opcode op; dstAST a; dstAST b;}}
  BinaryS{ opcode op; srcAST a; srcAST b;}
  BetweenS{ srcAST a; srcAST b; srcAST c;}} adt opcode{ AndOp{} OrOp{} LtOp{}}}
```

Fig. 1. ADTs for two small expression languages

of which are recursive), while dstAST has only three. In particular, the source language construct BetweenS(a, b, c), which denotes a < b < c, has to be desugared into a conjunction of two inequalities. Like case classes in Scala, data type variants in SYNTREC have named fields.

Specification. The first piece of user input required by the synthesizer is the specification of the program's intended behavior. In the case of desugar, we would like to specify that the desugared AST is semantically equivalent to the original AST, which can be expressed in SYNTREC using the following constraint:

$$\textbf{assert(}\ \ \textsf{srcInterpret (exp)} == \textsf{dstInterpret(desugar(exp))}\ \textbf{)}$$

This constraint states that interpreting an arbitrary source-language expression exp (bounded to some depth) must be equivalent to desugaring exp and interpreting the resulting expression in the destination language. Here, srcInterpret and dstInterpret are regular functions written in SYNTREC and defined recursively over the structure of the respective ASTs in a straightforward manner. As we explain in Sect. 3.4, our synthesizer contains a novel optimization called *inductive decomposition* that can take advantage of the structure of the above specification to significantly improve the scalability of the synthesis process.

Templates. The second piece of user input required by our system is a syntactic *template*, which describes the space of possible implementations. The template is intended to specify the high-level structure of the program, leaving low-level details for the system to figure out. In that respect, SYNTREC follows the SyGuS paradigm [2]; however, template languages used in existing SyGuS tools, such as SKETCH or Rosette, work poorly in the context of recursive ADT transformations.

For example, Fig. 2 shows a template for desugar written in SKETCH, the predecessor of SYNTREC. It is useful to understand this template as we will show, later, how the new language features in SYNTREC allow us to write the same template in a concise and reusable manner. This template uses three kinds of *synthesis constructs* already existing in SKETCH: a *choice* ($\textbf{choose}(e_1, ..., e_n)$) must be replaced with one of the expressions $e_1, \ldots, e_n$; a *hole* (??) must be replaced with an integer or a boolean constant; finally, a *generator* (such as rcons) can be thought of as a macro, which is inlined on use, allowing the synthesizer to make different choices for every invocation[1]. The task of the synthesizer is to

---

[1] Recursive generators, such as rcons, are unrolled up to a fixed depth, which is a parameter to our system.

```
dstAST desugar(srcAST src){                          generator dstAST rcons(fun e) {
  switch(src) {                                        if (??) return e();
  case NumS:                                           if (??) {
    return rcons(src.v);                                 int val = choose(e(), ??);
    ... /* Some cases are elided */                      return new NumD(v = val); }
  case BinaryS:                                         if (??) {
    dstAST a = desugar(src.a), b = desugar(src.b);       bit val = choose(e(), ??);
    return rcons(choose(a, b, src.op));                  return new BoolD(v = val);}
  case BetweenS:                                        if (??) {
    dstAST a = desugar(src.a), b = desugar(src.b),       dstAST a = rcons(e);
               c = desugar(src.c);                       dstAST b = rcons(e);
    return rcons(choose(a, b, c));                       opcode op = choose(e(), new AndOp(),...,
}}                                                                    new LtOp());
                                                         return new BinaryD(op = op, a= a, b = b);}
                                                     }
```

Fig. 2. Template for desugar in SKETCH

fill in every choice and hole in such a way that the resulting program satisfies the specification.

The template in Fig. 2 expresses the intuition that desugar should recursively traverse its input, src, replacing each node with some subtree from the destination language. These destination subtrees are created by calling the recursive, higher-order generator rcons (for "recursive constructor"). rcons(e) constructs a nondeterministically chosen variant of dstAST, whose fields, depending on their type, are obtained either by recursively invoking rcons, by invoking e (which is itself a generator), or by picking an integer or boolean constant. For example, one possible instantiation of the template rcons(choose(x, y, src.op))[2] can lead to new BinaryD(op = src.op, a = x, b = new NumD(5)). Note that the template for desugar provides no insight on how to actually encode each node of scrAST in terms of dstAST, which is left for the synthesizer to figure out. Despite containing so little information, the template is very verbose: in fact, more verbose than the full implementation! More importantly, this template cannot be reused for other synthesis problems, since it is specific to the variants and fields of the two data types. Expressing such a template in Rosette will be similarly verbose.

Reusable Templates. SYNTREC addresses this problem by extending the template language with *polymorphic synthesis constructs (PSCs)*, which essentially support parametrizing templates by the structure of data types they manipulate. As a result, in SYNTREC the end user can express the template for desugar with a single line of code:

```
dstAST desugar(srcAST src) { return recursiveReplacer(src, desugar);}
```

Here, recursiveReplacer is a reusable generator defined in a library; its code is shown in Fig. 3. When the user invokes recursiveReplacer(src, desugar), the body

---

[2] When an expression is passed as an argument to a higher-order function that expects a function parameter such as rcons, it is automatically casted to a *generator lambda* function. Hence, the expression will only be evaluated when the higher-order function calls the function parameter and each call can result in a different evaluation.

```
 1  generator T recursiveReplacer <T, Q>(Q src,
 2                         fun rec) {
 3      switch(src){
 4          case?:
 5              T[ ]  a = map(src.fields?, rec );
 6              return rcons(choose(a[??],
 7                         field (src )));
 8  }}}
 9  generator T rcons<T>(fun e) {
10      if (??) return e();
11      else return new cons?(rcons(e));
12  }
13  generator T  field <T,S>(S e) {
14      return (e.fields?) [??];
15  }
```

```
 1  dstAST desugar(srcAST src) {
 2      switch(src) {
 3          case NumS: return new NumD(v = src.v);
 4          case TrueS: return new BoolD(v = 1);
 5          case FalseS: return new BoolD(v = 0);
 6          case BinaryS:
 7              dstAST[2] a = {desugar(src.a), desugar(src.b)};
 8              return new BinaryD(op = src.op, a = a[1],
 9                         b = a[2]);
10          case BetweenS:
11              dstAST[3] a = {desugar(src.a), desugar(src.b),
12                         desugar(src.c)};
13              return new BinaryD(op = new AndOp(),
14              a = new BinaryD(op = new LtOp(), a = a[0],
15                         b = a[1])
16              b = new BinaryD(op = new LtOp(), a = a[1],
17                         b = a[2]));
18  }}
```

Fig. 3. Left: generic template for recursiveReplacer. Right: solution to the running example

of the generator is specialized to the surrounding context, resulting in a template very similar to the one in Fig. 2. Unlike the template in Fig. 2, however, recursiveReplacer is not specific to srcAST and dstAST, and can be reused with no modifications to synthesize desugaring functions for other languages, and even more general recursive ADT transformations. Crucially, even though the reusable template is much more concise than the SKETCH template, it does not increase the size of the search space that the synthesizer has to consider, since all the additional choices are resolved during type inference. Figure 3 also shows a compacted version of the solution for desugar, which SYNTREC synthesizes in about 8s. The rest of the section gives an overview of the PSCs used in Fig. 3.

Polymorphic Synthesis Constructs. Just like a regular synthesis construct, a PSC represents a set of potential programs, but the exact set depends on the context and is determined by the types of the arguments to a PSC and its expected return type. SYNTREC introduces four kinds of PSCs.

1. A **Polymorphic Generator** is a polymorphic version of a SKETCH generator. For example, recursiveReplacer is a polymorphic generator, parametrized by types T and Q. When the user invokes recursiveReplacer (src, desugar), T and Q are instantiated with dstAST and srcAST, respectively.
2. **Flexible Pattern Matching** (switch(x) case?: e) expands into pattern matching code specialized for the type of x. In our example, once Q in recursiveReplacer is instantiated with srcAST, the **case?** construct in Line 4 expands into five cases (**case NumS**, ..., **case BetweenS**) with the body of **case?** duplicated inside each of these cases.
3. **Field List** (e. **fields?**) expands into an array of all fields of type τ in a particular variant of e, where τ is derived from the context. Going back to Fig. 3, Line 5 inside recursiveReplacer maps a function rec over a field list src. **fields?**; in our example, rec is instantiated with desugar, which takes an input of type srcAST.

Hence, SYNTREC determines that src. fields? in this case denotes all fields of type srcAST. Note that this construct is expanded differently in each of the five cases that resulted from the expansion of **case?**. For example, inside **case NumS**, this construct expands into an empty array (NumS has no fields of type srcAST), while inside **case BetweenS**, it expands into the array {src.a, src.b, src.c}.

4. *Unknown Constructor* (**new cons?**(e_1, ..., e_n)) expands into a constructor for some variant of type τ, where τ is derived from the context, and uses the expressions $e_1, \ldots, e_n$ as the fields. In our example, the auxiliary generator rcons uses an unknown constructor in Line 11. When rcons is invoked in a context that expects an expression of type dstAST, this unknown constructor expands into **choose(new NumD(...), new BoolD(...), new BinaryD(...))**. If instead rcons is expected to return an expression of type opcode, then the unknown constructor expands into **choose(new AndOp(),...,new LtOp())**. If the expected type is an integer or a boolean, this construct expands into a regular SKETCH hole (**??**).

Even though the language provides only four *PSC*s, they can be combined in novel ways to create richer polymorphic constructs that can be used as library components. The generators field and rcons in Fig. 3 are two such components.

The field component expands into an arbitrary field of type τ, where τ is derived from the context. Its implementation uses the *field list PSC* to obtain the array of all fields of type τ, and then accesses a random element in this array using an integer hole. For example, if field (e) is used in a context where the type of e is BetweenS and the expected type is srcAST, then field (e) expands into {e.a, e.b, e.c}[**??**] which is semantically equivalent to **choose**(e.a, e.b, e.c).

The rcons component is a polymorphic version of the recursive constructor for dstAST in Fig. 2, and can produce ADT trees of any type up to a certain depth. Note that since rcons is a polymorphic generator, each call to

$$
\begin{aligned}
P &:= \{adt_i\}_i \ \{f_i\}_i \\
adt &:= \textbf{adt } name \{ \ variant_1 \ldots variant_n \ \} \\
variant &:= name \{l_1 : \tau_1 \ldots \ l_n : \tau_n\} \\
\theta &:= \tau \ | \ T \ | \ \theta[\,] \ | \ fun \ | \ \theta_1 \to \theta_2 \\
\tau &:= prim \ | \ name \ | \ \{l_i : \tau_i\}_{i<n} \\
&\quad | \ \sum name_i \{l_k^i : \tau_k^i\}_{k<n_i} \\
prim &:= \textbf{bit} \ | \ \textbf{int} \\
f &:= \bar{f} \ | \ \hat{f} \ | \ \hat{\hat{f}} \\
\bar{f} &:= \tau_{out} \ name \, (\{x_i : \tau_i\}_i) \quad e \\
\hat{f} &:= \textbf{generator } \tau_{out} \ name \, (\{x_i : \tau_i\}_i) \quad e \\
\hat{\hat{f}} &:= \textbf{generator } \theta_{out} \ name \langle\{T_i\}_i\rangle (\{x_i : \theta_i\}_i) \quad e \\
e &:= \bar{e} \ | \ \hat{e} \ | \ \hat{\hat{e}} \\
\bar{e} &:= x \ | \ \textbf{let } x : \theta = e_1 \textbf{ in } e_2 \ | \ f(e) \\
&\quad | \ \textbf{switch} \, (x) \, \{ \ \textbf{case } \ name_i : e_i \ \}_i \\
&\quad | \ e.l \ | \ \textbf{new } name(\{l_i = e_i\}_i) \\
&\quad | \ \{\{e_i\}_i\} \ | \ e_1[e_2] \ | \ \textbf{assert}(e) \\
\hat{e} &:= \textbf{??} \ | \ \textbf{choose}(\{e_i\}_i) | \ \hat{f}(e) \\
\hat{\hat{e}} &:= \hat{\hat{f}}(e) \ | \ \textbf{new cons?}(\{e_i\}_i) \\
&\quad | \ e.\textbf{fields?} \ | \ \textbf{switch}(x)\{\textbf{case?} : e\}
\end{aligned}
$$

Fig. 4. Kernel language

rcons in the argument to the unknown constructor (Line 11) is specialized based on the type required by that constructor and can make different nondeterministic choices. Similarly, it is possible to create other generic constructs such as iterators over arbitrary data structures. Components such as these are expected to be provided by expert users, while end users treat them in the same way as the built-in *PSC*s. The next section gives a formal account of the SYNTREC's language and the synthesis approach.

3   SYNTREC Formally

3.1   Language

Figure 4 shows a simple kernel language that captures the relevant features of SYNTREC. In this language, a program consists of a set of ADT declarations followed by a set of function declarations. The language distinguishes between a standard function $\overline{f}$, a generator $\hat{f}$ and a *polymorphic generator* $\hat{\hat{f}}$. Functions can be passed as parameters to other functions, but they are not entirely first-class citizens because they cannot be assigned to variables or returned from functions. Function parameters lack type annotations and are declared as type fun, but their types can be deduced from inference. Similarly, expressions are divided into standard expressions that does not contain any unknown choices ($\overline{e}$), existing synthesis constructs in SKETCH ($\hat{e}$), and the new *PSCs* ($\hat{\hat{e}}$). The language also has support for arrays with expressions for array creation ($\{e_1, e_2, ..., e_n\}$) and array access ($e_1[e_2]$). An array type is represented as $\theta[\,]$. In this formalism, we use the Greek letter τ to refer to a fully concrete type and θ to refer to a type that may involve type variables. The distinction between the two is important because *PSCs* can only be expanded when the types of their context are known. We formalize ADTs as tagged unions $\tau = \sum variant_i$, where each of the variants is a record type $variant_i = name_i \{l_k^i : \tau_k^i\}_{k<n_i}$. Note that ADTs in SYNTREC are not polymorphic. The notation $\{a_i\}_i$ is used to denote the $\{a_1, a_2, ...\}$.

3.2   Synthesis Approach

Given a user-written program $\hat{\hat{P}}$ that can potentially contain *PSCs*, choices and holes, and a specification, the synthesis problem is to find a program $\overline{P}$ in the language that only contains standard expressions ($\overline{e}$) and functions ($\overline{f}$). SYNTREC solves this problem using a two step approach as shown below:

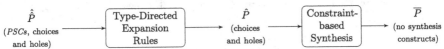

First, SYNTREC uses a set of expansion rules that uses bi-directional type checking to eliminate the *PSCs*. The result is a program that only contains choices and holes. The second step is to use a constraint-based approach to solve for these choices. The next subsections will present each of these steps in more detail.

3.3   Type-Directed Expansion Rules

We will now formalize the process of specializing and expanding the *PSCs* into sets of possible expressions. We should first note that the expansion and the specialization of the different *PSCs* interact in complex ways. For example, for the **case?** construct in the running example, the system cannot determine which cases to generate until it knows the type of src, which is only fixed once the *polymorphic generator* for recursiveReplacer is specialized to the calling context. On the other hand, if a *polymorphic generator* is invoked inside the body of a **case?** (like rcons in the running example), we may not know the types of the arguments until after the **case?** is expanded into separate cases. Because of this, type inference and expansion of the *PSCs* must happen in tandem.

We formalize the process of expanding *PSCs* using two different kinds of judgements. The *typing judgement* $\Gamma \vdash e : \theta$ determines the type of an expression by propagating information bottom-up from sub-expressions to larger expressions. On the other hand, *PSCs* cannot be type-checked in a bottom-up manner; instead, their types must be inferred from the context. The *expansion judgment* $\Gamma \vdash e \xrightarrow{\theta} e'$ expands an expression e involving *PSCs* into an expression e' that does not contain *PSCs* (but can contain choices and holes). In this judgment, θ is used to propagate information top-down and represents the type required in a given context; in other words, after this expansion, the typing judgement $\Gamma \vdash e' : \theta$ must hold. We are not the first to note that bi-directional typing [15] can be very useful in pruning the search space for synthesis [13,16], but we are the first to apply this in the context of constraint-based synthesis and in a language with user-provided definitions of program spaces.

$$FUN \quad \frac{\Gamma; \{x_i : \tau_i\}_{i<n} \vdash e \xrightarrow{\tau_o} e'}{\Gamma \vdash \tau_o \; f\left(\{x_i : \tau_i\}_{i<n}\right) e \xrightarrow{\perp} \tau_o \; f\left(\{x_i : \tau_i\}_{i<n}\right) e'}$$

$$FL \quad \frac{\Gamma \vdash e : \{l_i : \tau_i\}_{i<n} \quad \Gamma \vdash e \xrightarrow{\{l_i : \tau_i\}_{i<n}} e' \quad {}^*\{\tau_{i_j} = \tau_0\}_j \quad (\tau_0[\,] = \tau)}{\Gamma \vdash e.\textbf{fields?} \xrightarrow{\tau} \{\{e'.l_{i_j}\}_j\}}$$

$$FPM \quad \frac{\Gamma = \left(\Gamma'; x : \sum name_i \{l_k^i : \tau_k^i\}_{k<n_i}\right) \quad \left\{\left(\Gamma'; x : \{l_k^i : \tau_k^i\}_{k<n_i}\right) \vdash e \xrightarrow{\theta} e_i\right\}_i}{\Gamma \vdash \textbf{switch}\,(x)\,\{\ \textbf{case?} : e\ \} \xrightarrow{\theta} \textbf{switch}\,(x)\,\{\ \textbf{case}\ name_i : e_i\}_i}$$

$$UC1 \quad \frac{\tau = \Sigma name_i \{l_k^i : \tau_k^i\}_{k<n_i} \quad e_1 \xrightarrow{\tau_k^i} e_{1_k}^i \ldots e_m \xrightarrow{\tau_k^i} e_{m_k}^i}{\Gamma \vdash \textbf{new cons?}\,(e_1 \ldots e_m) \xrightarrow{\tau} \textbf{choose}\left(\left\{\textbf{new}\ name_i \left(\{l_k^i = \textbf{choose}\,(\{e_{r_k}^i\}_{r<m})\}_{k<n_i}\right)\right\}_i\right)}$$

$$UC2 \quad \frac{\tau = prim}{\Gamma \vdash \textbf{new cons?}\,(e_1 \ldots e_m) \xrightarrow{\tau} ??}$$

$$PG \quad \frac{\begin{array}{c}\theta_{out}\ \hat{f}\langle\{T_i\}\rangle\,(\{p_i : \theta_i\}_i)\ e \qquad \Gamma \vdash e_i : \tau_i^{in}\ \ for\ i<k \\ S = \mathrm{Unify}\left(\{(\theta_{out},\,\theta)\} \cup \{(\theta_i, \tau_i^{in})\}_{i<k}\right) \\ e_i \xrightarrow{S(\theta_i)} e_i'\ \ for\ i \leq k+n \qquad e[\{e_i'/p_i\}_i] \xrightarrow{S(\theta)} e'\end{array}}{\hat{f}\,(e_0 \ldots e_k \ldots e_{k+n}) \xrightarrow{\theta} e'}$$

Fig. 5. Expansion rules for various language constructs

The expansion rules for functions and *PSCs* are shown in Fig. 5. At the top level, given a program P, every function in P is transformed using the expansion rule FUN. The body of the function is expanded under the known output type of the function. The most interesting cases in the definition of the expansion judgment correspond to the *PSCs* as outlined below. The expansion rules for the other expressions are straightforward and are elided for brevity.

Field List. The rule FL shows how a *field list* is expanded. If the required type is an array of τ_0, then this *PSC* can be expanded into an array of all fields of type τ_0.

Flexible Pattern Matching. For each case, the body of **case?** is expanded while setting x to a different type corresponding to each variant $name_i \left\{ l_k^i : \tau_k^i \right\}_{k < n_i}$ as shown in the rule FPM. Here, the argument to **switch** is required to be a variable so that it can be used with a different type inside each of the different cases. Note that each case is expanded independently, so the synthesizer can make different choices for each e_i.

Unknown Constructor. If the required type is an ADT, the rule UC1 expands the expressions passed to the *unknown constructor* based on the type of each field of each variant of the ADT and uses the resulting expressions to initialize the fields in the relevant constructor. It returns a **choose** expression with all these constructors as the arguments. If the required type is a primitive type (int or bit), the unknown constructor is expanded into a SKETCH hole by the rule UC2.

Polymorphic Generator Calls. When the expansion encounters a call to a *polymorphic generator*, the generator will be expanded and specialized according to the PG rule. When a generator is called with arguments $\{e_i\}_i$, we can separate the arguments into expressions that can be typed using the standard typing judgement, and expressions such as **new cons?** (...) that cannot. In the rule, we assume, without loss of generality, that the first k expressions can be typed and the reminder cannot. The basic idea behind the expansion is as follows. First, the rule obtains the types of the first k arguments and unifies them with the types of the formal parameters of the function to get a type substitution S. The arguments to the original call are expanded with our improved knowledge of the types, and the body of the generator is then inlined and expanded in turn. The actual implementation also keeps track of how many times each generator has been inlined and replaces the generator invocation with **assert false** when the inlining bound has been reached.

The above expansion rules fail if a type variable is encountered in places where a concrete type is expected, and in such cases the system will throw an error. For example, expressions such as field (field (e)), where field is as defined in Fig. 3, cannot by type-checked in our system because the expected type of the inner field call cannot be determined using top-down type propagation.

3.4 Constraint-Based Synthesis

Once we have a program with a fixed number of integer unknowns, the synthesis problem can be encoded as a constraint $\exists \phi. \ \forall \sigma. \ P(\phi, \sigma)$ where ϕ is a *control vector* describing the set of choices that the synthesizer has to make, σ is the input state of the program, and $P(\phi, \sigma)$ is a predicate that is true if the program satisfies its specification under input σ and control ϕ. Our system follows the standard approach of unrolling loops and inlining recursive calls to derive P and uses counterexample guided inductive synthesis (CEGIS) to solve this doubly quantified problem [18]. For readers unfamiliar with this approach, the most relevant aspect from the point of view of this paper is that the doubly quantified problem is reduced to a sequence of inductive synthesis steps. At each step, the system generates a solution that works for a small set of inputs, and then checks if this solution is in fact correct for all inputs; otherwise, it generates a counter-example for the next inductive synthesis step.

Applying the standard approach can, however, be problematic in our context especially with regards to inlining recursive calls. For instance, consider the example from Sect. 2. Here, the function desugar that has to be synthesized is a recursive function. If we were to inline all the recursive calls to desugar, then a given concrete value for the input σ such as BetweenS(a = NumS(...), b = BinaryS(...), ...), will exercise multiple cases within desugar (BetweenS, NumS and BinaryS for the example). This is problematic in the context of CEGIS, because at each inductive synthesis step the synthesizer has to jointly solve for all these variants of desugar which greatly hinders scalability when the source language has many variants.

3.5   Inductive Decomposition

The goal of this section is to leverage the inductive specification to potentially avoid inlining the recursive calls to the synthesized function. This idea of treating the specification as an inductive hypothesis is well known in the deductive verification community where the goal is to solve the following problem: $\forall \sigma.\ P(\phi_0, \sigma)$. However, in our case, we want to apply this idea during the inductive synthesis step of CEGIS where the goal is to solve $\exists \phi.\ P(\phi, \sigma_0)$ which has not been explored before.

Definition 1 (Inductive Decomposition). *Suppose the specification is of the form $interp_s(e) = interp_d(trans(e))$ where trans is the function that needs to be synthesized. Let $trans(e')$ be a recursive call within $trans(e)$ where e' is strictly smaller term than e. Inductive Decomposition is defined as the following substitution: 1. Replace $trans(e')$ with a special expression $\boxed{e'}$. 2. When inlining function calls, apply the following rules for the evaluation of $\boxed{e'}$:*

$$interp_d(\boxed{e'}) \longrightarrow interp_s(e')$$
$$\boxed{e'}\ in\ any\ other\ context \longrightarrow trans(e')$$

i.e. Inductive Decomposition works by delaying the evaluation of a recursive $trans(e')$ call by replacing it with a placeholder that tracks the input e'. Then, if the algorithm encounters these placeholders when inlining $interp_d$ in the specification, it replaces them directly with $interp_s(e')$ which we know how to evaluate, thus, eliminating the need to inline the unknown $trans$ function. This replacement is sound because the specification states $interp_d(trans(e')) = interp_s(e')$. If the algorithm encounters the placeholders in any other context where the inductive specification can not be leveraged, it defaults to evaluating $trans(e')$.

Theorem 1. *Inductive Decomposition is sound and complete. In other words, if the specification is valid before the substitution, then it will be valid after the substitution and vice-versa.*

A proof of this theorem can be found in the tech report [6]. Although the Inductive Decomposition algorithm imposes restrictions on which recursive calls can be eliminated, it turns out that for many of the ADT transformation scenarios, the algorithm can totally eliminate all recursive calls to *trans*. For instance, in the running example, because of the inductive structure of dstInterpret , all placeholders for recursive desugar calls will occur only in the context of dstInterpret (desugar(e')) which can be replaced by srcInterpret (e') according to the algorithm. Thus, after the substitution, the desugar function is no longer recursive and moreover, the desugaring for the different variants can be synthesized separately. For the running example, we gain a 20X speedup using this optimization. Our system also implements several generalizations of the aforementioned optimization that are detailed in the tech report [6].

4 Evaluation

Benchmarks. We evaluated our approach on 23 benchmarks as shown in Fig. 6. All benchmarks along with the synthesized solutions can be found in the tech report [6]. Since there is no standard benchmark suite for morphism problems, we chose our benchmarks from common assignment problems (the lambda calculus ones), desugaring passes from SKETCH compiler and some standard data structure manipulations on trees and lists. The AST optimization benchmarks are from a system that synthesizes simplification rules for SMT solvers [17].

Templates. The templates for all our benchmarks use one of the four generic descriptions we have in the library. All benchmarks except arrAssertions , NegNorm and AST optimizations use a generalized version of the recursiveReplacer generator seen in Fig. 3 (the exact generator is in the tech report). This generator is also used as a template for problems that are very different from the desugaring benchmarks such as the list and the tree manipulation problems, illustrating how generic and reusable the templates can be. The arrAssertions benchmark differs slightly from the others as its ADT definitions have arrays of recursive fields and hence, we have a version of the recursive replacer that also recursively iterates over these arrays. The NegNorm benchmark requires a template that has nested pattern matching. Another interesting example of reusability of templates is the AST optimization benchmarks. All 5 benchmarks in this category are synthesized from a single library function. The template column in Fig. 6 shows the number of lines used in the template for each benchmark. Most benchmarks have a single line that calls the appropriate library description similar to the example in Sect. 2. Some benchmarks also specify additional components such as helper functions that are required for the transformation. Note that these additional components will also be required for other systems such as Leon and Synquid.

4.1 Experiments

Methodology. All experiments were run on a machine with forty 2.4 GHz Intel Xeon processors and 96 GB RAM. We ran each experiment 10 times and report the median.

Hypothesis 1: Synthesis of Complex Routines is Possible. Figure 6 shows the running times for all our benchmarks (T−opt column). SYNTREC can synthesize all but one benchmark very efficiently when run on a single core using less than 1 GB memory—19 out of 23 benchmarks take ≤1 min. Many of these benchmarks are beyond what can be synthesized by other tools like Leon, Rosette, and others and yet, SYNTREC can synthesize them just from very general templates. For instance, the IcB and IcP benchmarks are automatically discovering the Church encodings for boolean operations and pairs, respectively. The tc benchmark synthesizes an algorithm to produce type constraints for lambda calculus ASTs to be used to do type inference. The output of this algorithm is a conjunction of type equality constraints which is produced by traversing the AST. Several other desugaring benchmarks have specifications that involve complicated interpreters that keep track of state, for example. Some of these specifications are even undecidable and yet, SYNTREC can synthesize these benchmarks (up to bounded correctness guarantees). The figure also shows the size of the synthesized solution (code column)[3].

There is one benchmark (langState) that cannot be solved by SYNTREC using a single core. Even in this case, SYNTREC can synthesize the desugaring for 6 out of 7 variants in less than a minute. The unresolved variant requires generating expression terms that are very deep which exponentially increases the search space. Luckily, our solver is able to leverage multiple cores using the random concretization technique [7] to search the space of possible programs in parallel. The column T−parallel in Fig. 6 shows the running times for all benchmarks when run on 16 cores. SYNTREC can now synthesize all variants of the langState benchmark in about 9 min.

The results discussed so far are obtained for optimal search parameters for each of the benchmarks. We also run an experiment to randomly search for these parameters using the parallel search technique with 16 cores and report the results in the T−search column. Although these times are higher than when using the optimal parameters for each benchmark (T−parallel column), the difference is not huge for most benchmarks.

Hypothesis 2: The Inductive Decomposition Improves the Scalability. In this experiment, we run each benchmark with the *Inductive Decomposition* optimization disabled and the results are shown in Fig. 6 (T−unopt column). This experiment is run on a single core. First of all, the technique is not applicable for the AST optimization benchmarks because the functions to be synthesized are not recursive. Second, for three benchmarks—the λ-calculus ones and the

---

[3] Solution size is measured as the number of nodes in the AST representation of the solution.

	Bench	Description	template	code	T-opt	T-parallel	T-search	T-unopt
Desugar	lang	Running example	1	50	7.5	8.6	85.9	152.5
	langState	Running example with mutable state	1	62	$\perp$	527.2	1746.9	$\perp$
	regex	Desugaring regular expressions	1	22	2.0	3.3	9.1	3.3
	elimBool	Boolean operations to if else	1	21	1.5	2.9	7.5	2.4
	compAssign	Eliminates compound assignments	1	42	16.6	20.9	31.8	176.2
	langLarge	Desugaring a large language	1	126	61.2	58.0	49.7	$\perp$
	arrAssertions	Add out of bounds assertions	3	40	37.2	50.5	66.7	53.0
	NegNorm	Computes negation normal form	3	57	21.2	13.6	64.4	$\perp$
	lcB	Boolean operations to λ-calculus	1	55	43.1	47.4	40.6	47.4
	lcP	Pairs to λ-calculus	1	41	163.6	258.2	288.3	258.2
Analysis	tc	Type constraints for λ-calculus	8	41	168.9	68.0	201.9	68.0
AST optim	andLt	AST optimization 1	1	15	3.1	3.1	13.2	N/A
	andNot	AST optimization 2	1	6	2.6	3.0	13.0	N/A
	andOr	AST optimization 3	1	12	3.7	3.1	14.0	N/A
	plusEq	AST optimization 4	1	18	3.3	3.0	14.0	N/A
	mux	AST optimization 5	1	6	2.4	3.0	12.4	N/A
List	lIns	List insertion	1	12	1.5	2.3	2.2	2.1
	lDel	List deletion	2	14	4.0	4.6	4.1	3.1
	lUnion	Union of two lists	1	10	8.7	2.7	4.8	2.1
Tree	tIns	Binary search tree insertion	1	48	20.7	14.5	41.6	11.6
	tDel	Binary search tree deletion	4	63	224.8	227.4	286.1	298.9
	tDelMin	Binary search tree delete min	2	18	27.1	32.2	57.7	24.9
	tDelMax	Binary search tree delete max	2	18	25.9	30.8	54.4	25.9

Fig. 6. Benchmarks. All reported times are in seconds. $\perp$ stands for timeout (>45 min) and N/A stands for not applicable.

tc benchmark, we noticed that their specifications do not have the inductive structure and hence, the optimization never gets triggered.

But for the other benchmarks, it can be seen that *inductive decomposition* leads to a substantial speed-up on the bigger benchmarks. Three benchmarks time out (>45 min) and we found that langState times out even when run in parallel. In addition, without the optimization, all the different variants need to be synthesized together and hence, it is not possible to get partial solutions. The other benchmarks show an average speedup of 2X with two benchmarks having a speedup >10X. We found that for benchmarks that have very few variants, such as the list and the tree benchmarks, both versions perform almost similarly.

To evaluate how the performance depends on the number of variants in the initial AST, we considered the langLarge benchmark that synthesizes a desugaring for a source language with 15 variants into a destination language with just 4 variants. We started the benchmark with 3 variants in the source language while incrementally adding the additional variants and measured the run times both with the optimization enabled and disabled. The graph of run time against the number of variants is shown in Fig. 7. It can be seen that without the optimization the performance degrades very quickly and moreover, the unoptimized version times out (>45 min) when the number of variants is >11.

4.2 Comparison to Other Tools

We compared SYNTREC against three tools—Leon, Synquid and Rosette that can express our benchmarks. The list and the tree benchmarks are the typical benchmarks that Leon and Synquid can solve and they are faster than us on these benchmarks. However, this difference is mostly due to SYNTREC's final verification time. For these benchmarks, our verification is not at the state of the art because we use a very naive library for the set related functions used in their specifications. We also found that Leon and Synquid can synthesize some of our easy desugaring benchmarks that requires constructing relatively small ADTs like elimBool and regex in almost the same time as us. However, Leon and Synquid were not able to solve the harder desugaring problems including the running example. We should also note that this comparison is not totally apples-to-apples as Leon and Synquid are more automated than SYNTREC.

For comparison against Rosette, we should first note that since Rosette is also a SyGus solver, we had to write very verbose templates for each benchmark. But even then, we found that Rosette cannot get past the compilation stage because the solver gets bogged down by the large number of recursive calls requiring expansion. For the other smaller benchmarks that were able to get to the synthesis stage, we found that Rosette is either comparable or slower than SYNTREC. For example, the benchmark elimBool takes about 2 min in Rosette compared to 2 s in SYNTREC. We attribute these differences to the different solver level choices made by Rosette and SKETCH (which we used to built SYNTREC upon).

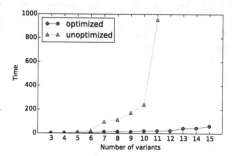

Fig. 7. Run time (in seconds) versus the number of variants of the source language for the langLarge benchmark with and without the optimization.

5   Related Work

There are many recent systems that synthesize recursive functions on algebraic data-types. Leon [3,8,9] and Synquid [16] are two systems that are very close to ours. Leon, developed by the LARA group at EPFL, is built on prior work on complete functional synthesis by the same group [10] and moreover, their recent work on Synthesis Modulo Recursive Functions [8] demonstrated a sound technique to synthesize provably correct recursive functions involving algebraic data types. Unlike our system, which relies on bounded checking to establish the correctness of candidates, their procedure is capable of synthesizing provably correct implementations. The tradeoff is the scalability of the system; Leon supports using arbitrary recursive predicates in the specification, but in practice it is limited by what is feasible to prove automatically. Verifying something like equivalence of lambda interpreters fully automatically is prohibitively expensive, which puts some of our benchmarks beyond the scope of their system.

Synquid [16], on the other hand, uses refinement types as a form of specification to efficiently synthesize programs. Like our system, Synquid also depends on bi-directional type checking to effectively prune the search space. But like Leon, it is also limited to decidable specifications. There has also been a lot of recent work on programming by example systems for synthesizing recursive programs [1,4,13,14]. All of these systems rely on explicit search with some systems like [13] using bi-directional typing to prune the search space and other systems like [1] using specialized data-structures to efficiently represent the space of implementations. However, they are limited to programming-by-example settings, and cannot handle our benchmarks, especially the desugaring ones.

Our work builds on a lot of previous work on SAT/SMT based synthesis from templates. Our implementation itself is built on top of the open source Sketch synthesis system [18]. However, several other solver-based synthesizers have been reported in the literature, such as Brahma [5]. More recently, the work on the solver aided language Rosette [20,21] has shown how to embed synthesis capabilities in a rich dynamic language and then how to leverage these features to produce synthesis-enabled embedded DSLs in the language. Rosette is a very expressive language and in principle can express all the benchmarks in our paper. However, Rosette is a dynamic language and lacks static type information, so in order to get the benefits of the high-level synthesis constructs presented in this paper, it would be necessary to re-implement all the machinery in this paper as an embedded DSL.

There is also some related work in the context of using polymorphism to enable re-usability in programming. [11] is one such approach where the authors describe a design pattern in Haskell that allows programmers to express the boilerplate code required for traversing recursive data structures in a reusable manner. This paper, on the other hand, focuses on supporting reusable templates in the context of synthesis which has not been explored before. Finally, the work on hole driven development [12] is also related in the way it uses types to gain information about the structure of the missing code. The key difference is that existing systems like Agda lack the kind of symbolic search capabilities present in our system, which allow it to search among the exponentially large set of expressions with the right structure for one that satisfies a deep semantic property like equivalence with respect to an interpreter.

6 Conclusion

The paper has shown that by combining type information from algebraic datatypes together with the novel Inductive Decomposition optimization, it is possible to efficiently synthesize complex functions based on pattern matching from very general templates, including desugaring functions for lambda calculus that implement non-trivial Church encodings.

Acknowledgments. We would like to thank the authors of Leon and Rosette for their help in comparing against their systems and the reviewers for their feedback. This research was supported by NSF award #1139056 (ExCAPE).

References

1. Albarghouthi, A., Gulwani, S., Kincaid, Z.: Recursive program synthesis. In: Sharygina, N., Veith, H. (eds.) CAV 2013. LNCS, vol. 8044, pp. 934–950. Springer, Heidelberg (2013). doi:10.1007/978-3-642-39799-8_67
2. Alur, R., Bodík, R., Juniwal, G., Martin, M.M.K., Raghothaman, M., Seshia, S.A., Singh, R., Solar-Lezama, A., Torlak, E., Udupa, A.: Syntax-guided synthesis. In: Formal Methods in Computer-Aided Design, FMCAD 2013, Portland, OR, USA, 20–23 October 2013, pp. 1–8 (2013)
3. Blanc, R., Kuncak, V., Kneuss, E., Suter, P.: An overview of the Leon verification system: verification by translation to recursive functions. In: Proceedings of the 4th Workshop on Scala, SCALA 2013, p. 1:1–1:10. ACM, New York (2013)
4. Feser, J.K., Chaudhuri, S., Dillig, I.: Synthesizing data structure transformations from input-output examples. In: Proceedings of the 36th ACM SIGPLAN Conference on Programming Language Design and Implementation, Portland, OR, USA, 15–17 June 2015, pp. 229–239 (2015)
5. Gulwani, S., Jha, S., Tiwari, A., Venkatesan, R.: Synthesis of loop-free programs. In: PLDI, pp. 62–73 (2011)
6. Inala, J.P., Qiu, X., Lerner, B., Solar-Lezama, A.: Type assisted synthesis of recursive transformers on algebraic data types (2015). CoRR, abs/1507.05527
7. Jeon, J., Qiu, X., Solar-Lezama, A., Foster, J.S.: Adaptive concretization for parallel program synthesis. In: Kroening, D., Păsăreanu, C.S. (eds.) CAV 2015. LNCS, vol. 9207, pp. 377–394. Springer, Heidelberg (2015). doi:10.1007/978-3-319-21668-3_22
8. Kneuss, E., Kuraj, I., Kuncak, V., Suter, P.: Synthesis modulo recursive functions. In: OOPSLA, pp. 407–426 (2013)
9. Kuncak, V.: Verifying and synthesizing software with recursive functions. In: Esparza, J., Fraigniaud, P., Husfeldt, T., Koutsoupias, E. (eds.) ICALP 2014. LNCS, vol. 8572, pp. 11–25. Springer, Heidelberg (2014). doi:10.1007/978-3-662-43948-7_2
10. Kuncak, V., Mayer, M., Piskac, R., Suter, P.: Complete functional synthesis. In: Proceedings of the 2010 ACM SIGPLAN Conference on Programming Language Design and Implementation, PLDI 2010, pp. 316–329 (2010)
11. Lämmel, R., Jones, S.P.: Scrap your boilerplate: a practical design pattern for generic programming. ACM SIGPLAN Not. **38**, 26–37 (2003)
12. Norell, U.: Dependently typed programming in Agda. In: Koopman, P., Plasmeijer, R., Swierstra, D. (eds.) AFP 2008. LNCS, vol. 5832, pp. 230–266. Springer, Heidelberg (2009). doi:10.1007/978-3-642-04652-0_5
13. Osera, P., Zdancewic, S.: Type-and-example-directed program synthesis. In: Proceedings of the 36th ACM SIGPLAN Conference on Programming Language Design and Implementation, Portland, OR, USA, 15–17 June 2015, pp. 619–630 (2015)
14. Perelman, D., Gulwani, S., Grossman, D., Provost, P.: Test-driven synthesis. In: PLDI, p. 43 (2014)
15. Pierce, B.C., Turner, D.N.: Local type inference. ACM Trans. Program. Lang. Syst. **22**(1), 1–44 (2000)
16. Polikarpova, N., Kuraj, I., Solar-Lezama, A.: Program synthesis from polymorphic refinement types. In: Proceedings of the 37th ACM SIGPLAN Conference on Programming Language Design and Implementation, PLDI 2016, pp. 522–538. ACM, New York (2016)

17. Singh, R., Solar-Lezama, A.: Swapper: a framework for automatic generation of formula simplifiers based on conditional rewrite rules. In: Formal Methods in Computer-Aided Design (2016)
18. Solar-Lezama, A.: Program synthesis by sketching. Ph.D. thesis, EECS Department, UC Berkeley (2008)
19. Solar-Lezama, A.: Open source sketch synthesizer (2012)
20. Torlak, E., Bodík, R.: Growing solver-aided languages with Rosette. In: Onward!, pp. 135–152 (2013)
21. Torlak, E., Bodík, R.: A lightweight symbolic virtual machine for solver-aided host languages. In: PLDI, p. 54 (2014)

Counterexample-Guided Model Synthesis

Mathias Preiner[(⊠)], Aina Niemetz, and Armin Biere

Johannes Kepler University, Linz, Austria
mathias.preiner@jku.at

Abstract. In this paper we present a new approach for solving quantified formulas in Satisfiability Modulo Theories (SMT), with a particular focus on the theory of fixed-size bit-vectors. We combine counterexample-guided quantifier instantiation with a syntax-guided synthesis approach, which allows us to synthesize both Skolem functions and terms for quantifier instantiations. Our approach employs two ground theory solvers to reason about quantified formulas. It neither relies on quantifier specific simplifications nor heuristic quantifier instantiation techniques, which makes it a simple yet effective approach for solving quantified formulas. We implemented our approach in our SMT solver Boolector and show in our experiments that our techniques are competitive compared to the state-of-the-art in solving quantified bit-vectors.

1 Introduction

Many techniques in hardware and software verification rely on quantifiers for describing properties of programs and circuits, e.g., universal safety properties, inferring program invariants [1], finding ranking functions [2], and synthesizing hardware and software [3,4]. Quantifiers further allow to define theory axioms to reason about a theory of interest not supported natively by an SMT solver.

The theory of fixed-size bit-vectors provides a natural way of encoding bit-precise semantics as found in hardware and software. In recent SMT competitions, the division for quantifier-free fixed-size bit-vectors was the most competitive with an increasing number of participants every year. Quantified bit-vector reasoning, however, even though a highly required feature, is still very challenging and did not get as much attention as the quantifier-free fragment. The complexity of deciding quantified bit-vector formulas is known to be NExpTime-hard and solvable in ExpSpace [5]. Its exact complexity, however, is still unknown.

While there exist several SMT solvers that efficiently reason about quantifier-free bit-vectors, only CVC4 [6], Z3 [7], and Yices [8] support the quantified bit-vector fragment. The SMT solver CVC4 employs counterexample-guided quantifier instantiation (CEGQI) [9], where a ground theory solver tries to find concrete values (counterexamples) for instantiating universal variables by generating models of the negated input formula. In Z3, an approach called model-based quantifier instantiation (MBQI) [10] is combined with a model finding procedure

Supported by Austrian Science Fund (FWF) under NFN Grant S11408-N23 (RiSE).

A. Legay and T. Margaria (Eds.): TACAS 2017, Part I, LNCS 10205, pp. 264–280, 2017.
DOI: 10.1007/978-3-662-54577-5_15

based on templates [11]. In contrast to only relying on concrete counterexamples as candidates for quantifier instantiation, MBQI additionally uses symbolic quantifier instantiation to generalize the counterexample by selecting ground terms to rule out more spurious models. The SMT solver Yices provides quantifier support limited to exists/forall problems [12] of the form $\exists \mathbf{x} \forall \mathbf{y}.P[\mathbf{x},\mathbf{y}]$. It employs two ground solver instances, one for checking the satisfiability of a set of generalizations and generating candidate solutions for the existential variables $\mathbf{x}$, and the other for checking if the candidate solution is correct. If the candidate model is not correct, a model-based generalization procedure refines the candidate models.

Recently, a different approach based on binary decision diagrams (BDD) was proposed in [13]. Experimental results of its prototype implementation Q3B show that it is competitive with current state-of-the-art SMT solvers. However, employing BDDs for solving quantified bit-vectors heavily relies on formula simplifications, variable ordering, and approximation techniques to reduce the size of the BDDs. If these techniques fail to substantially reduce the size of the BDDs this approach does not scale. Further, in most applications it is necessary to provide models in case of satisfiable problems. However, it is unclear if a bit-level BDD-based model can be lifted to produce more succinct word-level models.

In this paper, we combine a variant of CEGQI with a syntax-guided synthesis [14] approach to create a model finding algorithm called *counterexample-guided model synthesis* (CEGMS), which iteratively refines a synthesized candidate model. Unlike Z3, our approach synthesizes Skolem functions based on a set of ground instances without the need for specifying function or circuit templates up-front. Further, we can apply CEGMS to the negation of the formula in a parallel dual setting to synthesize quantifier instantiations that prove the unsatisfiability of the original problem. Our approach is a simple yet efficient technique that does not rely on quantifier specific simplifications, which have previously been found to be particularly useful [11]. Our experimental evaluation shows that our approach is competitive with the state-of-the-art in solving quantified bit-vectors. However, even though we implemented it in Boolector, an SMT solver for the theory of bit-vectors with arrays and uninterpreted functions, our techniques are not restricted to the theory of quantified bit-vectors.

2   Preliminaries

We assume the usual notions and terminology of first-order logic and primarily focus on the theory of *quantified fixed-size bit-vectors*. We only consider many-sorted languages, where bit-vectors of different size are interpreted as bit-vectors of different sorts.

Let Σ be a signature consisting of a set of function symbols $f : n_1, \ldots, n_k \rightarrow n$ with arity $k \geq 0$ and a set of bit-vector sorts with size $n, n_1, \ldots, n_k$. For the sake of simplicity and w.l.o.g., we assume that sort *Bool* is interpreted as a bit-vector of size one with constants $\top$ (1) and $\bot$ (0), and represent all predicate symbols as function symbols with a bit-vector of size one as the sort of the co-domain. We refer to function symbols occurring in Σ as *interpreted*, and those symbols not included in Σ as *uninterpreted*. A *bit-vector term* is either a bit-vector variable or an application of a bit-vector function of the form $f(t_1, \ldots, t_k)$, where $f \in \Sigma$ or $f \notin \Sigma$, and $t_1, \ldots, t_k$ are bit-vector terms. We denote bit-vector term t of size n as $t_{[n]}$ and define its *domain* as $\mathcal{BV}_{[n]}$, which consists of all *bit-vector values* of size n. Analogously, we represent a bit-vector value as an integer with its size as a subscript, e.g., $1_{[4]}$ for 0001 or $-1_{[4]}$ for 1111.

We assume the usual interpreted symbols for the theory of bit-vectors, e.g., $=_{[n]}, +_{[n]}, *_{[n]}, concat_{[n+m]}, <_{[n]}$, etc., and will omit the subscript specifying their bit-vector size if the context allows. We further interpret an $ite(c, t_0, t_1)$ as an *if-then-else* over bit-vector terms, where $ite(\top, t_0, t_1) = t_0$ and $ite(\bot, t_0, t_1) = t_1$.

In general, we refer to 0-arity function symbols as *constant* symbols, and denote them by a, b, and c. We use f and g for non-constant function symbols, P for predicates, x, y and z for variables, and t for arbitrary terms. We use symbols in bold font, e.g., $\mathbf{x}$, as a shorthand for tuple $(x_1, \ldots, x_k)$, and denote a formula (resp. term) that may contain variables $\mathbf{x}$ as $\varphi[\mathbf{x}]$ (resp. $t[\mathbf{x}]$). If a formula (resp. term) does not contain any variables we refer to it as *ground* formula (resp. term). We further use $\varphi[t/x]$ as a notation for *replacing* all occurrences of x in φ with a term t. Similarly, $\varphi[\mathbf{t}/\mathbf{x}]$ is used as a shorthand for $\varphi[t_1/x_1, \ldots, t_k/x_k]$.

Given a quantified formula $\varphi[\mathbf{x}, \mathbf{y}]$ with universal variables $\mathbf{x}$ and existential variables $\mathbf{y}$, *Skolemization* [15] eliminates all existential variables $\mathbf{y}$ by introducing *fresh* uninterpreted function symbols with arity ≥ 0 for the existential variables $\mathbf{y}$. For example, the *skolemized* form of formula $\exists y_1 \forall \mathbf{x} \exists y_2. P(y_1, \mathbf{x}, y_2)$ is $\forall \mathbf{x}. P(f_{y_1}, \mathbf{x}, f_{y_2}(\mathbf{x}))$, where f_{y_1} and f_{y_2} are fresh uninterpreted symbols, which we refer to as *Skolem symbols*. The subscript denotes the existential variable that was eliminated by the corresponding Skolem symbol. We write $skolemize(\varphi)$ for the application of Skolemization to formula φ, $var_\forall(\varphi)$ for the set of universal variables in φ, and $sym_{sk}(\varphi)$ for the set of Skolem symbols in φ.

A Σ-structure M maps each bit-vector sort of size n to its domain $\mathcal{BV}_{[n]}$, each function symbol $f : n_1, \ldots, n_k \to n \in \Sigma$ with arity $k > 0$ to a total function $M(f) : \mathcal{BV}_{[n_1]}, \ldots, \mathcal{BV}_{[n_k]} \to \mathcal{BV}_{[n]}$, and each constant symbol with size n to an element in $\mathcal{BV}_{[n]}$. We use $M' := M\{x \mapsto v\}$ to denote a Σ-structure M' that maps variable x to a value v of the same sort and is otherwise identical to M. The evaluation $M(x_{[n]})$ of a variable $x_{[n]}$ and $M(c_{[n]})$ of a constant c in M is an element in $\mathcal{BV}_{[n]}$. The evaluation of an arbitrary term t in M is denoted by $M[\![t]\!]$ and is recursively defined as follows. For a constant c (resp. variable x) $M[\![c]\!] = M(c)$ (resp. $M[\![x]\!] = M(x)$). A function symbol f is evaluated as $M[\![f(t_1, \ldots, t_k)]\!] = M(f)(M[\![t_1]\!], \ldots, M[\![t_k]\!])$. A Σ-structure M is a *model* of a formula φ if $M[\![\varphi]\!] = \top$. A formula is *satisfiable* if and only if it has a model.

3   Overview

In essence, our *counterexample-guided model synthesis* (CEGMS) approach for solving quantified bit-vector problems combines a variant of counterexample-guided quantifier instantiation (CEGQI) [9] with the syntax-guided synthesis

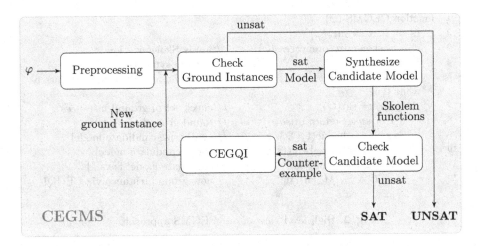

Fig. 1. Basic workflow of our CEGMS approach.

approach in [14] in order to synthesize Skolem functions. The general workflow of our approach is depicted in Fig. 1 and introduced as follows.

Given a quantified formula φ as input, CEGMS first applies Skolemization as a preprocessing step and initializes an empty set of ground instances. This empty set is, in the following, iteratively extended with ground instances of φ, generated via CEGQI. In each iteration, CEGMS first checks for a ground conflict by calling a ground theory solver instance on the set of ground instances. If the solver returns *unsatisfiable*, a ground conflict was found and the CEGMS procedure concludes with UNSAT. If the solver returns *satisfiable*, it produces a model for the Skolem symbols, which serves as a base for synthesizing a candidate model for all Skolem functions. If the candidate model is valid, the CEGMS procedure concludes with SAT. However, if the candidate model is invalid, the solver generates a counterexample, which is used to create a new ground instance of the formula via CEGQI. The CEGMS procedure terminates, when either a ground conflict occurs, or a valid candidate model is synthesized.

4   Counterexample-Guided Model Synthesis

The main refinement loop of our CEGMS approach is realized via CEGQI [9], a technique similar to the *generalization by substitution* approach described in [12], where a concrete counterexample to universal variables is used to create a ground instance of the formula, which then serves as a refinement for the candidate model. Similarly, every refinement step of our CEGMS approach produces a ground instance of the formula by instantiating its universal variables with a counter example if the synthesized candidate model is not valid. The counterexample corresponds to a concrete assignment to the universal variables for which the candidate model does not satisfy the formula. Figure 2 introduces the main algorithm of our CEGMS approach as follows.

```
1    function CEGMS (φ)
2        G := ⊤, x := var∀(φ)
3        φsk := skolemize(preprocess(φ))        // apply Skolemization
4        f := symsk(φsk)                        // Skolem symbols
5        φG := φsk[u/x]                         // ground φsk with fresh constants u
6        while true
7            r, MG := sat(G)                    // check set of ground instances
8            if r = unsat return unsat          // found ground conflict
9            MS := synthesize(f, G, MG, φG)     // synthesize candidate model
10           r, MC := sat(¬φG[MS(f)/f])         // check candidate model
11           if r = unsat return sat            // candidate model is valid
12           G := G ∧ φG[MC(u)/u]               // new ground instance via CEGQI
```

Fig. 2. High level view of our CEGMS approach.

Given a quantified bit-vector formula φ, we represent φ as a directed acyclic graph (DAG), with the Boolean layer expressed by means of *AND* and *NOT*. As a consequence, it is not possible to transform φ into negative normal form (NNF) and we therefore apply quantifier normalization as a preprocessing step to ensure that a quantifier does not occur in both negated and non-negated form. For the same reason, an *ite*-term is eliminated in case that a quantifier occurs in its condition. Note that if φ is not in NNF, it is sufficient to keep track of the polarities of the quantifiers, i.e., to count the number of negations from the root of the formula to the resp. quantifier, and flip the quantifier if the number of negations is odd. If a quantifier occurs negative and positive, the scope of the quantifier is duplicated, the quantification is flipped, and the negative occurrence is substituted with the new subgraph. Further note that preprocessing currently does not include any further simplification techniques such as miniscoping or destructive equality resolution (DER) [11].

After preprocessing, Skolemization is applied to the normalized formula, and all universal variables $\mathbf{x}$ in φ_{sk} are instantiated with fresh bit-vector constants $\mathbf{u}$ of the same sort. This yields ground formula φ_G. Initially, procedure CEGMS starts with an empty set of ground instances G, which is iteratively extended with new ground instances during the refinement loop.

In the first step of the loop, an SMT solver instance checks whether G contains a ground conflict (line 7). If this is the case, procedure CEGMS has found conflicting quantifier instantiations and concludes with *unsatisfiable*. Else, the SMT solver produces model M_G for all Skolem symbols in G, i.e., every Skolem constant is mapped to a bit-vector value, and every uninterpreted function corresponding to a Skolem function is mapped to a partial function mapping bit-vector values. Model M_G is used as a base for synthesizing a candidate model M_S that satisfies G. The synthesis of candidate models M_S will be introduced in more detail in the next section. In order to check if M_S is also a model that satisfies φ, we check with an additional SMT solver instance if there exists an assignment to constants $\mathbf{u}$ (corresponding to universal variables $\mathbf{x}$), such that candidate model M_S does not satisfy formula φ (line 10).

If the second SMT solver instance returns unsatisfiable, no such assignment to constants **u** exists and consequently, candidate model M_S is indeed a valid model for the Skolem functions and procedure CEGMS returns with *satisfiable*. Else, the SMT solver produces a concrete counterexample for constants **u**, for which candidate model M_S does not satisfy formula φ. This counterexample is used as a quantifier instantiation to create a new ground instance $g_i := \varphi_G[M_C(\mathbf{u})/\mathbf{u}]$, which is added to $G := G \wedge g_i$ as a refinement (line 12) and considered in the next iteration for synthesizing a candidate model. These steps are repeated until either a ground conflict is found or a valid candidate model was synthesized.

Our CEGMS procedure creates in the worst-case an unmanageable number of ground instances of the formula prior to finding either a ground conflict or a valid candidate model, infinitely many in case of infinite domains. In the bit-vector case, however, it produces in the worst-case exponentially many ground instances in the size of the domain. Since, given a bit-vector formula, there exist only finitely many such ground instances, procedure CEGMS will always terminate. Further, if CEGMS concludes with satisfiable, it returns with a model for the existential variables.

5   Synthesis of Candidate Models

In our CEGMS approach, based on a concrete model M_G we apply synthesis to find general models M_S to accelerate either finding a valid model or a ground conflict. Consider formula $\varphi := \forall xy \exists z . z = x + y$, its skolemized form $\varphi_{sk} := \forall xy . f_z(x, y) = x + y$, some ground instances $G := f_z(0,0) = 0 \wedge f_z(0,1) = 1 \wedge f_z(1,2) = 3$, and model $M_G := \{f_z(0,0) \mapsto 0, f_z(0,1) \mapsto 1, f_z(1,2) \mapsto 3\}$ that satisfies G. A simple approach for generating a Skolem function for f_z would be to represent model $M_G(f_z)$ as a lambda term $\lambda xy.ite(x = 0 \wedge y = 0, 0, ite(x = 0 \wedge y = 1, 1, ite(x = 1 \wedge y = 2, 3, 0)))$ with base case constant 0, and check if it is a valid Skolem function for f_z. If it is not valid, a counterexample is generated and a new ground instance is added via CEGQI to refine the set of ground instances G. However, this approach, in the worst-case, enumerates exponentially many ground instances until finding a valid candidate model. By introducing a modified version of a syntax-guided synthesis technique called *enumerative learning* [16], CEGMS is able to produce a more succinct and more general lambda term $\lambda xy . x + y$, which satisfies the ground instances G and formula φ_{sk}.

Enumerative learning as in [16] systematically enumerates expressions that can be built based on a given syntax and checks whether the generated expression conforms to a set of concrete test cases. These expressions are generated in increasing order of a specified complexity metric, such as, e.g., the size of the expression. The algorithm creates larger expressions by combining smaller ones of a given size, which is similar to the idea of dynamic programming. Each generated expression is evaluated on the concrete test cases, which yields a vector of values also denoted as *signature*. In order to reduce the number of enumerated expressions, the algorithm discards expressions with identical signatures, i.e., if two expressions produce the same signature the one generated first will be stored and the other one will be discarded. Figure 3 depicts a simplified version of the enumerative learning algorithm as employed in our CEGMS approach, while a more detailed description of the original algorithm can be found in [16].

```
1   function enumlearn (f, I, O, T, M)
2       S := ∅, E[1] := I, size = 0
3       while true
4           size := size + 1              // increase expression size to create
5           for t ∈ enumexps(size, O, E)  // enumerate all expressions of size size
6               s := eval(M, T[t/f])       // compute signature of t
7               if s ∉ S                   // expression not yet created
8                   S := S ∪ {s}           // cache signature
9                   if checksig(s) return t // t conforms to test cases T
10                  E[size] := E[size] ∪ {t} // store expression t
```

Fig. 3. Simplified version of enumerative learning [16] employed in CEGMS.

Given a Skolem symbol f, a set of inputs I, a set of operators O, a set of test cases T, and a model M, algorithm enumlearn attempts to synthesize a term t, such that $T[t/f]$ evaluates to true under model M. This is done by enumerating all terms t that can be built with inputs I and bit-vector operators O. Enumerating all expressions of a certain size (function enumexps) follows the original enumerative learning approach [16]. Given an expression size $size$ and a bit-vector operator o, the size is partitioned into partitions of size $k = arity(o)$, e.g., (1,3) (3,1) (2,2) for $size = 4$ and $k = 2$. Each partition $(s_1, \ldots, s_k)$ specifies the size s_i of expression e_i, and is used to create expressions of size $size$ with operator o, i.e., $\{o(e_1, \ldots, e_k) \mid (e_1, \ldots, e_k) \in E[s_1] \times \ldots \times E[s_k]\}$, where $E[s_i]$ corresponds to the set of expressions of size s_i. Initially, for $size = 1$, function enumexps enumerates inputs only, i.e., $E[1] = I$.

For each generated term t, a signature s is computed from a set of test cases T with function eval. In the original algorithm [16], set T contains concrete examples of the input/output relation of f, i.e., it defines a set of output values of f under some concrete input values. In our case, model $M(f)$ may be used as a test set T, since it contains a concrete input/output relation on some bit-vector values. However, we are not looking for a term t with that concrete input/output value behaviour, but a term t that at least satisfies the set of current ground instances G. Hence, we use G as our test set and create a signature s by evaluating every ground instance $g_i \in G[t/f]$, resulting in a tuple of Boolean constants, where the Boolean constant at position i corresponds to the value $M[\![g_i]\!]$ of ground instance $g_i \in G[t/f]$ under current model M. Procedure checksig returns true if signature s contains only the Boolean constant $\top$, i.e., if every ground instance $g_i \in G$ is satisfied.

As a consequence of using G rather than $M(f)$ as a test set T, the expression enumeration space is even more pruned since computing the signature of f

w.r.t. G yields more identical expressions (and consequently, more expressions get discarded). Note that the evaluation via function eval does not require additional SMT solver calls, since the value of ground instance $g_i \in G[t/f]$ can be computed via evaluating $M[\![g_i]\!]$.

Algorithm synthesize produces Skolem function candidates for every Skolem symbol $f \in \mathbf{f}$, as depicted in Fig. 4. Initially, a set of bit-vector operators O is selected, which consists of those operators appearing in formula φ_G. Note that we do not select all available bit-vector operators of the bit-vector theory in order to reduce the number of expressions to enumerate. The algorithm then selects a set of inputs I, consisting of the universal variables on which f depends and the constant values that occur in formula φ_G. Based on inputs I and operators O, a term t for Skolem symbol f is synthesized and stored in model M_S (lines 4–7). If algorithm enumlearn is not able to synthesize a term t, model $M_G(f)$ is used instead. This might happen if function enumlearn hits some predefined limit such as the maximum number of expressions enumerated.

```
1   function synthesize (f, G, M_G, φ_G)
2       M_S := M_G, O := ops(φ_G)              // choose operators O w.r.t. formula φ_G
3       for f ∈ f
4           I := inputs(f, φ_G)                // choose inputs for f
5           t := enumlearn(f, I, O, G, M_S)    // synthesize term t
6           if t ≠ null
7               M_S := M_S{f ↦ t}              // update model
8       return M_S
```

Fig. 4. Synthesis of candidate models in CEGMS.

In each iteration step of function synthesize, model M_S is updated if enumlearn succeeded in synthesizing a Skolem function. Thus, in the next iterations, previously synthesized Skolem functions are considered for evaluating candidate expressions in function enumlearn. This is crucial to guarantee that each synthesized Skolem function still satisfies the ground instances in G. Otherwise, M_S may not rule out every counterexample generated so far, and thus, validating the candidate model may result in a counterexample that was already produced in a previous refinement iteration. As a consequence, our CEGMS procedure would not terminate even for finite domains since it might get stuck in an infinite refinement loop while creating already existing ground instances.

The number of inputs and bit-vector operators used as base for algorithm enumlearn significantly affects the size of the enumeration space. Picking too many inputs and operators enumerates too many expressions and algorithm enumlearn will not find a candidate term in a reasonable time, whereas restricting the number of inputs and operators too much may not yield a candidate expression at all. In our implementation, we kept it simple and maintain a set of base operators $\{ite, \sim\}$, which gets extended with additional bit-vector operators occurring in the original formula. The set of inputs consists of the constant values occurring in the original formula and the universal variables on which a Skolem symbol depends. Finding more restrictions on the combination of inputs and bit-vector operators in order to reduce the size of the enumeration space is an important issue, but left to future work.

Example 1. Consider $\varphi := \forall x \exists y \, . \, (x < 0 \rightarrow y = -x) \wedge (x \geq 0 \rightarrow y = x)$, and its skolemized form $\forall x \, . \, (x < 0 \rightarrow f_y(x) = -x) \wedge (x \geq 0 \rightarrow f_y(x) = x)$, where y and consequently $f_y(x)$ corresponds to the absolute value function *abs(x)*. For synthesizing a candidate model for f_y, we first pick the set of inputs $I := \{x, 0\}$ and the set of operators $O := \{-, \sim, <, ite\}$ based on formula φ. Note that we omitted operators $\geq$ and $\rightarrow$ since they can be expressed by means of the other operators. The ground formula and its negation are defined as follows.

$$\varphi_G := (u < 0 \rightarrow f_y(u) = -u) \wedge (u \geq 0 \rightarrow f_y(u) = u)$$
$$\neg\varphi_G := (u < 0 \wedge f_y(u) \neq -u) \vee (u \geq 0 \wedge f_y(u) \neq u)$$

For every refinement round i, the table below shows the set of ground instances G, the synthesized candidate model $M(f_y)$, formula $\neg\varphi_G[M_S(f_y)/f_y]$ for checking the candidate model, and a counterexample M_C for constant u if the candidate model was not correct.

i	G	$M_S(f_y)$	$\neg\varphi_G[M_S(f_y)/f_y]$	$M_C(u)$
1	$\top$	$\lambda x.0$	$(u < 0 \wedge 0 \neq -u) \vee (u \geq 0 \wedge 0 \neq u)$	1
2	$f_y(1) = 1$	$\lambda x.x$	$(u < 0 \wedge u \neq -u) \vee (u \geq 0 \wedge u \neq u)$	-1
3	$f_y(-1) = 1$	$\lambda x.ite(x < 0, -x, x)$	$(u < 0 \wedge ite(x < 0, -u, u) \neq -u) \vee$ $(u \geq 0 \wedge ite(x < 0, -u, u) \neq u)$	-

In the first round, the algorithm starts with ground formula $G := \top$. Since any model of f_y satisfies G, for the sake of simplicity, we pick $\lambda x.0$ as candidate, resulting in counterexample $u = 1$, and refinement $\varphi_G[1/u] \equiv f_y(1) = 1$ is added to G. In the second round, lambda term $\lambda x.x$ is synthesized as candidate model for f_y since it satisfies $G := f_y(1) = 1$. However, this is still not a valid model for f_y and counterexample $u = -1$ is produced, which yields refinement $\varphi_G[-1/u] \equiv f_y(-1) = 1$. In the third and last round, $M_S(f_y) := \lambda x.ite(x < 0, -x, x)$ is synthesized and found to be a valid model since $\neg\varphi_G[M_S(f_y)/f_y]$ is unsatisfiable, and CEGMS concludes with satisfiable.

6   Dual Counterexample-Guided Model Synthesis

Our CEGMS approach is a model finding procedure that enables us to synthesize Skolem functions for satisfiable problems. However, for the unsatisfiable case we rely on CEGQI to find quantifier instantiations based on concrete counterexamples that produce conflicting ground instances. In practice, CEGQI is often successful in finding ground conflicts. However, it may happen that way too many quantifier instantiations have to be enumerated (in the worst-case exponentially many for finite domains, infinitely many for infinite domains). In order to obtain better (symbolic) candidates for quantifier instantiation, we exploit the concept of duality of the input formula and simultaneously apply our CEGMS approach to the original input and its negation (the *dual* formula).

Given a quantified formula φ and its negation, the dual formula $\neg\varphi$, e.g., $\varphi := \forall \mathbf{x} \exists \mathbf{y}.P[x, y]$ and $\neg\varphi := \exists \mathbf{x} \forall \mathbf{y}.\neg P[x, y]$. If $\neg\varphi$ is satisfiable, then there exists a model $M(\mathbf{x})$ to its existential variables $\mathbf{x}$ such that $\varphi[M(\mathbf{x})/\mathbf{x}, \mathbf{y}]$ is unsatisfiable. That is, a model in the dual formula $\neg\varphi$ can be used as a quantifier instantiation in the original formula φ to immediately produce a ground conflict. Similarly, if $\neg\varphi$ is unsatisfiable, then there exists no quantifier instantiation in φ such that φ is unsatisfiable. As a consequence, if we apply CEGMS to the dual formula and it is able to synthesize a valid candidate model, we obtain a quantifier instantiation that immediately produces a ground conflict in the original formula. Else, if our CEGMS procedure concludes with unsatisfiable on the dual formula, there exists no model to its existential variables and therefore, the original formula is satisfiable.

Dual CEGMS enables us to simultaneously search for models and quantifier instantiations, which is particularly useful in a parallel setting. Further, applying synthesis to produce quantifier instantiations via the dual formula allows us to create terms that are not necessarily ground instances of the original formula. This is particularly useful in cases where heuristic quantifier instantiation techniques based on E-matching [17] or model-based quantifier instantiation [10] struggle due to the fact that they typically select terms as candidates for quantifier instantiation that occur in some set of ground terms of the input formula, as illustrated by the following example.

Example 2. Consider the unsatisfiable formula $\varphi := \forall x \ . \ a * c + b * c \neq x * c$, where $x = a + b$ produces a ground conflict. Unfortunately, $a + b$ is not a ground instance of φ and is consequently not selected as a candidate by current state-of-the-art heuristic quantifier instantiation techniques. However, if we apply CEGMS to the dual formula $\forall abc \exists x \ . \ a * c + b * c = x * c$, we obtain $\lambda xyz.x + y$ as a model for Skolem symbol $f_x(a, b, c)$, which corresponds to the term $a + b$ if instantiated with (a, b, c). Selecting $a + b$ as a term for instantiating variable x in the original formula results in a conflicting ground instance, which immediately allows us to determine unsatisfiability.

Note that if CEGMS concludes unsatisfiable on the dual formula, we currently do not produce a model for the original formula. Generating a model would require further reasoning, e.g., proof reasoning, on the conflicting ground instances of the dual formula and is left to future work.

Further, dual CEGMS currently only utilizes the final result of applying CEGMS to the dual formula. Exchanging intermediate results (synthesized candidate models) between the original and the dual formula in order to prune the search is an interesting direction for future work.

In the context of quantified Boolean formulas (QBF), the duality of the given input has been previously successfully exploited to prune and consequently speed up the search in circuit-based QBF solvers [18]. In the context of SMT, in previous work we applied the concept of duality to optimize lemmas on demand approach for the theory of arrays in Boolector [19].

7   Experiments

We implemented our CEGMS technique and its dual version in our SMT solver Boolector [20], which supports the theory of bit-vectors combined with arrays and uninterpreted functions. We evaluated our approach on two sets of benchmarks (5029 in total). Set BV (191) contains all BV benchmarks of SMT-LIB [21], whereas set BV_{LNIRA} (4838) consists of all LIA, LRA, NIA, NRA benchmarks of SMT-LIB [21] translated into bit-vector problems by substituting every integer or real with a bit-vector of size 32, and every arithmetic operator with its signed bit-vector equivalent.

We evaluated four configurations of Boolector[1]: (1) **Btor**, the CEGMS version without synthesis, (2) **Btor+s**, the CEGMS version with synthesis enabled, (3) **Btor+d**, the dual CEGMS version without synthesis, (4) **Btor+ds**, the dual CEGMS version with synthesis enabled. We compared our approach to the current development versions of the state-of-the-art SMT solvers CVC4[2] [6] and Z3[3] [7], and the BDD-based approach implemented as a prototype called Q3B[4] [13]. The tool Q3B runs two processes with different approximation strategies in a parallel portfolio setting, where one process applies over-approximation and the other under-approximation. The dual CEGMS approach implemented in Boolector is realized with two parallel threads within the solver, one for the original formula and the other for the dual formula. Both threads do not exchange any information and run in a parallel portfolio setting.

All experiments were performed on a cluster with 30 nodes of 2.83GHz Intel Core 2 Quad machines with 8GB of memory using Ubuntu 14.04.5 LTS. We set the limits for each solver/benchmark pair to 7GB of memory and 1200 seconds of CPU time (not wall clock time). In case of a timeout, memory out, or an error, a penalty of 1200 seconds was added to the total CPU time.

Figure 5 illustrates the effect of our model synthesis approach by comparing configurations **Btor** and **Btor+s** on the BV and BV_{LNIRA} benchmark sets. On the BV benchmark set, **Btor+s** solves 22 more instances (21 satisfiable, 1 unsatisfiable) compared to **Btor**. The gain in the number of satisfiable instances is due to the fact that CEGMS is primarily a model finding procedure, which allows to find symbolic models instead of enumerating a possibly large number of bit-vector values, which seems to be crucial on these instances.

---

[1] Boolector commit 4f7837876cf9c28f42649b368eaffaf03c7e1357.
[2] CVC4 commit d19a95344fde1ea1ff7d784b2c4fc6d09f459899.
[3] Z3 commit 186afe7d10d4f0e5acf40f9b1f16a1f1c2d1706c.
[4] Q3B commit 68301686d36850ba782c4d0f9d58f8c4357e1461.

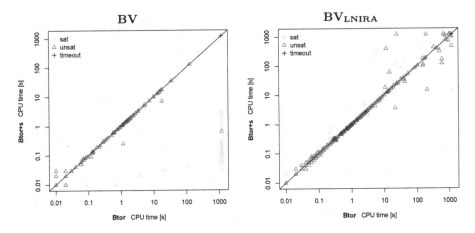

Fig. 5. Comparison of Boolector with model synthesis enabled (**Btor+s**) and disabled (**Btor**) on the BV and BV$_{LNIRA}$ benchmarks.

On set BV$_{LNIRA}$, however, **Btor+s** does not improve the overall number of solved instances, even though it solves two satisfiable instances more than **Btor**. Note that benchmark set BV$_{LNIRA}$ contains only a small number of satisfiable benchmarks (at most 12% = 575 benchmarks[5]), where configuration **Btor** already solves 465 instances without enabling model synthesis. For the remaining satisfiable instances, the enumeration space may still be too large to synthesize a model in reasonable time and may require more pruning by introducing more syntactical restrictions for algorithm *enumlearn* as discussed in Sect. 5.

Figure 6 shows the effect of model synthesis on the dual configurations **Btor+d** and **Btor+ds** on benchmark sets BV and BV$_{LNIRA}$. On the BV benchmark set, configuration **Btor+ds** is able to solve 10 more instances of which all are satisfiable. On the BV$_{LNIRA}$ benchmark set, compared to **Btor+d**, configuration **Btor+ds** is able to solve 132 more instances of which all are unsatisfiable. The significant increase is due to the successful synthesis of quantifier instantiations (133 cases).

Table 1 summarizes the results of all four configurations on both benchmark sets. Configuration **Btor+ds** clearly outperforms all other configurations w.r.t. the number of solved instances and runtime on both benchmark sets. Out of all 77 (517) satisfiable instances in set BV (BV$_{LNIRA}$) solved by **Btor+ds**, 32 (321) were solved by finding a ground conflict in the dual CEGMS approach. In case of configuration **Btor+d**, out of 67 (518) solved satisfiable instances, 44 (306) were solved by finding a ground conflict in the dual formula. As an interesting observation, 16 (53) of these instances were not solved by **Btor**. Note,

---

[5] Boolector, CVC4, Q3B, and Z3 combined solved 4263 unsatisfiable and 533 satisfiable instances, leaving only 42 instances unsolved.

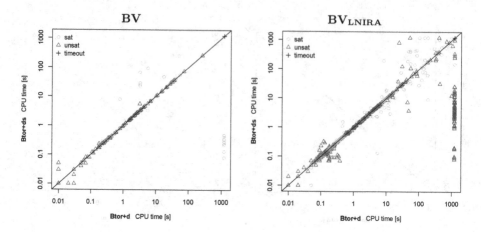

Fig. 6. Comparison of dual CEGMS with model synthesis enabled (**Btor+ds**) and disabled (**Btor+d**) on the BV and BV$_{LNIRA}$ benchmarks.

Table 1. Results for all configurations on the BV and BV$_{LNIRA}$ benchmarks.

	BV (191)					**BV**$_{LNIRA}$ (4838)				
	Solved	Sat	Unsat	Time [s]	Uniq	Solved	Sat	Unsat	Time [s]	Uniq
Btor	142	51	91	59529	0	4527	465	4062	389123	3
Btor+s	164	72	92	32996	0	4526	467	4059	390661	1
Btor+d	162	67	95	35877	0	4572	**518**	4054	342412	4
Btor+ds	**172**	**77**	**95**	**24163**	0	**4704**	517	**4187**	**187411**	**135**

however, that **Btor+d** is not able to construct a model for these instances due to the current limitations of our dual CEGMS approach as described in Sect. 6.

On the BV benchmark set, model synthesis significantly reduces the number of refinement iterations. Out of 142 commonly solved instances, **Btor+s** required 165 refinement iterations, whereas **Btor** required 664 refinements. On the 4522 commonly solved instances of the BV$_{LNIRA}$ benchmark set, **Btor+s** requires 5249 refinement iterations, whereas **Btor** requires 5174 refinements. The difference in the number of refinement iterations is due to the fact that enabling model synthesis may produce different counterexamples that requires the CEGMS procedure to sometimes create more refinements. However, as noted earlier, enabling model synthesis on set BV$_{LNIRA}$ does not improve the overall number of solved instances in the non-dual case.

We analyzed the terms produced by model synthesis for both **Btor+s** and **Btor+ds** on both benchmark sets. On the BV benchmark set, mainly terms of the form $\lambda \mathbf{x}.c$ and $\lambda \mathbf{x}.x_i$ with a bit-vector value c and $x_i \in \mathbf{x}$ have been synthesized. On the BV$_{LNIRA}$ benchmarks, additional terms of the form $\lambda \mathbf{x}.(x_i \; op \; x_j)$, $\lambda \mathbf{x}.(c \; op \; x_i)$, $\lambda \mathbf{x}. \sim(c*x_i))$ and $\lambda \mathbf{x}.(x_i + (c + \sim x_j))$ with a bit-vector operator op were synthesized. On these benchmarks, more complex terms did not occur.

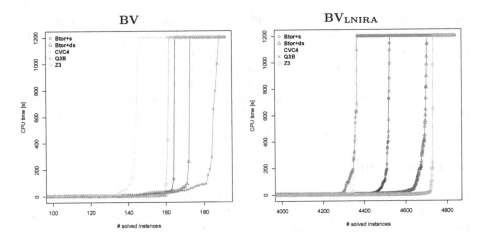

Fig. 7. Cactus plot of the runtime of all solvers on benchmark sets BV and BV$_{LNIRA}$.

Figure 7 depicts two cactus plots over the runtime of our best configuration **Btor+ds** and the solvers **CVC4**, **Q3B**, and **Z3** on the benchmark sets BV and BV$_{LNIRA}$. On both benchmark sets, configuration **Btor+ds** solves the second highest number of benchmarks after **Q3B** (BV) and **Z3** (BV$_{LNIRA}$). On both benchmark sets, a majority of the benchmarks seem to be trivial since they were solved by all solvers within one second.

Table 2 summarizes the results of all solvers on both benchmark sets. On the BV benchmark set, **Q3B** solves with 187 instances the highest number of benchmarks, followed by **Btor+ds** with a total of 172 solved instances. Out of all 19 benchmarks unsolved by **Btor+ds**, 9 benchmarks are solved by **Q3B** and **CVC4** through simplifications only. We expect Boolector to also benefit from introducing quantifier specific simplification techniques, which is left to future work. On the BV$_{LNIRA}$ set, **Z3** solves the most instances (4732) and **Btor+ds** again comes in second with 4704 solved instances. In terms of satisfiable instances, however, **Btor+ds** solves the highest number of instances (517). In terms of unsatisfiable instances, **Z3** clearly has an advantage due to its heuristic

Table 2. Results for all solvers on the BV and BV$_{LNIRA}$ benchmarks with a CPU time limit of 1200 seconds (not wall clock time).

	BV (191)					BV$_{LNIRA}$ (4838)				
	Solved	Sat	Unsat	Time [s]	Uniq	Solved	Sat	Unsat	Time [s]	Uniq
Btor+ds	172	77	**95**	24163	2	4704	**517**	4187	187411	**19**
CVC4	145	64	81	57652	0	4362	339	4023	580402	3
Q3B	**187**	**93**	94	**9086**	9	4367	327	4040	581252	5
Z3	161	69	92	36593	0	**4732**	476	**4256**	**130405**	11

quantifier instantiation techniques and solves 69 instances more than **Btor+ds**, out of which 66 were solved within 3 seconds. The BDD-based approach of **Q3B** does not scale as well on the BV_{LNIRA} set as on the BV set benchmark set and is even outperformed by **Btor+s**. Note that most of the benchmarks in BV_{LNIRA} involve more bit-vector arithmetic than the benchmarks in set BV.

Finally, considering **Btor+ds**, a wall clock time limit of 1200 seconds increases the number of solved instances of set BV_{LNIRA} by 11 (and by 6 for **Q3B**). On set BV, the number of solved instances does not increase.

8   Conclusion

We presented CEGMS, a new approach for handling quantifiers in SMT, which combines CEGQI with syntax-guided synthesis to synthesize Skolem functions. Further, by exploiting the duality of the input formula dual CEGMS enables us to synthesize terms for quantifier instantiation. We implemented CEGMS in our SMT solver Boolector. Our experimental results show that our technique is competitive with the state-of-the-art in solving quantified bit-vectors even though Boolector does not yet employ any quantifier specific simplification techniques. Such techniques, e.g., miniscoping or DER were found particularly useful in Z3. CEGMS employs two ground theory solvers to reason about arbitrarily quantified formulas. It is a simple yet effective technique, and there is still a lot of room for improvement. Model reconstruction from unsatisfiable dual formulas, symbolic quantifier instantiation by generalizing concrete counterexamples, and the combination of quantified bit-vectors with arrays and uninterpreted functions are interesting directions for future work. It might also be interesting to compare our approach to the work presented in [22–25].

Binary of Boolector, the set of translated benchmarks (BV_{LNIRA}) and all log files of our experimental evaluation can be found at http://fmv.jku.at/tacas17.

References

1. Gulwani, S., Srivastava, S., Venkatesan, R.: Constraint-based invariant inference over predicate abstraction. In: Jones, N.D., Müller-Olm, M. (eds.) VMCAI 2009. LNCS, vol. 5403, pp. 120–135. Springer, Heidelberg (2008). doi:10.1007/978-3-540-93900-9_13
2. Cook, B., Kroening, D., Rümmer, P., Wintersteiger, C.M.: Ranking function synthesis for bit-vector relations. In: Esparza, J., Majumdar, R. (eds.) TACAS 2010. LNCS, vol. 6015, pp. 236–250. Springer, Heidelberg (2010). doi:10.1007/978-3-642-12002-2_19
3. Srivastava, S., Gulwani, S., Foster, J.S.: From program verification to program synthesis. In: Hermenegildo, M.V., Palsberg, J. (eds.) Proceedings of the 37th ACM SIGPLAN-SIGACT Symposium on Principles of Programming Languages, POPL 2010, Madrid, Spain, 17–23 January 2010, pp. 313–326. ACM (2010)
4. Jobstmann, B., Bloem, R.: Optimizations for LTL synthesis. In: 6th International Conference on Formal Methods in Computer-Aided Design, FMCAD 2006, San Jose, California, USA, 12–16 November 2006, Proceedings, pp. 117–124. IEEE Computer Society (2006)

5. Kovásznai, G., Fröhlich, A., Biere, A.: Complexity of fixed-size bit-vector logics. Theory Comput. Syst. **59**(2), 323–376 (2016)
6. Barrett, C., Conway, C.L., Deters, M., Hadarean, L., Jovanović, D., King, T., Reynolds, A., Tinelli, C.: CVC4. In: Gopalakrishnan, G., Qadeer, S. (eds.) CAV 2011. LNCS, vol. 6806, pp. 171–177. Springer, Heidelberg (2011). doi:10.1007/978-3-642-22110-1_14
7. Moura, L., Bjørner, N.: Z3: an efficient SMT solver. In: Ramakrishnan, C.R., Rehof, J. (eds.) TACAS 2008. LNCS, vol. 4963, pp. 337–340. Springer, Heidelberg (2008). doi:10.1007/978-3-540-78800-3_24
8. Dutertre, B.: Yices 2.2. In: Biere, A., Bloem, R. (eds.) CAV 2014. LNCS, vol. 8559, pp. 737–744. Springer, Heidelberg (2014). doi:10.1007/978-3-319-08867-9_49
9. Reynolds, A., Deters, M., Kuncak, V., Tinelli, C., Barrett, C.: Counterexample-guided quantifier instantiation for synthesis in SMT. In: Kroening, D., Păsăreanu, C.S. (eds.) CAV 2015. LNCS, vol. 9207, pp. 198–216. Springer, Cham (2015). doi:10.1007/978-3-319-21668-3_12
10. Ge, Y., Moura, L.: Complete instantiation for quantified formulas in satisfiabiliby modulo theories. In: Bouajjani, A., Maler, O. (eds.) CAV 2009. LNCS, vol. 5643, pp. 306–320. Springer, Heidelberg (2009). doi:10.1007/978-3-642-02658-4_25
11. Wintersteiger, C.M., Hamadi, Y., de Moura, L.M.: Efficiently solving quantified bit-vector formulas. In: Bloem, R., Sharygina, N. (eds.) Proceedings of 10th International Conference on Formal Methods in Computer-Aided Design, FMCAD 2010, Lugano, Switzerland, 20–23 October, pp. 239–246. IEEE (2010)
12. Dutertre, B.: Solving exists/forall problems in Yices. In: Workshop on Satisfiability Modulo Theories (2015)
13. Jonáš, M., Strejček, J.: Solving quantified bit-vector formulas using binary decision diagrams. In: Creignou, N., Le Berre, D. (eds.) SAT 2016. LNCS, vol. 9710, pp. 267–283. Springer, Heidelberg (2016). doi:10.1007/978-3-319-40970-2_17
14. Alur, R., Bodík, R., Juniwal, G., Martin, M.M.K., Raghothaman, M., Seshia, S.A., Singh, R., Solar-Lezama, A., Torlak, E., Udupa, A.: Syntax-guided synthesis. In: Formal Methods in Computer-Aided Design, FMCAD 2013, Portland, OR, USA, 20–23 October 2013, pp. 1–8. IEEE (2013)
15. Robinson, J.A., Voronkov, A. (eds.): Handbook of Automated Reasoning, vol. 2s. Elsevier and MIT Press, Cambridge (2001)
16. Udupa, A., Raghavan, A., Deshmukh, J.V., Mador-Haim, S., Martin, M.M.K., Alur, R.: TRANSIT: specifying protocols with concolic snippets. In Boehm, H., Flanagan, C., eds.: ACM SIGPLAN Conference on Programming Language Design and Implementation, PLDI 2013, Seattle, WA, USA, 16–19 June 2013, pp. 287–296. ACM (2013)
17. Detlefs, D., Nelson, G., Saxe, J.B.: Simplify: a theorem prover for program checking. J. ACM **52**(3), 365–473 (2005)
18. Goultiaeva, A., Bacchus, F.: Exploiting QBF duality on a circuit representation. In: Fox, M., Poole, D. (eds.) Proceedings of the Twenty-Fourth AAAI Conference on Artificial Intelligence, AAAI 2010, Atlanta, Georgia, USA, 11–15 July 2010. AAAI Press (2010)
19. Niemetz, A., Preiner, M., Biere, A.: Turbo-charging lemmas on demand with don't care reasoning. In: Formal Methods in Computer-Aided Design, FMCAD 2014, Lausanne, Switzerland, 21–24 October 2014, pp. 179–186. IEEE (2014)
20. Niemetz, A., Preiner, M., Biere, A.: Boolector 2.0 system description. J. Satisfiability Boolean Model. Comput. **9**, 53–58 (2014) (2015, published)
21. Barrett, C., Fontaine, P., Tinelli, C.: The Satisfiability Modulo Theories Library (SMT-LIB) (2016). www.SMT-LIB.org

22. Fedyukovich, G., Gurfinkel, A., Sharygina, N.: Automated discovery of simulation between programs. In: Davis, M., Fehnker, A., McIver, A., Voronkov, A. (eds.) LPAR 2015. LNCS, vol. 9450, pp. 606–621. Springer, Heidelberg (2015). doi:10. 1007/978-3-662-48899-7_42
23. John, A.K., Chakraborty, S.: A layered algorithm for quantifier elimination from linear modular constraints. Formal Methods Syst. Des. **49**(3), 272–323 (2016)
24. Bjørner, N., Janota, M.: Playing with quantified satisfaction. In: Fehnker, A., McIver, A., Sutcliffe, G., Voronkov, A., (eds.) 20th International Conferences on Logic for Programming, Artificial Intelligence and Reasoning - Short Presentations, LPAR 2015. EPiC Series in Computing, Suva, Fiji, 24–28 November 2015, vol. 35, pp. 15–27. EasyChair (2015)
25. Farzan, A., Kincaid, Z.: Linear arithmetic satisfiability via strategy improvement. In: Kambhampati, S. (ed.) Proceedings of the Twenty-Fifth International Joint Conference on Artificial Intelligence, IJCAI 2016, New York, NY, USA, 9–15 July 2016, pp. 735–743. IJCAI/AAAI Press (2016)

Interpolation-Based GR(1) Assumptions Refinement

Davide G. Cavezza[✉] and Dalal Alrajeh

Imperial College London, London, UK
{d.cavezza15,dalal.alrajeh}@imperial.ac.uk

Abstract. This paper considers the problem of assumptions refinement in the context of unrealizable specifications for reactive systems. We propose a new counterstrategy-guided synthesis approach for GR(1) specifications based on Craig's interpolants. Our interpolation-based method identifies causes for unrealizability and computes assumptions that directly target unrealizable cores, without the need for user input. Thereby, we discuss how this property reduces the maximum number of steps needed to converge to realizability compared with other techniques. We describe properties of interpolants that yield helpful GR(1) assumptions and prove the soundness of the results. Finally, we demonstrate that our approach yields weaker assumptions than baseline techniques.

Keywords: Reactive synthesis · Assumption refinement · Interpolation

1 Introduction

Constructing formal specifications that capture user requirements precisely and from which implementations can be successfully derived is a difficult task [25]. Their imprecision often results from the conception of over-ideal systems, i.e., where the environment always behaves as expected [2,26]. Thus one of the challenges in building correct specifications is identifying sufficient assumptions over the environment under which a system would always be able to guarantee their satisfaction, in other words making a specification *realizable*.

This paper presents a new technique for automatically synthesizing assumptions over an adversarial environment for realizability assurance. More specifically, we develop a novel counterstrategy-guided synthesis procedure that iteratively generates assumption refinements, expressed in a fragment of Linear Temporal Logic (LTL) called *Generalized Reactivity (1)* (GR(1) for short), based on logical interpolation. *Craig interpolants* characterize automatically computable explanations for the inconsistency between Boolean formulae, in their shared alphabet. We exploit this feature to construct expressions that *explain* why a counterstrategy, and hence the environment, violates a guarantee, and whose negations form assumptions.

We demonstrate in our case study applications that our approach *directly targets unrealizable cores*, in the sense that by adding the assumptions returned at

© Springer-Verlag GmbH Germany 2017
A. Legay and T. Margaria (Eds.): TACAS 2017, Part I, LNCS 10205, pp. 281–297, 2017.
DOI: 10.1007/978-3-662-54577-5_16

each iteration, a specific subset of *minimally unfulfillable guarantees* [13] becomes realizable. Therefore each iteration takes a step closer to realizability. To characterize the scope of our approach we introduce the notion of fully-separable interpolants and prove the soundness of our computation when interpolants are fully separable. We further provide a discussion about the complexity of the proposed approach and its convergence, as well as the weakness of our refinements in comparison with those computed by existing techniques [3,4,27].

2   Related Work

Recent years have seen the development of effective counterstrategy-guided approaches to GR(1) assumptions refinement, notably [3,4,27]. Nonetheless those approaches depend significantly on users' knowledge of the problem domain and of the cause of unrealizability. The work in [27] requires users to specify a set of temporal logic templates as formulae with placeholders to be replaced with Boolean variables. Assumptions are then generated as instantiations of such templates that eliminate a given counterstrategy. This typically constrains the search space to only a subset of GR(1) formulae, which do not necessarily address the cause of unrealizability, and potentially eliminate viable solutions to the realizability problem. Similarly, the work in [3], although generating such templates automatically, requires users to provide a subset of variables for template instantiation. Unless the user knows the exact subset of variables that form the cause, this may yield assumptions that do not target the true cause of unrealizability, leading to refinements that needlessly over-constrain the environment. Our proposed method instead directly targets counter-strategies and unrealizable cores, and does not require users to provide variables for constructing refinements.

Other related work on assumption refinement includes those operating directly on game structures [12]. With regard to the parity game model used for controller synthesis (such as in [32,33]), the paper defines the concept of safety assumptions as sets of edges that have to be avoided by the environment, and the concept of fairness assumptions as sets of edges that have to be traversed by the environment infinitely often. The work devises an algorithm for finding minimal edge sets in order to ensure that the controller has a winning strategy. Our approach instead focuses on synthesizing general declarative temporal assertions whose inclusion has the effect of removing edges from the game structure, and directly targeting sources of unrealizability. The problem of synthesizing environment constraints has been tackled in the context of assume-guarantee reasoning for compositional model checking [15,21,31] to support compositional verification. In these, assumptions are typically expressed as LTSs and learning algorithms like $\mathcal{L}^*$ [5] are used to incrementally refine the environment assumptions needed in order to verify the satisfaction of properties.

Craig interpolants have been deployed in the context of abstraction refinement for verification in [18,19]. The differences with our work are in specification language and overall objective: they seek additional assertions for static analysis of programs, while we look for GR(1) refinements of systems specifications to enable their automated synthesis. The authors of [17] use interpolation to support the extraction of pre- and trigger-conditions of operations within event-driven systems to enable the 'satisfaction' of goals expressed within restricted fragment of LTL. Though different in objective, approach and class of properties, our technique can help in identifying specifications operationalizable by [17].

3 Background

Generalized Reactivity (1) Specifications. LTL [29] is a formalism widely used for specifying reactive systems. The syntax of LTL is defined over a finite non-empty set of propositional variables $\mathcal{V}$, the logical constants *true* and *false*, Boolean connectives, and operators $\mathbf{X}$ (next), $\mathbf{G}$ (always), $\mathbf{F}$ (eventually), $\mathbf{U}$ (until). Given a set of states Q and a labelling function $\lambda : Q \rightarrow 2^{\mathcal{V}}$, an LTL formula ϕ is interpreted over an infinite sequence of states $\sigma = q_0 q_1 ...$ in the standard way, and its language $\mathcal{L}(\phi)$ is the set of (infinite) state valuation sequences $w = \lambda(q_0)\lambda(q_1)...$ such that $w \models \phi$). We assume that the set $\mathcal{V}$ consists of two disjoint sets: *input variables* $\mathcal{X}$ and *output variables* $\mathcal{Y}$. We will use the expression $B(\mathcal{V})$ for a boolean expression (i.e., a logical expression without temporal operators) which uses variables in the set $\mathcal{V}$. We will also denote by $\mathbf{X}\mathcal{V}$ the set of expressions obtained by prepending a "next" operator to the variables in $\mathcal{V}$: this is equivalent to the set of primed versions of such variables [9].

Generalized Reactivity (1) specifications (written GR(1) for short) are a subset of LTL of the form $\phi^{\mathcal{E}} \rightarrow \phi^{\mathcal{S}}$ where $\phi^{\mathcal{E}}$ represents the assumptions of an environment and $\phi^{\mathcal{S}}$ the guarantees of a controller. The expression ϕ^{θ}, where $\theta \in \{\mathcal{E}, \mathcal{S}\}$, is specified as conjunction of the following: (1) a Boolean formula φ^{θ}_{init} of the form $B(\mathcal{X})$ if $\theta = \mathcal{E}$ and $B(\mathcal{V})$ otherwise, representing initial conditions; (2) a set of LTL formulae φ^{θ}_{inv} of the form $\mathbf{G}B(\mathcal{V} \cup \mathbf{X}\mathcal{X})$ if $\theta = \mathcal{E}$ and $\mathbf{G}B(\mathcal{V} \cup \mathbf{X}\mathcal{V})$ when $\theta = \mathcal{S}$, representing invariants; and (3) a set of LTL formulae φ^{θ}_{fair} of the form $\mathbf{GF}B(\mathcal{V})$ representing fairness conditions. We will sometimes indicate GR(1) specifications as a tuple $\langle \phi^{\mathcal{E}}, \phi^{\mathcal{S}} \rangle$ with $\phi^{\theta} = \{\varphi^{\theta}_{init}\} \cup \{\varphi^{\theta}_{inv}\} \cup \{\varphi^{\theta}_{fair}\}$.

A finite-state Moore transducer is a tuple $M = \langle Q, q_0, \mathcal{I}, \mathcal{O}, \rho, \delta \rangle$ where Q is a set of states, $q_0 \in Q$ is the initial state, $\rho : Q \times \mathcal{I} \rightarrow Q$ is the transition function, and $\delta : Q \rightarrow \mathcal{O}$ is the output function. Given an input sequence $w = i_0 i_1 ...$, a run of M is the sequence $\sigma = q_0 q_1 ...$ such that $q_{k+1} = \rho(q_k, i_k)$ for all $k \geq 0$. A run σ on input sequence $w \in \mathcal{I}^{\omega}$ produces an infinite word $M(w) = (\delta(q_0), i_0), (\delta(q_1), i_1)....$ The language of a Moore transducer M is $\mathcal{L}(M) = \{M(w) | w \in \mathcal{I}^{\omega}\}$, i.e., the infinite words generated by a sequence of inputs and the corresponding outputs over runs of M. A Moore transducer M is said to satisfy an LTL expression ϕ if $\mathcal{L}(M) \subseteq \mathcal{L}(\phi)$; in this case we also say that M is a model of ϕ and we denote it as $M \models \phi$. A GR(1) property ϕ is said to be realizable if there exists an M (representing a controller) such that $M \models \phi$.

Given a specification $\langle \phi^{\mathcal{E}}, \phi^{\mathcal{S}} \rangle$ that is unrealizable, we say that $\varphi^{\mathcal{S}} \subseteq \phi^{\mathcal{S}}$ is *minimally unfulfillable w.r.t. to* $\phi^{\mathcal{E}}$ iff the removal of any guarantee $g \in \varphi^{\mathcal{S}}$ makes $\langle \phi^{\mathcal{E}}, \varphi^{\mathcal{S}} \backslash \{g\} \rangle$ realizable [13]. Furthermore, an assumption $a \in \phi^{\mathcal{E}}$ is said to be *unhelpful w.r.t.* $\phi^{\mathcal{S}}$ if $\forall \varphi^{\mathcal{S}} \subseteq \phi^{\mathcal{S}}$. $\langle \phi^{\mathcal{E}}, \varphi^{\mathcal{S}} \rangle$ is realizable $\leftrightarrow \langle \phi^{\mathcal{E}} \backslash \{a\}, \varphi^{\mathcal{S}} \rangle$ is realizable. It is said to be *helpful* otherwise. Given a set of minimally unfulfillable guarantees φ^S w.r.t. $\phi^{\mathcal{E}}$, let $\varphi^{\mathcal{E}} \subseteq \phi^{\mathcal{E}}$ be a set of helpful assumptions for φ^S; the specification $\langle \varphi^{\mathcal{E}}, \varphi^S \rangle$ is called an *unrealizable core* [13].

If a specification ϕ over $\mathcal{V} = \mathcal{X} \cup \mathcal{Y}$ is unrealizable, an unrealizable core $\langle \varphi^{\mathcal{E}}, \varphi^S \rangle$ and an environment strategy (called a *counterstrategy*) can be computed [13,23]. A *counterstrategy* is defined as a Moore transducer $(S, s_{init}, 2^{\mathcal{Y}'}, 2^{\mathcal{X}}, \rho, \delta)$ that satisfies $\varphi^{\mathcal{E}}$ and violates φ^S [4]. It describes the inputs produced by an admissible environment in response to the output configuration yielded by the controller in order to force the violation of ϕ. The runs of a counterstrategy are called *plays*. The terms 'counterstrategy' and 'play' come from the game-theoretic algorithms used to reason about realizability [3,9,23]. The transition function ρ depends only on a subset of the output variables $\mathcal{Y}' \subseteq \mathcal{Y}$ [23]. We define a labelling function $\lambda' : S \to 2^{\mathcal{X} \cup \mathcal{Y}'}$ over states in the counterstrategy in this way: a propositional variable is in $\lambda'(s)$ if it is asserted in all the incoming transitions of s, while $\lambda'(s)$ is arbitrary for any s with no incoming transitions.

Interpolants. Craig interpolation was originally defined for first-order logic [16] and later for propositional logic [24]. No interpolation theorems have been proved for the general LTL. Extensions have been proposed recently for LTL fragments [20,22]. However these do not include GR(1) formulae and therefore are not applicable in our case. We use interpolation for propositional logic.

Formally, given an unsatisfiable conjunction of formulae $\alpha \wedge \beta$, a Craig interpolant I is a formula that is implied by α, is unsatisfiable in conjunction with β, and is defined on the common alphabet of α and β. We write $\mathcal{L}_\phi$ to denote the set of variables that occur in a formula ϕ (also called the *alphabet* of ϕ).

Definition 1 (Interpolant [24]). *Let α and β be two logical formulae such that their conjunction $\alpha \wedge \beta$ is unsatisfiable. Then there exists a third formula I, called* interpolant of α and β, *such that, $\alpha \to I$, $I \to \neg\beta$ and $\mathcal{L}_I \subseteq \mathcal{L}_\alpha \cap \mathcal{L}_\beta$.*

An interpolant can be considered as an over-approximation of α that is still unsatisfiable in conjunction with β. As stated in Craig's interpolation theorem, although an interpolant always exists, it is not unique. Several efficient algorithms have been proposed for interpolation in propositional logics. The resulting interpolant depends on the internal strategies of these algorithms (e.g., SAT solvers, theorem provers). Our approach is based on McMillan's interpolation algorithm described in [30] and implemented in MathSAT [14]. In brief, the algorithm considers a proof by resolution for the unsatisfiability of $\alpha \wedge \beta$.

4   Approach Overview

The general procedure is based on a sequence of realizability checks and counterstrategy computations, in the spirit of [3,27]. A specification $\langle \phi^{\mathcal{E}}, \phi^S \rangle$ is first checked for realizability. If it is unrealizable, a counterstrategy C and an unrealizable core $\langle \varphi^{\mathcal{E}}, \varphi^S \rangle$ are computed. The counterstrategy constitutes an example of environment behaviours that force the violation of the guarantees of $\varphi^{\mathcal{S}}$: therefore, the assumptions $\varphi^{\mathcal{E}}$ are refined by adding a GR(1) formula which is inconsistent with the counterstrategy. A set of such formulae Ψ is automatically computed by interpolating (α) the description of an environment behaviour in the counterstrategy, given by the assumptions and a sequence of state labellings in the counterstrategy; and (β) the guarantees, and by negating the interpolant. A formula $\psi_i \in \Psi$ is added to the original set of assumptions $\phi^{\mathcal{E}}$ and the procedure repeats the above steps recursively until realizability is achieved. Algorithm 1 describes this procedure schematically.

Algorithm 1. CounterstrategyGuidedRefinement procedure

Data: $\phi^{\mathcal{E}}$, assumptions
Data: $\phi^{\mathcal{S}}$, guarantees
Result: $\{\psi_i\}$, set of alternative assumption refinements such that $\phi^{\mathcal{E}} \wedge \psi_i \to \phi^{\mathcal{S}}$
  is realizable for every i

1   **if** *Satisfiable($\phi^{\mathcal{E}} \to \phi^{\mathcal{S}}$) & not Realizable($\phi^{\mathcal{E}} \to \phi^{\mathcal{S}}$)* **then**
2     $(\varphi^{\mathcal{E}}, \varphi^{\mathcal{S}}, C) :=$ **Counterstrategy**$(\phi^{\mathcal{E}}, \phi^{\mathcal{S}})$;
3     $\Psi :=$ **InterpolationBasedSynthesis**$(\varphi^{\mathcal{E}}, \varphi^{\mathcal{S}}, C)$;
4   **foreach** $\psi_i \in \Psi$ **do**
5   **foreach** $\psi'_j \in$ *CounterstrategyGuidedRefinement($\phi^{\mathcal{E}} \wedge \psi_i, \phi^{\mathcal{S}}$)* **do**
6   *refinements.add($\psi_i \wedge \psi'_j$)* ;
7   **end**
8   **end**
9   **return** *refinements*;
10 **else if** *Satisfiable($\phi^{\mathcal{E}} \to \phi^{\mathcal{S}}$) & Realizable($\phi^{\mathcal{E}} \to \phi^{\mathcal{S}}$)* **then**
11   **return** $\{true\}$;
12 **else**
13   **return** $\{false\}$;

The function **InterpolationBasedSynthesis** constitutes the core of our proposal (see Algorithm 2). It takes as inputs an unrealizable core and a counterstrategy and executes the computation of Ψ via interpolation. We give the details in the following section.

5   Interpolation-Based Synthesis

Each execution of **InterpolationBasedSynthesis** involves extracting temporal formulae that are satisfied by a single play of a counterstrategy (henceforth called *counterplay*), and obtaining refinements from its negation. It is sufficient to exclude a single counterplay of a counterstrategy to eliminate the entire counterstrategy from models of the assumption. Reasoning about counterplays has also some advantages, which are discussed in Sect. 8. For the purpose of this paper, we assume that the procedure **ExtractCounterplay** (line 1) extracts a counterplay π_C at random and consider metrics for selecting one in future work. A counterplay representing the violation of an initial condition or an invariant

---

Algorithm 2. InterpolationBasedSynthesis($\varphi^{\mathcal{E}}$, $\varphi^{\mathcal{S}}$, C)

Data: $\varphi^{\mathcal{E}}$, environment assumptions (in an unrealizable core)
Data: $\varphi^{\mathcal{S}}$, system guarantees (in an unrealizable core)
Data: C, counterstrategy
Result: Ψ, alternative assumptions eliminating the counterstrategy

1 $\pi_C :=$ **ExtractCounterplay**(C);
2 $u := 0$;
3 $\pi_{C,u} := \pi_C$;
4 $\Psi_{old} := \emptyset$;
5 *stopping_condition* := *true*;
6 **repeat**
7 | $[[\pi_{C,u}, \varphi_u^{\mathcal{E}}]] :=$ **TranslateCounterplayAssumptions**($\pi_{C,u}, \varphi^{\mathcal{E}}$);
8 | $[[\varphi_u^{\mathcal{S}}]] :=$ **TranslateGuarantees**($\pi_{C,u}, \varphi^{\mathcal{S}}$);
9 | $I_u :=$ **Interpolate**($[[\pi_{C,u}, \varphi_u^{\mathcal{E}}]], [[\varphi_u^{\mathcal{S}}]]$);
10 | **if** $I_u ==$ *false* or I_u is not fully-separable **then**
11 | | $\Psi := \{false\}$;
12 | | *stopping_condition* := *true*;
13 | **else**
14 | | $\mathcal{T}(I_u) :=$ **TranslateInterpolant**($\pi_{C,u}, I_u$);
15 | | $\Psi :=$ **ExtractDisjuncts**($\neg \mathcal{T}(I_u)$);
16 | | **if** $\pi_{C,u}$ is looping **then**
17 | | | **if** $\Psi \neq \Psi_{old}$ **then**
18 | | | | $\Psi_{old} := \Psi$;
19 | | | | $u := u + 1$;
20 | | | | $\pi_{C,u} :=$ **UnrollCounterplay**(π_C, u);
21 | | | | *stopping_condition* := *false*;
22 | | | **else**
23 | | | | *stopping_condition* := *true*;
24 | | | **end**
25 | | **end**
26 | **end**
27 **until** *stopping_condition*;
28 **return** Ψ;

---

guarantee is finite, while that of a fairness guarantee violation ends in a loop [28]. We call the latter a *looping counterplay*, and the loop an *ending loop*.

We distinguish four types of states that may appear in π_C: (a) the *initial state* $S^{init} = \{s^{init}\}$; (b) the *failing state* in a finite counterplay $S^{fail} = \{s^{fail}\}$ (c) *looping states* that include the states in ending loop, $S^{loop} = \{s_1^{loop}, \ldots, s_h^{loop}\}$, (d) *transient states* including all states between the initial state and the first failing state or loop state (exclusive) $S^{trans} = \{s_1^{trans}, \ldots, s_k^{trans}\}$. With this classification, a finite counterplay has the form $s^{init} s_1^{trans} \ldots s_k^{trans} s^{fail}$; whilst a looping counterplay has the form $s^{init} s_1^{trans} \ldots s_k^{trans} (s_1^{loop} \ldots s_h^{loop})^\omega$. The formulae in the next subsection also refer to a fifth set of states, called *unrolled states*, which represent replicates of looping states, and to the unrolling degree u. They are explored in Sect. 5.2. Each state in π_C is labelled with variables from the set $\mathcal{X} \cup \mathcal{Y}'$ defined in Sect. 3. The value of u is initialized to 0, and thus $\pi_{C,u}$ equates to π_C (lines 2–3).

The extraction of the counterplay occurs at the start of every call of the synthesis phase. The remaining steps described in this section are iteratively executed when the extracted counterplay is looping, and only once otherwise. In the former case, we will refer to the iteration as the *inner-cycle*, to distinguish it from the counterstrategy-guided refinement cycle.

5.1   Candidate Assumptions Computation

Refinements of environment assumptions are computed in four steps: (i) production of two inconsistent Boolean formulae from the counterplay and the unrealizable core, (ii) interpolation between the two Boolean formulae, (iii) translation of the interpolant into LTL, and (iv) negation of the translated interpolant.

Step (i) is executed by the functions **TranslateCounterplayAssumptions** and **TranslateGuarantees** (lines 7–8). The procedure employs the translation scheme in [7] for bounded model checking: it ensures that the obtained Boolean formula is satisfiable if and only if the play taken into account satisfies the LTL formula. The inclusion of assumptions in the counterplay translation is important in yielding an interpolant in the shared alphabet of assumptions and guarantees that explains why the assumptions violate the guarantees. Given a GR(1) formula in φ^θ over $\mathcal{V}$ and a counterplay $\pi_{C,u}$ with state space $S_\pi \in S$, its translation is a Boolean formula over the domain $\mathcal{V}(S_\pi)$ obtained by replicating every variable $p \in \mathcal{V}$ for every state $s \in S_\pi$; we denote by $p(s)$ the replica of p corresponding to state s, and by $\mathcal{V}(s)$ the subset of $\mathcal{V}(S_\pi)$ containing all the variables referring to state s. This step produces two formulae:

- $[[\pi_{C,u}, \varphi_u^{\mathcal{E}}]]$, which is a conjunction between the assumptions translation $[[\varphi_u^{\mathcal{E}}]]$ over $\pi_{C,u}$ and a formula representing the valuation of every $s \in S_\pi$ in $\pi_{C,u}$; the latter is a conjunctive formula containing a literal $p(s)$ (resp. $\neg p(s)$) for every $p \in \mathcal{X} \cup \mathcal{Y}'$ that is true (resp. false) in $\lambda'(s)$ (see end of Sect. 3);
- $[[\varphi_u^{\mathcal{S}}]]$ which is the guarantees translation over $\pi_{C,u}$.

The translations $[[\varphi_u^{\mathcal{E}}]]$ and $[[\varphi_u^{\mathcal{S}}]]$ are given in the extended version of this work [11]. Since by definition a counterplay π_C satisfies the assumptions and violates the guarantees, the formula $[[\pi_{C,u}, \varphi_u^{\mathcal{E}}]] \wedge [[\varphi_u^{\mathcal{S}}]]$ is unsatisfiable by construction. Therefore, there exists an interpolant for $[[\pi_{C,u}, \varphi_u^{\mathcal{E}}]]$ and $[[\varphi_u^{\mathcal{S}}]]$.

Step (ii) consists of the function **Interpolate** (line 9). The returned interpolant I_u is an over-approximation of $[[\pi_{C,u}, \varphi_u^{\mathcal{E}}]]$ which by definition implies the negation of $[[\varphi_u^{\mathcal{S}}]]$: it can be interpreted as a cause of the guarantees not being satisfied by the counterplay, and as such a characterization of a set of counterplays not satisfying the guarantees.

From such interpolant the procedure aims at extracting a set of refinements that fit the GR(1) format. In order to do this, the Boolean to temporal translation requires the interpolant to adhere a specific structure. This is embodied in the notion of *full-separability*. To formally define full-separability, we need first to define state-separability and I/O-separability.

Definition 2 (State-separable interpolant). *An interpolant I_u is said to be* state-separable *iff it can be expressed as*

$$\bigwedge_{s \in S_u} B_s(\mathcal{V}(s)) \tag{1}$$

where $B_s(\mathcal{V}(s))$ is a Boolean formula either equal to true *or expressed over variables in $\mathcal{V}(s)$ only.*

We will refer to each $B_s(\mathcal{V}(s))$ as a *state component* of the interpolant. In particular, a state component is equal to *true* if I_u does not use any variables from s. State-separability intuitively means that the subformulae of the interpolant involving a single state are linked by conjunctions. This means that in any model of the interpolant each state component must be itself *true*.

Definition 3 (I/O-separable Boolean expression). *A Boolean expression $B_s(\mathcal{V}(s))$ is said to be* I/O-separable *if it can be written as a conjunction of two subformulae containing only input and output variables respectively:*

$$B_s(\mathcal{V}(s)) = B_{s,\mathcal{X}}(\mathcal{X}(s)) \wedge B_{s,\mathcal{Y}}(\mathcal{Y}(s)) \tag{2}$$

We call $B_{s,\mathcal{X}}(\mathcal{X}(s))$ and $B_{s,\mathcal{Y}}(\mathcal{Y}(s))$ the *projections* of $B_s(\mathcal{V}(s))$ onto $\mathcal{X}$ and $\mathcal{Y}$ respectively. Any model of an I/O-separable Boolean expression satisfies the projections separately. We can now define full-separability of an interpolant.

Definition 4 (Fully-separable interpolant). *An interpolant is called* fully-separable *if it is state-separable and each of its state components is I/O-separable.*

An example of a fully-separable interpolant over $\mathcal{X} = \{a, b\}, \mathcal{Y} = \{c, d\}$ and states $S = \{s_0, s_1\}$ is $(a(s_0) \vee b(s_0)) \wedge c(s_0) \wedge \neg b(s_1)$; a non-fully-separable interpolant, instead, is $a(s_0) \vee a(s_1)$, since literals referring to different states are linked via a disjunction.

Remark 1. A particular class of fully-separable interpolants is that of fully conjunctive interpolants, where no disjunctions appear. Whether or not the resulting interpolant is conjunctive depends on the order in which the interpolation algorithm [30] chooses the root clauses for building the unsatisfiability proof. A sufficient condition for obtaining a fully-conjunctive interpolant is that such root clauses be single literals from $[[\pi_{C,u}, \varphi_u^{\mathcal{E}}]]$, and that the pivot variable in each resolution step belong to the shared alphabet of $[[\pi_{C,u}, \varphi_u^{\mathcal{E}}]]$ and $[[\varphi_u^{\mathcal{S}}]]$. (see [11,30] for details on the interpolation algorithm used).

Step (*iii*) consists of the function **TranslateInterpolant** (line 14). It converts a fully-separable interpolant $I_u = \bigwedge_{s \in S_u} B_s(\mathcal{V}(s))$ into the LTL formula

$$\mathcal{T}(I_u) = B_{\mathcal{X}}^{init}(\mathcal{X}) \wedge \bigwedge_{s \in S_u} \mathbf{F}\left(B_s(\mathcal{V}) \wedge B_{\mathrm{succ}(s),\mathcal{X}}(\mathbf{X}\mathcal{X})\right) \wedge$$

$$\mathbf{FG} \bigvee_{j=1}^{|S^{loop}|} \left(B_j^{loop}(\mathcal{V}) \wedge \bigwedge_{r=1}^{u} B_{j,r}^{unr}(\mathcal{V})\right) \tag{3}$$

where the expression $B_{\mathcal{X}}^{init}(\mathcal{X})$ is a shorthand for $B_{s^{init},\mathcal{X}}(\mathcal{X})$, $B_j^{loop}(\mathcal{V})$ for $B_{s_j^{loop}}(\mathcal{V})$ and $B_{j,r}^{unr}(\mathcal{V})$ for $B_{s_{j,r}^{unr}}(\mathcal{V})$. Formula (3) is formed from the single state components of I_u by replacing the variables in $\mathcal{V}(s)$ with the corresponding variables in $\mathcal{V}$ and by projecting the components onto the input variables where required by the GR(1) template. The translation consists of three units: a subformula describing the initial state, a conjunction of **F** formulae each containing two consecutive state components, and an **FG** formula; this unit consists of a disjunction over all the looping states, where each disjunct j groups the state components of all the replicas of state s_j^{loop}.

Formula (3) is guaranteed to hold in the counterplay π_C. Intuitively, since I_u is fully-separable by construction, $[[\pi_{C,u}, \varphi_u^{\mathcal{E}}]]$ implies each state component and its projections onto $\mathcal{X}$ and $\mathcal{Y}'$. A state component $B_s(\mathcal{V}(s))$ corresponds to a formula $B_s(\mathcal{V})$ satisfied by state s of the counterplay. Therefore, since the initial state satisfies $B^{init}(\mathcal{V})$, π_C satisfies $B_{\mathcal{X}}^{init}(\mathcal{X})$; since there are two consecutive states s and succ (s) that satisfy $B_s(\mathcal{V}(s))$ and $B_s(\mathcal{V}(\text{succ}\,(s)))$ respectively, π_C satisfies $\mathbf{F}\left(B_s(\mathcal{V}) \wedge B_{\text{succ}\,(s),\mathcal{X}}(\mathbf{X}\mathcal{X})\right)$. Finally, for the **FG** subformula, it is sufficient to observe that the looping state j satisfies the formula obtained from the state components referring to s_j^{loop} and $s_{j,r}^{unr}$: since the counterplay remains indefinitely in the looping state, there is a suffix of it where such formula is true for at least one j. Based on these considerations, we prove the following soundness property.

Theorem 1. *Let π_C be a counterplay and $\varphi^{\mathcal{E}}$ a set of assumptions satisfied in π_C, such that their Boolean translation $[[\pi_{C,u}, \varphi_u^{\mathcal{E}}]]$ implies I_u, and let I_u be a fully-separable interpolant. Then $\pi_C \models \mathcal{T}(I_u)$.*

The proof is in the extended version [11]. In the case a fully-separable interpolant is not generated from which $\mathcal{T}(I_u)$ can be constructed, the algorithm returns *false* as its candidate assumption. Otherwise, the approach proceeds to step (iv) (function **ExtractDisjuncts**, line 15) producing the candidate refinements by negating (3) and extracting the disjuncts in the resulting formula:

$$\neg B_{\mathcal{X}}^{init}(\mathcal{X}) \vee \bigvee_{s \in S_u} \mathbf{G}\neg \left(B_s(\mathcal{V}) \wedge B_{\text{succ}\,(s),\mathcal{X}}(\mathbf{X}\mathcal{X})\right) \vee$$

$$\mathbf{GF} \bigwedge_{j=1}^{|S^{loop}|} \neg \left(B_j^{loop}(\mathcal{V}) \wedge \bigwedge_{r=1}^{u} B_{j,r}^{unr}(\mathcal{V})\right) \tag{4}$$

Each disjunct above is a GR(1) candidate assumption which, by Theorem 1, ensures the exclusion of the counterplay π_C from the models of the assumptions.

5.2 Equivalence Checking and Unrolling

The equivalence checking of the produced candidates and the unrolling of the counterplay (lines 17–24) are only executed in case of a looping counterplay.

Thus in each iteration of the inner-cycle, our procedure checks whether the synthesized assumptions are equivalent to the assumptions ψ_{old} computed in the previous iteration. If not, the looping part of the counterplay is unrolled once (**UnrollCounterplay**, line 20) and the steps in Sect. 5.1–5.2 are repeated. If the equivalence condition is met, the synthesis procedure returns the last set of computed candidates as output.

Counterplay unrolling consists in making the first traversals of looping states explicit. It is achieved by augmenting a counterplay with replicates of the looping states. The number of unrollings is referred to as the *unrolling degree* u. Each unrolling yields a new set of states $S^{unr} = \{s_{1,1}^{unr}, \ldots, s_{h,1}^{unr}, \ldots, s_{1,u}^{unr}, \ldots,$ $s_{h,u}^{unr}\}$. An unrolled looping counterplay has the form $s^{init} s_1^{trans} \ldots s_k^{trans}$ $s_{1,1}^{unr} \ldots s_{h,1}^{unr} \ldots s_{1,u}^{unr} \ldots s_{h,u}^{unr} (s_1^{loop} \ldots s_k^{loop})^{\omega}$. Unrolling has two possible effects on the computed interpolant: on one hand, it can introduce new state components in the interpolant, which yield new invariant refinements according to (4); on the other hand, the interpolant can express a more specific characterization of looping states, which corresponds to a weaker fairness refinement in (4). These effects are both observed in our evaluation (see Sect. 7).

6   Convergence

Our procedure is guaranteed to terminate after a finite number of recursive calls. We discuss below the case of all computed interpolants being fully-separable. If not, the procedure terminates with a trivial assumption refinement *false*.

Theorem 2. *Given a satisfiable but unrealizable specification* $\langle \phi^{\mathcal{E}}, \phi^{\mathcal{S}} \rangle$ *Algorithm 1 terminates with a realizable specification* $\langle \phi^{\mathcal{E}'}, \phi^{\mathcal{S}} \rangle$.

To prove this, it is sufficient to show that both the recursion in Algorithm 1 and the iteration over unrollings in Algorithm 2 reach the respective termination conditions. In the following arguments, we will refer to the recursion tree of Algorithm 1. Each node is associated with the candidate assumption tested in one specific call of **CounterstrategyGuidedRefinements**. The root corresponds to the initial assumption; every internal node symbolizes an unrealizable assumptions refinement; the children of an internal node correspond to the alternative refinements that rule out the relevant counterstrategy. The leaves represent alternative realizable assumption refinements returned by the algorithm. We will show that this tree has finite depth and breadth.

Let us consider the number of children n_C of an internal node (the subscript C indicates the counterstrategy computed in that internal node). It consists of the maximum number of refinements that are generated from a single counterstrategy. Assuming that the maximum unrolling degree is finite (we will see that later in this section), denoted $u_{C,MAX}$, the maximum number of refinements generated from C can be computed by counting the maximum number of disjuncts in (4). Suppose $|S_{u_{C,MAX}}|$ denotes the number of distinct states in the unrolled counterplay, then $n_C \leq |S_{u_{C,MAX}}| + 2$: we count one initial condition, one fairness condition and $|S_{u_{C,MAX}}|$ invariants. Given that every node has a finite number of children, the breadth of each level in the tree is also finite.

We now consider the depth. The algorithm keeps refining a computed assumption until the property becomes realizable (in case the returned refinement is *false*, then the property is realizable, and therefore the algorithm reaches a *true* leaf). Given the soundness property, at each step every refinement excludes the latest computed counterstrategy; since this counterstrategy satisfies all the previously computed refinements by definition, the new refinement cannot be equivalent to any of the previous refinements along the same branch.

For the above reason, the depth d of the recursion tree is limited by the maximum number of existing GR(1) refinements modulo logical equivalence. The maximum number of initial conditions is $d_{init,MAX} = 2^{2^{|X|}}$, that is the number of all distinct Boolean expressions over the input variables. The maximum number of invariants is $d_{inv,MAX} = 2^{2^{|V|}+2^{|X|}}$; this corresponds to the maximum number of distinct B_s that can be present in the expression (4) times the number of distinct $B_{\text{succ}(s),X}$. Finally, the maximum number of distinct fairness assumptions is $d_{fair,MAX} = 2^{2^{|V|}}$ Therefore, the total depth d is bounded by the sum of these three quantities: $d \le d_{MAX} = d_{init,MAX} + d_{inv,MAX} + d_{fair,MAX}$.

Given the above, we conclude that the recursion tree is finite. This gives us a worst-case upper bound on the depth d of the recursion, which has a doubly exponential growth over $|V|$ — a general observation of counterstrategy-guided assumptions refinement strategies. It remains to show that the inner-cycle terminates in finite time. As mentioned in Sect. 5.2, each iteration can provide additional or weaker refinements with respect to the previous iteration. The termination condition holds when the current iteration does not yield new refinements with respect to the previous one. This is reached in the worst case after all distinct GR(1) refinements are generated. The computation is the same as the one for d: $u_{C,MAX} = d_{MAX}$.

7 Evaluation

We apply our approach to two benchmarks presented in [3,9,23]: a lift controller and ARM's AMBA-AHB protocol. The requirements analysis tool RATSY [8] is used to check unrealizability and compute counterstrategies. The SAT solver MathSAT [10,14] is used to compute interpolants. We implemented a translation module for GR(1) specifications and randomly extracted plays into a propositional logic format executable by MathSAT. For each case study, we report the maximum depth and breadth of the recursion tree, and an interpretation of some interesting refinements that are computed. Details are available at [1].

Table 1 provides a summary of both case studies. The columns **In** and **Out** contain the number of input and output variables in the specification alphabet respectively; **A** and **G** contain the number of assumptions and guarantees respectively; **MaxPlay** contains the maximum number of states in a counterplay among all the counterplays used in the refinement process; **MaxUnr** reports the maximum unrolling degree reached in any step of the approach before reaching the termination condition; **TreeDepth** corresponds to the depth of the recursion tree; **MaxAltRef** is the maximum number of alternative refinements computed to rule out any single counterstrategy (it corresponds to the maximum number of children of an internal node in the recursion tree); **#Ref** shows the total number of refinement sets computed that make the property realizable.

Table 1. Summary of refinement results on benchmarks

Specification	In	Out	A	G	MaxPlay	MaxUnr	TreeDepth	MaxAltRef	#Ref
Lift	3	3	7	12	2	2	1	3	3
AMBA02	7	16	10	66	4	2	3	6	17
AMBA04	11	23	16	97	7	1	2	2	8
AMBA08	19	36	28	157	18	1	7	2	80

7.1   Lift Controller

This case study (also used for controller synthesis problems [3,9]) involves the specification of a system comprising a lift controller. The lift moves between three floors. The environment consists of three buttons, whose states can be *pressed* or *unpressed*; the corresponding state is represented by three binary input variables $\{b_1, b_2, b_3\}$. The controller's state consists of three output variables $\{f_1, f_2, f_3\}$ which indicate at which floor the lift is. The assumptions are:

1. $\varphi^e_{init} = \neg b_1 \wedge \neg b_2 \wedge \neg b_3$
2. $\varphi^e_{1,i} = \mathbf{G}(b_i \wedge f_i \rightarrow \mathbf{X}\neg b_i)$
3. $\varphi^e_{2,i} = \mathbf{G}(b_i \wedge \neg f_i \rightarrow \mathbf{X}b_i)$

for $i \in \{1,2,3\}$. They state that the buttons are not pressed in the initial state (1); a pressed button transits to a non-pressed state when the lift arrives at the corresponding floor (2); and the button remains in the pressed state until the lift arrives at that floor (3). The guarantees are:

1. $\varphi^s_{init} = f_1 \wedge \neg f_2 \wedge \neg f_3$
2. $\varphi^s_1 = \mathbf{G}(\neg(f_1 \wedge f_2) \wedge \neg(f_2 \wedge f_3) \wedge \neg(f_1 \wedge f_3))$
3. $\varphi^s_{2,1} = \mathbf{G}(f_1 \rightarrow (\mathbf{X}f_1 \vee \mathbf{X}f_2))$
4. $\varphi^s_{2,2} = \mathbf{G}(f_2 \rightarrow (\mathbf{X}f_1 \vee \mathbf{X}f_2 \vee \mathbf{X}f_3))$
5. $\varphi^s_{2,3} = \mathbf{G}(f_3 \rightarrow (\mathbf{X}f_2 \vee \mathbf{X}f_3))$
6. $\varphi^s_3 = \mathbf{G}(((f_1 \wedge \mathbf{X}f_2) \vee (f_2 \wedge \mathbf{X}f_3) \vee (f_2 \wedge \mathbf{X}f_1) \vee (f_3 \wedge \mathbf{X}f_2)) \rightarrow (b_1 \vee b_2 \vee b_3))$
7. $\varphi^s_{4,i} = \mathbf{GF}(b_i \rightarrow f_i)$
8. $\varphi^s_{5,i} = \mathbf{GF}f_i$

for $i \in \{1,2,3\}$. They state that the lift starts from floor 1 (1); it can never be in two floors at the same time (2); it can move only between consecutive states (3–5), and moves only when at least a button is pressed (6); plays in which the environment keeps a button b_i pressed infinitely and the lift never reaches the corresponding f_i are forbidden (7); and that the lift is required to visit all the floors infinitely often (8). Given this specification, the fairness guarantee can be satisfied if the environment sets one of its b_i to 1 at least once.

The specification is unrealizable, since when the buttons (environment) stay indefinitely unpressed, the lift (controller) cannot move and therefore $\varphi^s_{5,2}$ and $\varphi^s_{5,3}$ are violated. The unrealizable core consists of the whole set of assumptions and the guarantees φ^s_{init}, $\varphi^s_{2,1}$, φ^s_3 and $\varphi^s_{5,2}$. From this core, RATSY computes the counterstrategy π_C in Fig. 1, which consists of a unique play. After translating the unrealizable core over the counterplay, the interpolant is $I_0 = \neg b_1(s_0) \wedge \neg b_2(s_0) \wedge \neg b_3(s_0)$, which corresponds to the GR(1) refinement $\neg b_1 \wedge \neg b_2 \wedge \neg b_3$. The first unrolling is performed yielding the interpolant $I_1 = \neg b_1(s_0) \wedge \neg b_2(s_0) \wedge \neg b_3(s_0) \wedge \neg b_1(s^{unr}_{1,1}) \wedge \neg b_2(s^{unr}_{1,1}) \wedge \neg b_3(s^{unr}_{1,1})$. By translating and negating this interpolant, we obtain the alternative refinements

1. $b_1 \vee b_2 \vee b_3$
2. $\mathbf{G}(\neg b_1 \wedge \neg b_2 \wedge \neg b_3 \rightarrow \mathbf{X}(b_1 \vee b_2 \vee b_3))$
3. $\mathbf{GF}(b_1 \vee b_2 \vee b_3)$

Notice that unrolling results in an interpolant containing an additional state component, thus allowing for more alternative refinements (see Sect. 5.2). Moreover, the new state component refers to an unrolled state, from which a new fairness refinement that is not inferable from I_0 is synthesized. The second unrolling produces equivalent refinements, and thereby the inner-cycle terminates.

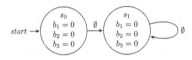

Fig. 1. Lift counterstrategy produced by RATSY. The labelling λ' is shown in each state. In this case the lift position plays no role in the environment's choice of next state, therefore $\mathcal{Y}' = \emptyset$.

Every candidate refinement computed by our approach is helpful. Moreover, each one solves the unrealizability problem for the original specification. Refinement (1) does this in a trivial way, since it contradicts the initial assumption contained in the specification. Notice that all the computed refinements force at least one of the buttons to be pressed at some point in any play of the environment. This corresponds to the refinement produced by the approach in [3].

7.2 AMBA-AHB Protocol

The *Advanced High-performance Bus (AHB)* is part of the *Advanced Microcontroller Bus Architecture (AMBA)* specification. It is an open-source communication protocol for on-chip devices through a shared bus. Devices are divided into *masters*, which initiate a communication, and *slaves*, which respond to requests. Multiple masters can request the bus simultaneously, but only one at a time can communicate through it. Masters and slaves constitute the environment, while the system is the bus arbiter implementing the protocol. The specification of the

AHB protocol is provided with RATSY. It is a GR(1) description of the protocol in [6], and formalized in [9]. We consider specifications for two, four and eight masters (AMBA02, AMBA04, AMBA08 respectively) which are realizable. To evaluate our approach, we remove the assumption **GF**_hready_ as done in [3, 27].

In all the variants, our approach was able to produce refinements that were semantically related to the removed assumption. In the AMBA02 case, one of the refinements is the invariant **G**($hready \vee$ **X**$hready$), which forces _hready_ to be true at least every two steps. The other refinements in all the AMBA0x variants involve the variable _hmaster_, which indicates the master that currently owns the bus. These refinements force _hmaster_ to change infinitely often. This corresponds to having _hready_ equal to _true_ infinitely often, since _hready_ must be true at any ownership switch according to the protocol [9].

The approach was further tested by extracting different counterplays from the same counterstrategy in the AMBA02 case. Every refinement produced within each synthesis call was helpful. We compared our results to those obtainable through [3, 27] when variables not contained in the interpolant are provided as input. The refinements **GF**($\neg$_hburst1_) and **GF**_hlock0_ (which are possible outputs of [3, 27] if the user chooses the corresponding templates/variables) remove the first counterstrategy; however neither is helpful, since even after their addition the corresponding set of minimally unfulfillable guarantees is still unrealizable.

8   Discussion

Targeting Unrealizable Cores. The evaluation shows that our approach automatically selects variables that need to be constrained in order to reach realizability. In particular, all the intermediate refinements eliminate precisely a cause of unrealizability, consisting of the set of minimally unfulfillable guarantees from which a counterstrategy has been computed. We note that the returned variables in the AMBA02 example (_hready_ and _hbusreq1_) are a subset of the variables that the authors in [3] suggest to use in order to instantiate the refinement templates.

Helpfulness of intermediate refinements is a desirable condition for reducing the convergence rate of the algorithm. When this holds, then the expected tree depth d (see Sect. 6) is reduced to $O(n_g)$, where n_g is the number of minimally unfulfillable subsets of guarantees. The application of our approach on the case studies consistently supports the attainment of this condition.

Number of Unrollings. We further define an upper bound to the number of unrollings needed to reach the termination condition as of Sect. 5.2. Every unrolling iteration produces an interpolant which is either the same as the previous iteration, or contains the description of one more state in the counterplay. In the worst case, without unrolling the interpolant describes just the initial state; after the first unrolling it contains a state component for the first transient state s_1^{trans}; it is iteratively strengthened by one more state component until it describes all the transient states and the first replica of the unrolled states $s_{j,1}^{unr}$ for each j. In the following unrolling step, the interpolant contains the component of $s_{1,2}^{unr}$, which is such that $\lambda'(s_{1,2}^{unr}) = \lambda'(s_{1,1}^{unr})$: interpolation produces an equivalent refinement to the previous step, and therefore the procedure terminates. The maximum number of unrollings before reaching the termination condition is: $u_{C,MAX} = |S|$ where $|S|$ is the number of states in π_C.

Comparison with Existing Approaches. Our approach extracts weaker refinements that those of [3]. The reason is that [3] uses templates that are true over all paths of a counterstrategy, while our approach requires them to be true in a single counterplay. More specifically, an invariant template used in [3] has the form $\mathbf{G}\neg q \vee \mathbf{X}\left(\bigwedge_{q' \in Next(q)} \neg q'\right)$, where q and q' indicate states in a counterstrategy and $Next(q)$ is the set of successor states of q; our approach extracts invariants of the form $\mathbf{G}\neg q \vee \neg q'$ for a $q' \in Next(q)$, which is implied by the former one, provided that they use the same variables set for q and q'.

We notice that in principle our approach may generate assumptions containing only output variables. This happens if some state component in the interpolant contains only output variables. Those are valid GR(1) formulae according to the definition, although hardly interpretable as constraints on the environment. Existing approaches circumvent the problem by allowing only input variables in their refinements [3,4]: however, in this way valid assumptions are also excluded. In our AMBA04 case study, one of the computed assumptions was $\mathbf{G}((\neg hmaster0 \wedge hbusreq1) \rightarrow \mathbf{X}(\neg hbusreq1))$, where $hmaster0 \in \mathcal{Y}$ and $hbusreq1 \in \mathcal{X}$. This assumption would not have been computed with that restriction.

9 Conclusions

We presented an interpolation-based approach for synthesizing weak environment assumptions for GR(1) specifications. Our approach exploits the information in counterstrategies and unrealizable cores to compute assumptions that directly target the cause of unrealizability. Compared to closely related approaches [3,27], our algorithm does not require the user to provide the set of variables upon which the assumptions are constructed. The case study applications show that our approach implicitly performs a variable selection that targets an unrealizable core, allowing for a quicker convergence to a realizable specification.

The final set of refinements is influenced by the choice of counterplay. We are investigating in our current work the effect of and criteria over the counterplay selection particularly on the full-separability of interpolants. Furthermore, since interpolants are over-approximations of the counterplays, the final specification is an under-approximation. In future work, we will explore the use of witnesses (winning strategies for the system) to counteract this effect. Finally, the applicability of our approach depends on the separability properties of the computed interpolants: further investigation is needed to characterize the conditions under which an interpolation algorithm returns fully-separable interpolants.

Acknowledgments. The support of the EPSRC HiPEDS CDT (EP/L016796/1) and Imperial College Junior Research Fellowship is gratefully acknowledged. We also thank our reviewers for their insightful comments and suggestions.

References

1. https://github.com/davidecavezza/TACAS17CaseStudies
2. Alrajeh, D., Kramer, J., van Lamsweerde, A., Russo, A., Uchitel, S.: Generating obstacle conditions for requirements completeness. In: ACM/IEEE 34th International Conference on Software Engineering, pp. 705–715 (2012)
3. Alur, R., Moarref, S., Topcu, U.: Counter-strategy guided refinement of GR(1) temporal logic specifications. In: Formal Methods in Computer-Aided Design, pp. 26–33 (2013)
4. Alur, R., Moarref, S., Topcu, U.: Pattern-based refinement of assume-guarantee specifications in reactive synthesis. In: Baier, C., Tinelli, C. (eds.) TACAS 2015. LNCS, vol. 9035, pp. 501–516. Springer, Heidelberg (2015). doi:10.1007/978-3-662-46681-0_49
5. Angluin, D.: Learning regular sets from queries and counterexamples. Inf. Comput. **75**(2), 87–106 (1987)
6. ARM Ltd.: AMBA-AHB specification. https://developer.arm.com/products/architecture/amba-protocol
7. Biere, A., Cimatti, A., Clarke, E.M., Strichman, O., Zhu, Y.: Bounded model checking. Adv. Comput. **58**, 117–148 (2003)
8. Bloem, R., Cimatti, A., Greimel, K., Hofferek, G., Könighofer, R., Roveri, M., Schuppan, V., Seeber, R.: RATSY – a new requirements analysis tool with synthesis. In: Touili, T., Cook, B., Jackson, P. (eds.) CAV 2010. LNCS, vol. 6174, pp. 425–429. Springer, Heidelberg (2010). doi:10.1007/978-3-642-14295-6_37
9. Bloem, R., Jobstmann, B., Piterman, N., Pnueli, A., Sa'Ar, Y.: Synthesis of reactive(1) designs. J. Comput. Syst. Sci. **78**(3), 911–938 (2012)
10. Bruttomesso, R., Cimatti, A., Franzén, A., Griggio, A., Sebastiani, R.: The MATH-SAT 4 SMT solver. In: Gupta, A., Malik, S. (eds.) CAV 2008. LNCS, vol. 5123, pp. 299–303. Springer, Heidelberg (2008). doi:10.1007/978-3-540-70545-1_28
11. Cavezza, D.G., Alrajeh, D.: Interpolation-based GR(1) assumptions refinement. CoRR abs/1611.07803 (2016), http://arXiv.org/abs/1611.07803
12. Chatterjee, K., Henzinger, T.A., Jobstmann, B.: Environment assumptions for synthesis. In: Breugel, F., Chechik, M. (eds.) CONCUR 2008. LNCS, vol. 5201, pp. 147–161. Springer, Heidelberg (2008). doi:10.1007/978-3-540-85361-9_14
13. Cimatti, A., Roveri, M., Schuppan, V., Tchaltsev, A.: Diagnostic information for realizability. In: Logozzo, F., Peled, D.A., Zuck, L.D. (eds.) VMCAI 2008. LNCS, vol. 4905, pp. 52–67. Springer, Heidelberg (2008). doi:10.1007/978-3-540-78163-9_9
14. Cimatti, A., Griggio, A., Sebastiani, R.: Efficient interpolant generation in satisfiability modulo theories. In: Ramakrishnan, C.R., Rehof, J. (eds.) TACAS 2008. LNCS, vol. 4963, pp. 397–412. Springer, Heidelberg (2008). doi:10.1007/978-3-540-78800-3_30
15. Cobleigh, J.M., Giannakopoulou, D., Păsăreanu, C.S.: Learning assumptions for compositional verification. In: Garavel, H., Hatcliff, J. (eds.) TACAS 2003. LNCS, vol. 2619, pp. 331–346. Springer, Heidelberg (2003). doi:10.1007/3-540-36577-X_24
16. Craig, W.: Three uses of the Herbrand-Gentzen theorem in relating model theory and proof theory. J. Symb. Logic **22**(03), 269–285 (1957)

17. Degiovanni, R., Alrajeh, D., Aguirre, N., Uchitel, S.: Automated goal operationalisation based on interpolation and SAT solving. In: ACM/IEEE 36th International Conference on Software Engineering, pp. 129–139 (2014)
18. D'Silva, V., Kroening, D., Weissenbacher, G.: A survey of automated techniques for formal software verification. IEEE Trans. Comput.-Aided Des. Integr. Circ. Syst. **27**(7), 1165–1178 (2008)
19. Esparza, J., Kiefer, S., Schwoon, S.: Abstraction refinement with craig interpolation and symbolic pushdown systems. In: Hermanns, H., Palsberg, J. (eds.) TACAS 2006. LNCS, vol. 3920, pp. 489–503. Springer, Heidelberg (2006). doi:10.1007/11691372_35
20. Gheerbrant, A., Cate, B.: Craig interpolation for linear temporal languages. In: Grädel, E., Kahle, R. (eds.) CSL 2009. LNCS, vol. 5771, pp. 287–301. Springer, Heidelberg (2009). doi:10.1007/978-3-642-04027-6_22
21. Gheorghiu Bobaru, M., Păsăreanu, C.S., Giannakopoulou, D.: Automated assume-guarantee reasoning by abstraction refinement. In: Gupta, A., Malik, S. (eds.) CAV 2008. LNCS, vol. 5123, pp. 135–148. Springer, Heidelberg (2008). doi:10.1007/978-3-540-70545-1_14
22. Kamide, N.: Interpolation theorems for some variants of LTL. Rep. Math. Logic **50**, 3–30 (2015)
23. Könighofer, R., Hofferek, G., Bloem, R.: Debugging formal specifications using simple counterstrategies. In: Formal Methods in Computer-Aided Design, pp. 152–159 (2009)
24. Krajíček, J.: Interpolation theorems, lower bounds for proof systems, and independence results for bounded arithmetic. J. Symb. Logic **62**(02), 457–486 (1997)
25. van Lamsweerde, A.: Requirements Engineering - From System Goals to UML Models to Software Specifications. Wiley, Hoboken (2009)
26. van Lamsweerde, A., Letier, E.: Handling obstacles in goal-oriented requirements engineering. IEEE Trans. Softw. Eng. **26**(10), 978–1005 (2000)
27. Li, W., Dworkin, L., Seshia, S.A.: Mining assumptions for synthesis. In: ACM/IEEE 9th International Conference on Formal Methods and Models for Codesign, pp. 43–50 (2011)
28. Li, W., Sadigh, D., Sastry, S.S., Seshia, S.A.: Synthesis for human-in-the-loop control systems. In: 20th International Conference on Tools and Algorithms for the Construction and Analysis of Systems, pp. 470–484 (2014)
29. Manna, Z., Pnueli, A.: The Temporal Logic of Reactive and Concurrent Systems. Springer, Heidelberg (1992)
30. McMillan, K.L.: Interpolation and SAT-based model checking. In: Hunt, W.A., Somenzi, F. (eds.) CAV 2003. LNCS, vol. 2725, pp. 1–13. Springer, Heidelberg (2003). doi:10.1007/978-3-540-45069-6_1
31. Păsăreanu, C., Dwyer, M., Huth, M.: Assume-guarantee model checking of software: a comparative case study. In: Dams, D., Gerth, R., Leue, S., Massink, M. (eds.) SPIN 1999. LNCS, vol. 1680, pp. 168–183. Springer, Heidelberg (1999). doi:10.1007/3-540-48234-2_14
32. Sohail, S., Somenzi, F.: Safety first: a two-stage algorithm for the synthesis of reactive systems. Int. J. Softw. Tools for Technol. Transfer **15**(5–6), 433–454 (2013)
33. Sohail, S., Somenzi, F., Ravi, K.: A hybrid algorithm for LTL games. In: Logozzo, F., Peled, D.A., Zuck, L.D. (eds.) VMCAI 2008. LNCS, vol. 4905, pp. 309–323. Springer, Heidelberg (2008). doi:10.1007/978-3-540-78163-9_26

Synthesis II

Connecting Program Synthesis and Reachability: Automatic Program Repair Using Test-Input Generation

ThanhVu Nguyen[1]([✉]), Westley Weimer[2], Deepak Kapur[3],
and Stephanie Forrest[3]

[1] University of Nebraska, Lincoln, NE, USA
tnguyen@cse.unl.edu
[2] University of Virginia, Charlottesville, VA, USA
weimer@virginia.edu
[3] University of New Mexico, Albuquerque, NM, USA
{kapur,forrest}@cs.unm.edu

Abstract. We prove that certain formulations of program synthesis and reachability are equivalent. Specifically, our constructive proof shows the reductions between the template-based synthesis problem, which generates a program in a pre-specified form, and the reachability problem, which decides the reachability of a program location. This establishes a link between the two research fields and allows for the transfer of techniques and results between them.

To demonstrate the equivalence, we develop a program repair prototype using reachability tools. We transform a buggy program and its required specification into a specific program containing a location reachable only when the original program can be repaired, and then apply an off-the-shelf test-input generation tool on the transformed program to find test values to reach the desired location. Those test values correspond to repairs for the original program. Preliminary results suggest that our approach compares favorably to other repair methods.

Keywords: Program synthesis · Program verification · Program reachability · Reduction proof · Automated program repair · Test-input generation

1 Introduction

Synthesis is the task of generating a program that meets a required specification. Verification is the task of validating program correctness with respect to a given specification. Both are long-standing problems in computer science, although there has been extensive work on program verification and comparatively less on program synthesis until recently. Over the past several years, certain verification techniques have been adopted to create programs, e.g., applying symbolic execution to synthesize program repairs [25, 26, 29, 32], suggesting the possibility that

© Springer-Verlag GmbH Germany 2017
A. Legay and T. Margaria (Eds.): TACAS 2017, Part I, LNCS 10205, pp. 301–318, 2017.
DOI: 10.1007/978-3-662-54577-5_17

these two problems may be "two sides of the same coin". Finding and formalizing this equivalence is valuable in both theory and practice: it allows comparisons between the complexities and underlying structures of the two problems, and it raises the possibility of additional cross-fertilization between two fields that are usually treated separately (e.g., it might enable approximations designed to solve one problem to be applied directly to the other).

This paper establishes a formal connection between certain formulations of program synthesis and verification. We focus on the *template-based synthesis* problem, which generates missing code for partially completed programs, and we view verification as a *reachability* problem, which checks if a program can reach an undesirable state. We then constructively prove that template-based synthesis and reachability are *equivalent*. We reduce a template-based synthesis problem, which consists of a program with parameterized templates to be synthesized and a test suite specification, to a program consisting of a specific location that is reachable only when those templates can be instantiated such that the program meets the given specification. To reduce reachability to synthesis, we transform a reachability instance consisting of a program and a given location into a synthesis instance that can be solved only when the location in the original problem is reachable. Thus, reachability solvers can be applied to synthesize code, and conversely, synthesis tools can be used to determine reachability.

To demonstrate the equivalence, we use the reduction to develop a new automatic program repair technique using an existing test-input generation tool. We view *program repair* as a special case of template-based synthesis in which "patch" code is generated so that it behaves correctly. We present a prototype tool called CETI that automatically repairs C programs that violate test-suite specifications. Given a test suite and a program failing at least one test in that suite, CETI first applies fault localization to obtain a list of ranked suspicious statements from the buggy program. For each suspicious statement, CETI transforms the buggy program and the information from its test suite into a program reachability instance. The reachability instance is a new program containing a special **if** branch, whose **then** branch is reachable only when the original program can be repaired by modifying the considered statement. By construction, any input value that allows the special location to be reached can map directly to a repair template instantiation that fixes the bug. To find a repair, CETI invokes an off-the-shelf automatic test-input generation tool on the transformed code to find test values that can reach the special branch location. These values correspond to changes that, when applied to the original program, cause it to pass the given test suite. This procedure is guaranteed to be sound, but it is not necessarily complete. That is, there may be bugs that the procedure cannot find repairs for, but all proposed repairs are guaranteed to be correct with respect to the given test suite. We evaluated CETI on the Tcas program [13], which has 41 seeded defects, and found that it repaired over 60%, which compares favorably with other state-of-the-art automated bug repair approaches.

To summarize, the main contributions of the paper include:

- *Equivalence Theorem:* We constructively prove that the problems of template-based program synthesis and reachability in program verification are equivalent. Even though these two problems are shown to be undecidable in general, the constructions allow heuristics solving one problem to be applied to the other.

– *Automatic Program Repair:* We present a new automatic program repair technique, which leverages the construction. The technique reduces the task of synthesizing program repairs to a reachability problem, where the results produced by a test-input generation tool correspond to a patch that repairs the original program. ·

– *Implementation and Evaluation:* We implement the repair algorithm in a prototype tool that automatically repairs C programs, and we evaluate it on a benchmark that has been targeted by multiple program repair algorithms. ·

2 Motivating Example

We give a concrete example of how the reduction from template-based synthesis to reachability can be used to repair a buggy program. Consider the buggy code shown in Fig. 1, a function excerpted from a traffic collision avoidance system [13]. The intended behavior of the function can be precisely described as: `is_upward(in,up,down)` = `in*100 + up > down`. The table in Fig. 1 gives a test suite describing the intended behavior. The buggy program fails two of the tests, which we propose to repair by synthesizing a patch.

We solve this synthesis problem by restricting ourselves to generating patches under predefined templates, e.g., synthesizing expressions involving program variables and unknown parameters, and then transforming this template-based synthesis problem into a reachability problem instance. In this approach, a template such as

$$\boxed{c_0} + \boxed{c_1}\, v_1 + \boxed{c_2}\, v_2$$

is a linear combination[1] of program variables v_i and unknown template parameters $\boxed{c_i}$. For clarity, we often denote template parameters with a box to

```
1  int is_upward(int in,int up,int down){
2    int bias , r;
3    if (in)
4      bias = down; //fix: bias = up + 100
5    else
6      bias = up;
7    if (bias > down)
8      r = 1;
9    else
10     r = 0;
11   return r;
12 }
```

Test	Inputs			Output		
	in	up	down	expected	observed	Passed?
1	1	0	100	0	0	✓
2	1	11	110	1	0	✗
3	0	100	50	1	1	✓
4	1	-20	60	1	0	✗
5	0	0	10	0	0	✓
6	0	0	-10	1	1	✓

Fig. 1. Example buggy program and test suite. CETI suggests replacing line 4 with the statement `bias = up + 100;` to repair the bug.

---

[1] More general templates (e.g., nonlinear polynomials) are also possible as shown in Sect. 3.4.

```
int c0,c1,c2,c3,c4; //global inputs          return r;
                                         }
int is_upwardP(int in,int up,int
       down){                            int main() {
   int bias, r;                            if(is_upwardP(1,0,100)    == 0 &&
   if (in)                                    is_upwardP(1,11,110)   == 1 &&
     bias =                                   is_upwardP(0,100,50)   == 1 &&
       c0+c1*bias+c2*in+c3*up+c4*down;       is_upwardP(1,-20,60)   == 1 &&
   else                                       is_upwardP(0,0,10)     == 0 &&
     bias = up;                               is_upwardP(0,0,-10)    == 1){
   if (bias > down)                           [L]
     r = 1;                               }
   else                                   return 0;
     r = 0;                             }
```

Fig. 2. The reachability problem instance derived from the buggy program and test suite in Fig. 1. Location L is reachable with values such as $c_0 = 100, c_1 = 0, c_2 = 0, c_3 = 1, c_4 = 0$. These values suggest using the statement bias = 100 + up; at Line 4 in the buggy program.

distinguish them from normal program elements. This template can be instantiated to yield concrete expressions such as $200 + 3v_1 + 4v_2$ via $c_0 = 200, c_1 = 3, c_2 = 4$. To repair Line 4 of Fig. 1, (bias = down;) with a linear template, we would replace Line 4 with:

$$\text{bias} = \boxed{c_0} + \boxed{c_1} * \text{bias} + \boxed{c_2} * \text{in} + \boxed{c_3} * \text{up} + \boxed{c_4} * \text{down};$$

where bias, in, up, and down are the variables in scope at Line 4 and the value of each c_i must be found. We propose to find them by constructing a special program reachability instance and then solving that instance.

The construction transforms the program, its test suite (Fig. 1), and the template statement into a reachability instance consisting of a program and target location. The first key idea is to derive a new program containing the template code with the template parameters $\boxed{c_i}$ represented explicitly as program variables c_i. This program defines the reachability instance, which must assign values to each c_i. The second key idea is that each test case is explicitly represented as a conditional expression. Recall that we seek a single synthesis solution (one set of values for c_i) that respects all tests. Each test is encoded as a conditional expression (a reachability constraint), and we take their conjunction, being careful to refer to the same c_i variables in each expression. In the example, we must find one repair that satisfies all six tests, not six separate repairs that each satisfy only one test.

The new program, shown in Fig. 2, contains a function is_upwardP that resembles the function is_upward in the original code but with Line 4 replaced by the template statement with each reference to a template parameter replaced by a reference to the corresponding new externally-defined program variable. The program also contains a starting function main, which encodes the inputs and expected outputs from the given test suite as the guards to the conditional statement leading to the target location L. Intuitively, the reachability problem instance asks if we can find values for each c_i that allow control flow to reach location L, which is only reachable iff all tests are satisfied.

This reachability instance can be given as input to any off-the-self test-input generation tool. Here, we use KLEE [8] to find value for each c_i. KLEE determines that the values $c_0 = 100, c_1 = 0, c_2 = 0, c_3 = 1, c_4 = 0$ allow control flow to reach location L. Finally, we map this solution back to the original program repair problem by applying the c_i values to the template

$$\texttt{bias} = \boxed{c_0} + \boxed{c_1} * \texttt{bias} + \boxed{c_2} * \texttt{in} + \boxed{c_3} * \texttt{up} + \boxed{c_4} * \texttt{down};$$

generating the statement:

$$\texttt{bias} = 100 + 0 * \texttt{bias} + 0 * \texttt{in} + 1 * \texttt{up} + 0 * \texttt{down};$$

which reduces to `bias = 100 + up`. Replacing the statement `bias = down` in the original program with the new statement `bias = 100 + up` produces a program that passes all of the test cases.

To summarize, a specific question (i.e., can the bug be repaired by applying template X to line Y of program P while satisfying test suite T?) is reduced to a single reachability instance, solvable using a reachability tool such as a test-input generator. This reduction is formally established in the next section.

3   Connecting Program Synthesis and Reachability

We establish the connection between the template-based formulation of program synthesis and the reachability problem in program verification. We first review these problems and then show their equivalence.

3.1   Preliminaries

We consider standard imperative programs in a language like C. The base language includes usual program constructs such as assignments, conditionals, loops, and functions. A function takes as input a (potentially empty) tuple of values and returns an output value. A function can call other functions, including itself. For simplicity, we equate a program P with its finite set of functions, including a special starting function main_P. For brevity, we write $P(c_i, \ldots, c_n) = y$ to denote that evaluating the function $\text{main}_P \in P$ on the input tuple $(c_i, \ldots, c_n)$ results in the value y. Program or function semantics are specified by a test suite consisting of a finite set of input/output pairs. When possible, we use c_i for concrete input values and v_i for formal parameters or variable names.

To simplify the presentation, we assume that the language also supports exceptions, admitting non-local control flow by raising and catching exceptions as in modern programming languages such as C++ and Java. We discuss how to remove this assumption in Sect. 3.3.

Template-Based Program Synthesis. *Program synthesis* aims to automatically generate program code to meet a required specification. The problem of synthesizing a complete program is generally undecidable [42], so many practical synthesis techniques operate on partially-complete programs, filling in well-structured gaps [1,36,39,41,43,44]. These techniques synthesize programs from specific grammars, forms, or templates and do not generate arbitrary code. A synthesis *template* expresses the shape of program constructs, but includes holes (sometimes called template parameters), as illustrated in the previous section. We refer to a program containing such templates as a *template program* and extend the base language to include a finite, fixed set of template parameters $\boxed{c_i}$ as shown earlier. Using the notation of contextual operational semantics, we write $P[c_0, \ldots, c_n]$ to denote the result of instantiating the template program P with template parameter values $c_0 \ldots c_n$. To find values for the parameters in a template program, many techniques (e.g., [1,41,43,44]) encode the program and its specification as a logical formula (e.g., using axiomatic semantics) and use a constraint solver such as SAT or SMT to find values for the parameters c_i that satisfy the formula. Instantiating the templates with those values produces a complete program that adheres to the required specification.

Definition 1. Template-based Program Synthesis Problem. *Given a template program Q with a finite set of template parameters $S = \{\boxed{c_1}, \ldots, \boxed{c_n}\}$ and a finite test suite of input/output pairs $T = \{(i_1, o_1), \ldots, (i_m, o_m)\}$, do there exist parameter values c_i such that $\forall(i, o) \in T \ . \ (Q[c_1, \ldots, c_n])(i) = o$?*

For example, the program in Fig. 1 with Line 4 replaced by bias $= \boxed{c_0} + \boxed{c_1} * \text{bias} + \boxed{c_2} * \text{in} + \boxed{c_3} * \text{up} + \boxed{c_4} * \text{down}$ is an instance of template-based synthesis. This program passes its test suite given in Fig. 1 using the solution $\{c_0 = 100, c_1 = 1, c_2 = 0, c_3 = 1, c_4 = 0\}$. The decision formulation of the problem asks if satisfying values $c_1 \ldots c_n$ exist; in this presentation we require that witnesses be produced.

Program Reachability. *Program reachability* is a classic problem which asks if a particular program state or location can be observed at run-time. It is not decidable in general, because it can encode the halting problem (cf. Rice's Theorem [35]). However, reachability remains a popular and well-studied verification problem in practice. In model checking [10], for example, reachability is used to determine whether program states representing undesirable behaviors could occur in practice. Another application area is test-input generation [9], which aims to produce test values to explore all reachable program locations.

Definition 2. Program Reachability Problem. *Given a program P, set of program variables $\{x_1, \ldots, x_n\}$ and target location L, do there exist input values c_i such that the execution of P with x_i initialized to c_i reaches L in a finite number of steps?*

For example, the program in Fig. 3 has a reachable location L using the solution $\{x = -20, y = -40\}$. Similar to the synthesis problem, the decision

```
//global inputs
int x, y;

int P(){
  if (2 * x == y)
    if (x > y + 10)
      [L]

  return 0;
}
```

```
int P_Q () {
  if (2*⬚x⬚ == ⬚y⬚)
    if (⬚x⬚ > ⬚y⬚+10)
      //loc L in P
      raise
           REACHED;

  return 0;
}
```

```
int main_Q () {
  //synthesize x, y
  int x = c_x;
  int y = c_y;
  try
    P_Q ();
  catch (REACHED)
    return 1;

  return 0;
}
```

Fig. 3. An instance of program reachability. Program P reaches location L using the solution $\{x = -20, y = -40\}$.

Fig. 4. Reducing the reachability example in Fig. 3 to a template-based synthesis program (i.e., synthesize assignments to c_x and c_y). The test suite of the reduced synthesis program is $Q() = 1$.

problem formulation of reachability merely asks if the input values $c_1, \ldots, c_n$ exist; in this presentation we require witnesses be produced.

3.2 Reducing Synthesis to Reachability

We present the constructive reduction from synthesis to reachability. The key to the reduction is a particular "gadget", which constructs a reachability instance that can be satisfied iff the synthesis problem can be solved.

Reduction: Let Q be a template program with a set of template parameters $S = \{\boxed{c_1}, \ldots, \boxed{c_n}\}$ and a set of finite tests $T = \{(i_1, o_1), \ldots\}$. We construct $\mathsf{GadgetS2R}(Q, S, T)$, which returns a new program P (the constructed reachability instance) with a special location L, as follows:

1. For every template parameter $\boxed{c_i}$, add a fresh global variable v_i. A solution to this reachability instance is an assignment of concrete values c_i to the variables v_i.
2. For every function $q \in Q$, define a similar function $q_P \in P$. The body of q_P is the same as q, but with every reference to a template parameter $\boxed{c_i}$ replaced with a reference to the corresponding new variable v_i.
3. P also contains a starting function main_P that encodes the specification information from the test suite T as a conjunctive expression e:

$$e = \bigwedge_{(i,o) \in T} \mathsf{main}_{QP}(i) = o$$

where main_{QP} is a function in P corresponding to the starting function main_Q in Q. In addition, the body of main_P is one conditional statement leading to a fresh target location L if and only if e is true. Thus, main_P has the form

```
int mainP() {
   if (e)
      [L]
}
```

4. The derived program P consists of the declaration of the new variables (Step 1), the functions q_P's (Step 2), and the starting function $main_P$ (Step 3).

Example: Figure 2 illustrates the reduction using the example from Fig. 1. The resulting reachability program can arrive at location L using the input $\{c_0 = 100, c_1 = 0, c_2 = 0, c_3 = 1, c_4 = 0\}$, which corresponds to a solution.

Reduction Correctness and Complexity: The correctness of GadgetS2R, which transforms synthesis to reachability, relies on two key invariants[2]. First, function calls in the derived program P have the same behavior as template functions in the original program Q. Second, location L is reachable if and only if values c_i can be assigned to variables v_i such that Q passes all of the tests.

The complexity of GadgetS2R is *linear* in both the program size and number of test cases of the input instance Q, S, T. The constructed program P consists of all functions in Q (with $|S|$ extra variables) and a starting function $main_P$ with an expression encoding the test suite T.

This reduction directly leads to the main result for this direction of the equivalence:

Theorem 1. *The template-based synthesis problem in Definition 1 is reducible to the reachability problem in Definition 2.*

3.3   Reducing Reachability to Synthesis

Here, we present the reduction from reachability to synthesis. The reduction also uses a particular gadget to construct a synthesis instance that can be solved iff the reachability instance can be determined.

Reduction: Let P be a program, L be a location in P, and $V = \{v_1, \ldots, v_n\}$ be global variables never directly assigned in P. We construct GadgetR2S(P, L, V), which returns a template program Q with template parameters S and a test suite T, as follows:

1. For every variable v_i, define a fresh template variable $\boxed{c_i}$. Let the set of template parameters S be the set containing each $\boxed{c_i}$.
2. For every function $p \in P$, define a derived function $p_Q \in Q$. Replace each function call to p with the corresponding call to p_Q. Replace each use of a variable v_i with a read from the corresponding template parameter $\boxed{c_i}$; remove all declarations of variables v_i.

---

[2] The full proof is given in the Appendix of [34].

3. Raise a unique exception REACHED, at the location in Q corresponding to the location L in P. As usual, when an exception is raised, control immediately jumps to the most recently-executed *try-catch* block matching that exception. The exception REACHED will be caught iff the location in Q corresponding to $L \in P$ would be reached.

4. Define a starting function main_Q that has no inputs and returns an integer value. Let main_{PQ} be the function in Q corresponding to the starting function main_P in P.

   – Insert *try-catch* construct that calls p_Q and returns the value 1 if the exception REACHED is caught.
   – At the end of main_Q, return the value 0.
   – Thus, main_Q has the form

   ```
   int mainQ() {
       try {
           mainPQ();
       } catch (REACHED) {
           return 1;
       }
       return 0;
   }
   ```

5. The derived program Q consists of the finite set of template parameters $S = \{\boxed{c_1}, \ldots, \boxed{c_n}\}$ (Step 1), functions p_Q's (Step 2), and the starting function main_Q (Step 4).

6. The test suite T for Q consists of exactly one test case $Q() = 1$, indicating the case when the exception REACHED is raised and caught.

Example: Figure 4 illustrates the reduction using the example from Fig. 3. The synthesized program can be satisfied by $c_0 = -20, c_1 = -40$, corresponding to the input $(x = -20, y = -40)$ which reaches L in Fig. 3.

The exception REACHED represents a unique signal to main_Q that the location L has been reached. Many modern languages support exceptions for handling special events, but they are not strictly necessary for the reduction to succeed. Other (potentially language-dependent) implementation techniques could also be employed. Or, we could use a tuple to represent the signal, e.g., returning (v, false) from a function that normally returns v if the location corresponding L has not been reached and $(1, \text{true})$ as soon as it has. BLAST [6], a model checker for C programs (which do not support exceptions), uses *goto* and labels to indicate when a desired location has been reached.

Reduction Correctness and Complexity: The correctness of the GadgetS2R, which transforms reachability to synthesis, depends on two key invariants[3]. First, for any c_i, execution in the derived template program Q with $\boxed{c_i} \mapsto c_i$ mirrors execution in P with $v_i \mapsto c_i$ up to the point when L is reached (if ever). Second, the exception REACHED is raised in Q iff location L is reachable in P.

---

[3] The full proof is given in the Appendix of [34].

The complexity of GadgetR2S is *linear* in the input instance P, L, v_i. The constructed program Q consists of all functions in P and a starting function $\text{main}Q$ having n template variables, where $n = |\{v_i\}|$.

This reduction directly leads to the main result for this direction of the equivalence:

Theorem 2. *The reachability problem in Definition 2 is reducible to the template-based synthesis problem in Definition 1.*

3.4   Synthesis ≡ Reachability

Together, the above two theorems establish the equivalence between the reachability problem in program verification and the template-based program synthesis.

Corollary 1. *The reachability problem in Definition 2 and the template-based synthesis problem in Definition 1 are linear-time reducible to each other.*

This equivalence is perhaps unsurprising as researchers have long assumed certain relations between program synthesis and verification (e.g., see Sect. 5). However, we believe that a proof of the equivalence is valuable. First, our proof, although straightforward, formally shows that both problems inhabit the same complexity class (e.g., the restricted formulation of synthesis in Definition 1 is as hard as the reachability problem in Definition 2). Second, although both problems are undecidable in the general case, the linear-time transformations allow existing approximations and ideas developed for one problem to apply to the other one. Third, in term of practicality, the equivalence allows for direct application of off-the-shelf reachability and verification tools to synthesize and repair programs. Our approach is not so different from verification works that transform the interested problems into SAT/SMT formulas to be solved by existing efficient solvers. Finally, this work can be extended to more complex classes of synthesis and repair problems. While we demonstrate the approach using linear templates, more general templates can be handled. For example, combinations of nonlinear polynomials can be considered using a priority subset of terms (e.g., $t_1 = x^2, t_2 = xy$, as demonstrated in nonlinear invariant generation [33]).

We hope that these results help raise fruitful cross-fertilization among program verification and synthesis fields that are usually treated separately. Because our reductions produce reachability problem instances that are rarely encountered by current verification techniques (e.g., with large guards), they may help refine existing tools or motivate optimizations in new directions. As an example, our bug repair prototype CETI (discussed in the next Section) has produced reachability instances that hit a crashing bug in KLEE that was confirmed to be important by the developers[4]. These hard instances might be used to evaluate and improve verification and synthesis tools (similar to benchmarks used in annual SAT[5] and SMT[6] competitions).

---

[4] http://mailman.ic.ac.uk/pipermail/klee-dev/2016-February/001278.html.
[5] SAT Competitions: http://www.satcompetition.org.
[6] SMT competitions: http://smtcomp.sourceforge.net/2016.

4   Program Repair Using Test-Input Generation

We use the equivalence to develop CETI (Correcting Errors using Test Inputs), a tool for automated program repair (a synthesis problem) using test-input generation techniques (which solves reachability problems). We define problem of program repair in terms of template-based program synthesis:

Definition 3 Program Repair Problem. *Given a program Q that fails at least one test in a finite test suite T and a finite set of parameterized templates S, does there exist a set of statements $\{s_i\} \subseteq Q$ and parameter values $c_1, \ldots, c_n$ for the templates in S such that s_i can be replaced with $S[c_1, \ldots, c_n]$ and the resulting program passes all tests in T?*

This repair problem thus allows edits to multiple program statements (e.g., we can replace both lines 4 and 10 in Fig. 1 with parameterized templates). The *single-edit* repair problem restricts the edits to one statement.

CETI implements the key ideas from Theorem 1 in Sect. 3.2 to transform this repair problem into a reachability task solvable by existing verification tools. Given a test suite and a buggy program that fails some test in the suite, CETI employs the statistical fault localization technique Tarantula [23] to identify particular code regions for synthesis, i.e., program statements likely related to the defect. Next, for each suspicious statement and synthesis template, CETI transforms the buggy program, the test suite, the statement and the template into a new program containing a location reachable only when the original program can be repaired. Thus, by default CETI considers single-edit repairs, but it can be modified to repair multiple lines by using k top-ranked suspicious statements (cf. Angelix [29]). Such an approach increases the search space and thus the computational burden placed on the reachability solver.

Our current implementation employs CIL [31] to parse and modify C programs using repair templates similar to those given in [25,32]. These templates allow modifying constants, expressions (such as the linear template shown in Sect. 2), and logical, comparisons, and arithmetic operators (such as changing $\|$ to &&, $\leq$ to $<$, or $+$ to $-$). Finally, we send the transformed program to the test-input generation tool KLEE, which produces test values that can reach the designated location. Such test input values, when combined with the synthesis template and the suspicious statement, correspond exactly to a patch that repairs the bug. CETI synthesizes correct-by-construction repairs, i.e., the repair, if found, is guaranteed to pass the test suite.

4.1   Evaluation

To evaluate CETI, we use the `Tcas` program from the SIR benchmark [13]. The program, which implements an aircraft traffic collision avoidance system, has 180 lines of code and 12 integer inputs. The program comes with a test suite of about 1608 tests and 41 faulty functions, consisting of seeded defects such as changed operators, incorrect constant values, missing code, and incorrect control flow. Among the programs in SIR, `Tcas` has the most introduced defects (41), and it has been used to benchmark modern bug repair techniques [12,26,32].

We manually modify `Tcas`, which normally prints its result on the screen, to instead return its output to its caller, e.g., `printf("output is %d\n",v)` becomes `return v`. For efficiency, many repair techniques initially consider a smaller number of tests in the suite and then verify candidate repairs on the entire suite [32]. In contrast, we use all available tests at all times to guarantee that any repair found by CETI is correct with respect to the test suite. We find that modern tools such as KLEE can handle the complex conditionals that encode such information efficiently and generate the desired solutions within seconds.

The behavior of CETI is controlled by customizable parameters. For the experiments described here, we consider the top $n = 80$ from the ranked list of suspicious statements and, then apply the predefined templates to these statements. For efficiency, we restrict synthesis parameters to be within certain value ranges: constant coefficients are confined to the integral range $[-100000, 100000]$ while the variable coefficients are drawn from the set $\{-1, 0, 1\}$.

Results. Table 1 shows the results with 41 buggy `Tcas` versions. These experiments were performed on a 32-core 2.60 GHz Intel Linux system with 128 GB of RAM. Column **Bug Type** describes the type of defect. *Incorrect Const* denotes a defect involving the use of the wrong constant, e.g., 700 instead of 600. *Incorrect Op* denotes a defect that uses the wrong operator for arithmetic, comparison, or logical calculations, e.g., $\geq$ instead of $>$. *Missing code* denotes defects that entirely lack an expression or statement, e.g., `a&&b` instead of `a&&b||c` or `return a` instead of `return a+b`. *Multiple* denotes defects caused by several actions such as missing code at a location and using an incorrect operator at another location. Column **T(s)** shows the time taken in seconds. Column **R-Prog** lists the number of reachability program instances that were generated and processed by KLEE. Column **Repair?** indicates whether a repair was found.

We were able to correct 26 of 41 defects, including multiple defects of different types. On average, CETI takes 22 seconds for each successful repair. The tool found 100% of repairs for which the required changes are single edits according to one of our predefined templates (e.g., generating arbitrary integer constants or changing operators at one location). In several cases, defects could be repaired in several ways. For example, defect v_{28} can be repaired by swapping the results of both branches of a conditional statement or by inverting the conditional guard. CETI also obtained unexpected repairs. For example, the bug in v_{13} is a comparison against an incorrect constant; the buggy code reads < 700 while the human-written patch reads < 600. Our generated repair of < 596 also passes all tests.

We were not able to repair 15 of 41 defects, each of which requires edits at multiple locations or the addition of code that is beyond the scope of the current set of templates. As expected, CETI takes longer for these programs because it tries all generated template programs before giving up. One common pattern among these programs is that the bug occurs in a macro definition,

Table 1. Repair results for 41 Tcas defects

	Bug type	R-Progs	T(s)	Repair?		Bug type	R-Progs	T(s)	Repair?
v1	incorrect op	6143	21	✓	v22	missing code	5553	175	–
v2	missing code	6993	27	✓	v23	missing code	5824	164	–
v3	incorrect op	8006	18	✓	v24	missing code	6050	231	–
v4	incorrect op	5900	27	✓	v25	incorrect op	5983	19	✓
v5	missing code	8440	394	–	v26	missing code	8004	195	–
v6	incorrect op	5872	19	✓	v27	missing code	8440	270	–
v7	incorrect const	7302	18	✓	v28	incorrect op	9072	11	✓
v8	incorrect const	6013	19	✓	v29	missing code	6914	195	–
v9	incorrect op	5938	24	✓	v30	missing code	6533	170	–
v10	incorrect op	7154	18	✓	v31	multiple	4302	16	✓
v11	multiple	6308	123	–	v32	multiple	4493	17	✓
v12	incorrect op	8442	25	✓	v33	multiple	9070	224	–
v13	incorrect const	7845	21	✓	v34	incorrect op	8442	75	✓
v14	incorrect const	1252	22	✓	v35	multiple	9070	184	–
v15	multiple	7760	258	–	v36	incorrect const	6334	10	✓
v16	incorrect const	5470	19	✓	v37	missing code	7523	174	–
v17	incorrect const	7302	12	✓	v38	missing code	7685	209	–
v18	incorrect const	7383	18	✓	v39	incorrect op	5983	20	✓
v19	incorrect const	6920	19	✓	v40	missing code	7364	136	–
v20	incorrect op	5938	19	✓	v41	missing code	5899	29	✓
v21	missing code	5939	31	✓					

e.g., `#define C = 100` instead of `#define C = 200`. Since the CIL front end automatically expands such macros, CETI would need to individually fix each use of the macro in order to succeed. This is an artifact of CIL, rather than a weakness inherent in our algorithm.

CETI, which repairs 26 of 41 Tcas defects, performs well compared to other reported results from repair tools on this benchmark program. GenProg, which finds edits by recombining existing code, can repair 11 of these defects [32, Table 5]. The technique of Debroy and Wong, which uses random mutation, can repair 9 defects [12, Table 2]. FoREnSiC, which uses the concolic execution in CREST, repairs 23 defects [26, Table 1]. SemFix out-performs CETI, repairing 34 defects [32, Table 5], but also uses fifty test cases instead of the entire suite of thousands[7]. Other repair techniques, including equivalence checking [26] and counterexample guided refinement [26], repair 15 and 16 defects, respectively.

Although CETI uses similar repair templates as both SemFix and FoREn-SiC, the repair processes are different. SemFix directly uses and customizes the

---

[7] Thus CETI's repairs, which pass the entire suite instead of just 50 selected tests, meet a higher standard. We were unable to obtain SemFix details, e.g., which 50 tests, online or from the authors.

KLEE symbolic execution engine, and FoRenSiC integrates concolic execution to analyze programs and SMT solving to generate repairs. In contrast, CETI eschews heavyweight analyses, and it simply generates a reachability instance. Indeed, our work is inspired by, and generalizes, these works, observing that the whole synthesis task can be offloaded with strong success in practice.

However, there is a trade-off: customizing a reachability solver to the task of program repair may increase the performance or the number of repairs found, but may also reduce the generality or ease-of-adoption of the overall technique. We note that our unoptimized tool CETI already outperforms published results for GenProg, Debroy and Wong, and FoRENSiC on this benchmark, and is competitive with SemFix.

Limitations. We require that the program behaves deterministically on the test cases and that the defect be reproducible. This limitation can be mitigated by running the test cases multiple times, but ultimately our technique is not applicable if the program is non-deterministic. We assume that the test cases encode all relevant program requirements. If adequate test cases are not available then the repair may not retain required functionality. Our formulation also encodes the test cases as inputs to a starting function (e.g., `main`) with a single expected output. This might not be feasible for certain types of specifications, such as liveness properties ("eventually" and "always") in temporal logic. The efficiency of CETI depends on fault localization to reduce the search space. The reachability or test-input generation tool used affects both the efficiency and the efficacy of CETI. For example, if the reachability tool uses a constraint solver that does not support data types such as string or arrays then we will not be able to repair program defects involving those types. Finally, we assume that the repair can be constructed from the provided repair templates.

The reduction in Sect. 3.2 can transform a finite space (buggy) program into an infinite space reachability problem (e.g., we hypothesize that a bounded loop guard $i \leq 10$ is buggy and try to synthesize a new guard using an unknown parameter $i \leq \boxed{c}$). However, this does not invalidate the theoretical or empirical results and the reduction is efficient in the program size and the number of tests. The reduction also might not be optimal if we use complex repair templates (e.g., involving many unknown parameters). In practice we do not need to synthesize many complex values for most defects and thus modern verification tools such as KLEE can solve these problems efficiently, as shown in our evaluation.

This paper concretely demonstrates the applicability of program reachability (test-input generation) to program synthesis (defect repair) but not the reverse direction of using program synthesis to solve reachability. Applying advances in automatic program repair to find test-inputs to reach nontrivial program locations remains future work.

5 Related Work

Program Synthesis and Verification. Researchers have long hypothesized about the relation between program synthesis and verification and proposed synthesis approaches using techniques or tools often used to verify programs such as constraint solving or model checking [1,43]. For example, Bodik and Solar-Lezama et al.'s work [39,40] on sketching defines the synthesis task as: $\exists c \,.\, \forall (i,o) \,.\, \in T \,.\, (P[c])(i) = o$ (similar to our template-based synthesis formulation in Definition 1) and solves the problem using a SAT solver. Other synthesis and program repair researches, e.g., [4,29,32,43,44], also use similar formulation to integrate verification tools, e.g., test-input generation, to synthesize desired programs. In general, such integrations are common in many ongoing synthesis works including the multi-disciplinary ExCAPE project [14] and the SyGuS competition [45], and have produced many practical and useful tools such as Sketch that generates low-level bit-stream programs [39], Autograder that provides feedback on programming homework [38], and FlashFill that constructs Excel macros [19,20].

The work presented in this paper is inspired by these works, and generalizes them by establishing a formal connection between synthesis and verification using the template-based synthesis and reachability formulations. We show that it is not just a coincident that the aforementioned synthesis works can exploit verification techniques, but that every template-based synthesis problem can be reduced to the reachability formulation in verification. Dually, we show the other direction that reduces reachability to template-based synthesis, so that every reachability problem can be solved using synthesis. Furthermore, our constructive proofs describe efficient algorithms to do such reductions.

Program Repair and Test-Input Generation. Due to the pressing demand for reliable software, automatic program repair has steadily gained research interests and produced many novel repair techniques. *Constraint-based* repair approaches, e.g., AFix [21], Angelix [29], SemFix [32], FoRenSiC [7], Gopinath et al. [18], Jobstmann et al. [22], generate constraints and solve them for patches that are correct by construction (i.e., guaranteed to adhere to a specification or pass a test suite). In contrast, *generate-and-validate* repair approaches, e.g., GenProg [46], Pachika [11], PAR [24], Debroy and Wong [12], Prophet [28], find multiple repair candidates (e.g., using stochastic search or invariant inferences) and verify them against given specifications.

The field of test-input generation has produced many practical techniques and tools to generate high coverage test data for complex software, e.g., fuzz testing [15,30], symbolic execution [8,9], concolic (combination of static and dynamic analyses) execution [16,37], and software model checking [5,6]. Companies and industrial research labs such as Microsoft, NASA, IBM, and Fujitsu have also developed test-input generation tools to test their own products [2,3,17,27]. Our work allows program repair and synthesis approaches directly apply these techniques and tools.

6   Conclusion

We constructively prove that the template-based program synthesis problem and the reachability problem in program verification are equivalent. This equivalence connects the two problems and enables the application of ideas, optimizations, and tools developed for one problem to the other. To demonstrate this, we develop CETI, a tool for automated program repair using test-input generation techniques that solve reachability problems. CETI transforms the task of synthesizing program repairs to a reachability problem, where the results produced by a test-input generation tool correspond to a patch that repairs the original program. Experimental case studies suggest that CETI has higher success rates than many other standard repair approaches.

Acknowledgments. This research was partially supported by NSF awards CCF 1248069, CNS 1619098, CNS 1619123, as well as AFOSR grant FA8750-11-2-0039 and DARPA grant FA8650-10-C-7089.

References

1. Alur, R., Bodik, R., Juniwal, G., Martin, M.M., Raghothaman, M., Seshia, S.A., Singh, R., Solar-Lezama, A., Torlak, E., Udupa, A.: Syntax-guided synthesis. Dependable Softw. Syst. Eng. **40**, 1–25 (2015)
2. Anand, S., Păsăreanu, C.S., Visser, W.: JPF–SE: a symbolic execution extension to Java PathFinder. In: Grumberg, O., Huth, M. (eds.) TACAS 2007. LNCS, vol. 4424, pp. 134–138. Springer, Heidelberg (2007). doi:10.1007/978-3-540-71209-1_12
3. Artzi, S., Kiezun, A., Dolby, J., Tip, F., Dig, D., Paradkar, A., Ernst, M.D.: Finding bugs in dynamic web applications. In: ISSTA, pp. 261–272. ACM (2008)
4. Attie, P., Cherri, A., Al Bab, K.D., Sakr, M., Saklawi, J.: Model and program repair via sat solving. In: MEMOCODE, pp. 148–157. IEEE (2015)
5. Ball, T., Rajamani, S.K.: The SLAM project: debugging system software via static analysis. In: POPL, pp. 1–3. ACM (2002)
6. Beyer, D., Henzinger, T.A., Jhala, R., Majumdar, R.: The software model checker BLAST. Soft. Tools Technol. Transf. **9**(5–6), 505–525 (2007)
7. Bloem, R., et al.: FoREnSiC – an automatic debugging environment for C programs. In: Biere, A., Nahir, A., Vos, T. (eds.) HVC 2012. LNCS, vol. 7857, pp. 260–265. Springer, Heidelberg (2013). doi:10.1007/978-3-642-39611-3_24
8. Cadar, C., Dunbar, D., Engler, D.R.: KLEE: unassisted and automatic generation of high-coverage tests for complex systems programs. In: OSDI, vol. 8, pp. 209–224. USENIX Association (2008)
9. Cadar, C., Sen, K.: Symbolic execution for software testing: three decades later. Commun. ACM **56**(2), 82–90 (2013)
10. Clarke, E.M., Grumberg, O., Peled, D.: Model Checking. MIT Press, Cambridge (1999)
11. Dallmeier, V., Zeller, A., Meyer, B.: Generating fixes from object behavior anomalies. In: ASE, pp. 550–554. IEEE (2009)
12. Debroy, V., Wong, W.E.: Using mutation to automatically suggest fixes for faulty programs. In: Software Testing, Verification and Validation, pp. 65–74. IEEE (2010)

13. Do, H., Elbaum, S., Rothermel, G.: Supporting controlled experimentation with testing techniques: an infrastructure and its potential impact. Empir. Softw. Eng. **10**(4), 405–435 (2005)
14. ExCAPE: Expeditions in computer augmented program engineering. http://excape.cis.upenn.edu. Accessed 19 Oct 2016
15. Forrester, J.E., Miller, B.P.: An empirical study of the robustness of Windows NT applications using random testing. In: USENIX Windows System Symposium, pp. 59–68 (2000)
16. Godefroid, P., Klarlund, N., Sen, K.: DART: directed automated random testing. PLDI **40**(6), 213–223 (2005)
17. Godefroid, P., Levin, M.Y., Molnar, D.A., et al.: Automated whitebox fuzz testing. In: Network and Distributed System Security Symposium, pp. 151–166 (2008)
18. Gopinath, D., Malik, M.Z., Khurshid, S.: Specification-based program repair using SAT. In: Abdulla, P.A., Leino, K.R.M. (eds.) TACAS 2011. LNCS, vol. 6605, pp. 173–188. Springer, Heidelberg (2011). doi:10.1007/978-3-642-19835-9_15
19. Gulwani, S.: Automating string processing in spreadsheets using input-output examples. In: POPL, pp. 317–330. ACM (2011)
20. Gulwani, S., Harris, W.R., Singh, R.: Spreadsheet data manipulation using examples. Commun. ACM **55**(8), 97–105 (2012)
21. Jin, G., Song, L., Zhang, W., Lu, S., Liblit, B.: Automated atomicity-violation fixing. In: PLDI, pp. 389–400. ACM (2011)
22. Jobstmann, B., Griesmayer, A., Bloem, R.: Program repair as a game. In: Etessami, K., Rajamani, S.K. (eds.) CAV 2005. LNCS, vol. 3576, pp. 226–238. Springer, Heidelberg (2005). doi:10.1007/11513988_23
23. Jones, J.A., Harrold, M.J.: Empirical evaluation of the Tarantula automatic fault-localization technique. In: ICSE, pp. 273–282. IEEE (2005)
24. Kim, D., Nam, J., Song, J., Kim, S.: Automatic patch generation learned from human-written patches. In: ICSE, pp. 802–811. ACM (2013)
25. Könighofer, R., Bloem, R.: Automated error localization and correction for imperative programs. In: FMCAD. IEEE (2011)
26. Könighofer, R., Bloem, R.: Repair with on-the-fly program analysis. In: Biere, A., Nahir, A., Vos, T. (eds.) HVC 2012. LNCS, vol. 7857, pp. 56–71. Springer, Heidelberg (2013). doi:10.1007/978-3-642-39611-3_11
27. Li, G., Ghosh, I., Rajan, S.P.: KLOVER: a symbolic execution and automatic test generation tool for C++ programs. In: Gopalakrishnan, G., Qadeer, S. (eds.) CAV 2011. LNCS, vol. 6806, pp. 609–615. Springer, Heidelberg (2011). doi:10.1007/978-3-642-22110-1_49
28. Long, F., Rinard, M.: Automatic patch generation by learning correct code. In: POPL, vol. 51, pp. 298–312. ACM (2016)
29. Mechtaev, S., Yi, J., Roychoudhury, A.: Angelix: scalable multiline program patch synthesis via symbolic analysis. In ICSE, pp. 691–701. ACM (2016)
30. Miller, B.P., Fredriksen, L., So, B.: An empirical study of the reliability of UNIX utilities. Commun. ACM **33**(12), 32–44 (1990)
31. Necula, G.C., McPeak, S., Rahul, S.P., Weimer, W.: CIL: intermediate language and tools for analysis and transformation of C programs. In: Horspool, R.N. (ed.) CC 2002. LNCS, vol. 2304, pp. 213–228. Springer, Heidelberg (2002). doi:10.1007/3-540-45937-5_16
32. Nguyen, H.D.T., Qi, D., Roychoudhury, A., Chandra, S., SemFix: program repair via semantic analysis. In: ICSE, pp. 772–781. ACM (2013)
33. Nguyen, T., Kapur, D., Weimer, W., Forrest, S.: Using dynamic analysis to discover polynomial and array invariants. In: ICSE, pp. 683–693. IEEE (2012)

34. Nguyen, T., Kapur, D., Weimer, W., Forrest, S.: Connecting program synthesis and reachability. Technical report, University of Nebraska, Lincoln, October 2016
35. Rice, H.: Classes of recursively enumerable sets and their decision problems. Trans. Am. Math. Soc. **74**(2), 358–366 (1953)
36. Saha, S., Garg, P., Madhusudan, P.: Alchemist: learning guarded affine functions. In: Kroening, D., Păsăreanu, C.S. (eds.) CAV 2015. LNCS, vol. 9206, pp. 440–446. Springer, Heidelberg (2015). doi:10.1007/978-3-319-21690-4_26
37. Sen, K., Agha, G.: CUTE and jCUTE: concolic unit testing and explicit path model-checking tools. In: Ball, T., Jones, R.B. (eds.) CAV 2006. LNCS, vol. 4144, pp. 419–423. Springer, Heidelberg (2006). doi:10.1007/11817963_38
38. Singh, R., Gulwani, S., Solar-Lezama, A.: Automated feedback generation for introductory programming assignments. In: PLDI, pp. 15–26. ACM (2013)
39. Solar-Lezama, A.: Program synthesis by sketching. Ph.D. thesis, University of California, Berkeley (2008)
40. Solar-Lezama, A., Arnold, G., Tancau, L., Bodík, R., Saraswat, V.A., Seshia, S.A.: Sketching stencils. In: PLDI, pp. 167–178. ACM (2007)
41. Solar-Lezama, A., Rabbah, R., Bodík, R., Ebcioğlu, K.: Programming by sketching for bit-streaming programs. PLDI **40**, 281–294 (2005)
42. Srivastava, S.: Satisfiability-based program reasoning and program synthesis. Ph.D. thesis, University of Maryland (2010)
43. Srivastava, S., Gulwani, S., Foster, J.S.: From program verification to program synthesis. In: POPL, pp. 313–326. ACM (2010)
44. Srivastava, S., Gulwani, S., Foster, J.S.: Template-based program verification and program synthesis. Soft. Tools Technol. Transf. **15**(5–6), 497–518 (2013)
45. SyGuS: Syntax-guided synthesis competition. www.sygus.org. Accessed 19 Oct 2016
46. Weimer, W., Nguyen, T., Le Goues, C., Forrest, S.: Automatically finding patches using genetic programming. In: ICSE, pp. 364–367. IEEE (2009)

Scaling Enumerative Program Synthesis via Divide and Conquer

Rajeev Alur, Arjun Radhakrishna$^{(\boxtimes)}$, and Abhishek Udupa

University of Pennsylvania, Philadelphia, USA
arjunrad@seas.upenn.edu

Abstract. Given a semantic constraint specified by a logical formula, and a syntactic constraint specified by a context-free grammar, the Syntax-Guided Synthesis (SyGuS) problem is to find an expression that satisfies both the syntactic and semantic constraints. An enumerative approach to solve this problem is to systematically generate all expressions from the syntactic space with some pruning, and has proved to be surprisingly competitive in the newly started competition of SyGuS solvers. It performs well on small to medium sized benchmarks, produces succinct expressions, and has the ability to generalize from input-output examples. However, its performance degrades drastically with the size of the smallest solution. To overcome this limitation, in this paper we propose an alternative approach to solve SyGuS instances.

The key idea is to employ a divide-and-conquer approach by separately enumerating (a) smaller expressions that are correct on subsets of inputs, and (b) predicates that distinguish these subsets. These expressions and predicates are then combined using decision trees to obtain an expression that is correct on all inputs. We view the problem of combining expressions and predicates as a multi-label decision tree learning problem. We propose a novel technique of associating a probability distribution over the set of labels that a sample can be labeled with. This enables us to use standard information-gain based heuristics to learn compact decision trees.

We report a prototype implementation EUSOLVER. Our tool is able to match the running times and the succinctness of solutions of both standard enumerative solver and the latest white-box solvers on most benchmarks from the SyGuS competition. In the 2016 edition of the SyGuS competition, EUSOLVER placed first in the general track and the programming-by-examples track, and placed second in the linear integer arithmetic track.

1 Introduction

The field of program synthesis relates to automated techniques that attempt to automatically generate programs from requirements that a programmer writes.

This research was supported by NSF Expeditions award CCF 1138996 and by the Simons Investigator award.

Abhishek Udupa—This work was done when the author was a student at the University of Pennsylvania. The author is currently employed at Microsoft Corp.

© Springer-Verlag GmbH Germany 2017
A. Legay and T. Margaria (Eds.): TACAS 2017, Part I, LNCS 10205, pp. 319–336, 2017.
DOI: 10.1007/978-3-662-54577-5_18

It has been applied to various domains such as program completion [21], program optimization, and automatic generation of programs from input-output examples [7], among others. Recently, Syntax-Guided Synthesis (SyGuS) has been proposed as a back-end exchange format and enabling technology for program synthesis [2]. The aim is to allow experts from different domains to model their synthesis problems as SyGuS instances, and leverage general purpose SyGuS solvers.

In the SyGuS approach, a synthesis task is specified using restrictions on both the form (syntax) and function (semantics) of the program to be synthesized: (a) The syntactic restrictions are given in terms of a context-free grammar from which a solution program may be drawn. (b) The semantic restrictions are encoded into a specification as an SMT formula. Most SyGuS solvers operate in two cooperating phases: a *learning phase* in which a candidate program is proposed, and a *verification phase* in which the proposal is checked against the specification. SyGuS solvers can be broadly categorized into two kinds: (a) black-box solvers, where the learning phase does not deal with the specification directly, but learns from constraints on how a potential solution should behave on sample inputs points [2,18,23]; and (b) white-box solvers, which attempt learn directly from the specification, generally using constraint solving techniques [3,17].

The enumerative solver [2] placed first and second in the SyGuS competition 2014 and 2015, respectively. It maintains a set of concrete input points, and in each iteration attempts to produce an expression that is correct on these concrete inputs. It does so by enumerating expressions from the grammar and checking if they are correct on the input points, while pruning away expressions that behave equivalently to already generated expressions. If an expression that is correct on the input points is found, it is verified against the full specification. If it is incorrect, a counter-example point is found and added to the set of input points.

Though the enumerative strategy works well when the solutions have small sizes, it does not scale well. The time take to explore all potential solutions up to a given size grows exponentially with the size. To overcome this scalability issue, we introduce a divide-and-conquer enumerative algorithm.

The divide-and-conquer enumerative approach is based on this insight: while the full solution expression to the synthesis problem may be large, the important individual parts are small. The individual parts we refer to here are: (a) *terms* which serve as the return value for the solution, and (b) *predicates* which serve as the conditionals that choose which term is the actual return value for a given input. For example, in the expression if $x \leq y$ then y else x, the terms are x and y, and the predicate is $x \leq y$. In this example, although the full expression has size 6, the individual terms have size 1 each, and the predicate has size 3. Hence, the divide-and-conquer enumerative approach only enumerates terms and predicates separately and attempts to combine them into a conditional expression.

To combine the different parts of a solution into a conditional expression, we use the technique of learning decision trees [4,16]. The input points maintained by the enumerative algorithm serve as the samples, the predicates enumerated serve as the attributes, and the terms serve as the labels. A term t is a valid label for a point pt if t is correct for pt. We use a simple multi-label decision tree learning algorithm to learn a decision tree that classifies the samples soundly, *i.e.*, for each point, following the edges corresponding to the attribute values (*i.e.*, predicates) leads to a label (*i.e.*, term) which is correct for the point.

To enhance the quality of the solutions obtained, we extend the basic divide-and-conquer algorithm to be an *anytime* algorithm, *i.e.*, the algorithm does not stop when the first solution is found, and instead continues enumerating terms and predicates in an attempt to produce more compact solutions. Decomposing the verification queries into *branch-level queries* helps in faster convergence.

Evaluation. We implemented the proposed algorithm in a tool EUSOLVER and evaluated it on benchmarks from the SyGuS competition. The tool was able to perform on par or better than existing solvers in most tracks of the 2016 SyGuS competition, placing first in the general and programming-by-example tracks, and second in the linear-integer-arithmetic track. In the general and linear-integer-arithmetic tracks, EUSOLVER's performance is comparable to the state-of-the-art solvers. However, in the programming-by-example track, EUSOLVER performs exceptionally well, solving 787 of the 852 benchmarks, while no other tool solved more than 39. This exceptional performance is due to EUSOLVER being able to generalize from examples like other enumerative approaches, while also being able to scale to larger solution sizes due to the divide-and-conquer approach.

Further, to test the anytime extension, we run EUSOLVER on 50 ICFP benchmarks with and without the extension. Note that no previous solver has been able to solve these ICFP benchmarks. We observed that the anytime extension of the algorithm was able to produce more compact solutions in 18 cases.

2   Illustrative Example

Consider a synthesis task to generate an expression e such that: (a) e is generated by the grammar from Fig. 1. (b) e when substituted for f, in the specification Φ, renders it true, where $\Phi \equiv \forall x, y : f(x, y) \geq x \wedge f(x, y) \geq y \wedge (f(x, y) = x \vee f(x, y) = y)$. Note that the specification constrains $f(x, y)$ to return maximum of x and y. Here, the smallest solution expression is if $x \leq y$ then y else x.

```
S ::= T | if (C) then T else T
T ::= 0 | 1 | x | y | T + T
C ::= T ≤ T | C ∧ C | ¬ C
```

Fig. 1. Grammar for linear integer expressions

Basic Enumerative Strategy. We explain the basic enumerative algorithm [23] using Table 1. The enumerative algorithm maintains a set of input points pts (initially empty), and proceeds in rounds. In each round, it proposes a candidate solution that is correct on all of pts. If this candidate is correct on all inputs, it is returned. Otherwise, a counter-example input point is added to pts.

The algorithm generates the candidate solution expression by enumerating expressions generated by the grammar in order of size. In the first round, the candidate expression proposed is the first expression generated (the expression 0) as pts is empty. Attempting to verify the correctness of this expression, yields a counter-example point $\{x \mapsto 1, y \mapsto 0\}$. In the second round, the expression

Table 1. Example run of the basic enumerative algorithm

Round no	Enumerated expressions	Candidate expression	Point added
1	0	0	$\{x \mapsto 1, y \mapsto 0\}$
2	0, 1	1	$\{x \mapsto 0, y \mapsto 2\}$
3	$0, 1, x, y, \ldots, x + y,$	$x + y$	$\{x \mapsto 1, y \mapsto 2\}$
...			
n	$0, \ldots,$ if $x \leq y$ then y else x	if $x \leq y$ then y else x	

0 is incorrect on the point, and the next expression to be correct on all of pts (the expression 1) is proposed. This fails to verify as well, and yields the counter-example point $\{x \mapsto 0, y \mapsto 2\}$. In the third round, all expressions of size 1 are incorrect on at least one point in pts, and the algorithm moves on to enumerate larger expressions. After several rounds, the algorithm eventually generates the expression if $x \leq y$ then y else x which the SMT solver verifies to be correct. In the full run, the basic enumerative strategy (algorithm presented in Sect. 3.1) generates a large number (in this case, hundreds) of expressions before generating the correct expression. In general, the number of generated expressions grows exponentially with the size of the smallest correct expression. Thus, the enumerative solver fails to scale to large solution sizes.

Divide and Conquer Enumeration. In the above example, though the solution is large, the individual components (terms x and y, and predicate $x \leq y$) are rather small and can be quickly enumerated. The divide-and-conquer approach enumerates terms and predicates separately, and attempts to combine them into a conditional expression. We explain this idea using an example (see Table 2).

Similar to the basic algorithm, the divide-and-conquer algorithm maintains a set of points pts, and works in rounds. The first two rounds are similar to the run of the basic algorithm. In contrast to the basic algorithm, the enumeration stops in the third round after 0, 1, x, and y are enumerated – the terms 1 and y are correct on $\{x \mapsto 1, y \mapsto 0\}$ and $\{x \mapsto 0, y \mapsto 2\}$, respectively, and thus together "cover" all of pts. Now, to propose an expression, the algorithm starts enumerating predicates until it finds a sufficient number of predicates to

Table 2. Example run of the divide-and-conquer enumerative algorithm

Round no	Enumerated terms	Enumerated predicates	Candidate expression	Point added
1	0	0	$\emptyset$	$\{x \mapsto 1, y \mapsto 0\}$
2	0, 1	1	$\emptyset$	$\{x \mapsto 0, y \mapsto 2\}$
3	$0, 1, x, y$	$0 \leq 0, \ldots 0 \leq y,$ $1 \leq 0, \ldots 1 \leq y$	if $1 \leq y$ then y else 1	$\{x \mapsto 2, y \mapsto 0\}$
4	$0, 1, x, y$	$0 \leq 0, \ldots x \leq y$	if $x \leq y$ then y else x	

generate a conditional expression using the previously enumerated terms. The terms and predicates are combined into conditional expression by learning decision trees (see Sect. 4.2). The candidate expression proposed in the third round is if $1 \leq y$ then y else x and the counter-example generated is $\{x \mapsto 2, y \mapsto 0\}$ (see table). Proceeding further, in the fourth round, the correct expression is generated. Note that this approach only generates 4 terms and 11 predicates in contrast to the basic approach which generates hundreds of expressions.

3   Problem Statement and Background

Let us fix the function to be synthesized f and its formal parameters params. We write range(f) to denote the range of f. The term *point* denotes a valuation of params, i.e., a point is an input to f.

Example 1. For the running example in this section, we consider a function to be synthesized f of type $\mathbb{Z} \times \mathbb{Z} \rightarrow \mathbb{Z}$ with the formal parameters params $= \{x, y\}$. Points are valuations of x and y. For example, $\{x \mapsto 1, y \mapsto 2\}$ is a point.

Specifications. SMT formulae have become the standard formalism for specifying semantic constraints for synthesis. In this paper, we fix an arbitrary theory $\mathcal{T}$ and denote by $\mathcal{T}$[symbols], the set of $\mathcal{T}$ terms over the set of symbols symbols. A *specification* Φ is a logical formula in a theory $\mathcal{T}$ over standard theory symbols and the function to be synthesized f. An expression e *satisfies* Φ ($e \models \Phi$) if instantiating the function to be synthesized f by e makes Φ valid.

Example 2. Continuing the running example, we define a specification $\Phi \equiv \forall x, y : f(x, y) \geq x \wedge f(x, y) \geq y \wedge f(x, y) = x \vee f(x, y) = y$. The specification states that f maps each pair x and y to a value that is at least as great as each of them and equal to one of them, i.e., the maximum of x and y.

Grammars. An *expression grammar* G is a tuple $\langle \mathcal{N}, S, \mathcal{R} \rangle$ where: (a) the set $\mathcal{N}$ is a set of non-terminal symbols, (b) the non-terminal $S \in \mathcal{N}$ is the initial non-terminal, (c) $\mathcal{R} \subseteq \mathcal{N} \times \mathcal{T}[\mathcal{N} \cup \text{params}]$ is a finite set of rewrite rules that map $\mathcal{N}$ to $\mathcal{T}$-expressions over non-terminals and formal parameters. We say that an expression e *rewrites to* an incomplete expression e' (written as $e \rightarrow_G e'$) if there exists a rule $R = (N, e'') \in \mathcal{R}$ and e' is obtained by replacing one occurrence of N in e by e''. Let $\rightarrow_G^*$ be the transitive closure of $\rightarrow$. We say that an expression $e \in \mathcal{T}[\text{params}]$ is *generated* by the grammar G (written as $e \in \llbracket G \rrbracket$) if $S \rightarrow_G^* e$. Note that we implicitly assume that all terms generated by the grammar have the right type, i.e., are of the type range(f).

Example 3. For the running example, we choose the following grammar. The set of non-terminals is given by $\mathcal{N} = \{S, T, C\}$ with the initial non-terminal being S. The rules of this grammar are $\{(S, T), (S, \text{if } C \text{ then } S \text{ else } S)\} \cup \{(T, x), (T, y), (T, 1), (T, 0), (T, T + T)\} \cup \{(C, T \leq T), (C, C \wedge C), (C, \neg C)\}$. This is the standard linear integer arithmetic grammar used for many SyGuS problems. This grammar is equivalent to the one from Fig. 1.

The Syntax-Guided Synthesis Problem. An instance of the SyGuS problem is given by a pair $\langle \Phi, G \rangle$ of specification and grammar. An expression e is a solution to the instance if $e \models \Phi$ and $e \in [\![G]\!]$.

Example 4. Continuing the running example, for the specification Φ from Example 2 and the grammar from Example 3, one of the solution expressions is given by $f(x, y) \equiv$ if $x \leq y$ then y else x.

From our definitions, it is clear that we restrict ourselves to a version of the SyGuS problem where there is exactly one unknown function to be synthesized, and the grammar does not contain let rules. Further, we assume that our specifications are *point-wise*. Intuitively, a specification is point-wise, if it only relates an input point to its output, and not the outputs of different inputs.

Here, we use a simple syntactic notion of point-wise specifications, which we call *plain separability*, for convenience. However, our techniques can be generalized to any notion of point-wise specifications. Formally, we say that a specification is *plainly separable* if it can be rewritten into a conjunctive normal form where each clause is either (a) a tautology, or (b) each appearing application of the function to be synthesized f has the same arguments.

Example 5. The specification for our running example $\Phi \equiv f(x, y) \geq x \wedge f(x, y) \geq y \wedge f(x, y) = x \vee f(x, y) = y$ is plainly separable. For example, this implies that the value of $f(1, 2)$ can be chosen irrespective of the value of f on any other point. On the other hand, a specification such as $f(x, y) = 1 \Rightarrow f(x + 1, y) = 1$ is neither plainly separable nor point-wise. The value of $f(1, 2)$ cannot be chosen independently of the value of $f(0, 2)$.

The above restrictions make the SyGuS problem significantly easier. However, a large fraction of problems do fall into this class. Several previous works address this class of problem (see, for example, [3,13,17]).

Plainly separable specifications allow us to define the notion of an expression e satisfying a specification Φ on a point pt. Formally, we say that $e \models \Phi \downarrow$ pt if e satisfies the specification obtained by replacing each clause C in Φ by $Prec_C(\text{pt}) \Rightarrow C$. Here, the premise $Prec_C(\text{pt})$ is given by $\bigwedge_{p \in \text{params}} Arg_C(p) = \text{pt}[p]$ where $Arg_C(p)$ is the actual argument corresponding to the formal parameter p in the unique invocation of f that occurs in C. We extend this definition to sets of points as follows: $e \models \Phi \downarrow$ pts $\Leftrightarrow \bigwedge_{\text{pt} \in \text{pts}} e \models \Phi \downarrow$ pt.

Example 6. For the specification Φ of the running example, the function given by $f(x, y) \equiv x + y$ is correct on the point $\{x \mapsto 0, y \mapsto 3\}$ and incorrect on the point $\{x \mapsto 1, y \mapsto 2\}$

3.1   The Enumerative Solver

The principal idea behind the enumerative solver is to enumerate all expressions from the given syntax with some pruning. Only expressions that are distinct with respect to a set of concrete input points are enumerated.

The full pseudo-code is given in Algorithm 1. Initially, the set of points is set to be empty at line 1. In each iteration, the algorithm calls the ENUMERATE procedure[1] which returns the next element

---

Algorithm 1 Enumerative Solver

Require: Grammar $G = \langle \mathcal{N}, S, \mathcal{R} \rangle$
Require: Specification Φ
Ensure: e s.t. $e \in [\![G]\!] \wedge e \models \Phi$
1: $\text{pts} \leftarrow \emptyset$
2: **while** true **do**
3:    **for** $e \in$ ENUMERATE(G, pts) **do**
4:       **if** $e \not\models \Phi \downarrow \text{pts}$ **then continue**
5:       $\text{cexpt} \leftarrow \text{verify}(e, \Phi)$
6:       **if** $\text{cexpt} = \bot$ **then return** e
7:       $\text{pts} \leftarrow \text{pts} \cup \text{cexpt}$

---

from a (possibly infinite) list of expressions such that no two expressions in this list evaluate to the same values at every point $\text{pt} \in \text{pts}$ (line 3). Every expression e in this list is then verified, first on the set of points (line 4) and then fully (line 5). If the expression e is correct, it is returned (line 6). Otherwise, we pick a counter-example input point (*i.e.*, an input on which e is incorrect) and add it to the set of points and repeat (line 7). A full description of the ENUMERATE procedure can be found in [2] and [23].

Theorem 1. *Given a* SyGuS *instance* (Φ, G) *with at least one solution expression, Algorithm 1 terminates and returns the smallest solution expression.*

Features and Limitations. The enumerative algorithm performs surprisingly well, considering its simplicity, on small to medium sized benchmarks (see [2,23]). Further, due to the guarantee of Theorem 1 that the enumerative approach produces small solutions, the algorithm is capable of generalizing from specifications that are input-output examples. However, enumeration quickly fails to scale with growing size of solutions. The time necessary for the enumerative solver to generate all expressions up to a given size grows exponentially with the size.

4   The Divide-and-Conquer Enumeration Algorithm

Conditional Expression Grammars. We introduce conditional expression grammars that separate an expression grammar into two grammars that generate: (a) the return value expression, and (b) the conditionals that decide which return value is chosen. These generated return values (terms) and conditionals (predicates) are combined using if-then-else conditional operators.

A *conditional expression grammar* is a pair of grammars $\langle G_T, G_P \rangle$ where: (a) the *term grammar* G_T is an expression grammar generating terms of type $\text{range}(f)$; and (b) the *predicate grammar* G_P is an expression grammar generating

---

[1] Note that ENUMERATE is a coprocedure. Unfamiliar readers may assume that each call to ENUMERATE returns the next expression from an infinite list of expressions.

boolean terms. The set of expressions $[\![\langle G_T, G_P\rangle]\!]$ generated by $\langle G_T, G_P\rangle$ is the smallest set of expressions $\mathcal{T}[\text{params}]$ such that: (a) $[\![G_T]\!] \subseteq [\![\langle G_T, G_P\rangle]\!]$, and (b) $e_1, e_2 \in [\![\langle G_T, G_P\rangle]\!] \wedge p \in [\![G_P]\!] \implies$ if p then e_1 else $e_2 \in [\![\langle G_T, G_P\rangle]\!]$. Most commonly occurring SyGuS grammars in practice can be rewritten as conditional expression grammars automatically.

Example 7. The grammar from Example 3 is easily decomposed into a conditional expression grammar $\langle G_T, G_P\rangle$ where: (a) the term grammar G_T contains only the non-terminal T, and the rules for rewriting T. (b) the predicate grammar G_P contains the two non-terminals $\{T, C\}$ and the associated rules.

Decision Trees. We use the concept of decision trees from machine learning literature to model conditional expressions. Informally, a decision tree DT maps *samples* to *labels*. Each internal node in a decision tree contains an *attribute* which may either hold or not for each sample, and each leaf node contains a label. In our setting, labels are terms, attributes are predicates, and samples are points.

To compute the label for a given point, we follow a path from the root of the decision tree to a leaf, taking the left (resp. right) child at each internal node if the attribute holds (resp. does not hold) for the sample. The required label is the label at the leaf. We do not formally define decision trees, but instead refer the reader to a standard text-book (see, for example, [4]).

Example 8. Figure 2 contains a decision tree in our setting, i.e., with attributes being predicates and labels being terms. To compute the associated label with the point $\mathsf{pt} \equiv \{x \mapsto 2, y \mapsto 0\}$: (a) we examine the predicate at the root node, i.e., $y \leq 0$ and follow the left child as the predicate hold for pt; (b) examine the predicate at the left child of the root node, i.e., $x \leq y$ and follow the right child as it does not hold; and (c) return the label of the leaf $x + y$.

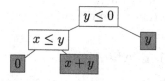

The expression $\mathsf{expr}(DT)$ corresponding to a decision tree DT is defined as: (a) the label of the root node if the tree is a single leaf node; and (b) if p then $\mathsf{expr}(DT_L)$ else $\mathsf{expr}(DT_Y)$ where p is the attribute of the root node, and DT_L and DT_Y are the left and right children, otherwise.

Fig. 2. Sample decision tree

Decision tree learning is a technique that learns a decision tree from a given set of samples. A decision tree learning procedure is given: (a) a set of samples (points), (b) a set of labels (terms), along with a function that maps a label to the subset of samples which it covers; and (c) a set of attributes (predicates). A sound decision tree learning algorithm returns a decision tree DT that classifies the points correctly, i.e., for every sample pt, the label associated with it by the decision tree covers the point. We use the notation LEARNDT to denote a generic, sound decision tree learning procedure. The exact procedure we use for decision tree learning is presented in Sect. 4.2.

4.1 Algorithm

Algorithm 2 presents the full divide-and-conquer enumeration algorithm for synthesis. Like Algorithm 1, the divide-and-conquer algorithm maintains a set of points pts, and in each iteration: (a) computes a candidate solution expression e (lines 3–10); (b) verifies and returns e if it is correct (lines 10 and 11); and (c) otherwise, adds the counter-example point into the set pts (line 12).

However, the key differences between Algorithms 2 and 1 are in the way the candidate solution expression e is generated. The generation of candidate expressions is accomplished in two steps.

Term Solving. Instead of searching for a single candidate expression that is correct on all points in pts, Algorithm 2 maintains a set of candidate terms terms. We say that a term t covers a point $pt \in$ pts if $t \models \Phi \downarrow pt$. The set of points that a term covers is computed and stored in cover$[t]$ (line 15). Note that the algorithm does not store terms that cover the same set of points as already generated terms (line 16). When the set of terms terms covers all the points in pts, i.e., for each $pt \in$ pts, there is at least one term that is correct on pt, the term enumeration is stopped (while-loop condition in line 4).

Unification and Decision Tree Learning. In the next step (lines 6–9), we generate a set of predicates preds that will be used as conditionals to combine the terms from terms into if-then-else expressions. In each iteration, we attempt to learn a decision tree that correctly labels each point $pt \in$ pts with a term t such that $pt \in$ cover$[t]$. If such a decision tree DT exists, the conditional expression expr(DT) is correct on all points, i.e., expr$(DT) \models \Phi \downarrow$ pts. If a decision tree does not exist, we generate additional terms and predicates and retry.

Algorithm 2 DCSolve: The divide-and-conquer enumeration algorithm

---

Require: Conditional expression grammar $G = \langle G_T, G_P \rangle$
Require: Specification Φ
Ensure: Expression e s.t. $e \in [\![G]\!] \wedge e \models \Phi$
 1: pts $\leftarrow \emptyset$
 2: **while** true **do**
 3:    terms $\leftarrow \emptyset$; preds $\leftarrow \emptyset$; cover $\leftarrow \emptyset$; $DT = \bot$
 4:    **while** $\bigcup_{t \in \text{terms}}$ cover$[t] \neq$ pts **do**   ▷ Term solver
 5:       terms $\leftarrow$ terms $\cup$ NextDistinctTerm(pts, terms, cover)
 6:    **while** $DT = \bot$ **do**   ▷ Unifier
 7:       terms $\leftarrow$ terms $\cup$ NextDistinctTerm(pts, terms, cover)
 8:       preds $\leftarrow$ preds $\cup$ Enumerate(G_P, pts)
 9:       $DT \leftarrow$ LearnDT(terms, preds)
10:    $e \leftarrow$ expr(DT); cexpt $\leftarrow$ verify(e, Φ) ▷ Verifier
11:    **if** cexpt $= \bot$ **then return** e
12:    pts $\leftarrow$ pts $\cup$ cexpt
13: **function** NextDistinctTerm(pts, terms, cover)
14:    **while** *True* **do**
15:       $t \leftarrow$ Enumerate(G_T, pts); cover$[t] \leftarrow \{$pt $\mid$ pt $\in$ pts $\wedge t \models \Phi \downarrow$ pt$\}$
16:       **if** $\forall t' \in$ terms : cover$[t] \neq$ cover$[t']$ **then return** t

---

Remark 1. In line 7, we generate additional terms even though terms is guaranteed to contain terms that cover all points. This is required to achieve semi-completeness, i.e., without this, the algorithm might not find a solution even if one exists.

Theorem 2. *Algorithm 2 is sound for the* SyGuS *problem. Further, assuming a sound and complete* LEARNDT *procedure, if there exists a solution expression, Algorithm 2 is guaranteed to find it.*

The proof of the above theorem is similar to the proof of soundness and partial-completeness for the original enumerative solver. The only additional assumption is that the LEARNDT decision tree learning procedure will return a decision tree if one exists. We present such a procedure in the next section.

4.2   Decision Tree Learning

The standard multi-label decision tree learning algorithm (based on ID3 [16]) is presented in Algorithm 3. The algorithm first checks if there exists a single label (i.e., term) t that applies to all the points (line 1). If so, it returns a decision tree with only a leaf node whose label is t (line 1). Otherwise, it picks the best predicate p to split on based on some heuristic (line 3). If no predicates are left, there exists no decision tree, and the algorithm returns $\perp$ (line 2). Otherwise, it recursively computes the left and right sub-trees for the set of points on which p holds and does not hold, respectively (lines 4 and 5). The final decision tree is returned as a tree with a root (with attribute p), and positive and negative edges to the roots of the left and right sub-trees, respectively.

Algorithm 3 Learning Decision Trees

Require: pts, terms, cover, preds
Ensure: Decision tree DT
 1: **if** $\exists t : \text{pts} \subseteq \text{cover}[t]$ **then return** $LeafNode[\mathcal{L} \leftarrow t]$
 2: **if** $\text{preds} = \emptyset$ **then return** $\perp$
 3: $p \leftarrow$ Pick predicate from preds
 4: $L \leftarrow$ LEARNDT$(\{\text{pt} \mid p[\text{pt}]\}, \text{terms}, \text{cover}, \text{preds} \setminus \{p\})$
 5: $R \leftarrow$ LEARNDT$(\{\text{pt} \mid \neg p[\text{pt}]\}, \text{terms}, \text{cover}, \text{preds} \setminus \{p\})$
 6: **return** $InternalNode[\mathcal{A} \leftarrow p, left \leftarrow L, right \leftarrow R]$

Information-Gain Heuristic. The choice of the predicate at line 3 influences the size of the decision tree learned by Algorithm 3, and hence, in our setting, the size of the solution expression generated by Algorithm 2. We use the classical information gain heuristic to pick the predicates. Informally, the information gain heuristic treats the label as a random variable, and chooses to split on the attribute knowing whose value will reveal the most information about the label. We do not describe all aspects of computing information gain, but refer the reader to any standard textbook on machine learning [4]. Given a set of points $pts' \subseteq pts$ the entropy $H(pts')$ is defined in terms of the probability $\mathbb{P}_{pts'}(label(pt) = t)$ of a point $pt \in pt'$ being labeled with the term t as

$$H(pts') = -\sum_t \mathbb{P}_{pts'}(label(pt) = t) \cdot \log_2 \mathbb{P}_{pts'}(label(pt) = t)$$

Further, given a predicate $p \in preds$, the information gain of p is defined as

$$G(p) = \frac{|pts_y|}{|pts|} \cdot H(pts_y) + \frac{|pts_n|}{|pts|} \cdot H(pts_n)$$

where $pts_y = \{pt \in pts \mid p[pt]\}$ and $pts_n = \{pt \in pts \mid \neg p[pt]\}$. Hence, at line 3, we compute the value $G(p)$ for each predicate in $preds$, and pick the one which maximizes $G(p)$.

We use conditional probabilities $\mathbb{P}_{pts'}(label(pt) = t \mid pt)$ to compute the probability $\mathbb{P}_{pts'}(label(pt) = t)$. The assumption we make about the prior distribution is that the likelihood of a given point pt being labeled by a given term t is proportional to the number of points in $cover[t]$. Formally, we define:

$$\mathbb{P}_{pts'}(label(pt) = t \mid pt) = \begin{cases} 0 & \text{if } pt \notin cover[t] \\ \dfrac{|cover[t] \cap pts'|}{\sum\limits_{t' \mid pt \in cover[t']} |cover[t'] \cap pts'|} & \text{if } pt \in cover[t] \end{cases}$$

Now, the unconditional probability of an arbitrary point being labeled with t is given by $\mathbb{P}_{pts'}(label(pt) = t) = \sum_{pt} \mathbb{P}_{pts'}(label(pt) = t \mid pt) \cdot \mathbb{P}_{pts'}(pt)$. Assuming a uniform distribution for picking points, we have that

$$\mathbb{P}_{pts'}(label(pt) = t) = \frac{1}{|pts|} \cdot \sum_{pt} \mathbb{P}_{pts'}(label(pt) = t \mid pt)$$

4.3   Extensions and Optimizations

The Anytime Extension. Algorithm 2 stops enumeration of terms and predicates as soon as it finds a single solution to the synthesis problem. However, there are cases where due to the lack of sufficiently good predicates, the decision tree and the resulting solution can be large (see Example 9). Instead, we can let the algorithm continue by generating more terms and predicates. This could lead to different, potentially smaller decision trees and solutions.

Example 9. Given the specification $(x \geq 0 \wedge y \geq 0) \Rightarrow (f(x,y) = 1 \Leftrightarrow x + y \leq 2)$ and a run of Algorithm 2 where the terms 0 and 1 are generated; the terms fully cover any set of points for this specification. Over a sequence of iterations the predicates are generated in order of size. Now, the predicates generated of size 3 include $x = 0$, $x = 1$, $x = 2$, $y \leq 2$, $y \leq 1$, and $y \leq 0$. With these predicates, the decision tree depicted in Fig. 3a is learned, and the corresponding conditional expression is correct for the specification. However, if the procedure continues to run after the first solution is generated, predicates of size 4 are generated. Among these predicates, the predicate $x + y \leq 2$ is also generated. With this additional predicate, the decision tree in Fig. 3b is generated, leading to the compact solution $f(x, y) \equiv$ if $x + y \leq 2$ then 1 else 0.

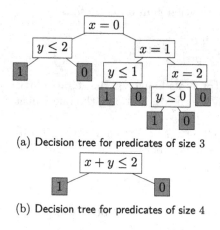

(a) Decision tree for predicates of size 3

(b) Decision tree for predicates of size 4

Fig. 3. Initial decision tree and the more compact version learned with the anytime extension for Example 9

Decision Tree Repair. In Algorithm 2, we discard the terms that cover the same set of points as already generated terms in line 16. However, these discarded terms may lead to better solutions than the already generated ones.

Example 10. Consider a run of the algorithm for the running example, where the set pts contains the points $\{x \mapsto 1, y \mapsto 0\}$ and $\{x \mapsto -1, y \mapsto 0\}$. Suppose the algorithm first generates the terms 0 and 1. These terms are each correct on one of the points and are added to terms. Next, the algorithm generates the terms x and y. However, these are not added to terms as x (resp. y) is correct on exactly the same set of points as 1 (resp. 0).

Suppose the algorithm also generates the predicate $x \leq y$ and learns the decision tree corresponding to the expression $e \equiv$ if $x \leq y$ then 0 else 1. Now, verifying this expression produces a counter-example point, say $\{x \mapsto 1, y \mapsto 2\}$. While the term 0, and correspondingly, the expression e is incorrect on this point, the term y which was discarded as an equivalent term to 0, is correct.

Hence, for a practical implementation of the algorithm we do not discard these terms and predicates, but store them separately in a map Eq : terms $\rightarrow$ $[\![G_T]\!]$ that maps the terms in terms to an additional set of equivalent terms. At lines 16, if the check for distinctness fails, we instead add the term t to the Eq map. Now, when the decision tree learning algorithm returns an expression that fails to verify and returns a counter-example, we attempt to replace terms and predicates in the decision tree with equivalent ones from the Eq map to make the decision tree behave correctly on the counter-example.

Example 11. Revisiting Example 10, instead of discarding the terms x and y, we store them into the Eq array, i.e., we set $Eq(0) = \{y\}$ and $Eq(1) = \{x\}$. Now, when the verification of the expression fails, with the counter-example point $\{x \mapsto 1, y \mapsto 2\}$, we check the term that is returned for the counter-example point–here, 0. Now, we check whether any term in $Eq(0)$ is correct on the counter-example point–here, the term y. If so, we replace the original term with the equivalent term that is additionally correct on the counter-example point and proceed with verification. Replacing 0 with y in the expression gives us if $x \leq y$ then y else 1. Another round of verification and decision tree repair will lead to replacing the term 1 with x, giving us the final correct solution.

Branch-Wise Verification. In Algorithm 2, and in most synthesis techniques, an incorrect candidate solution is used to generate one counter-example point. However, in the case of conditional expressions and point-wise specifications, each branch (i.e., leaf of the decision tree) can be verified separately. Verifying each branch involves rewriting the specification as in the point-wise verification defined in Sect. 3 – but instead of adding a premise to each clause asserting that the arguments to the function are equal to a point, we add a premise that asserts that the arguments satisfy all predicates along the path to the leaf. This gives us two separate advantages:

- We are able to generate multiple counter-examples from a single incorrect expression. This reduces the total number of iterations required, as well as the number of calls to the expensive decision tree learning algorithm.
- It reduces the complexity of each call to the verifier in terms of the size of the SMT formula to be checked. As verification procedures generally scale exponentially with respect to the size of the SMT formula, multiple simpler verification calls are often faster than one more complex call.

This optimization works very well along with the decision tree repair described above as we can verify and repair each branch of the decision tree separately.

Example 12. Consider the verification of the expression if $x \leq y$ then 0 else 1 for the running example. Instead of running the full expression through the verifier to obtain one counter-example point, we can verify the branches separately by checking the satisfiability of the formulae $x \leq y \wedge f(x,y) = 0 \wedge \neg\Phi$ and $\neg(x \leq y) \wedge f(x,y) = 1 \wedge \neg\Phi$. This gives us two separate counter-example points.

5 Evaluation

We built a prototype SyGuS solver named EUSOLVER that uses the divide-and-conquer enumerative algorithm. The tool consists of 6000 lines of Python code implementing the high-level enumeration and unification algorithms, and 3000 lines of C++ code implementing the decision tree learning. The code is written to be easily extensible and readable, and has not been optimized to any degree. All experiments were executed on the Starexec platform [22] where each benchmark is solved on a node with two 4-core 2.4 GHz Intel processors and 256 GB of RAM, with a timeout of 3600 s.

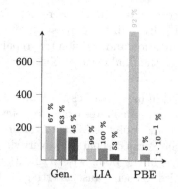

Fig. 4. Number of benchmarks solved per track for EUSOLVER (red), CVC4 (blue), and ESOLVER (green) (Color figure online)

Goals. We seek to empirically evaluate how our synthesis algorithm compares to other state-of-the-art synthesis techniques along the following dimensions: (a) *Performance:* How quickly can the algorithms arrive at a correct solution? (b) *Quality:* How *good* are the solutions produced by the algorithms? We use compactness of solutions as a metric for the quality of solutions. (c) *Effect of anytime extension:* How significant is the improvement in the quality of the solutions generated if the algorithm is given an additional (but fixed) time budget?

Benchmarks. We draw benchmarks from 3 tracks of the SyGuS competition 2016:[2]

(a) *General track.* The general track contains 309 benchmarks drawn from a wide variety of domains and applications.

(b) *Programming-by-example track.* The PBE track contains 852 benchmarks where, for each benchmark, the semantic specification is given by a set of input-output examples.

(c) *Linear-integer-arithmetic track.* The LIA track contains 73 benchmarks, each over the linear integer arithmetic theory, where the grammar is fixed to a standard grammar that generates conditional linear arithmetic expressions.

5.1   Discussion

Figures 5 and 4 plot the full results of running EUSOLVER on the benchmarks from the three categories. The plots also contain the results of 2 other state-of-the-art solvers: (a) the white-box solver CVC4-1.5.1 based on [17], and (b) the enumerative black-box solvers ESOLVER described in [2]

Performance. EUSOLVER was able to solve 206 of the 309 benchmarks in the general track and 72 of the 73 benchmarks in the PBE track. CVC4 solves 195 and 73 benchmarks in these categories, while ESOLVER solves 139 and 34. As Fig. 5 shows, the performance is comparable to both CVC4 and ESOLVER in both tracks, being only marginally slower in the LIA track. However, EUSOLVER performs exceptionally well on the PBE benchmarks, solving 787 while CVC4 solved 39 and ESOLVER solved 1. PBE benchmarks require the solver to generalize from input-output examples—EUSOLVER inherits this ability from the enumerative approach.

---

[2] The SyGuS competition 2016 included an addition track – the invariant generation track. However, the specifications in this track are not simply separable, and EUSOLVER falls back to the standard enumeration algorithm instead of the divide-and-conquer techniques described in this paper.

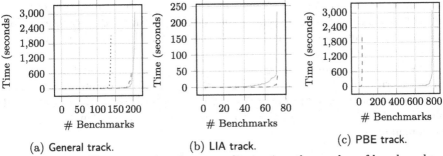

(a) General track.   (b) LIA track.   (c) PBE track.

Interpretation: For every point, the x-coordinate gives the number of benchmarks which are solved within the time indicated by the y-coordinate.

Fig. 5. Running times for ESOLVER (dotted), CVC4 (dashed), and EUSOLVER (solid).

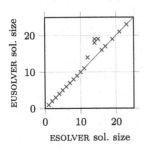

Fig. 6. Scatter plot of EUSOLVER and ESOLVER solution sizes.

However, the standard enumerative solver EUSOLVER is unable to solve these benchmarks due to the large solution sizes—EUSOLVER overcomes this hurdle with the divide-and-conquer approach.

Quality of Solutions. Figure 6 highlights the solution sizes produced by EUSOLVER and ESOLVER for the commonly solved benchmarks in the general track. EUSOLVER often matches the solution sizes produced by ESOLVER (108 of the 112 benchmarks). ESOLVER is guaranteed to produce the smallest solution possible. This shows that the divide-and-conquer approach does not significantly sacrifice solution quality for better performance.

Effect of Anytime Extension. We selected 50 ICFP benchmarks from the general track and use them to test the anytime extension described in Sect. 4.3. The ICFP benchmarks are synthesis tasks that were first proposed as a part of the ICFP programming contest 2013, which were then adapted to the SyGuS setting. To the best of our knowledge, no other SyGuS solver has been able to solve the ICFP benchmarks satisfactorily. For 18 of the 50 ICFP benchmarks, we were able to obtain a more compact solution by letting the algorithm continue execution after the first solution was discovered (Fig. 7). Further, the difference in the first and smallest solutions is sometimes significant—for example, in the case of the "icfp_118_100" benchmark, we see a reduction of 55%. An interesting phenomenon that we observed was that while the size of

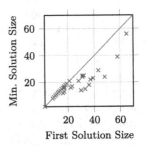

Fig. 7. Scatter plot of first vs. minimum size solutions with the anytime extension. Points below $x = y$ benefit from the anytime extension.

the decision tree almost always went down with time, the size of the solutions sometimes increased. This is because the algorithm generated larger terms and predicates over time, increasing the size of the labels and attributes in each node of the decision tree.

Overall, our experiments suggests that: (a) The DCSolve algorithm is able to quickly learn compact solutions, and generalizes well from input-output examples. (b) The anytime nature of DCSolve often reduces the size of the computed solution; (c) The DCSolve algorithm works competently on problems from different domains.

6   Concluding Remarks

Related Work. Program synthesis has seen a revived interest in the last decade, starting from the SKETCH framework [20,21] which proposed counterexample guided inductive synthesis (CEGIS). Most synthesis algorithms proposed in recent literature can be viewed as an instantiation of CEGIS. Synthesis of string manipulating programs using examples has found applications in Microsoft's FlashFill [7], and the ideas have been generalized in a meta-synthesis framework called FlashMeta [15]. Other recent work in the area of program synthesis have used type-theoretic approaches [9,14] for program completion and for generating code snippets. Synthesis of recursive programs and data structure manipulating code has also been studied extensively [1,5,12]. Lastly, synthesis techniques based on decision trees have been used to learn program invariants [6].

In the area of SyGuS, solvers based on enumerative search [23], stochastic search [2,19] and symbolic search [8,11] were among the first solvers developed. The SKETCH approach has also been used to develop SyGuS solvers [10]. Alchemist [18] is another solver that is quite competitive on benchmarks in the linear arithmetic domains. More recently, white box solvers like the CVC4 solver [17] and the unification based solver [3] have also been developed.

The enumerative synthesis algorithm used by ESOLVER [2,23] and the work on using decision trees for piece-wise functions [13] are perhaps the most closely related to the work described in this paper. We have already discussed at length the shortcomings of ESOLVER that our algorithm overcomes. The approach for learning piece-wise functions [13] also uses decision trees. While the presented framework is generic, the authors instantiate and evaluate it only for the linear arithmetic domain with a specific grammar. In DCSolve, neither the decision tree learning algorithm, nor the enumeration is domain-specific, making DCSolve a domain and grammar agnostic algorithm. The algorithm presented in [13] can easily learn large constants in the linear integer domain. This is something that enumerative approaches, including DCSolve, struggle to do. The heuristics used for decision tree learning are different; in [13], the authors use a heuristic based on hitting sets, while we use an information gain heuristic with cover-based priors.

Conclusion. This paper has presented a new enumerative algorithm to solve instances of the Syntax-Guided Synthesis (SyGuS) problem. The algorithm overcomes the shortcomings of a basic enumerative algorithm by using enumeration to only learn small expressions which are correct on subsets of the inputs. These expressions are then used to form a conditional expression using Boolean combinations of enumerated predicates using decision trees. We have demonstrated the performance and scalability of the algorithm by evaluating it on standard benchmarks, with exceptional performance on programming-by-example benchmarks. The algorithm is generic, efficient, produces compact solutions, and is *anytime* — in that continued execution can potentially produce more compact solutions.

References

1. Albarghouthi, A., Gulwani, S., Kincaid, Z.: Recursive program synthesis. In: Sharygina, N., Veith, H. (eds.) CAV 2013. LNCS, vol. 8044, pp. 934–950. Springer, Heidelberg (2013). doi:10.1007/978-3-642-39799-8_67
2. Alur, R., Bodík, R., Juniwal, G., Martin, M.M., Raghothaman, M., Seshia, S.A., Singh, R., Solar-Lezama, A., Torlak, E. and Udupa, A.: Syntax-guided synthesis. In: Formal Methods in Computer-Aided Design, FMCAD, Portland, OR, USA, 20–23 October, pp. 1–8 (2013)
3. Alur, R., Černý, P., Radhakrishna, A.: Synthesis through unification. In: Kroening, D., Păsăreanu, C.S. (eds.) CAV 2015. LNCS, vol. 9207, pp. 163–179. Springer, Heidelberg (2015). doi:10.1007/978-3-319-21668-3_10
4. Bishop, C.M.: Pattern Recognition and Machine Learning (Information Science and Statistics). Springer, New York (2006)
5. Feser, J.K., Chaudhuri, S., Dillig, I.: Synthesizing data structure transformations from input-output examples. In: Proceedings of the 36th ACM SIGPLAN Conference on Programming Language Design and Implementation, Portland, OR, USA, 15–17 June, pp. 229–239 (2015)
6. Garg, P., Neider, D., Madhusudan, P., Roth, D.: Learning invariants using decision trees and implication counterexamples. In: Proceedings of the 43rd Annual ACM SIGPLAN-SIGACT Symposium on Principles of Programming Languages, POPL 2016, St. Petersburg, FL, USA, 20–22 January, pp. 499–512 (2016)
7. Gulwani, S.: Automating string processing in spreadsheets using input-output examples. In: Proceedings of the 38th ACM SIGPLAN-SIGACT Symposium on Principles of Programming Languages, POPL 2011, Austin, TX, USA, 26–28 January, pp. 317–330 (2011)
8. Gulwani, S., Jha, S., Tiwari, A., Venkatesan, R.: Synthesis of loop-free programs. In: Proceedings of the 32nd ACM SIGPLAN Conference on Programming Language Design and Implementation, PLDI, San Jose, CA, USA, 4–8 June, pp. 62–73 (2011)
9. Gvero, T., Kuncak, V., Kuraj, I, Piskac, R.: Complete completion using types and weights. In: ACM SIGPLAN Conference on Programming Language Design and Implementation, PLDI 2013, Seattle, WA, USA, 16–19 June, pp. 27–38 (2013)
10. Jeon, J., Qiu, X., Solar-Lezama, A., Foster, J.S.: Adaptive concretization for parallel program synthesis. In: Kroening, D., Păsăreanu, C.S. (eds.) CAV 2015. LNCS, vol. 9207, pp. 377–394. Springer, Heidelberg (2015). doi:10.1007/978-3-319-21668-3_22

11. Jha, S., Gulwani, S., Seshia, S.A., Tiwari, A.: Oracle-guided component-based program synthesis. In: Proceedings of the 32nd ACM/IEEE International Conference on Software Engineering, ICSE 2010, Cape Town, South Africa, 1–8, vol. 1, pp. 215–224, May 2010

12. Kneuss, E., Kuraj, I., Kuncak, V., Suter, P.: Synthesis modulo recursive functions. In: Proceedings of the ACM SIGPLAN International Conference on Object Oriented Programming Systems Languages and Applications, OOPSLA 2013, Part of SPLASH, Indianapolis, IN, USA, 26–31 October, pp. 407–426 (2013)

13. Neider, D., Saha, S., Madhusudan, P.: Synthesizing piece-wise functions by learning classifiers. In: Chechik, M., Raskin, J.-F. (eds.) TACAS 2016. LNCS, vol. 9636, pp. 186–203. Springer, Heidelberg (2016). doi:10.1007/978-3-662-49674-9_11. Held as Part of the European Joint Conferences on Theory and Practice of Software, ETAPS 2016, Eindhoven, Netherlands, 2–8 April 2016, Proceedings

14. Osera, P.-M., Zdancewic, S: Type-and-example-directed program synthesis. In: Proceedings of the 36th ACM SIGPLAN Conference on Programming Language Design and Implementation, Portland, OR, USA, 15–17 June, pp. 619–630 (2015)

15. Polozov, O., Gulwani, S., FlashMeta: a framework for inductive program synthesis. In: Proceedings of the ACM SIGPLAN International Conference on Object-Oriented Programming, Systems, Languages, and Applications, OOPSLA 2015, Part of SLASH 2015 , Pittsburgh, PA, USA, 25–30 October, pp. 107–126 (2015)

16. Quinlan, J.R.: Induction of decision trees. Mach. Learn. 1(1), 81–106 (1986)

17. Reynolds, A., Deters, M., Kuncak, V., Tinelli, C., Barrett, C.: Counterexample-guided quantifier instantiation for synthesis in SMT. In: Kroening, D., Păsăreanu, C.S. (eds.) CAV 2015. LNCS, vol. 9207, pp. 198–216. Springer, Heidelberg (2015). doi:10.1007/978-3-319-21668-3_12

18. Saha, S., Garg, P., Madhusudan, P.: Alchemist: learning guarded affine functions. In: Kroening, D., Păsăreanu, C.S. (eds.) CAV 2015. LNCS, vol. 9206, pp. 440–446. Springer, Heidelberg (2015). doi:10.1007/978-3-319-21690-4_26

19. Schkufza, E., Sharma, R., Aiken, A.: Stochastic superoptimization. In: Architectural Support for Programming Languages and Operating Systems, ASPLOS 2013, Houston, TX, USA - 16–20 March, pp. 305–316 (2013)

20. Solar-Lezama, A., Tancau, L., Bodík, R., Seshia, S.A., Saraswat, V.A.: Combinatorial sketching for finite programs. In: Proceedings of the 12th International Conference on Architectural Support for Programming Languages and Operating Systems, ASPLOS 2006, San Jose, CA, USA, 21–25 October, pp. 404–415 (2006)

21. Solar-Lezama, A., Rabbah, R.M., Bodík, R., Ebcioğlu, K.: Programming by sketching for bit-streaming programs. In: Proceedings of the ACM SIGPLAN Conference on Programming Language Design and Implementation, Chicago, IL, USA, 12–15 June, pp. 281–294 (2005)

22. Stump, A., Sutcliffe, G., Tinelli, C.: Starexec: a cross-community infrastructure for logic solving. In: Automated Reasoning - 7th International Joint Conference, IJCAR 2014, Held as Part of the Vienna Summer of Logic, VSL 2014, Vienna, Austria, 1–22 July 2014, Proceedings, pp. 367–373 (2014). http://dx.doi.org/10.1007/978-3-319-08587-6_28.

23. Udupa, A., Raghavan, A., Deshmukh, J.V., Mador-Haim, S., Martin, M.M.K., Alur, R.: Transit: specifying protocols with concolic snippets. In: ACM SIGPLAN Conference on Programming Language Design and Implementation, PLDI 2013, Seattle, WA, USA, 16–19 June, pp. 287–296 (2013)

Towards Parallel Boolean Functional Synthesis

S. Akshay[1]([⊠]), Supratik Chakraborty[1]([⊠]),
Ajith K. John[2], and Shetal Shah[1]([⊠])

[1] IIT Bombay, Mumbai, India
{akshayss,supratik,shetals}@cse.iitb.ac.in
[2] HBNI, BARC, Mumbai, India

Abstract. Given a relational specification $\varphi(X, Y)$, where X and Y are sequences of input and output variables, we wish to synthesize each output as a function of the inputs such that the specification holds. This is called the Boolean functional synthesis problem and has applications in several areas. In this paper, we present the first parallel approach for solving this problem, using compositional and CEGAR-style reasoning as key building blocks. We show by means of extensive experiments that our approach outperforms existing tools on a large class of benchmarks.

1 Introduction

Given a relational specification of input-output behaviour, synthesizing outputs as functions of inputs is a key step in several applications, viz. program repair [14], program synthesis [28], adaptive control [25] etc. The synthesis problem is, in general, uncomputable. However, there are practically useful restrictions that render the problem solvable, e.g., if all inputs and outputs are Boolean, the problem is computable in principle. Nevertheless, functional synthesis may still require formidable computational effort, especially if there are a large number of variables and the overall specification is complex. This motivates us to investigate techniques for Boolean functional synthesis that work well in practice.

Formally, let X be a sequence of m input Boolean variables, and Y be a sequence of n output Boolean variables. A relational specification is a Boolean formula $\varphi(X, Y)$ that expresses a desired input-output relation. The goal in Boolean functional synthesis is to synthesize a function $F : \{0,1\}^m \to \{0,1\}^n$ that satisfies the specification. Thus, for every value of X, if there exists some value of Y such that $\varphi(X, Y) = 1$, we must also have $\varphi(X, F(X)) = 1$. For values of X that do not admit any value of Y such that $\varphi(X, Y) = 1$, the value of $F(X)$ is inconsequential. Such a function F is also referred to as a *Skolem function* for Y in $\varphi(X, Y)$ [15,22].

An interesting example of Boolean functional synthesis is the problem of integer factorization. Suppose Y_1 and Y_2 are n-bit unsigned integers, X is a $2n$-bit unsigned integer and $\times_{[n]}$ denotes n-bit unsigned multiplication. The relational specification $\varphi_{\mathsf{fact}}(X, Y_1, Y_2) \equiv ((X = Y_1 \times_{[n]} Y_2) \wedge (Y_1 \neq 1) \wedge (Y_2 \neq 1))$ specifies that Y_1 and Y_2 are non-trivial factors of X. This specification can be easily encoded as a Boolean relation. The corresponding synthesis problem requires

© Springer-Verlag GmbH Germany 2017
A. Legay and T. Margaria (Eds.): TACAS 2017, Part I, LNCS 10205, pp. 337–353, 2017.
DOI: 10.1007/978-3-662-54577-5_19

us to synthesize the factors Y_1 and Y_2 as functions of X, whenever X is non-prime. Note that this problem is known to be hard, and the strength of several cryptographic systems rely on this hardness.

Existing approaches to Boolean functional synthesis vary widely in their emphasis, ranging from purely theoretical treatments (viz. [3,6,7,10,20,23]) to those motivated by practical tool development (viz. [4,11,12,15,17,18,21,22,27–29]). A common aspect of these approaches is their focus on sequential algorithms for synthesis. In this paper, we present, to the best of our knowledge, the first parallel algorithm for Boolean functional synthesis. A key ingredient of our approach is a technique for solving the synthesis problem for a specification φ by composing solutions of synthesis problems corresponding to sub-formulas in φ. Since Boolean functions are often represented using DAG-like structures (such as circuits, AIGs [16], ROBDDs [1,8]), we assume w.l.o.g. that φ is given as a DAG. The DAG structure provides a natural decomposition of the original problem into sub-problems with a partial order of dependencies between them. We exploit this to design a parallel synthesis algorithm that has been implemented on a message passing cluster. Our initial experiments show that our algorithm significantly outperforms state-of-the-art techniques on several benchmarks.

Related Work: The earliest solutions to Boolean functional synthesis date back to Boole [6] and Lowenheim [20], who considered the problem in the context of Boolean unification. Subsequently, there have been several investigations into theoretical aspects of this problem (see e.g., [3,7,10,23]). More recently, there have been attempts to design practically efficient synthesis algorithms that scale to much larger problem sizes. In [22], a technique to synthesize Y from a proof of validity of $\forall X \exists Y \varphi(X, Y)$ was proposed. While this works well in several cases, not all specifications admit the validity of $\forall X \exists Y \varphi(X, Y)$. For example, $\forall X \exists Y \varphi_{\mathsf{fact}}(X, Y)$ is not valid in the factorization example. In [12,29], a synthesis approach based on functional composition was proposed. Unfortunately, this does not scale beyond small problem instances [11,15]. To address this drawback, a CEGAR based technique for synthesis from *factored* specifications was proposed in [15]. While this scales well if each factor in the specification depends on a small subset of variables, its performance degrades significantly if we have a few "large" factors, each involving many variables, or if there is significant sharing of variables across factors. In [21], Macii et al. implemented Boole's and Lowenheim's algorithms using ROBDDs and compared their performance on small to medium-sized benchmarks. Other algorithms for synthesis based on ROBDDs have been investigated in [4,17]. A recent work [11] adapts the functional composition approach to work with ROBDDs, and shows that this scales well for a class of benchmarks with pre-determined variable orders. However, finding a good variable order for an arbitrary relational specification is hard, and our experiments show that without prior knowledge of benchmark classes and corresponding good variable orders, the performance of [11] can degrade significantly. Techniques using *templates* [28] or *sketches* [27] have been found to be effective for synthesis when we have partial information about the set of candidate solutions. A framework for functional synthesis, focused on unbounded domains such as integer arithmetic, was proposed in [18]. This relies heavily on tailor-made smart heuristics that exploit specific form/structure of the relational specification.

2   Preliminaries

Let $X = (x_1, \ldots x_m)$ be the sequence of input variables, and $Y = (y_1, \ldots y_n)$ be the sequence of output variables in the specification $\varphi(X, Y)$. Abusing notation, we use X (resp. Y) to denote the set of elements in the sequence X (resp. Y), when there is no confusion. We use 1 and 0 to denote the Boolean constants true and false, respectively. A *literal* is either a variable or its complement. An assignment of values to variables *satisfies* a formula if it makes the formula true.

We assume that the specification $\varphi(X, Y)$ is represented as a rooted DAG, with internal nodes labeled by Boolean operators and leaves labeled by input/output literals and Boolean constants. If the operator labeling an internal node N has arity k, we assume that N has k ordered children. Figure 1 shows an example DAG, where the internal nodes are labeled by AND and

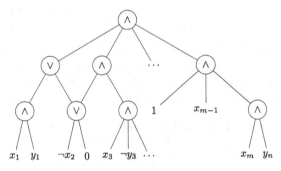

Fig. 1. DAG representing $\varphi(X, Y)$

OR operators of different arities. Each node N in such a DAG represents a Boolean formula $\Phi(N)$, which is inductively defined as follows. If N is a leaf, $\Phi(N)$ is the label of N. If N is an internal node labeled by op with arity k, and if the ordered children of N are $c_1, \ldots c_k$, then $\Phi(N)$ is op$(\Phi(c_1), \ldots \Phi(c_k))$. A DAG with root R is said to represent the formula $\Phi(R)$. Note that popular DAG representations of Boolean formulas, such as AIGs, ROBDDs and Boolean circuits, are special cases of this representation.

A k-ary Boolean function f is a mapping from $\{0, 1\}^k$ to $\{0, 1\}$, and can be viewed as the semantics of a Boolean formula with k variables. We use the terms "Boolean function" and "Boolean formula" interchangeably, using formulas mostly to refer to specifications. Given a Boolean formula φ and a Boolean function f, we use $\varphi[y \mapsto f]$ to denote the formula obtained by substituting every occurrence of the variable y in φ with f. The set of variables appearing in φ is called the *support* of φ. If f and g are Boolean functions, we say that f *abstracts* g and g *refines* f, if $g \rightarrow f$, where $\rightarrow$ denotes logical implication.

Given the specification $\varphi(X, Y)$, our goal is to synthesize the outputs $y_1, \ldots y_n$ as functions of X. Unlike some earlier work [5, 13, 22], we *do not assume the validity of* $\forall X \exists Y \; \varphi(X, Y)$. Thus, we allow the possibility that for some values of X, there may be no value of Y that satisfies $\varphi(X, Y)$. This allows us to accommodate some important classes of synthesis problems, viz. integer factorization. If $y_1 = f_1(X), \ldots y_n = f_n(X)$ is a solution to the synthesis problem, we say that $(f_1(X), \ldots f_n(X))$ *realizes* Y in $\varphi(X, Y)$. For notational clarity, we simply use $(f_1, \ldots f_n)$ instead of $(f_1(X), \ldots f_n(X))$ when X is clear from the context.

In general, an instance of the synthesis problem may not have a unique solution. The following proposition, stated in various forms in the literature, characterizes the space of all solutions, when we have one output variable y.

Proposition 1. *A function $f(X)$ realizes y in $\varphi(X, y)$ iff the following holds:*
$$\varphi[y \mapsto 1] \wedge \neg\varphi[y \mapsto 0] \quad \to \quad f(X) \text{ and } f(X) \quad \to \quad \varphi[y \mapsto 1] \vee \neg\varphi[y \mapsto 0].$$

As a corollary, both $\varphi[y \mapsto 1]$ and $\neg\varphi[y \mapsto 0]$ realize y in $\varphi(X, y)$. Proposition 1 can be easily extended when we have multiple output variables in Y. Let $\sqsubseteq$ be a total ordering of the variables in Y, and assume without loss of generality that $y_1 \sqsubseteq y_2 \sqsubseteq \cdots y_n$. Let $\overrightarrow{F}$ denote the vector of Boolean functions $(f_1(X), \ldots f_n(X))$. For $i \in \{1, \ldots n\}$, define $\varphi^{(i)}$ to be $\exists y_1 \ldots \exists y_{i-1} \varphi$, and $\varphi^{(i)}_{\overrightarrow{F}}$ to be $(\cdots(\varphi^{(i)}[y_{i+1} \mapsto f_{i+1}]) \cdots)[y_n \mapsto f_n]$, with the obvious modifications for $i = 1$ (no existential quantification) and $i = n$ (no substitution). The following proposition, once again implicit in the literature, characterizes the space of all solutions $\overrightarrow{F}$ that realize Y in $\varphi(X, Y)$.

Proposition 2. *The function vector $\overrightarrow{F} = (f_1(X), \ldots f_n(X))$ realizes $Y = (y_1, \ldots y_n)$ in $\varphi(X, Y)$ iff the following holds for every $i \in \{1, \ldots n\}$:*
$$\varphi^{(i)}_{\overrightarrow{F}}[y_i \mapsto 1] \wedge \neg\varphi^{(i)}_{\overrightarrow{F}}[y_i \mapsto 0] \to f_i(X), \text{ and } f_i(X) \to \varphi^{(i)}_{\overrightarrow{F}}[y_i \mapsto 1] \vee \neg\varphi^{(i)}_{\overrightarrow{F}}[y_i \mapsto 0].$$

Propositions 1 and 2 are effectively used in [11,12,15,29] to sequentially synthesize $y_1, \ldots y_n$ as functions of X. Specifically, output y_1 is first synthesized as a function $g_1(X, y_2, \ldots y_n)$. This is done by treating y_1 as the sole output and $X \cup \{y_2, \ldots y_n\}$ as the inputs in $\varphi(X, Y)$. By substituting g_1 for y_1 in φ, we obtain $\varphi^{(2)} \equiv \exists y_1 \varphi(X, Y)$. Output y_2 can then be synthesized as a function $g_2(X, y_3, \ldots y_n)$ by treating y_2 as the sole output and $X \cup \{y_3, \ldots y_n\}$ as the inputs in $\varphi^{(2)}$. Substituting g_2 for y_2 in $\varphi^{(2)}$ gives $\varphi^{(3)} \equiv \exists y_1 \exists y_2 \varphi(X, Y)$. This process is then repeated until we obtain y_n as a function $g_n(X)$. The desired functions $f_1(X), \ldots f_n(X)$ realizing $y_1, \ldots y_n$ can now be obtained by letting $f_n(X)$ be $g_n(X)$, and $f_i(X)$ be $(\cdots(g_i[y_{i+1} \mapsto f_{i+1}(X)]) \cdots)[y_n \mapsto f_n(X)]$, for all i from $n-1$ down to 1. Thus, given $\varphi(X, Y)$, it suffices to obtain $(g_1, \ldots g_n)$, where g_i has support $X \cup \{y_{i+1}, \ldots y_n\}$, in order to solve the synthesis problem. We therefore say that $(g_1, \ldots g_n)$ *effectively realizes* Y in $\varphi(X, Y)$, and focus on obtaining $(g_1, \ldots g_n)$.

Proposition 1 implies that for every $i \in \{1, \ldots n\}$, the function $g_i \equiv \varphi^{(i)}[y_i \mapsto 1]$ realizes y_i in $\varphi^{(i)}$. With this choice for g_i, it is easy to see that $\exists y_i \varphi^{(i)}$ (or $\varphi^{(i+1)}$) can be obtained as $\varphi^{(i)}[y_i \mapsto g_i] = \varphi^{(i)}[y_i \mapsto \varphi^{(i)}[y_i \mapsto 1]]$. While synthesis using quantifier elimination by such *self-substitution* [11] has been shown to scale for certain classes of specifications with pre-determined optimized variable orders, our experience shows that this incurs significant overheads for general specifications with unknown "good" variable orders. An alternative technique for synthesis from *factored* specification was proposed by John et al. [15], in which initial abstractions of $g_1, \ldots g_n$ are first computed quickly, and then a CEGAR-style [9] loop is used to refine these abstractions to correct Skolem functions. We use John et al.'s refinement technique as a black-box module in our work; more on this is discussed in Sect. 3.1.

Definition 1. *Given a specification* $\varphi(X, Y)$, *we define* $\Delta_{y_i}(\varphi)$ *to be the formula* $(\neg \exists y_1 \ldots y_{i-1} \varphi)[y_i \mapsto 0]$, *and* $\Gamma_{y_i}(\varphi)$ *to be the formula* $(\neg \exists y_1 \ldots y_{i-1} \varphi)[y_i \mapsto 1]$, *for all* $i \in \{1, \ldots n\}^1$. *We also define* $\overrightarrow{\Delta}(\varphi)$ *and* $\overrightarrow{\Gamma}(\varphi)$ *to be the vectors* $(\Delta_{y_1}(\varphi), \ldots \Delta_{y_n}(\varphi))$ *and* $(\Gamma_{y_1}(\varphi), \ldots \Gamma_{y_n}(\varphi))$ *respectively.*

If N is a node in the DAG representation of the specification, we abuse notation and use $\Delta_{y_i}(N)$ to denote $\Delta_{y_i}(\Phi(N))$, and similarly for $\Gamma_{y_i}(N)$, $\overrightarrow{\Delta}(N)$ and $\overrightarrow{\Gamma}(N)$. Furthermore, if both Y and N are clear from the context, we use Δ_i, Γ_i, $\overrightarrow{\Delta}$ and $\overrightarrow{\Gamma}$ instead of $\Delta_{y_i}(N), \Gamma_{y_i}(N), \overrightarrow{\Delta}(N)$ and $\overrightarrow{\Gamma}(N)$, respectively. It is easy to see that the supports of both Γ_i and Δ_i are (subsets of) $X \cup \{y_{i+1}, \ldots y_n\}$. Furthermore, it follows from Definition 1 that whenever Γ_i (resp. Δ_i) evaluates to 1, if the output y_i has the value 1 (resp. 0), then φ must evaluate to 0. Conversely, if Γ_i (resp. Δ_i) evaluates to 0, it doesn't hurt (as far as satisfiability of $\varphi(X, Y)$ is concerned) to assign the value 1 (resp. 0) to output y_i. This suggests that both $\neg \Gamma_i$ and Δ_i suffice to serve as the function $g_i(X, y_{i+1}, \ldots y_n)$ when synthesizing functions for multiple output variables. The following proposition, adapted from [15], follows immediately, where we have abused notation and used $\neg \overrightarrow{\Gamma}$ to denote $(\neg \Gamma_1, \ldots \neg \Gamma_n)$.

Proposition 3. *Given a specification* $\varphi(X, Y)$, *both* $\overrightarrow{\Delta}$ *and* $\neg \overrightarrow{\Gamma}$ *effectively realize* Y *in* $\varphi(X, Y)$.

Proposition 3 shows that it suffices to compute $\overrightarrow{\Delta}$ (or $\overrightarrow{\Gamma}$) from $\varphi(X, Y)$ in order to solve the synthesis problem. In the remainder of the paper, we show how to achieve this compositionally and in parallel by first computing refinements of Δ_i (resp. Γ_i) for all $i \in \{1, \ldots n\}$, and then using John et al.'s CEGAR-based technique [15] to abstract them to the desired Δ_i (resp. Γ_i). Throughout the paper, we use δ_i and γ_i to denote refinements of Δ_i and Γ_i respectively.

3 Exploiting Compositionality

Given a specification $\varphi(X, Y)$, one way to synthesize $y_1, \ldots y_n$ is to decompose $\varphi(X, Y)$ into sub-specifications, solve the synthesis problems for the sub-specifications in parallel, and compose the solutions to the sub-problems to obtain the overall solution. A DAG representation of $\varphi(X, Y)$ provides a natural recursive decomposition of the specification into sub-specifications. Hence, the key technical question relates to compositionality: how do we compose solutions to synthesis problems for sub-specifications to obtain a solution to the synthesis problem for the overall specification? This problem is not easy, and no state-of-the-art tool for Boolean functional synthesis uses such compositional reasoning.

---

^{1} In [15], equivalent formulas were called $Cb0_{y_i}(\varphi)$ and $Cb1_{y_i}(\varphi)$ respectively.

Our compositional solution to the synthesis problem is best explained in three steps. First, for a simple, yet representationally complete, class of DAGs representing $\varphi(X, Y)$, we present a lemma that allows us to do compositional synthesis at each node of such a DAG. Next, we show how to use this lemma to design a parallel synthesis algorithm. Finally, we extend our lemma, and hence the scope of our algorithm, to significantly more general classes of DAGs.

3.1 Compositional Synthesis in AND-OR DAGs

For simplicity of exposition, we first consider DAGs with internal nodes labeled by only AND and OR operators (of arbitrary arity). Figure 1 shows an example of such a DAG. Note that this class of DAGs is representationally complete for Boolean specifications, since every specification can be expressed in negation normal form (NNF). In the previous section, we saw that computing $\Delta_i(\varphi)$ or $\Gamma_i(\varphi)$ for all i in $\{1, \ldots n\}$ suffices for purposes of synthesis. The following lemma shows the relation between Δ_i and Γ_i at an internal node N in the DAG and the corresponding formulas at the node's children, say $c_1, \ldots c_k$.

Lemma 1 (Composition Lemma). *Let* $\Phi(N) = \mathsf{op}(\Phi(c_1), \ldots, \Phi(c_k))$, *where* $\mathsf{op} = \vee$ *or* $\mathsf{op} = \wedge$. *Then, for each* $1 \le i \le n$:

$$\left(\bigwedge_{j=1}^{k} \Delta_i(c_j) \right) \leftrightarrow \Delta_i(N) \quad and \quad \left(\bigwedge_{j=1}^{k} \Gamma_i(c_j) \right) \leftrightarrow \Gamma_i(N) \; if \; \mathsf{op} = \vee \quad (1)$$

$$\left(\bigvee_{j=1}^{k} \Delta_i(c_j) \right) \rightarrow \Delta_i(N) \quad and \quad \left(\bigvee_{j=1}^{k} \Gamma_i(c_j) \right) \rightarrow \Gamma_i(N) \; if \; \mathsf{op} = \wedge \quad (2)$$

The proof of this lemma can be found in [2]. Thus, if N is an OR-node, we obtain $\Delta_i(N)$ and $\Gamma_i(N)$ directly by conjoining Δ_i and Γ_i at its children. However, if N is an AND-node, disjoining the Δ_i and Γ_i at its children only gives refinements of $\Delta_i(N)$ and $\Gamma_i(N)$ (see Eq. (2)). Let us call these refinements $\delta_i(N)$ and $\gamma_i(N)$ respectively. To obtain $\Delta_i(N)$ and $\Gamma_i(N)$ exactly at AND-nodes, we must use the CEGAR technique developed in [15] to iteratively abstract $\delta_i(N)$ and $\gamma_i(N)$ obtained above. More on this is discussed below.

A CEGAR step involves constructing, for each i from 1 to n, a Boolean *error formula* Err_{δ_i} (resp. Err_{γ_i}) such that the error formula is unsatisfiable iff $\delta_i(N) \leftrightarrow \Delta_i(N)$ (resp. $\gamma_i(N) \leftrightarrow \Gamma_i(N)$). A SAT solver is then used to check the satisfiability of the error formula. If the formula is unsatisfiable, we are done; otherwise the satisfying assignment can be used to further abstract the respective refinement. This check-and-abstract step is then repeated in a loop until the error formulas become unsatisfiable. Following the approach outlined in [15], it can be shown that if we use $\mathsf{Err}_{\delta_i} \equiv \neg \delta_i \wedge \bigwedge_{j=1}^{i} (y_j \leftrightarrow \delta_j) \wedge \neg \varphi$ and $\mathsf{Err}_{\gamma_i} \equiv \neg \gamma_i \wedge \bigwedge_{j=1}^{i} (y_j \leftrightarrow \neg \gamma_j) \wedge \neg \varphi$, and perform CEGAR in order from $i = 1$ to $i = n$, it suffices to gives us Δ_i and Γ_i. For details of the CEGAR implementation, the reader is referred to [15]. The above discussion leads to a straightforward algorithm COMPUTE (shown as Algorithm 1) that computes $\overrightarrow{\Delta}(N)$ and $\overrightarrow{\Gamma}(N)$ for a node N, using $\overrightarrow{\Delta}(c_j)$ and $\overrightarrow{\Gamma}(c_j)$ for its children c_j. Here, we have assumed access to a black-box function PERFORM_CEGAR that implements the CEGAR step.

Algorithm 1. COMPUTE(NODE N)

Input: A DAG Node N labelled either AND or OR
Precondition: Children of N, if any, have their $\overrightarrow{\Delta}$ and $\overrightarrow{\Gamma}$ computed.
Output: $\overrightarrow{\Delta}(N), \overrightarrow{\Gamma}(N)$

1 **if** N is a leaf   // $\Phi(N)$ is a literal/constant; use Definition 1
2 **then**
3 | for all $y_i \in Y$, $\Delta_i(N) = \neg\exists y_1 \ldots y_{i-1}(\Phi(N))[y_i \mapsto 0]$;
4 | for all $y_i \in Y$, $\Gamma_i(N) = \neg\exists y_1 \ldots y_{i-1}(\Phi(N))[y_i \mapsto 1]$;

5 **else**
       // N is an internal node; let its children be $c_1, \ldots c_k$
6 | **if** N is an OR-node **then**
7 | | **for** each $y_i \in Y$ **do**
8 | | | $\Delta_i(N) := \Delta_i(c_1) \wedge \Delta_i(c_2) \ldots \wedge \Delta_i(c_k)$;
9 | | | $\Gamma_i(N) := \Gamma_i(c_1) \wedge \Gamma_i(c_2) \ldots \wedge \Gamma_i(c_k)$;

10 | **if** N is an AND-node **then**
11 | | **for** each $y_i \in Y$ **do**
12 | | | $\delta_i(N) := \Delta_i(c_1) \vee \Delta_i(c_2) \ldots \vee \Delta_i(c_k)$;   /* $\delta_i(N) \rightarrow \Delta_i(N)$ */
13 | | | $\gamma_i(N) := \Gamma_i(c_1) \vee \Gamma_i(c_2) \ldots \vee \Gamma_i(c_k)$;   /* $\gamma_i(N) \rightarrow \Gamma_i(N)$ */
14 | | $\left(\overrightarrow{\Delta}(N), \overrightarrow{\Gamma}(N)\right) = $ PERFORM_CEGAR$(N, (\delta_i(N), \gamma_i(N))_{y_i \in Y})$;

15 **return** $\left(\overrightarrow{\Delta}(N), \overrightarrow{\Gamma}(N)\right)$;

3.2 A Parallel Synthesis Algorithm

The DAG representation of $\varphi(X, Y)$ gives a natural, recursive decomposition of the specification, and also defines a partial order of dependencies between the corresponding synthesis sub-problems. Algorithm COMPUTE can be invoked in parallel on nodes in the DAG that are not ordered w.r.t. this partial order, as long as COMPUTE has already been invoked on their children. This suggests a simple parallel approach to Boolean functional synthesis. Algorithm PARSYN, shown below, implements this approach, and is motivated by a message-passing architecture. We consider a standard manager-worker configuration, where one out of available m cores acts as the manager, and the remaining $m - 1$ cores act as workers. All communication between the manager and workers is assumed to happen through explicit **send** and **receive** primitives.

    The manager uses a queue Q of ready-to-process nodes. Initially, Q is initialized with the leaf nodes in the DAG, and we maintain the invariant that all

---

Algorithm 2. PARSYN

Input: AND-OR DAG with root Rt representing $\varphi(X, Y)$ in NNF form
Output: $(g_1, \ldots g_n)$ that effectively realize Y in $\varphi(X, Y)$

```
/* Algorithm for Manager                                               */
```
1 Queue Q ;
```
  /* Invariant: Q has nodes that can be processed in parallel, i.e.,
     leaves or nodes whose children have their Δ⃗, Γ⃗ computed.        */
```
2 Insert all leaves of DAG into Q;
3 **while** *all DAG nodes not processed* **do**
4   **while** *a worker W is idle and Q is not empty* **do**
5   Node $N := Q.\text{front}()$;
6   **send** node N for processing to W;
7   **if** N has children $c_1, \ldots c_k$ **then send** $\vec{\Delta}(c_j), \vec{\Gamma}(c_j)$ for $1 \le j \le k$ to W;
8   **wait until** some worker W' processing node N' becomes free;
9   **receive** $\left(\vec{\Delta}, \vec{\Gamma}\right)$ from W', and store as $\left(\vec{\Delta}(N'), \vec{\Gamma}(N')\right)$;
10   Mark node N' as processed;
11   **for each** *parent node N'' of N'* **do**
12   **if** all children of N'' are processed **then** insert N'' into Q

```
/* All DAG nodes are processed; return ¬Γ⃗ or Δ⃗ from root Rt         */
```
13 **return** $(\neg\Gamma_1(Rt), \ldots \neg\Gamma_n(Rt))$ // or alternatively $(\Delta_1(Rt), \ldots \Delta_n(Rt))$

```
/* Algorithm for Worker W                                              */
```
14 **receive** node N to process, and $\vec{\Delta}(c_j), \vec{\Gamma}(c_j)$ for every child c_j of N, if any;
15 $\left(\vec{\Delta}, \vec{\Gamma}\right) := \text{COMPUTE}(N)$;
16 **send** $\left(\vec{\Delta}, \vec{\Gamma}\right)$ to Manager ;

---

nodes in Q can be processed in parallel. If there is an idle worker W and if Q is not empty, the manager assigns the node N at the front of Q to worker W for processing. If N is an internal DAG node, the manager also sends $\vec{\Delta}(c_j)$ and $\vec{\Gamma}(c_j)$ for every child c_j of N to W. If there are no idle workers or if Q is empty, the manager waits for a worker, say W', to finish processing its assigned node, say N'. When this happens, the manager stores the result sent by W' as $\vec{\Delta}(N')$ and $\vec{\Gamma}(N')$. It then inserts one or more parents N'' of N' in the queue Q, if all children of N'' have been processed. The above steps are repeatedly executed at the manager until all DAG nodes have been processed. The job of a worker W is relatively simple: on being assigned a node N, and on receiving $\vec{\Delta}(c_j)$ and $\vec{\Gamma}(c_j)$ for all children c_j of N, it simply executes Algorithm COMPUTE on N and returns $\left(\vec{\Delta}(N), \vec{\Gamma}(N)\right)$.

Note that Algorithm PARSYN is guaranteed to progress as long as all workers complete processing the nodes assigned to them in finite time. The partial order of dependencies between nodes ensures that when all workers are idle, either all nodes have already been processed, or at least one unprocessed node has $\vec{\Delta}$ and $\vec{\Gamma}$ computed for all its children, if any.

3.3   Extending the Composition Lemma and Algorithms

So far, we have considered DAGs in which all internal nodes were either AND- or OR-nodes. We now extend our results to more general DAGs. We do this by generalizing the Composition Lemma to arbitrary Boolean operators. Specifically, given the refinements $\delta_i(c_j)$ and $\gamma_i(c_j)$ at all children c_j of a node N, we show how to compose these to obtain $\delta_i(N)$ and $\gamma_i(N)$, when N is labeled by an arbitrary Boolean operator. Note that the CEGAR technique discussed in Sect. 3.1 can be used to abstract the refinements δ_i and γ_i to Δ_i and Γ_i respectively, at any node of interest. Therefore, with our generalized Composition Lemma, we can use compositional synthesis for specifications represented by general DAGs, even without computing Δ_i and Γ_i exactly at all DAG nodes. This gives an extremely powerful approach for parallel, compositional synthesis.

Let $\Phi(N) = \mathsf{op}(\Phi(c_1), \ldots \Phi(c_r))$, where op is an r-ary Boolean operator. For convenience of notation, we use $\neg N$ to denote $\neg\Phi(N)$, and similarly for other nodes, in the subsequent discussion. Suppose we are given $\delta_i(c_j)$, $\gamma_i(c_j)$, $\delta_i(\neg c_j)$ and $\gamma_i(\neg c_j)$, for $1 \le j \le r$ and for $1 \le i \le n$. We wish to compose these appropriately to compute $\delta_i(N)$, $\gamma_i(N)$, $\delta_i(\neg N)$ and $\gamma_i(\neg N)$ for $1 \le i \le n$. Once we have these refinements, we can adapt Algorithm 1 to work for node N, labeled by an arbitrary Boolean operator op.

To understand how composition works for op, consider the formula $\mathsf{op}(z_1, \ldots z_r)$, where $z_1, \ldots z_r$ are fresh Boolean variables. Clearly, $\Phi(N)$ can be viewed as $(\cdots (\mathsf{op}(z_1, \ldots z_r)[z_1 \mapsto \Phi(c_1)]) \cdots)[z_r \mapsto \Phi(c_r)]$. For simplicity of notation, we write op instead of $\mathsf{op}(z_1, \ldots, z_r)$ in the following discussion. W.l.o.g., let $z_1 \prec z_2 \prec \cdots \prec z_r$ be a total ordering of the variables $\{z_1, \ldots z_r\}$. Given $\prec$, suppose we compute the formulas $\delta_{z_l}(\mathsf{op})$, $\gamma_{z_l}(\mathsf{op})$, $\delta_{z_l}(\neg\mathsf{op})$ and $\gamma_{z_l}(\neg\mathsf{op})$ in negation normal form (NNF), for all $l \in \{1, \ldots r\}$. Note that these formulas have support $\{z_{l+1}, \ldots z_r\}$, and do not have variables in $X \cup Y$ in their support. We wish to ask if we can compose these formulas with $\delta_i(c_j)$, $\gamma_i(c_j)$, $\delta_i(\neg c_j)$ and $\gamma_i(\neg c_j)$ for $1 \le j \le r$ to compute $\delta_i(N)$, $\gamma_i(N)$, $\delta_i(\neg N)$ and $\gamma_i(\neg N)$, for all $i \in \{1, \ldots n\}$. It turns out that we can do this.

Recall that in NNF, negations appear (if at all) only on literals. Let $\Upsilon_{l,\mathsf{op}}$ be the formula obtained by replacing every literal $\neg z_s$ in the NNF of $\gamma_{z_l}(\mathsf{op})$ with a fresh variable $\overline{z_s}$. Similarly, let $\Omega_{l,\mathsf{op}}$ be obtained by replacing every literal $\neg z_s$ in the NNF of $\delta_{z_l}(\mathsf{op})$ with the fresh variable $\overline{z_s}$. The definitions of $\Upsilon_{l,\neg\mathsf{op}}$ and $\Omega_{l,\neg\mathsf{op}}$ are similar. Replacing $\neg z_s$ by a fresh variable $\overline{z_s}$ allows us to treat the literals z_s and $\neg z_s$ independently in the NNF of $\gamma_{z_l}(\mathsf{op})$ and $\delta_{z_l}(\mathsf{op})$. The ability to treat these independently turns out to be important when formulating the generalized Composition Lemma. Let $(\Upsilon_{l,\mathsf{op}}[z_s \mapsto \delta_i(\neg c_s)][\overline{z_s} \mapsto \delta_i(c_s)])_{s=l+1}^{r}$ denote the formula obtained by substituting $\delta_i(\neg c_s)$ for z_s and $\delta_i(c_s)$ for $\overline{z_s}$, for every $s \in \{l+1, \ldots r\}$, in $\Upsilon_{l,\mathsf{op}}$. The interpretation of $(\Omega_{l,\mathsf{op}}[z_s \mapsto \delta_i(\neg c_s)][\overline{z_s} \mapsto \delta_i(c_s)])_{s=l+1}^{r}$ is analogous. Our generalized Composition Lemma can now be stated as follows.

Lemma 2 (Generalized Composition Lemma). *Let* $\Phi(N) = \mathsf{op}(\Phi(c_1), \dots \Phi(c_r))$, *where* op *is an r-ary Boolean operator. For each* $1 \leq i \leq n$ *and* $1 \leq l \leq r$:

1. $\delta_i(c_l) \wedge (\Omega_{l,\mathsf{op}} [z_s \mapsto \delta_i(\neg c_s)] [\overline{z_s} \mapsto \delta_i(c_s)])_{s=l+1}^{r} \;\rightarrow\; \Delta_i(N)$
2. $\delta_i(\neg c_l) \wedge (\Upsilon_{l,\mathsf{op}} [z_s \mapsto \delta_i(\neg c_s)] [\overline{z_s} \mapsto \delta_i(c_s)])_{s=l+1}^{r} \;\rightarrow\; \Delta_i(N)$
3. $\gamma_i(c_l) \wedge (\Omega_{l,\mathsf{op}} [z_s \mapsto \gamma_i(\neg c_s)] [\overline{z_s} \mapsto \gamma_i(c_s)])_{s=l+1}^{r} \;\rightarrow\; \Gamma_i(N)$
4. $\gamma_i(\neg c_l) \wedge (\Upsilon_{l,\mathsf{op}} [z_s \mapsto \gamma_i(\neg c_s)] [\overline{z_s} \mapsto \gamma_i(c_s)])_{s=l+1}^{r} \;\rightarrow\; \Gamma_i(N)$

If we replace op *by* $\neg\mathsf{op}$ *above, we get refinements of* $\Delta_i(\neg N)$ *and* $\Gamma_i(\neg N)$.

The reader is referred to [2] for a proof of Lemma 2. We simply illustrate the idea behind the lemma with an example here. Suppose $\Phi(N) = \Phi(c_1) \wedge \neg\Phi(c_2) \wedge (\neg\Phi(c_3) \vee \Phi(c_4))$, where each $\Phi(c_j)$ is a Boolean function with support $X \cup \{y_1, \dots y_n\}$. We wish to compute a refinement of $\Delta_i(N)$, using refinements of $\Delta_i(c_j)$ and $\Delta_i(\neg c_j)$ for $j \in \{1, \dots 4\}$. Representing N as $\mathsf{op}(c_1, c_2, c_3, c_4)$, let $z_1, \dots z_4$ be fresh Boolean variables, not in $X \cup \{y_1, \dots y_n\}$; then $\mathsf{op}(z_1, z_2, z_3, z_4) = z_1 \wedge \neg z_2 \wedge (\neg z_3 \vee z_4)$. For ease of exposition, assume the ordering $z_1 \prec z_2 \prec z_3 \prec z_4$. By definition, $\Delta_{z_2}(\mathsf{op}) = (\neg \exists z_1 (z_1 \wedge \neg z_2 \wedge (\neg z_3 \vee z_4))) [z_2 \mapsto 0] = z_3 \wedge \neg z_4$, and suppose $\delta_{z_2}(\mathsf{op}) = \Delta_{z_2}(\mathsf{op})$. Replacing $\neg z_4$ by $\overline{z_4}$, we then get $\Omega_{2,\mathsf{op}} = z_3 \wedge \overline{z_4}$.

Recalling the definition of $\delta_{z_2}(\cdot)$, if we set $z_3 = 1$, $z_4 = 0$ and $z_2 = 0$, then op must evaluate to 0 regardless of the value of z_1. By substituting $\delta_i(\neg c_3)$ for z_3 and $\delta_i(c_4)$ for $\overline{z_4}$ in $\Omega_{2,\mathsf{op}}$, we get the formula $\delta_i(\neg c_3) \wedge \delta_i(c_4)$. Denote this formula by χ and note that its support is $X \cup \{y_{i+1}, \dots y_n\}$. Note also from the definition of $\delta_i(\cdot)$ that if χ evaluates to 1 for some assignment of values to $X \cup \{y_{i+1}, \dots y_n\}$ and if $y_i = 0$, then $\neg\Phi(c_3)$ evaluates to 0 and $\Phi(c_4)$ evaluates to 0, regardless of the values of $y_1, \dots y_{i-1}$. This means that $z_3 = 1$ and $z_4 = 0$, and hence $\delta_{z_2}(\mathsf{op}) = 1$. If z_2 (or $\Phi(c_2)$) can also be made to evaluate to 0 for the same assignment of values to $X \cup \{y_i, y_{i+1}, \dots y_n\}$, then $N = \mathsf{op}(c_1, \dots c_r)$ must evaluate to 0, regardless of the values of $\{y_1, \dots y_{i-1}\}$. Since $y_i = 0$, values assigned to $X \cup \{y_{i+1}, \dots y_n\}$ must therefore be a satisfying assignment of $\Delta_i(N)$. One way of having $\Phi(c_2)$ evaluate to 0 is to ensure that $\Delta_i(c_2)$ evaluates to 1 for the same assignment of values to $X \cup \{y_{i+1}, \dots y_n\}$ that satisfies χ. Therefore, we require the assignment of values to $X \cup \{y_{i+1}, \dots y_n\}$ to satisfy $\chi \wedge \Delta_i(c_2)$, or even $\chi \wedge \delta_i(c_2)$. Since $\chi = \delta_i(\neg c_3) \wedge \delta_i(c_4)$, we get $\delta_i(c_2) \wedge \delta_i(\neg c_3) \wedge \delta_i(c_4)$ as a refinement of $\Delta_i(N)$.

Applying the Generalized Composition Lemma: Lemma 2 suggests a way of compositionally obtaining $\delta_i(N)$, $\gamma_i(N)$, $\delta_i(\neg N)$ and $\gamma_i(\neg N)$ for an arbitrary Boolean operator op. Specifically, the disjunction of the left-hand sides of implications (1) and (2) in Lemma 2, disjoined over all $l \in \{1, \dots r\}$ and over all total orders ($\prec$) of $\{z_1, \dots z_r\}$, gives a refinement of $\Delta_i(N)$. A similar disjunction of the left-hand sides of implications (3) and (4) in Lemma 2 gives a refinement of $\Gamma_i(N)$. The cases of $\Delta_i(\neg N)$ and $\Gamma_i(\neg N)$ are similar. This suggests that for each operator op that appears as label of an internal DAG node, we can pre-compute a template of how to compose δ_i and γ_i at the children of the node to obtain δ_i and γ_i at the node itself. In fact, pre-computing this template for $op = \vee$ and $op = \wedge$ by disjoining as suggested above, gives us exactly the left-to-right implications, i.e., refinements of $\Delta_i(N)$ and $\Gamma_i(N)$, as given by Lemma 1. We present templates for some other common Boolean operators like *if-then-else* in [2].

Once we have pre-computed templates for composing δ_i and γ_i at children of a node N to get $\delta_i(N)$ and $\gamma_i(N)$, we can use these pre-computed templates in Algorithm 1, just as we did for AND-nodes. This allows us to apply compositional synthesis on general DAG representations of Boolean relational specifications.

Optimizations Using Partial Computations: Given δ_i and γ_i at children of a node N, we have shown above how to compute $\delta_i(N)$ and $\gamma_i(N)$. To compute $\Delta_i(N)$ and $\Gamma_i(N)$ exactly, we can use the CEGAR technique outlined in Sect. 3.1. While this is necessary at the root of the DAG, we need not compute $\Delta_i(N)$ and $\Gamma_i(N)$ exactly at each intermediate node. In fact, the generalized Composition Lemma allows us to proceed with $\delta_i(N)$ and $\gamma_i(N)$. This suggests some optimizations: (i) Instead of using the error formulas introduced in Sect. 3.1, that allow us to obtain $\Delta_i(N)$ and $\Gamma_i(N)$ exactly, we can use the error formula used in [15]. The error formula of [15] allows us to obtain some Skolem function for y_i (not necessarily $\Delta_i(N)$ or $\neg\Gamma_i(N)$) using the sub-specification $\Phi(N)$ corresponding to node N. We have found CEGAR based on this error formula to be more efficient in practice, while yielding refinements of $\Delta_i(N)$ and $\Gamma_i(N)$. In fact, we use this error formula in our implementation. (ii) We can introduce a *timeout* parameter, such that $\overrightarrow{\Delta}(N), \overrightarrow{\Gamma}(N)$ are computed exactly at each internal node until timeout happens. Subsequently, for the nodes still under process, we can simply combine δ_i and γ_i at their children using our pre-computed composition templates, and not invoke CEGAR at all. The only exception to this is at the root node of the DAG where CEGAR must be invoked.

4   Experimental Results

Experimental Methodology. We have implemented Algorithm 2 with the error formula from [15] used for CEGAR in Algorithm 1 (in function PER-FORM_CEGAR), as described at the end of Sect. 3.3. We call this implementation ParSyn in this section, and compare it with the following algorithms/tools: (i) CSk: This is based on the sequential algorithm for conjunctive formulas, presented in [15]. For non-conjunctive formulas, the algorithm in [15], and hence CSk, reduces to [12,29]. (ii) RSynth: The *RSynth* tool as described in [11]. (iii) Bloqqer: As prescribed in [22], we first generate special QRAT proofs using the preprocessing tool bloqqer, and then generate Boolean function vectors from the proofs using the qrat-trim tool.

Our implementation of ParSyn, available online at [26], makes extensive use of the ABC [19] library to represent and manipulate Boolean functions as AIGs. We also use the default SAT solver provided by ABC, which is a variant of MiniSAT. We present our evaluation on three different kinds of *benchmarks*.

1. *Disjunctive Decomposition Benchmarks*: Similar to [15], these benchmarks were generated by considering some of the larger sequential circuits in the HWMCC10 benchmark suite, and formulating the problem of disjunctively decomposing each circuit into components as a problem of synthesizing a vector of Boolean functions. Each generated benchmark is of the form $\exists Y \varphi(X, Y)$ where $\exists X (\exists Y \varphi(X, Y))$ is true. However, unlike [15], where each benchmark (if not already a conjunction of factors) had to be converted into factored form using Tseitin encoding (which introduced additional variables), we have used these benchmarks without Tseitin encoding.

2. *Arithmetic Benchmarks*: These benchmarks were taken from the work described in [11]. Specifically, the benchmarks considered are *floor*, *ceiling*, *decomposition*, *equalization* and *intermediate* (see [11] for details).

3. *Factorization Benchmarks*: We considered the integer factorization problem for different bit-widths, as discussed in Sect. 1.

For each arithmetic and factorization benchmark, we first specified the problem instance as an SMT formula and then used *Boolector* [24] to generate the Boolean version of the benchmark. For each arithmetic benchmark, three variants were generated by varying the bit-width of the arguments of arithmetic operators; specifically, we considered bit-widths of 32, 128 and 512. Similarly, for the factorization benchmark, we generated four variants, using 8, 10, 12 and 16 for the bit-width of the product. Further, as Bloqqer requires the input to be in qdimacs format and RSynth in cnf format, we converted each benchmark into qdimacs and cnf formats using Tseitin encoding [30]. All benchmarks and the procedure by which we generated them are detailed in [26].

Variable Ordering: We used the same ordering of variables for all algorithms. For each benchmark, the variables are ordered such that the variable which occurs in the transitive fan-in of the least number of nodes in the AIG representation of the specification, appears at the top. For RSynth this translated to an interleaving of most of the input and output variables.

Machine Details: All experiments were performed on a message-passing cluster, where each node had 20 cores and 64 GB main memory, each core being a 2.20 GHz Intel Xeon processor. The operating system was Cent OS 6.5. For CSk, Bloqqer, and RSynth, a single core on the cluster was used. For all comparisons, ParSyn was executed on 4 nodes using 5 cores each, so that we had both intra-node and inter-node communication. The maximum time given for execution was 3600 s, i.e., 1 h. We also restricted the total amount of main memory (across all cores) to be 16 GB. The metric used to compare the different algorithms was the time taken to synthesize Boolean functions.

Results. Our benchmark suite consisted of 27 disjunctive decomposition benchmarks, 15 arithmetic benchmarks and 4 factorization benchmarks. These benchmarks are fairly comprehensive in size i.e., the number of AIG nodes ($|SZ|$)

in the benchmark, and the number of variables ($|Y|$) for which Boolean functions are to be synthesized. Amongst disjunctive decomposition benchmarks, $|SZ|$ varied from 1390 to 58752 and $|Y|$ varied from 21 to 205. Amongst the arithmetic benchmarks, $|SZ|$ varied from 442 to 11253 and $|Y|$ varied from 31 to 1024. The factorization benchmarks are the smallest and the most complex of the benchmarks, with $|SZ|$ varying from 122 to 502 and $|Y|$ varying from 8 to 16.

We now present the performance of the various algorithms. On 4 of the 46 benchmarks, none of the tools succeeded. Of these, 3 belonged to the *intermediate* problem type in the arithmetic benchmarks, and the fourth one was the 16 bit factorization benchmark.

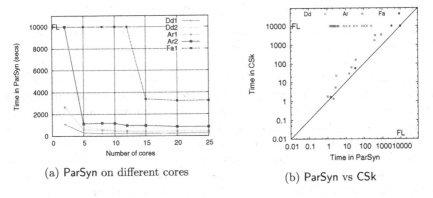

(a) ParSyn on different cores

(b) ParSyn vs CSk

Fig. 2. Legend: `Ar`: arithmetic, `Fa`: factorization, `Dd`: disjunctive decomposition. `FL`: benchmarks for which the corresponding algorithm was unsuccessful.

Effect of the Number of Cores. For this experiment, we chose 5 of the larger benchmarks. Of these, two benchmarks belonged to the disjunctive decomposition category, two belonged to the arithmetic benchmark category and one was the 12 bit factorization benchmark. The number of cores was varied from 2 to 25. With 2 cores, ParSyn behaves like a sequential algorithm with one core acting as the manager and the other as the worker with all computation happening at the worker core. Hence, with 2 cores, we see the effect of compositionality without parallelism. For number of cores > 2, the number of worker cores increase, and the computation load is shared across the worker cores.

Figure 2a shows the results of our evaluation. The topmost points indicated by `FL` are instances for which ParSyn timed out. We can see that, for all 5 benchmarks, the time taken to synthesize Boolean function vectors when the number of cores is 2 is considerable; in fact, ParSyn times out on three of the benchmarks. When we increase the number of cores we observe that (a) by synthesizing in parallel, we can now solve benchmarks for which we had timed out earlier, and (b) speedups of about 4–5 can be obtained with 5–15 cores. From 15 cores to 25 cores, the performance of the algorithm, however, is largely invariant and any further increase in cores does not result in further speed up.

To understand this, we examined the benchmarks and found that their AIG representations have more nodes close to the leaves than to the root (similar to the DAG in Fig. 1). The time taken to process a leaf or a node close to a leaf is typically much less than that for a node near the root. Furthermore, the dependencies between the nodes close to the root are such that at most one or two nodes can be processed in parallel leaving most of the cores unutilized. When the number of cores is increased from 2 to 5–15, the leaves and the nodes close to the leaves get processed in parallel, reducing the overall time taken by the algorithm. However, the time taken to process the nodes close to the root remains more or less the same and starts to dominate the total time taken. At this point, even if the number of cores is further increased, it does not significantly reduce the total time taken. This behaviour limits the speed-ups of our algorithm. For the remaining experiments, the number of cores used for ParSyn was 20.

ParSyn *vs* **CSk**: As can be seen from Fig. 2b, CSk ran successfully on only 12 of the 46 benchmarks, whereas ParSyn was successful on 39 benchmarks, timing out on 6 benchmarks and running out of memory on 1 benchmark. Of the benchmarks that CSk was successful on, 9 belonged to the arithmetic category, 2 to the factorization and 1 to the disjunctive decomposition category. On further examination, we found that factorization and arithmetic benchmarks (except the *intermediate* problems) were conjunctive formulae whereas disjunctive decomposition benchmarks were arbitrary Boolean formulas. Since CSk has been specially designed to handle conjunctive formulas, it is successful on some of these benchmarks. On the other hand, since disjunctive decomposition benchmarks are not conjunctive, CSk treats the entire formula as one factor, and the algorithm reduces to [12,29]. The performance hit is therefore not surprising; it has been shown in [15] and [11] that the algorithms of [12,29] do not scale to large benchmarks that are not conjunctions of small factors. In fact, among the disjunctive decomposition benchmarks, CSk was successful on only the smallest one.

ParSyn *vs* **RSynth:** As seen in Fig. 3a, RSynth was successful only on 3 of the 46 benchmarks; it timed out on 37 and ran out of memory on 6 benchmarks. The 3 benchmarks that RSynth was successful on were the smaller factorization benchmarks. Note that the arithmetic benchmarks used in [11] are semantically the same as the ones used in our experiments. In [11], custom variable orders were used to construct the ROBDDs, which resulted in compact ROBDDs. In our case, we use the variable ordering heuristic mentioned earlier, and include the considerable time taken to build BDDs from cnf representation. As mentioned in Sect. 1, if we know a better variable ordering, then the time taken can potentially reduce. However, we may not know the optimal variable order for an arbitrary specification in general. We also found the memory footprint of RSynth to be higher as indicated by the memory-outs. This is not surprising, as RSynth uses BDDs to represent Boolean formulas and it is well-known that BDDs can have large memory requirements.

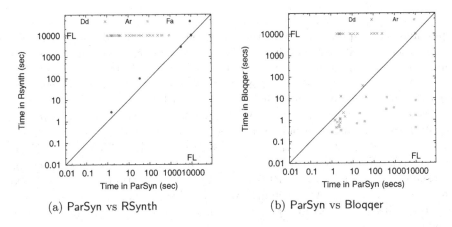

(a) ParSyn vs RSynth   (b) ParSyn vs Bloqqer

Fig. 3. Legend: `Ar`: arithmetic, `Fa`: factorization, `Dd`: disjunctive decomposition. `FL`: benchmarks for which the corresponding algorithm was unsuccessful.

ParSyn *vs Bloqqer:* Since Bloqqer cannot synthesize Boolean functions for formulas wherein $\forall X \exists Y \varphi(X, Y)$ is not *valid*, we restricted our comparison to only the disjunctive decomposition and arithmetic benchmarks, totalling 42 in number. From Fig. 3b, we can see that Bloqqer successfully synthesizes Boolean functions for 25 of the 42 benchmarks. For several benchmarks for which it is successful, it outperforms ParSyn. In line 14 of Algorithm 1, PERFORM_CEGAR makes extensive use of the SAT solver, and this is reflected in the time taken by ParSyn. However, for the remaining 17 benchmarks, Bloqqer gave a *Not Verified* message indicating that it could not synthesize Boolean functions for these benchmarks. In comparison, ParSyn was successful on most of these benchmarks.

Effect of Timeouts on ParSyn. Finally, we discuss the effect of the timeout optimization discussed in Sect. 3.3. Specifically, for 60 s (value set through a *timeout* parameter), starting from the leaves of the AIG representation of a specification, we synthesize exact Boolean functions for DAG nodes. After timeout, on the remaining intermediate nodes, we do not invoke the CEGAR step at all, except at the root node of the AIG.

This optimization enabled us to handle 3 more benchmarks, i.e., ParSyn with this optimization synthesized Boolean function vectors for all the *equalization* benchmarks (in <340 s). Interestingly, ParSyn without timeouts was unable to solve these problems. This can be explained by the fact that in these benchmarks many internal nodes required multiple iterations of the CEGAR loop to compute exact Boolean functions, which were, however, not needed to compute the solution at the root node.

5   Conclusion and Future Work

In this paper, we have presented the first parallel and compositional algorithm for complete Boolean functional synthesis from a relational specification. A key feature of our approach is that it is agnostic to the semantic variabilities of the input, and hence applies to a wide variety of benchmarks. In addition to the disjunctive decomposition of graphs and the arithmetic operation benchmarks, we considered the combinatorially hard problem of factorization and attempted to generate a functional characterization for it. We found that our implementation outperforms existing tools in a variety of benchmarks.

There are many avenues to extend our work. First, the ideas for compositional synthesis that we develop in this paper could potentially lead to parallel implementations of other synthesis tools, such as that described in [11]. Next, the factorization problem can be generalized to synthesis of inverse functions for classically hard one-way functions, as long as the function can be described efficiently by a circuit/AIG. Finally, we would like to explore improved ways of parallelizing our algorithm, perhaps exploiting features of specific classes of problems.

References

1. Akers, S.B.: Binary decision diagrams. IEEE Trans. Comput. **27**(6), 509–516 (1978). http://dx.doi.org/10.1109/TC.1978.1675141
2. Akshay, S., Chakraborty, S., John, A., Shah, S.: Towards Parallel Boolean Functional Synthesis. ArXiv e-prints (2017). CoRR abs/1703.01440
3. Baader, F.: On the complexity of Boolean unification. Technical report (1999)
4. Bañeres, D., Cortadella, J., Kishinevsky, M.: A recursive paradigm to solve Boolean relations. IEEE Trans. Comput. **58**(4), 512–527 (2009)
5. Benedetti, M.: sKizzo: a suite to evaluate and certify QBFs. In: Nieuwenhuis, R. (ed.) CADE 2005. LNCS (LNAI), vol. 3632, pp. 369–376. Springer, Heidelberg (2005). doi:10.1007/11532231_27
6. Boole, G.: The Mathematical Analysis of Logic. Philosophical Library (1847). https://books.google.co.in/books?id=zv4YAQAAIAAJ
7. Boudet, A., Jouannaud, J.P., Schmidt-Schauss, M.: Unification in Boolean rings and Abelian groups. J. Symb. Comput. **8**(5), 449–477 (1989). http://dx.doi.org/10.1016/S0747-7171(89)80054-9
8. Bryant, R.E.: Graph-based algorithms for Boolean function manipulation. IEEE Trans. Comput. **35**(8), 677–691 (1986). http://dx.doi.org/10.1109/TC.1986.1676819
9. Clarke, E., Grumberg, O., Jha, S., Lu, Y., Veith, H.: Counterexample-guided abstraction refinement for symbolic model checking. J. ACM **50**(5), 752–794 (2003)
10. Deschamps, J.P.: Parametric solutions of Boolean equations. Discret. Math. **3**(4), 333–342 (1972). http://dx.doi.org/10.1016/0012-365X(72)90090-8
11. Fried, D., Tabajara, L.M., Vardi, M.Y.: BDD-based Boolean functional synthesis. In: Chaudhuri, S., Farzan, A. (eds.) CAV 2016. LNCS, vol. 9780, pp. 402–421. Springer, Heidelberg (2016). doi:10.1007/978-3-319-41540-6_22
12. Jiang, J.-H.R.: Quantifier elimination via functional composition. In: Bouajjani, A., Maler, O. (eds.) CAV 2009. LNCS, vol. 5643, pp. 383–397. Springer, Heidelberg (2009). doi:10.1007/978-3-642-02658-4_30
13. Balabanov, V., Jiang, J.-H.R.: Resolution proofs and skolem functions in QBF evaluation and applications. In: Gopalakrishnan, G., Qadeer, S. (eds.) CAV 2011. LNCS, vol. 6806, pp. 149–164. Springer, Heidelberg (2011). doi:10.1007/978-3-642-22110-1_12

14. Jobstmann, B., Griesmayer, A., Bloem, R.: Program repair as a game. In: Etessami, K., Rajamani, S.K. (eds.) CAV 2005. LNCS, vol. 3576, pp. 226–238. Springer, Heidelberg (2005). doi:10.1007/11513988_23

15. John, A., Shah, S., Chakraborty, S., Trivedi, A., Akshay, S.: Skolem functions for factored formulas. In: FMCAD, pp. 73–80 (2015)

16. Kuehlmann, A., Paruthi, V., Krohm, F., Ganai, M.K.: Robust Boolean reasoning for equivalence checking and functional property verification. IEEE Trans. CAD of Integr. Circuits Syst. 21(12), 1377–1394 (2002). http://dblp.uni-trier.de/db/journals/tcad/tcad21.html#KuehlmannPKG02

17. Kukula, J.H., Shiple, T.R.: Building circuits from relations. In: Emerson, E.A., Sistla, A.P. (eds.) CAV 2000. LNCS, vol. 1855, pp. 113–123. Springer, Heidelberg (2000). doi:10.1007/10722167_12

18. Kuncak, V., Mayer, M., Piskac, R., Suter, P.: Complete functional synthesis. SIGPLAN Not. 45(6), 316–329 (2010)

19. Logic, B., Group, V.: ABC: A System for Sequential Synthesis and Verification. http://www.eecs.berkeley.edu/~alanmi/abc/

20. Lowenheim, L.: Über die Auflösung von Gleichungen in Logischen Gebietkalkul. Math. Ann. 68, 169–207 (1910)

21. Macii, E., Odasso, G., Poncino, M.: Comparing different Boolean unification algorithms. In: Proceedings of 32nd Asilomar Conference on Signals, Systems and Computers, pp. 17–29 (2006)

22. Marijn Heule, M.S., Biere, A.: Efficient extraction of Skolem functions from QRAT proofs. In: Proceedings of FMCAD (2014)

23. Martin, U., Nipkow, T.: Boolean unification - the story so far. J. Symb. Comput. 7(3–4), 275–293 (1989). http://dx.doi.org/10.1016/S0747-7171(89)80013-6

24. Niemetz, A., Preiner, M., Biere, A.: Boolector 2.0 system description. Satisfi. Boolean Model. Comput. 9, 53–58 (2014 (published 2015))

25. Ramadge, P.J., Wonham, W.M.: Supervisory control of a class of discrete event processes. SIAM J. Control Optim. 25(1), 206–230 (1987)

26. Akshay, S., Chakraborty, S., John, A., Shah, S.: Website for TACAS 2017 Experiments (2016). https://drive.google.com/drive/folders/0BwmvCTZAETPvVExUQkx6WVEtWWs

27. Solar-Lezama, A., Rabbah, R.M., Bodík, R., Ebcioglu, K.: Programming by sketching for bit-streaming programs. In: Proceedings of ACM SIGPLAN 2005 Conference on Programming Language Design and Implementation, Chicago, IL, USA, 12–15 June 2005, pp. 281–294 (2005)

28. Srivastava, S., Gulwani, S., Foster, J.S.: Template-based program verification and program synthesis. STTT 15(5–6), 497–518 (2013)

29. Trivedi, A.: Techniques in symbolic model checking. Master's thesis, Indian Institute of Technology Bombay, Mumbai, India (2003)

30. Tseitin, G.S.: On the complexity of derivation in propositional calculus. In: Structures in Constructive Mathematics and Mathematical Logic, Part II. Seminars in Mathematics, pp. 115–125 (1968)

Encodings of Bounded Synthesis

Peter Faymonville[1], Bernd Finkbeiner[1], Markus N. Rabe[2],
and Leander Tentrup[1(✉)]

[1] Saarland University, Saarbrücken, Germany
tentrup@react.uni-saarland.de
[2] University of California, Berkeley, USA

Abstract. The reactive synthesis problem is to compute a system satisfying a given specification in temporal logic. Bounded synthesis is the approach to bound the maximum size of the system that we accept as a solution to the reactive synthesis problem. As a result, bounded synthesis is decidable whenever the corresponding verification problem is decidable, and can be applied in settings where classic synthesis fails, such as in the synthesis of distributed systems. In this paper, we study the constraint solving problem behind bounded synthesis. We consider different reductions of the bounded synthesis problem of linear-time temporal logic (LTL) to constraint systems given as boolean formulas (SAT), quantified boolean formulas (QBF), and dependency quantified boolean formulas (DQBF). The reductions represent different trade-offs between conciseness and algorithmic efficiency. In the SAT encoding, both inputs and states of the system are represented explicitly; in QBF, inputs are symbolic and states are explicit; in DQBF, both inputs and states are symbolic. We evaluate the encodings systematically using benchmarks from the reactive synthesis competition (SYNTCOMP) and state-of-the-art solvers. Our key, and perhaps surprising, empirical finding is that QBF clearly dominates both SAT and DQBF.

1 Introduction

There has been a recent surge of new algorithms and tools for the synthesis of reactive systems from temporal specifications [5,9,14,15,19]. Roughly, these approaches can be classified into two categories: *game-based synthesis* [8] translates the specification into an deterministic automaton and subsequently determines the winner in a game played on the state graph of this automaton; *bounded synthesis* [25] constructs a constraint system that characterizes all systems, up to a fixed bound on the size of the system, that satisfy the specification.

The success of game-based synthesis is largely due to the fact that it is often possible to represent and analyze the game arena symbolically, in particular with BDDs (cf. [19]). As a result, it has been possible to scale synthesis to realistic benchmarks such as the AMBA bus protocol [3]. However, because the deterministic automaton often contains many more states than are needed by the

Supported by the European Research Council (ERC) Grant OSARES (No. 683300).

© Springer-Verlag GmbH Germany 2017
A. Legay and T. Margaria (Eds.): TACAS 2017, Part I, LNCS 10205, pp. 354–370, 2017.
DOI: 10.1007/978-3-662-54577-5_20

implementation, the synthesized systems are often unnecessarily (and impractically) large (cf. [11]). This problem is addressed by bounded synthesis, where an iteratively growing bound can ensure that the synthesized system is actually the smallest possible realization of the specification. However, bounded synthesis has not yet reached the same scalability as game-based synthesis. A likely explanation for the phenomenon is that the encoding of bounded synthesis into the constraint system is "less symbolic" than the BDD-based representation of the game arena. Even though bounded synthesis tools typically use powerful SMT solvers, a careful study of the standard encoding shows that both the states of the synthesized system and its inputs are enumerated explicitly [14].

The question arises whether it is the encodings that need to be improved, or whether the poor scalability points to a more fundamental flaw in the underlying solver technology. To answer this question, we reduce the bounded synthesis problem of linear-time temporal logic (LTL) to constraint systems given as boolean formulas (SAT), quantified boolean formulas (QBF), and dependency quantified boolean formulas (DQBF). The reductions are landmarks on the spectrum of symbolic vs. explicit encodings. All encodings represent the synthesized system in terms of its transition function, which identifies the successor state in terms of the current state and the input, and additionally in terms of an output function, which identifies the output signals in terms of the current state and the input, and annotation functions, which relate the states of the system to the states of a universal automaton representing the specification.

In the SAT encoding of the transition function, a separate boolean variable is used for every combination of a source state, an input signal, and a target state. The encoding is thus explicit in both the state and the input. In the QBF encoding, a universal quantification over the inputs is added, so that the encoding becomes symbolic in the inputs, while staying explicit in the states. Quantifying universally over the states, just like over the input signals, is not possible in QBF because the states occur twice in the transition function, as source and as target. Separate quantifiers over sources and targets would allow for models where, for example, the value of the output function differs, even though both the source state and the input are the same. In DQBF we can avoid such artifacts and obtain a "fully symbolic" encoding in both the states and the input.

We evaluate the encodings systematically using benchmarks from the reactive synthesis competition (SYNTCOMP) and state-of-the-art solvers. Our empirical finding is that QBF clearly dominates both SAT and DQBF. While the dominance of QBF over SAT fits with our intuition that a more symbolic encoding provides opportunities for optimization in the solver, the dominance of QBF over DQBF is surprising. This indicates that with the currently available solvers, the most symbolic encoding (DQBF) is *not* the best choice. Of course, with better DQBF solvers, this may change: our benchmarks identify opportunities for improvement for current DQBF solvers.

Related Work. The game-based approach to the synthesis of reactive systems dates back to Büchi and Landweber's seminal 1969 paper [8]. Modern implementations of this approach exploit symbolic representations of the game arena, using BDDs (cf. [19]) or decision procedures for the satisfiability of Boolean formulas (SAT-, QBF- and DQBF-solvers). We refer to [4] for a detailed comparison of the different methods.

Bounded synthesis belongs to the class of *Safraless decision procedures* [22]. Safraless synthesis algorithms avoid the translation of the specification into an equivalent deterministic automaton via Safra's determinization procedure. Instead, the specification is first translated into an equivalent universal co-Büchi automaton, whose language is then approximated in a sequence of deterministic safety automata, obtained by bounding the number of visits to rejecting states [25]. Most synthesis tools for full LTL, including Unbeast [9], and Acacia+ [5], are based on this idea.

Bounded synthesis [25] limits not only the number of visits to rejecting states, but also the number of states of the synthesized system itself. As a result, the bounded synthesis problem can be represented as a decidable constraint system, even in settings where the classic synthesis problem is undecidable, such as the synthesis of asynchronous and distributed systems (cf. [14]). There have been several proposals for encodings of bounded synthesis. The first encoding [13, 25] was based on first-order logic modulo finite integer arithmetic. Improvements to the original encoding include the representation of transition systems that are not necessarily input-preserving, and, hence, often significantly smaller [14], the lazy generation of the constraints from model checking runs [11], and specification rewriting and modular solving [21]. Recently, a SAT-based encoding was proposed [27]. Another SAT-based encoding [12] bounds, in addition to the number of states, also the number of loops. A QBF-based encoding has been used in the related problem of solving Petri games [10]. Petri games can be used to solve certain distributed synthesis problems. They have, however, a significantly simpler winning condition than the games resulting from LTL specifications.

This paper presents the first encodings of bounded synthesis based on QBF and DQBF, and the first comprehensive evaluation of the spectrum of encodings from SAT to DQBF with state-of-the-art solvers. The encodings are significantly more concise than the previous SAT-based encodings and provide opportunities for solvers to exploit the symbolic representation of inputs and states. The empirical evidence shows that, with current solvers, the QBF encoding is superior to the SAT and DQBF encodings. A further contribution of the paper are the benchmarks themselves, which pinpoint opportunities for the improvement of the solvers, in particular for DQBF.

2   Preliminaries

Given a finite set of variables V, we identify boolean assignments $\alpha : V \to \mathbb{B}$ as elements from the powerset of V, i.e., given V and α, then $\boldsymbol{v} = \{v \mid \alpha(v) = \top\} \in 2^V$ is a representation of α. We use $\mathbb{B}(V)$ to denote the set of propositional boolean formulas over the variables V.

LTL. Linear-time temporal logic (LTL) is the standard specification language for linear-time properties. Let Σ be a finite alphabet, i.e., a finite set of atomic propositions. The grammar of LTL is given by

$$\varphi ::= p \mid \neg\varphi \mid \varphi \vee \psi \mid \varphi \wedge \psi \mid \bigcirc\varphi \mid \varphi\,\mathcal{U}\,\psi \mid \varphi\,\mathcal{R}\,\psi,$$

where $p \in \Sigma$ is an atomic proposition. The abbreviations $true := p \vee \neg p$, $false := \neg true$, $\lozenge\varphi = true\,\mathcal{U}\,\varphi$, and $\square\varphi = false\,\mathcal{R}\,\varphi$ are defined as usual. We assume standard semantics and write $\sigma \vDash \varphi$ if $\sigma \in (2^\Sigma)^\omega$ satisfies φ. The language of φ, written $\mathcal{L}(\varphi)$, is the set of ω-words that satisfy φ.

Automata. A universal co-Büchi automaton $\mathcal{A}$ over finite alphabet Σ is a tuple $\langle Q, q_0, \delta, F \rangle$, where Q is a finite set of states, $q_0 \in Q$ the designated initial state, $\delta : Q \times 2^\Sigma \times Q$ is the transition relation, and $F \subseteq Q$ is the set of rejecting states. Given an infinite word $\sigma \in (2^\Sigma)^\omega$, a run of σ on $\mathcal{A}$ is an infinite path $q_0 q_1 q_2 \cdots \in Q^\omega$ where for all $i \geq 0$ it holds that $(q_i, \sigma_i, q_{i+1}) \in \delta$. A run is accepting, if it contains only finitely many rejecting states. $\mathcal{A}$ accepts a word σ, if *all* runs of σ on $\mathcal{A}$ are accepting. The language of $\mathcal{A}$, written $\mathcal{L}(\mathcal{A})$, is the set $\{\sigma \in (2^\Sigma)^\omega \mid \mathcal{A}$ accepts $\sigma\}$.

We represent automata as directed graphs with vertex set Q and a symbolic representation of the transition relation δ as propositional boolean formulas $\mathbb{B}(\Sigma)$. The rejecting states in F are marked by double lines.

Lemma 1. *Given an LTL formula φ, we can construct a universal co-Büchi automaton $\mathcal{A}_\varphi$ with $\mathcal{O}(2^{|\varphi|})$ states that accepts the language $\mathcal{L}(\varphi)$.*

Example 1. Consider the LTL formula $\psi = \square(r_1 \rightarrow \bigcirc\lozenge g_1) \wedge \square(r_2 \rightarrow \bigcirc\lozenge g_2) \wedge \square\neg(g_1 \wedge g_2)$. Whenever there is a request r_i, the corresponding grant g_i must be set eventually. Further, it is disallowed to set both grants simultaneously. The universal co-Büchi automaton $\mathcal{A}_\psi$ that accepts the same language as ψ is shown in Fig. 1(a).

Transition Systems. In the following, we partition the set of atomic propositions into a set I that contains propositions controllable by the environment and a set O that contains propositions controllable by the system. A transition system $\mathcal{T}$ is a tuple $\langle T, t_0, \tau \rangle$ where T is a finite set of states, $t_0 \in T$ is the designated initial state, and $\tau : T \times 2^I \rightarrow 2^O \times T$ is the transition function. The transition function τ maps a state t and a valuation of the inputs $i \in 2^I$ to a valuation of the outputs, also called *labeling*, and a next state t'. If the labeling produced by $\tau(t, i)$ is independent of i, we call $\mathcal{T}$ a state-labeled (or Moore) transition system and transition-labeled (or Mealy) otherwise. Formally, $\mathcal{T}$ is a state-labeled transition system if, given a state $t \in T$ and any $i \neq i' \in 2^I$ with $\tau(t, i) = (o, \_)$ and $\tau(t, i') = (o', \_)$ it holds that $o = o'$.

Given an infinite word $i_0 i_1 \cdots \in (2^I)^\omega$ over the inputs, $\mathcal{T}$ produces an infinite trace $(\{t_0\} \cup i_0 \cup o_0)(\{t_i\} \cup i_1 \cup o_1) \cdots \in (2^{T \cup I \cup O})^\omega$ where $\tau(t_j, i_j) = (o_j, t_{j+1})$ for every $j \geq 0$. A path $w \in (2^{I \cup O})^\omega$ is the projection of a trace to the atomic propositions. We denote the set of all paths generated by a transition system $\mathcal{T}$ as $Paths(\mathcal{T})$. A transition system realizes an LTL formula if $Paths(\mathcal{T}) \subseteq \mathcal{L}(\varphi)$.

Example 2. Figure 1(b) depicts the two-state (state-labeled) transition system $T_{arb} = \langle \{t_0, t_1\}, t_0, \tau \rangle$ with $\tau(t_0, i) = (\{g_1\}, t_1)$ and $\tau(t_1, i) = (\{g_2\}, t_0)$ for every $i \in 2^I$. The set of paths is $Paths(T) = (\{g_1\}\{g_2\})^\omega \cup (2^{\{i_1, i_2\}})^\omega$.

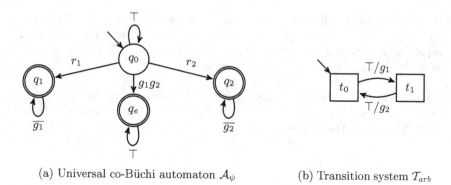

(a) Universal co-Büchi automaton $\mathcal{A}_\psi$ (b) Transition system T_{arb}

Fig. 1. A specification automaton over inputs r_1, r_2 and outputs g_1, g_2 and a realizing transition system.

3   Bounded Synthesis

Bounded synthesis [14] is a synthesis procedure for LTL specifications that produces size-optimal transition systems. A given LTL formula φ is translated into a universal co-Büchi automaton $\mathcal{A}$ that accepts the language $\mathcal{L}(\varphi)$. A transition system T realizes specification φ if, and only if, every trace generated by T is in the language $\mathcal{L}(\varphi)$. T is accepted by $\mathcal{A}$ if every path of the unique run graph, that is the product of T and $\mathcal{A}$, has only finitely many visits to rejecting states. This acceptance is witnessed by a bounded annotation on this product.

The bounded synthesis approach is to synthesize a transition system of bounded size n, by solving a constraint system that asserts the existence of a transition system and labeling function of T as well as a valid annotation. In this section we discuss how to construct a formula that represents that a *given* annotation is correct. We will use this formula as a building block for different bounded synthesis constraint systems in Sect. 4.

The product of a transition system $T = \langle T, t_0, \tau \rangle$ and a universal co-Büchi automaton $\mathcal{A} = \langle Q, q_0, \delta, F \rangle$ is a *run graph* $\mathcal{G} = \langle V, E \rangle$, where $V = T \times Q$ is the set of vertices and $E \subseteq V \times V$ is the edge relation with

$$((t, q), (t', q')) \in E \text{ iff } \exists i \in 2^I. \exists o \in 2^O. \tau(t, i) = (o, t') \text{ and } (q, i \cup o, q') \in \delta.$$

An annotation $\lambda : T \times Q \to \{\bot\} \cup \mathbb{N}$ is a function that maps nodes from the run graph to either unreachable $\bot$ or a natural number k. An annotation is valid if it satisfies the following conditions:

- the pair of initial states (t_0, q_0) is labeled by a natural number $(\lambda(t_0, q_0) \neq \perp)$, and
- if a pair of states (t, q) is annotated with a natural number $(\lambda(t, q) = k \neq \perp)$ then for every $i \in 2^I$ and $o \in 2^O$ with $\tau(t, i) = (o, t')$ and $(q, i \cup o, q') \in \delta$, the successor pair (t', q') is annotated with a greater number, which needs to be strictly greater if $q' \in F$ is rejecting. That is, $\lambda(t', q') \rhd_{q'} k$ where $\rhd_{q'} := >$ if $q' \in F$ and $\geq$ otherwise.

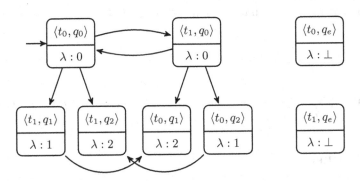

Fig. 2. Run graph of the automaton $\mathcal{A}_\psi$ and the two-state transition system $\mathcal{T}_{arb}$ from the earlier example (Fig. 1). The bottom node part displays a valid λ-annotation of the run graph.

Example 3. Figure 2 shows the run graph of $\mathcal{T}_{arb}$ and $\mathcal{A}_\psi$ from our earlier example (Fig. 1). Additionally, a valid annotation λ is provided at the second component of every node. One can verify that the annotation is correct by checking every edge individually. For example, the annotation has to increase from $\langle t_0, q_0 \rangle \to \langle t_1, q_2 \rangle$ and from $\langle t_0, q_2 \rangle \to \langle t_1, q_2 \rangle$ as q_2 is rejecting. As $\lambda(\langle t_0, q_0 \rangle) = 0$ and $\lambda(\langle t_0, q_2 \rangle) = 1$, it holds that $\lambda(\langle t_1, q_2 \rangle)$ must be at least 2.

Given $\mathcal{T}$, $\mathcal{A}$, and λ, we want to derive a propositional constraint that is satisfiable if, and only if, the annotation is valid. First, by the characterization above, we know that we can verify the annotation by local checks, i.e., we have to consider only one step in the product graph. To derive a propositional encoding, we encode $\mathcal{T}$, $\mathcal{A}$, and λ:

- $\mathcal{T} = \langle T, t_0, \tau \rangle$. We represent the transition function τ by one variable $o_{t,i}$ for every output proposition $o \in O$ and one variable $\tau_{t,i,t'}$ representing a transition form t to t'. Given $(t, t') \in T \times T$ and $i \in 2^I$, it holds that (1) $\tau_{t,i,t'}$ is true if, and only if, $\tau(t, i) = (\_, t')$, and (2) $o_{t,i}$ is true if, and only if, $\tau(t, i) = (o, \_)$ and $o \in o$.
- $\mathcal{A} = \langle Q, q_0, \delta, F \rangle$. We represent $\delta : (Q \times 2^{I \cup O} \times Q)$ as propositional formulas $\delta_{t,q,i,q'}$ over the output variables $o_{t,i}$. That is, an assignment o to the variables $o_{t,i}$ satisfies $\delta_{t,q,i,q'}$ iff $(q, i \cup o, q') \in \delta$.

- We first split the annotation λ into two parts: The first part $\lambda^{\mathbb{B}} : T \times Q \to \mathbb{B}$ represents the reachability constraint and the second part $\lambda^{\#} : T \times Q \to \mathbb{N}$ represents the bound. For every $t \in T$ and $q \in Q$ we introduce variables $\lambda^{\mathbb{B}}_{t,q}$ that we assign to be true iff the state pair is reachable from the initial state pair and a bit vector $\lambda^{\#}_{t,q}$ of length $\mathcal{O}(\log(|T| \cdot |Q|))$ that we assign the binary encoding of the value $\lambda(t, q)$.

Using the variables $o_{t,i}$, $\tau_{t,i,t'}$, $\lambda^{\mathbb{B}}_{t,q}$, and $\lambda^{\#}_{t,q}$ (which have a unique assignment for a given T, $\mathcal{A}$, and λ) as well as the propositional formulas $\delta_{t,q,i,q'}$, we construct a formula that represents that the annotation is valid:

$$\bigwedge_{q \in Q} \bigwedge_{t \in T} \left(\lambda^{\mathbb{B}}_{t,q} \to \bigwedge_{q' \in Q} \bigwedge_{i \in 2^I} \left(\delta_{t,q,i,q'} \to \bigwedge_{t' \in T} \left(\tau_{t,i,t'} \to \lambda^{\mathbb{B}}_{t',q'} \wedge \lambda^{\#}_{t',q'} \rhd_{q'} \lambda^{\#}_{t,q} \right) \right) \right)$$

Theorem 1 [14]. *Given T, $\mathcal{A}$, and an annotation λ. If the propositional encoding of T, $\mathcal{A}$, and λ satisfy the constraint system, then λ is a valid annotation.*

4   Encodings

Using the constraints developed in the last section for checking the validity of a given annotation, we now consider the problem of finding a transition system with a valid annotation.

   This section introduces four encodings, starting with the most explicit encoding and moving first to an input-symbolic variant, then to a input- and state-symbolic variant and then further to a "fully symbolic" variant which treats inputs, transition systems states and the specification automaton symbolically. The first encoding can be solved using a SAT solver, the second requires a QBF solver, and the remaining two encodings require a DQBF solver. We will indicate for each encoding the difficulty to switch from the decision variant of the problem (realizability) to the constructive variant of the problem (synthesis).

4.1   SAT: The Basic Encoding

The *basic encoding* of bounded synthesis follows almost immediately from the last section. Instead of checking that for given T, $\mathcal{A}$, and λ, the unique assignment to the variables satisfies the formula, we existentially quantify over the variables to find an assignment. We only have to add constraints that assert that the reachability information, represented in the variables $\lambda^{\mathbb{B}}_{t,q}$, is consistent, and that the transition relation, represented in the variables $\tau_{t,i,t'}$, provides at least one transition for every source state and every input. The consistency of the reachability annotation is given once we assert $\lambda^{\mathbb{B}}_{t_0,q_0}$, as the formula itself asserts that the $\lambda^{\mathbb{B}}_{t,q}$ annotations are consistent with the transition relation.

$$\exists\{\lambda^{\mathbb{B}}_{t,q}, \lambda^{\#}_{t,q} \mid t \in T, q \in Q\}$$

$$\exists\{\tau_{t,i,t'} \mid (t,t') \in T \times T, i \in 2^I\}$$

$$\exists\{o_{t,i} \mid o \in O, t \in T, i \in 2^I\}$$

$$\lambda^{\mathbb{B}}_{t_0,q_0} \wedge \bigwedge_{t \in T} \bigwedge_{i \in 2^I} \bigvee_{t' \in T} \tau_{t,i,t'}$$

$$\bigwedge_{q \in Q} \bigwedge_{t \in T} \left(\lambda^{\mathbb{B}}_{t,q} \to \bigwedge_{q' \in Q} \bigwedge_{i \in 2^I} \left(\delta_{t,q,i,q'} \to \bigwedge_{t' \in T} \left(\tau_{t,i,t'} \to \lambda^{\mathbb{B}}_{t',q'} \wedge \lambda^{\#}_{t',q'} \rhd_{q'} \lambda^{\#}_{t,q} \right) \right) \right)$$

Theorem 2. *The size of the constraint system is in* $\mathcal{O}(nm^2 \cdot 2^{|I|} \cdot (|\delta_{q,q'}| + n\log(nm)))$ *and the number of variables is in* $\mathcal{O}(n(m\log(nm) + 2^{|I|} \cdot (|O| + n)))$, *where* $n = |T|$ *and* $m = |Q|$.

Since we only quantify existentially over propositional variables, the encoding can be solved by a SAT solver. The synthesized transition system can be directly extracted from the satisfying assignment of the solver. For each state and each input, there is at least one true variable, indicating a possible successor. The variables $o_{t,i}$ indicate whether output o is given at state t for input i.

4.2 QBF: The Input-Symbolic Encoding

One immediate drawback of the encoding above is the explicit handling of the inputs in the existential quantifiers representing the transition relation τ and the outputs o, which introduces several variables for each possible input $i \in 2^I$. This leads to a constraint system that is exponential in the number of inputs, both in the size of the constraints and in the number of variables. Also, since all variables are quantified on the same level, some of the inherent structure of the problem is lost and the solver will have to assign a value to each propositional variable, which may lead to non-minimal solutions of τ and o due to unnecessary interdependencies.

By adding a universal quantification over the input variables, we obtain a quantified boolean formula (QBF) and avoid this exponential blow-up. In this encoding, the variables representing the λ-annotation remain in the outer existential quantifier - they cannot depend on the input. We then universally quantify over the valuations of the input propositions I (interpreted as variables in this encoding) before we existentially quantify over the remaining variables.

By the semantics of QBF, the innermost quantified variables, representing the transition function τ of $\mathcal{T}$, can be seen as boolean functions (Skolem functions) whose domain is the set of assignments to I. Indicating the dependency on the inputs in the quantifier hierarchy, we can now drop the indices i from the variables $\tau_{t,i,t'}$ and $o_{t,i}$. Further, we now represent $\delta : (Q \times 2^{I \cup O} \times Q)$ as propositional formulas $\delta_{t,q,q'}$ over the inputs I and output variables o_t (which depend on I) with the following property: an assignment $i \cup o$ satisfies $\delta_{t,q,q'}$ iff $(q, i \cup o, q') \in \delta$. We obtain the following formula for the input-symbolic encoding. (The gray box highlights the changes in the quantifier prefix compared to the previous encoding.)

$$\exists\{\lambda_{t,q}^{\mathbb{B}}, \lambda_{t,q}^{\#} \mid t \in T, q \in Q\}$$

$$\forall I$$

$$\exists\{\tau_{t,t'} \mid (t, t') \in T \times T\}$$

$$\exists\{o_t \mid o \in O, t \in T\}$$

$$\lambda_{t_0,q_0}^{\mathbb{B}} \wedge \bigwedge_{t \in T} \bigvee_{t' \in T} \tau_{t,t'}$$

$$\bigwedge_{q \in Q} \bigwedge_{t \in T} \left(\lambda_{t,q}^{\mathbb{B}} \rightarrow \bigwedge_{q' \in Q} \left(\delta_{t,q,q'} \rightarrow \bigwedge_{t' \in T} \left(\tau_{t,t'} \rightarrow \lambda_{t',q'}^{\mathbb{B}} \wedge \lambda_{t',q'}^{\#} \triangleright_{q'} \lambda_{t,q}^{\#} \right) \right) \right)$$

Theorem 3. *Let $n = |T|$ and $m = |Q|$. The size of the input-symbolic constraint system is in $\mathcal{O}(nm^2(|\delta_{q,q'}| + n\log(nm)))$. The number of existential and universal variables is in $\mathcal{O}(n(m\log(nm) + |O| + n))$ and $\mathcal{O}(|I|)$, respectively.*

The input-symbolic encoding is not only exponentially smaller (in $|I|$) than the basic encoding, but also enables the solver to exploit the dependency between I and the transition function τ. An additional property of this encoding that we use in the implementation is the following: If we fix the values of the λ-annotation, the resulting 2QBF query represents all transition systems that are possible with respect to the λ-annotation. Since the outermost variables are existentially quantified, their assignments (in case the formula is satisfiable) can be extracted easily, even from non-certifying QBF solvers. For synthesis, we thus employ a two-step approach. We first solve the complete encoding and, if the formula was satisfiable, extract the assignment of the annotation variables $\lambda_{t,q}^{\mathbb{B}}$ and $\lambda_{t,q}^{\#}$. In the second step we instantiate the formula by the satisfiable λ-annotation and solve the remaining formula with a certifying solver to generate boolean functions for the inner existential variables. Those can be then be translated into a realizing transition system.

4.3   DQBF/EPR: The State- and Input-Symbolic Encoding

The previous encoding shows how to describe the functional dependency between the inputs I and the transition function τ and outputs o as a quantifier alternation. The reactive synthesis problem, however, contains more functional dependencies that we can exploit.

In the following we describe an encoding that also treats the states of the system to generate symbolically. First, we change the definition of T slightly. Where before, T was the set of states of the transition system, we now consider T as the set of *state bits* of the transition system. Consequently, the state space of T is now 2^T and we consider the initial state to be the all-zero assignment to the variables T.

Since all variables depend on the state, we no longer have propositional variables. Instead, we quantify over the existence of boolean functions. Candidate logics for solving this query are dependency-quantified boolean formulas (DQBF) and the effective propositional fragment of first-order logic (EPR). While the existential quantification over functions is not immediately available in DQBF, we can encode them in a quadratic number of constraints, which is known as Ackermannization [7].

$$\exists\{\lambda_q^{\mathbb{B}}\colon 2^T \to \mathbb{B}, \lambda_q^{\#}\colon 2^T \to \mathbb{B}^b \mid q \in Q\}$$

$$\exists\tau\colon 2^T \times 2^I \to 2^T$$

$$\exists\{o\colon 2^T \times 2^I \to \mathbb{B} \mid o \in O\}$$

$$\forall I.\forall T, T'.$$

$$(T = 0 \to \lambda_{q_0}^{\mathbb{B}}(T))$$

$$\bigwedge_{q \in Q}\left(\lambda_q^{\mathbb{B}}(T) \to \bigwedge_{q' \in Q}\left(\delta_{q,q'} \wedge (\tau(T,I) \Rightarrow T') \to \lambda_{q'}^{\mathbb{B}}(T') \wedge \lambda_{q'}^{\#}(T') \rhd_{q'} \lambda_q^{\#}(T)\right)\right)$$

Theorem 4. *Let $n = |T|$ and $m = |Q|$. The size of the state-symbolic constraint system is in $\mathcal{O}(m^2(|\delta_{q,q}| + \log(nm)))$. The number of existential and universal variables is in $\mathcal{O}(n + m\log(nm) + |O|)$ and $\mathcal{O}(n + |I|)$, respectively.*

Encoding the states of the specification automaton. The last dependency that we consider here is the dependency on the state space of the specification automaton. As a precondition, we need a symbolic representation $\mathscr{A} = \langle Q, q_{\text{init}}, \delta, q_{\text{reject}}\rangle$ of a universal co-Büchi automaton over alphabet $I \cup O$, where Q is a set of variables whose valuations represent the state space, $q_{\text{init}} \in \mathbb{B}(Q)$ is a propositional formula representing the initial state, $\delta \in \mathbb{B}(Q, I \cup O, Q')$ is the transition relation $(q \cup i \cup o \cup q'$ satisfies δ iff $q \xrightarrow{i \cup o} q')$, and $q_{\text{reject}} \in \mathbb{B}(Q)$ is a formula representing the rejecting states.

$$\exists\lambda^{\mathbb{B}}\colon 2^T \times 2^Q \to \mathbb{B}, \lambda^{\#}\colon 2^T \times 2^Q \to \mathbb{B}^b$$

$$\exists\tau\colon 2^T \times 2^I \to 2^T$$

$$\exists\{o\colon 2^T \times 2^I \to \mathbb{B} \mid o \in O\}$$

$$\forall I.\forall T, T'.\forall Q, Q'.$$

$$(t_{\text{init}} \wedge q_{\text{init}} \to \lambda^{\mathbb{B}}(T, Q)) \wedge$$

$$\left(\lambda^{\mathbb{B}}(T, Q) \to \left(\delta \wedge (\tau(T,I) \Rightarrow T') \to \lambda^{\mathbb{B}}(T', Q') \wedge \lambda^{\#}(T', Q') \rhd_{q'_{\text{reject}}} \lambda^{\#}(T, Q)\right)\right)$$

Theorem 5. *Let $n = |T|$ and $m = |Q|$. The size of the state-symbolic constraint system is in $\mathcal{O}(n + m + |\delta| + \log(nm))$. The number of existential and universal variables is in $\mathcal{O}(\log n + |O|)$ and $\mathcal{O}(n + m + |I|)$, respectively.*

4.4   Comparison

Table 1 compares the sizes of the encodings presented in this paper. From the basic propositional encoding, we developed more symbolic encodings by making

Table 1. The table compares the encodings with respect to the number of variables and the size of the constraint system. We indicate the number of states of the transition system and the automaton by n and m, respectively.

	# existentials	# universals	Constraint size
Basic	$n(m\log(nm) + 2^{|I|} \cdot (|O| + n))$	-	$nm^2 \cdot 2^{|I|} \cdot (|\delta_{q,q'}| + n\log(nm))$
Input-symbolic	$n(m\log(nm) + |O| + n)$	$|I|$	$nm^2(|\delta_{q,q'}| + n\log(nm))$
State-symbolic	$n + m\log(nm) + |O|$	$n + |I|$	$m^2(|\delta_{q,q'}| + \log(nm))$
Symbolic	$\log n + |O|$	$n + m + |I|$	$n + m + |\delta| + \log(nm)$

dependencies explicit and employing Boolean functions. This conciseness, however, comes with the price of higher solving complexity. In the following section we study this tradeoff empirical.

5   Experimental Evaluation

5.1   Implementation

We implemented the encodings described in this paper in a tool called *BoSy*[1]. The LTL to automaton conversion is provided by the tool ltl3ba [1]. We reduce the number of counters and their size by only keeping them for automaton states within a rejecting strongly connected component, as proposed in [21]. The tool searches for a system implementation and a counter-strategy for the environment in parallel. An exponential search strategy is employed for the bound on the size of the transition system. In synthesis mode, we apply as a post-processing step circuit minimization provided by ABC [6].

For solving the non-symbolic encoding, we translate the propositional query to the DIMACS file format and solve it using the CryptoMiniSat SAT solver in version 5. The satisfying assignment is used to construct the realizing transition system.

The input-symbolic encoding is translated to the QDIMACS file format and is solved by a combination of the QBF preprocessor Bloqqer [2] and QBF solver RAReQS [18]. The solution extraction is implemented in two steps. For satisfiable queries, we first derive a top level (λ) assignment [26] and instantiate the QBF query using this assignment which results in a 2QBF query that represents transition systems that satisfy the specification. This is then solved using a certifying QBF solver, such as QuAbS [28], CADET [23], or CAQE [24]. Among those, QuAbS performed best and was used in the evaluation. The resulting resulting Skolem functions, represented as AIGER circuit, are transformed into a representation of the transition system.

The symbolic encodings are translated to DQDIMACS file format and solved by the DQBF solver iDQ [16]. Due to limited solver support, we have not implemented solution extraction.

---

[1] The tool is available at https://react.uni-saarland.de/tools/bosy/.

Table 2. Implementation matrix

	Basic	Input-symbolic	State-symbolic	Symbolic
Fragment	SAT	QBF	DQBF/EPR	DQBF/EPR
Mealy/Moore	●/●	●/●	●/●	●/●
Solution extraction	●	●	○	○

For comparison, we also implemented an SMT version using the classical encoding [14]. We also tested the state-symbolic and symbolic encoding with state-of-the art EPR solvers, but the solving times were not competitive. Table 2 gives an overview over the capabilities of the implemented encodings.

5.2 Setup and Benchmarks

For our experiments, we used a machine with a 3.6 GHz quad-core Intel Xeon processor and 32 GB of memory. The timeout and memout were set to 1 h and 8 GB, respectively. We use the LTL benchmark sets from the latest reactive synthesis competition (SYNTCOMP 2016) [17]. The benchmarks include a variety of arbiter specifications of increasing complexity, load balancers, buffers, detectors as well as benchmark suites from previously existing tools. Some of the benchmark classes are parameterized in the number of clients or masters, which allows scaling them for experimental purposes. In total, the realizability benchmark suite of SYNTCOMP 2016 consists of 195 benchmarks. We have additionally added six instances from scalable benchmark classes of this set to cover larger parameter values, resulting in a total size of 201 benchmarks for our benchmark set.

For comparison, we run the other two solves that participated in the SYNT-COMP 2016, that is Acacia [5], a game-based solver, and Party [20], a variant of the SMT bounded synthesis.

5.3 Realizability

In Table 3, we report results on realizability for all scalable instances from the aforementioned competition. We have omitted the results of our fully symbolic encoding from the table, since it could not solve a single instance of the selected benchmarks. The results from our own SMT encoding are also omitted, since they are very close to the results of the tool Party. Highlighted are those entries which reach the highest parameter value among the solvers and the best cumulative runtime within the class of instances.

An overall comparison of all realizability solvers on the full benchmark set is provided in Fig. 3. For the individual solvers, we track the number of instances solved by this solver within a certain time bound.

Table 3. Experimental results on selected scalable instances. Reported is the maximal parameter value k for which the instance could be solved and the cumulative solving time t (in seconds) up to this point.

instance	basic max k	basic sum t	input-sym max k	input-sym sum t	state-sym max k	state-sym sum t	Acacia max k	Acacia sum t	Party max k	Party sum t
simple-arbiter	7	1008.7	8	2.7	3	100.5	8	59.2	6	902.7
full-arbiter	4	2994.5	3	0.6	2	13.3	5	2683.4	3	111.7
roundrob-arbiter	4	143.1	4	227.0	2	11.0	4	345.6	4	19.2
loadfull	5	268.7	8	44.2	2	25.1	4	83.7	4	213.5
prio-abiter	4	176.5	4	1.6	2	0.4	6	701.2	3	69.0
loadcomp	5	36.9	6	639.4	3	432.1	5	387.8	5	212.7
genbuf	2	1840.3	2	2711.8	0	–	5	159.3	0	–
generalized-buffer	2	2093.8	2	3542.8	0	–	6	3194.8	2	792.5
load-balancer	5	1148.8	8	83.2	2	75.3	5	270.8	0	–
detector	6	1769.0	8	1010.7	3	239.4	8	261.6	5	370.3

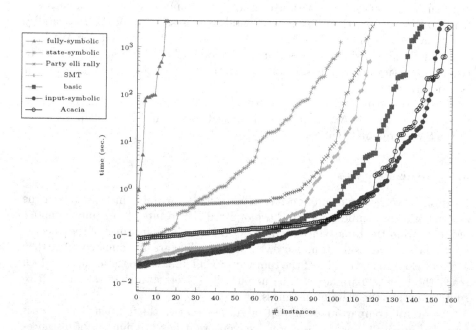

Fig. 3. Number of solved instances within 1 h among the 201 instances from SYNTCOMP 2016. The time axis has logarithmic scale.

5.4   Synthesis

To evaluate the different encodings in terms of their solutions to the synthesis problem and to compare with other competing tools, we measure the size of the provided solutions. In line with the rules of SYNTCOMP, the synthesized transition system is encoded as an AIGER circuit. The size of the result is measured in terms of the number of AND gates. In the comparisons, we only consider instances where both solvers in the comparison had a result. All resulting circuits have been minimized using ABC.

First, we compare in the scatter plot of Fig. 4 the propositional, non-symbolic encoding to the input-symbolic encoding. Since most points are below the diagonal and are therefore smaller than their counterparts, the input-symbolic solutions are better in size compared to the non-symbolic encoding.

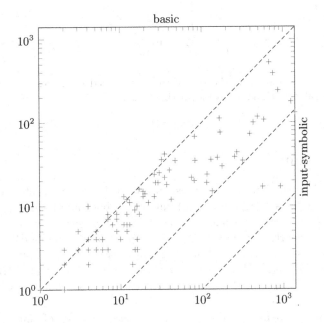

Fig. 4. Scatter plot comparing the size of the synthesized strategies between the basic (Sect. 4.1) and input-symbolic (Sect. 4.2) encoding. Both axes have logarithmic scale.

In Fig. 5, we compare our input-symbolic encoding against two competing tools. On the left, we observe that the solution sizes of our input-symbolic encoding are significantly better (observe the log-log scale) than the solutions provided by Acacia. The reason for the size difference is that the strategies of Acacia may depend on the current state of the specification automaton, as they are extracted from the resulting safety game. When comparing to the SMT-based Party tool, we again see a strict improvement in terms of strategy size, but not as significant as for Acacia.

We thus observe that the ability to universally quantify over the inputs and extract the transition system from the functional descriptions leads to advantages in terms of the size of the solution strategies.

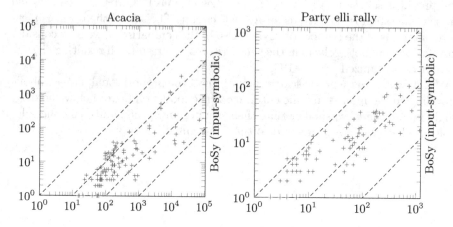

Fig. 5. Scatter plot comparing the size of the synthesized strategies of BoSy, Acacia, and Party elli rally. Both axes have logarithmic scale.

6 Conclusion

We have revisited the bounded synthesis problem [14] and presented alternative encodings into boolean formulas (SAT), quantified boolean formulas (QBF), and dependency-quantified boolean formulas (DQBF). Our evaluation shows that the QBF approach clearly dominates the SAT approach and the DQBF approach, and also previous approaches to bounded synthesis – both in terms of the number of instances solved and in the size of the solutions. This demonstrates that, while modern QBF-solvers effectively exploit the input-symbolic representation, current DQBF solvers cannot yet take similar advantage of the state-symbolic representation. The benchmarks obtained from the encodings of bounded synthesis problems should therefore be useful in improving current solvers, in particular for DQBF.

References

1. Babiak, T., Křetínský, M., Řehák, V., Strejček, J.: LTL to Büchi automata translation: fast and more deterministic. In: Flanagan, C., König, B. (eds.) TACAS 2012. LNCS, vol. 7214, pp. 95–109. Springer, Heidelberg (2012). doi:10.1007/978-3-642-28756-5_8
2. Biere, A., Lonsing, F., Seidl, M.: Blocked clause elimination for QBF. In: Bjørner, N., Sofronie-Stokkermans, V. (eds.) CADE 2011. LNCS (LNAI), vol. 6803, pp. 101–115. Springer, Heidelberg (2011). doi:10.1007/978-3-642-22438-6_10

3. Bloem, R., Galler, S.J., Jobstmann, B., Piterman, N., Pnueli, A., Weiglhofer, M.: Interactive presentation: automatic hardware synthesis from specifications: a case study. In: Proceedings of DATE, pp. 1188–1193. EDA Consortium, San Jose, CA, USA (2007)

4. Bloem, R., Könighofer, R., Seidl, M.: SAT-based synthesis methods for safety specs. In: McMillan, K.L., Rival, X. (eds.) VMCAI 2014. LNCS, vol. 8318, pp. 1–20. Springer, Heidelberg (2014). doi:10.1007/978-3-642-54013-4_1

5. Bohy, A., Bruyère, V., Filiot, E., Jin, N., Raskin, J.-F.: Acacia+, a tool for LTL synthesis. In: Madhusudan, P., Seshia, S.A. (eds.) CAV 2012. LNCS, vol. 7358, pp. 652–657. Springer, Heidelberg (2012). doi:10.1007/978-3-642-31424-7_45

6. Brayton, R., Mishchenko, A.: ABC: an academic industrial-strength verification tool. In: Touili, T., Cook, B., Jackson, P. (eds.) CAV 2010. LNCS, vol. 6174, pp. 24–40. Springer, Heidelberg (2010). doi:10.1007/978-3-642-14295-6_5

7. Bruttomesso, R., Cimatti, A., Franzén, A., Griggio, A., Santuari, A., Sebastiani, R.: To ackermann-ize or not to ackermann-ize? on efficiently handling uninterpreted function symbols in $SMT(\mathcal{EUF} \cup \mathcal{T})$. In: Hermann, M., Voronkov, A. (eds.) LPAR 2006. LNCS (LNAI), vol. 4246, pp. 557–571. Springer, Heidelberg (2006). doi:10.1007/11916277_38

8. Büchi, J.R., Landweber, L.H.: Solving sequential conditions by finite-state strategies. Trans. Am. Math. Soc. **138**, 295–311 (1969). http://www.jstor.org/stable/1994916

9. Ehlers, R.: Unbeast: symbolic bounded synthesis. In: Abdulla, P.A., Leino, K.R.M. (eds.) TACAS 2011. LNCS, vol. 6605, pp. 272–275. Springer, Heidelberg (2011). doi:10.1007/978-3-642-19835-9_25

10. Finkbeiner, B.: Bounded synthesis for petri games. In: Meyer, R., Platzer, A., Wehrheim, H. (eds.) Correct System Design. LNCS, vol. 9360, pp. 223–237. Springer, Heidelberg (2015). doi:10.1007/978-3-319-23506-6_15

11. Finkbeiner, B., Jacobs, S.: Lazy synthesis. In: Kuncak, V., Rybalchenko, A. (eds.) VMCAI 2012. LNCS, vol. 7148, pp. 219–234. Springer, Heidelberg (2012). doi:10.1007/978-3-642-27940-9_15

12. Finkbeiner, B., Klein, F.: Bounded cycle synthesis. In: Chaudhuri, S., Farzan, A. (eds.) CAV 2016. LNCS, vol. 9779, pp. 118–135. Springer, Heidelberg (2016). doi:10.1007/978-3-319-41528-4_7

13. Finkbeiner, B., Schewe, S.: SMT-based synthesis of distributed systems. In: Proceedings of AFM (2007)

14. Finkbeiner, B., Schewe, S.: Bounded synthesis. STTT **15**(5–6), 519–539 (2013)

15. Finkbeiner, B., Tentrup, L.: Detecting unrealizable specifications of distributed systems. In: Ábrahám, E., Havelund, K. (eds.) TACAS 2014. LNCS, vol. 8413, pp. 78–92. Springer, Heidelberg (2014). doi:10.1007/978-3-642-54862-8_6

16. Fröhlich, A., Kovásznai, G., Biere, A., Veith, H.: iDQ: Instantiation-based DQBF solving. In: Proceedings of POS@SAT. EPiC Series in Computing, vol. 27, pp. 103–116. EasyChair (2014)

17. Jacobs, S., Bloem, R., Brenguier, R., Khalimov, A., Klein, F., Könighofer, R., Kreber, J., Legg, A., Narodytska, N., Pérez, G.A., Raskin, J., Ryzhyk, L., Sankur, O., Seidl, M., Tentrup, L., Walker, A.: The 3rd reactive synthesis competition (SYNTCOMP 2016): Benchmarks, participants and results. In: Proceedings Fifth Workshop on Synthesis, SYNT@CAV 2016, Toronto, Canada, 17–18 July, 2016. EPTCS, vol. 229, pp. 149–177 (2016)

18. Janota, M., Klieber, W., Marques-Silva, J., Clarke, E.M.: Solving QBF with counterexample guided refinement. Artif. Intell. **234**, 1–25 (2016)

19. Jobstmann, B., Galler, S., Weiglhofer, M., Bloem, R.: Anzu: a tool for property synthesis. In: Damm, W., Hermanns, H. (eds.) CAV 2007. LNCS, vol. 4590, pp. 258–262. Springer, Heidelberg (2007). doi:10.1007/978-3-540-73368-3_29

20. Khalimov, A., Jacobs, S., Bloem, R.: PARTY parameterized synthesis of token rings. In: Sharygina, N., Veith, H. (eds.) CAV 2013. LNCS, vol. 8044, pp. 928–933. Springer, Heidelberg (2013). doi:10.1007/978-3-642-39799-8_66

21. Khalimov, A., Jacobs, S., Bloem, R.: Towards efficient parameterized synthesis. In: Giacobazzi, R., Berdine, J., Mastroeni, I. (eds.) VMCAI 2013. LNCS, vol. 7737, pp. 108–127. Springer, Heidelberg (2013). doi:10.1007/978-3-642-35873-9_9

22. Kupferman, O., Vardi, M.Y.: Safraless decision procedures. In: Proceedings of FOCS, pp. 531–542. IEEE Computer Society (2005)

23. Rabe, M.N., Seshia, S.A.: Incremental determinization. In: Creignou, N., Le Berre, D. (eds.) SAT 2016. LNCS, vol. 9710, pp. 375–392. Springer, Heidelberg (2016). doi:10.1007/978-3-319-40970-2_23

24. Rabe, M.N., Tentrup, L.: CAQE: a certifying QBF solver. In: Proceedings of FMCAD, pp. 136–143. IEEE (2015)

25. Schewe, S., Finkbeiner, B.: Bounded synthesis. In: Namjoshi, K.S., Yoneda, T., Higashino, T., Okamura, Y. (eds.) ATVA 2007. LNCS, vol. 4762, pp. 474–488. Springer, Heidelberg (2007). doi:10.1007/978-3-540-75596-8_33

26. Seidl, M., Könighofer, R.: Partial witnesses from preprocessed quantified boolean formulas. In: Proceedings of DATE, pp. 1–6. European Design and Automation Association (2014)

27. Shimakawa, M., Hagihara, S., Yonezaki, N.: Reducing bounded realizability analysis to reachability checking. In: Bojańczyk, M., Lasota, S., Potapov, I. (eds.) RP 2015. LNCS, vol. 9328, pp. 140–152. Springer, Heidelberg (2015). doi:10.1007/978-3-319-24537-9_13

28. Tentrup, L.: Solving QBF by abstraction. CoRR abs/1604.06752 (2016)

Tools

HQSpre – An Effective Preprocessor
for QBF and DQBF

Ralf Wimmer[(✉)], Sven Reimer, Paolo Marin, and Bernd Becker

Albert-Ludwigs-Universität Freiburg, Freiburg im Breisgau, Germany
{wimmer,reimer,marin,becker}@informatik.uni-freiburg.de

Abstract. We present our new preprocessor HQSPRE, a state-of-the-art tool for simplifying quantified Boolean formulas (QBFs) and the first available preprocessor for dependency quantified Boolean formulas (DQBFs). The latter are a generalization of QBFs, resulting from adding so-called Henkin-quantifiers to QBFs. HQSPRE applies most of the preprocessing techniques that have been proposed in the literature. It can be used both as a standalone tool and as a library. It is possible to tailor it towards different solver back-ends, e. g., to preserve the circuit structure of the formula when a non-CNF solver back-end is used. Extensive experiments show that HQSPRE allows QBF solvers to solve more benchmark instances and is able to decide more instances on its own than state-of-the-art tools. The same impact can be observed in the DQBF domain as well.

1 Introduction

Solvers for Boolean formulas have proven to be powerful tools for many applications, ranging from CAD, e. g., for formal verification [4] and circuit test [11], to artificial intelligence [33]. They are not only of academic interest, but have also gained acceptance in industry. While solvers for deciding satisfiability of quantifier-free propositional formulas (the famous SAT-problem [5]) have reached a certain level of maturity during the last years, solving quantified and dependency quantified Boolean formulas (QBFs and DQBFs [27], resp.) is still a hot topic in research. In particular, the last two decades have brought enormous progress in solving QBFs [16,19,25,29] and the last five years also in solving DQBFs [12,13,15]. With increasing improvements of solver technology also new applications have arisen which could not be handled (or only handled approximately) before, such as verification of partial designs [14,35], controller synthesis [7], and games with incomplete information [27].

One part of this success is due to improved solution methods not only based on depth-first search (the QDPLL algorithm) as implemented in solvers like

This work was supported by the German Research Council (DFG) as part of the project "Solving Dependency Quantified Boolean Formulas" and by the Sino-German Center for Research Promotion (CDZ) as part of the project CAP (GZ 1023).

© Springer-Verlag GmbH Germany 2017
A. Legay and T. Margaria (Eds.): TACAS 2017, Part I, LNCS 10205, pp. 373–390, 2017.
DOI: 10.1007/978-3-662-54577-5_21

DEPQBF [25], QUBE [16], and AQUA (see [32]), but also using quantifier elimination as applied by AIGSOLVE [29] and QUANTOR [2], counterexample-guided abstraction refinement, which is the principle underlying the solvers GHOSTQ [22], RAREQS [19], and QESTO [20], and further algorithms. Another protagonist are sophisticated preprocessing techniques. Their goal is to simplify the formula using algorithms of lower complexity (mostly polynomial) than the actual decision problem before the solver is called. This can reduce the overall computation time by orders of magnitude and, most interestingly, it can even make solving instances feasible which cannot be solved without preprocessing.

Many techniques have been proposed for preprocessing and implemented in different tools. One can distinguish between four main types of preprocessor routines: clause elimination, clause strengthening, variable elimination, and other formula modifications. We will discuss these categories and the corresponding techniques in Sect. 2.2. All of them yield an equisatisfiable formula, which is typically easier to solve than the original one.

Contribution. In this paper, we present the new tool HQSPRE, which supports most preprocessing techniques for QBFs and extends them to DQBFs. It is the first available tool for preprocessing DQBFs. The available QBF tools like SQUEEZEBF and BLOQQER only have a subset of these techniques available. HQSPRE can be used both as a standalone tool and as a library. It is designed to be easily extensible and adaptable to different solver back-ends. For instance, if the back-end solver is not CNF-based, but rather works on a circuit representation of the formula, the preprocessor takes care not to destroy this structure, e.g., by forbidding the application of clause elimination routines to clauses that encode circuit gates.

We provide an extensive experimental evaluation where we show that HQSPRE is state of the art: *(1)* it enables state-of-the-art QBF solvers (AIGSOLVE [29], AQUA [32], CAQE [38], DEPQBF [25], QESTO [20], and RAREQS [19]) to solve more instances in less time than using the alternative preprocessors SQUEEZEBF [17] and BLOQQER [6], and it is robust over different kinds of solvers; *(2)* HQSPRE is very effective on DQBFs as well, as it is able to solve directly or to simplify into QBFs many formulas, and lets DQBF solvers decide several more problems.

HQSPRE is available as an open source tool. The most recent version can be downloaded from:

https://projects.informatik.uni-freiburg.de/projects/dqbf/files.

Structure of this Paper. In the following section, we introduce the necessary foundations and describe the different preprocessing techniques and how they are implemented in HQSPRE. Section 3 contains the results of our experiments. Finally, in Sect. 4, we conclude this paper with an outlook on future work.

2   Preprocessing Techniques in HQSPRE

2.1   Foundations

Let V be a set of Boolean variables. We consider (dependency) quantified Boolean formulas in *prenex conjunctive normal form (PCNF)*: a quantifier-free Boolean formula is in CNF if it is a conjunction of clauses. A *clause* is a disjunction of literals, and a *literal* is either a variable $v \in V$ or its negation $\neg v$. We write clauses in the form $\{v_1, \ldots, v_n\}$ with literals v_i. A clause is called *unit* if it contains only one literal, and called *binary* if it contains two literals. We denote the size of a formula as the number of all literals in all clauses. A formula is in PCNF if it can be split into a quantifier prefix and a Boolean formula in CNF, the matrix of the formula.

Definition 1. *Let $V = \{v_1, \ldots, v_n\}$ be a set of Boolean variables and φ a quantifier-free Boolean formula over V. A quantified Boolean formula (QBF) ψ has the form $\psi = Q_1 v_1 \ldots Q_n v_n : \varphi$ with $Q_i \in \{\forall, \exists\}$ and $v_i \in V$ for $i = 1, \ldots, n$. $Q_1 v_1 \ldots Q_n v_n$ is called the* quantifier prefix *and φ the* matrix *of ψ.*

We denote universal variables with x, and existential ones with y. If the quantifier does not matter, we use v. Accordingly, ℓ is an arbitrary literal, $\ell^{\exists}$ a literal with an existential variable, and $\ell^{\forall}$ a universal literal. For a literal ℓ, we define $\mathrm{var}(\ell)$ as the corresponding variable, i.e., $\mathrm{var}(v) = \mathrm{var}(\neg v) = v$.

The quantifier prefix imposes a linear order on the variables. One can think of a QBF as a two-player game: one player assigns the existential variables, the other player the universal ones. The game proceeds turn-based according to the prefix from left to right: When it is the existential player's turn, he assigns the corresponding existential variable, and similarly for the universal player. The goal of the existential player is to satisfy the formula, the universal player wants to falsify it. The formula is satisfiable if the existential player has a winning strategy, i.e., if he can satisfy the formula no matter how the universal player assigns his variables.

Dependency quantified Boolean formulas are a generalization of QBFs. They are obtained syntactically by relaxing the requirement of a linearly ordered prefix and making the dependencies explicit, and semantically by restricting the knowledge of the players.

Definition 2. *Let $V = \{x_1, \ldots, x_n, y_1, \ldots, y_m\}$ be a set of Boolean variables and φ a quantifier-free Boolean formula over V in CNF. A dependency quantified Boolean formula (DQBF) Ψ has the form $\forall x_1 \ldots \forall x_n \exists y_1(D_{y_1}) \ldots \exists y_m(D_{y_m}) : \varphi$, where $D_{y_i} \subseteq \{x_1, \ldots, x_n\}$ for $i = 1, \ldots, m$ is the* dependency set *of y_i.*

In contrast to QBF, a DQBF can be considered as a game with partial information: The universal player assigns all universal variables in the beginning. The existential player assigns a value to each existential variable y based only on the assignment of the universal variables in the corresponding dependency set D_y.

A DQBF is equivalent to a QBF iff for all existential variables y, y' the condition $D_y \subseteq D_{y'}$ or $D_{y'} \subseteq D_y$ holds.

Algorithm 1. Outline of the main preprocessing routine. Note that after each routine, a fast formula simplification procedure is called. Universal reduction and subsumption checks are performed for each added or modified clause.

Preprocess((D)QBF $\psi = Q : \varphi$)	
begin	
$\quad$ simplify(ψ)	(1)
$\quad$ **repeat**	(2)
$\quad\quad$ **if** iteration $\leq$ gateConvLoops **then**	(3)
$\quad\quad\quad$ gates $\leftarrow$ gateDetection(ψ)	(4)
$\quad\quad\quad$ gateSubstitutionAndRewriting(ψ, gates); simplify(ψ)	(5)
$\quad\quad$ **end if**	(6)
$\quad\quad$ eliminateClauses(ψ); simplify(ψ) $\quad\lhd$ *Hidden/covered TE/SE/BCE*	(7)
$\quad\quad$ selfsubsumingResolution(ψ); simplify(ψ)	(8)
$\quad\quad$ variableEliminationByResolution(ψ); simplify(ψ)	(9)
$\quad\quad$ syntacticConstants(ψ); simplify(ψ)	(10)
$\quad\quad$ **if** first iteration **then**	(11)
$\quad\quad\quad$ semanticConstants(ψ); simplify(ψ)	(12)
$\quad\quad\quad$ trivialMatrixChecks(ψ)	(13)
$\quad\quad$ **end if**	(14)
$\quad\quad$ universalExpansion(ψ); simplify(ψ)	(15)
$\quad$ **until** ψ has not been changed anymore or ψ is decided	(16)
$\quad$ **return** ψ	(17)
end	

DQBFs are strictly more expressive than QBFs. While deciding satisfiability of QBFs is PSPACE complete [26], deciding DQBFs is NEXPTIME complete [27].

2.2 Preprocessing Techniques

The goal of preprocessing the formula before the actual solution process is to simplify the formula. Experience suggests that benefits of preprocessing increase with the difficulty of the decision problem. As mentioned already in the introduction, the techniques that we apply in our preprocessor HQSPRE can be grouped into four different classes: (1) variable elimination, (2) clause elimination, (3) clause strengthening, and (4) other formula modification routines. Due to space restrictions, we cannot provide all details of the techniques. For more information we refer the reader to the cited literature. We present more details for routines which (a) are not described or applied in the literature so far or (b) have interesting implementation details.

Algorithm 1 gives an overview of the main preprocessing routine which calls the different techniques in a loop until the formula does not change anymore.

Variable Elimination Routines. We define variable elimination routines as methods which are able to remove a variable v from the formula φ. The first kind of such techniques can eliminate v whenever we can fix the truth value of v and propagate it through φ using *Boolean constraint propagation (BCP)* [5]. Common techniques are the detection of *constant* and *pure* literals [5]. For efficiency reasons both kinds are usually only checked syntactically: a literal ℓ is constant if there exists a unit clause $\{\ell\}$ in φ, and a literal ℓ is pure if φ does not contain $\neg\ell$ in any clause. Both conditions can be easily generalized to (D)QBF [40].

We also apply a check for constants using another syntactic criterion over binary clauses. For this, we first determine the transitive implication closure, i.e., binary clauses of the form: $\{\neg\ell_1, \ell_2\}$, $\{\neg\ell_2, \ell_3\}$, $\{\neg\ell_3, \ell_4\}$, ..., $\{\neg\ell_{n-1}, \ell_n\}$, and $\{\neg\ell_n, \neg\ell_1\}$. These clauses represent a chain of implications: if ℓ_1 is assigned the truth value $\top$, we can deduce that also $\ell_2, \ell_3, \ell_4, \ldots, \ell_n$ get the truth value $\top$ in the example above, and this in turn implies that ℓ_1 has to get the truth value $\bot$, i.e., ℓ_1 implies $\neg\ell_1$, which is a contradiction. So the matrix will be unsatisfied, if we set ℓ_1 to $\top$. Hence, we can deduce $\neg\ell_1$ to be a constant literal.

Additionally, we use a SAT-based constant check as described in [30], which is able to detect constants semantically. For this the matrix φ is passed to an incremental SAT solver and it is determined whether $\varphi \wedge \ell$ is unsatisfiable. In this case, $\neg\ell$ is constant. This method reasons only over the matrix without consideration of the dependencies and can therefore be applied without any restrictions for (D)QBF. However, ignoring the quantifiers makes this method incomplete for (D)QBF.

Another well known variable elimination technique is the detection of *equivalences*, i.e., determining whether a literal ℓ_1 is logically equivalent to another literal ℓ_2. In this case, one of the variables can be eliminated by replacing all occurrences with the other one. In the (D)QBF case one has to take into account the quantifiers and the dependencies of the affected variables. A very efficient syntactic check to detect equivalent literals is to represent all binary clauses as a directed graph and to determine the strongly connected components (SCCs) within this graph. Every literal which is contained in such an SCC is equivalent to all other literals in the same component [9]. We refer to [40] for details.

The basic (syntactic) detection and propagation of constant and pure literals as well as equivalent literals can be (and were) implemented very efficiently and turned out to be a necessary feature to let preprocessing scale. Hence, in our implementation we apply these three methods[1] after each and every more complex technique until a fixed-point is reached. This is referred to as the `simplify()` method in Algorithm 1.

After eliminating unit, pure, and equivalent literals, we start the main preprocessing loop by applying *gate substitution* [10]. To do so, we first identify definitions of logical gates within the formula, which can, e.g., result from applying Tseitin transformation [39] to a circuit (see Algorithm 1, line 4). In particular, we seek for AND gates with an arbitrary number of inputs and 2-input XOR gates [29]. For both we allow arbitrary negations on both inputs and output.[2] As many (D)QBF instances result from applications with circuits, the number

---

[1] The syntactic constant detection using transitive implication chains is *not* included.

[2] Note, this covers also OR gates with arbitrarily negated inputs and output.

of detectable gates can be very large. Once a gate definition is found, the variable y_{out}, defining the gate output, is no longer needed. Instead y_{out} is replaced in each and every clause by its definition. The defining clauses can be deleted afterwards. This direct substitution often produces smaller formulas than eliminating y_{out} by resolution (see next paragraphs), but can nevertheless produce very large formulas in some cases. Hence, it is only performed if the formula does not grow above a user-given bound. It is important that this technique is applied early, since many other methods, in particular the clause elimination methods (see next section), might eliminate gate defining clauses. To overcome this issue we optionally apply the concept of frozen variables and clauses [23] for gate definitions, i. e., these variables and clauses are excluded from elimination methods (with the exception of unit, pure, and equivalent literal detection).

Lastly, there are techniques for the elimination of existential and universal variables applying resolution and universal expansion, respectively. For both, the QBF generalization can be found in [5], and the DQBF version in [40]. Generally speaking, both methods eliminate a variable at the cost of expanding the formula.

Variable elimination by resolution can be applied for any existential variable y depending on all universal variables. In this case, we obtain an equisatisfiable formula by adding all possible resolvents with the pivot y and removing all clauses containing y or $\neg y$. The resolution of a variable is performed if the estimated size of the formula does not grow beyond a threshold (which is usually set to zero, i. e., resolution is only performed if the formula does not grow).

We observed a special case of resolution which is efficiently identified and always leads to a smaller formula. Therefore, we perform these resolutions more frequently – namely during BCP and blocked clause elimination (see clause elimination routines). If an existential literal $\ell^\exists$ only occurs in exactly one binary clause $\{\ell^\exists, \ell\}$ ($\neg\ell^\exists$ can occur arbitrarily often), then resolution of the pivot literal $\ell^\exists$ yields resolvents in which $\neg\ell^\exists$ is replaced by ℓ w. r. t. the original clauses. In our implementation we simply remove the clause $\{\ell^\exists, \ell\}$ and replace $\neg\ell^\exists$ with ℓ in every clause. This procedure is sound as long as $\mathrm{var}(\ell)$ is also existential and $D_{\mathrm{var}(\ell)} \subseteq D_{\mathrm{var}(\ell^\exists)}$ or $\mathrm{var}(\ell)$ is universal and $\mathrm{var}(\ell^\exists)$ depends on it.

Universal expansion [8,40] of a universal variable x allows to remove x by introducing a copy y' for every existential variable y depending on x, which has to depend on the same variables as y. Therefore every clause in which y occurs has to be copied, too, such that y is replaced by y' in the copy. Every occurrence of x in the original part of the formula is now replaced by $\top$, and every occurrence in the copied part is replaced by $\bot$ (or vice versa) resulting in an equisatisfiable formula. In our DQBF benchmark set, the number of depending existential variables is often very large and therefore we obtain a huge blow-up of the formula. Hence, in our implementation we do not apply universal expansion for DQBF. In contrast, in QBF many benchmark classes have quite small universal quantifier blocks. In this case, it turns out that the elimination of a complete universal block is often very beneficial, whereas expansion of single variables in large blocks does have a rather small impact. Therefore, we try to expand blocks with small sizes (< 20). We always try to expand the whole block as long as the blow-up of the formula is at most 50% per variable. After each expansion step we also apply variable elimination by resolution in order to reduce the potential number of copied existential variables in the next steps as suggested in [8].

Clause Elimination Routines. As clause elimination routines [18] we understand techniques which eliminate a clause c such that deleting c yields an equisatisfiable formula.

The simplest form of clause elimination is *tautology elimination (TE)*: A clause $c \in \varphi$ is a tautology iff c contains both the literals ℓ and $\neg \ell$. Tautological clauses can be eliminated from φ. This condition is independent from the quantifier and hence can be applied for QBF and DQBF without any restrictions.

Another well-known technique is *subsumption elimination (SE)* [5]. A clause $c \in \varphi$ is subsumed if there exists another clause $c' \in \varphi$ such that the set of occurring literals in c' are a subset of those in c, i.e., if $\exists c' \in \varphi : c' \subseteq c$. In this case, c can be removed from φ. This technique is applied whenever new clauses are added to the formula and for each clause which was strengthened (see next section). Subsumption can be applied without any restrictions in the same manner for QBF as for DQBF as it yields a logically equivalent matrix.

Recently, *blocked clause elimination (BCE)* [21] has been intensively investigated. It was generalized to QBF in [6] and to DQBF in [40]. A clause $c \in \varphi$ is *blocked* if there is an existential literal $\ell^\exists \in c$ such that *every* resolvent with the pivot literal $\ell^\exists$ and the clause c is a tautology and the variable v which is responsible for the resolvent being a tautology is either universal and $\mathrm{var}(\ell^\exists)$ depends on v or v is existential and v's dependencies are a subset of $\mathrm{var}(\ell^\exists)$'s dependencies (in the QBF context this means that v is left of $\mathrm{var}(\ell^\exists)$ in the quantifier prefix). Such a blocked clause can be removed from φ without changing satisfiability. See the given literature for further details.

Furthermore, all clause elimination routines can be extended by adding so-called *hidden* and *covered* literals [18]. Simply speaking, these methods identify literals which can be added to c without changing satisfiability. These literals are added temporarily to c, obtaining a clause c'. TE, SE and BCE can be applied to c', resulting in *hidden/covered tautology/subsumption/blocked clause elimination* [18]. In case the checks were unsuccessful, the additional literals are removed. The intuition behind this literal addition is the following: The more literals a clause c contains, the more likely c is either a tautology, subsumed, or blocked. These methods are generalized to (D)QBF in [6,40], except for TE and SE with hidden/covered literals to DQBF. It is rather easy to see that these methods are sound, too; therefore we do not state an explicit proof here.

In our implementation we perform all clause elimination routines in a loop until a fixed-point is reached, i.e., until no further changes to the formula can be made (see Algorithm 1, line 7). To do so, we keep a queue of clause candidates, which are updated after removing a clause from the formula. Whenever a clause $c = \{\ell_1, \ldots, \ell_n\}$ has been removed, every clause in which at least one of the literals $\ell_1, \neg\ell_1, \ldots, \ell_n, \neg\ell_n$ occurs becomes a new candidate to be removed by one of the above methods.

Clause Strengthening Routines. Clause strengthening routines try to eliminate literals from a clause while preserving the truth value of the formula. We identify two main ways to do so.

Universal reduction (QBF [5], DQBF [1]) removes a universal literal $\ell^\forall$ from a clause $c \in \varphi$ if there are no existential literals $\ell^\exists$ in c that depend on $\ell^\forall$. In our implementation universal reduction is applied for every added clause as well as for every clause that was strengthened by self-subsuming resolution.

Self-subsuming resolution [10] identifies two clauses c_1 and c_2 with $\ell \in c_1$, $\neg\ell \in c_2$ and $c_2 \setminus \{\neg\ell\} \subseteq c_1 \setminus \{\ell\}$, i.e., c_2 "almost subsumes" c_1 with the exception of exactly one literal ℓ, which is contained in the opposite polarity. Resolution of c_1 and c_2 with the pivot literal ℓ leads to $c_r = c_1 \setminus \{\ell\}$. By adding c_r to the formula, c_1 is "self-subsumed" by c_r; therefore c_1 can be removed after this addition. Our implementation simply removes ℓ from c_1, which has the same effect. This technique leads to a logically equivalent matrix and is therefore independent of the quantification type and the dependencies of the variables; hence it can be applied to QBF and DQBF without any restrictions.

In our implementation, we iterate over all clauses in order to identify such self-subsumptions until a fixed-point is reached. To do so efficiently, we keep a queue of candidates that is updated after deleting a literal. Whenever a literal ℓ_i is removed from a clause $c = \{\ell_1, \ldots, \ell_n\}$, each clause containing at least one of $\neg\ell_1, \ldots, \neg\ell_{i-1}, \neg\ell_{i+1}, \ldots, \neg\ell_n$ is potentially self-subsuming with c.

Other Formula Modifications. As formula modifications we consider techniques which do not eliminate variables, literals or clauses, but which are able to identify properties that are helpful to decide the formula.

Whenever substituting a gate's output variable y_{out} with its definition is too costly, we apply *gate rewriting* [17] instead. It adds a new existential variable y'_{out} to the same quantifier block as y_{out}. For one implication direction of the Tseitin encoding of the gate, y_{out} is replaced by y'_{out}, thus delivering a double *Plaisted encoding* [31], and the occurrences of $\neg y_{\text{out}}$ in the (D)QBF are replaced by $\neg y'_{\text{out}}$. The purpose of this transformation is to favor detection of pure literals when the clauses including y_{out} evaluate to true and to increase the chance that clauses are blocked [6].

Dependency schemes [34] allow to identify dependencies of existential variables y on universal ones x as pseudo-dependencies. The dependencies are syntactically given by the order of the variables in prefix for QBFs and by the dependency sets for DQBFs. A dependency (x, y) is a pseudo-dependency, if it can be added or removed without altering the truth value of the formula. Since deciding whether a dependency is a pseudo-dependency is as hard as solving the formula itself [34,41], different sufficient criteria have been proposed, which are called dependency schemes.

During universal expansion (see variable elimination routines), we utilize the reflexive quadrangle resolution path dependency scheme [37,41], which is currently the most effective dependency scheme that is sound for both QBF and DQBF. Before expanding a universal variable x, we identify its pseudo-dependencies. All pseudo-dependencies of x do not have to be copied and neither have the clauses to be doubled in which only pseudo-dependencies and variables independent of x occur. This often leads to significantly smaller formulas after the expansion.

Lastly, we also apply SAT checks over the matrix in order to find *trivially (un)satisfied formulas*. A (D)QBF is trivially unsatisfied if the matrix φ is already unsatisfied for an arbitrary assignment of the universal variables. For this check, we use an assignment of the universal variables which satisfies the fewest clauses, i.e., we assign x to $\top$ if x occurs in fewer clauses than $\neg x$. A (D)QBF is trivially satisfied if, after removing each occurrence of a universal literal within the matrix φ, the resulting matrix φ' is satisfiable. Finally, if a formula does not contain any universal variables after universal expansion, we immediately employ a SAT solver for deciding the resulting formula.

2.3   Implementation Details

Our tool was implemented in C++ on a 64 bits Linux machine. We can handle the standard qdimacs and dqdimacs file formats and also provide a clause interface. We are able to convert each QBF into a DQBF and vice-versa in case the dependencies of the DQBF can be linearized into a QBF prefix.

We apply all described techniques in our preprocessor within a main loop until a fixed-point is reached, i.e., no further changes in the formula arise during the latest iteration. Some (costly) techniques, like `trivialMatrixChecks()`, which use a SAT solver, are applied only once. For all SAT-based techniques we use the SAT solver ANTOM [36]. Whenever a routine was able to decide the (D)QBF, we immediately exit the loop and return the result.

For an efficient access to all clauses in which a literal ℓ occurs, we keep complete occurrence lists for each literal. Furthermore, we redundantly hold for each literal ℓ a list of all binary clauses in which ℓ occurs, since many of our syntactic methods, such as gate and equivalence detection, employ binary clauses.

We re-use unused variable IDs, i.e., whenever a variable was removed, we mark the index as "open" and such that it can be re-used. This avoids very large variable IDs and gaps in the data structure, which is crucial during universal expansion where many existential variables are newly introduced as a copy.

We tested different data structures for clauses. Structures based on `std::set` have the advantage of sorted ranges, which is beneficial for, e.g., subsumption and hidden/covered literal addition, but comes with the downside of more expensive access and insertion costs. On the other hand, a `std::vector` has constant access time, but checking the occurence of a literal in a clause gets more expensive. To overcome this issue we implemented a data structure which marks already occuring literals in the current clause. This "seen" data structure is also implemented as a `std::vector` with the length of the maximal literal ID. By doing so, we have efficient access on clause data, and checking whether a literal occurs in the clause becomes very cheap. By using this structure, we have measured a speed-up compared to `std::set`-based clauses of up to a factor of 4.

3   Experimental Evaluation

3.1   QBF Instances

Setting. We evaluated the effectiveness of HQSPRE by comparing it against BLOQQER (Version 037) [6] and SQUEEZEBF [17] (we used QuBE 7.2, which includes SQUEEZEBF) regarding both the reduction of the input formula and the impact on several back-end solvers. Our new tool was run in two settings, its default one (HQSPRE) and HQSPRE$_g$, which preserves gate information. In BLOQQER and SQUEEZEBF two subsets of the techniques available in HQSPRE are implemented, for more details the interested reader is referred to [6] and [17], respectively.

We used the testset selected for the latest QBF Evaluation (QBFEval 2016 [32]), consisting of 825 formulas. We selected several state-of-the-art QBF solvers (AIGSOLVE [29], AQUA-F2V [32] CAQE v2 [38], DEPQBF v5.01 [25], GHOSTQ [19], QESTO v1.0 [20], and RAREQS v1.1 [19]) and observed the effects of HQSPRE and the other preprocessors on the solvers, which are based on different solving techniques. AIGSOLVE was also run in a modified version named AIG-HQS, where the built-in preprocessor was replaced with HQSPRE. This way, we can better evaluate how the preprocessors affect circuit-based solvers. The experiments were run on DALCO computing nodes, each having 2×8 Intel E5-2650v2 cores running at 2.6 GHz and providing 64 GB RAM. Each job[3] was run on a single core and limited to 600 s CPU time and 4 GB RAM. An overall consistency check reported no deviation in the results of different tools.

Comparing Pure Preprocessors. In Table 1 we evaluate the ability of the preprocessors to act as incomplete solvers and their efficiency. For each preprocessor under analysis, the number of formulas evaluated to true, to false, and of those on which the preprocessor fails are given; additionally, we specify the accumulated computation time needed to handle the testset. Whenever HQSPRE failed, the reason was the time limit; memory consumption was not an issue for our preprocessor. HQSPRE is the tool that solves the largest number of formulas and takes the least time on average to perform its transformations. HQSPRE$_g$ is the fastest tool as it applies clause elimination techniques only to those clauses that do not encode gate information. Additionally, it restricts variable elimination by resolution to variables that are not gate outputs.

---

[3] A job consists of preprocessing and, where applicable, solving one formula. To guarantee repeatability, the sub-job of preprocessing a formula was performed once for all the solvers.

Table 1. Number of QBF instances decided by different preprocessors.

	#sat	#unsat	#fails	Time (s)
sQueezeBF	73	64	53	47548.7
Bloqqer	177	171	44	41872.0
HQSpre$_g$	162	209	29	25660.6
HQSpre	236	242	31	32127.0

Formula Reduction. In Table 2, we show the main features of the formulas in the testset we used, and their counterparts after the transformation with the preprocessors under analysis. The average number of existential variables, universal variables, overall variables, clauses, and quantifier alternations are given in columns 2 to 6. The testsets obtained by using the tools under analysis are split into three sub-rows ("r", "s", and "f", resp.) to distinguish between reduced, solved, and failed instances, respectively. For the reduced instances we report

Table 2. Formula changes by preprocessing QBF: For each preprocessor, data is shown as "before → after" for just reduced formulas ("r"); for solved ("s") and failed ("f") instances we show their original size. At the bottom, the averages concern the subset made of the 233 instances all the preprocessors strictly reduced.

		∃-Vars	∀-Vars	Vars	Clauses	Q-alt
Original		23769	570	24339	85984	17.0
sQueezeBF	r	8748 → 3674	303 → 261	9051 → 3935	40907 → 25782	17.2 → 10.2
	s	77096	259	77355	167100	20.7
	f	65893	4573	70466	416385	4.6
Bloqqer	r	8729 → 3256	608 → 548	9336 → 3805	50015 → 28933	13.4 → 6.6
	s	25938	142	26080	55860	19.9
	f	154630	3584	158214	678207	28.9
HQSpre$_g$	r	9194 → 12027	943 → 889	10137 → 12916	37949 → 68601	12.9 → 8.8
	s	28303	104	28407	91853	22.4
	f	179367	1066	180433	714867	6.7
HQSpre	r	12775 → 13232	1317 → 1232	14092 → 14463	54693 → 99763	11.1 → 7.1
	s	25797	109	25905	81852	21.4
	f	104575	77	104652	468670	8.1
Original		7037	661	7698	29498	11.3
sQueezeBF		3695	566	4226	13889	7.4
Bloqqer		2389	584	2973	13628	6.7
HQSpre$_g$		15354	634	15988	89002	7.1
HQSpre		10572	619	11191	77491	7.0

the averages of the quantity shown in the header before and after preprocessing, whereas for the others we report the averages of the original formulas.

The number of remaining clauses and variables for HQSPRE are larger on average than for the competing preprocessors. This is mainly due to more aggressive universal expansion in HQSPRE leading to many copied existential variables and clauses. On the other hand, many instances can be decided only due to this aggressive expansion. This can also be seen from the average number of universal variables: for the solved formulas, the number of universal variables is significantly smaller for HQSPRE than for the other preprocessors.

At the bottom of Table 2, we also compare the numbers for all 233 instances which are neither solved nor failed for *all* applied preprocessors. Since the set of instances which are neither solved nor failed is different for each solver, this allows a better comparison of the size of the remaining formula. Also from this point of view, BLOQQER leads on average to the smallest formulas, but the difference to our preprocessor is not as large since many huge formulas for which BLOQQER fails but HQSPRE does not are excluded from this presentation. As our next experiments show, the remaining larger average size does not worsen the results when applying a QBF solver to the preprocessed formula.

Combination with QBF Solvers. In Table 3, we show the overall performance of the solvers when considering our testset in its original form and when transformed by the preprocessors under analysis. For each testset, we list the number of formulas to be solved, which excludes those already solved by the preprocessor and those where the preprocessor failed. For each solver and testset, the number of solved instances includes those already solved by the preprocessor.

At first glance, we notice that HQSPRE improves the state-of-the-art: for each solver, the number of solved instances is strictly higher compared to sQUEEZEBF and BLOQQER. CEGAR-based solvers (CAQE, RAREQS, and QESTO) take the greatest advantage from using HQSPRE compared to BLOQQER, whereas search-based ones (AQUA and DEPQBF) improve by a rather

Table 3. Overall results using the original QBF instances, preprocessed by BLOQQER, sQUEEZEBF, and HQSPRE. We give the number of solved instances together with the accumulated computation times in seconds. Best results for each tool are **highlighted**.

Solver	Original		sQUEEZEBF		BLOQQER		HQSPRE$_g$		HQSPRE	
	#	Time (s)	#	Time (s)	#	Time (s)	#	Time (s)	#	Time (s)
AQUA	330	306288	496	208396	574	163106	463	222542	**592**	**149602**
DEPQBF	434	243677	520	196531	585	157570	509	196605	**600**	**148303**
AIGSOLVE	532	188046	480	212830	518	194297	**559**	**171348**	544	175234
AIG-HQS	507	203696	440	239303	499	206756	**560**	**172549**	536	180341
CAQE	358	290370	534	195257	576	169814	485	213024	**637**	**132017**
RAREQS	337	300562	517	204385	615	144281	458	227326	**638**	**127443**
QESTO	360	291301	550	184821	606	148490	477	217943	**652**	**122782**

small number of solved instances. AIGSOLVE is the only solver which does not always take advantage from preprocessing: in most cases, its performance gets even degraded. This is mainly due to the underlying data structure of AIG-SOLVE: it uses AND-Inverter graphs (AIGs), which are basically a circuit representation. Since AIGSOLVE applies syntactic gate detection on the clauses, any preprocessing step destroying this structure is harmful to the solver. AIG-HQSbenefits most from our HQSPRE$_g$ variant, where gate defining clauses and variables are untouched, and both variants of AIGSOLVE simply work worse if coupled with general purpose CNF preprocessors. AIGSOLVE contains an integrated preprocessor, which is well optimized to the AIG-based back-end solver. Still, by using HQSPRE as additional front-end preprocessor, the number of solved instances increases. For the other preprocessors, results get worse because they destroy the gate information that AIGSOLVE can exploit. Note, that even though our preprocessor runs until a fixed-point is reached, a second independent run can change the results, since some methods are only applied at the very beginning and not in every pass through the main preprocessing loop.

Impact on QBF Solvers. In Table 4, we show the impact of the preprocessors on the solvers regarding their robustness. For each pair, we report as a negative number (left) the amount of formulas a solver is able to solve only without preprocessing, and as a positive number (right) the amount of those instances where the preprocessor is necessary for the solver to solve them. Large positive numbers show complementarity, negative numbers close to zero demonstrate good robustness. As a solver based on a circuit representation of the formula, AIGSOLVE shows the highest complementarity, whereas our gate-preserving preprocessor version HQSPRE$_g$ is the most robust one for this solver. For most solvers, HQSPRE is the most robust preprocessor; exceptions are DEPQBF, CAQE, and RAREQS whose techniques are less impaired by SQUEEZEBF.

Table 4. Positive and negative effect of preprocessing on QBF solvers. Best results for each QBF solver are **highlighted**.

	SQUEEZEBF		BLOQQER		HQSPRE$_g$		HQSPRE	
AQUA	**−8**	+174	−11	+255	−7	+140	−6	**+268**
DEPQBF	**−9**	+95	−15	+166	−21	+96	−19	**+185**
AIGSOLVE	−86	+34	−75	+61	**−36**	+63	−64	**+76**
AIG-HQS	−103	+36	−70	+62	**−32**	+85	−68	**+97**
CAQE	**−8**	+184	−13	+231	−11	+138	−10	**+289**
RAREQS	**−9**	+189	−16	+294	−12	+133	−12	**+313**
QESTO	−6	+196	−14	+260	−5	+122	**−3**	**+295**

3.2   DQBF Instances

Setting. We apply our preprocessor to DQBF benchmarks and use it as a front-end for the only two currently available solvers: HQS [15] and IDQ [13]. HQS is – like AIGSOLVE – an elimination-based solver using AIGs; IDQ is an instantiation-based approach using a SAT solver as back-end. Since HQSPRE is the first available preprocessor for DQBF, there are no competitors to compare with. We also apply the gate preserving version HQSPRE$_g$ for this test set. Since there is no standard benchmark set for DQBF we randomly selected 499 benchmarks of different size and difficulty from currently available benchmark sets: They encompass equivalence checking problems for incomplete circuits [12,13,15], and formulas resulting from the synthesis of safe controllers [7]. We used the DALCO computing nodes with the same limitations as in our QBF experiments.

Comparing Pure Preprocessors. Table 5 shows the ability of HQSPRE to act as an incomplete solver. Since no universal expansion is applied, on the one hand HQSPRE solved fewer instances compared to the QBF benchmarks set. On the other hand, HQSPRE could preprocess all instances within the given limits.

Table 5. Decided instances of different preprocessors for DQBF.

	#sat	#unsat	#fails	Time (s)
HQSPRE$_g$	7	60	0	29441.2
HQSPRE	5	71	0	162615.8

Formula Reduction. Table 6 shows the effect on the formula size for the DQBF instances in the same manner as in Table 2. Note, there are no quantifier blocks for DQBF, hence we cannot give the number of quantifier alternations. Instead, we state the number of dependencies ("deps"), which is the sum of the cardinalities of the dependency sets of the existential variables. The given number is the average over all concerned benchmarks. In the last rows, we state the numbers for the 407 commonly reduced, but not solved benchmarks.

Especially, the number of dependencies is significantly reduced for both variations. Since we do not apply any universal expansion the number of universal variables is almost unchanged – the small decrease is mainly caused by pure literal detection of universal variables. On the other hand, this strictly leads to smaller formulas in terms of variables, clauses, and dependencies. Notably, there are 18 instances with HQSPRE$_g$ and 20 instances with HQSPRE, respectively, for which the DQBF dependencies were linearized, i. e., the tools were able to convert the formula into an easier to solve QBF problem.

Table 6. Formula shrinking after preprocessing DQBF: For each preprocessing setting, data is shown as "before → after" for just reduced ("*r*") formulas, and for solved ("*s*") formulas we show their original size. At the bottom, the averages concern the subset made of the 407 instances all the preprocessors successfully reduce but not solve.

		∃-Vars	∀-Vars	Vars	Clauses	Deps
Original		367.7	70.5	438.3	1165.1	8425.8
HQSPRE$_g$	r	390.3 → 243.3	78.3 → 77.2	468.6 → 320.5	1187.9 → 883.7	9038.3 → 37.7
	s	222.3	20.4	242.7	1018.2	4476.7
HQSPRE	r	402.4 → 96.1	79.6 → 78.2	482.1 → 174.3	1229.9 → 540.7	9540.8 → 589.8
	s	174.5	19.9	194.4	804.1	2219.8
Original		407.1	81.9	489.0	1240.0	9544.8
HQSPRE$_g$		257.4	81.0	338.4	933.8	39.8
HQSPRE		97.2	80.6	177.8	543.6	612.4

Impact on DQBF Solvers. Finally, we passed the preprocessed formulas to the two DQBF solvers and compare them with the results for the original formula. For HQS we use two versions: the usual one (HQS) and a version where we have integrated HQSPRE$_g$ into the solver (HQS^I). This means that in the combination of HQSPRE and HQSPRE$_g$ with HQS^I the formula is actually preprocessed twice. The results are given in Table 7. As it can be seen, IDQ and HQS both significantly benefit from preprocessing. However, preprocessing the formula and feeding it into HQS in CNF form does not yield an optimal behavior of the solver compared to a tight integration as in HQS^I. The reason for this is that HQS does not apply gate detection on its own, which leads to much larger AIGs with more variables. Still, we can see that HQSPRE is effective: without preprocessing, only 223 instances are solved, with gate-preserving preprocessing, but without exploiting the gate information 326 instances, and with full preprocessing 351 instances are solved. However, the best results are obtained if we integrate the preprocessor into the solver such that the gate information extracted from the CNF is exploited when creating the AIG data structures of the solver. In this case, 456 instances get solved. Preprocessing the formula twice as in

Table 7. Overall results using the original DQBF instances and preprocessed by HQSPRE and HQSPRE$_g$. The accumulated computation times are given in seconds. Best results for each DQBF solver are **highlighted**.

Solver	Original		HQSPRE$_g$		HQSPRE	
	#	Time (s)	#	Time (s)	#	Time (s)
IDQ	151	214404	170	201165	**214**	**171676**
HQS	223	176222	326	108788	**351**	**93912**
HQS^I	**456**	**30946**	450	34621	228	164299

HQSPRE + HQS^I or HQSPRE$_g$ + HQS^I, causes an additional overhead and modifies the formula: Since some of the more expensive techniques like SAT-based constant detection are applied only once, preprocessing the formula twice leads not only to additional overhead, but also to a different formula.

We can conclude that HQSPRE is effective also for preprocessing DQBFs. For HQS as the back-end solver, it is of highest importance not only to preserve gate information, but also to integrate the preprocessor into the solver such that this information is exploited optimally.

4 Conclusion

We presented a new state-of-the-art tool HQSPRE for preprocessing QBF out-performing every tested competing tool by the number of solved instances as well as increasing the number of solved instances for each state-of-the-art QBF-solver using HQSPRE as front-end. Moreover our tool is able to preprocess DQBF formulas effectively and efficiently, being the first available DQBF preprocessor. An integrated version of the DQBF preprocessor clearly outperforms every other competing solver and preprocessor combination.

As future work we want to improve and enhance our gate detection methods. Namely, we want to support the Plaisted-Greenbaum encoding [31] and semantic gate detection. We like to develop an explicit gate and/or AIGER [3] interface, which also closes the gap between solver and applications in general. We also plan to expand our methodology portfolio by other well-known techniques like unit propagation look-ahead [24] (also sometimes referred to as failed literal detection) and vivification [28]. Moreover, we would like to extend our tool with Skolem and Herbrand functions in order to provide and preserve certificates. Lastly, our experimental results indicate that deciding DQBF is very efficient if we are able to transform the formula into a QBF. In order to decide whether a DQBF can be transformed into an equivalent QBF and which operations are needed to do so, a more intense utilization of dependency schemes is needed.

References

1. Balabanov, V., Chiang, H.K., Jiang, J.R.: Henkin quantifiers and Boolean for-mulae: a certification perspective of DQBF. Theoret. Comput. Sci. **523**, 86–100 (2014)
2. Biere, A.: Resolve and expand. In: Hoos, H.H., Mitchell, D.G. (eds.) SAT 2004. LNCS, vol. 3542, pp. 59–70. Springer, Heidelberg (2005). doi:10.1007/11527695_5
3. Biere, A.: Aiger format (2007). http://fmv.jku.at/aiger/
4. Biere, A., Cimatti, A., Clarke, E.M., Strichman, O., Zhu, Y.: Bounded model checking. Adv. Comput. **58**, 117–148 (2003)
5. Biere, A., Heule, M., van Maaren, H., Walsh, T. (eds.): Handbook of Satisfia-bility. Frontiers in Artificial Intelligence and Applications, vol. 185. IOS Press, Amsterdam (2008)
6. Biere, A., Lonsing, F., Seidl, M.: Blocked clause elimination for QBF. In: Bjørner, N., Sofronie-Stokkermans, V. (eds.) CADE 2011. LNCS (LNAI), vol. 6803, pp. 101–115. Springer, Heidelberg (2011). doi:10.1007/978-3-642-22438-6_10

7. Bloem, R., Könighofer, R., Seidl, M.: SAT-based synthesis methods for safety specs. In: McMillan, K.L., Rival, X. (eds.) VMCAI 2014. LNCS, vol. 8318, pp. 1–20. Springer, Heidelberg (2014). doi:10.1007/978-3-642-54013-4_1

8. Bubeck, U., Kleine Büning, H.: Bounded universal expansion for preprocessing QBF. In: Marques-Silva, J., Sakallah, K.A. (eds.) SAT 2007. LNCS, vol. 4501, pp. 244–257. Springer, Heidelberg (2007). doi:10.1007/978-3-540-72788-0_24

9. del Val, A.: Simplifying binary propositional theories into connected components twice as fast. In: Nieuwenhuis, R., Voronkov, A. (eds.) LPAR 2001. LNCS (LNAI), vol. 2250, pp. 392–406. Springer, Heidelberg (2001). doi:10.1007/3-540-45653-8_27

10. Eén, N., Biere, A.: Effective preprocessing in SAT through variable and clause elimination. In: Bacchus, F., Walsh, T. (eds.) SAT 2005. LNCS, vol. 3569, pp. 61–75. Springer, Heidelberg (2005). doi:10.1007/11499107_5

11. Eggersglüß, S., Drechsler, R.: A highly fault-efficient SAT-based ATPG flow. IEEE Des. Test Comput. **29**(4), 63–70 (2012)

12. Finkbeiner, B., Tentrup, L.: Fast DQBF refutation. In: Sinz, C., Egly, U. (eds.) SAT 2014. LNCS, vol. 8561, pp. 243–251. Springer, Cham (2014). doi:10.1007/978-3-319-09284-3_19

13. Fröhlich, A., Kovásznai, G., Biere, A., Veith, H.: iDQ: instantiation-based DQBF solving. In: Le Berre, D. (ed.) International Workshop on Pragmatics of SAT (POS). EPiC Series, vol. 27, pp. 103–116. EasyChair (2014)

14. Gitina, K., Reimer, S., Sauer, M., Wimmer, R., Scholl, C., Becker, B.: Equivalence checking of partial designs using dependency quantified Boolean formulae. In: Proceedings of ICCD, pp. 396–403. IEEE CS (2013)

15. Gitina, K., Wimmer, R., Reimer, S., Sauer, M., Scholl, C., Becker, B.: Solving DQBF through quantifier elimination. In: Proceedings of DATE, pp. 1617–1622. IEEE (2015)

16. Giunchiglia, E., Marin, P., Narizzano, M.: QuBE7.0. J. Satisf. Boolean Model. Comput. **7**(2–3), 83–88 (2010)

17. Giunchiglia, E., Marin, P., Narizzano, M.: sQueezeBF: an effective preprocessor for QBFs based on equivalence reasoning. In: Strichman, O., Szeider, S. (eds.) SAT 2010. LNCS, vol. 6175, pp. 85–98. Springer, Heidelberg (2010). doi:10.1007/978-3-642-14186-7_9

18. Heule, M., Järvisalo, M., Lonsing, F., Seidl, M., Biere, A.: Clause elimination for SAT and QSAT. J. Artif. Intell. Res. **53**, 127–168 (2015)

19. Janota, M., Klieber, W., Marques-Silva, J., Clarke, E.: Solving QBF with counterexample guided refinement. In: Cimatti, A., Sebastiani, R. (eds.) SAT 2012. LNCS, vol. 7317, pp. 114–128. Springer, Heidelberg (2012). doi:10.1007/978-3-642-31612-8_10

20. Janota, M., Marques-Silva, J.: Solving QBF by clause selection. In: Proceedings of IJCAI, pp. 325–331. AAAI Press (2015)

21. Järvisalo, M., Biere, A., Heule, M.: Blocked clause elimination. In: Esparza, J., Majumdar, R. (eds.) TACAS 2010. LNCS, vol. 6015, pp. 129–144. Springer, Heidelberg (2010). doi:10.1007/978-3-642-12002-2_10

22. Klieber, W., Sapra, S., Gao, S., Clarke, E.: A non-prenex, non-clausal QBF solver with game-state learning. In: Strichman, O., Szeider, S. (eds.) SAT 2010. LNCS, vol. 6175, pp. 128–142. Springer, Heidelberg (2010). doi:10.1007/978-3-642-14186-7_12

23. Kupferschmid, S., Lewis, M., Schubert, T., Becker, B.: Incremental preprocessing methods for use in BMC. Form. Methods Syst. Des. **39**(2), 185–204 (2011)

24. Li, C.M., Anbulagan, A.: Heuristics based on unit propagation for satisfiability problems. In: Proceedings of IJCAI, vol. 1, pp. 366–371. Morgan Kaufmann Publishers Inc. (1997)
25. Lonsing, F., Bacchus, F., Biere, A., Egly, U., Seidl, M.: Enhancing search-based QBF solving by dynamic blocked clause elimination. In: Davis, M., Fehnker, A., McIver, A., Voronkov, A. (eds.) LPAR 2015. LNCS, vol. 9450, pp. 418–433. Springer, Heidelberg (2015). doi:10.1007/978-3-662-48899-7_29
26. Meyer, A.R., Stockmeyer, L.J.: Word problems requiring exponential time: preliminary report. In: Proceedings of STOC, pp. 1–9. ACM Press (1973)
27. Peterson, G., Reif, J., Azhar, S.: Lower bounds for multiplayer non-cooperative games of incomplete information. Comput. Math. Appl. **41**(7–8), 957–992 (2001)
28. Piette, C., Hamadi, Y., Sais, L.: Vivifying propositional clausal formulae. In: Ghallab, M., Spyropoulos, C.D., Fakotakis, N., Avouris, N.M. (eds.) Proceedings of ECAI. Frontiers in Artificial Intelligence and Applications, vol. 178, pp. 525–529. IOS Press (2008)
29. Pigorsch, F., Scholl, C.: Exploiting structure in an AIG based QBF solver. In: Proceedings of DATE, pp. 1596–1601. IEEE (2009)
30. Pigorsch, F., Scholl, C.: An AIG-based QBF-solver using SAT for preprocessing. In: Sapatnekar, S.S. (ed.) Proceedings of DAC, pp. 170–175. ACM Press (2010)
31. Plaisted, D.A., Greenbaum, S.: A structure-preserving clause form translation. J. Symb. Comput. **2**(3), 293–304 (1986)
32. QBFEVAL2016. http://www.qbflib.org/event_page.php?year=2016
33. Rintanen, J., Heljanko, K., Niemelä, I.: Planning as satisfiability: parallel plans and algorithms for plan search. Artif. Intell. **170**(12–13), 1031–1080 (2006)
34. Samer, M., Szeider, S.: Backdoor sets of quantified Boolean formulas. J. Autom. Reason. **42**(1), 77–97 (2009)
35. Scholl, C., Becker, B.: Checking equivalence for partial implementations. In: Proceedings of DAC, pp. 238–243. ACM Press (2001)
36. Schubert, T., Reimer, S.: antom (2016). In: https://projects.informatik. uni-freiburg.de/projects/antom
37. Slivovsky, F., Szeider, S.: Soundness of Q-resolution with dependency schemes. Theoret. Comput. Sci. **612**, 83–101 (2016)
38. Tentrup, L., Rabe, M.N.: CAQE: a certifying QBF solver. In: Proceedings of FMCAD, pp. 136–143. IEEE (2015)
39. Tseitin, G.S.: On the complexity of derivation in propositional calculus. Stud. Constr. Math. Math. Log. Part **2**, 115–125 (1970)
40. Wimmer, R., Gitina, K., Nist, J., Scholl, C., Becker, B.: Preprocessing for DQBF. In: Heule, M., Weaver, S. (eds.) SAT 2015. LNCS, vol. 9340, pp. 173–190. Springer, Cham (2015). doi:10.1007/978-3-319-24318-4_13
41. Wimmer, R., Scholl, C., Wimmer, K., Becker, B.: Dependency schemes for DQBF. In: Creignou, N., Le Berre, D. (eds.) SAT 2016. LNCS, vol. 9710, pp. 473–489. Springer, Cham (2016). doi:10.1007/978-3-319-40970-2_29

RPP: Automatic Proof of Relational Properties by Self-composition

Lionel Blatter[1]([✉]), Nikolai Kosmatov[1], Pascale Le Gall[2], and Virgile Prevosto[1]

[1] Software Reliability and Security Laboratory, CEA, LIST,
91191 Gif-sur-Yvette, France
{lionel.blatter,nikolai.kosmatov,virgile.prevosto}@cea.fr
[2] Laboratoire de Mathématiques et Informatique pour la Complexité et les Systèmes,
CentraleSupélec, Université Paris-Saclay, 92295 Châtenay-Malabry, France
pascale.legall@centralesupelec.fr

Abstract. Self-composition provides a powerful theoretical approach to prove relational properties, i.e. properties relating several program executions, that has been applied to compare two runs of one or similar programs (in secure dataflow properties, code transformations, etc.). This tool demo paper presents RPP, an original implementation of self-composition for specification and verification of relational properties in C programs in the FRAMA-C platform. We consider a very general notion of relational properties invoking any finite number of function calls of possibly dissimilar functions with possible nested calls. The new tool allows the user to specify a relational property, to prove it in a completely automatic way using classic deductive verification, and to use it as a hypothesis in the proof of other properties that may rely on it.

Keywords: Self-composition · Relational properties · Deductive verification · Specification · FRAMA-C

1 Introduction

Modular deductive verification allows the user to prove that a function respects its formal specification. For a given function f, any individual call to f can be proved to respect the *contract* of f, that is, basically an implication: if the given *precondition* is true before the call, the given *postcondition* is true after it. However, some kinds of properties are not reduced to one function call. Indeed, it is frequently necessary to express a property that involves several functions or relates the results of several calls to the same function for different arguments. We call them *relational properties*.

Different theories and techniques have been proposed to deal with relational properties in different contexts. They include Relational Hoare Logic to show the equivalence of program transformations [5] or Cartesian Hoare Logic for k-safety properties [15]. Self-composition [2] is a theoretical approach to prove relational properties relating two execution traces. It reduces the verification of a relational

© Springer-Verlag GmbH Germany 2017
A. Legay and T. Margaria (Eds.): TACAS 2017, Part I, LNCS 10205, pp. 391–397, 2017.
DOI: 10.1007/978-3-662-54577-5_22

property to a standard verification problem of a new function. Self-composition techniques have been applied for verification of information flow properties [1,2] and properties of two equivalent-result object methods [14]. Relational properties can be expressed on Java pure methods [11] using the JML specification language. OpenJML [8] offers a partial support for deductive verification of relational properties. The purpose of the present work is to implement and extend self-composition for specification and verification of relational properties in the context of the ACSL specification language [4] and the deductive verification plugin WP of FRAMA-C [13]. We consider a large class of relational properties (universally quantified properties invoking any finite number of calls of possibly dissimilar functions with possibly nested calls), and propose an automatic solution allowing the user not only to prove a relational property, but also to use it as a hypothesis.

Motivation. The necessity to deal with relational properties in FRAMA-C has been faced in various verification projects. Recent work [6] reports on verification of continuous monotonic functions in an industrial case study on smart sensor software. The authors write: "After reviewing around twenty possible code analysis tools, we decided to use FRAMA-C, which fulfilled all our requirements (apart from the specifications involving the comparison of function calls)." The relational property in question is the monotonicity of a function (e.g., $x \leq y \Rightarrow f(x) \leq f(y)$). To deal with it in FRAMA-C, [6] applies a variation of self-composition consisting in a separate verification of an additional, manually created wrapper function simulating the calls to be compared.

Relational properties can often be useful to give an expressive specification of library functions or hardware-supported functions, when the source code is not available. In this case, relational properties are only specified and used to verify client code, but are not verified themselves. For instance, in the PISCO project[1], an industrial case study on verification of software using hardware-provided cryptographic primitives (PKCS#11 standard) required tying together different functions with properties such as Decrypt(Encrypt($Msg, PrivKey$), $PubKey$) = Msg. Other examples include properties of data structures, such as matrix transformations (e.g. $(A + B)^\mathsf{T} = A^\mathsf{T} + B^\mathsf{T}$ or $\det(A) = \det(A^\mathsf{T})$), the specification of Push and Pop over a stack [7], or parallel program specification (e.g., map(append(l_1, l_2)) = append(map(l_1), map(l_2)) in the MapReduce approach). A subclass of relational properties, *metamorphic properties*, relating multiple executions of the same function [12], are also used in a different context in order to address the oracle problem in software testing [16].

Manual application of self-composition or possible workarounds reduce the level of automation, can be error-prone and do not provide a complete automated link between three key components: *(i)* the property specification, *(ii)* its proof, and *(iii)* its usage as a hypothesis in other proofs. Thus, the lack of support for relational properties can be a major obstacle to a wider application of deductive verification in academic and industrial projects.

---

[1] http://www.systematic-paris-region.org/en/projets/pisco.

The contributions of this tool demo paper include:

- a new specification mechanism to formally express a relational property in ACSL;
- a fully-automated transformation into ACSL-annotated C code based on (an extension of) self-composition, that allows the user to prove such a property;
- a generation of an axiomatic definition and additional annotations that allow us to use a relational property as a hypothesis for the proof of other properties in a completely automatic and transparent way;
- an extension of self-composition to a large class of relational properties, including several calls of possibly dissimilar functions and possibly nested calls, and
- an implementation of this approach in a FRAMA-C plugin RPP with a sound integration of proof statuses of relational properties.

2   The Method and the Tool

2.1   Specification and Preprocessing of a Relational Property

The proposed solution is designed and implemented on top of FRAMA-C [13], a framework for analysis of C code developed at CEA LIST. FRAMA-C offers a specification language, called ACSL [4], and a deductive verification plugin, WP [3], that allow the user to specify the desired program properties as function contracts and to prove them. A typical ACSL function contract may include a precondition (**requires** clause stating a property supposed to hold before the function call) and a postcondition (**ensures** clause that should hold after the call), as well as a frame rule (**assigns** clause indicating which parts of the global program state the function is allowed to modify). An assertion (**assert** clause) can also specify a local property at any function statement.

Specification. To specify a relational property, we propose an extension of ACSL specification language with a new clause, **relational**. For technical, FRAMA-C-related, reasons, these clauses must be attached to a function contract. Thus, a property relating calls of different functions, such as R3 in Fig. 1a, must appear in the contract of the last function involved in the property, *i.e.* when all relevant functions are in scope. To refer to several function calls in such a property, we introduce a new construct \call(f,<args>) used to indicate the value returned by the call f(<args>) to f with arguments <args>. \call can be used recursively, i.e. a parameter of a called function can be the result of another function call. For example, properties R1, R2 at lines 2–3, 10–11 of Fig. 1a specify monotonicity of functions f1, f2, while property R3 at line 12–13 indicates that f1(x) is always less than f2(x).

Preprocessing and Proof Status Propagation. Since this new syntax is not supported by classic deductive verification tools, we have designed a code transformation, inspired by self-composition, allowing the user to prove the property with one of these tools.

```
1  /*@ assigns \nothing;
2     relational R1: ∀ int x1,x2;
3        x1 < x2 ⇒ \call(f1,x1) < \call(f1,x2);
4  */
5  int f1(int x){
6     return x + 1;
7  }
8
9  /*@ assigns \nothing;
10    relational R2: ∀ int x1, x2;
11       x1 < x2 ⇒ \call(f2,x1) < \call(f2,x2);
12    relational R3: ∀ int k;
13       \call(f1,k) < \call(f2,k);
14 */
15 int f2(int y){
16    return y + 2;
17 }
```

```
1  void relational_wrapper(int x1,int x2){
2     int tmp1 = 0;
3     int tmp2 = 0;
4     tmp1 = x1 + 1; // inlined f1(x1)
5     tmp2 = x2 + 1; // inlined f1(x2)
6  /*@ assert x1 < x2 ⇒ tmp1 < tmp2; */
7  }
8
9  /*@ axiomatic Relational_axiom{
10    logic int f1_acsl(int x);
11    lemma Relational_lemma: ∀ int x,y;
12       x < y ⇒ f1_acsl(x) < f1_acsl(y);
13    }
14 */
15
16 /*@ assigns \nothing;
17    behavior Relational_behavior:
18    ensures \result == f1_acsl(\old(x));
19 */
20 int f1(int x){
21    return x + 1;
22 }
23
24 ... // similar for f2
```

Fig. 1. (a) Two monotonic functions f1, f2 with three relational properties (file f.c), and (b) excerpt of their transformation by RPP for deductive verification

We illustrate the transformation for function f1 and property R1 (see Fig. 1a). The transformation result (Fig. 1b) consists of three parts. First, a new function, called *wrapper*, is generated. The wrapper function is inspired by the workaround proposed in [6] and self-composition. It inlines the function calls occurring in the relational property, records their results in local variables and states an assertion equivalent to the relational property (lines 1–7 in Fig. 1b). The proof of such an assertion is possible with a classic deductive verification tool (WP can prove it in this example).

However, a wrapper function is not sufficient if we need to use the relational property as a hypothesis in other proofs and to make their support fully automatic and transparent for the user. For this purpose, we generate an axiomatic definition (cf. **axiomatic** section at lines 9–14) to give a logical reformulation of the relational property as a lemma (cf. lines 11–12). This logical formulation can be used in subsequent proofs (as we illustrate below). Lemmas can refer to several function calls, but only for *logic* functions. Therefore, a logic counterpart (with _acsl suffix) is declareds for each C function involved in a relational property (cf. line 10). The ACSL function is partially specified *via* lemmas corresponding to the relational properties of the original C function. Note that the correspondence between f and f_acsl implies that f does not access global memory (neither for writing nor for reading). Indeed, since f_acsl is a pure logic function, it has no side effect and its result only depends on its parameters. Extending our approach for this case can rely on **assigns...\from...** clauses, similarly to what is proposed in [10], for adding to f_acsl parameters representing the relevant parts of the program state. This extension is left as future work.

Finally, to create a bridge between the C function and its logic counterpart, we add a postcondition (an **ensures** clause, placed in a separate **behavior** for readability) to state that they always return the same result (cf. line 18 relating f1 and f1_acsl).

To make the proposed solution as transparent as possible for the user and to ensure automatic propagation of proof statuses in the FRAMA-C property database [9], two additional rules are necessary. First, the postconditions making the link between C functions and their associated logic counterparts are always supposed valid (so the clause of line 18 is declared as valid). Second, the logic reformulation of a relational property in a lemma (lines 11–12) is declared valid[2] as soon as the assertion (line 6) at the end of the wrapper function is proved.

2.2   Implementation and Illustrative Examples

Implementation. A proof-of-concept implementation of the proposed technique has been realized in a FRAMA-C plugin RPP (Relational Property Prover). RPP works like a preprocessor for WP: after its execution on a project containing relational properties, the proof on the generated code proceeds like any other proof with WP [13]: proof obligations are generated and can be either discharged automatically by automatic theorem provers (e.g. Alt-Ergo, CVC4, Z3[3]) or proven interactively (e.g. in Coq[4]).

Thanks to the proposed code transformation no significant modification was required in FRAMA-C and WP. RPP currently supports relational properties of the form

$$\forall\ \texttt{<args1>}, \dots, \forall\ \texttt{<argsN>},$$
$$P(\ \texttt{<args1>}, \dots, \texttt{<argsN>}, \texttt{\textbackslash call}(\texttt{f\_1},\texttt{<args1>}), \dots, \texttt{\textbackslash call}(\texttt{f\_N},\texttt{<argsN>}))$$

for an arbitrary predicate P invoking $N \geq 1$ calls of non-recursive functions without side effects and complex data structures.

Illustrative Examples. After preprocessing with RPP, FRAMA-C/WP automatically validates properties R1–R3 of Fig. 1a by proving the assertions in the generated wrapper functions and by propagating proof statuses.

To show how relational properties can be used in another proof, consider properties Rg, Rh of Fig. 2a for slightly more complex functions (inspired by [6]) whose proof needs to use properties R1, R2. Thanks to their reformulation as lemmas and to the link between logic and C functions (cf. lines 11–12, 18 of Fig. 1b for f1), WP automatically proves the assertion at line 6 of Fig. 2b and validates property Rg as proven. The proof for Rh is similar.

---

[2] Technically, a special "valid under condition" status is used in this case in FRAMA-C.
[3] See, resp., https://alt-ergo.ocamlpro.com, http://cvc4.cs.nyu.edu, https://z3. codeplex.com/.
[4] See http://coq.inria.fr/.

```
1  /*@ relational R1: ∀ int x1,x2;           1  void relational_wrapper(int x1,int x2){
2    x1 < x2 ⇒ \call(f1,x1) < \call(f1,x2);  2    int tmp1 = 0;
3  */                                        3    int tmp2 = 0;
4  int f1(int x);                            4    tmp1 = f1(x1) + f2(x1); // g(x1)
5                                            5    tmp2 = f1(x2) + f2(x2); // g(x2)
6  /*@ relational R2: ∀ int x1,x2;           6  /*@ assert x1 < x2 ⇒ tmp1 < tmp2;*/
7    x1 < x2 ⇒ \call(f2,x1) < \call(f2,x2);  7  }
8  */                                        8
9  int f2(int x);                            9  /*@ axiomatic Relational_axiom{
10                                          10     logic int g_acsl(int x);
11 /*@ relational Rg: ∀ int x1,x2;          11     lemma relational_lemma: ∀ int x,y;
12   x1 < x2 ⇒ \call(g,x1) < \call(g,x2);   12     x < y ⇒ g_acsl(x) < g_acsl(y);
13 */                                       13     }
14 int g(int x){                            14 */
15   return f1(x)+f2(x);                    15
16 }                                        16 /*@ behavior Relational_behavior:
17                                          17    ensures \result == g_acsl(\old(x));
18 /*@ relational Rh: ∀ int x1,x2;          18 */
19   x1 < x2 ⇒ \call(h,x1) < \call(h,x2);   19 int g(int x){
20 */                                       20    return f1(x)+f2(x);
21 int h(int x){                            21 }
22   return f1(f2(x));                      22
23 }                                        23 ... // similar for h
```

Fig. 2. (a) Two monotonic functions g, h with two relational properties, and (b) extract of their transformation by RPP for deductive verification

Notice that in examples of Fig. 2, functions f1, f2 can be undefined since only their (relational) specification is required, which is suitable for specification of library or hardware-provided functions that cannot be specified without relational properties.

The RPP tool has also been successfully tested on several other examples such as cryptographic properties like $Decrypt(Encrypt(Msg, PrivKey), PubKey) = Msg$, squeeze lemma condition (i.e. $\forall x,\ f_1(x) \le f_2(x) \le f_3(x)$), median function properties (e.g. $\forall a, b, c,\ Med(a, b, c) = Med(a, c, b)$), properties of determinant for matrices of order 2 and 3 (e.g. $\det(A) = \det(A^\mathsf{T})$), matrix equations like $(A + B)^\mathsf{T} = A^\mathsf{T} + B^\mathsf{T}$, etc. Some of them include loops whose loop invariants are automatically transferred by RPP into the wrapper function to make possible its automatic proof.

3   Conclusion and Future Work

We proposed a novel technique for specification and proof of relational properties for C programs in FRAMA-C. We implemented it in a FRAMA-C plugin RPP and illustrated its capacity to treat a large range of examples coming from various industrial and academic projects that were suffering from the impossibility to express relational properties. One benefit of this approach is its capacity to rely on sound and mature verification tools like FRAMA-C/WP, thus allowing for automatic or interactive proof from the specified code. Thanks to an elegant transformation into auxiliary C code and logic definitions accompanied by a property status propagation, the user can treat complex relational properties and observe the results in a convenient and fully automatic manner. Another key benefit is that this approach is suitable for verification of programs relying on library or hardware-provided functions whose source code is not available.

Future work includes extending the tool to support complex data structures and functions with side-effects, support of recursive functions, studying other variants of generated code (e.g. avoiding function inlining in some cases), as well as further experiments on real-life programs.

Acknowledgment. Part of the research work leading to these results has received funding for DEWI project (www.dewi-project.eu) from the ARTEMIS Joint Undertaking under grant agreement No. 621353, and for the S3P project from French DGE and BPIFrance.

References

1. Barthe, G., Crespo, J.M., Kunz, C.: Product programs and relational program logics. J. Log. Algebr. Methods Program. **85**, 847–859 (2016)
2. Barthe, G., D'Argenio, P.R., Rezk, T.: Secure information flow by self-composition. Math. Struct. Comput. Sci. **21**, 1207–1252 (2011)
3. Baudin, P., Bobot, F., Correnson, L., Dargaye, Z.: WP Plugin Manual v1.0 (2016)
4. Baudin, P., Cuoq, P., Filliâtre, J.C., Marché, C., Monate, B., Moy, Y., Prevosto, V.: ACSL: ANSI/ISO C Specification Language (2016). http://frama-c.com/acsl.html
5. Benton, N.: Simple relational correctness proofs for static analyses and program transformations. In: POPL (2004)
6. Bishop, P.G., Bloomfield, R.E., Cyra, L.: Combining testing and proof to gain high assurance in software: a case study. In: ISSRE (2013)
7. Burghardt, J., Gerlach, J., Lapawczyk, T.: ACSL by Example (2016). http://www.fokus.fraunhofer.de/download/acsl_by_example
8. Cok, D.R.: OpenJML: software verification for Java 7 using JML, OpenJDK, and Eclipse. In: F-IDE (2014)
9. Correnson, L., Signoles, J.: Combining analyses for C program verification. In: Stoelinga, M., Pinger, R. (eds.) FMICS 2012. LNCS, vol. 7437, pp. 108–130. Springer, Heidelberg (2012). doi:10.1007/978-3-642-32469-7_8
10. Cuoq, P., Monate, B., Pacalet, A., Prevosto, V.: Functional dependencies of C functions via weakest pre-conditions. STTT **13**(5), 405–417 (2011)
11. Darvas, A., Müller, P.: Reasoning about method calls in JML specifications. FTfJP (2005)
12. Hui, Z.W., Huang, S.: A formal model for metamorphic relation decomposition. In: WCSE (2013)
13. Kirchner, F., Kosmatov, N., Prevosto, V., Signoles, J., Yakobowski, B.: Frama-C: a software analysis perspective. Form. Aspect Comput. **27**(3), 573–609 (2015). http://frama-c.com
14. Leino, K.R.M., Müller, P.: Verification of equivalent-results methods. In: Drossopoulou, S. (ed.) ESOP 2008. LNCS, vol. 4960, pp. 307–321. Springer, Heidelberg (2008). doi:10.1007/978-3-540-78739-6_24
15. Sousa, M., Dillig, I.: Cartesian hoare logic for verifying k-safety properties. In: PLDI (2016)
16. Weyuker, E.J.: On testing non-testable programs. Comput. J. **25**(4), 465–470 (1982)

autoCode4: Structural Controller Synthesis

Chih-Hong Cheng[1]([⊠]), Edward A. Lee[2], and Harald Ruess[1]

[1] fortiss - An-Institut Technische Universität München, Munich, Germany
cheng@fortiss.org
[2] EECS, UC Berkeley, Berkeley, USA

Abstract. autoCode4 synthesizes structured reactive controllers from realizable specifications in the GXW subset of linear temporal logic (LTL). Generated reactive controllers are expressed in terms of an intermediate synchronous dataflow (SDF) format, which is further translated, using an open interface, into SCADE/Lustre and Ptolemy II. Moreover, autoCode4 generates and maintains a traceability relation between individual requirements and generated code blocks, as mandated by current standards for certifying safety-critical control code.

1 Introduction

autoCode4 synthesizes structured and certifiable reactive controllers from a given realizable specification in the GXW [5] subset of linear temporal logic (LTL). It is released under the LGPLv3 open source license, and can be downloaded, including a hands-on tutorial, from

http://autocode4.sourceforge.net

autoCode4 is based on structural recursion of GXW input formulas [5] for generating synchronous dataflow (SDF) [12] controllers composed from a set of actors, and for maintaining the traceability between given specifications and the generated code blocks. The underlying synthesis algorithm [5] of autoCode4 differs considerably from previous approaches and tools for reactive synthesis [4,6,7,11,14,16,17]. In contrast to these prevailing automata-based approaches, autoCode4 generates a reactive controller in a structured actor language with high-level behavioral constructs and synchronous dataflow communication between connected actors. This choice of generating *structured controllers* is motivated by the fact that a subset of SDF is compatible with the underlying model of computation for state-of-the-practice design tools including LabVIEW[1] and SCADE[2]. Indeed, autoCode4 includes pre-defined code generators for Lustre/SCADE and for Ptolemy II [9], where C code or a hardware description, say, in Verilog, can be generated subsequently. Structured SDF controllers also support the integration of manually designed or legacy elements. Furthermore, the structure of the generated SDF controller is often instrumental in pinpointing

---

[1] http://www.ni.com/labview.
[2] http://www.ansys.com/Products/Embedded-Software/ANSYS-SCADE-Suite.

© Springer-Verlag GmbH Germany 2017
A. Legay and T. Margaria (Eds.): TACAS 2017, Part I, LNCS 10205, pp. 398–404, 2017.
DOI: 10.1007/978-3-662-54577-5_23

and isolating problematic (e.g. realizable but demonstrating undesired behavior) specifications for validating requirements.

autoCode4 supports the necessary interfaces for integration into existing development tool chains. In this way, autoCode4 has been embedded into the Ptolemy II [9] platform for the design, simulation, and code generation of cyber-physical systems. The open interfaces of autoCode4 are suitable for realizing additional code generators for, say, Matlab Simulink[3] or continuous function charts (IEC 61131-3). Moreover, requirement specification languages for embedded control systems, such as EARS [8], may be translated to the GXW input language of autoCode4.

autoCode4 is unique among reactive synthesis tools in that it explicitly maintains the traceability between individual requirements (as sub-specifications) and the generated controller code blocks. Such a traceability relation is mandated by current industrial standards for safety-related developments such IEC 61508 (e.g. industrial automation), DO-178C (aerospace), and ISO-26262 (automotive).

2 Structural Synthesis in a Nutshell

autoCode4 uses the GXW subset of linear temporal logic (LTL) as defined in [5] for specifying the input-output behavior of reactive controllers. This specification language supports a conjunction of input assumptions, invariance conditions on outputs, transition-like reactions of the form $\mathbf{G}(\text{input} \to \mathbf{X}^i \text{output})$, and reactions of the form $\mathbf{G}(\text{input} \to \mathbf{X}^i(\text{output}\,\mathbf{W}\,\text{release}))$, where input is an LTL formula whose validity is determined by the next i input valuations (e.g. falling edge (in $\wedge\,\mathbf{X}\,\neg\text{in}$)). The latter reaction formula states that if there is a temporal input event satisfying the constraint input, then the output constraint should hold on output events until there is a release event (or output always holds).

The operator $\mathbf{G}$ is the universal path quantifier, $\mathbf{X}^i$ abbreviates i consecutive next-steps, $\mathbf{W}$ denotes the *weak until* temporal operator, the constraint output contains no temporal operator, and the subformula release may contain certain numbers of consecutive next-steps but no other temporal operators. Output response to input events in GXW is *immediate* and, whenever an event occurs the specification excludes choices of the controller to select among multiple output options (such as setting either out1 or out2 to be true).

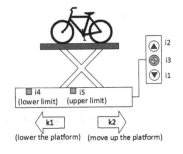

Fig. 1. A hydraulic lifting platform

The design of the GXW language has been guided by expressiveness, useability, and complexity considerations. We demonstrated the expressiveness of GXW by encoding of a large and rather diverse set of (Booleanized) control specifications from the domain of industrial automation [1,2]. On the other hand,

---

[3] http://www.mathworks.com/products/simulink/.

reactive synthesis for GXW is in PSPACE [5] compared to 2EXPTIME for full LTL. Moreover, the restrictions of GXW support the control designer by excluding non-causal, and commonly unrealizable, specifications, where output assignments are supposed to depend on future input values.

Structural synthesis [5] generates synchronous data flow [12] controllers from LTL specifications. Hereby, a controller is structurally composed from a set of interacting actors (behavior expressed in terms of Mealy machines). One of the main steps of the structural synthesis [5] involves checking for potentially conflicting constraints, from multiple sub-specifications, for the output assignments, and determining satisfiability of given invariance properties.

3   autoCode4 in Action

We illustrate the use of GXW by means of the simple example of controlling a hydraulic ramp as shown in Fig. 1 (cmp. with [2], Sect. 7.1.3, for similar scenarios). By pressing button i2 (up) the motor enables upward movement of the platform by setting output variable k2 to true. Button i3 (stop) stops the movement, and i1 (down) triggers the lowering of the hub by setting output variable k1 to true. Sensors i5 and i4 are used for detecting upper and lower limits. If i1 and i2 are simultaneously pressed, one needs to stop the movement. Finally, simultaneous triggering the motor in both directions (i.e., $G\neg(k1 \wedge k2)$) is disabled. The corresponding GXW specification is depicted in Fig. 2. Lines starting with "##" are comments, and a total of 8 GXW sub-specifications are listed. Sub-specifications are (implicitly) labeled, from top-to-bottom, by the indices 0 to 7.

```
## Driving a hydraulic lifting platform
## S0: When i2 is pressed, proceed upwards
[] ((i2 && !i1 && !i3) -> (k2 W (i5 || i1 || i3 || (i1 && i2))))
## S1: When i1 is pressed, proceed downwards
[] ((i1 && !i2 && !i3) -> (k1 W (i4 || i2 || i3 || (i1 && i2))))
## S2: forbidden to drive the motor both upwards and downwards
[] (!(k1 && k2))
## S3: When reaching the upper limit, disallow upward movement
[] (i5 -> !k2)
## S4: When reaching the lower limit, disallow downward movement
[] (i4 -> !k1)
## S5: When both up & down button are pressed, disallow movement
[] ((i1 && i2) -> (!k1 && !k2))
## S6: When stop is pressed, disallow movement
[] (i3 -> (!k1 && !k2))
## S7: Don't do any movement until i1 or i2 is pressed
((!k1 && !k2) W (i1 || i2))

INPUT i1, i2, i3, i4, i5
OUTPUT k1, k2
```

Fig. 2. GXW specification for hydraulic lifting platform

For the hydraulic lifting platform, Fig. 3 shows the resulting SDF controller synthesized under Ptolemy II. One may run interactive simulation or further use code generation features in Ptolemy II to automatically generate executable code in C or HDL. Due to space limits, we do not show the control structure within each block; instead we refer the reader to Fig. 4 for the corresponding Lustre implementation.

Now, we shortly comment on the requirement-to-implementation traceability using sub-specification S7: $(\neg k1 \wedge \neg k2)\mathbf{W}(i1 \vee i2)$ (the tool also allows generating a traceability report). In Fig. 3, an or-gate called event7 connects i1 and i2. The output of event7 is fed into an InUB-typed actor called Ctrl_7. The output of Ctrl_7 is negated (via Not_7k1 and Not_7k2) to influence output variables k1 and k2 respectively. One can observe that the specification index "7" can be identified in above mentioned blocks due to the naming convention.

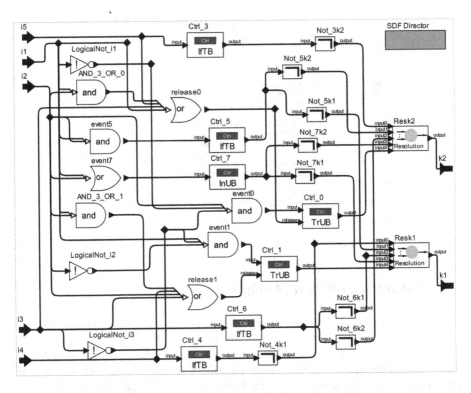

Fig. 3. Control realization as Ptolemy II models

autoCode4 may also generate reactive controllers in Lustre [13]. Figure 4 includes the Lustre v4 code generated from controlling the hydraulic lifting platform. The requirement-to-implementation traceability is similar to the Ptolemy II graphical representation in Fig. 3. Notice that parameterized blocks such as Res5 in Fig. 4 are instantiated twice. This kind of block reuse makes textual representations of generated code (i.e., define once, instantiate multiple times) highly compact.

```
node TrUB (input, release: bool) returns        node InUB (release: bool) returns (output: int);
(output: int);                                   var lock: bool;
var lock: bool;                                   let
let lock = if input and not release then true      lock = if release then false else true ->
       else if release then false               pre(lock);
       else false -> pre(lock);                    output = if release then 2
   output = if input and not release then 1         else 1 -> if pre(lock) then 1 else 2 ;
       else if release then 2                   node TernaryNot (input: int) returns (output:
       else 2 -> if pre(lock) then 1 else 2 ;   int);
tel                                              let output = if input = 1 then 0
node IfTB (input: bool) returns (output: int);      else if input = 0 then 1 else input;
let output = if input then 1 else 2;      tel    tel
node Res5 (input0, input1, input2, input3, input4: int; A: bool) returns (output: bool);
let
  output = if input0 = 1 or input1 = 1 or input2 = 1 or input3 = 1 or input4 = 1 then true
      else if input0 = 0 or input1 = 0 or input2 = 0 or input3 = 0 or input4 = 0 then false
      else A;
tel
node GXWcontroller(Gli1, Gli2, Gli3, Gli4, Gli5 : bool) returns (GOk1, GOk2: bool);
var
  Ctrl_4, Not_7k2, Ctrl_5, Ctrl_6, Not_6k1, Not_5k2, Ctrl_7, Not_7k1, Not_6k2,
  Ctrl_0, Not_4k1, Not_3k2, Ctrl_1, Not_5k1, Ctrl_3: int;
  Resk2, Resk1, event1, event0, release1, release0, event7, event5,
  AND_3_OR_0, AND_3_OR_1: bool;
let
  event0 = (Gli2 and (not Gli1) and (not Gli3));
  event1 = (Gli1 and (not Gli2) and (not Gli3));
  AND_3_OR_0 = (Gli1 and Gli2); release0 = (AND_3_OR_0 or Gli5 or Gli1 or Gli3);
  AND_3_OR_1 = (Gli1 and Gli2); release1 = (AND_3_OR_1 or Gli4 or Gli2 or Gli3);
  event7 = (Gli1 or Gli2);  event5 = (Gli1 and Gli2);
  Ctrl_0 = TrUB(event0 , release0); Ctrl_1 = TrUB(event1 , release1);
  Ctrl_3 = IfTB(Gli5); Ctrl_4 = IfTB(Gli4);
  Ctrl_5 = IfTB(event5); Ctrl_6 = IfTB(Gli3); Ctrl_7 = InUB(event7);
  Not_3k2 = TernaryNot(Ctrl_3);  Not_4k1 = TernaryNot(Ctrl_4);
  Not_5k1 = TernaryNot(Ctrl_5);  Not_5k2 = TernaryNot(Ctrl_5);
  Not_6k1 = TernaryNot(Ctrl_6);  Not_6k2 = TernaryNot(Ctrl_6);
  Not_7k2 = TernaryNot(Ctrl_7);  Not_7k1 = TernaryNot(Ctrl_7);
  Resk1 = Res5(Not_4k1, Ctrl_1, Not_5k1, Not_6k1, Not_7k1, false); GOk1 = Resk1;
  Resk2 = Res5(Ctrl_0, Not_3k2, Not_7k2, Not_5k2, Not_6k2, false); GOk2 = Resk2;
tel
```

Fig. 4. Control realization in Lustre format

4   autoCode4 Software Architecture

The software architecture of autoCode4 is depicted in Fig. 5 and follows the general outline of the structural synthesis algorithm as described [5]. Input specifications are analyzed and categorized by the specification analyzer, which also rejects non-GXW specifications. In our running example, S0 and S1 are of type TrUB (when event A triggers, do B until event C). S3, S4 and S5 are categorized as IfTB (when event A triggers, do B), S7 is InUB (initially, do A until B), and lastly, S2 is an invariance property.

Subsequently, Constraint Builder builds the corresponding SDF structure (via SDF Builder), which is not fully instantiated yet, and constructs a quantified Boolean formula with one quantifier alternation (2QBF) for resolving potential conflicts between individual sub-specifications. In this process, each sub-specification is associated with a set of actors; for example, formula S7 is associated with actors such as event7 or Ctrl_7. The engine can hash a set of actors that was instantiated previously, to enable actor reuse among multiple

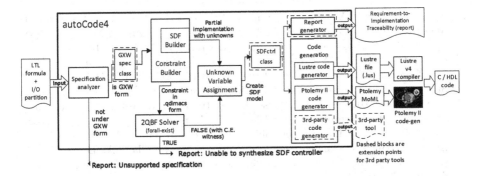

Fig. 5. System architecture of autoCode4, where dashed elements are extension points.

sub-specifications. Moreover, blocks such as Res5 in Fig. 4 are used for determining an output value A if none of the sub-specifications constrain such an output.

The generated 2QBF constraint is analyzed for potential conflicts on certain output variables from different sub-specifications, and for analyzing invariance properties. These constraints are of the form: $\exists$ A$_1$,..., A$_k$ $\forall$ system state s: (Env-Assumption(s) $\land$ SDF-dynamics(s)) $\rightarrow$ (No-output-conflict(s) $\land$ Invariance(s)). The open design choices are determined by witnesses for the existentially-quantified variables A$_1$,..., A$_k$, as specified in the previous step. Informally, the body of this formula encodes the condition: if the environment assumptions hold and the system adheres to the semantics of the SDF dynamics then there is no output conflict and the specified invariance properties hold. Our 2QBF solver implements an algorithm for alternating two Boolean satisfiability solvers [10] as in SAT4J [3]. It takes the negation of the constraint above with forall-exists top-level quantification. Therefore, whenever the 2QBF solver returns false, the generated counterexample determines a non-conflicting assignment for the uninstantiated variables. Using the definition of Resk1 and Resk2 in Fig. 4 in our running example, the variable A is set to false in both cases.

The internal SDF controller is stored using the class SDFctrl, and can be traversed for generating control code in Ptolemy II, Lustre, and other SDF-based languages. Finally, autoCode4 uses the Report generator for producing a requirement-to-implementation traceability report.

References

1. Online training material for PLC programming. http://plc-scada-dcs.blogspot.com/
2. CODESYS - Industrial IEC 61131-3 PLC programming framework. http://www.codesys.com/
3. Le Berre, D., Parrain, A.: The SAT4J library, release 2.2, system description. J. Satisf. Boolean Model. Comput. **7**, 59–64 (2010)

4. Bohy, A., Bruyère, V., Filiot, E., Jin, N., Raskin, J.-F.: Acacia+, a Tool for LTL Synthesis. In: Madhusudan, P., Seshia, S.A. (eds.) CAV 2012. LNCS, vol. 7358, pp. 652–657. Springer, Heidelberg (2012). doi:10.1007/978-3-642-31424-7_45

5. Cheng, C.-H., Hamza, Y., Ruess, H.: Structural synthesis for GXW specifications. In: Chaudhuri, S., Farzan, A. (eds.) CAV 2016. LNCS, vol. 9779, pp. 95–117. Springer, Cham (2016). doi:10.1007/978-3-319-41528-4_6

6. Cheng, C.-H., Huang, C.-H., Ruess, H., Stattelmann, S.: G4LTL-ST: automatic generation of PLC programs. In: Biere, A., Bloem, R. (eds.) CAV 2014. LNCS, vol. 8559, pp. 541–549. Springer, Cham (2014). doi:10.1007/978-3-319-08867-9_36

7. Ehlers, R.: Unbeast: symbolic bounded synthesis. In: Abdulla, P.A., Leino, K.R.M. (eds.) TACAS 2011. LNCS, vol. 6605, pp. 272–275. Springer, Heidelberg (2011). doi:10.1007/978-3-642-19835-9_25

8. Mavin, A., Wilkinson, P., Harwood, A., Novak, M.: Easy approach to requirements syntax (EARS). In: RE, pp. 317–322. IEEE (2009)

9. Ptolemaeus, C. (ed.): System Design, Modeling, and Simulation using Ptolemy II. Ptolemy.org, Berkeley (2014)

10. Janota, M., Marques-Silva, J.: abstraction-based algorithm for 2QBF. In: Sakallah, K.A., Simon, L. (eds.) SAT 2011. LNCS, vol. 6695, pp. 230–244. Springer, Heidelberg (2011). doi:10.1007/978-3-642-21581-0_19

11. Jobstmann, B., Galler, S., Weiglhofer, M., Bloem, R.: Anzu: a tool for property synthesis. In: Damm, W., Hermanns, H. (eds.) CAV 2007. LNCS, vol. 4590, pp. 258–262. Springer, Heidelberg (2007). doi:10.1007/978-3-540-73368-3_29

12. Lee, E.A., Messerschmitt, D.G.: Synchronous data flow. Proc. IEEE **75**(9), 1235–1245 (1987)

13. Halbwachs, N., Caspi, P., Raymond, P., Pilaud, D.: The synchronous data flow programming language LUSTRE. Proc. IEEE **79**(9), 1305–1320 (1987)

14. Piterman, N., Pnueli, A., Sa'ar, Y.: Synthesis of reactive(1) designs. In: Emerson, E.A., Namjoshi, K.S. (eds.) VMCAI 2006. LNCS, vol. 3855, pp. 364–380. Springer, Heidelberg (2005). doi:10.1007/11609773_24

15. Pnueli, A.: The temporal logic of programs. In: FOCS, pp. 46–57. IEEE (1977)

16. Pnueli, A., Rosner, R.: On the synthesis of a reactive module. In: POPL, pp. 179–190. IEEE (1989)

17. Schewe, S., Finkbeiner, B.: Bounded synthesis. In: Namjoshi, K.S., Yoneda, T., Higashino, T., Okamura, Y. (eds.) ATVA 2007. LNCS, vol. 4762, pp. 474–488. Springer, Heidelberg (2007). doi:10.1007/978-3-540-75596-8_33

Automata

Lazy Automata Techniques for WS1S

Tomáš Fiedor[1], Lukáš Holík[1], Petr Janků[1], Ondřej Lengál[1,2(✉)], and Tomáš Vojnar[1]

[1] FIT, Brno University of Technology, IT4Innovations Centre of Excellence, Brno, Czech Republic
lengal@fit.vutbr.cz

[2] Institute of Information Science, Academia Sinica, Taipei, Taiwan

Abstract. We present a new decision procedure for the logic WS1S. It originates from the classical approach, which first builds an automaton accepting all models of a formula and then tests whether its language is empty. The main novelty is to test the emptiness on the fly, while constructing a symbolic, term-based representation of the automaton, and prune the constructed state space from parts irrelevant to the test. The pruning is done by a generalization of two techniques used in antichain-based language inclusion and universality checking of finite automata: subsumption and early termination. The richer structure of the WS1S decision problem allows us, however, to elaborate on these techniques in novel ways. Our experiments show that the proposed approach can in many cases significantly outperform the classical decision procedure (implemented in the MONA tool) as well as recently proposed alternatives.

1 Introduction

Weak monadic second-order logic of one successor (WS1S) is a powerful language for reasoning about regular properties of finite words. It has found numerous uses, from software and hardware verification through controller synthesis to computational linguistics, and further on. Some more recent applications of WS1S include verification of pointer programs and deciding related logics [1–5] as well as synthesis from regular specifications [6]. Most of the successful applications were due to the tool MONA [7], which implements classical automata-based decision procedures for WS1S and WS2S (a generalization of WS1S to finite binary trees). The worst case complexity of WS1S is nonelementary [8] and, despite many optimizations implemented in MONA and other tools, the complexity sometimes strikes back. Authors of methods translating their problems to WS1S/WS2S are then forced to either find workarounds to circumvent the complexity blowup, such as in [2], or, often restricting the input of their approach, give up translating to WS1S/WS2S altogether [9].

The classical WS1S decision procedure builds an automaton A_φ accepting all models of the given formula φ in a form of finite words, and then tests A_φ for language emptiness. The bottleneck of the procedure is the size of A_φ, which can

© Springer-Verlag GmbH Germany 2017
A. Legay and T. Margaria (Eds.): TACAS 2017, Part I, LNCS 10205, pp. 407–425, 2017.
DOI: 10.1007/978-3-662-54577-5_24

be huge due to the fact that the derivation of A_φ involves many nested automata product constructions and complementation steps, preceded by determinization. The main point of this paper is to avoid the state-space explosion involved in the classical *explicit* construction by representing automata *symbolically* and testing the emptiness *on the fly*, while constructing A_φ, and by omitting the state space irrelevant to the emptiness test. This is done using two main principles: *lazy evaluation* and *subsumption-based pruning*. These principles have, to some degree, already appeared in the so-called antichain-based testing of language universality and inclusion of finite automata [10]. The richer structure of the WS1S decision problem allows us, however, to elaborate on these principles in novel ways and utilize their power even more.

Overview of Our Algorithm. Our algorithm originates in the classical WS1S decision procedure as implemented in MONA, in which models of formulae are encoded by finite words over a multi-track binary alphabet where each track corresponds to a variable of φ. In order to come closer to this view of formula models as words, we replace the input formula φ by a *language term* t_φ describing the language L_φ of all word encodings of its models.

In t_φ, the atomic formulae of φ are replaced by predefined automata accepting languages of their models. Boolean operators ($\wedge$, $\vee$, and $\neg$) are turned into the corresponding set operators ($\cup$, $\cap$, and complement) over the languages of models. An existential quantification $\exists X$ becomes a sequence of two operations. First, a projection π_X removes information about valuations of the quantified variable X from symbols of the alphabet. After the projection, the resulting language L may, however, encode some but not necessarily *all* encodings of the models. In particular, encodings with some specific numbers of trailing $\bar{0}$'s, used as a padding, may be missing. $\bar{0}$ here denotes the symbol with 0 in each track. To obtain a language containing *all* encodings of the models, L must be extended to include encodings with any number of trailing $\bar{0}$'s. This corresponds to taking the (right) $\bar{0}^*$-quotient of L, written $L - \bar{0}^*$, which is the set of all prefixes of words of L with the remaining suffix in $\bar{0}^*$. We give an example WS1S formula φ in (1) and its language term t_φ in (2). The dotted operators represent operators over language terms. See Fig. 2 for the automata

$$\varphi \equiv \exists X \colon \mathrm{Sing}(X) \wedge (\exists Y \colon Y = X + 1) \tag{1}$$

$A_{\mathrm{Sing}(X)}$ and $A_{Y=X+1}$.

$$t_\varphi \equiv \pi_X(\{A_{\mathrm{Sing}(X)} \mathbin{\dot{\cap}} (\pi_Y(A_{Y=X+1}) \mathbin{\dot{-}} \bar{0}^*)\}) \mathbin{\dot{-}} \bar{0}^* \tag{2}$$

The main novelty of our work is that we test emptiness of L_φ directly over t_φ. The term is used as a symbolic representation of the automata that would be explicitly constructed in the classical procedure: inductively to the terms structure, starting from the leaves and combining the automata of sub-terms by standard automata constructions that implement the term operators. Instead of first building automata and only then testing emptiness, we test it on the fly during the construction. This offers opportunities to prune out large portions of the state space that turn out not to be relevant for the test.

A sub-term t_ψ of t_φ, corresponding to a sub-formula ψ, represents final states of the automaton A_ψ accepting the language encoding models of ψ. Predecessors of the final states represented by t_ψ correspond to quotients of t_ψ. All states of $\mathcal{A}_\psi$ could hence be constructed by quotienting t_ψ until fixpoint. By working with terms, our procedure can often avoid building large parts of the automata when they are not necessary for answering the emptiness query. For instance, when testing emptiness of the language of a term $t_1 \cup t_2$, we adopt the *lazy app-roach* (in this particular case the so-called *short-circuit evaluation*) and first test emptiness of the language of t_1; if it is non-empty, we do not need to process t_2. Testing language emptiness of terms arising from quantified sub-formulae is more complicated since they translate to $-\bar{0}^*$ quotients. We evaluate the test on $t - \bar{0}^*$ by iterating the $-\bar{0}$ quotient from t. We either conclude with the positive result as soon as one of the iteration computes a term with a non-empty language, or with the negative one if the fixpoint of the quotient construction is reached. The fixpoint condition is that the so-far computed quotients *subsume* the newly constructed ones, where subsumption is a relation under-approximating inclu-sion of languages represented by terms. Subsumption is also used to prune the set of computed terms so that only an *antichain* of the terms maximal wrt subsumption is kept.

Besides lazy evaluation and subsumption, our approach can benefit from mul-tiple further optimizations. For example, it can be *combined* with the *explicit WS1S decision procedure*, which can be used to transform arbitrary sub-terms of t_φ to automata. These automata can then be rather small due to minimiza-tion, which cannot be applied in the on-the-fly approach (the automata can, however, also explode due to determinisation and product construction, hence this technique comes with a trade-off). We also propose a novel way of *utilising BDD-based encoding* of automata transition functions in the MONA style for computing quotients of terms. Finally, our method can exploit various methods of *logic-based pre-processing*, such as *anti-prenexing*, which, in our experience, can often significantly reduce the search space of fixpoint computations.

Experiments. We have implemented our decision procedure in a prototype tool called GASTON and compared its performance with other publicly available WS1S solvers on benchmarks from various sources. In the experiments, GASTON managed to win over all other solvers on various parametric families of WS1S formulae that were designed—mostly by authors of other tools—to stress-test WS1S solvers. Moreover, GASTON was able to significantly outperform MONA and other solvers on a number of formulae obtained from various formal verifi-cation tasks. This shows that our approach is applicable in practice and has a great potential to handle more complex formulae than those so far obtained in WS1S applications. We believe that the efficiency of our approach can be pushed much further, making WS1S scale enough for new classes of applications.

Related Work. As already mentioned above, MONA [7] is the usual tool of choice for deciding WS1S formulae. The efficiency of MONA stems from many opti-mizations, both higher-level (such as automata minimization, the encoding of first-order variables used in models, or the use of BDDs to encode the tran-sition relation of the automaton) as well as lower-level (e.g. optimizations of hash tables, etc.) [11,12]. Apart from MONA, there are other related tools based on the explicit automata procedure, such as JMOSEL [13] for a related logic M2L(Str), which implements several optimizations (such as second-order value numbering [14]) that allow it to outperform MONA on some benchmarks (MONA also provides an M2L(Str) interface on top of the WS1S decision procedure), or the procedure using symbolic finite automata of D'Antoni et al. in [15].

Our work was originally inspired by antichain techniques for checking universality and inclusion of finite automata [10,16,17], which use symbolic computation and subsumption to prune large state spaces arising from subset construction. In [18], which is a starting point for the current paper, we discussed a basic idea of generalizing these techniques to a WS1S decision procedure. In the current paper we have turned the idea of [18] to an algorithm efficient in practice by roughly the following steps: (1) reformulating the symbolic representation of automata from nested upward and downward closed sets of automata states to more intuitive language terms, (2) generalizing the procedure originally restricted to formulae in the prenex normal form to arbitrary formulae, (3) introduction of lazy evaluation, and (4) many other important optimizations.

Recently, a couple of logic-based approaches for deciding WS1S appeared. Ganzow and Kaiser [19] developed a new decision procedure for the weak monadic second-order logic on inductive structures, within their tool TOSS, which is even more general than WSkS. Their approach completely avoids automata; instead, it is based on Shelah's composition method. The TOSS tool is quite promising as it outperforms MONA on some of the benchmarks. It, however, lacks some features in order to perform meaningful comparison on benchmarks used in practice. Traytel [20], on the other hand, uses the classical decision procedure, recast in the framework of coalgebras. The work focuses on testing equivalence of a pair of formulae, which is performed by finding a bisimulation between derivatives of the formulae. While it is shown that it can outperform MONA on some simple artificial examples, the implementation is not optimized enough and is easily outperformed by the rest of the tools on other benchmarks.

2   Preliminaries on Languages and Automata

A *word* over a finite alphabet Σ is a finite sequence $w = a_1 \cdots a_n$, for $n \geq 0$, of symbols from Σ. Its i-th symbol a_i is denoted by $w[i]$. For $n = 0$, the word is the empty word ϵ. A language L is a set of words over Σ. We use the standard language operators of concatenation $L.L'$ and iteration L^*. The (right) quotient of a language L wrt the language L' is the language $L - L' = \{u \mid \exists v \in L' : uv \in L\}$. We abuse notation and write $L - w$ to denote $L - \{w\}$, for a word $w \in \Sigma^*$.

A *finite automaton* (FA) over an alphabet Σ is a quadruple $\mathcal{A} = (Q, \delta, I, F)$ where Q is a finite set of states, $\delta \subseteq Q \times \Sigma \times Q$ is a set of transitions, $I \subseteq Q$ is a set of *initial* states, and $F \subseteq Q$ is a set of *final* states. The *pre-image* of a state $q \in Q$ over $a \in \Sigma$ is the set of states $pre_{[a]}(q) = \{q' \mid (q', a, q) \in \delta\}$, and it is the set $pre_{[a]}(S) = \bigcup_{q \in S} pre_{[a]}(q)$ for a set of states S.

The language $\mathcal{L}(q)$ accepted *at* a state $q \in Q$ is the set of words that can be read along a run ending in q, i.e. all words $a_1 \cdots a_n$, for $n \geq 0$, such that δ

contains transitions $(q_0, a_1, q_1), \ldots, (q_{n-1}, a_n, q_n)$ with $q_0 \in I$ and $q_n = q$. The language $\mathcal{L}(\mathcal{A})$ of $\mathcal{A}$ is then the union $\bigcup_{q \in F} \mathcal{L}(q)$ of languages of its final states.

3   WS1S

In this section, we give a minimalistic introduction to the *weak monadic second-order logic of one successor* (WS1S) and outline its explicit decision procedure based on representing sets of models as regular languages and finite automata. See, for instance, Comon *et al.* [21] for a more thorough introduction.

3.1   Syntax and Semantics of WS1S

WS1S allows quantification over second-order *variables*, which we denote by upper-case letters $X, Y, \ldots$, that range over finite subsets of $\mathbb{N}_0$. Atomic formulae are of the form (i) $X \subseteq Y$, (ii) $\mathrm{Sing}(X)$, (iii) $X = \{0\}$, and (iv) $X = Y + 1$. Formulae are built from the atomic ones using the logical connectives $\land, \lor, \neg$, and the quantifier $\exists \mathcal{X}$ where $\mathcal{X}$ is a finite set of variables (we write $\exists X$ if $\mathcal{X}$ is a singleton $\{X\}$). A *model* of a WS1S formula $\varphi(\mathcal{X})$ with the set of free variables $\mathcal{X}$ is an assignment $\rho : \mathcal{X} \to 2^{\mathbb{N}_0}$ of the free variables $\mathcal{X}$ of φ to finite subsets of $\mathbb{N}_0$ for which the formula is *satisfied*, written $\rho \models \varphi$. Satisfaction of atomic formulae is defined as follows: (i) $\rho \models X \subseteq Y$ iff $\rho(X) \subseteq \rho(Y)$, (ii) $\rho \models \mathrm{Sing}(X)$ iff $\rho(X)$ is a singleton set, (iii) $\rho \models X = \{0\}$ iff $\rho(X) = \{0\}$, and (iv) $\rho \models X = Y + 1$ iff $\rho(X) = \{x\}, \rho(Y) = \{y\}$, and $x = y + 1$. Satisfaction for formulae obtained using Boolean connectives is defined as usual. A formula φ is *valid*, written $\models \varphi$, iff all assignments of its free variables to finite subsets of $\mathbb{N}_0$ are its models, and *satisfiable* if it has a model. Wlog we assume that each variable in a formula is quantified at most once.

3.2   Models as Words

Let $\mathcal{X}$ be a finite set of variables. A *symbol* τ over $\mathcal{X}$ is a mapping of all variables in $\mathcal{X}$ to the set $\{0, 1\}$, e.g. $\tau = \{X_1 \mapsto 0, X_2 \mapsto 1\}$ for $\mathcal{X} = \{X_1, X_2\}$, which we will write as $\tau = \begin{smallmatrix} X_1 : 0 \\ X_2 : 1 \end{smallmatrix}$ below. The set of all symbols over $\mathcal{X}$ is denoted as $\Sigma_{\mathcal{X}}$. We use $\bar{0}$ to denote the symbol in $\Sigma_{\mathcal{X}}$ that maps all variables to 0, i.e. $\bar{0} = \{X \mapsto 0 \mid X \in \mathcal{X}\}$.

An assignment $\rho : \mathcal{X} \to 2^{\mathbb{N}_0}$ may be encoded as a word w_ρ of symbols over $\mathcal{X}$ in the following way: w_ρ contains 1 in the $(i+1)$-st position of the row for X iff $i \in X$ in ρ. Notice that there exists an infinite number of encodings of ρ: the shortest encoding is w_ρ^s of the length $n + 1$, where n is the largest number appearing in any of the sets that is assigned to a variable of $\mathcal{X}$ in ρ, or -1 when all these sets are empty. The rest of the encodings are all those corresponding to w_ρ^s extended with an arbitrary number of $\bar{0}$'s appended to its end. For example, $\begin{smallmatrix} X_1 : 0 \\ X_2 : 1 \end{smallmatrix}, \begin{smallmatrix} X_1 : 00 \\ X_2 : 10 \end{smallmatrix}, \begin{smallmatrix} X_1 : 000 \\ X_2 : 100 \end{smallmatrix}, \begin{smallmatrix} X_1 : 000\ldots0 \\ X_2 : 100\ldots0 \end{smallmatrix}$ are all encodings of the assignment $\rho = \{X_1 \mapsto \emptyset, X_2 \mapsto \{0\}\}$. We use $\mathcal{L}(\varphi) \subseteq \Sigma_{\mathcal{X}}^*$ to denote the language of all encodings of a formula φ's models, where $\mathcal{X}$ are the free variables of φ.

For two sets $\mathcal{X}$ and $\mathcal{Y}$ of variables and any two symbols $\tau_1, \tau_2 \in \Sigma_{\mathcal{X}}$, we write $\tau_1 \sim_{\mathcal{Y}} \tau_2$ iff $\forall X \in \mathcal{X} \setminus \mathcal{Y} : \tau_1(X) = \tau_2(X)$, i.e. the two symbols differ (at most) in the values of variables in $\mathcal{Y}$. The relation $\sim_{\mathcal{Y}}$ is generalized to words such that $w_1 \sim_{\mathcal{Y}} w_2$ iff $|w_1| = |w_2|$ and $\forall 1 \leq i \leq |w_1| : w_1[i] \sim_{\mathcal{Y}} w_2[i]$. For a language $L \subseteq \Sigma_{\mathcal{X}}^*$, we define $\pi_{\mathcal{Y}}(L)$ as the language of words w that are $\sim_{\mathcal{Y}}$-equivalent with some word $w' \in L$. Seen from the point of view of encodings of sets of assignments, $\pi_{\mathcal{Y}}(L)$ encodes all assignments that may differ from those encoded by L (only) in the values of variables from $\mathcal{Y}$. If $\mathcal{Y}$ is disjoint with the free variables of φ, then $\pi_{\mathcal{Y}}(\mathcal{L}(\varphi))$ corresponds to the so-called *cylindrification* of $\mathcal{L}(\varphi)$, and if it is their subset, then $\pi_{\mathcal{Y}}(\mathcal{L}(\varphi))$ corresponds to the so-called *projection* [21]. We use π_Y to denote $\pi_{\{Y\}}$ for a variable Y.

Consider formulae over the set $\mathbb{V}$ of variables. Let $free(\varphi)$ be the set of free variables of φ, and let $\mathcal{L}^{\mathbb{V}}(\varphi) = \pi_{\mathbb{V} \setminus free(\varphi)}(\mathcal{L}(\varphi))$ be the language $\mathcal{L}(\varphi)$ cylindrified wrt those variables of $\mathbb{V}$ that are not free in φ. Let φ and ψ be formulae and assume that $\mathcal{L}^{\mathbb{V}}(\varphi)$

$$\mathcal{L}^{\mathbb{V}}(\varphi \vee \psi) = \mathcal{L}^{\mathbb{V}}(\varphi) \cup \mathcal{L}^{\mathbb{V}}(\psi) \quad (3)$$

$$\mathcal{L}^{\mathbb{V}}(\varphi \wedge \psi) = \mathcal{L}^{\mathbb{V}}(\varphi) \cap \mathcal{L}^{\mathbb{V}}(\psi) \quad (4)$$

$$\mathcal{L}^{\mathbb{V}}(\neg\varphi) = \Sigma_{\mathbb{V}}^* \setminus \mathcal{L}^{\mathbb{V}}(\varphi) \quad (5)$$

$$\mathcal{L}^{\mathbb{V}}(\exists \mathcal{X} : \varphi) = \pi_{\mathcal{X}}(\mathcal{L}^{\mathbb{V}}(\varphi)) - \bar{0}^* \quad (6)$$

and $\mathcal{L}^{\mathbb{V}}(\psi)$ are languages of encodings of their models cylindrified wrt $\mathbb{V}$. Languages of formulae obtained from φ and ψ using logical connectives are defined by Eqs. (3) to (6). Equations (3)–(5) above are straightforward: Boolean connectives translate to the corresponding set operators over the universe of encodings of assignments of variables in $\mathbb{V}$. Existential quantification $\exists \mathcal{X} : \varphi$ translates into a composition of two language transformations. First, $\pi_{\mathcal{X}}$ makes the valuations of variables of $\mathcal{X}$ arbitrary, which intuitively corresponds to forgetting everything about values of variables in $\mathcal{X}$ (notice that this is a different use of $\pi_{\mathcal{X}}$ than the cylindrification since here variables of $\mathcal{X}$ *are* free variables of φ). The second step, removing suffixes of $\bar{0}$'s from the model encodings, is necessary since $\pi_{\mathcal{X}}(\mathcal{L}^{\mathbb{V}}(\varphi))$ might be missing some encodings of models of $\exists \mathcal{X} : \varphi$. For example, suppose that $\mathbb{V} = \{X, Y\}$ and the only model of φ is $\{X \mapsto \{0\}, Y \mapsto \{1\}\}$, yielding $\mathcal{L}^{\mathbb{V}}(\varphi) = \begin{smallmatrix} X : 10 \\ Y : 01 \end{smallmatrix} \begin{smallmatrix} 0 \\ 0 \end{smallmatrix}^*$. Then $\pi_Y(\mathcal{L}^{\mathbb{V}}(\varphi)) = \begin{smallmatrix} X : 10 \\ Y : ?? \end{smallmatrix} \begin{smallmatrix} 0 \\ ? \end{smallmatrix}^*$ does not contain the shortest encoding $\begin{smallmatrix} X : 1 \\ Y : ? \end{smallmatrix}$ (where each '?' denotes an arbitrary value) of the only model $\{X \mapsto \{0\}\}$ of $\exists Y : \varphi$. It only contains its variants with at least one $\bar{0}$ appended to it. This generally happens for models of φ where the largest number in the value of the variable Y being eliminated is larger than maximum number found in the values of the free variables of $\exists Y : \varphi$. The role of the $-\bar{0}^*$ quotient is to include the missing encodings of models with a smaller number of trailing $\bar{0}$'s into the language.

The standard approach to decide satisfiability of a WS1S formula φ with the set of variables $\mathbb{V}$ is to construct an automaton $\mathcal{A}_\varphi$ accepting $\mathcal{L}^{\mathbb{V}}(\varphi)$ and check emptiness of its language. The construction starts with simple pre-defined automata $\mathcal{A}_\psi$ for φ's atomic formulae ψ (see Fig. 2 for examples of automata for selected atomic formulae and e.g. [21] for more details) accepting cylindrified languages $\mathcal{L}^{\mathbb{V}}(\psi)$ of models of ψ. These are simple regular languages. The construction then continues by inductively constructing automata $\mathcal{A}_{\varphi'}$ accepting languages $\mathcal{L}^{\mathbb{V}}(\varphi')$ of models for all other sub-formulae φ' of φ, using Eqs. (3)–(6)

above. The language operators used in the rules are implemented using standard automata-theoretic constructions (see [21]).

4 Satisfiability via Language Term Evaluation

This section introduces the basic version of our symbolic algorithm for deciding satisfiability of a WS1S formula φ with a set of variables $\mathbb{V}$. Its optimized version is the subject of the next section. To simplify presentation, we consider the particular case of *ground* formulae (i.e. formulae without free variables), for which satisfiability corresponds to validity. Satisfiability of a formula with free variables can be reduced to this case by prefixing it with existential quantification over the free variables. If φ is ground, the language $\mathcal{L}^{\mathbb{V}}(\varphi)$ is either $\Sigma^*_{\mathbb{V}}$ in the case φ is valid, or empty if φ is invalid. Then, to decide the validity of φ, it suffices to test if $\epsilon \in \mathcal{L}^{\mathbb{V}}(\varphi)$.

Our algorithm evaluates the so-called *language term* t_φ, a symbolic representation of the language $\mathcal{L}^{\mathbb{V}}(\varphi)$, whose structure reflects the construction of $\mathcal{A}_\varphi$. It is a (finite) term generated by the following grammar:

$$t ::= \mathcal{A} \mid t \mathbin{\text{\underline{$\cup$}}} t \mid t \mathbin{\text{\underline{$\cap$}}} t \mid \overline{t} \mid \pi_X(t) \mid t \mathbin{\underline{\text{---}}} \alpha \mid t \mathbin{\underline{\text{---}}} \alpha^* \mid T$$

where $\mathcal{A}$ is a finite automaton over the alphabet $\Sigma_{\mathbb{V}}$, α is a symbol $\tau \in \Sigma_{\mathbb{V}}$ or a set $S \subseteq \Sigma_{\mathbb{V}}$ of symbols, and T is a finite set of terms. We use marked variants of the operators to distinguish the syntax of language terms manipulated by our algorithm from the cases when we wish to denote the semantical meaning of the operators. A term of the form $t \mathbin{\underline{\text{---}}} \alpha^*$ is called a *star quotient*, or shortly a *star*, and a term $t \mathbin{\underline{\text{---}}} \tau$ is a *symbol quotient*. Both are also called *quotients*. The *language* $\mathcal{L}(t)$ *of a term* t is obtained by taking the languages of the automata in its leaves and combining them using the term operators. Terms with the same language are *language-equivalent*. The special terms T, having the form of a set, represent intermediate states of fixpoint computations used to eliminate star quotients. The language of a set T equals the *union* of the languages of its elements. The reason for having two ways of expressing a union of terms is a different treatment of $\mathbin{\text{\underline{$\cup$}}}$ and T, which will be discussed later. We use the standard notion of isomorphism of two terms, extended with having two set terms isomorphic iff they contain isomorphic elements.

A formula φ is initially transformed into the term t_φ by replacing every atomic sub-formula ψ in φ by the automaton $\mathcal{A}_\psi$ accepting $\mathcal{L}^{\mathbb{V}}(\psi)$, and by replacing the logical connectives with dotted term operators according to Eqs. (3)–(6) of Sect. 3.2. The core of our algorithm is evaluation of the ϵ-membership query $\epsilon \in t_\varphi$, which will also trigger further rewriting of the term.

The ϵ-membership query on a quotient-free term is evaluated using equivalences (7) to (12). Equivalences (7) to (11) reduce tests on terms to Boolean combinations of tests on their sub-terms and allow pushing the test towards the automata at the term's leaves. Equivalence (12) then reduces it to testing intersection of the initial states $I(\mathcal{A})$ and the final states $F(\mathcal{A})$ of an automaton.

$$\epsilon \in T \quad \text{iff} \quad \epsilon \in t \text{ for some } t \in T \quad (7)$$
$$\epsilon \in t \cup t' \quad \text{iff} \quad \epsilon \in t \text{ or } \epsilon \in t' \quad (8)$$
$$\epsilon \in t \cap t' \quad \text{iff} \quad \epsilon \in t \text{ and } \epsilon \in t' \quad (9)$$
$$\epsilon \in \overline{t} \quad \text{iff} \quad \text{not } \epsilon \in t \quad (10)$$
$$\epsilon \in \pi_{\mathcal{X}}(t) \quad \text{iff} \quad \epsilon \in t \quad (11)$$
$$\epsilon \in \mathcal{A} \quad \text{iff} \quad I(\mathcal{A}) \cap F(\mathcal{A}) \neq \emptyset \quad (12)$$

Equivalences (7) to (11) do not apply to quotients, which arise from quantified sub-formulae (cf. Eq. (6) in Sect. 3.2). A quotient is therefore (in the basic version) first rewritten into a language-equivalent quotient-free form. This rewriting corresponds to saturating the set of final states of an automaton in the explicit decision procedure with all states in their pre^*-image over $\overline{0}$. In our procedure, we use rules (13) and (14).

Rule (13) transforms the term into a form in which a star quotient is applied on a plain set of terms rather than on a projection. A star quotient

$$\pi_{\mathcal{X}}(T) \overset{\bullet}{-} \overline{0}^* \;\to\; \pi_{\mathcal{X}}(T \overset{\bullet}{-} \pi_{\mathcal{X}}(\overline{0})^*) \quad (13)$$

of a set is then eliminated using a fixpoint computation that saturates the set with all quotients of its elements wrt the set of symbols $S = \pi_{\mathcal{X}}(\overline{0})$. A single iteration is implemented using rule (14). There, $T \ominus S$ is the set $\{t \overset{\bullet}{-} \tau \mid t \in T \wedge \tau \in S\}$ of quotients

$$T \overset{\bullet}{-} S^* \;\to\; \begin{cases} T & \text{if } T \ominus S \sqsubseteq T \\ (T \cup (T \ominus S)) \overset{\bullet}{-} S^* & \text{otherwise} \end{cases} \quad (14)$$

of terms in T wrt symbols of S. (Note that (14) uses the identity $S^* = \{\epsilon\} \cup S^* S$.) Termination of the fixpoint computation is decided based on the subsumption relation $\sqsubseteq$, which is some relation that under-approximates language inclusion of terms. When the condition holds, then the language of T is stable wrt quotienting by S, i.e. $\mathcal{L}(T) = \mathcal{L}(T \overset{\bullet}{-} S^*)$. In the basic algorithm, we use term isomorphism for $\sqsubseteq$; later, we provide a more precise subsumption relation with a good trade-off between precision and cost. Note that an iteration of rule (14) can be implemented efficiently by the standard worklist algorithm, which extends T only with quotients $T' \ominus S$ of terms T' that were added to T in the previous iteration.

The set $T \ominus S$ introduces quotient terms of the form $t \overset{\bullet}{-} \tau$, for $\tau \in \Sigma_{\mathcal{V}}$, which also need to be eliminated to facilitate the ϵ-membership test. This is done using rewriting rules (15) to (19), where $pre_{[\tau]}(\mathcal{A})$ is $\mathcal{A}$ with its set of final states F replaced by $pre_{[\tau]}(F)$.

$$(t \cup t') \overset{\bullet}{-} \tau \;\to\; (t \overset{\bullet}{-} \tau) \cup (t' \overset{\bullet}{-} \tau) \quad (15)$$
$$(t \cap t') \overset{\bullet}{-} \tau \;\to\; (t \overset{\bullet}{-} \tau) \cap (t' \overset{\bullet}{-} \tau) \quad (16)$$
$$\overline{t} \overset{\bullet}{-} \tau \;\to\; \overline{t \overset{\bullet}{-} \tau} \quad (17)$$
$$\pi_{\mathcal{X}}(t) \overset{\bullet}{-} \tau \;\to\; \pi_{\mathcal{X}}(t \overset{\bullet}{-} \pi_{\mathcal{X}}(\tau)) \quad (18)$$
$$\mathcal{A} \overset{\bullet}{-} \tau \;\to\; pre_{[\tau]}(\mathcal{A}) \quad (19)$$

If t is quotient-free, then rules (15)–(18) applied to $t \overset{\bullet}{-} \tau$ push the symbol quotient down the structure of t towards the automata in the leaves, where it is eliminated by rule (19). Otherwise, if t is not quotient-free, it can be re-written using rules (13)–(19). In particular, if t is a star quotient of a quotient-free term, then the quotient-free form of t can be obtained by iterating rule (14), combined with rules (15)–(19) to transform the new terms in T into a quotient-free form.

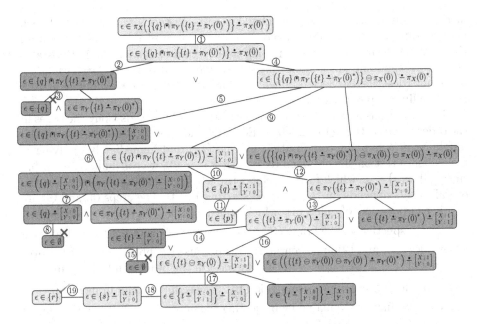

Fig. 1. Example of deciding validity of the formula $\varphi \equiv \exists X : \mathrm{Sing}(X) \wedge (\exists Y : Y = X + 1)$ (Color figure online)

Finally, terms with multiple quotients can be rewritten to the quotient-free form inductively to their structure. Every inductive step rewrites some star quotient of a quotient-free sub-term into the quotient-free form. Note that this procedure is bound to terminate since the terms generated by quotienting a star have the same structure as the original term, differing only in the states in their leaves. As the number of the states is finite, so is the number of the terms.

Example 1. We will show the workings of our procedure using an example of testing satisfiability of the formula $\varphi \equiv \exists X . \mathrm{Sing}(X) \wedge (\exists Y . Y = X + 1)$. We start by rewriting φ into a *term* t_φ representing its language $\mathcal{L}^V(\varphi)$:

$$t_\varphi \equiv \pi_X(\{\{q\} \mathbin{\cap} \pi_Y(\{t\} \mathbin{\overset{\bullet}{-}} \pi_Y(\bar{0})^*)\} \mathbin{\overset{\bullet}{-}} \pi_X(\bar{0})^*)$$

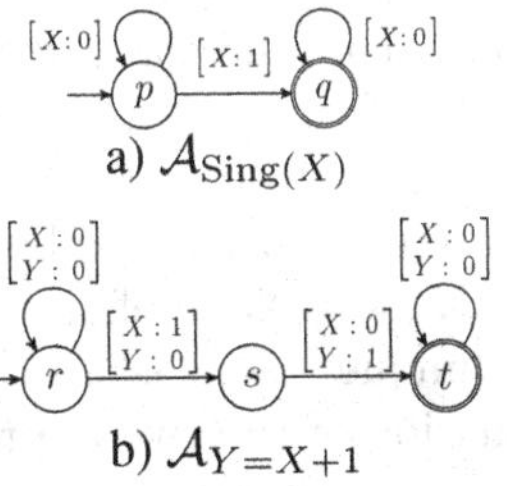

(we have already used rule (13) twice). In the example, a set R of states will denote an automaton obtained from $\mathcal{A}_{\mathrm{Sing}(X)}$ or $\mathcal{A}_{Y=X+1}$ (cf. Fig. 2) by setting the final states to R. Red nodes in the computation tree denote ϵ-membership tests that failed and green nodes those that succeeded. Grey nodes denote tests that were not evaluated.

As noted previously, it holds that $\models \varphi$ iff $\epsilon \in t_\varphi$. The sequence of computation steps for determining the ϵ-membership test is shown using the computation tree

Fig. 2. Example automata

in Fig. 1. The nodes contain ϵ-membership tests on terms and the test of each node is equivalent to a conjunction or disjunction of tests of its children. Leafs of the form $\epsilon \in R$ are evaluated as testing intersection of R with the initial states of the corresponding automaton. In the example, we also use the *lazy evaluation* technique (described in Sect. 5.2), which allows us to evaluate ϵ-membership tests on partially computed fixpoints.

The computation starts at the root of the tree and proceeds along the edges in the order given by their circled labels. Edges ② and ④ were obtained by a partial unfolding of a fixpoint computation by rule (14) and immediately applying ϵ-membership test on the obtained terms. After step ③, we conclude that $\epsilon \notin \{q\}$ since $\{p\} \cap \{q\} = \emptyset$, which further refutes the whole conjunction below ②, so the overall result depends on the sub-tree starting by ④. The steps ⑤ and ⑨ are another application of rule (14), which transforms $\pi_X(\bar{0})$ to the symbols $\begin{bmatrix} X:0 \\ Y:0 \end{bmatrix}$ and $\begin{bmatrix} X:1 \\ Y:0 \end{bmatrix}$ respectively. The branch ⑤ pushes the $\stackrel{\bullet}{-} \begin{bmatrix} X:0 \\ Y:0 \end{bmatrix}$ quotient to the leaf term using rules (16) and (9) and eventually fails because the predecessors of $\{q\}$ over the symbol $\begin{bmatrix} X:0 \\ Y:0 \end{bmatrix}$ in $\mathcal{A}_{\mathrm{Sing}(X)}$ is the empty set. On the other hand, the evaluation of the branch ⑨ continues using rule (16), succeeding in the branch ⑩. The branch ⑫ is further evaluated by projecting the quotient $\stackrel{\bullet}{-} \begin{bmatrix} X:1 \\ Y:0 \end{bmatrix}$ wrt Y (rule 18) and unfolding the inner star quotient zero times (⑭, failed) and once (⑯). The unfolding of one symbol eventually succeeds in step ⑲, which leads to concluding validity of φ. Note that thanks to the lazy evaluation, none of the fixpoint computations had to be fully unfolded.   □

5   An Efficient Algorithm

In this section, we show how to build an efficient algorithm based on the symbolic term rewriting approach from Sect. 4. The optimization opportunities offered by the symbolic approach are to a large degree orthogonal to those of the explicit approach. The main difference is in the available techniques for reducing the explored automata state space. While the explicit construction in MONA profits mainly from calling *automata minimization* after every step of the inductive construction, the symbolic algorithm can use generalized *subsumption* and *lazy evaluation*. None of the two approaches seems to be compatible with both these techniques (at least in their pure variant, disregarding the possibility of a combination of the two approaches discussed below).

Efficient data structures have a major impact on performance of the decision procedure. The efficiency of the explicit procedure implemented in MONA is to a large degree due to the BDD-based representation of automata transition relations. BDDs compactly represent transition functions over large alphabets and provide efficient implementation of operations needed in the explicit algorithm. Our symbolic algorithm can, on the other hand, benefit from a representation of terms as DAGs where all occurrences of the same sub-term are represented by a unique DAG node. Moreover, we assume the nodes to be associated with languages rather than with concrete terms (allowing the term associated with a node to change during its further processing, without a need to transform the DAG structure as long as the language of the term does not change).

We also show that despite our algorithm uses a completely different data structure than the explicit one, it can still exploit a BDD-based representation of transitions of the automata in the leaves of terms. Moreover, our symbolic algorithm can also be *combined* with the explicit algorithm. Particularly, it turns out that, sometimes, it pays off to translate to automata sub-formulae larger than the atomic ones. Our procedure can then be viewed as an extension of MONA that takes over once MONA stops managing. Lastly, optimizations on the level of formulae often have a huge impact on the performance of our algorithm. The technique that we found most helpful is the so-called *anti-prenexing*. We elaborate on all these optimizations in the rest of this section.

5.1   Subsumption

Our first technique for reducing the explored state space is based on the notion of *subsumption* between terms, which is similar to the subsumption used in antichain-based universality and inclusion checking over finite automata [10]. We define subsumption as the relation $\sqsubseteq_s$ on terms that is given by equivalences (20)–(25). Notice that, in rule (20), all terms of T are tested against all terms of T', while in rule (21), the left-hand side term t_1 is not tested against the right-hand side term t_2' (and similarly for t_2 and t_1').

The reason why $\uplus$ is order-sensitive is that the terms on different sides of the $\uplus$ are assumed to be built from automata with disjoint sets of states (originating from different sub-formulae of the original formula), and hence the sub-

$$T \sqsubseteq_s T' \text{ iff } \forall t \in T \ \exists t' \in T' : t \sqsubseteq_s t' \quad (20)$$

$$t_1 \uplus t_2 \sqsubseteq_s t_1' \uplus t_2' \text{ iff } t_1 \sqsubseteq_s t_1' \text{ and } t_2 \sqsubseteq_s t_2' \quad (21)$$

$$t_1 \cap t_2 \sqsubseteq_s t_1' \cap t_2' \text{ iff } t_1 \sqsubseteq_s t_1' \text{ and } t_2 \sqsubseteq_s t_2' \quad (22)$$

$$\overline{t} \sqsubseteq_s \overline{t'} \text{ iff } t \sqsupseteq_s t' \quad (23)$$

$$\pi_{\mathcal{X}}(t) \sqsubseteq_s \pi_{\mathcal{X}}(t') \text{ iff } t \sqsubseteq_s t' \quad (24)$$

$$\mathcal{A} \sqsubseteq_s \mathcal{A}' \text{ iff } F(\mathcal{A}) \subseteq F(\mathcal{A}') \quad (25)$$

sumption test on them can never conclude positively. The subsumption under-approximates language inclusion and can therefore be used for $\sqsubseteq$ in rule (14). It is far more precise than isomorphism and its use leads to an earlier termination of fixpoint computations.

Moreover, $\sqsubseteq_s$ can be used to prune star

$$T \to T \setminus \{t\} \quad \text{if there is } t' \in T \setminus \{t\} \text{ with } t \sqsubseteq_s t' \quad (26)$$

quotient terms $T \stackrel{\bullet}{-} S^*$ while preserving their language. Since the semantics of the set T is the union of the languages of its elements, then elements subsumed by others can be removed while preserving the language. T can thus be kept in the form of an *antichain* of $\sqsubseteq_s$-incomparable terms. The pruning corresponds to using the rewriting rule (26).

5.2   Lazy Evaluation

The top-down nature of our technique allows us to postpone evaluation of some of the computation branches in case the so-far evaluated part is sufficient for determining the result of the evaluated ϵ-membership or subsumption test. We call this optimization *lazy evaluation*. A basic variant of lazy evaluation *short-circuits* elimination of quotients from branches of ⊌ and ⋒. When testing whether $\epsilon \in t \uplus t'$ (rule (8)), we first evaluate, e.g., the test $\epsilon \in t$, and when it holds, we can completely avoid exploring t' and evaluating quotients there. When testing $\epsilon \in t \cap t'$, we can proceed analogously if one of the two terms is shown not to contain ϵ. Rules (21) and (22) offer similar opportunities for short-circuiting evaluation of subsumption of ⊌ and ⋒.

Let us note that subsumption is in a different position than ϵ-membership since correctness of our algorithm depends on the precision of the ϵ-membership test, but subsumption may be evaluated in any way that under-approximates inclusion of languages of terms (and over-approximates isomorphism in order to guarantee termination). Hence, ϵ-membership test must enforce eliminating quotients until it can conclude the result, while there is a choice in the case of the subsumption. If subsumption is tested on quotients, it can either eliminate them, or it can return the (safe) negative answer. However, this choice comes with a trade-off. Subsumption eliminating quotients is more expensive but also more precise. The higher precision allows better pruning of the state space and earlier termination of fixpoint computation, which, according to our empirical experience, pays off.

Lazy evaluation can also reduce the number of iterations of a star. The iterations can be computed *on demand*, only when required by the tests. The idea is to try to conclude a test $\epsilon \in T \overset{\bullet}{-} S^*$ based on the intermediate state T of the fixpoint computation. This can be done since $\mathcal{L}(T)$ always under-approximates $\mathcal{L}(T \overset{\bullet}{-} S^*)$, hence if $\epsilon \in \mathcal{L}(T)$, then $\epsilon \in \mathcal{L}(T \overset{\bullet}{-} S^*)$. Continuing the fixpoint computation is then unnecessary.

The above mechanism alone is, however, rather insufficient in the case of nested stars. Assume that an inner star fixpoint computation was terminated in a state $T \overset{\bullet}{-} S^*$ when ϵ was found in T for the first time. Every unfolding of an outer star then propagates $\overset{\bullet}{-}\tau$ quotients towards $T \overset{\bullet}{-} S^*$. We have, however, no way of eliminating it from $(T \overset{\bullet}{-} S^*) \overset{\bullet}{-} \tau$ other than finishing the unfolding of $T \overset{\bullet}{-} S^*$ first (which eliminates the inner star). The need to fully unfold $T \overset{\bullet}{-} S^*$ would render the earlier lazy evaluation of the ϵ-membership test worthless. To remove this deficiency, we need a way of eliminating the $\overset{\bullet}{-} \tau$ quotient from the intermediate state of $T \overset{\bullet}{-} S^*$.

The elimination is achieved by letting the star quotient $T \overset{\bullet}{-} S^*$ explicitly "publish" its intermediate state T using rule (27). The symbol $\succcurlyeq$ is read as *"is under-approximated by."* Rules (28)–(30) allow to conclude ϵ-membership and subsumption by testing the under-approximation on

$$T \overset{\bullet}{-} S^* \;\rightarrow\; T \overset{\bullet}{-} S^* \succcurlyeq T \quad (27)$$
$$\epsilon \in t \succcurlyeq t' \quad \text{if} \quad \epsilon \in t' \quad (28)$$
$$t \succcurlyeq T \not\sqsubseteq_s t' \quad \text{if} \quad T \not\sqsubseteq_s t' \quad (29)$$
$$t \succcurlyeq T \sqsupseteq_s t' \quad \text{if} \quad T \sqsupseteq_s t' \quad (30)$$

its right-hand side (notice the distinction between "if" and the "iff" used in the rules earlier).

Symbol quotients that come from the unfolding of an outer

$$(t \succcurlyeq T) \stackrel{\bullet}{-} S \;\rightarrow\; ((t \succcurlyeq T) \stackrel{\bullet}{-} S) \succcurlyeq T \ominus S \quad (31)$$

star can be evaluated on the approximation too using rule (31), which then applies the symbol-set quotient on the approximation T of the inner term t, and publishes the result on the right-hand side of $\succcurlyeq$. The left-hand side still remembers the original term $t \stackrel{\bullet}{-} S$.

Terms arising from rules (27) and (31) allow an efficient update in the case an inner term t spawns a new, more precise approximation. In the process, rule (32) is used to remove old outdated approximations.

We will explain the working of the rules and their effi-cient implementation on an evaluation from Example 1.

$$T \succcurlyeq T' \;\rightarrow\; T \quad (32)$$

Note that in Example 1, the partial unfoldings of the fixpoints that are tested for ϵ-membership are under-approximations of a star quotient term. For instance, branch ⑭ corresponds to testing ϵ-membership in the right-most approxima-tion of the term $\left((({\{t\}} \stackrel{\bullet}{-} \pi_Y(\bar{0})^*) \succcurlyeq \{t\}) \stackrel{\bullet}{-} \begin{bmatrix} X:1 \\ Y:0 \end{bmatrix} \right) \succcurlyeq \{t\} \stackrel{\bullet}{-} \begin{bmatrix} X:1 \\ Y:0 \end{bmatrix}$ by rule (28) (the branch determines that $\epsilon \notin \{t\} \stackrel{\bullet}{-} \begin{bmatrix} X:1 \\ Y:0 \end{bmatrix}$). The result of ⑭ cannot con-clude the top-level ϵ-membership test because $\{t\} \stackrel{\bullet}{-} \begin{bmatrix} X:1 \\ Y:0 \end{bmatrix}$ is just an under-approximation of $(\{t\} \stackrel{\bullet}{-} \pi_Y(\bar{0})^*) \stackrel{\bullet}{-} \begin{bmatrix} X:1 \\ Y:0 \end{bmatrix}$. Therefore, we need to compute a better approximation of the term and try to conclude the test on it. We compute it by first applying rule (32) twice to discard obsolete approximations ($\{t\}$ and $\{t\} \stackrel{\bullet}{-} \begin{bmatrix} X:1 \\ Y:0 \end{bmatrix}$), followed by applying rule (14) to replace $(\{t\} \stackrel{\bullet}{-} \pi_Y(\bar{0})^*) \stackrel{\bullet}{-} \begin{bmatrix} X:1 \\ Y:0 \end{bmatrix}$ with $(({\{t\}} \cup (\{t\} \ominus \pi_Y(\bar{0}))) \stackrel{\bullet}{-} \pi_Y(\bar{0})^*) \stackrel{\bullet}{-} \begin{bmatrix} X:1 \\ Y:0 \end{bmatrix}$. Let $\beta = \{t\} \cup (\{t\} \ominus \pi_Y(\bar{0}))$. Then, using rules (27) and (31), we can rewrite the term $(\beta \stackrel{\bullet}{-} \pi_Y(\bar{0})^*) \stackrel{\bullet}{-} \begin{bmatrix} X:1 \\ Y:0 \end{bmatrix}$ into $\left((\beta \stackrel{\bullet}{-} \pi_Y(\bar{0})^* \succcurlyeq \beta) \stackrel{\bullet}{-} \begin{bmatrix} X:1 \\ Y:0 \end{bmatrix} \right) \succcurlyeq \beta \ominus \begin{bmatrix} X:1 \\ Y:0 \end{bmatrix}$, where $\beta \ominus \begin{bmatrix} X:1 \\ Y:0 \end{bmatrix}$ is the approximation used in step ⑯, and re-evaluate the ϵ-membership test on it.

Implemented naïvely, the computation of subsequent approximations of fix-points would involve a lot of redundancy, e.g., in $\beta \stackrel{\bullet}{-} \begin{bmatrix} X:1 \\ Y:0 \end{bmatrix}$ we would need to recompute the term $\{t\} \stackrel{\bullet}{-} \begin{bmatrix} X:1 \\ Y:0 \end{bmatrix}$, which was already computed in step ⑮. The mechanism can, however, be implemented efficiently so that it completely avoids the redundant computations. Firstly, we can maintain a cache of already eval-uated terms and never evaluate the same term repeatedly. Secondly, suppose that a term $t \stackrel{\bullet}{-} S^*$ has been unfolded several times into intermediate states $(T_1 = \{t\}) \stackrel{\bullet}{-} S^*, T_2 \stackrel{\bullet}{-} S^*, \ldots, T_n \stackrel{\bullet}{-} S^*$. One more unfolding using (14) would rewrite $T_n \stackrel{\bullet}{-} S^*$ into $T_{n+1} = (T_n \cup (T_n \ominus S)) \stackrel{\bullet}{-} S^*$. When computing the set $T_n \ominus S$, however, we do not need to consider the whole set T_n, but only those elements that are in T_n and are not in T_{n-1} (since $T_n = T_{n-1} \cup (T_{n-1} \ominus S)$, all elements of $T_{n-1} \ominus S$ are already in T_n). Thirdly, in the DAG representation of terms described in Sect. 5.3, a term $(T \cup (T \ominus S)) \stackrel{\bullet}{-} S^* \succcurlyeq T \cup (T \ominus S)$ is repre-sented by the set of terms obtained by evaluating $T \ominus S$, a pointer to the term $T \stackrel{\bullet}{-} S^*$ (or rather to its associated DAG node), and the set of symbols S. The cost of keeping the history of quotienting together with the under-approximation (on the right-hand side of $\succcurlyeq$) is hence only a pointer and a set of symbols.

5.3   Efficient Data Structures

We describe two important techniques used in our implementation that concern
(1) representation of terms and (2) utilisation of BDD-based symbolic representation of transition functions of automata in the leaves of the terms.

Representation of Language Terms. We keep the term in the form of a DAG such
that all isomorphic instances of the same term are represented as a unique DAG
node, and, moreover, when a term is rewritten into a language-equivalent one,
it is still associated with the same DAG node. Newly computed sub-terms are
always first compared against the existing ones, and, if possible, associated with
an existing DAG node of an existing isomorphic term. The fact that isomorphic
terms are always represented by the same DAG node makes it possible to test
isomorphism of a new and previously processed term efficiently—it is enough to
test that their direct sub-terms are represented by identical DAG nodes (let us
note that we do not look for language equivalent terms because of the high cost
of such a check).

We also cache results of membership and subsumption queries. The key to the
cache is the identity of DAG nodes, not the represented sub-terms, which has the
advantage that results of tests over a term are available in the cache even after
it is rewritten according to $\rightarrow$ (as it is still represented by the same DAG node).
The cache together with the DAG representation is especially efficient when
evaluating a new subsumption or ϵ-membership test since although the result is
not in the cache, the results for its sub-terms often are. We also maintain the
cache of subsumptions closed under transitivity.

BDD-Based Symbolic Automata. Coping with large sets of symbols is central
for our algorithm. Notice that rules (14) and (18) compute a quotient for each
of the symbols in the set $\pi_{\mathcal{X}}(\tau)$ separately. Since the number of the symbols is
$2^{|\mathcal{X}|}$, this can easily make the computation infeasible.

MONA resolves this by using a BDD-based symbolic representation of transition relations of automata as follows: The alphabet symbols of the automata
are assignments of Boolean values to the free variables $X_1, \ldots, X_n$ of a formula. The transitions leading from a state q can be expressed as a function
$f_q : 2^{\{X_1, \ldots, X_n\}} \rightarrow Q$ from all assignments to states such that $(q, \tau, q') \in \delta_q$
iff $f_q(\tau) = q'$. The function f_q is encoded as a multi-terminal BDD (MTBDD)
with variables $X_1, \ldots, X_n$ and terminals from the set Q (essentially, it is a DAG
where a path from the root to a leaf encodes a set of transitions). The BDD `apply`
operation is then used to efficiently implement the computation of successors of
a state via a large set of symbols, and to facilitate essential constructions such as
product, determinization, and minimization. We use MONA to create automata
in leaves of our language terms. To fully utilize their BDD-based symbolic representation, we had to overcome the following two problems.

First, our algorithm computes predecessors of states, while the BDDs of
MONA are meant to compute successors. To use `apply` to compute backwards,
the BDDs would have to be turned into a representation of the inverted transition

function. This is costly and, according to our experience, prone to produce much larger BDDs. We have resolved this by only inverting the edges of the original BDDs and by implementing a variant of `apply` that runs upwards from the leaves of the original BDDs, against the direction of the original BDD edges. It cannot be as efficient as the normal `apply` because, unlike standard BDDs, the DAG that arises by inverting BDD edges is nondeterministic, which brings complications. Nevertheless, it still allows an efficient implementation of *pre* that works well in our implementation.

A more fundamental problem we are facing is that our algorithm can use `apply` to compute predecessors over the compact representation provided by BDDs only on the level of explicit automata in the leaves of terms. The symbols generated by projection during evaluation of complex terms must be, on the contrary, enumerated explicitly. For instance, the projection $\pi_{\mathcal{X}}(t)$ with $\mathcal{X} = \{X_1, \ldots, X_n\}$ generates 2^n symbols, with no obvious option for reduction. The idea to overcome this explosion is to treat nodes of BDDs as regular automata states. Intuitively, this means replacing words over $\Sigma_{\mathcal{X}}$ that encode models of formulae by words over the alphabet $\{0, 1\}$: every symbol $\tau \in \Sigma_{\mathcal{X}}$ is replaced by the *string* τ over $\{0, 1\}$. Then, instead of computing a quotient over, e.g., the set $\pi_{\mathcal{X}}(\bar{0})$ of the size 2^n, we compute only quotients over the 0's and 1's. Each quotienting takes us only one level down in the BDDs representing the transition relation of the automata in the leaves of the term. For every variable X_i, we obtain terms over nodes on the i-th level of the BDDs as -0 and -1 quotients of the terms at the level $i - 1$. The maximum number of terms in each level is thus 2^i. In the worst case, this causes roughly the same blow-up as when enumerating the "long" symbols. The advantage of this techniques is, however, that the blow-up can now be dramatically reduced by using subsumption to prune sets of terms on the individual BDD levels.

5.4   Combination of Symbolic and Explicit Algorithms

It is possible to replace sub-terms of a language term by a language-equivalent automaton built by the explicit algorithm before starting the symbolic algorithm. The main benefit of this is that the explicitly constructed automata have a simpler flat structure and can be minimized. The minimization, however, requires to explicitly construct the whole automaton, which might, despite the benefit of minimization, be a too large overhead. The combination hence represents a trade-off between the lazy evaluation and subsumption of the symbolic algorithm, and minimization and flat automata structure of the explicit one. The overall effect depends on the strategy of choice of the sub-formulae to be translated into automata, and, of course, on the efficiency of the implementation of the explicit algorithm (where we can leverage the extremely efficient implementation of MONA). We mention one particular strategy for choosing sub-formulae in Sect. 6.

5.5 Anti-prenexing

Before rewriting an input formula to a symbolic term, we pre-process the formula by moving quantifiers down by several language-preserving identities (which we call *anti-prenexing*). We, e.g., change $\exists X.\ (\varphi \wedge \psi)$ into $\varphi \wedge (\exists X.\ \psi)$ if X is not free in φ. Moving a quantifier down in the abstract syntax tree of a formula speeds up the fixpoint computation induced by the quantifier. In effect, one costlier fixpoint computation is replaced by several cheaper computations in the sub-formulae. This is almost always helpful since if the original fixpoint computation unfolds, e.g., a union of two terms, the two fixpoint computations obtained by anti-prenexing will each unfold only one operand of the union. The number of union terms in the original fixpoint is roughly the product of the numbers of terms in the simpler fixpoints. Further, in order to push quantifiers even deeper into the formula, we reorder the formula by several heuristics (e.g. group sub-formulae with free occurrences of the same variable in a large conjunction) and move negations down in the structure towards the leaves using De Morgan's laws.

6 Experiments

We have implemented the proposed approach in a prototype tool GASTON[1], Our tool uses the front-end of MONA to parse input formulae, to construct their abstract syntax trees, and also to construct automata for sub-formulae (as mentioned in Sect. 5.4). From several heuristics for choosing the sub-formulae to be converted to automata by MONA, we converged to converting only quantifier free sub-formulae and negations of innermost quantifiers to automata since MONA can usually handle them without any explosion. GASTON, together with all the benchmarks described below and their detailed results, is freely available [22].

We compared GASTON's performance with that of MONA, DWINA implementing our older approach [18], TOSS implementing the method of [19], and the

Table 1. UABE experiments

Formula	MONA		GASTON	
	Time	Space	Time	Space
a-a	**1.71**	30 253	>2m	>2m
ex10	**7.71**	131 835	12.67	82 236
ex11	4.40	2 393	**0.18**	4 156
ex12	**0.13**	2 591	6.31	68 159
ex13	**0.04**	2 601	1.19	16 883
ex16	**0.04**	3 384	0.28	3 960
ex17	3.52	165 173	**0.17**	3 952
ex18	**0.27**	19 463	>2m	>2m
ex2	0.18	26 565	**0.01**	1 841
ex20	1.46	1 077	**0.27**	12 266
ex21	**1.68**	30 253	>2m	>2m
ex4	**0.08**	6 797	0.50	22 442
ex6	**4.05**	27 903	22.69	132 848
ex7	0.90	857	**0.01**	594
ex8	7.69	106 555	**0.03**	1 624
ex9	**7.16**	586 447	9.41	412 417
fib.	**0.10**	8 128	24.19	126 688

implementations of the decision procedures of [20] and [15] (which we denote as COALG and SFA, respectively).[2] In our experiments, we consider formulae

---

[1] The name was chosen to pay homage to Gaston, an Africa-born brown fur seal who escaped the Prague Zoo during the floods in 2002 and made a heroic journey for freedom of over 300 km to Dresden. There he was caught and subsequently died due to exhaustion and infection.

[2] We are not comparing with JMOSEL [13] as we did not find it available on the Internet.

obtained from various formal verification tasks as well as parametric families of formulae designed to stress-test WS1S decision procedures.[3] We performed the experiments on a machine with the Intel Core i7-2600@3.4 GHz processor and 16 GiB RAM running Debian GNU/Linux.

Table 1 contains results of our experiments with formulae from the recent work [24] (denoted as UABE below), which uses WS1S to reason about programs with unbounded arrays. Table 2 gives results of our experiments with formulae derived from the WS1S-based shape analysis of [2] (denoted as Strand). In the table, we use

Table 2. Strand experiments

Formula	MONA		GASTON	
	Time	Space	Time	Space
bs-loop-else	0.05	14 469	0.04	2 138
bs-loop-if-else	0.19	61 883	**0.08**	3 207
bs-loop-if-if	0.38	127 552	**0.18**	5 428
sl-insert-after-loop	**0.01**	2 634	0.36	5 066
sl-insert-before-head	0.01	678	0.01	541
sl-insert-before-loop	0.01	1 448	0.01	656
sl-insert-in-loop	0.02	5 945	0.01	1 079
sl-reverse-after-loop	0.01	1 941	0.01	579
sl-search-in-loop	0.08	23 349	0.03	3 247

sl to denote Strand formulae over sorted lists and bs for formulae from verification of the bubble sort procedure. For this set of experiments, we considered MONA and GASTON only since the other tools were missing features (e.g., atomic predicates) needed to handle the formulae. In the UABE benchmark, GASTON was used with the last optimization of Sect. 5.3 (treating MTBDD nodes as automata states) to efficiently handle quantifiers over large numbers of variables. In particular, without the optimization, GASTON hit 11 more timeouts. On the other hand, this optimization was not efficient (and hence not used) in Strand.

The tables compare the overall time (in seconds) the tools needed to decide the formulae, and they also try to characterize the sizes of the generated state spaces. For the latter, we count the overall number of states of the generated automata for MONA, and the overall number of generated sub-terms for GASTON. The tables contain just a part of the results, more can be found in [22]. We use $>_{2m}$ in case the running time exceeded 2 min, oom to denote that the tool ran out of memory, $+k$ to denote that we added k quantifier alternations to the original benchmark, and N/A to denote that the benchmark requires some feature or atomic predicate unsupported by the given tool. On Strand, GASTON is mostly comparable, in two cases better, and in one case worse than MONA. On UABE, GASTON outperformed MONA on six out of twenty-three benchmarks, it was worse on ten formulae, and comparable on the rest. The results thus confirm that our approach can defeat MONA in practice.

---

[3] We note that GASTON currently does not perform well on formulae with many Boolean variables and M2L formulae appearing in benchmarks such as Secrets [11] or Strand2 [1,23], which are not included in our experiments. To handle such formulae, further optimizations of GASTON such as MONA's treatment of Boolean variables via a dedicated transition are needed.

The second part
of our experiments
concerns parametric
families of WS1S
formulae used for
evaluation in [15, 18,
19], and also para-
meterized versions
of selected UABE for-

Table 3. Experiments with parametric families of formulae

Benchmark	Src	MONA	DWINA	TOSS	COALG	SFA	GASTON
HornLeq	[15]	oom(18)	**0.03**	0.08	$>_{2m}$(08)	**0.03**	**0.01**
HornLeq (+3)	[15]	oom(18)	$>_{2m}$(11)	0.16	$>_{2m}$(07)	$>_{2m}$(11)	**0.01**
HornLeq (+4)	[15]	oom(18)	$>_{2m}$(13)	**0.04**	$>_{2m}$(06)	$>_{2m}$(11)	**0.01**
HornIn	[19]	oom(15)	$>_{2m}$(11)	0.07	$>_{2m}$(08)	$>_{2m}$(08)	**0.01**
HornTrans	[18]	86.43	$>_{2m}$(14)	N/A	N/A	38.56	**1.06**
SetSingle	[18]	oom(04)	$>_{2m}$(08)	0.10	N/A	$>_{2m}$(03)	**0.01**
Ex8	[24]	oom(08)	N/A	N/A	N/A	N/A	**0.15**
Ex11(10)	[24]	oom(14)	N/A	N/A	N/A	N/A	**1.62**

mulae [24]. Each of these families has one parameter (whose meaning is explained
in the respective works). Table 3 gives times needed to decide instances of the
formulae for the parameter having value 20. If the tools did not manage this
value of the parameter, we give in parentheses the highest value of the parameter for which the tools succeeded. More results are available in [22]. In this set of
experiments, GASTON managed to win over the other tools on many of their own
benchmark formulae. In the first six rows of Table 3, the superior efficiency of
GASTON was caused mainly by anti-prenexing. It turns out that this optimization of the input formula is universally effective. When run on anti-prenexed
formulae, the performance of the other tools was comparable to that of GAS-
TON. The last two benchmarks (parameterized versions of formulae from UABE)
show, however, that GASTON's performance does not stand on anti-prenexing
only. Despite that its effect here was negligable (similarly as for all the original
benchmarks from UABE and Strand), GASTON still clearly outperformed MONA.
We could not compare with other tools on these formulae due to a missing
support of the used features (e.g. constants).

Acknowledgement. We thank the anonymous reviewers for their helpful comments
on how to improve the presentation in this paper. This work was supported by the Czech
Science Foundation (projects 16-17538S and 16-24707Y), the BUT FIT project FIT-
S-17-4014, and the IT4IXS: IT4Innovations Excellence in Science project (LQ1602).

References

1. Madhusudan, P., Parlato, G., Qiu, X.: Decidable logics combining heap structures
   and data. In: POpPL 2011, pp. 611–622. ACM (2011)
2. Madhusudan, P., Qiu, X.: Efficient decision procedures for heaps using STRAND.
   In: Yahav, E. (ed.) SAS 2011. LNCS, vol. 6887, pp. 43–59. Springer, Heidelberg
   (2011). doi:10.1007/978-3-642-23702-7_8
3. Iosif, R., Rogalewicz, A., Šimáček, J.: The tree width of separation logic with
   recursive definitions. In: Bonacina, M.P. (ed.) CADE 2013. LNCS (LNAI), vol.
   7898, pp. 21–38. Springer, Heidelberg (2013). doi:10.1007/978-3-642-38574-2_2
4. Chin, W., David, C., Nguyen, H.H., Qin, S.: Automated verification of shape, size
   and bag properties via user-defined predicates in separation logic. Sci. Comput.
   Program. **77**(9), 1006–1036 (2012)
5. Zee, K., Kuncak, V., Rinard, M.C.: Full functional verification of linked data structures. In: POpPL 2008, pp. 349–361. ACM (2008)
6. Hamza, J., Jobstmann, B., Kuncak, V.: Synthesis for regular specifications over
   unbounded domains. In: FMCAD 2010, pp. 101–109. IEEE (2010)

7. Elgaard, J., Klarlund, N., Møller, A.: MONA 1.x: new techniques for WS1S and WS2S. In: Hu, A.J., Vardi, M.Y. (eds.) CAV 1998. LNCS, vol. 1427, pp. 516–520. Springer, Heidelberg (1998). doi:10.1007/BFb0028773

8. Meyer, A.R.: Weak monadic second order theory of successor is not elementary-recursive. In: Parikh, R. (ed.) Logic Colloquium. LNM, vol. 453, pp. 132–154. Springer, Heidelberg (1972). doi:10.1007/BFb0064872

9. Wies, T., Muñiz, M., Kuncak, V.: An efficient decision procedure for imperative tree data structures. In: Bjørner, N., Sofronie-Stokkermans, V. (eds.) CADE 2011. LNCS (LNAI), vol. 6803, pp. 476–491. Springer, Heidelberg (2011). doi:10.1007/978-3-642-22438-6_36

10. De Wulf, M., Doyen, L., Henzinger, T.A., Raskin, J.-F.: Antichains: a new algorithm for checking universality of finite automata. In: Ball, T., Jones, R.B. (eds.) CAV 2006. LNCS, vol. 4144, pp. 17–30. Springer, Heidelberg (2006). doi:10.1007/11817963_5

11. Klarlund, N., Møller, A., Schwartzbach, M.I.: MONA implementation secrets. Int. J. Found. Comput. Sci. 13(4), 571–586 (2002)

12. Klarlund, N.: A theory of restrictions for logics and automata. In: Halbwachs, N., Peled, D. (eds.) CAV 1999. LNCS, vol. 1633, pp. 406–417. Springer, Heidelberg (1999). doi:10.1007/3-540-48683-6_35

13. Topnik, C., Wilhelm, E., Margaria, T., Steffen, B.: jMosel: a stand-alone tool and jABC plugin for M2L(Str). In: Valmari, A. (ed.) SPIN 2006. LNCS, vol. 3925, pp. 293–298. Springer, Heidelberg (2006). doi:10.1007/11691617_18

14. Margaria, T., Steffen, B., Topnik, C.: Second-order value numbering. In: Proceedings of GraMoT 2010, ECEASST, vol. 30, pp. 1–15. EASST (2010)

15. D'Antoni, L., Veanes, M.: Minimization of symbolic automata. In: Proceedings of POPL 2014, pp. 541–554 (2014)

16. Doyen, L., Raskin, J.-F.: Antichain algorithms for finite automata. In: Esparza, J., Majumdar, R. (eds.) TACAS 2010. LNCS, vol. 6015, pp. 2–22. Springer, Heidelberg (2010). doi:10.1007/978-3-642-12002-2_2

17. Abdulla, P.A., Chen, Y.-F., Holík, L., Mayr, R., Vojnar, T.: When simulation meets antichains (on checking language inclusion of NFAs). In: Esparza, J., Majumdar, R. (eds.) TACAS 2010. LNCS, vol. 6015, pp. 158–174. Springer, Heidelberg (2010). doi:10.1007/978-3-642-12002-2_14

18. Fiedor, T., Holík, L., Lengál, O., Vojnar, T.: Nested Antichains for WS1S. In: Baier, C., Tinelli, C. (eds.) TACAS 2015. LNCS, vol. 9035, pp. 658–674. Springer, Heidelberg (2015). doi:10.1007/978-3-662-46681-0_59

19. Ganzow, T., Kaiser, Ł.: New algorithm for weak monadic second-order logic on inductive structures. In: Dawar, A., Veith, H. (eds.) CSL 2010. LNCS, vol. 6247, pp. 366–380. Springer, Heidelberg (2010). doi:10.1007/978-3-642-15205-4_29

20. Traytel, D.: A coalgebraic decision procedure for WS1S. In: 24th EACSL Annual Conference on Computer Science Logic (CSL 2015), Leibniz International Proceedings in Informatics (LIPIcs), vol. 41, pp. 487–503. Schloss Dagstuhl-Leibniz-Zentrum fuer Informatik, Dagstuhl, Germany (2015)

21. Comon, H., Dauchet, M., Gilleron, R., Löding, C., Jacquemard, F., Lugiez, D., Tison, S., Tommasi, M.: Tree Automata Techniques and Applications (2008). http://tata.gforge.inria.fr/

22. Fiedor, T., Holík, L., Janků, P., Lengál, O., Vojnar, T.: GASTON (2016). http://www.fit.vutbr.cz/research/groups/verifit/tools/gaston/

23. Madhusudan, P., Parlato, G., Qiu, X.: Strand benchmark. http://web.engr.illinois.edu/qiu2/strand/. Accessed 29 Jan 2014

24. Zhou, M., He, F., Wang, B., Gu, M., Sun, J.: Array theory of bounded elements and its applications. J. Autom. Reason. 52(4), 379–405 (2014)

From LTL and Limit-Deterministic Büchi Automata to Deterministic Parity Automata

Javier Esparza[1], Jan Křetínský[1(✉)], Jean-François Raskin[2],
and Salomon Sickert[1]

[1] Technische Universität München, Munich, Germany
{esparza,jan.kretinsky,sickert}@in.tum.de
[2] Université libre de Bruxelles, Brussels, Belgium
jraskin@ulb.ac.be

Abstract. Controller synthesis for general linear temporal logic (LTL) objectives is a challenging task. The standard approach involves translating the LTL objective into a deterministic parity automaton (DPA) by means of the Safra-Piterman construction. One of the challenges is the size of the DPA, which often grows very fast in practice, and can reach double exponential size in the length of the LTL formula. In this paper we describe a single exponential translation from limit-deterministic Büchi automata (LDBA) to DPA, and show that it can be concatenated with a recent efficient translation from LTL to LDBA to yield a double exponential, "Safraless" LTL-to-DPA construction. We also report on an implementation, a comparison with the SPOT library, and performance on several sets of formulas, including instances from the 2016 SyntComp competition.

1 Introduction

Limit-deterministic Büchi automata (LDBA, also known as semi-deterministic Büchi automata) were introduced by Courcoubetis and Yannakakis (based on previous work by Vardi) to solve the qualitative probabilistic model-checking problem: Decide if the executions of a Markov chain or Markov Decision Process satisfy a given LTL formula with probability 1 [Var85, VW86, CY95]. The problem faced by these authors was that fully nondeterministic Büchi automata (NBAs), which are as expressible as LTL, and more, cannot be used for probabilistic model checking, and deterministic Büchi automata (DBA) are less expressive than LTL. The solution was to introduce LDBAs as a model in-between: as expressive as NBAs, but deterministic enough.

After these papers, LDBAs received little attention. The alternative path of translating the LTL formula into an equivalent fully deterministic Rabin

This work is partially funded by the DFG Research Training Group "PUMA: Programm- und Modell-Analyse" (GRK 1480), DFG project "Verified Model Checkers", the ERC Starting Grant (279499: inVEST), and the Czech Science Foundation, grant No. P202/12/G061.

A. Legay and T. Margaria (Eds.): TACAS 2017, Part I, LNCS 10205, pp. 426–442, 2017.
DOI: 10.1007/978-3-662-54577-5_25

automaton using Safra's construction [Saf88] was considered a better option, mostly because it also solves the quantitative probabilistic model-checking problem (computing the probability of the executions that satisfy a formula). However, recent papers have shown that LDBAs were unjustly forgotten. Blahoudek *et al.* have shown that LDBAs are easy to complement [BHS+16]. Kini and Viswanathan have given a single exponential translation of $LTL_{\backslash \mathbf{GU}}$ to LDBA [KV15]. Finally, Sickert *et al.* describe in [SEJK16] a double exponential translation for full LTL that can also be applied to the quantitative case, and behaves better than Safra's construction in practice.

In this paper we add to this trend by showing that LDBAs are also attractive for synthesis. The standard solution to the synthesis problem with LTL objectives consists of translating the LTL formula into a deterministic parity automaton (DPA) with the help of the Safra-Piterman construction [Pit07]. While limit-determinism is not "deterministic enough" for the synthesis problem, we introduce a conceptually simple and worst-case optimal translation LDBA→DPA. Our translation bears some similarities with that of [Fin15] where, however, a Muller acceptance condition is used. This condition can also be phrased as a Rabin condition, but not as a parity condition. Moreover, the way of tracking all possible states and finite runs differs.

Together with the translation LTL→LDBA of [SEJK16], our construction provides a "Safraless", procedure to obtain a DPA from an LTL formula. However, the direct concatenation of the two constructions does not yield an algorithm of optimal complexity: the LTL→LDBA translation is double exponential (and there is a double-exponential lower bound), and so for the LTL→DPA translation we only obtain a triple exponential bound. In the second part of the paper we solve this problem. We show that the LDBAs derived from LTL formulas satisfy a special property, and prove that for such automata the concatenation of the two constructions remains double exponential. To the best of our knowledge, this is the first double exponential "Safraless" LTL→DPA procedure. (Another asymptotically optimal "Safraless" procedure for determinization of Büchi automata with Rabin automata as target has been presented in [FKVW15].)

In the third and final part, we report on the performance of an implementation of our LTL→LDBA→DPA construction, and compare it with algorithms implemented in the SPOT library [DLLF+16]. Note that it is not possible to force SPOT to always produce DPA, sometimes it produces a deterministic generalized Büchi automaton (DGBA). The reason is that DGBA are often smaller than DPA (if they exist) and game-solving algorithms for DGBA are not less efficient than for DPA. Therefore, also our implementation may produce DGBA in some cases. We show that our implementation outperforms SPOT for several sets of parametric formulas and formulas used in synthesis examples taken from the SyntComp 2016 competition, and remains competitive for randomly generated formulas.

Structure of the Paper. Section 2 introduces the necessary preliminaries about automata. Section 3 defines the translation LDBA→DPA. Section 4 shows how to compose of LTL→LDBA and LDBA→DPA in such a way that the resulting DPA is at most doubly exponential in the size of the LTL formula. Section 5 reports on the experimental evaluation of this worst-case optimal translation, and Sect. 6 contains our conclusions. Several proofs and more details on the implementation can be found in [EKRS17].

2 Preliminaries

Büchi Automata. A (nondeterministic) ω-word automaton A with Büchi acceptance condition (NBA) is a tuple $(Q, q_0, \Sigma, \delta, \alpha)$ where Q is a finite set of states, $q_0 \in Q$ is the *initial* state, Σ is a finite alphabet, $\delta \subseteq Q \times \Sigma \times Q$ is the transition relation, and $\alpha \subseteq \delta$ is the set of *accepting* transitions[1]. W.l.o.g. we assume that δ is total in the following sense: for all $q \in Q$, for all $\sigma \in \Sigma$, there exists $q' \in Q$ such that $(q, \sigma, q') \in \delta$. A is *deterministic* if for all $q \in Q$, for all $\sigma \in \Sigma$, there exists a unique $q' \in Q$ such that $(q, \sigma, q') \in \delta$. When δ is deterministic and total, it can be equivalently seen as a function $\delta : Q \times \Sigma \to Q$. Given $S \subseteq Q$ and $\sigma \in \Sigma$, let $\mathsf{post}_\delta^\sigma(S) = \{q' \mid \exists q \in S \cdot (q, \sigma, q') \in \delta\}$.

A *run* of A on a ω-word $w : \mathbb{N} \to \Sigma$ is a ω-sequence of states $\rho : \mathbb{N} \to Q$ such that $\rho(0) = q_0$ and for all positions $i \in \mathbb{N}$, we have that $(\rho(i), w(i), \rho(i+1)) \in \delta$. A run ρ is *accepting* if there are infinitely many positions $i \in \mathbb{N}$ such that $(\rho(i), w(i), \rho(i+1)) \in \alpha$. The *language* defined by A, denoted by $\mathsf{L}(A)$, is the set of ω-words w for which A has an accepting run.

A *limit-deterministic Büchi automaton* (LDBA) is a Büchi automaton $A = (Q, q_0, \Sigma, \delta, \alpha)$ such that there exists a subset $Q_d \subseteq Q$ satisfying the three following properties:

1. $\alpha \subseteq Q_d \times \Sigma \times Q_d$, i.e. all accepting transitions are transitions within Q_d;
2. $\forall q \in Q_d \cdot \forall \sigma \in \Sigma \cdot \forall q_1, q_2 \in Q \cdot (q, \sigma, q_1) \in \delta \wedge (q, \sigma, q_2) \in \delta \to q_1 = q_2$, i.e. the transition relation δ is deterministic within Q_d;
3. $\forall q \in Q_d \cdot \forall \sigma \in \Sigma \cdot \forall q' \in Q \cdot (q, \sigma, q') \in \delta \to q' \in Q_d$, i.e. Q_d is a trap (when Q_d is entered it is never left).

W.l.o.g. we assume that $q_0 \in Q \setminus Q_d$, and we denote $Q \setminus Q_d$ by $\overline{Q_d}$. Courcoubetis and Yannakakis show that for every ω-regular language $\mathcal{L}$, there exists an LDBA A such that $\mathsf{L}(A) = \mathcal{L}$ [CY95]. That is, LDBAs are as expressive as NBAs. An example of LDBA is given in Fig. 1. Note that the language accepted by this LDBA cannot be recognized by a deterministic Büchi automaton.

Parity Automata. A deterministic ω-word automaton A with *parity* acceptance condition (DPA) is a tuple $(Q, q_0, \Sigma, \delta, p)$, defined as for deterministic Büchi automata with the exception of the acceptance condition p, which is now

---

[1] Here, we consider automata on infinite words with acceptance conditions based on transitions. It is well known that there are linear translations from automata with acceptance conditions defined on transitions to automata with acceptance conditions defined on states, and vice-versa.

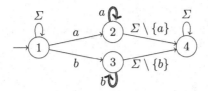

Fig. 1. An LDBA for the LTL language **FG**$a \vee$ **FG**b. The behavior of A is deterministic within the subset of states $Q_d = \{2, 3, 4\}$ which is a trap, the set of accepting transitions are depicted in bold face and they are defined only between states of Q_d.

a function assigning an integer in $\{1, 2, \ldots, d\}$, called a *color*, to each transition in the automaton. Colors are naturally ordered by the order on integers.

Given a run ρ over a word w, the infinite sequence of colors traversed by the run ρ is noted $p(\rho)$ and is equal to $p(\rho(0), w(0), \rho(1))\ p((\rho(1), w(1), \rho(2)) \ldots$ $p(\rho(n), w(n), \rho(n+1)) \ldots$. A run ρ is *accepting* if the minimal color that appears infinitely often along $p(\rho)$ is *even*. The *language* defined by A, denoted by $\mathsf{L}(A)$ is the set of ω-words w for which A has an accepting run.

While deterministic Büchi automata are not expressively complete for the class of ω-regular languages, DPAs are complete for ω-regular languages: for every ω-regular language $\mathcal{L}$ there exists a DPA A such that $\mathsf{L}(A) = \mathcal{L}$, see e.g. [Pit07].

3 From LDBA to DPA

3.1 Run DAGs and Their Coloring

Run DAG. A nondeterministic automaton A may have several (even an infinite number of) runs on a given ω-word w. As in [KV01], we represent this set of runs by means of a directed acyclic graph structure called the *run DAG* of A on w. Given an LDBA $A = (Q, Q_d, q_0, \Sigma, \delta, \alpha)$, this graph $G_w = (V, E)$ has a set of vertices $V \subseteq Q \times \mathbb{N}$ and edges $E \subseteq V \times V$ defined as follows:

- $V = \bigcup_{i \in \mathbb{N}} V_i$, where the sets V_i are defined inductively:
  - $V_0 = \{(q_0, 0)\}$, and for all $i \geq 1$,
  - $V_i = \{(q, i) \mid \exists (q', i-1) \in V_{i-1} : (q', w(i), q) \in \delta\}$;
- $E = \{((q, i), (q', i+1)) \in V_i \times V_{i+1} \mid (q, w(i), q') \in \delta\}$.

We denote by V_i^d the set $V_i \cap (Q_d \times \{i\})$ that contains the subset of vertices of layer i that are associated with states in Q_d.

Observe that all the paths of G_w that start from $(q_0, 0)$ are runs of A on w, and, conversely, each run ρ of A on w corresponds exactly to one path in G_w that starts from $(q_0, 0)$. So, we call *runs* the paths in the run DAG G_w. In particular, we say that an infinite path $v_0 v_1 \ldots v_n \ldots$ of G_w is an accepting run if there are infinitely many positions $i \in \mathbb{N}$ such that $v_i = (q, i)$, $v_{i+1} = (q', i+1)$, and $(q, w(i), q') \in \alpha$. Clearly, w is accepted by A if and only if there is an accepting run in G_w. We denote by $\rho(0..n) = v_0 v_1 \ldots v_n$ the prefix of length $n+1$ of the run ρ.

Ordering of Runs. A function Ord $: Q \rightarrow \{1, 2, \ldots, |Q_d|, +\infty\}$ is called an *ordering* of the states of A w.r.t. Q_d if Ord defines a strict total order on the state from Q_d, and maps each state $q \in \overline{Q_d}$ to $+\infty$, i.e.:

- for all $q \in \overline{Q_d}$, Ord$(q) = +\infty$,
- for all $q \in Q_d$, Ord$(q) \neq +\infty$, and
- for all $q, q' \in Q_d$, Ord$(q) = $ Ord(q') implies $q = q'$.

We extend Ord to vertices in G_w as follows: Ord$((q, i)) = $ Ord(q).

Starting from Ord, we define the following pre-order on the set of run prefixes of the run DAG G_w. Let $\rho(0..n) = v_0 v_1 \ldots v_n \ldots$ and $\rho'(0..n) = v'_0 v'_1 \ldots v'_n \ldots$ be two run prefixes of length $n + 1$, we write $\rho(0..n) \sqsubseteq \rho'(0..n)$, if $\rho(0..n)$ is *smaller than* $\rho'(0..n)$, which is defined as:

- for all i, $0 \leq i \leq n$, Ord$(\rho(i)) = $ Ord$(\rho'(i))$, or
- there exists i, $0 \leq i \leq n$, such that:
  - Ord$(\rho(i)) < $ Ord$(\rho'(i))$, and
  - for all j, $0 \leq j < i$, Ord$(\rho(j)) = $ Ord$(\rho'(j))$.

This is extended to (infinite) runs as: $\rho \sqsubseteq \rho'$ iff for all $i \geq 0 \cdot$ Ord$(\rho(0..i)) \sqsubseteq$ Ord$(\rho'(0..i))$.

Remark 1. If A accepts a word w, then A has a $\sqsubseteq$-smallest accepting run for w.

We use the $\sqsubseteq$-relation on run prefixes to order the vertices of V_i that belong to Q_d: for two different vertices $v = (q, i) \in V_i$ and $v' = (q', i) \in V_i$, v is $\sqsubseteq_i$-smaller than v', if there is a run prefix of G_w that ends up in v which is $\sqsubseteq$-smaller than all the run prefixes that ends up in v', which induces a total order among the vertices of V_i^d because the states in Q_d are totally ordered by the function Ord.

Lemma 1. *For all $i \geq 0$, for two different vertices $v = (q, i), v' = (q', i) \in V_i^d$, then either $v \sqsubseteq_i v'$ or $v' \sqsubseteq_i v$, i.e., $\sqsubseteq_i$ is a total order on V_i^d.*

Indexing Vertices. The index of a vertex $v = (q, i) \in V_i$ such that $q \in Q_d$, denoted by Ind$_i(v)$, is a value in $\{1, 2, \ldots, |Q_d|\}$ that denotes its order in V_i^d according to $\sqsubseteq_i$ (the $\sqsubseteq_i$-smallest element has index 1). For $i \geq 0$, we identify two important sets of vertices:

- Dec(V_i^d) is the set of vertices $v \in V_i^d$ such that there exists a vertex $v' \in V_{i+1}^d$: $(v, v') \in E$ and Ind$_{i+1}(v') < $ Ind$_i(v)$, i.e. the set of vertices in V_i^d whose (unique) successor in V_{i+1}^d has a smaller index value.
- Acc(V_i^d) is the set of vertices $v = (q, i) \in V_i^d$ such that there exists $v' = (q', i+1) \in V_{i+1}^d$: $(v, v') \in E$ and $(q, w(i), q') \in \alpha$, i.e. the set of vertices in V_i^d that are the source of an accepting transition on $w(i)$.

Remark 2. Along a run, the index of vertices can only decrease. As the function $\mathsf{Ind}(\cdot)$ has a finite range, the index along a run has to eventually stabilize.

Assigning Colors. The set of colors that are used for coloring the levels of the run DAG G_w is $\{1, 2, \ldots, 2 \cdot |Q_d| + 1\}$. We associate a color with each transition from level i to level $i + 1$ according to the following set of cases:

1. if $\mathsf{Dec}(V_i^d) = \emptyset$ and $\mathsf{Acc}(V_i^d) \neq \emptyset$, the color is $2 \cdot \min_{v \in \mathsf{Acc}(V_i^d)} \mathsf{Ind}_i(v)$.
2. if $\mathsf{Dec}(V_i^d) \neq \emptyset$ and $\mathsf{Acc}(V_i^d) = \emptyset$, the color is $2 \cdot \min_{v \in \mathsf{Dec}(V_i^d)} \mathsf{Ind}_i(v) - 1$.
3. if $\mathsf{Dec}(V_i^d) \neq \emptyset$ and $\mathsf{Acc}(V_i^d) \neq \emptyset$, the color is defined as the minimal color among
   - $c_{\mathsf{odd}} = 2 \cdot \min_{v \in \mathsf{Dec}(V_i^d)} \mathsf{Ind}_i(v) - 1$, and
   - $c_{\mathsf{even}} = 2 \cdot \min_{v \in \mathsf{Acc}(V_i^d)} \mathsf{Ind}_i(v)$.
4. if $\mathsf{Dec}(V_i^d) = \mathsf{Acc}(V_i^d) = \emptyset$, the color is $2 \cdot |Q_q| + 1$.

The intuition behind this coloring is as follows: the coloring tracks runs in Q_d (only those are potentially accepting as $\alpha \subseteq Q_d \times \Sigma \times Q_d$) and tries to produce an even color that corresponds to the smallest index of an accepting run. If in level i the run DAG has an outgoing transition that is accepting, then this is a *positive event*, as a consequence the color emitted is *even* and it is a function of the smallest index of a vertex associated with an accepting transition from V_i to V_{i+1}. Runs in Q_d are deterministic but they can merge with *smaller* runs. When this happens, this is considered as a *negative event* because the even colors that have been emitted by the run that merges with the smaller run should not be taken into account anymore. As a consequence an odd color is emitted in order to cancel all the (good) even colors that were generated by the run that merges with the smaller one. In that case the odd color is function of the smallest index of a run vertex in V_i whose run merges with a smaller vertex in V_{i+1}. Those two first cases are handled by cases 1 and 2 of the case study above. When both situations happen at the same time, then the color is determined by the minimum of the two colors assigned to the positive and the negative events. This is handled by case 3 above. And finally, when there is no accepting transition from V_i to V_{i+1} and no merging, the largest odd color is emitted as indicated by case 4 above.

According to this intuition, we define the *color summary* of the run DAG G_w as the minimal color that appears infinitely often along the transitions between its levels. Because of the deterministic behavior of the automaton in Q_d, each run can only merge at most $|Q_d| - 1$ times with a smaller one (the size of the range of the function $\mathsf{Ind}(\cdot)$ minus one), and as a consequence of the definition of the above coloring, we know that, on word accepted by A, the smallest accepting run will eventually generate infinitely many (good) even colors that are never trumped by smaller odd colors.

Example 1. The left part of Fig. 2 depicts the run DAG of the limit-deterministic automaton of Fig. 1 on the word $w = abb(ab)^\omega$. Each path in this graph represents a run of the automaton on this word. The coloring of the run DAG follows the

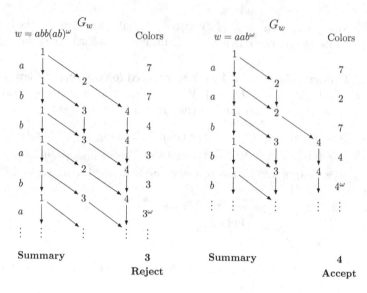

Fig. 2. The run DAGs automaton of Fig. 1 on the word $w = (ab)^\omega$ given on the left, and on the word $w = aab^\omega$ given on the right, together with their colorings.

coloring rules defined above. Between level 0 and level 1, the color is equal to $7 = 2|Q_d| + 1$, as no accepting edge is taken from level 0 to level 1 and no run merges (within Q_d). The color 7 is also emitted from level 1 to level 2 for the same reason. The color 4 is emitted from level 2 to level 3 because the accepting edge $(3, b, 3)$ is taken and the index of state 3 in level 2 is equal to 2 (state 4 has index 1 as it is the end point of the smallest run prefix within Q_d). The color 3 is emitted from level 3 to level 4 because the run that goes from 3 to 4 merges with the smaller run that goes from 4 to 4. In order to cancel the even colors emitted by the run that goes from 3 to 4, color 3 is emitted. It cancels the even color 4 emitted before by this run. Afterwards, colors 3 is emitted forever. The color summary is 3 showing that there is no accepting run in the run DAG.

The right part of Fig. 2 depicts the run DAG of the limit deterministic automaton of Fig. 1 on the word $w = aab^\omega$. The coloring of the run DAG follows the coloring rules defined above. Between levels 0 and 1, color 7 is emitted because no accepting edge is crossed. To the next level, we see the accepting edge $(2, a, 2)$ and color $2 \cdot 1 = 2$ is emitted. Upon reading the first b, we see again 7 since there is neither any accepting edge seen nor any merging takes place. Afterwards, each b causes an accepting edge $(3, b, 3)$ to be taken. While the smallest run, which visits 4 forever, is not accepting, the second smallest run that visits 3 forever is accepting. As 3 has index 2 in all the levels below level 3, the color is forever equal to 4. The color summary of the run is thus equal to $2 \cdot 2 = 4$ and this shows that word $w = aab^\omega$ is accepted by our limit deterministic automaton of Fig. 1.

The following theorem tells us that the color summary (the minimal color that appears infinitely often) can be used to identify run DAGs that contain accepting runs. The proof can be found in [EKRS17, Appendix A].

Theorem 1. *The color summary of the run DAG G_w is even if and only if there is an accepting run in G_w.*

3.2   Construction of the DPA

From an LDBA $A = (Q, Q_d, q_0, \Sigma, \delta, \alpha)$ and an ordering function Ord $: Q \rightarrow \{1, 2, \ldots, |Q_d|, +\infty\}$ compatible with Q_d, we construct a deterministic parity automaton $B = (Q^B, q_0^B, \Sigma, \delta^B, p)$ that, on a word w, constructs the levels of the run DAG G_w and the coloring of previous section. Theorem 1 tells us that such an automaton accepts the same language as A.

First, we need some notations. Given a finite set S, we note $\mathcal{P}(S)$ the set of its subsets, and $\mathcal{OP}(S)$ the set of its totally ordered subsets. So if $(s, <) \in \mathcal{OP}(S)$ then $s \subseteq S$ and $< \subseteq s \times s$ is a total strict order on s. For $e \in s$, we denote by $\mathrm{Ind}_{(s,<)}(e)$ the position of $e \in s$ among the elements in s for the total strict order $<$, with the convention that the index of the $<$-minimum element is equal to 1. The deterministic parity automaton $B = (Q^B, q_0^B, \Sigma, \delta^B, p)$ is defined as follows.

States and Initial State. The set of states is $Q^B = \mathcal{P}(\overline{Q_d}) \times \mathcal{OP}(Q_d)$, i.e. a state of B is a pair $(s, (t, <))$ where s is a set of states outside Q_d, and t is an ordered subset of Q_d. The ordering reflects the relative index of each state within t. The initial state is $q_0^B = (\{q_0\}, (\{\}, \{\}))$.

Transition Function. Let $(s_1, (t_1, <_1))$ be a state in Q^B, and $\sigma \in \Sigma$. Then $\delta^B((s_1, (t_1, <_1))) = (s_2, (t_2, <_2))$ where:

- $s_2 = \mathrm{post}_\delta^\sigma(s_1) \cap \overline{Q_d}$;
- $t_2 = \mathrm{post}_\delta^\sigma(s_1 \cup t_1) \cap Q_d$;
- $<_2$ is defined from $<_1$ and Ord as follows: $\forall q_1, q_2 \in t_2$: $q_1 <_2 q_2$ iff:
  1. **either,** $\neg \exists q_1' \in t_1 : q_1 = \delta(q_1', \sigma)$, and $\neg \exists q_2' \in t_1 : q_2 = \delta(q_2', \sigma)$, and $\mathrm{Ord}(q_1) < \mathrm{Ord}(q_2)$,
     i.e. none has a predecessor in Q_d, then they are ordered using Ord;
  2. **or,** $\exists q_1' \in t_1 : q_1 = \delta(q_1', \sigma)$, and $\neg \exists q_2' \in t_1 : q_2 = \delta(q_2', \sigma)$,
     i.e. q_1 has a σ-predecessor in Q_d, and q_2 not;
  3. **or** $\exists q_1' \in t_1 : q_1 = \delta(q_1', \sigma)$, and $\exists q_2' \in t_1 : q_2 = \delta(q_2', \sigma)$, and $\min_{<_1}\{q_1' \in t_1 \mid q_1 = \delta(q_1', \sigma)\} < \min_{<_1}\{q_2' \in t_1 \mid q_2 = \delta(q_2', \sigma)\}$,
     i.e. both have a predecessor in Q_d, and they are ordered according to the order of their minimal parents.

Coloring. To define the coloring of edges in the deterministic automaton, we need to identify the states $q \in t_1$ in a transition $(s_1, (t_1, <_1)) \xrightarrow{\sigma} (s_2, (t_2, <_2))$ whose indices decrease when going from t_1 to t_2. Those are defined as follows:

$$\mathrm{Dec}(t_1) = \{q_1 \in t_1 \mid \mathrm{Ind}_{(t_2, <_2)}(\delta(q_1, \sigma)) < \mathrm{Ind}_{(t_1, <_1)}(q_1)\}.$$

Additionally, let $\text{Acc}(t_1) = \{q \mid \exists q' \in t_2 : (q, \sigma, q') \in \alpha\}$ denote the subset of states in t_1 that are the source of an accepting transition.

We assign a color to each transition $(s_1, (t_1, <_1)) \to^\sigma (s_2, (t_2, <_2))$ as follows:

1. if $\text{Dec}(t_1) = \emptyset$ and $\text{Acc}(t_1) \neq \emptyset$, the color is $2 \cdot \min_{q \in \text{Acc}(t_1)} \text{Ind}_{(t_1, <_1)}(q)$.
2. if $\text{Dec}(t_1) \neq \emptyset$ and $\text{Acc}(t_1) = \emptyset$, the color is $2 \cdot \min_{q \in \text{Dec}(t_1)} \text{Ind}_{(t_1, <_1)}(q) - 1$.
3. if $\text{Dec}(t_1) \neq \emptyset$ and $\text{Acc}(t_1) \neq \emptyset$, the color is defined as the minimal color among
   - $c_{odd} = 2 \cdot \min_{q \in \text{Dec}(t_1)} \text{Ind}_{(t_1, <_1)}(q) - 1$, and
   - $c_{even} = 2 \cdot \min_{q \in \text{Acc}(t_1)} \text{Ind}_{(t_1, <_1)}(q)$.
4. if $\text{Dec}(t_1) = \text{Acc}(t_1) = \emptyset$, the color is $2 \cdot |Q_q| + 1$.

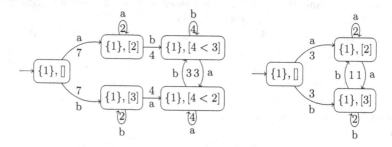

Fig. 3. Left: DPA that accepts the LTL language $\mathbf{FG}a \vee \mathbf{FG}b$, edges are decorated with a natural number that specifies its color. Right: A reduced DPA.

Example 2. The DPA of Fig. 3 is the automaton that is obtained by applying the construction LDBA→DPA defined above to the LDBA of Fig. 1 that recognizes the LTL language $\mathbf{FG}a \vee \mathbf{FG}b$. The figure only shows the reachable states of this construction. As specified in the construction above, states of DPA are labelled with a subset of $\overline{Q_d}$ and a ordered subset of Q_d of the original NBA. As an illustration of the definitions above, let us explain the color of edges from state $(\{1\}, [4, 3])$ to itself on letter b. When the NBA is in state 1, 3 or 4 and letter b is read, then the next state of the automaton is again 1, 3 or 4. Note also that there are no runs that are merging in that case. As a consequence, the color that is emitted is even and equal to the index of the smallest state that is the target of an accepting transition. In this case, this is state 3 and its index is 2. This is the justification for the color 4 on the edge. On the other hand, if letter a is read from state $(\{1\}, [4, 3])$, then the automaton moves to states $(\{1\}, [4, 2])$. The state 3 is mapped to state 4 and there is a run merging which induces that the color emitted is odd and equal to 3. This 3 trumps all the 4's that were possibly emitted from state $(\{1\}, [4, 3])$ before.

Theorem 2. *The language defined by the deterministic parity automaton B is equal to the language defined by the limit deterministic automaton A, i.e.* $L(A) = L(B)$.

Proof. Let $w \in \Sigma^\omega$ and G_w be the run DAG of A on w. It is easy to show by induction that the sequence of colors that occur along G_w is equal to the sequence of colors defined by the run of the automaton B on w. By Theorem 1, the language of automaton B is thus equal to the language of automaton A. □

3.3 Complexity Analysis

Upper Bound. Let $n = |Q|$ be the size of the LDBA and let $n_d = |Q_d|$ be the size of the accepting component. We can bound the number of different orderings using the series of reciprocals of factorials (with e being Euler's number):

$$|\mathcal{OP}(Q_d)| = \sum_{i=0}^{n_d} \frac{n_d!}{(n_d - i)!} \leq n_d \cdot n_d! \cdot \sum_{i=0}^{\infty} \frac{1}{i!} = e \cdot n_d \cdot n_d! \in \mathcal{O}(2^{n \cdot \log n})$$

Thus the obtained DPA has $\mathcal{O}(2^n \cdot 2^{n \cdot \log n}) = 2^{\mathcal{O}(n \cdot \log n)}$ states and $\mathcal{O}(n)$ colours.

Lower Bound. We obtain a matching lower bound by strengthening Theorem 8 from [Löd99]:

Lemma 2. *There exists a family* $(L_n)_{n \geq 2}$ *of languages* $(L_n$ *over an alphabet of n letters) such that for every n the language L_n can be recognized by a limit-deterministic Büchi automaton with $3n + 2$ states but can not be recognized by a deterministic Parity automaton with less than $n!$ states.*

Proof. The proof of Theorem 8 from [Löd99] constructs a non-deterministic Büchi automaton of exactly this size and which is in fact limit-deterministic.

Assume there exists a deterministic Parity automata for L_n with $m < n!$ states. Since parity automata are closed under complementation, we can obtain a parity automaton and hence also a Rabin automaton of size m for $\overline{L_n}$ and thus a Streett automaton of size m for L_n, a contradiction to Theorem 8 of [Löd99]. □

Corollary 1. *Every translation from limit-deterministic Büchi automata of size n to deterministic parity yields automata with $2^{\Omega(n \log n)}$ states in the worst case.*

4 From LTL to Parity in $2^{2^{\mathcal{O}(n)}}$

In [SEJK16] we present a LTL→LDBA translation. Given a formula φ of size n, the translation produces an asymptotically optimal LDBA with $2^{2^{\mathcal{O}(n)}}$ states. The straightforward composition of this translation with the single exponential LDBA→DPA translation of the previous section is only guaranteed to be triple exponential, while the Safra-Piterman construction produces a DPA of at most doubly exponential size. In this section we describe a modified composition that yields a double exponential DPA. To the best of our knowledge this is the first translation of the whole LTL to deterministic parity automata that is asymptotically optimal and does not use Safra's construction.

The section is divided into two parts. In the first part, we explain and illustrate a redundancy occurring in our LDBA→DPA translation, responsible for the undesired extra exponential. We also describe an optimization that removes this redundancy when the LDBA satisfies some conditions. In the second part, we show these conditions are satisfied on the products of the LTL→LDBA translation, which in turn guarantees a doubly exponential LTL→DPA procedure.

4.1   An Improved Construction

We can view the second component of a state of the DPA as a sequence of states of the LDBA, ordered by their indices. Since there are $2^{2^{\mathcal{O}(n)}}$ states of the LDBA for an LTL formula of length n, the number of such sequences is

$$2^{2^{\mathcal{O}(n)}}! = 2^{2^{2^{\mathcal{O}(n)}}}$$

If only the length of the sequences (the maximum index) were bounded by 2^n, the number of such sequences would be smaller than the number of functions $2^n \to 2^{2^{\mathcal{O}(n)}}$ which is

$$(2^{2^{\mathcal{O}(n)}})^{2^n} = 2^{2^{\mathcal{O}(n)} \cdot 2^n} = 2^{2^{\mathcal{O}(n)}}$$

Fix an LDBA with set of states Q. Assume the existence of an *oracle*: a list of statements of the form $L(q) \subseteq \bigcup_{q' \in Q_q} L(q')$ where $q \in Q$ and $Q_q \subseteq Q$. We use the oracle to define a mapping that associates to each run DAG G_w a "reduced DAG" G_w^*, defined as the result of iteratively performing the following four-step operation:

- Find the first V_i in the current DAG such that the sequence $(v_1, i) \sqsubset (v_2, i) \sqsubset \cdots \sqsubset (v_{n_i}, i)$ of vertices of V_i^d contains a vertex (v_k, i) for which the oracle ensures

$$L(v_k) \subseteq \bigcup_{j<k} L(v_j) \tag{$*$}$$

  We call (v_k, i) a *redundant vertex*.
- Remove (v_k, i) from the sequence, and otherwise keep the ordering $\sqsubseteq_i$ unchanged (thus decreasing the index of vertices (v, ℓ) with $\ell > k$).
- Redirect transitions leading from vertices in V_{i-1} to (v_k, i) so that they lead to the smallest vertex (v_1, i) of V_i.
- Remove any vertices (if any) that are no longer reachable from vertices of V_1.

We define the color summary of G_w^* in exactly the same way as the color summary of G_w. The DAG G_w^* satisfies the following crucial property, whose proof can be found in [EKRS17, Appendix B]:

Proposition 1. *The color summary of the run DAG G_w^* is even if and only if there is an accepting run in G_w.*

The mapping on DAGs induces a reduced DPA as follows. The states are the pairs $(s, (t, <))$ such that $(t, <)$ does not contain redundant vertices. There is a transition $(s_1, (t_1, <)) \xrightarrow{a} (s_2, (t_2, <))$ with color c iff there is a word w and an index i such that $(s_1, (t_1, <))$ and $(s_2, (t_2, <))$ correspond to the i-th and $(i+1)$-th levels of G_w^*, and a and c are the letter and color of the step between these levels in G_w^*. Observe that the set of transitions is independent of the words chosen to define them.

The equivalence between the initial DPA $\mathcal{A}$ and the reduced DPA $\mathcal{A}_r$ follows immediately from Proposition 1: $\mathcal{A}$ accepts w iff G_w contains an accepting run iff the color summary of G_w^* is even iff $\mathcal{A}_r$ accepts w.

Example 3. Consider the LDBA of Fig. 1 and an oracle given by $\mathsf{L}(4) = \emptyset$, ensuring $\mathsf{L}(4) \subseteq \bigcup_{i \in I} \mathsf{L}(i)$ for any $I \subseteq Q$. Then 4 is always redundant and merged, removing the two rightmost states of the DPA of Fig. 3(left), resulting in the DPA of Fig. 3(right). However, for the sake of technical convenience, we shall refrain from removing a redundant vertex when it is the smallest one (with index 1).

Since the construction of the reduced DPA is parametrized by an oracle, the obvious question is how to obtain an oracle that does not involve applying an expensive language inclusion test. Let us give a first example in which an oracle can be easily obtained:

Example 4. Consider an LDBA where each state $v = \{s_1, \ldots, s_k\}$ arose from some powerset construction on an NBA in such a way that $\mathsf{L}(\{s_1, \ldots, s_k\}) = \mathsf{L}(s_1) \cup \cdots \mathsf{L}(s_k)$. An oracle can, for instance, allow us to merge whenever $v_k \subseteq \bigcup_{j<k} v_j$, which is a sound syntactic approximation of language inclusion. This motivates the following formal generalization.

Let $\mathcal{L}_B = \{L_i \mid i \in B\}$ be a finite set of languages, called *base* languages. We call $\mathcal{L}_C := \{\bigcup \mathcal{L} \mid \mathcal{L} \subseteq \mathcal{L}_B\}$ the join-semilattice of *composed* languages. We shall assume an LDBA with some $\mathcal{L}_B$ such that $\mathsf{L}(q) \in \mathcal{L}_C$ for every state q. We say that such an LDBA *has a base* $\mathcal{L}_B$. In other words, every state recognizes a union of some base languages. (Note that every automaton has a base of at most linear size.) Whenever we have states v_j recognizing $\bigcup_{i \in I_j} L_i$ with $I_j \subseteq B$ for every j, the oracle allows us to merge vertices v_k satisfying $I_k \subseteq \bigcup_{j<k} I_j$. Intuitively, the oracle declares a vertex redundant whenever the simple syntactic check on the indices allows for that.

Let $V_1 = \bigcup_{i \in I_1} L_i, \cdots V_j = \bigcup_{i \in I_j} L_i$ be a sequence of languages of $\mathcal{L}_C$ where the reduction has been applied and there are no more redundant vertices. The maximum length of such a sequence is given already by the base $\mathcal{L}_B$ and we denote it *width*$(\mathcal{L}_B)$.

Lemma 3. *For any $\mathcal{L}_B$, we have width$(\mathcal{L}_B) \leq |\mathcal{L}_B| + 1$.*

Proof. We provide an injective mapping of languages in the sequence (except for V_1) into B. Since $I_2 \not\subseteq I_1$, there is some $i \in I_2 \setminus I_1$ and we map V_2 to this i. In general, since $I_k \not\subseteq \bigcup_{j=1}^{k-1} I_j$, we also have $i \in I_k \setminus \bigcup_{j=1}^{k-1} I_j$ and we map V_k to this i.   □

On the one hand, the transformation of LDBA to DPA without the reduction yields $2^{\mathcal{O}(|Q| \cdot \log |Q|)}$ states. On the other hand, we can now show that the second component of reduced LDBA with a base can be exponentially smaller. Further, let us assume the LDBA is *initial-deterministic*, meaning that $\delta \cap (\overline{Q_d} \times \Sigma \times \overline{Q_d})$ is deterministic, thus not resulting in blowup in the first component.

Corollary 2. *For every initial-deterministic LDBA with base of size m, there is an equivalent DPA with $2^{\mathcal{O}(m^2)}$ states.*

Proof. The number of composed languages is $\mathcal{L}_C = 2^m$. Therefore, the LDBA has at most 2^m (non-equivalent) states. Hence the construction produces at most

$$|\mathcal{L}_C| \cdot |\mathcal{L}_C|^{\mathcal{O}(width(\mathcal{L}_B))} = 2^m \cdot (2^m)^{\mathcal{O}(m)} = 2^{\mathcal{O}(m^2)}$$

states since the LDBA is initial-deterministic, causing no blowup in the first component.   □

4.2   Bases for LDBAs Obtained from LTL Formulas

We prove that the width for LDBA arising from the LTL transformation is only singly exponential in the formula size. To this end, we need to recall a property of the LTL→LDBA translation of [SEJK16]. Since partial evaluation of formulas plays a major role in the translation, we introduce the following definition. Given an LTL formula φ and sets T and F of LTL formulas, let $\varphi[T, F]$ denote the result of substituting **tt** (true) for each occurrence of a formula of T in φ, and similarly **ff** (false) for formulas of F. The following property of the translation is proven in [EKRS17, Appendix C].

Proposition 2. *For every LTL formula φ, every state s of the LDBA of [SEJK16] is labelled by an LTL formula $label(s)$ such that (i) $\mathsf{L}(s) = \mathsf{L}(label(s))$ and (ii) $label(s)$ is a Boolean combination of subformulas of $\varphi[T_s, F_s]$ for some T_s and F_s. Moreover, the LDBA is initial-deterministic.*

As a consequence, we can bound the corresponding base:

Corollary 3. *For every LTL formula φ, the LDBA of [SEJK16] for φ has a base of size $2^{\mathcal{O}(|\varphi|)}$.*

Proof. Firstly, we focus on states using the same $\varphi[T_s, F_s]$. The language of each state can be defined by a Boolean formula over $\mathcal{O}(|\varphi|)$ atoms. Since every Boolean formula can be expressed in the disjunctive normal form, its language is a union of the conjuncts. The conjunctions thus form a base for these states.

There are exponentially many different conjunction in the number of atoms. Hence the base is of singly exponential size $2^{\mathcal{O}(|\varphi|)}$ as well.

Secondly, observe that there are only $2^{\mathcal{O}(|\varphi|)}$ different formulas $\varphi[T_s, F_s]$ and thus only $2^{\mathcal{O}(|\varphi|)}$ different sets of atoms. Altogether, the size is bounded by

$$2^{\mathcal{O}(|\varphi|)} \cdot 2^{\mathcal{O}(|\varphi|)} = 2^{\mathcal{O}(|\varphi|)}$$

$\square$

Theorem 3. *For every LTL formula φ, there is a DPA with $2^{2^{\mathcal{O}(|\varphi|)}}$ states.*

Proof. The LDBA for φ has base of singly exponential size $2^{\mathcal{O}(|\varphi|)}$ by Corollary 3 and is initial-deterministic by Proposition 2. Therefore, by Corollary 2, the size of the DPA is doubly exponential, in fact

$$2^{(2^{\mathcal{O}(|\varphi|)})^2} = 2^{2^{\mathcal{O}(|\varphi|)}}$$

$\square$

This matches the lower bound $2^{2^{\Omega(n)}}$ by [KR10] as well as the upper bound by the Safra-Piterman approach. Finally, note that while the breakpoint constructions in [SEJK16] is analogous to Safra's vertical merging, the merging introduced here is analogous to Safra's horizontal merging.

5   Experimental Evaluation

We evaluate the performance of our construction on several datasets taken from [BKS13, DWDMR08, SEJK16] and several Temporal Logic Synthesis Format (TLSF) specifications [JBB+16] of the SyntComp 2016 competition.

We use the size of the constructed deterministic automaton as an indicator for the overall performance of the synthesis procedure. In [ST03] it is argued that the degree of determinism of the automaton is a better predictor for performance in model-checking problems; however, this parameter is not applicable for synthesis problems, which require deterministic automata.

We compare two versions of our implementation (with and without optimizations, see below) with the algorithms of Spot [DLLF+16]. Each tool is given 64 GB of memory and 10 min. Increasing time to 10 hours does not change the results. More precisely, we compare the following three setups:

S. (ltl2tgba, 2.1.1) - Spot [DLLF+16] implements a version of the Safra-Piterman determinization procedure [Red12] with several optimizations.

L2P and L2P′. (ltl2dpa, 1.0.0) - L2P is the construction of this paper, available at https://www7.in.tum.de/~sickert/projects/ltl2dpa. L2P′ adds two optimizations. First, the tool translates both the formula and its negation to DPAs A_1, A_2, complements A_2 to yield $\overline{A}_2$, and picks the smaller of A_1, A_2. Further, we apply the simplification routines of Spot (ltlfilt and autfilt, respectively).

We consider three groups of benachmarks:

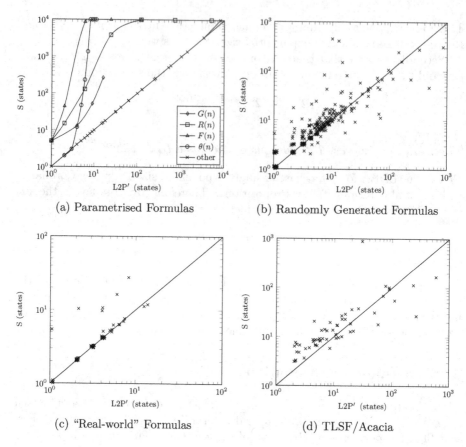

(a) Parametrised Formulas   (b) Randomly Generated Formulas

(c) "Real-world" Formulas   (d) TLSF/Acacia

Fig. 4. Comparison of Spot and our implementation using the best configurations. Timeouts are denoted by setting the size of the automaton to the maximum.

Parametric Formulas. 10 benchmarks from [BKS13, SEJK16]). In six cases S and L2P′ produce identical results. The other four are

$$R(n) = \bigwedge_{i=1}^{n}(\mathbf{GF}p_i \vee \mathbf{FG}p_{i+1}) \qquad G(n) = (\bigwedge_{i=1}^{n}\mathbf{GF}p_i) \to (\bigwedge_{i=1}^{n}\mathbf{GF}q_i)$$
$$\theta(n) = \neg((\bigwedge_{i=1}^{n}\mathbf{GF}p_i) \to \mathbf{G}(q \to \mathbf{F}r)) \quad F(n) = \bigwedge_{i=1}^{n}(\mathbf{GF}p_i \to \mathbf{GF}q_i)$$

for which the results are shown in (Fig. 4a). Additionally, we consider the "*f*" formulas from [SEJK16] (Table 1). Observe that L2P′ performs clearly better, and the gap between the tools grows when the parameter increases.

Randomly Generated Formulas from [BKS13] (Fig. 4b).

Real Data. Formulas taken from case studies and synthesis competitions—the intended domain of application of our approach. Figure 4c and d show results for the real-world formulas of [BKS13] and the TLSF specifications contained in the Acacia set of [JBB+16]. Table 1 shows results for LTL formulas expressing properties of Szymanski's protocol [DWDMR08], and for the generalised buffer benchmark of Acacia.

Table 1. Number of states and number of used colours in parenthesis for the constructed automata. Timeouts are marked with t.

	$f(1,0)$	$f(1,2)$	$f(1,4)$	$f(2,0)$	$f(2,2)$	zn	zp1	zp2	zp3	Buffer
S	18(6)	141(8)	2062(8)	208(12)	883(12)	t	t	t	t	t
L2P	12(8)	114(9)	332(15)	144(14)	4732(19)	t	t	t	t	1425(27)
L2P'	12(8)	78(7)	271(11)	106(9)	1904(15)	32(6)	42(6)	111(12)	97(12)	435(4)

Average Compression Ratios. The geometric average compression ratio for a benchmark suite B is defined as $\prod_{\varphi \in B} (n_\varphi^S / n_\varphi^{L2P'})^{1/|B|}$, where n_φ^S and $n_\varphi^{L2P'}$ denote the number of states of the automata produced by Spot and L2P', respectively. The ratios in our experiments (excluding benchmarks where Spot times out) are: 1.14 for random formulas, 1.12 for the real-world formulas of [BKS13], and 1.35 for the formulas of Acacia.

6   Conclusion

We have presented a simple, "Safraless", and asymptotically optimal translation from LTL and LDBA to deterministic parity automata. Furthermore, the translation is suitable for an on-the-fly implementation. The resulting automata are substantially smaller than those produced by the SPOT library for formulas obtained from synthesis specifications, and have comparable or smaller size for other benchmarks. In future work we want to investigate the performance of the translation as part of a synthesis toolchain.

Acknowledgments. The authors want to thank Michael Luttenberger for helpful discussions and the anonymous reviewers for constructive feedback.

References

[BHS+16] Blahoudek, F., Heizmann, M., Schewe, S., Strejček, J., Tsai, M.-H.: Complementing semi-deterministic Büchi automata. In: Chechik, M., Raskin, J.-F. (eds.) TACAS 2016. LNCS, vol. 9636, pp. 770–787. Springer, Heidelberg (2016). doi:10.1007/978-3-662-49674-9_49

[BKS13] Blahoudek, F., Křetínský, M., Strejček, J.: Comparison of LTL to deterministic rabin automata translators. In: McMillan, K., Middeldorp, A., Voronkov, A. (eds.) LPAR 2013. LNCS, vol. 8312, pp. 164–172. Springer, Heidelberg (2013). doi:10.1007/978-3-642-45221-5_12

[CY95] Courcoubetis, C., Yannakakis, M.: The complexity of probabilistic verification. J. ACM **42**(4), 857–907 (1995)

[DLLF+16] Duret-Lutz, A., Lewkowicz, A., Fauchille, A., Michaud, T., Renault, É., Xu, L.: Spot 2.0 — a framework for LTL and ω-automata manipulation. In: Artho, C., Legay, A., Peled, D. (eds.) ATVA 2016. LNCS, vol. 9938, pp. 122–129. Springer, Heidelberg (2016). doi:10.1007/978-3-319-46520-3_8

[DWDMR08] Wulf, M., Doyen, L., Maquet, N., Raskin, J.-F.: Antichains: alternative algorithms for LTL satisfiability and model-checking. In: Ramakrishnan, C.R., Rehof, J. (eds.) TACAS 2008. LNCS, vol. 4963, pp. 63–77. Springer, Heidelberg (2008). doi:10.1007/978-3-540-78800-3_6

[EKRS17] Esparza, J., Křetínský, J., Raskin, J.-F., Sickert, S.: From LTL and limit-deterministic Büchi automata to deterministic parity automata. Technical report, https://arxiv.org/abs/1701.06103 (2017)

[Fin15] Finkbeiner, B.: Automata, games, and verification (2015). https://www.react.uni-saarland.de/teaching/automata-games-verification-15/downloads/notes.pdf

[FKVW15] Fogarty, S., Kupferman, O., Vardi, M.Y., Wilke, T.: Profile trees for Büchi word automata, with application to determinization. Inf. Comput. 245, 136–151 (2015)

[JBB+16] Jacobs, S., Bloem, R., Brenguier, R., Khalimov, A., Klein, F., Könighofer, R., Kreber, J., Legg, A., Narodytska, N., Perez, G.A., Raskin, J.-F., Ryzhyk, L., Sankur, O., Seidl, M., Tentrup, L., Walker, A.: The 3rd reactive synthesis competition (SYNTCOMP 2016): benchmarks, participants & results. CoRR, abs/1609.00507 (2016)

[KR10] Kupferman, O., Rosenberg, A.: The blow-up in translating LTL to deterministic automata. In: Meyden, R., Smaus, J.-G. (eds.) MoChArt 2010. LNCS (LNAI), vol. 6572, pp. 85–94. Springer, Heidelberg (2011). doi:10.1007/978-3-642-20674-0_6

[KV01] Kupferman, O., Vardi, M.Y.: Weak alternating automata are not that weak. ACM Trans. Comput. Log. 2(3), 408–429 (2001)

[KV15] Kini, D., Viswanathan, M.: Limit deterministic and probabilistic automata for LTL\GU. In: Baier, C., Tinelli, C. (eds.) TACAS 2015. LNCS, vol. 9035, pp. 628–642. Springer, Heidelberg (2015). doi:10.1007/978-3-662-46681-0_57

[Löd99] Löding, C.: Optimal bounds for transformations of ω-automata. In: Rangan, C.P., Raman, V., Ramanujam, R. (eds.) FSTTCS 1999. LNCS, vol. 1738, pp. 97–109. Springer, Heidelberg (1999). doi:10.1007/3-540-46691-6_8

[Pit07] Piterman, N.: From nondeterministic Büchi and Streett automata to deterministic parity automata. Logical Methods Comput. Sci. 3(3:5), 1–21 (2007)

[Red12] Redziejowski, R.R.: An improved construction of deterministic omega-automaton using derivatives. Fundam. Inform. 119(3–4), 393–406 (2012)

[Saf88] Safra, S.: On the complexity of omega-automata. In: FOCS, pp. 319–327 (1988)

[SEJK16] Sickert, S., Esparza, J., Jaax, S., Křetínský, J.: Limit-deterministic Büchi automata for linear temporal logic. In: Chaudhuri, S., Farzan, A. (eds.) CAV 2016. LNCS, vol. 9780, pp. 312–332. Springer, Heidelberg (2016). doi:10.1007/978-3-319-41540-6_17

[ST03] Sebastiani, R., Tonetta, S.: "More deterministic" vs. "smaller" Büchi automata for efficient LTL model checking. In: Geist, D., Tronci, E. (eds.) CHARME 2003. LNCS, vol. 2860, pp. 126–140. Springer, Heidelberg (2003). doi:10.1007/978-3-540-39724-3_12

[Var85] Vardi, M.Y.: Automatic verification of probabilistic concurrent finite-state programs. In: FOCS, pp. 327–338 (1985)

[VW86] Vardi, M.Y., Wolper, P.: An automata-theoretic approach to automatic program verification (preliminary report). In: LICS, pp. 332–344 (1986)

Index Appearance Record for Transforming Rabin Automata into Parity Automata

Jan Křetínský[(✉)], Tobias Meggendorfer, Clara Waldmann,
and Maximilian Weininger

Technical University of Munich, Munich, Germany
jan.kretinsky@tum.de

Abstract. Transforming deterministic ω-automata into deterministic parity automata is traditionally done using variants of appearance records. We present a more efficient variant of this approach, tailored to Rabin automata, and several optimizations applicable to all appearance records. We compare the methods experimentally and find out that our method produces smaller automata than previous approaches. Moreover, the experiments demonstrate the potential of our method for LTL synthesis, using LTL-to-Rabin translators. It leads to significantly smaller parity automata when compared to state-of-the-art approaches on complex formulae.

1 Introduction

Constructing correct-by-design systems from specifications given in linear temporal logic (LTL) [Pnu77] is a classical problem [PR89], called *LTL synthesis*. The automata-theoretic solution to this problem is to translate the LTL formula to a deterministic automaton and solve the corresponding game on the automaton. Although different kinds of automata can be used, a reasonable choice would be parity automata (DPA) due to the practical efficiency of parity game solvers [FL09, ML16] and the fact they allow for optimal memoryless strategies. The bottleneck is thus to create a reasonably small DPA. The classical way to transform LTL formulae into DPA is to first create a non-deterministic Büchi automaton (NBA) and then determinize it, as implemented in ltl2dstar [KB06]. Since determinization procedures [Pit06, Sch09] based on Safra's construction [Saf88] are practically inefficient, many alternative approaches to LTL synthesis arose, trying to avoid determinization and/or focusing on fragments of LTL, e.g. [KV05, PPS06, AL04]. However, new results on translating LTL directly and efficiently into deterministic automata [KE12, EK14] open new possibilities for the automata-theoretic approach. Indeed, tools such as Rabinizer [KK14] or LTL3DRA [BBKS13] can produce practically small deterministic Rabin automata (DRA). Consequently, the task is to efficiently transform DRA into DPA, which is the aim of this paper.

Transformations of deterministic automata into DPA are mostly based on *appearance records* [GH82]. For instance, for deterministic Muller automata, we

© Springer-Verlag GmbH Germany 2017
A. Legay and T. Margaria (Eds.): TACAS 2017, Part I, LNCS 10205, pp. 443–460, 2017.
DOI: 10.1007/978-3-662-54577-5_26

want to track which states appear infinitely often and which do not. In order to do that, the *state appearance record* keeps a permutation of the states, ordered according to their most recent visits, see e.g. [Sch01]. In contrast, for deterministic Streett automata (DSA) we only want to track which *sets* of states are visited infinitely often and which not. Consequently, *index appearance record* (IAR) keeps a permutation of these sets of interest instead, which are typically very few. Such a transformation has been given first in [Saf92] from DSA to DRA only (not DPA, which is a subclass of DRA). Fortunately, this construction can be further modified into a transformation of DSA to DPA, as shown in [Löd99b].

Since (1) DRA and DSA are syntactically the same, recognizing the complement languages of each other, and (2) DPA can be complemented without any cost, one can apply the IAR of [Löd99b] to DRA, too. However, we design another IAR, which is more natural from the DRA point of view, as opposed to the DSA perspective taken in [Löd99b]. This is in spirit more similar to a sketch of a construction suggested in [FEK11]. Surprisingly, we have found that the DRA perspective yields an algorithm producing considerably smaller automata than the DSA perspective.

Our contribution in this paper is as follows:

- We provide an IAR construction transforming DRA to DPA.
- We present optimizations applicable to all appearance records.
- We evaluate all the unoptimized and optimized versions of our IAR and the IAR of [Löd99b] experimentally, in comparison to the procedure implemented in GOAL [TTH13].
- We compare our approach LTL $\xrightarrow{\text{Rabinizer}}$ DRA $\xrightarrow{\text{optimized IAR}}$ DPA to the state-of-the-art translation of LTL to DPA by Spot 2.1 [DLLF+16], which mixes the construction of [Red12] with some optimizations of `ltl2dstar` [KB06] and of their own. The experiments show that for more complex formulae our method produces smaller automata.

2   Preliminaries on ω-automata

We recall basic definitions of ω-automata and establish some notation.

2.1   Alphabets and Words

An *alphabet* is any finite set Σ. The elements of Σ are called *letters*. A *word* is a (possibly infinite) sequence of letters. The set of all infinite words is denoted by Σ^ω. A set of words $\mathcal{L} \subseteq \Sigma^\omega$ is called *(infinite) language*. The i-th letter of a word $w \in \Sigma^\omega$ is denoted by w_i, i.e. $w = w_0 w_1 \dots$.

2.2   Transition Systems

A *deterministic transition system* (DTS) $\mathcal{T}$ is given by a tuple (Q, Σ, δ, q_0) where Q is a set of states, Σ is an alphabet, δ is a *transition function* $\delta : Q \times \Sigma \to Q$ which may be partial (due to technical reasons) and $q_0 \in Q$ is the *initial state*.

The transition function induces the *set of transitions* $\Delta = \{\langle q, a, q'\rangle \mid q \in Q, a \in \Sigma, q' = \delta(p, a)\}$. For a transition $t = \langle q, a, q'\rangle \in \Delta$ we say that t *starts at* q, *moves under* a and *ends in* q'. A sequence of transitions ρ is a *run* of a DTS $\mathcal{T}$ on a word $w \in \Sigma^\omega$ if ρ_0 starts at q_0, ρ_i moves under w_i for each $i \geq 0$ and ρ_{i+1} starts at the same state as ρ_i ends for each $i \geq 0$. We write $\mathcal{T}(w)$ to denote the unique run of $\mathcal{T}$ on w, if it exists. A transition t *occurs* in ρ if there is some i with $\rho_i = t$. By $\mathrm{Inf}(\rho)$ we denote the set of all transitions occurring infinitely often in ρ. Additionally, we extend Inf to words by defining $\mathrm{Inf}_\mathcal{T}(w) = \mathrm{Inf}(\mathcal{T}(w))$ if $\mathcal{T}$ has a run on w. If $\mathcal{T}$ is clear from the context, we write $\mathrm{Inf}(w)$ for $\mathrm{Inf}_\mathcal{T}(w)$.

2.3   Acceptance Conditions and ω-automata

An *acceptance condition* for $\mathcal{T}$ is a positive Boolean formula over the formal variables $V_\Delta = \{\mathrm{Inf}(T), \mathrm{Fin}(T) \mid T \subseteq \Delta\}$. Acceptance conditions are interpreted over runs as follows. Given a run ρ of $\mathcal{T}$ and such an acceptance condition α, we consider the truth assignment that sets the variable $\mathrm{Inf}(T)$ to true iff ρ visits (some transition of) T infinitely often, i.e. $\mathrm{Inf}(\rho) \cap T \neq \emptyset$. Dually, $\mathrm{Fin}(T)$ is set to true iff ρ visits every transition in T finitely often, i.e. $\mathrm{Inf}(\rho) \cap T = \emptyset$. A run ρ satisfies α if this truth-assignment evaluates α to true.

A *deterministic ω-automaton* over Σ is a tuple $\mathcal{A} = (Q, \Sigma, \delta, q_0, \alpha)$, where (Q, Σ, δ, q_0) is a DTS and α is an acceptance condition for it. An automaton $\mathcal{A}$ *accepts* a word $w \in \Sigma^\omega$ if the run of the automaton on w satisfies α. The language of $\mathcal{A}$, denoted by $\mathcal{L}(\mathcal{A})$, is the set of words accepted by $\mathcal{A}$. An acceptance condition α is a

- *Rabin condition* $\{(F_i, I_i)\}_{i=1}^k$ if $\alpha = \bigvee_{i=1}^k (\mathrm{Fin}(F_i) \wedge \mathrm{Inf}(I_i))$. Each (F_i, I_i) is called a *Rabin pair*, where the F_i and I_i are called the *prohibited set* and the *required set* respectively.
- *generalized Rabin condition* $\{(F_i, \{I_i^j\}_{j=1}^{k_i})\}_{i=1}^k$ if the acceptance condition is of the form $\alpha = \bigvee_{i=1}^n (\mathrm{Fin}(F_i) \wedge \bigwedge_{j=1}^{k_i} \mathrm{Inf}(I_j^k))$. This generalizes the Rabin condition, where each $k_i = 1$. Furthermore, every generalized Rabin automaton can be de-generalized into an equivalent Rabin automaton, which however may incur an exponential blow-up [KE12].
- *Streett condition* $\{(F_i, I_i)\}_{i=1}^k$ if $\alpha = \bigwedge_{i=1}^k (\mathrm{Inf}(F_i) \vee \mathrm{Fin}(I_i))$. Note that the Streett condition is exactly the negation of the Rabin condition and thus an automaton with a Rabin condition can be interpreted as a Streett automaton recognizing exactly the complement language.
- *Rabin chain condition* $\{(F_i, I_i)\}_{i=1}^k$ if it is a Rabin condition and $F_1 \subseteq I_1 \subseteq \cdots \subseteq F_k \subseteq I_k$. A Rabin chain condition is equivalent to a *parity condition*, specified by a priority assignment $\lambda : \Delta \to \mathbb{N}$. Such a parity condition is satisfied by a run ρ iff the maximum priority of all infinitely often visited transitions $\max\{\lambda(q) \mid q \in \mathrm{Inf}(\rho)\}$ is even.

A deterministic Rabin, generalized Rabin, Street or parity automaton is a deterministic ω-automaton with an acceptance condition of the corresponding kind. In the rest of the paper we use the corresponding abbreviations DRA, DGRA, DSA and DPA.

Furthermore, given a DRA with an acceptance set $\{(F_i, I_i)\}_{i=1}^k$ and a word $w \in \Sigma^\omega$, we write $\mathcal{F}_{\inf} = \{F_i \mid F_i \cap \mathrm{Inf}(w) \neq \emptyset\}$ and $\mathcal{I}_{\inf} = \{I_i \mid I_i \cap \mathrm{Inf}(w) \neq \emptyset\}$ to denote the set of all infinitely often visited prohibited and required sets, respectively.

3   Index Appearance Record

In order to translate (state-based acceptance) Muller automata to parity automata, a construction called *latest appearance record* has been devised[1]. In essence, the constructed state space consists of permutations of all states in the original automaton. In each transition, the state which has just been visited is moved to the front of the permutation. From this, one can deduce the set of all infinitely often visited states by investigating which states change their position in the permutation infinitely often along the run of the word. Such a constraint can be encoded as parity condition.

However, this approach comes with a very fast growing state space, as the amount of permutations grows exponentially. Moreover, applying this idea to transition based acceptance leads to even faster growth, as there usually are a lot more transitions than states. In contrast to Muller automata, the exact set of infinitely often visited transitions is not needed to decide acceptance of a word by a Rabin automaton. It is sufficient to know which of the prohibited and required *sets* are visited infinitely often. Hence, *index appearance record* uses the indices of the Rabin pairs instead of particular states in the permutation construction. This provides enough information to decide acceptance.

We introduce some formalities regarding permutations: For a given $n \in \mathbb{N}$, we use Π^n to denote the set of all permutations of $N = \{1, \ldots, n\}$, i.e. the set of all bijective functions $\pi : N \to N$. We identify π with its canonical representation as a vector $(\pi(1), \ldots, \pi(n))$. In the following, we will often say "the position of F_i in π" or similar to refer to the position of i in a particular π, i.e. $\pi^{-1}(i)$. With this, we define our variant of the index appearance record construction. Note that in contrast to previous constructions, ours is transition based, which also has a positive effect on the size of the produced automata, as discussed in our experimental results.

Definition 1 (Transition-based index appearance record for Rabin automata). *Let* $\mathcal{R} = (Q, \Sigma, \delta, q_0, \{(F_i, I_i)\}_{i=1}^k)$ *be a Rabin automaton. Then the* index appearance record automaton $\mathrm{IAR}(\mathcal{R}) = (\tilde{Q}, \Sigma, \tilde{\delta}, \tilde{q}_0, \lambda)$ *is defined as the parity automaton with*

- $\tilde{Q} = Q \times \Pi^k$.
- $\tilde{q}_0 = (q_0, (1, \ldots, k))$.
- $\tilde{\delta}((q, \pi), a) = (\delta(q, a), \pi')$ *where* π' *is the permutation obtained from* π *by moving all indices of* prohibited *sets visited by the transition* $t = \langle q, a, \delta(q, a) \rangle$

---

[1] Originally, it appeared in an unpublished report of McNaughton under the name "order vector with hit".

to the front. Formally, let $\mathsf{Move} = \{i \mid t \in F_{\pi(i)}\}$ be the set of positions of currently visited prohibited sets. If $\mathsf{Move} = \emptyset$, define $\pi' = \pi$, otherwise let $n = |\mathsf{Move}|$ and $\mathsf{Move} = \{i_1, \ldots, i_n\}$. With this

$$\pi'(j) = \begin{cases} i_j & if\ j \leq n \\ \pi(j - n + |\{i \in \mathsf{Move} \mid i \leq j\}|) & otherwise. \end{cases}$$

- To define the priority assignment, we first introduce some auxiliary notation. For a transition $\tilde{t} = \langle (q, \pi), a, (q', \pi') \rangle$ and its corresponding transition $\langle q, a, q' \rangle$ in the original automaton, let

$$\mathrm{maxInd}(\tilde{t}) = \max(\{\pi^{-1}(i) \mid t \in F_i \cup I_i\} \cup \{0\})$$

be the maximal position of acceptance pair in π visited by t (or 0 if none is visited). Using this, define the priority assignment as follows:

$$\lambda(\tilde{t}) := \begin{cases} 1 & if\ \mathrm{maxInd}(\tilde{t}) = 0, \\ 2 \cdot \mathrm{maxInd}(\tilde{t}) & if\ t \in I_{\pi(\mathrm{maxInd}(\tilde{t}))} \setminus F_{\pi(\mathrm{maxInd}(\tilde{t}))} \\ 2 \cdot \mathrm{maxInd}(\tilde{t}) + 1 & otherwise,\ i.e.\ if\ t \in F_{\pi(\mathrm{maxInd}(\tilde{t}))}. \end{cases}$$

When a transition visits multiple prohibited sets, they can be moved to the front of the appearance record in arbitrary order. As an optimization we choose existing states as successors whenever possible.

Before formally proving correctness, i.e. that $\mathrm{IAR}(\mathcal{R})$ recognizes the same language as $\mathcal{R}$, we provide a small example in Fig. 1 and explain the general intuition behind the construction. For a given run, all prohibited sets which are visited infinitely often will eventually be "in front" of all those only seen finitely often: After some finite number of steps, none of the finitely often visited ones will be seen any more. Taking another sufficiently large amount of steps, every infinitely often visited set has been seen again and all their indices have been moved to the front.

Lemma 1. Let $w \in \Sigma^\omega$ be a word on which $\mathrm{IAR}(\mathcal{R})$ has a run $\tilde{\rho}$. Then, the positions of all finitely often visited prohibited sets stabilize after a finite number of steps, i.e. their positions are identical in all infinitely often visited states. Moreover, for any i, j with $F_i \in \mathcal{F}_{\inf}$, $F_j \notin \mathcal{F}_{\inf}$ we have that the position of F_i is smaller than the position of F_j in every infinitely often visited state.

Proof. The position of any F_i only changes in two different ways:

- Either F_i itself has been visited and thus is moved to the front,
- or some $F_{i'}$ with a position greater than the one of F_i has been visited and is moved to the front, increasing the position of F_i.

Let ρ be the run of $\mathcal{R}$ on w. (We prove the existence of such a run in [KMWW17, Lemma 3].) Assume that F_i is visited finitely often in some run ρ, i.e. there is a step in the run from which on F_i is never visited again. As the amount of

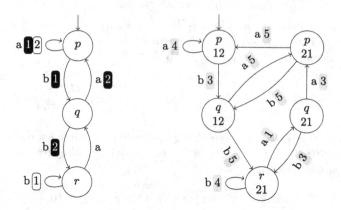

Fig. 1. An example DRA and its resulting IAR DPA. For the Rabin automaton, a number in a white box next to a transition indicates that this transition is a required one of that Rabin pair. A black shape dually indicates membership in the corresponding prohibited set. For example, with $t = \langle p, a, p \rangle$ we have $t \in F_1$ and $t \in I_2$. In the IAR construction, we shorten the notation for permutations to save space, so $p, 12$ corresponds to $(p, (1, 2))$. The priority of a transition is written next to the transitions letter.

positions is bounded, the second case may only occur finitely often after this step and the position of F_i eventually remains constant. As F_i was chosen arbitrarily, we conclude that all finitely often visited F_i are eventually moved to the right and remain on their position. Trivially, all infinitely often visited F_i move to the left, proving the claim.   □

As an immediate consequence we see that if some transition $(q, a, q') \in F_i$ is visited infinitely often, then every F_j with a smaller position than F_i in q is also visited infinitely often:

Corollary 1. *Let $\tilde{t} \in \mathrm{Inf}_{\mathrm{IAR}(\mathcal{R})}(w)$ be an infinitely often visited transition with its corresponding transition $t \in F_{\pi(i)}$ for some i. Then $\forall j \leq i.F_{\pi(j)} \in \mathcal{F}_{\inf}$.*

Looking back at the definition of the priority function, the central idea of correctness can be outlined as follows. For every I_i which is visited infinitely often we can distinguish two cases:

- F_i is visited finitely often. Then the position of the pair is greater than the one of every $F_j \in \mathcal{F}_{\inf}$. Hence the priority of every transition $\tilde{t}$ with corresponding transition $t \in I_i$ is both even and bigger than every odd priority seen infinitely often along the run.
- F_i is visited infinitely often, i.e. after each visit of I_i, F_i is eventually visited. As argued in the proof of Lemma 1, the position of F_i can only increase until it is visited again. Hence every visit of I_i which yields an even parity is followed by a visit of F_i yielding an odd parity which is strictly greater.

Using this intuition, we formally show correctness of the construction in [KMWW17, Appendix A.1].

Theorem 1. *For any DRA $\mathcal{R}$ we have that $\mathcal{L}(\mathrm{IAR}(\mathcal{R})) = \mathcal{L}(\mathcal{R})$.*

Proposition 1 (Complexity). *For every DRA $\mathcal{R}$ with n states and k Rabin pairs, the constructed automaton $\mathrm{IAR}(\mathcal{R})$ has at most $n \cdot k!$ states and $2k + 1$ priorities.*

Moreover, using the [Löd99a], one can show that this is essentially optimal. There exists a family $\{\mathcal{L}_n\}_{n \geq 2}$ of languages such that for every n the language L_n can be recognized by a DRA with $O(n)$ states and $O(n)$ pairs, but cannot be recognized by a DPA with less than $n!$ states. For details, see [KMWW17, Appendix A.2].

Remark 1 (Comparison to previous IAR). Our construction is similar to the index appearance record of [Löd99b] in that it keeps the information about the current state and a permutation of pairs, implementing the appearance record. However, from the point of view of Streett automata, it is very natural to keep two pointers into the permutation, indicating the currently extreme positions of both types of sets in the accpetance condition. Indeed, this way we can keep track of all conjuncts of the form $\mathrm{Inf}(I_j) \implies \mathrm{Inf}(F_j)$. This is also the approach that [Löd99b] takes. In contrast, we have no pointers at all. From the Rabin point of view, it is more natural to keep track of the prohibited sets only and the respective pointer is hidden in the information about the current state *together* with the current permutation. Additionally, the pointer for the required set is hidden into the acceptance status of transitions. In the transition-based setting, it is not necessary to remember the visit of a required set in the state-space; it is sufficient to emit the respective priority upon seeing this *during* the transition when we know both the source and target states. The absence of these pointers results in better performance.

Remark 2 (Using IAR for DGRA). The straightforward way to translate a DGRA to DPA is to first de-generalize the DGRA and then apply the presented IAR construction. However, one can also apply the IAR idea to directly translate from DGRA to DPA: Instead of only tracking the pair indices, one could incorporate all F_i and I_i^j into the appearance permutation. With the same reasoning as above, a parity condition can be used to decide acceptance.

This approach yields a correct algorithm, but compared to de-generalization combined with IAR, the state space grows much larger. Indeed, given a DGRA with n states and k accepting pairs with l_i required sets each, the de-generalized DRA has at most $n \cdot \prod_{i=1}^{k} l_i$ states and k pairs, hence the resulting parity automaton has at most $k! \cdot n \cdot \prod_{i=1}^{k} l_i$ states and $2k+1$ priorities. Applying the mentioned specific construction gives $n \cdot (\sum_{i=1}^{k}(l_i+1))!$ states and $2 \cdot (\sum_{i=1}^{k}(l_i+1))+1$ priorities. A simple induction on k suffices to show that the worst case upper bound for the specific construction is always larger. We conjecture that this behaviour also shows in real-world applications.

4   Optimizations

In general, many states generated by the IAR procedure are often superfluous and could be omitted. In the following, we present several optimizations of our construction, which aim to do so. Moreover, these optimizations can be applied also to the IAR construction of [Löd99b] and in a slightly adjusted way also to the standard SAR [Sch01]. Further, although the optimizations are transition-based, they can be of course easily adapted to the state-based setting. Due to space constraints, the correctness proofs can be found in [KMWW17, Appendix A.3].

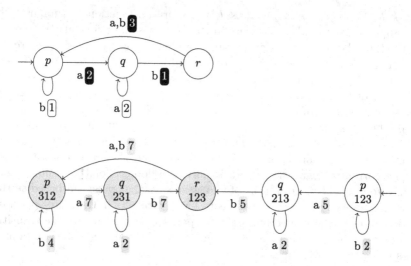

Fig. 2. Example of a suboptimal initial permutation, using the same notation as in Fig. 1. Only the shaded states are constructed when choosing a better initial permutation.

4.1   Choosing an Initial Permutation

The first observation is that the arbitrary choice of $(1, \ldots, k)$ as initial permutation can lead to suboptimal results. It may happen that several states of the resulting automaton are visited at most once by every run before some "recurrent" permutation is reached. These states enlarge the state-space unnecessarily, as demonstrated in Fig. 2. Indeed, when choosing $(p, (3, 1, 2))$ instead of $(p, (1, 2, 3))$ as the initial state in the example, only the shaded states are built during the construction, while the language of the resulting automaton is still equal to that of the input DRA.

We overload the IAR algorithm to be parametrized by the starting permutation, i.e. we write $\mathrm{IAR}(\mathcal{R}, \pi_0)$ to denote the IAR construction applied to the DRA $\mathcal{R}$ starting with permutation π_0.

Theorem 2. *For an arbitrary Rabin automaton $\mathcal{R}$ with k pairs we have that $\mathcal{L}(\mathrm{IAR}(\mathcal{R})) = \mathcal{L}(\mathrm{IAR}(\mathcal{R}, \pi_0))$ for all $\pi_0 \in \Pi^k$.*

How to choose a "good" initial permutation is deferred to Sect. 4.3, as it is intertwined with the algorithm presented in the following section.

4.2 SCC Decomposition

Acceptance of a word by an ω-automaton only depends on the set of states visited infinitely often by its run. This set of states is *strongly connected* on the underlying graph structure, i.e. starting from any state in the set, any other state can be reached with finitely many steps. In general, any strongly connected set belongs to exactly one *strongly connected component* (SCC). Therefore, for a fixed SCC, only the Rabin pairs with required sets intersecting this SCC are relevant.

Using this we can restrict ourselves to the Rabin pairs that can possibly accept in that SCC while processing it. This reduces the number of indices we need to track in the appearance record for each SCC, which can lead to significant savings.

For readability, we introduce some abbreviations. Given a DRA $\mathcal{R} = (Q, \Sigma, \delta, q_0, \{(F_i, I_i)\}_{j=1}^k)$ and a set of states $S \subseteq Q$ we write $\delta \restriction S : S \times \Sigma \to S$ to denote the restriction of δ to S, i.e. $\delta \restriction S(q, a) = \delta(q, a)$ if $\delta(q, a) \in S$ and undefined otherwise. Analogously, we define $\Delta \restriction S = \Delta \cap S \times \Sigma \times S$ as the set of transitions in the restricted automaton. Consequently, we define the restriction of the whole automaton $\mathcal{R}$ to the set of states S using $q \in S$ as initial state by

$$\mathcal{R} \restriction_q S = (S, \Sigma, \delta \restriction S, q, \{(F_i \cap (\Delta \restriction S), I_i \cap (\Delta \restriction S)) \mid I_i \cap (\Delta \restriction S) \neq \emptyset\}).$$

Furthermore, we call a SCC of an automaton *transient*, if it is a singleton set without a self-loop. This means that it is visited at most once by any run and it is not of interest for acceptance. Finally, we use ε to denote the "empty" permutation (of length 0).

Using this notation, we describe the optimized IAR construction, denoted IAR* in Algorithm 1. The algorithm decomposes the DRA into its SCCs, applies the formerly introduced IAR procedure to each sub-automaton separately and finally connects the resulting DPAs back together.

As we apply the IAR construction to each SCC separately, we have to choose the initial permutation for each state of those SCCs. Theorem 2 shows that for a particular initial state, correctness of IAR does not depend on the chosen permutation. We therefore delegate the choice to a function PICKPERM and prove correctness of the optimized algorithm independent of this function, allowing for further optimizations. We present an optimal definition of PICKPERM in the next subsection.

Figure 3 shows an example application and the obtained savings of the construction. Pair 1 is only relevant for acceptance in the SCC $\{p\}$, but in the unoptimized construction it still changes the permutations in the part of the

Input : A DRA $\mathcal{R} = (Q, \Sigma, \delta, q_0, \{(F_i, I_i)\}_{j=1}^k)$

Output: A DPA recognizing the same language as $\mathcal{R}$

```
1  Q* ← {}, δ* ← {}, λ* ≡ 1
2  foreach SCC S in R do
3  │    if S transient or {i | Ii ∩ Δ ↾ S ≠ ∅} = ∅ then // SCC not relevant
4  │    │    Add S × {ε} to Q*
5  │    │    foreach q ∈ S, a ∈ Σ such that (δ ↾ S)(q, a) is defined do
6  │    │    │    Let q' = δ(q, a)
7  │    │    │    Set δ*((q, ε), a) = (q', ε) and λ*(⟨(q, ε), a, (q', ε)⟩) = 1
8  │    │    end
9  │    else // SCC relevant, apply IAR to the sub-automaton
10 │    │    Pick a starting state q ∈ S
11 │    │    (Qs, Σ, δs, (q, π), λs) ← IAR(R ↾q S, PICKPERM(q, S))
12 │    │    Update Q*, δ* and λ* with Qs, δs and λs, respectively
13 │    end
14 end
   // Connect all SCCs
15 foreach (q, π) ∈ Q* and a ∈ Σ s.t. q' = δ(q, a) in different SCC of R than q do
16 │    Pick a π' with (q', π') ∈ Q*
17 │    Set δ*((q, π), a) = (q', π')
18 end
```

Algorithm 1. The optimized IAR construction IAR*

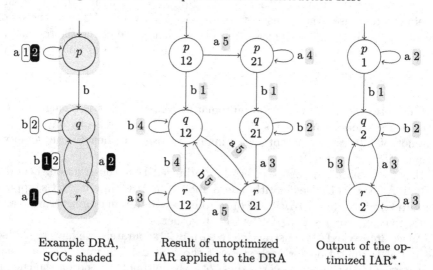

Example DRA,   Result of unoptimized   Output of the op-
SCCs shaded   IAR applied to the DRA   timized IAR*.

Fig. 3. Example application of Algorithm 1

automaton constructed from $\{q, r\}$, as e.g. the transition $\langle r, b, q \rangle$ is contained in F_1. Similarly, pair 2 is tracked in $\{p\}$ while actually not being relevant. The optimized version yields improvements in both state-space size and amount of priorities.

Theorem 3. *For any DRA $\mathcal{R}$ we have that $\mathcal{L}(\text{IAR}^*(\mathcal{R})) = \mathcal{L}(\mathcal{R})$, independent of* PICKPERM.

4.3 Optimal Choice of the Initial Permutation

In Fig. 2 we provided a scalable example where the choice of the initial permutation can significantly reduce the size of the generated automaton. In this subsection, we explain a procedure yielding a permutation which minimizes the state space of the automaton generated by IAR*.

First, we recall that PICKPERM is only invoked when processing a particular (non-transient) SCC of the input automaton. Consequently, we can restrict ourselves to only deal with Rabin automata forming a single SCC. Let now $\mathcal{R}$ be such an automaton. While IAR$(\mathcal{R}, \pi_0)$ may contain multiple SCCs, we show that it contains exactly one bottom SCC (BSCC), i.e. a SCC without outgoing edges. Additionally, this BSCC is the only SCC which contains all states of the original automaton $\mathcal{R}$ in the first component of its states.

Theorem 4. *Let $\mathcal{R} = (Q, \Sigma, \delta, q_0, \{(F_i, I_i)\}_{i=1}^{k})$ be a Rabin automaton that is strongly connected. For a fixed $\pi_0 \in \Pi^k$, IAR$(\mathcal{R}, \pi_0)$ contains exactly one BSCC S and for every SCC S' we have that $S = S'$ iff $Q = \{q \mid \exists \pi \in \Pi^k.(q, \pi) \in S'\}$. Furthermore the BSCCs for different π_0 are isomorphic.*

The proof can be found in [KMWW17, Appendix A.4]. This result makes defining an optimal choice of PICKPERM straightforward. By the theorem, there always is a BSCC of the same size, independent of PICKPERM. If (q_0, π) is in the BSCC of some IAR$(\mathcal{R}, \pi_0)$, IAR$(\mathcal{R}, \pi)$ will generate the same BSCC and no other states. Hence, we define PICKPERM(q, S) to return any permutation such that (q, π) lies in the corresponding BSCC. As a trivial consequence of the theorem, this choice is optimal in terms of the state-space size of the generated automaton. In our implementation, we start exploring the state space using an arbitrary initial permutation and then prune all states which do not belong into the respective BSCC.

5 Experimental Results

In this section, we compare variants of our new approach to the established tools. All of the benchmarks have been run on a Linux 4.4.3-gentoo x64 virtual machine with 3.0 GHz per core. We implemented our construction as part of Rabinizer [KK14] and used the 64 bit Oracle JDK 1.8.0_102 as JVM for our experiments.

5.1 DRA to DPA Translation

We present comparisons of different approaches to translate DRA into DPA. As there are to our knowledge no "standard" DRA datasets for this kind of comparison, we use Spot's tool `randaut` to produce various Rabin automata. All executions in this chapter ran with a time-out of five minutes.

We consider both our basic method IAR of Sect. 3 and the optimized version IAR* of Sect. 4. We compare our methods to GOAL[2] [TTH13] and the Streett-based construction StreetIAR of [Löd99b]. As we are not aware of any implementations of StreetIAR, we implemented it ourselves in Haskell[3]. Both of these constructions are using state-based acceptance. In order to allow for a fair comparison, we therefore also implemented sbIAR, a variant of our construction working directly with state-based acceptance[4] in Haskell (See footnote 3), too. Additionally, we combine every tool with Spot's multi-purpose post-processing[5] and denote this by a subscript P (for post-processing), e.g. IAR* combined with this post-processing is written IAR$^*_P$.

In Table 1 we present a comparison between GOAL, StreettIAR and our unoptimized state-based implementation sbIAR. Additionally, since GOAL does not perform too well, we also include its post-processed variant GOAL$_P$. For comparison, we also include our optimized variant IAR$^*_P$. As test data, we use 1000 state-based DRA over 4 atomic propositions with 5 to 15 states, a transition density of 0.05 and 2 to 3 Rabin pairs[6]. We use Spot's tool `autfilt` to gather the statistics. Failures denote either time-outs, out of memory errors or invalid results, e.g. automata which could not be read by `autfilt`, which sometimes occurred with GOAL.

Table 1. Comparison of the DRA to DPA translations on 1000 randomly generated DRAs. First, we compare the cases where all tools finished successfully, according to the average size, the number of SCCs and the run-time. Second, we give the percentage each tool produces an automaton with the least number of states, and failures, respectively.

		GOAL	GOAL$_P$	StreettIAR	sbIAR	IAR$^*_P$
Avg.	#states	1054	281	18.4	15.4	8.83
	#SCC	73.2	19.2	4.97	4.33	1.61
	time (s)	11.7	15.7	0.02	0.02	0.99
Smallest (%)		15.5	37.8	7.7	15.5	95.9
Failure (%)		8.6	11.9	0	0	0

---

[2] `gc batch"\$nba = load -c HOAF /dev/stdin; \$dpa = convert -t dpw \$nba; save \$dpa -c HOAF /dev/stdout;"`, executed with OpenJDK IcedTea 2.6.6, java version 1.7.0_101.

[3] Compiled with GHC 7.10.3.

[4] We also proved correctness for the direct construction, the proof can be obtained by trivial modifications of the proofs in this paper.

[5] `autfilt --deterministic --generic --small --high`.

[6] `randaut 4 --seed=0 -Q 5..15 --acceptance="Rabin 2..3"--density=0.05 -- deterministic --acc-probability 0.2 --state-based-acceptance --hoaf - n1000`. The acceptance probability parameter denotes the chance of a particular transition belonging to a Rabin pair.

From the results in Table 1 we observe that on this dataset all appearance-record variants drastically outperform GOAL. We remark that IAR* performs even better compared to GOAL if more SCCs are involved. However, for reasonably complex automata, virtually every execution of GOAL timed out or crashed, making more specific experiments difficult. Already for the automata in Table 1 with 5–15 states, GOAL regularly consumed around 3 GB of memory and needed roughly 10 seconds to complete on average, whereas our methods only used a few hundred MB and less than a second. We could not find a dataset where GOAL showed a significant advantage over our new methods. Therefore, we exclude GOAL from further experiments. The remaining methods are investigated more thoroughly in the next experiment.

Table 2. Comparison of StreettIAR and (sb)IAR on 1000 randomly generated DRAs. We use the same definitions as in Table 1.

		StreettIAR	sbIAR	StreettIAR$_P^*$	sbIAR$_P^*$	IAR$_P^*$
Avg.	#states	4959	1568	4175	1081	833
	#SCC	63.8	42.5	1.35	1.35	1.35
	time (s)	1.86	0.34	39.47	3.11	3.38
Smallest (%)		0	0	0.4	5.90	95.1
Failure (%)		1.3	0	1.4	0	0

In Table 2 we compare StreettIAR to sbIAR on more complex input automata to demonstrate the advantages of our new method compared to the existing StreettIAR construction. We consider the methods both in the basic setting and with post-processing and optimizations. Note that as the presented optimizations are applicable to appearance records in general, we also added them to our implementation of StreettIAR. Its optimized version is denoted by StreettIAR*. Again, we include our best (transition-based) variant IAR$_P^*$ for reference. The dataset now contains DRA with 20 to 30 states[7].

StreettIAR is significantly outperformed by our new methods in this experiment. This is quite surprising, considering that both methods essentially follow the same idea of index appearance records, only from different perspectives. The difference is partially due to Remark 1. Besides, we have observed that the discrepancy between StreettIAR and IAR is closely linked to the amount of acceptance pairs. After increasing the number of pairs further, the gap between the two approaches grows dramatically. For instance, on a dataset of automata with 8 states and 8 Rabin pairs, the IAR construction yielded automata roughly an order of magnitude smaller: sbIAR needed less than three hundred states

---

[7] `randaut 4 --seed=0 -Q 20..30 --acceptance="Rabin 6"--density=0.05 --acc -probability=0.2 --deterministic --state-based-acceptance --hoaf-n1000.`

compared to StreettIAR needing over three thousand. Applying the post-processing does not remedy the situation.

Table 3. Evaluation of the presented optimizations on 1000 randomly generated DRAs, again using the same definitions as in Table 1. No tool failed for any of the input automata.

		sbIAR	sbIAR$_P^*$	IAR	IAR$_P$	IAR*	IAR$_P^*$
Avg.	#states	3431	2530	1668	1655	1302	1296
	#SCC	24.8	1.14	8.98	3.5	1.43	1.43
	Time (s)	0.77	11.47	1.09	48.3	76.5	95.7
Smallest (%)		0	0	38.3	48.30	76.5	95.7

Finally, we demonstrate the significance of the transition-based acceptance and our optimizations in Table 3. To evaluate the impact of our improvements, we compare the unoptimized IAR procedure and its post-processed counterpart to the optimized IAR* and IAR$_P^*$. Furthermore, we also include our state-based version in its basic (sbIAR) and best (sIAR$_P^*$ [8]) form. We run these algorithms on a dataset of DRA with 20 states each[9].

Spot's generic post-processing algorithms often yield sizeable gains, but they are marginal compared to the effect of our optimizations on this dataset. Our optimizations are thus not only significantly beneficial, but also irreplacable by general purpose optimizations. We furthermore want to highlight the reduction of SCCs. As a final remark, we emphasize the improvements due to the adoption of transition-based acceptance, halving the size of the automata.

5.2 Linear Temporal Logic

Motivated by the previous results we concatenated IAR* with Rabinizers LTL-to-DRA translation, obtaining an LTL-to-DPA translation. We compare this approach to the established tool `ltl2tgba` of Spot, which can also produce DPA[10]. We use Spot's comparison tool `ltlcross` in order to produce the results. Unfortunately, this tool sometimes crashes caused by too many acceptance sets[11]. We alleviated this problem by splitting our datasets into smaller chunks. Time-outs are set to 15 min.

---

[8] We use `autfilt --state-based-acceptance` to convert the transition based input DRA to state based.

[9] `randaut 4 --seed=0 -Q 20 --acceptance="Rabin 5"--acc-probability=0.05--density=0.1 --deterministic --hoaf -n1000`.

[10] By specifying `--deterministic --generic` on the command line.

[11] Around 20 acceptance sets. The exact error message emitted is `-terminate called after throwing an instance of 'std::runtime_error' what(): Too many acceptance sets used`.

First, we compare the two tools on random LTL formulae. We use `randltl` and `ltlfilt` to generate pure LTL formulae[12]. The test results are outlined in Table 4. On average, our methods are comparable to `ltl2tgba`, even outperforming it slightly in the number of states.

Note that the averages have to be compared carefully. As the constructions used by `ltl2tgba` are fundamentally different from ours, there are some formulae where we outperform `ltl2tgba` by orders of magnitude and similarly in the other direction. We conjecture that on some formulae `ltl2tgba` has an edge merely due to its rewriting together with numerous pre- and post-processing steps, whereas our method profits from Rabinizer, which can produce smaller deterministic automata also for very complex formulae. On many dataset we tested, median state count over all formulae (including timeouts) is better for our methods. For more detail, see the histogram in [KMWW17, Appendix B, Fig. 4].

Table 4. Comparison of `ltl2tgba` to Rabinizer + IAR$_P^*$ on 2000 LTL formulae.

		Rabinizer + IAR$_P^*$	`ltl2tgba`
Avg.	#states	6.60	7.89
	#acc	2.31	1.79
	#SCC	4.49	4.69
	Timeouts	22	0

To give more insight in the difference between the approaches, we list several classes of formulae where our technique performs particularly well. For instance, for fairness-like constraints our toolchain produces significantly smaller automata than `ltl2tgba`, see Table 5. Further examples, previously investigated in e.g. [KE12, BBKS13, EK14] can be found in [KMWW17, Appendix B, Table 6], including formulae of the GR(1) fragment [PPS06]. Additionally, our method is performing better on many practical formulae, for instance complex formulae from SPEC PATTERN [DAC99][13].

6   Conclusion

We have presented a new version of index appearance record. In comparison to the standard Streett-based approach, our new Rabin-based approach produces significantly smaller automata. Besides, it has a significant potential for LTL synthesis. For more complex formulae, it makes use of high efficiency of Rabinizer

---

[12] `randltl -n2000 5 --tree-size=20..25 --seed=0 --simplify=3 -p --ltl -priorities' ap=3, false=1,true=1,not=1,F=1,G=1,X=1,equiv=1,implies=1, xor=0,R=0,U=1,W=0,M=0,and=1,or=1' | ltlfilt --unabbreviate="eiMRW"`.

[13] Spec Patterns: Property Pattern Mappings for LTL. http://patterns.projects.cis.ksu. edu/documentation/patterns/ltl.shtml.

Table 5. Fairness formulae: $Fairness(k) = \bigwedge_{i=1}^{k}(\mathbf{G}\,\mathbf{F}\,a_i \Rightarrow \mathbf{G}\,\mathbf{F}\,b_i)$

	Rabinizer+IAR$_P^*$			ltl2tgba		
Formula	States	Acc	SCCs	States	Acc	SCCs
$Fairness(1)$	2	4	1	5	4	3
$Fairness(2)$	12	9	1	44	8	9
$Fairness(3)$	1431	17	1	8607	20	546

and thus avoids the blow-up in many cases, compared to determinization-based methods.

Since we only provided the method for DRA we want to further investigate whether it can be extended to DGRA more efficiently than by de-generalization. Besides, a more targeted post-processing of the state space and the priority function is desirable. For instance, in order to decrease the total number of used priorities, all non-accepting SCCs can be assigned any odd priority that is already required elsewhere instead of the one suggested by the algorithm. Further, one can adopt optimizations of Spot as well as consider optimizations taking the automaton topology more into account. The whole tool-chain will then be integrated into Rabinizer. Finally, in order to estimate the effect on LTL synthesis more precisely, we shall link our tool chain to parity-game solvers and apply it to realistic case studies.

Acknowledgment. This work is partially funded by the DFG project "Verified Model Checkers" and by the Czech Science Foundation, grant No. P202/12/G061.

References

[AL04]   Alur, R., La Torre, S.: Deterministic generators and games for LTL fragments. ACM Trans. Comput. Log. **5**(1), 1–25 (2004)

[BBKS13] Babiak, T., Blahoudek, F., Křetínský, M., Strejček, J.: Effective translation of LTL to deterministic Rabin automata: beyond the (F,G)-fragment. In: Hung, D., Ogawa, M. (eds.) ATVA 2013. LNCS, vol. 8172, pp. 24–39. Springer, Heidelberg (2013). doi:10.1007/978-3-319-02444-8_4

[DAC99] Dwyer, M.B., Avrunin, G.S., Corbett, J.C.: Patterns in property specifications for finite-state verification. In: ICSE, pp. 411–420 (1999)

[DLLF+16] Duret-Lutz, A., Lewkowicz, A., Fauchille, A., Michaud, T., Renault, É., Xu, L.: Spot 2.0 — a framework for LTL and ω-automata manipulation. In: Artho, C., Legay, A., Peled, D. (eds.) ATVA 2016. LNCS, vol. 9938, pp. 122–129. Springer, Heidelberg (2016). doi:10.1007/978-3-319-46520-3_8

[EK14]   Esparza, J., Křetínský, J.: From LTL to deterministic automata: a safraless compositional approach. In: Biere, A., Bloem, R. (eds.) CAV 2014. LNCS, vol. 8559, pp. 192–208. Springer, Heidelberg (2014). doi:10.1007/978-3-319-08867-9_13

[FEK11] Finkbeiner, B., Ehlers, R., Kupriyanov, A: Automata, games, and verification (2011). https://www.react.uni-saarland.de/teaching/automata-games-verification-11/downloads/ps9.pdf. Accessed 30 Aug 2016

[FL09] Friedmann, O., Lange, M.: Solving parity games in practice. In: Liu, Z., Ravn, A.P. (eds.) ATVA 2009. LNCS, vol. 5799, pp. 182–196. Springer, Heidelberg (2009). doi:10.1007/978-3-642-04761-9_15

[GH82] Gurevich, T., Harrington, L.: Trees, automata, and games. In: STOC, pp. •60–65 (1982)

[KB06] Klein, J., Baier, C.: Experiments with deterministic ω-automata for formulas of linear temporal logic. Theoret. Comput. Sci. **363**(2), 182–195 (2006)

[KE12] Křetínský, J., Esparza, J.: Deterministic Automata for the (F,G)-fragment of LTL. In: Madhusudan, P., Seshia, S.A. (eds.) CAV 2012. LNCS, vol. 7358, pp. 7–22. Springer, Heidelberg (2012). doi:10.1007/978-3-642-31424-7_7

[KK14] Komárková, Z., Křetínský, J.: Rabinizer 3: safraless translation of LTL to small deterministic automata. In: Cassez, F., Raskin, J.-F. (eds.) ATVA 2014. LNCS, vol. 8837, pp. 235–241. Springer, Heidelberg (2014). doi:10.1007/978-3-319-11936-6_17

[KMWW17] Křetínský, J., Meggendorfer, T., Waldmann, C., Weininger, M.: Index appearance record for transforming Rabin automata into parity automata. Technical report abs/1701.05738, arXiv.org (2017)

[KV05] Orna Kupferman and Moshe Y. Vardi. Safraless decision procedures. In FOCS, pp. 531–542, (2005)

[Löd99a] Löding, C.: Optimal bounds for transformations of ω-automata. In: Rangan, C.P., Raman, V., Ramanujam, R. (eds.) FSTTCS 1999. LNCS, vol. 1738, pp. 97–109. Springer, Heidelberg (1999). doi:10.1007/3-540-46691-6_8

[Löd99b] Löding, C.: Methods for the transformation of automata: complexity and connection to second order logic. Master's thesis, Institute of Computer Science and Applied Mathematics, Christian-Albrechts-University of Kiel, Germany (1999)

[ML16] Meyer, P.J., Luttenberger, M.: Solving mean-payoff games on the GPU. In: Artho, C., Legay, A., Peled, D. (eds.) ATVA 2016. LNCS, vol. 9938, pp. 262–267. Springer, Heidelberg (2016). doi:10.1007/978-3-319-46520-3_17

[Pit06] Piterman, N.: From nondeterministic Buchi and Streett automata to deterministic parity automata. In: LICS, pp. 255–264 (2006)

[Pnu77] Pnueli, A.: The temporal logic of programs. In: FOCS, pp. 46–57 (1977)

[PPS06] Piterman, N., Pnueli, A., Sa'ar, Y.: Synthesis of Reactive(1) Designs. In: Emerson, E.A., Namjoshi, K.S. (eds.) VMCAI 2006. LNCS, vol. 3855, pp. 364–380. Springer, Heidelberg (2005). doi:10.1007/11609773_24

[PR89] Pnueli, A., Rosner, R.: On the synthesis of a reactive module. In: POPL, pp. 179–190 (1989)

[Red12] Redziejowski, R.R.: An improved construction of deterministic omega-automaton using derivatives. Fundam. Inform. **119**(3–4), 393–406 (2012)

[Saf88] Safra, S.: On the complexity of omega-automata. In: FOCS, pp. 319–327 (1988)

[Saf92] Safra, S.: Exponential determinization for omega-automata with strong-fairness acceptance condition (extended abstract). In: STOC, pp. 275–282 (1992)

[Sch01] Schwoon, S.: Determinization and complementation of Streett automata. In: Grädel, E., Thomas, W., Wilke, T. (eds.) Automata Logics, and Infinite Games. LNCS, vol. 2500, pp. 79–91. Springer, Heidelberg (2002). doi:10.1007/3-540-36387-4_5

[Sch09] Schewe, S.: Tighter bounds for the determinisation of Büchi automata. In: Alfaro, L. (ed.) FoSSaCS 2009. LNCS, vol. 5504, pp. 167–181. Springer, Heidelberg (2009). doi:10.1007/978-3-642-00596-1_13

[TTH13] Tsai, M.-H., Tsay, Y.-K., Hwang, Y.-S.: GOAL for Games, Omega-Automata, and Logics. In: Sharygina, N., Veith, H. (eds.) CAV 2013. LNCS, vol. 8044, pp. 883–889. Springer, Heidelberg (2013). doi:10.1007/978-3-642-39799-8_62

Minimization of Visibly Pushdown Automata Using Partial Max-SAT

Matthias Heizmann, Christian Schilling$^{(\boxtimes)}$, and Daniel Tischner

University of Freiburg, Freiburg, Germany
`schillic@informatik.uni-freiburg.de`

Abstract. We consider the problem of state-space reduction for nondeterministic weakly-hierarchical visibly pushdown automata (VPA). VPA recognize a robust and algorithmically tractable fragment of context-free languages that is natural for modeling programs.

We define an equivalence relation that is sufficient for language-preserving quotienting of VPA. Our definition allows to merge states that have different behavior, as long as they show the same behavior for reachable equivalent stacks. We encode the existence of such a relation as a Boolean partial maximum satisfiability (PMax-SAT) problem and present an algorithm that quickly finds satisfying assignments. These assignments are sub-optimal solutions to the PMax-SAT problem but can still lead to a significant reduction of states.

We integrated our method in the automata-based software verifier ULTIMATE AUTOMIZER and show performance improvements on benchmarks from the software verification competition SV-COMP.

1 Introduction

The class of visibly pushdown languages (VPL) [6] lies properly between the regular and the context-free languages. VPL enjoy most desirable properties of regular languages (closure under Boolean operations and decision procedures for, e.g., the equivalence problem). They are well-suited for representing data that have both a linear and a hierarchical ordering, e.g., procedural programs [4,22,24,37] and XML documents [31,33,34,38].

The corresponding automaton model is called *visibly pushdown automaton* (VPA). It extends the finite automaton model with a stack of restricted access by requiring that the input symbol specifies the stack action – a call (resp. return) symbol implies a push (resp. pop) operation, and an internal symbol ignores the stack. In this paper, we consider a notion of VPA where a call always pushes the current state on the stack. These VPA are called weakly-hierarchical VPA [7].

Size reduction of automata is an active research topic [2,3,8,9,14,15,32] that is theoretically appealing and has practical relevance: smaller automata require less memory and speed up automata-based tools [21,23,27,29]. In this paper, we present a size reduction technique for a general class of (nondeterministic) VPA that is different from classes that were considered in previous approaches [5,13,30]. An extended version of this paper is available [26].

© Springer-Verlag GmbH Germany 2017
A. Legay and T. Margaria (Eds.): TACAS 2017, Part I, LNCS 10205, pp. 461–478, 2017.
DOI: 10.1007/978-3-662-54577-5_27

It is well-known that for deterministic finite automata the unique minimal automaton can be obtained by quotienting (i.e., merging equivalent states), and there exists an efficient algorithm for this purpose [28]. VPA do not have a canonical minimum [5]. For other automaton classes that lack this property, the usual approach is to find equivalence relations that are sufficient for quotienting [1,3,18]. The main difficulty of a quotienting approach for VPA is that two states may behave similarly given one stack but differently given another stack, and as the number of stacks is usually infinite, one cannot simply compare the behaviors for each of them.

1.1 Motivating Examples

We now present three observations. The first observation is our key insight and shows that VPA have interesting properties that we can exploit. The other observations show that VPA have intricate properties that make quotienting nontrivial. For convenience, we use a for internal, c for call, and r for return symbols, and we omit transitions to the sink state.

Exploiting Unreachable Stacks Allows Merging States. Consider the VPA in Fig. 1(a). The states q_1 and q_2 have the same behavior for the internal symbol a but different behaviors for the return symbol r with stack symbol q_0: Namely, state q_1 leads to the accepting state while q_2 has no respective return transition. However, in q_2 it is generally impossible to take a return transition with stack symbol q_0 since q_2 can only be reached with an empty stack. Thus the behavior for the stack symbol q_0 is "undefined" and we can merge q_1 and q_2 without changing the language. The resulting VPA is depicted in Fig. 1(b).

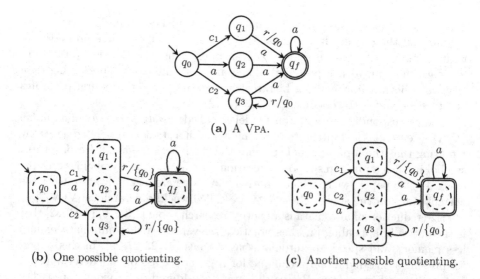

(a) A VPA.

(b) One possible quotienting.

(c) Another possible quotienting.

Fig. 1. A VPA and two possible quotientings due to unreachable stacks.

Merging States Requires a Transitive Relation. Using the same argument as above, we can also merge the states q_2 and q_3; the result is depicted in Fig. 1(c). For finite automata, mergeability of states is transitive. However, here we cannot merge all three states q_1, q_2, and q_3 without changing the language because q_1 and q_3 have different behaviors for stack symbol q_0. For VPA, we have to check compatibility for each pair of states.

Merging States Means Merging Stack Symbols. Consider the VPA in Fig. 2(a). Since for (weakly-hierarchical) VPA, stack symbols are states, merging the states q_1 and q_2 implicitly merges the stack symbols q_1 and q_2 as well. After merging we receive the VPA in Fig. 2(b) which recognizes a different language (e.g., it accepts the word $a_1 c r_2$).

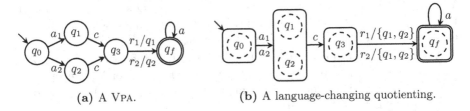

(a) A VPA.   (b) A language-changing quotienting.

Fig. 2. A VPA where quotienting of states leads to quotienting of stack symbols.

1.2 Our Approach

We define an equivalence relation over VPA states for quotienting that is language-preserving. This equivalence relation exploits our key observation, namely that we can merge states if they have the same behavior on equivalent reachable stacks, even if they have different behavior in general (Sect. 3). We show an encoding of such a relation as a Boolean partial maximum satisfiability (PMax-SAT) instance (Sect. 4). In order to solve these instances efficiently, we propose a greedy algorithm that finds suboptimal solutions (Sect. 5.1). As a proof of concept, we implemented the algorithm and evaluated it in the context of the automata-based software verifier ULTIMATE AUTOMIZER [23,25] (Sect. 5.2).

2 Visibly Pushdown Automata

In this section, we recall the basic definitions for visibly pushdown automata [6] and quotienting. After that, we characterize when an automaton is *live*.

2.1 Preliminaries

Alphabet. A *(visibly pushdown) alphabet* $\Sigma = \Sigma_i \uplus \Sigma_c \uplus \Sigma_r$ is a partition consisting of three finite sets of *internal* (Σ_i), *call* (Σ_c), and *return* (Σ_r) symbols.

A *word* is a sequence of symbols. We denote the set of finite words over alphabet Σ by Σ^* and the empty word by ε. As a convention we use a for internal, c for call, and r for return symbols, x for any type of symbol, and v, w for words.

The set of *well-matched* words over Σ, $WM(\Sigma)$, is the smallest set satisfying: (1) $\varepsilon \in WM(\Sigma)$; (2) if $w \in WM(\Sigma)$, so is wa for $a \in \Sigma_i$; and if $v, w \in WM(\Sigma)$, so is $vcwr$ for $cr \in \Sigma_c \cdot \Sigma_r$, and we call symbols c and r *matching*. Given a word over Σ, for any return symbol we can uniquely determine whether the symbol is matching. The set of *matched-return* words, $MR(\Sigma)$, consists of all words where each return symbol is matching. Clearly, $WM(\Sigma)$ is a subset of $MR(\Sigma)$.

Visibly Pushdown Automaton. A *visibly pushdown automaton* (VPA) is a tuple $\mathcal{A} = (Q, \Sigma, \bot, \Delta, Q_0, F)$ with a finite set of states Q, a visibly pushdown alphabet Σ, a bottom-of-stack symbol $\bot \notin Q$, a transition relation $\Delta = (\Delta_i, \Delta_c, \Delta_r)$ consisting of internal transitions $\Delta_i \subseteq Q \times \Sigma_i \times Q$, call transitions $\Delta_c \subseteq Q \times \Sigma_c \times Q$, and return transitions $\Delta_r \subseteq Q \times \Sigma_r \times Q \times Q$, a nonempty set of initial states $Q_0 \subseteq Q$, and a set of accepting states $F \subseteq Q$.

A *stack* σ is a word over $St \stackrel{\text{def}}{=} \{\bot\} \cdot Q^*$. We write $\sigma[i]$ for the i-th symbol of σ. A *configuration* is a pair $(q, \sigma) \in Q \times St$. A *run* $\rho_{\mathcal{A}}(w)$ of VPA $\mathcal{A}$ on word $w = x_1 x_2 \cdots \in \Sigma^*$ is a sequence of configurations $(q_0, \sigma_0)(q_1, \sigma_1) \cdots$ according to the following rules (for $i \geq 0$):

1. If $x_{i+1} \in \Sigma_i$ then $(q_i, x_{i+1}, q_{i+1}) \in \Delta_i$ and $\sigma_{i+1} = \sigma_i$.
2. If $x_{i+1} \in \Sigma_c$ then $(q_i, x_{i+1}, q_{i+1}) \in \Delta_c$ and $\sigma_{i+1} = \sigma_i \cdot q_i$.
3. If $x_{i+1} \in \Sigma_r$ then $(q_i, x_{i+1}, \hat{q}, q_{i+1}) \in \Delta_r$ and $\sigma_i = \sigma_{i+1} \cdot \hat{q}$.

A run is *initial* if $(q_0, \sigma_0) \in Q_0 \times \{\bot\}$. A configuration (q, σ) is *reachable* if there exists some initial run $\rho = (q_0, \sigma_0)(q_1, \sigma_1) \cdots$ such that $(q_i, \sigma_i) = (q, \sigma)$ for some $i \geq 0$, and *unreachable* otherwise. Similarly, we say that a stack σ is reachable (resp. unreachable) for state q if (q, σ) is reachable (resp. unreachable). A run of length n is *accepting* if $q_n \in F$. A word $w \in \Sigma^*$ is *accepted* if some initial run $\rho_{\mathcal{A}}(w)$ is accepting. The *language* recognized by a VPA $\mathcal{A}$ is defined as $L(\mathcal{A}) \stackrel{\text{def}}{=} \{w \mid w$ is accepted by $\mathcal{A}\}$. A VPA is *deterministic* if it has one initial state and the transition relation is functional.

A *finite automaton* (FA) is a VPA where $\Sigma_c = \Sigma_r = \emptyset$.

Remark 1. We use a variant of VPA that deviates from the VPA model by Alur and Madhusudan [6] in two ways: (1) We forbid return transitions when the stack is empty, i.e., the automata accept only matched-return words; this assumption is also used in other works [30, 35]. (2) We consider *weakly-hierarchical* VPA where a call transition implicitly pushes the current state on the stack; this assumption is also a common assumption [13, 30]; every VPA can be converted to weakly-hierarchical form with $2|Q||\Sigma|$ states [7].

Both assumptions are natural in the context of computer programs: The call stack can never be empty, and return transitions always lead back to the respective program location after the corresponding call.

Quotienting. For an equivalence relation over some set S, we denote the equivalence class of element e by $[e]$; analogously, lifted to sets, let $[T] \stackrel{\text{def}}{=} \{[e] \mid e \in T\}$.

Given a VPA $\mathcal{A} = (Q, \Sigma, \bot, (\Delta_i, \Delta_c, \Delta_r), Q_0, F)$ and an equivalence relation $\equiv \subseteq Q \times Q$ on states, the *quotient* VPA is the VPA $\mathcal{A}/_{\equiv} \stackrel{\text{def}}{=} ([Q], \Sigma, \bot, \Delta', [Q_0], [F])$ with $\Delta' = (\Delta'_i, \Delta'_c, \Delta'_r)$ and

- $\Delta'_i = \{([p], a, [p']) \mid \exists (q, a, q') \in \Delta_i . q \in [p], q' \in [p']\}$,
- $\Delta'_c = \{([p], c, [p']) \mid \exists (q, c, q') \in \Delta_c . q \in [p], q' \in [p']\}$, and
- $\Delta'_r = \{([p], r, [\hat{p}], [p']) \mid \exists (q, r, \hat{q}, q') \in \Delta_r . q \in [p], q' \in [p'], \hat{q} \in [\hat{p}]\}$.

Quotienting is the process of merging states from the same equivalence class to obtain the quotient VPA; this implicitly means merging stack symbols, too.

2.2   Live Visibly Pushdown Automata

Let $Q_\bot \stackrel{\text{def}}{=} Q \cup \{\bot\}$ be the *stack alphabet*. The function $top : St \to Q_\bot$ returns the topmost symbol of a stack:

$$top(\sigma) \stackrel{\text{def}}{=} \begin{cases} \bot & \sigma = \bot \\ q & \sigma = \sigma' \cdot q \text{ for some } \sigma' \in St \end{cases}$$

Given a state q, the function $tops : Q \to 2^{Q_\bot}$ returns the topmost symbols of all reachable stacks σ for q (i.e., reachable configurations (q, σ)):

$$tops(q) \stackrel{\text{def}}{=} \{top(\sigma) \mid \exists \sigma \in St . (q, \sigma) \text{ is reachable}\}$$

For seeing that $tops$ is computable, consider a VPA $\mathcal{A} = (Q, \Sigma, \bot, \Delta, Q_0, F)$. The function $tops$ is the smallest function $f : Q \to 2^{Q_\bot}$ satisfying:

1. $q \in Q_0 \implies \bot \in f(q)$
2. $\hat{q} \in f(q), (q, a, q') \in \Delta_i \implies \hat{q} \in f(q')$
3. (q, σ) reachable for some σ, $(q, c, q') \in \Delta_c \implies q \in f(q')$
4. $\hat{q} \in f(q), (q, r, \hat{q}, q') \in \Delta_r \implies f(\hat{q}) \subseteq f(q')$

We call a VPA *live* if the following holds. For each state q and for each internal and call symbol x there is at least one outgoing transition (q, x, q') to some state q'; additionally, for each return symbol r and state $\hat{q}$ there is at least one outgoing return transition $(q, \hat{q}, r, q')$ to some state q' if and only if $\hat{q} \in tops(q)$.

Note that a live VPA has a total transition relation in a weaker sense: There are outgoing return transitions from state q if and only if the respective transition can be taken in at least one run. That is, we forbid return transitions when no corresponding configuration is reachable. Every VPA can be converted to live form by adding one sink state.

Remark 2. For live VPA $\mathcal{A}$, a run $\rho_{\mathcal{A}}(w)$ on word w can only "get stuck" in an empty-stack configuration, i.e., if $w = v_1 r v_2$ with $r \in \Sigma_r$ such that $\rho_{\mathcal{A}}(v_1) = (q_0, \sigma_0) \cdots (q_k, \bot)$ for some $q_k \in Q$. If $w \in MR(\Sigma)$, no run gets stuck.

For the remainder of the paper, we fix a live VPA $\mathcal{A} = (Q, \Sigma, \bot, \Delta, Q_0, F)$. We sometimes refer to this VPA as the *input automaton*.

3 A Quotienting Relation for VPA

In this section, we define an equivalence relation on the states of a VPA that is useful for quotienting, i.e., whose respective quotient VPA is language-preserving.

We first need the notion of *closure under successors* for each kind of symbol. Let $R \subseteq Q \times Q$ be a binary relation over states and let $p, q, \hat{p}, \hat{q} \in Q$ be states. We say that R is

- *closed under internal successors for* (p, q) if for each internal symbol $a \in \Sigma_i$
  - for all $(p, a, p') \in \Delta_i$ there exists $(q, a, q') \in \Delta_i$ s.t. $(p', q') \in R$ and
  - for all $(q, a, q') \in \Delta_i$ there exists $(p, a, p') \in \Delta_i$ s.t. $(p', q') \in R$,
- *closed under call successors for* (p, q) if for each call symbol $c \in \Sigma_c$
  - for all $(p, c, p') \in \Delta_c$ there exists $(q, c, q') \in \Delta_c$ s.t. $(p', q') \in R$ and
  - for all $(q, c, q') \in \Delta_c$ there exists $(p, c, p') \in \Delta_c$ s.t. $(p', q') \in R$,
- *closed under return successors for* $(p, q, \hat{p}, \hat{q})$ if for each return symbol $r \in \Sigma_r$
  - for all $(p, r, \hat{p}, p') \in \Delta_r$ there exists $(q, r, \hat{q}, q') \in \Delta_r$ s.t. $(p', q') \in R$ and
  - for all $(q, r, \hat{q}, q') \in \Delta_r$ there exists $(p, r, \hat{p}, p') \in \Delta_r$ s.t. $(p', q') \in R$.

We are ready to present an equivalence relation that is useful for quotienting using a fixpoint characterization.

Definition 1 (Reachability-aware quotienting relation). *Let $\mathcal{A}$ be a VPA and $R \subseteq Q \times Q$ be an equivalence relation over states. We say that R is a RAQ relation if for each pair of states $(p, q) \in R$ the following constraints hold.*

(i) State p is accepting if and only if state q is accepting ($p \in F \iff q \in F$).
(ii) R is closed under internal successors for (p, q).
(iii) R is closed under call successors for (p, q).
(iv) For each pair of states (resp. topmost stack symbols) $(\hat{p}, \hat{q}) \in R$,
  - *R is closed under return successors for $(p, q, \hat{p}, \hat{q})$, or*
  - *no configuration (q, σ_q) with $\hat{q} = top(\sigma_q)$ is reachable, or*
  - *no configuration (p, σ_p) with $\hat{p} = top(\sigma_p)$ is reachable.*

Remark 3. "No configuration (q, σ_q) with $\hat{q} = top(\sigma_q)$ is reachable" is equivalent to "$\hat{q} \notin tops(q)$". The equality relation $\{(q, q) \mid q \in Q\}$ is a RAQ relation for any VPA; the respective quotient VPA is isomorphic to the input automaton.

Example 1. Consider again the VPA from Fig. 1(a). We claim that the relation $R \stackrel{\text{def}}{=} \{(q, q) \mid q \in Q\} \cup \{(q_1, q_2), (q_2, q_1)\}$ is a RAQ relation. Note that it corresponds to the quotient VPA from Fig. 1(b). First we observe that R is an equivalence relation. We check the remaining constraints only for the two pairs (q_1, q_2) and (q_2, q_1). Both states are not accepting. Relation R is closed under internal (here: a) and call (here: none, i.e., implicitly leading to a sink) successors. The return transition constraint is satisfied because in state q_2 no stack with topmost symbol q_0 is reachable ($q_0 \notin tops(q_2)$).

We want to use a RAQ relation for language-preserving quotienting. For this purpose we need to make sure that unreachable configurations in Definition 1 do not enable accepting runs that are not possible in the original VPA. In the remainder of this section, we show that this is indeed the case.

Given an equivalence relation $R \subseteq Q \times Q$ on states, we call a stack σ the R-quotienting of some stack σ' of the same height if either $\sigma = \sigma' = \bot$ or for all $i = 2, \ldots, |\sigma|$ each symbol $\sigma[i]$ is the equivalence class of $\sigma'[i]$, i.e., $\sigma'[i] \in [\sigma[i]]$. We write $\sigma' \in [\sigma]$ in this case. (We compare stacks only for $i \geq 2$ because the first stack symbol is always $\bot$.)

Lemma 1 (Corresponding run). *Let $\mathcal{A}$ be a VPA and $\equiv$ be some RAQ relation for $\mathcal{A}$. Then for any matched-return word w and respective run*

$$\rho_{\mathcal{A}/\equiv}(w) = ([p_0], \bot) \cdots ([p_n], [\sigma_n])$$

with $p_0 \in Q_0$ in $\mathcal{A}/\equiv$ there is some corresponding run

$$\rho_{\mathcal{A}}(w) = (q'_0, \bot) \cdots (q'_n, \sigma'_n)$$

in $\mathcal{A}$ such that $q'_i \in [p_i]$ and $\sigma'_i \in [\sigma_i]$ for all $i \geq 0$, and furthermore $q'_0 \in Q_0$.

Proof. The proof is by induction on the length of w. The case for $w = \varepsilon$ is trivial. Now assume $w' = w \cdot x$ for $x \in \Sigma$ and fix some run $\rho_{\mathcal{A}/\equiv}(w') = ([p_0], \bot) \cdots ([p_n], [\sigma_n]) \cdot ([p_{n+1}], [\sigma_{n+1}])$. The hypothesis ensures that there exists a corresponding run for the prefix $\rho_{\mathcal{A}}(w) = (q'_0, \bot) \cdots (q'_n, \sigma'_n)$ s.t. $q'_n \in [p_n]$ and $\sigma'_n \in [\sigma_n]$. We will extend this run in each of the three cases for symbol x.

(1) If $x \in \Sigma_i$, then, since there is a transition $([p_n], x, [p_{n+1}]) \in \Delta_{i/\equiv}$, there exist some states $q''_n \in [p_n]$ and $q''_{n+1} \in [p_{n+1}]$ s.t. $(q''_n, x, q''_{n+1}) \in \Delta_i$ (from the definition of quotienting). Using that $\equiv$ is closed under internal successors, there also exists a target state $q'_{n+1} \in [p_{n+1}]$ s.t. $(q'_n, x, q'_{n+1}) \in \Delta_i$. Additionally, because $x \in \Sigma_i$, we have that $\sigma'_{n+1} = \sigma'_n \in [\sigma_n] = [\sigma_{n+1}]$ by the hypothesis.

(2) If $x \in \Sigma_c$, a similar argument holds, only this time the stack changes. We have that $\sigma'_{n+1} = \sigma'_n \cdot q'_n \in [\sigma_n \cdot p_n] = [\sigma_{n+1}]$ by the hypothesis.

(3) If $x \in \Sigma_r$, then the configuration (q'_n, σ'_n) is reachable (witnessed by the run $\rho_{\mathcal{A}}(w)$). Since $\equiv$ is closed under return successors for all states in $[p_n]$ (modulo unreachable configurations), for each top-of-stack symbol $\hat{q} \in [top(\sigma'_n)]$ s.t. $(q'_n, \sigma'' \cdot \hat{q})$ is reachable for some stack σ'' there exists a corresponding return transition $(q'_n, x, \hat{q}, q'_{n+1}) \in \Delta_r$ with $q'_{n+1} \in [p_{n+1}]$; in particular, this holds for $\hat{q} = top(\sigma'_n)$. Recall that $\mathcal{A}$ is assumed to be live, which ensures that every return transition that exists in the quotient VPA has such a witness. The stack property $\sigma'_{n+1} \in [\sigma_{n+1}]$ follows from the hypothesis. $\square$

From the above lemma we can conclude that quotienting with a RAQ relation preserves the language.

Theorem 1 (Language preservation of quotienting). *Let $\mathcal{A}$ be a VPA and let $\equiv$ be a RAQ relation on the states of $\mathcal{A}$. Then $L(\mathcal{A}) = L(\mathcal{A}/\equiv)$.*

Proof. Clearly, $L(\mathcal{A}) \subseteq L(\mathcal{A}/_\equiv)$ for any equivalence relation $\equiv$. We show the other inclusion by means of a contradiction.

Assume there exists a word w s.t. $w \in L(\mathcal{A}/_\equiv) \setminus L(\mathcal{A})$. By assumption, in $\mathcal{A}/_\equiv$ there is an initial accepting run $\rho_{\mathcal{A}/_\equiv}(w)$. Then, by Lemma 1, there is a corresponding run $\rho_{\mathcal{A}}(w)$, and furthermore this run is initial.

The run $\rho_{\mathcal{A}}(w)$ is also accepting by the property that $[p] \in [F]$ if and only if $q \in F$ for all $q \in [p]$ (cf. Property (i) of a RAQ relation). $\qquad\square$

4   Computing Quotienting Relations

In Sect. 3, we introduced the notion of a RAQ relation and showed how we can use it to minimize VPA while preserving the language. In this section, we show how we can compute a RAQ relation. For this purpose, we provide an encoding as a partial maximum satisfiability problem (PMax-SAT). From a (in fact, any) solution, i.e., satisfying assignment, we can synthesize a RAQ relation. While this does not result in the coarsest RAQ relation possible, the relation obtained is locally optimal, i.e., there is no coarser RAQ relation that is a strict superset.

4.1   Computing RAQ Relations

Note that in general there are many possible instantiations of a RAQ relation, e.g., the trivial equality relation which is not helpful for minimization. Since we are interested in reducing the number of states, we prefer coarser relations over finer relations.

To obtain a coarse relation, we describe an encoding of the RAQ relation constraints as an instance of the PMax-SAT problem [12,19]. Such a problem consists of a propositional logic formula in conjunctive normal form with each clause being marked as either *hard* or *soft*. The task is to find a truth assignment such that all hard clauses are satisfied and the number of the satisfied soft clauses is maximal.

SAT Encoding. For the moment, we ignore soft clauses and provide a standard SAT encoding of the constraints. The encoding has the property that any satisfying assignment induces a valid RAQ relation $\equiv$.

Let true and false be the Boolean constants. We need $\mathcal{O}(n^2)$ variables of the form $X_{\{p,q\}}$ where p and q are states of the input automaton. The idea is that $p \equiv q$ holds if we assign the value true to $X_{\{p,q\}}$. (We ignore the order of p and q as $\equiv$ must be symmetric.) We express the constraints from Definition 1 as follows.

Consider the constraint (i). For each pair of states (p, q) not satisfying the constraint we introduce the clause

$$\neg X_{\{p,q\}}. \tag{1}$$

Consider the constraints (ii), (iii), (iv). For each transition $(p, a, p') \in \Delta_i$, $(p, c, p') \in \Delta_c$, and $(p, r, \hat{p}, p') \in \Delta_r$ and all states q and $\hat{q}$ we respectively construct one of the following clauses.

$$\neg X_{\{p,q\}} \vee (X_{\{p',q_1^a\}} \vee \cdots \vee X_{\{p',q_{k_a}^a\}}) \tag{2}$$

$$\neg X_{\{p,q\}} \vee (X_{\{p',q_1^c\}} \vee \cdots \vee X_{\{p',q_{k_c}^c\}}) \tag{3}$$

$$\neg X_{\{p,q\}} \vee \neg X_{\{\hat{p},\hat{q}\}} \vee (X_{\{p',q_1^r\}} \vee \cdots \vee X_{\{p',q_{k_r}^r\}}) \tag{4}$$

Here the q_i^a / q_i^c are the respective a/c-successors of q and the q_i^r are the r-successors of q with stack symbol $\hat{q}$. To account for the unreachable configuration relaxation, we may omit return transition clauses (4) where $\hat{p} \notin tops(p)$ or $\hat{q} \notin tops(q)$.

We also need to express that $\equiv$ is an equivalence relation, i.e., we need additional reflexivity clauses

$$X_{\{q_1,q_1\}} \tag{5}$$

and transitivity clauses

$$\neg X_{\{q_1,q_2\}} \vee \neg X_{\{q_2,q_3\}} \vee X_{\{q_1,q_3\}} \tag{6}$$

for any distinct states q_1, q_2, q_3 (assuming there are least three states). Recall that our variables already ensure symmetry.

Let Φ be the conjunction of all clauses of the form (1), (2), (3), (4), (5), and (6). All assignments satisfying Φ represent valid RAQ relations.

However, we know that the assignment

$$X_{\{p,q\}} \mapsto \begin{cases} \text{true} & p = q \\ \text{false} & \text{otherwise} \end{cases}$$

corresponding to the equality relation is always trivially satisfying. Such an assignment is not suited for our needs. We consider an assignment *optimal* if it represents a RAQ relation with a coarsest partition.

PMax-SAT Encoding. We now describe an extension of the SAT encoding to a PMax-SAT encoding. In this setting, we can enforce that the number of variables that are assigned the value true is maximal.

As an addition to Φ, we add for every two states p, q with $p \neq q$ the clause

$$X_{\{p,q\}} \tag{7}$$

and finally we consider all old clauses, i.e., clauses of the form (1)–(6), as hard clauses and all clauses of the form (7) as soft clauses.

4.2   Locally Maximal RAQ Relation

Note that an assignment obtained from the PMax-SAT encoding does not necessarily give us a coarsest RAQ relation. Consider a VPA with seven states $q_0, \ldots, q_6$ and the partition $\{\{q_0, q_1, q_2, q_3\}, \{q_4\}, \{q_5\}, \{q_6\}\}$. Here we set six variables to true (all pairs of states from the first set). However, the partition $\{\{q_0, q_1, q_2\}, \{q_3, q_4\}, \{q_5, q_6\}\}$ is coarser, and yet we only set five variables to true.

Despite not finding the globally maximal solution, we can establish local maximality.

Theorem 2 (Local maximum). *A satisfying assignment of the* PMax-SAT *instance corresponds to a RAQ relation such that no strict superset of the relation is also a RAQ relation.*

Proof. It is clear from the construction that in the obtained assignment, no further variable $X_{\{p,q\}}$ can be assigned the value true. Each such variable determines membership of the symmetric pairs (p, q) and (q, p) in the RAQ relation. $\square$

5   Experimental Evaluation

In this section, we report on our implementation and its potential in practice.

5.1   Implementation

Initially, we apply the following preprocessing steps for reducing the complexity. First, we remove unreachable and dead states and make the VPA live for return transitions (we do not require that the VPA is total for internal or call transitions). Second, we immediately replace variables $X_{\{p\}}$ by true (reflexivity). Third, we construct an initial partition of the states and replace variables $X_{\{p,q\}}$ by false if p and q are not in the same block. This partition is the coarsest fixpoint of a simple partition refinement such that states in the same block have the same acceptance status, the same outgoing internal and call symbols, and, if all states in a block have a unique successor under an internal/call symbol, those successors are in the same block (cf. Definition 1 and Hopcroft's algorithm [28]).

Optimally solving a PMax-SAT instance is an NP-complete problem. Expectedly, a straightforward implementation of the algorithm presented in Sect. 4 using an off-the-shelf PMax-SAT solver does not scale to interesting problems (see also the extended version [26]). Therefore, we implemented a domain-specific greedy PMax-SAT solver that only maximizes the satisfied soft clauses locally.

Our solver is interactive, i.e., clauses are added one after another, and propagation is applied immediately. After adding the last clause, the solver chooses some unset variable and first sets it to true optimistically. Theorem 2 still holds with this strategy. Apart from that, the solver follows the standard DPLL algorithm and uses no further enhancements found in modern SAT solvers.

Remark 4. If the VPA is deterministic, we obtain a Horn clause system. Then the above algorithm never needs to backtrack for more than one level, as the remaining clauses can always be satisfied by assigning false to the variables.

The main limitation of the approach is the memory consumption. Clearly, the majority of clauses are those expressing transitivity. Therefore, we implemented and integrated a solver for the theory of equality: When a variable $X_{\{p,q\}}$ is set to true, this solver returns all variables that must also be set to true for consistency. That allowed us to omit the transitivity clauses (see [26] for details).

5.2 Experiments

Our evaluation consists of three parts. First, we evaluate the impact of our minimization on an verifier ULTIMATE AUTOMIZER. Second, we evaluate the performance of our minimization on automata that were produced by ULTIMATE AUTOMIZER. Third, we evaluate the performance of our minimization on a set of random automata. All experiments are performed on a PC with an Intel i7 3.60 GHz CPU running Linux.

Impact on the software verifier Ultimate Automizer. The software verifier ULTIMATE AUTOMIZER [23] follows an automata-based approach [25] in which sets of program traces are represented by automata. The approach can be seen as a CEGAR-style algorithm in which an abstraction is iteratively refined. This abstraction is represented as a weakly-hierarchical VPA where the automaton stack only keeps track of the states from where function calls were triggered.

For our evaluation, we run ULTIMATE AUTOMIZER on a set of C programs in two different modes. In the mode "No minimization" no automata minimization is applied. In the mode "Minimization" we apply our minimization in each iteration of the CEGAR loop to the abstraction if it has less than 10,000 states. (In cases where the abstraction has more than 10,000 states the minimization can be too slow to pay off on average.)

As benchmarks we took C programs from the repository of the SV-COMP 2016 [10] and let ULTIMATE AUTOMIZER analyze if the error location is reachable. In this repository the folders `systemc` and `eca-rers2012` contain programs that use function calls (hence the VPA contain calls and returns) and in whose analysis the automata sizes are a bottleneck for ULTIMATE AUTOMIZER. We randomly picked 100 files from the `eca-rers2012` folder and took all 65 files from the `systemc` folder. The timeout of ULTIMATE AUTOMIZER was set to 300 s and the available memory was restricted to 4 GiB.

The results are given in Table 1. Our minimization increases the number of programs that are successfully analyzed from 66 to 78. On programs that are successfully analyzed in both modes, the mode using minimization is slightly faster. Hence, the additional cost due to minimization is more than compensated by savings in other operations on the (now smaller) VPA on average.

Evaluation on automata from Ultimate Automizer. To evaluate the performance of our minimization algorithm in more details, we applied it to a benchmark set that consists of 1026 VPA produced by ULTIMATE AUTOMIZER. All

Table 1. Performance of ULTIMATE AUTOMIZER with and without minimization. Column # shows the number of successful reachability analyses (out of 165), average run time is given in milliseconds, average removal shows the states removed for all iterations, and the last column shows the relative number of iterations where minimization was employed. The first two rows contain the data for those programs where both modes succeeded, and the third row contains the data for those programs where only the minimization mode succeeded.

Mode	Set	#	∅ Time total	∅ Time minimization	∅ Removal	% Iterations with minimization
No minimization	Both	66	16085	–	–	–
Minimization			15564	2649	3077	75
Minimization	Exclusive	12	101985	61384	8472	76

Table 2. Performance of our algorithm on automata produced by ULTIMATE AUTOMIZER (see also Fig. 3). We aggregate the data for all automata whose number of states is in a certain interval. Column # shows the number of automata, #nd shows the number of nondeterministic automata, and the other data is reported as average. The next seven columns show information about the input automata. The run time is given in milliseconds. The last two columns show the number of variables and clauses passed to the PMax-SAT solver.

$|Q|$ (interval)	#	#nd	$|Q|$	$|\Sigma_i|$	$|\Sigma_c|$	$|\Sigma_r|$	$|\Delta_i|$	$|\Delta_c|$	$|\Delta_r|$	Time	$|Var|$	$|Cls|$
$[22; 250]$	102	46	149	29	4	4	131	13	75	130	1440	35375
$[250; 1000]$	158	64	554	83	11	11	533	43	105	607	8363	53016
$[1000; 4000]$	161	27	2053	413	34	34	2188	170	345	2536	36865	170256
$[4000; 16000]$	127	6	8530	1535	152	150	9293	625	889	31481	161214	244007
$[16000; 34114]$	48	5	21755	2133	203	202	25348	603	1137	32129	361866	813549

automata from this set contain call and return transitions and do not contain any dead ends (states from which no accepting state is reachable). Details on the construction of these automata can be found in the extended version [26]

We ran our implementation on these automata using a timeout of 300 s and a memory limit of 4 GiB. Within the resource bounds we were able to minimize 596 of the automata. Details about these automata and the minimization run are presented in Table 2. In the table we grouped automata according to their size. For instance, the first row aggregates the data of all automata that have up to 250 states. The table shows that we were able to minimize automata up to a five-digit number of states and that automata that have a few thousand states can be minimized within seconds. Figure 3 shows the sizes of the minimization results. The first four graphs compare the sizes of input and output in terms of states and transitions. The fourth graph shows that the (partly) significant size reduction is not only due to "intraprocedural" merges, but that also the number of return transitions is reduced. The last two graphs show that the relative size

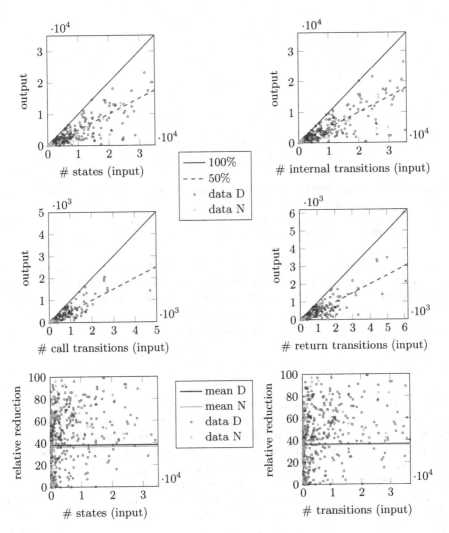

Fig. 3. Minimization results on automata produced by ULTIMATE AUTOMIZER (see also Table 2). D(N) stands for (non-)deterministic automata.

reduction is higher on larger automata. The reason is that small automata in ULTIMATE AUTOMIZER tend to have similarities to the control flow graph of a program, which is usually already minimal.

Evaluation on Random Automata. The automata produced by ULTIMATE AUTOMIZER have relatively large alphabets (according to Table 2 there are on average less than 10 states per symbol) and are extremely sparse (on average less than 1.5 transitions per state). To investigate the applicability of our approach to VPA without such structure, we also evaluate it on random

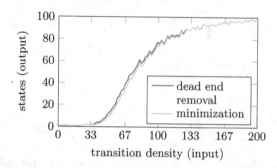

Fig. 4. Minimization results on random VPA with 100 states, of which 50% are accepting, and with one internal, call, and return symbol each. Return transitions are each inserted with 50 random stack symbols. The transition density is increased in steps of 2%. Each data point stems from 500 random automata.

nondeterministic VPA. We use a generalization of the random Büchi automata model by Tabakov and Vardi [36] to VPA (see the extended version [26] for details). Figure 4 shows that our algorithm can remove some states on top of removing dead ends for lower transition densities, but overall it seems more appropriate to automata that have some structure.

6   Related Work

Alur *et al.* [5] show that a canonical minimal VPA does not exist in general. They propose the *single entry*-VPA (SEVPA) model, a special VPA of equivalent expressiveness with the following constraints: Each state and call symbol is assigned to one of k modules, and each module has a unique entry state which is the target of all respective call transitions. This is enough structure to obtain the unique minimal k-SEVPA from any given k-SEVPA by quotienting.

Kumar *et al.* [30] extend the idea to *modular* VPA. Here the requirement of having a unique entry per module is overcome, but more structure must be fixed to preserve a unique minimum – most notably the restriction to weakly-hierarchical VPA and the return alphabet being a singleton.

Chervet and Walukiewicz [13] generalize the above classes to *call driven automata*. They show that general VPA can be exponentially more succinct than the three classes presented. Additionally, they propose another class called *block* VPA for which a unique minimum exists that is at most quadratic in the size of some minimal (general) VPA. However, to find it, the "right" partition into modules must be chosen, for which no efficient algorithm is known.

All above VPA classes have in common that the languages recognized are subsets of $WM(\Sigma)$, the states are partitioned into modules, and the minimal automaton (respecting the partition) can be found by quotienting. While the latter is an enjoyable property from the algorithmic view, the constraints limit practical applicability: Even under the assumption that the input VPA recognizes a well-matched language, if it does not meet the constraints, it must first be converted to the respective form. This conversion generally introduces an exponential blow-up in the number of states. In contrast, our procedure assumes only weakly-hierarchical VPA accepting matched-return words. In general, a weakly-hierarchical VPA can be obtained with only a linear blow-up. (In ULTIMATE AUTOMIZER the automata already have this form.)

Consider the k-SEVPA in Fig. 5. It has k modules $\{q_1\}, \ldots, \{q_k\}$ (and the default module $\{q_0, q_f\}$). This is the minimal k-SEVPA recognizing the language with the given modules. Our algorithm will (always) merge all singleton modules into one state, resulting in a (minimal) three-state VPA.

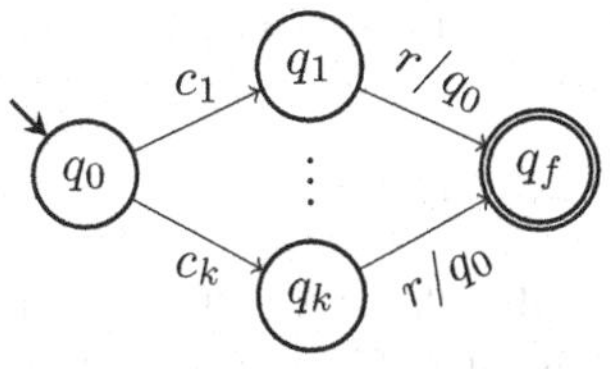

Caralp et al. [11] present a polynomial trimming procedure for VPA. The task is to ensure

Fig. 5. A parametric k-SEVPA.

that every configuration exhibited in the VPA is both reachable and co-reachable. Such a procedure may add new states. We follow the opposite direction and exploit untrimmed configurations to reduce the number of states.

Ehlers [17] provides a SAT encoding of the question "does there exist an equivalent Büchi automaton (BA) of size $n - 1$". Baarir and Duret-Lutz [8,9] extend the idea to so-called *transition-based generalized* BA. Since the search is global, on the one hand, such a query can be used iteratively to obtain a reduced BA after each step and some globally minimal BA upon termination; on the other hand, global search leaves little structure to the solver.

Geldenhuys et al. [20] also use a SAT encoding to reduce the state-space of nondeterministic FA. The first step is to construct the minimal deterministic FA $\mathcal{B}$. Then the solver symbolically guesses a candidate FA of a fixed size and checks that the automaton resulting from the subset construction applied to the candidate is isomorphic to $\mathcal{B}$. If the formula is unsatisfiable, the candidate size must be increased. Determinization may incur an exponential blow-up, and the resulting automaton is not always (but often) minimal.

In contrast to the above works, our PMax-SAT encoding consists of constraints about a quotienting relation (which always exists) that is polynomial in the size of the VPA. We do not find a minimal VPA, but our technique can be applied to VPA of practical relevance (the authors report results for automata with less than 20 states), in particular using our greedy algorithm.

Restricted to FA, the definition of a RAQ relation coincides with direct bisimulation [16,18]. This has two consequences. First, for FA, we can omit the transitivity clauses because a direct bisimulation is always transitive. Second, our algorithm always produces the (unique) maximal direct bisimulation. This can be seen as follows. If two states p and q bisimulate each other, then $X_{\{p,q\}}$ can be assigned true: since we are looking for a maximal assignment, we will assign this value. If p and q do not bisimulate each other, then in any satisfying assignment $X_{\{p,q\}}$ must be false. Alternatively, one can also say that our algorithm searches for *some* maximal fixpoint, which is unique for direct bisimulation.

For FA, it is well-known that minimization based on direct simulation yields smaller automata compared to direct bisimulation (i.e., the induced equivalence relation is coarser) [18]. Two states can be merged if they simulate each other. Our PMax-SAT encoding can be generalized to direct simulation by making the variables non-symmetric, i.e., using both $X_{p,q}$ and $X_{q,p}$ and adapting the clauses in a straightforward way. This increases the complexity by a polynomial.

References

1. Abdulla, P.A., Chen, Y., Holík, L., Vojnar, T.: Mediating for reduction (on minimizing alternating Büchi automata). In: FSTTCS, LIPIcs, vol. 4, pp. 1–12. Schloss Dagstuhl - Leibniz-Zentrum fuer Informatik (2009)
2. Abel, A., Reineke, J.: MeMin: SAT-based exact minimization of incompletely specified mealy machines. In: ICCAD, pp. 94–101. IEEE (2015)
3. Almeida, R., Holík, L., Mayr, R.: Reduction of nondeterministic tree automata. In: Chechik, M., Raskin, J.-F. (eds.) TACAS 2016. LNCS, vol. 9636, pp. 717–735. Springer, Heidelberg (2016). doi:10.1007/978-3-662-49674-9_46
4. Alur, R., Bouajjani, A., Esparza, J.: Model checking procedural programs. In: Handbook of Model Checking. Springer, Heidelberg (2017, to appear)
5. Alur, R., Kumar, V., Madhusudan, P., Viswanathan, M.: Congruences for visibly pushdown languages. In: Caires, L., Italiano, G.F., Monteiro, L., Palamidessi, C., Yung, M. (eds.) ICALP 2005. LNCS, vol. 3580, pp. 1102–1114. Springer, Heidelberg (2005). doi:10.1007/11523468_89
6. Alur, R., Madhusudan, P.: Visibly pushdown languages. In: STOC, pp. 202–211. ACM (2004)
7. Alur, R., Madhusudan, P.: Adding nesting structure to words. J. ACM 56(3) (2009). Article No. 16
8. Baarir, S., Duret-Lutz, A.: Mechanizing the minimization of deterministic generalized Büchi automata. In: Ábrahám, E., Palamidessi, C. (eds.) FORTE 2014. LNCS, vol. 8461, pp. 266–283. Springer, Heidelberg (2014). doi:10.1007/978-3-662-43613-4_17
9. Baarir, S., Duret-Lutz, A.: SAT-based minimization of deterministic ω-automata. In: Davis, M., Fehnker, A., McIver, A., Voronkov, A. (eds.) LPAR 2015. LNCS, vol. 9450, pp. 79–87. Springer, Heidelberg (2015). doi:10.1007/978-3-662-48899-7_6
10. Beyer, D.: Reliable and reproducible competition results with BenchExec and witnesses (report on SV-COMP 2016). In: Chechik, M., Raskin, J.-F. (eds.) TACAS 2016. LNCS, vol. 9636, pp. 887–904. Springer, Heidelberg (2016). doi:10.1007/978-3-662-49674-9_55
11. Caralp, M., Reynier, P.-A., Talbot, J.-M.: Trimming visibly pushdown automata. In: Konstantinidis, S. (ed.) CIAA 2013. LNCS, vol. 7982, pp. 84–96. Springer, Heidelberg (2013). doi:10.1007/978-3-642-39274-0_9
12. Cha, B., Iwama, K., Kambayashi, Y., Miyazaki, S.: Local search algorithms for partial MAXSAT. In: AAAI/IAAI, pp. 263–268. AAAI Press/The MIT Press (1997)
13. Chervet, P., Walukiewicz, I.: Minimizing variants of visibly pushdown automata. In: Kučera, L., Kučera, A. (eds.) MFCS 2007. LNCS, vol. 4708, pp. 135–146. Springer, Heidelberg (2007). doi:10.1007/978-3-540-74456-6_14
14. Clemente, L.: Büchi automata can have smaller quotients. In: Aceto, L., Henzinger, M., Sgall, J. (eds.) ICALP 2011. LNCS, vol. 6756, pp. 258–270. Springer, Heidelberg (2011). doi:10.1007/978-3-642-22012-8_20

15. D'Antoni, L., Veanes, M.: Minimization of symbolic automata. In: POPL, pp. 541–554. ACM (2014)
16. Dill, D.L., Hu, A.J., Wong-Toi, H.: Checking for language inclusion using simulation preorders. In: Larsen, K.G., Skou, A. (eds.) CAV 1991. LNCS, vol. 575, pp. 255–265. Springer, Heidelberg (1992). doi:10.1007/3-540-55179-4_25
17. Ehlers, R.: Minimising deterministic Büchi automata precisely using SAT solving. In: Strichman, O., Szeider, S. (eds.) SAT 2010. LNCS, vol. 6175, pp. 326–332. Springer, Heidelberg (2010). doi:10.1007/978-3-642-14186-7_28
18. Etessami, K., Wilke, T., Schuller, R.A.: Fair simulation relations, parity games, and state space reduction for Büchi automata. SIAM J. Comput. **34**(5), 1159–1175 (2005)
19. Fu, Z., Malik, S.: On solving the partial MAX-SAT problem. In: Biere, A., Gomes, C.P. (eds.) SAT 2006. LNCS, vol. 4121, pp. 252–265. Springer, Heidelberg (2006). doi:10.1007/11814948_25
20. Geldenhuys, J., Merwe, B., Zijl, L.: Reducing nondeterministic finite automata with SAT solvers. In: Yli-Jyrä, A., Kornai, A., Sakarovitch, J., Watson, B. (eds.) FSMNLP 2009. LNCS (LNAI), vol. 6062, pp. 81–92. Springer, Heidelberg (2010). doi:10.1007/978-3-642-14684-8_9
21. Habermehl, P., Holík, L., Rogalewicz, A., Simácek, J., Vojnar, T.: Forest automata for verification of heap manipulation. Formal Methods Syst. Des. **41**(1), 83–106 (2012)
22. Harris, W.R., Jha, S., Reps, T.: Secure programming via visibly pushdown safety games. In: Madhusudan, P., Seshia, S.A. (eds.) CAV 2012. LNCS, vol. 7358, pp. 581–598. Springer, Heidelberg (2012). doi:10.1007/978-3-642-31424-7_41
23. Heizmann, M., Dietsch, D., Greitschus, M., Leike, J., Musa, B., Schätzle, C., Podelski, A.: Ultimate automizer with two-track proofs. In: Chechik, M., Raskin, J.-F. (eds.) TACAS 2016. LNCS, vol. 9636, pp. 950–953. Springer, Heidelberg (2016). doi:10.1007/978-3-662-49674-9_68
24. Heizmann, M., Hoenicke, J., Podelski, A.: Nested interpolants. In: POPL, pp. 471–482. ACM (2010)
25. Heizmann, M., Hoenicke, J., Podelski, A.: Software model checking for people who love automata. In: Sharygina, N., Veith, H. (eds.) CAV 2013. LNCS, vol. 8044, pp. 36–52. Springer, Heidelberg (2013). doi:10.1007/978-3-642-39799-8_2
26. Heizmann, M., Schilling, C., Tischner, D.: Minimization of visibly pushdown automata using partial Max-SAT, vol. abs/1701.05160 (2017)
27. Holzmann, G.J., Puri, A.: A minimized automaton representation of reachable states. STTT **2**(3), 270–278 (1999)
28. Hopcroft, J.E.: An n log n algorithm for minimizing states in a finite automaton. In: Theory of Machines and Computations, pp. 189–196. Academic Press (1971)
29. Klarlund, N., Møller, A., Schwartzbach, M.I.: MONA implementation secrets. Int. J. Found. Comput. Sci. **13**(4), 571–586 (2002)
30. Kumar, V., Madhusudan, P., Viswanathan, M.: Minimization, learning, and conformance testing of boolean programs. In: Baier, C., Hermanns, H. (eds.) CONCUR 2006. LNCS, vol. 4137, pp. 203–217. Springer, Heidelberg (2006). doi:10.1007/11817949_14
31. Kumar, V., Madhusudan, P., Viswanathan, M.: Visibly pushdown automata for streaming XML. In: WWW, pp. 1053–1062. ACM (2007)
32. Mayr, R., Clemente, L.: Advanced automata minimization. In: POPL, pp. 63–74. ACM (2013)
33. Mozafari, B., Zeng, K., Zaniolo, C.: High-performance complex event processing over XML streams. In: SIGMOD Conference, pp. 253–264. ACM (2012)

34. Pitcher, C.: Visibly pushdown expression effects for XML stream processing. Programming Language Technologies for XML **1060**, 1–14 (2005)
35. Srba, J.: Beyond language equivalence on visibly pushdown automata. Logical Methods Comput. Sci. **5**(1) (2009)
36. Tabakov, D., Vardi, M.Y.: Experimental evaluation of classical automata constructions. In: Sutcliffe, G., Voronkov, A. (eds.) LPAR 2005. LNCS (LNAI), vol. 3835, pp. 396–411. Springer, Heidelberg (2005). doi:10.1007/11591191_28
37. Thakur, A., Lim, J., Lal, A., Burton, A., Driscoll, E., Elder, M., Andersen, T., Reps, T.: Directed proof generation for machine code. In: Touili, T., Cook, B., Jackson, P. (eds.) CAV 2010. LNCS, vol. 6174, pp. 288–305. Springer, Heidelberg (2010). doi:10.1007/978-3-642-14295-6_27
38. Thomo, A., Venkatesh, S., Ye, Y.Y.: Visibly pushdown transducers for approximate validation of streaming XML. In: Hartmann, S., Kern-Isberner, G. (eds.) FoIKS 2008. LNCS, vol. 4932, pp. 219–238. Springer, Heidelberg (2008). doi:10.1007/978-3-540-77684-0_16

Concurrency and Bisimulation

CSimpl: A Rely-Guarantee-Based Framework for Verifying Concurrent Programs

David Sanán[1]([⊠]), Yongwang Zhao[1,2], Zhe Hou[1], Fuyuan Zhang[1], Alwen Tiu[1], and Yang Liu[1]

[1] School of Computer Science and Engineering, Nanyang Technological University, Singapore, Singapore
sanan@ntu.edu.sg
[2] School of Computer Science and Engineering, Beihang University, Beijing, China

Abstract. It is essential to deal with the interference of the environment between programs in concurrent program verification. This has led to the development of concurrent program reasoning techniques such as rely-guarantee. However, the source code of the programs to be verified often involves language features such as exceptions and procedures which are not supported by the existing mechanizations of those concurrent reasoning techniques. Schirmer et al. have solved a similar problem for sequential programs by developing a verification framework in the Isabelle/HOL theorem prover called Simpl, which provides a rich sequential language that can encode most of the features in real world programming languages. However Simpl only aims to verify sequential programs, and it does not support the specification nor the verification of concurrent programs. In this paper we introduce CSimpl, an extension of Simpl with concurrency-oriented language features and verification techniques. We prove the compositionality of the CSimpl semantics and we provide inference rules for the language constructors to reason about CSimpl programs using rely-guarantee, showing that the inference rules are sound w.r.t. the language semantics. Finally, we run a case study where we use CSimpl to specify and prove functional correctness of an abstract communication model of the XtratuM partitioning separation micro-kernel.

1 Introduction

In the past two decades, formal methods have been successfully applied in the verification of many critical systems. To improve confidence on the reliability of computer systems, verification of functional correctness and security properties is applied not only at the specification level [19], but also at the implementation [9] or even at the machine code level [5]. Verification of the implementation requires modelling languages that are able to capture the features in programming languages such as exceptions and procedure calls. Verification of sequential programs at implementation and machine code level has gained much attention both in academia and in industry [11], and now there is a reasonably strong tool support in this area [10,15]. However, nowadays critical and high-assurance systems are often designed for multi-core architectures where multiple processes

© Springer-Verlag GmbH Germany 2017
A. Legay and T. Margaria (Eds.): TACAS 2017, Part I, LNCS 10205, pp. 481–498, 2017.
DOI: 10.1007/978-3-662-54577-5_28

run in parallel, but verification techniques and tools for concurrent programs are relatively less developed than those for sequential programs.

In order to tackle the verification of concurrent programs, first Owicki and Gries's work [14] introduced techniques for the verification of parallel programs. Later Jones [4] introduced the rely-guarantee method to improve Owicki and Gries's method by allowing compositional verification. The Owicki-Gries method has been mechanized in the Isabelle/HOL theorem prover in [13], and Jones's rely-guarantee method has been mechanized in Isabelle/HOL in [12] which follows the specification in [17]. Also, [1] models in Isabelle/HOL an algebraic specification of rely-guarantee. Although the languages used in previous mechanizations of the above mentioned methods are suitable for verifying system specifications, many implementations cannot be directly captured in those mechanizations. Therefore there is a need to develop a richer modelling language to accurately capture the behaviour of programs at the implementation level.

Simpl [15] is a while-language that supports most of the features of real world programming languages. The syntax and semantics of Simpl are modelled in Isabelle/HOL and Simpl has been used in the verification of seL4 source code [9]. However, its design aims only at reasoning about sequential programs, consequently, this language lacks constructors for parallel composition of programs. Moreover, its proof system is based on Hoare Logic, also for the verification of sequential languages, which cannot be used for reasoning about concurrent programs.

Building on the Simpl framework and the rely-guarantee method, we develop a formal verification framework in Isabelle/HOL, called CSimpl, for verifying partial correctness of high-assurance concurrent systems. The main contributions of this paper are as below:

(1) We extend Simpl using the notion of computation [12,17] to introduce parallelism in two layers: the bottom layer is the execution of sequential Simpl programs extended with a synchronization primitive Await over shared variables; and the top layer is the parallel execution of the bottom layer programs by means of a parallel composition operator. While existing rely-guarantee methods are mechanized for reasoning about abstract specification languages [12,13], our method goes one step further and covers most of the features of system programming languages such as exceptions, procedures, and pointers, among others.

(2) We define a compositional semantics of rely-guarantee for CSimpl. We also provide a set of inference rules for the rely-guarantee proof system and we prove that they are sound w.r.t. the semantics. The rich expressibility of CSimpl means that the number of inference rules of the rely-guarantee proof system is much higher than the work in [12] and their complexity is significantly increased. The CSimpl semantics, the rely-guarantee proof system specification and its soundness proof comprise more than 15k lines of proof and specification in Isabelle/HOL and Isar[1].

---

[1] Due to space reasons we only show some excerpts of the semantics and proofs, the whole model can be found at: http://securify.scse.ntu.edu.sg/MicroVer/CSimpl.

(3) As a case study, we specify in CSimpl two XtratuM [3] services for queuing inter-partition communication and we prove the correctness of an invariant on the queuing communication structure. Inter-partition communication is the mechanism used to implement information flow and is critical in proving event-based non-interference. XtratuM is a separation micro-kernel for space and time partitioning of applications. XtratuM supports multi-core architectures, being able to run several instances of the micro-kernel in parallel in multiple cores. Using our new rely-guarantee proof system, we prove that the specification of the inter-partition communication services correctly introduces and removes messages in the communication channel. The specification and the proofs comprise 3500 lines of formalization. To the best of our knowledge, this is the first attempt on the verification of separation micro-kernels targeting multi-core architectures. Other works such as [18–20] verify functional correctness and non-interference for sequential micro-kernels, and the work in [2] focuses on the verification of sequential applications using the ARINC standard.

2   CSimpl Language

2.1   Simpl Overview

Schirmer introduces in [15] a verification framework for imperative sequential programs developed in Isabelle/HOL. The verification framework includes a generic imperative language, called Simpl, which is composed of the necessary constructors to capture most of the features present in common sequential languages, such as conditional branching, loops, abrupt termination and exceptions, assertions, mutually recursive functions, expressions with side effects, and non-determinism. Additionally, Simpl can express memory related features like the memory heap, pointers, and pointers to functions. The Simpl verification framework also includes a Floyd/Hoare-like logic to reason about partial and total correctness, and on top of it, the framework implements a verification condition generator (VCG) to ease the verification process.

In order to capture all aspects of abrupt termination, assertions, and function calls, the program state 's in Simpl is modelled in Isabelle/HOL as a datatype xstate (shown in Fig. 1), which is composed of four different constructors: Normal 's, representing a regular execution; Fault 'f, representing a failed assertion; Abrupt 's, representing an exceptional state; and Stuck, representing a state where a call to a non-defined function is made. Additionally, the semantics requires an environment Γ containing procedure definitions, i.e., a partial function from the set 'p of procedure names to the body of the procedures. Both features regarding the state and procedures definitions are used in CSimpl.

2.2   CSimpl Syntax

The syntax of CSimpl is shown in Fig. 1. CSimpl extends Simpl by adding two constructors for concurrency: Await, which takes two parameters cond and body,

```
type_synonym 's bexp = "'s set"
datatype ('s, 'p, 'f) com =
  Skip | Throw | Basic "'s ⇒ 's" | Spec "('s × 's) set"
  | Seq "('s ,'p, 'f) com" "('s,'p, 'f) com"
  | Cond "'s bexp" "('s,'p,'f) com"  "('s,'p,'f) com"
  | While "'s bexp" "('s,'p,'f) com" | Call "'p"
  | DynCom "'s ⇒ ('s,'p,'f) com"
  | Guard "'f" "'s bexp" "('s,'p,'f) com"
  | Catch "('s,'p,'f) com" "('s,'p,'f) com"
  | Await "'s bexp" "('s,'p,'f) Simpl.com"
datatype ('s,'f) xstate = Normal 's | Abrupt 's | Fault 'f | Stuck
type_synonym ('s,'p,'f) config = "('s,'p,'f)com × ('s,'f) xstate"
type_synonym ('s,'p,'f) body = "'p ⇒ ('s,'p,'f) com option"
type_synonym ('s,'p,'f) par_Simpl = "('s,'p,'f) com  list"
```

Fig. 1. Syntax and state definition of the CSimpl language

and Parallel Composition. Await allows synchronization of processes under the boolean condition cond and then it atomically executes body, which is a pure sequential Simpl program. This allows us to use Hoare logic for sequential programs and the original Simpl VCG in the verification of the atomic blocks. Parallel composition happens at the top layer (root program), and it can not be nested with other constructors like in the approach followed in [7]. Therefore, a parallel program launches n sequential programs that are executed concurrently and that do not create new concurrent threads. A parallel program is defined as a list of sequential programs. Since we are aiming the verification of programs without dynamic creation of process, this approach is not a problem for our goal and simplify the mechanization.

CSimpl's syntax, following the syntax of Simpl, is defined in terms of states, of type 's; a set of fault types, of type 'f; and a set of procedure names of type 'p. The constructor Skip indicates program termination; Seq s1 s2, Cond b c1 c2, and While b c are respectively the standard constructors for sequential, conditional, and loop statements. Throw and Throw c1 c2 are the complements for abrupt termination of programs of Skip and Seq c1 c2, and they allow to model exceptions. Call p invokes procedure p; Guard f g c represents assertions, where c is executed if the guard g holds in the current state, fault of type 'f is raised otherwise. Finally, Spec r and DynCom cs respectively introduce a nondeterministic behavior expressed by relation r, and a state dependent dynamic command transformation which is used to model blocks and functions with arguments.

2.3   CSimpl Semantics

The small-step operational semantics of CSimpl is a predicate inductively defined based on an environment for procedures Γ and a pair of component configurations $((P,s), (P',s'))$ where the program P in the state s, transits to the program P' and the state s'. It is represented as $\Gamma \vdash_c (P,s) \to (P',s')$, where c indicates it is a step transition in CSimpl. A CSimpl component configuration is defined as a tuple (P,s) where P is a CSimpl program and s is of type xstate. A component configuration (p,s) is called final if p = Skip or p = Throw and there exists a state s' such that $s =$ Normal s'. A final configuration cannot progress to another configuration.

CSimpl extends Simpl with rules for synchronization on shared variables, Await, and the parallel computation shown below. For space reason we only provide the small-step semantics rules Await and AwaitAb for the Await command (Fig. 2). The rest are similar to those defined in [15].

$$\frac{s \in b \quad \Gamma_{\neg a} \vdash \langle c, \text{Normal } s \rangle \Rightarrow t}{\Gamma \vdash_c (\text{Await } b\ p, \text{Normal } s) \to (\text{Skip}, t)} \text{ AWAIT} \qquad \frac{}{\Gamma \vdash_c (P, \text{Normal } s) \to_e (P, t)} \text{ ENV}$$

$$\frac{s \in b \quad \Gamma_{\neg a} \vdash \langle c, \text{Normal } s \rangle \Rightarrow t \quad t = \text{Abrupt } t'}{\Gamma \vdash_c (\text{Await } b\ p, \text{Normal } s) \to (\text{Throw}, \text{Normal } t')} \text{ AWAITAB} \qquad \frac{\forall s'. s \neq \text{Normal } s'}{\Gamma \vdash_c (P, s) \to_e (P, s)} \text{ ENV\_N}$$

$$\frac{i < \text{length } Ps \quad \Gamma \vdash_c (Ps!i, s) \to (r, t)}{\Gamma \vdash_p (Ps, s) \to (Ps[i := r], t)} \text{ PAR} \qquad \frac{}{\Gamma \vdash_p (Ps, \text{Normal } s) \to_e (Ps, \text{Normal } t)} \text{ P\_ENV}$$

Fig. 2. Small step and environment CSimpl semantic rules

The Await rules leverage Simpl's big step semantics to atomically transit from the initial configuration (p,s) to the next state t resulting from the execution of p from s and it is expressed as $\Gamma \vdash \langle p, s \rangle \Rightarrow t$. The two rules express the situation where from a current state s satisfying the synchronization condition. The atomic program in Simpl ends in a state t that can be an abrupt state as a result of an exception thrown in the sequential program for the rule AwaitAb, or any other possible state for the rule Await. This distinction is necessary since a Simpl program can finish in an Abrupt state, however the small-step semantics does not use the state Abrupt. Instead, a CSimpl program finishes in an exception state when the last configuration of a computation is a pair composed of the program Throw, together with a Normal state. Note that big step transitions use sequential Simpl programs, therefore the environment in the atomic step has to be a function from procedure names to Simpl programs, which do not contain Await instructions (for the same reason the body of Await cannot contain nested Await neither). $\Gamma_{\neg a}$ translates bodies of procedures in Γ into Simpl programs if they do not contain any Await instruction, removing from Γ those procedures containing Await instructions.

A Parallel CSimpl configuration is defined as a tuple (Ps,s) where Ps is a list of CSimpl programs and s is of type xstate. Parallel CSimpl semantics is inductively defined by means of rule PAR in Fig. 2. A parallel configuration (Ps,s) transits to another parallel configuration (Ps[i:=r], s') when there is a program i in Ps such that $\Gamma \vdash_c (Ps!i,s) \rightarrow (r,s')$. It is represented with $\Gamma \vdash_p (Ps,\ s) \rightarrow (Ps[i:=r],\ s')$. Similarly to component configurations, a parallel CSimpl configuration $(\mathtt{xs},\mathtt{s})$ is called final if $\mathtt{xs}$ is not empty and every component configuration $(\mathtt{xs}!i, s)$, with i smaller than the length of $\mathtt{xs}$, is final. $Ps!i$ means accessing the i element in the list Ps, whilst $Ps[i := r]$ means substitute the i element in Ps for r.

Together with the semantic representing component transitions, it is necessary to define semantics for environment transitions. They are inductively defined using rules Env and Env_n in Fig. 2, where e is to express that it is an environment transition. CSimpl semantics for components can transit from a Normal state to a different type. However it is not possible to transit from a non Normal state to a different type of state, i.e. $\Gamma \vdash_p$ (P, Stuck) $\rightarrow$ (P', Normal t). Moreover, the component semantics always transits from a configuration (p,s) with p = Skip and $\nexists s'.s = $ Normal s' to a final transition (Skip,s). Therefore, the environment at the sequential layer needs to model this behaviour in the rules Env and Env_n in order to make the semantics at the parallel layer compositional. Environment transitions at the parallel level are defined in such a way that they can transit from a Normal state to another Normal state as shown in rule P_ENV in Fig. 2.

3   Rely-Guarantee for CSimpl

The rely-guarantee [7] method extends the specification of a program with two relations R and G characterizing, respectively, how the environment interferes with the program (Rely) and how the program modifies the environment (Guarantee). Therefore a specification for the verification of parallel systems using rely-guarantee is composed of four elements: precondition, postcondition, rely, and guarantee.

In order to take into account CSimpl state specification xstate (which can take multiple forms to express different execution issues), the semantic for procedure calls, and the dual postcondition for normal or exception termination, the rely-guarantee specification and proof rules need to be modified accordingly. In the proof system itself, a total of 8 new rules have been added to the work in [12] to deal with all the language constructors present in CSimpl. Finally, soundness of the axiomatic rules for the proof system w.r.t. the rely-guarantee specification of validity is proven. The multiple forms of states makes the proof considerably more complex and larger than the work in [12]. While the work in [12] consists of around 2300 lines of proofs and specification, the current work consists of more than 13000 lines of proofs and specification.

3.1   Definition of Computation for CSimpl

The formal validity of a rely-guarantee tuple in this work is based on the definition of computation, which is the set of all possible sequences of configurations resulting of transiting the component or the environment, starting from an initial configuration.

Definition 1 (Sequential Component Computation). *A computation is a tuple* $(\Gamma, \texttt{confs})$ *where* Γ *is an environment for procedures and* $\texttt{confs}$ *is a list of sequential configurations. The set of possible computations* $\texttt{cptn}$ *is inductively defined as follows:*

- $(\Gamma, [(P,s)]) \in cptn$
- *if* $\Gamma \vdash_c (P,s) \rightarrow_e (P,t)$ *and* $(\Gamma, (P, t)\#xs) \in cptn$ *then* $(\Gamma, (P,s)\#(P,t)\#xs)$ $\in cptn$
- *if* $\Gamma \vdash_c (P,s) \rightarrow (Q,t)$ *and* $(\Gamma, (Q, t)\#xs) \in cptn$ *then* $(\Gamma, (P,s)\#(Q,t)\#xs)$ $\in cptn$

Definition 2 (cp Γ P s). *The set of possible computations of an environment for procedures* Γ *starting from an initial configuration* (P, s) *is the set of tuples* (Γ, l) *such that* $l!0 = (P, s)$ *and* $(\Gamma, l) \in cptn$.

The set of parallel computations $\texttt{par\_cp}$ is defined similarly to $\texttt{cp}$ using parallel configurations and the semantic rules for parallel and environment step transitions.

Definition 3 ($\propto$). *Conjoin [17] represented by* $\propto$, *defines an equivalence relation between a parallel computation* p *of* n *CSimpl components and a list clist of* n *component computations, where for all* $i < n.$ $clist!i = (\Gamma_i, cptn_i)$. $(\Gamma, p) \propto$ *clist iff:*

- *for all* $i < n$, *length* $cptn_i = lenght\ p$ *and* $\Gamma_i = \Gamma$.
- *for all* $i < n$ *and* $k < length\ p$, $cptn_i!k = (c_i^k, s_i^k)$ *and* $p!k = (cs, s)$ *with* $cs!i = c_i^k$ *and* $s = s_i^k$.
- *for all* k *such that* $k + 1 < length\ p$, *if* $\Gamma \vdash_p p!k \rightarrow_e p!(k + 1)$, *then for all* $i < n$, $\Gamma_i \vdash cptn_i!k \rightarrow_e cptn_i!(k+1)$; *if* $\Gamma \vdash_p p!k \rightarrow p!(k+1)$ *then there exists an* $i < n$ *where* $\Gamma_i \vdash cptn_i!k \rightarrow (cptn_i)!(k+1)$ *and* $\forall j.\ j \neq i \longrightarrow$ $\Gamma_j \vdash cptn_j!k \rightarrow_e cptn_j!(k+1)$.

The last condition of conjoin states that for any step k in p, if k is an environment step in p, then k is also an environment step in all $cptn_i$; and if it is a component step, then there is some $cptn_i$ where k is a component step and for any other $cptn_j$, with $j \neq i$, k is an environment step.

Lemma 1 (Parallel computation as component computation).

$$xs \neq [] \implies par\_cp\ \Gamma xs\ s = \{(\Gamma_1, c).\Gamma_1 = \Gamma \wedge (\exists clist.(length\ clist) = (length\ xs) \wedge$$
$$(\forall i < lenght\ clist.(clist!i) \in cp\Gamma(xs!i)s) \wedge (\Gamma, c) \propto clist)\}$$

Lemma 1 states that given a parallel configuration $(\texttt{xs}, \texttt{s})$ such that $\texttt{xs}$ is not empty ($[]$), then for any parallel computation $(\Gamma, \texttt{c})$ starting from $(\texttt{xs}, \texttt{s})$ there is a list of component computations $\texttt{clist}$ with the same length of $\texttt{xs}$ and $(\Gamma, \texttt{c}) \propto clist$. That is, the execution of a parallel number of components $xs_0 \ldots xs_n$ can be expressed as the execution of one single component xs_i, with i smaller than n, where the execution of any other component xs_j is simulated by a component environment transition, with j smaller than n and different than i. The right and left implications of the equality in Lemma 1 are proven first by induction on the parallel computation and then by cases on the type of parallel and component events using conjoin.

3.2 Validity of Formulas for Rely-Guarantee in CSimpl

Based on the rely-guarantee definitions, we define the validity of a rely-guarantee tuple from the set of all possible computations from an initial configuration. This uses the notions of *assumption* of preconditions and the environment, and *commitment* of the component and the postcondition.

Definition 4 (assum(pre, rely)). *The assumption of a predicate pre and an environment relation rely for an environment of procedures Γ is the set of component computations $(\Gamma, cptn)$ such that $cptn!0 = Normal\ s$ and $s \in pre$, and for any step transition in the computation $\Gamma \vdash_c cptn!k \rightarrow_e cptn!(k+1)$, where $k+1 < lenght\ cptn$, $cptn!k = (p_k, s_k)$, and $cptn!(k+1) = (p_{k+1}, s_{k+1})$ then $(s_k, s_{k+1}) \in rely$.*

The predicate *assum* represents the set of component computations $(\Gamma, cptn)$, such that the state component of the initial configuration of the computation is a Normal state satisfying *pre*. Also, in any transition of the environment $\Gamma \vdash_c cptn!k \rightarrow_e cptn!(k+1)$, the states of the configurations $cptn!k$ and $cptn!(k+1)$ belong to the rely relation.

To take advantage of automatic methods such as model checking, and following the original notion of validity for Hoare triples in Simpl, the commitment assumes that the last configuration in a computation does not end in a Fault state belonging to the set F, which is a set of non-reachable states previously calculated using external tools. Then the commitment is the set of computations such that component transitions belong to the *guarantee* relation, and that their last configuration are final (therefore with the program state equal to Skip or Throw) with the state component belonging to q or a.

Definition 5 (comm(guar, (q, a)) F). *The commitment of a relation guar, a pair of predicates (q, a), and a set of Fault states F, for an environment of procedures Γ, is the set of component computations $(\Gamma, cptn)$ such that if $cptn!(length\ l - 1) = (l_p, l_s)$ and there is not a fault f such that $l_s = Fault\ f$ and $f \in F$, then (1) if for any component transition in the computation $\Gamma \vdash_c cptn!k \rightarrow cptn!(k+1)$ where $k < length\ cptn$, $cptn!k = (p_k, s_k)$, and $cptn!(k+1) = (p_{k+1}, s_{k+1})$ then $(s_k, s_{k+1}) \in guar$, and (2) if l is final then $l_s = Normal\ l'_s$ and if $l_p = Skip$ then $l'_s \in q$ and if $l_p = Throw$ then $l'_s \in a$.*

Definition 6 (com_validity). *Validity of a specification of a component P w.r.t. a precondition p, postcondition (q, a), a rely relation R, a guarantee relation G, an environment of procedures Γ, and a set F of Faults, is represented as $\Gamma \models_{/F} P\ sat[p, R, G, q, a]$ iff for all s, cp Γ P $s \cap assum(p, R) \subseteq comm(G(q, a))\ F$.*

Following [15], we use a set of procedure specifications Θ that are used during the procedure verification. The set of procedure specifications Θ, is a tuple which elements represent a procedure name and its specification in terms of precondition, rely and guarantee relations, and postcondition. Note that procedures in specifications belonging to Θ do not need to match the procedures defined in the environment Γ.

Definition 7 (com_cvalidity). *CValidity of a specification of a component P w.r.t. a precondition p, postcondition (q,a), a rely relation R, a guarantee relation G, an environment of procedures Γ, a specification of procedures Θ, and a set F of Faults, represented as $\Gamma, \Theta \models_{/F} P\ sat[p, R, G, q, a]$ iff for all tuples $(c, p', R', G', q', a') \in \Theta$ such that $\Gamma \models_{/F} (Call\ c)\ sat[p', R', G', q', a']$ then $\Gamma \models_{/F} P\ sat[p, R, G, q, a]$.*

Validity and CValidity for parallel computations are respectively represented by $\Gamma \models_{/F} P\ SAT[p, R, G, q, a]$ and $\Gamma, \Theta \models_{/F} P\ SAT[p, R, G, q, a]$. They are defined similarly to the ones for computation of components, using the definitions of computation, assumption, and commitment for parallel programs. We omit these definitions due to space reasons. Theorem 1 shows compositionality of validity of parallel rely-guarantee specifications.

Theorem 1 (validity_compositionality).
$\forall i < length\ xs.\Gamma, \Theta \models_{/F} C(xs!i) sat\ [P(xs!i), R(xs!i), G(xs!i), Q(xs!i), A(xs!i)] \longrightarrow$
(1) $\forall i < length\ xs.\ R_p \cup (\bigcup j \in \{j.\ j < length\ xs \wedge j \neq i\}.\ G(xs!j) \subseteq R(xs!i)) \longrightarrow$
(2) $\bigcup j < length\ xs.\ G(xs!j) \subseteq G_p \longrightarrow$ (3) $p \subseteq (\bigcap i < length\ xs.\ P(xs!i)) \longrightarrow$
(4) $(\bigcap i < length\ xs.\ (Q(xs!i))) \subseteq q \longrightarrow$ (5) $(\bigcap i < length\ xs.\ (A(xs!i))) \subseteq a \longrightarrow$
$\Gamma, \Theta \models_{/F} ParCom\ xs\ SAT\ [p, R_p, G_p, q, a].$

Therefore, to show that a parallel rely-guarantee specification is true, it is only necessary to prove rely-guarantee validity for each one of the single components and that (1) the rely of individual components is implied by the parallel rely and the union of the guarantee relations of the other individual components of the parallel system, (2) the union of the guarantee relations of the component specifications implies the guarantee relation for the parallel specification, (3) the precondition of the parallel specification is included in all the component specifications, (4) the intersection of all the normal postconditions of the component specifications is included in the normal postcondition of the parallel specification, (5) the union of the abrupt postcondition of all the component specifications is included in the abrupt postcondition of the parallel specification. Theorem 1 is proven using Lemma 1 and the definition of parallel validity of a rely-guarantee specification.

3.3   Inference Rules of the Proof System

The rely-guarantee proof system for CSimpl extends the previous mechanization of the logic in [12] with eight more inference rules. There are a total of fifteen rules, one for each language constructor, plus the consequence rule. Figure 3 shows those rules that are either new or substantially changed w.r.t. the work in [12]. Rules Skip, and Throw are added to handle program termination for normal and abrupt termination respectively. Since Skip deals with normal termination it requires the normal postcondition to be stable w.r.t. the rely relation, whilst in the case of Throw is the abrupt postcondition which has to be stable w.r.t. the rely relation. Similarly, Catch is the complement of the sequential rule for abrupt termination. In CSimpl, composition of programs can finish on an

$$\frac{\begin{array}{l} Sta\,p\,R \quad Sta\,q\,R \quad p \subseteq \{s.f\,s \in q\} \\ \forall s\,t.s \in p \wedge (t = f\,s) \longrightarrow (Normal\,s, Normal\,s) \in G \end{array}}{\Gamma, \Theta \vdash_{/F} Basic\,f\,\textbf{sat}\,[p,R,G,q,a]}\ \text{Basic}$$

$$\frac{\begin{array}{l} Sta\,p\,R \quad Sta\,q\,R \\ p \subseteq \{s.(\forall t.(s,t) \in r \longrightarrow t \in q) \wedge (\exists t.(s,t) \in r)\} \\ \forall s\,t.s \in p \wedge (s,t) \in r \longrightarrow (Normal\,s, Normal\,s) \in G \end{array}}{\Gamma, \Theta \vdash_{/F} Spec\,r\,\textbf{sat}\,[p,R,G,q,a]}\ \text{Spec}$$

$$\frac{\begin{array}{l} Sta\,a\,R \\ \forall s.(Normal\,s, Normal\,s) \in G \end{array}}{\Gamma, \Theta \vdash_{/F} Throw\,\textbf{sat}\,[a,R,G,q,a]}\ \text{Throw} \qquad \frac{\begin{array}{l} Sta\,q\,R \\ \forall s.(Normal\,s, Normal\,s) \in G \end{array}}{\Gamma, \Theta \vdash_{/F} Skip\,\textbf{sat}\,[q,R,G,q,a]}\ \text{Skip}$$

$$\frac{\begin{array}{l} Sta\,p\,R \quad Sta\,q\,R \quad Sta\,a\,R \\ \forall V.\Gamma_{\neg a}, \{\} \vdash_{/F} (p \cap b \cap \{V\})c \\ \{s.(Normal\,V, Normal\,s) \in G\} \cap q, \\ \{s.(Normal\,V, Normal\,s) \in G\} \cap a \end{array}}{\Gamma, \Theta \vdash_{/F} Await\,b\,c\,\textbf{sat}\,[p,R,G,q,a]}\ \text{AW} \qquad \frac{\begin{array}{l} \Gamma, \Theta \vdash_{/F} c\,\textbf{sat}\,[p \cap g, R, G, q, a] \\ Sta\,(p \cap g)R \\ \forall s.(Normal\,s, Normal\,s) \in G \end{array}}{\Gamma, \Theta \vdash_{/F} Guard\,f\,g\,c\,\textbf{sat}\,[p \cap g, R, G, q, a]}\ \text{GD}$$

$$\frac{\begin{array}{l} \Gamma, \Theta \vdash_{/F} c1\,\textbf{sat}\,[p,R,G,q,r] \\ \Gamma, O \vdash_{/F} c2\,\textbf{sat}\,[r,R,G,q,a] \\ Sta\,(p \cap g)R \quad Sta\,(a \cap g)R \\ \forall s.(Normal\,s, Normal\,s) \in G \end{array}}{\Gamma, O \vdash_{/F} Catch\,c1\,c2\,\textbf{sat}\,[p,R,G,q,a]}\ \text{Catch} \qquad \frac{\begin{array}{l} \Gamma, \Theta \vdash_{/F} c1\,\textbf{sat}\,[p,R,G,r,a] \\ \Gamma, \Theta \vdash_{/F} c2\,\textbf{sat}\,[r,R,G,q,a] \\ Sta\,(p \cap g)R \quad Sta\,(a \cap g)R \\ \forall s.(Normal\,s, Normal\,s) \in G \end{array}}{\Gamma, \Theta \vdash_{/F} Seq\,c1\,c2\,\textbf{sat}\,[p,R,G,q,a]}\ \text{Seq}$$

$$\frac{\begin{array}{l} \Gamma, \Theta \vdash_{/F} c\,\textbf{sat}\,[p \cap g, R, G, q, a] \\ Sta\,(p \cap g)R \quad f \in F \\ \forall s.(Normal\,s, Normal\,s) \in G \end{array}}{\Gamma, \Theta \vdash_{/F} Guard\,f\,g\,c\,\textbf{sat}\,[p,R,G,q,a]}\ \text{G} \qquad \frac{\begin{array}{l} \Gamma, \Theta \vdash_{/F} the(\Gamma\,c)\,\textbf{sat}\,[p \cap g, R, G, q, a] \\ Sta\,(p \cap g)R \quad c \in dom\,\Gamma \\ \forall s.(Normal\,s, Normal\,s) \in G \end{array}}{\Gamma, \Theta \vdash_{/F} Call\,c\,\textbf{sat}\,[p,R,G,q,a]}\ \text{C}$$

$$\frac{\begin{array}{l} \forall s \in p.\Gamma, \Theta \vdash_{/F} c\,s\,\textbf{sat}\,[p \cap g, R, G, q, a] \\ Sta\,p\,R \quad \forall s.(Normal\,s, Normal\,s) \in G \end{array}}{\Gamma, \Theta \vdash_{/F} DynCom\,c\,\textbf{sat}\,[p,R,G,q,a]}\ \text{DynCom}$$

$$\frac{\begin{array}{l} \forall i<xs.R \cup (\bigcup j \in \{j.j<xs \wedge j \neq i\}.(Guar(xs!j))) \subseteq Rely(xs!i) \\ (\bigcup j<length\,xs.(Guard(xs!j))) \subseteq G \quad p \subseteq (\bigcap i<length\,xs.Pre(xs!i)) \\ (\bigcap j<length\,xs.(Post(xs!j))) \subseteq q \quad (\bigcup j<length\,xs.(Abr(xs!j))) \subseteq a \\ \forall i<xs.\Gamma, \Theta \vdash_{/F} Com(xs!i)\,\textbf{sat}\,[Pre(xs!i), Rely(xs!i), Guar(xs!i), Post(xs!i), Abr(xs!i)] \end{array}}{\Gamma, \Theta \vdash_{/F} xs\,\textbf{SAT}\,[p,R,G,q,a]}\ \text{Comp}$$

Fig. 3. Rely-guarantee proof rules for CSimpl

abrupt state without executing the second program. Hence it is necessary stability of the abrupt postcondition w.r.t. the *rely* relation. Similarly, the Catch rule requires stability of the normal postcondition with rely. We say that a predicate p is stable w.r.t. a relation R, Sta p R, if given two states s, s', such that p s is true and $(s, s') \in R$, then s' is also true in p.

The Await rule requires Hoare satisfiability of the sequential program representing its body, which is represented following traditional Hoare triplet notation $\{p\}c\{q\}$. In this case the postcondition is given as a pair to capture normal and abrupt termination. See [15] for more details on sequential Simpl program verification. Since the Hoare program can finish in either a normal state or an abrupt state, it is necessary that both postconditions are stable. The precondition should also be stable to remain unchanged under environment transitions. Since every component transition has to belong to the guarantee relation, we add this constraint into the Hoare triple, binding the initial states from the precondition to the final states of both the normal and abrupt postconditions.

The rest of rules can be deduced intuitively from their semantics adding stability of the precondition for non-terminal commands, e.g., if for branching and call for non-recursive procedure calls; and adding also stability of the normal postcondition for commands modifying the state.

Finally COMP is the rule for parallel composition. To apply compositionality, the rule is applied over a tuple xs composed of a sequential component *Com* and rely-guarantee specification, i.e. $Pre, Rely, Guarantee, Post$ for *Com*. The rule follows [12] taking abrupt termination into consideration, since this is an exception state, and not all the individual computations may be in an exception state. Therefore, whilst we require that the intersection of all component postconditions is included in the postcondition of the parallel program, for abrupt termination we only require that the union of abrupt postconditions is in the parallel program.

3.4 Soundness of the Proof System

We prove that the set of inference rules in the proof system is sound w.r.t. the definition of validity for parallel systems. The proof is carried out in two steps, first we prove that the inference rules for single components are sound.

Theorem 2 (comp_rgsound).
$$\Gamma, \Theta \vdash_{/F} c \ sat \ [p, R, G, q, a] \longrightarrow \Gamma, \Theta \models_{/F} c \ sat \ [p, R, G, q, a]$$

This is proved by induction on the inference rules. Axioms, i.e., those rules without assumptions on the proof system induction, are proven based on the notion of stability and the fact that any computation starting from them only has one component step. Therefore we prove that the stability rule preserves the precondition under any environment step. We then show that the component step preserves the commitment.

The semantics for computation makes it cumbersome to prove the soundness for those CSimpl constructors whose semantic is recursively defined, such as Seq,

Catch, and While. Soundness for these constructors are proven using a modular notion of computation [17] and the equivalence of both types of computation. The modular computation serializes the recursive specification of computation for the CSimpl constructors. This alternative semantics for computation unfolds the computation of CSimpl constructors. Soundness for these constructors is proven based on the different cases these rules provide. The modular computation for CSimpl extends the one provided in [12] with rules for the new language constructors, and new rules for seq and while, considering that the program in a final configurations can be Skip or Throw. The constructors If and Call, for non-recursive function calls, are proven similarly to the axioms based on the existence of a first component step for non-final configurations. After applying the component transition, we prove the correctness by the inductive step.

Recursive procedure calls require to consider the maximum number of nested function calls invoked by an execution and we do not currently provide a rule for them. cptn serializes the small step semantics removing scopes, which does not allow to prove soundness of recursive procedure calls. Nevertheless, it is possible to provide such a rule for recursive procedure calls, by extending the modular computation, with a parameter n representing the limit of nested procedures for which the computation is valid. Also, the semantics for validity must be extended to express that a formula is valid when it invokes at least n nested function calls by intersecting the assumptions in com_validity with the set of modular computations with limit n. Soundness of recursive procedure calls can be proven similarly to [15], by monotonicity of the extended computation in n and equality of the semantics.

Finally we show soundness of the proof system for the parallel composition of programs using Theorems 1 and 2.

Theorem 3 (par_rgsound).
$$\Gamma, \Theta \vdash_{/F} Ps\ SAT\ [p, R, G, q, a] \longrightarrow \Gamma, \Theta \models_{/F} (ParCom\ Ps)\ SAT\ [p, R, G, q, a]$$

4   Case Study

We apply the proof system for the specification and the verification of two XtratuM services for inter-partition communication. The XtratuM separation micro-kernel [3] provides spatial and temporal partitioning of applications. In a separation micro-kernel, different partitions are executed in separated memory domains, and the only allowed communication among partitions is by means of static dedicated channels explicitly defined between two or more partitions. XtratuM provides, among others services to communicate partitions through channels, partitions health-monitoring, and a static cyclic scheduler. In this case study we provide a very abstract CSimpl specification of the services to send and receive messages using queuing channels in a parallel architecture, where the XtratuM micro-kernel is executed in several cores of a multi-core processor. Using the rely-guarantee proof system introduced in Sect. 3 we prove: (1) that the services correctly introduce and remove elements in the queues associated with each communication channel and (2) that the number of elements in the queues do not exceed the channel maximum capacity. The specification and proofs are comprised of more than 3500 lines of specification.

4.1 Queuing Inter-Partition Communication Description

Queuing inter-partition communication services allow partitions to escape from the isolated environment that XtratuM provides, allowing them to send and receive messages to/from other partitions using communication channels by means of dedicated ports assigned to partitions. A communication channel is an entity storing the communication data and the source and destination ports involved in the communication.

XtratuM implements two types of communication: sampling and queuing communication. While the former only allows to store one message, and it is multicasting, i.e., a channel has one source port and a list of destination ports. The latter allows to store many messages in a bounded buffer implemented as a queue, and only allows peer to peer communication, i.e., the channel has one source port and one destination port. Channels and ports are classified according to the type of communication. Therefore, a channel and a port can be of type sampling or queuing, and a sampling channel can only allocate sampling ports, and vice-verse. The services have as input a port to/from which the message is sent/received, and the message to be sent in the case of the sending service. Prior to modifying the queue, the services check whether the input values are consistent, e.g., the port which receives the message belongs to the partition, or it is a source or destination port depending on the invoked service.

4.2 State and Specification Definition

The state definition provides global and local variables. Global variables represent those variables shared by multiple instances of the micro-kernel, they hold the data for inter-partition communication, partitions, and the partition scheduler. Since we are targeting only queuing inter-partition communication, the components for the scheduler and partitions contain the necessary information for those services. The scheduler is highly abstracted and only contains information about the partition that is currently being executed, and therefore invoking the service; partitions only contain the list of assigned ports to the partition. The communication datatype includes the specification of channels and ports. A channel is defined as a datatype with the two possible types of channels, having as parameters the source and destination ports, and the message shared between the partitions, for which the queue is abstracted in the model as a multiset. The queuing channel also has a parameter indicating the maximum size of the channel buffer. Messages are modelled just as an abstract entity.

```
record com = ports :: "port_id ⇀ port" channels :: "chan_id ⇀ channel"
record vars = p_' :: "part_id ⇀ partition"   c_' :: "com"
              s_' :: "scheduler list"   l_' ::"locals list"
```

In the model, ´l, ´c, ´s, and ´p access the locals, communication, scheduler, and partition component of the state, respectively. Local variables for each process are a structure with the necessary variables for the input and output parameters of the services. One of the limitations of rely-guarantee is that the relations lose track of the sequence of executed operations. To solve this, verification of the concurrent increment of a variable, or adding/removing elements from a set like in this example, requires using additional variables to help tracking the changes [17]. In our model, we include a variable of type `Message option` that is initialized to None, and when a message is correctly sent or received the model assigns it to the variable. Our state abstracts and maps XtratuM global structures `xmcCommChannelTab`, and `xmcCommChannelPorts`, storing channel and port data, into the components of ´c and `xmcPartition`, storing partition data, into ´p respectively.

The parallel execution of services is modelled parametrically on the number of processes, which is defined as a fixed natural number within a Isabelle/HOL locale [8]. Each service is modelled as a procedure that is also parametrized by the process being executed; this allows that each specific procedure only accesses its local variables. The function Γ is generated by assigning a unique name for each service using a fold higher order function and assigning to each parametrized service name the corresponding parametrized body of the service. The parametrized event `receive` is shown below.

```
definition receive_q_message_i where "receive_q_message_i i ≡
(IF (¬ (ex_port_id ´c ((pt (( ´1)!i))))) ∨
    (¬ (port_q (the ((ports ´c) (pt ( ´1!i)))))) ∨
    (¬ (port_dest (the ((ports ´c) (pt ( ´1!i)))))) ∨
    (¬ port_in_part   ´p (( ´s)!i) (the ((ports ´c) (pt ( ´1!i))))) THEN
      ´1 :== ´1[i:=(( ´1!i)(|ret_msg := None|))]
  ELSE AWAIT True
    IF_s port_empty (pt (( ´1)!i)) ´c THEN
      ´1 :==_s ´1[i:=(( ´1!i)(|ret_msg := None|))]
    ELSE
      ´1 :==_s ´1[i:=(( ´1!i) (|ret_msg := port_get_msg (pt ( ´1!i)) ´c |))];;_s
      ´c :==_s port_rem_msg (pt ( ´1!i)) (the (ret_msg ( ´1!i))) ´c ;;_s
      ´1 :==_s ´1[i:=(( ´1!i) (|aux_msg := (ret_msg ( ´1!i)) |))] FI FI)"
```

The services abstract the low level behaviour of the Xtratum functions. They first check parameters validity, and then carries out the insertion/extraction of the message to/from the queue. Atomic blocks abstract XtratuM's mutexes for mutual exclusion. Validation of correctness of the model w.r.t. the implementation is carried out at this stage by inspecting the code. For the `ReceiveQueuingPort` model, the event first checks that the accessed port exists in the current communication state, that it is a queuing and destination port, and that the partition that it belongs to the partition being executed. If any parameter is not valid then the service finishes returning None, otherwise it performs the operations over the channel queue after checking whether the queue is not empty for event `receive`, or not full for event `send`. The statements in the body of the Await statement are IF_s and $:==_s$. This is because the body of the `Await` is a sequential `Simpl` program and when embedded into a `CSimpl` program needs to modify the syntax. Event `SendQueuingPort` is modeled similarly.

4.3   Verification

For the parallel verification, we specify the rely and guarantee relations for the receive and send services. This relations are parameterized by a variable i, which refers to the ith process. We show the rely relation, the guarantee relation is similar to this, only differing in that local variables for any process j different than i will not be modified.

definition Rely where "Rely B i≡
```
{(x,y). (∃x1 y1. x=Normal x1 ∧ y=Normal y1 ∧ s_' x1 = s_' y1 ∧
    (1_' x1)!i = (1_' y1)!i ∧ ports (c_' x1) =  ports (c_' y1) ∧
    p_' x1 = p_' y1 ∧ (x1 ∈ Invariant B ⟶ y1 ∈ Invariant B)) } "
```

Since parallel programs do not change others programs' local variables, the i element in the list of local variables is not changed by the rely. Also, ports, partitions, and the scheduler are not changed by any service, therefore the rely relation does not change them. Finally, if the initial state of the relation preserves the invariant, it also preserves the shape of the channel's queues, then so does the final state of the relation.

The invariant establishes consistency of the port and channel structures that must be preserved by the services. Its most important specification is **channel_spec** which preserves the specification of the queue for every defined channel in the state.

definition channel_spec where "channel_spec B ≡
```
{ ∀c_id c. (channels ´c) c_id = Some c ⟶
    chan_get_msgs c = (B c_id + chan_sent_msgs c_id ´c ´1) -
      chan_rec_msgs c_id ´c ´1 ∧
    (size (chan_get_msgs c) ≤ chan_get_max_bufs c) ∧
    chan_rec_mes c_id ´c ´1) ⊆# B c_id + chan_sent_msgs c_id ´c ´1 }"
```

channel_spec checks that the multiset modelling the queue for each defined c_id is equal to its initial value, which is given by B c_id; those messages correctly sent are pushed into the queue by the service; and that the received messages are popped out of the queue. chan_sent\rec_msgs gets for each c_id the multiset with the auxiliary variables different than None, meaning that the service has modified the queue for that channel. Also, for consistency of the multiset, the invariant needs to ensure that removed messages are a subset of the added messages.

Lemma 2 (Send_Rec_Correct).
```
n>0 ⟹ Γ,{} ⊢/{} (COBEGIN SCHEME [0 ≤ i < n]
  (ex_service i, pre_i B i, Rely B i, Guar B i, Post_Arinc B, {True})
  COEND) SAT [Pre_Arinc B, {(x,y). x = y}, {True}, Post_Arinc B, {True}]
```

Lemma 2 proves the property on the parallel execution of the services. **ex_service** is a sequence of nested ifs controlling the call to the services, each if guarded by a local variable that indicates which service is invoked in each parallel process. In the parallel program, the identity relation indicates that the parallel environment does not change the state, being therefore a closed system, i.e., there is not any environment at the parallel level. The guarantee relation is the universal set in which everything can be modified. The precondition `Pre_Arinc B` defines the invariant and auxiliary variables initialization to `None`. The precondition for each process `pre_i B i` sets the initial value for the auxiliary variable, the initial values of the channel queues, and it defines the invariant that is preserved by the postcondition for the normal termination `Post_Arinc B`. The abrupt postcondition is the universal set since we do not have any abrupt termination in this specification.

The proof obligations for the parallel rule are proven immediately after unfolding the definitions of the precondition, postcondition, and rely and guarantee relations. After applying the parallel rule on the parallel execution of the n components, it is necessary to prove that the parametrized `execute_service` satisfies the postcondition using the rely-guarantee rules for components. Once the `conditional` and `call` rules have been applied on `execute_service`, only the proof of the verification of each service body is left. Both send and receive services are similarly proven.

To prove the body of the services, it is necessary to apply the conditional rule to generate the proof obligations for the execution of two branches of the `if`. The first corresponds to the case in which the service is not invoked with the appropriate parameters and is immediately proven after apply the `Basic` rule since it does not modify any channel or auxiliary variable. For the second branch, after invoking `Await`, the sequential Simpl program representing its body is automatically unfolded using Simpl's VCG. The resulting goal, now without any embedded Simpl specification, is solved by proving that the state after removing or inserting a message from/to the channel associated to the input port, and after assigning the removed/inserted message to the auxiliary variable, satisfies `channel_spec`. We use some auxiliary lemmas to prove it: first, that the modification of the auxiliary variable in a component does not modify the sets `chan_sent_msgs` and `chan_rec_msgs` for any channel other than the one associated to the port the service access; second, that the modification of a variable only modifies one of these sets. Using these auxiliary lemmas the postcondition is proven immediately by applying the properties over multisets.

5   Conclusions and Future Work

In this work we have presented CSimpl, a framework for specifying concurrent programs and verifying their partial correctness using rely-guarantee. This framework allows us to specify programs written in a large subset of the C language. Currently we are working also on axiomatic separation rules for the proof system following works on separation logic and rely-guarantee [6,16]. This will help to cope with local variables and to hide global variables, thus improving scalability of the approach. There are, however, some aspects where this framework can be improved. First, we can introduce deadlock freedom and weak total correctness, which enable us to reason about termination of programs. Second, we can provide VCG tactics to achieve a higher level of automation. Currently, the language supports annotation to provide loop invariant, but the soundness of annotated rules is yet to be proven. Third, it is also desirable to have completeness of the proof system to introduce properties proven at the language and semantics levels. The complexity of proving completeness make us to consider this as future work. Finally, the current proof system do not include a rule for recursive procedure calls, but our framework can be easily extended to support it, with minimal modifications on the rules already proven.

Acknowledgement. This research is supported (in part) by the National Research Foundation, Prime Ministers Office, Singapore under its National Cybersecurity R&D Program (Award No. NRF2014NCR-NCR001-30) and administered by the National Cybersecurity R & D Directorate.

References

1. Armstrong, A., Gomes, V.B.F., Struth, G.: Algebraic principles for rely-guarantee style concurrency verification tools. In: Jones, C., Pihlajasaari, P., Sun, J. (eds.) FM 2014. LNCS, vol. 8442, pp. 78–93. Springer, Heidelberg (2014). doi:10.1007/978-3-319-06410-9_6
2. de la Cámara, P., Mar Gallardo, M., Merino, P.: Model extraction for ARINC 653 based avionics software. In: Bošnački, D., Edelkamp, S. (eds.) SPIN 2007. LNCS, vol. 4595, pp. 243–262. Springer, Heidelberg (2007). doi:10.1007/978-3-540-73370-6_16
3. Carrascosa, E., Coronel, J., Masmano, M., Balbastre, P., Crespo, A.: XtratuM hypervisor redesign for LEON4 multicore processor. SIGBED Rev. **11**(2), 27–31 (2014)
4. Coleman, J.W., Jones, C.B.: A structural proof of the soundness of rely/guarantee rules. J. Logic Comput. **17**(4), 807–841 (2007)
5. Dam, M., Guanciale, R., Khakpour, N., Nemati, H., Schwarz, O.: Formal verification of information flow security for a simple arm-based separation kernel. In: Proceedings of the 2013 ACM SIGSAC Conference on Computer & Communications Security, CCS 1913, pp. 223–234. ACM, New York (2013)
6. Feng, X.: Local rely-guarantee reasoning. SIGPLAN Not. **44**(1), 315–327 (2009)
7. Jones, C.B.: Development methods for computer programs including a notion of interference. Ph.D. thesis. Oxford University, June 1981
8. Kammüller, F., Wenzel, M., Paulson, L.C.: Locales a sectioning concept for Isabelle. In: Bertot, Y., Dowek, G., Théry, L., Hirschowitz, A., Paulin, C. (eds.) TPHOLs 1999. LNCS, vol. 1690, pp. 149–165. Springer, Heidelberg (1999). doi:10.1007/3-540-48256-3_11
9. Klein, G., Elphinstone, K., Heiser, G., Andronick, J., Cock, D., Derrin, P., Elkaduwe, D., Engelhardt, K., Kolanski, R., Norrish, M., Sewell, T., Tuch, H., Winwood, S.: seL4: Formal verification of an OS kernel. In: Proceedings of the ACM SIGOPS 22nd Symposium on Operating Systems Principles (SOSP), pp. 207–220. ACM, New York (2009)
10. Myreen, M.O., Gordon, M.J.C., Slind, K.: Machine-code verification for multiple architectures: an application of decompilation into logic. In: Proceedings of the 2008 International Conference on Formal Methods in Computer-Aided Design, FMCAD 2008, pp. 20:1–20:8. IEEE Press, Piscataway (2008)

11. Newcombe, C., Rath, T., Zhang, F., Munteanu, B., Brooker, M., Deardeuff, M.: How Amazon web services uses formal methods. Commun. ACM **58**(4), 66–73 (2015)
12. Nieto, L.P.: The rely-guarantee method in Isabelle/HOL. In: Degano, P. (ed.) ESOP 2003. LNCS, vol. 2618, pp. 348–362. Springer, Heidelberg (2003). doi:10.1007/3-540-36575-3_24
13. Nipkow, T., Nieto, L.P.: Owicki/Gries in Isabelle/HOL. In: Finance, J.-P. (ed.) FASE 1999. LNCS, vol. 1577, pp. 188–203. Springer, Heidelberg (1999). doi:10.1007/978-3-540-49020-3_13
14. Owicki, S., Gries, D.: An axiomatic proof technique for parallel programs I. Acta Informatica **6**(4), 319–340 (1976)
15. Schirmer, N.: Verification of sequential imperative programs in Isabelle/HOL. Ph.D. thesis, Technischen Universitat Munchen (2006)
16. Vafeiadis, V., Parkinson, M.: A marriage of rely/guarantee and separation logic. In: Caires, L., Vasconcelos, V.T. (eds.) CONCUR 2007. LNCS, vol. 4703, pp. 256–271. Springer, Heidelberg (2007). doi:10.1007/978-3-540-74407-8_18
17. Xu, Q., de Roever, W.P., He, J.: The rely-guarantee method for verifying shared variable concurrent programs. Formal Aspects Comput. **9**(2), 149–174 (1997)
18. Zhao, Y., Yang, Z., Sanán, D., Liu, Y.: Event-based formalization of safety-critical operating system standards: an experience report on ARINC 653 using event-B. In: Proceedings of IEEE 26th International Symposium on Software Reliability Engineering (ISSRE), pp. 281–292 November 2015
19. Zhao, Y., Sanán, D., Zhang, F., Liu, Y.: Formal specification and analysis of partitioning operating systems by integrating ontology and refinement. IEEE Trans. Industr. Inf. **12**(4), 1321–1331 (2016)
20. Zhao, Y., Sanán, D., Zhang, F., Liu, Y.: Reasoning about information flow security of separation kernels with channel-based communication. In: Chechik, M., Raskin, J.-F. (eds.) TACAS 2016. LNCS, vol. 9636, pp. 791–810. Springer, Heidelberg (2016). doi:10.1007/978-3-662-49674-9_50

Fair Termination for Parameterized Probabilistic Concurrent Systems

Ondřej Lengál[1], Anthony W. Lin[2(✉)], Rupak Majumdar[3],
and Philipp Rümmer[4]

[1] FIT, Brno University of Technology, Brno, Czech Republic
lengal@fit.vutbr.cz
[2] Department of Computer Science, University of Oxford, Oxford, UK
anthony.lin@cs.ox.ac.uk
[3] MPI-SWS Kaiserslautern, Kaiserslautern, Germany
[4] Uppsala University, Uppsala, Sweden

Abstract. We consider the problem of automatically verifying that a parameterized family of probabilistic concurrent systems terminates with probability one for all instances against adversarial schedulers. A parameterized family defines an infinite-state system: for each number n, the family consists of an instance with n finite-state processes. In contrast to safety, the parameterized verification of liveness is currently still considered extremely challenging especially in the presence of probabilities in the model. One major challenge is to provide a sufficiently powerful symbolic framework. One well-known symbolic framework for the parameterized verification of non-probabilistic concurrent systems is *regular model checking*. Although the framework was recently extended to probabilistic systems, incorporating fairness in the framework—often crucial for verifying termination—has been especially difficult due to the presence of an infinite number of fairness constraints (one for each process). Our main contribution is a systematic, regularity-preserving, encoding of *finitary fairness* (a realistic notion of fairness proposed by Alur and Henzinger) in the framework of regular model checking for probabilistic parameterized systems. Our encoding reduces termination with finitary fairness to verifying parameterized termination *without fairness* over probabilistic systems in regular model checking (for which a verification framework already exists). We show that our algorithm could verify termination for many interesting examples from distributed algorithms (Herman's protocol) and evolutionary biology (Moran process, cell cycle switch), which do not hold under the standard notion of fairness. To the best of our knowledge, our algorithm is the first fully-automatic method that can prove termination for these examples.

1 Introduction

In parameterized probabilistic concurrent systems, a population of *agents*, each typically modeled as a finite-state probabilistic program, run concurrently in discrete time and update their states based on probabilistic transition rules.

© Springer-Verlag GmbH Germany 2017
A. Legay and T. Margaria (Eds.): TACAS 2017, Part I, LNCS 10205, pp. 499–517, 2017.
DOI: 10.1007/978-3-662-54577-5_29

The interaction is governed by an underlying *topology*, which determines which agents can interact in one step, and a *scheduler*, which picks the specific agents involved in the interaction. Concurrent probabilistic systems arise as models of distributed algorithms [25, 29, 31, 34, 38], where each agent is a processor, the interaction between processors is determined by a communication topology, and the processor can update its internal state based on the communication as well as randomization. In each step, the scheduler adversarially chooses a processor to run. Concurrent probabilistic populations also arise in agent-based population models in biology [35], wherein an agent can represent an allele, a cell, or a species, and the interaction between agents describes how these entities evolve over time. For a population of a fixed size, there is a rich theory of probabilistic verification [1, 7, 20, 48] based on finite-state Markov decision processes (MDPs). Verification questions for population models, however, ask if a property holds for populations of *all* sizes: even if each agent is finite-state, the family of all processes (for each population size) is an infinite-state MDP. Indeed, for many simple population models, one can show that the verification question is undecidable, even for reachability or safety properties in the non-probabilistic setting [6, 11, 22]. Consequently, the verification question for populations requires techniques beyond finite-state probabilistic verification, and requires symbolic techniques to represent potentially infinite sets of states.

One well-known symbolic framework for verifying parameterized non-probabilistic concurrent systems is *regular model checking* [3, 4, 13, 41, 42, 47], where states of a population are modeled using words over a suitable alphabet, sets of states are represented as regular languages, and the transition relation is defined as a regular transducer. From parameterized verification of non-probabilistic processes, it is known that regular languages provide a robust symbolic representation of infinite sets, and automata-theoretic algorithms provide the basis of checking safety or termination properties.

In this paper, we consider the problem of verifying that a given parameterized family of probabilistic concurrent systems *almost surely terminates*, i.e., reaches certain final states with probability 1 from each initial state regardless of the behaviour of the schedulers. Termination is a fundamental property when verifying parameterized probabilistic systems. Since termination typically, however, fails without imposing certain *fairness* conditions on the scheduler, it is crucial to be able to incorporate fairness assumptions into a termination analysis. Therefore, although the framework of regular model checking has recently been extended for proving termination (without fairness) over parameterized probabilistic concurrent systems [36], it still cannot be used to prove termination for many interesting parameterized probabilistic concurrent systems.

What notion of fairness should we consider for proving termination for parameterized probabilistic concurrent systems? To answer this question, one would naturally start by looking at standard notions of fairness in probabilistic model checking [7], which asserts that every process must be chosen infinitely often. However, this notion seems to be too weak to prove termination for many of our examples, notably Herman's self-stabilizing protocol [29] in an asynchronous setting, and population models from biology (e.g. Moran's process [35]). The standard notion of fairness gives rise to a rather unintuitive and unrealistic strategy for the scheduler, which could delay an enabled process for as long as it desires while still being fair (see [15, Example 8] and the Herman's protocol example in Sect. 3). For this reason, we propose to consider Alur and Henzinger's [5] *finitary fairness*—a stronger notion of fairness that allows the scheduler to delaying executing an enabled process in an infinite run for at most k steps, for some unknown but fixed bound $k \in \mathbb{N}$. Alur and Henzinger argued that this fairness notion is more realistic in practice, but it is not as restrictive as the notion of k-*fairness*, which fixes the bound k a priori. In addition, it should be noted that finitary fairness is strictly weaker than probabilistic fairness (scheduler chooses processes randomly) for almost-sure termination over finite MDPs and parameterized probabilistic systems (an infinite family of finite MDPs). We will show in this paper that there are many interesting examples of parameterized probabilistic concurrent systems for which termination is satisfied under finitary fairness, but *not* under the most general notion of fairness.

Contributions. Our main contribution is a systematic, regularity-preserving, encoding of finitary fairness in the framework of regular model checking for parameterized probabilistic concurrent systems. More precisely, our encoding reduces the problem of verifying almost sure termination under finitary fairness to almost sure termination *without fairness* in regular model checking, for which a verification framework exists [36].

In general, the difficulty with finding an encoding of fairness is how to deal with an infinite number of fairness requirements (one for each process) in a systematic and regularity-preserving manner. There are known encodings of general notions of fairness in regular model checking, e.g., by using a token that is passed to the next process (with respect to some ordering of the processes) when the current process is executed, and ensuring that the first process holds the token and passes it to the right infinitely many times (e.g. see [4,42]). However, these encodings do not work in our case for several reasons. Firstly, they do not take into account the unknown upper bound (from finitary fairness) within which time a process has to be executed. Adapting these encodings to finitary fairness would require *the use of unbounded counters*, which do not preserve regularity. Secondly, such encodings would yield the problem of verifying an almost-sure Rabin property (of the form $\Box \Diamond A \wedge \Diamond B$ in LTL notation, where A and B are regular sets). Although we could reduce this to an almost-sure termination property by means of product automata construction (i.e. by first converting the formula to deterministic Rabin automaton), the target set B in the resulting termination property $\Diamond B$ (consisting of configurations in strongly connected components satisfying some properties) is *not* necessarily regular.

Instead, we revisit the well-known *abstract program transformation* in the setting of non-probabilistic concurrent systems [26] encoding fairness into the program by associating to each process an unbounded counter that acts as an "alarm clock", which will "set off" if an enabled process has not been chosen by the scheduler for "too long." This abstract program transformation has been adapted by Alur and Henzinger [5] in the case of finitary fairness by additionally incorporating an extra counter n that stores the unknown upper bound and resetting the value of a counter belonging to a chosen process to the "default value" n. Our contributions are as follows:

1. We show how Alur and Henzinger's program transformation could be adapted to the setting of probabilistic parameterized concurrent systems (infinite family of finite MDPs). This involves constructing a new parameterization of the system (using the idea of weakly finite systems) and a proof that the transformation preserves reachability probabilities.
2. We show how the resulting abstract program transformation could be made concrete in the setting of regular model checking *without using automata models beyond regular automata*.
3. We have implemented this transformation in FAIRYTAIL. Combined with the existing algorithm [36] for verifying almost sure termination (without fairness) in regular model checking, we have successfully verified a number of models obtained from distributed algorithms and biological systems including Herman's protocol [29], Moran processes in a linear array [35,40], and the cell cycle switch model [17] on ring and line topologies. To the best of our knowledge, our algorithm is the first fully-automatic method that can prove termination for these examples.

Related Work. There are few techniques for automatic verification of liveness properties of parameterized probabilistic programs. Almost sure verification of probabilistic finite-state programs goes back to Pnueli and co-workers [28,45]. Esparza et al. [23] generalize the reasoning to weakly finite programs, and describe a heuristic to guess a *terminating pattern* by constructing a nondeterministic program from a given probabilistic program and a terminating pattern candidate. This allows them to exploit model checkers and termination provers for nondeterministic programs. More recently, Lin and Rümmer [36] consider unconditional termination for parameterized probabilistic programs. While our work builds on these techniques, our main contribution is the incorporation of fairness in regular model checking of probabilistic programs, which was not considered before.

Fairness for concurrent probabilistic systems was considered by Vardi [48] and by Hart et al. [28], and generalized later [8,21,45]. The focus was, however, on a fixed number of processes. The notion of fairness through explicit scheduling was developed by Olderog and Apt [43]. More recently, notions of fairness for infinitary control (i.e., where an infinite number of processes can be created) was considered by Hoenicke, Olderog, and Podelski [30,44].

Martingale techniques have been used to prove termination of sequential, infinite-state, probabilistic programs [18,19,24,32,39]. These results are not comparable to our results, as they do not consider unbounded families of fairness constraints nor communication topologies.

2   Preliminaries

General Notations: For any two given real numbers $i \leq j$, we use a standard notation (with an extra subscript) to denote real intervals, e.g., $[i, j]_{\mathbb{R}} = \{k \in \mathbb{R} : i \leq k \leq j\}$ and $(i, j]_{\mathbb{R}} = \{k \in \mathbb{R} : i < k \leq j\}$. We will denote intervals over integers by removing the subscript, i.e., $[i, j] = [i, j]_{\mathbb{R}} \cap \mathbb{Z}$. Given a set S, we use S^* to denote the set of all finite sequences of elements from S. The set S^* always includes the empty sequence, which we denote by ϵ. We use S^+ to denote the set $S^* \setminus \{\epsilon\}$. Given two sets of words S_1, S_2, we use $S_1 \cdot S_2$ to denote the set $\{v \cdot w : v \in S_1, w \in S_2\}$ of words formed by concatenating words from S_1 with words from S_2. Given two relations $R_1, R_2 \subseteq S \times S$, we define their composition as $R_1 \circ R_2 = \{(s_1, s_3) : \exists s_2((s_1, s_2) \in R_1 \wedge (s_2, s_3) \in R_2)\}$.

Transition Systems: We fix the (countably infinite) set AP of *atomic propositions*. Let ACT be a finite set of *action symbols*. A *transition system* over ACT is a tuple $\mathfrak{S} = \langle S; \{\rightarrow_a\}_{a \in \mathsf{ACT}}, \ell \rangle$, where S is a set of *configurations*, $\rightarrow_a \subseteq S \times S$ is a binary relation over S, and $\ell : \mathsf{AP} \rightarrow 2^S$ maps atomic propositions to sets of configurations (we omit ℓ if it is not important). We use $\rightarrow$ to denote the relation $\left(\bigcup_{a \in \mathsf{ACT}} \rightarrow_a \right)$. The notation $\rightarrow^+$ (resp. $\rightarrow^*$) is used to denote the transitive (resp. transitive-reflexive) closure of $\rightarrow$. We say that a sequence $s_1 \rightarrow \cdots \rightarrow s_n$ is a *path* (or *run*) in $\mathfrak{S}$ (or in $\rightarrow$). Given two paths $\pi_1 : s_1 \rightarrow^* s_2$ and $\pi_2 : s_2 \rightarrow^* s_3$ in $\rightarrow$, we may concatenate them to obtain $\pi_1 \odot \pi_2$ (by gluing together s_2). We call π_1 a *prefix* of $\pi_1 \odot \pi_2$. For each $S' \subseteq S$ we use the notations $pre_{\rightarrow}(S')$ and $post_{\rightarrow}(S')$ to denote the pre/post image of S' under $\rightarrow$. That is, $pre_{\rightarrow}(S') = \{p \in S : \exists q \in S'(p \rightarrow q)\}$ and $post_{\rightarrow}(S') = \{q \in S : \exists p \in S'(p \rightarrow q)\}$.

Words and Automata: We assume basic familiarity with finite word automata. Fix a finite alphabet Σ. For each finite word $w = w_1 \ldots w_n \in \Sigma^*$, we write $w[i, j]$, where $1 \leq i \leq j \leq n$, to denote the segment $w_i \ldots w_j$. Given an automaton $\mathcal{A} = (\Sigma, Q, \delta, q_0, F)$, a run of $\mathcal{A}$ on w is a function $\rho : \{0, \ldots, n\} \rightarrow Q$ with $\rho(0) = q_0$ that obeys the transition relation δ. We may also denote the run ρ by the word $\rho(0) \cdots \rho(n)$ over the alphabet Q. The run ρ is said to be *accepting* if $\rho(n) \in F$, in which case we say that w is *accepted* by $\mathcal{A}$. The language $L(\mathcal{A})$ of $\mathcal{A}$ is the set of words in Σ^* accepted by $\mathcal{A}$.

Reachability Games: We recall some basic concepts on 2-player reachability games (see e.g. [27, Chapter 2] on games with 1-accepting conditions). An *arena* is a transition system $\mathfrak{S} = \langle S = V_1 \cup V_2; \rightarrow_1, \rightarrow_2 \rangle$, where S (i.e. the set of "game configurations") is partitioned into two disjoint sets V_1 and V_2 such that $pre_{\rightarrow_i}(S) \subseteq V_i$ for each $i \in \{1, 2\}$. The transition relation $\rightarrow_i$ denotes the actions of Player i. Similarly, for each $i \in \{1, 2\}$, the configurations V_i are controlled by Player i. In the following, Player 1 will also be called "Scheduler," and Player 2 "Process". Given a set $I_0 \subseteq S$ of initial configurations and a set $F \subseteq S$ of final (a.k.a. target) configurations, the goal of Player 2 is to reach F from I_0, while the goal of Player 1 is to avoid it. More formally, a *strategy* for Player i is a partial function $f : S^*V_i \to S$ such that, for each $v \in S^*$ and $p \in V_i$, if vp is a path in $\mathfrak{S}$ and p is not a dead end (i.e., $p \to_i q$ for some q), then $f(vp)$ is defined in such a way that $p \to_i f(vp)$. Given a strategy f_i for Player $i \in \{1,2\}$ and an initial configuration $s_0 \in S$, we can define a unique (finite or infinite) path in $\mathfrak{S}$ such that $\pi : s_0 \to_{j_1} s_1 \to_{j_2} \cdots$ where $s_{j_{k+1}} = f_i(s_0 s_1 \ldots s_{j_k})$ for $i \in \{1,2\}$ is the (unique) configuration s.t. $s_{j_k} \in V_i$. Player 2 *wins* iff some configuration in F appears in π, or if the path is finite and the last configuration belongs to Player 1. Player 1 *wins* iff Player 2 does not win; we say Player 2 *loses*. A strategy f for Player i is *winning* from I_0 if for each strategy g of Player $3 - i$, the unique path in $\mathfrak{S}$ from each $s_0 \in I_0$ witnesses a win for Player i. Such games (a.k.a. *reachability games*) are *determined* (see e.g. [27, Proposition 2.21]): either Player 1 has a winning strategy or Player 2 has a winning strategy.

Convention. *For notational simplicity, w.l.o.g., we make the following assumptions on our reachability games. They suffice for the purpose of proving liveness for parameterised systems.*

(A0) *Arenas are strictly alternating, i.e., a move made by a player does not take the game back to her configuration ($post_{\to_i}(S) \cap V_i = \emptyset$, for each $i \in \{1,2\}$).*

(A1) *Initial and final configurations belong to Player 1, i.e., $I_0, F \subseteq V_1$*

(A2) *Non-final configurations are not dead ends: $\forall x \in S \setminus F, \exists y : x \to_1 y \vee x \to_2 y$.*

Markov Chains: A (discrete-time) *Markov chain* (a.k.a. *DTMC*) is a structure of the form $\mathfrak{S} = \langle S; \delta, \ell \rangle$ where S is a set of configurations, δ is a function that associates a configuration $s \in S$ with a probability distribution over a sample space $D \subseteq S$ (i.e. the probability of going to a certain configuration from s), and $\ell : AP \to 2^S$ maps atomic propositions to subsets of S. In what follows, we will assume that each $\delta(s)$ is a discrete probability distribution with a finite sample space. This assumption allows us to simplify our notation: a DTMC $\langle S; \delta, \ell \rangle$ can be seen as a transition system $\langle S; \to, \ell \rangle$ with a transition probability function δ mapping a transition $t = (s, s') \in \to$ to a value $\delta(t) \in (0, 1]$ such that $\sum_{s' \in post(s)} \delta((s, s')) = 1$. That is, transitions with zero probabilities are removed from $\to$. We will write $s \xrightarrow{p} s'$ to denote $s \to s'$ and that $\delta((s, s')) = p$. The *underlying transition graph* of a DTMC $\langle S; \delta, \ell \rangle$ is the transition system $\langle S; \to, \ell \rangle$ with δ omitted. Given a finite path $\pi = s_0 \to \cdots \to s_n$ from the initial configuration $s_0 \in S$, let Run_π be the set of all finite/infinite paths with π as a prefix, i.e., of the form $\pi \odot \pi'$ for some finite/infinite path π'. Given a set $F \subseteq S$ of target configurations, the probability $\text{Prob}_\mathfrak{S}(s_0 \models \Diamond F)$ (the subscript $\mathfrak{S}$ may be omitted when understood) of reaching F from s_0 in $\mathfrak{S}$ can be defined using a standard cylinder construction (see e.g. [33]) as follows. For each finite path $\pi = s_0 \to \cdots \to s_n$ in $\mathfrak{S}$ from s_0, we set Run_π to be a basic cylinder, to which we associate the probability $\text{Prob}(Run_\pi) = \prod_{i=0}^{n-1} \delta((s_i, s_{i+1}))$. This gives rise to

. a unique probability measure for the σ-algebra over the set of all runs from s_0. The probability $\text{Prob}(s_0 \models \Diamond F)$ is then the probability of the event F containing all paths in $\mathfrak{G}$ with some "accepting" finite path as a prefix, i.e., a finite path from s_0 ending in some configuration in F. In general, given an LTL formula φ over AP, the event containing all paths from s_0 in $\mathfrak{G}$ satisfying φ is measurable [48] and its probability value $\text{Prob}(s_0 \models \varphi)$ is well-defined.

Notation: Whenever understood, we will omit mention of ℓ from $\langle S; \delta, \ell \rangle$.

3   Abstract Models of Probabilistic Concurrent Programs

In this section, we recall the notion of Markov Decision Processes (MDPs) and fair MDPs [7]. These serve as our abstract models of probabilistic concurrent programs. We then define the notion of finitary fairness [5] and discuss its basic properties in the setting of MDPs.

3.1   Markov Decision Processes

A *Markov decision process (MDP)* is a strictly alternating arena $\mathfrak{G} = \langle S = V_1 \cup V_2; \rightarrow_1, \rightarrow_2 \rangle$ such that $\langle S; \rightarrow_2 \rangle$ is a DTMC, i.e., $\rightarrow_2$ is associated with some transition probability function, and that the atomic propositions are not important. Intuitively, the transition relation $\rightarrow_1$ is nondeterministic (controlled by a "demonic" scheduler), whereas the transition relation $\rightarrow_2$ is probabilistic. By definition of arenas, the configurations of the MDPs are partitioned into the set V_1 of *nondeterministic states* (controlled by Scheduler) and the set V_2 of *probabilistic states*. Formally, $pre_{\rightarrow_1}(S) \cap pre_{\rightarrow_2}(S) = \emptyset$. Each Scheduler's strategy[1] $f : S^* V_1 \rightarrow S$ gives rise to an infinite-state DTMC with the underlying transition system $\mathfrak{G}_f = \langle S'; \rightarrow_3, \ell \rangle$ and the transition probability function δ' defined as follows. Here, S' is the set of all finite/infinite paths π from s_0. For each state $s' \in S$ and each path π from s_0 ending in some state $s \in S$, we define $\pi \rightarrow_3 \pi s'$ iff: (1) if $s \in V_1$ is a nondeterministic state, then $f(\pi) = s'$, and (2) if $s \in V_2$ is a probabilistic state, then $s \rightarrow_2 s'$. Intuitively, $\mathfrak{G}_f$ is an unfolding of the game arena $\mathfrak{G}$ (i.e. a disjoint union of trees) where branching only occurs on probabilistic states. Transitions $\pi \rightarrow_3 \pi s'$ satisfying Case (1) have the probability $\delta'((\pi, \pi s')) = 1$; otherwise, its probability is $\delta'((\pi, \pi s')) = \delta((s, s'))$. We let ℓ be a function mapping each subset $X \subseteq S$ (used as an atomic proposition) to the set of all finite paths in $\mathfrak{G}_f$ from s_0 to X. Since $\mathfrak{G}_f$ is a DTMC, given an LTL formula φ over subsets of S as atomic propositions, the probability $\text{Prob}_{\mathfrak{G}_f}(s_0 \models \varphi)$ of satisfying φ in $\mathfrak{G}$ from s_0 under the scheduler f is well-defined. In particular, $\text{Prob}_{\mathfrak{G}_f}(s_0 \models \Diamond F)$ is the probability of reaching F from s_0 in $\mathfrak{G}$ under the scheduler f. The probability $\text{Prob}_{\mathfrak{G},\mathcal{C}}(s_0 \models \varphi)$ of satisfying φ from s_0 in the MDP $\mathfrak{G}$ under a class $\mathcal{C}$ of schedulers is defined to be the infimum of the set of all probabilities $\text{Prob}_{\mathfrak{G}_f}(s_0 \models \varphi)$ over all $f \in \mathcal{C}$. We will omit mention of $\mathcal{C}$ when it denotes the class of all schedulers.

---

[1] Also called "scheduler" or "adversary" for short.

An MDP is *weakly-finite* [23] if from each configuration, the set of all configurations that are reachable from it (in the underlying transition system of the MDP) is finite. Note that the state space of weakly-finite MDPs can be infinite. The restriction of weak finiteness is another way of defining the notion of *parameterized systems*, which are an infinite family of finite-state systems. Weakly-finite MDPs capture many interesting probabilistic concurrent systems in which each process is finite-state; this is the case for many probabilistic distributed protocols.

3.2   Fair Markov Decision Processes

A *fair Markov decision process (FMDP)* is a structure of the form $\mathfrak{S} = \langle S = V_1 \cup V_2; \rightarrow_1, \rightarrow_2, \mathfrak{C}, \mathfrak{J} \rangle$, where $\langle S = V_1 \cup V_2; \rightarrow_1, \rightarrow_2 \rangle$ is an MDP, $\mathfrak{J}$ is a weak fairness (a.k.a. *justice*) requirement, and $\mathfrak{C}$ is a strong fairness (a.k.a. *compassion*) requirement. More precisely, a *weak fairness requirement* is a set (at most countably infinite) of *atomic weak fairness requirements* of the form $\Diamond \Box A \Rightarrow \Box \Diamond B$, for some $A, B \subseteq S$. Here, the $\Box$ and $\Diamond$ modalities are the standard "always" and "eventually" LTL operators. The set A (resp. B) will be called the *premise* (resp. *consequence*). Intuitively, if A is interpreted as "Process 1 is waiting to move" and B as "Process 1 is chosen", then this fairness requirement may be read as: at no point can Process 1 be continuously waiting to move without being chosen. In addition, a *strong fairness requirement* is a set (again, at most countably infinite) of *atomic strong fairness requirements* of the form $\Box \Diamond A \Rightarrow \Box \Diamond B$, for some $A, B \subseteq S$. Using the above example, a strong fairness requirement reads: if Process 1 is waiting to move infinitely often, then it is chosen infinitely often. As before, the set A (resp. B) will be called the *premise* (resp. *consequence*). In the following, when it is clear whether a fairness requirement is a justice or a compassion, we will denote it by the pair (A, B) of premise and consequence.

Given an FMDP $\mathfrak{S} = \langle S = V_1 \cup V_2; \rightarrow_1, \rightarrow_2, \mathfrak{C}, \mathfrak{J} \rangle$, a configuration $s_0 \in S$, and a scheduler f, since each atomic fairness requirement is an LTL formula and there are at most countably many atomic fairness requirements, the set of paths from s_0 in the DTMC $\mathfrak{S}_f$ induced by f satisfying $\mathfrak{C}$ and $\mathfrak{J}$ is measurable. We say that a scheduler f is $\mathfrak{S}$-*fair* if $\mathrm{Prob}_{\mathfrak{S}_f}(s_0 \models \mathfrak{C} \wedge \mathfrak{J}) = 1$ for every initial configuration s_0. The fairness conditions $(\mathfrak{C}, \mathfrak{J})$ are *realizable* in $\mathfrak{S}$ if there exists at least one $\mathfrak{S}$-fair scheduler.

A natural fairness notion we consider in this paper is *process fairness*, which asserts that each process is chosen infinitely often. For this notion of fairness, we can assume that the consequence B of each atomic fairness requirement asserts that a particular process is chosen. We make one simplifying assumption: *each process is always enabled* (i.e., can always be chosen by the scheduler). This assumption is reasonable since we can always introduce an idle transition for each process. Under this assumption, we have that *from each $v_1 \in V_1$, there exists a transition $v_1 \rightarrow_1 v_2$ for some $v_2 \in B$*. This implies that our fairness conditions are always realizable and that the probability $\mathrm{Prob}_{\mathfrak{S},c}(E)$ of event E over the set of all $\mathfrak{S}$-fair schedulers is well-defined.

3.3   Finitary Fairness

Given an FMDP $\mathfrak{S} = \langle S = V_1 \cup V_2; \to_1, \to_2, \mathfrak{C}, \mathfrak{J} \rangle$, a configuration $s_0 \in S$, and a number $k \in \mathbb{N}$, we say that a scheduler f is $\mathfrak{S}$-k-fair (or k-fair whenever $\mathfrak{S}$ is understood) if for each atomic fairness requirement (A, B):

1. if (A, B) is justice, then (the underlying graph of) $\mathfrak{S}_f$ contains no path π of length k satisfying the LTL formula $\Box(A \wedge \neg B)$.
2. if (A, B) is compassion, then $\mathfrak{S}_f$ contains no path π satisfying the LTL formula $\psi_k \wedge \Box \neg B$, where $\psi_0 := true$ and $\psi_i := \Diamond(A \wedge \psi_{i-1})$ for each $i > 0$.

In other words, a premise in a justice requirement cannot be satisfied for k *consecutive* steps without satisfying a consequence, while a premise in a compassion requirement cannot be satisfied for k (not necessarily consecutive) steps without satisfying a consequence. A scheduler is said to be *finitary fair (fin-fair)* if it is k-fair for some k. The fairness conditions $(\mathfrak{C}, \mathfrak{J})$ are said to be *finitary-realizable (fin-realizable)* in $\mathfrak{S}$ if there exists at least one fin-fair scheduler. Under this assumption, the probability $\text{Prob}_{\mathfrak{S}, \mathcal{C}}(E)$ of an event E over the set $\mathcal{C}$ of all fin-fair schedulers is well-defined. In what follows, for an FMDP $\mathfrak{S}$, we will simply denote $\text{Prob}_{\mathfrak{S}, \mathcal{C}}(E)$ as $\text{Prob}_{\mathfrak{S}}(E)$. In this paper, we propose to study *termination of probabilistic concurrent programs under finitary fairness*, i.e., to determine whether $\text{Prob}_{\mathfrak{S}, \mathcal{C}}(s_0 \models \Diamond F) = 1$, where $\mathcal{C}$ is the class of all fin-fair schedulers.

The following proposition states one special property of weakly-finite MDPs.

Proposition 1. *Let $\mathfrak{S}$ and $\mathfrak{S}'$ be two weakly-finite fair MDPs with identical underlying transition systems (but possibly different probability values). For each set F of final states, and each initial configuration s_0, it is the case that $\text{Prob}_{\mathfrak{S}}(s_0 \models \Diamond F) = 1$ iff $\text{Prob}_{\mathfrak{S}'}(s_0 \models \Diamond F) = 1$.*

By Proposition 1, when dealing with almost-sure finitary-fair termination of weakly-finite MDPs, we only care whether a transition has a zero or a non-zero probability, i.e., if it is non-zero, then the exact value is irrelevant. Incidentally, the same also holds for other properties including almost-sure termination without fairness and qualitative temporal specifications [28, 36, 45]. *For this reason, we may simply omit these probability values from our symbolic representation of weakly-finite MDPs, which we will do from the next section onwards.*

3.4   Herman's Protocol

Herman's protocol [29] is a distributed self-stabilization algorithm for a population of processes organized in a ring. The *correct* configurations are those where exactly one process holds a token. If, through some error, the ring enters an *erroneous* configuration (in which multiple processes hold tokens), Herman's protocol ensures that the system will *self-stabilize*: it will almost surely go back to a configuration with only one token.

Let us discuss how the protocol works in more detail. Fix $N \geq 3$ processors organized in a ring. If a chosen process does not hold a token, then it can perform an idle transition (i.e. do nothing). If a chosen process holds a token, then it can keep holding the token with probability $\frac{1}{2}$ or pass it on to its clockwise neighbor (the process $(i+1)$ mod N, for processes numbered $0, \ldots, N-1$) with probability $\frac{1}{2}$. If a process currently holds a token and receives another token from its (counter-clockwise) neighbor, then the two tokens are merged[2] into one, leaving the process with one token.

Formally, Hermann's protocol can be modeled as a weakly-finite Markov decision process whose states are vectors in $\{\bot, \top\}^*$. For each N, the state of the protocol is described by a bitvector of N bits, with the i-th bit being one iff the i-th process holds a token. From a state $\mathbf{v}$, the scheduler picks a process $i \in \{0, \ldots, N-1\}$. Given a chosen process i, the new state remains $\mathbf{v}$ if the chosen process i did not hold a token ($\mathbf{v}(i) = \bot$). If $\mathbf{v}(i) = \top$, the new state is $\mathbf{v}$ with probability $\frac{1}{2}$ and $\mathbf{v} \oplus e_i \oplus e_{(i+1) \bmod N}$ with probability $\frac{1}{2}$. Here, e_i denotes a vector with $\top$ in the i-th position and $\bot$ everywhere else, and $\oplus$ is the XOR operation. We want to ensure that, starting from an arbitrary initial assignment of tokens, any population self-stabilizes with probability one.

Process fairness for Herman's protocol is a set of N atomic fairness requirements, each asserting that the process i is executed infinitely often, for each $i \in \{1, \ldots, N\}$. Unfortunately, Herman's protocol does *not* terminate with probability one against some fair schedulers. To see this, consider the start state $s_0 = (\top, \bot, \top)$. Let us call the token held by Process 0 "the first token", and the token held by Process 2 "the second token". Define a *round* as the following sequence of moves by the scheduler: keep choosing the process that holds the first token until it passes the token to the right, and do the same to the same to the second token. For example, the two configurations obtained after completing the first and second rounds from s_0 are, respectively, $(\top, \top, \bot)$ and $(\bot, \top, \top)$. To see that the scheduler is fair, for each integer $i > 0$, the probability that the i-th round is not completed is 0 since the probability that one of the tokens will be kept at the same process for an infinite amount of time is 0. Therefore, the probability that some round is not completed is also 0. Completing two rounds ensure that all the processes are picked. Therefore, every process will be chosen with probability 1. On the other hand, observe that correct configurations are not seen in the induced DTMC, showing that self-stabilization holds with probability 0 under this scheduler.

Herman's protocol can be shown to self-stabilize with probability one under all fin-fair schedulers, which can be proved by our fully-automatic verification algorithm (presented later in the paper).

---

[2] Herman [29] describes a more general protocol in which tokens can be merged/destroyed with some probability. We consider this restriction for simplicity of presentation.

4   Regular Model Checking: A Symbolic Framework

In this section, we recall *regular model checking* (see e.g. [3,42,46]), a symbolic framework for specifying infinite-state systems based on finite automata and regular transducers and developing automatic verification (semi-)algorithms.

A transition system $\mathfrak{S} = \langle S = V_1 \cup V_2; \rightarrow_1, \rightarrow_2 \rangle$ is specified in the framework as a regular language S (e.g. as a regular expression over some alphabet Σ), and two "regular relations" $\rightarrow_1, \rightarrow_2 \subseteq \Sigma^* \times \Sigma^*$. For simplicity, in the following we will assume that $S = \Sigma^*$. How do we specify regular relations? One standard way is to restrict to length-preserving relations (i.e. the relation may only contain a pair of words of the same length) and specify such relations as regular languages over the alphabet $\Sigma \times \Sigma$. There is, then, a simple one-to-one correspondence between the set of words over $\Sigma \times \Sigma$ and the set of all pairs of words over Σ of the same length. This can be achieved by mapping a pair (v, w) of words Σ with $|v| = |w| = n$ to a word $v \otimes w$, defined as $(v_1, w_1)(v_2, w_2) \cdots (v_n, w_n)$ whenever $v = v_1 \cdots v_n$ and $w = w_1 \cdots w_n$.

Proving that a property φ holds over a transition system $\mathfrak{S}$ is done "in a regular way,", by finding a "regular proof" for the property. For example, if φ asserts that the set *Bad* of bad states can never be reached, then a regular proof amounts to finding an inductive invariant *Inv* in the form of a regular language [3,42] that does not intersect with *Bad*, i.e., $Bad \cap Inv = \emptyset$, $S_0 \subseteq Inv$ (S_0 is a regular set of initial states), and $post_\rightarrow(Inv) \subseteq Inv$, where $\rightarrow = \rightarrow_1 \cup \rightarrow_2$. Since regular languages are effectively closed under boolean operations and taking pre/post images w.r.t. regular transducers, an algorithm for verifying the correctness of a given regular proof can be obtained by using language inclusion algorithms for regular automata, e.g., [2,14]. The framework of regular proofs is incomplete in general since it could happen that there is a proof, but no regular proof. The pathological cases when only non-regular proofs exist do not, however, seem to frequently occur in practice, e.g., see [3,9,10,12,16,37,41,42,47].

The framework of regular proofs has been extended to deal with almost-sure termination for weakly-finite probabilistic concurrent programs in [36]. We briefly summarise the main idea, since we reduce the fair termination problem to their setting. By Proposition 1, the actual probability values do not matter in proving almost-sure termination. For this reason, we may specify a weakly-finite MDP $\mathfrak{S} = \langle S = V_1 \cup V_2; \rightarrow_1, \rightarrow_2 \rangle$ as a regular specification in the same way as we specify a non-probabilistic transition system in our regular specification language. Given an MDP $\mathfrak{S} = \langle S = V_1 \cup V_2; \rightarrow_1, \rightarrow_2 \rangle$, a set $I_0 \subseteq V_1$ of initial configurations, and a set $F \subseteq V_1$ of final configurations, a regular proof for $\mathrm{Prob}(s_0 \models F) = 1$ for each $s_0 \in I_0$ is a pair $\langle Inv, \prec \rangle$ consisting of a regular inductive invariant $Inv \subseteq S$ and a regular relation $\prec \subseteq S \times S$ such that:

1. $I_0 \subseteq Inv$ and $post_\rightarrow(Inv) \subseteq Inv$.
2. $\prec$ is a strict preorder on S, i.e., it is irreflexive ($\forall s \in S : s \not\prec s$) and transitive ($\forall s, s', s'' \in S : s \prec s' \wedge s' \prec s'' \rightarrow s \prec s''$).
3. Irrespective of the nondeterministic transitions from any configuration in *Inv*, there is a probabilistic transition to a configuration in *Inv* that decreases its rank with respect to $\prec$:

$$\forall x \in Inv \setminus F, y \in S \setminus F : \quad ((x \to_1 y) \Rightarrow (\exists z \in Inv : (y \to_2 z) \wedge x \succ z)).$$

An automata-theoretic algorithm can then be devised for checking the above verification conditions with respect to a given regular proof [36].

Example 1 (**Herman's protocol, continued**). We provide a regular encoding of Herman's protocol. The configurations are words over the alphabet $\{\top, \bot, \overline{\top}, \overline{\bot}\}$, where $\top$ (resp. $\bot$) signifies that a process holds (resp. does not hold) a token, while overlining the character signifies that the process is chosen by the scheduler. We set $\Sigma = \{\top, \bot\}$. The set S_0 of initial configurations is $\Sigma^* \top \Sigma^*$, i.e., at least one process holds a token. The set of final configurations is $\bot^* \top \bot^*$, i.e., there is only a single token in the system. The actions of the scheduler is to choose a process; this can be expressed as the regular expression $I^*((\top, \overline{\top}) + (\bot, \overline{\bot}))I^*$, where I denotes the regular language $(\top, \top) + (\bot, \bot)$. The probabilistic actions can be expressed as a union of the following three regular expressions:

$$I^*((\overline{\top}, \top) + (\overline{\bot}, \bot))I^* \qquad \qquad \text{(idle)}$$
$$I^*(\overline{\top}, \bot)((\bot, \top)) + (\top, \top))I^*, \quad ((\bot, \top) + (\top, \top))I^*(\overline{\top}, \bot)) \qquad \text{(\textbf{pass token right})}$$

5   Handling Fairness Requirements

We now describe the main result of the paper: a general method for embedding finitary fairness into regular model checking for probabilistic concurrent systems.

5.1   Regular Specifications of Fairness

When a complex system or a distributed protocol is being modelled in regular model checking, it is often necessary to add an *infinite* number of fairness requirements. This is because such a system admits a finite but arbitrary number of agents or processes, each with its own fairness requirement (e.g. that the process should be executed infinitely often). For this reason, it is not enough to simply express the fairness requirements as a finite set of pairs of regular languages (one for the premise, and one for the consequence). We describe a regular way of specifying infinitely many fairness constraints. Our presentation is a generalisation of the regular specification of fairness from [4,42].

The general idea is to define a "regular function" $\mathcal{T}$ that maps a configuration $s = s_1 \cdots s_n \in S$ to a word $w = w_1 \cdots w_n$ such that w_i contains: (1) a bit b_i indicating whether s is in the premise of the i-th fairness requirement, (2) a bit b_i' indicating whether s is in the consequence of the i-th fairness requirement, and (3) a bit t indicating whether the i-th fairness requirement is justice or compassion. Such a regular specification of fairness allows an infinite number of fairness constraints since S is potentially infinite (i.e., containing words of unbounded lengths), though only the first $|s|$ fairness requirements matter for a word $s \in S$. This is sufficient for weakly-finite MDPs since the set of reachable configurations from any given configuration s is finite and so, among the infinite number of fairness constraints, only finitely many are distinguishable.

The regular function can be defined by a letter-to-letter tranducer with input alphabet Σ and output alphabet $\Gamma := \{0,1\} \times \{0,1\} \times \{0,1\}$. Without loss of generality, we assume that the i-th letter in the output of every input word of $\mathcal{T}$ agree on the third bit (i.e., whether the fairness requirement is justice or compassion is well-defined): for every $s, s' \in S$ and $i \in \mathbb{N}$, if $\mathcal{T}(s)[i] = (a,b,c)$ and $\mathcal{T}(s')[i] = (a',b',c')$, then $c = c'$. Observe this condition on $\mathcal{T}$ can be algorithmically checked by using a simple automata-theoretic method: find two accepted words in which in some position their third bits differ.

In this case, $\mathcal{T}$ gives rise to compassion requirements $\mathfrak{C}$ and justice requirements $\mathfrak{J}$ by associating the i-th position in all output words by a unique fairness constraint. More precisely, let $A_i = \{s : \mathcal{T}(s)[i] = (1,j,t), \text{ for some } j,t \in \{0,1\}\}$ and $B_i = \{s : \mathcal{T}(s)[i] = (j,1,t), \text{ for some } j,t \in \{0,1\}\}$. Define: (i) $\mathfrak{J} = \{\Diamond\Box A_i \Rightarrow \Box\Diamond B_i : \mathcal{T}(s)[i] = (i,j,0), \text{ for some } s \in S, \text{ for some } j \in \{0,1\}\}$, (ii) $\mathfrak{C} = \{\Box\Diamond A_i \Rightarrow \Box\Diamond B_i : \mathcal{T}(s)[i] = (i,j,1), \text{ for some } s \in S, \text{ for some } j \in \{0,1\}\}$. Therefore, by Proposition 1, our regular fairness specification allows us to define weakly-finite fair MDPs $\langle S = V_1 \cup V_2; \to_1, \to_2, \mathfrak{C}, \mathfrak{J}\rangle$. In the following, we shall call such fair MDPs *regular*.

Our main theorem is a regularity-preserving reduction from proving almost sure termination for regular FMDPs (under finitary fairness) to proving almost sure termination for regular MDPs (without fairness).

Theorem 1. *Let* $\mathfrak{S} = \langle S = V_1 \cup V_2; \to_1, \to_2, \mathfrak{C}, \mathfrak{J}\rangle$ *be a regular representation of an FMDP, $I_0 \subseteq V_1$ be a regular set of initial configurations, and $F \subseteq V_1$ be a regular set of final configurations. Then one can compute a regular presentation of MDP* $\mathfrak{S}' = \langle S = V_1' \cup V_2'; \leadsto_1, \leadsto_2 \rangle$ *and two regular sets $I_0', F' \subseteq V_1'$ such that it holds that if $\mathfrak{C}$ and $\mathfrak{J}$ are realizable, then $Prob_{\mathfrak{S}'}(I_0' \models \Diamond F') = 1$ iff $Prob_{\mathfrak{S}}(I_0 \models \Diamond F) = 1$.*

5.2   Abstract Program Transformation

Before proving Theorem 1, let us first recall an abstract program transformation *à la* Alur and Henzinger [5], which encodes finitary fairness into a program using integer counter variables. Intuitively, we reserve one variable for each atomic fairness condition as an "alarm clock" that will set off if its corresponding process has not been executed for a long time, and one global variable n that acts as a *default* value to reset a clock to as soon as the corresponding process is executed. Although Alur and Henzinger [5] did not discuss about probabilistic programs, their transformation can be easily adapted to the setting of MDPs, though correctness still has to be proven.

We now elaborate on the details of the transformation. Given an FMDP $\mathfrak{S} = \langle S = V_1 \cup V_2; \to_1, \to_2, \mathfrak{C}, \mathfrak{J}\rangle$ with a probability distribution δ, the transformation will produce an MDP $\mathfrak{S}' = \langle S = V_1' \cup V_2'; \leadsto_1, \leadsto_2 \rangle$ with a probability distribution δ' as follows. Introduce a set $\mathcal{V}$ of "counter" variables that range over natural numbers: x_j (for each $j \in \mathfrak{J}$), y_c (for each $c \in \mathfrak{C}$), and n. Let $\mathfrak{F}$ be the set of all valuations f mapping each variable in $\mathcal{V}$ to a natural number such that $f(x_j), f(y_c) \leq f(n)$ for each $j \in \mathfrak{J}$ and $c \in \mathfrak{C}$. We define $V_1' = V_1 \times \mathfrak{F}$ and

$V_2' = V_2 \times \mathfrak{F}$. We now define the transition relation $\leadsto_i$ such that $(s, f) \leadsto_i (s', f')$ if $s \to_i s'$ and

- for each $z \in \mathcal{V}$, $f(z) > 0$,
- $f'(n) := f(n)$,
- x_j (for $j = (A, B) \in \mathfrak{J}$) and y_c (for $c = (A, B) \in \mathfrak{C}$) change as follows:

$$f'(x_j) = \begin{cases} f(x_j) - 1 & \text{if } s \in A \cap \overline{B} \\ f(n) & \text{if } s \in \overline{A} \cup B \end{cases} \qquad f'(y_c) = \begin{cases} f(n) & \text{if } s \in \overline{A} \cap \overline{B} \\ f(y_c) - 1 & \text{if } s \in A \cap \overline{B} \\ f(n) & \text{if } s \in B \end{cases}$$

($\overline{A}$ denotes the set-complement of A). Finally, we define the probability distribution δ' underlying $\leadsto_2$ as $\delta'((s, f), (s', f')) = \delta(s, s')$ whenever $s \in V_2$.

Lemma 1. *If $\mathfrak{S}$ is a weakly-finite FMDP, then $\mathfrak{S}'$ is weakly-finite.*

Intuitively, the variables x_j's and y_c's keep track of how long the scheduler has delayed choosing an enabled process, while the variable n (unchanged once the initial configuration of the MDP is fixed) aims to ensure that the scheduler is n-fair. Since n is a variable (not a constant), the resulting MDP $\mathfrak{S}'$ captures precisely the behaviour of $\mathfrak{S}$ under fin-fair schedulers.

We next state a correctness lemma for the transformation (proof in the full version). To this end, given a set $S_0 \subseteq S$ of initial configurations in $\mathfrak{S}$, we define:

- $S_0' := S_0 \times \mathfrak{F}_=$, where $\mathfrak{F}_=$ contains functions $f \in \mathfrak{F}$ such that $f(x_j) = f(y_c) = f(n)$ for each $j \in \mathfrak{J}$ and $c \in \mathfrak{C}$.
- $F' = (F \times \mathfrak{F}_{>0}) \cup (S \times \mathfrak{F}_0)$, where $\mathfrak{F}_0$ contains all $f \in \mathfrak{F}$ such that $f(x_j) = 0$ for some $j \in \mathfrak{J}$ or $f(y_c) = 0$ for some $c \in \mathfrak{C}$ (i.e. one of the alarms has been triggered), and $\mathfrak{F}_{>0} := \mathfrak{F} \setminus \mathfrak{F}_0$.

Lemma 2 (Correctness). *For weakly-finite fair MDPs $\mathfrak{S}$, it is the case that $Prob_{\mathfrak{S}}(S_0 \models \Diamond F) = Prob_{\mathfrak{S}'}(S_0' \models \Diamond F')$.*

These two lemmas immediately imply Theorem 1.

5.3   Finitary Fairness in Regular Model Checking

We now show how to implement the aforementioned abstract program transformation in our regular model checking framework. Fix a regular presentation of an FMDP $\mathfrak{S} = \langle S = V_1 \cup V_2; \to_1, \to_2, \mathfrak{C}, \mathfrak{J} \rangle$, which includes two automata over the alphabet $\Sigma \times \Sigma$ representing $\to_1$ and $\to_2$, and an automaton over the alphabet $\Sigma \times \Gamma$ representing the regular specification of the fairness conditions $\mathfrak{C}$ and $\mathfrak{J}$. [Recall that $\Gamma := \{0, 1\} \times \{0, 1\} \times \{0, 1\}$.] We describe the construction of $\leadsto_1$ (the construction for $\leadsto_2$ is similar). Let $\mathcal{A} = (\Sigma \times \Sigma, Q, \Delta, q_0, F)$ be an automaton representing $\to_1$ and $\mathcal{A}^f = (\Sigma \times \Gamma, Q^f, \Delta^f, q_0^f, F^f)$ be an automaton representing the regular specification of fairness. The construction of the automaton for $\leadsto_1$ has two stages.

Stage 1: Compute an Intermediate Automaton. The intermediate automaton $\mathcal{B}$ will have the alphabet $\Sigma' := (\Sigma \times \Sigma) \cup \Gamma$ and recognize a subset of $((\Sigma \times \Sigma)\Gamma)^*$. Intuitively, on input $(a, b) \in \Sigma \times \Sigma$, the automaton $\mathcal{B}$ simultaneously runs both $\mathcal{A}$ and $\mathcal{A}^f$. Here, the automaton $\mathcal{A}^f$ will nondeterministically guess a letter $c \in \Gamma$ and make a transition on the letter (a, c). The automaton $\mathcal{B}$, then, immediately consumes the letter c. This process is repeated until both $\mathcal{A}$ and $\mathcal{A}^f$ accept. More precisely, the automaton is defined as $\mathcal{B} := (\Sigma', Q^B, \Delta^B, q_0^B, F^B)$ where:

- $Q^B = Q \times Q^f \times (\Gamma \cup \{?\})$, $q_0^B = (q_0, q_0^f, ?)$, and $F^B = F \times F^f \times \{?\}$
- Δ_B has the following transitions:
  - $((p_1, q_1^f, ?), (a, b), (p_2, q_2^f, c))$ if $(p_1, (a, b), p_2) \in \Delta$ and $(q_1^f, (a, c), q_2^f) \in \Delta^f$.
  - $((p, q^f, c), c, (p, q^f, ?))$ for each $c \in \Gamma$.

Stage 2: Regular Substitution of Letters in Γ. Define the following regular languages

- (Identity) ID $:= (1, 1)^+(?, ?)^*$,
- (Decrement) DEC $:= (1, 1)^*(1, ?)(?, ?)^*$, and
- (Reset) RES $:= (1, 1)^+(?, 1)^*$.

Define the regular substitution σ mapping letters in Γ to regular languages:

- if (x, y, z) is $(i, 1, j)$ or $(0, i, 0)$ (for $i, j \in \{0, 1\}$), then $\sigma((x, y, z)) = $ RES.
- if (x, y, z) is of the form $(1, 0, i)$ (for some $i \in \{0, 1\}$), then $\sigma((x, y, z)) = $ DEC.
- define $\sigma((0, 0, 1)) = $ ID.

We then apply the regular substitution σ to the letters Γ appearing in our intermediate automaton $\mathcal{B}$. The resulting automaton implements the desired automaton for $\leadsto_1$.

Finishing Off the Rest of the Construction. Computing S_0', F' is easy. Define S_0' to be the set of all words $a_1 w_1 a_2 w_2 \cdots a_m w_m$—where $a_i \in \Sigma$ and $w_i \in 1^+$ for each $i \in \{1, \ldots, m\}$—such that $a_1 \cdots a_m \in S_0$. Similarly, define F' to be the set of all words $a_1 w_1 a_2 w_2 \cdots a_m w_m$—where $a_i \in \Sigma$ and $w_i \in 1^+?^* \cup ?^+$ for each $i \in \{1, \ldots, m\}$—such that $a_1 \cdots a_m \in F$ or $w_i \in ?^+$ for some $i \in \{1, \ldots, m\}$. Regular automata for these sets could be easily constructed given automata for S_0 and F.

Example 2 (**Herman's protocol**)**.** We encode process fairness in the following way. The counters use the unary encoding, their values represented as the lengths of sequences of 1's padded on the right by the symbol ? (crucial to keep the transducers length-preserving). For example, the number 3 is represented by any word of the form $111?^*$. Define $\mathcal{X} = 1^*?^*$, i.e., the set of all valid counters. The set of initial configurations can be expressed using the regular expression $(\Sigma \cdot \mathcal{X})^*(\top \cdot \mathcal{X})(\Sigma \cdot \mathcal{X})^*$, i.e., counters for all processes are initialized to an arbitrary value. The set of final configurations is now $(\bot \cdot \mathcal{X})^*(\top \cdot \mathcal{X})(\bot \cdot \mathcal{X})^* \cup (\Sigma \cdot \mathcal{X})^*(\Sigma \cdot ?^*)(\Sigma \cdot \mathcal{X})^*$, i.e., either there is exactly one token in the system, or (at least) one counter has reached 0. Scheduler now also performs operations on the counters for processes: for a chosen process, the counter is reset, for other processes, the counter is decremented. This can be expressed as the language $(I \cdot \text{DEC})^* (((\bot, \overline{\bot}) + (\top, \overline{\top})) \cdot \text{RES}) (I \cdot \text{DEC})^*$. Actions of the protocol are the same as in the original encoding and the values of counters are left unmodified:

$$(I \cdot \text{ID})^* (((\overline{\bot}, \bot) + (\overline{\top}, \top)) \cdot \text{ID}) (I \cdot \text{ID})^* \quad \textbf{(idle)}$$

$$(I \cdot \text{ID})^* ((\overline{\top}, \bot) \cdot \text{ID}) (((\bot, \top) + (\top, \top)) \cdot \text{ID}) (I \cdot \text{ID})^* \quad \textbf{(pass token right}_1\textbf{)}$$

$$(((\bot, \top) + (\top, \top)) \cdot \text{ID}) (I \cdot \text{ID})^* ((\overline{\top}, \bot) \cdot \text{ID}) \quad \textbf{(pass token right}_2\textbf{)}$$

At this point, we can use existing tools for checking termination (without fairness constraints), e.g. [36]. Indeed, we can automatically check that the system after reduction terminates with probability one, thus proving that Herman's protocol fairly terminates with probability one (under finitary process-fair schedulers).

6   Implementation and Experiments

The approach presented in this paper has been implemented in the tool FAIRY-TAIL.[3] For evaluation, we extracted models of a number of probabilistic parameterized systems. The tool receives a system with fairness conditions and transforms it into a system without fairness conditions, where fairness of the original system is encoded using counters. For solving liveness in the output transformed system, we use SLRP [36] (in the *incremental liveness proofs* setting) as the underlying liveness checker for parameterized systems.

Table 1 shows the results of our experiments. The times given are the wall clock times for the individual benchmarks on a PC with 4 Quad-Core AMD Opteron 8389 processors with Java heap memory limited to 64 GiB. The time included translation of the system into a system without fairness (always less than 1 s) and the runtime of SLRP.

We consider two versions of *Herman's protocol* and two topologies. *Moran process*, is a model of genetic drift [40] with individuals of $N \geq 2$ types. When an individual is chosen by the scheduler, it can either idle or infect a neighbor. The

Table 1. Times of analyses of probabilistic paremeterised systems. The timeout was set to 10 h (timeout is denoted as T/O).

Case study	Time
Herman's protocol (merge, line)	3.64 s
Herman's protocol (annih., line)	4.33 s
Herman's protocol (merge, ring)	4.31 s
Herman's protocol (annih., ring)	4.61 s
Moran process (2 types, line)	2 m 48 s
Moran process (3 types, line)	56 m 14 s
Cell cycle switch (1 types, line)	43.94 s
Cell cycle switch (2 types, line)	9 h 46 m
Clustering (2 types, line)	10 m 30 s
Clustering (3 types, line)	T/O
Coin game ($k = 3$, clique)	1 m 0 s

model of *cell cycle switch* is a simplification of the model of [17]. Individuals can be committed to a decision from $N \geq 1$ types. An individual neighboring another one not sharing the same decision can make him *undecided*, or persuade an undecided individual to commit to his decision. *Clustering* considers a population model of alleles of $N \geq 2$ (resp. 3) types on a line, that can change

---

[3] https://github.com/uuverifiers/autosat/tree/master/Fairness.

position with their neighbours of a different type. *Coin game* is a population protocol where every agent has one of two types of coins. If an agent is chosen by the scheduler, it can change its coin to the one held by the majority of k other randomly selected agents.

In our experiments, we verify that a given property holds under every finitary process-fair scheduler with probability one. For *clustering*, the property is that the system eventually reaches a configuration with N clusters of the same type, while for the other population protocols, the property is that the system reaches a stable configuration.

The experiments show that our encoding of fairness into systems is viable and can be used for verification of parameterized systems with fairness by their reduction to systems without fairness. On the other hand, when the size of the regular proof is large, we observe that the problem for the underlying solver gets significantly more difficult (as can be seen on the example of *clustering* for three types of alleles). We conjecture that the performance can be improved significantly by making the solver take into account the (not arbitrary) structure of the problem, which we leave for future work.

Future Work. We leave the reader with several research challenges. A natural question is how to deal with non-finitary fairness for parameterized probabilistic concurrent systems in general and in the framework of regular model checking. Secondly, since there are numerous examples of population models over more complex topologies (e.g. grids), how do you deal with termination and fair termination over such models in the parameterized setting?

Acknowledgement. We thank anonymous reviewers and Dave Parker for their helpful feedback. This work was supported by the Czech Science Foundation (project 16-24707Y), the BUT FIT project FIT-S-17-4014, the IT4IXS: IT4Innovations Excellence in Science project (LQ1602), Yale-NUS Starting Grant, the European Research Council under ERC Grant Agreement No. 610150, and Swedish Research Council (2014-5484).

References

1. PRISM website (referred in July 2015). http://www.prismmodelchecker.org/
2. Abdulla, P.A., Chen, Y.-F., Holík, L., Mayr, R., Vojnar, T.: When simulation meets antichains. In: Esparza, J., Majumdar, R. (eds.) TACAS 2010. LNCS, vol. 6015, pp. 158–174. Springer, Heidelberg (2010). doi:10.1007/978-3-642-12002-2_14
3. Abdulla, P.A.: Regular model checking. STTT **14**(2), 109–118 (2012)
4. Abdulla, P.A., Jonsson, B., Nilsson, M., d'Orso, J., Saksena, M.: Regular model checking for LTL (MSO). STTT **14**(2), 223–241 (2012)
5. Alur, R., Henzinger, T.A.: Finitary fairness. ACM Trans. Program. Lang. Syst. **20**(6), 1171–1194 (1998)
6. Apt, K.R., Kozen, D.: Limits for automatic verification of finite-state concurrent systems. Inf. Process. Lett. **22**(6), 307–309 (1986)
7. Baier, C., Katoen, J.-P.: Principles of Model Checking. MIT Press, Cambridge (2008)

8. Baier, C., Kwiatkowska, M.Z.: On the verification of qualitative properties of probabilistic processes under fairness constraints. Inf. Process. Lett. **66**(2), 71–79 (1998)
9. Bardin, S., Finkel, A., Leroux, J., Petrucci, L.: FAST: acceleration from theory to practice. STTT **10**(5), 401–424 (2008)
10. Bardin, S., Finkel, A., Leroux, J., Schnoebelen, P.: Flat acceleration in symbolic model checking. In: Peled, D.A., Tsay, Y.-K. (eds.) ATVA 2005. LNCS, vol. 3707, pp. 474–488. Springer, Heidelberg (2005). doi:10.1007/11562948_35
11. Bertrand, N., Fournier, P.: Parameterized verification of many identical probabilistic timed processes. In: FSTTCS 2013, LIPIcs, vol. 24, pp. 501–513. Schloss Dagstuhl - Leibniz-Zentrum fuer Informatik (2013)
12. Boigelot, B., Herbreteau, F.: The power of hybrid acceleration. In: Ball, T., Jones, R.B. (eds.) CAV 2006. LNCS, vol. 4144, pp. 438–451. Springer, Heidelberg (2006). doi:10.1007/11817963_40
13. Boigelot, B., Legay, A., Wolper, P.: Iterating transducers in the large. In: Hunt, W.A., Somenzi, F. (eds.) CAV 2003. LNCS, vol. 2725, pp. 223–235. Springer, Heidelberg (2003). doi:10.1007/978-3-540-45069-6_24
14. Bonchi, F., Pous, D.: Checking NFA equivalence with bisimulations up to congruence. In: POPL 2013, pp. 457–468. ACM (2013)
15. Bonnet, R., Kiefer, S., Lin, A.W.: Analysis of probabilistic basic parallel processes. In: Muscholl, A. (ed.) FoSSaCS 2014. LNCS, vol. 8412, pp. 43–57. Springer, Heidelberg (2014). doi:10.1007/978-3-642-54830-7_3
16. Bouajjani, A., Habermehl, P., Rogalewicz, A., Vojnar, T.: Abstract regular (tree) model checking. STTT **14**(2), 167–191 (2012)
17. Cardelli, L., Csikász-Nagy, A.: The cell cycle switch computes approximate majority. Sci. Rep. **2**(656) (2012)
18. Chakarov, A., Sankaranarayanan, S.: Probabilistic program analysis with martingales. In: Sharygina, N., Veith, H. (eds.) CAV 2013. LNCS, vol. 8044, pp. 511–526. Springer, Heidelberg (2013). doi:10.1007/978-3-642-39799-8_34
19. Chakarov, A., Voronin, Y.-L., Sankaranarayanan, S.: Deductive proofs of almost sure persistence and recurrence properties. In: Chechik, M., Raskin, J.-F. (eds.) TACAS 2016. LNCS, vol. 9636, pp. 260–279. Springer, Heidelberg (2016). doi:10.1007/978-3-662-49674-9_15
20. Courcoubetis, C., Yannakakis, M.: Minimum and maximum delay problems in real-time systems. Form. Methods Syst. Des. **1**(4), 385–415 (1992)
21. Alfaro, L.: Temporal logics for the specification of performance and reliability. In: Reischuk, R., Morvan, M. (eds.) STACS 1997. LNCS, vol. 1200, pp. 165–176. Springer, Heidelberg (1997). doi:10.1007/BFb0023457
22. Esparza, J.: Parameterized verification of crowds of anonymous processes. Dependable Softw. Syst. Eng. **45**, 59–71 (2016)
23. Esparza, J., Gaiser, A., Kiefer, S.: Proving termination of probabilistic programs using patterns. In: Madhusudan, P., Seshia, S.A. (eds.) CAV 2012. LNCS, vol. 7358, pp. 123–138. Springer, Heidelberg (2012). doi:10.1007/978-3-642-31424-7_14
24. Ferrer Fioriti, L.M., Hermanns, H.: Probabilistic termination: soundness, completeness, and compositionality. In: POPL 2015, pp. 489–501. ACM (2015)
25. Fokkink, W.: Distributed Algorithms. MIT Press, Cambridge (2013)
26. Francez, N.: Fairness. Springer, New York (1986)
27. Grädel, E., Thomas, W., Wilke, T. (eds.): Automata, Logics, and Infinite Games: A Guide to Current Research. Lecture Notes in Computer Science, vol. 2500. Springer, Heidelberg (2002). [Outcome of a Dagstuhl seminar, February 2001]
28. Hart, S., Sharir, M., Pnueli, A.: Termination of probabilistic concurrent program. ACM Trans. Program. Lang. Syst. **5**(3), 356–380 (1983)

29. Herman, T.: Probabilistic self-stabilization. Inf. Process. Lett. **35**(2), 63–67 (1990)
30. Hoenicke, J., Olderog, E.-R., Podelski, A.: Fairness for dynamic control. In: Esparza, J., Majumdar, R. (eds.) TACAS 2010. LNCS, vol. 6015, pp. 251–265. Springer, Heidelberg (2010). doi:10.1007/978-3-642-12002-2_20
31. Israeli, A., Jalfon, M.: Token management schemes and random walks yield self-stabilizing mutual exclusion. In: PODC, pp. 119–131 (1990)
32. Kaminski, B.L., Katoen, J.-P., Matheja, C., Olmedo, F.: Weakest precondition reasoning for expected run-times of probabilistic programs. In: Thiemann, P. (ed.) ESOP 2016. LNCS, vol. 9632, pp. 364–389. Springer, Heidelberg (2016). doi:10.1007/978-3-662-49498-1_15
33. Kwiatkowska, M.Z.: Model checking for probability and time: from theory to practice. In: LICS, p. 351 (2003)
34. Lehmann, D., Rabin, M.: On the advantage of free choice: a symmetric and fully distributed solution to the dining philosophers problem (extended abstract). In: POPL, pp. 133–138 (1981)
35. Lieberman, E., Hauert, C., Nowak, M.A.: Evolutionary dynamics on graphs. Nature **433**(7023), 312–316 (2005)
36. Lin, A.W., Rümmer, P.: Liveness of randomised parameterised systems under arbitrary schedulers. In: Chaudhuri, S., Farzan, A. (eds.) CAV 2016. LNCS, vol. 9780, pp. 112–133. Springer, Heidelberg (2016). doi:10.1007/978-3-319-41540-6_7
37. Lin, A.W.: Accelerating tree-automatic relations. In: FSTTCS, pp. 313–324 (2012)
38. Lynch, N.A., Saias, I., Segala, R.: Proving time bounds for randomized distributed algorithms. In: PODC, pp. 314–323 (1994)
39. Monniaux, D.: An abstract analysis of the probabilistic termination of programs. In: Cousot, P. (ed.) SAS 2001. LNCS, vol. 2126, pp. 111–126. Springer, Heidelberg (2001). doi:10.1007/3-540-47764-0_7
40. Moran, P.A.P.: Random processes in genetics. Math. Proc. Camb. Philos. Soc. **54**(1), 60–71 (1958)
41. Neider, D., Jansen, N.: Regular model checking using solver technologies and automata learning. In: Brat, G., Rungta, N., Venet, A. (eds.) NFM 2013. LNCS, vol. 7871, pp. 16–31. Springer, Heidelberg (2013). doi:10.1007/978-3-642-38088-4_2
42. Nilsson, M.: Regular model checking. Ph.D. thesis, Uppsala Universitet (2005)
43. Olderog, E.-R., Apt, K.R.: Fairness in parallel programs: the transformational approach. ACM Trans. Program. Lang. Syst. **10**(3), 420–455 (1988)
44. Olderog, E.-R., Podelski, A.: Explicit fair scheduling for dynamic control. In: Dams, D., Hannemann, U., Steffen, M. (eds.) Concurrency, Compositionality, and Correctness. LNCS, vol. 5930, pp. 96–117. Springer, Heidelberg (2010). doi:10.1007/978-3-642-11512-7_7
45. Pnueli, A., Zuck, L.D.: Verification of multiprocess probabilistic protocols. Distrib. Comput. **1**(1), 53–72 (1986)
46. To, A.W.: Model checking infinite-state systems: generic and specific approaches. Ph.D. thesis, LFCS, School of Informatics, University of Edinburgh (2010)
47. To, A.W., Libkin, L.: Algorithmic metatheorems for decidable LTL model checking over infinite systems. In: Ong, L. (ed.) FoSSaCS 2010. LNCS, vol. 6014, pp. 221–236. Springer, Heidelberg (2010). doi:10.1007/978-3-642-12032-9_16
48. Vardi, M.Y.: Automatic verification of probabilistic concurrent finite-state programs. In: FOCS, pp. 327–338 (1985)

Forward Bisimulations for Nondeterministic Symbolic Finite Automata

Loris D'Antoni[1] and Margus Veanes[2(✉)]

[1] University of Wisconsin, Madison, USA
loris@cs.wisc.edu
[2] Microsoft Research, Redmond, USA
margus@microsoft.com

Abstract. Symbolic automata allow transitions to carry predicates over rich alphabet theories, such as linear arithmetic, and therefore extend classic automata to operate over infinite alphabets, such as the set of rational numbers. Existing automata algorithms rely on the alphabet being finite, and generalizing them to the symbolic setting is not a trivial task. In our earlier work, we proposed new techniques for minimizing deterministic symbolic automata and, in this paper, we generalize these techniques and study the foundational problem of computing forward bisimulations of nondeterministic symbolic finite automata. We propose three algorithms. Our first algorithm generalizes Moore's algorithm for minimizing deterministic automata. Our second algorithm generalizes Hopcroft's algorithm for minimizing deterministic automata. Since the first two algorithms have quadratic complexity in the number of states and transitions in the automaton, we propose a third algorithm that only requires a number of iterations that is linearithmic in the number of states and transitions at the cost of an exponential worst-case complexity in the number of distinct predicates appearing in the automaton. We implement our algorithms and evaluate them on 3,625 nondeterministic symbolic automata from real-world applications.

1 Introduction

Finite automata are used in many applications in software engineering, including software verification [8] and text processing [3]. Despite their many applications, finite automata suffer from a major drawback: in the most common forms they can only handle finite and small alphabets. Symbolic automata allow transitions to carry predicates over a specified alphabet theory, such as linear arithmetic, and therefore extend finite automata to operate over infinite alphabets, such as the set of rational numbers [13]. Symbolic automata are therefore more general and succinct than their finite-alphabet counterparts. Traditional algorithms for finite automata do not always generalize to the symbolic setting, making the design of algorithms for symbolic automata challenging. A notable example appears in [11]: while allowing finite state automata transitions to read multiple adjacent inputs does not add expressiveness, in the symbolic case this extension makes problems such as checking equivalence undecidable.

© Springer-Verlag GmbH Germany 2017
A. Legay and T. Margaria (Eds.): TACAS 2017, Part I, LNCS 10205, pp. 518–534, 2017.
DOI: 10.1007/978-3-662-54577-5_30

Symbolic finite automata (s-FA) are closed under Boolean operations and enjoy decidable equivalence if the alphabet theory forms a decidable Boolean algebra [13]. s-FAs have been used in combination with symbolic transducers to analyze complex string and list-manipulating programs [12,16]. In these applications it is crucial to keep the automata "small" and, in our previous work, we proposed algorithms for minimizing deterministic s-FAs [13]. However, no algorithms have been proposed to reduce the state space of nondeterministic s-FAs (s-NFAs). While computing minimal nondeterministic automata is a hard problem [18], several techniques have been proposed to produce "small enough" automata. These algorithms compute bisimulations over the state space and use them to collapse bisimilar states [2,26]. In this paper, we study the problem of computing forward bisimulations for s-NFAs.

While the problem of computing forward bisimulations has been studied for classic NFAs, it is not easy to adapt these algorithms to s-NFAs. Most efficient automata algorithms view the size of the alphabet as a constant and use data structures that are optimized for this view [2]. We propose three new algorithms for computing forward bisimulation of s-NFAs. First, we extend the classic Moore's algorithm for minimizing deterministic finite automata [25] and define an algorithm that operates in quadratic time. We then adapt our previous algorithm for minimizing deterministic s-FAs [13] to the problem of computing forward bisimulations and show that a natural implementation leads to a quadratic running time algorithm. Finally, we adapt a technique proposed by Abdulla et al. [2] to our setting, and propose a new symbolic data-structure that allows us to perform only a number of iterations that is linearithmic in the number of states and transitions. However, this improved state complexity comes at the cost of an exponential complexity in the number of distinct predicates appearing in the automaton. We compare the performance of the three algorithms on 3,625 s-FAs obtained from regular expressions and NFAs appearing in verification applications and show that, unlike for the case of deterministic s-FAs, no algorithm strictly outperforms the other ones.

Contributions. In summary, our contributions are:

- a formal study of the notion of forward bisimulations for s-FAs and their relation to state reduction for nondeterministic s-FAs (Sect. 3);
- three algorithms for computing forward bisimulations (Sects. 4, 5 and 6);
- an implementation and a comprehensive evaluation of the algorithms on 3,625 s-FAs obtained from real-world applications (Sect. 7).

2   Effective Boolean Algebras and s-NFAs

We define the notion of effective Boolean algebra and symbolic finite automata. An *effective Boolean algebra* $\mathcal{A}$ has components $(U, \Psi, \llbracket\_\rrbracket, \bot, \top, \vee, \wedge, \neg)$. U is a set called the *universe*. Ψ is a set of *predicates* closed under the Boolean connectives and $\bot, \top \in \Psi$. The *denotation function* $\llbracket\_\rrbracket : \Psi \to 2^U$ is such that, $\llbracket\bot\rrbracket = \emptyset$, $\llbracket\top\rrbracket = U$, for all $\varphi, \psi \in \Psi$, $\llbracket\varphi \vee \psi\rrbracket = \llbracket\varphi\rrbracket \cup \llbracket\psi\rrbracket$, $\llbracket\varphi \wedge \psi\rrbracket = \llbracket\varphi\rrbracket \cap \llbracket\psi\rrbracket$, and

$[\![\neg\varphi]\!] = U \setminus [\![\varphi]\!]$. For $\varphi \in \Psi$, we write $\mathbf{SAT}(\varphi)$ when $[\![\varphi]\!] \neq \emptyset$ and say that φ is *satisfiable*. $\mathcal{A}$ is *decidable* if $\mathbf{SAT}$ is decidable.

Intuitively, such an algebra is represented programmatically as an API with corresponding methods implementing the Boolean operations and the denotation function. We are primarily going to use the following two effective Boolean algebras in the examples, but the techniques in the paper are fully generic.

$2^{\mathbf{bv}k}$ is the powerset algebra whose domain is the finite set $\mathrm{BV}k$, for some $k > 0$, consisting of all non-negative integers smaller than 2^k—i.e., all k-bit bit-vectors. A predicate is represented by a Binary Decision Diagram (BDD) of depth k.[1] Boolean operations correspond directly to BDD operations and $\bot$ is the BDD representing the empty set. The denotation $[\![\beta]\!]$ of a BDD β is the set of all integers n such that a binary representation of n corresponds to a solution of β.

$\mathbf{int}[k]$ is an algebra for small finite alphabets of the form $\Sigma = \{0, \dots, 32k - 1\}$. A predicate φ is an array of k unsigned 32-bit integers, $\varphi = [a_1, \dots, a_k]$, and for all $i \in \Sigma$: $i \in [\![\varphi]\!]$ iff in the integer $a_{i/32+1}$ the bit in position i mod 32 is 1. Boolean operations can be performed efficiently using bit-vector operations. For example, the conjunction $[a_1, \dots, a_k] \wedge [b_1, \dots, b_k]$ corresponds to $[a_1 \& b_1, \dots, a_k \& b_k]$, where $\&$ is the bit-wise and of two integers.

We can now define symbolic finite automata. Intuitively, a symbolic finite automaton is a finite automaton over a symbolic alphabet, where edge labels are replaced by predicates. In order to preserve the classical Boolean closure operations (intersection, complement, and union) over languages, the predicates must also form a Boolean algebra. Since the core topic of the paper is about *nondeterministic* automata we adopt the convention often used in studies of NFAs [10, 22, 28] that an automaton has a *set* of initial states rather than a single initial state as used in other literature on automata theory [21].

Definition 1. A *symbolic nondeterministic finite automaton (s-NFA)* M is a tuple $(\mathcal{A}, Q, I, F, \Delta)$ where $\mathcal{A}$ is an effective Boolean algebra, called the *alphabet*, Q is a finite set of *states*, $I \subseteq Q$ is the set of *initial states*, $F \subseteq Q$ is the set of *final states*, and $\Delta \subseteq Q \times \Psi_{\mathcal{A}} \times Q$ is a finite set of *moves* or *transitions*.

Elements of $U_{\mathcal{A}}$ are called *characters* and finite sequences of characters, elements of $U_{\mathcal{A}}^*$, are called *words*; ϵ denotes the empty word. A move $\rho = (p, \varphi, q) \in \Delta$ is also denoted by $p \xrightarrow{\varphi}_M q$ (or $p \xrightarrow{\varphi} q$ when M is clear from the context), where p is the *source* state, q is the *target* state, and φ is the *guard* or *predicate* of the move. Given a character $a \in U_{\mathcal{A}}$, an *a-move* of M is a tuple (p, a, q) such that $p \xrightarrow{\varphi}_M q$ and $a \in [\![\varphi]\!]$, also denoted $p \xrightarrow{a}_M q$ (or $p \xrightarrow{a} q$ when M is clear). In the following let $M = (\mathcal{A}, Q, I, F, \Delta)$ be an s-NFA.

Definition 2. Given a state $p \in Q$, the *(right) language of p in M*, denoted $\mathscr{L}(p, M)$, is the set of all $w = [a_i]_{i=1}^k \in U_{\mathcal{A}}^*$ such that, either $w = \epsilon$ and $p \in F$, or

---

[1] Let the variable order of the BDD be the reverse bit order of the binary representation of a number, i.e., the most significant bit has the lowest ordinal, etc.

$w \neq \epsilon$ and there exist $p_{i-1} \xrightarrow{a_i}_M p_i$ for $1 \leq i \leq k$, such that $p_0 = p$, and $p_k \in F$. The *language of* M is $\mathscr{L}(M) \stackrel{\text{def}}{=} \bigcup_{q \in I} \mathscr{L}(q, M)$. Two states p and q of M are *indistinguishable* if $\mathscr{L}(p, M) = \mathscr{L}(q, M)$. Two s-NFAs M and N are *equivalent* if $\mathscr{L}(M) = \mathscr{L}(N)$.

The following terminology is used to characterize various key properties of M. A state $p \in Q$ is called *complete* if for all $a \in U_A$ there exists an a-move from p, p is *partial* otherwise. A move is *feasible* if its guard is satisfiable.

- M is *deterministic*: $|I| = 1$ and whenever $p \xrightarrow{a} q$ and $p \xrightarrow{a} q'$ then $q = q'$.
- M is *complete*: all states of M are complete; M is *partial*, otherwise.
- M is *clean*: all moves of M are feasible.
- M is *normalized*: for all $(p, \varphi, q), (p, \psi, q) \in \Delta$: $\varphi = \psi$.
- M is *minimal*: there exists no equivalent s-NFA with fewer states.

In the following, we always assume that M is clean. If E is an equivalence relation over Q, then, for $q \in Q$, $q_{/E}$ denotes the E-equivalence class containing q, for $X \subseteq Q$, $X_{/E}$ denotes $\{q_{/E} \mid q \in X\}$. The E-*quotient* of M is the s-NFA

$$M_{/E} \stackrel{\text{def}}{=} (A, Q_{/E}, I_{/E}, F_{/E}, \{(p_{/E}, \varphi, q_{/E}) \mid (p, \varphi, q) \in \Delta\})$$

3   Forward Bisimulations

Here we adapt the notion of forward bisimulation to s-NFAs. Below, consider a fixed s-NFA $M = (A, Q, I, F, \Delta)$.

Definition 3. Let $E \subseteq Q \times Q$ be an equivalence relation. E is a *forward bisimulation on* M when, for all $(p, q) \in E$, if $p \in F$ then $q \in F$, and, for all $a \in U_A$ and $p' \in Q$, if $p \xrightarrow{a} p'$ then there exists $q' \in p'_{/E}$ such that $q \xrightarrow{a} q'$.

If E is a forward bisimulation on M then the quotient $M_{/E}$ preserves the language of all states in M, as stated formally by Theorem 1, as a generalization of the same property known in the classical case when the alphabet is finite.

Theorem 1. *Let E be a forward bisimulation on M. Then, for all states q of M, $\mathscr{L}(q, M) = \mathscr{L}(q_{/E}, M_{/E})$.*

Proof. We prove the statement $\phi(w)$ by induction over $|w|$ for $w \in U_A^*$:

$$\phi(w) : \forall p \in Q_M(w \in \mathscr{L}(p, M) \Leftrightarrow w \in \mathscr{L}(p_{/E}, M_{/E}))$$

The base case $|w| = 0$ follows from the property of the forward bisimulation E on M that if $p \in F$ then $p_{/E} \subseteq F$ and by definition of E-quotient of M that its set of final states is $F_{/E}$.

For the induction case assume that $\phi(w)$ holds as the IH. Let $a \in U_A$. We prove $\phi(a \cdot w)$. Fix $p \in Q_M$.

$$
\begin{aligned}
a \cdot w \in \mathscr{L}(p, M) &\Leftrightarrow \exists q \in Q \text{ such that } (p \xrightarrow{a}_M q, \ w \in \mathscr{L}(q, M)) \\
&\overset{\text{by IH}}{\Leftrightarrow} \exists q \in Q \text{ such that } (p \xrightarrow{a}_M q, \ w \in \mathscr{L}(q_{/E}, M_{/E})) \\
&\overset{(*)}{\Leftrightarrow} \exists q \in Q \text{ such that } (p_{/E} \xrightarrow{a}_{M_{/E}} q_{/E}, \ w \in \mathscr{L}(q_{/E}, M_{/E})) \\
&\Leftrightarrow a \cdot w \in \mathscr{L}(p_{/E}, M_{/E})
\end{aligned}
$$

Proof of $(*)$:

$(\Rightarrow)$: If $p \xrightarrow{a}_M q$ then there is $(p, \varphi, q) \in \Delta_M$ such that $a \in [\![\varphi]\!]$. By definition of $M_{/E}$, there is $(p_{/E}, \varphi, q_{/E}) \in \Delta_{M_{/E}}$, hence $p_{/E} \xrightarrow{a}_{M_{/E}} q_{/E}$.

$(\Leftarrow)$: Fix a q such that $p_{/E} \xrightarrow{a}_{M_{/E}} q_{/E}$ and $w \in \mathscr{L}(q_{/E}, M_{/E})$. By definition of $\Delta_{M_{/E}}$ there exists a transition (p_1, α, q_1) in Δ_M where $a \in [\![\alpha]\!]$ and $p_{1/E} = p_{/E}$ and $q_{1/E} = q_{/E}$, so $p_1 \xrightarrow{a}_M q_1$. By the assumption that E is a bisimulation on M it follows that there exists $q' \in q_{1/E}$ such that $p \xrightarrow{a}_M q'$. But $q_{1/E} = q_{/E}$, so $q'_{/E} = q_{/E}$ and therefore $\exists q' \in Q$ such that $(p \xrightarrow{a}_M q', \ w \in \mathscr{L}(q'_{/E}, M_{/E}))$. $\boxtimes$

Corollary 1. *Let E be a forward bisimulation on M. Then $\mathscr{L}(M) = \mathscr{L}(M_{/E})$.*

For a deterministic s-NFA M one can efficiently compute the *coarsest* forward bisimulation relation $\equiv_M$ over Q_M defined by indistinguishability of states, in order to construct $M_{/\equiv_M}$ as the minimal canonical (up to equivalence of predicates) deterministic s-NFA that is equivalent to M [13, Theorem 2]. The nondeterministic case is much more difficult because there exists, in general, no canonical minimal NFA [22] for a given regular language.

Our aim in this paper is to study algorithms for computing forward bisimulations for s-NFAs. Once a forward bisimulation E has been computed for an s-NFA M, it can be applied, according to Corollary 1, to build the equivalent E-quotient $M_{/E}$ with reduced number of states, $M_{/E}$ need not be minimal though.

4   Symbolic Partition Refinement

We start by presenting the high-level idea of symbolic partition refinement for forward bisimulations as an abstract algorithm. Let the given s-NFA be $M = (A, Q, I, F, \Delta)$. It is convenient to view Δ, without loss of generality, as a function from $Q \times Q$ to Ψ_A, and we also lift the definition over its second argument to subsets $S \subseteq Q$ of states,

$$
\Delta(p, q) \overset{\text{def}}{=} \bigvee_{(p, \varphi, q) \in \Delta} \varphi, \qquad \Delta(p, S) \overset{\text{def}}{=} \bigvee_{q \in S} \Delta(p, q),
$$

where the predicates are effectively constructed using $\vee_A$. Essentially, this view of Δ corresponds to M being normalized, where all pairs (p, q) such that there is no transition from p to q have $\Delta(p, q) = \bigvee \emptyset \overset{\text{def}}{=} \bot$, else the guard of the transition from p to q is $\Delta(p, q)$. The predicate $\Delta(p, S)$ denotes the set of all those characters that transition from p to some state in S.

M is assumed to be nontrivial, so that both F and $Q \backslash F$ are nonempty. We construct partitions $\mathcal{P}_i$ of Q such that $\mathcal{P}_i$ is a *refinement* of $\mathcal{P}_{i-1}$ for $i \geq 1$, i.e., each block in $\mathcal{P}_i$ is a subset of some block in $\mathcal{P}_{i-1}$. Initially let

$$\mathcal{P}_0 = \{Q\}, \ \mathcal{P}_1 = \{F, Q \backslash F\}.$$

For a partition $\mathcal{P}$ of Q define $\sim_{\mathcal{P}}$ as the following equivalence relation over Q:

$$p \sim_{\mathcal{P}} q \overset{\text{def}}{=} \exists B \in \mathcal{P} \text{ such that } (p, q \in B).$$

Let $\sim_i \overset{\text{def}}{=} \sim_{\mathcal{P}_i}$. The partition $\mathcal{P}_i$ is refined until $\mathcal{P}_{n+1} = \mathcal{P}_n$ for some $n \geq 1$. Each such refinement step maintains the invariant (1) for $i \geq 1$ and $p, q \in Q$:[2]

$$p \sim_{i+1} q \iff p \sim_i q \text{ and for all } B \in \mathcal{P}_i : [\![\Delta(p, B)]\!] = [\![\Delta(q, B)]\!] \tag{1}$$

Under the assumption that $\mathcal{A}$ is decidable, $[\![\Delta(p, B)]\!] = [\![\Delta(q, B)]\!]$ can be decided by checking that $\Delta(p, B) \not\Leftrightarrow \Delta(q, B)$ is *unsatisfiable*.[3] So $\mathcal{P}_{i+1}$ can be computed effectively from $\mathcal{P}_i$ and iterating this step provides an abstract algorithm for computing the fixpoint $\sim_M \overset{\text{def}}{=} \sim_{\mathcal{P}_n}$ such that $\mathcal{P}_{n+1} = \mathcal{P}_n$.

Theorem 2. $\sim_M$ *is the coarsest forward bisimulation on* M.

Proof. Let $\sim \ = \ \sim_M$. We show first that $\sim$ is a forward bisimulation on M by way of contradiction. Suppose that $\sim$ is not a forward bisimulation on M. Since $p \sim_1 q$ iff $p, q \in F$ or $p, q \notin F$, and $\sim$ refines $\sim_1$, the condition that for $p \sim q$ if $p \in F$ then $q \in F$ holds. Therefore, there must exists $p \sim q$ such that for some $a \in U_{\mathcal{A}}$ and $p' \in Q$ we have $p \overset{a}{\to} p'$, while for all q' such that $q \overset{a}{\to} q'$ we have $q' \not\sim p'$. Hence there is $B \in \mathcal{P}_i$ for some $i \geq 1$, namely $B = p'_{/\sim}$, such that $a \in [\![\Delta(p, B)]\!]$ but $a \notin [\![\Delta(q, B)]\!]$, so $[\![\Delta(p, B)]\!] \neq [\![\Delta(q, B)]\!]$. But then $p \not\sim_{i+1} q$, contradicting that $p \sim q$. So $\sim$ is a forward bisimulation on M.

Next, consider any bisimulation $\simeq$ on M. We show that $\simeq \ \subseteq \ \sim_i$ for all $i \geq 1$.

Base case. Suppose $p \simeq q$. If $p \in F$ then $q \in F$, by Definition 3, and, since $\simeq$ is an equivalence relation, symmetrically, if $p \notin F$ then $q \notin F$. So $p \sim_1 q$.

Induction case. Assume as the IH that $\simeq \ \subseteq \ \sim_i$. We prove that $\simeq \ \subseteq \ \sim_{i+1}$. Suppose $p \simeq q$. We show that $p \sim_{i+1} q$. By using the IH, we have that $p \sim_i q$. By using Eq. (1), we need to show that for all $B \in \mathcal{P}_i$, $[\![\Delta(p, B)]\!] = [\![\Delta(q, B)]\!]$. By way of contradiction, suppose there exists $B \in \mathcal{P}_i$ such that $[\![\Delta(p, B)]\!] \neq [\![\Delta(q, B)]\!]$. Then, w.l.o.g., there exists $a \in U_{\mathcal{A}}$ and $p' \in B$ such that $p \overset{a}{\to} p'$, and for all $q' \in Q$ if $q \overset{a}{\to} q'$ then $q' \notin B$, i.e., $q' \not\sim_i p'$, and by using the contrapositive of the IH ($\sim_i \ \subseteq \ \not\simeq$) we have $q' \not\simeq p'$. But then $p \overset{a}{\to} p'$ while there is no $q' \in p'_{/\simeq}$ such that $q \overset{a}{\to} q'$, contradicting, by Definition 3, that $p \simeq q$. Thus, for all $B \in \mathcal{P}_i$, $[\![\Delta(p, B)]\!] = [\![\Delta(q, B)]\!]$. So $p \sim_{i+1} q$.

It follows that $\simeq \ \subseteq \ \sim$ which proves that $\sim$ is coarsest. $\boxtimes$

---

[2] One can view one iteration of refinement from $\mathcal{P}_i$ to $\mathcal{P}_{i+1}$ as computing $\not\sim_{i+1}$ from $\not\sim_i$, which is often how Moore's algorithm is presented for DFAs.

[3] $\varphi \Leftrightarrow \psi$ is defined as $((\varphi \lor \neg \psi) \land (\neg \varphi \lor \psi))$ and $\varphi \not\Leftrightarrow \psi$ stands for $\neg(\varphi \Leftrightarrow \psi)$.

```
1  SimpleBisimSFA(M = (A, Q, I, F, Δ)) ≝
2    P := {F, Q\F}  //initial partition
3    W := {F, Q\F}  //workset
4    while (W ≠ ∅)
5      pull R from W  //choose a splitter candidate
6      while (exists B in P and q, r in B such that SAT(Δ(q, R) ∧ ¬Δ(r, R)))
7        let D = {p ∈ B | SAT(Δ(p, R) ∧ Δ(q, R) ∧ ¬Δ(r, R))}
8        P := (P \ {B}) ∪ {D, B\D}  //refine the partition
9        W := (W\{B}) ∪ {D, B\D}  //update the workset
10   return ∼P
```

```
1  GreedyBisimSFA(M = (A, Q, I, F, Δ)) ≝
2    P := {F, Q\F}  //initial partition
3    W := {if (|F| ≤ |Q\F|) then F else Q\F}  //workset
4    SUPER(F) := Q; SUPER(Q\F) := Q  //SUPER(B) is the superblock of B
5    while (W ≠ ∅)
6      pull R from W  //choose a splitter candidate
7      let R' = SUPER(R)\R
8      while (exists B in P and q, r in B such that
9        SAT(Δ(q, R) ∧ ¬Δ(r, R)) or SAT(Δ(q, R') ∧ ¬Δ(r, R')))
10       let D = if SAT(Δ(q, R) ∧ ¬Δ(r, R))
11              then {p ∈ B | SAT(Δ(p, R) ∧ Δ(q, R) ∧ ¬Δ(r, R))}
12              else {p ∈ B | SAT(Δ(p, R') ∧ Δ(q, R') ∧ ¬Δ(r, R'))}
13       P := (P\{B}) ∪ {D, B\D}  //refine P
14       if (B ∈ W) then  //add both parts into the workset
15         W := (W\{B}) ∪ {D, B\D}
16         SUPER(D) := SUPER(B);  //SUPER(B) remains the superblock of B parts
17         SUPER(B\D) := SUPER(B)
18       else  //add only the smaller of the two parts into the workset
19         W := W ∪ {if (|D| ≤ |B\D|) then D else B\D}
20         SUPER(D) := B;  //B becomes the superblock of both parts
21         SUPER(B\D) := B
22   return ∼P
```

Fig. 1. Simple and greedy algorithms for computing $\sim_M$.

A simple algorithm for computing $\sim_M$ is shown in Fig. 1. It differs from the abstract algorithm in that the partition is refined in smaller increments, rather than in large parallel refinement steps corresponding to Eq. (1). The order of such steps does not matter as long as progress is made at each step.

Theorem 3. *SimpleBisimSFA(M) computes* $\sim_M$.

Proof (outline). The key observation is the following: if $[\![\Delta(q, B)]\!] \neq [\![\Delta(r, B)]\!]$ holds for some $q \sim_P r$ and $B \in P$ and B has been split into $\{B_i\}_{i=1}^n$ before it has been chosen from the workset then $[\![\Delta(q, B_i)]\!] \neq [\![\Delta(r, B_i)]\!]$ for some i, or else $[\![\Delta(q, B)]\!] = \bigcup_i [\![\Delta(q, B_i)]\!] = \bigcup_i [\![\Delta(r, B_i)]\!] = [\![\Delta(r, B)]\!]$. In other words, even if B has not yet been used as a splitter, the fact that $q \nsim_M r$ holds will be detected at some later point using one of the blocks B_i because all subblocks are added to the workset W.

The splitting of B into D and $B\backslash D$ requires some explanation. First note that $q \in D$ and $r \in B\backslash D$, so both new blocks are nonempty. Second, pick any $p \in D$ and any $s \in B\backslash D$. We need to show that $[\![\Delta(p, R)]\!] \neq [\![\Delta(s, R)]\!]$ to justify the split. We know that $\mathbf{SAT}(\Delta(p, R) \wedge \Delta(q, R) \wedge \neg\Delta(r, R))$ holds. Thus, if $\Delta(p, R)$ were equivalent to $\Delta(s, R)$ then $\mathbf{SAT}(\Delta(s, R) \wedge \Delta(q, R) \wedge \neg\Delta(r, R))$ would also hold, contradicting that $s \notin D$.

It follows that upon termination, when $W = \emptyset$, $\mathcal{P}$ cannot be refined further and thus $\sim_{\mathcal{P}} = \sim_M$.   ⊠

Complexity. If the complexity of checking satisfiability of predicates of size ℓ is $f(\ell)$, then *SimpleBisimSFA(M)* has complexity $\mathcal{O}(mnf(n\ell))$, where m is the number of transitions in the input s-FA, n is the number of states, and ℓ is the size of the largest predicate in the input s-FA.[4] Since we check satisfiability by taking the union of all predicates in multiple transition (e.g., $\Delta(q, R)$), satisfiability checks are performed on predicates of size $\mathcal{O}(n\ell)$.

5   Greedy Symbolic Partition Refinement

We can improve the simple algorithm by incorporating Hoprcoft's "keep the smaller half" partition refinement strategy [19]. This strategy is also reused in Paige-Tarjan's relational coarsest partition algorithm [26]. Hopcroft's strategy is generalized to symbolic alphabets in [13] by incorporating the idea of using symmetric differences of character predicates during partition refinement, instead of single characters, as illustrated also in the simple algorithm. Here we further generalize the algorithm from [13] to s-NFAs. The algorithm can also be seen as a generalization of Paige-Tarjan's relational coarsest partition algorithm from computing the coarsest forward bisimulation of an NFA to that of an s-NFA.

The greedy algorithm is shown in Fig. 1. The computation of partition $\mathcal{P}$ is altered in such a way that whenever a block B (that is no longer, or never was, in the workset W) is split into D and $B\backslash D$, only the smaller of the two halves is added to the workset. In order to preserve correctness, the original $\mathbf{SAT}$ condition involving R must be augmented with a corresponding condition involving $R' = \text{SUPER}(R)\backslash R$, where $\text{SUPER}(R)$ is the block that contained R before splitting. This means that the other half will also participate in the splitting process. The gain is how efficiently the information computed for a block is reused in the computation. The core difference to the deterministic case [13] is that if M is deterministic then the use of R' is redundant, i.e., the $\mathbf{SAT}$ check holds for R iff it holds for $\text{SUPER}(R)\backslash R$, so the superblock mapping is not needed.

---

[4] This bound is obtained using the same amortized complexity argument used for Moore's minimization algorithm [25].

Example 1. This example illustrates why the additional **SAT**-checks on SUPER(R)\$R$ are needed in the greedy algorithm, when M is nondeterministic. Let M be the NFA in Fig. 2, where $U_A = \{a\}$. Then initially $W = \{\{f\}\}$ and $\mathcal{P} = \{\{q, r\}, \{f\}\}$. So, in the first itera-tion $R = \{f\}$. Let $R' = \text{SUPER}(R)\backslash R = \{q, r\}$.

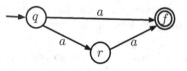

Fig. 2. Sample NFA.

The only candidate block for B is $\{q, r\}$. **SAT**($\Delta(q, R) \wedge \neg\Delta(r, R)$) fails because $[\![\Delta(q, R)]\!] = [\![\Delta(r, R)]\!] = \{a\}$, while $[\![\Delta(q, R')]\!] = \{a\}$ and $[\![\Delta(r, R')]\!] = \emptyset$. Thus, if **SAT**($\Delta(q, R') \wedge \neg\Delta(r, R')$) was omitted then the algorithm would return $\sim\{\{q,r\},\{f\}\}$ but $q \nsim_M r$. ⊠

Theorem 4. *GreedyBisimSFA(M) computes $\sim_M$.*

Proof (outline). The justification behind splitting of B into D and $B\backslash D$ based on R or SUPER(R)\R is analogous to the argument provided in the proof of Theorem 3. We show that no splits are missed due to the additional optimization.

In the case a block B in W has not yet been used as a splitter, its original superblock $B^s = \text{SUPER}(B)$ must be kept as the superblock of the new sub-blocks D and $B\backslash D$. This implies that blocks $B^s\backslash D$ and $B^s\backslash(B\backslash D)$ serve as the replacement candidate splitters for the block $B^s\backslash B$. In the case a block B is not in W, its use as a splitter is already covered, and it serves as the superblock for its subblocks D and $B\backslash D$, i.e., SUPER(D) = B and SUPER($B\backslash D$) = B, which implies that SUPER(D)\$D$ = $B\backslash D$ and SUPER($B\backslash D$)\$(B\backslash D)$ = D. ⊠

Complexity. If the complexity of checking satisfiability of predicates of size ℓ is $f(\ell)$, the naive implementation of *GreedyBisimSFA(M)* presented in Fig. 1, which explicitly computes $\Delta(r, \text{SUPER}(R)\backslash R)$, has complexity $\mathcal{O}(mnf(n\ell))$, with m as the number of transitions in the input s-FA and n as the number of states. Even though only the small block is added to added to W after a split, both blocks are eventually visited. Therefore, we still have a quadratic complexity as n and m are multiplied. In the next section, we discuss a different data structure that yields a different complexity for the greedy algorithm in Fig. 1.

6   Counting Symbolic Partition Refinement

We want to avoid explicit computation of $\Delta(p, \text{SUPER}(R)\backslash R)$ in the greedy algo-rithm. We investigate a method that can reuse the computation performed for SUPER(R) and R in order to calculate $\Delta(p, \text{SUPER}(R)\backslash R)$. We consider a *sym-bolic bag* datastructure that, by using predicates in Ψ_A, provides a finite partition for U_A and maps each part in the partition into a natural number. A (symbolic) bag σ denotes a function $[\![\sigma]\!]$ from U_A to $\mathbb{N}$ that has a *finite* range. All elements that map to the same number effectively define a part or block of the partition. For $p \in Q$ and $S \subseteq Q$ let *Bag(p, S)* be a bag such that, for all $a \in U_A$,

$$[\![Bag(p, S)]\!](a) = |\{q \in S \mid p \xrightarrow{a} q\}|.$$

In other words, in addition to encoding if a character a can reach S from p, the bag also encodes, to *how many different target states*. Let Set be a function that transforms bags σ to predicates in $\Psi_{\mathcal{A}}$ such that

$$[\![Set(\sigma)]\!] = \{a \in U_{\mathcal{A}} \mid [\![\sigma]\!](a) > 0\}$$

In particular $[\![Set(Bag(p, S))]\!] = [\![\Delta(p, S)]\!]$. A bag can be implemented effectively in several ways and we defer the discussion of such choices to below. We assume that there is an effective difference operation $\sigma \doteq \tau$ over bags such that, for all $a \in U_{\mathcal{A}}$, given $m \doteq n \overset{\text{def}}{=} \max(0, m - n)$, $[\![\sigma \doteq \tau]\!](a) = [\![\sigma]\!](a) \doteq [\![\tau]\!](a)$. So

$$[\![\Delta(p, \textsc{super}(R)\backslash R)]\!] = [\![Set(Bag(p, \textsc{super}(R)) \doteq Bag(p, R))]\!].$$

This shows that each $\Delta(p, X)$ in the greedy algorithm can be represented using a symbolic bag. The potential advantage is, provided that we can efficiently implement the difference and the Set operations, that in the computation of $Bag(p, \textsc{super}(R)) \doteq Bag(p, R)$ we can reuse the prior computations of $Bag(p, \textsc{super}(R))$ and $Bag(p, R)$, and therefore do not need $\textsc{super}(R)\backslash R$.

We call the instance of the greedy algorithm that uses symbolic bags, the *counting* algorithm or *CountingBisimSFA*. The counting algorithm is a generalization of the bisimulation based minimization algorithm of NFAs [2] from using algebraic decision diagrams (ADDs) [4] and binary decision diagrams (BDDs) [9] for representing multisets ands sets of characters, to symbolic bags and predicates. If the size of the alphabet is $k = 2^p$ then p is the depth or the number of bits required in the ADDs. An open problem for symbolic bags is to maintain an equally efficient data structure. Although theoretically p is bounded by the number of predicates in the s-NFA, the actual computation of those bits and their relationship to the predicates of the s-NFA requires that the s-NFA is first transformed into an NFA. However, the NFA transformation has complexity $O(2^p)$. This factor is also reflected in the complexity of the algorithm in [2] that is $O(km \log n)$ with k, m and n as above.

Implementation. We define symbolic bags over $\mathcal{A}$, denoted $Bag_{\mathcal{A}}$, as the least set of expressions that satisfies the following conditions.

- If $n \in \mathbb{N}$ then $\boldsymbol{nat}(n) \in Bag_{\mathcal{A}}$.
- If $\varphi \in \Psi_{\mathcal{A}}$ and $\sigma, \tau \in Bag_{\mathcal{A}}$ then $\boldsymbol{ite}(\varphi, \sigma, \tau) \in Bag_{\mathcal{A}}$.

The denotation of a bag σ is a function $[\![\sigma]\!] : U_{\mathcal{A}} \to \mathbb{N}$ such that, for all $a \in U_{\mathcal{A}}$,

$$[\![\boldsymbol{nat}(n)]\!](a) \overset{\text{def}}{=} n, \quad [\![\boldsymbol{ite}(\varphi, \sigma, \tau)]\!](a) \overset{\text{def}}{=} \begin{cases} [\![\sigma]\!](a), \text{ if } a \in [\![\varphi]\!]; \\ [\![\tau]\!](a), \text{ otherwise.} \end{cases}$$

We say that a symbolic bag is *clean* if all paths from the root to any of its leaves is satisfiable. In our operations over bags we maintain cleanness. An operator $\diamond$, such as $+$ or $\doteq$, over $\mathbb{N}$ is lifted to bags as follows.

$$\sigma \diamond \tau \stackrel{\text{def}}{=} \sigma \diamond_\top \tau$$

$$\boldsymbol{nat}(m) \diamond_\gamma \boldsymbol{nat}(n) \stackrel{\text{def}}{=} \boldsymbol{nat}(m \diamond n)$$

$$\boldsymbol{ite}(\varphi, \sigma, \tau) \diamond_\gamma \rho \stackrel{\text{def}}{=} \boldsymbol{ite}(\varphi, \sigma \diamond_{\gamma \wedge \varphi} \rho, \tau \diamond_{\gamma \wedge \neg \varphi} \rho)$$

$$\boldsymbol{nat}(n) \diamond_\gamma \boldsymbol{ite}(\varphi, \sigma, \tau) \stackrel{\text{def}}{=} \begin{cases} \boldsymbol{nat}(n) \diamond_\gamma \tau, & \text{if not } \mathbf{SAT}(\gamma \wedge \varphi); \\ \boldsymbol{nat}(n) \diamond_\gamma \sigma, & \text{else if not } \mathbf{SAT}(\gamma \wedge \neg \varphi); \\ \boldsymbol{ite}(\varphi, \boldsymbol{nat}(n) \diamond_{\gamma \wedge \varphi} \sigma, \boldsymbol{nat}(n) \diamond_{\gamma \wedge \neg \varphi} \tau), & \text{otherwise.} \end{cases}$$

Cleaning of the result is done incrementally during construction by passing the context condition γ with the operator $\diamond_\gamma$. Observe that if $\alpha \wedge \beta$ is unsatisfiable (i.e., $[\![\alpha]\!] \cap [\![\beta]\!] = \emptyset$) then α implies $\neg\beta$ (i.e., $[\![\alpha]\!] \subseteq [\![\neg\beta]\!]$). For all $p, q \in Q$ let

$$Bag(p, q) \stackrel{\text{def}}{=} \begin{cases} \boldsymbol{ite}(\Delta(p, q), \boldsymbol{nat}(1), \boldsymbol{nat}(0)), & \text{if } \Delta(p, q) \neq \bot; \\ \boldsymbol{nat}(0), & \text{otherwise.} \end{cases}$$

Let $Bag(p, R) \stackrel{\text{def}}{=} \sum_{q \in R} Bag(p, q)$. One additional simplification that is performed is that if $[\![\sigma]\!] = [\![\tau]\!]$ then the expression $\boldsymbol{ite}(\varphi, \sigma, \tau)$ is simplified to σ. The $Set(\sigma)$ operation replaces each non-zero leaf in σ with $\top$ and each zero leaf in σ with $\bot$, assuming, w.l.o.g., that $\mathcal{A}$ has the corresponding operator $\boldsymbol{ite}(\varphi, \psi, \gamma)$ with the expected semantics that $[\![\boldsymbol{ite}(\varphi, \psi, \gamma)]\!] = [\![(\varphi \wedge \psi) \vee (\neg\varphi \wedge \gamma)]\!]$.

Example 2. Consider an s-NFA M with alphabet $\mathcal{A}$ such that $U_\mathcal{A} = \mathbb{N}$ that has the following transitions from a given state p: $\{p \xrightarrow{\phi_2} q_2, p \xrightarrow{\phi_3} q_3, p \xrightarrow{\phi_6} q_6\}$ where ϕ_k for $k \geq 1$ is a predicate such that $n \in [\![\phi_k]\!]$ iff n is divisible by k. In the following $\boldsymbol{ite}(\varphi, l, r)$ is depicted with φ as the node, l as the left subtree, and r as the right subtree. Let $R = \{q_2, q_3, q_6\}$. Then $Bag(p, R) = Bag(p, q_2) + Bag(p, q_3) + Bag(p, q_6)$ is computed as follows:

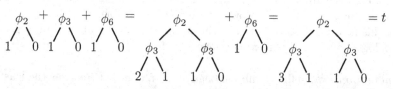

In the second addition, all the branch conditions of the leaves of the first tree, other than the first branch, become unsatisfiable with the condition ϕ_6. Only the very first branch condition $\phi_2 \wedge \phi_3$ is consistent (in this case equivalent) with ϕ_6 while $\boldsymbol{nat}(0)$ is the identity. Hence $\boldsymbol{nat}(3) = \boldsymbol{nat}(2) + \boldsymbol{nat}(1)$ in t. ⊠

Complexity. In this implementation, $\Delta(r, B)$ is represented by $Set(Bag(r, B))$, and $\Delta(r, \text{SUPER}(R) \backslash R)$ can be computed from $Bag(r, \text{SUPER}(R))$ and $Bag(r, R)$ without having to iterate over the automaton transitions. However, in the worst case, at each step in the algorithm, the Bag data structure can have exponential size in p, the number of distinct predicates in the s-FA. Using a similar amortized complexity argument to that used by Hopcroft's algorithm for minimizing DFAs [20], we have that, if we ignore the cost of computing the bag data structure, the algorithm has complexity $\mathcal{O}(m \log n)$. In summary, if the complexity of checking satisfiability of predicates of size ℓ is $f(\ell)$, the counting implementation of $GreedyBisimSFA(M)$ presented in Fig. 1 has complexity $\mathcal{O}(2^p m \log n f(n\ell))$, where m is the number of transitions in the input s-FA and n is the number of states, and p is the number of distinct predicates in the automaton. Concretely, while this implementation helps reducing the number of iterations over the automaton transitions, it suffers from an extra cost that is a function of the alphabet complexity and of the predicates appearing in the automaton. Notice, that in the case of finite alphabets 2^p is exactly the size of the alphabet and this problem does not exist [2]. This is another remarkable case of how adapting classic algorithms to the symbolic setting is not always possible.

7   Evaluation

We evaluate our algorithms on two sets of benchmarks. We report the state reduction obtained using forward bisimulations and, for each algorithm, we compare the running times and the number of explored blocks. We use Simple to denote the algorithm presented at the top of Fig. 1, Greedy to denote the algorithm presented in Sect. 5, and Count to denote the counting based algorithm described in Sect. 6. As a sanity check, we assured that all the algorithms computed the same results. All the experiments were run on a 4-core Intel i7-2600 CPU 3.40 GHz, with 8 GB of RAM.

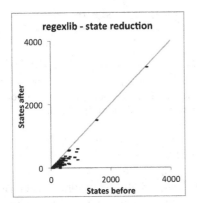
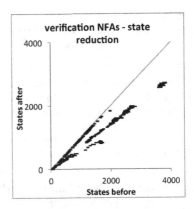

Fig. 3. State reduction for the two benchmark sets.

Regexlib. We collected the s-NFAs over the alphabet 2^{BV16} resulting from converting 2,625 regular expressions appearing in http://regexlib.com/. This website contains a library of crowd-sourced regular expressions for tasks such as detecting URLs, emails, and phone numbers. These s-NFAs have 1 to 3,174 states, 1 to 10,670 transitions, and have an average of 2 transitions per state. These benchmarks operate over very large alphabets and can only be handled symbolically. We use the algebra 2^{BVk}.

Verification s-NFAs. We collected 1,000 s-NFAs over small alphabets (2-40 symbols) appearing in verification applications from [8]. These s-NFAs are generated from the steps of abstract regular model checking while verifying the bakery algorithm, a producer-consumer system, bubble sort, an algorithm that reverses a circular list, and a Petri net model of the readers/writers protocol. These s-FAs have 4 to 3,782 states, 7 to 18,670 transitions, and have an average of 4.1 transitions per state. Given the small size of the alphabets, these automata are quite dense. We represent the alphabet using the algebra **int**[k].

State Reduction. Figure 3 shows the state reduction obtained by our algorithm. Each point (x, y) in the figure shows that an automaton with x states was reduced to an equivalent automaton with y states. On average, the number of states reduces by 14% and 19% for the regexlib benchmarks and the verification NFAs respectively.

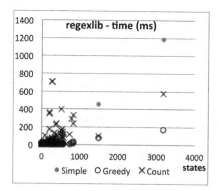 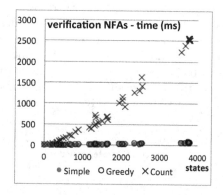

Fig. 4. Running times of three algorithms on regular expression from www.regexlib. com and on NFAs from verification applications. In the second plot, we do not show data points that are very close to each other to make the figure readable.

Runtime. Figure 4 shows the running times of the algorithms on each benchmark s-FA. For the regexlib s-FAs, most automata take less than 1ms to complete causing the same running time for the three algorithms on 2528 benchmarks. In general, the Greedy algorithm is slightly faster than the other two algorithms and the Count algorithm is at times slower than both the other two algorithms (93 cases total), on relatively small cases. On two large instances (1,502 and 3,174 states, 1,502 and 10,670 transitions) the Greedy and Count algorithms clearly outperform the Simple algorithm.

For s-FAs from [8], the algorithms Simple and Greedy, have very comparable performances (Greedy is, on average, 6 ms slower than Simple). The Count algorithm is slower than both these algorithms in 90% of the cases and has the same performance in the remaining 10% of the cases.

In both experiments, almost all the computation time of the Count algorithm is spent manipulating the counting data structure presented in Sect. 6. In summary, the Count algorithm, despite having $m \log n$ complexity, is consistently slower than the other two algorithms and the slowdown is due to the complexity of manipulating the counting data structure.

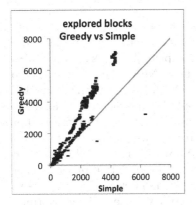 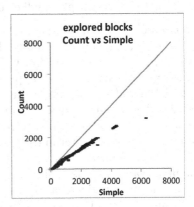

Fig. 5. Ratio of number of explored blocks between the simple algorithm and the other algorithms.

Explored Blocks. We measure the number of blocks pushed into the worklist W for the different algorithms. Figure 5 shows the ratio between the explored blocks of the Simple algorithm and the other two algorithms. As expected from the theoretical complexities, the Count algorithm consistently explores fewer blocks than the Simple algorithm. As we observed in Fig. 4, this is not enough to achieve better speedups. The Greedy algorithm often explores more blocks than the other two algorithms. This is because $R' = \text{SUPER}(R)\backslash R$ of a set R is explored even in the cases where R' has already been split into subsets. In this case, the simple algorithm will only explore the splits and not the original set, while the Greedy algorithm will explore both R' as well as its splits.

8   Related Work

Minimization of Deterministic Automata. Automata minimization algorithms have been studied and analyzed extensively in several different aspects. Moore's and Hopcroft's algorithms [20,25] are the two most common algorithms for minimizing DFAs. Both of these algorithms compute forward bisimulations over DFAs and can be implemented with complexity $O(kn \log n)$ (where k is the size of the alphabet). This bound is tight [5–7]. The two algorithms, although in different ways, iteratively refine a partition of the set of states until the forward bisimulation is computed. In the case of DFAs, the equivalence relation induced by the bisimulation relation produces a minimal and canonical DFA. In our earlier work, we extended Hopcroft's algorithm to work with symbolic alphabets [13] and showed how, for deterministic s-FAs, the algorithm can be implemented in $\mathcal{O}(m \log n f(nl))$ for automata with m transitions, n states, and predicates of size l. Here $f(x)$ is the cost of checking satisfiability of predicates of size x. The algorithm proposed in [13] is similar to the greedy algorithm in Fig. 1. The main difference is in the necessity to use SUPER$(R)\setminus R$ in the **SAT** checks and that this seemingly small change has drastic complexity implications.

Minimization and State Reduction in Nondeterministic Automata. In the case of NFAs, there exists no canonical minimal automaton and the problem of finding a minimal NFA is known to be PSPACE complete [24]. It is shown in [18] that it is not even possible to efficiently approximate NFA minimization. The original search based algorithm for minimizing NFAs is known as the Kameda-Weiner method [22]. A generalization of the Kameda-Weiner method based on atoms of regular languages [10] was recently introduced in [28]. Most practical approaches for computing small nondeterministic automata use notions of state reductions that do not always produce a minimal NFAs [2]. These techniques are based on computing various kinds of simulation and bisimulation relations. The set of most common such relations has been described in detail and extended to Büchi automata in [23]. In this paper, we are only concerned with performing state reduction by computing forward bisimulations.

Abdulla et al. were the first to observe that forward bisimulation for NFAs could be computed with complexity $\mathcal{O}(km \log n)$ by keeping track of the number of states each symbol can reach from a certain part of a partition [2]. In their paper, they also proposed an efficient implementation based on BDDs and algebraic decision diagrams for the special case in which the alphabet is a set of bit-vectors. The techniques proposed in [2] are tailored for finite alphabets and the goal of our paper is extending them to arbitrary alphabets that form a decidable Boolean algebra. In this paper, we propose an extension based on our symbolic bag data structure and experimentally show that, unlike for the case of finite alphabets, the counting algorithm is not practical.

Recently, Geldenhuys et al. have proposed a technique for reducing the size of certain classes of NFAs using SAT solvers [17]. In this technique, a SAT formula is used to describe the existence of an NFA that is equivalent to the original one, but has at most k states. Applying these techniques to symbolic automata is an interesting research direction.

Automata with Predicates. The concept of automata with predicates instead of concrete symbols was first mentioned in [31] and was first discussed in [29] in the context of natural language processing. Since then s-FAs have been studied extensively and we have seen algorithms for minimizing deterministic s-FAs [13] and deterministic s-FAs over trees [14], and extensions of classic logic results to s-FAs [15]. To the best of our knowledge, the problem of reducing the states and efficiently computing forward bisimulations for nondeterministic s-FAs has not been studied before. The term symbolic automata is sometimes used to refer to automata over finite alphabets where the state space is represented using BDDs [27]. This meaning is different from the one described in this paper.

AutomataDotNet. This is an open source Microsoft Automata project [1] that is an extension of the automata toolkit originally introduced in [30]. The source code (written in C#) of all the algorithms discussed in this paper as well as the source code of the experiments discussed in Sect. 7 are available in [1].

Acknowledgements. Loris D'Antoni performed part of this work while visiting Microsoft Research, Redmond. We thank Zachary Kincaid for his feedback.

References

1. AutomataDotNet (2015). https://github.com/AutomataDotNet/
2. Abdulla, P.A., Deneux, J., Kaati, L., Nilsson, M.: Minimization of nondeterministic automata with large alphabets. In: Farré, J., Litovsky, I., Schmitz, S. (eds.) CIAA 2005. LNCS, vol. 3845, pp. 31–42. Springer, Heidelberg (2006). doi:10. 1007/11605157_3
3. Alur, R., D'Antoni, L., Raghothaman, M.: Drex: a declarative language for efficiently evaluating regular string transformations. SIGPLAN Not. **50**(1), 125–137 (2015)
4. Bahar, R.I., Frohm, E.A., Gaona, C.M., Hachtel, G.D., Macii, E., Pardo, A., Somenzi, F.: Algebraic decision diagrams and their applications. Form. Methods Syst. Des. **10**(2/3), 171–206 (1997)
5. Berstel, J., Boasson, L., Carton, O.: Hopcroft's automaton minimization algorithm and Sturmian words. In: DMTCS 2008, pp. 355–366 (2008)
6. Berstel, J., Carton, O.: On the complexity of Hopcroft's state minimization algorithm. In: Domaratzki, M., Okhotin, A., Salomaa, K., Yu, S. (eds.) CIAA 2004. LNCS, vol. 3317, pp. 35–44. Springer, Heidelberg (2005). doi:10.1007/ 978-3-540-30500-2_4
7. Blum, N.: An $0(n \log n)$ implementation of the standard method for minimizing n-state finite automata. Inf. Process. Lett. **57**, 65–69 (1996)
8. Bouajjani, A., Habermehl, P., Vojnar, T.: Abstract regular model checking. In: Alur, R., Peled, D.A. (eds.) CAV 2004. LNCS, vol. 3114, pp. 372–386. Springer, Heidelberg (2004). doi:10.1007/978-3-540-27813-9_29
9. Bryant, R.E.: Graph-based algorithms for boolean function manipulation. IEEE Trans. Comput. **35**(8), 677–691 (1986)
10. Brzozowski, J., Tamm, H.: Theory of átomata. Theoret. Comput. Sci. **539**, 13–27 (2014)
11. D'Antoni, L., Veanes, M.: Equivalence of extended symbolic finite transducers. In: Sharygina, N., Veith, H. (eds.) CAV 2013. LNCS, vol. 8044, pp. 624–639. Springer, Heidelberg (2013). doi:10.1007/978-3-642-39799-8_41
12. D'Antoni, L., Veanes, M.: Static analysis of string encoders and decoders. In: Giacobbazzi, R., Berdine, J., Mastroeni, I. (eds.) VMCAI 2013. LNCS, vol. 7737, pp. 209–228. Springer, Heidelberg (2013). doi:10.1007/978-3-642-35873-9_14
13. D'Antoni, L., Veanes, M.: Minimization of symbolic automata. In: Proceedings of the 41st ACM SIGPLAN-SIGACT Symposium on Principles of Programming Languages, (POPL 2014), pp. 541–553. ACM (2014)
14. D'Antoni, L., Veanes, M.: Minimization of symbolic tree automata. In: Proceedings of the 31st Annual ACM/IEEE Symposium on Logic in Computer Science. ACM (2016)
15. D'Antoni, L., Veanes, M.: Monadic second-order logic on finite sequences. In: Proceedings of the 44th ACM SIGPLAN-SIGACT Symposium on Principles of Programming Languages, (POPL 2017). ACM (2017)

16. D'Antoni, L., Veanes, M., Livshits, B., Molnar, D.: Fast: a transducer-based language for tree manipulation. ACM Trans. Program. Lang. Syst. **38**(1), 1–32 (2015)
17. Geldenhuys, J., Merwe, B., Zijl, L.: Reducing nondeterministic finite automata with SAT solvers. In: Yli-Jyrä, A., Kornai, A., Sakarovitch, J., Watson, B. (eds.) FSMNLP 2009. LNCS (LNAI), vol. 6062, pp. 81–92. Springer, Heidelberg (2010). doi:10.1007/978-3-642-14684-8_9
18. Gramlich, G., Schnitger, G.: Minimizing NFA's and regular expressions. In: Diekert, V., Durand, B. (eds.) STACS 2005. LNCS, vol. 3404, pp. 399–411. Springer, Heidelberg (2005). doi:10.1007/978-3-540-31856-9_33
19. Hopcroft, J.: An $n\log n$ algorithm for minimizing states in a finite automaton. In: Kohavi, Z. (ed.) Proceedings of International Symposium Technion, Theory of machines and computations, 1971, Haifa, pp. 189–196. Academic Press, New York (1971)
20. Hopcroft, J.E., Ullman, J.D.: Formal Languages and Their Relation to Automata. Addison-Wesley Longman Publishing Co., Inc., Boston (1969)
21. Hopcroft, J.E., Ullman, J.D.: Introduction to Automata Theory, Languages, and Computation. Addison Wesley, Boston (1979)
22. Kameda, T., Weiner, P.: On the state minimization of nondeterministic finite automata. IEEE Trans. Comput. **C-19**(7), 617–627 (1970)
23. Mayr, R., Clemente, L.: Advanced automata minimization. In: POPL 2013, pp. 63–74 (2013)
24. Meyer, A.R., Stockmeyer, L.J.: The equivalence problem for regular expressions with squaring requires exponential space. In: Proceedings of the 13th Annual Symposium on Switching and Automata Theory (SWAT 1972), pp. 125–129. IEEE (1972)
25. Moore, E.F.: Gedanken-experiments on sequential machines. Autom. Stud. Ann. Math. Stud. **34**, 129–153 (1956)
26. Paige, R., Tarjan, R.E.: Three partition refinement algorithms. SIAM J. Comput. **16**(6), 973–989 (1987)
27. Rozier, K.Y., Vardi, M.Y.: A multi-encoding approach for LTL symbolic satisfiability checking. In: Butler, M., Schulte, W. (eds.) FM 2011. LNCS, vol. 6664, pp. 417–431. Springer, Heidelberg (2011). doi:10.1007/978-3-642-21437-0_31
28. Tamm, H.: New interpretation and generalization of the Kameda-Weiner method. In: Chatzigiannakis, I., Mitzenmacher, M., Rabani, Y., Sangiorgi, D. (eds.) ICALP 2016. LIPIcs, vol. 55, pp. 116:1–116:12. Schloss Dagstuhl - Leibniz-Zentrum fuer Informatik, Wadern (2016)
29. van Noord, G., Gerdemann, D.: Finite state transducers with predicates and identities. Grammars **4**(3), 263–286 (2001)
30. Veanes, M., Bjørner, N.: Symbolic automata: the toolkit. In: Flanagan, C., König, B. (eds.) TACAS 2012. LNCS, vol. 7214, pp. 472–477. Springer, Heidelberg (2012). doi:10.1007/978-3-642-28756-5_33
31. Watson, B.W.: Implementing and using finite automata toolkits. In: Extended Finite State Models of Language, pp. 19–36. Cambridge University Press, New York (1999)

Up-To Techniques for Weighted Systems

Filippo Bonchi[1], Barbara König[2(✉)], and Sebastian Küpper[2]

[1] ENS Lyon, Lyon, France
[2] Universität Duisburg-Essen, Duisburg, Germany
barbara_koenig@uni-due.de

Abstract. We show how up-to techniques for (bi-)similarity can be used in the setting of weighted systems. The problems we consider are language equivalence, language inclusion and the threshold problem (also known as universality problem) for weighted automata. We build a bisimulation relation on the fly and work up-to congruence and up-to similarity. This requires to determine whether a pair of vectors (over a semiring) is in the congruence closure of a given relation of vectors. This problem is considered for rings and l-monoids, for the latter we provide a rewriting algorithm and show its confluence and termination. We then explain how to apply these up-to techniques to weighted automata and provide runtime results.

1 Introduction

Language equivalence of deterministic automata can be checked by means of the bisimulation proof principle. For non-deterministic automata, this principle is sound but not complete: to use bisimulation, one first has to determinize the automaton, via the so-called powerset construction. Since the determinized automaton might be much larger than the original non-deterministic one, several algorithms [1,9,13,23] have been proposed to perform the determization on the fly and to avoid exploring a huge portion of states. Among these, the algorithm in [9] that exploits *up-to techniques* is particularly relevant for our work.

Up-to techniques have been introduced by Robin Milner in his seminal work on CCS [18] and, since then, they proved useful, if not essential, in numerous proofs about concurrent systems (see [19] for a list of references). According to the standard definition a relation R is a bisimulation whenever two states x, y in R can simulate each other, resulting in a pair x', y' that is still in R. An up-to technique allows to replace the latter R by a larger relation $f(R)$ which contains more pairs and hence allows to cut off bisimulation proofs and work with much smaller relations.

Here we focus on up-to techniques in a quantitative setting: weighted systems, especially weighted automata over arbitrary semirings. Some examples of up-to techniques for weighted systems already appeared in [8,20], that study up-to techniques from the abstract perspective of coalgebras.

Research partially supported by DFG project BEMEGA and ANR-16-CE25-0011 REPAS.

A. Legay and T. Margaria (Eds.): TACAS 2017, Part I, LNCS 10205, pp. 535–552, 2017.
DOI: 10.1007/978-3-662-54577-5_31

Although up-to techniques for weighted systems have already received some attentions, their relevance for algorithms to perform behavioural analysis has never been studied properly. This is the main aim of our paper: we give a uniform class of algorithms exploiting up-to techniques to solve the problems of equivalence, inclusion and universality, which, in the weighted setting, asks whether the weight of all words is below some given threshold. In particular we show how to implement these techniques and we perform runtime experiments.

The key ingredient to algorithmically exploit up-to techniques is a procedure to decide, given x, y, R as above, whether x, y belongs to $f(R)$. For a non-deterministic automaton (NFA) with state space S, the algorithm in [9] uses as sub-routine a rewriting system to check whether two sets of states $S, S' \in \mathcal{P}(X)$ – representing states of the determinised automaton – belong to $c(R)$, the congruence closure of R.

For NFA, the congruence closure is taken with respect to the structure of join semi-lattices $(\mathcal{P}(X), \cup, \emptyset)$, carried by the state space of a determinized automaton. For weighted automata, rather than join semi-lattices, we need to consider the congruence closure for *semimodules* (which resemble vector spaces, but are defined over semirings instead of fields). Indeed, an analogon of the powerset construction for weighted automata results in a sort of "determinised automaton" (called in [6] linear weighted automaton) whose states are vectors with values in the underlying semiring.

Our first issue is to find a procedure to check whether two vectors belong to the congruence closure (with respect to semimodules) of a given relation. We face this problem for different semirings, especially rings and l-monoids. For l-monoids we adapt the rewriting procedure for the non-deterministic case [9] and show its confluence and termination, which guarantees a unique normal form as a representative for each equivalence class. Confluence holds in general and termination can be shown for certain semirings, such as the tropical semiring (also known as the (min, +)-semiring).

Reasoning up-to congruence is sound for language equivalence, but not for inclusion. For the latter, we need the precongruence closure that, in the case of l-monoids, can be checked with a simple modification of the rewriting procedure. Inspired by [1], we further combine this technique with a certain notion of weighted *similarity*, a preorder that entails language inclusion and can be computed in polynomial time.

We then show how to apply our up-to techniques to language equivalence and inclusion checks for weighted automata. For some interesting semirings, such as the tropical semiring, these problems are known to be undecidable [17]. But based on the inclusion algorithm we can develop an algorithm which solves the universality (also called threshold) problem for the tropical semiring over the natural numbers. This problem is known to be PSPACE-complete and we give detailed runtime results that compare our up-to threshold algorithm with one previously introduced in [3].

2   Preliminaries

In this section we recall all the algebraic structures we intend to work with and, in particular, spaces of vectors over these structures.

A *semiring* is a tuple $\mathbb{S} = (S, +, \cdot, 0, 1)$ where $(S, +, 0)$ is a commutative monoid, $(S, \cdot, 1)$ is a monoid, 0 *annihilates* $\cdot$ (i.e., $0 \cdot s_1 = 0 = s_1 \cdot 0$) and $\cdot$ *distributes over* $+$ (i.e., $(s_1 + s_2) \cdot s_3 = s_1 \cdot s_3 + s_2 \cdot s_3$ and $s_3 \cdot (s_1 + s_2) = s_3 \cdot s_1 + s_3 \cdot s_2$). A *ring* is a semiring equipped with inverses for $+$.

Let $(L, \sqsubseteq)$ be a partially ordered set. If for all pairs of elements $\ell_1, \ell_2 \in L$ the infimum $\ell_1 \sqcap \ell_2$ and the supremum $\ell_1 \sqcup \ell_2$ exist (wrt. the order $\sqsubseteq$), it is a *lattice*. If $(\ell_1 \sqcup \ell_2) \sqcap \ell_3 = (\ell_1 \sqcap \ell_3) \sqcup (\ell_2 \sqcap \ell_3)$ for all $\ell_1, \ell_2, \ell_3 \in L$, it is called *distributive*. It is *complete* if suprema and infima of arbitrary subsets exist. Every complete distributive lattice is a semiring $(L, \sqcup, \sqcap, \bot, \top)$, where $\bot, \top$ are the infimum and supremum of L.

Let $(L, \sqsubseteq)$ be a lattice and $(L, \cdot, 1)$ be a monoid. If $\cdot$ distributes over $\sqcup$, we call $(L, \sqcup, \cdot)$ an *l-monoid*. Moreover, if L has a $\bot$-element 0 that annihilates $\cdot$, we call $(L, \sqcup, \cdot)$ *bounded*. and it is then a semiring $(L, \sqcup, \cdot, 0, 1)$ It is called *completely distributive* if $(L, \sqsubseteq)$ is complete and multiplication distributes over arbitrary suprema. Observe that every completely distributive *l*-monoid is bounded.[1] It is called *integral* if $\top = 1$.

Example 2.1. *The tropical semiring is the structure* $\mathbb{T} = (\mathbb{R}_0^+ \cup \{\infty\}, \min, +, \infty, 0)$.[2] $\mathbb{T}$ *is a distributive l-monoid for the lattice* $(\mathbb{R}_0^+ \cup \{\infty\}, \geq)$.

Another example for a distributive l-monoid is $\mathbb{M} = ([0, 1], \max, \cdot, 0, 1)$, *which is based on the lattice* $([0, 1], \leq)$.

The l-monoid $\mathbb{M}$ *is isomorphic to* $\mathbb{T}$ *via the isomorphism* $\varphi \colon \mathbb{T} \to \mathbb{M}, x \mapsto 2^{-x}$.

Hereafter, we will sometimes identify the semiring $\mathbb{S}$ with the underlying set S. For the sake of readability, we will only consider commutative semirings, i.e., semirings where multiplication is commutative.

For a semiring $\mathbb{S}$ and a finite set X, an $\mathbb{S}$-*vector of dimension* X is a mapping $v \colon X \to \mathbb{S}$. The set of all such vectors is denoted by $\mathbb{S}^X$ and is called a *semimodule*.

For notational convenience, we assume that $X = \{1, 2, \ldots, |X|\}$ and we write a vector v as a column vector. For X and Y finite sets, an $\mathbb{S}$-*matrix of dimension* $X \times Y$ is a mapping $M \colon X \times Y \to \mathbb{S}$. The set of all such matrices is denoted by $\mathbb{S}^{X \times Y}$. $M[x, y]$ $(v[x])$ denotes the (x, y)-th entry of M (x-th entry of v). Furthermore $v \cdot s$ denotes the multiplication of a vector with a scalar s and $v_1 + v_2$ is the componentwise addition.

Given a set V of $\mathbb{S}$-vectors, a *linear combination* of vectors in V is a vector $v_1 \cdot s_1 + \cdots + v_n \cdot s_n$, where $v_1, \ldots, v_n \in V$, $s_1, \ldots, s_n \in \mathbb{S}$. A subset of $\mathbb{S}^X$ that is closed under linear combinations is called a *(sub-)semimodule*.

Henceforward we will always require *l*-monoids to be completely distributive: this ensures that we have a residuation operation defined as follows.

---

[1] Completely distributive *l*-monoids are often referred to as *unital quantales*.

[2] We will sometimes use min as an infix operator (i.e., $a \min b$).

Definition 2.2. *The residuation operation for a completely distributive l-monoid* $\mathbb{L}$ *is defined for all* $\ell_1, \ell_2 \in \mathbb{L}$ *as* $\ell_1 \to \ell_2 = \bigsqcup\{\ell \in \mathbb{L} \mid \ell_1 \cdot \ell \sqsubseteq \ell_2\}$, *also called residuum of* ℓ_1, ℓ_2. *We extend this to* $\mathbb{L}$*-vectors, replacing* ℓ_1, ℓ_2 *by* $v_1, v_2 \in \mathbb{L}^X$.

Example 2.3. *Recall* $\mathbb{T}$, $\mathbb{M}$ *in Example 2.1. For* $\ell_1, \ell_2 \in \mathbb{T}$ *we have* $\ell_1 \to \ell_2 = \min\{\ell \in \mathbb{R}_0^+ \cup \{\infty\} \mid \ell_1 + \ell \geq \ell_2\} = \ell_2 \dot{-} \ell_1$ *(modified subtraction). For* $\ell_1, \ell_2 \in \mathbb{M}$, *we have* $\ell_1 \to \ell_2 = \max\{\ell \in [0,1] \mid \ell_1 \cdot \ell \leq \ell_2\} = \min\{1, \frac{\ell_2}{\ell_1}\}$.

Another example where the residuation operation can be easily characterized is any boolean algebra $(\mathbb{B}, \vee, \wedge, 0, 1)$. *For* $\ell_1, \ell_2 \in \mathbb{B}$ *we have* $\ell_1 \to \ell_2 = \neg \ell_1 \vee \ell_2$.

We will assume that all relevant operations of any semiring under consideration (addition, multiplication, in the case of l-monoids residuation) are computable.

3   Congruence Closure

As explained in the introduction, the key ingredient for exploiting up-to techniques in Sect. 4 is an algorithmic procedure to check whether two vectors belong to the congruence closure of a given relation of vectors.

3.1   Problem Statement

Let X be a finite set and let $\mathbb{S}$ be a semiring. A relation $R \subseteq \mathbb{S}^X \times \mathbb{S}^X$ is a *congruence* if it is an equivalence and *closed under linear combinations*, that is, for each $(v_1, v_1'), (v_2, v_2') \subseteq R$ and each scalar $s \in \mathbb{S}$, $(v_1 + v_2, v_1' + v_2') \in R$ and $(v_1 \cdot s, v_1' \cdot s) \in R$. The *congruence closure* $c(R)$ of a relation R over a semiring $\mathbb{S}$ is the smallest congruence $R' \subseteq \mathbb{S}^X \times \mathbb{S}^X$ such that $R \subseteq R'$. Alternatively, two vectors $v, v' \in \mathbb{S}^X$ are in $c(R)$ whenever this can be derived via the rules in Table 1.

Table 1. Proof rules for the congruence closure

$$(\text{REL})\ \frac{v\,R\,w}{v\,c(R)\,w} \qquad (\text{REFL})\ \frac{}{v\,c(R)\,v} \qquad (\text{SYM})\ \frac{v\,c(R)\,w}{w\,c(R)\,v}$$

$$(\text{TRANS})\ \frac{u\,c(R)\,v \quad v\,c(R)\,w}{u\,c(R)\,w} \qquad (\text{SCA})\ \frac{v\,c(R)\,w}{v\cdot s\,c(R)\,w\cdot s}\ \text{ where } s \in \mathbb{S}$$

$$(\text{PLUS})\ \frac{v_1\,c(R)\,v_1' \quad v_2\,c(R)\,v_2'}{v_1 + v_2\,c(R)\,v_1' + v_2'}$$

Given a finite $R \subseteq \mathbb{S}^X \times \mathbb{S}^X$ and $v, w \in \mathbb{S}^X$, we aim to determine if $(v, w) \in c(R)$.

In [9], Bonchi and Pous presented a procedure to compute the congruence closure for the two-valued boolean semiring $B = \{0, 1\}$. The purpose of this section is to generalise the procedure towards more general semirings, such as rings and l-monoids.

3.2   Congruence Closure for Rings

A simple case to start our analysis is the congruence closure of a ring. It is kind of folklore (see e.g. [10,21]) that a submodules[3] can be used to represent a congruences. In particular we write $[V]$ to denote the submodule generated by a set of vectors V.

Proposition 3.1. *Let $\mathbb{I}$ be a ring and X be a finite set. Let $R \subseteq \mathbb{I}^X \times \mathbb{I}^X$ be a relation and let $(v, v') \in \mathbb{I}^X \times \mathbb{I}^X$ be a pair of vectors. We construct a generating set for a submodule of $\mathbb{I}^X$ by defining $U_R = \{u - u' \mid (u, u') \in R\}$. Then $(v, v') \in c(R)$ iff $v - v' \in [U_R]$.*

This yields an algorithm for a congruence check whenever we have a n algorithm to solve linear equations, e.g. for fields. If the ring is not a field, it might still be possible to embed it into a field. In this case we can solve e.g. the language equivalence problem (Sect. 4.1) for weighted automata in the field and the results are also valid in the ring. Similarly, the procedure can be used for probabilistic automata which can be seen as weighted automata over the reals.

3.3   Congruence Closure for l-Monoids

Rewriting and Normal Forms. Our method to determine if a pair of vectors is in the congruence closure is to employ a rewriting algorithm that rewrites both vectors to a normal form. These coincide iff the vectors are related by the congruence closure.

Definition 3.2 (Rewriting and normal forms). *Let $\mathbb{L}$ be an integral l-monoid and let $R \subseteq \mathbb{L}^X \times \mathbb{L}^X$ be a finite relation.*

We define a set of rewriting rules $\mathcal{R}$ as follows: For each pair of vectors $(v, v') \in R$, we obtain two rewriting rules $v \mapsto v \sqcup v'$ and $v' \mapsto v \sqcup v'$.

A rewriting step works as follows: given a vector v and a rewriting rule $l \mapsto r$, we compute the residuum $l \to v$ and, provided $v \sqsubseteq (v \sqcup r \cdot (l \to v))$, the rewriting rule is applicable and v rewrites to $v \sqcup r \cdot (l \to v)$ (symbolically: $v \leadsto v \sqcup r \cdot (l \to v)$). A vector v is in normal form wrt. R, provided there exists no rule that is applicable to v.

Example 3.3. *In order to illustrate how rewriting works, we work in $\mathbb{T}$, set $X = \{1, 2\}$ (two dimensions) and take the relation $R = \{(\binom{\infty}{0}, \binom{0}{\infty})\} \subseteq \mathbb{T}^2 \times \mathbb{T}^2$, relating the two unit vectors, and the vector $v = \binom{\infty}{3}$. This yields a rule $l = \binom{\infty}{0} \mapsto r = \binom{0}{0}$. We obtain $l \to v = 3$ and hence $v \leadsto v \sqcup r \cdot (l \to v) = \binom{\infty}{3} \min (\binom{0}{0} + 3) = \binom{3}{3}$.*

It is worth to observe that when $\mathbb{L}$ is the boolean semiring, the above procedure coincides with the one in [9]. The rewriting relation satisfies some simple properties:

---

[3] A sub-semimodule for a ring is called submodule.

Lemma 3.4. *(i) If $v \rightsquigarrow v'$ and $v \sqsubseteq w$, then $v' \sqsubseteq w$ or there exists w' s.t. $w \rightsquigarrow w'$ and $v' \sqsubseteq w'$.*

(ii) Whenever $v \rightsquigarrow v'$ and w is any vector, there exists a vector u s.t. $v \sqcup w \rightsquigarrow u \sqsupseteq v' \sqcup w$ or $v \sqcup w = v' \sqcup w$.

We now have to prove the following three statements: (i) Our technique is sound, i.e. whenever two vectors have the same normal form wrt. R, they are in $c(R)$. (ii) Our technique is complete, i.e. whenever two vectors are in $c(R)$, they have the same normal form wrt. R. (iii) Our algorithm to compute normal forms terminates.

We will show (i) and prove that (ii) follows from (iii). Afterwards we will discuss sufficient conditions and examples where (iii) holds.

Theorem 3.5. *Whenever there exists a vector v, such that two vectors v_1, v_2 both rewrite to $\overline{v}$, i.e., $v_1 \rightsquigarrow^* \overline{v}$, $v_2 \rightsquigarrow^* \overline{v}$, then $(v_1, v_2) \in c(R)$.*

Proof. We will show that if v rewrites to v' via a rule $l \mapsto r$, then $(v, v') \in c(R)$.

Since $l \mapsto r$ is a rewriting rule we have that $l = w$, $r = w \sqcup w'$ for $(w, w') \in R$ or $(w', w) \in R$. In both cases $w = w \sqcup w \; c(R) \; w \sqcup w'$ due to the definition of congruence closure, using rules (PLUS), (REL) and (REFL), as well as (SYM) in case $(w', w) \in R$. Hence $l \; c(R) \; r$. This implies that $l \cdot (l \to v) \; c(R) \; r \cdot (l \to v)$ (SCA) and furthermore $v \sqcup l \cdot (l \to v) \; c(R) \; v \sqcup r \cdot (l \to v)$ (PLUS). Since $l \cdot (l \to v) \sqsubseteq v$ we have $v \sqcup l \cdot (l \to v) = v$ and hence $v \; c(R) \; v'$. $\square$

This concludes the proof of soundness, we will go on proving completeness.

Lemma 3.6. *Assume we have a rewriting system that always terminates. Then the local Church-Rosser property holds. That is whenever $v \rightsquigarrow v_1$ and $v \rightsquigarrow v_2$, there exists a vector v' such that $v_1 \rightsquigarrow^* v'$ and $v_2 \rightsquigarrow^* v'$.*

If a rewriting system terminates and the local Church-Rosser property holds, the system is automatically confluent [12]. In this case, every vector v is as associated with a unique normal form, written $\Downarrow_R v$ or simply $\Downarrow v$ where $v \rightsquigarrow^* \Downarrow v \not\rightsquigarrow$.

Furthermore, due to Lemma 3.4.(i) we know that $\Downarrow$ is monotone, i.e., $v \sqsubseteq v'$ implies $\Downarrow v \sqsubseteq \Downarrow v'$. This also implies $\Downarrow (v \sqcup v') \sqsupseteq (\Downarrow v) \sqcup (\Downarrow v')$.

Lemma 3.7. *For all $v \in \mathbb{L}^X, \ell \in \mathbb{L}$ we have that if $v \rightsquigarrow v'$, then $v \cdot \ell \rightsquigarrow v''$ for some $v'' \sqsupseteq v' \cdot \ell$ or $v \cdot \ell = v' \cdot \ell$. In particular, if rewriting terminates, we have $(\Downarrow v) \cdot \ell \sqsubseteq \Downarrow (v \cdot \ell)$.*

Now we have all the necessary ingredients to show that the technique is complete, provided the computation of a normal form terminates.

Theorem 3.8. *Assume that rewriting terminates. If $v \; c(R) \; v'$ then $\Downarrow v = \Downarrow v'$.*

Termination. One technique to prove termination is given in Corollary 3.10: it suffices to show that the supremum of all the elements reachable via $\leadsto$ is included in the congruence class. First we need the following result.

Proposition 3.9. *If* $v\ c(R)\ \overline{v}$, *then* $v \leadsto^* v'$ *where* $v' \sqsupseteq v \sqcup \overline{v}$.

Now take $\overline{v} = \bigsqcup\{\hat{v} \mid v \leadsto^* \hat{v}\}$. By the above proposition if $v\ c(R)\ \overline{v}$, then $v' = \overline{v}$ and $v \leadsto^* \overline{v}$. Since $\leadsto$ is irreflexive, $\overline{v} \not\leadsto$. If we assume that rule application is fair, we can guarantee that $\overline{v}$ is eventually reached in every rewriting sequence.

Corollary 3.10. *If* $v\ c(R)\ \bigsqcup\{\hat{v} \mid v \leadsto^* \hat{v}\}$, *then the rewriting algorithm termi-nates, assuming that every rule that remains applicable is eventually applied.*

Termination for Specific l-Monoids. We now study the l-monoid $\mathbb{M} = ([0,1], \max, \cdot, 0, 1)$ from Example 2.1 and show that the rewriting algorithm ter-minates for this l-monoid. For the proof we mainly use the pigeon-hole principle and exploit the total ordering of the underlying lattice. Since $\mathbb{M}$ is isomorphic to $\mathbb{T}$, we obtain termination for the tropical semiring as a corollary.

Theorem 3.11. *The rewriting algorithm terminates for the l-monoids* $\mathbb{M}$ *and* $\mathbb{T}$.

These results provide an effective procedure for checking congruence closure over the tropical semiring. We will mainly apply them to weighted automata, but expect that they can be useful to solve other problems. For instance, in [7], we show an interesting connection to the shortest path problem.

Termination for Lattices. We next turn to lattices and give a sufficient condi-tion for termination on lattices. Obviously, rewriting terminates for lattices for which the ascending chain condition holds (i.e., every ascending chain eventually becomes stationary), but one can go beyond that.

In this section, we assume a completely distributive lattice $\mathbb{L}$ and a boolean algebra $\mathbb{B}$ such that the orders of $\mathbb{L}$ and $\mathbb{B}$, as well as the infima coincides. Suprema need not coincide. Thus, whenever there is ambiguity, we will add the index $\mathbb{B}$ or $\mathbb{L}$ to the operator. For the negation of a given $x \in \mathbb{B}$, we write $\neg x$. One way to obtain such a boolean algebra – in particular one where the suprema coincide as well – is via Funayama's theorem, see [5].

We want to show that if $\mathbb{L}$ approximates $\mathbb{B}$ "well enough", the rewriting algorithm terminates for $\mathbb{L}$.

Theorem 3.12. *The approximation of an element* $\ell \in \mathbb{B}$ *in the lattice* $\mathbb{L}$ *is defined as* $\lfloor \ell \rfloor = \bigsqcup_{\mathbb{L}}\{\ell' \in \mathbb{L} \mid \ell' \leq \ell\}$.

Let $\mathcal{R}$ *be a rewriting system for vectors in* $\mathbb{L}^X$. *Whenever the set* $L(l,x) = \{\ell \in \mathbb{L} \mid \lfloor \neg l[x] \rfloor \sqsubseteq \ell \sqsubseteq \neg l[x]\}$ *is finite for all rules* $(l \mapsto r) \in \mathcal{R}$ *and all* $x \in X$, *rewriting terminates.*

Note that $\lfloor \neg \ell \rfloor = \lfloor \ell \to_{\mathbb{B}} 0 \rfloor = \ell \to_{\mathbb{L}} 0$. Hence the theorem says that there should be only finitely many elements between the negation of an element in the lattice and the negation of the same element in the boolean algebra. As a simple corollary we obtain that the rewriting algorithm terminates for all boolean algebras.

4   Up-To Techniques for Weighted Automata

In this section we present applications of our congruence closure method. More specifically, we investigate weighted automata and present up-to techniques both for the language equivalence and the inclusion problem, which are variants of the efficient up-to based algorithm presented in [9]. For the tropical semiring we also give a procedure for solving the threshold problem, based on the language inclusion algorithm.

4.1   Language Equivalence for Weighted Automata

We turn our attention towards weighted automata and their languages.

A *weighted automaton* over the semiring $\mathbb{S}$ and alphabet A is a triple (X, o, t) where X is a finite set of states, $t = (t_a \colon X \to \mathbb{S}^X)_{a \in A}$ is an A-indexed set of transition functions and $o \colon X \to \mathbb{S}$ is the output function. Intuitively $t_a(x)(y) = s$ means that the states x can make a transition to y with letter $a \in A$ and weight $s \in \mathbb{S}$ (sometimes written as $x \xrightarrow{a,s} y$). The functions t_a can be represented as $X \times X$-matrices with values in $\mathbb{S}$ and o as a row vector of dimension X. Given a vector $v \in \mathbb{S}^X$, we use $t_a(v)$ to denote the vector obtained by multiplying the matrix t_a by v and $o(v)$ to denote the scalar in $\mathbb{S}$ obtained by multiplying the row vector o by the column vector v.

A *weighted language* is a function $\varphi \colon A^* \to \mathbb{S}$, where A^* is the set of all words over A. We will use ε to denote the empty word and aw the concatenation of a letter $a \in A$ with the word $w \in A^*$. Every weighted automaton is associated with a function $[\![-]\!] \colon \mathbb{S}^X \to \mathbb{S}^{A^*}$ mapping each vector into its *accepted language*. For all $v \in \mathbb{S}^X$, $a \in A$ and $w \in A^*$, this is defined as

$$[\![v]\!](\varepsilon) = o(v) \qquad [\![v]\!](aw) = [\![t_a(v)]\!](w).$$

Two vectors $v_1, v_2 \in \mathbb{S}^X$ are called *language equivalent*, written $v_1 \sim v_2$ iff $[\![v_1]\!] = [\![v_2]\!]$.[4] The problem of checking language equivalence in weighted automata for an arbitrary semiring is undecidable: for the tropical semiring this was shown by Krob in [17]; the proof was later simplified in [3]. However, for several semirings the problem is decidable, for instance for all (complete and distributive) lattices. For finite non-deterministic automata, i.e., automata weighted over the boolean semiring, Bonchi and Pous introduced in [9] the algorithm HKC. The name stems from the fact that the algorithm extends the procedure of Hopcroft and Karp [15] with congruence closure.

Figure 1 shows the extension of HKC to weighted automata over an arbitrary semiring: the code is the same as the one in [9], apart from the fact that, rather

---

[4] The accepted notions of language and language equivalence can be given for states rather than for vectors by assigning to each state $x \in X$ the corresponding unit vector $e_x \in \mathbb{S}^X$. On the other hand, when weighted automata are given with an initial vector i – which is often the case in literature – one can define the language of an automaton as $[\![i]\!]$.

HKC (v_1, v_2)

```
(1)  R := ∅;  todo := ∅
(2)  insert (v₁, v₂) into todo
(3)  while todo is not empty do
     (3.1)   extract (v'₁, v'₂) from todo
     (3.2)   if (v'₁, v'₂) ∈ c(R) then continue
     (3.3)   if o(v'₁) ≠ o(v'₂) then return false
     (3.4)   for all a ∈ A,
                  insert (tₐ(v'₁), tₐ(v'₂)) into todo
     (3.5)   insert (v'₁, v'₂) into R
(4)  return true
```

Fig. 1. Algorithm to check the equivalence of vectors $v_1, v_2 \in \mathbb{S}^X$ for a weighted automata (X, o, t).

than exploring sets of states, the algorithm works with vectors in $\mathbb{S}^X$. The check at step (3.2) can be performed with the procedures discussed in Sect. 3.

Below we prove that the algorithm is sound and complete, but termination can fail in two ways: either the check at step (3.2) does not terminate, or the while loop at step (3) does not. For the tropical semiring we have seen that the check at step (3.2) can be effectively performed by rewriting (Theorem 3.11). Therefore, due to Krob's undecidability result, the while loop at step (3) may not terminate. For (distributive) lattices, we have shown termination of rewriting under some additional constraints (Theorem 3.12); moreover the loop at (3) will always terminate, because from a given finite set of lattice elements only finitely many lattice elements can be constructed using infimum and supremum [16].

To prove soundness of HKC, we introduce the notions of simulation and bisimulation up-to. Let $Rel_{\mathbb{S}^X}$ be the complete lattice of relations over $\mathbb{S}^X$ and $b_1 \colon Rel_{\mathbb{S}^X} \to Rel_{\mathbb{S}^X}$ be the monotone map defined for all $R \subseteq \mathbb{S}^X \times \mathbb{S}^X$ as

$$b_1(R) = \{(v_1, v_2) \mid o(v_1) = o(v_2) \text{ and for all } a \in A, (t_a(v_1), t_a(v_2)) \in R\}$$

Definition 4.1. *A relation $R \subseteq \mathbb{S}^X \times \mathbb{S}^X$ is a b_1-simulation if $R \subseteq b_1(R)$, i.e., for all $(v_1, v_2) \in R$: (i) $o(v_1) = o(v_2)$; (ii) for all $a \in A$, $(t_a(v_1), t_a(v_2)) \in R$.*

For a monotone map $f \colon Rel_{\mathbb{S}^X} \to Rel_{\mathbb{S}^X}$, a b_1-simulation up-to f is a relation R such that $R \subseteq b_1(f(R))$.

It is easy to show (see e.g. [19]) that b_1-simulation provides a sound and complete proof technique for $\sim$. On the other hand, not all functions f can be used as sound up-to techniques. HKC exploits the monotone function $c \colon Rel_{\mathbb{S}^X} \to Rel_{\mathbb{S}^X}$ mapping each relation R to its congruence closure $c(R)$.

Proposition 4.2. *Let $v_1, v_2 \in \mathbb{S}^X$. It holds that $v_1 \sim v_2$ iff there exists a b_1-simulation R such that $(v_1, v_2) \in R$ iff there exists a b_1-simulation up-to c R such that $(v_1, v_2) \in R$.*

With this result, it is easy to prove the correctness of the algorithm.

Theorem 4.3. *Whenever HKC terminates, it returns true iff $[\![v_1]\!] = [\![v_2]\!]$.*

Proof. Observe that $R \subseteq b_1(c(R) \cup todo)$ is an invariant for the while loop at step (3).

If HKC returns *true* then *todo* is empty and thus $R \subseteq b_1(c(R))$, i.e., R is a b_1-simulation up-to c. By Proposition 4.2, $v_1 \sim v_2$.

Whenever HKC returns false, it encounters a pair $(v_1', v_2') \in todo$ such that $o(v_1') \neq o(v_2')$. Observe that for all pairs $(v_1', v_2') \in todo$, there exists a word $w = a_1 a_2 \ldots a_n \in A^*$ such that $v_1' = t_{a_n}(\ldots t_{a_2}(t_{a_1}(v_1)))$ and $v_2' = t_{a_n}(\ldots t_{a_2}(t_{a_1}(v_2)))$. Therefore $[\![v_1]\!](w) = [\![v_1']\!](\varepsilon) = o(v_1') \neq o(v_2') = [\![v_2']\!](\varepsilon) = [\![v_2]\!](w)$. $\qquad\square$

4.2 Language Inclusion

Whenever a semiring $\mathbb{S}$ carries a partial order $\sqsubseteq$, one can be interested in checking language inclusion of the states of a weighted automata (X, o, t). More generally, given $v_1, v_2 \in \mathbb{S}^X$, we say that the language of v_1 is included in the language of v_2 (written $v_1 \precsim v_2$) iff $[\![v_1]\!](w) \sqsubseteq [\![v_2]\!](w)$ for all $w \in A^*$.

The algorithm HKC can be slightly modified to check language inclusion, resulting in algorithm HKP: steps (3.2) and (3.3) are replaced by

```
(3.2)    if (v₁',v₂') ∈ p(R) then continue
(3.3)    if o(v₁') ⋢ o(v₂') then return false
```

where $p\colon Rel_{\mathbb{S}^X} \to Rel_{\mathbb{S}^X}$ is the monotone function assigning to each relation R its pre-congruence closure $p(R)$.

The precongruence closure is defined as the closure of R under $\sqsubseteq$, transitivity and linear combination. That is, in the rules of Table 1 $c(R)$ is replaced by $p(R)$, rule (Sym) is removed and rule (Refl) is replaced by rule (Ord) on the right. $\quad$ (ORD) $\dfrac{v \sqsubseteq v'}{v \; p(R) \; v'}$

The soundness of the modified algorithm can be proved in the same way as for HKC by replacing c by p and b_1 by $b_2\colon Rel_{\mathbb{S}^X} \to Rel_{\mathbb{S}^X}$ defined for all $R \subseteq \mathbb{S}^X \times \mathbb{S}^X$ as

$$b_2(R) = \{(v_1, v_2) \mid o(v_1) \sqsubseteq o(v_2) \text{ and for all } a \in A, \ (t_a(v_1), t_a(v_1)) \in R\}.$$

However, the soundness of up-to reasoning is guaranteed only if $\sqsubseteq$ is a precongruence, that is $p(\sqsubseteq)$ is contained in $\sqsubseteq$.

Theorem 4.4. *Let $\mathbb{S}$ be a semiring equipped with a precongruence $\sqsubseteq$. Whenever HKP(v_1, v_2) terminates, it returns true if and only if $v_1 \precsim v_2$.*

In order for HKP to be effective, we need a procedure to compute p. When $\mathbb{S}$ is an integral l-monoid, we can check $(v, v') \in p(R)$ via a variation of the congruence check, using a rewriting system as in Sect. 3.3.

Proposition 4.5. *Let* $\mathbb{L}$ *be an integral l-monoid and let* $R \subseteq \mathbb{L}^X \times \mathbb{L}^X$ *be a relation.*

The set of rules $\mathcal{R}$ *is defined as* $\{v' \mapsto v \sqcup v' \mid (v, v') \in R\}$.[5] *Rewriting steps are defined as in Definition 3.2. If the rewriting algorithm terminates, then for all* $v, v' \in \mathbb{L}^X$, $(v, v') \in p(R)$ *iff* $\Downarrow v' \geq v$ *(where, as usual,* $\Downarrow v'$ *denotes the normal form of* v').

Observe that Theorems 3.11 and 3.12 guarantee termination for certain specific *l*-monoids. In particular, termination for the tropical semiring will be pivotal henceforward.

4.3 Threshold Problem for Automata over the Tropical Semiring

Language inclusion for weighted automata over the tropical semiring is not decidable, because language equivalence is not. However, the algorithm that we have introduced in the previous section can be used to solve the so called *threshold problem* over the tropical semiring of natural numbers $(\mathbb{N}_0 \cup \{\infty\}, \min, +, \infty, 0)$. The problem is to check whether for a given threshold $T \in \mathbb{N}_0$, a vector of states of a weighted automaton $v \in (\mathbb{N}_0 \cup \{\infty\})^X$ satisfies the threshold T, i.e. $[\![v]\!](w) \leq T$ for all $w \in A^*$.

Note that this problem is also known as the *universality problem*: universality for non-deterministic automata can be easily reduced to it, by taking weight 0 for each transition and setting $T = 0$ for the threshold.

This problem – which is known to be PSPACE-complete [3] – can be reduced to language inclusion by adding a new state t with output $o(t) = T$ and a 0 self-loop for each letter $a \in A$. Then we check whether the language of v includes the language of the unit vector e_t.

It is worth to note that in $(\mathbb{N}_0 \cup \{\infty\}, \min, +, \infty, 0)$ the ordering $\sqsubseteq$ is actually $\geq$, the reversed ordering on natural numbers. Therefore to solve the threshold problem, we need to check $e_t \precsim v$.

The reader can easily concoct an example where HKP may not terminate. However, it has already been observed in [3] that it is a sound reasoning technique to replace every vector entry larger than T by ∞. To formalise this result, we will first introduce an abstraction mapping $\mathcal{A}$ and then state our modified algorithm:

Definition 4.6. *Let a threshold* $T \in \mathbb{N}_0$ *be given. We define the abstraction* $\mathcal{A} : \mathbb{N}_0 \cup \{\infty\} \to \mathbb{N}_0 \cup \{\infty\}$ *according to* $\mathcal{A}(s) = s$ *if* $s \leq T$ *and* $\mathcal{A}(s) = \infty$ *otherwise. The definition extends elementwise to vectors in* $(\mathbb{N}_0 \cup \{\infty\})^X$.

With this definition, we call $\text{HKP}_\mathcal{A}$, the algorithm obtained from HKP by replacing step (3.4) with the following:

```
(3.4)    for all a ∈ A
            insert (t_a(v'_1), A(t_a(v'_2))) into todo
```

---

[5] Whenever $v \leq v'$, the rule can be omitted, since it is never applicable.

Now to check whether a certain vector v satisfies the threshold of T, it is enough to run $\mathrm{HKP}_{\mathcal{A}}(e_t, v)$ where e_t is the unit vector for t as defined above.

The soundness of the proposed algorithm can be shown in essentially the same way as for HKP but using a novel up-to technique to take care of the abstraction $\mathcal{A}$. For the completeness, we need the following additional result.

Lemma 4.7. *For all vectors* $v \in (\mathbb{N}_0 \cup \{\infty\})^X$ *it holds that (i)* $\mathcal{A}(t_a(\mathcal{A}(v))) = \mathcal{A}(t_a(v))$; *(ii)* $\mathcal{A}(o(\mathcal{A}(v))) = \mathcal{A}(o(v))$.

Theorem 4.8. $\mathrm{HKP}_{\mathcal{A}}(e_t, v_1)$ *always terminates. Moreover* $\mathrm{HKP}_{\mathcal{A}}(e_t, v_1)$ *returns true iff* $[\![v_1]\!](w) \leq T$ *for all* $w \in A^*$.

4.4   Exploiting Similarity

For checking language inclusion of non-deterministic automaton it is often convenient to precompute a *similarity* relation that allows to immediately skip some pairs of states [1]. This idea can be readapted to weighted automata over an l-monoid by using the following notion.

Definition 4.9. *Let* (X, o, t) *be a weighted automaton. A relation* $R \subseteq \mathbb{S}^X \times \mathbb{S}^X$ *on unit vectors is called a* simulation relation *whenever for all* $(v, v') \in R$ *(i)* $o(v) \sqsubseteq o(v')$; *(ii) for all* $a \in A$, *there exists a pair* (u, u') *that is a linear combination of vector pairs in* R *and furthermore* $t_a(v) \sqsubseteq u$, $u' \sqsubseteq t_a(v')$.

Similarity, *written* $\preceq$, *is the greatest simulation relation.*

Lemma 4.10. *Simulation implies language inclusion, i.e.* $\preceq$ *is included in* $\mathrel{\underset{\sim}{\sqsubseteq}}$.

Similarity over an l-monoid can be computed with the algorithm in Fig. 2. Even though the relation is not symmetric, the method is conceptually close to the traditional partition refinement algorithm to compute bisimilarity. Starting from the cross-product of all states, the algorithm first eliminates all pairs of

SIM (X, o, t)

```
(1)     R := {(v,v') ∈ S^X × S^X | v,v' are unit vectors}
(2)     R' := ∅
(3)     for all (v,v') ∈ R
   (3.1) if o(v) ⋢ o(v') then R := R \ {(v,v')}
(4)     while R ≠ R'
   (4.1) R' := R
   (4.2) for all a ∈ A
       (4.2.1)   for all (v,v') ∈ R
           (4.2.1.1)   u := ⨆{v₁ · (v₂ → t_a(v')) | (v₁,v₂) ∈ R}
           (4.2.1.2)   if t_a(v) ⋢ u then R := R \ {(v,v')}
(5)     return R
```

Fig. 2. Algorithm to compute similarity ($\preceq$) for a weighted automaton (X, o, t).

states where the first state does not have a smaller-or-equal output than the second one and then continuously removes all pairs of states that do not meet the second requirement for a simulation relation, until the relation does not change anymore.

Lemma 4.11. *SIM computes $\preceq$.*

Lemma 4.12. *The runtime complexity of SIM when applied to an automaton over state set X and alphabet A is polynomial, assuming constant time complexity for all semiring operations (supremum, multiplication, residuation).*

Once $\preceq$ is known, it can be exploited by HKP and HKP$_A$. To be completely formal in the proofs, it is convenient to define two novel algorithm – called HKP$'$ and HKP$'_A$ – which are obtained from HKP and HKP$_A$ by replacing step (3.2) by

> (3.2) if $(v'_1, v'_2) \in p'(R)$ then continue

where $p'(R)$ is defined for all relations R as $p'(R) = p(R \cup \preceq)$. The following two results state the correctness of the two algorithms.

Lemma 4.13. *Let $\mathbb{S}$ be a semiring equipped with a precongruence $\sqsubseteq$. Whenever HKP$'(v_1, v_2)$ terminates, it returns true iff $v_1 \precsim v_2$.*

Lemma 4.14. *HKP$'_A(e_t, v_1)$ always terminates. Moreover HKP$'_A(e_t, v_1)$ returns true iff $[\![v_1]\!](w) \leq T$ for all $w \in A^*$.*

4.5 An Exponential Pruning

To illustrate the benefits of up-to techniques, we show an example where HKP$'_A$ exponentially prunes the exploration space by exploiting the technique p'. We compare HKP$'_A$ against ABK in Fig. 3, that can be thought as an adaptation of the algorithm proposed in [3] to the notation used in this paper.

ABK(v_0)

```
(1)     todo := {v₀}
(2)     P := ∅
(3)     while todo ≠ ∅
  (3.1) extract v from todo
  (3.2) if v ∈ P then continue
  (3.3) if o(v) ≰ T then return false
  (3.4) for all a ∈ A insert A(tₐ(v)) into todo
  (3.5) insert v into P
(4)     return true
```

Fig. 3. Algorithm to check whether a vector v_0 of a weighted automata (X, o, t) satisfies the threshold $T \in \mathbb{N}_0$

Consider the family of automata over the tropical semiring in Fig. 4 and assume that $T = n$. By taking as initial vector $e_x \sqcup e_y$ (i.e., the vector mapping x and y to 0 and all other states to ∞), the automaton clearly does not respect the threshold, but this can be observed only for words longer than n.

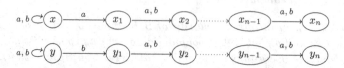

Fig. 4. Examples where $\mathsf{HKP}'_\mathcal{A}$ exponentially improves over ABK. Output weight is always 0, transition weight is always 1.

First, for ABK the runtime is exponential. This happens, since every word up to length n produces a different weight vector. For a word w of length m state x_i has weight m iff the i-last letter of the word is a, similarly state y_i has weight m iff the i-last letter is b. All other weights are ∞. For instance, the weights for word aab are given below.

x	x_1	x_2	x_3	x_4	$\cdots$	y	y_1	y_2	y_3	y_4	$\cdots$
3	∞	3	3	∞	$\cdots$	3	3	∞	∞	∞	$\cdots$

Now we compare with $\mathsf{HKP}'_\mathcal{A}$. Observe that $x_i \preceq x$, $y_i \preceq y$ for all i. (Remember that since the order is reversed, a lower weight simulates a higher weight.) Hence, we obtain rewriting rules that allow to replace an ∞-entry in x_i and y_i by m for all i. (Since both entries x and y are m, we can always apply this rule.) In the example above this leads to a vector where every entry is 3.

Hence it turns out that for all words of the same length, the corresponding vectors are all in the precongruence relation with each other – as they share the same normal form – and we only have to consider exactly one word of each length. Therefore, only linearly many words are considered and the runtime is polynomial.

5   Runtime Results for the Threshold Problem

We now discuss runtime results for the threshold problem for weighted automata over the tropical semiring of the natural numbers. We compare the following three algorithms: the algorithm without up-to technique (ABK) algorithm in Fig. 3, the algorithm that works up-to precongruence (HKP$_\mathcal{A}$), explained in Sect. 4.3, and the algorithm that additionally exploits pre-computed similarity (HKP$'_\mathcal{A}$), introduced in Sect. 4.4. This precomputation step is relatively costly and is included in the runtime results below.

Table 2. Runtime results on randomly generated automata

$(\lvert X\rvert, T)$	Algo	Runtime (millisec.)			Size of R/P			Size of $\preceq$		
		50%	90%	99%	50%	90%	99%	50%	90%	99%
(3,10)	HKP$'_\mathcal{A}$	2	8	20	5	14	33	0	2	4
	HKP$_\mathcal{A}$	1	3	14	5	14	34	-	-	-
	ABK	1	3	13	6	28	92	-	-	-
(3,15)	HKP$'_\mathcal{A}$	3	17	127	11	34	100	0	2	4
	HKP$_\mathcal{A}$	2	16	126	11	34	100	-	-	-
	ABK	2	17	90	18	119	373	-	-	-
(3,20)	HKP$'_\mathcal{A}$	6	65	393	18	70	174	0	2	4
	HKP$_\mathcal{A}$	4	64	466	18	71	192	-	-	-
	ABK	5	79	315	55	364	825	-	-	-
(6,10)	HKP$'_\mathcal{A}$	21	227	1862	18	106	302	0	2	12
	HKP$_\mathcal{A}$	8	217	1858	19	106	302	-	-	-
	ABK	9	286	2045	40	693	2183	-	-	-
(6,15)	HKP$'_\mathcal{A}$	90	2547	12344	65	353	750	0	2	11
	HKP$_\mathcal{A}$	84	2560	12328	65	353	750	-	-	-
	ABK	88	4063	20987	346	3082	7270	-	-	-
(6,20)	HKP$'_\mathcal{A}$	239	7541	59922	111	589	1681	0	3	11
	HKP$_\mathcal{A}$	234	7613	60360	111	589	1681	-	-	-
	ABK	253	16240	103804	702	6140	14126	-	-	-
(9,10)	HKP$'_\mathcal{A}$	274	9634	73369	98	582	1501	0	3	21
	HKP$_\mathcal{A}$	236	9581	72833	99	582	1501	-	-	-
	ABK	232	17825	99332	536	6336	14956	-	-	-
(9,15)	HKP$'_\mathcal{A}$	1709	71509	301033	256	1517	3319	0	3	19
	HKP$_\mathcal{A}$	1681	70587	301018	256	1517	3319	-	-	-
	ABK	919	112323	515386	1436	14889	28818	-	-	-
(9,20)	HKP$'_\mathcal{A}$	3885	168826	874259	407	2347	5086	0	3	20
	HKP$_\mathcal{A}$	3838	168947	872647	407	2347	5086	-	-	-
	ABK	1744	301253	1617813	2171	22713	48735	-	-	-
(12,10)	HKP$'_\mathcal{A}$	1866	93271	560824	247	1586	3668	0	7	31
	HKP$_\mathcal{A}$	1800	92490	560837	251	1586	3668	-	-	-
	ABK	1067	189058	889949	1342	18129	37387	-	-	-
(12,15)	HKP$'_\mathcal{A}$	5127	363530	1971541	423	3001	6743	0	7	35
	HKP$_\mathcal{A}$	5010	362908	1968865	423	3001	6743	-	-	-
	ABK	1418	509455	2349335	1672	27225	55627	-	-	-
(12,20)	HKP$'_\mathcal{A}$	15101	789324	3622374	744	4489	9027	0	6	32
	HKP$_\mathcal{A}$	15013	787119	3623393	744	4489	9027	-	-	-
	ABK	4169	1385929	4773543	3297	43756	80712	-	-	-

We performed the following experiment: for certain values of $|X|$ (size of state set) and of T (threshold) we generated random automata. The alphabet size was randomly chosen between 1 and 5. For each pair of states and alphabet symbol, the probability of having an edge with finite weight is 90%. (We chose this high number, since otherwise the threshold is almost never respected and the algorithms return false almost immediately due to absence of a transition for a given letter. With our choice instead, the algorithms need many steps and the threshold is satisfied in 14% of the cases.) In case the weight is different from ∞, a random weight from the set $\{0, \ldots, 10\}$ is assigned.

For each pair $(|X|, T)$ we generated 1000 automata. The runtime results can be seen in Table 2. We considered the 50%, 90% and 99% percentiles: the 50% percentile is the median and the 90% percentile means that 90% of the runs were faster and 10% slower than the time given in the respective field. Analogously for the 99% percentile.

Apart from the runtime we also measured the size of the relation R (or P in the case of ABK) and the size of the similarity $\preceq$ (in case of HKP'_A). The program was written in C# and executed on an Intel Core 2 Quad CPU Q9550 at 2.83 GHz with 4 GB RAM, running Windows 10.

First note that, as expected, HKP_A and HKP'_A always produce much smaller relations than ABK. However, they introduce some overhead, due to rewriting for checking $p(R)$, and due to the computation of similarity, which is clearly seen for the 50% percentile. However, if we look at the larger parameters and at the 90% and 99% percentiles (which measure the worst-case performance), HKP_A and HKP'_A gain the upper hand in terms of runtime.

Note also that while in the example above similarity played a large role, this is not the case for the random examples. Here similarity (not counting the reflexive pairs) is usually quite small. This means that similarity does not lead to savings, only in very few cases does the size of R decrease for HKP'_A. But this also means that the computation of $\preceq$ is not very costly and hence the runtime of HKP_A is quite similar to the runtime of HKP'_A. We believe that for weighted automata arising from concrete problems, the similarity relation will usually be larger and promise better runtimes. Note also that similarity is independent of the initial vector and the threshold and if one wants to ask several threshold questions for the same automaton, it has to be computed only once.

6   Conclusion and Future Work

In this work, we have investigated up-to techniques for weighted automata, including methods to determine the congruence closure for semimodules.

Related Work: Related work on up-to techniques has already been discussed in the introduction. For the language equivalence problem for weighted automata we are mainly aware of the algorithm presented in [4], which is a partition refinement algorithm and which already uses a kind of up-to technique: it can eliminate certain vectors which arise as linear combinations of other vectors. The paper [22] considers simulation for weighted automata, but not in connection to up-to techniques.

Congruence closure for term rewriting has been investigated in [11].

Our examples mainly involved the tropical semiring (and related semirings). Hence there are relations to work by Aceto et al. [2] who presented an equational theory for the tropical semiring and related semirings, as well as Gaubert and Plus [14] who discuss several reasons to be interested in the tropical semiring and present solution methods for several types of linear equation systems.

Future Work: As we have seen in the experiments on the threshold problem, our techniques greatly reduce the size of the relations. However, the reduction in runtime is less significant, which is due to the overhead for the computation of similarity and the rewriting procedure. There is still a substantial improvement for the worst-case running times (90% and 99% percentiles). So far, the algorithms, especially algorithm SIM for computing similarity, are not very sophisticated and we believe that there is further potential for optimization.

Acknowledgements. We would like to thank Paweł Sobociński and Damien Pous for interesting discussions on the topic of this paper. Furthermore we express our thanks to Issai Zaks for his help with the runtime results.

References

1. Abdulla, P.A., Chen, Y.-F., Holík, L., Mayr, R., Vojnar, T.: When simulation meets antichains. In: Esparza, J., Majumdar, R. (eds.) TACAS 2010. LNCS, vol. 6015, pp. 158–174. Springer, Heidelberg (2010). doi:10.1007/978-3-642-12002-2_14
2. Aceto, L., Ésik, Z., Ingólfsdóttir, A.: Equational theories of tropical semirings. Theor. Comput. Sci. **298**(3), 417–469 (2003). Foundations of Software Science and Computation Structures
3. Almagor, S., Boker, U., Kupferman, O.: What's decidable about weighted automata? In: Bultan, T., Hsiung, P.-A. (eds.) ATVA 2011. LNCS, vol. 6996, pp. 482–491. Springer, Heidelberg (2011). doi:10.1007/978-3-642-24372-1_37
4. Béal, M.-P., Lombardy, S., Sakarovitch, J.: Conjugacy and equivalence of weighted automata and functional transducers. In: Grigoriev, D., Harrison, J., Hirsch, E.A. (eds.) CSR 2006. LNCS, vol. 3967, pp. 58–69. Springer, Heidelberg (2006). doi:10.1007/11753728_9
5. Bezhanishvili, G., Gabelaia, D., Jibladze, M.: Funayama's theorem revisited. Algebra Univers. **70**(3), 271–286 (2013)
6. Bonchi, F., Bonsangue, M.M., Boreale, M., Rutten, J.J.M.M., Silva, A.: A coalgebraic perspective on linear weighted automata. Inf. Comput. **211**, 77–105 (2012)
7. Bonchi, F., König, B., Küpper, S.: Up-to techniques for weighted systems (extended version) arXiv:1701.05001 (2017)
8. Bonchi, F., Petrisan, D., Pous, D., Rot, J.: Coinduction up-to in a fibrational setting. In: Henzinger, T.A., Miller, D. (eds.) Proceedings of CSL-LICS 2014, pp. 20:1–20:9. ACM (2014)
9. Bonchi, F., Pous, D.: Checking NFA equivalence with bisimulations up to congruence. In: Proceedings of POPL 2013, pp. 457–468. ACM (2013)

10. Boreale, M.: Weighted bisimulation in linear algebraic form. In: Bravetti, M., Zavattaro, G. (eds.) CONCUR 2009. LNCS, vol. 5710, pp. 163–177. Springer, Heidelberg (2009). doi:10.1007/978-3-642-04081-8_12

11. Cyrluk, D., Lincoln, P., Shankar, N.: On Shostak's decision procedure for combinations of theories. In: McRobbie, M.A., Slaney, J.K. (eds.) CADE 1996. LNCS, vol. 1104, pp. 463–477. Springer, Heidelberg (1996). doi:10.1007/3-540-61511-3_107

12. Dershowitz, N., Jouannaud, J.-P.: Rewrite systems. In: van Leeuwen, J. (ed.) Formal Models and Semantics, Handbook of Theoretical Computer Science, vol. B, pp. 243–320. Elsevier (1990)

13. Doyen, L., Raskin, J.-F.: Antichain algorithms for finite automata. In: Esparza, J., Majumdar, R. (eds.) TACAS 2010. LNCS, vol. 6015, pp. 2–22. Springer, Heidelberg (2010). doi:10.1007/978-3-642-12002-2_2

14. Gaubert, S., Plus, M.: Methods and applications of (max,+) linear algebra. In: Reischuk, R., Morvan, M. (eds.) STACS 1997. LNCS, vol. 1200, pp. 261–282. Springer, Heidelberg (1997). doi:10.1007/BFb0023465

15. Hopcroft, J.E., Karp, R.M.: A linear algorithm for testing equivalence of finite automata. Technical report TR 114, Cornell University (1971)

16. König, B., Küpper, S.: A generalized partition refinement algorithm, instantiated to language equivalence checking for weighted automata. Soft Comput. 1–18 (2016). http://link.springer.com/article/10.1007/s00500-016-2363-z

17. Krob, D.: The equality problem for rational series with multiplicities in the tropical semiring is undecidable. Int. J. Algebra Comput. 4(3), 405–425 (1994)

18. Milner, R.: Communication and Concurrency. Prentice Hall, Upper Saddle River (1989)

19. Pous, D., Sangiorgi, D.: Enhancements of the coinductive proof method. In: Sangiorgi, D., Rutten, J. (eds.) Advanced Topics in Bisimulation and Coinduction. Cambridge University Press, Cambridge (2011)

20. Rot, J., Bonchi, F., Bonsangue, M., Pous, D., Rutten, J., Silva, A.: Enhanced coalgebraic bisimulation. Math. Struct. Comput. Sci. 1–29 (2015). https://www.cambridge.org/core/journals/mathematical-structures-in-computer-science/article/div-classtitleenhanced-coalgebraic-bisimulationdiv/C588A590E7DB3A73F1C86487D0F8DE19

21. Stark, E.W.: On behaviour equivalence for probabilistic i/o automata and its relationship to probabilistic bisimulation. J. Automata Lang. Comb. 8(2), 361–395 (2003)

22. Urabe, N., Hasuo, I.: Generic forward and backward simulations III: quantitative simulations by matrices. In: Baldan, P., Gorla, D. (eds.) CONCUR 2014. LNCS, vol. 8704, pp. 451–466. Springer, Heidelberg (2014). doi:10.1007/978-3-662-44584-6_31

23. Wulf, M., Doyen, L., Henzinger, T.A., Raskin, J.-F.: Antichains: a new algorithm for checking universality of finite automata. In: Ball, T., Jones, R.B. (eds.) CAV 2006. LNCS, vol. 4144, pp. 17–30. Springer, Heidelberg (2006). doi:10.1007/11817963_5

Hybrid Systems

Rigorous Simulation-Based Analysis of Linear Hybrid Systems

Stanley Bak[1]([✉]) and Parasara Sridhar Duggirala[2]

[1] Air Force Research Laboratory, Dayton, USA
stanley.bak@gmail.com
[2] University of Connecticut, Mansfield, USA
psd@uconn.edu

Abstract. Design analysis of Cyber-Physical Systems (CPS) with complex continuous and discrete behaviors, in-practice, relies heavily on numerical simulations. While useful for evaluation and debugging, such analysis is often incomplete owing to the nondeterminism in the discrete transitions and the uncountability of the continuous space. In this paper, we present a precise notion of simulations for CPS called simulation-equivalent reachability, which includes all the states that can be reached by any simulation. While this notion is weaker than traditional reachability, we present a technique that performs simulation-equivalent reachability in an efficient, scalable, and theoretically sound and complete manner. For achieving this, we describe two improvements, namely *invariant constraint propagation* for handling invariants and *on-demand successor deaggregation* for handling discrete transitions. We use our tool implementation of the approach, **HyLAA** (**Hy**brid **L**inear **A**utomata **A**nalyzer), to evaluate the improvements, and demonstrate computing the simulation-equivalent reachable set for a replicated helicopter systems with over 1000 dimensions in about 10 min.

1 Introduction

Cyber-Physical Systems (CPS) that involve interaction between a system's software and the physical world can be naturally modeled using the framework of hybrid automata [4,29]. A common industrial practice to design and debug these systems is to use a model-based design framework such as Simulink or Modelica, which produces concrete traces of system behavior. An engineer uses a combination of his or her intuition about potential edge cases and sampled simulations to try and find behaviors that violate the safety specification. While performing large numbers of simulations can be extremely useful, the space of possible simulations is often infinite, and so simulations can miss critical error cases. For large and complex models, with high numbers of dimensions, the amount of coverage provided by simulations decreases further, increasing the chances of missing a simulation that violates safety.

DISTRIBUTION A. Approved for public release; Distribution unlimited. (Approval AFRL PA #88ABW-2016-5197, 18 OCT 2016).

A. Legay and T. Margaria (Eds.): TACAS 2017, Part I, LNCS 10205, pp. 555–572, 2017.
DOI: 10.1007/978-3-662-54577-5_32

In this work, we add rigor to such simulation-based analysis and compute what we call the *simulation-equivalent reachable set*. To do this, we build upon a recently proposed method [18] that exploits the superposition property of linear systems by combining the information from selected individual simulations to reason about an unbounded number of simulations. We extend this approach to analyze a general linear hybrid system, and provide an analysis method which is exact, *with respect to a particular simulation algorithm*. Upon termination, if our algorithm infers that the system is safe, then no simulation enters the unsafe set; if our algorithm infers that the system is unsafe, a counter-example trace is provided. One of the main reasons to present an alternative notion of reachability is fundamentally driven by the desire to generate counterexamples which are of high importance during the debugging phase of design analysis. Additionally, while simulation-equivalent reachability is a bit weaker than traditional reachability, the simplifications enable analysis which is more scalable, as well as sound and complete. The contributions of this paper are as follows.

1. We formally state the simulation-equivalent reachability problem and provide a sound and complete algorithm for its computation.
2. We present two new improvements, first, for reducing the number of constraints in handling invariants, and second, for aggregating and deaggregating sets after discrete transitions, without losing simulation-equivalence.
3. We present an accuracy-equivalent comparison with traditional reachability algorithms, and evaluate the proposed techniques in a new tool called **HyLAA** (**Hy**brid **L**inear **A**utomata **A**nalyzer).

Related Approaches: Verification techniques for hybrid automata can be classified into two main categories: flow-pipe construction [13] and deductive verification [24,31]. Flow-pipe construction methods, which are more closely related to this paper, are typically classified by the complexity allowed by their continuous dynamics. Existing techniques can handle systems where continuous dynamics are restricted to be timers [5,10], piecewise constants [21,26], linear [23,25], and general nonlinear expressions [2,12]. In this context, our approach fits in with the class of tools used to analyze *linear systems*. The proposed method differs, however, in that our analysis is sound and complete for simulation-equivalent reachability, and can provide concrete counterexamples if the system violates the safety specification. Systems with complex dynamics are sometimes analyzed using hybridization [6,14]. In hybridization, complex dynamics are simplified as a hybrid system with simpler dynamics and nondeterministic inputs, where the inputs account for the simplification errors.

Simulations have also been leveraged before to perform more formal analysis of hybrid systems. One approach studies the effects of perturbations of the initial state on the divergence of trajectories [15–17,20]. These approaches are different from the way HyLAA uses simulations, in that they reason about tubes of states around individual simulations. Other falsification methods use a metric to determine how close a particular simulation is to violating a formal specification [19], and then apply a global optimization routine to generate new simulation inputs which try to optimize the metric, essentially trying to generate simulations that are closer to a violation [9,30]. While often better than purely random Monte Carlo simulation, this class of approaches is incomplete and so may still miss error trajectories.

2   Preliminaries

States and vectors are elements in $\mathbb{R}^n$ are denoted as x and v. Given a sequence $seq = s_1, s_2, \ldots$, the ith element in the sequence is denoted as $seq[i]$. In this work, we use the following mathematical notation of a linear hybrid automata.

Definition 1. *A linear hybrid automaton is defined to be a tuple $\langle Loc, X, Flow, Inv, Trans, Guard \rangle$ where:*

Loc is a finite set of locations (also called modes).
$X \subseteq \mathbb{R}^n$ is the state space of the behaviors.
Flow: Loc $\rightarrow$ AffineDeq(X) assigns an affine differential equation $\dot{x} = A_l x + B_l$ for location l of the hybrid automaton.
Inv: Loc $\rightarrow 2^{\mathbb{R}^n}$ assigns an invariant set for each location of the hybrid automaton.
Trans $\subseteq$ Loc $\times$ Loc is the set of discrete transitions.
Guard: Trans $\rightarrow 2^{\mathbb{R}^n}$ defines the set of states where a discrete transition is enabled. For a linear hybrid automaton, the invariants and guards are given as a conjunction of linear constraints.

The *initial set of states* Θ is a subset of *Loc* $\times 2^{\mathbb{R}^n}$, where second element in the pair is a conjunction of linear constraints. An *initial state* q_0 is a pair (Loc_0, x_0), such that $x_0 \in X$, and $(Loc_0, x_0) \in \Theta$. Unsafe states are indicated by having a set of error modes, $U \subseteq Loc$.

Definition 2. *Given a hybrid automaton and an initial set of states Θ, an execution of the hybrid automaton is a sequence of trajectories and actions $\tau_0 a_1 \tau_1 a_2 \ldots$ such that (i) the first state of τ_0 denoted as q_0 is in the initial set, i.e., $q_0 = (Loc_0, x_0) \in \Theta$, (ii) each τ_i is the solution of the differential equation of the corresponding location Loc_i, (iii) all the states in the trajectory τ_i respect the invariant of the location Loc_i, and (iv) the state of the trajectory before each action a_i satisfies Guard(a_i).*

The set of states encountered by all executions that conform to the above semantics is called the *reachable set*. For linear systems, the closed form expression for the trajectories is given as $\tau_i(t) = e^{A_l t} \tau(0) + \int_0^t e^{A_l (t-\mu)} B_l d\mu$ where A_l and B_l define the affine dynamics of the mode. Instead of computing the reachable set of states, we compute the set of states which can be reached by a fixed simulation algorithm. We now precisely define the semantics for a simulation of hybrid automata that we will use in this paper.

Definition 3. *A sequence* $\rho_H(q_0, h) = q_0, q_1, q_2, \ldots,$ *where each* $q_i = (Loc_i, x_i),$ *is a* (q_0, h)-*simulation of the hybrid automaton* H *with initial set* Θ *if and only if* $q_0 \in \Theta$ *and each pair* (q_i, q_{i+1}) *corresponds to either: (i) a continuous trajectory in location* Loc_i *with* $Loc_i = Loc_{i+1}$ *such that a trajectory starting from* x_i *would reach* x_{i+1} *after exactly* h *time units with* $x_i \in Inv(Loc_i)$, *or (ii) a discrete transition from* Loc_i *to* Loc_{i+1} *(with* $Loc_{i-1} = Loc_i$*) where* $\exists a \in Trans$ *such that* $x_i = x_{i+1}$, $x_i \in Guard(a)$ *and* $x_{i+1} \in Inv(Loc_{i+1})$. *Bounded-time variants of these simulations, with time bound* T, *are called* (q_0, h, T)-*simulations.*

For simulations, h is called the *step size* and T is called *time bound*. While talking about the continuous or discrete behaviors of simulations, we abuse notation and use x_i, the continuous component of the state instead of q_i. Notice that the simulation engine given in Definition 3 does not check if the invariant is violated for the entire time interval, but only at a given time instance. Also, the discrete transitions are only enabled at time instances that are multiples of h. To avoid Zeno behaviors, the simulation engine forces that the system should spend at least h time units in each mode. Hence, if two consecutive states x_i and x_{i+1} corresponds to a continuous trajectory of the hybrid automaton, it is not necessary that $x_{i+1} \in Inv(Loc_i)$. If a guard is enabled and the invariant is still true, or if multiple guards are enabled, the simulation engine can make a nondeterministic choice. We call the set of states encountered by all simulations which conform to this definition the *simulation-equivalent reachable set*.

Condition (ii) in the semantics of simulations permits a discrete transition to be taken even if the invariant condition of the predecessor mode is false. This is necessary to handle the common case where a guard is the complement of an invariant, and a sampled simulation jumps over the guard boundary during a single step. If these types of behaviors are not desired, the guard can be explicitly strengthened with the invariant of the originating mode. For readers familiar with the simulation engines in standard tools like Simulink or Modelica, the defined simulation sequences do not perform special algorithms to isolate *zero crossings*, and the transitions are not necessarily *urgent*.

Definition 4. *A given simulation* $\rho_H(q_0, h)$ *is said to be safe with respect to an unsafe set of locations* U *if and only if* $\forall q_i = (Loc_i, x_i) \in \rho_H(q_0, h), Loc_i \notin U.$ *Safety for bounded time simulations are defined similarly.*

Definition 5. *A hybrid automaton* H *with initial set* Θ, *time bound* T, *and unsafe set of locations* U *is said to be safe with respect to its simulations if all simulations starting from* Θ *for bounded time* T *are safe.*

Definition 6. *Given any initial state* x_0, *vectors* $v_1, \ldots, v_m$ *where* $v_i \in \mathbb{R}^n$, *scalars* $\alpha_1, \ldots, \alpha_m$, *the trajectories of linear differential equations in a given location* τ *always satisfy*

$$\tau(x_0 + \Sigma_{i=1}^m \alpha_i v_i, t) = \tau(x_0, t) + \Sigma_{i=1}^m \alpha_i(\tau(x_0 + v_i, t) - \tau(x_0, t)).$$

We exploit the superposition property of linear systems in order to compute the simulation-equivalent reachable set of states for a linear hybrid system. An illustration of the superposition principle for two vectors is shown in Fig. 1. Before describing the algorithm for computing the reachable set, we finally introduce the data structure called a *generalized star* that is used to represent the reachable set of states.

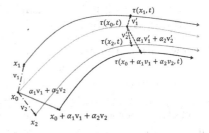

Fig. 1. Observe that the state reached at time t from $x_0 + v_1 + v_2$ is identical to $\tau_i(x_0, t) + (\tau_i(x_0 + v_1, t) - \tau_i(x_0, t)) + (\tau_i(x_0 + v_2, t) - \tau_i(x_0, t))$.

Definition 7. *A generalized star (or simply star)* Θ *is a tuple* $\langle c, V, P \rangle$ *where* $c \in \mathbb{R}^n$ *is called the* center, $V = \{v_1, v_2, \ldots, v_m\}$ *is a set of* m $(\leq n)$ *vectors in* $\mathbb{R}^n$ *called the* basis vectors, *and* $P : \mathbb{R}^n \to \{\top, \bot\}$ *is a predicate.*

A generalized star Θ *defines a subset of* $\mathbb{R}^n$ *as follows.*

$$[\![\Theta]\!] = \{x \mid \exists \bar{\alpha} = [\alpha_1, \ldots, \alpha_m]^T \text{ such that } x = c + \Sigma_{i=1}^n \alpha_i v_i \text{ and } P(\bar{\alpha}) = \top\}$$

Sometimes we will refer to both Θ *and* $[\![\Theta]\!]$ *as* Θ.

In this paper, we consider predicates P which are conjunctions of linear constraints, in order to be able to use linear programming for several key operations on stars such as checking if a point is in a star.

Example 1. Consider a set $\Theta \subset \mathbb{R}^2$ given as $\Theta \triangleq \{(x, y) | x \in [2, 3], y \in [2, 3]\}$. The given set Θ can be represented as a generalized star in multiple ways. One way of representing the set is given as $\langle c, V, P \rangle$ where $c = (2.5, 2.5)$, $V = \{[0, 1]^T, [0, 1]^T\}$ and $P \triangleq -0.5 \leq \alpha_1 \leq 0.5 \wedge -0.5 \leq \alpha_2 \leq 0.5$. That is, the set Θ is represented as a star with center $(2.5, 2.5)$ with vectors as the orthonormal vectors in the Cartesian plane and predicate where the components along the basis vectors are restricted by the set $[-0.5, 0.5] \times [-0.5, 0.5]$.

Operations on Generalized Stars: In this paper we restrict our attention to stars with predicates that are conjunctions of linear inequalities. As generalized stars are used to represent the reachable set of states, one has to perform operations such as basis transformation, intersection, and union. For stars with linear predicates, one can perform *basis and center transformation* by changing the center to another center, the basis vectors to a new basis vector set (with same rank), and perform matrix multiplication.

Given two stars $S_1 \triangleq \langle c, V, P_1 \rangle$ and $S_2 \triangleq \langle c, V, P_2 \rangle$ the set intersection of two stars is obtained as $S_\cap \triangleq \langle c, V, P_1 \wedge P_2 \rangle$ and their *aggregation* as $S_{agg} = \langle c, V, P_{agg} \rangle$ where $P_1 \vee P_2 \Rightarrow P_{agg}$. For computing P_{agg} one can choose several *template directions*, compute the maximum and minimum values along each direction using linear programming.

2.1   Reachable Set Computation for Linear Dynamical Systems Using Simulations

We now outline the algorithm that computes the reachable set of states for continuous dynamics on which we base our approach. Owing to space limitations, we briefly describe the algorithm here, and note that a longer explanation and proof of correctness is available in prior work [18]. At its crux, the algorithm exploits the superposition principle of linear systems and computes the reachable states using a generalized star representation. For an n-dimensional system, this algorithm requires at most $n + 1$ simulations.

Given an initial set $\Theta \triangleq \langle c, V, P \rangle$ with $V = \{v_1, v_2, \ldots, v_m\}(m \leq n)$, the algorithm performs a simulation starting from c (denoted as $\rho(c, h, k)$), and $\forall 1 \leq j \leq n$, performs a simulation from $c + v_j$ (denoted as $\rho(c + v_j, h, k)$). For a given time instance $i \cdot h$, the reachable set denoted as $Reach_i(\Theta)$ is defined as $\langle c_i, V_i, P \rangle$ where $c_i = \rho(c, h, k)[i]$ and $V_i = \langle v_1', v_2', \ldots, v_m' \rangle$ where $\forall 1 \leq j \leq m, v_j' = \rho(c + v_j, h, k)[i] - \rho(c, h, k)[i]$. Notice that the predicate does not change for the reachable set, but only the center and the basis vectors are changed.

> **input** : Initial Set: $\Theta = \langle c, V, P \rangle$, time step: h, time bound: $k \cdot h$
> **output** : $Reach(\Theta) = Reach_0(\Theta), \ldots, Reach_k(\Theta)$
> 1 **for** *each i from 0 to k* **do**
> 2 $\quad$ $c_i \leftarrow \rho(c, h, k)[i]$;
> 3 $\quad$ **for** *each $v_j \in V$* **do**
> 4 $\quad\quad$ $|$ $v_j' \leftarrow \rho(c + v_j, h, k)[i] - c_i$;
> 5 $\quad$ **end**
> 6 $\quad$ $V_i \leftarrow \{v_1', \ldots, v_m'\}$;
> 7 $\quad$ $Reach_i(\Theta) \leftarrow \langle c_i, V_i, P \rangle$;
> 8 $\quad$ Append $Reach_i(\Theta)$ to $Reach(\Theta)$;
> 9 **end**
> 10 **return** $Reach(\Theta)$;

Algorithm 1. Algorithm that computes the reachable set at time instances $i \cdot h$ from $n + 1$ simulations.

An illustration of this reachable set computation is shown in Fig. 2. Here, as the system is 2-dimensional, a total number of three simulations are performed, one from *center c* and one from $c + v_1$ and one from $c + v_2$. The reachable set after time $i \cdot h$ is given as the star with center $c' = \rho(c, h, k)[i]$, basis vectors $v_1' = \rho(c + v_1, h, k)[i] - \rho(c, h, k)[i]$, and $v_2' = \rho(c + v_2, h, k)[i] - \rho(c, h, k)[i]$ and the same predicate P as the given in the initial set.

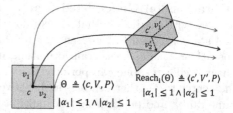

Fig. 2. Illustration of the reachable set using sample simulations and generalized star representation. Notice that in the star representation, the predicate that defines the reachable set is same as that of the initial set.

Remark 1. Observe that the reachable set computation described in Algorithm 1 is not dependent on the predicate of the initial set. Therefore, if the given initial set $\Theta \triangleq \langle c, V, P \rangle$ is changed to $\langle c, V, P' \rangle$, the reachable set computed in line 7 changes from $\langle c_i, V_i, P \rangle$ to $\langle c_i, V_i, P' \rangle$. This key observation helps us in proposing new techniques for handling invariants and discrete transitions.

Assumptions: Since our method for reasoning about states reachable in the continuous space uses numerical simulations and superposition, we make a few key assumptions. First, the numerical computations performed by our algorithm are exact (we do not track floating-point errors through the computations). Second, the underlying ODE simulation engine provides an exact result. We believe that these assumptions are reasonable, because in practice, most of the system designers accept that numerical simulations are a very close approximation to a model's true behavior, and using numerical simulations requires the same assumptions. A user concerned about the inaccuracy of numerical simulation can either use validated simulations [1] or compute the linear ODE solution as a matrix exponential to an arbitrary degree of precision.

3   Constraint Propagation for Invariants

The goal of this paper is to perform simulation-equivalent reachability for hybrid automata. While Algorithm 1 computes reachable set for a dynamical system, it does not take into account the invariant and the discrete transitions. An earlier extension of Algorithm 1 for hybrid systems propose handling the invariants by performing $Reach_i \cap Inv(l)$ where $Inv(l)$ is the invariant of the current mode [18].

Although sound, such procedure would result in an overapproximation, but not a simulation-equivalent reachable set. Consider the illustration in Fig. 3 depicting reachable sets $Reach_i$ and $Reach_{i+1}$ and their overlap with the invariant of the current mode. If one considers the executions that visit $Reach_i \cap Inv(l)$, one can only reach the states labeled as $ActualReach_{i+1}(\Theta)$. To avoid such overapproximations, we present an algorithm that performs constraint propagation for computing the reachable set while respecting the invariant.

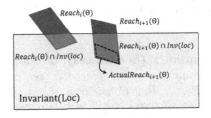

Fig. 3. Figure depicting the overapproximation of the reachable set computed by performing $Reach_i \cap Inv(l)$ without invariant propagation.

We exploit the observation made in Remark 1 for performing constraint propagation. Consider the scenario where $Reach_i$ contains states that satisfy the invariant and states that violate the invariant. For accurately computing the reachable set for all the future iterations, one must only consider the states originating from $Reach_i \cap Inv(l)$. Given $Reach_i = \langle c_i, V_i, P \rangle$, we perform center and basis transformation on $Inv(l)$ to represent it as a star with center c_i and basis V_i such that $Inv(l) = \langle c_i, V_i, Q_i \rangle$. Hence, $Reach_i \cap Inv(l) = \langle c_i, V_i, P \wedge Q_i \rangle$. From the correctness of Algorithm 1, it follows that the simulations reaching $\langle c_i, V_i, P \wedge Q_i \rangle$ should originate from $\Theta' \subseteq \Theta$ where $\Theta' = \langle c, V, P \wedge Q_i \rangle$.

For the time instances $j > i$, since the simulations should visit $\langle c_i, V_i, P \wedge Q_i \rangle$, they should originate from $\Theta' = \langle c, V, P \wedge Q_i \rangle$. This implies that the constraints Q_i should be added to the predicate in $Reach_j$. Therefore, for every instance i, we propagate the constraints Q_i for all future time instances. The reachable set at time instance j accumulates the constraints from time instances $0, 1, \ldots, j-1$ and updates the predicate with the conjunction of these constraints. We call this technique as *invariant constraint propagation*. This procedure is formally presented in Algorithm 2 and its correctness is given in Theorems 2 and 1.

---

input : Initial Set: $\Theta = \langle c, V, P \rangle$, time step: h, time bound: $k \cdot h$, Invariant: Inv
output : $Reach(\Theta) = Reach_0(\Theta), \ldots, Reach_k(\Theta)$ that respect the invariant
1   $ConstraintsList \leftarrow \emptyset$;
2   $AccumulatedConstraints \leftarrow \top$;
3   $R \leftarrow \mathsf{Alg1}(\Theta, h, k)$;
4 **for** *each i from 1 to k* **do**
5     $R_i = \langle c_i, V_i, P_i \rangle \leftarrow R[i]$;
6     $Q_i \leftarrow \mathsf{Tranformation}(Inv, c_i, V_i)$;
7     $AccumulatedConstraints \leftarrow AccumulatedConstraints \wedge Q_i$;
8     $R_i \leftarrow \langle c_i, V_i, P \wedge AccumulatedConstraints \rangle$;
9   Append R_i to $Reach(\Theta)$;
10   Append Q_i to $ConstraintsList$;
11 **end**
12 **return** $(Reach(\Theta), ConstraintsList)$;

Algorithm 2. Algorithm that computes the reachable set at time instances $i \cdot h$ from $n + 1$ simulations and respects the invariant.

Theorem 1 (Soundness). *Consider initial set $\Theta \triangleq \langle c, V, P \rangle$, time bound $k \cdot h$, invariant Inv, and reachable set computed by Algorithm 2 as $Reach(\Theta) = R_0, R_1, \ldots, R_k$. Consider a simulation $x_0, x_1, \ldots, x_j$ where $j \leq k$ such that $x_0 \in \Theta$, and $\forall 0 \leq i \leq j, x_i \in Inv$, then we have $\forall 0 \leq i \leq j, x_i \in R_i$.*

Proof. Consider the initial state $x_0 \in \Theta \cap Inv$, it automatically follows that $x_0 \in \langle c_0, V_0, P \wedge Q_0 \rangle$, where Q_0 is computed in line 6 in the first iteration of the loop (lines 4–11). Hence, it follows that $\forall i > 0, x_i \in \langle c_i, V_i, P \wedge Q_0 \rangle$.

Consider $x_i, 0 < i \leq k$, the ith state in the simulation that respects invariant. Therefore, we have that $\forall m < i, x_m \in Inv$. Consider $Q_0, Q_1, \ldots, Q_{i-1}$ be the clauses computed in line 6 for the iterations $0, 1, \ldots, i-1$ of the loop respectively. Since $\forall m \leq i, x_m \in Inv$, if follows that $x_m \in \langle c_m, V_m, P \wedge Q_m \rangle$. Therefore, the simulation should originate in $\langle c, V, P \wedge Q_0 \wedge Q_1 \wedge \ldots \wedge Q_i \rangle$. Hence, $x_i \in \langle c_i, V_i, P \wedge Q_0 \wedge Q_1 \wedge \ldots \wedge Q_i \rangle$. Therefore, $x_i \in R_i$.

Theorem 2 (Completeness). *Given an initial set $\Theta \overset{\Delta}{=} \langle c, V, P \rangle$, dynamics A, B, time bound $k \cdot h$, invariant Inv, and the reachable set computed as $Reach(\Theta) = R_0, R_1, \ldots, R_k$ by Algorithm 2, we have $\forall 0 \leq j \leq k$, given any $x_j \in R_j$, the simulation $x_0, x_1, \ldots, x_j$ that reaches x_j is such that $x_0 \in \Theta$ and $\forall 0 \leq i \leq j, x_i \in Inv$.*

Proof. Consider the reachable set $Reach(\Theta) = R_0, R_1, \ldots, R_k$ computed by Algorithm 2 and an element $x_j \in R_j$. Consider the simulation $x_0, x_1, \ldots, x_j$ be a simulation that reaches x_j. Let $Q_0, Q_1, \ldots, Q_j$ represents the constraints computed in line 6 for the iterations $0, 1, \ldots, j$ of the loop from lines 4–11 respectively. Since $x_j \in R_j \overset{\Delta}{=} \langle c_j, V_j, P \wedge Q_0 \wedge Q_1 \wedge \ldots \wedge Q_j \rangle$, it follows that the simulation should origin from $\Theta' = \langle c, V, P \wedge Q_0 \wedge Q_1 \wedge \ldots \wedge Q_j \rangle$. This simulation therefore respects the invariant at time instances $m \leq j$ as $\Theta' \subseteq \langle c, V, P \wedge Q_m \rangle$. Therefore the simulation $x_0, x_1, \ldots, x_j$ is indeed a valid simulation.

Discussion: Theorems 2 and 1 establish that the reachable set returned by Algorithm 2 only contains all the states that are reachable by a simulation that respects the invariant. One potential drawback of the constraint propagation is that the number of clauses can increase linearly with the number of steps in the simulation. We mitigate this by performing three optimizations. First, we do not add any constraints if $Reach_i \subseteq Inv(l)$ because in such instances $P \Rightarrow Q_i$. Second, a constraint Q_i is added to the list of constraints only if it is strictly stronger than the existing constraints. Formally, Q_i is added if and only if $\neg (P \wedge Q_0 \wedge Q_1 \wedge \ldots \wedge Q_{i-1} \Rightarrow Q_i)$. Third, we remove the redundant constraints, i.e., a constraint Q_j is dropped from the list if $(P \bigwedge_{i=1 \ldots k}^{i \neq j} Q_i) \Rightarrow Q_j$. In practice, we observe that these optimizations drastically reduce the number of constraints to an almost constant.

4   Discrete Transitions and Reachable Set Computation

In this section, we discuss computing the simulation-equivalent reachable set for a given hybrid automaton across discrete transitions.

4.1   Guards

Algorithm 3, which computes the set of states obtained after a discrete transition takes an input the set of reachable states computed by Algorithm 1 (which does not take into account the invariant), and the list of constraints that needed to be added to predicates for respecting the invariants $ConstraintsList$ computed by Algorithm 2. The algorithm for checking discrete transition *does not* consider the first element R_0 in the sequence $R_0, R_1, \ldots, R_k$. This is because the simulations generated enforce that at least a minimum time h is spent in each mode of the hybrid automaton. Given $1 \leq i \leq k$, the set of state in R_i that can be reached by simulations that respect the invariants for time instances $0, 1, \ldots, i - 1$ is

---

Input : Reachable set R obtained from Algorithm 1, List of constraints
            ConstraintsList from Algorithm 2
Output: *NextReach*, a list of stars that take the discrete transition.
1 *ConstraintsList* $\triangleq Q_0, Q_1, \ldots, Q_k$; $R \triangleq R_0, R_1, \ldots, R_k$;
2 *NextReach* $\leftarrow \emptyset$;
3 **for** *each i from 1 to k* **do**
4     $R_i = \langle c_i, V_i, P \rangle \leftarrow R[i]$;
5     $R_i' \leftarrow \langle c_i, V_i, P \wedge Q_0 \wedge \ldots \wedge Q_{i-1} \rangle$;
6   **for** *each guard G_a for a discrete transition a* **do**
7   **if** $G_a \cap R_i' \neq \emptyset$ **then**
8 | append $R_i' \cap G_a$ to *NextReach*;
9   **end**
10   **end**
11 **end**
12 **return** *NextReach*;

Algorithm 3. Computing the states after discrete transitions.

computed by adding the constraints $Q_0, Q_1, \ldots, Q_{i-1}$ to the predicate. This new set is assigned as R_i' in line 5. Notice that the number of constraints added for R_i does not include Q_i. This is because the discrete transition can be taken even when the state does not satisfy the invariant of the current location. The correctness of Algorithm 3 is given in Theorem 3

Theorem 3 (Correctness). *Given a reachable set* $R = R_0, R_1, \ldots, R_k$ *from initial set* Θ *computed by Algorithm 1, and the list of constraints* $Q_0, Q_1, \ldots, Q_k$ *computed by Algorithm 2, the following statements about* *NextReach returned by Algorithm 3 are true.*

1. *$\forall S \in NextReach, \forall x \in S, \exists \rho = x_0, x_1, \ldots, x_m, x$ such that $x_0 \in \Theta$ and ρ is a valid simulation.*
2. *For any valid simulation $\rho = x_0, x_1, \ldots, x_m, x_{m+1}$ starting from Θ, such that $\forall 0 \leq i \leq m, x_i \in Inv$, and $x_{m+1} \in G_a$, $\exists R \in NextReach$ such that $x_{m+1} \in R$.*

Proof. Consider $S \in NextReach$ and $x \in S$, we have that $\exists R_0, R_1, \ldots, R_m, R_{m+1}$ and constraints $Q_0, Q_1, \ldots, Q_{m+1}$ such that $S = \langle c_{m+1}, V_{m+1}, P \wedge Q_0 \wedge \ldots \wedge Q_m \rangle$. Therefore, it follows that $x \in \langle c_{m+1}, V_{m+1}, P \wedge Q_0 \wedge \ldots \wedge Q_m \rangle$, therefore, there exists a simulation $x_0, \ldots, x_m, x$ such that $0 \leq i \leq m, x_i \in Inv$. and $x_0 \in \Theta$.

Next, consider a simulation $\rho = x_0, x_1, \ldots, x_m, x_{m+1}$, where $\forall 0 \leq i \leq m, x_i \in Inv$, $x_{m+1} \in G_a$ for some a, it follows that $x_i \in \langle c_i, V_i, P \wedge Q_0 \wedge \ldots \wedge Q_i \rangle$. Hence $x_{m+1} \in \langle c_{m+1}, V_{m+1}, P \wedge Q_0 \wedge \ldots \wedge Q_m \rangle$. From Algorithm 3, it follows that $\langle c_{m+1}, V_{m+1}, P \wedge Q_0 \wedge \ldots \wedge Q_m \rangle \in NextReach$. Therefore $\exists R \in NextReach$ such that $x_{m+1} \in R$.

4.2 Algorithm for Computing Simulation-Equivalent Reachable Set

Algorithm 4 that computes the simulation-equivalent reachable set for hybrid automata uses Algorithms 2 and 3 as sub-routines for handling invariants and

---

input : Initial set Θ, Hybrid automaton H, Time bound $k \cdot h$, Unsafe locations U.
output : *ReachSet* as the set of reachable states.

1 *queueStars* $\leftarrow \emptyset$; append Θ to *queueStars*; *ReachSet* $\leftarrow \emptyset$;
2 **while** *queueStars is not empty* **do**
3     $S \leftarrow$ dequeue(*queueStars*);
4   **if** $S.loc \in U$ **then**
5 | **return** (**Unsafe**, execution leading to S);
6   **end**
7     $R \leftarrow$ SimulationsReachableSet(S);
8     $(R', ConstraintsList) \leftarrow$ InvariantTrimming(R);
9   *ReachSet* $\leftarrow$ *ReachSet* $\cup R'$;
10   *nextRegions* $\leftarrow$ discreteTrans(R, *ConstraintsList*);
11   append *nextRegions* to *queueStars*;
12 **end**
13 **return** (**Safe**, *ReachSet*);

Algorithm 4. Algorithm that computes bounded time simulation equivalent reachable set.

discrete transitions respectively. The set of initial states for each mode are stored in the queue called *queueStars*. The algorithm first computes the reachable set using $n + 1$ simulations by calling SimulationsReachableSet (Algorithm 1). Next, calling the InvariantTrimming procedure (Algorithm 2) uses the invariant of the mode to return the set of states that respect the invariant (R') and the corresponding list of constraints for each set in the sequence (*ConstraintsList*). The call to discreteTrans then produces the initial states for the next mode, which get added to *queueStars*. The correctness of Algorithm 4 follows from the correctness of Algorithms 2 and 3.

4.3 Aggregation and Deaggregation

A component of many flow-pipe construction methods is the aggregation of states that result from a discrete transition. This is often necessary because multiple regions in the reachable set have the guard enabled resulting in several regions being added to the *nextRegions* queue. Over multiple discrete transitions, this can cause an exponential blowup in the number of states in *queueStars*.

The drawback of aggregation is that it introduces conservativeness in the reachability analysis. In general, a single convex set cannot exactly capture the union of two or more convex sets, so an overapproximation of the union is the only sound option. If the reachable set from an aggregated star reaches an unsafe mode, the user cannot discern whether this is because of overapproximation due to aggregation or if it corresponds to an unsafe simulation of the system.

For this reason, we propose a new aggregation and deaggregation approach. By default, we aggregate all the stars that make a discrete transition into to the same mode as S_{agg} and compute the reachable set of S_{agg}. If S_{agg} reaches a state when a guard is enabled, we deaggregate the star by splitting it into two stars. If S_{agg} is an aggregation of $S_1, S_2, \ldots S_w$, then the two new stars are aggregations of $S_1, \ldots, S_{w/2}$ and of $S_{w/2+1}, \ldots, S_w$ respectively. This process can repeat recursively if the new stars intersect the guard.

If $m \cdot h$ time units have elapsed before S_{agg} reaches a guard, the component stars skip the first m steps in the reachable set computation and checking for discrete transitions. This is because if S_{agg} did not reach any guard until m steps, then its component stars also did not reach any guard. However, one has to propagate the constraints from the invariants for all the deaggregated stars. This approach ensures that whenever a discrete transition is taken, there exists an unaggregated star for which the discrete transition is enabled. Therefore, if an unsafe mode is reached, there exists a simulation trace of the system that starts from initial set and reaches the unsafe mode, thus maintaining simulation-equivalence.

5   Implementation and Evaluation

The proposed simulation-equivalent algorithm has been implemented in a tool named HyLAA that is mostly written in Python, although computational libraries are used which may be written in other languages. Simulations are performed using scipy's odeint function, which can handle stiff and non-stiff differential equations using the FORTRAN library odepack's lsoda solver. Linear programming is performed using the GLPK library, and matrix operations are performed using numpy. HyLAA can produce static visualizations of the reachable set and live animations during the reachable set computation (that can be exported as videos) using matplotlib. The following experiments were performed using the model generation capability within the Hyst [7] tool, and hypy [8] was used to script together the the model generation with the tool execution. The measurements were performed using a 2.30 GHz Intel i5-5300U CPU with 16 GB RAM.

5.1   Scalability

We performed scalability measurement on a replicated version of the helicopter benchmark available on SpaceEx website[1]. This model consists of a 28 dimensional helicopter plus controller system, along with a time dimension. We used the x8_over_time_large variant of the benchmark, considering the same initial states, step size, and time bound.

We emphasize that we tried to explicitly control for the accuracy of the result in the comparison, which is not straightforward as different approaches use different parameters. From a preliminary analysis, we observed the x_8 variable always stays below 0.45, so we used this as a metric for accuracy. By adding a transition to unsafe mode if $x_8 \geq 0.45$, we tuned tool parameters until the condition was on the verge of being violated. For SpaceEx [23], we found that a flowpipe-tolerance of 0.0304 was safe for the stc scenario [22], whereas

---

[1] http://spaceex.imag.fr/news/helicopter-example-posted-39.

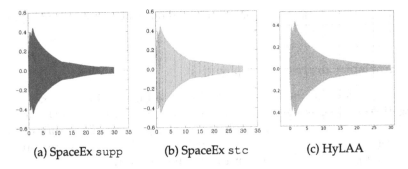

(a) SpaceEx supp   (b) SpaceEx stc   (c) HyLAA

Fig. 4. Plots of x_8 over time for the helicopter system show the selected accuracy settings result in similar plots. This remained true for replicated variants.

0.5222 was safe for the supp scenario [28]. Furthermore, increasing these parameters by 0.0001 would cause forbidden error states to be reached. We also attempted to use Flow*'s [12] linear ODE mode, although failed to find a set of parameters for which the accuracy condition was satisfied. For HyLAA, we used the default simulation parameters used by odeint, absolute tolerance and relative tolerance of $1.49 \cdot 10^{-8}$, and no error states were reached. Then, for the actual runtime measurements, we removed the error states while keeping each tool's accuracy parameters. This results in a plot of the reachable set of states that is qualitatively similar, as shown in Fig. 4.

We replicated the 28-dimensional helicopter multiple times within the same model, and measured the runtime of the reachability computation. The results are shown in Fig. 5. The simulation-equivalent approach outperforms the two SpaceEx scenarios on this model, and is capable of analyzing a 449 dimensional system (16 replicated helicopters plus time) in under a minute, and a system with 1009 dimensions (36 helicopters) in about 10 min. It is important to be aware that SpaceEx's analysis is a guaranteed overapproximation (subject to floating-point error), whereas HyLAA's correctness is subject to the accuracy of

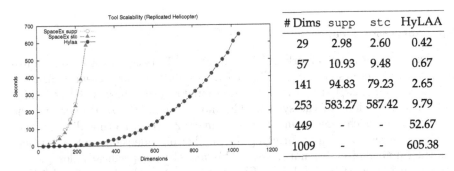

# Dims	supp	stc	HyLAA
29	2.98	2.60	0.42
57	10.93	9.48	0.67
141	94.83	79.23	2.65
253	583.27	587.42	9.79
449	-	-	52.67
1009	-	-	605.38

Fig. 5. The runtime for the $n + 1$ simulation continuous-post operation in HyLAA is generally faster than SpaceEx's supp and stc methods.

the underlying simulations, and only reasons about states at exact multiples of the time step.

5.2   Invariant Constraint Propagation

We next provide a simple evaluation of the importance of invariant constraint propagation as well as our proposed optimization. Consider a 2-D harmonic oscillator, a single-mode system with $\dot{x} = y$ and $\dot{y} = -x$. Trajectories of this system rotate clockwise around the origin. The initial set of states are $x \in [-6, -5]$ and $y \in [0, 0.1]$, and the invariant is $0 \leq y \leq 5.1$.

This system is designed so that most of the trajectories actually get trimmed away because of the invariant. Reachability analysis of this system was performed using SpaceEx's stc scenario, Flow*, and HyLAA, and is shown in Fig. 6. Here, SpaceEx removes states which violate the invariant after computing states reachable by the continuous dynamics, which is sound, but results in an overapproximation. Flow* uses domain contraction of Taylor models [12] to trim invariant-violating states, and its result appears correct. HyLAA performs invariant constraint propagation, and also produces a correct result. The table shows the number of constraints in the final star when using HyLAA, with and without the invariant constraint trimming optimization.

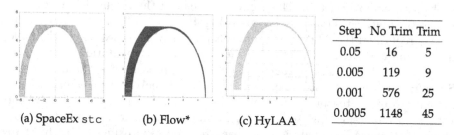

Step	No Trim	Trim
0.05	16	5
0.005	119	9
0.001	576	25
0.0005	1148	45

(a) SpaceEx stc   (b) Flow*   (c) HyLAA

Fig. 6. The harmonic oscillator system with invariant $0 \leq y \leq 5.1$ demonstrates the benefit of invariant constraint propagation.

5.3   Successor Deaggregation

We next consider a benchmark which models the effects of backlash on an automotive drivetrain system [3, 27]. This a 7-dimensional linear system, which can be scaled as large as desired by adding additional rotating masses, each of which adds two dimensions to the system. The model has a PID controller and the reference input is changed from -5 to 5 at time 0.2. We add a time dimension to generate the reference input, bringing the number of dimensions to $8 + 2\theta$ where θ is the number of additional masses. This model was specifically designed to stress guard intersection, and SpaceEx was noted as not being able to finish on smallest version of the benchmark, without shrinking the initial set to 5% of its original size.

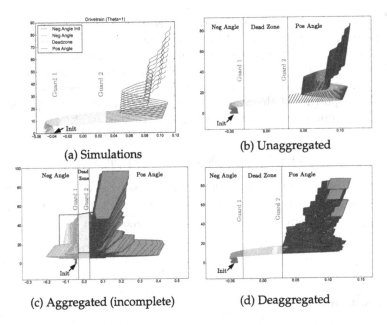

(a) Simulations

(b) Unaggregated

(c) Aggregated (incomplete)

(d) Deaggregated

Fig. 7. Projections of x_3 versus x_1 for the 10-dimensional drivetrain system. While complete aggregation fails to complete for this model, using deaggregation produces a similar plot to the unaggregated method in less time. (Color figure online)

Plots of the reachable set of states are shown in Fig. 7 for $\theta = 1$. The system starts in the `NegAngle` mode (green). After 0.2 s, the reference trajectory changes from -5 to 5 (cyan). Then, the system's trajectories reach the `DeadZone` mode (orange), and finally end in the `PosAngle` mode (magenta). Similar to SpaceEx, HyLAA did not complete reachable set computation with full aggregation (without deaggregation). The reason is that aggregation introduces overapproximation error which leads the approach to examine states that are not actually reachable. In this system, the aggregated star introduces new spurious discrete transitions from the `DeadZone` mode back to the `NegAngle` mode, leading to additional error when further discrete transitions are taken. Essentially, the computation explores spurious sequences of discrete transitions. The deaggregation method, however, splits aggregated states upon reaching a discrete transition, ensuring that every sequence of modes explored corresponds to a true simulation of the system. The result is closer to the exact unaggregated case, although using less computation time. A video of HyLAA's visualization of this computation is available online[2].

To evaluate the effect of the deaggregatation approach, Table 1 shows the runtime as we increased the number of rotating masses. Notice that times can actually go down for some higher-dimensional versions of the benchmark, as the extra rotating masses can cause the generalized star to cross the guard boundary at a more orthogonal angle, reducing the number of stars in the successor mode.

---

[2] http://stanleybak.com/hylaa/.

For example, in the unaggregated 10-d case, there are 24 successor stars after the second guard, compared with 13 successor stars in the 12-d case. Generally, deaggregation provides improvement over no aggregation, although the benefits are reduced in higher dimensions. This is because in these cases even a small amount of aggregation often causes enough error to reach new locations, resulting in immediate splitting of the aggregated star, which shows the importance of finding good template directions for aggregation [11].

Table 1. Drivetrain benchmark runtimes.

# Dims	10	12	14	16	18	20	24	30	42
Deaggregated	25.70	44.94	24.71	131.82	47.72	267.71	450.42	331.57	516.21
Unaggregated	112.94	79.24	98.63	145.87	214.80	409.55	561.47	384.55	672.60

6   Conclusion

In this paper, we introduced the notion of simulation-equivalent reachability analysis, and provided a sound and complete algorithm for its computation. We do not believe this type of approach is at odds with traditional hybrid automata reachability computation, as the goal for both methods is to improve the state of practice of system design from an incomplete analysis based on simulations towards more rigorous approaches. Furthermore, the proposed enhancements, the elimination of accumulated invariant constraints and on-demand successor deaggregation, may be applied to both methods.

The advantage of the simulation-equivalent approach is increased scalability, which makes it applicable to larger CPS models. Furthermore, the approach and tool implementation generate concrete traces whenever a simulation can violate the system specification, making it useful to system engineers who may not have a formal methods background.

References

1. Computer Assisted Proofs in Dynamic Groups (CAPD). http://capd.ii.uj.edu.pl/index.php
2. Althoff, M.: An introduction to CORA. In: Proceedings of the Workshop on Applied Verification for Continuous and Hybrid Systems (2015)
3. Althoff, M., Krogh, B.H.: Avoiding geometric intersection operations in reachability analysis of hybrid systems. In: Hybrid Systems: Computation and Control, pp. 45–54 (2012)
4. Alur, R., Courcoubetis, C., Halbwachs, N., Henzinger, T.A., Ho, P.-H., Nicollin, X., Olivero, A., Sifakis, J., Yovine, S.: The algorithmic analysis of hybrid systems. Theoret. Comput. Sci. **138**, 3–34 (1995)

5. Alur, R., Dill, D.L.: A theory of timed automata. Theoret. Comput. Sci. **126**, 183–235 (1994)
6. Bak, S., Bogomolov, S., Henzinger, T.A., Johnson, T.T., Prakash, P.: Scalable static hybridization methods for analysis of nonlinear systems. In: Proceedings of the 19th International Conference on Hybrid Systems: Computation and Control, HSCC 2016, pp. 155–164. ACM, New York (2016)
7. Bak, S., Bogomolov, S., Johnson, T.T.: HYST: a source transformation and translation tool for hybrid automaton models. In: 18th International Conference on Hybrid Systems: Computation and Control, Seattle, Washington. ACM, April 2015
8. Bak, S., Bogomolov, S., Schilling, C.: High-level hybrid systems analysis with hypy. In: ARCH 2016: Proceedings of the 3rd Workshop on Applied Verification for Continuous and Hybrid Systems (2016)
9. Balkan, A., Tabuada, P., Deshmukh, J.V., Jin, X., Kapinski, J.: Underminer: a framework for automatically identifying non-converging behaviors in black box system models. In: Proceedings of the 13th International Conference on Embedded Software, p. 7. ACM (2016)
10. Bengtsson, J., Larsen, K., Larsson, F., Pettersson, P., Yi, W.: UPPAAL—a tool suite for automatic verification of real-time systems. In: Alur, R., Henzinger, T.A., Sontag, E.D. (eds.) HS 1995. LNCS, vol. 1066, pp. 232–243. Springer, Heidelberg (1996). doi:10.1007/BFb0020949
11. Chen, X., Ábrahám, E.: Choice of directions for the approximation of reachable sets for hybrid systems. In: Moreno-Díaz, R., Pichler, F., Quesada-Arencibia, A. (eds.) EUROCAST 2011. LNCS, vol. 6927, pp. 535–542. Springer, Heidelberg (2012). doi:10.1007/978-3-642-27549-4_69
12. Chen, X., Abraham, E., Sankaranarayanan, S.: Taylor model flowpipe construction for non-linear hybrid systems. In: 2013 IEEE 34th Real-Time Systems Symposium, pp. 183–192 (2012)
13. Chutinan, A., Krogh, B.H.: Computational techniques for hybrid system verification. IEEE Trans. Autom. Control **48**(1), 64–75 (2003)
14. Dang, T., Le Guernic, C., Maler, O.: Computing reachable states for nonlinear biological models. In: Degano, P., Gorrieri, R. (eds.) CMSB 2009. LNCS, vol. 5688, pp. 126–141. Springer, Heidelberg (2009). doi:10.1007/978-3-642-03845-7_9
15. Donzé, A., Maler, O.: Systematic simulation using sensitivity analysis. In: Bemporad, A., Bicchi, A., Buttazzo, G. (eds.) HSCC 2007. LNCS, vol. 4416, pp. 174–189. Springer, Heidelberg (2007). doi:10.1007/978-3-540-71493-4_16
16. Duggirala, P.S., Mitra, S., Viswanathan, M.: Verification of annotated models from executions. In: Proceedings of the 13th International Conference on Embedded Software (EMSOFT), Montreal, Canada (2013)
17. Duggirala, P.S., Mitra, S., Viswanathan, M., Potok, M.: C2E2: a verification tool for stateflow models. In: Baier, C., Tinelli, C. (eds.) TACAS 2015. LNCS, vol. 9035, pp. 68–82. Springer, Heidelberg (2015). doi:10.1007/978-3-662-46681-0_5
18. Duggirala, P.S., Viswanathan, M.: Parsimonious, simulation based verification of linear systems. In: Chaudhuri, S., Farzan, A. (eds.) CAV 2016. LNCS, vol. 9779, pp. 477–494. Springer, Heidelberg (2016). doi:10.1007/978-3-319-41528-4_26
19. Fainekos, G.E., Pappas, G.J.: Robustness of temporal logic specifications for continuous-time signals. Theoret. Comput. Sci. **410**(42), 4262–4291 (2009)
20. Fan, C., Kapinski, J., Jin, X., Mitra, S.: Locally optimal reach set over-approximation for nonlinear systems. In: Proceedings of the 13th International Conference on Embedded Software, p. 6. ACM (2016)
21. Frehse, G.: PHAVer: algorithmic verification of hybrid systems past hytech. In: HSCC, pp. 258–273 (2005)

22. Frehse, G., Kateja, R., Le Guernic, C.: Flowpipe approximation, clustering in space-time. In: Proceedings of Hybrid Systems: Computation and Control (HSCC 2013), pp. 203–212. ACM (2013)
23. Frehse, G., Le Guernic, C., Donzé, A., Cotton, S., Ray, R., Lebeltel, O., Ripado, R., Girard, A., Dang, T., Maler, O.: SpaceEx: scalable verification of hybrid systems. In: Gopalakrishnan, G., Qadeer, S. (eds.) CAV 2011. LNCS, vol. 6806, pp. 379–395. Springer, Heidelberg (2011). doi:10.1007/978-3-642-22110-1_30
24. Fulton, N., Mitsch, S., Quesel, J.-D., Völp, M., Platzer, A.: KeYmaera X: an axiomatic tactical theorem prover for hybrid systems. In: Felty, A.P., Middeldorp, A. (eds.) CADE 2015. LNCS (LNAI), vol. 9195, pp. 527–538. Springer, Heidelberg (2015). doi:10.1007/978-3-319-21401-6_36
25. Girard, A.: Reachability of uncertain linear systems using zonotopes. In: Morari, M., Thiele, L. (eds.) HSCC 2005. LNCS, vol. 3414, pp. 291–305. Springer, Heidelberg (2005). doi:10.1007/978-3-540-31954-2_19
26. Henzinger, T.A., Ho, P.-H., Wong-Toi, H.: HyTech: a model checker for hybrid systems. In: Grumberg, O. (ed.) CAV 1997. LNCS, vol. 1254, pp. 460–463. Springer, Heidelberg (1997). doi:10.1007/3-540-63166-6_48
27. Lagerberg, A.: A benchmark on hybrid control of an automotive powertrain with backlash. Technical report (2007)
28. Le Guernic, C., Girard, A.: Reachability analysis of hybrid systems using support functions. In: Bouajjani, A., Maler, O. (eds.) CAV 2009. LNCS, vol. 5643, pp. 540–554. Springer, Heidelberg (2009). doi:10.1007/978-3-642-02658-4_40
29. Maler, O., Manna, Z., Pnueli, A.: Prom timed to hybrid systems. In: Bakker, J.W., Huizing, C., Roever, W.P., Rozenberg, G. (eds.) REX 1991. LNCS, vol. 600, pp. 447–484. Springer, Heidelberg (1992). doi:10.1007/BFb0032003
30. Nghiem, T., Sankaranarayanan, S., Fainekos, G., Ivancić, F., Gupta, A., Pappas, G.J.: Monte-Carlo techniques for falsification of temporal properties of non-linear hybrid systems. In: 2010 Proceedings of the 13th ACM International Conference on Hybrid Systems: Computation and Control, pp. 211–220. ACM (2010)
31. Platzer, A.: Differential dynamic logic for hybrid systems. J. Autom. Reason. **41**(2), 143–189 (2008)

HARE: A Hybrid Abstraction Refinement Engine for Verifying Non-linear Hybrid Automata

Nima Roohi[1]([✉]), Pavithra Prabhakar[2], and Mahesh Viswanathan[1]

[1] Department of Computer Science, University of Illinois at Urbana-Champaign, Urbana, USA
{roohi2,vmahesh}@illinois.edu
[2] Department of Computer Science, Kansas State University, Manhattan, USA
pprabhakar@ksu.edu

Abstract. HARE (Hybrid Abstraction-Refinement Engine) is a counterexample guided abstraction-refinement (CEGAR) based tool to verify safety properties of hybrid automata, whose continuous dynamics in each mode is non-linear, but initial values, invariants, and transition relations are specified using polyhedral constraints. HARE works by abstracting non-linear hybrid automata into hybrid automata with polyhedral inclusion dynamics, and uses dReach to validate counterexamples. We show that the CEGAR framework forming the theoretical basis of HARE, makes provable progress in each iteration of the abstraction-refinement loop. The current HARE tool is a significant advance on previous versions of HARE—it considers a richer class of abstract models (polyhedral flows as opposed to rectangular flows), and can be applied to a larger class of concrete models (non-linear hybrid automata as opposed to affine hybrid automata). These advances have led to better performance results for a wider class of examples. We report an experimental comparison of HARE against other state of the art tools for affine models (SpaceEx, PHAVer, and SpaceEx AGAR) and non-linear models (FLOW*, HSolver, and C2E2).

1 Introduction

Abstractions play an important role in the verification of cyber-physical systems, where complex continuous dynamics are abstracted into simpler dynamics that are amenable to automated analysis. This is because the general problem of safety verification is undecidable even for very simple class of continuous dynamics [2,4,20,25,32]. The success of the abstraction based method depends on finding the right abstraction, which can be difficult. One approach that tries to address this issue is the counter example guided abstraction refinement (CEGAR) framework [9] that tries to automatically discover the right abstraction through a process of progressive refinement based on analyzing spurious counter examples in abstract models. CEGAR has been found to be useful in a number of contexts [6,12,21,22], including hybrid systems [3,10,11,14,17,23,30,31].

© Springer-Verlag GmbH Germany 2017
A. Legay and T. Margaria (Eds.): TACAS 2017, Part I, LNCS 10205, pp. 573–588, 2017.
DOI: 10.1007/978-3-662-54577-5_33

In this paper, we present the tool HARE, which is a CEGAR based tool for safety verification of hybrid automata with non-linear hybrid systems. The input to HARE is the parallel composition of one or more hybrid automata, where the continuous dynamics in each control mode is described by non-linear ordinary differential equations, while the initial values, invariants, and transition relations are specified using polyhedral constraints. HARE abstracts such models into hybrid automata with polyhedral inclusion dynamics, i.e., in the abstract model, in each mode, the derivative of the continuous variables with respect to time is constrained to belong to a polyhedral set. In this sense, HARE is different from the other CEGAR based tool for non-linear hybrid systems, namely, HSolver [28], which abstracts hybrid automata by finite discrete transition systems. To perform validation of counter examples, HARE uses dReach and the δ-satisfiability procedure of dReal.

The tool described in this paper, is a significant improvement over the version reported in [29]. First, the old version only verified affine hybrid automata. The new version also considers non-linear dynamics. Second, the old version used rectangular automata to abstract concrete models. The new version uses polyhedral hybrid automata. We have observed a marked improvement in running time due to the change in abstract models—there are fewer refinement iterations on many examples because of the use of polyhedral hybrid automata. Third, the tool has been made robust. The implementation has migrated to C++ from Scala to improve its running time. We have changed some of the 3rd party tools that HARE uses internally. All these changes have enabled HARE to handle a larger class of examples (including more affine hybrid automata), with a faster running time (see results reported in Sect. 6). We have compared the performance of HARE against a number of state of the art model checkers for affine hybrid automata and non-linear hybrid automata— SpaceEx [19], PHAVer [18], SpaceEx AGAR [7], HSolver [28], C2E2 [16], and FLOW* [8]. We also compare against the old version of HARE [29]. We show that the new tool successfully proves safety when the others fail, and the running time is comparable to the other tools (see Sect. 6). A virtual machine for the new HARE, along with examples and scripts can be downloaded from https://uofi.box.com/v/HARE.

The rest of the paper is organized as follows. We introduce basic definitions and notation in Sect. 3. Our CEGAR framework, algorithms for abstraction, counter example validation, and refinement, that form the theoretical basis for HARE, are described in Sect. 4. The tool architecture and its internals are presented in Sect. 5, and Sect. 6 reports our experimental results.

2   Related Work

Doyen *et al.* consider rectangular abstractions for safety verification of affine hybrid systems in [15]. However, their refinement is not guided by counter example analysis. Instead, a reachable unsafe location in the abstract system is determined, and the invariant of the corresponding concrete location is split to ensure certain optimality criteria on the resulting rectangular dynamics. This, in general, may not lead to abstract counter example elimination, as in our CEGAR algorithm. We believe that the refinement algorithms of the two papers are incomparable—one may perform better than the other on certain examples. Empirical evaluations could provide some insights into the merits of the approaches, however, the implementation of the algorithm in [15] was not available for comparison at the time of writing the paper.

Bogomolov *et al.* consider polyhedral inclusion dynamics as abstract models of affine hybrid systems for CEGAR in [7]. Their abstraction merges the locations, and refinement corresponds to splitting the locations. Hence, the CEGAR loop ends with the original automaton in a finite number of steps, if safety is not proved by then. Our algorithm splits the invariants of the locations, and hence, explores finer abstractions. Our method is orthogonal to that of [7], and can be used in conjunction with [7] to further refine the abstractions.

Nellen *et al.* use CEGAR in [26] to model check chemical plants controlled by programmable logic controllers. They assume that the dynamics of the system in each location is given by *conditional* ODEs, and their abstraction consists of choosing a subset of these conditional ODEs. The refinement consists of adding some of these conditional ODEs based on an unsafe location in a counter example. The method does not ensure counter example elimination in successive iterations. Their prototype tool does not automate the refinement step, in that the inputs to the refinements need to be provided manually. Hence, we did not experimentally compare with this tool.

Zutshi *et al.* propose a CEGAR-based search in [33] to find violations of safety properties. Here they consider the problem of finding a concrete counter example and use CEGAR to guide the search of the same. We instead use CEGAR to prove safety—the absence of such concrete counter examples.

3 Preliminaries

Numbers. Let $\mathbb{N}$, $\mathbb{Q}$, and $\mathbb{R}$ denote the set of *natural, rational,* and *real* numbers, respectively. Similarly, $\mathbb{N}_+$, $\mathbb{Q}_+$, and $\mathbb{R}_+$ are respectively the set of *positive* natural, rational, and real numbers, and $\mathbb{Q}_{\geq 0}$ and $\mathbb{R}_{\geq 0}$ are respectively the set of *non-negative* rational and real numbers. For any $n \in \mathbb{N}$ we define $[n] = \{0, 1, \ldots, n-1\}$.

Sets and Functions. For any sets A and B, $|A|$ is the size of A (the number of elements in A), 2^A is the power set of A, $A \times B$ is the Cartesian product of A and B, and B^A (similarly $A \to B$) is the set of all functions from A to B. In order to make the notations simpler, for any $n, m \in \mathbb{N}$, by A^n and $A^{n \times m}$, we mean $A^{[n]}$ and $A^{[n] \times [m]}$. The latter represents matrices of dimension $n \times m$ with elements from A. For any $f \in A \to B$ and set $C \subseteq A$, $f(C) = \{f(c) \mid c \in C\}$. Similarly, for any $\pi = a_1, a_2, \ldots, a_n$, a sequence of elements in A, we define $f(\pi)$ to be $f(a_1), f(a_2), \ldots, f(a_n)$.

Polytopes. For any set of variables X, a function $c \in \mathbb{R}^X$, and a constant $b \in \mathbb{R}$, $\Sigma_{x \in X} c_x x \leq b$ is an *affine constraint* over the variables in X. A *polyhedron* is a conjunction of finite number of affine constraints. Every polyhedron P over X, defines a set of points in $\mathbb{R}^X$, namely the set of points that satisfy all constraints of P. We only consider non-strict inequalities, therefore P always defines a closed set. For any point $\nu \in \mathbb{R}^X$, $\nu \in P$ means ν satisfies all the constraints in P. A polyhedron that defines a bounded set is called *polytope*. We denote the set of all polytopes over X by $\mathbb{P}^X$.

3.1 Hybrid Automata

In this section, we present hybrid automata models for representing concrete and abstract hybrid systems.

Definition 1 (Hybrid Automata). *A hybrid automata $\mathcal{H}$ is a tuple $(Q, X, I, F, E, Q^{init}, Q^{bad})$ in which*

- *Q is a non-empty finite set of locations.*
- *X is a non-empty finite set of variables. We let $V := \mathbb{R}^X$ be the set of all possible valuations of variables in X. We also let X' to be the set of primed variables ($X \cap X' = \emptyset$ and $|X| = |X'|$). For every variable $x \in X$ we use x' to denote the corresponding variable in X'.*
- *$I \in Q \to \mathbb{P}^X$ maps each location to a polytope over $\mathbb{R}^X$ as invariant of that location.*
- *$F \in Q \to 2^{V \times V}$ maps each location q to the set of possible flows of that location. Each element in this set is a pair $(\nu, \dot{\nu})$. Intuitively it means, if the current continuous state is ν then $\dot{\nu}$ is a possible direction field.*
- *E is a set of edges of the form $e = (s, d, r)$ where*
  - *$s, d \in Q$ are respectively source and destination of e,*
  - *$r \in \mathbb{P}^{X \cup X'}$ specifies relation of valuations before and after taking edge e as the reset relation.*

  We let $G(e) := \exists X' \bullet r$ to be guard of e, as the set of valuations for which the reset relation is non-empty (note that $G(e)$ can be represented by a polytope in $\mathbb{P}^X$). We use $S(e)$, $D(e)$ and $R(e)$, to denote different elements of guard e.
- *$Q^{init}, Q^{bad} \subseteq Q$ are respectively sets of initial and unsafe locations.*

We denote different elements of $\mathcal{H}$ by adding a subscript to their names. For example, we use $X_{\mathcal{H}}$ to denote the set of variables of $\mathcal{H}$. We may omit the subscript whenever it is clear from the context.

In this paper, we use *non-linear hybrid automata* to specify a concrete system. In this class of automata, for any location $q \in Q$, $F(q)$ is specified by a *continuous* (possibly nonlinear) function f of type $I(q) \to V$. More precisely, $F(q) := \{(\nu, f(\nu)) \mid \nu \in I(q)\}$. Therefore, $F(q)$ defines exactly one direction for any valuation in the invariant of that location. We abuse the notation and write $F(q) = f$ when it causes no confusion. Next, in this paper, we use *polyhedral hybrid automata* to specify abstract systems. In this class of automata, for any location $q \in Q$, $F(q)$ is specified by a polytope $P \in \mathbb{P}^X$. More precisely, $F(q) := \{(\nu, \dot{\nu}) \mid \nu \in I(q) \wedge \dot{\nu} \in P\}$. Therefore, $F(q)$ is independent of the current valuation. We abuse the notation and write $F(q) = P$ when it causes no confusion. Note that affine hybrid automata and rectangular automata which we used in [29] for specifying concrete and abstract systems, are subclasses of non-linear automata and polyhedral automata we use in this paper.

The semantics of a hybrid automaton $\mathcal{H}$ is defined using an infinite transition system $[\![\mathcal{H}]\!]$ in the usual way. $S_{[\![\mathcal{H}]\!]} := Q \times V$ is the state set of $[\![\mathcal{H}]\!]$. For any two states $(q_1, \nu_1), (q_2, \nu_2) \in S_{[\![\mathcal{H}]\!]}$, we write $(q_1, \nu_1) \xrightarrow{t} (q_2, \nu_2)$ iff $q_1 = q_2$ and ν_1 goes to ν_2 at non-negative time t according to the continuous dynamics of location q_1. We also write $(q_1, \nu_1) \xrightarrow{e} (q_2, \nu_2)$ iff q_1 and q_2 are source and destination of the edge e and ν_1 and ν_2 satisfies invariants of source and destination locations as well as the transition relation. Finally, we use $S_{[\![\mathcal{H}]\!]}^{\mathsf{init}}$ and $S_{[\![\mathcal{H}]\!]}^{\mathsf{bad}}$ to refer to the set of initial and unsafe states respectively.

A *trajectory* is a sequence $\tau = s_0, (t_0, e_0), s_1, (t_1, e_1), s_2, (t_2, e_2), \ldots, s_n$ such that for any $i < n$ there is a state s_i' such that $s_i \xrightarrow{t_i} s_i' \xrightarrow{e_i} s_{i+1}$. We define τ_0 to be the initial state s_0 and τ_{st} to be final state s_n. For any hybrid automaton $\mathcal{H}$, the *reachability problem* asks whether or not $\mathcal{H}$ has a trajectory τ such that $\tau_0 \in S_{[\![\mathcal{H}]\!]}^{\mathsf{init}}$ and $\tau_{\mathsf{st}} \in S_{[\![\mathcal{H}]\!]}^{\mathsf{bad}}$. If the answer is positive, we say the $\mathcal{H}$ is *unsafe*. Otherwise, we say the $\mathcal{H}$ is *safe*.

For any hybrid automaton $\mathcal{H}$, set of states $S \subseteq S_{[\![\mathcal{H}]\!]}$, and edge $e \in E_\mathcal{H}$ we define the following functions:

- $\mathsf{dpost}_\mathcal{H}^e(S) = \{s' \mid \exists s \in S \bullet s \xrightarrow{e} s'\}$. Discrete post of S in $\mathcal{H}$ with respect to e is the set of states reachable from S after taking e.
- $\mathsf{dpre}_\mathcal{H}^e(S) = \{s \mid \exists s' \in S \bullet s \xrightarrow{e} s'\}$. Discrete pre of S in $\mathcal{H}$ with respect to e is the set of states that can reach a state in S after taking e.
- $\mathsf{cpost}_\mathcal{H}(S) = \{s' \mid \exists s \in S, t \in \mathbb{R}_{\geq 0} \bullet s \xrightarrow{t} s'\}$. Continuous post of S in $\mathcal{H}$ is the set of states reachable from S in an arbitrary amount of time using dynamics specified for the source locations.
- $\mathsf{cpre}_\mathcal{H}(S) = \{s \mid \exists s' \in S, t \in \mathbb{R}_{\geq 0} \bullet s \xrightarrow{t} s'\}$ Continuous pre of S in $\mathcal{H}$ is the set of states that can reach a state in S in an arbitrary amount of time using dynamics specified for the source locations.

4   CEGAR Algorithm for Safety Verification of Non-linear Automata

Every CEGAR-based algorithm has four main parts [9]: 1. abstracting the concrete system, 2. model checking the abstract system, 3. validating the abstract counter example, and 4. refining the abstract system. We explain parts of our algorithm regarding each of these parts in this section. Algorithm 1 shows at a very high level what the steps of our algorithm are.

Algorithm 1. High level steps of our CEGAR algorithm

Input: C a non-linear automaton   ▷ C is called concrete hybrid automaton. Def 1
Output: Whether or not C is safe   ▷ this is the reachability problem.
  1. Add a self-loop to every location of C
  2. $P \leftarrow$ the initial partition of invariants in C ▷ Sec 4.1
  3. $A \leftarrow \alpha(C, P)$ ▷ A is called abstract hybrid automaton. Def 3
  4. $\tau = O^{\text{Poly}}(A)$ ▷ O^{Poly} model checks polyhedral automata. Sec 4.2
  5.   ▷ τ is an annotated counter example. Sec 4.2
  6. **while** $\tau \neq \emptyset$ **do**   ▷ while abstract system is unsafe
  7.   **if** τ is valid in C **then return** 'unsafe'   ▷ Sec 4.3
  8. $(q, p) \leftarrow$ abstract location that should be split   ▷ Sec 4.3
  9. $p_1, p_2 \leftarrow$ sets that should be separated in (q, p) ▷ Sec 4.3
 10.   refine $P(q)$ such that p_1 and p_2 gets separated   ▷ Sec 4.3
 11. $A \leftarrow \alpha(C, P)$ ▷ Sec 4.1
 12. $\tau = O^{\text{Poly}}(A)$ ▷ Sec 4.2
 13. **end while**
 14. **return** 'safe'

For technical reasons (see Sect. 4.1 of [29]), we assume that in the concrete hybrid automaton, each location has a self loop transition that ensures that the duration between successive discrete steps is bounded. This assumption also makes defining the refinement step technically easier.

4.1 Abstraction

Input to our algorithm is a non-linear automaton C which we call the *concrete* hybrid automaton. The first step is to construct an *abstract* hybrid automaton A which is a polyhedral automaton. The abstract hybrid automaton A is obtained from the concrete hybrid automaton C, by splitting the invariant of any location $q \in Q_C$ into a finite number of cells of type $\mathbb{P}^X$ and defining an abstract location for each of these cells which over-approximates the non-linear dynamics in the cell by polyhedral dynamics. Definitions 2 and 3 formalizes the way an abstraction A is constructed from C. Note that the construction guarantees that the behavior of A *over-approximates* behavior of C and therefore if A is found to be safe, C is guaranteed to be safe as well.

Definition 2 (Invariant Partitions). *For any hybrid automaton C and function $P \in Q \to 2^{\mathbb{P}^X}$ we say P partitions invariants of C iff the following conditions hold for any location $q \in Q$:*

- *$\bigcup P(q) = I(q)$, which means union of cells in $P(q)$ covers invariant of q.*
- *For any $p_1, p_2 \in P(q)$, $p_1 \neq p_2$ implies p_1 and p_2 have disjoint interior[1].*

Definition 3 (Abstraction Using Invariant Partitioning). *For any non-linear automaton C and invariant partition $P \in Q \to 2^{\mathbb{P}^X}$, $\alpha(C, P)$ returns polyhedral automaton A which is defined below:*

- $Q_A = \{(q, p) \mid q \in Q_C \wedge p \in P(q)\}$, $- X_A = X_C$,
- $Q_A^{\text{init}} = \{(q, p) \in Q_A \mid q \in Q_C^{\text{init}}\}$, $- I_A((q, p)) = p$,

---

[1] Interior of a polytope is obtained by making all its corresponding constraints strict.

- $Q_{\mathcal{A}}^{\mathsf{bad}} = \{(q,p) \in Q_{\mathcal{A}} \mid q \in Q_{\mathcal{C}}^{\mathsf{bad}}\}$,
- $E_{\mathcal{A}} = \{((s,p_1),(d,p_2),g,j,r) \mid (s,d,g,j,r) \in E_{\mathcal{C}} \wedge (s,p_1),(d,p_2) \in Q_{\mathcal{A}}\}$, and
- $F_{\mathcal{A}}((q,p),\nu) = \mathsf{polyhull}(\bigcup_{\nu \in p} F_{\mathcal{C}}(q,\nu))$, where for any bounded set $S \subset \mathbb{R}^{\mathsf{X}}$, $\mathsf{polyhull}(S)$ is a polytope W such that $\forall \nu \in S \bullet \nu \in W$ and for any sequence of bounded sets $S_1, S_2, \ldots$, if the maximum distance of any two points in S_n converges to 0 then the maximum distance of any two points in the image of this sequence under $\mathsf{polyhull}$ converges to 0 as well.

In addition, we define function $\gamma_{\mathcal{A}}$ to map 1. every state in $[\![\mathcal{A}]\!]$ to a state in $[\![\mathcal{C}]\!]$, and 2. every edge in $E_{\mathcal{A}}$ to an edge in $E_{\mathcal{C}}$. Formally, for any $s = ((q,p),\nu) \in S_{[\![\mathcal{A}]\!]}$ and $e = ((q_1,p_1),(q_2,p_2),r) \in E_{\mathcal{A}}$, we define $\gamma_{\mathcal{A}}(s)$ to be (q,ν) and $\gamma_{\mathcal{A}}(e)$ to be (q_1,q_2,r).

When $F_{\mathcal{C}}(q)$ is an affine dynamic, there is unique minimum polytope for $F_{\mathcal{A}}((q,p))$ that can be constructed exactly and efficiently. However, if the concrete flow is non-linear, abstraction even using the minimum rectangular hull might be very expensive. In our current implementation, when the flow is non-linear, we first find the rectangular hull for $I_{\mathcal{C}}(q)$ and then use interval arithmetic to find a rectangular set that contains $F_{\mathcal{A}}((q,p))$ as specified in Definition 3.

4.2 Counter Example and Model Checking Polyhedral Automata

After an abstract hybrid automaton is constructed (initially and after any refinement), we have to model check it. In this section we define the notion of a counter example and annotation of a counter example, which we assume is returned by the abstract model checker O^{Poly} when it finds that the input hybrid automaton is unsafe.

Definition 4. *For any hybrid automaton $\mathcal{H}$, a* counter example *is a path $e_1, \ldots, e_n$ such that $Se_1 \in Q^{\mathsf{init}}$ and $De_n \in Q^{\mathsf{bad}}$.*

Definition 5. *A* counter example *π is called* valid *in $\mathcal{H}$ iff $\mathcal{H}$ has a trajectory τ and τ has the same sequence of edges as π. A counter example that is not valid is called* spurious.

Definition 6. *An* annotation *for a counter example $\pi = e_1, \ldots, e_n$ of hybrid automaton $\mathcal{H}$ is a sequence $\tau = S_0 \to S_0' \xrightarrow{e_1} S_1 \to S_1' \xrightarrow{e_2} \cdots \xrightarrow{e_n} S_n \to S_n'$ such that the following conditions hold:*

1. $\forall 0 \leq i \leq n \bullet \emptyset \neq S_i, S_i' \subseteq S_{[\![\mathcal{H}]\!]}$,
2. $\forall 0 \leq i \leq n \bullet S_i = \mathsf{cpre}_{\mathcal{H}}(S_i')$,
3. $\forall 0 \leq i < n \bullet S_i' = \mathsf{dpre}_{\mathcal{H}}^{e_{i+1}}(S_{i+1})$,
4. $S_n' = S_{[\![\mathcal{H}]\!]}^{\mathsf{bad}} \cap (\{De_n\} \times V_{\mathcal{H}})$.

Condition 1 means that each S_i and S_i' in τ are a non-empty set of states. Conditions 2 and 3 mean that sets of states in τ are computed using backward reachability. Finally, condition 4 means that S_n' is the set of unsafe states in destination of e_n. Note that these conditions completely specify $S_0, \ldots, S_n$ and

$S'_0, \ldots, S'_n$ from $e_1, \ldots, e_n$ and $\mathcal{H}$. Also, every S_i and S'_i is a subset of states corresponding to exactly one location.

In this paper, we assume to have access to an oracle O^{Poly} that can correctly answer reachability problems when the hybrid automata are restricted to be polyhedral automata. If no unsafe location of $\mathcal{A}$ is reachable from an initial location of it, $O^{\text{Poly}}(\mathcal{A})$ returns 'safe'. Otherwise, it returns an annotated counter example of $\mathcal{A}$.

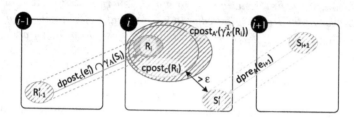

Fig. 1. Validation and refinement. There are three locations: $i-1$, i, and $i+1$. S_{i+1} and S'_i are elements of annotated counter example τ. R'_{i-1}, R_i, and $\text{cpost}_C(R_i)$ are computed when τ is validated. i is the smallest index for which $\text{cpost}_C(R_i)$ and $\gamma_\mathcal{A}(S'_i)$ are separated. Hence we need to refine $\mathcal{A}$ in location i. Refinement should be done in such a way that for the result of refinement $\mathcal{A}'$ we have $\text{cpost}_{\mathcal{A}'}(\gamma_{\mathcal{A}'}^{-1}(R_i)) \cap \gamma_{\mathcal{A}'}(S'_i) = \emptyset$ (γ^{-1} is the preimage of γ).

4.3   Validating Abstract Counterexamples and Refinement

For any invariant partition P and non-linear automaton C, if $O^{\text{Poly}}(\mathcal{A})$ (for $\mathcal{A} = \alpha(C, P)$) returns 'safe', we know C is safe. So the algorithm returns C is 'safe' and terminates. On the other hand, if O^{Poly} finds $\mathcal{A}$ to be unsafe it returns an annotated counter example τ of $\mathcal{A}$. Since $\mathcal{A}$ is an over-approximation of C, we cannot be certain at this point that C is also unsafe. More precisely, if π is the path in τ, we do not know whether $\gamma_\mathcal{A}(\pi)$ is a valid counter example in C or it is spurious. Therefore, we need to validate τ in order to determine if it corresponds to any actual run from an initial location to an unsafe location in C.

To validate τ, an annotated counter example of $\mathcal{A} = \alpha(C, P)$, we run τ on C. More precisely, we create a sequence $\tau' = R_0 \rightarrow R'_0 \xrightarrow{e'_1} R_1 \rightarrow \cdots \xrightarrow{e'_n} R_n \rightarrow R'_n$ where

1. $e'_i = \gamma_\mathcal{A}(e_i)$,
2. $R_0 = \gamma_\mathcal{A}(S_0)$,
3. $R'_i = \text{cpost}_C(R_i) \cap \gamma_\mathcal{A}(S'_i)$,
4. $R_i = \text{dpost}_C^{e'_i}(R'_{i-1}) \cap \gamma_\mathcal{A}(S_i)$.

We proved the following proposition and lemma in [29].

Proposition 7. $R'_n = \emptyset$ in τ' implies there exists i such that 1. $R'_i = \emptyset$, 2. $R_i \neq \emptyset$, 3. $\forall j < i \cdot R_j, R'_j \neq \emptyset$, and 4. $\text{cpost}_C(R_i)$ and $\gamma_\mathcal{A}(S'_i)$ are nonempty disjoint sets.

Lemma 8. *The counter example $\pi' = e'_1, \ldots, e'_n$ of C is valid iff $R'_n \neq \emptyset$.*

Refinement. Suppose the counterexample τ is spurious. There is a smallest index i such that $R'_i = \emptyset$. We will refine the location $(q, p) = De_i$ of $\mathcal{A}$ by refining its invariant p. We know from Proposition 7, $\mathsf{cpost}_C(R_i) \cap \gamma_{\mathcal{A}}(S'_i) = \emptyset$. However, the corresponding sets in the abstract system $\mathcal{A}$ are not disjoint, that is, $\mathsf{cpost}_{\mathcal{A}}(\gamma_{\mathcal{A}}^{-1}(R_i)) \cap S'_i \neq \emptyset$ (γ^{-1} is the preimage of γ). Our refinement strategy is to find a partition for the location (q, p) such that in the refined model $R = \alpha(C, P')$ (for some P'), S'_i is not reachable from R_i (Fig. 1). Let us denote by $\mathcal{C}_{q,p}$ the restriction of C to the single location q with invariant p, *i.e.*, $\mathcal{C}_{q,p}$ has only one location q whose flow and invariant is the same as that of (q, p) in $\mathcal{A}$, and only transitions whose source and destination is q. We will say that an invariant partition P_r of $\mathcal{C}_{q,p}$ *separates* R_i from S'_i iff in the automaton $\mathcal{A}_1 = \alpha(\mathcal{C}_{q,p}, P_r)$, $\mathsf{reach}_{\mathcal{A}_1}(\gamma_{\mathcal{A}_1}^{-1}(R_i)) \cap \gamma_{\mathcal{A}_1}^{-1}(\gamma_{\mathcal{A}}(S'_i)) = \emptyset$. In other words, the states corresponding to S'_i in $\mathcal{A}_1$ are not reachable from $\gamma_{\mathcal{A}_1}^{-1}(R_i)$ in $\mathcal{A}_1$. Our refinement strategy will refine $\mathcal{A}$ by partitioning the control location (q, p) by the invariant partition P_r. Using results from [27], we observed [29] that such a partition P_r always exists. We also showed that such a refinement strategy ensures that any abstract counter example appears only finitely many times in the CEGAR loop.

The previous discussion, relies on the fact that we can compute $\mathsf{cpost}(.)$ exactly. Unfortunately this is not possible for the class of hybrid automaton we are considering. We use δ-complete decision procedures available through dReach and dReal to check whether R'_n will be empty for some n. If dReach returns unsat, we know the $R'_n = \emptyset$, and we can conclude that the counter example is spurious. However, if dReach returns δ-sat, we know δ-perturbation of the *syntax* of the formula defining R'_n makes it satisfiable. But this does not imply that R'_n itself isnon-empty. Hence, it is possible that because of our use of dReach for counter example validation, we may not be able to detect spurious counter examples.

5   Tool's Architecture

Figure 2 shows the flow and architecture of HARE. It also identifies 3rd party libraries/tools that are internally used by HARE at different steps. We use Z3 [13] to check if a fix-point is reached in the abstract system model-checking, and also to check whether an unsafe state is reached. We use Boost Interval Arithmetic Library (IAL) [1] to abstract non-linear dynamics. We use dReach to validate a counter example (the validation a counter example of length n involves at most n invocations of dReach). Note that dReach calls dReal, internally. Also, dReach/dReal are not available in the form of libraries. Therefore, HARE executes dReach as a separate process and communicates with it through files. Finally, we use Parma Polyhedra Library (PPL) [5] to manipulate symbolic abstract states. This includes, computing discrete/continuous abstract posts, constructing annotated counter examples, finding rectangular hull of a polytope, abstracting affine flows, and checking if a parallelly composed location/edge has non-empty

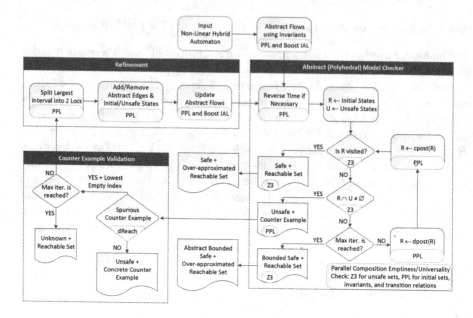

Fig. 2. Flow chart of HARE's CEGAR loop

invariant/transition relation. Compared to the old version of HARE in [29], we have replaced SpaceEx with dReach, since SpaceEx does not support non-linear dynamics. Also, we have implemented everything in C++ instead of Scala to improve performance.

The abstract model checker in HARE has a parameter direction with possible values forward and backward. It specifies whether the tool should perform forward or backward reachability. But PPL can only compute cpost and not cpre. This is the reason for the step "Reverse Time If Necessary". There is an optional integer parameter max-iter for each of the abstract and concrete model checkers. If the maximum number of iterations is reached in the abstract model checker, it returns bounded-safe as an answer. If abstract model checker returns this answer to the concrete model checker, abstract bounded safe will be returned as a result. If the maximum number of iterations is reached in the concrete model checker, it returns unknown as the answer. In addition to Safe or Unsafe, the user can also ask HARE to produce a counter-example, an annotated-counter-example, or the reachable-set. Clearly, the first two will only be produced if the system is found to be unsafe and the last one will only output the *abstract* reachable states. Note that abstract model checker can be directly called by user.

The model to be checked along with all the options for the model checker are specified in a single human readable text file according to INFO Parser from Boost Property Tree Library [24]. Every model, contains one or more hybrid automata and the safety problem is considered for their parallel composition which is constructed on the fly. Continuous variables can be read by all hybrid automata. If the file specifies polyhedral automata, each hybrid automaton can write to all variables through transition relations and flow. On the other hand, if the file specifies a non-linear automaton, different hybrid automata can still write to a common variable through transition relations, but flow of a variable should be defined in exactly one hybrid automaton. Initial and unsafe states are specified after all hybrid automata using zero or more polyhedra for each composed location. Each edge has an optional label. If it is specified, it means that edge must be synced with an edge from other hybrid automata in the file. Otherwise, it will be interleaved. If a specified label does not end with '?', '!', or '!!', synchronization will be among all hybrid automata in the file (*i.e.* each hybrid automaton must take an edge with the exact same label). Characters '?', '!', and '!!' are used to specify input/output hybrid automata, where '?' is for an input edge, '!' is for an output edge, and '!!' is for a broadcast edge. Character '*' at the beginning of a location name means that location is transient and time cannot pass inside that location. Allowing transient locations in the model has three benefits 1. neither abstract nor concrete model checker will waste time by computing continuous post in transient locations, 2. the result automata will have one less variable, and 3. the model will be easier to understand. Finally, the current interface to the tool is only through the command line.

6   Experimental Results

The new version of HARE is available from https://uofi.box.com/v/HARE; the old version of the tool can be downloaded from https://uofi.box.com/cegar-hare-tacas-2016. Examples and scripts for running the examples can also be found on the links. Both these links contain a virtual machine to make repeatability straightforward.

We have run HARE with different set of examples with both affine and non-linear dynamics. Brief explanations of the affine benchmarks can be found in [29]. Table 1 contains the results for the affine examples. We compare the performance of HARE, its old version in [29], SpaceEx [19], PHAVer [18], and SpaceEx AGAR [7]s[2]. The first two tools are affine hybrid automata model checkers that are not CEGAR based, while the last is a CEGAR based tool for concurrent hybrid automata[3]. In the past [29], we also reported the performance of HSolver [28] on affine examples. However, since it performed poorly on affine examples, we have not included it for comparison in Table 1.

The new version of HARE proved all examples are safe, while the old version could not do this for four examples. Also the new version is faster on all examples, except one. SpaceEx almost never reached a fixed point. PHAVer could prove safety for only half of the examples, and it did it faster than new version of HARE in only one case. Abstraction in SpaceEx AGAR appears to be a very expensive

---

[2] By SpaceEx we mean SpaceEx with Supp as its scenario and by PHAVer we mean SpaceEx with PHAVer as its scenario.

[3] It is called "Assume Guarantee Abstraction Refinement" in [7].

operation—in four examples, the initial abstraction was not constructed even after 600 s (10 min) and we terminated the execution. Also, in three examples we could not find any set of locations that does not cause the tool to crash right at the beginning. Among 8 examples that worked for SpaceEx AGAR, it could prove safety for 5 of them and it was always slower than new version of HARE.

Table 1. Comparing HARE with its old version in [29] and other tools for affine dynamics. Dim. is the number of continuous variables. Size is the number of locations/edges in the input (concrete) model. Iters. is the number of iterations in our CEGAR loop before proving safety. FP. tells whether or not a tool reached a fixed-point. If a tool does not reach a fixed-point then even if it says the system is safe, the answer may not be true. As explained in [29], sometimes SpaceEx tells it reached a fixed-point, but before that it generates a warning that its result may not be complete. We continue to consider those cases as SpaceEx has not reached a fixed-point. Merged Locs. is the number of locations we initially merged for SpaceEx AGAR. Columns old and new for HARE contain results from the previous and current version of this tool. All times are in seconds and all examples were run on a laptop with Intel i5 2.50 GHz CPU and 6 GB of RAM.

Model	Dim.	Size	HARE						SpaceEx			PHAVer			SpaceEx AGAR			
			Time		Iters.		Safe		Time	FP.	Safe	Time	FP.	Safe	Merged Locs.	Time	FP.	Safe
			old	new	old	new	old	new										
Tank 16	3	3 / 6	<1	<1	1	1	✓	✓	3	✗	✗	1414	✗	✓	2	1133	✗	✓
Tank 17	3	3 / 6	<1	<1	1	1	✓	✓	5	✗	✓	1309	✗	✓	2	1041	✗	✓
Satellite 03	4	64 / 198	91	<1	1	1	✗	✓	<1	✗	✗	1804	✗	✗	28	>600	---	---
Satellite 04	4	100 / 307	<1	<1	1	1	✓	✓	<1	✗	✓	<1	✓	✓	91	49	✓	✓
Satellite 11	4	576 / 1735	1	<1	1	1	✓	✓	<1	✗	✓	<1	✓	✓	449	>600	---	---
Satellite 15	4	1296 / 3895	2	<1	1	1	✓	✓	<1	✗	✓	<1	✓	✓	264	>600	---	---
Heater 03	3	4 / 6	>600	54	---	1	---	✓	84	✗	✓	<1	✓	✗	---	---	---	---
Heater 05	3	4 / 6	<1	58	1	38	✗	✓	61	✗	✓	<1	✓	✗	---	---	---	---
Heater 09	3	4 / 6	<1	80	1	15	✗	✓	42	✗	✗	<1	✓	✗	---	---	---	---
Nav 01	4	25 / 80	9	18	11	11	✓	✓	<1	✓	✓	<1	✓	✓	21	5	✓	✓
Nav 08	4	16 / 48	7	<1	13	1	✓	✓	685	✗	✓	<1	✓	✓	10	<1	✓	✓
Nav 09	4	16 / 48	7	<1	10	1	✓	✓	<1	✗	✗	<1	✓	✗	4	<1	✓	✗
Nav 13	4	9 / 18	8	<1	15	1	✓	✓	<1	✗	✓	<1	✓	✓	4	<1	✓	✓
Nav 19	4	33 / 97	29	<1	17	1	✓	✓	2	✗	✓	<1	✓	✓	11	<1	✓	✓

Table 2 contains results of comparing HARE with C2E2 [16], HSolver [28], and FLOW* [8] on nonlinear examples. Note that HARE and HSolver support proving safety for unbounded time and unbounded number of discrete transitions. But both C2E2 and FLOW* require bounded time and bounded number of discrete transitions. Also none of these two tools check whether the computed (unbounded) reachable set so far is a fixed-point. Therefore, no matter how big the time-bound is set, proving safety for this time bound in these tools does not guarantee unbounded time safety. In our experience, we set the bound for discrete number of transitions large enough so none of the tools reported maximum number of discrete transitions are reached. For the first 5 examples, we set the time bound equal to 1000 in C2E2 and HSolver. For the last example, the time bound is 10 in all tools. HARE always finished faster than C2E2. On three examples HARE is faster than FLOW* and only in one example it is slower. On 3 examples HARE proved safety faster than HSolver, and in 2 examples HSolver was faster. HSolver comes with an example named circuit (not reported in

Table 2). The size of hybrid automaton in this example is small, but it has constants of the order 10^{12}, which turns out to be too big for C2E2 and dReach and trigger a bug in these two tools (and hence HARE). Only HSolver proves safety of this example. Finally, in our experiments, dReach performs much faster for the affine dynamics. Non-linear examples are also available at link for the new version of HARE we mentioned earlier.

Table 2. Comparing running time of HARE with other tools for non-linear dynamics. Dim. is the number of continuous variables. Size is the number of locations/edges in the input (concrete) model. Reached Abst. Size is the number of locations/edges in the final abstract model that are reached in HARE right before safety is proved. Time Bound is 10 for the "Sinusoid" model in all four tools. For all the other examples, there is no time bound in both HARE and HSolver. In other word, HARE and HSolver prove unbounded time safety for all but the last example. C2E2 and FLOW* on the other hand, require finite time bound, and we set it to be 1000 (except for the "Sinusoid" model which is 10). We have terminated all the runs that took more than 600 s (10 min). HSolver requires bounded invariants. So in the first four examples, we put 100 as an upper bound and −100 for as a lower bound of unbounded variables. FLOW* does not support trigonometric functions and C2E2 encounters an internal error on one of the examples. All times are in seconds and all examples were run on a laptop with Intel i5 2.50 GHz CPU and 6 GB of RAM.

| Model | Dim. | Size | HARE | | C2E2 | HSolver | FLOW* |
			Reached Abst. Size	Time Bound	Time	Time	Time	Time
Van der Pol	2	1 / 0	26 / 194	∞	< 1	56	3*	> 600
Jet Engine	2	1 / 0	189 / 1330	∞	55	56	2*	> 600
Cardiac Cell	2	2 / 2	249 / 1783	∞	16	50	< 1*	25
Cardiac Control	3	2 / 2	270 / 3974	∞	153	> 600	> 600*	41
Clock	3	1 / 0	9 / 56	∞	< 1	---	< 1	< 1
Sinusoid	2	1 / 0	32 / 62	10	< 1	1	7	---

6.1 Unbounded Invariants

The first 4 examples in Table 2 are taken from C2E2. Tools like C2E2 and FLOW* that try to compute the reachable set as precisely as possible, tend not to specify invariants. On the other hand, tools like HARE and HSolver that perform refinement by partitioning the state space tend to require bounded invariants. Another reason for HARE to prefer bounded invariants is that dReach, which HARE uses internally, only works for bounded variables. We had a few options to bound the invariants in those examples. The first option is to bound the invariants using large enough numbers (just like what we did for HSolver). This means we are guessing the invariant. If the guessed invariants are all closed sets, one can verify the guess by setting closure of complement of it as the unsafe states. If the unsafe states are not reachable then the guess is valid. Note that since HARE computes over-approximation of unsafe states, it is possible that HARE incorrectly says a guessed invariant is invalid. The second option is to first use tools like C2E2 or FLOW* and find a coarse invariant for all locations. Note that since these tools have bounded number of discrete transitions and they do not check for fixpoint, one might still need to verify that invariants obtained using C2E2 or FLOW* are valid. The third option, which we have used for the current implementation, is noticing that the only part of the implementation that requires invariant to be bounded is where dReach is called. If this tool is called with an unbounded variable, then it will quickly raise an exception and terminate. In other words, it will terminate without saying that the counter example is valid. We take *not saying valid* as saying *invalid*. This approach makes it possible to use dReach even when invariants are not bounded. Note that during validation of a counter example of length larger than one, it is possible that only invariants after some step k are unbounded. Our current approach guarantees all variables are bounded when dReach is called for indices k or smaller. An example of such a system, *Automatic lane change system (driver assist)* that comes with C2E2. It is a system with affine dynamics and 10 unsafe sets. HARE proved unbounded safety for all these sets in about 190 s. During this time, dReach encountered exception in almost every iteration. But eventually, the abstract model checker reached a fixed point and found the system to be safe, so dReach was not called again. C2E2 needs to prove safety for each of these sets separately and it took this tool about 1163 s to prove them all when the time bound is set to 1000. HSolver and FLOW* could not prove safety for any of these sets within 600 s (10 min)[4]. A fourth option is one where we initially partition the state space blindly for a small number of times first, and then start the actual CEGAR loop. We used this option in all four examples in Table 2 from C2E2.

7   Conclusion

We presented a new version of the CEGAR-based model checker for non-linear hybrid systems called HARE. This version is a significant improvement over the previous version of HARE that was reported in [29]. First, HARE can now verify non-linear hybrid automata instead of hybrid automata with affine dynamics and rectangular constraints. Second, HARE now uses *polyhedral hybrid automata* as abstractions as opposed to rectangular hybrid automata. Finally, the implementation has been optimized. These changes have enabled the tool to handle a larger class of examples, in faster time. These observations have been substantiated by our experimental results reported here. While the use of dReach for counter example validation has improved the performance for affine hybrid automaton, our experiments show that dReach performs poorly for counter examples for non-linear automata (when compared with C2E2). In the future, we plan to explore if we can use C2E2 (instead of dReach) for counter example validation.

Acknowledgement. We gratefully acknowledge the support of the following grants— Nima Roohi was partially supported by NSF CNS 1329991; Pavithra Prabhakar was partially supported by NSF CAREER Award 1552668; and Mahesh Viswanathan was partially supported by NSF CCF 1422798 and AFOSR FA9950-15-1-0059.

---

[4] Time bound for HSolver and HARE are set to be the same. Similarly, time bound for FLOW* and C2E2 are set to be the same.

References

1. Boost Interval Arithmetic Library. http://www.boost.org/doc/libs/1_62_0/libs/numeric/interval/doc/interval.htm. Accessed 19 Oct 2016
2. Alur, R., Courcoubetis, C., Halbwachs, N., Henzinger, T.A., Ho, P.H., Nicollin, X., Olivero, A., Sifakis, J., Yovine, S.: The algorithmic analysis of hybrid systems. TCS **138**(1), 3–34 (1995)
3. Alur, R., Dang, T., Ivančić, F.: Predicate abstraction for reachability analysis of hybrid systems. ACM Trans. Embed. Comput. Syst. **5**(1), 152–199 (2006)
4. Asarin, E., Maler, O., Pnueli, A.: Reachability analysis of dynamical systems having piecewise-constant derivatives. TCS **138**(1), 35–65 (1995)
5. Bagnara, R., Hill, P.M., Zaffanella, E.: The Parma Polyhedra Library: toward a complete set of numerical abstractions for the analysis and verification of hardware and software systems. Sci. Comput. Program. **72**(1–2), 3–21 (2008)
6. Ball, T., Rajamani, S.K.: Bebop: a symbolic model checker for boolean programs. In: Havelund, K., Penix, J., Visser, W. (eds.) SPIN 2000. LNCS, vol. 1885, pp. 113–130. Springer, Heidelberg (2000). doi:10.1007/10722468_7
7. Bogomolov, S., Frehse, G., Greitschus, M., Grosu, R., Pasareanu, C., Podelski, A., Strump, T.: Assume-guarantee abstraction refinement meets hybrid systems. In: Yahav, E. (ed.) HVC 2014. LNCS, vol. 8855, pp. 116–131. Springer, Heidelberg (2014). doi:10.1007/978-3-319-13338-6_10
8. Chen, X., Ábrahám, E., Sankaranarayanan, S.: Flow*: an analyzer for non-linear hybrid systems. In: Sharygina, N., Veith, H. (eds.) CAV 2013. LNCS, vol. 8044, pp. 258–263. Springer, Heidelberg (2013). doi:10.1007/978-3-642-39799-8_18
9. Clarke, E., Grumberg, O., Jha, S., Lu, Y., Veith, H.: Counterexample-guided abstraction refinement. In: Emerson, E.A., Sistla, A.P. (eds.) CAV 2000. LNCS, vol. 1855, pp. 154–169. Springer, Heidelberg (2000). doi:10.1007/10722167_15
10. Clarke, E., Fehnker, A., Han, Z., Krogh, B., Ouaknine, J., Stursberg, O., Theobald, M.: Abstraction and counterexample-guided refinement in model checking of hybrid systems. JFCS **14**(4), 583–604 (2003)
11. Clarke, E., Fehnker, A., Han, Z., Krogh, B., Stursberg, O., Theobald, M.: Verification of hybrid systems based on counterexample-guided abstraction refinement. In: Garavel, H., Hatcliff, J. (eds.) TACAS 2003. LNCS, vol. 2619, pp. 192–207. Springer, Heidelberg (2003). doi:10.1007/3-540-36577-X_14
12. Corbett, J., Dwyer, M., Hatcliff, J., Laubach, S., Pasareanu, C., Zheng, H.: Bandera: extracting finite-state models from Java source code. In: ICSE, pp. 439–448 (2000)
13. Moura, L., Bjørner, N.: Z3: an efficient SMT solver. In: Ramakrishnan, C.R., Rehof, J. (eds.) TACAS 2008. LNCS, vol. 4963, pp. 337–340. Springer, Heidelberg (2008). doi:10.1007/978-3-540-78800-3_24
14. Dierks, H., Kupferschmid, S., Larsen, K.G.: Automatic abstraction refinement for timed automata. In: Raskin, J.-F., Thiagarajan, P.S. (eds.) FORMATS 2007. LNCS, vol. 4763, pp. 114–129. Springer, Heidelberg (2007). doi:10.1007/978-3-540-75454-1_10
15. Doyen, L., Henzinger, T.A., Raskin, J.-F.: Automatic rectangular refinement of affine hybrid systems. In: Pettersson, P., Yi, W. (eds.) FORMATS 2005. LNCS, vol. 3829, pp. 144–161. Springer, Heidelberg (2005). doi:10.1007/11603009_13
16. Duggirala, P.S., Mitra, S., Viswanathan, M., Potok, M.: C2E2: a verification tool for stateflow models. In: Baier, C., Tinelli, C. (eds.) TACAS 2015. LNCS, vol. 9035, pp. 68–82. Springer, Heidelberg (2015). doi:10.1007/978-3-662-46681-0_5

17. Fehnker, A., Clarke, E., Jha, S., Krogh, B.: Refining abstractions of hybrid systems using counterexample fragments. HSCC **2005**, 242–257 (2005)
18. Frehse, G.: PHAVer: algorithmic verification of hybrid systems past HyTech. In: Morari, M., Thiele, L. (eds.) HSCC 2005. LNCS, vol. 3414, pp. 258–273. Springer, Heidelberg (2005). doi:10.1007/978-3-540-31954-2_17
19. Frehse, G., et al.: SpaceEx: scalable verification of hybrid systems. In: Gopalakrishnan, G., Qadeer, S. (eds.) CAV 2011. LNCS, vol. 6806, pp. 379–395. Springer, Heidelberg (2011). doi:10.1007/978-3-642-22110-1_30
20. Henzinger, T.A., Kopke, P.W., Puri, A., Varaiya, P.: What's decidable about hybrid automata? J. Comput. Syst. Sci. 373–382 (1995). ACM Press
21. Henzinger, T.A., Jhala, R., Majumdar, R., Sutre, G.: Lazy abstraction. SIGPLAN Not. **37**(1), 58–70 (2002). doi:10.1145/565816.503279
22. Holzmann, G., Smith, M.: Automating software feature verification. Bell Labs Tech. J. **5**(2), 72–87 (2000)
23. Jha, S.K., Krogh, B.H., Weimer, J.E., Clarke, E.M.: Reachability for linear hybrid automata using iterative relaxation abstraction. In: Bemporad, A., Bicchi, A., Buttazzo, G. (eds.) HSCC 2007. LNCS, vol. 4416, pp. 287–300. Springer, Heidelberg (2007). doi:10.1007/978-3-540-71493-4_24
24. Kalicinski, M., Redl, S.: Boost Property Tree (2016). http://www.boost.org/doc/libs/1_62_0/doc/html/property_tree.html
25. Mysore, V., Pnueli, A.: Refining the undecidability frontier of hybrid automata. In: Sarukkai, S., Sen, S. (eds.) FSTTCS 2005. LNCS, vol. 3821, pp. 261–272. Springer, Heidelberg (2005). doi:10.1007/11590156_21
26. Nellen, J., Ábrahám, E., Wolters, B.: A CEGAR tool for the reachability analysis of PLC-controlled plants using hybrid automata. In: Bouabana-Tebibel, T., Rubin, S.H. (eds.) Formalisms for Reuse and Systems Integration. AISC, vol. 346, pp. 55–78. Springer, Heidelberg (2015). doi:10.1007/978-3-319-16577-6_3
27. Puri, A., Borkar, V.S., Varaiya, P.: Epsilon-approximation of differential inclusions. In: Hybrid Systems III: Verification and Control, pp. 362–376 (1995)
28. Ratschan, S., She, Z.: Safety verification of hybrid systems by constraint propagation based abstraction refinement. ACM Trans. Embed. Comput. Syst. **6**(1), 8 (2007)
29. Roohi, N., Prabhakar, P., Viswanathan, M.: Hybridization based CEGAR for hybrid automata with affine dynamics. In: Chechik, M., Raskin, J.-F. (eds.) TACAS 2016. LNCS, vol. 9636, pp. 752–769. Springer, Heidelberg (2016). doi:10.1007/978-3-662-49674-9_48
30. Segelken, M.: Abstraction and counterexample-guided construction of ω-automata for model checking of step-discrete linear hybrid models. In: Damm, W., Hermanns, H. (eds.) CAV 2007. LNCS, vol. 4590, pp. 433–448. Springer, Heidelberg (2007). doi:10.1007/978-3-540-73368-3_46
31. Sorea, M.: Lazy approximation for dense real-time systems. In: Lakhnech, Y., Yovine, S. (eds.) FORMATS/FTRTFT-2004. LNCS, vol. 3253, pp. 363–378. Springer, Heidelberg (2004). doi:10.1007/978-3-540-30206-3_25
32. Vladimerou, V., Prabhakar, P., Viswanathan, M., Dullerud, G.: STORMED hybrid systems. In: Aceto, L., Damgård, I., Goldberg, L.A., Halldórsson, M.M., Ingólfsdóttir, A., Walukiewicz, I. (eds.) ICALP 2008. LNCS, vol. 5126, pp. 136–147. Springer, Heidelberg (2008). doi:10.1007/978-3-540-70583-3_12
33. Zutshi, A., Deshmukh, J.V., Sankaranarayanan, S., Kapinski, J.: Multiple shooting, CEGAR-based falsification for hybrid systems. In: Proceedings of 14th International Conference on Embedded Software (2014)

Counterexample-Guided Refinement
of Template Polyhedra

Sergiy Bogomolov[1,2], Goran Frehse[3], Mirco Giacobbe[2(✉)],
and Thomas A. Henzinger[2]

[1] Australian National University, Canberra, Australia
[2] IST Austria, Klosterneuburg, Austria
mirco.giacobbe@ist.ac.at
[3] University of Grenoble Alpes - Verimag, Grenoble, France

Abstract. Template polyhedra generalize intervals and octagons to polyhedra whose facets are orthogonal to a given set of arbitrary directions. They have been employed in the abstract interpretation of programs and, with particular success, in the reachability analysis of hybrid automata. While previously, the choice of directions has been left to the user or a heuristic, we present a method for the automatic discovery of directions that generalize and eliminate spurious counterexamples. We show that for the class of convex hybrid automata, i.e., hybrid automata with (possibly nonlinear) convex constraints on derivatives, such directions always exist and can be found using convex optimization. We embed our method inside a CEGAR loop, thus enabling the time-unbounded reachability analysis of an important and richer class of hybrid automata than was previously possible. We evaluate our method on several benchmarks, demonstrating also its superior efficiency for the special case of linear hybrid automata.

1 Introduction

Template polyhedra are convex polyhedra whose defining halfspaces are orthogonal to a template, i.e., a finite set of directions. In other words, they are those conjunctions of linear inequalities where all coefficients are fixed and constants can vary. Template polyhedra naturally generalize geometrical representations like intervals or octagons, yet maintain low computational cost for several set operations. Template polyhedra have been employed for the abstract interpretation of programs [17,38], but in particular they have recently gained popularity with the abstract interpretation of hybrid automata [12,18,25,27,37], i.e., the extension of finite automata with continuous dynamics [26]. In fact, verification of hybrid automata via template polyhedra has shown promise in practice [8,13,20,23,35], in spite of the theoretical undecidability even for the reachability question [29].

This research was supported in part by the Austrian Science Fund (FWF) under grants S11402-N23 (RiSE/SHiNE) and Z211-N23 (Wittgenstein Award), by the European Commission under grant 643921 (UnCoVerCPS) and by the ARC project DP140104219 (Robust AI Planning for Hybrid Systems).

A. Legay and T. Margaria (Eds.): TACAS 2017, Part I, LNCS 10205, pp. 589–606, 2017.
DOI: 10.1007/978-3-662-54577-5_34

In this paper, we develop a novel abstraction refinement procedure for template polyhedra and we evaluate its use in the time-unbounded reachability analysis of hybrid automata.

Efficiency often comes at the price of precision, and template polyhedra are no exception. The precision is sensitive to the choice of template and a bad one might cause several problems. First, even computing the tightest of the template polyhedra around a set won't necessarily bring to an exact representation. This holds for linear sets, think about using intervals or octagons for representing arbitrary polyhedra, and for non linear sets, think about using any finite set of directions for representing ellipses or parabolae. Second, template polyhedra suffer from the so called wrapping effect, that is to say that even if you represent initial and guard constraints of a hybrid automaton precisely, discrete transitions and time elapse might make new directions necessary. Think about representing a box using intervals, applying a slight rotation, and representing it again using intervals. Thus the question is: how do you choose the template?

The current approaches for the abstract interpretation by means of template polyhedra are affected by multiple problems. First, they do not guarantee avoidance of spurious counterexamples. In fact, they either assume a priori fixed templates or derive directions from initial and guard constraints [37,38]. The online refinement techniques focus on improving local errors rather than inductively eliminating and generalizing whole paths [6,22]. Counterexample-guided methods have been developed, but not for template polyhedra [4,7,15,19]. Second, they partition and bound the time domain. Differential equations are in general hard to solve, thus time partitioning is often necessary [23,25]. Efforts in taking larger time intervals have been made, but not for unbounded time [24]. Third, the approaches to the analysis of non-linear systems do not handle template refinement, even offline. The abstraction refinement of Bernstein and Taylor expansion-based approximations relies on global parameters that are hard to infer from counterexamples [12,13,18,20,39].

We propose a method which, for the first time, discovers template directions from spurious counterexamples and adds to the template a few of them at a time. Let us look at a refinement workflow. Initially, we search for a spurious counterexample using a fixed (and possibly empty) template. Once such a counterexample is found, we extract an inductive sequence of halfspace interpolants, i.e., Craig's interpolants that consist of single linear inequalities [2]. We take their outward pointing directions and we add them to the template. Such directions eliminate the counterexample and generalize to all other counterexamples with the same switching sequence and any (and possibly unbounded) time elapse. We repeat the procedure in CEGAR fashion [16].

We target the time-unbounded reachability analysis of convex hybrid automata (CHA), i.e., hybrid automata whose flow constraints consist of differential inclusions (on derivatives only) and all constraints (flow, guards, and invariants) are (possibly non-linear) closed convex sets, and the special cases of linear hybrid automata (LHA) and quadratic hybrid automata (QHA). A large class of systems belongs to CHA, e.g., timed systems with convex non-linear clock drifts, or can be approximated as CHA, e.g., systems with Gaussian disturbances truncated by elliptic sets. The reachability analysis of LHA has a long history [5], while for QHA or beyond only bounded reachability analysis has been explored [11,14].

We show that (i) for every CHA halfspace interpolants suitable for refinement always exist and that (ii) they can be computed efficiently using convex optimization [10], in particular using linear programming for LHA and second-order conic programming for QHA. We implement a tool based of this technology and evaluate it on several linear and quadratic benchmarks, comparing (favorably) against PHAVer where that tool applies [21,23], namely LHA. This gives the following new results. First, we enable the use of template polyhedra for the abstract interpretation and the abstraction refinement of CHA, thus enabling the efficient time-unbounded reachability analysis for the full class where efficient convex optimizers are available, namely QHA. Second, we achieve greater practical performance against the state-of-the-art techniques for the time-unbounded reachability of even LHA. We evaluate our tool on multiple scaling and linear and non-linear variants of three different benchmarks, namely Fischer's protocol [31], the TTEthernet protocol [9], and an adaptive cruise controller [30].

In summary, our contribution is threefold. First, we develop the first complete counterexample-guided procedure for the discovery of template directions. Second, we enable, for the first time, abstraction refinement for the time-unbounded reachability analysis for all CHA. Third, we build an efficient tool for the new class of time-unbounded QHA verification, which shows superior performance also for the special case of LHA.

2 Motivating Example

Consider a system with two real-valued variables x and y whose dynamics follows some differential equation, which in turn is discontinuously switched by an automaton with three modes. Figure 1 shows such an example. The trajectory

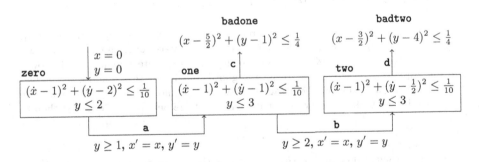

Fig. 1. A CHA with two variables x and y, three good modes zero, one, and two, two bad modes badone and badtwo, and four switches a, b, c, and d. The good modes have three different relative speeds for x and y with an additional spherical drift. All invariants, the jump guards of a and of b are linear and the jump guards of c and of d are spherical.

starts in the origin and enters mode zero and follows any differential equation whose derivative is $\dot{x} = 1$ and $\dot{y} = 2$ with possibly some drift in the ball of radius $10^{-\frac{1}{2}}$ around this value. The invariant allows the trajectory to stay in mode zero as long as $y \leq 2$. The trajectory can take a if $y \geq 1$ and switch to mode one, where the derivative of y halves. The dynamics continues similarly on mode one, switch c, and mode two, and similarly can take a switch to badone and badtwo when the respective guards are satisfied. We know that there does not exists a trajectory that leads to one of the bad modes, namely the system is *safe*. We want to prove it automatically by means of template polyhedra.

The set of states that are respectively reachable on modes zero, one, and two are the cones spanned by the points that enter the mode and take any possible trajectory, as respectively depicted in Fig. 2 in three shades on gray. We abstract the whole systems by representing each of these sets using template polyhedra. But first, we need to discover a suitable template. In fact, different templates produce different abstractions and not all of them can prove safety. Figure 2 shows three different such abstractions (striped polyhedra), but (a) and (b) hit the guards (dashed circled) to the bad modes while only (c) accomplishes the task. Our goal is to construct a good template like in (c).

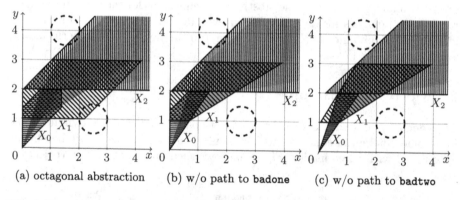

(a) octagonal abstraction   (b) w/o path to badone   (c) w/o path to badtwo

Fig. 2. Template-polyhedral abstraction refinement for the CHA in Fig. 1. In dark gray, gray, and light gray the points reachable on the modes zero, one, and two, resp., and the striped polyhedra X_0, X_1, and X_2 are the resp. template polyhedra. The lower and the upper dashed circles are, resp., the guards of the switches c and d to the bad modes. The variant (a) show the octagonal abstraction, and (b) and (c) show resp. the results of the templates obtained after refinement of the paths to badone and then to badtwo.

We begin with abstraction (a) which uses the octagonal template, i.e., the 8 orthogonal directions to the facets of an octagon. The abstract interpreter will produce several abstract paths (sequences of pairs of modes and polyhedra interleaved by switches) among which will occur the path zero, a, one, c, badone, for the regions $X_0, X_1 \subseteq \mathbb{R}^n$ where $X_0 = \text{init}_{\text{zero}}$ abstracts the flow on zero, and $X_1 = \text{post}_a(X_0)$ abstracts the flow on one (see Fig. 2a). This path reaches a bad mode, but it is spurious, namely it does not have a concrete counterpart. We prove it by computing a sequence of halfspace interpolants, i.e., two half-spaces H_0 and H_1 such that $\text{init}_{\texttt{zero}} \subseteq H_0$ and $\text{post}_{\texttt{a}}(H_0) \subseteq H_1$ and H_1 does not intersect with the guard of the switch $\texttt{c}$ (see Fig. 3b). The outward pointing directions d_0 and d_1 of H_0 and H_1 are the directions that generalize and eliminate all counterexamples with the switching sequence $\texttt{zero, a, one, c, badone}$ (see Fig. 3c). We add them to the template and we recompute the abstraction, obtaining a necessarily different counterexample (see Fig. 2b). We repeat and eventually obtain Fig. 2c, finally proving the safety of the hybrid automaton.

In the next section we define the modeling and the (template-polyhedral) abstraction framework for CHA. In Sect. 4 we present our interpolant-based refinement technique and in Sect. 5 we phrase it as a convex optimization problem. In Sect. 6 we instantiate it to QHA and in Sect. 7 we show our experimental results.

3   Template-Polyhedral Abstractions for Convex Systems

Hybrid automata extend finite automata adding constraints on the (discrete and continuous) dynamics of a set of real variables [26]. Convex hybrid automata (CHA) are the class whose constraint define non-linear convex sets that exclusively constrain either variables or variable derivatives, as it is the case for the well-know class of linear hybrid automata (LHA) [26], which is thus generalized by CHA.

Definition 1 (Convex hybrid automata). *A convex hybrid automaton $\mathcal{H}$ with n real-valued variables consists of a finite directed multigraph (V, E) where the vertices $v \in V$ are called control modes and the edges $e \in E$ are called control switches. Each $v \in V$ is decorated by an initial constraint $Z_v \subseteq \mathbb{R}^n$, an invariant constraint $I_v \subseteq \mathbb{R}^n$, and a flow constraint $F_v \subseteq \mathbb{R}^n$, each $e \in E$ is decorated by a jump constraint $J_e \subseteq \mathbb{R}^{2n}$, and all constraints define closed convex sets.*

A finite *control path* $v_0, e_1, v_1, \ldots, e_k, v_k$ of the CHA $\mathcal{H}$ is a path of the control graph of $\mathcal{H}$, i.e., for all $0 \leq i \leq k$ it holds that $v_i \in V$ and for all $1 \leq i \leq k$ it holds that $e_i \in E$ and is a switch with source v_{i-1} and destination v_i. When a control path is clear from the context, we abbreviate any object indexed by v_i or e_i as the same object indexed by i, e.g., we abbreviate F_{v_i} as F_i. The semantics associates modes to points $x \in \mathbb{R}^n$. For every two points $x, x' \in \mathbb{R}^n$, for every control mode $v \in V$ we say that x' is a *v-successor* of x if there exists a derivable function $f \colon \mathbb{R}_{\geq 0} \to \mathbb{R}^n$ and a time delay $\delta \in \mathbb{R}_{\geq 0}$ such that $f(0) = x$, $f(\delta) = x'$, and for all $0 \leq \gamma \leq \delta$ it holds that $\dot{f}(\gamma) \in F_v$ and $f(\gamma) \in I_v$, and for every control switch $e \in E$ we say that x' is an *e-successor* of x if $(x, x') \in J_e$.

Definition 2 ($\mathcal{H}$-feasibility). *A finite control path $v_0, e_1, v_1, \ldots, e_k, v_k$ is $\mathcal{H}$-feasible if for some $x_0, x'_0, x_1, x'_1, \ldots, x_k, x'_k \in \mathbb{R}^n$ it holds that $x_0 \in Z_0$, and for all $0 \leq i \leq k$, x'_i is a v_i-successor of x_i and x_i is a e_i-successor of x'_{i-1}.*

The semantics of $\mathcal{H}$ is the maximal set of $\mathcal{H}$-feasible paths. A mode $v \in V$ is *reachable* if there exists an $\mathcal{H}$-feasible control path whose last mode is v, and a point $x' \in \mathbb{R}^n$ is reachable on v if x' is the last point of a sequence as in Definition 2.

The abstraction associates modes to regions of $\mathbb{R}^n$ into abstract paths whose elements are related by the init and post operator of an abstraction structure $\mathcal{A}$.

Definition 3 (Abstraction structure). *An abstraction structure $\mathcal{A}$ for the CHA $\mathcal{H}$ consists of an init operator $\mathsf{init}_v \in \wp(\mathbb{R}^n)$ for every $v \in V$ and of a post operator $\mathsf{post}_e \colon \wp(\mathbb{R}^n) \to \wp(\mathbb{R}^n)$ for every $e \in E$.*

Similarly as for $\mathcal{H}$, a control path with an abstract counterpart is called $\mathcal{A}$-feasible.

Definition 4 ($\mathcal{A}$-feasibility). *A finite control path $v_0, e_1, v_1, \ldots, e_k, v_k$ is $\mathcal{A}$-feasible if for some non-empty sets $X_0, X_1, \ldots, X_k \subseteq \mathbb{R}^n$ holds that $X_0 = \mathsf{init}_0$ and for all $1 \leq i \leq k$, $X_i = \mathsf{post}_i(X_{i-1})$.*

An $\mathcal{A}$-feasible path is *genuine* if it is also $\mathcal{H}$-feasible, and *spurious* otherwise. An abstraction structure $\mathcal{A}$ is *sound* if all $\mathcal{H}$-feasible control paths are $\mathcal{A}$-feasible.

The *support function* [36] in direction $d \in \mathbb{R}^n$ of a convex set $X \subseteq \mathbb{R}^n$ is

$$\rho_X(d) \overset{\text{def}}{=} \sup\{d \cdot x \mid x \in X\}. \tag{1}$$

The support function of X characterizes the template polyhedron [25,38] of X for the template $\Delta \subseteq \mathbb{R}^n$ (a finite set). We call it the Δ-*polyhedron* of X, that is

$$\bigcap_{d \in \Delta} \{x \in \mathbb{R}^n \mid d \cdot x \leq \rho_X(d)\}. \tag{2}$$

We aim at computing template polyhedra for the (continuous) flow and the (discrete) jump post operators (and their compositions) of the hybrid automaton. The *flow operator* of mode $v \in V$ gives the points reachable by time elapse on v:[1]

$$\mathsf{flow}_v(X) \overset{\text{def}}{=} (X \oplus \mathsf{coni}\, F_v) \cap I_v. \tag{3}$$

The *jump operator* of switch $e \in E$ gives the points reachable through e:[2]

$$\mathsf{jump}_e(X) \overset{\text{def}}{=} [0_{n \times n}\ I_n] \left(\left(\begin{bmatrix} I_n \\ 0_{n \times n} \end{bmatrix} X \oplus \begin{bmatrix} 0_{n \times n} \\ I_n \end{bmatrix} \mathbb{R}^n \right) \cap J_e \right). \tag{4}$$

Flow and jump operators are an exact symbolical characterization for the semantics of CHA, and follow as an extension of the symbolic analysis of LHA [26].

---

[1] For $X \subseteq \mathbb{R}^n$, $\mathsf{coni}\, X$ denotes the conical combination $\{0\} \cup \{\alpha x \mid \alpha > 0 \wedge x \in X\}$ and for $Y \subseteq \mathbb{R}^n$, $X \oplus Y$ denotes the Minkowski sum $\{x + y \mid x \in X \wedge y \in Y\}$.
[2] For $M \in \mathbb{R}^{m \times n}$ and $X \subseteq \mathbb{R}^n$, MX denotes the linear transformation $\{Mx \mid x \in X\}$.

Lemma 1. *For every CHA $\mathcal{H}$ and every set $X \subseteq \mathbb{R}^n$ it holds that (i) $x' \in$ flow$_v(X)$ if and only if x' is a v-successor of some $x \in X$ for every control mode $v \in V$ and (ii) $x' \in$ jump$_e(X)$ if and only if x' is a e-successor of some $x \in X$ for every control switch $e \in E$.*

The exact symbolic analysis of CHA has in general high complexity, as it requires eliminating quantifiers, and possibly from formulae that contain non-linear constraints. For this reason we approximate them using template polyhedra.

The template-polyhedral abstraction computes the template polyhedra of the flow and jump operators above and, in our definition, using a different template for each mode, given by the *precision function* prec: $V \to \wp(\mathbb{R}^n)$.

Definition 5 (Template-polyhedral abstraction). *The template-polyhedral abstraction for the CHA $\mathcal{H}$ and the precision function* prec: $V \to \wp(\mathbb{R}^n)$ *is the abstraction structure where the init operator* init$_v$ *is the* prec(v)*-polyhedron of* flow$_v(Z_v)$, *and the post operator* post$_e(X)$ *is the* prec(t)*-polyhedron of* flow$_t \circ$ jump$_e(X)$ *where $t \in V$ is the destination of e.*

It is well-know that the template-polyhedral abstraction constructs a conservative over-approximation for linear systems [38], and the same holds for CHA.

Theorem 1. *For every CHA $\mathcal{H}$ and every precision function* prec *the template-polyhedral abstraction for $\mathcal{H}$ and* prec *is sound.*

The obvious difficulty is in finding a precision function that is suitable for proving or disproving reachability. In the next section, we show how to form one such automatically by means of counter-example guided abstraction refinement.

4   Refining the Template-Polyhedral Abstraction

A counter-example guided abstraction refinement (CEGAR) loop [16] for a hybrid automaton $\mathcal{H}$ and a set of bad modes T consists of an abstractor and a refiner interacting with each other. At each iteration i, the *abstractor* takes an abstraction structure $\mathcal{A}_i$ and attempts to construct the finite state machine that recognizes all $\mathcal{A}_i$-feasible paths. If it terminates and it does not find a counterexample, i.e., a path leading to a bad mode, then it returns no. Otherwise, it passes $\mathcal{A}_i$ and a set of counterexamples W_i to the refiner. The *refiner* attempts to construct an abstraction structure $\mathcal{A}_{i+1}$ that refines $\mathcal{A}_i$ and eliminates all counterexamples in W_i. If it fails, then it reports yes and a set $\bar{W}_i \subseteq W_i$ of genuine counterexamples. Otherwise, it passes $\mathcal{A}_{i+1}$ to the abstractor.

The above procedure is sound (upon termination), provided $\mathcal{A}_i$ is sound, in the sense that if it reports no then no mode in T is reachable. It is complete (upon termination), namely if it reports yes then some mode in T is reachable, if it returns an abstraction $\mathcal{A}_{i+1}$ that is locally complete w.r.t. W_i when one exists.

Local completeness. An abstraction structure $\mathcal{A}$ for the CHA $\mathcal{H}$ is locally complete w.r.t. the set W of control paths of $\mathcal{H}$ if all $\mathcal{H}$-infeasible control paths in W are $\mathcal{A}$-infeasible.

Moreover, if it ensures local completeness w.r.t. $\cup\{W_j | 0 \leq j \leq i\}$, then it ensures progress of the procedure if the counterexamples are given one by one.

Whenever we find a spurious counterexample, we augment the precision of the modes along the path with additional template directions, so to make it $\mathcal{A}$-infeasible. First of all, we start with finding a sequence of Craig's interpolants and only Craig's interpolants that are halfspaces [2]. Formally, let $w = v_0, e_1, v_1, \ldots, e_k, v_k$ be a control path of $\mathcal{H}$, then a sequence of *halfspace interpolants* for w is a sequence of sets $H_0, H_1, \ldots, H_k \subseteq \mathbb{R}^n$ such that each element is either the universe, a closed halfspace, or the empty set and

$$\text{flow}_0(Z_0) \subseteq H_0, \text{flow}_1 \circ \text{jump}_1(H_0) \subseteq H_1, \ldots, \text{flow}_k \circ \text{jump}_k(H_{k-1}) \subseteq H_k, \quad (5)$$

and $H_k \subseteq \emptyset$. If such sequence exists, then the path is clearly $\mathcal{H}$-infeasible. Conversely, it is not trivial that for every $\mathcal{H}$-infeasible path such sequence exists.

Lemma 2. *For every CHA $\mathcal{H}$ and every control path w of $\mathcal{H}$ it holds that w is $\mathcal{H}$-infeasible if (and only if)[3] there exists a sequence $H_0, H_1, \ldots, H_k \subseteq \mathbb{R}^n$ of halfspace interpolants for w as in Eq. 5.*

Indeed, existence relies on further technical conditions that are out of the scope of this paper [36]. With this in mind, simply assuming all non-linear constraints to be bounded (e.g., Fig. 1) ensures existence, yet without preventing time-unbounded reachability. Computing interpolants is the subject of the next section.

The refining directions are the outward pointing directions of the halfspace interpolants, respectively for each mode along the path. In fact, it is enough to observe that every abstraction we obtain after adding such directions also satisfy

$$\text{init}_0 \subseteq H_0, \text{post}_1(H_0) \subseteq H_1, \ldots, \text{post}_k(H_{k-1}) \subseteq H_k. \quad (6)$$

Figure 3 shows such an example. The path is the one leading to badone from the CHA of Fig. 1, which is spurious with octagonal template (see Fig. 3a), and, in fact, a sequence H_0 and H_1 of halfspace interpolants exists (see Fig. 3b). The halfspace H_1 is disjoint from the guard of c (dashed circle) and includes the points reachable from H_0 (light gray), which in its turn includes the points reachable from Z_{zero}, i.e., $\text{flow}_{\text{zero}}(Z_{\text{zero}}) \subseteq H_0$, $\text{flow}_{\text{one}} \circ \text{jump}_a(H_0) \subseteq H_1$, and $\text{jump}_c(H_1) \subseteq \emptyset$. Taking the supporting halfspaces in the same directions preserves these inclusions, hence adding d_0 to prec(zero) and d_1 to prec(one) causes $\text{init}_{\text{zero}} \subseteq H_0$, $\text{post}_a(H_0) \subseteq H_1$, and $\text{post}_c(H_1) \subseteq \emptyset$. Thus d_0 and d_1 eliminate the counterexample, and regardless of whether prec contains further directions (see Fig. 3c).

---

[3] We exclude the pathological cases of disjoint convex sets w/o separating hyperplane.

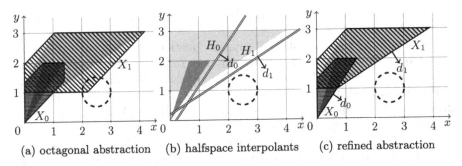

(a) octagonal abstraction   (b) halfspace interpolants   (c) refined abstraction

Fig. 3. Refinement for the control path `zero, a, one, b, badone` of the CHA in Fig. 1. In dark gray, the points reachable on mode `zero`. In (a), (b), and (c), in light gray are the points reachable on mode `one` resp. from X_0, H_0, and X_0. In (a) the spurious path, in (b) the interpolants, and in (c) the abstraction with the outward pointing directions.

Definition 6 (Template-polyhedral refinement). *Let $\mathcal{H}$ be a CHA and let $w = v_0, e_1, v_1, \ldots, e_k, v_k$ be a control path. Define the precision function* prec *such that for some (if one exists) sequence of halfspace interpolants $H_0, H_1, \ldots, H_k \subseteq \mathbb{R}^n$ for w as in Eq. 5 then for all $0 \le i \le k$ set $d_i \in$ prec(v_i) where d_i is the outward pointing direction of H_i. We define the template-polyhedral refinement for $\mathcal{H}$ and w as the template-polyhedral abstraction for $\mathcal{H}$ and* prec.

Local completeness w.r.t. a single path easily generalizes to local completeness w.r.t. multiple paths by taking the union of the discovered directions.

Theorem 2. *For every CHA $\mathcal{H}$ and every set W of finite control paths of $\mathcal{H}$ the union[4] over all $w \in W$ of the template-polyhedral refinements for $\mathcal{H}$ and w is locally complete w.r.t. W.*

Summarizing, we search for abstract counterexamples and we accumulate all outward pointing directions of the respective halfspace interpolants. If either the abstractor finds a fixpoint or interpolation fails, then we obtain a sound and complete answer. In the following section, we show how to compute init and post operators and sequences of halfspace interpolants by using convex optimization.

5   Craig's Interpolation as Convex Optimization

The support function is a central actor both in abstraction, as it defines template polyhedra, and refinement, as it gives a powerful formalism to talk about inclusion in halfspaces and separation of convex sets. In either case, the sets we deal with are arbitrary compositions of flow and jump operators, which in their turn are compositions of Minkowski sums, linear transformations, conical combinations, and intersections. We characterize the support functions of such

---

[4] The union of the abstractions $\mathcal{A}_1, \ldots, \mathcal{A}_i$ for $\mathcal{H}$ and resp. the precisions prec$_1$, $\ldots$, prec$_i$ is the abstraction for $\mathcal{H}$ and the precision $\lambda v.$prec$_1(v) \cup \cdots \cup$ prec$_i(v)$.

operations as convex programs, with the aim of characterizing abstraction and refinement as convex programs.

We present a characterization of support functions that is compositional for the set operations above. The *classic* support function representation framework[5] offers a very similar machinery [25], but it suffers from the following shortcomings. First, it requires the operand sets in Minkowski sums and intersections to be compact (i.e., closed and bounded) and boundedness cannot be easily relaxed, e.g., $\rho_{\mathbb{R}^n}(d) + \rho_\emptyset(d) = +\infty - \infty$ while $\rho_{\mathbb{R}^n \oplus \emptyset}(d) = -\infty$ for every $d \neq 0$. Since we aim at time-unbounded reachability, is would be too restrictive to assume boundedness. Second, substituting boundedness with nonemptiness might cause uncorrect results, e.g., for the sets $A = \{(x,y) \mid x \leq -1\}$, $B = \{(x,y) \mid x \geq 1\}$, and the direction $c = (0,1)$ we obtain $\inf\{\rho_A(c-a) + \rho_B(a)\} = +\infty$, while $\rho_{A \cap B}(c) = -\infty$. We relax both the assumptions of boundedness and nonemptiness by characterizing the support function $\rho_X(d)$ with a convex program

$$\begin{aligned} \text{minimize } & \bar{\rho}_X(\lambda) \\ \text{subject to } & (\lambda, d) \in \Lambda_X, \end{aligned} \tag{7}$$

with objective function $\bar{\rho}_X : \mathbb{R}^m \to \mathbb{R}$ and constraint $\Lambda_X \subseteq \mathbb{R}^{m+n}$. The minimum of $\bar{\rho}_X(\lambda)$ over λ characterizes $\rho_X(d)$ for directions in which X is bounded, while Λ_X characterizes boundedness. This is encapsulated by the notion of duality.

Duality. Let $X \subseteq \mathbb{R}^n$ be a nonempty closed convex set. The convex program of Eq. 7 is *dual* to ρ_X if for all $d \in \mathbb{R}^n$ it holds that
  (i) $\rho_X(d) = +\infty$ if and only if there does not exist λ such that $(\lambda, d) \in \Lambda_X$,
  (ii) $\rho_X(d) < +\infty$ if and only if $\rho_X(d) = \min\{\bar{\rho}_X(\lambda) \mid (\lambda, d) \in \Lambda_X\}$.

We define inductive rules for constructing dual convex programs for the support functions of set operations, provided dual convex programs for their operands (whose instantiation for sets defined by symbolic constraints is subject of Sect. 6):

$$\begin{aligned} \bar{\rho}_{X \oplus Y}(\lambda, \mu) &\overset{\text{def}}{=} \bar{\rho}_X(\lambda) + \bar{\rho}_Y(\mu), \\ \Lambda_{X \oplus Y} &\overset{\text{def}}{=} \{(\lambda, \mu, d) \mid (\lambda, d) \in \Lambda_X, (\mu, d) \in \Lambda_Y\}, \end{aligned} \tag{8}$$

$$\begin{aligned} \bar{\rho}_{MX}(\lambda) &\overset{\text{def}}{=} \bar{\rho}_X(\lambda), \\ \Lambda_{MX} &\overset{\text{def}}{=} \{(\lambda, d) \mid (\lambda, M^\mathsf{T} d) \in \Lambda_X\}, \end{aligned} \tag{9}$$

$$\begin{aligned} \bar{\rho}_{\text{coni } X}(\lambda) &\overset{\text{def}}{=} 0, \\ \Lambda_{\text{coni } X} &\overset{\text{def}}{=} \{(\lambda, d) \mid \bar{\rho}_X(\lambda) \leq 0, (\lambda, d) \in \Lambda_X\}, \end{aligned} \tag{10}$$

$$\begin{aligned} \bar{\rho}_{X \cap Y}(\lambda, \mu) &\overset{\text{def}}{=} \bar{\rho}_X(\lambda) + \bar{\rho}_Y(\mu), \text{ and} \\ \Lambda_{X \cap Y} &\overset{\text{def}}{=} \{(\lambda, \mu, a, d) \mid (\lambda, a) \in \Lambda_X, (\mu, d - a) \in \Lambda_Y\}. \end{aligned} \tag{11}$$

---

[5] $\rho_{X \oplus Y}(d) = \rho_X(d) + \rho_Y(d)$, $\rho_{MX}(d) = \rho_X(M^\mathsf{T} d)$, and $\rho_{X \cap Y}(d) = \inf\{\rho_X(a) + \rho_Y(d - a)\}$.

Nevertheless, duality is not sufficient to characterize operations producing the empty set. Considering the examples above, the constraint $\Lambda_{\mathbb{R}^n \oplus \emptyset}$ is infeasible for every direction $d \neq 0$ and the constraint $\Lambda_{A \cap B}$ is infeasible for direction c, contradicting (i). However, it suffices that the convex program is unbounded for at least $d = 0$, providing an alternative for deciding emptiness beforehand.

Alternativity. The convex program of Eq. 7 is *alternative* to $\rho_\emptyset$ if for every $\epsilon < 0$ there exists $(\lambda, 0) \in \Lambda_\emptyset$ such that $\bar{\rho}_\emptyset(\lambda) \leq \epsilon$.

Altogether, we compute the support of X in direction d as follows. We decide whether there exists a negative solution in direction 0. If so we return $-\infty$, otherwise we decide whether Λ_X is infeasible in direction d. If so we return $+\infty$, otherwise we solve the convex program. This is permitted on any combination of the set operations above, as our construction preserves duality and alternativity.

Lemma 3. *Let $X, Y \subseteq \mathbb{R}^n$ be closed convex sets. If the convex programs for $\bar{\rho}_X, \Lambda_X$ and $\bar{\rho}_Y, \Lambda_Y$ are dual and alternative to resp. ρ_X and ρ_Y then the convex programs for Eqs. 8, 9, and 10 are dual and alternative to the respective support functions. If either X and Y intersect or they admit a separating hyperplane then also the convex program for Eq. 11 is dual and alternative to $\rho_{X \cap Y}$.*

In addition, the construction allows us to inductively extract separating hyperplanes and therefore sequences of halfspace interpolants.

The emptiness check or more generally deciding whether a support function is below a threshold permits us to inductively extract interpolants. For each of the four set operation we wish first to prove inclusion within a given halfspace (or the empty set) H and then to find a second halfspace H' which interpolates the operand. For instance, for an intersection $X \cap Y$ such that $X \cap Y \subseteq H$, we wish to find a H' such that $X \subseteq H'$ and $H' \cap Y \subseteq H$. Indeed, we just need their outward pointing directions, and our construction carries this information.

Lemma 4. *Let $X, Y \subseteq \mathbb{R}^n$ be closed convex sets. Let the convex programs for $\bar{\rho}_X, \Lambda_X$ and $\bar{\rho}_Y, \Lambda_Y$ be dual and alternative to ρ_X and ρ_Y. Let H be the set $\{x \in \mathbb{R}^n \mid d \cdot x \leq \epsilon\}$, which is empty if and only if $d = 0$ and $\epsilon < 0$.*

- *If either X and Y are both nonempty or H is empty then for every $(\lambda^\star, \mu^\star, d) \in \Lambda_{X \oplus Y}$ such that $\bar{\rho}_{X \oplus Y}(\lambda^\star, \mu^\star) \leq \epsilon$ there exists $H' = \{x \in \mathbb{R}^n \mid d \cdot x \leq \epsilon'\}$ such that $\bar{\rho}_X(\lambda^\star) \leq \epsilon'$ and $H' \oplus Y \subseteq H$.*
- *If either X is nonempty or H is empty then for every $(\lambda^\star, d) \in \Lambda_{MX}$ such that $\bar{\rho}_{MX}(\lambda^\star) \leq \epsilon$ there exists $H' = \{x \in \mathbb{R}^n \mid (M^\mathsf{T} d) \cdot x \leq \epsilon'\}$ such that $\bar{\rho}_X(\lambda^\star) \leq \epsilon'$ and $MH' \subseteq H$.*
- *For every $(\lambda^\star, d) \in \Lambda_{\text{coni} X}$ such that $\bar{\rho}_{\text{coni} X}(\lambda^\star) \leq \epsilon$ there exists $H' = \{x \in \mathbb{R}^n \mid d \cdot x \leq \epsilon'\}$ such that $\bar{\rho}_X(\lambda^\star) \leq \epsilon'$ and $\text{coni} H' \subseteq H$.*
- *If either X and Y intersect or H is empty and they admit a separating hyperplane then for every $(\lambda^\star, \mu^\star, a^\star, d) \in \Lambda_{X \cap Y}$ such that $\bar{\rho}_{X \cap Y}(\lambda^\star, \mu^\star) \leq \epsilon$ there exists $H' = \{x \in \mathbb{R}^n \mid a^\star \cdot x \leq \epsilon'\}$ such that $\bar{\rho}_X(\lambda^\star) \leq \epsilon'$ and $H' \cap Y \subseteq H$.*

We can extract the outward pointing directions by looking at the arguments instantiated by an emptiness check. Inductively, if d is the outward pointing direction of H, then the outward pointing direction of H' is d for the Minkowski sum, $M^\mathsf{T}d$ for the linear transformation, d for the conical combination, and a for the intersection. As a result, we can extract sequences of interpolants for arbitrary combinations of basic set operations from one single emptiness check.

We build such a construction for arbitrary sequences of flow and jump operators induced by control paths. More concretely, let $w = v_0, e_1, v_1, \ldots, e_k, v_k$ be a control path of some CHA $\mathcal{H}$ then the *path operator* of w is

$$P_w \stackrel{\text{def}}{=} \text{flow}_k \circ \text{jump}_k \circ \cdots \circ \text{flow}_1 \circ \text{jump}_1 \circ \text{flow}_0(Z_0). \tag{12}$$

Similarly to Lemma 2, we assume every path operator to be either nonempty or to admit a separating hyperplane at some intersection. By applying the above rules, we construct the convex program for the support function of P_w as follows:

$$
\begin{aligned}
\text{minimize} \quad & \bar{\rho}_{Z_0}(\lambda_{Z_0}) + \sum_{i=1}^{k} \bar{\rho}_{J_i}(\lambda_{J_i}) + \sum_{i=0}^{k} \bar{\rho}_{I_i}(\lambda_{I_i}) \\
\text{subject to} \quad & (\lambda_{Z_0}, a_0 - b_0) && \in \Lambda_{Z_0}, \\
& (\lambda_{J_i}, \left[-a_{i-1}, a_i - b_i\right]^\mathsf{T}) && \in \Lambda_{J_i} && \text{for each } i \in [1..k], \\
& \bar{\rho}_{F_i}(\lambda_{F_i}, a_i - b_i) && \leq 0 && \text{for each } i \in [0..k], \\
& (\lambda_{F_i}, a_i - b_i) && \in \Lambda_{F_i} && \text{for each } i \in [0..k], \\
& (\lambda_{I_i}, b_i) && \in \Lambda_{I_i} && \text{for each } i \in [0..k], \\
& a_k && = d.
\end{aligned}
\tag{13}
$$

Duality and alternativity is preserved, therefore we can use such construction to compute the support functions for init and post (which are special cases of path).

Lemma 5. *For every CHA $\mathcal{H}$, every control path w of $\mathcal{H}$, if the convex programs for every constraint X along the path are dual and alternative to ρ_X then the convex program in Eq. 13 is dual and alternative to ρ_{P_w}.*

We identify the arguments that determine a suitable sequence of halfspace interpolants after the emptiness check.

Lemma 6. *For every CHA $\mathcal{H}$, every control path w of $\mathcal{H}$, every $\epsilon < 0$, and every $(\lambda^\star, 0) \in \Lambda_{P_w}$ whose projection on $a_0, a_1, \ldots, a_k$ is $a_0^\star, a_1^\star, \ldots, a_k^\star \in \mathbb{R}^n$, if the convex programs for the constraints X along the path are dual and alternative to ρ_X then $\bar{\rho}_{P_w}(\lambda^\star) \leq \epsilon$ if and only if $a_0^\star, a_1^\star, \ldots, a_k^\star$ are the outward pointing directions of a sequence of halfspace interpolants $H_0, H_1, \ldots, H_k$ for w as in Eq. 5.*

In summary, we search by convex optimization for an argument for which the convex program of Eq. 13 for $d = 0$ has negative solution. If so, the argument $a_i^\star$ for the parameter a_i is the outward pointing direction for the interpolant at mode v_i. Adding $a_i^\star$ to $\text{prec}(v_i)$ eliminates the spurious counterexample w.

In this section, we have built a refiner for every spurious path of every CHA, assuming dual and alternative convex programs for the constraints along the path. In the following section, we discuss such functions and show how to instantiate interpolation for the special case of quadratic hybrid automata.

6   Abstraction Refinement for Quadratic Systems

The interpolation technique in Sect. 5 relies on the notions of duality and alternativity. Duality and alternativity are preserved by Minkowski sum, linear transformation, conical combination, and intersection, but whether they hold in the first place depends on the constraint of the automaton. We discuss these properties for (convex) quadratic programs, and we show their implications to the classes of quadratic and linear hybrid automata.

Closed convex quadratic sets are sets of the form $\bigcap_{i=1}^m \{x \in \mathbb{R}^n \mid xQ_ix^\mathsf{T} + p_i^\mathsf{T}x \le r_i\}$ where $Q_1,\ldots,Q_m \in \mathbb{R}^{n\times n}$ are positive semidefinite matrices of coefficients, $p_1,\ldots,p_m \in \mathbb{R}^n$ are vectors of coefficients, and $r_1,\ldots,r_m \in \mathbb{R}$ are constants. Closed convex quadratic sets characterize quadratic hybrid automata.

Definition 7 (Quadratic hybrid automata). *A quadratic hybrid automaton (QHA) is a CHA whose constraints define closed convex quadratic sets.*

The support function of a convex quadratic set is a quadratically constrained (convex) quadratic program, which is known to cast to second-order conic programming (SOCP) [3]. We cast the support function to an optimization problem over a (rotated) second-order cone and we take its dual [3], so obtaining

$$\begin{aligned}
&\text{minimize } r_1\lambda_1 + \cdots + r_m\lambda_m \\
&\text{subject to } p_1\lambda_1 + L_1^\mathsf{T}\mu_1 + \cdots + p_m\lambda_m + L_m^\mathsf{T}\mu_m = d, \\
&\quad\quad \lambda_1 \ge \|\mu_1\|_2^2,\ldots,\lambda_m \ge \|\mu_m\|_2^2,
\end{aligned} \tag{14}$$

where $L_1,\ldots,L_m$ are the Cholesky decompositions of $Q_1,\ldots,Q_m$ respectively, and $\lambda_1,\ldots,\lambda_m \in \mathbb{R}$ and $\mu_1,\ldots,\mu_m \in \mathbb{R}^n$ are the optimization arguments. Under the regularity conditions for non-linear optimization, e.g., Slater's condition, duality and alternativity hold [3,10]. Encodings that do not need such conditions exist [34], but are not discussed in this paper.

Every algorithm that solves feasibility and optimization of SOCP solves init and post computation and halfspace interpolation for QHA, thus enabling their template-polyhedral abstraction and abstraction refinement.

Theorem 3. *Let $\mathcal{H}$ be a QHA with n variables and m inequalities. Let the time complexity of SOCP be $\mathsf{socp}(\alpha,\beta,\gamma)$ for α variables, β equalities, and γ cones.*

- *Init and post operators time complexity is $p \times \mathsf{socp}(n \times m, n, m)$ where $p = \max\{|\mathsf{prec}(v)| \mid v \in V\}$ for the precision function prec.*
- *Refinement time complexity is $c \times \mathsf{socp}(n \times m, n \times k, m \times k)$ where $c = |W|$ and $k = \max\{|w| \mid w \in W\}$ for the set of counterexamples W.*

Nevertheless, the complexity SOCP remains an open problem on the Turing machine, while it is known to be in NP∩coNP on the real number model [34]. On the other hand, several efficient (but incomplete) numerical procedures are available, therefore in practice we can obtain support functions and interpolants, but with weaker guarantees. We are in a better position for the case of linear hybrid automata (LHA) [26], i.e., the special case of QHA where all constraints define polyhedra. For linear hybrid automata, the program of Eq. 14 is always a linear program, i.e., all cones are positive orthants, where duality holds, alternativity is given by Farkas' lemma, and time complexity is polynomial. Hence, for LHA, init operator, post operator, and refinement time complexities are as well polynomial.

7   Experimental Evaluation

We evaluate our algorithms on three main classes of benchmarks, namely Fischer's protocol [31], an adaptive cruise controller [30], and the TTEthernet protocol [9]. For each class, we consider a linear version and a non-linear version, as well as for each a safe version and an unsafe version.

Fischer's protocol is a time based protocol of mutual exclusion between processes. The protocol is correct if two processes are never in the critical section at the same time. For the linear version, the flow constraints are given by $\frac{1}{2} \leq \dot{x}_1 \leq \frac{3}{2}, \ldots, \frac{1}{2} \leq \dot{x}_m \leq \frac{3}{2}$, where x_i is the clock of the i-th process, and for the non-linear case, $\sqrt{\dot{x}_1^2 + \cdots + \dot{x}_m^2} \leq 1$. We verify the linear version up to 5 processes and the non-linear version up to 3 processes.

The adaptive cruise controller is a distributed system for safety distance of platoon of cars. Each car either cruises or recovers by slowing down. The relative velocity has a drift $|\dot{x} - \dot{x}_{1dr}| \leq \frac{1}{2}$ when cruising and $|\dot{x} - \dot{x}_{1dr} + \varepsilon| \leq \frac{1}{2}$ when recovering, where x and x_{1dr} are the positions of each car the car in front, resp., and ε is the slow-down. We check for car crashes in platoons up to 7 cars.

Finally, we consider the TTEthernet protocol for the remote synchronization of possibly drifted clocks distributed over multiple components. Similarly to previous case studies, we consider flows defined in terms of intervals and unit balls for linear and non-linear cases, respectively. We verify both linear and non-linear systems with 3, 5, 9, and 17 components.

We implemented a CEGAR loop based on our procedure in C++ and conducted the following experiments on a machine with 2.6 GHz CPU and 4 GB of dedicated RAM. We use the GLPK for solving LPs and MOSEK for solving SOCPs [1,33]. We executed our tool under the *empty* strategy and the *octagonal* strategy. With the empty strategy, the initial precision is empty, which means that the very first abstraction computation consists of a simple exploration of the control graph. With the octagonal strategy, the precision at every mode consists of the octagonal template, with a total of $2|V|n^2$ directions over all modes. For all linear instances, we compared against PHAVer [21] (SpaceEx v0.9.8c with PHAVer scenario).

Table 1 shows the results. The empty strategy has on average the best runtime and always outperforms PHAVer. It also outperforms the octagonal strategy for most of the instances. Both strategies spend most of the time in the first phase

Table 1. Results of the experimental evaluation. Empty and octagonal indicate the initial precision. #spu is number of discovered spurious counterexamples, #dir is the number of discovered directions (empty case) or initial directions + discovered directions (octagonal case). cgr is the total time spent in unsuccessful abstractions (with spurious counterexample), itp is the total time spent in discovering halfspace interpolants, ver is the time spent in successful abstractions. oot indicates out of time (24 h), oom indicates out of memory (4 Gb), and dash indicates unsupported. The benchmark names are structured as follows. fsr indicates Fischer's protocol, acc indicates adaptive cruise controller, tte indicates TTEthernet, lnr indicates linear, qdr indicates quadratic, the following number indicates the number of components, and sf and usf resp. indicate safe and unsafe.

Benchmark	Empty					Octagonal					PHAVer
	#spu	#dir	cgr [s]	itp [s]	ver [s]	#spu	#dir	cgr [s]	itp [s]	ver [s]	time [s]
fsr_lnr_2_sf	5	8	0.06	0.02	≈0	0	256 + 0	0.11	0	0.11	≈0
fsr_lnr_3_sf	41	69	1.12	0.02	0.02	12	3456 + 12	5.55	≈0	0.50	1.25
fsr_lnr_4_sf	259	440	33.16	0.29	0.14	221	32768 + 221	1190	0.07	23.06	135
fsr_lnr_5_sf	1379	2335	857	2.08	0.76	oot	256k	oot	oot	oot	78807
fsr_lnr_2_usf	0	0	≈0	0	≈0	0	256 + 0	0	0	0.12	≈0
fsr_lnr_3_usf	0	0	0.03	0	0.03	0	3456 + 0	0	0	0.37	1.01
fsr_lnr_4_usf	0	0	0.06	0	0.06	0	32768 + 0	0	0	1.67	300
fsr_lnr_5_usf	0	0	0.16	0	0.16	0	256k + 0	0	0	13.63	oom
fsr_qdr_2_sf	5	8	5.13	0.10	1.32	0	256 + 0	0	0	8.18	-
fsr_qdr_3_sf	41	69	226	0.44	9.04	12	3456 + 12	3599	0.15	886	-
fsr_qdr_2_usf	0	0	0.66	0	0.66	0	256 + 0	0	0	6.40	-
fsr_qdr_3_usf	0	0	1.76	0	1.76	0	3456 + 0	0	0	26.67	-
acc_lnr_2_sf	2	2	≈0	≈0	≈0	0	32 + 0	0	0	≈0	≈0
acc_lnr_3_sf	8	8	0.04	≈0	≈0	0	144 + 0	0	0	0.19	0.03
acc_lnr_4_sf	24	24	0.39	≈0	0.02	0	512 + 0	0	0	0.87	0.53
acc_lnr_5_sf	64	64	0.94	≈0	0.12	oot	1600	oot	oot	oot	21.78
acc_lnr_6_sf	160	160	42.12	0.07	0.74	oot	4608	oot	oot	oot	1455
acc_lnr_7_sf	384	384	569	0.13	4.22	oot	12544	oot	oot	oot	oot
acc_lnr_2_usf	1	1	≈0	≈0	≈0	0	32 + 0	0	0	≈0	≈0
acc_lnr_3_usf	2	2	≈0	≈0	≈0	0	144 + 0	0	0	0.05	≈0
acc_lnr_4_usf	3	3	≈0	≈0	≈0	0	512 + 0	0	0	0.37	0.18
acc_lnr_5_usf	4	4	≈0	≈0	≈0	0	1600 + 0	0	0	0.61	22.51
acc_lnr_6_usf	5	5	0.06	≈0	0.04	0	4608 + 0	0	0	1.23	4621
acc_lnr_7_usf	6	6	0.17	≈0	0.06	0	12544 + 0	0	0	2.87	oot
tte_lnr_3_sf	17	18	≈0	≈0	≈0	oot	864	oot	oot	oot	oot
tte_lnr_5_sf	49	50	0.32	≈0	≈0	oot	2400	oot	oot	oot	oot
tte_lnr_9_sf	161	162	3.47	≈0	0.06	oot	7776	oot	oot	oot	oot
tte_lnr_17_sf	577	578	239	0.06	1.27	oot	27774	oot	oot	oot	oot
tte_lnr_3_usf	18	24	0.26	≈0	0.05	0	864 + 0	0	0	0.42	oot
tte_lnr_5_usf	60	80	0.85	≈0	0.02	0	2400 + 0	0	0	0.95	oot
tte_lnr_9_usf	216	288	15.65	≈0	0.26	0	7776 + 0	0	0	4.36	oot
tte_lnr_17_usf	816	1088	1722	0.35	8.68	0	27774 + 0	0	0	109	oot
tte_qdr_3_sf	17	18	8.30	0.38	1.36	oot	864	oot	oot	oot	-
tte_qdr_5_sf	49	50	56.31	1.25	4.01	oot	2400	oot	oot	oot	-
tte_qdr_9_sf	161	162	492	3.94	12.29	oot	7776	oot	oot	oot	-
tte_qdr_17_sf	577	578	3325	12.79	47.49	oot	27774	oot	oot	oot	-
tte_qdr_3_usf	18	24	3.65	0.21	0.60	0	864 + 0	0	0	6.33	-
tte_qdr_5_usf	60	80	37.99	0.66	1.82	0	2400 + 0	0	0	21.68	-
tte_qdr_9_usf	216	288	514	2.61	7.32	0	7776 + 0	0	0	58.27	-
tte_qdr_17_usf	816	1088	15515	18.28	58.95	0	27774 + 0	0	0	78.19	-

(CEGAR iterations ending in a spurious counterexample), and take a very short time for the final verification step. For Fischer's protocol the octagonal strategy is always slower than the empty. For the other benchmarks the difference is less stunning, in particular for the unsafe cases of the TTEthernet benchmarks, where the first phase penalizes considerably. On the other hand, we can observe that, under the assumption that we are not aware of the safety of the systems, our method shows to be the most scalable. The octagonal strategy tends to run out of time because the higher number of directions causes the generation of bigger and bigger abstract regions. In fact, we have verified that for these instances a spurious counter-example is never found. The same argument likely holds for PHAVer, as its dump shows that new symbolic states are always found. Not surprisingly, for QHA the performance is generally worse than for LHA.

In summary, template polyhedra coupled with our abstraction refinement technique are faster than the exact polyhedral reachability analysis. Noteworthy is how negligible is the time required in the final verification step on all instances. Our tool recomputes the whole abstraction after every refinement phase, as all our efforts have been strictly focused on implementing an efficient template refinement. The final time sets a lower bound for the verification time achievable by an incremental abstraction. Furthermore, we could observe that inferring small template sets plays an important role in the convergence of the whole analysis.

8   Conclusion

We have presented the first template refinement technique that iteratively derives template directions from spurious counterexamples. These directions eliminate all counterexamples that pass through the same switching sequence, independently of any time delays. These directions can refute further spurious paths, so that a small number of directions may suffice to show safety. This is supported by our experiments, which terminate with small templates in all cases. Our procedure can be implemented efficiently for LHA and QHA using convex optimization, and in principle it applies to every CHA. Our implementation outperforms polyhedral reachability (PHAVer), and yet has room for further substantial improvement since the abstraction is constructed from scratch at each iteration and could be made incremental [28,32]. In terms of modeling power, extending template refinement to affine or general polynomial systems also brings further challenges, as the reachable regions lose the convexity property, thus requiring more powerful techniques for halfspace interpolation [2].

References

1. GLPK (GNU linear programming kit). www.gnu.org/software/glpk
2. Albarghouthi, A., McMillan, K.L.: Beautiful interpolants. In: Sharygina, N., Veith, H. (eds.) CAV 2013. LNCS, vol. 8044, pp. 313–329. Springer, Heidelberg (2013). doi:10.1007/978-3-642-39799-8_22

3. Alizadeh, F., Goldfarb, D.: Second-order cone programming. Math. Program. **95**(1), 3–51 (2003)
4. Alur, R., Dang, T., Ivančić, F.: Counter-example guided predicate abstraction of hybrid systems. In: Garavel, H., Hatcliff, J. (eds.) TACAS 2003. LNCS, vol. 2619, pp. 208–223. Springer, Heidelberg (2003). doi:10.1007/3-540-36577-X_15
5. Alur, R., Henzinger, T.A., Ho, P.: Automatic symbolic verification of embedded systems. In: RTSS. IEEE Computer Society (1993)
6. Asarin, E., Dang, T., Maler, O., Testylier, R.: Using redundant constraints for refinement. In: Bouajjani, A., Chin, W.-N. (eds.) ATVA 2010. LNCS, vol. 6252, pp. 37–51. Springer, Heidelberg (2010). doi:10.1007/978-3-642-15643-4_5
7. Bogomolov, S., Frehse, G., Greitschus, M., Grosu, R., Pasareanu, C., Podelski, A., Strump, T.: Assume-guarantee abstraction refinement meets hybrid systems. In: Yahav, E. (ed.) HVC 2014. LNCS, vol. 8855, pp. 116–131. Springer, Heidelberg (2014). doi:10.1007/978-3-319-13338-6_10
8. Bogomolov, S., Frehse, G., Grosu, R., Ladan, H., Podelski, A., Wehrle, M.: A box-based distance between regions for guiding the reachability analysis of SpaceEx. In: Madhusudan, P., Seshia, S.A. (eds.) CAV 2012. LNCS, vol. 7358, pp. 479–494. Springer, Heidelberg (2012). doi:10.1007/978-3-642-31424-7_35
9. Bogomolov, S., Herrera, C., Steiner, W.: Benchmark for verification of fault-tolerant clock synchronization algorithms. In: ARCH (2016)
10. Boyd, S., Vandenberghe, L.: Convex Optimization. Cambridge University Press, Cambridge (2004)
11. Bu, L., Zhao, J., Li, X.: Path-oriented reachability verification of a class of nonlinear hybrid automata using convex programming. In: Barthe, G., Hermenegildo, M. (eds.) VMCAI 2010. LNCS, vol. 5944, pp. 78–94. Springer, Heidelberg (2010). doi:10.1007/978-3-642-11319-2_9
12. Chen, X., Ábrahám, E., Sankaranarayanan, S.: Taylor model flowpipe construction for non-linear hybrid systems. In: RTSS (2012)
13. Chen, X., Ábrahám, E., Sankaranarayanan, S.: Flow*: an analyzer for non-linear hybrid systems. In: Sharygina, N., Veith, H. (eds.) CAV 2013. LNCS, vol. 8044, pp. 258–263. Springer, Heidelberg (2013). doi:10.1007/978-3-642-39799-8_18
14. Cimatti, A., Mover, S., Tonetta, S.: A quantifier-free SMT encoding of non-linear hybrid automata. In: FMCAD (2012)
15. Clarke, E.M., Fehnker, A., Han, Z., Krogh, B.H., Ouaknine, J., Stursberg, O., Theobald, M.: Abstraction and counterexample-guided refinement in model checking of hybrid systems. Int. J. Found. Comput. Sci. **14**, 583–604 (2003)
16. Clarke, E., Grumberg, O., Jha, S., Lu, Y., Veith, H.: Counterexample-guided abstraction refinement. In: Emerson, E.A., Sistla, A.P. (eds.) CAV 2000. LNCS, vol. 1855, pp. 154–169. Springer, Heidelberg (2000). doi:10.1007/10722167_15
17. Cousot, P., Cousot, R.: Abstract interpretation: a unified lattice model for static analysis of programs by construction or approximation of fixpoints. In: POPL (1977)
18. Dang, T., Salinas, D.: Image computation for polynomial dynamical systems using the Bernstein expansion. In: Bouajjani, A., Maler, O. (eds.) CAV 2009. LNCS, vol. 5643, pp. 219–232. Springer, Heidelberg (2009). doi:10.1007/978-3-642-02658-4_19
19. Doyen, L., Henzinger, T.A., Raskin, J.-F.: Automatic rectangular refinement of affine hybrid systems. In: Pettersson, P., Yi, W. (eds.) FORMATS 2005. LNCS, vol. 3829, pp. 144–161. Springer, Heidelberg (2005). doi:10.1007/11603009_13
20. Dreossi, T., Dang, T., Piazza, C.: Parallelotope bundles for polynomial reachability. In: HSCC (2016)

21. Frehse, G.: PHAVer: algorithmic verification of hybrid systems past HyTech. In: Morari, M., Thiele, L. (eds.) HSCC 2005. LNCS, vol. 3414, pp. 258–273. Springer, Heidelberg (2005). doi:10.1007/978-3-540-31954-2_17

22. Frehse, G., Bogomolov, S., Greitschus, M., Strump, T., Podelski, A.: Eliminating spurious transitions in reachability with support functions. In: HSCC (2015)

23. Frehse, G., et al.: SpaceEx: scalable verification of hybrid systems. In: Gopalakrishnan, G., Qadeer, S. (eds.) CAV 2011. LNCS, vol. 6806, pp. 379–395. Springer, Heidelberg (2011). doi:10.1007/978-3-642-22110-1_30

24. Frehse, G., Kateja, R., Guernic, C.L.: Flowpipe approximation and clustering in space-time. In: HSCC (2013)

25. Guernic, C., Girard, A.: Reachability analysis of hybrid systems using support functions. In: Bouajjani, A., Maler, O. (eds.) CAV 2009. LNCS, vol. 5643, pp. 540–554. Springer, Heidelberg (2009). doi:10.1007/978-3-642-02658-4_40

26. Henzinger, T.A.: The theory of hybrid automata. In: LICS (1996)

27. Henzinger, T.A., Ho, P.-H.: A note on abstract interpretation strategies for hybrid automata. In: Antsaklis, P., Kohn, W., Nerode, A., Sastry, S. (eds.) HS 1994. LNCS, vol. 999, pp. 252–264. Springer, Heidelberg (1995). doi:10.1007/3-540-60472-3_13

28. Henzinger, T.A., Jhala, R., Majumdar, R., Sutre, G.: Lazy abstraction. In: POPL (2002)

29. Henzinger, T.A., Kopke, P.W., Puri, A., Varaiya, P.: What's decidable about hybrid automata? In: STOC (1995)

30. Jha, S.K., Krogh, B.H., Weimer, J.E., Clarke, E.M.: Reachability for linear hybrid automata using iterative relaxation abstraction. In: Bemporad, A., Bicchi, A., Buttazzo, G. (eds.) HSCC 2007. LNCS, vol. 4416, pp. 287–300. Springer, Heidelberg (2007). doi:10.1007/978-3-540-71493-4_24

31. Lamport, L.: A fast mutual exclusion algorithm. ACM Trans. Comput. Syst. (TOCS) 5(1), 1–11 (1987)

32. McMillan, K.L.: Lazy abstraction with interpolants. In: Ball, T., Jones, R.B. (eds.) CAV 2006. LNCS, vol. 4144, pp. 123–136. Springer, Heidelberg (2006). doi:10.1007/11817963_14

33. MOSEK ApS: The MOSEK C optimizer API manual, Version 7.1 (Revision 53) (2015). http://docs.mosek.com/7.1/capi/

34. Ramana, M.V.: An exact duality theory for semidefinite programming and its complexity implications. Math. Program. 77, 129–162 (1997)

35. Ray, R., Gurung, A., Das, B., Bartocci, E., Bogomolov, S., Grosu, R.: XSpeed: accelerating reachability analysis on multi-core processors. In: Piterman, N. (ed.) HVC 2015. LNCS, vol. 9434, pp. 3–18. Springer, Heidelberg (2015). doi:10.1007/978-3-319-26287-1_1

36. Rockafellar, R.T.: Convex Analysis. Princeton University Press, Princeton (1970)

37. Sankaranarayanan, S., Dang, T., Ivančić, F.: Symbolic model checking of hybrid systems using template polyhedra. In: Ramakrishnan, C.R., Rehof, J. (eds.) TACAS 2008. LNCS, vol. 4963, pp. 188–202. Springer, Heidelberg (2008). doi:10.1007/978-3-540-78800-3_14

38. Sankaranarayanan, S., Sipma, H.B., Manna, Z.: Scalable analysis of linear systems using mathematical programming. In: Cousot, R. (ed.) VMCAI 2005. LNCS, vol. 3385, pp. 25–41. Springer, Heidelberg (2005). doi:10.1007/978-3-540-30579-8_2

39. Ben Sassi, M.A., Testylier, R., Dang, T., Girard, A.: Reachability analysis of polynomial systems using linear programming relaxations. In: Chakraborty, S., Mukund, M. (eds.) ATVA 2012. LNCS, vol. 7561, pp. 137–151. Springer, Heidelberg (2012). doi:10.1007/978-3-642-33386-6_12

Author Index

Printed in the United States
By Bookmasters